Mander Portman W

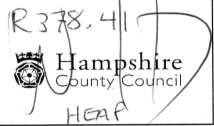

UNIVERSITY DEGREE COURSE OFFERS

The essential guide to winning
your place at university

Brian Heap

42nd edition

UNIVERSITY DEGREE COURSE OFFERS – HEAP 2012

In order to ensure that *University Degree Course Offers* retains its reputation as the definitive guide for students wishing to study at UK universities and other higher education institutions, thousands of questionnaires are distributed, months of research and analysis are undertaken, and painstaking data checking and proofing are carried out.

Every effort has been made to maintain absolute accuracy in providing course information and to ensure that the entire book is as up-to-date as possible. However, changes are constantly taking place in higher education so it is important for readers to check carefully with prospectuses and websites before submitting their applications. The author, compilers and publishers cannot be held responsible for any inaccuracies in information supplied to them by third parties or contained in resources and websites listed in the book.

We hope you find this 42nd edition useful, and would welcome your feedback as to how we can ensure the 43rd edition is even better.

Author Brian Heap
Advertising Sales Crimson Publishing Services.
Contact Lee Scott or Simon Connor on 020 8334 1781 or email info@crimsonpublishingservices.co.uk

This 42nd edition published in 2011 by Trotman Publishing an imprint of Crimson Publishing Ltd, Westminster House, Kew Road, Richmond, Surrey, TW9 2ND
www.trotman.co.uk

A CIP record for this book is available from the British Library

ISBN 978 1 84455 419 5

Typeset by RefineCatch Limited, Bungay, Suffolk
Printed and bound in the UK by Ashford Colour Press, Gosport, Hants

Founded in 1973, **Mander Portman Woodward (MPW)** is one of the UK's best known groups of independent sixth-form colleges with centres in London, Birmingham and Cambridge. It offers over 40 subjects at AS and A2 with no restrictions on subject combinations and a maximum class size of eight.

MPW has one of the highest numbers of university placements each year of any independent school in the country. It has developed considerable expertise over the years in the field of applications strategy and is frequently consulted by students facing some of the more daunting challenges that may arise in areas such as getting into Oxbridge, Medicine or Law. This expertise is available to a wider audience in the form of **Getting Into** guides on higher education and the seminars that are run for sixth-formers at its London centre. We are grateful to Trotman for publishing the Guides and hope that this latest edition of **University Degree Course Offers** will prove as popular and useful as ever.

If you would like to know more about MPW or Getting Into guides, please telephone us on 020 7835 1355 or visit our website, www.mpw.co.uk.

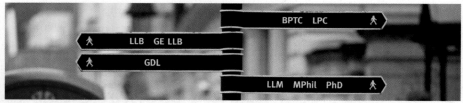

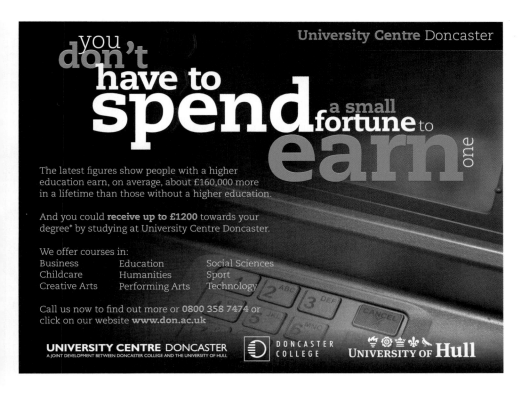

Apply **NOW** to study on the beautiful south coast of England.

A great place to live... A great place to study

Some of the Degree programmes we run in conjunction with our associate universities are:

- Applied Art and Design FdA/BA (Hons)
- Business Computing FdSc
- Business and Management FdA
- Computing and Networking FdSc
- Computer Games Technology FdSc
- Computer Generated Imagery FdSc/BSc (Hons)
- Creative Multimedia Design FdA
- Early Years FdA
- Electronics and Engineering HNC/FdSc
- Finance and Law FdA

- Marketing Communications FdA
- Music and Sound Technology FdSc
- Performing Arts FdA
- Popular Music FdA
- Professional Culinary Arts FdA
- Public Services FdA
- Radio Production FdA
- Teacher Training PGCE/BA (Hons)
- Tourism Management FdA

If you would like to know more about Higher Education at The College visit:

www.thecollege.co.uk/highereducation

Call The College helpline on **01202 205205**

or contact the HE Unit on **01202 205180**

or email us: **heunit@bpc.ac.uk**

Aspire • Achieve • Succeed

Be a name
not a number...

PRIFYSGOL CYMRU
Y Drindod Dewi Sant

UNIVERSITY OF WALES
Trinity Saint David

0300 500 1822
www.tsd.ac.uk

QUOTES

'Degree Course Offers ... will keep aspirations realistic'
www.newteachers.tes.co.uk, 2011

'An extremely useful guide ...'
Woodhouse Grove School, 2010

'Look out for Brian Heap's excellent books on choosing higher education courses'
Carre's Grammar School, 2010

'Degree Course Offers by Brian Heap – not to be missed. Invaluable'
Maidstone Grammar School, 2010

'Degree Course Offers ... a really good resource'
www.positive-parents.com, 2009
'The guru of university choice'
The Times, 2007

'For those of you going through Clearing, an absolute must is the Degree Course Offers book. This guide operates subject by subject and gives you each university's requirements, standard offers and, most importantly, "course features"'
The Independent, August 2007

'Brian Heap, the guru of university admissions'
The Independent, September 2007

'I would like to take this opportunity to congratulate you in maintaining the quality and currency of the information in your guide. We are aware of its wide range and its reputation for impartiality'
University Senior Assistant Registrar, 2007

'Degree Course Offers is probably the UK's longest running and best known reference work on the subject'
www.universityadvice.co.uk, 2005

'This guide contains useful, practical information for all university applicants and those advising them. I heartily recommend it'
Dr John Dunford, General Secretary, Association of School and College Leaders, 2005

'An invaluable guide to helping students and their advisers find their way through the maze of degree courses currently on offer'
Kath Wright, President, Association for Careers Education and Guidance, 2005

'No one is better informed or more experienced than Brian Heap in mediating this range of information to university and college applicants'
Careers Education and Guidance, October 2005

'The course-listings bible'
The Guardian, June 2005

'After consulting this you won't be able to say "I didn't know!" For every school library'
The Teacher, Nov 2003

'A must buy ... one of the best single reference sources to degree course offers available'
Career Guidance Today, July 2003

'The most comprehensive guide is Degree Course Offers by Brian Heap'
John Clare in The Daily Telegraph, April 2003

CONTENTS

AUTHOR'S ACKNOWLEDGEMENTS

This year, again, I must record my gratitude for the invaluable and extended support received from my daughter Jane Heap of Putney High School (Head of Careers), who has provided additional research and advice in the compilation of this edition.

I acknowledge gratefully the efforts of the many university and college registrars, schools liaison staff, faculty and departmental heads and admissions tutors in providing information about their admissions policies and courses. I appreciate, especially, the information and generosity of time given by admissions staff in the many universities and colleges who respond each year to the questionnaire research for *University Degree Course Offers*.

In particular, I should like to thank Tony Charlton, Caroline Russell and Jenny Vowles at UCAS, Sarah Hannaford of the University of Cambridge Admissions Office, Clare Woodcock of the University of Oxford Public Relations Office and Lee Hennessy, Deputy Head of Admissions at the University of Bath, for providing me with up-to-date information on admissions procedures. Additionally, my thanks are due to the Higher Education Statistics Agency (HESA) for the use of data in *Destinations of Leavers from Higher Education 2007/8*.

In addition I am also grateful to those admissions tutors, teachers and their pupils who have sent me interview reports and other information which has provided useful supplementary data for the book.

I also wish to thank the many readers and university staff who have contributed information on courses and places to study. Such information adds to a valuable store of knowledge which can be passed on, thereby creating a better understanding of mutual difficulties.

Finally, I should like to thank my wife Rita for her administrative help (and patience!) through 42 years of publication.

Brian Heap BA DA (Manc) ATD
March 2011

ABOUT THIS BOOK

University Degree Course Offers for 40 years has been a first-stop reference for university and college applicants choosing their courses in higher education by providing information from official sources about how to choose courses and how admissions tutors select students.

For 2012/13 higher education applicants, this new annual edition of *University Degree Course Offers* again aims to provide the latest possible information from universities to help equip them to obtain a degree course place in a fiercely competitive applications process. This level of competition will make it essential for every applicant to research carefully courses and institutions. Latest statistics show that over 210,000 applicants were not able to obtain university places for entry in 2010 and, because of the huge and increasing number of applicants and cuts in the number of places, the same will happen to applicants planning entry in 2012.

This cannot be stressed enough. There are many students who restrict their applications to a small number of well-known universities. They must realise that in doing so they are very likely to receive rejections from all of them. Applicants must spread their choices across a wide range of institutions.

Many universities and colleges have a limited number of places and are setting their offers higher for places on their courses in 2012 and 2013. How do applicants decide on a strategy to find a place on a degree course? There are more than 1000 separate degree subjects and over 18,000 Joint and Combined Honours courses so how can applicants choose a course that is right for them, especially at a time of recession and employment difficulties? What can applicants do to find a course place and a university or college that is right for them?

University Degree Course Offers 2012 is intended to help applicants find their way through these problems by providing the latest possible information about university course offers from official sources, and by giving guidance and information about:

- **Degree courses** – what Honours level courses involve, the range and differences between them, and what applicants need to consider when choosing and deciding on subjects and courses
- **Universities and higher education colleges** – the range and differences between universities and colleges, and the questions applicants might ask when deciding where to study
- **Typical A/AS grade/UCAS points offers** (listed in points order in the Subject Tables in **Chapter 8**) for 2012 entry to Honours degree courses in universities and colleges, with additional Appendix data for applicants with IB, the Progression and Advanced Diplomas, the Extended Project, Scottish Highers, the Welsh Baccalaureate, the Irish Leaving Certificate and international qualifications
- **The UCAS applications process** – what to do, when to do it and how to prepare the personal statement in the UCAS application
- **Universities' and colleges' admissions policies** – how admissions tutors select students
- **Which universities, colleges and courses use admissions tests for entry**
- **Finance, fees and sources of help**
- **Graduate destinations data for each subject area**
- **Action after results day** – and what to do if your grades don't match your offer
- **Entry to UK universities and higher education colleges for international students**

University Degree Course Offers provides essential information for all students preparing to go into higher education in 2012, covering all stages of researching, planning, deciding and applying to courses and universities. To provide the latest possible information the book is compiled each year between October and March for publication in May and includes important data from the many universities and colleges responding to questionnaires each year.

Every effort is made to ensure the book is as up to date as possible. Nevertheless, the increased demand for places and cuts in the number of places available are expected to lead to offers changes during 2012/13, and after prospectuses have been published. Some institutions may also discontinue courses as a result of government cuts and the changes in tuition fees. It will be essential for applicants to check institutions' websites **frequently** to find out any changes in offers, course availability and requirements. If you have any queries, contact admissions staff without delay to find out the latest information as institutions, for many courses, will be looking for a very close, if not precise, match between their requirements and what you offer in your application, qualifications and grades.

University Degree Course Offers 2012 is your starting point for moving on into higher education and planning ahead. Used in conjunction with *Choosing Your Degree Course & University* and *University Scholarships, Awards & Bursaries* (see Appendix 5) it will take you through all the stages in choosing the course and place of study which is right for you.

Brian Heap
May 2011

Every effort has been made to maintain absolute accuracy in providing course information and to ensure that the entire book is as up-to-date as possible. However, changes are constantly taking place in higher education so it is important for readers to check carefully with prospectuses and websites before submitting their applications.

YOUR FIRST DECISIONS

HIGHER EDUCATION OR NOT?

Why do you want to go on to higher education? If you are taking GCE Advanced (AL) and Advanced Subsidiary (AS) qualifications, the International Baccalaureate, Scottish Highers and Advanced Highers, the Welsh Baccalaureate, the Cambridge Pre-U or the new Advanced Diploma this is an important question to ask. Last year there were 697,351 applicants, with 487,329 acceptances, for full-time first degree and diploma courses in the United Kingdom. However, higher education is just one of two options you have. Increasingly, with the shortage of university places, full-time employment is the other option and it's important to remember that higher education is not necessarily the best option for everyone, but it should not be rejected lightly. Higher education has the advantage however of opening many doors and giving you opportunities for work and leisure that otherwise you might not have. Also, very often and quite accidentally, it can lead into careers that you might not have considered before.

Choosing your AS/A-levels (or equivalent qualifications) is done on the basis of your best subjects and those which you find most interesting. However, leading universities (and, especially, those with popular and competitive courses) may seek a grouping of subjects with 'academic weight'. Usually at least two AS/A-level 'academic' subjects are preferred.

In some cases the following may not be regarded as strong academic subjects: accounting, art and design, business studies, communication studies, dance, design and technology, drama/theatre studies, film studies, health and social care, home economics, information and communication, leisure studies, media studies, music technology, performance studies, performing arts, photography, physical education, sports studies, technology, travel and tourism.

If you are taking two or more of these subjects at AS/A-level you should check with your preferred universities whether they will be accepted for your chosen course before you apply.

Most courses in higher education lead to a degree or a diploma and for either you will have to make a subject choice. This can be difficult because the universities alone offer over 1200 degree subjects and over 50,000 course combinations within the UCAS scheme. You have two main options:

A Choosing a course that is either similar to, or the same as, one (or more) of your examination subjects, or related to an interest outside the school curriculum, such as Anthropology, American Studies, Archaeology. See **Section A** below.

B Choosing a course in preparation for a future career, for example Medicine, Architecture, Engineering. See **Section B** below and also **Appendix 4**.

SECTION A

Choosing your course by examination subjects

Deciding your degree or diploma course on the basis of your A-level (or equivalent) subjects is a reasonably safe option since you are already familiar with the subjects themselves and what they involve. Inevitably, long-term career prospects will be of some concern, especially in a period of economic recession. However, it is important to remember that a degree in higher education gives you many skills, including for example, those for critical thinking, assessment and research and, for many occupations, the degree subject is often not as important as the degree itself. If you are taking science subjects, they can lead naturally on to a range of scientific careers, although many scientists follow non-science careers such as law and accountancy. If you are taking arts or social science subjects, remember that specialist training for most non-scientific careers often starts once you have your degree.

When choosing your degree course by examination subjects it is important to consider the subjects you are taking at A-level (or equivalent) as universities may 'require' or 'prefer' certain subjects for entry to some courses. To make sure you have the right subjects, check the course subject requirements in university/college prospectuses and on their websites. Many universities, especially those giving high level offers, have increasingly detailed A-level requirements, so it is very important that you find out the latest information. This also applies to GCSE subjects and grade requirements. When choosing AS-level subjects, students sometimes prefer to select those with a similar subject base, for example four science subjects, or four arts, or four humanities subjects. However, some institutions welcome one, or even two, contrasting subjects, even for specialist courses such as Medicine, providing the required subjects are also offered.

Subjects do not stand on their own, in isolation. Each subject you are taking is one of a much larger family. Each has many similarities to subjects studied in degree and diploma courses that you might never have considered, so before you decide finally on taking a subject to degree level read through the list of A-level subjects below, each followed by examples of degree courses in the same subject field which will give you some idea of degree courses with similarities to the subjects you might be taking. (These lists are also useful if you have to consider alternative courses after the examination results are published!)

Accounting Accountancy, Accounting, Actuarial Mathematics, Banking and Finance, Business Studies (Finance), Economics, Finance Investment and Risk, Financial Mathematics, Financial Software Engineering, Management Sciences, Mathematics. See also **Section B**.

Ancient history Archaeology, Biblical Studies, Classical Greek, Classics and Classical Civilisation, Latin, Middle and Near Eastern Studies.

Arabic Arabic. See also **Languages** below.

Archaeology Ancient History, Anthropology, Archaeological Sciences, Archaeology, Bioarchaeology, Classical Civilisation, Conservation of Objects in Museums and Archaeology, Egyptology, Geology, History, Marine Archaeology, Viking Studies. See also **Section B**.

Art and design Art, Fine Art, Furniture Design, Graphic Design, Photography, Textile Design, Theatre Design, Three Dimensional Design, Typography and Graphic Communication. See also **Section B**.

Bengali Bengali. See also **Languages** below.

Biblical Hebrew Hebrew, Religious Studies, Theology.

Biology Agricultural Sciences, Animal Behaviour, Audiology, Bioinformatics, Biological Sciences, Biology, Biomedical Sciences, Biotechnology, Dental Hygiene, Ecology and Conservation, Environmental Sciences, Genetics, Human Embryology, Infection and Immunity, Life Sciences, Medicine, Microbiology, Molecular Sciences, Natural Sciences, Physiology, Plant Biology, Veterinary Science, Zoology. See also **Section B**.

Business Accounting, Banking, Business Management, Business Statistics, Computing, Economics, Entrepreneurship, Finance, Hospitality Management, Human Resource Management, Information Systems, Logistics, Management Sciences, Marketing, Mathematics, Publishing, Retail Management, Transport Management, Web Design and Development. See also **Section B**.

Chemistry Biochemistry, Cancer Biology, Chemical Engineering, Chemical Physics, Chemistry, Dentistry, Environmental Sciences, Fire Engineering, Forensic Sciences, Medicinal Chemistry, Medicine, Microbiology, Natural Sciences, Nutritional Biochemistry, Pharmacology, Pharmacy, Veterinary Science, Virology and Immunology. See also **Section B**.

Chinese Chinese. See also **Languages** below.

Classics and classical civilisation Ancient History, Archaeology, Classical Studies, Classics, Greek (Classical), Latin.

Communication studies Advertising, Communication Studies, Drama, Education, English Language, Information and Library Studies, Journalism, Languages, Linguistics, Media and Communications, Psychology, Public Relations, Publishing, Speech Sciences. See also **Section B**.

UNDERGRADUATE

Get yourself on course

at Bath Spa University

With a wide range of courses and quality teaching, your path to future success starts here.

Make the first move

visit **bathspa.ac.uk**

or call **01225 875 875**

Computing Artificial Intelligence, Business Information Systems, Computer Engineering, Computer Science, Computing, Cybernetics, E-Commerce, Electronic Engineering, Games Technology, Intelligent Product Design, Multimedia Systems Engineering, Network Management and Security, Robotics, Software Engineering. See also **Section B**.

Critical thinking (Check acceptability with universities and colleges: subject may not be included in offers.)

Dance Arts Management, Ballet Education, Choreography, Dance, Drama, Education, Music, Musical Theatre, Performance Management, Performing Arts, Sport and Exercise, Street Arts, Theatre and Performance, Theatre Arts, Writing Directing and Performance. See also **Section B**.

Design technology Food Technology, Manufacturing Engineering, Product Design, Sport Equipment Design, Systems and Control. See also **Section B**.

Drama and theatre studies Acting, Community Drama, Costume Production, Creative Writing, Dance, Drama, Education Studies, English Comedy: Writing and Performance, International Theatre, Music, Performing Arts, Scenic Arts, Scriptwriting, Set Design, Stage Management, Theatre Arts, Theatre Practice. See also **Section B**.

Dutch Dutch. See also **Languages** below.

Economics Accountancy, Banking, Business Administration, Business Economics, Business Studies, Development Studies, Economics, Estate Management, Finance, Management Science, Mathematics, Political Economy, Politics, Quantity Surveying, Sociology, Statistics.

Electronics Computing, Electronics, Engineering (Aeronautical, Aerospace, Communication, Computer, Software, Systems), Mechatronics, Medical Electronics, Multimedia Technology, Technology. See also **Section B**.

English language and literature Communication Studies, Comparative Literature, Creative Writing, Drama, Education, English Language, English Literature, Information and Library Studies/Management, Journalism, Linguistics, Media Writing, Philosophy, Publishing, Scottish Literature, Scriptwriting, Theatre Studies.

Environmental sciences Biological Sciences, Biology, Earth Sciences, Ecology, Environment and Planning, Environmental Management, Environmental Sciences, Forestry, Geography, Geology, Land Management, Marine Biology, Meteorology, Oceanography, Outdoor Education, Plant Sciences, Sustainable Development, Wastes Management, Water Science, Wildlife Biology, Wildlife Conservation, Zoology.

French French, International Business Studies, International Hospitality Management, Law with French Law. See also **Languages** below.

General studies (Check acceptability with universities and colleges: subject may not be included in offers.)

Geography Development Studies, Earth Sciences, Environmental Policy, Environmental Sciences, Estate Management, Forestry, Geographical Information Science, Geography, Geology, Land Economy, Meteorology, Oceanography, Surveying, Town and Country Planning, Urban Studies, Water Science.

Geology Earth Sciences, Geography, Geology, Geophysical Sciences, Geosciences, Meteorology, Mining Engineering, Natural Sciences, Oceanography, Palaeontology and Evolution, Planetary Sciences, Water and Environmental Management. See also **Section B**.

German German, International Business Studies, International Hospitality Management, Law with German Law. See also **Languages** below.

Government/Politics Development Studies, Economics, Global Politics, Government, History, Human Rights, Industrial Relations, International Politics, Law, Peace Studies, Politics, Public Administration, Social and Political Science, Social Policy, Sociology, Strategic Studies, War Studies.

Gujarati Gujarati. See also **Languages** below.

Health and social care Early Childhood Studies, Environmental Health, Health and Social Care, Health Promotion, Health Psychology, Health Sciences, Health Studies, Nursing, Nutrition, Public Health, Social Sciences, Social Work, Sport and Health, Working with Children and Young People, Youth and Community Work. See also **Section B**.

History African Studies, American Studies, Ancient History, Archaeology, Art History, Classical Civilisations, Classical Studies, Education, Egyptology, Fashion and Dress History, History, International Relations, Law, Literature, Medieval Studies, Museum and Heritage Studies, Philosophy, Politics, Russian Studies, Scandinavian Studies, Scottish History, Social and Economic History, Theology and Religious Studies, Victorian Studies.

Home economics Culinary Arts Management, Design and Technology Education, Food and Consumer Management, Food Science, Home Economics (Food Design and Technology), Hospitality Management, Nutrition.

Information and communication technology Business Information Systems, Communications Systems Design, Communications Technology, Digital Communications, Electrical and Electronic Engineering, Geographic Information Science, Information and Library Studies, Information Management, Information Sciences, Information Systems, Internet Engineering, Mobile Computing, Multimedia Computing, Telecommunications Engineering. See also **Section B**.

Italian Italian. See also **Languages** below.

Japanese Japanese. See also **Languages** below.

Languages Languages, Modern Languages, Translating and Interpreting. **NB** Apart from French and German – and Spanish for some universities – it is not usually necessary to have completed an A-level language course before studying the many languages (over 60) offered at degree level. Many universities provide opportunities to study a language in a wide range of degree courses. See also **the Erasmus programme** details in **Chapter 5**.

Law Criminal Justice, Criminology, European Business Law, Human Rights, International Business, International Relations, Law, Legal Studies, Police Sciences, Social Sciences, Sociology, Youth Justice. See also **Section B**.

Leisure studies Adventure Tourism Management, Countryside Recreation and Tourism, Equine Business Management, Events Management, Fitness and Health, Health and Leisure Studies, Hospitality and Leisure Management, Leisure Marketing, Outdoor Leadership, Personal Fitness Training, Sport and Leisure Management, Sport Leisure and Culture, Sports Education, Tourism Management, Tourism Marketing.

Mathematics Accountancy, Actuarial Mathematics, Aeronautical Engineering, Astrophysics, Business Management, Chemical Engineering, Civil Engineering, Computational Science, Computer Systems Engineering, Control Systems Engineering, Cybernetics, Economics, Engineering Science, Ergonomics, Financial Mathematics, Further and Additional Mathematics, Geophysics, Management Science, Materials Science and Technology, Mechanical Engineering, Meteorology, Naval Architecture, Physics, Quantity Surveying, Statistics, Systems Analysis, Telecommunications.

Media studies Advertising, Animation, Broadcasting, Communication Studies, Creative Writing, English, Film and Television Studies, Journalism, Mass Communication, Media courses, Media Culture and Society, Media Production, Media Technology, Multimedia, Photography, Publishing, Radio Production and Communication, Society Culture and Media, Translation Media and French/Spanish, Web and Broadcasting. See also **Section B**.

Modern Greek Greek. See also **Languages** above.

Modern Hebrew Hebrew. See also **Languages** above.

Music Audio and Music Production, Creative Music Technology, Education, Music, Music Broadcasting, Music Informatics, Music Management, Music Systems Engineering, Musical Theatre, Musician, Performance Arts, Popular and World Musics, Sonic Arts. See also **Section B**.

Persian Persian. See also **Languages** above.

Philosophy Classical Studies, Cultural Studies, Divinity, Educational Studies, Ethics, History of Ideas, History of Science, Law, Mathematics, Natural Sciences, Philosophy, Politics Philosophy and Economics, Psychology, Religious Studies, Social Sciences, Theology.

Physics Aeronautical Engineering, Architecture, Astronomy, Astrophysics, Automotive Engineering, Biomedical Engineering, Biophysics, Chemical Physics, Civil Engineering, Communications Engineering, Computer Science, Cybernetics, Education, Electrical/Electronic Engineering, Engineering Science, Ergonomics, Geophysics, Materials Science and Technology, Mechanical Engineering, Medical Physics, Meteorology, Nanotechnology, Naval Architecture, Oceanography, Optometry, Photonics, Planetary Science, Quantum Informatics, Radiography, Renewable Energy, Telecommunications Engineering.

Polish Polish. See also **Languages** above.

Portuguese Portuguese. See also **Languages** above.

Psychology Advertising, Animal Behaviour, Anthropology, Artificial Intelligence, Behavioural Science, Childhood Strudies, Cognitive Science, Counselling Studies, Criminology, Education, Human Resource Management, Marketing, Neuroscience, Nursing, Politics, Psychology, Social Sciences, Sociology, Speech and Language Therapy. See also **Section B**.

Punjabi Punjabi. See also **Languages** above.

Religious studies Abrahamic Religions (Christianity, Islam and Judaism), Anthropology, Archaeology, Biblical Studies, Christian Youth Work, Comparative Religion, Divinity, Education, Ethics, History of Art, International Relations, Islamic Studies, Jewish Studies, Philosophy, Psychology, Religious Studies, Social Policy, Theology.

Russian Russian. See also **Languages** above.

Sport and physical education Chiropractic, Coaching Science, Community Sport Development, Dance Studies, Exercise and Health, Exercise Science, Fitness Science, Football Studies, Golf Studies, Osteopathy,

Outdoor Pursuits, Physical Education, Physiotherapy, Sport and Exercise Science, Sport and Health, Sport Coaching, Sport Equipment Design, Sport Management, Sport Marketing, Teaching (Primary) (Secondary).

Statistics Actuarial Studies, Business Analysis, Business Studies, Informatics, Management Sciences, Statistics. See also Mathematics above and **Section B** Mathematics-related careers.

Travel and tourism See **Section B**.

Turkish Turkish. See also **Languages** above.

Urdu Urdu. See also **Languages** above.

SECTION B
Choosing your course by career interests

An alternative strategy for deciding on the subject of your degree or diploma course is to relate it to your career interests. However, even though you may have set your mind on a particular career, it is important to remember that sometimes there are others which are very similar to your planned career. The following lists give examples of career areas, each followed by examples of degree subjects in the subject field.

Accountancy Accountancy, Accounting, Actuarial Science, Banking, Business Studies, Economics, Finance and Business, Finance and Investment, Financial Services, Management Science, Real Estate Management, Risk Management.

Actuarial work Actuarial Mathematics, Actuarial Science, Actuarial Studies, Financial Mathematics, Risk Analysis and Insurance.

Agricultural careers Agri-Business, Agricultural Engineering, Agriculture, Animal Sciences, Aquaculture and Fishery Sciences, Conservation and Habitat Management, Countryside Management, Crop Science, Ecology, Environmental Science, Estate Management, Forestry, Horticulture, Landscape Management, Plant Sciences, Rural Resource Management, Soil Science, Wildlife Management.

Animal careers Agricultural Sciences, Animal Behaviour and Welfare, Biological Sciences, Bioveterinary Science, Equine Management/Science/Studies, Veterinary Nursing, Veterinary Practice Management, Veterinary Science, Zoology.

Archaeology Ancient History, Anthropology, Archaeology, Bioarchaeology, Classical Civilisation and Classics, Egyptology, Geography, History, History of Art and Architecture, Viking Studies.

Architecture Architectural Design, Architectural Technology, Architecture, Building, Building Conservation, City and Regional Planning, Civil Engineering, Conservation and Restoration, Construction Engineering and Management, Interior Architecture, Stained Glass Restoration and Conservation, Structural Engineering.

Art and Design Careers Advertising, Animation, Architecture, Art, Design, Digital Media Design, Education (Art), Fashion and Textiles, Fine Art, Games Art and Design, Glassware, Graphic Design, Illustration, Industrial Design, Jewellery, Landscape Architecture, Photography, Stained Glass, Three Dimensional Design.

Astronomy Astronomy, Astrophysics, Mathematics, Natural Sciences, Planetary Geology, Physics, Quantum and Cosmological Physics, Space Science, Space Technology and Planetary Exploration.

Audiology Audiology, Education of the Deaf, Human Communication, Nursing, Speech and Language Therapy.

Banking/Insurance Accountancy, Actuarial Sciences, Banking, Business Studies, Economics, Financial Services, Insurance, Real Estate Management, Risk Management.

Biology-related careers Agricultural Sciences, Animal Sciences, Biochemistry, Biological Sciences, Biology, Biomedical Sciences, Biotechnology, Cell Biology, Ecology, Education, Environmental Biology, Environmental Sciences, Freshwater Science, Genetics, Immunology, Life Sciences, Marine Biology, Medical Biochemistry, Medicine, Microbiology, Molecular Biology, Natural Sciences, Oceanography, Pharmacy, Plant Science, Physiology, Wildlife Conservation.

Inspiring...
Fulfilling...
Enjoyable...

The Bournemouth and Poole College is a leading provider of Further and Higher Education and we focus on providing you with the skills, knowledge and confidence to improve your future prospects, either for continued study or employability.

We have an impressive range of courses and qualifications and if you choose to study a Higher Education course you are investing in your future, boosting your skills, employability and earning power.

Impressive benefits...

As a student at The Bournemouth and Poole College you will enjoy learning in a creative, supportive and welcoming environment. The College is exceptionally well resourced within each of the specialist faculties, and our staff are highly experienced professionals, with a great deal of subject expertise and knowledge.

Our courses are endorsed and designed in partnership with employers, which means that you have the confidence of learning the right skills that employers want to see in their workforce. Indeed, an integral part of your course will be a work placement or work based project, designed to give you invaluable experience to support your learning.

The majority of our Foundation Degrees are awarded by associate universities (mainly Bournemouth University). This means that as a student enrolled onto one of our Higher Education courses you are automatically entitled to utilise the facilities and resources at the partner university.

Living and learning...
having fun...

This part of Dorset is a great place to live, and a great place to learn. There is everything you would expect from a thriving and lively coastal resort, lots of shopping, entertainment, good restaurants, fantastic beaches and a buzzing nightlife.

This part of the south coast is also within easy reach of London (approx 2 hours by car or train), and within minutes you can be at the World Heritage Jurassic Coast or in the New Forest National Park.

There are many cultural avenues to explore, including excellent libraries, galleries and museums, plus theatres and cinemas. The Bournemouth International Centre and Poole's Lighthouse are both venues with a full calendar of shows and events, including many national tours for music gigs, comedy and leading shows.

For when you are not studying, you are welcome to join the Students' Union where you can get involved with events, social and leisure activities organised by The College's SU team or those at the partner university.

High Tech Digital Design Centre

Last Autumn saw the launch of the new Digital Design Centre a state of the art digital design learning space, created in response to the new national skills strategy. Working with Bournemouth University we enjoy an excellent reputation for our Computer Generated Imagery technologies and creating this space gives our students their own dedicated learning environment.

CGI Modelling and Animation

Claire is on the second year of the Foundation Degree at The Bournemouth and Poole College, which has an excellent reputation for this specialism.

Claire commented, *"I really liked the sound of the course, and it was something I had always wanted to do! The course is very practical and hands on which is great and I really enjoy the creative side of it. They are a good crowd of people to work with and the lecturers are supportive and encourage us to do well. It's great studying in the new Digital Design Centre which is a fantastic facility and resource for HE students. Generally the course is hard work but also great fun. I am not sure whether I will do the Top-up, but I would like to work on animated films when I'm qualified."*

www.thecollege.co.uk/highereducation   Aspire • Achieve • Succeed
The College helpline: 01202 205205   HE Unit: 01202 205180   Email: heunit@bpc.ac.uk

Book Publishing Advertising, Business Studies, Communications, Creative Writing, Illustration, Journalism, Media Communication, Photography, Printing, Publishing, Science Communication, Web and Multimedia.

Brewing and Distilling Biochemistry, Brewing and Distilling, Chemistry, Food Science and Technology, Viticulture and Oenology.

Broadcasting Audio Video and Digital Broadcast Engineering, Broadcast Documentary, Broadcast Media, Broadcast Technology and Production, Digital Media, Electronic Engineering (Broadcast Systems), Film and TV Broadcasting, Media and Communications Studies, Media Production, Multimedia, Music Broadcasting, Outside Broadcast Technology, Radio Journalism, Television Studio Production, TV Production, Video and Broadcasting.

Building Architecture, Building Conservation, Building Services Engineering, Building Studies, Building Surveying, Civil Engineering, Estate Management, General Practice Surveying, Land Surveying, Quantity Surveying.

Business Accountancy, Advertising, Banking, Business Administration, Business Analysis, Business Studies, Business Systems, E-Commerce, Economics, Estate Management, European Business, Hospitality Management, Housing Management, Human Resource Management, Industrial Relations, Insurance, Logistics, Management Sciences, Marketing, Property Development, Public Relations, Publishing, Supply Chain Management, Transport Management, Tourism.

Cartography Geographic Information Systems, Geographical Information Science, Geography, Land Surveying.

Catering Consumer Studies, Culinary Arts Management, Dietetics, Food Science, Hospitality Management, International and Hospitality Business Management, Nutrition.

Chemistry-related careers Agricultural Science, Biochemistry, Botany, Ceramics, Chemical Engineering, Chemistry, Colour Chemistry, Education, Environmental Sciences, Geochemistry, Materials Science and Technology, Medical Chemistry, Nanotechnology, Natural Sciences, Pharmacology, Pharmacy, Physiology, Technologies (for example Food, Plastics).

Computing Artificial Intelligence, Bioinformatics, Business Computing, Business Studies, Computer Engineering, Computer Games Development, Computer Science, Computers, Electronics and Communications, Digital Forensics and System Security, Electronic Engineering, Games Design, Information and Communication Technology, Internet Computing, Mathematics, Multimedia Computing, Physics, Software Systems, Telecommunications, Virtual Reality Design.

Construction Architectural Technology, Architecture, Building, Building Services Engineering, Civil Engineering, Construction Management, Fire Risk Engineering, Landscape Architecture, Quantity Surveying, Surveying, Town and Country Planning.

Dance Ballet Education, Choreography, Dance, Drama, Movement Studies, Performance/Performing Arts, Physical Education, Theatre Studies.

Dentistry Biochemistry, Dental Materials, Dental Technician, Dentistry, Equine Dentistry, Medicine, Nursing, Oral Health Sciences, Pharmacy.

Drama Dance, Drama, Education, Movement Studies, Musical Theatre, Scenic Arts, Teaching, Theatre Management.

Education Ballet Education, British Sign Language, Childhood Studies, Coach Education, Deaf Studies, Early Years Education, Education Studies, Education with QTS, Education without QTS, Music Education, Physical Education, Primary Education, Psychology, Secondary Education, Social Work, Special Educational Needs, Speech and Language Therapy, Sport and Exercise, Teaching, Technology for Teaching and Learning, Youth Studies.

Electronics Automotive Electronics, Avionics, Computer Systems, Computer Technology, Computing, Digital Electronics, Digital Media Technology, Electronic Design, Electronic Engineering, Electronics, Information Systems, Internet Engineering, Mechatronics, Medical Electronics, Motorsport Electronic Systems, Multimedia Computing, Software Development, Sound Engineering.

Engineering Engineering (including Aeronautical, Aerospace, Chemical, Civil, Computing, Control, Electrical, Electronics, Energy, Environmental, Food Process, Manufacturing, Mechanical, Motorsport, Nuclear, Product Design, Software, Telecommunications Electronics), Geology and Geotechnics, Horology, Mathematics, Physics.

Estate Management Architecture, Building, Civil Engineering, Economics, Estate Management, Forestry, Housing Studies, Landscape Architecture, Property Development, Real Estate Management, Town and Country Planning.

Food Science and Technology Biochemistry, Brewing and Distilling, Chemistry, Culinary Arts, Dietetics, Food and Consumer Studies, Food Safety Management, Food Science and Technology, Food Supply Chain Management, Fresh Produce Management, Hospitality and Food Management, Nutrition, Public Health Nutrition, Viticulture and Oenology.

Forestry Arboriculture, Biological Sciences, Countryside Management, Ecology, Environmental Science, Forestry, Horticulture, Plant Sciences, Rural Resource Management, Tropical Forestry, Urban Forestry.

Furniture Design Furniture Design, Furniture Production, History of Art and Design, Three Dimensional Design, Timber Technology.

Geology-related careers Chemistry, Earth Sciences, Engineering (Civil, Minerals), Environmental Sciences, Geochemistry, Geography, Geology, Land Surveying, Oceanography, Soil Science.

Graphic Design Advertising, Graphic Design, Photography, Printing, Web Design.

Health and Safety careers Biomedical Informatics, Biomedical Sciences, Community and Health Studies, Environmental Health, Exercise and Health Science, Fire Science Engineering, Health and Social Care, Health Management, Health Promotion, Health Psychology, Health Sciences, Holistic Therapy, Nursing, Occupational Safety and Health, Paramedic Science, Public Health, Public Services Management. (See also **Medical careers**.)

Horticulture Agriculture, Botany, Crop Science, Horticulture, Landscape Architecture, Plant Science, Soil Science.

Hospitality Management Business and Management, Culinary Arts Management, Events and Facilities Management, Food Science, Food Technology, Heritage Management, Hospitality Management, Human Resource Management, International Hospitality Management, Leisure Services Management, Licensed Retail Management, Spa Management, Travel and Tourism Management.

Housing Architecture, Estate Management, General Practice Surveying, Housing, Social Administration, Town and Country Planning.

Law Business Law, Commercial Law, Consumer Law, Criminal Justice, Criminology, European Law, Government and Politics, International History, Land Management, Law, Legal Studies, Politics, Sociology.

Leisure and Recreation Adventure Tourism, Airline and Airport Management, Business Travel and Tourism, Community Arts, Countryside Management, Dance, Drama, Event Management, Fitness Science, Hospitality Management, International Tourism Management, Leisure Management, Movement Studies, Music, Physical Education, Sport and Leisure Management, Sport Development, Sports Management, Theatre Studies, Travel and Tourism.

Library and Information Management Administration, Business Information Systems, Digital Media, Education Studies, Information and Communication Studies, Information and Library Studies, Information Management, Information Sciences and Technology, Management and Marketing, Media and Cultural Studies, Media Communications, Museum and Galleries Studies, Publishing.

Marketing Advertising, Business Studies, Consumer Science, E-Marketing, Health Promotion, International Business, Marketing, Psychology, Public Relations, Retail Management, Sports Development, Travel and Tourism.

Materials Science/Metallurgy Automotive Materials, Chemistry, Engineering, Glass Science and Technology, Materials Science and Technology, Mineral Surveying, Physics, Polymer Science, Sports Materials, Textile Science.

Mathematics-related careers Accountancy, Actuarial Science, Astronomy, Banking, Business Decision Mathematics, Business Studies, Computer Studies, Economics, Education, Engineering, Financial Mathematics, Mathematical Physics, Mathematics, Physics, Quantity Surveying, Statistics.

Media careers Advertising, Broadcasting, Communications, Computer Graphics, Creative Writing, Film/Video Production, Journalism, Media, Multimedia, Photography, Public Relations, Psychology, Visual Communication.

Medical careers Anatomy, Biochemistry, Biological Sciences, Biomedical Sciences, Chiropractic, Dentistry, Genetics, Human Physiology, Immunology, Medical Engineering, Medical Sciences/Medicine, Nursing, Occupational Therapy, Orthoptics, Osteopathy, Pathology and Microbiology, Pharmacology, Pharmacy, Physiotherapy, Radiography, Speech and Language Therapy, Sports Biomedicine, Virology.

Music Commercial Music, Creative Music Technology, Digital Music, Drama, Folk and Traditional Music, Music, Music Composition, Music Education, Music Industry Management, Music Performance, Music Production, Music Studies, Musical Theatre, Performance/Performing Arts, Popular Music, Sonic Arts, Sound and Multimedia Technology, Theatre Studies.

Nautical careers Marine Engineering, Marine Studies, Nautical Studies, Naval Architecture, Oceanography, Offshore Engineering, Ship Science.

Naval Architecture Boat Design, Marine Engineering, Marine Studies, Naval Architecture, Offshore Engineering, Ship Science, Yacht and Powercraft Design, Yacht Production.

Nursing Anatomy, Applied Biology, Biochemistry, Biological Sciences, Biology, Dentistry, Education, Environmental Health and Community Studies, Health Studies, Human Biology, Medicine, Midwifery, Nursing, Occupational Therapy, Orthoptics, Physiotherapy, Podiatry, Psychology, Radiography, Social Administration, Speech and Language Therapy, Veterinary Nursing. (See also **Medical careers**.)

Nutrition Dietetics, Food Science and Technology, Health Promotion, Human Nutrition, Nursing, Nutrition, Sport and Fitness.

Occupational Therapy Art, Nursing, Occupational Therapy, Orthoptics, Physiotherapy, Psychology, Social Sciences, Speech and Language Therapy.

Optometry Applied Physics, Optometry, Orthoptics, Physics.

Photography/Film/TV Animation, Communication Studies (some courses), Digital Video Design, Documentary Communications, Film and Media, Graphic Art, Media Studies, Moving Image, Multimedia, Photography.

Physics-related careers Applied Physics, Astronomy, Astrophysics, Avionics and Space Systems, Education, Electronics, Engineering (Civil, Electrical, Mechanical), Laser Physics, Mathematical Physics, Medical Instrumentation, Molecular Physics, Nanotechnology, Natural Sciences, Optometry, Physics, Planetary and Space Physics, Quantum and Cosmological Physics, Theoretical Physics.

Physiotherapy Chiropractic, Exercise Science, Nursing, Orthoptics, Osteopathy, Physical Education, Physiotherapy, Sport and Exercise, Sports Rehabilitation.

Production Technology Engineering (Mechanical, Manufacturing), Materials Science.

Property and Valuation Management Architecture, Building Surveying, Estate Agency, Property Investment and Finance, Property Management and Valuation, Quantity Surveying, Real Estate Management, Residential Property, Urban Land Economics.

Psychology Advertising, Animal Sciences, Anthropology, Applied Social Studies, Behavioural Science, Business, Cognitive Science, Criminology, Early Childhood Studies, Education, Human Resource Management, Human Sciences, Linguistics, Marketing, Neuroscience, Occupational Therapy, Psychology (Clinical, Developmental, Educational, Experimental, Forensic, Health, Occupational, Social, Sports), Psychosocial Sciences, Public Relations, Social Sciences, Sociology.

Public Administration Applied Social Studies, Business Studies, Public Administration, Public Policy Investment and Management, Public Services, Social Administration, Social Policy, Youth Studies.

Quantity Surveying Architecture, Building, Civil Engineering, Construction and Commercial Management Surveying Technology, Environmental Construction Surveying, Quantity Surveying, Surveying (Building, Land, Quantity and Valuation).

Radiography Anatomy, Audiology, Biological Sciences, Clinical Photography, Diagnostic Imaging, Diagnostic Radiography, Digital Imaging, Imaging Science and Technology, Medical Imaging, Moving Image, Nursing, Orthoptics, Photography, Physics, Physiology, Physiotherapy, Radiography, Radiotherapy, Therapeutic Radiography.

Silversmithing/Jewellery Design Silversmithing and Jewellery, Silversmithing Goldsmithing and Jewellery, Silversmithing Metalwork and Jewellery, Three Dimensional Design.

Social Work Abuse Studies, Applied Social Science, Community Work, Counselling Studies, Early Childhood Studies, Education, Health and Social Care, Human Rights, Journalism, Law, Nursing, Playwork, Politics and Government, Psychology, Public Administration, Religious Studies, Social Administration, Social Policy, Social Work, Sociology, Town and Country Planning, Youth Studies.

Speech and Language Therapy Audiology, Education (Special Education), Linguistics, Nursing, Occupational Therapy, Psychology, Radiography, Speech and Language Therapy.

Sport and Physical Education Coaching Sciences, Exercise Sciences, Fitness Science, Health and Fitness Management, Leisure and Recreation Management, Physical Education, Sport and Recreational Studies, Sport Journalism, Sports Psychology, Sports Science, Sports Studies.

Statistics Business Studies, Economics, Informatics, Mathematics, Operational Research, Population Sciences, Statistics.

Surveying Building Surveying, General Practice Surveying, Property Development, Quantity Surveying, Real Estate Management.

Technology Audio Technology, Dental Technology, Design Technology, Food Science and Technology, Football Technology, Logistics Technology, Medical Technology, Music Studio Technology, Paper Science, Polymer Science, Product Design Technology, Sports Technology, Technology for Teaching and Learning, Timber Technology.

Textile Design Applied Art and Design, Art, Clothing Studies, Fashion Design, Interior Design, Textile Design (Embroidery, Constructive Textiles, Printed Textiles), Textile Management.

Theatre Design Drama, Interior Design, Leisure and Recreational Studies, Theatre Design, Theatre Management, Theatre Studies.

Three Dimensional Design Architecture, Industrial Design, Interior Design, Theatre Design, Three Dimensional Design.

Town and Regional Planning Architecture, Architecture and Planning, City and Regional Planning, Environmental Planning, Estate Management, Geography, Housing, Land Economy, Planning and Development, Population Sciences, Property Planning and Development, Spatial Planning, Statistics, Sustainable Development, Town and Regional Planning, Transport Management, Urban and Regional Planning.

Transport Air Transport Engineering, Air Transport Operations, Air Transport with Pilot Training, Business Studies, Civil and Transportation Engineering, Cruise Operations Management, Industrial Design Transport, Logistics, Planning with Transport, Supply Chain Management, Sustainable Transport Design, Town and Regional Planning, Urban Planning Design and Management.

Typography and Graphic Communication Design (Graphic and Typographic Design), Digital Graphics, Fine Art (Print and Digital Media), Graphic Communication and Typography, Graphic Design, Illustration, Illustration and Print, Printmaking, Publication Design, Publishing, Visual Communication.

Veterinary careers Agricultural Sciences, Agriculture, Anatomical Science, Animal Behaviour and Welfare, Animal Sciences, Bioveterinary Sciences, Equine Dentistry, Equine Science, Medicine, Pharmacology, Pharmacy, Veterinary Medicine, Veterinary Nursing, Veterinary Practice Management, Zoology.

COURSE TYPES AND DIFFERENCES

You will then need to decide on the type of course you want to follow. The way in which Honours degree courses are arranged differs between institutions. For example, a subject might be offered as a single subject course (a Single Honours degree), or as a two-subject course (a Joint Honours degree), or as one of two, three or four subjects (a Combined Honours degree) or a major–minor degree (75% and 25% of each subject respectively). The chapter **University Course Profiles** gives more information about the different types of courses and provides for each university a resumé of the ways their courses are structured and the range of courses they offer.

Courses in the same subject at different universities and colleges can have different subject requirements so it is important to check the acceptability of your GCE A/AS and GCSE subjects (or equivalent) for all your preferred courses. Specific GCE A/AS-levels, and in some cases, GCSE subjects, may be stipulated. (See also **Chapter 7** and **Appendix 1** for information on the International Baccalaureate, Scottish Highers/ Advanced Highers, the Welsh Baccalaureate, the Cambridge Pre-U Diploma, the Advanced Diploma, the Extended Project Qualification and the Irish Leaving Certificate, and **Appendix 2** for international qualifications.)

SANDWICH COURSES AND PROFESSIONAL PLACEMENTS

One variation on Single Honours courses is that of the sandwich course, in which students will spend part of their degree course on professional, industrial or commercial placements. Media coverage on student debt and the introduction of tuition fees (see **Chapter 2**) highlight the importance of sandwich courses. Many sandwich and placement courses are on offer, in which industrial, commercial and public sector placements take place, usually, in the third year of a four-year degree course. There is also a Work-Based Learning (WBL) programme, which Chester University established several years ago, with some other institutions following suit, in which students take a WBL module in the second year of their degree course. This involves a placement lasting a few weeks when students can have the opportunity to try out possible careers. Other universities and colleges may offer longer placements of periods of six months with different employers for students taking vocational courses.

However, the most structured arrangements are known as 'professional placements' which a number of universities offer and which are very advantageous to students (see the subject tables in **Chapter 8** and university/college websites and prospectuses). Although placements in some fields such as health, social care, education may be unpaid, in most cases a salary is paid. Where a placement is unpaid the placement period is shorter – 30 weeks – to allow students time to undertake paid work. It is important to note that during the placement year students' tuition fees will be reduced by 50% except for those on one-year courses on the Erasmus programme (see **Chapter 5**) when no fees are paid but student loans will still apply.

The advantages of sandwich courses are quite considerable although students should be aware that in the present period of recession safeguards are necessary when selecting courses and universities. While students can arrange their own placement, with the approval of their Head of Department, it is more usual for university staff to make contacts with firms and to recommend students. With the present cutbacks, however, some firms may be less likely to take on students or to pay them during their placement. This is an important issue to raise with admissions tutors before applying and it is important also to find out how your studies would continue if placements are not possible. To help you to consider the advantages of sandwich courses, included below are views of some students, employers and university staff. They could well help you decide whether a four-year sandwich course is, for you, preferable to a three-year full-time degree.

Students report...

'I was able to earn £15,000 during my year out and £4000 during my three-month vacation with the same firm.' (**Bath** Engineering)

'There's really no other better way to find out what you want to do for your future career than having tried it for a year.' (**Aston** Human Resources Management)

'It was a welcome break in formal university education: I met some great people including students from other universities.' (**Kingston** Biochemistry)

'Having experienced a year in a working environment, I am more confident and more employable than students without this experience.' (**Aston** Business Studies)

'At Sanolfi in Toulouse, I learned to think on my feet – no two days were the same.' (**Aston** European Studies)

'I have seen how an organisation works at first-hand, learned how academic skills may be applied in a working environment, become proficient in the use of various software, acquired new skills in interpersonal relationships and communications and used my period away to realign my career perspectives.' (**Aston** European Studies)

'I was working alongside graduate employees and the firm offered me a job when I graduated.' (**Bath** Mathematics)

Employers, too, gain from having students ...
'We meet a lot of enthusiastic potential recruits who bring new ideas into the firm, and we can offer them commercially sponsored help for their final year project.'

'The quality of this student has remained high throughout the year. He will do well for his next employer, whoever that may be. However, I sincerely hope that it will be with us.'

University staff advise ...
'We refer to sandwich courses as professional placements, not "work experience" which is a phrase we reserve for short non-professional experiences, for example summer or pre-university jobs. The opportunity is available to all students but their success in gaining a good placement depends on academic ability.' (**Bath**)

'Where a placement year is optional, those who opt for it are more likely to be awarded a First or an Upper Second compared to those who don't, not because they are given more marks for doing it, but because they always seem to have added context and motivation for their final year.' (**Aston**)

When choosing your sandwich course, check with the university (a) that the institution will guarantee a list of employers (b) whether placement experience counts towards the final degree result (c) that placements are paid (d) that placements are validated by professional bodies. Finally, once you start on the course, remember that your first-year academic performance will be taken into account by potential employers. Now read on!

What do employers require when considering students?
Aston (Biol) Successful second year undergraduates; (Bus) Number of UCAS points, degree programme, any prior experience; (Eng) UCAS points scores and expected degree classification; (Mech Eng) Students interviewed and selected by the company according to student ability, what they are studying and specific needs of the job. **Bath** (Chem) 'Good students': Upper Second or above and non-international students (those without work visas). Students with strong vivisection views rejected; (Mech Elec Eng) Subject-based, eg electronics, aerospace, computing and electrical engineering; (Mech Eng) Good communication, IT and social skills; (Maths) Interest in positions of responsibility, teamwork, integrity, self-motivation, analytical ability, communication, recent work experience, knowledge of the company, desire to work for the company; GCSE maths/English A/B, AL 300 UCAS points minimum (excluding general studies), predicted 2.1; (Phys) Many organisations have cut-offs regarding students' first-year performance (eg must be heading for a 2.1 although some require better than this), some need students to be particularly good in some areas (eg lab work, computer programming), many require UK nationality with minimum residency condition. **Brunel** Requirements not usually specified except for IT jobs since they need technical skills. **Cardiff (UWIC)** (Clsrm Asst) Criminal Records Bureau (CRB) checks. **Kingston** (Bus Law) Theoretical knowledge and a stated interest in certain areas (eg finance, human resources, marketing, sales, IT), excellent communication skills, teamwork, ability to prioritise, time management and a professional attitude; (Sci) Grades are rarely mentioned: it's usually a specific module or course requirement undertaken by the students that they are looking for, as well as a good attitude, motivation, initiative: a good all-rounder. **Loughborough** (Civ Eng) Target specific courses.

What are the advantages of placements to the students?
Aston (Biol) Many take jobs with their placement employers (eg NHS), gaining valuable research and clinical experience; (Bus) Graduate job offers, sponsorship through the final year of the course, gym

membership, staff discounts; (Eng) Some students are fast-tracked into full-time employment and, in some cases, have been given higher starting salaries as a result of the placement with the company; (Mech Eng) Offers of full-time employment on graduation, bursaries for their final year of study, final year projects following placements, better class of degree. **Bath** (Chem) Sponsorships for final year project work, offers of full-time employment, PhD offers and work-to-study courses, industrial references, establishment of prizes; (Maths) Sponsorship in the second year, graduate employment, bonuses during placement, travel abroad during placement, sponsorship during final year; (Phys) Job offers on graduation, sponsored final year, improved study skills for final year, job market awareness, career decisions. **Brunel** Higher percentage of students get Firsts, many students get a job offer from the placement provider, higher salaries often paid to sandwich course students, some students get exemptions from professional exams, eg ACCA, ACA and IMechE. **Cardiff (UWIC)** (Clsrm Asst) Good experience in team work, classroom experience, coaching, mentoring: decisions made whether or not to follow a teaching career. **Kingston** (Bus Law) Sponsorships fewer these days but students return with more confidence and maturity and better able to complete their final year; 60% receive job offers on completion of a successful placement; (Sci) Full-time employment on graduation and occasionally part-time work in the final year; many students are encouraged to write their final year dissertation whilst on placement and benefit from the company's support, subject matter and validation. **Loughborough** (Civ Eng) Most students are sponsored by their firms and perform better in their final examinations; (Prod Des) Final year bursary for some students, offer of employment by the sponsor and a final year design project for the sponsor.

MATURE APPLICANTS

There are a great many mature students following first degree courses in UK universities and colleges. The following is a list of key points a group of mature students found useful in exploring and deciding on a university course.

- Check with your nearest university or college to find out about the courses they can offer, for example degrees, diplomas, full-time, part-time.
- Some institutions will require examination passes in some subjects, others may not.
- An age limit may apply for some vocational courses, for example Medicine, Dentistry and Teaching.
- If entry requirements are an obstacle, prospective students should approach their local colleges for information on Access or Open College courses. These courses are fast-growing in number and popularity, offering adults an alternative route into higher education other than A-levels. They are usually developed jointly by colleges of further education and the local higher education institution.
- Demands of the course – how much time will be required for study? What are the assignments and the deadlines to be met? How is your work assessed – unseen examinations, continuous assessment, practicals?
- The demands on finance – cost of the course – loan needed – loss of earnings – drop in income if changing to another career – travel requirements – accommodation – need to work part-time for income?
- The availability and suitability of the course – geographical location – competition for places – where it will lead – student support services, for example childcare, library.
- What benefits will you derive? Fulfilment, transferable skills, social contacts, sense of achievement, enjoyment, self-esteem, career enhancement?
- Why would employers want to recruit you? Ability to adapt to the work scene, realistic and balanced approach, mature attitude to work?
- Why would employers not want to recruit you? Salary expectations, inability to fit in with younger colleagues, limited mobility? However, some employers particularly welcome older graduates: Civil Service, local authorities, Health Service, religious, charitable and voluntary organisations, teaching, social/probation work, careers work, housing.

MODULAR COURSES AND CREDIT ACCUMULATION AND TRANSFER SCHEMES (CATS)

Courses can also differ considerably not only in their content but in how they are organised. Many universities and colleges of higher education have modularised their courses which means you can choose modules of different subjects, and 'build' your course within specified 'pathways' with the help and approval of your course tutor. It also means that you are likely to be assessed after completing each module, rather than in your last year for all your previous years' learning. In almost every course the options and modules offered include some which reflect the research interests of individual members of staff. In some courses subsidiary subjects are available as minor courses alongside a Single Honours course. In an increasing number of courses these additional subjects include a European language, and the importance of this cannot be over-emphasised with the United Kingdom's membership of the European Union. Such links are also reinforced by way of the Erasmus Programme (see **Chapter 5**) which enables university students to apply for courses in Europe for periods of up to a year, some of the courses being taught in English. Many institutions have introduced credit accumulation and transfer schemes (CATS). These allow students to be awarded credits for modules or units of study they have successfully completed which are accumulated towards a certificate, diploma or degree. They can also put their completed modules towards higher education study in other universities or colleges. Students wanting to transfer their credits should talk to the admissions office of the university they want to enter as there may be additional special subjects or module requirements for the degree they want to study.

FOUNDATION DEGREES AND FOUNDATION COURSES

Foundation courses, not be confused with Foundation degrees, normally require two years' full-time study, or longer for part-time study. They are also often taught in local colleges and may be taken part-time to allow students to continue to work. In comparison a Foundation degree can lead into the second or final year of related Honours degree courses when offered by the university validating the Foundation degree. Two-year Higher National Diplomas will also qualify for entry into the second or final year of degree courses. These, too, are often offered at universities as well as colleges of further education and partnership colleges linked to universities.

Part-time degrees and lifelong learning or distance learning courses are also often available and details of these can be found on university websites and in prospectuses. Some universities publish separate prospectuses for part-time courses.

NEXT STEPS

When choosing your course remember that one course is not better than another – it is just different. The best course for you is the one which best suits you. To give some indication of the differences between courses, see **Chapter 3** and also *Choosing Your Degree Course & University*, the companion book to *Heap 2012: University Degree Course Offers* (see **Appendix 5**). After provisionally choosing your courses, read the prospectuses again carefully to be sure that you understand what is included in the three, four or more years of study. Each institution differs in its course content even though the course titles may be the same and courses differ in other ways, for example:

- methods of assessment (eg unseen examinations, continuous assessment, project work, dissertations)
- contact time with tutors
- how they are taught (for example, frequency and size of lectures, seminars)
- practicals; field work requirements
- library, computing, laboratory and studio facilities
- amount of free study time available.

These are useful points of comparison between courses in different institutions when you are on an open day visit or making final course choices. Other important factors to consider when comparing courses include the availability of opportunities for studying and working abroad during your course, professional body accreditation of courses leading to certain professional careers (see **Appendix 4**) and in the career destinations of their graduates.

Once you have chosen your course subject(s) and the type of course you want to follow, the next step is to find out about the universities and colleges offering courses in your subject area, how much a higher education course will cost you and what financial help is available. The next chapter, **University Choice and Finance** provides information to help you do this.

TAKING A GAP YEAR

Choosing your course is the first decision you need to make, the second is choosing your university and then, for an increasing number, the third is deciding whether or not to take a Gap Year. But there lies the problem. Because of the very large number of things to do and places to go, you'll find that you almost need a Gap Year to choose the right one (although a read through *Your Gap Year* by Susan Griffith (see **Appendix 5**) is a good place to start)!

Planning ahead is important but, in the end, bear in mind that you might be overtaken by events, not least in failing to get the grades you need for a place on the course or at the university you were counting on. This could mean repeating A-levels and re-applying, which in turn could mean waiting for interviews and offers and, possibly, deferring the start of your 'gap' until February or March.

Once you have decided to go, however, it's a question of whether you will go under your own steam or through a Gap Year agency. Unless you are streetwise, or preferably 'world wise', then an agency offers several advantages. Some agencies may cover a broad field of opportunities whilst others will focus on a specific region and activity, such as the African Conservation Experience, offering animal and plant conservation work in game and nature reserves in southern Africa.

When making the choice, some students will always prefer a 'do-it-yourself' arrangement. However, there are many advantages to going through specialist agencies. Not only can they offer a choice of destinations and opportunities but also they can provide a lot of essential and helpful advice before your departure on issues such as health precautions and insurance. Support is also available in the case of accidents or illnesses when a link can be established between the agency and parents.

Finally in order to enhance your next university or college application, applying for a job for the year could be an even better option than spending a year travelling. Not only will it provide you with some financial security but it will also introduce you to the world of work, which could be more challenging than the Inca Trail!

CHOOSING YOUR UNIVERSITY OR COLLEGE
Location, reputation and Open Days

For many applicants the choice of university or college is probably the main priority, with location being a key factor. However, many students have little or no knowledge of regional geography and have no concept of where universities are located: one student thought that Bangor University (situated in North Wales) was located at Bognor on England's south coast!

Some institutions – probably those nearest home or those farthest away – will be rejected quickly. In addition to the region, location and immediate surroundings of a university or college, applicants have their own individual priorities – perhaps a hectic city life or, alternatively, a quiet life in the country! But university isn't all about studying, so it's not a bad idea to link your leisure interests with what the university or college can offer or with the opportunities available in the locality. Many applicants have theatrical, musical or artistic interests while others have sporting interests and achievements ranging from basketball, cricket and football to riding, rowing, sailing, mountaineering, and even fishing for England!

Some other decisions about your choice of university or college, however, could be made for the wrong reasons. Many students, for example, talk about 'reputation' or base their decisions on league tables. Reputations are fairly clear-cut in the case of some institutions. Oxford and Cambridge are both top world-class universities in which all courses have been established for many years and are supported by first class facilities. In other universities certain subjects are predominant, such as the social sciences at the London School of Economics, and the sciences and technologies at Imperial London.

Many other leading universities in the UK are also very strong in some subjects but not necessarily in all. This is why it is wrong to conclude that a 'university has a good reputation' – most universities are not necessarily good at everything! In seeking advice, you should also be a little wary of school staff who will usually always claim that their own university or college has a 'good reputation'. Teachers obviously can provide good advice on the courses and the general atmosphere of their own institution, but they are not in a good position to make comparisons with other universities.

The best way to find out about universities and colleges and the courses that interest you is to visit your preferred institutions. Open Days provide the opportunity to talk to staff and students although, with thousands of students wandering round campuses, it may be difficult to meet and talk to the right people. Also, many institutions hold Open Days during vacations when many students are away which means that you may only hear talks from the staff, and not have any opportunity to meet students. However, it is often possible to visit a university or college in your own time and simply 'walk in'. Alternatively, a letter to the head of department requesting a visit could enable you to get a closer look at the subject facilities. But failing this, you will be invited automatically to visit when you receive an offer and then you can meet the students in the department.

ACTION POINTS
Before deciding on your preferred universities and courses check out the following points:

Teaching staff
How do the students react to their tutors? Do staff have a flair and enthusiasm for their subject? Are they approachable? Do they mark your work regularly and is the feedback helpful, or are you left to get on with your own work with very little direction? What are the research interests of the staff?

Teaching styles

How will you be taught, for example, lectures, seminars, tutorials? Are lectures popular? If not, why not? How much on-line learning will you have? How much time will you be expected to work on your own? If there are field courses, how often are they arranged and are they compulsory? How much will they cost?

Facilities

Are the facilities of a high standard and easily available? Is the laboratory equipment 'state of the art' or just adequate? Are the libraries well-stocked with software packages, books and journals? What are the computing facilities? Is there plenty of space to study or do rooms and workspaces become overcrowded? Do students have to pay for any materials?

New students

Are there induction courses for new students? What student services and facilities are available? Is it possible to buy second-hand copies of set books?

Work placements

Are work placements an optional or compulsory part of the course? Who arranges them? Are the placements popular? Do they count towards your degree? Are work placements paid? How long are they?

Transferable skills

Transferable skills are now regarded as important by all future employers. Does the department provide training in communication skills, teamwork, time-management and information technology as part of the degree course?

Accommodation

How easy is it to find accommodation? Where are the halls of residence? Are they conveniently located for libraries and lecture theatres? Are they self-catering? Alternatively, what is the cost of meals in the university refectory? Which types of student accommodation are the most popular? What is the annual cost of accommodation? If there is more than one campus, is a shuttle-bus service provided?

Costs

Find out the costs of materials, accommodation and travel in addition to tuition fees (see below) and your own personal needs. What are the opportunities for earning money, on or off campus? Does the department or faculty have any rules about part-time employment?

FINANCE: WHAT WILL IT COST AND WHAT HELP IS THERE?
Tuition fees and other costs

Tuition fees are charged for degree courses in England, Wales and Northern Ireland. The level of tuition fees for courses has in the past been decided annually and has varied between institutions. However as a result of recent Government decisions a rise in the cost of tuition fees is planned to come into effect for students commencing courses in 2012. Maintenance grants and loans will still be available

Specific details of the charges to be made by individual universities will not be available until later in the year, and will be published on websites, but depending on the popularity of universities and certain courses the maximum charge will be £9000, although some institutions will charge a lower level of fees of up to £6000. In the past students domiciled in Scotland have received free tuition although tuition fees may be introduced for Scottish universities and decisions are awaited.

Students starting their courses in 2012 should check university and college websites, and websites listed in this section, for the latest information about fees, as this was not available at the time this book went to press.

You may also have additional charges, depending on your course of study. For example, studio fees for Art courses could reach £300 per year, while for other courses, such as Architecture, Science and Engineering, there could be charges for equipment. Additionally, there could also be charges for fieldwork trips, study abroad and vacation courses. To find out your likely yearly course costs, in addition to your tuition fees, check with your subject department.

Also, check your fee status if you are planning a sandwich course involving either unpaid or paid placements. You can receive a salary of up to £12,000 doing a one-year placement but if you earn more than this you'll need to check your fee status carefully with your finance officer and consult the relevant websites listed below.

Loans Students will not have to pay tuition fees before starting their courses or while they are studying. Depending on their household income, students either have their tuition fees paid or they will be able to take out a student loan to pay for their fees. Loan repayments are made only after graduation and currently when annual earnings are more than £15,000. From 2012 the earnings threshold for making loan repayments will increase to £21,000 per year and this figure will be reviewed annually.

University scholarships These are usually merit-based and are often competitive although some universities offer valuable scholarships to any new entrant who has achieved top grades at A-level. Scholarships vary considerably and are often subject-specific, offered through faculties or departments, so check the availability of any awards with the subject departmental head. Additionally, there are often music, choral and organ awards, and scholarships and bursaries for sporting achievement. Entry scholarships are offered by several universities which normally stipulate that the applicant must place the university as their first choice and achieve the specified high grades. Changes in bursaries and scholarships take place every year so it is important to check university and college websites.

University bursaries These are usually paid in cases of financial need: all universities charging course fees are obliged to offer some bursaries to students receiving maintenance grants. The term 'bursary' is usually used to denote an award to students requiring financial assistance or who are disadvantaged in various ways. Universities are committed to fair access to all students from lower income backgrounds and individual universities and colleges have bursaries, trust funds and sponsorships for those students receiving maintenance grants, although reports suggest that many such students fail to claim the money due to them. These non-repayable awards are linked to the size of the maintenance grant students receive and vary between universities.

Living costs

Most students spend their first year in university accommodation. This is usually the highest single cost in a typical weekly budget and the costs will vary considerably between universities. Rooms may be single or shared and include catering or self-catering arrangements. Outside university in the private sector additional costs are likely to include heating, electricity, hot water and water rates.

In addition, other living expenses will need to be considered. These include insurance, healthcare, food, books and stationery, photocopying, computing and telephone calls, clothes and toiletries, local travel, travel to and from university, entertainment, socialising and sport or leisure activities.

Help towards living costs

Maintenance grants These government grants are available but depend on the student's household income. They are paid on a sliding scale to students where the family income is (currently) between £25,000 and £42,600: the maximum grant is £3250 per annum for 2012. These grants are not repayable. Loans to help towards living costs are also available, and details of these are found on the websites listed below. In addition, price reductions are often available for students at some shops, restaurants, cinemas, museums and galleries. Contact the University Student Union before or when you arrive to find out more about these arrangements.

Other financial support

Many major organisations also provide financial help to those in various categories. These include the Lawrence Atwell's Charity for refugee young people from low income backgrounds, the Prince's Trust for disadvantaged young people aged between 14 and 25, and grants of up to £2000 for the disabled from the Snowdon Award Scheme.

Similarly, many scholarships are also offered by professional, commercial and other organisations. These include the armed services and the engineering professional organisations, particularly those specialising in civil or mechanical engineering, and also the Institute of Materials, Minerals and Mining. There are also sponsorships in which the student joins a firm on leaving school, combining university study with work experience and with an almost guaranteed offer of full-time employment on graduation. And there is the alternative route of taking a sandwich course and being placed with a firm for a year on full pay, often up to £14,000 (see **Chapter 1**).

Some universities also offer additional bursaries to encourage applications from the locality. These may be available to students applying from partner schools or colleges and living in certain postcode areas, in some cases to the brothers and sisters of current students at the university, or to students who have been in care or are homeless. These awards are not repayable.

In addition, students on some health-related courses, for example Dental Hygiene, Nursing, Occupational Therapy, Physiotherapy, Radiography will be eligible for NHS bursaries. Other bursaries are also payable for programmes funded through the General Social Care Council and also for shortage subjects for those on teacher training courses.

After starting the course, Access to Learning funds are available to help students in financial hardship or through emergency payments for unexpected financial crises. Hardship funds are also offered in very special cases, particularly to students with children or to single parents, mature students and, in particular, to students with disabilities who may also claim Disability Living Allowance. These payments are made in instalments or as a lump sum or as a short-term loan.

Useful websites   Students from England www.direct.gov.uk/studentfinance
Students from Scotland www.student-support-saas.gov.uk
Students from Wales www.studentfinancewales.co.uk
Students from Northern Ireland www.studentfinanceni.co.uk

For comprehensive finance information see the useful websites above, *University Scholarships, Awards and Bursaries* and other sources listed in **Appendix 5**.

INFORMATION SOURCES

Prospectuses, websites and Open Days are key sources of the information you need to decide where to study and at the back of this book a directory of institutions is provided, with full contact details, for you to use in your research. Other sources of information include the books and websites listed in **Appendix 5**, the professional associations listed in **Appendix 4**, and the websites given in the subject tables in **Chapter 8**. It is important to take time to find out as much as you can about your preferred universities, colleges and courses, and to explore their similarities and differences. The following chapter **University Course Profiles** gives you information about the types of courses offered by each university and how they are organised. This is important information that you need to know when choosing your university or college because those factors affect, for example, the amount of choice you have in what you study, and the opportunities you have for sandwich placements (see **Chapter 1**). You therefore need to read **Chapter 3** to give you an insight into universities so that you can find the one that is right for you.

3

UNIVERSITY COURSE PROFILES

UNIVERSITIES AND THEIR COURSES

Choosing a degree subject is one step of the way to higher education (see **Chapter 1**), choosing a university or college is the next stage (see **Chapter 2** and directory of institutions on page 593). However, in addition to such features as location, entry requirements, accommodation, students' facilities and the subjects offered, many universities differ in the way they organise and teach their courses. The course profiles which follow aim to identify the main course features of each of the universities and to provide some brief notes about the types of courses they offer and how they differ.

Although universities have their own distinct identities and course characteristics, they have many similarities. Apart from full-time and sandwich courses, one-year foundation courses are also offered in many subjects which can help the student to either convert or build on existing qualifications to enable them to start an Honours degree programme. All universities also offer one-year international foundation courses for overseas students to provide a preliminary introduction to courses and often to provide English language tuition.

COURSE PROFILES

Aberdeen Students applying for the MA degree in Arts and Social Sciences are admitted to a degree rather than a subject. Students select from a range of courses in the first year, leading up to the final choice of subject and Honours course in the fourth year. The BSc degree is also flexible but within the Science framework. Engineering students follow a common core course in Years 1 and 2, specialising in Year 3. There is less flexibility, however, in some vocational courses such as Accountancy, Law, Medicine and Dentistry. For some degree programmes, highly qualified applicants may be admitted to the second year of the course. Other courses cover Divinity and Theology, Education and Music.

Abertay Dundee Courses have a strong vocational bias and are offered in the Schools of Arts, Media and Computing, Creative Technologies, Business, Contemporary Sciences and Social and Health Sciences. Four-year courses are offered on a modular basis. Sandwich courses may be either thick (one-year placement) or thin (two six-month placements) and placements are usually at the end of the second and/or third years.

Aberystwyth The University offers Single, Joint and major/minor Honours courses on a modular basis. In Part 1 (Year 1) core topics related to the chosen subject are studied alongside optional subjects. This arrangement allows some flexibility for change when choosing final degree subjects in Part 2 (Years 2 and 3). Some students take a year in industry or commerce between Years 2 and 3. Courses include Accountancy, Agriculture, the Arts and Humanities, Business, Economics, Computer Science, Education, Law, Languages, Management and Marketing, Mathematics, the Sciences, Sport, Theatre and TV Studies, and Welsh and Celtic Studies.

Anglia Ruskin Courses are modular which enables students to choose from a range of subject topics in addition to the compulsory subject core modules. Single and Combined Honours courses are offered in the Faculties of Arts, Law and Social Sciences, Science and Technology, Health and Social Care, Education, and in the Business School. Many programmes have a strong vocational focus, with some opportunities to study abroad.

Arts London The University is Europe's largest institution offering courses in Art and Design, Communication and Performing Arts, focusing on creativity and practice in a large number of specialist fields.

Aston The University offers modular courses in Single Honours degrees (one subject), Joint Honours (two subjects, usually in related areas) and in Combined Honours and interdisciplinary studies in which programmes are organised across different subjects. Combined Honours courses may be weighted

50%–50%, and major/minor programmes weighted 67% for the major element and 33% for the minor. A distinctive feature of Aston is that most degrees allow students to spend the third year on a one-year sandwich placement; 70% of students follow sandwich courses or study-abroad programmes, leading to a high percentage of employed graduates. Courses are taught in the Schools of Engineering and Applied Science, Languages and Social Sciences, Life and Health Sciences and in the Aston Business School.

Bangor Modular courses are offered in Single and Joint Honours programmes. A broad and flexible programme is taken in Level 1 (Year 1) with the opportunity to study modules outside the chosen subject including a language. This is followed by greater specialisation in Levels 2 and 3. Courses include Agriculture and Forestry, Arts subjects, Business and Management, Computer Science and Electronics, Creative Studies, Education, Archaeology, History, Law, Health Studies, Languages, Music, Psychology, Biological Sciences, Chemistry, Ocean Sciences, Geography, Social Sciences, Sport and Religious Studies. Contrary to popular belief, two-thirds of the students come from outside Wales and all courses are taught in English.

Bath The academic year is divided into two semesters with Single and Combined Honours degrees composed of core units and optional units, allowing students some flexibility in shaping their courses with 10–12 units taken each year. A central feature of all programmes is the opportunity to take a sandwich course as part of the degree: this is usually taken as either one 12-month placement or two periods of six months. Courses are offered in the Faculties of Engineering and Design, Humanities and Social Sciences, Science, Sport and the School of Management.

Bath Spa Most courses – for Single awards, specialised awards and Combined awards – are part of a flexible modular scheme with students taking six modules each year. Some modules are compulsory but there is a good range of optional modules. The wide range of courses on offer include Biology, Business and Management, Creative Studies, Cultural Studies, Dance, Drama, Education, English Literature, Food Studies, Geography, Health Studies, History, Media Communications, Music, Psychology, Sociology and Study of Religions.

Bedfordshire This university offers BA and BSc undergraduate, Foundation and Extended degrees in Advertising, Marketing and Communications, Art and Design, Biosciences, Business, Computing, Journalism, Law, Media, Nursing, Psychology, Social Sciences, Sport and Leisure and Tourism. Most of the courses are vocational, some of which offer a placement year in industry or commerce.

Birmingham Courses cover Arts subjects (including Drama), Social Sciences, Business and Commerce, Education, Engineering, Law, Life and Environmental Sciences, Medicine and Dentistry and Health Sciences. Single subject and Joint Honours courses are offered. In Joint Honours courses the two chosen subjects may have common ground or can be very disparate, for example technology and a modern language. Some major/minor combinations are also possible. The modular system provides opportunities for students to study a subject outside their main degree.

Birmingham City Courses are offered through the Birmingham Institute of Art and Design, the Business School, the School of Computing, the School of Jewellery and the Faculties of the Built Environment, Education, Health and Community Care, Law, Humanities and Social Sciences and the Technology Innovation Centre. Many courses have a vocational focus and include sandwich placements. Music is offered through the Birmingham Conservatoire, a music college of international standing. There is also an extensive International Exchange Programme, with many courses abroad being taught in English.

Bolton Modular Single and Combined Honours courses are available, with many offering vocational or professional content and work experience elements. Courses include Art and Design, Built Environment, Business Studies, Computing and Electronics, Cultural and Creative Studies, Education, Engineering, Health and Social Studies, Product Design, Psychology and Sport, Leisure and Tourism. Teaching and learning take place through a mixture of lectures, practicals, seminars and small tutorial groups.

Bournemouth The University offers undergraduate degrees leading to BA, BSc and LLB. The programmes, which are mainly vocational and include sandwich placements, often carry professional recognition. The academic schools cover Arts and Humanities, Business and Management, Design, Food and Nutrition, Law, Media and Communications, Technology, Tourism, Sport and Hospitality.

Bradford Single, Joint and major/minor Honours degree courses are offered, many of which are vocational, leading to professional accreditation, and include sandwich placements in industry and commerce. Other courses offer work-shadowing placements. Language options are available to all students irrespective of their chosen degree course. Subjects are taught in the Schools of Computing, Informatics and Media, The School of Engineering Design and Technology, The School of Health Studies, The School of Life Sciences, The School of Management, The School of Social and International Studies and The School of Lifelong Education and Development.

Brighton BA, BSc and BEng courses are offered, 90% with industrial placements including some in Europe, the USA and Canada. Courses include Accounting, Art and Architecture, Business, Education and Sport, Health, Law, Information Sciences and Science and Engineering. Brighton and Sussex Medical School students are based at the Falmer campus for the first two years, with academic and clinical studies integrated from Year 1, and thereafter in the education centre at the Royal Sussex County Hospital in Brighton.

Bristol The University offers Single and Joint Honours programmes, mostly of three or four years and, except for Dentistry, Medicine and Veterinary Science, they are based on a modular structure. Students on Single Honours courses have open units allowing optional choices from a range of subjects. Lectures play an important part in teaching and are supported by tutorials and seminars which, in Arts and Social Sciences, tend to dominate the final year. Other subject areas offered in Sciences and Engineering (some courses include a year abroad), Arts, Social Sciences and Law.

Bristol UWE The University offers Single and Joint Honours courses organised on a modular basis which gives flexibility in the choice of options. Many courses include sandwich placements and, in addition, students have the opportunity to undertake a period of study in another EU country. The language centre is open to all students. Courses cover a full range of subjects in the Faculties of Media and Design, Applied Sciences, Built Environment, Computing, Education, Engineering and Mathematical Sciences, Health and Social Care, Humanities, Law, Languages and Social Sciences, the Bristol Business School and Hartpury College (offering Agricultural and Equine Business courses).

Brunel All courses are made up of self-contained modules enabling students, within their scheme of studies, to choose a broad range of topics or greater specialisation as they prefer. Some modern language modules may be taken, depending on the timetable of the chosen subjects. Almost all degree courses are available in a three-year full-time mode or in four-year thick or thin sandwich courses which combine academic work with industrial experience. Some exchange schemes also operate in Europe and the USA. Degree programmes are offered in the Schools of Arts (Drama, English, Media), Business, Engineering and Design, Health Sciences and Social Care, Information Systems, Law, Social Sciences and Sport and Education.

Buckingham The University is an educational charity with its main income provided by the students who pay full tuition fees. A unique feature is the two-year degree programme which starts in January although some courses start in September and may extend to 2¼ years, and some last three years. Courses are offered in Business, Humanities, Law, International Studies and Sciences.

Bucks New Courses are focused on vocational studies in a wide range of subjects in three main groups. These cover Creativity and Culture (Art, Design, Music and Media), Enterprise and Innovation (Business, Computing, Law, Human Sciences and Sport) and Society and Health (Health and Social Care and Nursing).

Cambridge The University offers undergraduate courses in Arts and Sciences and postgraduate degree programmes. Three-year degree courses (Triposes) provide a broad introduction to the subject followed by options at a later stage, and are divided into Part 1 (one or two years) and Part 2. In some Science and Engineering courses there is a fourth year (Part 3). In college-based teaching sessions (supervisions), essays are set for discussion to support university lectures, seminars and practicals.

Canterbury Christ Church A wide range of BA and BSc courses are on offer in addition to a wide choice of combined courses. Most of these courses are offered at the Canterbury campus and include Primary Education and Law, Arts and Social Science and Science subjects. Nursing and other paramedical courses are also offered at the Medway campus at Chatham, Visual and Performing Arts are studied at Folkestone and Music and some Business courses are taken at the Broadstairs campus.

Cardiff All students taking the very flexible BA degree study three subjects in the first year and then follow a Single or Joint Honours course in their chosen subject(s), or a degree in the additional subject. Similarly, BSc Econ courses offer the option to transfer to an alternative degree course at the end of Year 1, depending on the subjects originally chosen. Many degree schemes have a vocational and professional content with a period of attachment in industry, and there are well established links with universities abroad. Degrees schemes are offered by 26 Schools covering Architecture and Planning, Arts and Humanities subjects, Business, Computer Science, Earth, Ocean and Planetary Sciences, Engineering, Healthcare Studies, Law, Media Studies, Medicine, Dentistry and Nursing, Music, Optometry, Pharmacy, Psychology, Religious Studies, Sciences, Social Sciences and Welsh Studies.

Central Lancashire The University has five Faculties (Cultural, Legal, Social Studies, Health, Science). Subjects are taught in a series of modules which gives maximum flexibility in the final choice of degree course. Students may specialise or keep their options open with a choice of Single Honours, Joint or Combined Honours, or they can choose three subjects in Year 1 and reduce to two in the second and third years. Some sandwich courses are offered.

Chester Single and Combined Honours courses are offered in a wide range of subjects on the Chester campus. Subjects offered include Art and Design, Drama and Theatre Studies, Business and Social Studies courses and Nutrition and Health Care. The Warrington campus offers well established courses in Media (Radio, TV, Music) and Journalism in addition to Computer Science and Sports courses.

Chichester Degree subjects can be studied in major, joint or minor programmes. All undergraduate courses comprise a number of individual short course units/modules, taught and assessed separately. Each degree course consists of compulsory and optional modules enabling students to follow their own interests. BA courses are offered in a range of subjects covering Dance, Education, English, Fine Art, History, Media Studies, Music, Performing Arts, Sports Studies and Theology at Chichester, and Business, Education and Tourism at the Bognor Regis campus.

City The University offers a wide range of three-year and four-year programmes leading to degrees in Business and Management, Communication, Computing, Engineering and Mathematical Sciences, Health Sciences, Law, Nursing and Social Sciences. Some Schools and Departments provide a common first year, allowing students to make a final decision on their degree course at the end of the first year. Some sandwich courses are optional, others compulsory. Students in some subject areas may apply to study abroad.

Coventry Courses are offered in the Schools of Art and Design, Business, Environment and Society (including Law, Geography and Social Science), Engineering and Computing (including mathematical sciences) and Health and Life Sciences. Many courses are industry linked and offer sandwich placements in industry and commerce, with some opportunities to study abroad. Individual programmes of study are usually made up of compulsory modules, core options from a prescribed list and free choice modules.

Creative Arts Foundation and Honours degree courses are offered covering Art and Design, Architecture, Media and Communications.

Cumbria Courses cover Art, Design, Media and Performance, Arts, Humanities and Social Science, Business, IT and Law, Education, Health and Social Care, Natural Resources and Outdoor Studies and Sport.

De Montfort Courses cover Art and Design, Business and Management, Computing Sciences, Creative Technologies, Dance and Drama, Engineering, Health and Society, Humanities, Law, Life Sciences and Music. Single Honours programmes are offered together with sandwich courses and an extensive Joint Honours programme in which two subjects are chosen to be studied equally. Courses are modular, some assessed by coursework only, or by a combination of coursework and examination and a few by examination only. It is possible to change a selected module early in the year.

Derby Courses in Derby are offered across three subject areas – Arts, Design and Technology, Business and Education, Health and Sciences, whilst at the Buxton campus Foundation degrees and Higher National Diploma courses are offered as well as some BA and BSc degrees. There is also a comprehensive Joint Honours programme offering two subjects and Combined Honours courses with a choice of up to three subjects. Major/minor courses are also available.

Dundee Courses are offered in Accountancy, Architecture and Planning, Art and Design, Arts, Education, Engineering, Law, Medicine and Dentistry, Nursing, Sciences and Social Sciences. A flexible modular system is offered in which Arts and Social Science students have a choice of up to three or four subjects in Year 1 leading to greater specialisation as students progress through the next three years. A similar system applies to courses in Life Sciences and Physical Sciences. In Engineering a common core curriculum operates in Level 1 and in the first half of Level 2.

Durham A collegiate university with 15 colleges including two colleges at the Queen's campus at Stockton. Degree options include Single and Joint Honours courses to which subsidiary subjects can be added. There are named routes in Natural Sciences and courses in Combined Arts and Social Sciences in which students may design their own degree course by choosing several subjects from a wide range. Courses include the Arts, Business, Computer Science, Education, Engineering, Law, Medicine, Science and Social Science.

East Anglia There are 24 Schools of Study spanning the Arts, Humanities, Biological Sciences, Business, Computing Sciences, Social Sciences, Health Professions, Mathematics, World Art Studies and Meteorology. Many Schools are interdisciplinary or multidisciplinary, allowing students to combine a specialist study with complementary subjects and optional units. Some courses include study abroad in Europe, North America and Australasia. There is also the University Language Programme offering all undergraduate students 'non-credit' language courses with a choice from nine modern languages and British Sign Language.

East London The University offers Single Honours and Combined Honours programmes. Courses provide a flexibility of choice and are based on a modular structure with compulsory and optional course units. Courses include Architecture, Art and Design, Business, Computing, Engineering, Health Sciences, Humanities, Law, Media, Social Sciences, Sciences and Sport. A very large number of extended degrees are also available for applicants who do not have the normal university entrance requirements.

Edge Hill The University has three-year programmes including Business, English, Film, Geographical Sciences, History, Law, Media, Midwifery, Nursing, Performance Studies, Social and Psychological Sciences, Sport and Teacher Training.

Edinburgh Courses are offered in Humanities and the Social Sciences, Medicine and Veterinary Medicine and in Science and Engineering. Depending on the choice of degree, three or more subjects are taken in the first year followed by second level courses in at least two of these subjects in Year 2, thus allowing a range of subjects to be studied at degree level. There is a considerable choice of subjects although there may be restrictions in the case of high-demand subjects such as English, Economics and Psychology. General or Ordinary degrees take three years and Honours degrees take four years. Joint Honours degrees are also offered.

Edinburgh Napier Students choose between Single and Joint (two subject) degrees and customised degrees which can include a range of subjects. Courses are offered in Accounting, Economics and Financial Services, Business, Management, Languages and Law, Computing, Creative Industries, Engineering and the Built Environment, Life Sciences, Nursing, Social Sciences and Tourism and Hospitality.

Essex Undergraduate departments are grouped in Schools of Study covering Humanities and Comparative Studies, Social Sciences, Law and Sciences and Engineering. In Year 1 students take four or five courses including modules for their chosen degree. In Year 2 they may follow their chosen degree or choose another degree, including combined and joint courses. The four-year BA and some Law degrees include a year abroad and/or industrial placements. Degree schemes in Health, Business and the Performing Arts are also offered at the Southend campus.

Exeter The university has six schools of study: Business, Engineering Maths and Physical Sciences, Humanities, Life and Environmental Sciences, Social Sciences and International Studies and the Peninsula Medical School. In some courses it is possible to study for up to a year in Europe, North America, Australia or New Zealand. Some subjects including Mining Engineering, Geology and Law can be taken at the Cornwall campus at Penryn.

Glamorgan Many of the courses are vocational and can be studied as Single or Joint Honours courses or major/minor degrees. Courses are offered in the fields of Art and Design, Built Environment, Business, Computing and Mathematics, Education, Engineering, English and Creative Writing, Geography and the Environment, Health Sciences, Life and Physical Sciences, Humanities and Social Sciences, Law, Policing and Crime, Media and Drama Studies and Sport.

Glasgow Applicants choose a Faculty and a degree from the Faculties of Arts, Education, Engineering, Law, Business and Social Sciences, Medicine, Science and Veterinary Medicine. Flexible arrangements allow students to build their own degree programme from all the courses on offer. Honours degrees normally take four years, with the decision for Honours taken at the end of Year 2 (not automatic). General degrees take three years except for those involving a foreign language. Creative, Cultural, Environmental, Health and Scottish Studies can also be taken at the Crichton campus in Dumfries.

Glasgow Caledonian The University offers a wide range of vocational full-time and sandwich courses organised in the Schools of the Built and Natural Environment, Computing and Engineering, Health and Social Care, Law and Social Sciences, Life Sciences, Nursing, Midwifery and Community Health and the Caledonian Business School.

Gloucestershire Courses are made up of individual study units (modules). Some are compulsory for the chosen course but other modules can be chosen from other subjects. There are three main Faculties: Arts and Education, Business and Social Sciences and Environment and Leisure. Modular, Single and Joint Honours courses are offered, many with work placements and some with exchange schemes with institutions in the USA. Many students are home-based.

Glyndŵr This new university in North Wales (Wrexham) offers a range of courses covering Art and Design, Business, Computing and Communications Technology, Education and Community, Health, Social Sciences, Social Care and Sport and Exercise Sciences, Humanities and Science and Technology.

Greenwich Courses include Architecture and Construction, Business, Chemical and Life Sciences, Computing and Mathematical Sciences, Earth and Environmental Sciences, Education and Training, Engineering, Languages, Health and Social Care, Humanities and Social Sciences and Law. There is also a flexible and comprehensive Combined Honours degree programme offering two joint subjects of equal weight or, alternatively, major/minor combinations.

Heriot-Watt The year is divided into three ten-week terms with four modules taken each term. The six Schools cover the Built Environment, Engineering and Physical Sciences, Management and Languages, Mathematical and Computer Sciences, Textiles and Design and Life Sciences.

Hertfordshire Honours degree courses, including sandwich degrees, are offered including Art and Design, Astronomy and Astrophysics, Business, Computer Science, Education, Engineering, Humanities, Law, Life and Physical Sciences, Geography, Music, Sport, Nursing and Health subjects, Psychology and Social Studies and many courses are vocational. There is also an extensive combined modular programme in which students choose three subjects in Year 1, followed by specialisation in Years 2 and 3.

Huddersfield The modular approach to study provides a flexible structure to all courses which are offered as full-time or sandwich options. All students also have the opportunity to study a modern language either as a minor option or by studying part-time through the Modern Languages Centre. Most courses are vocational and include such subjects as Accountancy and Business, Architecture, Art and Design, Computing, Education, Engineering, Geography and Environmental Sciences, Food Sciences, Hospitality and Tourism, Human and Health Sciences, Law, Marketing, Music and Sciences.

Hull All full-time courses are made up of core and optional modules with a free elective scheme which allows students to take one module each year outside their main subject. A 'Languages for All' programme is available for all students irrespective of their degree course subject. The wide range of subjects offered include Arts and Humanities, Business, Computing, Drama, Economics, Education, Engineering, Law, Medicine (Hull York Medical School), Music, Nursing, Physical Sciences, Social Sciences and Sport. The Scarborough campus also offers a wide range of courses.

Imperial London The University offers world-class programmes in Science, Medicine, Engineering and Management. Joint Honours courses and degree courses abroad with a year abroad are also available.

Science courses are offered primarily in one principal subject, but flexibility is provided by the possibility to transfer at the end of the first year and by the choice of optional subjects in the later years of the course. A Humanities programme is also open to all students with a wide range of options whilst the Tanaka Business School offers Management courses which form an integral part of undergraduate degrees.

Keele Flexibility is provided through either interdisciplinary Single Honours degrees, bringing together a number of topics in an integrated form, or Dual Honours degrees in which two principal subjects are studied to degree level to the same depth as a Single Honours course. In addition, all students take a first-year course in Complementary Studies and may also study a foreign language. Courses are offered in Arts subjects, Biosciences and Physical Sciences, Economics, Education, Law, Management Science, Media, Music and Social Sciences.

Kent Single Honours courses can include the option of taking up to 25% of the degree in another subject, or to change the focus of a degree at the end of the year. Two subjects are studied on a 50/50 basis in Joint Honours courses and there are also major/minor Honours degrees. Degrees include Accountancy and Business courses, Arts subjects, Biological and Physical Sciences, Computer Science, Drama and Theatre and Film Studies, Languages, Law, Music Technology, Pharmacy, Psychology, Religious Studies and Social Sciences.

Kingston Single and Joint Honours courses are offered within a modular structure, with the opportunity to take a language option in French, German, Italian, Japanese, Mandarin Chinese, Russian or Spanish. Several courses are available as a minor field, for example, Business, which adds an extra dimension to the chosen degree. Subjects are offered in Architecture, Art, Design and Music, Arts and Social Sciences, Business, Computing, Earth Sciences, Economics, Education, Engineering, Humanities, Law, Life Sciences, Mathematics, Health and Social Care Sciences, Media, Performance Studies, Pharmacy, Social Sciences and Surveying. Exchange schemes are offered with 72 universities in Europe and five in the USA.

Lancaster The University is collegiate with each student being a member of one of the eight colleges. Each college has its own social activities and events. The degree programme is split into Part 1 (Year 1) and Part 2 (Years 2 and 3). Students study up to three subjects in Year 1 and then choose to major in one or a combination of subjects in Years 2 and 3. Single and joint courses are offered in a wide range of subjects, for example, Business, Computer Science, Engineering, Finance, Languages, Mathematics, Medicine, Natural Sciences, Music, Politics and Psychology. There are study opportunities abroad in the USA and Canada, the Far East and Australasia.

Leeds A very wide range of courses are on offer in most subject areas (Leeds is a pioneer of Joint Honours degrees). In the first year, Joint Honours students normally divide their time equally between three subjects, with a wide choice of the third or elective subject in the first year. In many cases, students can transfer to a different course at the end of the first year and delay their final choice of degree. A wide range of subjects is offered in Arts and Humanities, Medicine and Dentistry, Theatre and Performance, Science and Engineering, Social Sciences and in the Business School.

Leeds Met Many of the degrees are vocational with links to industry and commerce. Courses are modular with core studies and optional modules. Degree programmes are offered in the Faculties of Arts and Society, Information and Technology, Health, Sport and Recreation, the Leslie Silver International Faculty and the Leeds Business School.

Leicester Single Honours courses are offered in all the main disciplines and are taken by 75% of students. The main subject of study may be supported by one or two supplementary subjects taken in the first, and sometimes the second, year. Joint Honours courses are also offered. A three-year Combined Studies degree is also available in which three subjects are studied, one taken for two years only. Apart from Medicine, all programmes have a common modular structure with compulsory modules and a wide choice of optional modules.

Lincoln There are Faculties of Art, Architecture and Design, Business and Law, Health, Life and Social Sciences, Media, Humanities and Technology. Single and Joint subject degrees are offered on a modular basis, with some subjects offering the chance to study abroad.

Liverpool The University offers degrees in the Faculties of Arts, Engineering, Medicine, Science, Social and Environmental Studies and Veterinary Science. Apart from courses with a clinical component, programmes are modular. In some cases they include placements in industry or in another country whilst a 'Languages for All' scheme offers European languages. A Combined Honours programme in Arts gives students the chance to choose three subjects in Year 1, reducing to two subjects in Years 2 and 3. A similar Combined Honours course in Social and Environmental Studies is also offered.

Liverpool Hope Single Honours courses leading to degrees of BA and BSc are offered and there is also a wide range of options by way of two combined subjects. Courses include Business, Computing, Dance, Drama, Education, English, Environmental Management, Film Studies, Fine Art and Design, Geography, Health, History, Human Biology, Law, Leisure, Marketing, Mathematics, Media, Music, Politics, Psychology, Sports Studies, Theology and Religious Studies and Tourism.

Liverpool John Moores Courses are offered in the Faculties of Business, Law and Languages, Education, Community and Leisure, Health and Applied Social Sciences, Media, Arts and Social Science, Science and Technology and the Environment. The majority of courses provide the opportunity for work-based learning or for a year-long industrial placement.

London (Birk) Part-time evening courses are offered for mature students wishing to read for first and higher degrees. Courses are offered in the Faculties of Arts, Science, Social Science and Continuing Education.

London (Central Sch SpDr) The School offers a broad range of courses in the Theatre Arts. It is also linked to the Webber Douglas Academy of Dramatic Art to provide a range of courses leading to careers in classical and contemporary theatre, film and TV. Courses include Acting, Costume Construction, Stage Design, Prop Making, Puppetry, Stage Management, Theatre Lighting and Sound Design.

London (Court) A leading centre for the study of the history of art and conservation located in central London. Small class-size teaching.

London (Gold) Programmes include Art, Drama and Media, the Arts, Education and Social Sciences. Like most London University degrees, the majority of undergraduate degrees are made up of course units giving some flexibility. Twelve units are taken over three years.

London (Hey) Nine BA courses are offered in Philosophy and Theology and a Foundation degree in Pastoral Mission. Some part-time undergraduate courses available. The supportive and learning environment is enhanced by one-to-one tutorials for all students throughout their courses.

London (Inst in Paris) A Single Honours course in French Studies is offered to English-speaking applicants who study in France for the whole of their course. The course is taught almost entirely in French. Students graduate after their three year course with a University of London BA.

London (King's) The College offers more than 200 degree programmes in the Faculties of Arts and Humanities, Biomedical and Health Sciences, Law, Nursing and Midwifery, and Physical Sciences; Social Science and Public Policy, and Medicine and Dentistry at the Guy's or King's Denmark Hill and St Thomas's campuses. The degree course structure varies with the subject chosen and consists of Single Honours (one subject), Joint Honours (two subjects), Combined Honours (a choice of over 60 programmes) and major/minor courses.

London (QM) The College offers courses in the Arts and Humanities, Biological and Physical Sciences, Business Management and Economics, Computer Science, Engineering, Languages, Materials Science, Mathematics, Medicine and Social Sciences. In most subjects, students choose compulsory and optional course units which allow for some flexibility in planning a course to suit individual interests.

London (RH) The College offers Single, Joint and major/minor Honours degrees in three Faculties – Arts, History and Social Sciences, and Science. Study abroad is a feature of many courses and all students can compete for international exchanges.

London (RVC) Courses are offered in Veterinary Medicine and Bioveterinary Sciences; the latter does not qualify graduates to practise as veterinary surgeons. There is also a Veterinary Gateway course and a four-year Veterinary Nursing programme.

London (St George's) A 'Health Sciences' university located in south London. Courses are offered in Biomedical Informatics, Biomedical Science, Medicine, Physiotherapy and Diagnostic and Therapeutic Radiography.

London (Sch Pharm) The School offers the Master of Pharmacy degree. Except for hospital and extra-mural projects, all the teaching takes place on the Bloomsbury campus.

London (SOAS) This is the only higher education institution in the UK specialising in the study of Asia, Africa and the Near and Middle East. Single subject degrees include compulsory and optional units, with two-thirds of the total units studied in the chosen subject and the remaining units or 'floaters' from a complementary course offered at SOAS or another college of the University. In addition, two-subject degrees give great flexibility in the choice of units, enabling students to personalise their degrees to match their interests.

London (UCL) Subjects are organised in Faculties – Arts and Humanities, Social and Historical Sciences (with a flexible course unit system), Fine Art (the Slade School), Law, Built Environment (the Bartlett), Engineering Sciences, Mathematical and Physical Sciences and Life Sciences. In addition, there is the School of Medicine. The School of Slavonic and East European Studies also offers degrees which focus on developing a high level of proficiency in speaking, writing and understanding the chosen language.

London LSE The School offers courses not only in Economics and Political Science but also in a wide range of other Social Science subjects taught in 19 Departments. Programmes are offered as Single Honours, Joint Honours or major/minor courses. All undergraduates study a compulsory course (LSE 100) in Year 1.

London Met Single and Joint Honours courses are made up of compulsory and optional modules allowing students some flexibility to follow their particular interests. Courses are offered in Accountancy and Business, Art and Architecture, Arts, Humanities and Languages, Computing, Economics and Finance, Education, Health and Human Sciences and Law.

London South Bank Subject areas cover Arts and Human Sciences including Law and Psychology, Business, Computing and Information Management, Engineering, Science and the Built Environment and Health and Social Care. All courses have flexible modes of study and many vocational courses offer sandwich placements.

Loughborough Academic programmes cover Art and Design, Business, Chemistry, Computer Science, Economics, Engineering, Mathematics, Politics and International Relations, Humanities, Sciences, Social Science and Sport. Degree programmes combine compulsory and optional modules and some transfers between courses are possible. Additional language study is possible in French, German or Spanish (including beginners' courses), for students on most courses. Sandwich degree courses with a year's paid work experience in industry result in high graduate employment. World-class sporting facilities and an unrivalled reputation in sporting success attract applicants at junior international level and above.

Manchester The University offers Single and Joint Honours courses which are divided into course units, some of which are compulsory and others optional, and some are taken from a choice of subjects offered by other Schools and Faculties. A comprehensive Combined Studies degree enables students to choose course units from Arts, Humanities, Social Sciences and Sciences, and this provides the flexibility for students to alter the emphasis of their studies from year to year. Degree programmes are offered in the Faculties of Engineering and Physical Sciences, Humanities, Life Sciences and Medical and Human Sciences.

Manchester Met Degree programmes are offered in the Faculties of Art and Design, Community Studies and Education, Food, Clothing and Hospitality Management, Humanities, Law and Social Science, Science and Engineering and the Manchester Metropolitan Business School. A large number of courses involve industrial and commercial placements. It is also possible to take Combined Honours degrees selecting a combination of two or three subjects. Many programmes have a modular structure with compulsory and optional core modules.

Middlesex Single and Joint Honours courses are offered on a modular basis, most programmes having an optional work placement. Courses cover Art and Design, Arts subjects, Biological and Health Sciences,

Business and Management, Computing and IT, Dance, Drama and Music, Social Sciences and Teaching and Education.

Newcastle Degree programmes are available in the Faculties of Arts, Biological Sciences, Business and Law, Engineering, Medical Sciences, Physical Sciences and Social Sciences. Single, Joint and Combined Honours programmes are offered, in some cases providing students with the opportunity either to defer their choice of final degree or to transfer to other subjects at a later stage. In the Combined Studies BA and BSc courses it is possible to combine the study of up to three different subjects.

Newport The University consists of seven Schools – Art and Design, Humanities, Business, Computing and Engineering, Social Studies, Education and the Centre for Community and Lifelong Learning. Courses include Single and Joint Honours and major/minor studies; they vary in structure but many are based on a modular system.

Northampton Courses are offered in seven schools: Applied Sciences (Computing, Mechanical and Electrical/Electronic Engineering), Business, Education, Health, Social Sciences, Arts (including Fine Art and Design) and Land-based subjects at Moulton College. Courses are offered as Single, Combined and Joint Honours programmes.

Northumbria A wide range of courses is offered with an emphasis on vocational studies, including Art and Design, Arts subjects, Built Environment, Business and Financial Management, Computing, Education and Sport, Engineering, Health and Social Care, Humanities, Languages, Law, Mathematics, Nursing and Midwifery, Psychology and Sciences. Single and Joint Honours courses are offered, and a Combined Honours course allows a choice of up to three subjects.

Nottingham Single and Joint Honours courses are available, with some sandwich courses. Programmes are modular with compulsory and optional modules, the latter giving some flexibility in the selection of topics from outside the chosen subject field. Degree programmes are offered in the Faculties of Arts, Business, Engineering, Law, Medicine and Health Sciences, Science and Social Sciences.

Nottingham Trent Degree programmes are offered in a range of subjects covering Animal, Rural and Environmental Sciences, Architecture, Arts and Humanities, Art and Design, Business, Education, Law, Sciences and Technology and Social Sciences. Many courses are vocational with industrial and commercial placements and some students are also able to spend a semester (half an academic year) studying at a partner university in Europe, the USA or Australia.

Open University Degree and diploma courses are offered in the following subject areas: Arts and Humanities, Business and Management, Childhood and Youth, Computing and ICT, Education, Engineering and Technology, Environmental Development and International Studies, Health and Social Care, Languages, Law, Mathematics and Statistics, Psychology, Science and Social Sciences. Students study at home and are sent learning materials by the OU, maintaining contact with their tutors by email, post and telephone.

Oxford Candidates apply to a college and for a Single or Joint Honours programme. Courses are offered with a core element plus a variety of options. Weekly contact with a college tutor assists students to tailor their courses to suit personal interests. Arts students are examined twice, once in the first year (Preliminary examinations) and at the end of the course (Final Honours School). Science students are similarly examined although in some subjects examinations also take place in the second year.

Oxford Brookes Single Honours courses are offered with modules chosen from a field of study or, alternatively, Combined Honours courses in which two subjects are chosen. These subjects may be in related or unrelated subjects. There is also a Combined Studies degree in which students 'build' their own degree by taking approved modules from a range of the subjects offered by the University.

Plymouth A broad portfolio of degree courses is available including Medicine at the Peninsula Medical School – a partnership with Exeter University. Other courses cover Agriculture, Art and Design, Biological and Physical Sciences, Built Environment, Business and Financial Management, Computing, Drama, Education, Engineering, Health and Social Sciences, Humanities, Languages, Law, Marine Studies, Mathematics and Sport Studies. Single Honours courses are offered with many vocational programmes offering work placements.

Portsmouth The Faculties of Creative and Cultural Industries, Humanities and Social Sciences, Science, Technology and the Portsmouth Business School offer Single and Joint Honours courses. Sandwich programmes are also available in many subjects and there is also an opportunity for all students to learn a foreign language. Many courses are planned on a modular basis which allows students to defer specialisation until after their first year.

Queen Margaret The five main areas at this new university (2007) now based on a purpose-built campus outside Edinburgh, cover Business and Enterprise, Health, Media and Social Sciences, Drama and the Creative Industries. All courses focus on vocational careers.

Queen's Belfast The academic year is divided into two semesters of 15 weeks each (12 teaching weeks and three examination weeks), with degree courses (pathways) normally taken over three years of full-time study. Six modules are taken each year (three in each semester) and, in theory, a degree can involve any combination of six Level 1 modules. Single, Joint and Combined Honours courses are offered and, in addition, major/minor combinations; some courses include sandwich placements. Courses cover Agriculture and Food Science, Education, Engineering, Humanities and Social Sciences, Management and Economics, Law and Medicine and Health Sciences.

Reading Faculties of Arts and Humanities and Economics and Social Sciences provide flexible arrangements for students. A teaching system operates in Year 1 in which students can take modules in their chosen subject and in two or three other subjects. At the end of the first year they may transfer from Single Honours to Joint Honours courses or change to another subject.

Robert Gordon The University offers a wide range of vocational courses including Accountancy and Business, Architecture, Art and Design, Computer Science, Engineering, Law, Nursing, Occupational Therapy, Pharmacy, Physiotherapy, Radiography, Sciences, Social Sciences and Sports Science. Many courses offer work placements and there are some opportunities to study abroad in Europe, Canada and the USA.

Roehampton London's only campus university, managing its academic programmes in eight Schools – Arts and Business, Social Sciences and Computing, Education Studies, English and Modern Languages, Humanities and Cultural Studies, Initial Teacher Education, Sports Science and Psychological and Therapeutic Studies. All programmes operate within a modular and semester-based structure.

St Andrews A very wide range of subjects is offered across the Faculties of Arts, Divinity, Medicine and Science. A flexible programme is offered in the first two years when students take several subjects. The decision of Honours degree subject is made at the end of Year 2 when students choose between Single or Joint Honours degrees for the next two years. A broadly-based General degree programme is also offered lasting three years. After two years of a General degree programme students may transfer onto a named Honours degree programme if they meet the requirements of the department(s).

Salford The University offers BA, BSc and BEng degrees with teaching methods depending on the degree (they are equally likely to accept students with BTECs and Access qualifications as well as those with A-levels). There is a wide range of professionally accredited programmes many involving work placements. All undergraduates may study a foreign language. Subjects include Accountancy and Business, Art and Design, Computer Science, Drama, Engineering, Humanities, Journalism, Leisure and Tourism, Languages, Music, Nursing, Physiotherapy, Psychology, Sciences, Social Sciences and Sport Science.

Sheffield The teaching year consists of two semesters (two periods of 15 weeks). Courses are fully modular, with the exceptions of Dentistry and Medicine. Students register for a named degree course which has a number of core modules, some optional modules chosen from a prescribed range of topics and some unrestricted modules chosen from any at the University. Programmes offered include Accounting and Business, Arts and Humanities, Computer Science, Engineering and Materials Science, Languages, Law, Nursing, Psychology, Sciences, Social Sciences and Town and Country Planning.

Sheffield Hallam A large number of vocational courses are offered in addition to those in Arts, Humanities and Social Sciences. The University is the largest provider of sandwich courses in the UK with most courses offering work placements, usually between the second and third years. Most students are able to study an additional language from French, German, Italian, Spanish and Japanese.

Southampton A wide range of courses is offered in the Faculties of Law, Arts and Social Sciences, Engineering, Science and Mathematics and Medicine, Health and Life Sciences. Programmes are generally for three years. All students have the chance to study a language as part of their degree and there are many opportunities for students to study abroad or on Erasmus-Socrates exchange programmes whether or not they are studying modern languages.

Southampton Solent Courses are offered in the Faculties of Technology, Media, Arts and Society and the Southampton Business School. Subjects cover Art and Design, Business and Finance including Accountancy, Marketing and Personnel, Computing, Construction, Engineering and Technology, the Environment, Human and Social Sciences and Law, Leisure, Sport and Tourism, Maritime Studies and Media, Film and Journalism.

Staffordshire The Stafford campus focuses on courses in Computing, Engineering, Technology and Health Studies whilst at Stoke programmes are offered in Art and Design, Law, Business, Humanities, Social Sciences and Science subjects. Single and Joint Honours awards are available, some of which are for four years and include a work placement year. Part-time courses are also offered.

Stirling A flexible system operates in which students can delay their final degree choice until midway through the course. The University year is divided into two 15-week semesters, from September to December and February to May with a reading/study block and exams at the end of each semester. Innovative February entry is possible to some degree programmes. There are 250 degree combinations with the opportunity to study a range of disciplines in the first two years. In addition to Single and Combined Honours degrees, there is a General degree which allows for greater breadth of choice. Subjects range across the Arts, Social Sciences and Sciences.

Strathclyde A credit-based modular system operates with a good degree of flexibility in course choices. The University offers many vocational courses in the Faculties of Engineering, Science and the Strathclyde Business School. There are also degree programmes in Arts subjects, Education, Law and the Social Sciences.

Sunderland There are two campuses, City Campus in Sunderland and Sir Tom Cowie Campus across the river, and five Schools of study: Arts, Media and Culture, Business, Computer Science and Technology and Single, Joint Honours and sandwich courses with strong links with industry. A modular programme provides maximum flexibility in choosing appropriate subjects. Some placements are possible in Canada, USA, Australia, New Zealand, India and Europe and there is a large number of mature and local students.

Surrey Degree programmes are offered in the Arts, Biomedical and Molecular Sciences, Electronics and Physical Sciences, Engineering, Health and Medical Sciences, Human Sciences and Management. Some 80% of students spend a professional training year as part of their course and in some cases there are placements abroad. There is also a part-time BSc degree in Professional Development through work-based learning.

Sussex Teaching is structured around five Schools of study, the Brighton and Sussex Medical School and the Science and Technology Policy Research Unit. Courses cover a wide range of subjects in Humanities, Life Sciences, Science and Technology, Social Sciences and Cultural Studies. Students are registered in a School depending on the degree taken. The flexible structure allows students to interrupt their degree programme to take a year out.

Swansea Courses are offered in Arts and Social Sciences, Business, Economics and Law, Engineering, Languages, Medicine and Health Sciences and Science. Degree courses are modular with the opportunity to take some subjects outside the chosen degree course. Part-time degrees are available and study abroad arrangements are possible in several subject areas.

Swansea Met This new university consists of three main faculties. The faculty of Applied Design and Engineering offers a broad spectrum of courses from Automotive Engineering to Multimedia. The Faculty of Art and Design established 150 years ago is a major centre for art and crafts in Wales. The Faculty of Humanities comprises Schools of Business, Education, Health Sciences, Humanities, the Performing Arts, Leisure, Tourism and Recreation.

Teesside Single and Combined Honours degrees are offered with the major subject occupying two thirds of the course and the minor option one third. There is a wide choice of vocational courses, many with sandwich arrangements in industry, commerce and the professions. Courses are offered in the Arts, Business, Engineering, Law, Media, Social Sciences and Sport with large Schools of Health and Social Care and Computing and Mathematics. There is a high mature student intake.

Trinity Saint David Courses are offered in the Humanities, Business and Management, Education, Art, Design, the Performing Arts, and the Social Sciences. Check the University website for the latest information (www.trinitysaintdavid.ac.uk).

Ulster Faculties of Arts, Business and Management, Engineering and Built Environment, Life and Health Sciences and Social Sciences offer a wide range of courses. There are various styles of learning supported by formal lectures and many courses include periods of work placement.

Warwick Courses are offered by Departments in the Faculty of Arts, Science and Social Studies, the Warwick Business School, the Warwick Institute of Education and the Warwick Medical School. Students may choose single subject degrees or combine several subjects in a joint degree. Options offered in each course provide flexibility in the choice of subjects although courses are not fully modularised. Many degrees offer the opportunity to study abroad and work placements on some science courses.

West London Subjects offered cover Business, Management and Law, Tourism, Hospitality and Leisure, Music, Media and Creative Technologies and Health and Human Sciences. Credit-rated Single and Joint Honours courses are offered, many with year-long work placements between Years 2 and 3. There are some study-abroad arrangements in Europe, Canada and the USA and there is a large mature student intake.

West Scotland The University is located on four campuses at Ayr, Dumfries, Hamilton and Paisley and is a leading provider of vocational education in the region. It offers industry-relevant and career-focused courses, and many programmes include periods of paid work placements. There are also some European and US study opportunities. Courses are offered in the Business School and the Schools of Computing, Education, Engineering and Science, Health, Nursing and Midwifery and Media, Language and Music.

Westminster Courses include Architecture and the Built Environment, Biosciences, Business Management, Complementary Therapies, Computer Sciences, Electronics, English and Linguistics, Languages, Law, Media and Arts and Design and Psychology and Social Sciences. Undergraduate courses are modular and taught over two semesters. The University has a broad network of partnerships within the EU which enables students to include a period of study abroad as part of their degree.

Winchester Single and two-subject courses are offered consisting of either one subject, or two subjects studied equally (a Joint Honours degree) or a 75%–25% split by way of a main and subsidiary subject Honours degree. Courses are offered in American Studies, Archaeology, Business, Dance, Drama and Performance, Education, English and Creative Writing, Film Studies, History, Journalism and Media Studies, Psychology, Sport Science, Theology and Tourism.

Wolverhampton A large number of specialist and Joint Honours degrees are offered and many have work placements at home or abroad. Except for courses linked to specific professional requirements, programmes are modular providing flexibility of choice. Courses include Art and Design, Humanities, Business Studies, Computer Science, Education, Engineering, Environmental Studies, Health Studies, Law, Media, Nursing, Sciences and Social Studies.

Worcester The courses are grouped into six institutes: Health and Society, Humanities and Creative Arts, Science and the Environment, Sport and Exercise Science, the Worcester Business School and Education.

York Thirty departments and centres cover a range of subjects in the arts, social sciences, technology and medicine. The 'Languages for All' programme enables any student to take a course in any one of 14 languages, in addition to which there are several opportunities to build a period abroad into a degree course. Courses offered include Archaeology, Arts subjects, Computer Science, Economics, Education, Electronics, Health Sciences, Languages, Management, Medicine, Music, Psychology, Sciences and Social Sciences.

Be a name...

A lifetime experience…

Great Courses… that develop your professional and personal skills

Small campuses in Carmarthen and Lampeter… with all you need in one place

Friendly atmosphere… where you won't be lost in a crowd

Scholarships available… to help you make ends meet

Fantastic location… with excellent facilities, and spectacular countryside and coastline

Excellent student life… with an active Students' Union that gets you involved in university life

Great Courses

The University offers a range of courses – from those aiming for specific vocations, for example Archaeology or Teaching, to programmes leading to a range of suitable employment opportunities e.g. English, Classics and History, which combine academic knowledge with a range of the transferable skills that employers seeks.

//Life's going well at the University. The lectures are good and the social activities are fun. I love living on the campus and having some independence.//

Ashley Joseph
BA Physical Education

Our campuses

Our campuses in Carmarthen and Lampeter are excellent places to live and study. Both sites are based around the original nineteenth century college buildings and comprise beautiful landscaped grounds with modern and well-equipped buildings. Each campus has accommodation, learning resources, a lively Students' Union, catering and sports facilities on site so that there is no need for a long daily commute, saving you both time and money.

PRIFYSGOL CYMRU
Y Drindod Dewi Sant

UNIVERSITY OF WALES
Trinity Saint David

0300 500 1822
www.tsd.ac.uk

not a number

A friendly atmosphere

Our campuses and location foster a close-knit and friendly atmosphere and you will get to know other students from other courses and year groups. The range of clubs and societies - sports and others - encourages this and means that there is plenty to do outside of lectures and your academic work.

Fantastic location

Our campuses and excellent links with the local community mean that students quickly settle in and make friends, both within the University and outside. Both our campuses are surrounded by green fields and there are a host of opportunities for outdoor recreation such as hill walking, mountain biking, canoeing, coasteering, and surfing as well as visits to sites of historical and cultural interest. The additional advantages of living in West Wales is that the cost of living is much lower than in many urban areas, which means that your student loan may go further, while crime rates are amongst some of the lowest in the UK, allowing you a greater sense of personal freedom.

Scholarships available

The University has a number of scholarships and bursaries available to provide extra financial support for students.

Excellent student life

The Students' Union works across both campuses to enhance your social, cultural and academic experience.

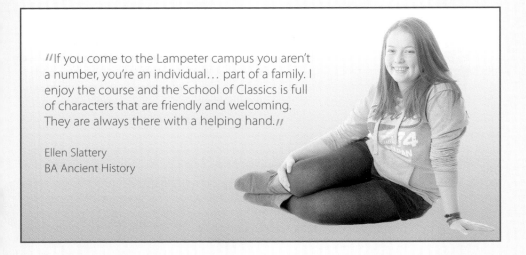

//If you come to the Lampeter campus you aren't a number, you're an individual... part of a family. I enjoy the course and the School of Classics is full of characters that are friendly and welcoming. They are always there with a helping hand.//

Ellen Slattery
BA Ancient History

York St John The Faculties of Education and Theology, Business and Communication, Health and Life Sciences and Art offer a range of specialist degrees and Joint Honours courses are offered in Business, Management, Languages and Linguistics, Peace Studies, Health Studies, Counselling, Design, Education, Information Technology, Occupational Therapy, Physiotherapy, Psychology, Sport and Theology.

COLLEGES AND THEIR COURSES

In addition to the large numbers of universities offering degree courses, there are over 100 colleges admitting several thousands of students, each on full degree courses. These include University Colleges, University Centres, Colleges of Further and Higher Education and specialist colleges of Agriculture and Horticulture, Art, Drama, and Music: see the directory of institutions at the back of the book. Larger institutions will offer a range of Single subject, Joint and Combined Honours degree courses leading to BA, BSc and BEd degrees whilst the smaller colleges may only offer one or two degree programmes. A large number, however, also provide full or part-time Foundation degrees which can lead to Honours degree courses. These colleges are listed in the subject tables. The next chapter **University Admissions** outlines how universities select applicants for their courses and it provides information for each university relating to key points of their admissions policies.

4

UNIVERSITY ADMISSIONS

ADMISSIONS POLICIES

Although the UCAS application process is standard for all undergraduate Honours degree courses (see **Chapter 5**) the admissions policies adopted by individual departments in universities and colleges often differ, depending on the popularity of the course and the quality of applicants. There are, however, common areas of agreement concerning applications, in particular the acceptance of the different qualifying examinations being offered. Apart from a diverse range of international qualifications, A-level grades, the International Baccalaureate (IB) and BTEC have been the common currency of selection linked with the UCAS Tariff points system for many years, although some very popular universities and courses do not make points offers, preferring to set their entry standards in the grades awarded in specific subjects.

Most universities are still making decisions on the timing and introduction of the new A* grades, although this year an A* grade has been stipulated in over 6000 offers. Most, if not all, institutions accept recent qualifications such as the Advanced Diplomas, the Extended Project Qualification and the Cambridge Pre-U Diploma although there may be some additional requirements depending on the degrees applied for when specified subjects may be required. A-levels in general studies and critical thinking are nearly always taken into account when selecting applicants although they rarely form part of an offer. Key Skills may also be noted by selectors and for some courses they could be worth up to 20 Tariff points. BTEC is also acceptable with two passes for some Foundation courses to full distinction for some competitive degree programmes. However, it should also be noted that a number of universities and degree courses also have general entry requirements which include GCSE grade C or above in English and mathematics.

Interview policies vary considerably and, in most cases, simply will be based on the information on the UCAS application with the personal statement being highly important for many courses. Candidates receiving offers will be invited to visit their universities. Interviews are usual for Medicine, Dentistry, Veterinary Science, Art, Social Work and for Teaching courses and inevitable for Dance, Drama and Music (see **Chapter 6**). Mature students (defined as those over 21 on entry) are often interviewed. Normal published offers may not apply to mature students. In all universities certain courses require Criminal Records Bureau (CRB) checks or medical examinations; students should check these requirements before applying for courses.

Deferred entry is acceptable in almost all cases although many universities ask that the intention to take a Gap Year should be included on the application if firm arrangements have been made. It is worth noting, however, that there may well be fewer places available on a subsequent course for students wanting to defer. Several universities have advised that if a student fails to achieve the grades required for an offer, they may still be awarded a place; however they may receive a changed offer for an alternative course. Many universities are also prepared to provide feedback on the results of unsuccessful applications.

In addition, all universities have a number of schemes in place to enable admissions tutors to identify and make offers to applicants who, for example, may have had their education affected by circumstances outside their control. A major initiative is Widening Participation in which various schemes can assist school and college students in getting into university. These programmes focus on specific groups of students and communities including:

- Students from low participation areas
- Low-performing schools and colleges or those without a strong history of progression to higher education

- Students with disabilities
- People living in deprived geographical areas, including deprived rural areas
- Students from black or ethnic minority backgrounds
- Students from the lower socio-economic groups 4–8 including mature learners
- Students requiring financial assistance or who are disadvantaged in various ways
- Families with little or no experience of higher education
- Students from homes with low household incomes
- Students returning to study after a period of time spent away
- Students from state schools.

Students who feel that they might qualify for Widening Participation programmes should find out from their school or college about the schemes offered by universities including their local university. In addition to the general information above, universities have emphasised certain aspects of their selection procedures and these are listed below. Even so, applicants are strongly advised to check prospectuses and websites for up-to-date information on admissions and, in particular, any entrance test to be taken (see also **Chapter 6**).

UNIVERSITIES' ADMISSIONS INFORMATION

The following information provides a selection of relevant aspects of universities' admissions policies and practice. Although the information on alternative qualifications to A-levels such as the Cambridge Pre-U Diploma, the Advanced Diploma, BTEC qualifications, Key Skills and Access courses is not always published in prospectuses, it is usually available on universities' websites. While it can be assumed that applicants will be considered and accepted with these alternative qualifications, depending on the requirements for individual degree programmes, it is important to check with university admissions staff **before** you make your application that your qualifications will meet their requirements. Applicants whose first language is not English should refer to **Chapter 9** for details of the English Language entry requirements.

Applicants for places at popular universities of for popular courses cannot assume that they will receive an offer even if their predicted grades are the same or higher than a stated standard offer.

Aberdeen Selectors look for evidence of subject knowledge and understanding, commitment, motivation and responsibility, and the ability to cope with a university education.

Abertay Dundee The University will not use admissions tests for entry in 2012, and only some applicants are interviewed – for courses in Nursing, Ethical Hacking and Computer Arts.

Aberystwyth The University states that it is important that applications are made by the initial closing date of 15 January. They cannot guarantee to consider late applications. The number of applicants considerably exceeds the number of places for Drama and Theatre Studies courses. Offers will be made on the basis of the application form and interviews are required for some subjects. Decisions are made within four weeks of receiving the application and all those receiving an offer will be invited to visit the University. Applicants are advised not to depend on clearing as there is very limited flexibility in August.

Anglia Ruskin The University interviews all applicants for Art and Design, Education, Nursing, Physiotherapy, Social Work, Midwifery and Television and Media Studies. Some applicants are interviewed for Business. A maths test is also used for some Education (ITT) courses. The University is happy to give advice and guidance about the admissions process: email admissions@anglia.ac.uk.

Arts London In addition to formally qualified applicants, the University welcomes applications from candidates without formal qualifications who can demonstrate equivalent skills, knowledge and ability gained from work or life experience.

Aston There are no entrance tests in the selection process and offers are not normally made simply on the basis of UCAS points. Interviews are only used in special cases, for example, mature students, or those with non-standard entry qualifications. Most courses include a one-year placement as part of the degree.

This is normally paid, and also has a reduced tuition fee and placement bursary. Aston is one of only four UK universities with more than 50% of students taking sandwich courses or year-abroad programmes. Applications from high-achieving students taking Applied A-levels are welcomed and all degree programmes will consider a single award Applied A-level in place of a third A-level subject. For all degree programmes, except those in the School of Health and Life Sciences, a relevant Applied A-level double award plus one relevant A-level will normally be accepted. BTEC awards are acceptable and a mix of BTEC and A-levels welcomed. High-achieving Level 3 Diploma students in relevant subjects will be considered. Key skills will be taken into account but will not be included in offers; Access programmes are accepted.

Bangor Applications welcomed from students taking validated Access courses and 14–19 Diplomas in specified subjects.

Bath Some departments interview promising applicants; those not receiving an offer can obtain feedback on the reasons for their rejection. Students are encouraged to take the Extended Project and to provide details on their personal statement. Students taking the Advanced Diploma should check the requirements of individual degree courses. Applicants who are re-sitting A-levels will not be accepted on Economics and Business Management Courses.

Bath Spa All eligible candidates are interviewed for the following courses: Art & Design, Broadcast Media, Creative Media Practice, Music and Performing Arts, Publishing. All applicants will be invited to visit the University after receiving an offer. Gap Years are acceptable.

Birmingham Courses are academic and 75% of the personal statement should relate to the proposed course of study. General studies A-level is accepted for some degree courses. Most subjects of the Advanced Diploma will be acceptable for most courses, although an A-level will also be required for some courses. The Extended Project will not be included in the University's offers. Some applicants are interviewed, for example for Medicine, Dentistry and for Social Work. The University uses LNAT (see Chapter 6) as its admissions test for Law applicants. Gap Years are acceptable and should be mentioned on the UCAS application or as soon as arrangements have been made. Decisions on offers are normally made within four to six weeks of receiving the application.

Birmingham City Some applicants will be called to interview and others invited to the Department before an offer is made. If the required grades of an offer are not achieved it may still be possible to be accepted on to a course. Deferred entry is acceptable.

Bolton Applicants are advised to apply through UCAS as early as possible. The University welcomes the AL and AS general studies and also Key Skills at Level 3. If admissions staff consider that the course applied for is not suitable then an offer for an alternative course may be made. The academic reference should highlight academic skills, attendance and punctuality, time management skills and any contributions to extra-curricular activities. Dissatisfied applicants should contact the Head of Marketing and Recruitment with details of their application.

Bournemouth The personal statement is regarded as an important aspect of the application process. Some subject areas may require applicants to attend for interview. Deferred entry is acceptable.

Bradford It is not anticipated that the A* grade will be used in any offers. Candidates will not be accepted on to any degree course purely on the basis of AS-level results (including the double award) although two AS-levels or an AS double award may be accepted instead of a non-essential A-level. Low offers may be made to applicants showing considerable promise in academic or in other areas. Offers are normally based on the UCAS Tariff. The University accepts a range of alternative qualifications and takes a very positive view on the value of the new Advanced Diploma. These qualifications will be considered on a course-by-course basis.

Brighton The University welcomes applications from students with qualifications and experience other than traditional A-levels. The Advanced Diploma, Access courses and BTEC are acceptable alternative qualifications.

Brighton and Sussex (MS) The School welcomes candidates offering A*, or predicted to achieve A*, and will account for this level of achievement when the school shortlists for interview. The same policy applies to applicants offering the Extended Project.

Bristol Decisions on applications may be delayed due to the volume of applications. A* grades may be included in the offers for some applicants depending on the application, the subject and the competition for places. Students choosing to take the Extended Project may receive two offers, one which includes the Extended Project, for example, AAA, or AAB plus the Extended Project. Requirements for the Advanced Diploma will be set by individual departments. Up to two Applied A-levels will be accepted with an A-level. Some admissions tutors take unit grade information into account in making an offer while others may specify unit grades in their offers. Deferred entry is acceptable but intention to defer should be indicated in the personal statement, giving information about your plans. However, in some cases the number of places available might be limited and higher offers may be made. An interview is required for an offer for Medicine, Dentistry, Veterinary Science, Drama, Engineering Design and Veterinary Nursing, but not all applicants are interviewed. LNAT (see **Chapter 6**) is used for admission to the Law programmes. Applicants who are re-sitting A-levels or who are re-applying will not be given offers for Medicine, Dentistry or Law. Advice to applicants can be found on www.bristol.ac.uk/study.

Bristol UWE Typical offers are made for each degree programme although these offers may vary between applicants since selection is based on individual merit. Students applying for courses 'subject to approval' or 'subject to validation' will be kept informed of the latest developments. Many offers will be made in terms of Tariff points.

Brunel All applicants are interviewed for Design, Electrical Engineering, Social Work and Education courses. All offers for degree courses are for three A-levels and either one AS-level or the Extended Project. If an applicant has not been able to take a fourth subject at AS-level, or complete a Project, this should be indicated in the application; offers will then be made for three A-levels (or equivalent). For some courses, students who have re-sat A-levels and/or re-applied for the course will be given a higher offer then the standard entry requirements. The University accepts relevant Advanced Diplomas (see www.brunel.ac.uk).

Buckingham Candidates apply through UCAS in the normal way or directly with a paper application obtainable from the University. Applicants may be invited for interview.

Bucks New It may be possible to transfer to the University from another university under the Credit Accumulation and Transfer Scheme (CATS), and to gain exemptions from part of the course if the student has CATS credit points from their relevant previous study. Transfer from full-time to part-time study is possible. BTEC qualifications are acceptable. Admissions tests will be used for entry to Nursing and Social Work courses.

Cambridge Currently, the standard offer is A*AA but the subject in which the A* is to be achieved in unlikely to be specified. All Colleges modify offers to take account of individual circumstances, for example, lower offers may be made to students applying through the Cambridge Special Access Scheme – see the University's website. Self-discipline, motivation and commitment are required together with the ability to think critically and independently, plus passion or, at the very least, real enthusiasm for the chosen course. If examination predictions are good then the chance of admission may be better than one in four. Applicants are encouraged to take the Extended Project although it will not be a requirement of any offer. Although AS and AL critical thinking and general studies are acceptable as a fourth AS or A-level subject, neither is considered acceptable as a third A-level. The Advanced Engineering Diploma is the only Advanced Diploma with adequate preparation for a Cambridge course and will be accepted for Engineering if applicants have an AL physics and the new Level 3 Certificate in Mathematics for Engineering within the Specialist Learning component. For many courses admissions tests are used – and written work may be required – so it is very important to check the university website and prospectus well before completing the application to find out exactly what is needed for entry. See **Chapter 6**, and also www.cam.ac.uk/admissions/undergraduate/tests and www.admissionstests. cambridgeassment.org.uk.

Canterbury Christ Church The personal statement and school references are regarded as highly important. Applicants for Teaching and Health-related courses must show evidence on their application of relevant experience. If they do not, they will be rejected without interview. Other subjects, including Geography, History and Music also interview candidates.

Cardiff Applicants are required to take only three A-levels for degree courses. Deferred entry is acceptable. The 14–19 Diploma is an acceptable qualification for entry. Key Skills should be mentioned in an application but will not form part of an offer.

Central Lancashire The University looks for grades C/D plus Additional Specialist Learning for applicants with the new Advanced Diplomas. Grades B/C will be required from students with the Progression Diploma.

Chester Interviews and workshops are required for some courses to support applications. General studies at A-level is acceptable for entry to courses in addition to other A-levels.

Chichester Early application is advised for popular courses such as Dance, Physical Education, Primary Education, Teaching and Sports Therapy. Deferred entry applications are not considered for PGCE courses. Teaching applicants should have spent a minimum of two weeks observing/helping out in a state school within two years of applying. Significant experience is also required for applicants for Social Work courses. Applicants taking a Level 3 Diploma will be considered for entry to the relevant course. Dance, Music and Performing Arts applicants will be required to prepare a set piece in advance and to perform it in front of a group. Decisions on applications are normally made within two weeks, and, except for some courses where interviews are required (see **Chapter 6**) most decisions are made on the basis of the application form. Some applicants will be interviewed for Teacher Training, Physical Education, Social Work, Dance, Fine Art, Music, Musical Theatre, Drama, Performing Arts and Childhood Studies courses. Chichester uses more grade-based offers than UCAS Tariff points offers for entry.

City It is hoped that applicants will have taken four AS-level subjects in Year 13, one of which is a contrasting subject.

Coventry The University welcomes applications from those with significant work or life experience who do not necessarily meet the published academic requirements for the course. Applicants will be required to demonstrate evidence of motivation, potential and knowledge of the subject. Some candidates will be required to attend interviews depending on their course choice. 2012 applicants wishing to defer entry to 2013 will not be accepted.

Creative Arts Interviews and portfolios are required for all courses. There is no minimum age requirement for entry to undergraduate courses.

Cumbria Candidates without GCSE English, Mathematics or Science at Grade C or above (which are required for some courses) take an equivalency test at the University. The new Diploma qualification is acceptable for some subjects and will be recognised as equivalent to 3.5 A-levels with a possible total Tariff score of 300 points. Key Skills at Level 3 may be allowed to contribute up to 20 UCAS Tariff points towards meeting the conditions of an offer.

Derby The Level 2 Diploma is regarded as equivalent to GCSEs and the Level 3 Diploma to A-levels. Students without formal qualifications can take an Access course or the Modular Foundation course to gain entry to degree programmes.

Dundee Decisions for non-interviewing courses are usually made within five working days. Admissions tests and interviews are required for Medicine and Dentistry. Applicants taking qualifications in subjects other than A-levels should contact the subject department for details of entry requirements. The University considers applicants re-sitting A-levels on an individual basis.

De Montfort Selection criteria depend on the chosen course. Some courses require a personal interview and/or examination of portfolios.

Durham Since September 2010 a number of changes have been introduced to the Durham admissions policy.

(a) Successful applicants will be informed of the decision on their application before a college is allocated. See www.durham.ac.uk/undergraduate/apply/process
(b) Students applying for more than one type of course or institution may submit a substitute personal statement of the same length as the original personal statement on the UCAS form. See www.durham.ac.uk/undergraduate/apply/personalstatement

(c)   Durham has reviewed their policy towards the A* grade at A-level. In brief an A* will be required for Mathematical Sciences but for no other programmes. See www.durham.ac.uk/undergraduate/apply/faqs/?/faqno=1985

(d)   In addition the following factors are reviewed: A-level or equivalent grades, GCSE performance, the personal statement, the school/college reference, motivation for the chosen degree programme, independence of thought and working, skills derived from non-academic activities eg sport, the arts, and voluntary and community work.

East Anglia Offers are normally made in terms of three A-levels although applicants with two A-levels and AS-levels are welcome. Critical Thinking and General Studies A-levels are not accepted for most courses. Interviews are necessary for some courses. Deferred entry is acceptable.

East London Candidates are advised to apply as soon as possible and results are normally announced within seven days. Some students may be called for interview and in some cases an essay or a portfolio may be required. The interviewers will be looking for evidence of a real interest in the chosen subject. Rejected applicants may receive an offer of a place on an Extended degree or another course.

Edge Hill With the exception of courses in Journalism, Animation, Media (Film and TV), TV Production courses, Performing Arts and Social and Psychological Sciences, Teacher Training, Nursing and Midwifery, most decisions are made without an interview, those applicants made offers being invited to visit the University. The new Advanced Diploma is accepted as equivalent to three A-levels.

Edinburgh The results of applications may be delayed until the deadline and all applications have been received. All offers will be expressed in grades not Tariff points. Decisions have yet to be made on the timing of the introduction of the new A* grade. Applicants offering the new Advanced Diploma in Engineering, IT or Society, Health and Development may be considered for entry to programmes in Engineering, Computing, Nursing or Social Work.

Edinburgh Napier Offers are normally based on the UCAS Tariff point system. The normal offers may not apply to candidates over 21 who should contact the admissions tutor for details. Interviews may be required for some courses.

Essex Candidates are required to have two full A-levels or equivalent although students taking two A-levels, or re-sitting some subjects may get a higher offer. All departments accept general studies and critical thinking. Key Skills at Level 3 can be used as part of the points total providing they do not overlap with other qualifications (eg numeracy or A-level Mathematics). Unit grades are not used as standard procedure. Additional aptitude tests are not used. Interviews may be required for some subjects.

Exeter The University welcomes applications that offer a greater breadth of experience both academically and vocationally. Key indicators include predicted and achieved academic performance in Level 2 and 3 qualifications; candidates normally would be expected to take four AS-levels followed by three A-levels in Year 13. The personal statement should cover the reasons for your course choice and how the course relates to your current or previous studies and experience. It should also give evidence of your motivation to study at a higher level, details of work experience or positions of responsibility and what you have gained from these. The University supports the introduction of the new qualifications including the Advanced Diplomas, the Extended Project and the Cambridge Pre-U Diploma. Deferred applications are acceptable but the number of places for deferred applicants for popular courses can be limited and in some cases higher offers may be made.

Glamorgan Candidates applying for the Excellence Award must submit their applications by the 15 January deadline. Key Skills points can contribute to the overall Tariff point requirement.

Glasgow Candidates are strongly advised to meet the deadlines for applications. Normally all subjects apart from Dentistry, Education (for the BEd Primary programme), Medicine, Veterinary Medicine, Social Sciences and Law accept applications after the 15 January deadline, but this is not guaranteed and will depend on the pressure on places and the academic qualifications of the applicant. Offers are made from early to late March. The University does not interview students to all faculties, some exceptions being the Medical and Veterinary Sciences, Music, Education and Technological Education. Deferrred entry is not guaranteed for all subjects (eg Dentistry, Veterinary Medicine and Primary Education): check with the University.

Glasgow Caledonian Nursing and Health courses interview applicants. An additional admissions test is required for Social Work and Journalism courses. Applicants who are considering deferred entry should contact the admissions tutor before applying.

Gloucestershire Students failing to meet the UCAS Tariff requirements may be eligible for entry based on life or work experience following an interview. Entry with the Advanced Diploma, BTEC, NVQ Level 3 and Access to Higher Education qualifications is acceptable.

Glyndŵr The general requirement for entry to most degree courses is 200 UCAS points and 100 points for Foundation degrees. UCAS points may be counted from a wide variety of qualifications. Applications are also welcomed from candidates who do not possess the standard qualifications but who can demonstrate their capacity to pursue the course successfully. Entrance can be based on past experience, skills, organisational capabilities and the potential to succeed. Interviews for some courses are essential including Education, Nursing and Social Work. Portfolios are required for Art and Design courses and an audition is required for Theatre and Performance.

Greenwich The University operates a Credit Accumulation and Transfer Scheme (CATS). This means that normally a full-time undergraduate student earns 120 credits for each academic year they successfully complete, and most degrees require a total of 360 credits. CATS make it easier for students to transfer their credits from one university to another, and to move between programmes of the University. Candidates are reminded to apply early since popular courses fill up quickly. Interviews are held for some courses. Those who are rejected may receive an offer for an alternative course.

Heriot-Watt In order to give candidates as much flexibility as possible, many will receive offers for both first and second year entry. Although one of these will be the main offer, candidates accepting this can easily change their main offer to the alternative year if they subsequently want to do so. Applicants are interviewed for some programmes.

Hertfordshire Applicants wanting to take a Gap Year should finalise their arrangements before asking for deferment and accepting a place. Once a place has been accepted for the following year it will not be possible to change their application for entry to the current year. They would need to withdraw their application and apply again through Clearing.

Huddersfield The University welcomes a wide range of qualifications. Some students will be called for interview. Students wishing to defer entry should state their intention on their application. It is advisable to have finalised arrangements for a Gap Year before accepting an offer for deferment.

Hull A wide range of qualifications are accepted for entry to degree courses. Applications are also welcomed from those who can demonstrate Level 3 work-based learning such as Advanced Apprenticeships and NVQ 3. Bridging study may be recommended by way of a foundation year. Most courses welcome applications for deferred entry although this should be stated on the application. Deferred entry is not available for Nursing courses.

Imperial London Except for courses where three specific A-levels are required for admission, candidates with two A-levels and two AS-levels will normally be considered equally with other candidates offering three A-levels. The College considers candidates with the Advanced Engineering Diploma if they also have A levels in specified subjects which meet the College's entry requirements. Applicants for entry to Year 2 of some courses can also be considered if they have completed the first year of a comparable degree at another institution with a high level of achievement, but they need to contact the relevant department before applying. A College Admissions and Appeals and Complaints procedure is available to applicants dissatisfied with the way their application has been considered. Applicants should note the College's policy on dress, health and safety published on its website. An offer for an alternative course may be made to rejected applicants.

Keele Conditional offers are normally made in grades for Medicine, Pharmacy and Physiotherapy. For other subjects offers are usually made in Tariff points and include points for Key Skills at Level 3, stand-alone AS-levels and Advanced Extension Awards. The Advanced Diploma is accepted as equivalent to three A-levels and general studies is also accepted as a condition of an offer. Applicants are normally required to be currently undertaking some formal study before starting a course, but if this is not possible the University may make an offer for a Foundation course.

Kent The University accepts a wide range of qualifications. For mature students and those without the required qualifications Foundation course offers may be made. Applicants returning to study after a long break are advised to contact the admissions staff before making a UCAS application. Deferred entry is acceptable but should be mentioned on the application. The University regards the personal statement as important and recommends that applicants research their chosen courses thoroughly, and show an understanding of the curriculum.

Kingston Admissions staff look carefully at each applicant's academic record, references and personal statement. Some courses require interviews where selectors look for evidence of the applicant's intellectual capacity, course knowledge and enthusiasm. Punctuality and a smart appearance could be important.

Lancaster The University welcomes applications from students wishing to defer entry. General studies is acceptable for the majority of courses. Schools and colleges should include clearly in their references the range of programmes available to their students, whether students are required to sit AS-level examinations if they are continuing the subject to A-level, and whether it is school policy to list AS-level results on the UCAS application. Admissions tutors accept a range of qualifications for entry. Some candidates are interviewed before an offer is made, but most are invited to an informal post-offer Open Day which can involve an interview or discussion with an admissions tutor.

Leeds The University welcomes students who do not come straight from school or college or who wish to defer entry. It also welcomes the increased breadth of post-16 qualifications. Some courses do not accept AL general studies or critical thinking.

Leeds Met Most offers are made in UCAS points, and interviews are held before an offer is made for some courses. Deferred entry is acceptable although applicants should be aware that some courses may change slightly each year. Students without the required qualifications may provide a 'portfolio of achievement', giving, for example, information about their work experience and their reasons for applying for the course, and also providing references.

Leicester Most courses do not interview applicants although invitations to visit the University will follow any offers made. Most offers are made on the basis of three A-levels although in some cases two A-levels and two AS-levels may be accepted. The University welcomes the Extended Project which should be mentioned in the personal statement. The Advanced Diploma and the Cambridge Pre-U Diploma are also acceptable qualifications. Applications from suitably qualified students are also considered for second year entry. Contact the subject department for further information.

Lincoln On some courses, notably Art and Design and Architecture, an interview with a portfolio is sometimes required before an offer can be made. The University accepts a wide range of qualifications but students without the standard entry requirements may still be offered a place on the basis of prior experience and qualifications.

Liverpool Most departments will invite applicants to visit the University before or after an offer is made. Some departments require interviews. Offers are normally based on three A-levels or equivalent (a wide range of qualifications is accepted). Some programmes will accept two A-levels and two AS-levels.

Liverpool Hope Students who are invited for audition or interview are encouraged to bring their Records of Achievement.

Liverpool John Moores The personal statement is regarded as highly important and students are advised to include all relevant interests and work experience. The University welcomes a wide range of entry qualifications. If an applicant fails to receive an offer for their chosen course then an offer for an alternative course may be made.

London (Birk) Applications are made on-line. For details contact the Registry at www.bbk.ac.uk.

London (Court) History, history of art, English and modern European languages are the most relevant A-level subjects for the one BA course in History of Art, but applications will be considered from those studying other subjects. Art offered at A-level should normally include a history of art paper. The ability to read foreign languages is a particular asset. The offer of BBB is flexible.

London (Gold) While offers are stipulated for courses, candidates are assessed individually and may receive an offer lower than the published grades. Some applicants are interviewed, in particular those for Art and Design degrees for which examples of current art and design work are required before interview. Applicants requiring deferred entry (which may or may not be acceptable depending on the course) should contact the admissions tutor before applying. International students applying for the BA in Design, or the MEng/BEng in Design and Innovation who are unable to attend for interview are asked to send photographs and explanations of their work.

London (Hey) When considering applications Heythrop takes note of applicants' current and predicted performance at A-level, their ability to study at the relevant level, to take increasing responsibility for their own learning and their motivation to engage intellectually with issues in theology and philosophy.

London (King's) Applicants will normally have taken four AS-level subjects and pursued three of these at A-level. However, departments will also consider those who have taken five AS-levels and passed only two of these at A-level. Applicants may take all their examinations at the end of Year 13 without prejudice. Conditional offers may include the fourth AS-level, a high grade possibly compensating for a failure to obtain the right grade in one of the A-level subjects. AS and A-level general studies and critical thinking are not accepted although the grade achieved may be considered when the required grades of an offer have not been met. Applicants are not required to take aptitude tests, except for Dentistry, Law and Medicine. Deferred entry is acceptable.

London (QM) It is possible for students to join undergraduate degree programmes at the beginning of the second and sometimes the third year. Those wishing to transfer their degree studies from another UK higher education institution may be considered but should contact the subject department before applying to obtain approval.

London (RH) Applicants likely to meet the entry requirements may be called for interview or invited to an Open Day. International students may be asked to submit an example of academic work or other exercise although it would be preferable if they could visit the campus. Interviews are not intended to be nerve-wracking or daunting but rather a chance to assess the candidate's potential. In Music there may be an audition, in Drama a workshop session, and in Modern Languages some conversation in the appropriate language. Candidates who fail to meet the requirements of their offer may still be offered a place, particularly if they shone at interview.

London (RVC) Applications for deferred entry are considered but the offer conditions must be met in the same academic year as the application. Applicants holding offers from RVC who fall slightly below the grades required are always reconsidered and may be offered entry if places are available.

London (St George's) Interviews and admissions test are required for most courses. Once admitted students are not allowed to change courses.

London (Sch Pharm) Applicants are recommended to write a supplementary personal statement explaining their interest in studying Pharmacy. The statement should be sent directly to the admissions tutor before the interview. Qualified applicants are required to attend for interview.

London (SOAS) Offers may be made without an interview and particular attention is paid to past and predicted academic performance. SOAS is happy to consider deferred entry which should be stated on the UCAS application.

London (UCL) UCL welcomes applications from students proposing to spend a pre-university year engaged in constructive activity in the UK or abroad. About 9% of UCL's undergraduates take a Gap Year. Those wanting to enter the second or third year of a degree programme should make early contact with the relevant subject department to obtain approval. Applications are assessed on the basis of the personal statement, the referee's report and the predicted academic performance. UCL is one of the few universities that interviews a significant proportion of its applicants. The programme for the day varies but will include a talk about the subject, a tour of the campus, a discussion with current students and the interview itself. Interviews vary, some being subject-based, others focusing on motivation and communication skills. Decisions on admission are final and there is normally no right of appeal.

London LSE While many other qualifications are considered in the selection of applicants, the vast majority of applicants are expected to have taken four AS-level subjects, followed by three at A-level. Applicants will not be penalised if they have not been able to take the normal number of AS and AL subjects but referees should advise on such circumstances. Applicants normally offer A-levels in LSE's preferred subjects which do not include AS/AL accounting, art and design, business studies, communication studies, design and technology, drama and theatre studies (for some departments), home economics, ICT, law, media studies, music technology, sports studies, travel and tourism. The A* grade may be used for the 2012 entry – check with departments. The Advanced Diploma in Society Health and Development will be considered with one A-level in the additional/specialist learning component plus one free-standing additional A-level in a preferred subject. Competition is particularly high for the Accounting and Finance, Economics, Law, and Management courses. Predicted grades on the application will not guarantee an offer of a place. Applications are often held in a 'gathered field' (candidates are informed) and decisions made only when all on-time applications have been received. All first-year students follow a new course in their degree programme 'Understanding the causes of things'(LSE 100) which actively challenges them to analyse questions of current public concern and to develop their critical skills. Some applicants will be asked to take an entrance examination (held in March each year), which lasts for three hours and consists of a précis of an English language text, essays on general discussion topics and tests of mathematical understanding. Sample papers are available from web pages from January to March. It is unlikely that there will be any course vacancies when the A-level results are published.

London Met Applicants may be required to sit a test or to submit a portfolio of work.

London South Bank Applicants not achieving the grades required for their chosen course should contact the University which may still be able to make an offer of a place. All applicants are interviewed for Nursing, Allied Health Professions and Architecture courses.

Loughborough The University will not use admissions tests for entry in 2012. It does not differentiate between applicants taking A-levels for the first time or re-sitting subjects. The Advanced Diploma is acceptable for most undergraduate degrees (see below) although for some degrees applicants may be asked to achieve an A-level in an appropriate subject or relevant Additional Specialist Learning. In most cases offers are based on the application following an invitation to visit the University. All applicants are interviewed prior to making an offer for Aeronautical and Automotive Engineering, Information Science, Design and Technology, Civil Engineering and Art and Design. Transfers between courses may be possible providing that the required entry requirements have been achieved. The following Advanced Diploma subjects are accepted for some courses:

Business, Administration and Finance Diploma Business and Management, Economics, History and International Relations, Information Science, Politics.

Construction Diploma Architectural Engineering, Commercial Management and Quantity Surveying, Geography.

Creative and Media Diploma Business and Management, Design and Technology, Drama, English, Ergonomics, History and International Relations, Information Science, Politics, Psychology, Social Sciences.

Engineering Diploma Chemistry, Computer Science, Design and Technology, all Engineering subjects, Mathematics.

Environmental and Land-Based Studies Diploma Architectural Engineering, Commercial Management and Quantity Surveying, Geography.

IT Diploma Architectural Engineering, Business and Management, Chemistry, Commercial Management and Quantity Surveying, Computer Science, Design and Technology, Drama, Economics, Electronic and Electrical Engineering, English, Ergonomics, Geography, History and International Relations, Information Science, Mathematics, Politics, Psychology, Social Sciences.

Manufacturing and Product Design Diploma Design and Technology, Manufacturing Engineering, Materials Engineering.

The University's admissions and associated policies are available on its website: www.lboro.ac.uk/admin/ar/admissions/sacop/index.htm.

Manchester Entry requirements are set at course level: check course requirements at www.manchester. ac.uk/undergraduate/courses for latest information. Methods of assessing applications vary between courses and may involve interviews, supporting information and aptitude tests. Unit grades normally will not form part of the offer, except for Mathematics programmes. Candidates who fail to achieve the required grades of an offer should not automatically assume that they have been rejected. In the case of failure to obtain a place on a course it should not be assumed that a department will consider a re-application for a course.

Manchester Met Admissions staff look for personal statements showing evidence of the applicants' motivation and commitment to their chosen courses, work or voluntary experience relevant to any chosen career, and extra-curricular activities, achievements and interests which are relevant to the chosen courses.

Middlesex Some courses start in January (see www.mdx.uk/janstart).

Newcastle In general, offers will be made in grades to be achieved, not in Tariff points. A and AS-level critical thinking and in some cases general studies will be considered. The Advanced Diploma is welcomed although it may not be acceptable for some courses. Offers will also be made for the Cambridge Pre-U Diploma, together with other specified subjects.

Newman (UC) Basic literacy and numeracy tests are required for Humanities, Primary Education and English. A written test is set for applicants to Youth and Community Work.

Newport Interviews and auditions are held for applicants to Art, Media and Design courses.

Northampton Achievement in Key Skills units counts towards the final UCAS Tariff points score.

Northumbria Interviews are compulsory for courses in Architecture, most courses in Art and Design and courses in Health and Teaching. There are no admissions tests.

Nottingham Although grade predictions may match the offers published for the course there is no guarantee that an offer can be made.

Nottingham Trent The UCAS personal statement is seen as a key part of the application process; the University website provides a guide on its possible content and preparation.

Open University There are no formal entry qualifications for admission to courses.

Oxford The University will not use the A* grade when making offers for 2011 entry but will review this policy in time to advise those applying for 2012 entry. All A-levels except general studies are approved for admissions purposes but specific subject requirements must be met. If applicants have taken the Extended Project (EP), the University will not make it a condition for an offer but it does recognise its potential value to applicants for study at the University and encourages applicants to use their experience of the EP when writing their personal statements, especially if their EP topic is related to their chosen degree course. The Advanced Diploma in Engineering will be accepted for Engineering courses provided candidates obtain both an A-level in Physics and the new Level 3 Certificate in Mathematics for Engineering.

Oxford Brookes For all applications considerable emphasis is placed on the personal statement. Referees are requested to give reasons for their statements, for example, whether predicted grades are based on the results of studies at the end of Year 12, how applicants' skills have been assessed. Fine Art applicants wishing to take a Gap Year should contact the admissions tutor before applying.

Plymouth The University looks for evidence in the UCAS personal statement of your understanding of the course, good numeracy and literacy skills, motivation and commitment, work experience or placement or voluntary work, especially if it is relevant to your course, any sponsorships or placements you have applied for, and your possible plans for a Gap Year.

Portsmouth For some courses applicants will be expected to attend an interview as part of the selection process. The University accepts the principle of credit transfer and wherever possible, recognition will be given to prior learning in order to facilitate admission with advanced standing. It also welcomes applications from those taking the Advanced Diploma: one A-level will be required in most cases. The Extended Project is not a requirement but may be taken into consideration.

Queen Margaret Applicants are interviewed for some courses including Physiotherapy and Speech Sciences.

Queen's Belfast Applications for admission to full-time undergraduate courses are made through UCAS except for courses in Midwifery and Nursing. These should be made direct to the University's School of Nursing and Midwifery (see www.qub.ac.uk). Interviews are essential for Medicine and Dentistry.

Reading For some courses admissions tutors may interview before making an offer, and in a few programmes, they may make an offer of a place which is dependent on passing the interview. The University welcomes evidence of Key Skills in students' portfolios, and will take them into account when making offers, although points from Key Skills will not be included in the standard offers.

Robert Gordon Interviews are held for some courses, for example Social Work.

Roehampton Applicants successfully achieving the new Level 3 Advanced Diplomas will be considered for entry onto degrees in closely related subjects. For entry to other subjects, each application will be judged taking the applicant's entire academic record into account and on its own merit.

St Andrews The University highlights the importance of the personal statement and the quality of this is likely to decide which applicants receive offers. It looks for well-organised, well-written statements which include information about the applicants, their interests, relevant work experience, any voluntary work, ideas about career choice and, importantly, their reasons for their choice of course. Admissions tutors prefer candidates to achieve their grades at the first sitting, and if they re-apply, to upgrade their academic attainment if that was the main reason for UCAS rejection. Only candidates for Medicine A100 are interviewed; no other subjects interview as a matter of course.

Salford The University is committed to widening participation; it does not make lower offers on the basis of educational or social disadvantage.

Sheffield Qualifications already achieved (including GCSEs), predicted grades and personal statements are the most important parts in assessing an application. Interviews are not a pre-requisite of admission however some departments do interview to further assess the motivation and personal qualities of applicants. Departments that interview include Medicine, Dentistry, Orthoptics, Human Communication Science and Social Work.

Sheffield Hallam An intensive six-week preparation course in mathematics is offered, equivalent to GCSE maths, to applicants who are unable to meet the entrance requirements for their chosen course.

Southampton The University looks for a well-considered personal statement, focusing on your reasons for choosing a particular course, the skills you would bring to it, information about any relevant work experience, your career ideas, your personal interests related to the course, and your thoughts about 'what makes you stand out in a crowd'.

Southampton Solent Admissions staff look for applicants' reasons for their course choice, and for evidence of their abilities and ambitions.

Staffordshire The University provides an on-line workbook for helping applicants to prepare their personal statements.

Stirling It is essential to include in the personal statement your reasons for choosing your specified course. The University also looks for evidence of your transferable skills, for example communication skills, teamwork, and how you acquired these, for example through work experience, voluntary work, academic studies, hobbies and general life experience.

Strathclyde Formal interviews are required for some Faculty of Education courses; informal interviews are held by some Science and Engineering courses.

Suffolk (Univ Campus) Applications from students studying Diploma qualifications are welcomed and the Progression, Advanced and Extended Diplomas are considered to meet the minimum entry requirements for university study. Depending on which course the student applies for, and which Diploma they are studying, specific Additional and Specific Learning or other qualifications may also be required.

Sunderland The University holds informal interviews for certain courses, when applicants will be asked to present their portfolio, or to give an audition, or to talk about themselves and why they want to study for that particular course.

Surrey The University is willing to consider deferring an application for one year, providing it considers that this will benefit the applicant's studies. Contact the admissions staff if you are considering deferred entry.

Sussex Apart from Social Work and Medicine, interviews at Sussex are increasingly unusual, but some departments may ask for examples of written work or for an additional reference. Mature students submitting a strong application but without the relevant qualifications will probably be asked to attend an interview and submit an essay of up to 1500 words on their chosen subject.

Swansea Admissions test is required for Medicine. Selectors take into account the candidate's ability to contribute to the cultural, sporting and social life of the University.

Swansea Met For many courses an interview is an important part of the selection process.

Teesside Interviews are held for a wide range of courses, and successful applicants are given an individualised offer. Each course accepts a minimum of 20 UCAS Tariff points for Level 3 Key Skills.

Trinity Saint David The University guarantees to give equal consideration to all applicants irrespective of when their applications are received. Applicants who successfully complete the residential Wales Summer School at Lampeter, Aberystwyth or Carmarthen are offered a place on an appropriate course of study on completion of their current school or college course.

Ulster Applicants seeking admission to any of the following courses should use the University's direct entry form: BSc courses in Community Nursing, Specialist Nursing Practice, Nursing Sciences, and Health Sciences, the Certificate in Information Technology and Professional Development for Women and the Diploma in Telematics and Management Studies.

Warwick The University welcomes the introduction of the A* grade and is monitoring developments. Students taking the Advanced Diploma will be considered if they are taking subjects closely aligned to the chosen degree courses, and they must also take appropriate additional specialised learning options: they are advised to contact the admissions team before making their application. Advice on the completion of the application is available on www.warwick.ac.uk/go/study. Feedback can be provided if requested for candidates whose application has been rejected.

West London The University accepts each of the new 14–19 Diplomas as qualification for entry on to all of its undergraduate courses, providing the UCAS Tariff points achieved by applicants match or exceed the UCAS Tariff points listed in the course entry requirements. The University welcomes applicants with the Extended Project, and offers an Extended Project module to students in Years 12 and 13 in the school holidays. It is also possible to transfer credits achieved at another university to a course at Thames Valley.

West Scotland Applications to Nursing and Midwifery courses are not made through UCAS but through the Centralised Applications to Nursing and Midwifery Training Clearing House (CATCH): contact the University for details.

Westminster Interviews are usually only required for Media, Art and Design and Complementary Therapy courses. The University accepts transfers into Years 1, 2 or 3 of a full-time degree programme if students have studied similar units to the chosen Westminster course, and have passed Year 1 and Year 2, each with 120 credits.

Winchester The following programmes require applicants to take a second subject at Level 1: Childhood, Youth and Community Studies; Education Studies; Education Studies (Early Childhood); Film Studies; Media Studies; Politics and Global Studies; Psychology; Theology and Religious Studies. Second subjects can be contrasting or complementary.

Wolverhampton Admissions staff make decisions on the basis of the application, and may invite applicants for interview or audition. If an applicant cannot meet the entry requirements for the chosen course, the University may offer an alternative course, or give the applicant feedback about why it was unable to offer a place.

Worcester The University advises applicants to consider their personal statements carefully. It advises them to include their reasons for their choice of degree programme, their career plans, their outside interests and work experience, and any other information they consider relevant. Applicants who are not accepted are not necessarily rejected: they may receive a 'changed programme' offer which they need not accept if they prefer to enter Clearing.

York The University welcomes applicants with the Advanced Diploma, and Departments will consider applicants studying any of the following Diplomas: Construction and the Built Environment, Creative and Media, IT, and Society, Health and Development.

York St John Interviews are compulsory for the following courses: Primary Education, Occupational Therapy, Physiotherapy, Product Design, Fine Art and Counselling.

5 | APPLICATIONS

ENTRY REQUIREMENTS

Before applying to universities and colleges, be sure that you have the required subjects and qualifications for entry to your chosen course. Details of entry requirements are available direct from the universities and colleges. You will need to check:

(i) the general entry requirements for courses.
(ii) any specific subject requirements to enter a particular course, for example, study of specified GCE A- and/or AS-levels, Scottish Highers/Advanced Highers, GCSEs, Scottish Standard Grades, or BTEC qualifications (for example, National Diploma, National Certificate). The course requirements are set out in prospectuses and on websites.
(iii) any age, health, Criminal Records Bureau (CRB) clearance or other requirements for entry to particular courses and universities and colleges. For entry to some specific courses such as Medicine and Nursing, offers are made subject to health screening for hepatitis B, for example, and immunisation requirements. Owing to Government regulations, some universities will insist on a minimum age at entry of 18 years. Check university and college websites and prospectuses for these particular course requirements.
(iv) admissions tests required by a number of universities for a range of subjects, including Dentistry, Law, Medicine and Veterinary Science/Medicine. Offers of places made by these universities are dependent on an applicant's performance in the relevant test. It is important to find out full details about universities' course requirements for possible admissions tests well before submitting the UCAS application and to make all the necessary arrangements for registering and taking any required admissions tests. See **Chapter 6** and check university/college and admissions tests websites for the latest information.

Potential applicants should ask the advice of teachers, careers advisers and university and college advisers before submitting their application.

APPLICATIONS FOR UNIVERSITY AND COLLEGE COURSES THROUGH UCAS

UCAS, the organisation responsible for managing applications to higher education courses in the UK, deals with applications for admission to full-time and sandwich first degrees, Foundation degrees, Diploma of Higher Education and Higher National Diploma courses and some full-time Higher National Certificate courses in nearly all universities (but not the Open University), university colleges, colleges and institutes of higher education, specialist colleges and some further education colleges.

The UCAS application process

Full details of application procedures and all course information can be found on the UCAS website. Other information is also available in the *UCAS Guide to Getting Into University and College* and other UCAS publications (available from www.ucasbooks.com or from UCAS Media, PO Box 130, Cheltenham GL52 3ZF, tel 01242 544610).

Applications are made online at www.ucas.com using **UCAS Apply**. This is a secure web-based application system, which has been designed for all applicants whether they are applying through a UCAS-registered centre, such as a school or college, or applying independently from anywhere in the world.

Applications can be sent to UCAS from mid-September. The first deadline is 15 October for applications to Oxford or Cambridge Universities and applications for courses in Medicine, Dentistry and Veterinary Science/Medicine. The deadline for UK and EU applicants to apply for all other courses is 15 January, except for some Art and Design courses that have a 24 March deadline. You can still apply after these deadlines up to 30 June, but institutions may not be able to consider you.

On the UCAS application, you have up to five course choices unless you are applying for Dentistry, Medicine or Veterinary Science/Medicine. For these courses only four choices are permitted.

It is important to note that some universities (for example Cambridge) now require their applicants to complete a Supplementary Application Questionnaire after they have received your UCAS application. Check the websites of your listed universities for their latest application information.

Each university or college makes any offer through the UCAS system. UCAS does not make offers, or recruit on behalf of universities and colleges. It does not advise applicants on their choice of subject although it does publish material which applicants may find useful.

Applicants may receive an 'unconditional' offer in the case of those who already hold the required qualifications, or, for those awaiting examination results, a 'conditional' offer or a rejection. When all decisions have been received from universities or colleges, applicants may finally hold up to two offers: a first choice (firm) offer and an insurance offer. Applicants who have made five choices and have no offers or have declined any offers received can use **UCAS Extra**. Applicants are told when they become eligible for **UCAS Extra** and can apply online for one further course at a time using **UCAS Track** at www. ucas.com. **UCAS Extra** runs from 24 February until 4 July. Courses available in **UCAS Extra** will be highlighted on **Course Search** at www.ucas.com. Applicants not placed through this system will be eligible to contact institutions with vacancies in **Clearing** from mid-July.

Confirmation starts on the day when the A-level examination results are released. **Clearing** vacancy lists are also published on A-level results day. Applicants meeting the conditions of their offers for their firm choice will receive confirmation from their university or college and may still be accepted even if their results are slightly lower than those stipulated in the original offer. If rejected by their firm choice university/college, applicants will have their places confirmed by their insurance choice institution providing they have obtained the right grades. Applicants who are unsuccessful with both their institutions will be eligible to go into **Clearing** in which they can select an appropriate course in the same or a different institution where places are available. Each year up to 40,000 applicants obtain places through **Clearing**, and over 5500 applicants found a place though **Extra** last year.

UCAS timetable

Mid-September 2011	UCAS begins accepting applications.
15 October	Deadline for UCAS to receive applications to Oxford University or the University of Cambridge, and applications to courses in Medicine, Dentistry or Veterinary Medicine/Science.
15 January 2012	Deadline for UCAS to receive applications from UK and EU applicants for all other courses, except for some Art and Design courses that have a 24 March deadline. Visit **Course Search** at www.ucas.com to find out whether Art and Design courses have a 15 January or 24 March deadline.
16 January–30 June	Applications received by UCAS are forwarded to the institutions for consideration at their discretion. Applications received after 30 June are processed through **Clearing**.
24 February–4 July	Applicants who have made five choices and have no offers or who have declined any offers received can use **UCAS Extra** to apply for one further course at a time on **UCAS Track** at www.ucas.com. Institutions will show which courses have vacancies in **UCAS Extra** on the UCAS website. Details of the **UCAS Extra** service will be included in the *Applicant Welcome Guide* sent to applicants.
24 March	Deadline for UCAS to receive applications for some Art and Design courses. Visit **Course Search** at www.ucas.com to find out whether Art and Design courses have a 15 January or 24 March deadline.
9 May	Applicants who have received all their decisions from universities and colleges by the end of March are asked to reply to their offers by this date.
7 June	Applicants receiving decisions from all their choices by 9 May must reply to their offers by this date.
30 June	Last date for receiving applications. Applications received after this date are entered directly into **Clearing**. In mid-July **Clearing** starts.
4 August	Scottish SQA results published.

16 August   GCE A-level and AS-level results published. **Clearing** vacancy information available. (See **What To Do on Results Day … and After** below.)

PLEASE NOTE

- You are not required to reply to any university/college offers until you have received your last decision.
- Do not send a firm acceptance to more than one offer.
- Do not try to alter a firm acceptance.
- Send a Cancel slip to, or phone, UCAS at once if you decide not to go to university/college this year.
- Remember to tell the institutions and UCAS if you change your address, or change your examination board(s), subjects or arrangements.

Information on the special arrangements for applications for Law, Medicine and Dentistry can be found under separate headings in Chapter 6.

APPLICATIONS FOR MUSIC COURSES AT CONSERVATOIRES

The Conservatoires UK Admissions Service (CUKAS) handles applications for practical Music courses. Applications can be made simultaneously to a maximum of six of the conservatoires listed below and simultaneous applications can also be made to both UCAS and CUKAS. Full details of CUKAS are given on www.cukas.ac.uk. The conservatoires taking part in this online admissions system are:

- Birmingham Conservatoire www.conservatoire.uce.ac.uk
- Leeds College of Music www.lcm.ac.uk
- Royal College of Music www.rcm.ac.uk
- Royal Northern College of Music www.rncm.ac.uk
- Royal Scottish Academy of Music and Drama www.rsamd.ac.uk
- Royal Welsh College of Music and Drama www.rwcmd.ac.uk
- Trinity Laban Conservatoire of Music and Dance www.tcm.ac.uk

See also the **Music** table of interview requirements/tests in **Chapter 6**.

APPLICATIONS FOR TEACHER TRAINING COURSES

Applicants intending to start a course of initial teacher training in England leading to Qualified Teacher Status have to be provisionally registered with the General Teaching Council of England (GTCE). Check www.gtce.org.uk for full details. See also www.gttr.ac.uk/students/beforeyouapply and www.tda.gov.uk for full details of applying for undergraduate (and postgraduate) training courses. Students in Wales and Northern Ireland should also check with this website; Scottish students should check www.gtcs.org.uk.

THE UCAS APPLICATION

Two important aspects of the UCAS application concern Sections 3 and 10. In Section 3 all your university/college choices (a maximum of five) are to be listed, but remember that you should not mix your subjects. For example, in popular subject areas such as English, History or Physiotherapy, it is safer to show total commitment by applying for all courses in the same subject and not to include second and/or third subject alternatives on the form. (See advice in separate tables in **Chapter 8** for **Medicine**, **Dentistry** and **Veterinary Science/Medicine**.)

A brief glance at the subject tables in **Chapter 8** will give you some idea of the popularity of various courses. In principle, institutions want the best applicants available so if there are large numbers of applicants the offers made will be higher. For Medicine and a number of other courses, offers in terms of A-level grades are now reaching AAA or A* grades, and often with additional AS-levels. Conversely, for the less popular subjects such as Chemistry or Manufacturing Engineering, the offers can be much lower – down to CCC, but with many more applicants expected in 2011 for entry in 2012, typical offers for many courses have increased significantly.

Similarly, some institutions are more popular (not necessarily better) than others. Again, this popularity can be judged easily in the tables in **Chapter 8**: the higher the offer, the more popular the institution. Popular universities often are located in attractive towns or cities such as Bristol, Exeter, Warwick, Bath or York. Additionally, some institutions have established a good 'reputation' for various reasons, for example, Oxford, Cambridge and Durham. Conversely and unfortunately, some universities have confused applicants with unfamiliar names and no immediate identity as to their location, such as De Montfort and Brunel. More students would apply to these excellent institutions if they knew where they were situated! Because of the intense competition for places at the popular universities, applications to five of them could result in rejections from all of them! (If you are not good enough for one of them you won't be good enough for the other four!) Spread your choice of institutions.

When you have chosen your courses and your institutions, look again at the offers made and compare these with the grades projected by your teachers on your UCAS reference. It is most important to maximise your chances of a place by choosing institutions which might make you a range of offers. When all universities have considered your application you can hold only two offers (one firm and one insurance offer) and naturally it is preferable for one to be lower than the other in case you do not achieve the offer grades or equivalent points for your first choice of university or college.

The other section of the UCAS application that deserves careful thought is Section 10 (the personal statement). This seems simple enough but it is the only part of the application where you can put in a personal bid for a place! In short, you are asked to give relevant background information about yourself, your interests and your choice of course and career. Give yourself plenty of time to prepare Section 10 – if you have a Record of Achievement you could use it as a guide – as this part of your application could make all the difference to getting an offer or not.

Motivation to undertake your chosen course is very important. You can show this by giving details of any work experience and work shadowing you have done (and for History courses, for example, details of visits to places of historical interest). It is a good idea to begin your statement with such evidence and explain how your interest in your chosen subject has developed. In the subject tables in **Chapter 8** under **Advice to applicants and planning the UCAS personal statement**, advice is given on what you might include in Section 10. You should also include various activities in which you have been involved in the last three or four years. Get your parents and other members of the family to refresh your memory – it is easy to forget something quite important. You might consider planning out this section in a series of sub-sections – and if you have a lot to say, be brief. The sub-sections can include:

- **School activities** Are you a prefect, chairperson or treasurer of a society? Are you involved in supervisory duties of any kind? Are you in a school team? Which team? For how long? (Remember, team means any team: sports, chess, debating, even business.)
- **Intellectual activities** Have you attended any field or lecture courses in your main subjects? Where? When? Have you taken part in any school visits? Do you play in the school orchestra or have you taken part in a school drama production – on or off stage? Do you go to the theatre, art galleries or concerts?
- **Out-of-school activities** This category might cover many of the topics above, but it could also include any community or voluntary work you do, or Duke of Edinburgh's Awards, the Combined Cadet Force (CCF), sport, music and drama activities etc. The countries you have visited might also be mentioned – for example, any exchange visits with friends living abroad.
- **Work experience** Details of part-time, holiday or Saturday jobs could be included here, particularly if they have some connection with your chosen course. Some applicants plan ahead and arrange to visit firms and discuss career interests with various people who already work in their chosen field. For some courses such as Veterinary Science, work experience is essential, and it certainly helps for others, for example Medicine and Business courses.
- **Key Skills** These cover numeracy, communication and information technology (the basics) and also advanced skills involving teamwork, problem solving and improving your own learning. If you are not offering the Key Skills Certificate then evidence of your strengths in these areas may be mentioned in the school or college reference or you may include examples in your personal statement relating to your out-of-school activities.

Finally, plan your personal statement carefully. You may write short statements if you wish. It is not essential to write in prose except perhaps if you are applying for English or language courses in which case your statement will be judged grammatically! Take a copy to use as a trial and a copy of your complete application to keep by you for reference if you are called for interview. Almost certainly you will be questioned on what you have written.

Admissions tutors always stress the importance of the confidential report from your head teacher or form tutors. Most schools and colleges will make some effort to find out why you want to apply for a particular course, but if they do not ask, do not take it for granted that they will know! Consequently, although you have the opportunity to write about your interests on the form, it is still a good idea to tell your teachers about them. Also, if you have to work at home under difficult conditions or if you have any medical problem, your teachers must be told since these points should be mentioned on the report.

Deferred entry
Although application is usually made in the autumn of the year preceding the proposed year of entry, admissions tutors may be prepared to consider an application made two years before entry, so that the applicant can, perhaps, gain work experience or spend a period abroad. Policies on deferred entry may differ from department to department, so you should check with admissions tutors before applying. Simply remember that there is no guarantee that you will get the grades you need or a place at the university of your first choice at the first attempt! If not, you may need to repeat A-levels and try again. It may be better not to apply for deferred entry until you are certain in August of your grades and your place.

APPLICATIONS TO THE UNIVERSITY OF CAMBRIDGE
The University recently announced changes to its applications process so you will need to check with its Admissions Office or on www.cam.ac.uk/admissions/undergraduate/apply for the latest information. If you are a UK or EU applicant, you now need only complete the UCAS application. You will then receive an email from the University, confirming the arrival of your application and giving you the website address of their online Supplementary Application Questionnaire (SAQ) which you will then need to complete and return by the specified date.

Your UCAS application listing Cambridge as one of your university choices must be sent to UCAS by 15 October. If you are applying for Medicine or Veterinary Medicine you must include your BMAT registration with your application. You can indicate your choice of college or make an Open application if you have no preference. Open applicants are allocated by a computer program to colleges that have had fewer applicants per place for your chosen subject.

The Cambridge Special Access Scheme (CSAS) is also available for applicants whose schooling has been disrupted or disadvantaged. You need to complete a CSAS application by 15 October but discuss this with your school/college higher education adviser and check with the UCAS website for more information. Interviews take place in Cambridge in the first three weeks of December, although some may be a little earlier. Many of the University's colleges use tests as part of the selection process for specific courses and written work also may be requested before interview. This practice, however, varies between colleges and subjects. See the University website and **Chapter 6** for information you need to know before completing and submitting your application.

In January applicants receive either an offer conditional upon certain grades in examinations to be taken the following summer, or a rejection. Alternatively, you may be placed in a pool for further consideration. About one in five applicants are pooled and one in four receive an offer. Decisions are made on the basis of academic record, reference, personal statement, submitted work/test results and interviews. The conditions set are grades to be obtained in examinations such as A-levels, Scottish Highers/Advanced Highers or the International Baccalaureate. Offers made by some Cambridge University colleges may also include Sixth Term Examination Papers (STEP) in mathematics (see **Chapter 6** under *Mathematics*). The STEPs are taken in June and copies of past papers and full details are available from www.admissionstests.cambridgeassessment.org.uk.

College policies
All colleges which admit undergraduates use the selection procedures described in **Chapter 6**. However, there will be some minor variations between the various colleges, within each college and also between

subjects. Further information about the policies of any particular college can be found in the Cambridge Undergraduate Prospectus and may also be obtained from the admissions tutor of the college concerned. No college operates a quota system for any subject except Medicine and Veterinary Medicine, for which there are strict quotas for the University from which places are allocated to each college.

Full details of the admissions procedures are contained in the current Cambridge Undergraduate Prospectus. Copies of the prospectus are available from Cambridge Admissions Office, Fitzwilliam House, 32 Trumpington Street, Cambridge CB2 1QY, or via the website www.cam.ac.uk/admissions.

APPLICATIONS TO THE UNIVERSITY OF OXFORD

Application procedures to Oxford are similar to all other universities except that candidates applying to Oxford must submit a UCAS application by 15 October 2011 for those applying for entry in October 2012 or for deferred entry in October 2013. Admissions are carried out on a college basis: candidates can name a college of preference and may be allocated second and third preference colleges, but if they do not have a specific college in mind, they can make an open application. This means that they will be allocated a college by the Admissions Office computer which takes account of their chosen course and the approximate number of applicants per place that each college has received that year (and gender in the case of the one women-only college).

For some subjects at some colleges at Oxford, applicants are required to sit aptitude or admissions tests (for example, the History Aptitude Test, the National Admissions Test for Law (LNAT) and the BioMedical Admissions Test (BMAT)) or to provide essays or a portfolio for interview. Specimen test questions are published on the website. See **Chapter 6** for more information and see www.ox.ac.uk/admissions/ undergraduatecourses/howtoapply for full details. All candidates are considered carefully on their individual merits. Tutors take into account a range of information from the candidate's application including details of their academic record and the reference in order to assess a candidate's suitability and potential for his or her proposed course. Candidates applying for some courses may be required to submit samples of marked school work by early November, and/or to take a short written test when they are in Oxford for interview (see **Chapter 6**). The majority of candidates applying to Oxford are invited for interview at the beginning of December and this is an integral part of the selection procedure. Candidates will be interviewed at their college of preference and also may be interviewed by other colleges. Colleges co-operate and pool candidates to ensure that the most able candidates are offered places. Successful candidates who have not completed their school-leaving examinations will be made conditional offers based on their forthcoming examinations such as A-levels, Scottish Highers, Advanced Highers, International Baccalaureate, European Baccalaureate and other European and international qualifications. Decisions are notified to candidates via UCAS by the end of January. Candidates are welcome to attend Open Days which are held at all of the colleges and a number of departments, usually during the summer term or in September.

Common Framework

The University and Colleges have agreed to a Common Framework for Colleges and Faculties (see www. admissions.ox.ac.uk/news/common_framework.shtml) which lays down key principles and procedures for undergraduate admissions. The Common Framework is designed to make admissions more transparent, improve methods of assessing candidates and ensure that selection is unaffected by the applicant's choice of college. Colleges will continue to have the final say over whom they admit but they will be guided by the central banding of candidates by faculties based on the whole range of information arising from the selection process. This information may include results from pre-interview tests, written work, school qualifications and/or predicted school-leaving grades, interviews and contextual information about a candidate's educational background.

Where a college wishes to offer a place to a candidate below the 'selection threshold', it will be required to explain the reasons to the relevant faculty with reference to the agreed admissions criteria.

APPLICATIONS TO IRISH UNIVERSITIES

All applications to universities in the Republic of Ireland are made through the Central Application Office, Tower House, Eglinton Street, Galway, Ireland; see www.cao.ie or telephone 091 509 800. The Central Application Office website gives full details of all 44 institutions and details of the application procedure.

Applications are made by 1 February. Individual institutions publish details of their entry requirements for courses, but unlike applications through UCAS in the UK, no conditional offers are made. Applicants are judged purely on their academic ability except for the Royal College of Surgeons which also requires a school reference and a personal statement. The results are published in August when institutions make their offers and when successful students are required to accept or decline the offer.

APPLICATIONS TO COMMONWEALTH UNIVERSITIES
Details of universities in 38 commonwealth countries (all charge fees) are published on www.acu.ac.uk or for Australia (www.students.idp.com) and Canada (www.studyincanada.com).

APPLICATIONS TO AMERICAN UNIVERSITIES
There are over 2000 universities and colleges offering degree course programmes in the USA; some institutions are independent and others state-controlled. Unlike the UK, however, where UCAS control nearly all university and college applications, it is necessary to apply separately to all American universities. Most American universities will expect applicants to have A-levels or IB qualifications and in addition, usually require students to complete a School Assessment Test (SAT) covering mathematical and verbal reasoning abilities. In some cases applicants may be required to take SAT II tests which are based on specific subjects. Tests can be taken at centres in the UK: see www.collegeboard.com.

Unlike the usual specialised subject degrees at UK universities, 'Liberal Arts programmes' in the USA have considerable breadth and flexibility, although subjects requiring greater specialised knowledge such as Medicine and Law require further study at Medical or Law School.

Because of the complexities of an application to American universities, such as financial implications, visas etc, students should initially refer to www.fulbright.co.uk. It is also important to be able to identify the differences between and the quality of institutions and a valuable guide can be sourced through www.petersons.com (*General Guides to Colleges, Scholarships and Admissions*) or see *Barrons Guide*.

THE ERASMUS PROGRAMME
Many universities in the UK have formal agreements with partner institutions in Europe through the Erasmus Programme which enables UK university students to apply for courses in Europe for periods up to one year. Some of these courses are taught in English and students can receive help with accommodation and other expenses through the Erasmus Student Grant scheme.

The Erasmus Programme is for undergraduates in all subject areas who would like to study or do a work placement for three to twelve months as part of their degree course in one of 30 other European countries. Most universities offer it although it is not available with every course so students are advised to check with their chosen universities before making an application. Students do not pay any fees to the European university they visit and those who go for the full academic year (24 weeks) have their UK tuition fees waived.

AND FINALLY ... BEFORE YOU SEND IN YOUR APPLICATION
CHECK that you have passes at Grade C or higher in the GCSE (or equivalent) subjects required for the course at the institutions to which you are applying. FAILURE TO HAVE THE RIGHT GCSE SUBJECTS OR THE RIGHT NUMBER OF GRADE C PASSES OR HIGHER IN GCSE WILL RESULT IN A REJECTION.

CHECK that you are taking (or have taken) the GCE A- and AS-level (or equivalent) subjects required for the course at the institution to which you are applying. FAILURE TO BE TAKING OR HAVE TAKEN THE RIGHT A-levels WILL ALSO RESULT IN A REJECTION.

CHECK that the GCE A-levels and other qualifications you are taking will be accepted for the course for which you are applying. Some subjects and institutions do not stipulate any specific A-levels, only that you are required to offer two or three subjects at GCE A-level. In the view of some admissions tutors NOT ALL GCE A-levels CARRY THE SAME WEIGHT (see **Chapter 1**).

CHECK that you can meet the requirements for all relevant admissions/interview tests.

CHECK that you have made all the necessary arrangements for sitting any required admissions tests.

CHECK that you can meet any age, health and CRB requirements for entry to your listed courses.

WHAT TO DO ON RESULTS DAY … AND AFTER

BE AT HOME! Do not arrange to be away when your results are published. If you do not achieve the grades you require, you will need to follow an alternative course of action and make decisions that could affect your life during the next few years. Do not expect others to make these decisions for you. If you achieve the grades or points which have been offered you will receive confirmation of a place, but this may take a few days to reach you. Once your place is confirmed contact the accommodation office at the university or college and inform them that you will need a place in a hall of residence or other accommodation.

If you achieve grades or points higher than your conditional firm (CF) choice you can reconsider where and what to study by registering with UCAS to use the **Adjustment in Track** process. This is available from A-level results day until 31 August and you have five days to register and secure an alternative course. You must check very carefully all the **Adjustment** information on the UCAS website (www.ucas.com) before changing your CF choice to make sure you are eligible and that a vacancy is available. There is no guarantee of a vacancy on a course you are aiming for, and it is very unlikely that competitive courses will have places. If you decide definitely to change courses advise the university or college immediately, but check with www.ucas.com and your school/college adviser for the latest information.

If your grades or points are higher than you expected and you are not holding any offers you can telephone or e-mail the admissions tutor at the universities and colleges which rejected you and request that they might reconsider you.

If you just miss your offers then telephone or email the universities and colleges to see if they can still offer you a place. ALWAYS HAVE YOUR UCAS REFERENCE NUMBER AVAILABLE WHEN YOU CALL. Their decisions may take a few days. You should check the universities and colleges in your order of preference. Your first choice must reject you before you contact your second choice.

If you have not applied to any university or college earlier in the year then you can apply through the **Clearing** scheme which runs from the middle of July. Check the tables in **Chapter 8** to identify which institutions normally make offers matching your results, then telephone or email the institution to see if they have any vacancies before completing your **Clearing** form.

If you learn finally that you do not have a place you will receive automatically a **Clearing** form to enable you to re-apply. Before you complete this form follow the instructions above.

If an institution has vacancies they will ask you for your grades. If they can consider you they will ask you for your **Clearing** form. You can only be considered by one institution at a time.

If you have to re-apply for a place, check the vacancies on the UCAS website (www.ucas.com), in the national press and through your local careers office. If there are vacancies in your subject, check with the university or college that these vacancies have not been taken.

REMEMBER – There are many thousands of students just like you. Admissions tutors have a mammoth task checking how many students will be taking up their places since not all students whose grades match their offers finally decide to do so!

IF YOU HAVE AN OFFER AND THE RIGHT GRADES BUT ARE NOT ACCEPTING THAT OR AN ALTERNATIVE PLACE – TELL THE UNIVERSITY OR COLLEGE. Someone else is waiting for your place! If you are applying for a place through **Clearing** it may even be late September before you know you have a place so BE PATIENT AND STAY CALM!

Good luck!

ADMISSIONS TESTS, SELECTION OF APPLICANTS AND INTERVIEWS

The selection of applicants by universities and colleges takes many forms. However, with rising numbers of applicants for places (especially in the popular subjects) and increasing numbers of students with high grades, greater importance is now attached not only to applicants' predicted A-level grades and GCSE attainments, but also to other aspects of their applications, especially the school reference and the personal statement and, for some courses and some institutions, performance at interview, and performance in admissions tests.

ADMISSIONS TESTS

Admissions tests are now increasingly used for undergraduate entry to specific courses and specific institutions. These include national subject-based tests such as LNAT, BMAT and UKCAT (see below) which are used for selecting applicants for entry to specified courses at particular institutions in subjects such as Law, Medicine, Dentistry and Veterinary Sciences. Admissions tests are also set by individual universities and colleges (or commercial organisations on their behalf) for entry, again, to particular courses in the individual institutions. Examples of these include the Thinking Skills Assessment (TSA) used by, for example, many Cambridge University colleges, and the Health Professions Aptitude Test (HPAT) used by Ulster University for entry to some health-related courses. Other examples include the subject-based admissions tests used by many universities and colleges for entry to particular courses in subjects such as Art, Dance, Construction, Design, Drama and other Performance-based courses, Education and Teacher Training, Economics, Engineering, Journalism, Languages, Music, Nursing and Social Work.

Admissions tests are usually taken before or at interview and, except for courses requiring auditions or portfolio inspections, they are generally timed, unseen, written, or on-line tests. They can be used on their own, or alongside other selection methods used by university and college admissions staff, including:

- Questionnaires or tests to be completed by applicants prior to interview and/or offer
- Examples of school work to be submitted prior to interview and/or offer
- Written tests at interview
- Mathematical tests at interview
- Practical tests at interview
- A response to a passage at interview
- Performance-based tests (for example, for Music, Dance, Drama).

Applicants should find out early from university prospectuses and websites whether admissions tests are required for entry to their preferred courses, and if so, what these will be, and the arrangements for taking them. This is important, especially for Oxford and Cambridge applicants as many of their courses and colleges also require submission of marked written work done in Years 12 or 13 at school or college.

Here is a list of commonly used admissions tests, and this is followed by degree subject lists showing subject-based and individual institutions' admissions tests.

English
English Literature Admissions Test (ELAT)
The ELAT is a pre-interview admissions test for applicants to English courses at the University of Oxford (see the ELAT pages on the Cambridge Assessment website www.admissionstests.cambridgeassessment.org.uk).

Health Professions
Health Professions Admissions Test (HPAT)
The HPAT is used by the University of Ulster for entry to Dietetics, Occupational Therapy, Physiotherapy, Podiatry, Radiography and Speech and Language Therapies.

History
History Aptitude Test (HAT)
The HAT is a two-hour test sat by all candidates applying for History courses at Oxford University (see *History* below). See www.history.ox.ac.uk.

Law
Cambridge Law Test
This is a new paper-based, one-hour, one-question test designed and used by most of the Cambridge University Colleges with Law applicants who are called for interview. No prior knowledge of law is required for the test. See www.law.cam.ac.uk/admissions/cambridge-law-test.php for full details.

National Admissions Test for Law (LNAT)
The LNAT is an on-screen test for applicants to specified undergraduate Law programmes at the Birmingham, Bristol, Durham, Glasgow, Leeds, London (King's), (UCL), Nottingham and Oxford universities. (See *Law* below, and **Law** in the subject tables in **Chapter 8**.) Applicants need to check universities' websites and the LNAT website (www.lnat.ac.uk) for the UCAS codes for courses requiring applicants to sit the LNAT. (**NB** Cambridge does not now require Law applicants to take the LNAT but see above and the Cambridge entry under *Law* below.) Details of LNAT (which includes multiple-choice and essay questions), practice papers, registration dates, test dates, test centres and fees are all available on the LNAT website.

Mathematics
Sixth Term Examination Paper (STEP)
Applicants with offers for Mathematics courses at Cambridge and Warwick universities are usually required to take STEP. Bristol and Oxford Universities, and Imperial London also encourage applicants for their Mathematics courses to take STEP. For details, see the STEP pages on the Cambridge Assessment website (www.admissionstests.cambridgeassesssment.org.uk).

Medicine, Dentistry, Veterinary Science/Medicine, and related subjects
The BioMedical Admissions Test (BMAT)
This is a pen-and-paper admissions test taken by undergraduate applicants to specified Medicine, Veterinary Science/Medicine courses at Cambridge and Oxford universities, and at Imperial London, London (RVC) and London (UCL). Imperial London also requires BMAT for entry to Biomedical Science, and Pharmacology with Translational Medical Science; BMAT is also a requirement for entry to Biomedical Sciences at Oxford University. A list of the courses requiring BMAT is available on the BMAT pages of the Cambridge Assessment website (www.admissionstests.cambridgeassessment.org.uk) and also on university websites and in their prospectuses. It is important to note BMAT's early closing date for entries and also the test dates. The two-hour test consists of three sections:

- Aptitude and skills
- Scientific knowledge and application
- Writing task.

Applicants sit the test only once and pay one entry fee no matter how many courses they apply for. However, if they re-apply to universities the following year they will need to re-take the BMAT and pay another fee. Past question papers are available (see website) and an official study guide *Preparing for the BMAT* is also available at www.pearsonschoolsandfecolleges.co.uk. Results of the BMAT are first sent to the universities, and then to the BMAT test centres. Candidates need to contact their test centres direct for their results. See *Dentistry*, *Medicine* and *Veterinary Science/Medicine* below and relevant subject tables in **Chapter 8**.

The UK Clinical Aptitude Test (UKCAT)
The UKCAT is a clinical aptitude test used by the majority of medical and dental schools in the selection of applicants for Medicine and Dentistry, alongside their existing selection processes, for undergraduate entry. The tests are not curriculum-based and do not have a science component. No revision is necessary; there is no textbook and no course of instruction. In the first instance, the UKCAT is a test of cognitive skills involving problem-solving and critical reasoning. With over 150 test centres, it is an on-screen test (not paper-based), and is marked electronically. Some bursaries are available to help towards the cost of the test. Further details (including the most recent list of universities requiring applicants to sit the UKCAT) are found on the website www.ukcat.ac.uk. See also the **Dentistry** and **Medicine** subject tables in **Chapter 8**, the entries for *Dentistry* and *Medicine* below, and **Chapter 5** for application details. See www.ukcat.ac.uk.

Modern and Medieval Languages
The Modern and Medieval Languages Test (MML)
This written test is used by the University of Cambridge for selecting applicants for entry to courses involving modern and medieval languages. See www.mml.cam.ac.uk/prospectus/undergrad/applying/test.html.

General Admissions Test
Thinking Skills Assessment (TSA)
The TSA is a 90-minute multiple choice test consisting of 50 questions which test applicants' critical thinking and problem-solving skills. It is used at or before interview by applicants for some courses at Cambridge University by some colleges, by University College London for applicants to European Social and Political Studies, and by Oxford University for entry to several courses (see below and see the TSA web pages on www.admissionstests.cambridgeassessment.org.uk).

DEGREE SUBJECT LISTS OF UNIVERSITIES AND COLLEGES USING TESTS AND ASSESSMENTS
Many universities and colleges set their own tests for specific subjects so it is important to check the websites for your preferred institutions and courses for the latest information about their applications and selection processes. The following list provides a guide to the subjects and institutions requiring admissions tests and other forms of assessment.

Accountancy
Buckingham Written test for non-English-speaking applicants.
Lancaster (Acc, Audt Fin) Ernst & Young assessment.
Leeds (Acc Law) LNAT.

Anglo Saxon, Norse and Celtic
Cambridge *Interview only:* Fitzwilliam, Girton, Murray Edwards, St Edmund's, St John's; *Test at interview:* Hughes Hall, Lucy Cavendish, Wolfson; School/College essays: all other colleges offering the subject. Check www.cam.ac.uk/admissions/undergraduate/apply/tests.html.

Animal Management
Kirklees (Coll) Mature applicants screening test.

Anthropology
Cambridge See Archaeology.
Oxford See Archaeology.

Arabic
Oxford Language aptitude or translation test
Salford (Arbc Engl Transl Interp – for native speakers of Arabic) Applicants may be required to sit Arabic or English language tests.

Archaeology
Bournemouth Test for mature applicants.

Cambridge (Arch Anth) *Interview only:* Jesus; College-set Essay: Newnham, Peterhouse, St Catharine's; *Test at interview:* Clare, Emmanuel, Girton, Hughes Hall, King's, Lucy Cavendish, Robinson, St Edmunds; Preparatory study/assignment before interview: Churchill, Robinson, Trinity; *School/ college essays:* Christ's, Churchill, Corpus Christi, Downing, Fitzwilliam, Gonville & Caius, Homerton, Magdalene, Murray Edwards, Pembroke, Queens', Robinson, St John's, Selwyn, Sidney Sussex, Trinity Hall. Check www.cam.ac.uk/admissions/undergraduate/apply/tests.html.

Oxford (Arch Anth) *All colleges offering the subject:* Two recent marked essays are required, preferably in different subjects, plus a statement of no more than 300 words setting out your understanding of the relations between archaeology and social, cultural and biological anthropology required before interview. No written test at interview. Check www.admissions.ox.ac.uk/tests.

Oxford (Class Arch Anc Hist) *All colleges offering the subject:* Two recent marked essays are required. No written test at interview. Check www.admissions.ox.ac.uk/tests.

Architecture

Bradford (Coll Univ Centre) Questionnaire and samples of work before interview. Literacy and numeracy test at interview.

Cambridge *Interview only:* Downing, Girton, King's, Queens', Robinson, Sidney Sussex, Trinity Hall; *Test at interview:* Jesus, Lucy Cavendish, Pembroke, Trinity; Preparatory study/assignment at/before interview: Clare, Emmanuel, Fitzwilliam, Magdalene, Murray Edwards, St Edmund's, Selwyn, Wolfson; Project: Peterhouse; *School/college essays:* Churchill, Clare, Gonville & Caius, Newnham, St John's. **NB All colleges offering course require a portfolio of recent work at interview.** Check www.cam.ac.uk/admissions/undergraduate/apply/tests.html.

Cardiff (also Archit Eng) Samples of work to be sent before interview.

Dundee Samples of work required before interview.

Huddersfield Portfolio of work required.

Liverpool The interview will be based on the portfolio of work.

London Met Portfolio of work required.

London South Bank Samples of work to be sent before interview.

Nottingham Trent Examples of work are required.

Sheffield Art portfolio required for applicants without A-level art.

Westminster Samples of work required before interview.

Art and Design

Bournemouth (Comp Vis Animat) Maths, logic and life-drawing tests at interview, and portfolio of work required.

Bournemouth Arts (UC) Practical test.

Creative Arts Tests.

Oxford (Fine Art) *All colleges offering the subject:* No written work required. Portfolio to be submitted by mid-November. Drawing examination. Two drawings in pencil or pencil and ink from a number of possible subjects. Check www.admissions.ox.ac.uk/tests.

Oxford and Cherwell Valley (Coll) A drawing examination is taken by all candidates who are interviewed (two drawings in pencil or pen and ink).

Ravensbourne Verbal examination. (Animat) Written test.

Westminster (Fash Mrchnds Mgt) Interview and numeracy test.

Asian and Middle Eastern Studies

Cambridge *Interview only:* St Edmund's; *Test at interview:* Girton (depending on subject), Fitzwilliam, Hughes Hall, Lucy Cavendish, Magdalene (depending on subject), Murray Edwards (depending on subject), Robinson, Sidney Sussex (depending on subject), Trinity Hall (depending on subject); *Preparatory study at/before interview:* Robinson, St John's, Selwyn; *School/college essays:* Christ's, Churchill, Clare, Corpus Christie, Downing, Emmanuel, Fitzwilliam, Girton, Gonville & Caius, Homerton, Jesus, King's, Magdalene, Murray Edwards, Newnham, Pembroke, Peterhouse, Queens', St Catharine's, St John's, Trinity, Trinity Hall, Wolfson. Check www.cam.ac.uk/admissions/undergraduate/apply/tests.html.

Biochemistry
London South Bank Degree subject-based test at interview.
Oxford *All colleges offering the subject:* No written work required. No written tests. Check www. admissions.ox.ac.uk/tests

Biological Sciences
London South Bank Degree subject-based test at interview.
Nottingham Trent Essay set.
Oxford *All colleges offering the subject:* No written work or written tests required. Check www.ox.ac.uk/ tests.

Biomedical Sciences
Hull (Coll) Essay.
Imperial London BMAT.
Nottingham Trent Essay.
Oxford BMAT is required for entry into all colleges. Check www.medsci.ox.ac.uk/study/bms.
Portsmouth Test of motivation and knowledge of the subject, the degree and careers to which it leads.

Bioveterinary Science
London (RVC) BMAT is not required for entry but applicants wanting to be considered for Merit Scholarships will have to take BMAT.

Broadcast Technology
Birmingham City Mature students to take English and mathematics tests.
Ravensbourne Written test.

Building/Construction
Bradford (Coll Univ Centre) Questionnaire before interview, literacy and numeracy tests at interview.
London South Bank (Bld Serv Eng) Degree subject-based test and numeracy test at interview.

Business Courses
Arts London (CFash) School work to be submitted before interview. Degree subject-based test and numeracy test at interview.
Bolton Literacy and numeracy tests.
Bradford (Coll Univ Centre) Written test.
Buckingham English test for applicants without English as a first language.
Farnborough (CT) Written test.
Newcastle Some short-listed applicants will be given a variety of assessment tests at interview.
Nottingham Trent Short-listed applicants are invited to a day-long business style assessment.
Westminster (Fash Mrchnds Mgt) Interview and numeracy test.

Celtic
Oxford Language aptitude or translation test.

Chemistry
London South Bank Degree subject-based test.
Oxford *All colleges offering the subject:* No written work and no written tests required. Check www. admissions.ox.ac.uk/tests.

Classical Studies
Birmingham Language aptitude test for students without a language at GCSE.

Classics (See also *Archaeology*)
Cambridge *Test at interview:* Clare, Corpus Christi, Fitzwilliam, Girton, Hughes Hall, Lucy Cavendish, Newnham, St Catharine's, St Edmund's, St John's, Wolfson; *Preparatory study at/before interview:* Downing, Emmanuel, Jesus, Magdelene, Murray Edwards, Newnham, Peterhouse, Sidney Sussex; *School/college essays:* Christ's, Churchill, Clare, Corpus Christi, Downing, Emmanuel, Fitzwilliam,

Girton, Gonville & Caius, Homerton, Jesus, King's, Magdalene, Murray Edwards, Newnham, Pembroke, Peterhouse, Queen's, Robinson, St Catharine's, St Edmund's, St John's, Selwyn, Sidney Sussex, Trinity, Trinity Hall. Check www.cam.ac.uk/admissions/undergraduate/apply/tests.html.

Oxford *All colleges offering the subject:* Two recently marked essays required, normally in areas related to Classics. Written tests at interview. Check www.admissions.ox.ac.uk/tests.

Classics and English
Oxford *All colleges offering the subject:* The ELAT and the Classics test. Two pieces of written work, relevant to either Classics or English also required. Check www.admissions.ox.ac.uk/tests.

Classics and Modern Languages
Oxford *All colleges offering the subject:* Classics and Modern Languages tests; two Classics essays and two modern language essays also required, one in the chosen language. Check with www.admissions. ox.ac.uk/tests.

Classics and Oriental Studies
Oxford *All colleges offering the subject:* Classics test; also language aptitude test for applicants planning to study Arabic, Hebrew, Persian or Turkish as main language; two pieces written work also required, at least one on classical topic. Check www.admissions.ox.ac.uk/tests.

Communication Studies
Buckingham English test for non-native-English-speaking applicants.
Cardiff Short essay.

Computer Science
Abertay Dundee (Comp Arts) Portfolio of work required. Practical tests at interview.
Blackburn (Coll Univ Centre) Questionnaire and tests before interview.
Cambridge *Interview only:* Magdalene, Girton, St Catharine's, Sidney Sussex, Wolfson; *Test at interview:* Churchill, Downing, Homerton, Hughes Hall, Peterhouse Trinity; Thinking Skills Assessment at interview: Christ's, Clare, Corpus Christi, Emmanuel, Fitzwilliam, Gonville & Caius, Jesus, King's, Lucy Cavendish, Murray Edwards, Newnham, Pembroke, Peterhouse, Queens', Robinson, St Edmund's, St John's, Selwyn, Trinity Hall; *Preparatory study at/before interview:* Clare, Gonville & Caius, King's, Robinson. **NB** STEP used for conditional offers. Check www.cam.ac.uk/admissions/undergraduate/ apply/tests.html.
Central Lancashire Test for Foundation course applicants.
Cumbria Literacy test at interview.
Liverpool John Moores Questionnaire before interview. Literacy test at interview.
London (Gold) Degree subject-based test.
London (QM) Mathematical test at interview.
Oxford *All colleges offering the subject:* Maths aptitude test. See also *Mathematics* below. Check www. admissions.ox.ac.uk/tests.

Counselling
Hull (Coll) Written test.

Czech
Oxford Language aptitude or translation test.

Dance
Chichester (Perf Arts) Group practical test.
Liverpool (LIPA) See **Dance/Dance Studies** in **Chapter 8** (Interview advice and questions).

Dental Nursing
Portsmouth (Dntl Nurs; Dntl Hyg Dntl Thera) Interview.

Dietetics
London Met Interview and essay.
Ulster Health Professions Admissions Test: see above, www.hpat.org.uk and www.ulster.ac.uk before completing the UCAS application.

Drama
Central Lancashire Written papers and/or tests.
De Montfort Written papers and/or tests.
Liverpool (LIPA) (Perf Arts (Actg)) Applicants will be expected to perform one devised piece, one Shakespearean piece and a song plus a short review of a performance they have seen recently.
London (Central Sch SpDr) Written papers and/or tests.
London (RH) Written work required at interview. At interview the University looks for students who are mentally agile and versatile who enjoy reading as well as taking part in productions.
Royal Welsh (CMusDr) Written papers and/or tests.

Earth Sciences (Geology)
Oxford All Colleges offering the subject: No essays required. No written tests at interview; no written work for interview. Check www.admissions.ox.ac.uk/tests.

Economics
Buckingham English test for non-native-English-speaking applicants.
Cambridge *Interview only:* Clare, Girton, Selwyn; *Test at interview:* Corpus Christi, Downing (mathematical test), Gonville & Caius, Homerton, Hughes Hall, Lucy Cavendish, Pembroke, Robinson, Sidney Sussex, Wolfson; *Thinking Skills Assessment:* Fitzwilliam, Jesus, King's, Newnham, Peterhouse, Queens', St Edmund's, St John's; *Preparatory study at/before interview:* Christ's, Churchill, Emmanuel, Fitzwilliam, Jesus, King's, Magdalene, Murray Edwards, Newnham, St Catherine's, St John's; College-set essay/work: Peterhouse, St John's, Trinity Hall; *School/college essays:* Christ's, Churchill, Homerton, Magdalene, Newnham, Robinson. Check www.cam.ac.uk/admissions/undergraduate/apply/tests.html.
Lancaster Workshop.
London LSE Has its own admissions test (the LSE Entrance Examination) which is used for some applicants with non-standard backgrounds. The test is not subject or course-specific.
Oxford (Econ Mgt) *All colleges offering the subject:* Thinking Skills Assessment (Oxford University). Check www.admissions.ox.ac.uk/tests, and also www.admissionstests.cambridgeassessment.org.uk.

Education Studies (See also *Teacher Training*)
Anglia Ruskin Numeracy tests.
Cambridge *Interview only:* Clare, Fitzwilliam, Girton, Jesus, Murray Edwards, St Edmund's, St John's, Selwyn; *Test at interview:* Churchill (depending on subject), Downing (depending on subject), Homerton (depending on subject), Hughes Hall, Lucy Cavendish, Magdalene (depending on subjects), Trinity Hall, Wolfson; *Preparatory study at/before interview:* Churchill, Emmanuel, Homerton, Magdalene, Robinson, Trinity Hall; College-set essay: Emmanuel; *School/college essays:* Christ's, Churchill, Downing, Gonville & Caius, Homerton, Magdalene, Queens', Trinity Hall. Check www.cam.ac.uk/admissions/undergraduate/apply/tests.html.
Cumbria (Science and Education) Literacy test.
Durham (Primary Teaching) Key skills tests at interview.
Newman (UC) Basic numeracy and literacy tests.

Engineering
Birmingham City Mature students without GCSE English and/or mathematics are required to take a literacy and/or numeracy test. (Snd Eng Prod) Mature students to take English and mathematics tests.
Blackburn (Coll Univ Centre) Questionnaire and tests before interview.
Bristol (Eng Des) A-level-based test.
Cambridge *Interview only:* Corpus Christi, Girton, Murray Edwards, St Catharine's; *Test at interview:* Churchill, Downing (maths test), Fitzwilliam, Gonville & Caius, Hughes Hall, King's (problem-solving), Lucy Cavendish, Magdalene, Newham, Peterhouse, Robinson, St John's (maths test), Trinity; *Thinking Skills Assessment:* Christ's, Clare, Emmanuel, Gonville & Caius, Homerton, Jesus, King's, Lucy Cavendish, Newnham, Pembroke, Queens', St Edmund's, Selwyn, Sidney Sussex, Trinity Hall, Wolfson; *Preparatory study at/before interview:* Clare, St John's (and possible STEP requirement). Check www.cam.ac.uk/admissions/undergraduate/apply/tests.html.
Kingston (Aircrft Eng) Numeracy and basic physics test.

London South Bank (Bld Serv Eng; Civ Eng; Elec Eng; Mech Eng) Degree subject-based test and numeracy test at interview.

Oxford (Eng Sci; Eng Comp Sci; Eng Econ Mgt) *All colleges offering the subjects:* No written work or written tests required. Check www.admissions.ox.ac.uk/tests.

Southampton Literacy and numeracy tests for foundation course applicants.

Southampton Solent Mathematical test at interview.

Suffolk (Univ Campus) (Civ Eng, Elec Electron Eng, Mech Eng courses) Interviews.

English

Anglia Ruskin Samples of written work required.

Birmingham City Samples of work required.

Blackpool and Fylde (Coll) Samples of work before interview.

Bristol Samples of work required.

Buckingham English test for non-native-English-speaking applicants.

Cambridge *Test at interview:* Churchill, Clare, Corpus Christi, Downing, Emmanuel, Fitzwilliam, Girton, Homerton, Hughes Hall, Jesus, King's, Lucy Cavendish, Magdalene, Murray Edwards, Newnham, Pembroke, Peterhouse, Queens', Robinson, St Catharine's, St Edmund's, St John's, Selwyn, Sidney Sussex, Trinity, Trinity Hall, Wolfson; *Preparatory study at/before interview:* Christ's, Churchill, Clare, Corpus Christi, Emmanuel, Fitzwilliam, Jesus, Newnham, Robinson, Selwyn, Sidney Sussex; *School/ college essays:* Christ's, Churchill, Clare, Corpus Christi, Emmanuel, Fitzwilliam, Girton, Homerton, Jesus, King's, Magdalene, Murray Edwards, Newnham, Peterhouse, Queens', Robinson, St Catharine's, St John's, Selwyn, Sidney Sussex, Trinity, Trinity Hall. Check www.cam.ac.uk/admissions/ undergraduate/apply/tests.html.

Cardiff Short essay.

London (King's) Applicants to prepare a short literary text before interview.

London (UCL) After interview applicants are asked to write a critical commentary on an unseen passage of prose or verse.

Newport (Creative Writing) Samples of creative writing before interview.

Oxford Check www.admissions.ox.ac.uk/tests. (Engl Lang Lit) *All colleges offering the subject:* ELAT and one recent marked essay. (Engl Modn Langs) *All colleges offering the subject:* Modern Language(s) test, one recent marked essay.

Portsmouth (Engl Crea Writ; Crea Writ Dr) All applicants will be required to submit a short piece of creative writing to the admissions office. This should be between 400 and 500 words long and should include the following words and use each one twice: shell, flicker, knit, coin, compose, lark, stream, root. All the words must be used and each word must be used in a different context and/ or with a different meaning on each occasion. Language should be used imaginatively and accurately.

Southampton Examples of written work required from Access students.

Equine Science

Lincoln Applicants are required to show that they can ride to BHS Level 2 or equivalent.

European and Middle Eastern Languages (See also Modern and Medieval Languages)

Oxford *All colleges offering the subject:* Language aptitude test, modern language test, TSA. Check www.admissions.ox.ac.uk/tests.

European Studies

London (Gold) Informal conversation in the relevant language (French, German or Spanish).

Film Production

Birmingham City (Film Prod Tech) Mature students to take English and mathematics tests.

Film Studies

Bournemouth (Script) A 20-page screen-play required before interview.

Bournemouth Arts (UC) Portfolio. Practical test of short film stills.

Creative Arts Portfolio at interview.

Liverpool John Moores Questionnaire and test before interview.

Newport Portfolio of work.

Roehampton Essays taken to interview and discussed.
Westminster Questionnaire to be completed and samples of work required before interview.

Fine Art
Oxford *All colleges offering the subject:* Specimen drawing examination paper available on website. Check www.admissions.ox.ac.uk/tests.

Geography
Cambridge Cambridge *Interview only:* Christ's, Downing, St Edmund's, St John's; *Test at interview:* Hughes Hall, Lucy Cavendish, Murray Edwards, Wolfson; *Preparatory study at/before interview:* Churchill, Clare, Corpus Christi, Emmanuel, Fitzwilliam, Girton, Homerton, King's, Newnham, Robinson, St Catharine's, Selwyn; *School/college essays:* Churchill, Clare, Corpus Christi, Emmanuel, Fitzwilliam, Girton, Gonville & Caius, Homerton, Jesus, King's, Magdalene, Murray Edwards, Newnham, Queens', Robinson, Sidney Sussex, Trinity, Trinity Hall. Check www.cam.ac.uk/admissions/undergraduate/apply/tests.html.
Cardiff Test for some joint courses.
Oxford *All colleges offering the subject:* No test. Check www.admissions.ox.ac.uk/tests.

German (See also *Modern and Medieval Languages*)
Aston Written test at interview.
Liverpool John Moores Written test at interview.

History
Bangor Samples of work only required from mature applicants without conventional qualifications.
Buckingham English test for non-native-English-speaking applicants.
Cambridge *Test at interview:* Hughes Hall, Lucy Cavendish, Newnham, Pembroke, Peterhouse, Robinson, St Edmund's, St John's, Sidney Sussex, Wolfson; *Thinking Skills Assessment:* St John's; *Preparatory study at/before interview:* Christ's, Churchill, Clare, Corpus Christi, Downing, Emmanuel, Fitzwilliam, Girton, Homerton, Murray Edwards, Newnham, Pembroke, Queens', Robinson, St Catharine's, St John's, Selwyn, Sidney Sussex, Trinity; *School/college essays:* Christ's, Churchill, Clare, Corpus Christi, Downing, Emmanuel, Fitzwilliam, Girton, Gonville & Caius, Homerton, Jesus, King's, Magdalene, Murray Edwards, Newnham, Pembroke, Peterhouse, Queens', Robinson, St Catharine's, Selwyn, Sidney Sussex, Trinity, Trinity Hall, Wolfson. Check www.cam.ac.uk/admissions/undergraduate/apply/tests.html.
Liverpool Test for mature applicants.
Liverpool John Moores Mature students not in education must submit an essay.
London (Gold) Samples of written work from non-standard applicants and from those without academic qualifications.
Oxford Check www.admissions.ox.ac.uk/tests. (Hist (Anc Modn)(Hist Econ)) *All colleges offering the subject:* History Aptitude Test. (Hist Modn Langs) History Aptitude Test and Modern Language Test. (Hist Pol) No test. Those called for interview send an essay by end of November.
Roehampton Essays taken to interview and discussed.

History of Art
Cambridge *Interview only:* Fitzwilliam, Robinson, Selwyn; *Test at interview:* Hughes Hall, Lucy Cavendish, St Edmund's, Wolfson; *School/college essays:* Christ's, Churchill, Clare, Corpus Christie, Downing, Emmanuel, Girton, Gonville & Caius, Homerton, Jesus, King's, Magdalene, Murray Edwards, Newnham, Pembroke, Peterhouse, Queens', St John's, Sidney Sussex, Trinity, Trinity Hall. Check www.cam.ac.uk.admissions/ undergraduate/apply/tests.html.
Oxford *All colleges offering the subject:* Two pieces required: (a) a marked essay from an A-level or equivalent course, and (b) a brief account of no more than 750 words responding to an item of art or design to which the applicant has had first-hand access with a photograph or photocopy of the item provided if possible. No written test at interview although the applicant may be presented with photographs or artefacts for discussion at interview. Submitted written work may also be discussed at interview. Check www.admissions.ox.ac.uk/tests.

Human Sciences
Oxford *All colleges offering the subject:* Two recent marked essays or project reports, relevant to the Human Sciences course, written as part of the school or college course. No written test at interview.

Italian (see also *Medieval and Modern Languages*)
Cardiff Test for some joint courses.

Journalism (see also *Media Studies*)
Kent Written test.
Nottingham Trent Written test.

Land Economy

Cambridge *Interview only:* Christ's, Downing, Girton, Gonville & Caius, Pembroke, Queens', St Catharine's, St John's, Selwyn, Sidney Sussex, Trinity Hall; *Test at interview:* Hughes Hall, Lucy Cavendish, Wolfson; *Thinking Skills Assessment:* Jesus, Lucy Cavendish, Newnham, Robinson, St Edmund's; *Preparatory study at/before interview:* Fitzwilliam (written test prior to interview), Jesus, Magdalene, Trinity; *School/college essays:* Clare, Fitzwilliam, Homerton, Magdalene, Murray Edwards, Newnham. Check www.cam.ac.uk/admissions/undergraduate/apply/tests.html.

Law

The following universities require applicants to take the LNAT for specified Law courses: **Birmingham**, **Bristol**, **Durham**, **Glasgow**, **Leeds**, **London (King's)**, **(UCL)**, **Nottingham**, **Oxford.** Check university websites and www.lnat.ac.uk; see also **Chapter 6** and the **Law** subject table in **Chapter 8**. (**NB** After 2009, LNAT is not required for entry to **Cambridge**.)

Birmingham City Questionnaire to be completed and an IQ test.
Bradford (Coll Univ Centre) Academic tests at interview for mature students.
Bolton Own diagnostic test used (logic and reasoning).
Bristol Check with the Law Department for LNAT requirements.
Cambridge *Test at interview:* Churchill, Hughes Hall, St Edmund's, Wolfson; *Cambridge Law Test:* Christ's, Clare, Corpus Christi, Downing, Emmanuel, Fitzwilliam, Girton, Gonville & Caius, Homerton, Jesus, King's, Lucy Cavendish, Magdalene, Murray Edwards, Newnham, Pembroke, Peterhouse, Queens', Robinson, St Catharine's, St John's, Selwyn, Sidney Sussex, Trinity, Trinity Hall; *Preparatory study at/ before interview:* Christ's, Corpus Christi, Emmanuel, Homerton, Jesus, King's, Magdalene, Newnham, Pembroke, Selwyn, Sidney Sussex, St John's, Trinity, Trinity Hall. Separate tests at interview: Hughes Hall, St Edmund's, Wolfson. *School/college essays:* Emmanuel, Magdalene, Wolfson. Check www. cam.ac.uk/admissions/undergraduate/apply/tests.html.
Oxford *All colleges offering the subject:* All applicants take the LNAT. (Law Law St Euro) LNAT plus, at interview, a short oral test in the modern language for students taking a joint language, except for those taking European Legal Studies. No other written work required except for Harris Manchester College. Check www.admissions.ox.ac.uk/tests.

Linguistics

Cambridge *Interview only:* Christ's, Homerton, King's, Robinson, Wolfson; *Test at interview:* Churchill, Fitzwilliam, Girton, Jesus, Magdelene, St Johns; *Preparatory study at/before interview:* Churchill, Robinson, Sidney Sussex, Trinity. *School/college essays:* Churchill, Clare, Corpus Christi, Downing, Emmanuel, Gonville & Caius, Murray Edwards, Newnham, Peterhouse, Selwyn, Sidney Sussex, St John's, Trinity, Trinity Hall; *Contact the College:* Hughes Hall, Lucy Cavendish, Pembroke, Queens', St Catharine's, St Edmund's. Check www.cam.ac.uk/admissions/undergraduate/apply/tests.html.

Materials Science

Oxford (Mat Sci) (Mat Econ Mgt) No written work required. No written test at interview. Check www. admissions.ox.ac.uk/tests.

Mathematics

Cambridge *Test at interview:* Christ's, Churchill, Corpus Christi, Downing, Girton, Homerton, Hughes Hall, King's, Lucy Cavendish, Magdalene, Murray Edwards, Robinson, St Edmunds, St John's, Trinity; Maths STEP: Christ's, Churchill, Clare, Corpus Christi, Downing, Emmanuel, Fitzwilliam, Girton, Gonville & Caius, Homerton, Jesus, King's, Lucy Cavendish, Magdalene, Murray Edwards, Newnham, Pembroke, Peterhouse, Queens', Robinson, St Catharine's, St John's, Selwyn, Sidney Sussex, Trinity, Trinity Hall; *Preparatory study at/before interview:* King's, Newnham. Check www.cam.ac.uk/admissions/ undergraduate/apply/tests.html.

Liverpool John Moores Literacy and numeracy tests.
Oxford (Maths; Maths Comp Sci; Maths Stats) *All colleges offering the subjects:* Mathematics Aptitude Test. Overseas candidates unable to attend for interview may be required to submit written work; (Maths Phil) *All colleges offering the subject:* Mathematics Aptitude Test; two essays showing capacity for reasoned argument and clear writing, not expected to be on a philosophical subject. Check www.admissions.ox.ac.uk/interviews/tests.

Media Studies
Blackpool and Fylde (Coll) Samples of work before interview.
Bolton Samples of work at interview.
Bournemouth 250-word essay.
Bournemouth and Poole (Coll) Degree subject-based test at interview.
Brighton (Spo Jrnl) Test for those called to interview: contact admissions tutor.
City Spelling, punctuation, grammar, general knowledge tests and an essay assignment. Tests on current affairs and use of English.
Coventry Interview and portfolio.
Edinburgh Napier (Jrnl) Samples of work before interview.
Glasgow Caledonian Written test at interview.
Hull (Coll) Essay required before interview.
Liverpool John Moores Questionnaire to be completed before interview. Degree subject-based test at interview.
London Met Mathematics and written English test.
Newport Portfolio of work.
Westminster Questionnaire to be completed before interview.

Medicine
NB Most medical schools require applicants to sit the UK Clinical Aptitude Test (UKCAT) or the BioMedical Admissions Test (BMAT) or, for graduate entry, the Graduate Australian Medical Schools Admissions Test (GAMSAT) for specified Medicine courses. Applicants are advised to check the websites of all universities and medical schools offering Medicine for their latest admissions requirements, including admissions and aptitude tests, to check the UKCAT website www.ukcat.ac.uk or the BMAT pages on www.admissionstests.cambridgeassessment.org.uk, (and for graduate entry www.gamsat.co.uk) for the latest information.

BMAT is required by:
Cambridge Christ's, Churchill, Clare, Corpus Christi, Downing, Emmanuel, Fitzwilliam, Girton, Gonville & Caius, Jesus, King's, Lucy Cavendish, Magdalene, Murray Edwards, Newnham, Pembroke, Peterhouse, Queens', Robinson, St Catharine's, St Edmund's, St John's, Selwyn, Sidney Sussex, Trinity, Trinity Hall, Wolfson. Check www.cam.ac.uk/admissions/undergraduate/apply/tests.html.
Imperial London (Six-year course) BMAT.
London (UCL) (Six year course) BMAT.
Oxford.

Modern and Medieval Languages (See also Asian and Middle Eastern Studies, Oriental Studies and separate languages)
Bangor Offer may be lowered after interview.
Cambridge *Test at interview:* Christ's, Churchill, Clare, Corpus Christi, Downing, Emmanuel, Fitzwilliam, Girton, Gonville & Caius, Homerton, Hughes Hall, Jesus, King's, Lucy Cavendish, Magdalene, Murray Edwards, Newnham, Pembroke, Peterhouse, Queens', Robinson, St Catharine's, St Edmund's, St John's, Selwyn, Sidney Sussex, Trinity Hall, Wolfson; *Preparatory study at/before interview:* Churchill, Clare, Emmanuel, Homerton, Jesus, Magdalene, Murray Edwards, Newnham, Pembroke, Peterhouse, Queens', Robinson, St Edmund's, St John's, Selwyn, Trinity, Trinity Hall; *School/college essays:* Christ's, Churchill, Corpus Christi, Downing, Emmanuel, Gonville & Caius, Homerton, Jesus, King's, Magdalene, Murray Edwards, Newnham, Pembroke, Peterhouse, Queens', Robinson, St Catharine's, St Edmund's, St John's, Selwyn, Trinity, Trinity Hall. Check www.cam.ac.uk/admissions/undergraduate/apply/tests.html.
Liverpool The interview lasts approximately 20 minutes with part in the language(s) to be studied. Occasionally the applicant may be asked to sit a short grammar test.

Oxford Check course requirements carefully on the University website and check test requirements on www.admissions.ox.ac.uk/tests. (Modn Langs) *All colleges offering the subjects:* Modern Languages Test(s). Two marked essays for each language being studied. (Modn Lang Ling) *All colleges offering the subject:* Language Aptitude Test and Modern Language Test. (Euro Mid E Langs) *All colleges offering the subject:* Language Aptitude Test and Modern Language Test. Two recent marked essays, one in the European language.

Music

Bangor Candidates offered the option of an audition.

Birmingham City Some subject-based and practical tests.

Cambridge *Test at interview:* Clare, Downing, Fitzwilliam, Girton, Gonville & Caius, Homerton, Hughes Hall, Jesus, King's, Lucy Cavendish, Magdalene, Murray Edwards, Newnham, Pembroke, Peterhouse, Queens', Robinson, St Catharine's, St Edmunds, St John's (possible keyboard test), Selwyn, Trinity, Trinity Hall; *Preparatory study at/before interview:* Churchill, Clare, Emmanuel, Newnham, Robinson, St Edmund's, Sidney Sussex, Wolfson; *School/college essays:* Christ's, Churchill, Corpus Christi, Downing, Emmanuel, Fitzwilliam, Girton, Gonville & Caius, Homerton, Jesus, King's, Magdalene, Murray Edwards, Newnham, Pembroke, Peterhouse, Queens', Robinson, St Catharine's, St John's, Selwyn, Sidney Sussex, Trinity, Trinity Hall. Check www.cam.ac.uk/admissions/undergraduate/apply/tests.html.

Coventry Proforma used prior to interview. Some students rejected at this stage.

Edinburgh Napier Audition and theory test.

Leeds (CMus) (Jazz; Mus; Pop Mus St) In-house theory test to determine level of musical theory ability.

Liverpool Candidates may be asked to undertake a variety of aural tests, the performance of a prepared piece of music and some sight-reading when called for interview.

London (Gold) Degree subject-based test.

London (RAcMus) (BMus) 50-minute written test; possible keyboard and aural skills test.

TABLE OF INTERVIEW REQUIREMENTS FOR MUSIC COURSES

Key   P = Performance   A = Aural
K = Keyboard tests   H = Harmony and Counterpoint (Written)
E = Essay   X = Extracts for analysis or 'guessing the composer', dates etc.
S = Sight-singing

Bangor* PAX (bring example)	**Liverpool** PK
Barnsley (Coll) A	**Liverpool Hope** PKH
Bath Spa PKXA	**London (Gold)** PKH
Birmingham PSKHXA	**London (King's)** PASK
Birmingham City PAH	**London (RAcMus)** PKHX
Bristol PSKHEXA	**London (RCMus)** PKEXH
Cambridge (Hom)* PKE (bring example)	**London (RH)** PHEXA
Cardiff PE	**Oxford** PHAK
Chichester P	**Roehampton** PKH
City PASKE	**Royal Scottish (RSAMD)** PSA
Colchester (Inst) PKSX	**Royal Welsh (CMus/Dr)** PSA
Derby PE	**Salford** PKEH
Durham PKXA	**Sheffield** PEAH
East Anglia PKHEXA	**South Birmingham (Coll)** P
Edinburgh PKHEA	**Southampton** P
Glasgow PS	**Surrey** PH or X
Huddersfield PH	**Ulster** P
Lancaster PAH	**Wolverhampton** PE
Leeds PX	**York** PEKHX

* Examples may include essays, harmony and counterpoint compositions. Performance tests/auditions are standard practice for Music courses in all universities and colleges.

London Met Performance tests and essay.

Oxford *All colleges offering the subject:* One marked sample of harmony and/or counterpoint and two marked essays on any areas or aspects of music. Candidates may submit a portfolio of compositions (these are non-returnable). Performance tests at interview; Check www.admissions.ox.ac.uk/tests.

West London (Mus Tech) Students required to produce a portfolio of work. (Mus Perf) Students attend an audition: see www.tvu.ac.uk.

Natural Sciences (Biological Sciences)

Cambridge *Interview only:* Churchill, Corpus Christi, Downing, Fitzwilliam, Girton, Jesus, King's, Newnham, Pembroke, St Catharine's, Selwyn; *Test at interview:* Homerton, Hughes Hall, Lucy Cavendish, Magdalene, Murray Edwards, Robinson, St Edmund's, St John's, Trinity; *Thinking Skills Assessment:* Clare, Emmanuel, Gonville & Caius, Peterhouse, Queens', St Edmund's, Trinity Hall, Wolfson; *Preparatory study at/before interview:* Emmanuel, Homerton, Magdalene, Robinson; *School/college essays:* Christ's (or project work), Peterhouse, Robinson. Check www.cam.ac.uk/admissions/undergraduate/apply/tests.html.

Natural Sciences (Physical Sciences)

Cambridge *Interview only:* Christ's, Churchill, Fitzwilliam, Girton, Jesus, Pembroke, St Catharine's, Selwyn; *Test at interview:* Corpus Christi, Downing (mathematical test), Homerton, Hughes Hall, Lucy Cavendish, Magdalene, Robinson, St John's, Trinity; *Thinking Skills Assessment:* Clare, Emmanuel, Gonville & Caius, King's, Murray Edwards, Newnham, Peterhouse, Queens', St Edmund's, Trinity Hall, Wolfson; *Preparatory study at/before interview:* Emmanuel (for Chemistry), Homerton; *School/college essays:* Murray Edwards. Check www.cam.ac.uk/admissions/undergraduate/apply/tests.html.

Nursing

Birmingham City Literacy and numeracy tests at interview.

Bolton Literacy test.

Bristol UWE Questionnaire/test before interview.

Bucks New Tests for BSc and DipHE Nursing.

City Written test.

Derby Literacy and numeracy tests at interview.

Dundee Literacy test.

East Anglia Tests.

Liverpool A group of candidates is given a task to undertake during which applicants are assessed for their ability to work in a team, maturity, communication skills and their level of involvement.

London South Bank (Nurs A, C, MH) Literacy and numeracy tests at interview.

Suffolk (Univ Campus) Interview and tests.

West London Numeracy and literacy tests.

Wolverhampton Tests.

York Literacy and numeracy tests.

Occupational Therapy

Bristol UWE Questionnaire/test before interview.

Ulster Health Professions Admissions Test: see www.hpat.org.uk and www.ulster.ac.uk before completing the UCAS application.

Optometry

Bradford (Coll Univ Centre) Literacy and numeracy tests.

Oriental Studies

Cambridge See Asian and Middle Eastern Studies.

Oxford *All colleges offering the subject:* Language Aptitude Test. Two essays, preferably of different kinds. Essays in a European language are acceptable. No prior knowledge of Oriental languages required. Occasional written tests. Check the University website and prospectuses and www.admissions.ox.ac.uk/tests.

Osteopathy
British Sch Ost At interview, A-level, literacy, numeracy, logic and reasoning-based tests plus a practical aptitude test.

Paramedic Science
Coventry Fitness and literacy test.

Pharmacology/Pharmaceutical Sciences
Imperial London (Pharmacology and Translational Medical Sciences) BMAT.
Portsmouth Test of motivation, knowledge of the subject, of the degree course and the careers to which it leads.

Pharmacy
Liverpool John Moores Literacy and numeracy tests.
Portsmouth (A-level students) Test of motivation and knowledge of Pharmacy as a profession. (Other applicants) Test of chemistry and biology, plus literacy and numeracy tests.

Philosophy
Cambridge *Test at interview:* Christ's, Churchill, Clare, Corpus Christi, Downing, Emmanuel, Fitzwilliam, Girton, Gonville & Caius, Homerton, Hughes Hall, Jesus, King's, Lucy Cavendish, Magdalene, Newnham, Pembroke, Peterhouse, Queens', Robinson, St Catharine's, St Edmund's, St John's, Selwyn, Sidney Sussex, Trinity, Trinity Hall, Wolfson; *School/college essays:* Churchill, Downing, Emmanuel, Homerton, Magdalene, Peterhouse, St Catharine's, Trinity. Check www.cam.ac.uk/admissions/undergraduate/apply/tests.html.
Leeds Written test at interview.
Liverpool Samples of written work may be requested in cases where there is a question of the applicant's ability to cope with the academic skills required of them.
London (UCL) Written test at interview.
Oxford *All colleges offering the subjects:* (Phil Modn Langs) Philosophy and Modern Languages tests; two pieces of written work required. (Phil Theol) Philosophy test and two pieces of written work; (Phil Pol Econ (PPE)) Thinking Skills Assessment (Oxford University); no written work required. Check course pages on University website and www.admissions.ox.ac.uk/tests.
Warwick Written test at interview.

Physical Education
Chichester Physical test.
Liverpool John Moores Literacy and numeracy tests and gym assessment.

Physics
Oxford *All colleges offering the subject:* Physics Aptitude test; no written work required. Check www.admissions.ox.ac.uk/tests.

Physics and Philosophy
Oxford *All colleges offering the subject:* Physics Aptitude test; two pieces of written work required.

Physiological Sciences/Physiology
Oxford Physiological Sciences, Physiology and Philosophy, and Physiology and Psychology has been replaced by the new Biomedical Sciences course. For details of how to apply and admissions test check the course pages on the University website and www.admissions. ox.ac.uk/tests.

Physiotherapy
East Anglia Tests.
Liverpool A group of candidates is given a task to undertake, during which they are assessed for their ability to work in a team, maturity, communication skills and their level of involvement.
Robert Gordon Practical testing varies from year to year.
Ulster Health Professions Admissions Test (see www.hpat.org.uk and www.ulster.ac.uk before completing the UCAS application).

Podiatry
Ulster Health Professions Admissions Test (see www.hpat.ac.uk and www.ulster.ac.uk before completing the UCAS application).

Politics
Buckingham English test for non-native-English-speaking applicants.
Cambridge *Test at interview:* Churchill, Jesus, Lucy Cavendish, Robinson, St John's, Sidney Sussex; *Thinking Skills Assessment:* Clare, Gonville & Caius, King's, Newnham, Queens', St John's; Preparatory work at/before interview: Emmanuel, Magdalene, Murray Edwards, Newnham, Robinson, Sidney Sussex; *School/college essays:* Christ's, Churchill, Corpus Christi, Downing, Emmanuel, Fitzwilliam, Girton, Gonville & Caius, Homerton, Jesus, King's, Magdalene, Murray Edwards, Newnham, Pembroke, Robinson, St Edmund's, St John's, Selwyn, Sidney Sussex, Trinity, Trinity Hall (College-set essay), Wolfson. Check www.cam.ac.uk/admissions/undergraduate/apply/tests.html.
Kent Written test.
Liverpool John Moores Mature students not in education must submit an essay.
London (Gold) Essays from current A/AS-level course to be submitted before interview.
Oxford See (Philosopy, Politics and Economics PPE) under Philosophy above.

Psychology
Bangor Access course entry students may be asked to submit an essay.
Birmingham Written tests at interview.
Liverpool John Moores Written tests at interview.
London (UCL) Questionnaire to be completed.
Manchester Written tests at interview.
Oxford (Expmtl Psy) *All colleges offering the subject:* Thinking Skills Assessment test (Oxford University); no written work required. See www.admissions.ox.ac.uk/tests. (Psy Phil Physiol) From 2011 this course is replaced by the Biomedical Sciences course. For details of admissions requirements see the course pages on the University website and also www.admissions.ox.ac.uk/tests.
Roehampton Questionnaire before interview; test at interview.

Radiography
Liverpool (Diag Radiog Radiothera) The group of candidates is given a task to undertake, during which they are assessed for their ability to work in a team, maturity, communication skills and their level of involvement.
Ulster Health Professions Admissions Test: see www.hpat.org.uk and www.ulster.ac.uk before completing the UCAS application.

Retail Store Management
Hull (Coll) Literacy and numeracy tests.

Social Policy
London LSE Two essays to be submitted before interview.

Social Work
Anglia Ruskin Samples of written work required.
Bangor Written test at interview.
Birmingham Written test at interview.
Birmingham City Some tests are set at interview.
Bristol UWE Questionnaire before interview.
Brunel Written test at interview.
Bucks New Tests.
De Montfort Written test at interview.
Derby Literacy and numeracy tests at interview.
Dundee Literacy test.
Durham New (Coll) Written test at interview.
East Anglia Test.

London (Gold) Written test at interview. Questions on social work practice and the applicant's experience of working in the social work/social care field.
London Met Pre-interview literacy test and if successful, an interview.
London South Bank Literacy and numeracy tests.
Manchester Met (Yth Commun Wk) Tests.
NEW (Coll) Test.
Newman (UC) (Yth Commun Wk) Written test.
Portsmouth Test.
Sheffield Literacy and numeracy tests.
Stirling Tests.
Suffolk (Univ Campus) Interview and test.
Wolverhampton Tests.

Sociology
Leeds Copy of written work requested.
London Met Where appropriate separate tests in comprehension and mathematical skills that will be used to help us reach a decision.

Speech Sciences
Manchester Met Two essays and a questionnaire.
Sheffield Listening test and problem-solving.
Ulster Health Professions Admissions Test: see www.hpat.org.uk and www.ulster.ac.uk before completing the UCAS application.

Sports Sciences/Studies
Nottingham Trent (Spo Hrs Mgt) Riding test.

Stage Management
Hull (Coll) Essay.

Teacher Training
Anglia Ruskin Literacy test at interview; maths test for some courses.
Bath Spa Written test at interview.
Brighton Written test at interview.
Bristol UWE Literacy and mathematical tests at interview.
Brunel Literacy, mathematical and practical tests depending on subject.
Cardiff (UWIC) Literacy and numeracy test.
Chester Literacy and numeracy tests.
Chichester Written test at interview.
Cumbria Written test at interview.
De Montfort Written test at interview.
Dundee Literacy and numeracy tests.
Durham Key Skills test.
Gloucestershire Mathematical test at interview. Written test at interview.
Liverpool John Moores Written test at interview. Mathematical and diagnostic tests on interview day.
London South Bank Literacy and numeracy tests.
Newman (UC) Basic literacy and numeracy tests for QTS and other courses.
Nottingham Trent Practical presentation. Written test at interview.
Plymouth Mathematical test at interview. Written test at interview.
Roehampton Written test at interview.
St Mary's Twickenham (UC) Literacy and mathematical tests at interview. Practical tests for PE applicants.
Winchester Literacy test at interview.
Worcester Written test at interview.

Theology and Religious Studies
Cambridge *Test at interview:* Clare, Corpus Christi, Fitzwilliam, Hughes Hall, Lucy Cavendish, St Edmund's; Preparatory work at/before interview: Corpus Christi, Emmanuel, Girton, Jesus, Magdalene, Newnham,

Selwyn; *School/college essays:* Christ's, Clare, Corpus Christi, Downing, Emmanuel, Fitzwilliam, Girton, Gonville & Caius, Homerton, Jesus, King's, Magdalene, Murray Edwards, Newnham, Pembroke, Peterhouse, Queens', Robinson, St Catharine's, St John's, Selwyn, Sidney Sussex, Trinity, Trinity Hall, Wolfson. Check www.cam.ac.uk/admissions/undergraduate/apply/tests.html.

Oxford *All colleges offering the subject:* (Theol) No test; two pieces written work required. (Theol Orntl St) Oriental Studies Language Aptitude Test for candidates planning to study Islam or Judaism; two pieces written work required. Check www.admissions.ox.ac.uk/tests.

Veterinary Science/Medicine

Cambridge BMAT: Churchill, Clare, Downing, Emmanuel, Fitzwilliam, Girton, Gonville & Caius, Jesus, Lucy Cavendish, Magdalene, Murray Edwards, Newnham, Pembroke, Queens', Robinson, St Catharine's, St Edmund's, St John's, Selwyn, Sidney Sussex, Trinity Hall, Wolfson; Preparatory work at/before interview: Emmanuel, Robinson. Check www.cam.ac.uk/admissions/undergraduate/apply/tests.html.

Liverpool Candidates are asked to write an essay on a veterinary topic prior to interview.

London (RVC) BMAT (see www.admissionstests.cambridgeassessment.org.uk and www.rvc.ac.uk).

Myerscough (Coll) (Vet Nurs) Subject-based test at interview.

SELECTION OF APPLICANTS

University and college departmental admissions tutors are responsible for selecting candidates, basing their decisions on the policies of acceptable qualifications established by each institution and, where required, applicants' performance in admissions tests. There is little doubt that academic achievement, aptitude and promise are the most important factors although other subsidiary factors may be taken into consideration. The outline which follows provides information on the way in which candidates are selected for degree and diploma courses:

- Grades obtained by the applicant in GCE, A-level and AS-level examinations and the range of subjects studied may be considered.

- Applicant's performance in aptitude and admissions tests, as required by universities and colleges.

- Academic record of the applicant throughout his or her school career, especially up to A-level and AS-levels, Highers, Advanced Highers or other qualifications and the choice of subjects. If you are taking general studies at A-level or AS-level confirm with the admissions tutor that this is acceptable.

- Time taken by the applicant to obtain good grades at GCSE/Standard Grade and A-level and AS-levels/Highers/Advanced Highers.

- Forecast or the examination results of the applicant at A-level and AS-level and head teacher's report.

- The applicant's intellectual development; evidence of ability and motivation to follow the chosen course.

- The applicant's range of interests, both in and out of school; aspects of character and personality.

- The vocational interests, knowledge and experience of the applicant particularly if they are choosing vocational courses.

INTERVIEWS

Fewer applicants are now interviewed than in the past but even if you are not called you should make an effort to visit your chosen universities and/or colleges before you accept any offer. Interviews may be arranged simply to give you a chance to see the institution and the department and to meet the staff and students. Alternatively, interviews may be an important part of the selection procedure for specific courses such as Law, Medicine and Teaching. If they are, you need to prepare yourself well. Most interviews last approximately 20–30 minutes and you may be interviewed by more than one person. For practical subjects such as Music and Drama almost certainly you will be asked to perform, and for artistic subjects, to take examples of your work. For some courses you may also have a written or other test at interview (see above).

How best can you prepare yourself?

Firstly, as one applicant advised, 'Go to the interview – at least you'll see the place.'

Secondly, on the question of dress, try to turn up looking smart (it may not matter, but it can't be wrong).

Two previous applicants were more specific: 'Dress smartly but sensibly so you are comfortable for travelling and walking round the campus.'

More general advice is also important:
- 'Prepare well – interviewers are never impressed by applicants who only sit there with no willingness to take part.'
- 'Read up the prospectus and course details. Know how their course differs from any others you have applied for and be able to say why you prefer theirs.'
- 'They always ask if you have any questions to ask them: prepare some!' For example, How many students are admitted to the course each year? What are the job prospects for graduates? How easy is it to change from your chosen course to a related course?

Questions which you could ask might focus on the ways in which work is assessed, the content of the course, field work, work experience, teaching methods, accommodation and, especially for vocational courses, contacts with industry, commerce or the professions. However, don't ask questions which are already answered in the prospectus!

These are only a few suggestions and other questions may come to mind during the interview which, above all, should be a two-way flow of information. It is also important to keep a copy of your UCAS application (especially Section 10) for reference since your interview will probably start with a question about something you have written.

Usually interviewers will want to know why you have chosen the subject and why you have chosen their particular institution. They will want to see how motivated you are, how much care you have taken in choosing your subject, how much you know about your subject, what books you have read. If you have chosen a vocational course they will want to find out how much you know about the career it leads to, and whether you have visited any places of work or had any work experience. If your chosen subject is also an A-level subject you will be asked about your course and the aspects of the course you like the most.

Try to relax. For some people interviews can be an ordeal; most interviewers know this and will make allowances. The following extract from the Oxford prospectus will give you some idea of what admissions tutors look for:

- 'Interviews serve various purposes and no two groups of tutors will conduct them in the same way or give them exactly the same weight. Most tutors wish to discover whether a candidate has done more than absorb passively what he/she has been taught. They try to ascertain the nature and strength of candidates' intellectual interests and their capacity for independent development. They are also likely to ask about applicants' other interests outside their school curriculum. This is partly because between two candidates of equal academic merit, preference will be given to the one who has the livelier interests or activities, and partly because it is easier to learn about candidates when they talk about what interests them most.'
- 'Interviews are in no sense hostile interrogations. Those candidates who show themselves to be honest, thoughtful and unpretentious will be regarded more favourably than those who try to impress or take the view that it is safest to say as little as possible. We do not expect candidates to be invariably mature and judicious.'

In the tables in **Chapter 8** (Selection interviews, Interview advice and questions and Reasons for rejection) you will also find examples of questions which have been asked in recent years for which you might prepare, and non-academic reasons why applicants have been rejected! Chapter 5, **Applications,** provides a guide through the process of applying to your chosen universities and courses and highlights key points for your action.

The subject tables in the next chapter represent the core of the book, listing degree courses offered by all UK universities and colleges. These tables are designed to provide you with the information you need so that you can match your abilities and interests with your chosen degree subject, prepare your application and find out how applicants are selected for courses.

At the top of each table there is a brief overview of the subject area, together with a selection of websites for organisations that can provide relevant careers or course information. This is then followed by the subject tables themselves in which information is provided in sequence under the following headings.

Course offers information
- Subject requirements/preferences (GCSE/A-level/other requirements)
- NB Offers statement
- Your target offers and examples of courses provided by each institution
- Alternative offers

Examples of Foundation degrees in the subject field

Choosing your course
- Some course features
- Universities and colleges teaching quality
- Top universities and colleges (research)
- Examples of sandwich degree courses

Admissions information
- Number of applicants per place
- Advice to applicants and planning the UCAS personal statement
- Misconceptions about this course
- Selection interviews
- Interview advice and questions
- Reasons for rejection (non-academic)

After-results advice
- Offers to applicants repeating A-levels

Graduate destinations and employment
- Career note

Other degree subjects for consideration

When selecting a degree course it is important to try to judge the points score or grades that you are likely to achieve and compare them with the offers listed under **Your target offers and examples of courses provided by each institution**. However, even though you might be capable of achieving the indicated grades or UCAS Tariff points, it is important to note that these are likely to be the minimum grades or points required and that there is no guarantee that you will receive an offer: other factors in your application, such as the personal statement, references, and admissions test performance will be taken into consideration (see also **Chapters 4** and **6**).

University departments frequently adjust their offers, depending on the numbers of candidates applying, so you must not assume that the offers and policies published now will necessarily apply to courses starting in 2012 or thereafter. In 2011 there are many more changes than usual because of the high number of applicants to universities and colleges, and competition for places in 2012 for many courses is likely to be keen. Nevertheless, even though offers may change during the 2011/12 application cycle, you can assume that the offers published in this book represent the typical academic levels at which you should aim.

Below are explanations of the information given under the headings in the subject tables. It is important that you read these carefully so that you understand how they can help you to choose and apply for courses that are right for you.

COURSE OFFERS INFORMATION

Subject requirements/preferences

Brief information is given on the GCSE and A-level requirements. Note that for the Dentistry, Medicine and Veterinary Sciences/Medicine courses A-level subject requirements are stated on the individual institutions' offers line as their A-level requirements are more complex than for other subjects. Other requirements are sometimes specified, where these are relevant to the course subject area, for example, medical requirements for health-related courses and Criminal Records Bureau (CRB) clearance. Check prospectuses and websites of universities and colleges for course requirements. The following statement appears in all subject tables:

NB In 2012 universities and colleges will differ in their use of GCE AL/AS unit grade information, A* grades, the Extended Project (EPQ), the Advanced Diploma and the Cambridge Pre-U when considering applicants and making offers. An EPQ may be accepted in place of an AS subject. Check websites of universities and colleges for the latest offers information.

However, pressure on places available from increasing numbers of applicants in recent years has created a situation in which universities are constantly reviewing and often changing their offers in mid-cycle. The reader therefore should regard the published offers in most cases as minimum requirements.

Your target offers and examples of courses provided by each institution

Universities and colleges offering degree courses in the subject area are listed in descending order according to the number of UCAS Tariff points and/or A-level grades they are likely to require applicants to achieve. The UCAS Tariff points total is listed down the left-hand side of the page, and to the right appear all the institutions (in alphabetical order) likely to make offers in this Tariff point range. (Information on the UCAS Tariff is given in **Appendix 1** and guidance on how to calculate your offers is provided on the inside back cover of this book. Please also read the information in the **Important Note** box below.)

The courses included on the offers line are examples of the courses available in the subject field at that university or college. You will need to check prospectuses and websites for a complete list of the institution's single, joint, combined or major/minor degree courses available in the subject. For each institution listed, the following information may be given.

Name of institution

Note that the name of an institution's university college or campus may be given in brackets after the institution title, for example London (King's) or Kent (Medway Sch Pharm). Where the institution is not a university, further information about its status may also be given to indicate the type of college – for example (UC) to mean University College or (CAg) to mean College of Agriculture. This is to help readers to differentiate between the types of colleges and to help them identify any specialisation a college may have, for example art or agriculture. A full list of abbreviations used is given under the heading **INSTITUTION ABBREVIATIONS** later in this chapter.

Grades/points offer

After the institution's name, a line of offers information is given, showing a typical offer made by the institution for the courses indicated in brackets at the end of the line. Offers, however, may vary between applicants and the published grades and/or points offers should be regarded as targets to aim for and not necessarily the actual grades or points required. Offers may be reduced after the publication of A-level results, particularly if a university or college is left with spare places. However, individual course offers listed in the Tables in **Chapter 8** are abridged and should be used as a first source of reference and comparison only. It is not possible to publish all the variables relevant to each offer: applicants must check prospectuses and websites for full details of all offers and courses.

Depending on the details given by institutions, the offers may provide information as follows:

- **Grades** The specific grades, or average grades, required at GCE A-level or at A-level plus AS-level or, if specified, EPQ for the listed courses. (NB Graded offers may require specific grades for specific subjects.) A-level grades are always presented in capital letters; AS-levels and EPQ grades are shown in lower case – so the offer BBBc would indicate three grade Bs at A-level, plus an additional EPQ or AS-level at grade c. Where necessary, the abbreviation 'AL' is used to indicate A-level, 'AS' to indicate AS-level and EPQ to indicate that an Extended Project Qualification is part of the offer. Offers are usually shown in terms of three A-level grades although some institutions accept two grades with the same points total or, alternatively, two A-level grades accompanied by AS-level grades. Two AS-levels may generally be regarded as equivalent to one A-level, and one Double Award A-level as equivalent to two standard A-levels.

NB Unit grade and module information, now introduced into the admissions system, is most likely to be required by universities where a course is competitive, or where taking a specific unit is necessary or desirable for entry. Check with institutions' websites for their latest information.

- **UCAS Tariff points** A, AS-levels, International Baccalaureate (IB), Scottish Highers, the Advanced Diploma and a range of other qualifications have a unit value in the UCAS Tariff system (see **The UCAS Tariff Points Table** in **Appendix 1**). Where a range of Tariff points is shown, for example 220–180 points, offers are usually made within this points range for these specified courses. Note that, in some cases, an institution may require a points score which is higher than the specified grade offer given. This can be for a number of reasons – for example, you may not be offering the standard subjects that would have been stipulated in a grades offer. In such cases additional points may be added by way of AS-levels, Key Skills etc.

A Tariff point offer will not usually discriminate between the final year exam subjects being taken by the applicant unless otherwise stated, although certain GCSE subjects may be stipulated eg English or mathematics.

Admission tutors have the unenviable task of trying to assess the number of applicants who will apply for their courses against the number of places available and so judging the offers to be made. It is therefore important when reading the offers tables to be aware that variations occur each year. Lower offers or equivalents may be made to disadvantaged students, mature and international applicants.

The offers published in this edition therefore are based on admission policies operating in January 2011. They are targets to be achieved and in the case of popular courses at popular universities they should be regarded as minimum entry qualifications.

See **Chapter 4** for information from universities about their admissions policies including, for example, information about their expected use of A*, unit grades, the Advanced Diploma, the Extended Project and the Cambridge Pre-U in their offers for applicants. See **Appendix 1** for **The UCAS 2012 Entry Tariff Points** tables.

- **Admissions tests for Law, Medicine and Veterinary Science/Medicine** Where admissions tests form part of a university's offer for any of these subjects, this is indicated on the offers line in the subject tables for the relevant university. This is shown by '+LNAT' (for Law), '+BMAT' or '+UKCAT' (for Medicine), and '+BMAT' (for Veterinary Science/Medicine). For example, the offers lines could read as follows:

  Edinburgh – AAAb +UKCAT (inc AL chem+1 from maths/phys/biol; AS biol min) (Medicine 5/6 yrs) (IB 37 pts HL 766)
  London (King's) – AAAb +LNAT (Law) (IB 38 pts HL 555–554)
  London (RVC) – AAA +BMAT (inc AL chem+biol+1 other) (Vet Med)

  Entry and admissions tests will be required for 2012 by a number of institutions for a wide range of subjects: see **Chapter 6** and the subject tables in **Chapter 8** for more information and check university websites and prospectuses.

COURSE TITLE(S)

After the offer, an abbreviated form of the course title(s) to which the offers information refers is provided, also in brackets. The abbreviations used (see **COURSE ABBREVIATIONS** at the end of this chapter) closely relate to the course titles shown in the institutions' prospectuses. When the course gives the opportunity to study abroad (for example, in Continental Europe, Australia, North America) the abbreviated name of the relevant country is shown after the abbreviated course title. For example:

Lancaster – AAB 340 pts (Env Sci N Am/Aus; MChem Env Chem Abrd) (IB 30 pts)

When experience in industry is provided as part of the course (not necessarily a sandwich course) this can be indicated on the offers line by including 'Ind' after the abbreviated course title. For example:

Bristol – ABB (Pharmacol; Pharmacol Ind) (IB 34 pts)

Sometimes the information in the offers line relates to more than one course (see **Plymouth** below). In such cases, each course title is separated with a semicolon.

Plymouth – 300 pts (MEng Civ Eng; Civ Cstl Eng)

When a number of joint courses exist in combination with a major subject, they may be presented using a list separated by slashes – for example '(Euro Mgt with Fr/Ger/Ital/Span)' indicates European Management with French or German or Italian or Spanish. Some titles may be followed by the word 'courses' – for example, (Geog courses):

St Andrews – AAB (Theol St; Bib St courses) (IB 30 pts)

This means that the information on the offers line refers not only to the Single Honours course in Theological Studies, but also to the range of Biblical Studies courses. For some institutions with extensive Combined Honours programmes, the information given on the offers line may specify (Comb Hons) or (Comb courses).

Courses awaiting validation are usually publicised in prospectuses and on websites. However, these are not included in the tables in **Chapter 8** since there is no guarantee that they will run. You should check with the university that a non-validated course will be available.

To help you understand the information provided under the 'UCAS Tariff points requirements' heading, the box below provides a few examples with their meaning explained underneath.

OFFERS LINES EXPLAINED

320 pts [University/College name] – BBCc **or** BBccc (Fr Ger)
For the joint course in French and German, the University requires grades of BBC (280 pts) at A-level plus AS-level grade c (40 pts) making a total of 320 points or, alternatively, BB (200 pts) at A-level plus AS-level grades ccc (120 pts), making the same total.

320 pts [University/College name] – 320 pts BBC +AS/EPQ c (Biomed Sci (Genet))
For the Biomedical Sciences course specialising in Genetics the University requires 320 pts, typically from 3 A-levels, together with either one AS-level or Extended Project Qualification (EPQ). The typical offer will be BBC at A-level plus c in either an AS-level or an EPQ.

220 pts [University/College name] – 220–280 pts (Geography)
For Geography, the University usually requires 220 UCAS Tariff points, but offers may range up to 280 UCAS Tariff points.

IB offers

A selection of IB points offers appears at the end of some university/subject entries. For comparison of entry requirements, applicants with IB qualifications should check the A-level offers required for their course and then refer to **Appendix 1** which gives the revised IB UCAS points Tariff for 2012 entry. The figures under this subheading indicate the number or range of International Baccalaureate (IB) Diploma points likely to be requested in an offer. A range of points indicates variations between Single and Joint Honours courses. Applicants should check with the universities for any requirements for points gained from specific Higher Level subjects. Applicants offering the IB should check with prospectuses and websites and, if in doubt, contact admissions tutors for the latest information on IB offers.

Rel	Relations		**Sctr**	Sector
Relgn	Religion		**Sculp**	Sculpture
Relig	Religious		**Sdlry**	Saddlery
Reltd	Related		**SE**	South East
Rem Sens	Remote Sensing		**Sec**	Secretarial
Ren	Renaissance		**Semicond**	Semiconductor
Renew	Renewable		**SEN**	Special Educational Needs
Rep	Representation		**Serb Cro**	Serbo-Croat
Reqd	Required		**Serv**	Services
Res	Resources		**Set**	Settings
Resid	Residential		**Sfc**	Surface
Resoln	Resolution		**Sfty**	Safety
Resp	Response		**Sgnl**	Signal
Restor	Restoration		**Ship**	Shipping
Rev	Revenue		**Simul**	Simulation
Rflxgy	Reflexology		**Sit Lrng**	Situated Learning
Rgby	Rugby		**Sk**	Skills
Rgstrn	Registration		**Slf**	Self
Rl	Real		**Sln**	Salon
Rlblty	Reliability		**Slov**	Slovak/Slovene/Slavonic
Rlwy	Railway		**Sls**	Sales
Rmnc	Romance		**Sml**	Small
Rnwl	Renewal		**Smt**	Smart
Robot	Robotics		**Smtc**	Semitic
Rom	Roman		**Snc**	Sonic
Romn	Romanian		**Snd**	Sound
Rsch	Research		**Sndtrk**	Soundtrack
Rspnsb	Responsibility		**Sndwch**	Sandwich
Rsprty	Respiratory		**Sng**	Song
Rsrt	Resort		**Soc**	Social
Rstrnt	Restaurant		**Sociol**	Sociology
Rtl	Retail		**SocioLeg**	Socio-Legal
Rts	Rights		**Socling**	Sociolinguistics
Rur	Rural		**Soft**	Software
Russ	Russian		**Sol**	Solution(s)
Rvr	River		**Soty**	Society
			Sov	Soviet
S	Secondary		**Sp**	Speech
Sansk	Sanskrit		**Span**	Spanish
S As	South Asian		**Spat**	Spatial
Sat	Satellite		**Spc**	Space
Sbstnce	Substance		**SPD**	Surface Pattern Design
Scand	Scandinavian		**Spec**	Special/Specialisms/
Schlstc	Scholastic			Specialist
Schm	Scheme		**Spec Efcts**	Special Effects
Sci	Science/Scientific		**Sply**	Supply
Scnc	Scenic		**Spn**	Spain
Scngrph	Scenographic/Scenography		**Spo**	Sports
Scot	Scottish		**Spowr**	Sportswear
Scr	Secure		**Sprtd**	Supported
Script	Scriptwriting		**Sprtng**	Supporting
Scrn	Screen		**Sqntl**	Sequential
Scrnwrit	Sreenwriting		**Srf**	Surf/Surfing
Scrts	Securities		**Srgy**	Surgery
Scrty	Security		**SS**	Solid-state

St	Studies	Tr	Trade
St Reg	State Registration	Tr Stands	Trading Standards
Stats	Statistics	Trad	Traditional
Std	Studio	Trans	Transport(ation)
Stg	Stage	Transat	Transatlantic
Stgs	Settings	Transnl Med Sci	Translational Medical Science
Stnds	Standards	Transl	Translation
STQ	Scottish Teaching Qualification	Trav	Travel
Str	Stringed	Trfgrs	Turfgrass
Strat	Strategic/Strategy	Trg	Training
Strg	Strength	Trnrs	Trainers
Strt	Street	Trpcl	Tropical
Struct	Structural/Structures	Trpl	Triple
Stt	State	Trstrl	Terrestrial
Surf	Surface	Tstmnt	Testament
Surv	Surveying	Ttl	Total
Sust	Sustainability/Sustainable	Turk	Turkish
Swed	Swedish	Twn	Town
Swli	Swahili	Typo	Typographical/Typography
Sxlty	Sexuality		
Sys	System(s)	Ukr	Ukrainian
Systmtc	Systematic	Un	Union
		Undwtr	Underwater
Tap	Tapestry	Unif	Unified
Tax Rev	Taxation and Revenue	Up	Upland
Tbtn	Tibetan	Urb	Urban
Tcnqs	Techniques	USA	United States of America
Teach	Teaching	Util	Utilities/Utilisation
Tech	Technology/Technician/ Technical		
		Val	Valuation
Technol	Technological	Vcl	Vocal
TEFL	Teaching English as a Foreign Language	Veh	Vehicle
		Vntr	Venture
Telecomm	Telecommunications	Vib	Vibration
Ter	Terrestial	Vict	Victorian
TESOL	Teaching English to Speakers of Other Languages	Vid	Video
		Viet	Vietnamese
Testmt	Testament	Virol	Virology
Tex	Textiles	Vis	Visual/Visualisation
Thea	Theatre	Vit	Viticulture
Theol	Theology	Vkg	Viking
Theor	Theory/Theoretical	Vnu	Venue
Ther	Therapeutic	Voc	Vocational
Thera	Therapy	Vol	Voluntary
Tht	Thought	Vrtbrt	Vertebrate
Tiss	Tissue	Vrtl Rlty	Virtual Reality
Tlrg	Tailoring	Vsn	Vision
Tm	Time	Vstr	Visitor
Tmbr	Timber		
Tnnl	Tunnel/Tunnelling	Wdlnd	Woodland
Tns	Tennis	Welf	Welfare
Topog	Topographical	Wk	Work
Tour	Tourism	Wkg	Working
Tox	Toxicology	Wlbng	Well-being
TQ	Teaching Qualification	Wldlf	Wildlife

Wls	Wales	**Wvn**	Woven
Wmnswr	Womenswear	**www**	World Wide Web
Wn	Wine		
Wrbl	Wearable	**Ycht**	Yacht
Writ	Writing/Writer	**Ychtg**	Yachting
Wrld	World	**Yng**	Young
Wrlss	Wireless	**Yth**	Youth
Wst	Waste(s)		
Wstn	Western	**Zool**	Zoology
Wtr	Water		
Wtrspo	Watersports	**3D**	Three-dimensional

ACCOUNTANCY/ACCOUNTING

(see also **Finance**)

Accountancy and Accounting degree courses include accounting, finance, economics, law, management, qualitative methods and information technology. Many, but not all, Accountancy and Accounting degrees give exemptions from the examinations of some or all of the accountancy professional bodies. Single Honours courses are more likely to give full exemptions, while Joint Honours courses are more likely to lead to partial exemptions. Students should check with universities and colleges which professional bodies offer exemptions for their courses before applying. Most courses are strongly vocational and many offer sandwich placements or opportunities to study Accountancy/Accounting with a second subject. Many graduates entering careers in accountancy will do so after taking degree courses in other subjects although in all cases further study is necessary to qualify as an accountant.

Useful websites www.acca.co.uk; www.cimaglobal.org.uk; www.cipfa.org.uk; www.tax.org.uk; www.icaew.com; www.bized.co.uk.

NB The points totals shown to the left of the institutions are for ease of reference only. It must not be assumed that Tariff points are always used by institutions or that they can be substituted for an offer in grades. The level of an offer is not necessarily indicative of the quality of a course.

COURSE OFFERS INFORMATION

Subject requirements/preferences **GCSE** English and mathematics required: popular universities may specify grades. **AL** Mathematics or accounting required or preferred for some courses. Business studies accepted for some courses.

NB In 2012 universities and colleges will differ in their use of GCE AL/AS unit grade information, A* grades, the Extended Project (EPQ), the Advanced Diploma and the Cambridge Pre-U examination when considering applicants and making offers. An EPQ may be accepted in place of an AS subject. Check websites of universities and colleges for the latest offers information. Increasing numbers of applicants in 2012/13 could result in higher offers.

Your target offers and examples of courses provided by each institution
390 pts **Warwick** – AAAb–A*AA (Acc Fin) (IB 38 pts)
370 pts **Keele** – 370 pts (Acc Fin) (IB 28–30 pts)
360 pts **Bath** – AAA (Acc Fin) (IB 36 pts HL maths 5–6)
Bristol – AAA–ABB (Econ Acc) (IB 37–34 pts)
City – AAA (Acc Fin) (IB 35 pts)
Edinburgh – AAA (Law Acc; Econ Acc)
Exeter – AAA–ABB (Acc Ldrshp) (IB 36–33 pts)
Lancaster – AAA–AAB (Acc Adt Fin) (IB 36 pts)
Manchester – AAA (Acc) (IB 37–35 pts)
Newcastle – AAA–AAB (Acc Fin) (IB 34–38 pts)
340 pts **Birmingham** – AAB–ABBc (Acc Fin) (IB 34 pts)
Bristol – AAB–ABB (Acc Fin) (IB 35–34 pts)
Cardiff – AAB (Acc Fin) (IB 35 pts)
City – AAB (Econ Acc) (IB 35 pts)
Glasgow – AAB–AAA (Acc Fin) (IB 34 pts)

Kent – AAB (Law Acc Fin) (IB 36 ps)
Lancaster – AAB (Acc Fin Comp Sci) (IB 34 pts)
Leeds – AAB (Acc Law) (IB 38 pts)
London (RH) – AAB (Mgt Acc) (IB 35 pts)
London LSE – AAB (Acc Fin) (IB 37 pts HL 666)
Loughborough – AAB-AAA (Maths Acc Fin Mgt) (IB 34 pts HL 6 maths)
Manchester – AAB (Acc Fin) (IB 35–37 pts)
Nottingham – AAB (Fin Acc Mgt) (IB 34 pts)
Queen's Belfast – AAB-ABBa (Acc; Acc Fr/Ger/Span)
Reading – AAB (Acc Econ) (IB 34 pts)
Sheffield – AAB-ABB (Acc Fin Mgt Econ) (IB 33 pts)
Southampton – AAB (Mgt Sci Acc) (IB 34 pts)
Ulster – 340 pts (Acc Mark; Acc)

320 pts **Aston** – 320–340 pts (Acc Mgt) (IB 34 pts)
Bournemouth – 320 pts (Acc Fin; Acc Tax; Acc Law; Acc Bus)
Durham – ABB (Acc Fin)
Keele – 320–360 pts inc BB/AB (Acc)
Kent – 320 pts inc AB (Acc Fin) (IB 35 pts HL 16 pts)
Kingston – 320 pts (Acc Fin)
Lancaster – ABB (Acc Fin Maths) (IB 30 pts)
Liverpool – ABB (Acc) (IB 32 pts)
London (QM) – 320 pts (Maths Fin Acc) (IB 34 pts)
Newcastle – ABB-AAB (Acc Stats) (IB 32–34 pts)
Sheffield – ABB-BBB (Acc Fin Mgt Inf Mgt; Acc Fin Mgt Maths)
Strathclyde – ABB (Acc Bus Law)
Surrey – ABB 320 pts (Acc Fin) (IB 34 pts)
Swansea – ABB (Acc Fin)
Ulster – ABB (Law Acc)
York – ABB (Acc Bus Fin Mgt) (IB 34 pts)

300 pts **Aberystwyth** – 260–300 pts (Acc Fin) (IB 27 pts)
Brunel – 3AL **or** 350 pts 3AL+AS 300 pts (Bus Mgt (Acc)) (IB 32 pts.)
Coventry – 300 pts (Acc)
East Anglia – BBB-BBC (Acc Mgt) (IB 32–30 pts)
Edinburgh – BBB-AAA (Acc Fin)
Edinburgh Napier – 300 pts 2nd year entry (Acc courses) (IB 30 pts)
Essex – 300 pts (Acc Fin) (IB 29 pts)
Heriot-Watt – ABC-BBC 2nd yr entry (Acc Fin)
Huddersfield – 300 pts (Acc Fin Serv; Law Acc)
Northumbria – 300 pts (Acc) (IB 26 pts)
Portsmouth – 300 pts (Accounting; Acc Fin; Acc Bus)
Swansea – BBB (Bus Mgt Acc)
Westminster – BBB (Acc Bus Mgt) (IB 28 pts)

280 pts **Birmingham City** – (Acc; Acc joint courses)
Bradford – BBC (Acc Fin)
Brighton – BBC (Acc Fin) (IB 30 pts)
Bristol UWE – 280–340 pts (Acc Fin) (IB 24–28 pts)
Brunel – BBC (Fin Acc) (IB 32–33 pts)
Central Lancashire – 280–300 pts (Acc)
De Montfort – 280 pts (Acc Fin) (IB 30 pts)
Edge Hill – 280 pts (Accountancy)
Gloucestershire – 280–300 pts (Acc Fin Mgt)
Heriot-Watt – ABC-BBC (Acc Bus Law)
Hertfordshire – 280 pts (Acc Langs) (IB 28 pts)
Huddersfield – 280 pts (Acc)
Hull – 280 pts (Acc)

London South Bank – 280 pts (Acc Fin)
Nottingham Trent – 280 pts (Acc Fin) (IB 25 pts)
Oxford Brookes – BBC (Acc Fin) (IB 30 pts)
Salford – 280 pts (Fin Acc) (IB 28 pts)
Stirling – BBC 1st year entry (Acc courses) (IB 30 pts)
Worcester – 280 pts (Bus Entr Acc)

260 pts **Aberdeen** – BCC 2nd yr entry (Acc)
Bangor – 260–300 pts (Acc Fin; Acc Bank; Acc Econ)
Bolton – 260 pts (Acc courses; Acc Bus Mgt; Acc Law; Acc Maths)
BPP (UC) – 260 pts (Prof Acc)
Cardiff (UWIC) – 260 pts (Acc)
Central Lancashire – 260 pts (Acc Int Bus)
Dundee – BCC (Acc App Comp) (IB 30 pts)
Glasgow Caledonian – CCC (Accountancy) (IB 24 pts)
Greenwich – 260 pts (Acc Fin)
Heriot-Watt – BCC 260 pts 1st yr entry (Acc Fin)
Lincoln – 260 pts (Acc Fin; Acc Mark)
Liverpool John Moores – 260 pts (Acc Fin) (IB 26 pts)
Staffordshire – BCC 260 pts (Acc Fin) (IB 26 pts)
Winchester – 260–300 pts (Acc Fin) (IB 25 pts)

240 pts **Aberdeen** – CCC **or** aabb 1st yr entry (Acc) (IB 30 pts)
Bradford (Coll Univ Centre) – 2 A2 GCEs 240 pts (Acc Law)
Buckingham – 240–200 pts (Acc Fin Mgt)
Canterbury Christ Church – CCC (Mark Acc)
Cardiff (UWIC) – 240 pts (Acc Fin)
Chichester – CCC (Acc Fin)
De Montfort – 240 pts (Acc Mark; Acc; Acc Joint Hons)
Dundee – CCC (Int Acc) (IB 29 pts)
Glamorgan – 240–280 pts (Acc Fin; Foren Acc; Int Acc)
Liverpool Hope – 240-280 pts (Accounting)
London Met – 240 pts (Acc Bank)
Manchester Met – 240 pts (Acc Fin) (IB 28 pts)
Middlesex – 240–280 pts (Bus Acc)
Newport – 240 pts (Acc Fin; Acc Law; Acc Econ)
Plymouth – 240 pts (Acc Fin)
Robert Gordon – CCC (Acc Fin) (IB 20 pts)
Sheffield Hallam – 240 pts (Acc Fin Mgt)
Teesside – 240 pts (Acc Fin) (IB 30 pts)
Wolverhampton – 240 pts (Bus Acc; Acc Fin)

220 pts **Chester** – 220–260 pts (Acc Fin)
Leeds Met – 220 pts (Acc Fin) (IB 24 pts)
London Met – 220 pts (Acc Fin)
Northampton – 220–260 pts (Acc courses) (IB 24 pts)
Southampton Solent – 220 pts (Acc)

200 pts **Anglia Ruskin** – (Acc Fin)
Bucks New – 200–240 pts (Acc Fin)
Canterbury Christ Church – 200 pts (Bus St Acc)
East London – 200 pts (Acc Law; Acc; Acc Bus Econ)
Glyndŵr – 200 pts (Bus Acc)
West London – 200 pts (Acc Fin)
Wolverhampton – 200 pts (Acc Law)

180 pts **Derby** – 180–240 pts (Acc Joint)

160 pts **Bedfordshire** – 160–240 pts (Acc)
Bradford (Coll Univ Centre) – 2 A2 GCEs (not General Studies) 160 pts (Accountancy)
London South Bank – 160 pts (Acc Mark)

Swansea Met – 160 pts (Bus Fin)
West Scotland – CC (Acc)
120 pts **Swansea Met** – 120 pts (Acc)
80 pts **London (Birk)** – for under 21s (over 21s varies) p/t (Acc Mgt)

Alternative offers
See **Chapter 7** and **Appendix 1** for grades/UCAS Tariff points information for the International Baccalaureate, Scottish Highers/Advanced Highers, the Welsh Baccalaureate, the Irish Leaving Certificate, the Cambridge Pre-U Diploma, the Advanced Diploma and the Extended Project.

EXAMPLES OF FOUNDATION DEGREES IN THE SUBJECT FIELD
Aberdeen (Coll); Adam Smith (Coll); Anniesland (Coll); Ayr (Coll); Banff and Buchan (Coll); Blackburn (Coll Univ Centre); Blackpool and Fylde (Coll); Bournemouth; Cardiff (UWIC); Central Lancashire; Cornwall (Coll); Croydon (Coll); Darlington (Coll); Doncaster (Coll Univ Centre); Glamorgan; Glyndŵr; Hertfordshire; Highbury Portsmouth (Coll); Kensington Bus (Coll); Lambeth (Coll); Langside (Coll); Leeds Met; London Met; London South Bank; Manchester (Coll); Northampton; Northbrook (Coll); Plymouth; Salford; Southampton Solent; Suffolk (Univ Campus); West Cheshire (Coll); Westminster Kingsway (Coll); Wirral Met (Coll).

CHOOSING YOUR COURSE (SEE ALSO CH. 1)
Some course features
Anglia Ruskin Course can be started in February
Aston Third year spent in paid professional placement; experience can count towards professional recognition by major accounting bodies.
Exeter Courses can include a year of study or a combination of study and work placement in Europe or in North America, Japan or China.
Lancaster (Acc Adt Fin) Up to 18 months spent on salaried placement with Ernst & Young; first year bursary paid to all students.
London LSE A broad course, focusing on both accounting and its applications in different management areas. Options in first year depend on students' level of mathematics.
Portsmouth Professional mentoring scheme, pairing Level 2 and 3 students with practising accountant.

Universities and colleges teaching quality See www.qaa.ac.uk; http://unistats.direct.gov.uk.

Top research universities and colleges (RAE 2008) (Accounting and Finance) Bangor; Essex; Exeter; Bristol; Glasgow; Stirling; Bristol UWE; Dundee; Huddersfield.

Examples of sandwich degree courses Aston; Bath; Birmingham City; Bournemouth; Bradford; Brighton; Bristol UWE; Brunel; City; Coventry; De Montfort; Derby; Exeter; Glamorgan; Gloucestershire; Greenwich; Hertfordshire; Huddersfield; Lancaster; Leeds Met; Loughborough; Middlesex; Nottingham Trent; Plymouth; Portsmouth; Sheffield Hallam; Staffordshire; Swansea Met; Teesside; Ulster; West Scotland; Westminster; Wolverhampton; Worcester.

ADMISSIONS INFORMATION
Number of applicants per place (approx) Bath 7; Birmingham 12; Bristol 12; Dundee 5; East Anglia 17; Essex 7; Exeter 18; Glasgow 10; Heriot-Watt 7; Hull 8; Kent 10; Lancaster 20; Leeds 25; London LSE 17; Loughborough 12; Manchester 22; Oxford Brookes 9; Salford 8; Sheffield 40; Southampton 13; Staffordshire 3; Stirling 20; Strathclyde 10; Ulster 10; Warwick 14.

Advice to applicants and planning the UCAS personal statement Universities look for good numerical and communication skills, interest in the business and financial world, teamwork, problem-solving and computing experience. On the UCAS application you should be able to demonstrate your interest and understanding of accountancy and to give details of any work experience or work shadowing undertaken. Try to arrange meetings with accountants, or work shadowing or work experience in accountants' offices, commercial or industrial firms, town halls, banks or insurance companies and describe the work you have done. Obtain information from the main accountancy

BSc (Hons) Professional Accounting

Your first step to a successful accounting career

BPP is a specialist in accountancy education – teaching more global accountancy prize-winning professionals than any other institution. Study your degree with BPP, and we will balance the development of your technical competence with intellectual and practical skills, as well as awarding you with exemptions to some of your future professional exams.

BPP tutors bring their professional experience into the classroom, immersing you in the latest industry and commercial developments. The real world application of your academic learning means when you graduate, you're ready to hit the ground running.

Course details

Length of programme: 2-7 years

Start dates: January & September

Study Centres: London (City), Manchester*, Birmingham* and online

Admission requirements: 260 UCAS points plus a minimum grade C in GCSE Maths and English

Each year, we train over 30,000 accounting professionals who consistently outperform the market in their exams

For more information on starting your accounting career with a BPP degree, visit: **www.bpp.com/ug** tel: **0845 077 5036**

* Subject to validation

professional bodies (see **Appendix 4**). Refer to current affairs which have stimulated your interest from articles in the Financial Times, The Economist or the business and financial sections of the weekend press. **Bath** Gap Year welcomed. Extra-curricular activities important and should be described on the personal statement. There should be no gaps in your chronological history. **Brunel** (Bus Mgt (Acc)) Extended Project qualification accepted in place of AS-level; AL critical thinking and general studies acceptable. **Lancaster** (Acc Adt Fin) Selected UCAS applicants complete supplementary application form and on-line test. They may then be invited to a selection workshop.

Misconceptions about this course Many students believe incorrectly that you need to be a brilliant mathematician. However, you do have to be numerate and enjoy numbers (see Subject requirements/preferences). Many under-estimate the need for a high level of attention to detail. **Buckingham** Some students think it's a maths course. **Salford** Some applicants believe the course is limited to financial knowledge when it also provides an all-round training in management skills.

Selection interviews Yes West London; **Some** Abertay Dundee, Aberystwyth, Anglia Ruskin, Buckingham, Cardiff, Cardiff (UWIC), De Montfort, Dundee, East Anglia, Kent, Lincoln, Liverpool John Moores, London LSE, Staffordshire, Stirling, Sunderland, Wolverhampton; **No** Bristol.

Interview advice and questions Be prepared to answer questions about why you have chosen the course, the qualities needed to be an accountant, and why you think you have these qualities! You should also be able to discuss any work experience you have done and to describe the differences in the work of chartered, certified, public finance and management accountants. See also **Chapter 6**. **Buckingham** Students from a non-English-speaking background are asked to write an essay. If their maths results are weak they may be asked to do a simple arithmetic test. Mature students with no formal qualifications are usually interviewed and questioned about their work experience.

Reasons for rejection (non-academic) Poor English. Lack of interest in the subject because they realise they have chosen the wrong course! No clear motivation. Course details not researched.

London South Bank Punctuality, neatness, enthusiasm and desire to come to London South Bank not evident.

AFTER-RESULTS ADVICE

Offers to applicants repeating A-levels **Higher** Brunel, Glasgow Caledonian, Hull, Manchester Met; **Possibly higher** Brighton, Central Lancashire, East Anglia, Leeds, Newcastle, Oxford Brookes, Sheffield Hallam; **Same** Abertay Dundee, Aberystwyth, Anglia Ruskin, Bangor, Birmingham City, Bolton, Bradford, Buckingham, Cardiff, Cardiff (UWIC), Chichester, De Montfort, Derby, Dundee, Durham, East London, Edinburgh Napier, Glasgow, Heriot-Watt, Huddersfield, Liverpool John Moores, Loughborough, Northumbria, Portsmouth, Salford, Staffordshire, Stirling, Swansea Met, West London, West Scotland, Wolverhampton.

GRADUATE DESTINATIONS AND EMPLOYMENT (2007/8 HESA)

Graduates surveyed 2870 **Employed** 1140 **In further study** 305 **Assumed unemployed** 355

Career note Most Accountancy/Accounting graduates enter careers in finance. Further study is required to qualify as accountants.

OTHER DEGREE SUBJECTS FOR CONSIDERATION

Actuarial Studies; Banking; Business Studies; Economics; Financial Services; Insurance; International Securities and Investment Banking; Mathematics; Quantity Surveying; Statistics.

ACTUARIAL SCIENCE/STUDIES

Actuaries deal with the evaluation and management of financial risks, particularly those associated with insurance companies and pension funds. Although Actuarial Science/Studies degrees are vocational and give full or partial exemptions from some of the examinations of the Institute and Faculty of Actuaries, students are not necessarily committed to a career as an actuary on graduation. However, many graduates go on to be actuary trainees, leading to one of the highest-paid careers.

Useful websites www.actuaries.org.uk; www.soa.org; www.beanactuary.org.

NB The points totals shown to the left of the institutions are for ease of reference only. It must not be assumed that Tariff points are always used by institutions or that they can be substituted for an offer in grades. The level of an offer is not necessarily indicative of the quality of a course.

COURSE OFFERS INFORMATION

Subject requirements/preferences **GCSE** Most institutions require grades A or B in mathematics. **AL** Mathematics at a specified grade required.

NB In 2012 universities and colleges will differ in their use of GCE AL/AS unit grade information, A* grades, the Extended Project (EPQ), the Advanced Diploma and the Cambridge Pre-U examination when considering applicants and making offers. An EPQ may be accepted in place of an AS subject. Check websites of universities and colleges for the latest offers information.

Your target offers and examples of courses provided by each institution

420 pts **Queen's Belfast** – AAAa (Act Sci Rsk Mgt)
360 pts **City** – AAA (Act Sci) (IB 35 pts)
        London LSE – AAA (App Stats Act Sci) (IB 38 pts HL 17 pts)
        Manchester – A*AA–AAB (Act Sci Maths)
        Southampton – AAA inc A maths **or** AAB (inc f. maths) (Maths Act Sci) (IB 36 pts HL 6)
340 pts **East Anglia** – AAB–ABB (Act Sci) (IB 33–32 pts HL maths 7)
        Heriot-Watt – AAB (inc A maths) 2nd year entry (Act Sci)
        Keele – AAB (Act Sci)
        Kent – 340 pts (Act Sci Ind) (IB 35 pts HL maths 6)
        Leeds – AAB (Act Maths) (IB 34 pts HL maths 6)

320 pts Heriot-Watt – ABB (inc A maths) 1st yr entry (Act Sci)
260 pts Kingston – 260–280 pts (Act Maths Stats) (IB 26–28 pts)
240 pts City – CCC (Act Sci 4 yr inc Fdn)

Alternative offers
See **Chapter 7** and **Appendix 1** for grades/UCAS Tariff points information for the International Baccalaureate, Scottish Highers/Advanced Highers, the Welsh Baccalaureate, the Irish Leaving Certificate, the Cambridge Pre-U Diploma, the Advanced Diploma and the Extended Project.

CHOOSING YOUR COURSE (SEE ALSO CH. 1)

Some course features
Heriot-Watt Opportunities for industrial placements or year abroad. University has active Students' Actuarial Society.
Kent Core actuarial modules taught by qualified actuaries. Optional year in industry in Year 3.
London LSE The Actuarial Science degree and the BSc Business Mathematics and Statistics degree have the same first year. Transfer between the two courses possible in Year 2.
Queen's Belfast Nine-month placement in Year 3 in either an actuarial or risk management setting in mainland UK, Ireland, the US or mainland Europe.
Southampton Both courses offer some exemptions from the examinations of the Institute of Actuaries.

Universities and colleges teaching quality See http://unistats.direct.gov.uk; www.qaa.ac.uk.

Examples of sandwich degree courses City; East Anglia; Kent; Queen's Belfast.

ADMISSIONS INFORMATION

Number of applicants per place (approx) City 6; Heriot-Watt 5; Kent 6; London LSE 9; Southampton (Maths Act Sci) 9, (Econ Act Sci) 8; Swansea 9.

Advice to applicants and planning the UCAS personal statement Demonstrate your knowledge of this career and its training, and mention any contacts you have made with an actuary. (See **Appendix 4** for contact details of professional associations for further information.) Any work experience or shadowing in insurance companies should be mentioned, together with what you have learned about the problems facing actuaries. It is important to show motivation and sheer determination for training as an actuary which is long and tough (up to three or four years after graduation). Mathematical flair, an ability to communicate and an interest in business are paramount.

Misconceptions about this course There is a general lack of understanding of actuaries' career training and of the career itself.

Selection interviews Some Heriot-Watt, Kent, Southampton, Swansea.

Interview advice and questions In view of the demanding nature of the training, it is important to have spent some time discussing this career with an actuary in practice. Questions, therefore, may focus on the roles of the actuary and the qualities you have to succeed. You should also be ready to field questions about your Advanced Level mathematics course and the aspects of it you most enjoy. See also **Chapter 6**. **Swansea** The interview does not determine who will be accepted or rejected, only the level of the offer made.

Reasons for rejection (non-academic) Kent Poor language skills.

AFTER-RESULTS ADVICE

Offers to applicants repeating A-levels Higher City; **Same** Heriot-Watt, Southampton.

GRADUATE DESTINATIONS AND EMPLOYMENT (2007/8 HESA)

See **Finance**.

Career note Graduates commonly enter careers in finance, many taking further examinations to qualify as actuaries.

OTHER DEGREE SUBJECTS FOR CONSIDERATION

Accountancy; Banking; Business Studies; Economics; Financial Risk Management; Financial Services; Insurance; Mathematics; Money, Banking and Finance; Statistics.

AFRICAN AND CARIBBEAN STUDIES

(see also **Languages**)

African Studies courses tend to be multi-disciplinary, covering several subject areas and can include anthropology, history, geography, sociology, social psychology and languages. Most courses focus on Africa and African languages (Amharic (Ethiopia), Hausa (Nigeria), Somali (Horn of Africa), Swahili (Somalia and Mozambique), Yoruba (Nigeria, Sierra Leone, Ghana and Senegal), and Zulu (South Africa)).

Useful websites www.britishmuseum.org; www.africanstudies.org; www.black-history-month.co.uk.

NB The points totals shown to the left of the institutions are for ease of reference only. It must not be assumed that Tariff points are always used by institutions or that they can be substituted for an offer in grades. The level of an offer is not necessarily indicative of the quality of a course.

COURSE OFFERS INFORMATION

Subject requirements/preferences **GCSE** Grade A–C in mathematics and English may be required. **AL** For language courses a language subject or demonstrated proficiency in a language is required.

NB In 2012 universities and colleges will differ in their use of GCE AL/AS unit grade information, A* grades, the Extended Project (EPQ), the Advanced Diploma and the Cambridge Pre-U examination when considering applicants and making offers. An EPQ may be accepted in place of an AS subject. Check websites of universities and colleges for the latest offers information.

Your target offers and examples of courses provided by each institution
320 pts **Birmingham** – ABB–BBB (Af St joint courses) (IB 32 pts)
　　　　 London (SOAS) – ABB (Af St courses) (IB 34 pts HL 555)
300 pts **Birmingham** – BBB–BCC (Af St) (IB 30–32 pts)
260 pts **London Met** – 260 pts (Carib St Educ St) (IB 28 pts)

Alternative offers
See **Chapter 7** and **Appendix 1** for grades/UCAS Tariff points information for the International Baccalaureate, Scottish Highers/Advanced Highers, the Welsh Baccalaureate, the Irish Leaving Certificate, the Cambridge Pre-U Diploma, the Advanced Diploma and the Extended Project.

CHOOSING YOUR COURSE (SEE ALSO CH. 1)

Some course features
Birmingham A broad multi-disciplinary degree, offering Single and Joint Honours courses.
London (SOAS) Six African languages taught at undergraduate level; students have some flexibility in constructing their own course of study.
London Met One-semester or one-year placement in the West Indies.

Universities and colleges teaching quality See www.qaa.ac.uk; http://unistats.direct.gov.uk.

Top research universities and colleges (RAE 2008) (Middle Eastern and African Studies) Cambridge; Oxford; Edinburgh; London (SOAS); Durham.

ADMISSIONS INFORMATION

Number of applicants per place (approx) Birmingham 5.

Advice to applicants and planning the UCAS personal statement Describe any visits you have made to African or Caribbean countries, and why you wish to study this subject. Embassies in London may be able to provide information about the history, geography, politics, economics and the culture of the countries in which you are interested. Keep up-to-date with political developments in Africa or Caribbean countries. Discuss any aspects which interest you.

Interview advice and questions Questions are likely on your choice of country or geographical region, your knowledge of it and your awareness of some of the political, economic and social problems that exist. See also **Chapter 6**.

AFTER-RESULTS ADVICE
Offers to applicants repeating A-levels Higher Information not available from institutions.

GRADUATE DESTINATIONS AND EMPLOYMENT (2007/8 HESA)
Graduates surveyed 15 **Employed** 5 **In further study** 5 **Assumed unemployed** 0

Career note The language skills and knowledge acquired in African Studies courses, particularly when combined with periods of study in Africa, are relevant to a wide range of careers.

OTHER DEGREE SUBJECTS FOR CONSIDERATION
Anthropology; Geography; History; Languages; Sociology.

AGRICULTURAL SCIENCES/AGRICULTURE

(including **Agricultural Business Management, Aquaculture, Countryside Conservation, Crop Science** and **Rural Resources Management**; see also **Animal Sciences, Food Science/Studies and Technology, Forestry, Horticulture, Landscape Architecture, Surveying, Zoology**)

Courses in Agriculture recognise that modern farming practice requires sound technical and scientific knowledge, together with appropriate management skills, and most courses focus to a greater or lesser extent on all these requirements. Your choice of course depends on your particular interest and aims: some courses will give greater priority than others to practical application. Many students will come from an agricultural background and work experience will be necessary for most institutions.

Useful websites www.defra.gov.uk; www.naturalengland.org.uk; www.ccw.gov.uk; www.rase.org.uk; www.scienceyear.com; www.iah.bbsrc.ac.uk; www.lantra.co.uk; www.nfuonline.com; www.nfyfc.org. uk; www.iagre.org; www.afuturein.com.

NB The points totals shown to the left of the institutions are for ease of reference only. It must not be assumed that Tariff points are always used by institutions or that they can be substituted for an offer in grades. The level of an offer is not necessarily indicative of the quality of a course.

COURSE OFFERS INFORMATION
Subject requirements/preferences GCSE English and mathematics usually required; chemistry sometimes required. Practical experience may be required. **AL** One or two maths/biological science subjects may be required or preferred. Geography may be accepted as a science subject. Similar requirements apply for Agricultural Business Management courses. (Crop Science) Two science subjects may be required. (Countryside Management) Geography or biology preferred.

NB In 2012 universities and colleges will differ in their use of GCE AL/AS unit grade information, A* grades, the Extended Project (EPQ), the Advanced Diploma and the Cambridge Pre-U examination when considering applicants and making offers. An EPQ may be accepted in place of an AS subject. Check websites of universities and colleges for the latest offers information. Note that many agricultural courses are offered at colleges on sites separate from the universities.

Your target offers and examples of courses provided by each institution
320 pts Newcastle – 320 pts (Rur St) (IB 28-30 pts)
Stirling – ABB 2nd year entry (Aquacult)

300 pts   **Newcastle** – BBB (Cntry Mgt) (IB 30 pts)
           Queen's Belfast – BBB (Agric Tech)
           Reading – 300 pts (Agric) (IB 29 pts HL 655)
           Royal (CAg) – 300 pts (Rur Lnd Mgt)
           Stirling – BBB 2nd year entry (Cons Mgt) (IB 26 pts)
280 pts   **Harper Adams (UC)** – 280 pts (Rur Ent Lnd Mgt)
           Newcastle – BBC–BCC (Anim Prod Sci) (IB 28 pts)
           Nottingham – BBC–BCC (Crop Sci) (IB 28 pts)
           Stirling – BBC 1st year entry (Aqua)
240 pts   **Aberystwyth** – 240 pts (Cntry Recr Tour) (IB 28 pts)
           Bangor – 240–260 pts (Agric Cons Env) (IB 28 pts)
           Harper Adams (UC) – 240 pts (Agric courses (8))
           Royal (CAg) – (Int Eqn Agric Bus Mgt) (IB 26–28 pts)
           Sparsholt (Coll) – 240 pts (Aquacult Fish Mgt)
220 pts   **Aberystwyth** – (Agric Anim Sci) (IB 24 pts)
           Harper Adams (UC) – 220–240 pts (Cntry Env Mgt)
           Myerscough (Coll) – 220 pts (Agric; Sportsturf Sci Mgt)
           Nottingham Trent – 220 pts (Wldlf Cons)
210 pts   **Aberystwyth** – (Agric Bus St) (IB 28 pts)
200 pts   **Aberystwyth** – (Agric Cntry Mgt) (IB 24 pts)
           Writtle (Coll) – 200–360 pts (Agric courses)
160 pts   **Greenwich** – 160 pts (Int Agric) (IB 24 pts)
           SAC (Scottish CAg) – CC (Agri Sci; Agric; Rur Bus Mgt (Agric); Cntry Mgt; Rur Bus Mgt courses; Grn Tech)

           Myerscough (Coll) – (Mach Mgt Log) Check with College

Alternative offers
See **Chapter 7** and **Appendix 1** for grades/UCAS Tariff points information for the International Baccalaureate, Scottish Highers/Advanced Highers, the Welsh Baccalaureate, the Irish Leaving Certificate, the Cambridge Pre-U Diploma, the Advanced Diploma and the Extended Project.

EXAMPLES OF FOUNDATION DEGREES IN THE SUBJECT FIELD
Aberystwyth; Askham Bryan (Coll); Bath; Bath City (Coll); Bath Spa; Berkshire (CAg); Bishop Burton (Coll); Bournemouth; Bridgend (Coll); Brighton; Bucks New; CAFRE; Cumbria; Duchy (Coll); East Anglia; Easton (Coll); Greenwich; Guildford (Coll); Hadlow (Coll); Harper Adams (UC); Hertfordshire; Kingston Maurward (Coll); Lincoln; Manchester (Coll); Moulton (Coll); Myerscough (Coll); Northampton; Northop (Coll); Nottingham Trent; Oatridge (Coll); Oxford Brookes; Plymouth; Reaseheath (Coll); Royal (CAg); South Staffordshire (Coll); Sparsholt (Coll); Suffolk (Univ Campus); Sunderland; Warwickshire (Coll); Wiltshire (Coll); Wolverhampton; Writtle (Coll).

CHOOSING YOUR COURSE (SEE ALSO CH. 1)
Some course features
Other universities offer a very wide choice of courses including many specialisms associated with land use including Forest and Woodland Management (**Cumbria**, **Worcester**), Garden Design (**Greenwich**), Wildlife Conservation (**Kent**, **Plymouth**).

Aberystwyth (Agric) Nine months of work experience in third year.
Bristol UWE (Cons Cntry Mgt) Range of optional modules allow students to develop interests in, for example, woodland management.
Greenwich (Int Agric) Worldwide focus on agriculture science and practice, business, trade, development and sustainability; placement opportunities in the UK, Europe and the US, with study tours in UK and Europe.
Harper Adams (UC) (Rur Ent Lnd Mgt) Course includes surveying, valuation, law, taxation, the rural economy (including woodlands and field sports management), business finance, and agriculture and the environment. Options include languages and property investment.
Newcastle Choice of degree deferred to third year.
Nottingham Trent During optional fourth year students can take a Certificate in European Studies. Second modern language at Grade B required.
Reading Wide range of optional modules in every year includes subjects from other departments, for example languages, business entrepreneurship, international development.
Royal (CAg) (Int Eqn Agric Bus Mgt) Twenty-week work placement in second year; links with the Westphalian Riding School.

Universities and colleges teaching quality See www.qaa.ac.uk; http://unistats.direct.gov.uk.

Top research universities and colleges (RAE 2008) (Agriculture, Veterinary and Food Science) Warwick; Aberdeen; Nottingham; Leeds; Reading (Food Biosciences); London (RVC); Aberystwyth; Glasgow; Edinburgh; Stirling; Cambridge; Liverpool; Newcastle; Bristol UWE; Bangor.

Examples of sandwich degree courses Aberystwyth; Bangor; Harper Adams (UC); Nottingham Trent; Plymouth; Royal (CAg); Sparsholt (Coll).

ADMISSIONS INFORMATION
Number of applicants per place (approx) Aberystwyth (Agric courses) 2–3; Bangor (Agric Cons Env) 4; Newcastle 6; Nottingham 4; Royal (CAg) (Agric) 2.

Advice to applicants and planning the UCAS personal statement First-hand farming experience is essential for some courses and obviously important for all. Check prospectuses and websites. Describe the work done. Details of experience of work with agricultural or food farms (production and laboratory work), garden centres, even with landscape architects, could be appropriate. Keep up-to-date with European agricultural and fishing policies and mention any interests you have in these areas. Read farming magazines and discuss any articles which have interested you. You may even have had first-hand experience of the serious problems facing farmers. Interest or experience in practical conservation work. Ability to work both independently or as a member of a team is important. (See **Appendix 4**.)

Selection interviews Some Bangor, Bishop Burton (Coll), Derby, Edinburgh, Harper Adams (UC), Queen's Belfast, Royal (CAg).

Interview advice and questions Agriculture is in the news, especially in relation to the use of farming land for growing bio-fuel crops, the rapidly rising prices of fertilisers, world food shortages and the problems faced by UK dairy farmers. You should be up-to-date with political and scientific issues concerning the farming community in general and how these problems might be resolved. You are likely to be questioned on your own farming background (if relevant) and your farming experience. Questions asked in the past have included: What special agricultural interests do you have? What types of farms have you worked on? What farming publications do you read and which agricultural shows have you visited? What is meant by the term 'sustainable development'? What is the UK Biodiversity Action Plan? Are farmers custodians of the countryside? What are the potential sources of non-fossil-fuel electricity generation? See also **Chapter 6**. **Bangor** (Agric Cons Env) No tests at interview. **Derby** (Cntry Mgt) Discussion about fieldwork experience.

Reasons for rejection (non-academic) Insufficient motivation. Too immature. Unlikely to integrate well. Lack of practical experience with crops or animals.

AFTER-RESULTS ADVICE
Offers to applicants repeating A-levels Possibly higher Newcastle (Agric); **Same** Bangor (Agric Cons Env), Derby, Harper Adams (UC), Nottingham, Royal (CAg), Writtle (Coll).

GRADUATE DESTINATIONS AND EMPLOYMENT (2007/8 HESA)
Agriculture graduates surveyed 650 **Employed** 315 **In further study** 60 **Assumed unemployed** 65

Agricultural Science graduates surveyed 20 **Employed** 5 **In further study** 5 **Assumed unemployed** 5

Career note The majority of graduates entered the agricultural industry whilst others moved into manufacturing, the wholesale and retail trades and property development.

OTHER DEGREE SUBJECTS FOR CONSIDERATION
Agroforestry; Animal Sciences; Biochemistry; Biological Sciences; Biology; Biotechnology; Chemistry; Conservation Management; Crop Science; Ecology (Biological Sciences); Environmental Sciences; Estate Management (Surveying); Food Science and Technology; Forestry; Horticulture; Land Surveying; Landscape Architecture; Plant Sciences; Veterinary Science; Zoology.

AMERICAN STUDIES
(see also **Latin American Studies**)

Courses normally cover American history, politics and literature, although there are opportunities to study specialist fields such as drama, film studies, history of art, linguistics, politics or sociology. In some universities a year, term or semester spent in the USA (or Canada) is compulsory or optional whilst at other institutions the course lasts three years without a placement abroad.

Useful websites www.historynet.com; www.americansc.org.uk; www.theasa.net.

NB The points totals shown to the left of the institutions are for ease of reference only. It must not be assumed that Tariff points are always used by institutions or that they can be substituted for an offer in grades. The level of an offer is not necessarily indicative of the quality of a course.

COURSE OFFERS INFORMATION
Subject requirements/preferences GCSE Specific grades in some subjects may be specified by some popular universities. **AL** English, a modern language, humanities or social science subjects preferred.

NB In 2012 universities and colleges will differ in their use of GCE AL/AS unit grade information, A* grades, the Extended Project (EPQ), the Advanced Diploma and the Cambridge Pre-U examination when considering applicants and making offers. An EPQ may be accepted in place of an AS subject. Check websites of universities and colleges for the latest offers information.

Your target offers and examples of courses provided by each institution

380 pts	**Warwick** – AABc (Hist Lit Cult Am) (IB 36 pts)
320 pts	**Birmingham** – AAB–ABB (Engl Am Cdn St) (IB 34–36 pts)
	Dundee – ABB 2nd yr entry (Am St courses) (IB 29 pts)
	East Anglia – BBB–BBC (Am Lit Crea Writ) (IB 30–31 pts)
	Essex – ABB–BBB 320–300 pts (Am (US St) Film) (IB 32 pts)
	Kent – 320 pts (Am St (Lit)) (IB 33 pts)
	Leicester – ABB–BBB (Am St Yr USA) (IB 30 pts)
	Loughborough – ABB (Engl N Am Lit Film) (IB 34 pts)
	Manchester – ABB (Am St) (IB 33 pts)
	Nottingham – ABB (Am Engl St) (IB 32–34 pts)
	Sussex – ABB–BBB (Am St courses) (IB 32–34 pts)
300 pts	**East Anglia** – BBB (Am Hist Pol) (IB 31 pts HL hist 5)
	Hull – 300–260 pts (Am St)
	Leicester – BBB (Hist Am St) (IB 34 pts)
	Liverpool – BBB–BBC (Compar Am St) (IB 30 pts)
	London (Gold) – BBB (Engl Am Lit)
	Manchester – BBB (Am Lat Am St) (IB 32 pts)
	Nottingham – ABC–BBB (Am St Lat Am St) (IB 32 pts)
	Swansea – BBB (Am St courses) (IB 32 pts)
280 pts	**Glamorgan** – 280 pts (Am St Comb Hons)
	Manchester Met – 280 pts (Engl Am Lit)
260 pts	**Dundee** – BCC 1st yr entry (Am St courses) (IB 29 pts)
	Hull – 260–280 pts (Am St Hist; Am St Phil; Am St Fr/Ger/Ital/Span)
	Keele – 260–320 pts (Am St) (IB 28–32 pts)
	London Met – 260 pts (Carib St courses)
	Winchester – 260–300 pts (Am St Am Film)
240 pts	**Central Lancashire** – 240–260 pts (Am St) (IB 28 pts)
	Hull – 240–280 pts (Am St Relig)
	Lincoln – 240–280 pts (Am St courses)
	Portsmouth – 240–300 pts (Am St courses) (IB 24 pts)
	Ulster – 240 pts (Am St courses)
	Winchester – 240–260 pts (Am St Bus Mgt) (IB 24 pts)
220 pts	**Sunderland** – 220–360 pts (Am St comb courses)
	Winchester – 220–260 pts (Am St Film Cnma Tech)
	York St John – 220–260 pts (Am St courses) (IB 24 pts)
200 pts	**Canterbury Christ Church** – 200 pts (Am St courses)
	Worcester – 200–240 pts (Am St courses)
180 pts	**Derby** – 180 pts (Am St courses)

Alternative offers

See **Chapter 7** and **Appendix 1** for grades/UCAS Tariff points information for the International Baccalaureate, Scottish Highers/Advanced Highers, the Welsh Baccalaureate, the Irish Leaving Certificate, the Cambridge Pre-U Diploma, the Advanced Diploma and the Extended Project.

CHOOSING YOUR COURSE (SEE ALSO CH. 1)
Some course features
Canterbury Christ Church American Studies is available as Single Honours and Joint or Combined Honours courses. Opportunity to spend either a semester or a year in the US.

East Anglia Students on four-year programme spend third year at American, Australian or Canadian university and are eligible for local education authority financial support.
Kent (Am St courses) Students spending a third year at an American university do not pay American tuition fees – only travel and living costs.
Liverpool An inter-disciplinary course covering North America, Latin America and the Caribbean. Option to learn Spanish or Portuguese from scratch, or to combine study of AL French, Spanish or Portuguese to degree level.
Manchester (Am St) Course covers the history, literature, film, politics and popular culture of the United States. Opportunity to study in US university for one or two semesters.
Nottingham (Am St courses) Part-time (4–7 yrs) study is also available.
Ulster Programme combines study of American history, literature, film, politics, music and cultural studies in an area study of the US.

Universities and colleges teaching quality See www.qaa.ac.uk; http://unistats.direct.gov.uk.

Top research universities and colleges (RAE 2008) Sussex; Birmingham; East Anglia; Nottingham; London (King's).

ADMISSIONS INFORMATION

Number of applicants per place (approx) Birmingham 4; Dundee 5; East Anglia 7; Essex 6; Hull 15; Keele 7; Leicester 7; Manchester 6; Nottingham 12; Swansea 2; Warwick 14.

Advice to applicants and planning the UCAS personal statement Visits to America should be described, and any knowledge or interests you have of the history, politics, economics and the culture of the USA should be included on the UCAS application. The US Embassy in London may be a useful source of information. American magazines and newspapers are good reference sources and also give a good insight to life in the USA. Applicants should demonstrate an intelligent interest in both North American literature and history in their personal statement. Tell us why you are excited and interested in the subject: at least half of your personal statement should focus on how and why your interest has developed, for example through extra-curricular reading, projects, films, academic study. **Manchester** Due to the detailed nature of entry requirements for American Studies courses, we are unable to include full details in the prospectus. For complete and up-to-date information on our entry requirements for these courses, please visit our website at www.manchester.ac.uk/ugcourses.

Misconceptions about this course Swansea Some candidates feel that American Studies is a soft option. While we study many topics which students find interesting, we are very much a humanities-based degree course incorporating more traditional subjects like history, literature and English. Our graduates also find that they are employable in the same jobs as those students taking other degrees.

Selection interviews Yes Birmingham, Dundee, East Anglia, Hull, Sussex, Winchester; **Some** Derby, Kent, Warwick.

Interview advice and questions Courses often focus on history and literature so expect some questions on any American literature you have read and also on aspects of American history, arts and culture. You may also be questioned on visits you have made to America (or Canada) and your impressions. Current political issues might also be raised, so keep up-to-date with the political scene. See also **Chapter 6**. **Birmingham** Access course and mature students are interviewed and also those students with strong applications but whose achieved grades do not meet entrance requirements. **Derby** The purpose of the interview is to help applicants understand the interdisciplinary nature of the course. **East Anglia** Admissions tutors want to see how up-to-date is the applicant's knowledge of American culture. **Swansea** Our interviews are very informal, giving students the chance to ask questions about the course.

Reasons for rejection (non-academic) If personal reasons prevent year of study in America. **Birmingham** Lack of commitment to the course. **Swansea** Lack of knowledge covering literature, history and politics.

AFTER-RESULTS ADVICE

Offers to applicants repeating A-levels **Higher** Essex, Warwick, Winchester; **Possibly higher** Nottingham; **Same** Birmingham, Derby, Dundee, East Anglia, Hull, Swansea.

GRADUATE DESTINATIONS AND EMPLOYMENT (2007/8 HESA)

Graduates surveyed 555 **Employed** 270 **In further study** 85 **Assumed unemployed** 55

Career note All non-scientific careers are open to graduates. Start your career planning during your degree course and obtain work experience.

OTHER DEGREE SUBJECTS FOR CONSIDERATION

Business Studies; Cultural Studies; English Literature; Film Studies; Government; History; International History; International Relations; Latin-American Literature/Studies; Politics.

ANATOMICAL SCIENCE/ANATOMY

(see also **Biological Sciences, Physiology**)

Anatomy is the study of the structures of living creatures, from the sub-cellular level to the whole individual, and relates structure to function in the adult and during embryonic development.

Useful websites www.scienceyear.com; www.innerbody.com; www.instantanatomy.net

NB The points totals shown to the left of the institutions are for ease of reference only. It must not be assumed that Tariff points are always used by institutions or that they can be substituted for an offer in grades. The level of an offer is not necessarily indicative of the quality of a course.

COURSE OFFERS INFORMATION

Subject requirements/preferences GCSE Mathematics usually required. **AL** One or two mathematics/science subjects usually required; biology and chemistry preferred.

NB In 2012 universities and colleges will differ in their use of GCE AL/AS unit grade information, A* grades, the Extended Project (EPQ), the Advanced Diploma and the Cambridge Pre-U examination when considering applicants and making offers. An EPQ may be accepted in place of an AS subject. Check websites of universities and colleges for the latest offers information.

Your target offers and examples of courses provided by each institution

360 pts **London (UCL)** – AAAe–AABe (Anat Dev Biol) (IB 36–38 pts)

340 pts **Cardiff** – AAB–ABB (Biomed Sci (Anat)) (IB 34 pts)

London (King's) – AAB+AS (Anat Hum Sci) (IB 34 pts)

Manchester – AAB–BBB (Anat Sci Ind/Prof Exp/Modn Lang) (IB 35 pts)

320 pts **Bristol** – ABB (Anat Sci Vet Anat) (IB 33 pts HL 665)

Dundee – ABB 2nd yr entry (Anat Physiol Sci) (IB 34 pts HL 665)

Glasgow – ABB (Anat) (IB 32 pts)

Liverpool – ABB–AAB (Anat Hum Biol) (IB 32 pts)

260 pts **Dundee** – BCC 1st yr entry (Anat Sci) (IB 30 pts)

Alternative offers

See **Chapter 7** and **Appendix 1** for grades/UCAS Tariff points information for the International Baccalaureate, Scottish Highers/Advanced Highers, the Welsh Baccalaureate, the Irish Leaving Certificate, the Cambridge Pre-U Diploma, the Advanced Diploma and the Extended Project.

CHOOSING YOUR COURSE (SEE ALSO CH. 1)

Some course features

Bristol (Anat Sci; Hum Muscskel Sci) Focus on mammalian anatomy involving dissection. (Anat Sci Vet Anat) Focus on anatomy and physiology of domestic mammals (eg dogs, horses). All courses can lead to further study in, for example, medicine, veterinary medicine.

Cardiff A common Biosciences first year programme (with the chance to change degrees) with following years centred on human anatomy, with dissection.

Dundee Emphasis on human anatomy.

Glasgow Students may be eligible for one-year research placement, registering for an MSci degree in Anatomy.

Liverpool Practical degree involving dissection and module choices from Biomedical and Biological Sciences and Psychology.

Manchester Anatomy part of Life Sciences programme, with common first year and options to change between degree courses.

Universities and colleges teaching quality See www.qaa.ac.uk; http://unistats.direct.gov.uk.

Top research universities and colleges (RAE 2008) See **Biological Sciences**.

Examples of sandwich degree courses Bristol; Cardiff; Glasgow; Manchester.

ADMISSIONS INFORMATION

Number of applicants per place (approx) Bristol 10; Cardiff 8; Dundee 6; Liverpool 7.

Advice to applicants and planning the UCAS personal statement Give reasons for your interest in this subject (usually stemming from school work in biology). Discuss any articles in medical and other scientific journals which have attracted your attention and any new developments in medicine related to anatomical science.

Selection interviews **Yes** Liverpool (Offer subject to interview); **Some** Cardiff, Dundee; **No** Bristol.

Interview advice and questions Questions are likely on your particular interests in biology and anatomy, why you wish to study the subject and your future career intentions. See also **Chapter 6**.

Reasons for rejection (non-academic) **Liverpool** Unfocused applications with no evidence of basic knowledge of the course.

AFTER-RESULTS ADVICE

Offers to applicants repeating A-levels **Higher** Bristol, Dundee; **Possibly higher** Liverpool; **Same** Cardiff.

GRADUATE DESTINATIONS AND EMPLOYMENT (2007/8 HESA)

Including Pathology and Physiology

Graduates surveyed 2735 **Employed** 1445 **In further study** 495 **Assumed unemployed** 195

Career note The subject leads to a range of careers in various laboratories, in government establishments, the NHS, pharmaceutical and food industries. It can also lead to postgraduate studies in physiotherapy, nursing, osteopathy and, in exceptional cases, in medicine, dentistry and veterinary science.

OTHER DEGREE SUBJECTS FOR CONSIDERATION

Biological Sciences; Biology; Genetics; Microbiology; Neuroscience; Osteopathy; Physiology; Physiotherapy.

ANIMAL SCIENCES

(including **Equine Science/Studies** and **Wildlife Conservation**; see also **Agricultural Sciences/ Agriculture, Biological Sciences, Biology, Physiology, Psychology, Veterinary Science/Medicine, Zoology**)

Animal Sciences is a broad-based subject involving both farm and companion animals. The range of specialisms is reflected in the table of courses below and can focus on animal nutrition and health, animal biology, behaviour, ecology and welfare. In addition, many courses specialise in equine

science, studies and management. **NB** It is important to note that Bioveterinary Science graduates are not qualified to practise as vets (see **Veterinary Sciences/Medicine**).

Useful websites www.rspca.org.uk; www.iah.bbsrc.ac.uk; www.bhs.org.uk; www.wwf.org.uk; www.bsas.org.uk.

NB The points totals shown to the left of the institutions are for ease of reference only. It must not be assumed that Tariff points are always used by institutions or that they can be substituted for an offer in grades. The level of an offer is not necessarily indicative of the quality of a course.

COURSE OFFERS INFORMATION

Subject requirements/preferences GCSE Mathematics/science subjects required. Also check any weight limits on equitation modules. **AL** One or two science subjects required for scientific courses, biology and chemistry preferred.

NB In 2012 universities and colleges will differ in their use of GCE AL/AS unit grade information, A* grades, the Extended Project (EPQ), the Advanced Diploma and the Cambridge Pre-U examination when considering applicants and making offers. An EPQ may be accepted in place of an AS subject. Check websites of universities and colleges for the latest offers information.

Your target offers and examples of courses provided by each institution
380 pts **Cambridge** – A*AA college offers may vary (Nat Sci) (IB 38–42 pts HL 766-777)
340 pts **Sheffield** – AAB (Anim Bhv MBiolSci) (IB 35 pts)
320 pts **Bristol** – ABB (Anat Sci Vet Anat) (IB 34 pts HL 665)
　　　　　Exeter – ABB-BBB (Anim Bhv) (IB 34–30 pts)
　　　　　Kent – 320 pts (Wldlf Cons) (IB 33 pts)
　　　　　Sheffield – ABB (Anim Bhv BSc) (IB 33 pts.)

300 pts **Aberdeen** – BBB 300 pts 2nd yr entry (Anim Ecol; Wldlf Mgt)

Glasgow – BBB (inc chem+biol+maths/phys) (Vet Biosci) (IB 32 pts)

Harper Adams (UC) – BBB (Anim Sci; Biovet Sci)

London (RVC) – See **Advice to applicants and planning the UCAS personal statement** below BBB (Biovet Sci BSc) (HL 555)

Newcastle – BBB–BBC (Anim Sci (Cmpn Anim St) (Lvstk Tech)) (IB 30–32 pts)

Reading – 300 pts (Anim Sci) (IB 30 pts HL 655)

280 pts **Aberystwyth** – (Anim Sci) (IB 28 pts)

Bristol – BBC (inc BB biol+chem) (Vet Nurs Biovet Sci) (IB 30 pts)

Bristol UWE – 280 pts (Eqn Dntl Sci)

Gloucestershire – 280 pts (Anim Biol)

Lincoln – (inc biol) 280 pts (Biovet Sci)

Nottingham – BBB–BBC (Anim Sci) (IB 30 pts)

Plymouth – 280–320 pts (Anim Bhv Welf)

260 pts **Lincoln** – 260 pts (Eqn Sci) (IB 30 pts)

Liverpool John Moores – 260–300 pts (Anim Bhv; Wldlf Cons)

Staffordshire – 260 pts (Anim Biol Cons)

240 pts **Aberdeen** – CCC 1st yr entry (Anim Ecol; Wldlf Mgt)

Aberystwyth – 240 pts (Eqn Hum Spo Sci) (IB 28 pts)

Anglia Ruskin – 240 pts (Anim Bhv Psy)

Bristol UWE – 240–280 pts (inc biol) (Biovet Sci) (IB 24 pts)

Canterbury Christ Church – 240 pts (Anim Sci)

Chester – 240–200 pts (Anim Bhv courses)

Cumbria – 240 pts (Anim Cons Sci) (IB 24 pts)

Glamorgan – 240–280 pts (Int Wldlf Biol)

Hadlow (Coll) – 240 pts (Anim Cons Biodiv; App Bhv Sci Welf; Anim Mgt; Eqn Mgt)

Harper Adams (UC) – 240 pts (Anim Hlth Welf)

Royal (CAg) – 240 pts (Agric (Anim Mgt); Eqn Mgt)

Worcester – 240–280 pts (Anim Biol)

220 pts **Aberystwyth** – (Agric Anim Sci) (IB 24 pts)

Bristol UWE – 220–240 pts (Anim Bhv Welf)

Lincoln – 220–240 pts (Anim Bhv Sci) (IB 30 pts)

Myerscough (Coll) – 220 pts (Anim Bhv Welf; Eqn Sci Mgt Bhv Welf; Eqn Sci Mgt Phys)

Northampton – 220–260 pts (Eqn St)

Warwickshire (Coll) – 220 pts (Eqn Sci; Eqn St; Spo Sci (Eqn Hum))

200 pts **Bristol UWE** – 200–240 pts (Eqn Sci) (IB 24 pts)

Northampton – 200-240 pts (App Anim St)

Reaseheath (Coll) – 200–240 pts (Anim Mgt)

Salford – 200 pts (Wldlf Prac Cons)

Wolverhampton – 200–260 pts (Anim Bhv Wldlf Cons; Anim Mgt; Eqn Spo Sci)

Writtle (Coll) – 200–360 pts (Eqn Spo Thera)

180 pts **Salford** – 180–200 pts (Wldlf Cons Zoo Biol)

Writtle (Coll) – 180 pts (Eqn St)

160 pts **Greenwich** – 160 pts (Anim Cons Biodiv) (IB 24 pts)

SAC (Scottish CAg) – CC (App Anim Sci)

140 pts **Bishop Burton (Coll)** – 140 pts (Eqn Sci; App Anim Sci)

120 pts **Sparsholt (Coll)** – DD 120 pts (Anim Mgt; Cons Wldlf Mgt)

Alternative offers

See **Chapter 7** and **Appendix 1** for grades/UCAS Tariff points information for the International Baccalaureate, Scottish Highers/Advanced Highers, the Welsh Baccalaureate, the Irish Leaving Certificate, the Cambridge Pre-U Diploma, the Advanced Diploma and the Extended Project.

EXAMPLES OF FOUNDATION DEGREES IN THE SUBJECT FIELD

Aberystwyth; Abingdon and Witney (Coll); Askham Bryan (Coll); Berkshire (CAg); Bicton (Coll); Bishop Burton (Coll); Bournemouth; Bridgwater (Coll); Brighton; Brooksby Melton (Coll); Bucks New; CAFRE;

Chester; Cornwall (Coll); Craven (Coll); Derby; Duchy (Coll); East Anglia; Easton (Coll); Greenwich; Guildford (Coll); Hadlow (Coll); Harper Adams (UC); Kingston Maurward (Coll); Leeds City (Coll); Lincoln; Moulton (Coll); Myerscough (Coll); Northampton; Nottingham Trent; Otley (Coll); Plymouth; Reaseheath (Coll); Shuttleworth (Coll); Solihull (Coll); Sparsholt (Coll); Warwickshire (Coll); Weston (Coll); Wiltshire (Coll); Worcester; Writtle (Coll).

CHOOSING YOUR COURSE (SEE ALSO CH. 1)

Some course features

Aberdeen Field courses in land use and zoology compulsory. Opportunities for expeditions, volunteering work overseas and year-out placements. All students carry out work experience.

Bristol UWE (Anim Sci) A science-based programme focusing on anatomy, physiology, health, nutrition and welfare, and including, eg animal management, equine husbandry, animal psychology with work experience.

Newcastle Range of Animal Science courses with a common first year followed by specialisation in, eg Companion Animal Studies or Livestock Technology.

Nottingham Trent First animal degree in UK specialising in exotic animals.

Oxford Brookes (Eqn Sci) Practical and vocational course with range of opportunities in second year to study in Europe or the US or Canada or Australia.

Writtle (Coll) (Anim Sci) Common first year with Animal Management degree focusing on development of practical husbandry in each of the three major animal groups (farm animals, horses and companion animals). Business skills also important.

Universities and colleges teaching quality See www.qaa.ac.uk; http://unistats.direct.gov.uk.

Top research universities and colleges (RAE 2008) See **Agricultural Sciences/Agriculture** and **Biological Sciences**.

Examples of sandwich degree courses Aberystwyth; Edinburgh Napier; Harper Adams (UC); Nottingham Trent; Royal (CAg); Warwickshire (Coll).

ADMISSIONS INFORMATION

Number of applicants per place (approx) Aberystwyth 6; Bristol 8; Harper Adams (UC) 5; Leeds 6; Newcastle (all courses) 9; Nottingham 6; Nottingham Trent (Eqn Spo Sci) 4; Reading 10; Royal (CAg) 4.

Advice to applicants and planning the UCAS personal statement Describe any work you have done with animals which generated your interest in this subject. Work experience in veterinary practices, on farms or with agricultural firms would be useful. Read agricultural/scientific journals for updates on animal nutrition or breeding. For Equine courses, details of practical experience with horses (eg BHS examinations, Pony Club tests) should be included. **London (RVC)** BMAT is not required for entry but applicants wanting to be considered for the Merit Scholarships will have to take BMAT.

Misconceptions about this course Students are not always aware that horse studies courses cover science, business management, nutrition, health and breeding. **Bishop Burton (Coll)** (Eqn Sci) Some students wrongly believe that riding skills and a science background are not required for this course which, in fact, is heavily focused on the scientific principles and practice of horse management.

Selection interviews Yes Bristol, Cumbria (usually), Lincoln, Newcastle, Nottingham (depends on application), Plymouth, Royal (CAg), SAC (Scottish CAg), Writtle (Coll); **Some** Anglia Ruskin, Bishop Burton (Coll), Bristol UWE, Harper Adams (UC), Stirling.

Interview advice and questions Questions are likely about your experience with animals and your reasons for wishing to follow this science-based subject. Other questions asked in recent years have included: What do your parents think about your choice of course? What are your views on battery hens and the rearing of veal calves? The causes of blue-tongue disease, foot and mouth disease and BSE may also feature. **Equine courses** students should check the level of riding ability expected (eg BHS Level 2 or PC B-test level). Check the amount of riding, jumping and competition work on the course. (see also **Chapter 6**) **Lincoln** (Eqn Spo Sci) Applicants required to show that they can ride to BHS Level 2. Experience with animals in general.

Reasons for rejection (non-academic) Uncertainty as to why applicants chose the course. Too immature. Unlikely to integrate well.

AFTER-RESULTS ADVICE
Offers to applicants repeating A-levels Possibly higher Nottingham; **Same** Anglia Ruskin, Bishop Burton (Coll), Bristol UWE, Chester, Harper Adams (UC), Liverpool John Moores, Royal (CAg), Stirling.

GRADUATE DESTINATIONS AND EMPLOYMENT (2007/8 HESA)
Graduates surveyed 450 **Employed** 185 **In further study** 80 **Assumed unemployed** 50

Career note The majority of graduates obtained work with animals whilst others moved towards business and administration careers. This is a specialised subject area and undergraduates should start early to make contacts with organisations and gain work experience.

OTHER DEGREE SUBJECTS FOR CONSIDERATION
Agriculture; Biological Sciences; Biology; Food Science; Natural Sciences; Veterinary Science; Zoology.

ANTHROPOLOGY
(including Social Anthropology; see also Archaeology, Sociology)

Anthropology is the study of people's behaviour, beliefs and institutions and the diverse societies in which they live, and is concerned with the biological evolution of human beings. It also involves our relationships with other primates, the structure of communities and the effects of diet and disease on human groups. Alternatively, social or cultural anthropology covers aspects of social behaviour in respect of family, kinship, marriage, gender, religion, political structures, law, psychology and language.

Useful websites www.britishmuseum.org; www.therai.org.uk.

NB The points totals shown to the left of the institutions are for ease of reference only. It must not be assumed that Tariff points are always used by institutions or that they can be substituted for an offer in grades. The level of an offer is not necessarily indicative of the quality of a course.

COURSE OFFERS INFORMATION
Subject requirements/preferences GCSE English and mathematics usually required. A foreign language may be required. **AL** Biology and geography preferred for some biological anthropological courses. (Social Anthropology) No specific subjects required except London LSE; see prospectus and website.

NB In 2012 universities and colleges will differ in their use of GCE AL/AS unit grade information, A* grades, the Extended Project (EPQ), the Advanced Diploma and the Cambridge Pre-U examination when considering applicants and making offers. An EPQ may be accepted in place of an AS subject. Check websites of universities and colleges for the latest offers information.

Your target offers and examples of courses provided by each institution
380 pts Cambridge – A*AA college offers may vary (Arch Anth) (IB 38–42 pts)
360 pts Durham – AAA (Nat Sci (Anth)) (IB 37 pts)
       London (UCL) – AABe (Arch Anth) (IB 38 pts)
       Oxford – AAA (Arch Anth) (IB 38–42 pts)
350 pts Brunel – Contact admissions office (Psy Anth)
340 pts Bristol – AAB–BBB (Arch Anth Sci MSci) (IB 35–32 pts HL 666–665)
       Durham – AAB 340 pts (Anthropology) (IB 34 pts HL 17–19 pts)
       East Anglia – AAB-BBB (Arch Anth Art Hist) (IB 31-33 pts)
       Kent – AAB 340 pts (Anth Jap) (IB 33 pts HL 16 pts)
       London (SOAS) – AAA (Soc Anth) (IB 38 pts HL 666)

St Andrews – AAB–AAA (Soc Anth courses) (IB 32 pts)
Sussex – AAB–BBB (Anth courses) (IB 32–36 pts)
320 pts **Dundee** – ABB 2nd year entry (Foren Anth) (IB 34 pts)
Durham – ABB (Anth and Sociol) (IB 34 pts HL 17–19 pts)
Exeter – AAB–BBB (Arch Anth/For Sci) (IB 32–39 pts)
Kent – 320–300 pts (Arch Anth) (IB 31 pts)
London (Gold) – ABB (Hist Anth) (IB 32 pts HL 766)
London LSE – ABB (Soc Anth) (IB 37 pts HL 666)
Manchester – ABB (Arch Anth) (IB 33 pts)
Southampton – ABB–BBBb (App Soc Sci (Anth)) (IB 32 pts)
300 pts **Birmingham** – BBB–BBC (Anth joint courses) (IB 30–32 pts)
Bristol – BBB–BCC (Arch Anth Sci BSc) (IB 32–29 pts)
Brunel – BCC +AS/EPQ c 300 pts (Anth courses except under **350 pts**) (IB 32 pts)
Durham – BBB (Biol Anth)
Edinburgh – BBB (Soc Anth courses) (IB 35 pts HL 555)
Kent – 300 pts (Soc Anth) (IB 33 pts)
Liverpool – BBB (Evol Anth) (IB 30 pts)
London (Gold) – BBB (Anth Sociol) (IB 32 pts)
Queen's Belfast – BBB–BBCb (Soc Anth courses)
280 pts **Oxford Brookes** – BBB–BBcc (Anth courses) (IB 31 pts)
Roehampton – 280–340 pts (Anth; Biol Anth courses)
260 pts **Dundee** – BCC 1st year entry (Foren Anth) (IB 32 pts)
Hull – 260–300 pts (Sociol Anth courses)
Liverpool John Moores – 260–300 pts (Foren Anth) (IB 24 pts)
240 pts **Aberdeen** – CCC (Anth courses) (IB 30 pts)
200 pts **East London** – 200 pts (Anth Comb courses) (IB 24 pts)
London Met – 200 pts (Soc Anth) (IB 24 pts)
180 pts **Trinity Saint David** – 180–240 pts (Anth)

Alternative offers
See **Chapter 7** and **Appendix 1** for grades/UCAS Tariff points information for the International Baccalaureate, Scottish Highers/Advanced Highers, the Welsh Baccalaureate, the Irish Leaving Certificate, the Cambridge Pre-U Diploma, the Advanced Diploma and the Extended Project.

CHOOSING YOUR COURSE (SEE ALSO CH. 1)

Some course features
Birmingham A broad course taught in the Centre of West African Studies.
Durham A wide choice of social and biological anthropology courses including Joint and Combined Honours and a route via Natural Sciences.
East London (Anth Ntv Am St) The degree includes one year in the University of New Mexico.
Kent The course covers both biological and social aspects of anthropology.
Liverpool (Evol Anth) Unique course focusing on human evolution, evolutionary psychology and hominid palaeontology.
Sussex Opportunities for overseas placements.

Universities and colleges teaching quality See www.qaa.ac.uk; http://unistats.direct.gov.uk.

Top research universities and colleges (RAE 2008) Cambridge; London (SOAS); London LSE; Roehampton; London (UCL); Sussex; Queen's Belfast; Aberdeen; London (Gold); Oxford; Edinburgh; St Andrews; Manchester.

Examples of sandwich degree courses Brunel; Liverpool John Moores; Oxford Brookes.

ADMISSIONS INFORMATION

Number of applicants per place (approx) Cambridge 2; Durham 14; Hull 11; Kent 6; Liverpool John Moores 4; London (Gold) 7; London (SOAS) 10; London (UCL) 3; London LSE 9; Manchester 5; Oxford Brookes 8; Queen's Belfast 10; Southampton 6; Sussex 10.

Advice to applicants and planning the UCAS personal statement Visits to museums should be discussed, for example, museums of anthropology (London, Oxford, Cambridge). Describe any aspect of the subject which interests you (including books you have read) and how you have pursued this interest. Give details of any overseas travel. Give reasons for choosing course: since this is not a school subject, you will need to convince the selectors of your knowledge and interest. **Oxford** See **Archaeology**.

Selection interviews Yes Cambridge, Dundee (Foren Anth), East Anglia, Hull, London (Gold) (mature students), London (UCL) (mature students), Oxford (88% (Successsful applicants 29%)), Oxford Brookes; **Some** London LSE, Roehampton; **No** Bristol.

Interview advice and questions This is a broad subject and questions will tend to emerge as a result of your interests in aspects of anthropology or social anthropology and your comments on your personal statement. Past questions have included: What stresses are there among the nomads of the North African desert? What is a society? What is speech? If you dug up a stone axe what could you learn from it? What are the values created by a capitalist society? Discuss the role of women since the beginning of this century. **Cambridge** See **Chapter 6** and Archaeology. **Oxford** See **Chapter 6** and **Archaeology**.

Reasons for rejection (non-academic) Lack of commitment. Inability to deal with a more philosophical (less positivist) approach to knowledge.

AFTER-RESULTS ADVICE
Offers to applicants repeating A-levels Possibly higher Oxford Brookes; **Same** Cambridge, Durham, East Anglia, Liverpool John Moores, London (UCL), Roehampton.

GRADUATE DESTINATIONS AND EMPLOYMENT (2007/8 HESA)
Graduates surveyed 515 **Employed** 185 **In further study** 120 **Assumed unemployed** 55

Career note All non-scientific careers are open to graduates. However, career planning should start early and efforts made to contact employers and gain work experience.

OTHER DEGREE SUBJECTS FOR CONSIDERATION
Archaeology; Egyptology; Heritage Studies; History; Human Sciences; Political Science; Psychology; Religious Studies; Social Science; Sociology.

ARABIC AND ANCIENT NEAR AND MIDDLE EASTERN STUDIES

Arabic is one of the world's most widely used languages, spoken by more than 300 million people in 21 countries in the Middle East and countries right across north Africa. Links between Britain and Arabic-speaking countries have increased considerably in recent years and most of the larger UK organisations with offices in the Middle East have only a relatively small pool of Arabic-speaking graduates from which to recruit future employees each year. Islamic Studies focuses on a faith which has much in common with Christianity and Judaism, is the second largest religion in the world, extending from Africa to the East Indies, and is focused on the Middle East.

Useful websites www.cilt.org.uk; www.iol.org.uk; www.bbc.co.uk/languages; www.language advantage.com; www.languagematters.co.uk; www.reed.co.uk/multilingual; www.metimes.com; www.merip.org; www.memri.org; www.mei.edu.

NB The points totals shown to the left of the institutions are for ease of reference only. It must not be assumed that Tariff points are always used by institutions or that they can be substituted for an offer in grades. The level of an offer is not necessarily indicative of the quality of a course.

COURSE OFFERS INFORMATION

Subject requirements/preferences GCSE English, mathematics and a foreign language usually required. A high grade in Arabic may be required. **AL** A modern language is usually required or preferred.

NB In 2012 universities and colleges will differ in their use of GCE AL/AS unit grade information, A* grades, the Extended Project (EPQ), the Advanced Diploma and the Cambridge Pre-U examination when considering applicants and making offers. An EPQ may be accepted in place of an AS subject. Check websites of universities and colleges for the latest offers information.

Your target offers and examples of courses provided by each institution
380 pts **Cambridge** – A*AA college offers may vary (As Mid E St (Arbc)) (IB 38–42 pts)
360 pts **Durham** – AAA (Comb Arts (Arbc)) (IB 38 pts)
        Edinburgh – check with admissions tutor AAA (Arbc courses) (IB 34 pts)
        Oxford – AAA (Turk courses) (IB 38–40 pts)
        St Andrews – AAA (Arbc Int Rel) (IB 38 pts)
340 pts **Durham** – AAB (Modn Langs (Arbc))
        London (King's) – ABBe (Turk Modn Gk St) (IB 36 pts)
        St Andrews – AAB (Arbc Mid E St) (IB 32 pts)
320 pts **Exeter** – ABB–BBB (Arbc Persn) (IB 32–29 pts)
        Leeds – ABB–BBB (Arbc courses)
        Liverpool – ABB (Egyptology) (IB 34 pts)
        London (SOAS) – ABB (Heb Isrl St) (IB 34 pts HL 555)
        Manchester – ABB–BBC (Jew St Heb St) (IB 32–30 pts)
        Swansea – ABB–BBB (Egypt)
300 pts **Edinburgh** – BBB (Mid E St) (IB 34 pts)
        Leeds – BBB (Mid E St) (IB 32 pts HL 15 pts)
280 pts **Salford** – 280 pts (Arbc Engl Transl Interp (for native Arabic speakers: contact admissions
        tutor))

        London (Birk) – Check with admissions tutor (Arabic courses)

Alternative offers
See **Chapter 7** and **Appendix 1** for grades/UCAS Tariff points information for the International Baccalaureate, Scottish Highers/Advanced Highers, the Welsh Baccalaureate, the Irish Leaving Certificate, the Cambridge Pre-U Diploma, the Advanced Diploma and the Extended Project.

CHOOSING YOUR COURSE (SEE ALSO CH. 1)

Some course features
Edinburgh (Arbc) Students usually spend part of their third year in Cairo.
Exeter Single and Combined Honours Arabic courses provide a strong language base combined with study of the culture, literature and history. All four-year Arabic students spend their second year in, eg Morocco, Egypt, Damascus or Jordan.
Leeds (Mid E St) Course focuses on the culture, politics and economy of the region. No knowledge is needed; an Arabic option is available.
Liverpool (Egypt) Course covers the language, archaeology and history of Ancient Egypt, together with a study of Egyptian art, religion and society.
Salford The only Arabic/English translation and interpreting course.

Universities and colleges teaching quality See www.qaa.ac.uk; http://unistats.direct.gov.uk.

Top research universities and colleges (RAE 2008) (Middle Eastern and African Studies) Cambridge; Oxford; Edinburgh; London (SOAS); Durham.

ADMISSIONS INFORMATION

Number of applicants per place (approx) Cambridge 3; Leeds 6; London (SOAS) 5; Salford 5.

Advice to applicants and planning the UCAS personal statement Describe any visits to, or your experience of living in, Arabic-speaking countries. Develop a knowledge of Middle Eastern cultures, history and politics and mention these topics on the UCAS application. Provide evidence of language-learning skills and experience. **Salford** Students whose first language is Arabic are normally expected to have passed their secondary school leaving certificate and to demonstrate an acceptable command of English. English-speaking and European applicants should also be able to speak Arabic.

Selection interviews Yes Cambridge, Exeter, Leeds, Oxford; **Some** Salford.

Interview advice and questions You will need to be able to justify your reasons for wanting to study Arabic or other languages and to discuss your interest in, and awareness of, cultural, social and political aspects of the Middle East. **Cambridge** See **Chapter 6** under **Modern and Medieval Languages**. **Oxford** See **Chapter 6** under **Modern and Medieval Languages**. **Salford** (Arbc Engl Transl Interp) Applicants may be required to sit Arabic language tests. See also **Chapter 6**.

AFTER-RESULTS ADVICE
Offers to applicants repeating A-levels Higher Leeds, St Andrews; **Same** Exeter, Salford.

GRADUATE DESTINATIONS AND EMPLOYMENT (2007/8 HESA)
Graduates surveyed 75 **Employed** 30 **In further study** 15 **Assumed unemployed** 10

Career note Most graduates entered business and administrative work, in some cases closely linked to their language studies.

OTHER DEGREE SUBJECTS FOR CONSIDERATION
Anthropology; Archaeology; Classical Studies; Hebrew; History; Persian; Politics; Turkish.

ARCHAEOLOGY

(see also Anthropology, Classical Studies/Classical Civilisation, History (Ancient))

Courses in Archaeology differ between institutions but the majority focus on the archaeology of Europe, the Mediterranean and Middle Eastern countries and on the close examination of discoveries of pre-historic communities and ancient, medieval and post-medieval societies. Hands-on experience is involved in all courses as well as a close study of the history of the artefacts themselves and, in some courses, an appreciation of the application of science.

Useful websites www.britarch.ac.uk; www.english-heritage.org.uk; www.prehistoric.org.uk; www.britishmuseum.org; www.archaeologists.net.

NB The points totals shown to the left of the institutions are for ease of reference only. It must not be assumed that Tariff points are always used by institutions or that they can be substituted for an offer in grades. The level of an offer is not necessarily indicative of the quality of a course.

COURSE OFFERS INFORMATION
Subject requirements/preferences GCSE English and mathematics or science usually required for BSc courses. **AL** History, geography, English or a science subject may be preferred for some courses and two science subjects for Archaeological Science courses.

NB In 2012 universities and colleges will differ in their use of GCE AL/AS unit grade information, A* grades, the Extended Project (EPQ), the Advanced Diploma and the Cambridge Pre-U examination when considering applicants and making offers. An EPQ may be accepted in place of an AS subject. Check websites of universities and colleges for the latest offers information.

Your target offers and examples of courses provided by each institution
380 pts Cambridge – A*AA college offers may vary (Arch Anth) (IB 38–42 pts)
360 pts Durham – AAA (Comb Soc Sci (Arch)) (IB 38 pts)

London (UCL) – AABe (Arch Anth) (IB 38 pts)
Oxford – AAA (Arch Anth) (IB 38–42 pts)
Warwick – ABBc–BBBc (Anc Hist Class Arch) (IB 32–36 pts)
340 pts **Bristol** – AAB–BBB (Palae Evol) (IB 36 pts HL 665–666)
Durham – AAB–ABB (Anc Hist Arch) (IB 32 pts)
East Anglia – AAB–ABB (Hist Land Arch) (IB 32–34 pts)
London (UCL) – AAB+AS – ABB+AS (Arch courses) (IB 34 pts)
Newcastle – AAB–BBC (Anc Hist Arch) (IB 30–35 pts)
St Andrews – AAB (Anc Hist Arch) (IB 36 pts)
320 pts **Birmingham** – ABB (Arch Anc Hist) (IB 30–32 pts)
Cardiff – ABB–BBB (Arch courses)
Exeter – ABB–BBB (Arch courses) (IB 32–29 pts)
Glasgow – ABB–BBB (Arch courses) (IB 32–30 pts)
Kent – 320–300 pts (Arch Anth) (IB 31 pts)
Leicester – ABB (Geog Arch) (IB 32 pts)
Liverpool – ABB (Egyptology) (IB 34 pts)
London (King's) – ABB+AS (Class Arch) (IB 36 pts)
Manchester – ABB–BBB (Anc Hist Arch) (IB 33–32 pts)
Nottingham – ABB–BBC (Arch Hist)
Sheffield – ABB (Arch courses) (IB 33 pts)
Swansea – ABB–BBB (Egypt)
York – ABB (Hist Arch) (IB 32 pts)
300 pts **Birmingham** – ABB–BBB (Arch) (IB 30–32 pts)
Bournemouth – 300 pts (Arch Anth Foren Sci)
Bristol – BBB–BCC (Arch Anth Sci BSc) (IB 32–29 pts)
Edinburgh – check with Admissions Tutor BBB (Scot Ethnol Arch) (IB 34 pts HL 555)
Hull – 300 pts (Hist Arch)
Kent – 300–340 pts (Class Arch St courses) (IB 33 pts)
Leicester – BBB (Hist Arch) (IB 34 pts)
Liverpool – BBB (Egypt Arch) (IB 30 pts)
Queen's Belfast – BBB–BCCb (Arch Ir Celt) (IB 29 pts)
Reading – 300–360 pts (Arch courses) (IB 30 pts)
Southampton – AAB–BBB (Arch Hist) (IB 34 pts)
280 pts **Bristol** – BBC–BBB 280 pts (Arch) (IB 32–39 pts)
Leicester – BBC–BCC (Arch Comb courses)
London (SOAS) – BBC (Hist Art Arch courses) (IB 30 pts)
260 pts **Bradford** – 260–280 pts (Foren Arch Sci) (IB 28 pts)
Hull – 260–320 pts (Arch Mediev Hist)
240 pts **Aberdeen** – CCC 240 pts (Scot Arch) (IB 28 pts)
Bangor – 240–280 pts (Welsh Hist Arch) (IB 28 pts)
Central Lancashire – 240–220 pts (Arch courses) (IB 26 pts)
Chester – 240–280 pts (Arch courses) (IB 24 pts)
Portsmouth – 240–300 pts (Pal Evol)
Worcester – 240–280 pts (Arch Herit St courses)
220 pts **Winchester** – 220–260 pts (Arch courses) (IB 24 pts)
200 pts **Trinity Saint David** – 200–260 pts (Arch (Prac) (Wrld Cult)) (IB 26 pts)
120 pts **Peterborough (Reg Coll)** – 120 pts (Arch Land Hist)
80 pts **London (Birk)** – for under 21s (over 21s varies) p/t (Archaeology)

Alternative offers

See **Chapter 7** and **Appendix 1** for grades/UCAS Tariff points information for the International Baccalaureate, Scottish Highers/Advanced Highers, the Welsh Baccalaureate, the Irish Leaving Certificate, the Cambridge Pre-U Diploma, the Advanced Diploma and the Extended Project.

EXAMPLES OF FOUNDATION DEGREES IN THE SUBJECT FIELD
Bournemouth; Cornwall (Coll).

CHOOSING YOUR COURSE (SEE ALSO CH. 1)
Some course features
Bangor (Herit Arch Hist) Focus on historical and archaeological evidence and its use in the heritage industry.
Bournemouth (Fld Arch) Focuses on a practical training for a career in archaeology.
Glasgow (Arch) A study of Scottish archaeology and field projects in Britain, Europe and the Mediterranean.
Leicester (Arch) Option to study another subject outside Archaeology in Year 1.
London (SOAS) Wide range of Archaeology courses, many with languages and History of Art.
York Archaeology courses provide wide range of options and opportunity to spend a term in another discipline, for example History, Biology.

Universities and colleges teaching quality See www.qaa.ac.uk; http://unistats.direct.gov.uk.

Top research universities and colleges (RAE 2008) Durham; Reading; Oxford; Cambridge; Liverpool; London (UCL); Leicester; Southampton; Sheffield; York; Queen's Belfast; Exeter; Nottingham.

Examples of sandwich degree courses Bradford.

ADMISSIONS INFORMATION
Number of applicants per place (approx) Birmingham 5; Bradford 4; Bristol 7; Cambridge 2; Cardiff 6; Durham 6; Leicester 6; Liverpool 12; London (UCL) 5; Manchester (Anc Hist Arch) 15, (Arch) 4; Newcastle 14; Nottingham 11; Sheffield 5; Southampton 6; Trinity Saint David 2; York 3.

Advice to applicants and planning the UCAS personal statement First-hand experience of digs and other field work should be described. The Council for British Archaeology (see **Appendix 4**) can provide information on where digs are taking place. Describe any interests in fossils and museum visits as well as details of visits to current archaeological sites. Your local university archaeological department or central library will also provide information on contacts in your local area (each county council employs an archaeological officer). Since this is not a school subject, the selectors will be looking for good reasons for your choice of subject. Gain practical field experience and discuss this in the personal statement. Show your serious commitment to archaeology through your out-of-school activities (fieldwork, museum experience) (see **Chapter 6**). (See also **Anthropology** and **Appendix 4**.) **Cambridge** Most colleges require a school/college essay.

Misconceptions about this course Bristol We are not an élitist course: 75% of applicants and students come from state schools and non-traditional backgrounds. **Liverpool** (Egypt) Some students would have been better advised looking at courses in Archaeology or Ancient History and Archaeology which offer major pathways in the study of Ancient Egypt.

Selection interviews Yes Bangor, Bournemouth, Bradford, Cambridge, Durham, East Anglia, Glasgow, Liverpool, London (UCL), Newcastle, Nottingham, Oxford (Arch) 30%, (Class Arch Anc Hist) 23%, Southampton, Swansea, Trinity Saint David; **Some** Birmingham, Bristol, Cardiff, York.

Interview advice and questions Questions will be asked about any experience you have had in visiting archaeological sites or taking part in digs. Past questions have included: How would you interpret archaeological evidence, for example a pile of flints, coins? What is stratification? How would you date archaeological remains? What recent archaeological discoveries have been made? How did you become interested in archaeology? With which archaeological sites in the UK are you familiar? See also **Chapter 6**. **Birmingham** Questions may cover recent archaeological events. **Cambridge** (see **Chapter 6**). **Oxford** (see **Chapter 6**). Interviews involve artefacts, maps and other material to be interpreted. Successful entrants average 30.7%. **York** What are your views on the archaeology programmes on TV? What would you do with a spare weekend?

Reasons for rejection (non-academic) (Mature students) Inability to cope with essay-writing and exams. **Bournemouth** Health and fitness important for excavations. **Liverpool** (Egypt) Applicant misguided on choice of course – Egyptology used to fill a gap on the UCAS application.

AFTER-RESULTS ADVICE
Offers to applicants repeating A-levels **Same** Birmingham, Bradford, Cambridge, Chester, Durham, East Anglia, Leicester, Liverpool, London (UCL), Sheffield, Trinity Saint David, Winchester.

GRADUATE DESTINATIONS AND EMPLOYMENT (2007/8 HESA)
Graduates surveyed 645 **Employed** 180 **In further study** 190 **Assumed unemployed** 95

Career note Vocational opportunities closely linked to this subject are limited. However, some graduates aim for positions in local authorities, libraries and museums. A number of organisations covering water boards, forestry, civil engineering and surveying also employ field archaeologists.

OTHER DEGREE SUBJECTS FOR CONSIDERATION
Ancient History; Anthropology; Classical Studies; Classics; Geology; Heritage Studies; History; History of Art and Architecture; Medieval History.

ARCHITECTURE
(including **Architectural Technology** and **Architectural Engineering**; see also **Art and Design (Product and Industrial Design), Building and Construction**)

Courses in Architecture provide a broad education consisting of technological subjects covering structures, construction, materials and environmental studies. Project-based design work is an integral part of all courses and in addition, history and social studies will also be incorporated into degree programmes. After completing the first three years leading to a BA (Hons), students aiming for full professional status take a further two-year course leading to eg, the BArch, MArch degrees or Diploma and after a year in an architect's practice, the final professional examinations are taken.

Useful websites www.ciat.org.uk; www.architecture.com; www.rias.org.uk; www.archrecord. construction.com.

NB The points totals shown to the left of the institutions are for ease of reference only. It must not be assumed that Tariff points are always used by institutions or that they can be substituted for an offer in grades. The level of an offer is not necessarily indicative of the quality of a course.

COURSE OFFERS INFORMATION
Subject requirements/preferences **GCSE** English and mathematics, in some cases at certain grades, are required in all cases. A science subject may also be required. **AL** Mathematics and/or physics required or preferred for some courses. Art and design may be preferable to design and technology. Art is sometimes a requirement and many schools of architecture prefer it; a portfolio of art work is often requested and, in some cases, a drawing test will be set.

NB In 2012 universities and colleges will differ in their use of GCE AL/AS unit grade information, A* grades, the Extended Project (EPQ), the Advanced Diploma and the Cambridge Pre-U examination when considering applicants and making offers. An EPQ may be accepted in place of an AS subject. Check websites of universities and colleges for the latest offers information.

Your target offers and examples of courses provided by each institution
380 pts **Cambridge** – A*AA college offers may vary (Architecture) (IB 38–42 pts)
360 pts **Bath** – A*AA (Archit) (IB 36–38 pts HL maths 6)
    Cardiff – AAA (Archit St) (IB 35 pts)
    Glasgow (SA) – AAA–ABB (Archit)
    Liverpool – AAA (Archit) (IB 35 pts)
    Manchester – AAA (Archit) (IB 36 pts)
    Manchester Met – AAA (Archit) (IB 36 pts)
    Newcastle – AAA (Archit St) (IB 37 pts HL art 6)
    Nottingham – AAA (Archit Env Des) (IB 36 pts)

Sheffield – AAA + portfolio (Archit Land) (IB 37 pts)
Southampton – AAA (Civ Eng Archit) (IB 36 pts)

340 pts **Bristol UWE** – 340 pts (Archit Env Eng)
City – AAA-AAB 340–360 pts (Civ Eng Archit MEng/BEng) (IB 32 pts)
Leeds – AAB (Archit Eng Int)
London (UCL) – ABBe (Archit) (IB 34 pts)
Oxford Brookes – portfolio + interview AAB (Int Archit) (IB 32–34 pts)
Strathclyde – ABB (Archit Eng MEng) (IB 36 pts HL maths phys 6)

320 pts **Birmingham City** – 320 pts (Archit) (IB 31 pts)
Brighton – ABB offers may vary (Archit) (IB 34pts)
Glasgow – ABB 320 pts (MEng Civ Eng Archit) (IB 32 pts)
Heriot-Watt – AAB 2nd yr entry (MEng/BEng/BSc Archit Eng) (IB 35 pts)
Kent – 320 pts (Inter Archit) (IB 33 pts HL 15 pts)
Kingston – 320 pts (Archit)
Lincoln – 320 pts (Archit)
Northumbria – ABB (Archit) (IB 27 pts)
Plymouth – 320 pts (Archit) (IB 30 pts)
Queen's Belfast – ABB (Archit) (IB 29 pts HL 655)
Strathclyde – ABB (Archit St) (IB 34 pts)
Westminster – ABB 320 pts (Archit (Urb Des)) (IB 28 pts)

300 pts **Archit Assoc Sch London** – BBB 300 pts (Archit)
Bristol UWE – 300–360 pts (Archit Plan) (IB 24–32 pts)
Central Lancashire – 300 pts (Archit) (IB 32 pts)
Coventry – 300 pts (Archit)
Dundee – 300 pts (Archit St) (IB 30 pts)
Edinburgh – BBB (Archit Hist courses) (IB 30 pts)
Edinburgh (CA) – BBB (Arch; Arch Crea Cult Env)
Glasgow – BBB 300 pts (BEng Civ Eng Archit)
Huddersfield – 300 pts (Archit Tech) (IB 28–26 pts)
Leeds Met – 300 pts (Archit)
Liverpool John Moores – 300 pts inc AL art **or** sci B (Archit)
Nottingham Trent – 300 pts (Architecture) (IB 28 pts)
Sheffield Hallam – 300 pts (Archit Env Des)
Strathclyde – BBB (Archit Eng BEng) (IB 32 pts HL maths phys 55)
Ulster – 300 pts (Architecture) (IB 25 pts)

285 pts **Cardiff (UWIC)** – 285 pts (Archit Des Tech)

280 pts **Brighton** – BBC offers may vary (Archit Tech) (IB 28 pts)
City – 280 pts (Civ Eng Archit BEng) (IB 38 pts)
De Montfort – 280 pts (Archit) (IB 30 pts)
Heriot-Watt – BBC 1st yr entry (Archit Eng MEng/BEng/BSc) (IB 29 pts)
London Met – 280 pts (Archit St) (IB 32 pts)
Salford – 280 pts (Archit Tech)
Sheffield Hallam – 280 pts (Archit Tech)

260 pts **Bristol UWE** – 260–280 pts (Archit Tech Des) (IB 24–28 pts)
Central Lancashire – 260 pts (Archit Tech) (IB 26 pts)
Creative Arts – 260 pts (Archit) (IB 28 pts)
Northumbria – 260 pts (Archit Tech) (IB 24 pts)
Nottingham Trent – 260 pts (Archit Tech) (IB 28 pts)
Plymouth – 260 pts (Archit Tech Env) (IB 26 pts)
Portsmouth – 260–320 pts (Archit) (IB 28 pts)
Ulster – 260 pts (Archit Tech Mgt) (IB 24 pts)

240 pts **Anglia Ruskin** – 240 pts (Archit) (IB 26 pts)
Bolton – 240 pts (Archit Tech) (IB 30 pts)
Edinburgh Napier – 240 pts (Archit Tech)

For a quick reference offers calculator, fold out the inside back cover.

Greenwich – 240 pts (Archit) (IB 24 pts)
Leeds Met – 240 pts (Archit Tech)
Liverpool John Moores – 240 pts (Archit Tech)
Plymouth – 240 pts (Archit Des Struct) (IB 28 pts)
Robert Gordon – CCC (Architecture) (IB 30 pts)
220 pts **Anglia Ruskin** – 220 pts (Archit Tech) (IB 26 pts)
Birmingham City – 220 pts (Archit Tech)
Coventry – 220 pts (Archit Des Tech)
East London – 220–260 pts (Archit)
London South Bank – 220 pts (Archit Tech) (IB 24 pts)
Northampton – 220–260 pts (Archit Tech) (IB 24 pts)
200 pts **Glyndŵr** – 200 pts (Archit Des Tech)
Wolverhampton – 200 pts (Archit Des Tech; Int Archit Prop Dev)
180 pts **Derby** – 180–240 pts (Archit Tech Prac) (IB 26 pts)
160 pts **London South Bank** – 160 pts (Archit Eng) (IB 24 pts)
120 pts **Southampton Solent** – 120 pts (Archit Tech)
80 pts **Arts London** – 80 pts (Archit (Spc Objs))
Bournemouth Arts (UC) – 80 pts (Archit)

Alternative offers
See **Chapter 7** and **Appendix 1** for grades/UCAS Tariff points information for the International Baccalaureate, Scottish Highers/Advanced Highers, the Welsh Baccalaureate, the Irish Leaving Certificate, the Cambridge Pre-U Diploma, the Advanced Diploma and the Extended Project.

EXAMPLES OF FOUNDATION DEGREES IN THE SUBJECT FIELD
Bolton; Bournemouth; Brighton; Derby; Huddersfield; Northumbria; Oldham (Coll); West London.

CHOOSING YOUR COURSE (SEE ALSO CH. 1)
Some course features
Architecture is a broad subject combining the vocational with the academic. To practise as an architect it is important to check that your chosen courses follow the requirements of the Royal Institute of British Architects (see **Appendix 4**).

Bath Four-year full-time thin sandwich BSc degree with second and third-year placements, and opportunity for third-year Erasmus exchange at a European school of architecture.
Edinburgh Wide range of Architecture-related courses delivered jointly by University and Edinburgh College of Art. Choice of three-year BA or four-year MA Architecture course, both with options to proceed to MArch degree which completes RIBA/ARB Part 2 qualification for architects.
Huddersfield (Archit (Int)) Course focuses on the built environment in the developing world, with extensive overseas field work.
Northumbria Project work, management skills in architectural design, field study visits and strong links with Interior Design programme central to this full-time course.
Oxford Brookes (Archit) Wide-ranging three-year full-time course, with teaching centred on the design studio, technology, practice and historical and theoretical approaches to architecture. Department has open-studio culture.
Westminster Modular course with 75% core modules, 25% options. Choice of modules determines choice of a general or special pathway degree.

Universities and colleges teaching quality See www.qaa.ac.uk; http://unistats.direct.gov.uk.

Top research universities and colleges (RAE 2008) (Architecture and Built Environment) Cambridge; London (UCL); Sheffield; Liverpool; Loughborough; Bath; Reading; Edinburgh.

Examples of sandwich degree courses Bath; Brighton; Bristol UWE; Cardiff; De Montfort; Dundee; Glasgow (SA); Huddersfield; Leeds Met; London South Bank; Northumbria; Nottingham Trent; Plymouth; Queen's Belfast; Sheffield Hallam; Ulster.

ADMISSIONS INFORMATION

Number of applicants per place (approx) Archit Assoc Sch London 2; Bath 13; Cambridge 8; Cardiff 12; Cardiff (UWIC) 2; Creative Arts 4; Dundee 6; Edinburgh 18; Glasgow 16; London (UCL) 16; London Met 13; Manchester Met 25; Newcastle 11; Nottingham 30; Oxford Brookes 15; Queen's Belfast 9; Robert Gordon 8; Sheffield 20; Southampton 10; Strathclyde 10.

Advice to applicants and planning the UCAS personal statement You should describe any visits to historical or modern architectural sites and give your opinions. Contact architects in your area and try to obtain work shadowing or work experience in their practices. Describe any such work you have done. Develop a portfolio of drawings and sketches of buildings and parts of buildings (you will probably need this for your interview). Show evidence of your reading on the history of architecture in Britain and modern architecture throughout the world. Discuss your preferences among the work of leading 20th century world architects (see **Chapter 5**). (See **Appendix 4**.) **Cambridge** Check college requirement for preparatory work.

Misconceptions about this course Some applicants believe that Architectural Technology is the same as Architecture. Some students confuse Architecture with Architectural Engineering.

Selection interviews The majority of universities and colleges interview or inspect portfolios for Architecture and most require a portfolio of art work. **Yes** Archit Assoc Sch London, Bradford, Brighton, Cambridge, Cardiff, Coventry, Derby, Dundee, East London, Edinburgh, Huddersfield, Kingston, Liverpool, London (UCL), London South Bank, Newcastle, Nottingham, Sheffield; **Some** Anglia Ruskin, Cardiff (UWIC).

Interview advice and questions Most Architecture departments will expect to see evidence of your ability to draw; portfolios are often requested at interview and, in some cases, drawing tests are set prior to the interview. You should have a real awareness of architecture with some knowledge of historical styles as well as examples of modern architecture. If you have gained some work experience then you will be asked to describe the work done in the architect's office and any site visits you have made. Questions in the past have included the following: What is the role of the architect in society? Is the London Eye an eyesore? Discuss one historic and one 20th century building you admire. Who is your favourite architect? What sort of buildings do you want to design? How do you make a place peaceful? How would you reduce crime through architecture? Do you like the University buildings? Do you read any architectural journals? Which? What is the role of an architectural technologist? See also **Chapter 5**. **Archit Assoc Sch London** The interview assesses the student's potential and ability to benefit from the course. Every portfolio we see at interview will be different; sketches, models, photographs and paintings all help to build up a picture of the student's interests. Detailed portfolio guidelines are available on the website. **Cambridge** Candidates who have taken, or are going to take, A-level art should bring with them their portfolio of work (GCSE work is not required). All candidates, including those who are not taking A-level art, should bring photographs of any three-dimensional material. Those not taught art should bring a sketch book (for us to assess drawing abilities) and analytical drawings of a new and old (pre-1900) building and a natural and human-made artefact. We are interested to see any graphic work in any medium that you would like to show us – please do not feel you should restrict your samples to only those with architectural reference. All evidence of sketching ability is helpful to us. (NB All colleges at Cambridge and other university Departments of Architecture will seek similar evidence.) **Sheffield** Art portfolio required for those without AL/GCSE art.

Reasons for rejection (non-academic) Weak evidence of creative skills. Folio of art work does not give sufficient evidence of design creativity. Insufficient evidence of interest in architecture. Unwillingness to try freehand sketching. **Archit Assoc Sch London** Poor standard of work in the portfolio.

AFTER-RESULTS ADVICE

Offers to applicants repeating A-levels Higher Huddersfield; **Possibly higher** Brighton, De Montfort, Glasgow, Newcastle; **Same** Archit Assoc Sch London, Bath, Birmingham City, Cambridge, Cardiff, Cardiff (UWIC), Creative Arts, Derby, Dundee, Greenwich, Kingston, Liverpool John Moores, London Met, London South Bank, Manchester Met, Nottingham, Nottingham Trent, Oxford Brookes, Queen's Belfast, Robert Gordon, Sheffield.

For a quick reference offers calculator, fold out the inside back cover.

GRADUATE DESTINATIONS AND EMPLOYMENT (2007/8 HESA)
Graduates surveyed 1855 **Employed** 780 **In further study** 370 **Assumed unemployed** 250

Career note Further study is needed to enter architecture as a profession. Opportunities exist in local government or private practice – areas include planning, housing, environmental and conservation fields. Architectural technicians support the work of architects and may be involved in project management, design presentations and submissions to planning authorities.

OTHER DEGREE SUBJECTS FOR CONSIDERATION
Architectural Engineering; Building; Building Surveying; Civil Engineering; Construction; Heritage Management; History of Art and Architecture; Housing; Interior Architecture; Interior Design; Landscape Architecture; Property Development; Quantity Surveying; Surveying; Town and Country Planning; Urban Studies.

ART and DESIGN (General)

(including **Animation, Conservation** and **Restoration**; see also **Art and Design (Graphic Design), Art and Design (3D Design), Combined Courses, Communication Studies/Communication, Drama, Media Studies, Photography**)

Art and Design and all specialisms remain one of the most popular subjects. This table provides a list of Art and Design courses that cover a wide range of creative activities. Many of the courses listed in this table cover aspects of fine art, graphic or three dimensional design, but to a less specialised extent than those listed in the other Art and Design tables. Travel and visits to art galleries and museums are strongly recommended by many universities and colleges. Note that for entry to Art and Design courses it is often necessary to follow an Art and Design Foundation course first: check with your chosen institution.

Art and Design degree courses cover a wide range of subjects. These are grouped together in the following six tables:

**Art and Design (General),
Art and Design (Fashion and Textiles),
Art and Design (Fine Art),
Art and Design (Graphic Design),
Art and Design (Product and Industrial Design),
Art and Design (Three Dimensional Design)**.
(**History of Art** and **Photography** are listed in separate tables.)

Useful websites www.artscouncil.org.uk; www.designcouncil.org.uk; www.britart.com; www. theatredesign.org.uk; www.worldofinteriors.co.uk; www.artefactantiques.com; www.arts.ac.uk; www. dandad.org; www.csd.org.uk; www.yourcreativefuture.org.uk.

NB The points totals shown to the left of the institutions are for ease of reference only. It must not be assumed that Tariff points are always used by institutions or that they can be substituted for an offer in grades. The level of an offer is not necessarily indicative of the quality of a course.

COURSE OFFERS INFORMATION
Subject requirements/preferences Entry requirements for Art and Design courses vary between institutions and courses (check prospectuses and websites). Most courses require an Art and Design Foundation course. **AL** grades or points may be required plus five **GCSE** subjects at grades A–C, or a recognised equivalent. A portfolio of work demonstrating potential and visual awareness will also be required. **AL** (Design Technology) Design technology or a physical science may be required or preferred. (Creative Arts courses) Music/art/drama may be required.

NB In 2012 universities and colleges will differ in their use of GCE AL/AS unit grade information, A* grades, the Extended Project (EPQ), the Advanced Diploma and the Cambridge Pre-U

examination when considering applicants and making offers. An EPQ may be accepted in place of an AS subject. Check websites of universities and colleges for the latest offers information.

Your target offers and examples of courses provided by each institution

360 pts **Glasgow (SA)** – AAA–ABB (Des (Vis Comm))

340 pts **Reading** – AAB–ABBb (Art Psy) (HL 666)

320 pts **Dundee** – ABB 320 pts 2nd yr entry (Art Phil Contemp Prac) (IB 34 pts)
Lancaster – ABB 300–320 pts (Crea Arts courses) (IB 28 pts)
Reading – 3AL **or** 340 pts 3AL+AS 320 pts (Art Phil) (HL 655)

300 pts **Kent** – 300 pts (Art Film)

280 pts **Glamorgan** – 280–300 pts (Animat courses)
Kent – 280 pts (Vis Perf Arts)
Leeds – BBC (Tech Des Colour)
London (Gold) – BBC (Des Innov; Des)
Newman (UC) – 280–300 pts (P Educ Arts (QTS))
Reading – 280–300 pts (Art Film Thea)

260 pts **Newman (UC)** – 260 pts (Art Des)

240 pts **Bath Spa** – 240–300 pts (Crea Arts; Art)
Bolton – 240 pts (Animat Illus)
Cumbria – 240 pts (Contemp App Arts)
De Montfort – 240 pts (Animat Des)
Dundee – CCC 240 pts 1st yr entry (Art Phil Contemp Prac)
Glamorgan – 240–280 pts (Animat)
Lincoln – 240 pts (Animat; Cons Restor)
Manchester Met – 240 pts (Interact Arts)
Newport – 240–260 pts (Crea Thera Educ; Animat)
Suffolk (Univ Campus) – 240 pts (Des)
Wolverhampton – 240 pts (Animat)

220 pts **Falmouth (UC)** – 220 pts (Crea Evnts Mgt)
Hull – 220–260 pts (Des Tech)
Middlesex – 220 pts (Animat)
Staffordshire – 220 pts (Animat) (IB 28 pts)
Worcester – 220–260 pts (Art Des; Animat)

200 pts **Bolton** – 200 pts (Art Des)
Bucks New – 200 pts (Art)
Central Lancashire – interview 200–250 pts (Contemp Vis Arts (Hist Theor))
Glamorgan – 200–240 pts (Art Prac)
Glyndŵr – 200 pts (Des; Animat)
Hereford (CA) – 200 pts (Animat; Contemp App Arts; Illus)
Hull – 200–240 pts (Dig Arts; Des Dig Media)
Portsmouth – 200–280 pts (Comp Animat; Animat)
Salford – 200 pts (Des Dig Media; Des Fut; Vis Arts)
Southampton Solent – 200 pts (Animat)
Swansea Met – 200 pts (Des Adv)

180 pts **Dundee** – 180 pts (Art Des Fdn) (IB 24 pts)
Kingston – 180–220 pts (Des St)
Northampton – 180–220 pts (Crea Des Mark)
Sunderland – 180 pts (Art Des)

160 pts **Bath Spa** – 160–200 pts (App Art Des)
Bishop Grosseteste (UC) – CC (Educ St Art QTS)
Bournemouth Arts (UC) – 160 pts (Arts Evnt Mgt)
Creative Arts – 160–200 pts (App Arts; Arts Animat)
Glasgow (SA) – CC (Vis Comm)
Middlesex – 160 pts (Des Inter App Arts)
Ulster – 160 pts (Art Des; Des Vis Comm)

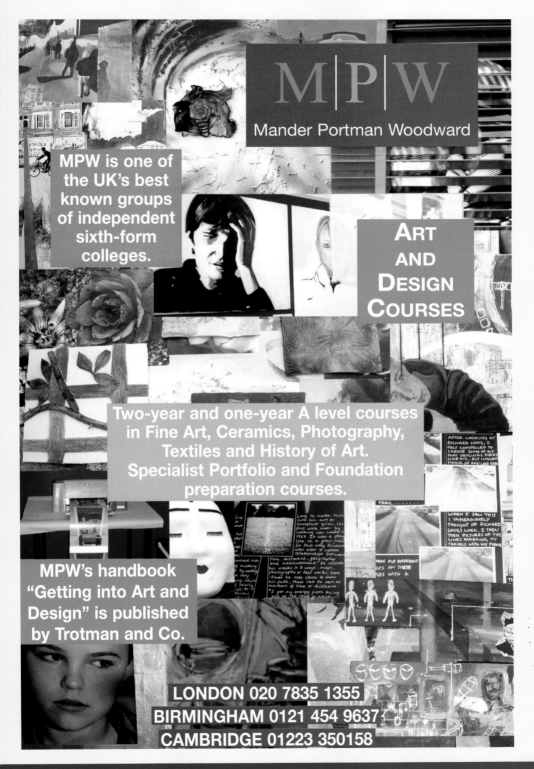

West London – 160 pts (Dig Animat)
Westminster – 160 pts (Illus; Animat)
100 pts and below or other selection criteria (Foundation course, interview and portfolio inspection)
    Bournemouth and Poole (Coll) – one year top-up degree check with School (Appl Art Des BA (Hons))

Anglia Ruskin; Archit Assoc Sch London; Arts London; Arts London (Camberwell CA); Arts London (CFash); Arts London (Chelsea CAD); Bath Spa; Bedfordshire; Bournemouth Arts (UC); Brighton; Bristol UWE; Colchester (Inst); Creative Arts; Cumbria; Derby; Doncaster (Coll Univ Centre); East London; Edge Hill; Edinburgh (CA); Falmouth (UC); Glamorgan; Gloucestershire; Hull (Coll); Kingston; Leeds (CAD); Leeds Met; Lincoln; London (Gold); London Met; London South Bank; Loughborough; Manchester (Coll); Middlesex; NEW (Coll); Newcastle (Coll); Northbrook (Coll); Norwich (UCA); Nottingham New (Coll); Nottingham Trent; Portsmouth; Reading; Sheffield Hallam; Sir Gâr (Coll); Suffolk (Univ Campus); Swansea Met; Warwickshire (Coll); Westminster.

Alternative offers
See **Chapter 7** and **Appendix 1** for grades/UCAS Tariff points information for the International Baccalaureate, Scottish Highers/Advanced Highers, the Welsh Baccalaureate, the Irish Leaving Certificate, the Cambridge Pre-U Diploma, the Advanced Diploma and the Extended Project.

EXAMPLES OF FOUNDATION DEGREES IN THE SUBJECT FIELD
Arts London; Blackburn (Coll Univ Centre); Blackpool and Fylde (Coll); Bournemouth; Bournemouth and Poole (Coll); Bournemouth Arts (UC); Brighton; Bristol City (Coll); Burnley (Coll); Cardiff; Cavendish (Coll); Chesterfield (Coll); Cleveland (CAD); Colchester (Inst); Cornwall (Coll); Creative Arts; Croydon (Coll); Darlington (Coll); De Montfort; Derby; Doncaster (Coll Univ Centre); Essex; Glyndŵr; Grimsby (IFHE); Hereford (CA); Hertfordshire; Hopwood Hall (Coll); Huddersfield; Hugh Baird (Coll); Hull (Coll); Huntingdon (Reg Coll); K (Coll); Kirklees (Coll); Leeds (CAD); Leeds Met; Leicester (Coll); London Met; Manchester (Coll); Mid-Cheshire (Coll); Milton Keynes (Coll); Newcastle (Coll); Newham (CFE); Newport; North West Kent (Coll); Northumberland (Coll); Norwich (UCA); Nottingham New (Coll); Oldham (Coll); Plymouth (CA); Preston (Coll); Ravensbourne; Richmond-upon-Thames (Coll); Runshaw (Coll); St Helens (Coll); Shrewsbury (CAT); South Devon (Coll); South Kent (Coll); South Nottingham (Coll); South Tyneside (Coll); Stafford (Coll); Staffordshire Reg Fed (SURF); Sussex Coast Hastings (Coll); Sussex Downs (Coll); Tameside (Coll); Truro (Coll); West Anglia (Coll); West Herts (Coll); West London; Weston (Coll); Weymouth (Coll); Wiltshire (Coll); Winchester; Writtle (Coll); York St John; Yorkshire Coast (CFHE).

CHOOSING YOUR COURSE (SEE ALSO CH. 1)
Some course features
Bournemouth Course includes specialist units in art practice, visual studies and aesthetic theory.
Dundee Course includes digital film making, photography, sound design, sonic art, performance, web art and interactive media.
Lancaster Two arts disciplines chosen from art, creative writing, music and theatre studies.
London (Gold) This interdisciplinary course includes contemporary design practice, design and art theory, literature, sociology, philosophy, anthropology and material culture with strong emphasis on studio practice.
Loughborough Graphic communication and illustration are two alternative routes in the Visual Communication course.
Teesside (Decr Arts Inter) Unique studio-based course focussing on decorative interior crafts and surface application working with paint, glass, ceramics, wood, metal and plastics; also includes project management and developing software applications for production processes.

Top research universities and colleges (RAE 2008) Loughborough (Design Technology); Reading (Typographic/Graphic Communication); Lancaster; Newcastle; Westminster; London (UCL); Brighton; Bournemouth; Oxford; Cardiff (UWIC); Newport.

Art & Design
at Hull and Harrogate College

HC UK Hull College Group

Higher Education

The Hull College Group is regarded nationally and internationally for its excellence as a specialist creative centre for Higher Education including the Hull School of Art and Design (founded 1861). The range of programmes includes, Foundation Degrees, BA (Hons) and Masters in Art and Design disciplines including Illustration, Graphic Design, Fashion, Media and Photography.

Engagement with creative industries is high on our agenda so that graduates can experience real work with significant companies on most programmes. The Hull College Group offers a friendly and creative environment in which to study, small teaching groups and easy access to a full range of specialist facilities.

Hull Campus:
01482 480970
Or visit:
www.artdesignhull.ac.uk

Harrogate Campus:
01423 878211
Or visit:
www.harrogate.ac.uk/HE

ADMISSIONS INFORMATION

Number of applicants per place (approx) Arts London (Camberwell CA) 2; Arts London (Chelsea CAD) 2; Birmingham 20; Birmingham City 10; Colchester (Inst) 4; Cumbria 5; Derby 4; Dundee 5; Falmouth (UC) 4; Glamorgan 7; Gloucestershire 8; Leeds (CAD) 5; London (Gold) 10; Manchester Met 10; Newman (UC) 5; Northampton (Crea Des Mark) 5; Norwich (UCA) 3; Nottingham Trent 25; Portsmouth 3; Sheffield Hallam 15; Southampton Solent 1; Sunderland 8; Teesside 2; York St John 3.

Admissions tutors' advice Ulster Candidates should be able to communicate clearly and through discussion, to show an awareness of current developments, and to convey enthusiasm for their chosen subject.

Advice to applicants and planning the UCAS personal statement Admissions tutors look for a wide interest in aspects of art and design. Discuss the type of work and the range of media you have explored through your studies to date. Refer to visits to art galleries and museums and give your opinions of the styles of painting and sculpture, both historical and present-day. Mention art-related hobbies. Good drawing skills and sketchbook work, creative and analytical thinking will be needed. See also **Appendix 4**.

Misconceptions about this course Kent (Vis Perf Arts) It is not a fine arts course. **Nottingham Trent** School sixth formers are often unaware of the importance of a level zero or Foundation course preceding BA Art and Design courses.

Selection interviews Most courses (see under **Interview advice and questions**) **Yes** Creative Arts, Dundee, Nottingham Trent, West London; **Some** Staffordshire.

Interview advice and questions All courses require a portfolio inspection. Admissions tutors will want to see both breadth and depth in the applicant's work and evidence of strong self-motivation. They will also be interested to see any sketchbooks or notebooks. However, they do not wish to see similar work over and over again! A logical, ordered presentation helps considerably. Large work, especially three-dimensional work, can be presented by way of photographs. Video or film work should be edited to a running time of no more than 15 minutes. Examples of written work may also be provided. Past questions have included: How often do you visit art galleries and exhibitions? Discuss the last exhibition you visited. What are the reactions of your parents to your choice of course and career? How do they link up with art? Do you feel that modern art has anything to contribute to society compared with earlier art? Is a brick a work of art? Show signs of life – no apathy! Be eager and enthusiastic. See also **Chapter 6**.

Reasons for rejection (non-academic) Lack of enthusiasm for design issues or to acquire design skills. Poorly presented practical work. Lack of interest or enthusiasm in contemporary visual arts. Lack of knowledge and experience of the art and design industry.

AFTER-RESULTS ADVICE
Offers to applicants repeating A-levels **Possibly higher** Brighton; **Same** Birmingham City, Canterbury Christ Church, Chester, Chichester, Colchester (Inst), Creative Arts, Dundee, Leeds, Lincoln, Liverpool Hope, Newcastle, Nottingham Trent, Portsmouth, Staffordshire, Sunderland, West London, Wolverhampton, York St John.

GRADUATE DESTINATIONS AND EMPLOYMENT (2007/8 HESA)
Graduates surveyed 8950 **Employed** 4185 **In further study** 615 **Assumed unemployed** 1230

Career note Many Art and Design courses are linked to specific career paths which are achieved through freelance consultancy work or studio work. Some enter teaching and many find other areas such as retail and management fields. Opportunities for fashion and graphic design specialists exceed those of the other areas of art and design. Opportunities in industrial and product design and 3D design are likely to be limited and dependent on the contacts that students establish during their degree courses. Only a very limited number of students committed to painting and sculpture can expect to succeed without seeking alternative employment.

OTHER DEGREE SUBJECTS FOR CONSIDERATION
Animation; Architecture; Art Gallery Management; Communication Studies; Computer Studies; Education; Film Studies; History of Art; Media Studies; Photography; see other **Art and Design** tables.

ART and DESIGN (Fashion and Textiles)
(including Surface Design)

Fashion Design courses involve drawing and design, research, pattern cutting and garment construction for clothing for men, women and children. Courses may also cover design for textiles, commercial production and marketing. Some institutions have particularly good contacts with industry and are able to arrange sponsorships for students.

Useful websites www.fashion.net; www.londonfashionweek.co.uk; www.texi.org; www.yourcreative future.org.uk.

NB The points totals shown to the left of the institutions are for ease of reference only. It must not be assumed that Tariff points are always used by institutions or that they can be substituted for an offer in grades. The level of an offer is not necessarily indicative of the quality of a course.

COURSE OFFERS INFORMATION
Subject requirements/preferences **AL** Textiles or textile science and technology may be required.

NB In 2012 universities and colleges will differ in their use of GCE AL/AS unit grade information, A* grades, the Extended Project (EPQ), the Advanced Diploma and the Cambridge Pre-U examination when considering applicants and making offers. An EPQ may be accepted in

place of an AS subject. Check websites of universities and colleges for the latest offers information.

Your target offers and examples of courses provided by each institution
360 pts   **Glasgow (SA)** – AAA–AAB (Fash Tex)
320 pts   **Manchester** – ABB–ABC (Tex Sci Tech) (IB 34–33 pts)
          Southampton/Winchester (SA) – ABB (Fash Mark) (IB 32 pts)
300 pts   **Leeds** – BBB–BBC (Tex Des) (IB 30 pts)
          Manchester – ABC (Tex Tech (Bus Mgt)) (IB 32 pts)
          Northumbria – 300 pts (Fash Mark)
          Nottingham Trent – 300 pts (Fash Mark Brnd; Fash Comm Prom)
280 pts   **Birmingham City** – 280 pts (Fash Des courses)
          Brighton – BBC (Fash Drs Hist) (IB 28 pts)
          Glamorgan – 280 pts (Fash Des; Fash Prom; Cstm Constr Scrn Stg)
          London (Central Sch SpDr) – BBC (Thea Prac (Cstm Constr) (Pptry) (Perf Arts) (Prod))
          Manchester Met – 280 pts (Int Fash Mark) (IB 30 pts)
          Northumbria – 280 pts (Fash)
          Nottingham Trent – 280 pts (Fash Des)
          Westminster – BBC 280 pts (Fash Merch Mgt)
260 pts   **Heriot-Watt** – BBC (Fash Tech)
          Huddersfield – 260 pts (Fash Des Tex)
          Sheffield Hallam – 260 pts (Fash Des)
          Southampton Solent – 260 pts (Writ Fash Cult)
240 pts   **Coventry** – 240 pts (Fash; Fash Accs)
          De Montfort – 240 pts (Fash Cont Des; Rtl Buy (Fash) (Tex); Fash Des; Fash Tech; Tex Des; Fash Fabs Accs)
          Dundee – CCC (Tex Des Fdn)
          Glasgow Caledonian – CCC (Fash Mark)
          Hertfordshire – 240 pts (Fashion)
          Lincoln – 240 pts (Fash St)
          Manchester Met – 240 pts (Fash; Tex Des Fash; Embr; Fash Des Tech)
          Newport – 240–260 pts (Fash Des)
          Nottingham Trent – 240–280 pts (Tex Des)
220 pts   **Anglia Ruskin** – 220 pts (Fash Des)
          Bournemouth – 220 pts (Fash Tex)
          Bradford (Coll Univ Centre) – 220 pts (Fash Des)
          Creative Arts – 220 pts (Fash Jrnl)
          Glasgow Caledonian – CCD (Fash Bus)
          Heriot-Watt – CCD (Fash Comm; Fash Wmnswr; Fash Mnswr; Fash)
          Northampton – 220–260 pts (Fash Mark; Fash; Fash (Ftwr Accs); Sfc Des Prntd Tex)
          Queen Margaret – 220 pts (Cstm Des Constr) (IB 28 pts)
200 pts   **Bolton** – 200 pts (Tex Sfc Des)
          Creative Arts – 200 pts (Fash Atel; Tex Fash Int; Fash Prom Imag)
          Hereford (CA) – 200 pts (Tex Des)
          Manchester Met – 200 pts (Tex)
          Portsmouth – 200–280 pts (Fash Tex Des Ent)
          Salford – 200 pts (Fash) (IB 26 pts)
          Staffordshire – 200 pts (Tex Sfc; Sfc Pattn Des)
          Swansea Met – 200–340 pts (Sfc Pattn (Tex Fash); Sfc Pattn (Tex Inter))
          Wolverhampton – 200 pts (Fash Tex)
180 pts   **Derby** – 180–240 pts (Tex Des; Fash St)
          Dundee – 180 pts (Fash St)
          Robert Gordon – BCC (Fsh Mgt) (IB 27 pts)
160 pts   **Bournemouth Arts (UC)** – 160 pts (Fash St)
          Cardiff (UWIC) – 160 pts (Fash Inter Art Tex)

Central Lancashire – 160–200 pts (Dig Des Fash; E Fash Des; Fash Prom Styl; Fash Brnd Mgt)
East London – 160 pts (Prtd Tex Des)
Leeds Met – 160 pts (Des App Tex)
Robert Gordon – CC (Fash Des) (IB 24 pts)
South Essex (Coll) – 160 pts (Fash Des)
Southampton Solent – 160 pts (Fash Graph; Fash PR)
UHI Millennium Inst – CC (Contemp Tex)
Ulster – 160 pts (Tex Fash Des)
West London – 160 pts (Fash Tex)

120 pts **Basingstoke (CT)** – 120 pts (Tex Fash)
Cleveland (CAD) – 120–100 pts (Tex Sfc Des)
Northbrook (Coll) – 120 pts (Fash Des; Fash Media Prom; Tex Des)
Stockport (Coll) – 120–240 pts (Des Vis Arts (Sfc Des))

100 pts and below or other selection criteria (Foundation course, interview and portfolio inspection)
Loughborough – Direct entry from A-levels also considered (minimum 320 pts) Pre-degree course preferred prior to entry (Tex (Multim Tex) (Prnt Tex) (Wv Tex))
Yorkshire Coast (CFHE) – Check with College (Costume Design)

Arts London (CFash); Arts London (Wimb CA); Bath Spa; Birmingham City; Birmingham City (Coll); Bournemouth; Brighton; Bristol UWE; Bucks New; Chesterfield (Coll); Colchester (Inst); Coventry; Croydon (Coll); Doncaster (Coll Univ Centre); East London; Edinburgh (CA); Falmouth (UC); Glamorgan; Great Yarmouth (Coll); Havering (Coll); Kingston; Leeds (CAD); Leeds Met; Leicester (Coll); Lincoln; Liverpool John Moores; Loughborough; Manchester (Coll); Menai (Coll); Mid-Cheshire (Coll); Middlesex; NEW (Coll); Newcastle (Coll); Northampton; Nottingham New (Coll); Plymouth; Ravensbourne; Robert Gordon; Sir Gâr (Coll); Somerset (CAT); Southampton/Winchester (SA); Staffordshire Reg Fed (SURF); West Anglia (Coll); West London; Westminster; York (Coll).

Alternative offers
See **Chapter 7** and **Appendix 1** for grades/UCAS Tariff points information for the International Baccalaureate, Scottish Highers/Advanced Highers, the Welsh Baccalaureate, the Irish Leaving Certificate, the Cambridge Pre-U Diploma, the Advanced Diploma and the Extended Project.

EXAMPLES OF FOUNDATION DEGREES IN THE SUBJECT FIELD
Arts London (CFash); Barnfield (Coll); Bath City (Coll); Bath Spa; Bedfordshire; Blackburn (Coll Univ Centre); Bournemouth Arts (UC); Brighton; Bristol UWE; Chesterfield (Coll); Cleveland (CAD); Colchester (Inst); Cornwall (Coll); Creative Arts; Croydon (Coll); Derby; Exeter (Coll); Hereford (CT); Hertfordshire; Hull (Coll); Kent; Kirklees (Coll); Leeds Met; Leicester (Coll); Liverpool (CmC); London Met; Manchester (Coll); Mid-Cheshire (Coll); Newcastle (Coll); Newport; Nottingham New (Coll); Plymouth City (Coll); Sheffield (Coll); South Essex (Coll); Suffolk (Univ Campus); West Anglia (Coll).

CHOOSING YOUR COURSE (SEE ALSO CH. 1)
Some course features
Universities and colleges offer a very wide range of specialist and individual subjects. In each case programmes will differ, often depending on the specialist interests of teaching staff. When considering specialist courses, eg Fashion Retail Management, Fashion Embroidery, Fashion Journalism, choose only named courses since a number of institutions claim to offer these subjects but only as a minor study.

Universities and colleges teaching quality See www.qaa.ac.uk; http://unistats.direct.gov.uk.

Top research universities and colleges (RAE 2008) See **Art and Design (General)**.

Examples of sandwich degree courses Brighton; Central Lancashire; De Montfort; Glasgow Caledonian; Huddersfield; Leeds; Manchester Met; Northumbria; Nottingham Trent; Southampton Solent; Westminster.

ADMISSIONS INFORMATION

Number of applicants per place (approx) Arts London 5; Arts London (CFash) (Fash Mgt) 20; Birmingham City (Tex Des) 4; Bournemouth Arts (UC) 6; Brighton 6; Bristol UWE 4; Central Lancashire 4; Creative Arts 8; De Montfort 5; Derby (Tex Des) 2; Essex 2; Heriot-Watt 6; Huddersfield 4; Kingston 5; Leeds (CAD) 4; Liverpool John Moores 6; London (Gold) 5; Loughborough 5; Manchester Met 3; Middlesex 5; Northampton 4; Northumbria 8; Nottingham Trent 8, (Tex Des) 3; Southampton 4; Southampton/Winchester (SA) 3; Staffordshire 3; Wolverhampton 2.

Advice to applicants and planning the UCAS personal statement A well-written legible statement is sought, clearly stating an interest in fashion and how prior education and work experience relate to your application. You should describe any visits to exhibitions, and importantly, your views and opinions. Describe any work you have done ('making' and 'doing' skills, if any, for example, pattern cutting, sewing) or work observation in textile firms, fashion houses, even visits to costume departments in theatres can be useful. These contacts and visits should be described in detail, showing your knowledge of the types of fabrics and production processes. Give opinions on trends in haute couture, and show awareness of the work of others. Provide evidence of materials handling (see also **Appendix 4**). Show good knowledge of the contemporary fashion scene. See also **Art and Design (Graphic Design)**.

Misconceptions about this course Some students expect the Fashion degree to include textiles; (Tex) Some applicants feel that it's necessary to have experience in textiles – this is not the case. The qualities sought in the portfolio are analytical drawing, good colour sense and a sensitivity to materials.

Selection interviews Most institutions interview and require a portfolio of work. You should be familiar with current fashion trends and the work of leading designers.

Interview advice and questions Questions mostly originate from student's portfolio. See also **Art and Design (General)** and **Chapter 6**. **Birmingham City** (Tex Des) What do you expect to achieve from a degree in Fashion? **Creative Arts** Describe in detail a specific item in your portfolio and why it was selected.

Reasons for rejection (non-academic) Portfolio work not up to standard. Not enough research. Not articulate at interview. Lack of sense of humour, and inflexibility. Narrow perspective. Lack of resourcefulness, self-motivation and organisation. Complacency, lack of verbal, written and self-presentation skills. Not enough experience in designing or making clothes. See also **Art and Design (General)**.

AFTER-RESULTS ADVICE

Offers to applicants repeating A-levels **Same** Birmingham City, Bournemouth Arts (UC), Creative Arts, Huddersfield, Manchester Met, Nottingham Trent, South Essex (Coll), Staffordshire.

GRADUATE DESTINATIONS AND EMPLOYMENT (2007/8 HESA)

See **Art and Design (General)**.

Career note See **Art and Design (General)**.

OTHER DEGREE SUBJECTS FOR CONSIDERATION

History of Art; Retail Management; Theatre Design.

ART and DESIGN (Fine Art)

(including **Printing, Printmaking** and **Sculpture**; see also **Art and Design (Graphic Design), Photography**)

Fine Art courses can involve a range of activities such as painting, illustration and sculpture and often fine art media – electronic media, film, video, photography and print – although course options will vary between institutions. As in the case of most Art degrees, admission to courses usually requires a one-year Foundation Art course before applying.

Useful websites www.artcyclopedia.com; www.fine-art.com; www.nationalgallery.org.uk; www.britisharts.co.uk; www.tate.org.uk; www.yourcreativefuture.org.uk.

NB The points totals shown to the left of the institutions are for ease of reference only. It must not be assumed that Tariff points are always used by institutions or that they can be substituted for an offer in grades. The level of an offer is not necessarily indicative of the quality of a course.

COURSE OFFERS INFORMATION

Subject requirements/preferences See **Art and Design (General) Course offers information**.

NB In 2012 universities and colleges will differ in their use of GCE AL/AS unit grade information, A* grades, the Extended Project (EPQ), the Advanced Diploma and the Cambridge Pre-U examination when considering applicants and making offers. An EPQ may be accepted in place of an AS subject. Check websites of universities and colleges for the latest offers information.

Your target offers and examples of courses provided by each institution

360 pts **Glasgow (SA)** – AAA–AAB (Fine Art (Sculp Env Art); Fine Art (Pntg/Prtg))
Oxford – AAA (Fine Art) (IB 38–40 pts)
320 pts **Dundee** – ABB 320 pts 2nd yr entry (Art Phil Contemp Prac) (IB 34 pts)
Glasgow (SA) – ABB (Fine Art (Photo))
London (UCL/Slade SA) – BBBe (Fine Art) (IB 32 pts)
Southampton – ABB (Fine Art) (32 pts)
300 pts **Edinburgh** – BBB–AAA (Fine Art)
Edinburgh (CA) – BBB (Fine Art)
Leeds – BBB (Fine Art) (IB 32 pts)
Newcastle – BBB–BCC (Fine Art) (IB 28–30 pts HL 555+)
280 pts **Birmingham City** – 280 pts (Fine Art)
Gloucestershire – 280 pts (Fine Art Pntg Drg; Fine Art Photo)
Kent – 280 pts inc BC (Fine Art)
Reading – 280–300 pts (Art Hist Art Archit)
260 pts **Aberystwyth** – 260 pts (Fine Art courses) (IB 29 pts)
Gloucestershire – 260 pts (Fine Art)
Lancaster – BCC 260 pts (Fine Art) (IB 27 pts)
Liverpool Hope – 260 pts (Fine Art)
Northumbria – 260 pts (Fine Art)
240 pts **Chichester** – BCD 240–280 pts (Fine Art courses) (IB 28 pts)
Coventry – 240 pts (Fine Art)
Cumbria – 240 pts (Fine Art)
De Montfort – 240 pts (Fine Art)
Dundee – CCC 240 pts 1st yr entry (Art Phil Contemp Prac)
Hertfordshire – 240 pts (Fine Art)
Huddersfield – 240–300 pts (Fine Art courses)
Lincoln – 240 pts (Fine Art)
London Met – 240 pts (Fine Art courses)
Manchester Met – 240 pts (Fine Art)

Newport – 240–260 pts (Fine Art)
Nottingham Trent – 240 pts (Fine Art)
Plymouth – 240 pts (Fine Art Art Hist; Fine Art)
Sheffield Hallam – 240 pts (Contemp Fine Art)
York St John – 240 pts (Fine Art courses)
220 pts **Anglia Ruskin** – 220 pts (Fine Art)
Blackburn (Coll Univ Centre) – CCD 220 pts (Fine Art (Integ Media))
Chester – 220–260 pts (Fine Art) (IB 24 pts)
Falmouth (UC) – 220 pts (Fine Art)
Northampton – 220 pts (Fine Art; Fine Art Pntg Drg)
Oxford Brookes – CCD/CCcc/CDcc (Fine Art)
Staffordshire – 220 pts (Fine Art joint courses) (IB 28 pts)
Teesside – 220–260 pts (Fine Art)
Worcester – 220–260 pts (Fine Art Prac)
205 pts **Reading** – 205 pts (Fine Art (Post Fdn))
200 pts **Bolton** – 200 pts (Fine Arts)
Canterbury Christ Church – 200 pts (Fine App Arts)
Glyndŵr – 200 pts (Fine Art)
Hereford (CA) – 200 pts (Fine Art)
Middlesex – 200–240 pts (Fine Art)
Portsmouth – 200–280 pts (Fine Art)
Southampton Solent – 200 pts (Fine Art)
Suffolk (Univ Campus) – 200 pts (Fine Art; Fine Art Prac)
Swansea Met – 200 pts (Fine Art (Combined Media); Fine Art (Pntg Drg))
Wolverhampton – 200 pts (Photo)
180 pts **Derby** – 180–240 pts (Fine Art)
Dundee – 180 pts (Fine Art)
Stamford New (Coll) – 180 pts (Fine Art)
160 pts **Blackpool and Fylde (Coll)** – 160 pts (Fine Art Prof Prac)
Bournemouth Arts (UC) – 160 pts (Fine Art)
Colchester (Inst) – 160 pts (Art Des (Fine Art))
Creative Arts – 160 pts (Fine Art courses)
Grimsby (IFHE) – 160 pts (Fine App Arts)
Kingston – 160 pts (Fine Art)
Robert Gordon – 160–180 pts (Pntg; Prtg; Sculp)
South Essex (Coll) – 160 pts (Fine Art)
Swindon (Coll) – 160–200 pts (Fine Art)
Ulster – 160 pts (Fine App Arts)
Yorkshire Coast (CFHE) – 160 pts (Fine Art)
140 pts **Sunderland** – 140 pts (Fine Art)
100 pts and below or other selection criteria (Foundation course, interview and portfolio inspection)
Brighton – offers may vary (Crit Fine Art Prac)

Arts London; Arts London (Camberwell CA); Arts London (Chelsea CAD); Arts London (Wimb CA); Barking (Coll); Bath Spa; Bedfordshire; Bradford (Coll Univ Centre); Brighton; Bristol UWE; Bucks New; Cardiff (UWIC); Central Lancashire; Colchester (Inst); Cornwall (Coll); Coventry; Creative Arts; Croydon (Coll); De Montfort; Doncaster (Coll Univ Centre); East London; Edinburgh (CA); Glamorgan; Glyndŵr; Havering (Coll); Hopwood Hall (Coll); Kingston; Kirklees (Coll); Leeds (CAD); Leeds Met; Liverpool (CmC); Liverpool John Moores; London (Gold); Loughborough; Manchester Met; Middlesex; NEW (Coll); North Warwickshire and Hinckley (Coll); Northbrook (Coll); Norwich (UCA); Nottingham; Reading; St Helens (Coll); Salford; Sheffield (Coll); Sir Gâr (Coll); Solihull (Coll); South Essex (Coll); South Nottingham (Coll); Southgate (Coll); Staffordshire Reg Fed (SURF); Stourbridge (Coll); Stranmillis (UC); Suffolk (Univ Campus); Swansea Met; Swindon (Coll); Trinity Saint David;

Tyne Met (Coll); UHI Millennium Inst; Walsall (Coll); Warwickshire (Coll); West Anglia (Coll); West London; West Thames (Coll); Westminster; Wirral Met (Coll).

Alternative offers
See **Chapter 7** and **Appendix 1** for grades/UCAS Tariff points information for the International Baccalaureate, Scottish Highers/Advanced Highers, the Welsh Baccalaureate, the Irish Leaving Certificate, the Cambridge Pre-U Diploma, the Advanced Diploma and the Extended Project.

EXAMPLES OF FOUNDATION DEGREES IN THE SUBJECT FIELD
All are practical workshop courses. Arts London; Bath Spa; Bedfordshire; Blackpool and Fylde (Coll); Brighton; Bristol UWE; Central Bedfordshire (Coll); Cornwall (Coll); Creative Arts; De Montfort; Exeter (Coll); Glyndŵr; Greenwich; Hereford (CA); Huddersfield; Leeds Met; Leicester (Coll); Liverpool (CmC); Llandrillo Cymru (Coll); Newcastle (Coll); Plymouth; Plymouth (CA); Sheffield (Coll); Somerset (CAT); South Tyneside (Coll); Southgate (Coll); Suffolk (Univ Campus); Sunderland; Sunderland City (Coll); Tyne Met (Coll); West London.

CHOOSING YOUR COURSE (SEE ALSO CH. 1)
Universities and colleges teaching quality See www.qaa.ac.uk; http://unistats.direct.gov.uk.

Top research universities and colleges (RAE 2008) See **Art and Design (General)**.

ADMISSIONS INFORMATION
Number of applicants per place (approx) Arts London (Chelsea CAD) 5; Arts London (Wimb CA) (Sculp) 3; Bath Spa 8; Birmingham City 6; Bournemouth Arts (UC) 6; Bristol UWE 3; Cardiff (UWIC) 3; Central Lancashire 4; Cleveland (CAD) 2; Creative Arts 2; Cumbria 4; De Montfort 5; Derby 3; Dundee 5; Gloucestershire 5; Hertfordshire 6; Hull (Scarborough) 2; Hull (Coll) 2; Kingston 9; Lincoln 4; Liverpool John Moores 3; London (Gold) 10; London (UCL) 26; London Met 11; Loughborough 4; Manchester Met 4; Middlesex 3; Newcastle 30; Northampton 3; Northumbria 4; Norwich (UCA) 3; Nottingham Trent 5; Portsmouth 6; Robert Gordon 5; Sheffield Hallam 4; Solihull (Coll) 4; Southampton 3; Staffordshire 3; Sunderland 3; UHI Millennium Inst 2; Wirral Met (Coll) 3.

Advice to applicants and planning the UCAS personal statement Since this is a subject area that can be researched easily in art galleries, you should discuss not only your own style of work and your preferred subjects but also your opinions on various art forms, styles and periods. Keep up-to-date with public opinion on controversial issues. Give your reasons for wishing to pursue a course in Fine Art. Visits to galleries and related hobbies, for example reading, cinema, music, literature should be mentioned. Show the nature of your external involvement in art. (See also **Appendix 4**.) **Oxford** No deferred applications are accepted for this course; successful applicants average 11.5%.

Misconceptions about this course That Fine Art is simply art and design. Sixth form applicants are often unaware of the importance of a Foundation Art course before starting a degree programme. **Bournemouth Arts (UC)** Applicants need to make the distinction between fine art and illustration.

Selection interviews Most institutions interview and require a portfolio of work. **Yes** Arts London (Chelsea CAD) (interviews with portfolios and essays), Oxford (Fine Art) 12%.

Interview advice and questions Questions asked on portfolio of work. Be prepared to answer questions on your stated opinions on your UCAS application and on current art trends and controversial topics reported in the press. Discussion covering the applicant's engagement with contemporary fine art practice. Visits to exhibitions, galleries etc. Ambitions for their own work. How do you perceive the world in a visual sense? Who is your favourite living artist and why? See also **Art and Design (General)** and **Chapter 6**. **UHI Millennium Inst** Applicants are asked to produce a drawing in response to a set topic.

Reasons for rejection (non-academic) Lack of a fine art specialist portfolio. No intellectual grasp of the subject – only interested in techniques.

AFTER-RESULTS ADVICE

Offers to applicants repeating A-levels **Same** Anglia Ruskin, Arts London, Birmingham City, Cumbria, Manchester Met, Nottingham Trent, Staffordshire, Sunderland, UHI Millennium Inst.

GRADUATE DESTINATIONS AND EMPLOYMENT (2007/8 HESA)

Graduates surveyed 2620 **Employed** 915 **In further study** 320 **Assumed unemployed** 335

Career note See **Art and Design (General)**.

OTHER DEGREE SUBJECTS FOR CONSIDERATION

Art Gallery Management; History of Art; see other **Art and Design** tables.

ART and DESIGN (Graphic Design)

(including Advertising, Design, Graphic Communication, Illustration and Visual Communication; see also Art and Design (General), Art and Design (Fine Art), Film, Radio, Video and TV Studies)

Graphic Design ranges from the design of websites, books, magazines and newspapers to packaging and advertisements. Visual communication uses symbols as teaching aids and also includes TV graphics. An Art Foundation course is usually taken before entry to degree courses.

Useful websites www.graphicdesign.about.com; www.graphic-design.com; www.allgraphicdesign. com; www.yourcreativefuture.org.uk.

NB The points totals shown to the left of the institutions are for ease of reference only. It must not be assumed that Tariff points are always used by institutions or that they can be substituted for an offer in grades. The level of an offer is not necessarily indicative of the quality of a course.

COURSE OFFERS INFORMATION

Subject requirements/preferences See **Art and Design (General) Course offers information**.

NB In 2012 universities and colleges will differ in their use of GCE AL/AS unit grade information, A* grades, the Extended Project (EPQ), the Advanced Diploma and the Cambridge Pre-U examination when considering applicants and making offers. An EPQ may be accepted in place of an AS subject. Check websites of universities and colleges for the latest offers information.

Your target offers and examples of courses provided by each institution
320 pts **Southampton** – ABB (Graph Arts) (IB 32 pts HL 16)
300 pts **Leeds** – BBB (N Media) (IB 32 pts)
         Reading – 300–330 pts (Graph Comm)
         Teesside – 300 pts (Graph Arts (Mtn Graph); Graph Des (Illus))
         Worcester – 220–300 pts (Graph Des)
280 pts **Birmingham City** – 280 pts (Vis Comm (Graph Comm) (Illus) (Mov Imag) (Photo))
         Glamorgan – 280 pts (Graph Comm)
         Northumbria – 280 pts (Graph Des)
         Nottingham Trent – 280 pts (Graph Des)
         Suffolk (Univ Campus) – 280 pts (Graph Des; Graph Des Graph Illus; Graph Des Mtn Graph)
260 pts **Gloucestershire** – 260 pts (Adv; Graph Des)
         Liverpool John Moores – 260 pts (Graph Des Illus)
         Sheffield Hallam – 260 pts (Graph Des courses)
240 pts **Coventry** – 240 pts (Graph Des; Illus Animat; Illus Graph)
         Cumbria – 240 pts (Graph Des)
         De Montfort – 240 pts (Graph Des; Graph Des Illus; Graph Des Photo; Graph Des Interact Media)
         Edinburgh Napier – 240 pts (Graph Des)
         Hertfordshire – 240 pts (Graph Des Illus)

Huddersfield – 240 pts (Illus; Adv Des)
Lincoln – 240 pts (Contemp Lns Media courses; Graph Des; Graph Des Illus; Graph Des Contemp Lns Media)
London Met – 240 pts (Graph Des)
Manchester Met – 240-280 pts (Illus Animat)
Newport – 240–280 pts (Graph Des; Adv Des)
Plymouth – 240 pts (Graph Comm Typo)
Salford – 240 pts (Graph Des)
Wolverhampton – 240 pts (Graph Comm; Graph Comm Illus)

230 pts **Greenwich** – 230 pts (Graph Dig Des)

220 pts **Anglia Ruskin** – 220 pts (Graph Des; Illus Animat; Graph Web Des)
Bradford (Coll Univ Centre) – 220 pts (Graph Des Illus Dig Media)
Middlesex – 200 pts (Illus)
Northampton – 220–260 pts (Graph Arts (Mtn Graph))

200 pts **Creative Arts** – 200 pts (Graph Des; Graph Comm; Adv Brnd Comm)
Hereford (CA) – 200 pts (Graph Media Des; Illus)
Hull (Coll) – 200 pts (Graph Des; Illus)
Portsmouth – 200–280 pts (Illus; Graph Des)
Salford – 200 pts inc Art C (Adv Des)
Southampton Solent – 200 pts (Graph Des)
Staffordshire – 200 pts (Graph Des)
Swansea Met – 200 pts (Graph Des; Illus)
Westminster – BB (Graph Inf Des)

180 pts **Derby** – 180–240 pts (Vis Comm (Graph Des))
Dundee – 180 pts (Graph Des) (IB 24 pts)
Stamford New (Coll) – 180 pts (Graph Des)

160 pts **Bedfordshire** – 160 pts (Adv Des)
Blackpool and Fylde (Coll) – 160 pts (Graph Des)
Bournemouth Arts (UC) – 160 pts (Graph Des; Illus)
Colchester (Inst) – 160 pts (Art Des (Graph Media))
East London – 160 pts (Graph Des; Illus)
Glasgow (SA) – CC (Vis Comm)
Robert Gordon – CC (Graph Des) (IB 24 pts)
Sunderland – 160 pts (Graph Comm; Illus Des)
Swindon (Coll) – 160–200 pts (Graph Des; Illus)
Ulster – 160 pts (Des Vis Comm)

120 pts **Northbrook (Coll)** – 120 pts (Comm Des)

100 pts and below or other selection criteria (Foundation course, interview and portfolio inspection)
Blackpool and Fylde (Coll) – check with College (Illus)
South Essex (Coll) – contact Admissions Tutor (Graph Des)

Arts London; Bath Spa; Blackburn (Coll Univ Centre); Bradford; Brighton; Bristol City (Coll); Bristol UWE; Bucks New; Cardiff (UWIC); Central Lancashire; Colchester (Inst); Coventry; Croydon (Coll); Cumbria; Doncaster (Coll Univ Centre); Edinburgh (CA); Falmouth (UC); Gloucestershire (Coll); Greenwich; Grimsby (IFHE); Havering (Coll); Hertfordshire; Hopwood Hall (Coll); Kent; Kingston; Leeds (CAD); Leeds Met; Liverpool John Moores; Llandrillo Cymru (Coll); Loughborough; Manchester (Coll); Mid-Cheshire (Coll); NEW (Coll); Northbrook (Coll); Norwich (UCA); Plymouth (CA); Ravensbourne; Rotherham (CAT); Sir Gâr (Coll); Solihull (Coll); Somerset (CAT); South Essex (Coll); South Nottingham (Coll); Southampton/ Winchester (SA); Southwark (Coll); St Helens (Coll); Stockport (Coll); Suffolk (Univ Campus); Swansea Met; Tyne Met (Coll); Warwickshire (Coll); West Anglia (Coll); West London; West Thames (Coll); Westminster; Wigan and Leigh (Coll); Wiltshire (Coll); Worcester; Yorkshire Coast (CFHE).

Alternative offers
See **Chapter 7** and **Appendix 1** for grades/UCAS Tariff points information for the International Baccalaureate, Scottish Highers/Advanced Highers, the Welsh Baccalaureate, the Irish Leaving Certificate, the Cambridge Pre-U Diploma, the Advanced Diploma and the Extended Project.

EXAMPLES OF FOUNDATION DEGREES IN THE SUBJECT FIELD
Arts London; Bath Spa; Bedfordshire; Bournemouth; Brighton; Bristol City (Coll); Bucks New; Cardiff (UWIC); Chichester; Cleveland (CAD); Cornwall (Coll); Creative Arts; Cumbria; Durham New (Coll); Exeter (Coll); Greenwich; Hereford (CA); Hertfordshire; Kingston; Kirklees (Coll); Leeds (CAD); Leicester (Coll); Mid-Cheshire (Coll); Middlesex; Newcastle (Coll); Norwich (UCA); Plymouth (CA); Rotherham (CAT); Sheffield (Coll); Somerset (CAT); South Tyneside (Coll); Southwark (Coll); St Helens (Coll); Staffordshire Reg Fed (SURF); Suffolk (Univ Campus).

CHOOSING YOUR COURSE (SEE ALSO CH. 1)
Some course features
These courses offer a wide range of specialisms; check the course contents before selecting.

Universities and colleges teaching quality See www.qaa.ac.uk; http://unistats.direct.gov.uk.

Top research universities and colleges (RAE 2008) See **Art and Design (General)**.

Examples of sandwich degree courses Aberystwyth; Arts London; Huddersfield; Kingston; Northumbria; Sheffield Hallam; Staffordshire; Teesside.

ADMISSIONS INFORMATION
Number of applicants per place (approx) Anglia Ruskin (Illus) 3; Arts London 4; Bath Spa 9; Blackburn (Coll Univ Centre) 2; Bournemouth Arts (UC) 6; Bristol UWE 4; Cardiff (UWIC) 5; Central Lancashire 5; Colchester (Inst) 3; Coventry 6; Creative Arts 5; Derby 5; Edinburgh Napier 7; Glamorgan 3; Hertfordshire 6; Kingston 8; Lincoln 5; Liverpool John Moores 7; Loughborough 5; Manchester Met 8; Middlesex 3; Northampton 3; Northumbria 8; Norwich (UCA) 4; Nottingham Trent 6; Ravensbourne 9; Solihull (Coll) 3; South Essex (Coll) 2; Southampton 6; Staffordshire 3; Swansea Met 10; Teesside 5; Wolverhampton 5.

Advice to applicants and planning the UCAS personal statement Discuss your special interest in this field and any commercial applications that have impressed you. Discuss the work you are enjoying at present and the range of media that you have explored. Show your interests in travel, architecture, the arts, literature, film, current affairs (see also **Appendix 4** for contact details of relevant professional associations). Awareness of the place of design in society.

Misconceptions about this course Bath Spa Some students think that they can start the course from A-levels, that a course in Illustration is simply 'doing small drawings' and that Graphic Design is a soft option with little academic work.

Selection interviews All institutions interview and require a portfolio of work.

Interview advice and questions Questions may be asked on recent trends in graphic design from the points of view of methods and designers and, particularly, art and the computer. Questions are usually asked on applicant's portfolio of work. See also **Art and Design (General)** and **Chapter 6**. **Nottingham Trent** Why Graphic Design? Why this course? Describe a piece of graphic design which has succeeded.

Reasons for rejection (non-academic) Not enough work in portfolio. Inability to think imaginatively. Lack of interest in the arts in general. Lack of drive. Tutor's statement indicating problems. Poorly constructed personal statement. Inability to talk about your work. Lack of knowledge about the chosen course. See also **Art and Design (General)**.

AFTER-RESULTS ADVICE
Offers to applicants repeating A-levels Same Bath Spa, Blackpool and Fylde (Coll), Bournemouth Arts (UC), Cardiff (UWIC), Creative Arts, Lincoln, Manchester Met, Nottingham Trent, Salford, South Essex (Coll), Staffordshire.

GRADUATE DESTINATIONS AND EMPLOYMENT (2007/8 HESA)

See Art and **Design (General)**.

Career note Graphic Design students are probably the most fortunate in terms of the range of career opportunities open to them on graduation. These include advertising, book and magazine illustration, film, interactive media design, typography, packaging, photography and work in publishing and television. See also **Art and Design (General)**.

OTHER DEGREE SUBJECTS FOR CONSIDERATION

Art Gallery Management; Film and Video Production; History of Art; Multimedia Design, Photography and Digital Imaging. See also other **Art and Design** tables.

ART and DESIGN (Product and Industrial Design)

(including Design Technology, Footwear Design, Furniture Design, Interior Architecture, Interior Design, Product Design, Theatre Design and Transport Design; see also Architecture, Art and Design (3D Design))

The field of industrial design is extensive and degree studies are usually preceded by an Art Foundation course. Product Design is one of the most common courses in which technological studies (involving materials and methods of production) are integrated with creative design in the production of a range of household and industrial products. Other courses on offer include Furniture Design, Interior, Theatre, Museum and Exhibition, Automotive and Transport Design. It should be noted that some Product Design courses have an engineering bias: see **Subject requirements/preferences** below.

These are stimulating courses but graduate opportunities in this field are very limited. Good courses will have good industrial contacts for sandwich courses or shorter work placements – check with course leaders (or students) before applying.

Useful websites www.ergonomics.org.uk; www.yourcreativefuture.org.uk; www.productdesignforums.com; www.carbodydesign.com; www.shoe-design.com.

NB The points totals shown to the left of the institutions are for ease of reference only. It must not be assumed that Tariff points are always used by institutions or that they can be substituted for an offer in grades. The level of an offer is not necessarily indicative of the quality of a course.

COURSE OFFERS INFORMATION

Subject requirements/preferences AL Check Product Design, Industrial Design and Engineering Design course requirements since these will often require mathematics and/or physics.

NB In 2012 universities and colleges will differ in their use of GCE AL/AS unit grade information, A* grades, the Extended Project (EPQ), the Advanced Diploma and the Cambridge Pre-U examination when considering applicants and making offers. An EPQ may be accepted in place of an AS subject. Check websites of universities and colleges for the latest offers information.

Your target offers and examples of courses provided by each institution

360 pts Glasgow (SA) – AAA–ABB (Prod Des; Des (Inter Des))
340 pts Strathclyde – AAB (Prod Des Eng MEng) (IB 36 pts)
320 pts Brunel – BBC +AS/EPQ c 320 pts (Prod Des) (IB 31 pts)
        Glasgow – ABB (Prod Des Eng BEng)
        Leeds – ABB (Prod Des) (IB 34 pts HL 16 pts)
        Nottingham – ABB (Prod Des Manuf MEng)
        Queen's Belfast – ABB (Prod Des Dev MEng)

Strathclyde – ABB (Prod Eng Mgt BEng) (IB 32 pts)
Sussex – ABB–BBC (Prod Des) (IB 30–34 pts)
300 pts **Aston** – BBB 280–320 pts (Sust Prod Des) (IB 29 pts)
Bournemouth – 300 pts (Soft Prod Des; Prod Des)
Brighton – BBB 300 pts offers may vary (Sust Prod Des Prof Experience) (IB 32 pts)
Brunel – BBB (Prod Des Eng) (IB 30 pts)
Liverpool – BBB–BBC (Eng Prod Des) (IB 32 pts HL 555)
Nottingham Trent – 300 pts (Inter Archit Des)
285 pts **Cardiff (UWIC)** – 285 pts (Prod Des)
Kingston – 285 pts (Prod Des)
280 pts **Birmingham City** – 280 pts (Inter Des)
Brunel – BBC +AS/EPQ c 280–320 pts (Ind Des Tech) (IB 32 pts)
Leeds – BBC (Des Tech Mgt) (IB 30 pts)
Leeds Met – 280–300 pts (Inter Archit Des)
London Met – 280 pts (Inter Archit Des)
Loughborough – 280–300 pts (Ind Des Tech) (IB 32 pts)
Nottingham – BBC (Prod Des Manuf BEng) (IB 30–32 pts)
Nottingham Trent – 280 pts (Prod Des)
Queen's Belfast – BBC (Prod Des Dev BEng)
Staffordshire – 280 pts (Prod Des Tech) (IB 28 pts)
260 pts **Aston** – 260–300 pts (Electron Prod Des)
De Montfort – 260 pts (Prod Des BSc)
Glamorgan – 260 pts (TV Film Set Des)
Manchester Met – 260–300 pts (Inter Des)
Northumbria – 260 pts (Prod Des Tech)
Salford – 260 pts (Prod Des) (IB 26 pts)
Swansea – 260–300 pts (Prod Des Eng BEng)
Ulster – 260 pts (Tech Des)
West Scotland – BCC (Prod Des Dev)
245 pts **Edinburgh Napier** – CCC 245 pts (Prod Des Eng)
240 pts **Bolton** – 240 pts (Prod Des courses)
Bristol UWE – 240–300 pts (Prod Des Tech)
Central Lancashire – Portfolio interview required 240–300 pts (Inter Des)
Coventry – 240 pts (Auto Trans Des; Ind Prod Des; Spo Prod Des; Prod Des Toy)
De Montfort – 240 pts (Inter Des; Prod Furn Des; Ftwr Des)
Dundee – CCC (Prod Des)
Edinburgh Napier – 240 pts (Inter Archit)
Glamorgan – 240–280 pts (Inter Des)
Hertfordshire – 240 pts (Prod Des; Ind Des)
Huddersfield – 240–300 pts (Inter Des; Prod Des (3D Animat); Exhib Rtl Des; Prod Des
(Child Prod Toys) (Sust Des); Prod Innov Des Dev)
Liverpool John Moores – 240 pts (Prod Des Eng)
London Met – 240 pts (Inter Des Tech; Prod Des)
Middlesex – 240–260 pts (Prod Des; Inter Archit Des)
Sheffield Hallam – 240–260 pts (Prod Des Furn; Prod Des)
Teesside – 240–280 pts (Inter Archit Des; Prod Des (Contemp Lfstl Furn) (Ind Trans))
Wolverhampton – 240 pts (Inter Des; Prod Des)
230 pts **Creative Arts** – 230–260 pts (Inter Archit Des)
220 pts **Anglia Ruskin** – 220 pts (Inter Des)
Hull – 220-260 pts (Med Prod Des)
Manchester Met – 220–240 pts (Prod Des Tech) (IB 26 pts)
Northampton – 220–260 pts (Prod Des; Inter Des)
Portsmouth – 220–320 pts (Inter Des)
Swansea Met – 220 pts (Prod Des)
Teesside – 220–260 pts (Prod Des (Mark))

200 pts **Bangor** – 200–220 pts (Prod Des)
Bolton – 200 pts (Inter Des)
Bradford – 200–240 pts (Prod Des)
Creative Arts – 200 pts (Prod Des Sust Fut; Prod Des)
East London – 200 pts (Prod Des; Prod Des Fut)
Glyndŵr – 200 pts (Mtrspo Des Mgt)
London Met – 200 pts (Furn Prod Des)
London South Bank – CDD 200 pts (Prod Des)
Portsmouth – 200 pts (Prod Des Innov; Prod Des Modn Mat)
Salford – 200 pts (Inter Des)
Suffolk (Univ Campus) – 200 pts (Inter Des)
York St John – 200–220 pts (Prod Des courses)

180 pts **Derby** – 180–240 pts (Prod Des)
Greenwich – 180–240 pts (Des Tech Educ)
Liverpool (LIPA) – 180 pts (Thea Perf Des)
Sunderland – 180 pts (Inter Des)

160 pts **Bedfordshire** – 160–240 pts (Inter Des)
Robert Gordon – CC (Prod Des) (IB 24 pts)
South Essex (Coll) – 160 pts (Inter Des)
Southampton Solent – 160 pts (Inter Des (Decr); Prod Des)

140 pts **Sheffield Hallam** – 140 pts (Des Tech)

100 pts and below or other selection criteria (Foundation course, interview and portfolio inspection)
Arts London; Arts London (Chelsea CAD); Arts London (Wimb CA); Barking (Coll); Bath Spa; Bolton; Bournemouth Arts (UC); Brighton; Bucks New; Cardiff (UWIC); Cleveland (CAD); Colchester (Inst); Croydon (Coll); De Montfort; Derby; Dundee; Easton (Coll); Edinburgh (CA); Falmouth (UC); Forth Valley (Coll); Glasgow Caledonian; Glasgow Met (Coll); Hereford (CA); Heriot-Watt; Hertfordshire; Huddersfield; Kingston; Kirklees (Coll); Leeds (CAD); Lincoln; London South Bank; NEW (Coll); Ravensbourne; Royal Welsh (CMusDr); Shrewsbury (CAT); South Essex (Coll); Southampton Solent; Teesside; West Scotland.

Alternative offers
See **Chapter 7** and **Appendix 1** for grades/UCAS Tariff points information for the International Baccalaureate, Scottish Highers/Advanced Highers, the Welsh Baccalaureate, the Irish Leaving Certificate, the Cambridge Pre-U Diploma, the Advanced Diploma and the Extended Project.

EXAMPLES OF FOUNDATION DEGREES IN THE SUBJECT FIELD
Arts London; Barking (Coll); Bath Spa; Bedfordshire; Bishop Burton (Coll); Blackburn (Coll Univ Centre); Bournemouth Arts (UC); Bristol City (Coll); Bristol UWE; Bucks New; Cornwall (Coll); Croydon (Coll); Greenwich; Kirklees (Coll); Leeds (CAD); Leicester (Coll); London Met; Plymouth (CA); Rose Bruford (Coll); Somerset (CAT); South Devon (Coll); Swansea Met; West London.

CHOOSING YOUR COURSE (SEE ALSO CH. 1)
Some course features
Note that there is an engineering element in some Product Design courses, and several specifically lead to an Engineering degree. Many are accredited by the Institution of Engineering Designers (see **Appendix 4**).

Universities and colleges teaching quality See www.qaa.ac.uk; http://unistats.direct.gov.uk.

Top research universities and colleges (RAE 2008) See **Art and Design (General)**.

Examples of sandwich degree courses Aston; Bournemouth; Bradford; Brighton; Bristol UWE; Brunel; De Montfort; East London; Hertfordshire; Huddersfield; Lincoln; Liverpool John Moores; London South Bank; Manchester Met; Middlesex; Nottingham Trent; Portsmouth; Robert Gordon; Sheffield Hallam; Staffordshire; Sunderland; Sussex; West Scotland.

ADMISSIONS INFORMATION

Number of applicants per place (approx) Arts London 2; Arts London (Chelsea CAD) 2; Arts London (Wimb CA) 2; Aston 6; Bath Spa 4; Birmingham City (Inter Des) 9; Bolton 1; Brunel 4; Cardiff (UWIC) 6; Central Lancashire 7; Colchester (Inst) 4; Coventry 5; Creative Arts 4; De Montfort 5; Derby 2; Edinburgh Napier 6; Loughborough 9; Manchester Met 2; Middlesex (Inter Archit Des) 4; Northampton (Prod Des) 2; Northumbria 4; Nottingham Trent (Inter Archit Des) 7, (Prod Des) 5; Portsmouth 3; Ravensbourne (Inter Des) 4, (Prod Des) 7; Salford 6; Sheffield 4; Shrewsbury (CAT) 6; Staffordshire 3; Swansea Met 3; Teesside 3.

Advice to applicants and planning the UCAS personal statement Your knowledge of design in all fields should be described, including any special interests you may have, for example in domestic, rail and road aspects of design, and visits to exhibitions, motor shows. **School/college reference:** tutors should make it clear that the applicant's knowledge, experience and attitude match the chosen course – not simply higher education in general. Admissions tutors look for knowledge of interior design and interior architecture, experience in 3D-design projects (which include problem-solving and sculptural demands), model-making experience in diverse materials, experience with 2D illustration and colour work, and knowledge of computer-aided design. Photography is also helpful, and also model-making and CAD/computer skills. See also **Art and Design (Graphic Design)**.

Misconceptions about this course Theatre Design is sometimes confused with Theatre Architecture or an academic course in Theatre Studies. **Birmingham City** (Inter Des) Some applicants believe that it is an interior decorating course (carpets and curtains). **Lincoln** (Musm Exhib Des) This is a design course, not a museum course. **Portsmouth** (Inter Des) Some students think that this is about interior decorating after Laurence Llewelyn-Bowen!

Selection interviews Most institutions will interview and require a portfolio of work. **Yes** Brunel, Cardiff (UWIC), Dundee; **Some** Salford, Staffordshire.

Interview advice and questions Applicants' portfolios of art work form an important talking-point throughout the interview. Applicants should be able to discuss examples of current design and new developments in the field and answer questions on the aspects of industrial design which interest them. See also **Art and Design (General)** and **Chapter 6**. **Creative Arts** No tests. Discuss any visits to modern buildings and new developments, eg British Museum Great Court or the Louvre Pyramid.

Reasons for rejection (non-academic) Not hungry enough! Mature students without formal qualifications may not be able to demonstrate the necessary mathematical or engineering skills. Poor quality and organisation of portfolio. Lack of interest. Inappropriate dress. Lack of enthusiasm. Insufficient portfolio work (eg exercises instead of projects). Lack of historical knowledge of interior design. Weak oral communication. See also **Art and Design (General)**. **Creative Arts** Not enough 3D model-making. Poor sketching and drawing.

AFTER-RESULTS ADVICE

Offers to applicants repeating A-levels **Same** Birmingham City, Bournemouth, Creative Arts, Nottingham Trent, Salford, Staffordshire.

GRADUATE DESTINATIONS AND EMPLOYMENT (2007/8 HESA)

See **Art and Design (General)**.

Career note See **Art and Design (General)**.

OTHER DEGREE SUBJECTS FOR CONSIDERATION

Architectural Studies; Architecture; Art Gallery Management; Design (Manufacturing Systems); History of Art; Manufacturing Engineering; Multimedia and Communication Design and subjects in other **Art and Design** tables.

ART and DESIGN (3D Design)

(including **Ceramics, Design Crafts, Glassmaking, Jewellery, Metalwork, Silversmithing, Plastics and Woodwork**; see also **Art and Design (General), Art and Design (Product and Industrial Design)**)

This group of courses covers mainly three dimensional design work, focusing on creative design involving jewellery, silverware, ceramics, glass, wood and plastics. Some institutions offer broad three dimensional studies courses while others provide the opportunity to study very specialised subjects such as stained glass, gemology and horology. Students normally take an Art Foundation course before their degree level studies.

Useful websites www.ergonomics.org.uk; www.yourcreativefuture.org.uk; www.top3D.net; www.glassassociation.org.uk; www.bja.org.uk; www.cpaceramics.com.

NB The points totals shown to the left of the institutions are for ease of reference only. It must not be assumed that Tariff points are always used by institutions or that they can be substituted for an offer in grades. The level of an offer is not necessarily indicative of the quality of a course.

COURSE OFFERS INFORMATION

Subject requirements/preferences See **Art and Design (General)** Course offers information.

NB In 2012 universities and colleges will differ in their use of GCE AL/AS unit grade information, A* grades, the Extended Project (EPQ), the Advanced Diploma and the Cambridge Pre-U examination when considering applicants and making offers. An EPQ may be accepted in place of an AS subject. Check websites of universities and colleges for the latest offers information.

Your target offers and examples of courses provided by each institution

360 pts	**Glasgow (SA)** – AAA–ABB (Des Silver Jewel)
280 pts	**Birmingham City** – 280 pts (Jewel Silver)
	Northumbria – 280 pts (3D Des)
240 pts	**Bath Spa** – 240-300 pts (Crea Arts (Cer))
	Coventry – 240 pts (3D Des)
	De Montfort – 240 pts (Furn Des)
	Hertfordshire – 240 pts (3D Gms Art)
	Lincoln – 240 pts (Jewel Obj)
	Manchester Met – 240–280 pts (3D Des)
	Plymouth – 240 pts (3D Des; 3D Des (Des Mkr) (Furn Inter Des))
	Sheffield Hallam – 240 pts (Mtl Jewel)
	Staffordshire – 240–280 pts (Dig Film 3D Animat Tech)
	Suffolk (Univ Campus) – 240 pts (Des)
220 pts	**Falmouth (UC)** – 220 pts (3D Des)
200 pts	**Glyndŵr** – 200 pts (Des Decr Arts; App Arts)
	Hereford (CA) – 200 pts (Jewel Des)
	Portsmouth – 200–280 pts (3D Des)
	Swansea Met – 200 pts (Fine Art (3D and Sculp Prac))
	Wolverhampton – 200 pts (App Arts)
180 pts	**Dundee** – 180 pts (Jewel Metal Des)
	Sunderland – 180–220 pts (Glass Ceram)
	Swansea Met – 180 pts (3D Comp Animat)
160 pts	**Bournemouth Arts (UC)** – 160 pts (Modelmaking)
	Bucks New – 160–200 pts (3D Contemp Crfts Prods)
	Glasgow (SA) – CC (Vis Comm)
	Leeds Met – 160 pts (Des Furn)
	Robert Gordon – 160–180 pts (3D Des (Ceram Gls Jewel))
	Swansea Met – 160–360 pts (Archit Gls)

For a quick reference offers calculator, fold out the inside back cover.

100 pts and below or other selection criteria (Foundation course, interview and portfolio inspection)

Bournemouth and Poole (Coll) – one year top-up degree check with School (3D Comp Gen Img BSc (Hons))

Anglia Ruskin; Arts London; Arts London (Camberwell CA); Barking (Coll); Bath Spa; Bedfordshire; Bradford (Coll Univ Centre); Brighton; Bucks New; Central Lancashire; Colchester (Inst); Cornwall (Coll); Creative Arts; Croydon (Coll); Dundee; East London; Edinburgh (CA); Greenwich; Havering (Coll); Hereford (CA); Leeds (CAD); Lincoln; Loughborough; Manchester (Coll); Menai (Coll); Middlesex; NEW (Coll); Northampton; Northbrook (Coll); Northumbria; Nottingham New (Coll); Ravensbourne; Robert Gordon; Staffordshire Reg Fed (SURF); Stockport (Coll); Teesside; Warwickshire (Coll); York St John.

Alternative offers

See **Chapter 7** and **Appendix 1** for grades/UCAS Tariff points information for the International Baccalaureate, Scottish Highers/Advanced Highers, the Welsh Baccalaureate, the Irish Leaving Certificate, the Cambridge Pre-U Diploma, the Advanced Diploma and the Extended Project.

EXAMPLES OF FOUNDATION DEGREES IN THE SUBJECT FIELD

Barking (Coll); Bedfordshire; Bournemouth and Poole (Coll); Bournemouth Arts (UC); Brighton; Cleveland (CAD); Croydon (Coll); Cumbria; East Anglia; East London; Hereford (CA); Hertfordshire; London Met; Manchester (Coll); Newcastle (Coll); Plymouth; Plymouth (CA); South Devon (Coll); South Essex (Coll); Truro (Coll); Writtle (Coll).

CHOOSING YOUR COURSE (SEE ALSO CH. 1)

Some course features

Other courses specialise in ceramics, glassware, jewellery and silversmithing.

Manchester Met Four-year course offers a business option.
Plymouth Opportunity for European study exchange or work placement for 12 weeks in Year 2.
Sheffield Hallam Students work with precious and non-precious metals, mixed media, wood, plastics and paper; opportunities to learn a language.
Staffordshire (Dig Film 3D Animat Tech) Course covers 3D modelling, creating and editing digital video, animation, 2D graphics, post-production work and a year-long project merging filmed footage with 3D objects.
Ulster Live projects undertaken in all three years of course. Furniture Design covers public, contract, domestic and street furniture.
Wolverhampton Seven specialised courses.

Universities and colleges teaching quality See www.qaa.ac.uk; http://unistats.direct.gov.uk.

Top research universities and colleges (RAE 2008) See **Art and Design (General)**.

ADMISSIONS INFORMATION

Number of applicants per place (approx) Arts London (Ceram) 2; Arts London (Camberwell CA) 2, (Ceram) 3, (Jewel) 2; Bath Spa 3; Birmingham City 4, (Jewel) 5; Brighton 3; Creative Arts 4; De Montfort 3; Dundee 5; Manchester Met 5; Middlesex (3D Des) 4, (Jewel) 4; Portsmouth 3; Ravensbourne Total of 110 first-choice applicants.

Advice to applicants and planning the UCAS personal statement Describe your art studies and your experience of different types of materials used. Discuss your special interest in your chosen field. Compare your work with that of professional artists and designers and describe your visits to museums, art galleries, exhibitions etc. Submit a portfolio of recent work to demonstrate drawing skills, visual awareness, creativity and innovation, showing examples of 3D work in photographic or model form. See also **Art and Design (Graphic Design)**.

Selection interviews All institutions will interview and require a portfolio of work.

Interview advice and questions Questions focus on the art work presented in the student's portfolio. See also **Art and Design (General)** and **Chapter 6**.

Reasons for rejection (non-academic) Lack of pride in their work. No ideas. See also **Art and Design (General)**.

AFTER-RESULTS ADVICE
Offers to applicants repeating A-levels Same Brighton, Creative Arts, Dundee, Manchester Met.

GRADUATE DESTINATIONS AND EMPLOYMENT (2007/8 HESA)
See **Art and Design (General)**.

Career note See **Art and Design (General)**.

OTHER DEGREE SUBJECTS FOR CONSIDERATION
Design Technology; see other **Art and Design** tables.

ASIA-PACIFIC STUDIES
(including **East** and **South Asian Studies**; see also **Chinese, Japanese, Languages**)

These courses focus on the study of the cultures and the languages of this region of the world, such as Korean, Sanskrit, Thai, Vietnamese.

Useful websites www.dur.ac.uk/oriental.museum; www.bubl.ac.uk; www.asia-alliance.org; www.bacsuk.org.uk.

NB The points totals shown to the left of the institutions are for ease of reference only. It must not be assumed that Tariff points are always used by institutions or that they can be substituted for an offer in grades. The level of an offer is not necessarily indicative of the quality of a course.

COURSE OFFERS INFORMATION
Subject requirements/preferences GCSE A language subject grade A–C. **AL** A language or a second joint subject may be required.

NB In 2012 universities and colleges will differ in their use of GCE AL/AS unit grade information, A* grades, the Extended Project (EPQ), the Advanced Diploma and the Cambridge Pre-U examination when considering applicants and making offers. An EPQ may be accepted in place of an AS subject. Check websites of universities and colleges for the latest offers information.

Your target offers and examples of courses provided by each institution
380 pts **Cambridge** – A*AA college offers may vary (As Mid E St) (IB 39–42 pts)
360 pts **Oxford** – AAA (Japanese) (IB 38–40 pts)
320 pts **Leeds** – ABB (As Pacif St Chin/Jap) (IB 32 pts HL 15 pts)
　　　　London (SOAS) – ABB (Sansk/Burm/Hindi/Nepali/Thai/Viet/Chin/Jap/Kor courses) (IB 34 pts HL 555)
　　　　Sheffield – ABB (Kor St; E As St; Chin St courses; Jap St)
300 pts **Edinburgh** – BBB (Sansk Gk) (IB 34 pts)
　　　　Leeds – ABC/BBB (Thai SE As St) (IB 32 pts)
200 pts **Central Lancashire** – 200–240 pts (As Pacif St)

Alternative offers
See **Chapter 7** and **Appendix 1** for grades/UCAS Tariff points information for the International Baccalaureate, Scottish Highers/Advanced Highers, the Welsh Baccalaureate, the Irish Leaving Certificate, the Cambridge Pre-U Diploma, the Advanced Diploma and the Extended Project.

CHOOSING YOUR COURSE (SEE ALSO CH. 1)

Some course features

Central Lancashire A sandwich course covering business, politics and Asian languages – Chinese and Japanese.

Leeds (As Pacif St courses) Courses deal mainly with the region's politics, economics and culture. Single Honours, major and Joint courses available.

Manchester Course focuses on religious, social and cultural traditions and issues in South Asia and provides an opportunity to learn a South Asian language.

Universities and colleges teaching quality See www.qaa.ac.uk; http://unistats.direct.gov.uk.

Top research universities and colleges (RAE 2008) London (SOAS); Oxford; Cambridge; Leeds; Manchester; Sheffield.

Examples of sandwich degree courses Central Lancashire.

ADMISSIONS INFORMATION

Number of applicants per place (approx) London (SOAS) 4, (Thai) 2, (Burm) 1.

Advice to applicants and planning the UCAS personal statement Connections with, and visits to, South and South East Asia should be mentioned. You should give some indication of what impressed you and your reasons for wishing to study these subjects. An awareness of the geography, culture and politics of the area also should be shown on the UCAS application. Show your skills in learning a foreign language (if choosing a language course), interest in current affairs of the region, experience of travel and self-discipline.

Selection interviews Yes Cambridge, Manchester, Oxford (Orntl St) 26%.

Interview advice and questions General questions are usually asked that relate to applicants' reasons for choosing degree courses in this subject area and to their background knowledge of the various cultures. See also **Chapter 6**.

GRADUATE DESTINATIONS AND EMPLOYMENT (2007/8 HESA)

Graduates surveyed 40 **Employed** 20 **In further study** 5 **Assumed unemployed** 5

Career note Graduates enter a wide range of careers covering business and administration, retail work, education, transport, finance, community and social services. Work experience during undergraduate years will help students to focus their interests. Many courses have a language bias or are taught jointly with other subjects. Graduates may have opportunities of using their languages in a range of occupations.

OTHER DEGREE SUBJECTS FOR CONSIDERATION

Anthropology; Development Studies; Far Eastern Languages; Geography; History; International Relations; Politics; Social Studies.

ASTRONOMY and ASTROPHYSICS

(including **Planetary Science** and **Space Science**; see also **Geology/Geological Sciences, Physics**)

All Astronomy-related degrees are built on a core of mathematics and physics which, in the first two years, is augmented by an introduction to the theory and practice of astronomy or astrophysics. Astronomy emphasises observational aspects of the science and includes a study of the planetary system whilst Astrophysics tends to pursue the subject from a more theoretical stand-point. Courses often combine Mathematics or Physics with Astronomy.

Useful websites www.ras.org.uk; www.scicentral.com; www.iop.org.

NB The points totals shown to the left of the institutions are for ease of reference only. It must not be assumed that Tariff points are always used by institutions or that they can be substituted for an offer in grades. The level of an offer is not necessarily indicative of the quality of a course.

COURSE OFFERS INFORMATION

Subject requirements/preferences GCSE English and a foreign language may be required by some universities; specified grades may be stipulated for some subjects. **AL** Mathematics and physics usually required.

NB In 2012 universities and colleges will differ in their use of GCE AL/AS unit grade information, A* grades, the Extended Project (EPQ), the Advanced Diploma and the Cambridge Pre-U examination when considering applicants and making offers. An EPQ may be accepted in place of an AS subject. Check websites of universities and colleges for the latest offers information.

Your target offers and examples of courses provided by each institution

380 pts **Cambridge** – A*AA college offers may vary (Nat Sci (Astro)) (IB 38–42 pts HL 776–777)
Manchester – A*AA–AAA (Phys Astro) (IB 37–33 pts)

360 pts **Bristol** – AAA–AAB (Phys Astro) (IB 37–35 pts HL maths phys 6)
Durham – AAA–AAB (Phys Astron) (IB 37 pts HL 6 maths phys)
Leeds – AAA–AAB (Phys Astro MPhys) (IB 33 pts)
Leicester – AAA–ABB (Phys Planet Sci) (IB 34 pts)
Liverpool – AAA–ABB (Astro MPhys) (IB 27 pts HL maths phys 6)
London (King's) – AABe (Phys Astro) (IB 36 pts HL maths phys 5)
London (UCL) – AABe–ABBe (Astro) (IB 34–36 pts)
Nottingham – AAA–AAB (Phys Astron) (IB 34–36 pts HL maths 6 +65)
St Andrews – AAA (Astro) (IB 36 pts)
Surrey – AAA–AAB (Spc Tech Planet Explor MEng)

340 pts **Cardiff** – AAB (Astro MPhys) (IB 32pts)
Edinburgh – AAB (Astro MPhys) (IB 32 pts)
Exeter – AAB–ABB (Phys Astro) (IB 30 pts, IB 34–31 pts)
Lancaster – AAB–AAA 340–360 pts (Phys Astro Spc Sci BSc) (IB 34–36 pts)
Leicester – AAB (Phys Astro MPhys) (IB 32–34 pts)

University of Central Lancashire

Traditional Physics and Astronomy in a Modern University

The University of Central Lancashire (UCLan) in Preston, named top modern university in the north west by the Times, has a long association with the traditional subjects of physics and astronomy; Jeremiah Horrocks first observed the Transit of Venus in 1639 from just outside Preston, and the University's roots date back to 1828. Today we offer flexible accredited degree programmes, enabling students to select the most appropriate subjects for their needs. UCLan's Jeremiah Horrocks Institute (JHI) brings together research staff and students with interests in Solar Physics, Stellar Astrophysics, Extragalactic Astrophysics and Soft Matter Physics.

No less than 85 percent of the astronomy and physics research at UCLan has been judged to be of international standing.

Our degree programmes are based on a common first year - students can then bias their studies towards subjects that interest them, and also adjust the relative amounts of practical, mathematical and theoretical content. Classes are relatively small, so you will find it easy to get to know staff and students. Courses are delivered as a mix of lectures, tutorials, seminars, problem classes, laboratory work, observatory experiments, individual project work and group work. Final year MPhys students undertake a large project and have the opportunity to spend a semester in one of the research groups.

Students may study abroad and are encouraged to participate in exchanges through the ERASMUS programme. Our third year physics groups often include EU students completing their degrees in the UK. Exchanges outside the EU are also allowed.

We offer a range of specialist physics laboratories and our projects laboratory is equipped to study nuclear physics, optics and spectroscopy, image processing, microcomputer interfacing, laser physics and nano-structured soft-matter physics. Astrophysics is taught at the University's Alston Observatory, which overlooks the Ribble Valley. The Observatory has recently been re-equipped with a digital planetarium, and has a mix of ancient and modern telescopes. The spectacular Wilfred Hall 15-inch astrographic refractor (WHT) built by Grubb in the 1890s is on loan from the RAS. The Multiple Aperture Telescope has one of the largest total apertures available in the UK.

The JHI collaborates with NASA on the Solar Dynamics Observatory project, leads the UK involvement in the Southern African Large Telescope, is a founding partner of the Commonwealth Cosmology Initiative, is a member of the European Space Infrared telescope for Cosmology and Astrophysics Instrument consortium, is a partner in the Radial Velocity Experiment and is a co-investigator of the Herschel Astrophysical Terahertz Large Area Survey. The condensed matter group focuses on new technological areas - nano-structured soft materials and biologically inspired materials, which will lead to the design of materials of the future.

At UCLan, the teaching of cutting-edge concepts and their recent applications, together with transferable skills, will equip you for success in your future employment or research ambitions.

www.uclan.ac.uk/ceps

London (RH) – AAB (Astrophysics) (IB 34 pts HL maths phys 6–7)
Queen's Belfast – AAB (Phys Astro MSci)
Southampton – AAB (Phys Spc Sci) (IB 36–34 pts)
Sussex – AAB–BBB (Astro) (IB 32–36 pts)
York – AAB (Phys Astro MPhys) (IB 34 pts)
320 pts **Birmingham** – AAA–ABB (Phys Astron) (IB 32–36 pts)
Edinburgh – ABB (Astro BSc)
Glasgow – ABB (Astron) (IB 32 pts)
Liverpool – ABB–BBB (Phys Astron) (IB 26 pts)
London (QM) – 320 pts (Astro MSci) (IB 34 pts HL maths phys 6)
Loughborough – ABB (Cosmo Phys)
Sheffield – ABB–BBB (Maths Astron) (IB 32–33 pts)
Surrey – ABB (Spc Tech Planet Explor BEng) (IB 28 pts)
York – ABB (Phys Astro BSc)
300 pts **Cardiff** – 300 pts (Phys Astron BSc) (IB 28 pts)
Keele – 300–320 pts (Astro)
Kent – 300 pts (Astron Spc Sci Astro) (IB 33 pts)
Liverpool John Moores – BBB (Phys Astron) (IB 24–28 pts)
London (QM) – 300 pts (Astro BSc) (IB 32 pts HL maths phys 6)
Salford – 300 pts (Phys Spc Tech MPhys)
280 pts **Aberystwyth** – 280 pts (Spc Sci Robot) (IB 27 pts)
Central Lancashire – 280–320 pts (Astro)
Hertfordshire – 280 pts (Astro) (IB 24 pts)
Queen's Belfast – BBC (Phys Astro BSc)
260 pts **Salford** – 260 pts (Phys Spc Tech BSc) (IB 27 pts)
240 pts **Aberystwyth** – 240–280 pts (Phys Planet Spc Phys) (IB 29 pts)
Hull – 240–300 pts (Phys Astro)
200 pts **Glamorgan** – 200 pts (Astron)
120 pts **Sussex** – DD (Phys Astron inc Fdn Yr 4 yr)

Liverpool John Moores – Check with university (Astro MPhys)

Alternative offers
See **Chapter 7** and **Appendix 1** for grades/UCAS Tariff points information for the International Baccalaureate, Scottish Highers/Advanced Highers, the Welsh Baccalaureate, the Irish Leaving Certificate, the Cambridge Pre-U Diploma, the Advanced Diploma and the Extended Project.

CHOOSING YOUR COURSE (SEE ALSO CH. 1)
Some course features
Aberystwyth New Astrophysics course designed for students with a general interest in astronomy; it includes core physics modules and broader modules in cosmology and galactic astronomy; progression possible to MPhys degree.
Glamorgan Course provides practical experience of observational astronomy and training in astrophysical techniques, with an astronomy field school in the Algarve.
Kent Course includes involvment in space missions and work on Hubble Telescope data and an exchange programme in Year 3 in the USA.
London (QM) Astronomy and Astrophysics programmes are similar and transfer is possible up to the final year.
Surrey (Spc Tech Planet Explor) Courses include hands-on spacecraft engineering, have a strong international focus with close ties with space industries and European Space Agency; opportunities for a professional training year. Surrey is the only university building complete satellites.

Universities and colleges teaching quality www.qaa.ac.uk; http://unistats.direct.gov.uk.

Top research universities and colleges (RAE 2008) See **Physics**.

Examples of sandwich degree courses Hertfordshire; Kingston; Nottingham Trent; Surrey.

ADMISSIONS INFORMATION

Number of applicants per place (approx) Bristol 8; Cardiff 6; Durham 3; Hertfordshire 5; Leicester 12; London (QM) 6; London (RH) 6; London (UCL) 5; Newcastle 7; Southampton 6.

Advice to applicants and planning the UCAS personal statement Books and magazines you have read on astronomy and astrophysics are an obvious source of information. Describe your interests and why you have chosen this subject. Visits to observatories would also be important. (See also **Appendix 4**.) **York** Advanced Diploma not generally accepted.

Misconceptions about this course Career opportunities are not as limited as some students think. These courses involve an extensive study of maths and physics, opening many opportunities for graduates such as geodesy, rocket and satellite studies and engineering specialisms.

Selection interviews Yes Bristol, Cambridge, London (UCL), Newcastle; **Some** Cardiff.

Interview advice and questions You will probably be questioned on your study of physics and the aspects of the subject you most enjoy. Questions in the past have included: Can you name a recent development in physics which will be important in the future? Describe a physics experiment, indicating any errors and exactly what it was intended to prove. Explain weightlessness. What is a black hole? What are the latest discoveries in space? See also **Chapter 6**. **Southampton** Entrance examination for year abroad courses.

AFTER-RESULTS ADVICE

Offers to applicants repeating A-levels Higher St Andrews; **Same** Cardiff, Durham, London (UCL), Newcastle.

GRADUATE DESTINATIONS AND EMPLOYMENT (2007/8 HESA)
Graduates surveyed 180 **Employed** 40 **In further study** 75 **Assumed unemployed** 25

Career note The number of posts for professional astronomers is limited although some technological posts are occasionally offered in observatories. However, degree courses include extensive mathematics and physics so many graduates can look towards related fields including telecommunications and electronics.

OTHER DEGREE SUBJECTS FOR CONSIDERATION
Aeronautical/Aerospace Engineering; Computer Science; Earth Sciences; Geology; Geophysics; Mathematics; Meteorology; Mineral Sciences; Oceanography; Physics.

BIOCHEMISTRY

(see also **Biological Sciences, Chemistry, Food Science/Studies and Technology, Pharmacy and Pharmaceutical Sciences**)

Biochemistry is the study of life processes at molecular level. Most courses are extremely flexible and have common first years. Modules could include genetics, immunology, blood biochemistry, physiology and biotechnology. The option to choose other courses in the subject field features at many universities. Many courses allow for a placement in industry in the UK or in Europe or North America.

Useful websites www.biochemistry.org; www.scienceyear.com; www.bioworld.com; www.arjournals.annualreviews.org; see also **Biological Sciences** and **Biology**.

NB The points totals shown to the left of the institutions are for ease of reference only. It must not be assumed that Tariff points are always used by institutions or that they can be substituted for an offer in grades. The level of an offer is not necessarily indicative of the quality of a course.

COURSE OFFERS INFORMATION

Subject requirements/preferences GCSE English, mathematics and science usually required; leading universities often stipulate A–B grades. **AL** Chemistry required and biology usually preferred; one or two mathematics/science subjects required.

NB In 2012 universities and colleges will differ in their use of GCE AL/AS unit grade information, A* grades, the Extended Project (EPQ), the Advanced Diploma and the Cambridge Pre-U examination when considering applicants and making offers. An EPQ may be accepted in place of an AS subject. Check websites of universities and colleges for the latest offers information.

Your target offers and examples of courses provided by each institution

380 pts **Cambridge** – A*AA College offers may vary (Nat Sci (Biochem)) (IB 38–42 pts HL 766–777)
360 pts **Aston** – AAA-AAB (Biol Chem)
    Bristol – AAA-ABB (Bioch Mol Biol Biotech) (IB 35 pts)
    East Anglia – AAA-AAB (Bioch Aus/N Am) (IB 33–34 pts HL 666)
    Edinburgh – Check with Ad tutor AAA-ABB 360-320 pts (Biochem) (IB 37-32 pts)
    London (UCL) – AAA+AS-AAB+AS (Bioch) (IB 36-38 pts)
    Oxford – AAA (Mol Cell Bioch) (IB 39 pts)
340 pts **Bath** – AAB (Bioch Eng MEng) (IB 34 pts HL chem 6)
    Birmingham – AAB-BBB (Bioch) (IB 32–34 pts)
    Cardiff – AAB-ABB 340-320 pts (Biochemistry) (IB 34 pts)
    Exeter – AAB-BBB (Biochem) (IB 34–29 pts)
    Imperial London – AAB (Bioch Yr Ind) (IB 38 pts)
    Leeds – AAB-BBB (Med Bioch) (IB 36-32 pts HL 15-17 pts)
    London (King's) – ABB+AS (Bioch) (IB 34 pts HL chem 5)
    Manchester – AAB-BBB (Med Bioch) (IB 32–35 pts)
    Nottingham – AAB-BBB (Bioch Mol Med) (IB 32–34 pts)
    St Andrews – AAB (Bioch) (IB 32 pts)
    Sheffield – AAB-ABB (Med Bioch) (IB 33 pts)
320 pts **Aberdeen** – ABB 2nd yr entry (Bioch Biobus) (IB 28 pts)
    Bath – ABB (Bioch) (IB 34 pts HL chem 6)
    Birmingham – ABB-BBBb (Bioch Biotech; Med Bioch)
    Dundee – ABB 2nd year entry (Bioch Physiol Sci) (IB 34 pts)
    Durham – AAB-ABB (Mol Biol Bioch) (IB 34 pts)
    East Anglia – ABB-BBB (Bioch Euro) (IB 31-32 pts HL 555)
    Glasgow – ABB (Med Bioch) (IB 32 pts)
    Heriot-Watt – ABB 2nd yr entry (Chem Bioch)
    Lancaster – ABB (Biomed Genet)
    Leicester – ABB-BBB (Med Bioch) (IB 32-34 pts)
    Liverpool – ABB-BBB (Bioch Yr Ind/Rsch) (IB 33-30 pts)
    London (RH) – ABB (Med Bioch) (IB 34 pts)
    Newcastle – ABB (Bioch) (IB 32-35 pts HL biol chem 6)
    Nottingham – ABB-BBB (Neuro Bioch) (IB 32 pts)
    Reading – 320 pts (Bioch) (IB 30 pts)
    Southampton – ABB-BBB (Bioch) (IB 32 pts)
    Surrey – ABB-BBB (Bioch (Med) (Neuro) (Pharmacol) (Tox)) (IB 34-32 pts)
    Sussex – ABB-BBB 320-300 pts (Biochem) (IB 34 pts)
    Warwick – ABB-BBB (Bioch) (IB 32-34 pts)
    York – ABB (Bioch Yr Euro) (IB 32 pts)
300 pts **Aberdeen** – BBB 1st year entry (Bioch)
    Aberystwyth – (Bioch (Genet Bioch)) (IB 26 pts HL chem 5)
    Heriot-Watt – BBB 1st yr entry (Chem Bioch; Brew Distil)
    Keele – inc BC (Bioch courses) (IB 26-28 pts)
    Lancaster – BBB (Bioch Genet) (IB 29 pts)
    London (QM) – 300 pts (Bioch) (IB 28-32 pts)
    Nottingham – BBB-BBC (Nutr Biochem) (IB 28-32 pts)
    Queen's Belfast – BBB (Biochem) (IB 28 pts HL 555)
    Strathclyde – BBB (Nat Sci) (IB 28 pts)
    Swansea – ABB 300-320 pts (Bioch)

280 pts **Brunel** – BBC (Biomed Sci (Bioch)) (IB 30 pts HL 5 biol)
Essex – 280–240 pts (Biochem) (IB 30–26 pts)
Kent – BBC–BBB (Bioch Euro) (IB 31–33 pts HL 14–15 pts)
Strathclyde – BBC (Bioch Pharmacol)
Swansea – 280 pts (Med Bioch)
260 pts **Bradford** – 260 pts (Med Bioch)
Dundee – BCC 1st year entry (Bioch Physiol Sci) (IB 30 pts)
Liverpool John Moores – 260–300 pts (Bioch; Bioch Foren Sci)
Nottingham Trent – 260 pts (Bioch)
Portsmouth – 260 pts (Bioch Gnm Sci)
Sheffield Hallam – 260 pts (Bioch)
Staffordshire – 260 pts (Bioch Microbiol) (IB 28 pts)
Strathclyde – BCC (Bioch Immun; Bioch Microbiol)
240 pts **Aberdeen** – 240 pts (Bioch (Immun))
Dundee – BCC 1st yr entry (Bioch) (IB 30 pts)
Hertfordshire – 240 pts (Bioch; Bioch Euro)
Huddersfield – 240 pts (Bioch; Med Bioch)
Liverpool John Moores – (Med Bioch)
London Met – 240 pts (Biochem)
Salford – 240 pts (Bioch USA) (IB 34 pts)
220 pts **Westminster** – CCD (Bioch) (IB 26 pts)
200 pts **East London** – 200 pts (Biochem)
Kingston – 200 pts (Bioch; Med Bioch)
Lancaster – 200-280 pts (Bioch)
London South Bank – 200 pts (Bioch)
Wolverhampton – 200–260 pts (Biochem)
160 pts **Sussex** – CC (Biosci inc Fdn Yr) (IB 28 pts)
140 pts **West Scotland** – CD (App Bioch)
80 pts **London (Birk)** – for under 21s (over 21s varies) p/t (Bioch Sci)

Alternative offers
See **Chapter 7** and **Appendix 1** for grades/UCAS Tariff points information for the International Baccalaureate, Scottish Highers/Advanced Highers, the Welsh Baccalaureate, the Irish Leaving Certificate, the Cambridge Pre-U Diploma, the Advanced Diploma and the Extended Project.

EXAMPLES OF FOUNDATION DEGREES IN THE SUBJECT FIELD
Truro (Coll).

CHOOSING YOUR COURSE (SEE ALSO CH. 1)
Some course features
Birmingham (Bioch) A range of Biochemistry programmes offers specialisation in several fields.
Bristol (Bioch) A choice to include a period of industrial placement is made in Year 2 from any one of the Biochemistry courses.
East Anglia (Bioch) Options to study for a year in Australia, Europe or North America.
Imperial London Biochemistry and Biotechnology students follow a similar programme with specialisations in Year 3.
Lancaster (Bioch) Option to study one other non-scientific subject in Year 1.
Leeds Biochemistry and the course with Molecular Biology have a common first year, with the choice of degree made in Year 2.
Sussex (Bioch) Option to study French, German or Spanish.
Wolverhampton (Bioch) Joint courses and an optional year's placement are offered.

Universities and colleges teaching quality See www.qaa.ac.uk; http://unistats.direct.gov.uk.

Top research universities and colleges (RAE 2008) See **Biological Sciences**.

Examples of sandwich degree courses Bath; Bristol; Bristol UWE; Brunel; Cardiff; East London; Essex; Hertfordshire; Huddersfield; Kent; Kingston; Leeds; Liverpool John Moores; London South Bank; Manchester; Nottingham Trent; Salford; Sheffield Hallam; Surrey; Sussex; West Scotland; Wolverhampton; York.

ADMISSIONS INFORMATION

Number of applicants per place (approx) Aberystwyth 5; Bath 7; Birmingham 5; Bradford 7; Bristol 10; Cardiff 6; Dundee 6; Durham 6; East Anglia 10; East London 5; Edinburgh 8; Essex 5; Imperial London 6; Keele 7; Leeds 10; Leicester (Med Bioch) 5; London (RH) 8; London (UCL) 8; Newcastle 7; Nottingham 14; Salford 4; Southampton 8; Staffordshire 6; Strathclyde 7; Surrey 3; Warwick 6; York 6.

Advice to applicants and planning the UCAS personal statement It is important to show by reading scientific journals that you have interests in chemistry and biology beyond the exam syllabus. Focus on one or two aspects of biochemistry that interest you. Attend scientific lectures (often arranged by universities on open days), find some work experience if possible, and use these to show your understanding of what biochemistry is. Give evidence of your communication skills and time management (see **Appendix 4**). **Oxford** No written or work tests; successful entrants 42.7%. Further information may be obtained from the Institute of Biology and the Royal Society of Chemistry.

Misconceptions about this course York Students feel that being taught by two departments could be a problem but actually it increases their options.

Selection interviews Yes Birmingham (Clearing only), Bradford, Brunel, Cambridge, East London, Keele (mature students only), Kingston, Leeds, London (RH), London (UCL), London South Bank, Oxford (38%), Portsmouth (mature students only), Surrey, Warwick; **Some** Aberystwyth (mature students only), Bath, Cardiff, East Anglia, Liverpool John Moores, Salford, Sheffield, Staffordshire, Wolverhampton.

Interview advice and questions Questions will be asked on your study of chemistry and biology and any special interests. They will also probe your understanding of what a course in Biochemistry involves and the special features offered by the university. In the past questions have been asked covering Mendel, genetics, RNA and DNA. See also **Chapter 6**. **Liverpool John Moores** Informal interviews. It would be useful to bring samples of coursework to the interview.

Reasons for rejection (non-academic) Borderline grades plus poor motivation. Failure to turn up for interviews or answer correspondence. Inability to discuss subject. Not compatible with A-level predictions or references. **Birmingham** Lack of total commitment to Biochemistry, for example intention to transfer to Medicine without completing the course.

AFTER-RESULTS ADVICE

Offers to applicants repeating A-levels Higher East Anglia, Leeds, Leicester, Nottingham, St Andrews, Strathclyde, Surrey, Warwick; **Possibly higher** Bath, Bristol, Brunel, Keele, Kent, Lancaster, Newcastle; **Same** Aberystwyth, Birmingham, Bradford, Cardiff, Dundee, Durham, Heriot-Watt, Hull, Liverpool, Liverpool John Moores, London (RH), London (UCL), Salford, Sheffield, Staffordshire, Wolverhampton, York.

GRADUATE DESTINATIONS AND EMPLOYMENT (2007/8 HESA)

Including Biophysics and Molecular Biology

Graduates surveyed 1315 **Employed** 380 **In further study** 525 **Assumed unemployed** 150

Career note Biochemistry courses involve several specialities which offer a range of job opportunities. These include the application of biochemistry in industrial, medical and clinical areas with additional openings in pharmaceuticals and agricultural work, environmental science and in toxicology.

OTHER DEGREE SUBJECTS FOR CONSIDERATION

Agricultural Sciences; Agriculture; Biological Sciences; Biology; Biotechnology; Botany; Brewing; Chemistry; Food Science; Genetics; Medical Sciences; Medicine; Microbiology; Neuroscience; Nursing; Nutrition; Pharmaceutical Sciences; Pharmacology; Pharmacy; Plant Science.

BIOLOGICAL SCIENCES

(including **Biomedical Science, Ecology, Forensic Science, Immunology, Neurosciences** and **Virology**; see also **Anatomical Science/Anatomy, Animal Sciences, Biochemistry, Biology, Biotechnology, Environmental Sciences/Studies, Genetics, Medicine, Microbiology, Natural Sciences, Nursing and Midwifery, Pharmacology, Plant Sciences, Psychology, Zoology**)

Biological Science (in some universities referred to as Biosciences) is a fast-moving, rapidly expanding and wide subject area, ranging from, for example, conservation biology to molecular genetics. Boundaries between separate subjects are blurring and this is reflected in the content and variety of the courses offered. Many universities offer a common first year allowing final decisions to be made later in the course. Since most subjects are research-based, students undertake their own projects in the final year.

Useful websites http://bsi. immunology.org; www.ibms.org; www.scienceyear.com; www.scicentral. com; www.forensic.gov.uk; www.bbsrc.ac.uk; see also **Biochemistry** and **Biology**.

NB The points totals shown to the left of the institutions are for ease of reference only. It must not be assumed that Tariff points are always used by institutions or that they can be substituted for an offer in grades. The level of an offer is not necessarily indicative of the quality of a course.

COURSE OFFERS INFORMATION

Subject requirements/preferences GCSE English, mathematics and science usually required. Grades AB often stipulated by popular universities. **AL** Chemistry required plus one or two other mathematics/science subjects, biology preferred. (Ecology) Biology and one other science subject may be required or preferred. (Neuroscience) Mathematics/science subjects with chemistry and/or biology required or preferred. **London (St George's)** (Biol Inform) Computer science, mathematics and/or science advantageous.

NB In 2012 universities and colleges will differ in their use of GCE AL/AS unit grade information, A* grades, the Extended Project (EPQ), the Advanced Diploma and the Cambridge Pre-U examination when considering applicants and making offers. An EPQ may be accepted in place of an AS subject. Check websites of universities and colleges for the latest offers information.

Your target offers and examples of courses provided by each institution
410 pts **Imperial London** – AAAb (Biomed Sci)
380 pts **Cambridge** – A*AAcollege offers may vary (Educ Biol Sci) (IB 38–42 pts)
 Edinburgh – A*AA 2nd yr entry (Immun) (IB 38 pts)
 London (UCL) – AAAe–AABe (Biomed Sci) (IB 36–38 pts)
360 pts **East Anglia** – AAA–AAB (Ecol N Am/Aus) (IB 33–34 pts)
 Edinburgh – AAA–ABB (Ecol) (IB 37–32 pts)
 Leeds – AAA–BBB (Hum Physiol) (IB 32 pts)
 London (UCL) – AAA–AAB (Neuro) (IB 36–38 pts)
 Oxford – AAA (Biol Sci) (IB 38–42 pts)
340 pts **Birmingham** – AAB–BBB (Med Sci) (IB 32–34 pts)
 Cardiff – AAB–ABB (Biomed Sci; Biomed Sci (Anat) (Neuro) (Physiol); Ecol)
 Exeter – AAB–BBB (Biol Sci; Hum Biosci) (IB 34–29 pts)
 Heriot-Watt – AAB 2nd yr entry (Biol Sci)
 Imperial London – AAB (Ecol Env Biol) (IB 38 pts)
 Lancaster – AAB 340 pts (Ecol Abrd)
 Leeds – AAB (Neuro) (IB 35 pts)
 Leicester – AAB (Biol Sci MBiol) (IB 34 pts)
 London (King's) – ABB+AS (Neuro) (IB 34 pts)
 Manchester – AAB–ABC (Biomed Mat Sci courses) (IB 32 pts)
 Newcastle – AAB (Biomed Sci) (IB 34 pts)
 St Andrews – AAB–ABB (Mol Biol; Ecol Cons)

Sheffield – AAB–ABB (Biomed Sci) (IB 33 pts)
Sussex – AAB–ABB (Med Neuro) (IB 32–36 pts)

320 pts **Aberdeen** – ABB 2nd yr entry (Biol)
Aston – ABB–BBB (Biomed Sci) (IB 33 pts)
Bournemouth – 320 pts (Foren Sci)
Bristol – ABB (Virol Immun) (IB 33–30 pts HL 665)
Bristol UWE – 320–280 pts (Biomed courses; Foren Sci)
Dundee – ABB 2nd yr entry (Bio Chem Drug Dscvry) (IB 34 pts)
Durham – AAB–ABB (Ecol) (IB 28 pts)
East Anglia – ABB–BBB (Biomed) (IB 31–32 pts)
Edinburgh – Check with Ad Tutor ABB–AAA 1st yr entry (Ecol Sci) (IB 32–37 pts)
Glasgow – ABB (Neuro) (IB 32 pts)
Lancaster – ABB (Ecol) (IB 30 pts)
Leeds – ABB–BBB (Ecol) (IB 32 pts)
Leicester – ABB–BBB (Biol Sci (Genet) (Microbiol) (Physiol Pharmacol)) (IB 32–34 pts)
Liverpool – ABB–BBB (Lf Sci App Med) (IB 33–30 pts HL 6/5 biol chem)
London (RH) – AAB–BBB (Ecol Env) (IB 34 pts)
Newcastle – ABB (Biomed Sci + Med Microbiol) (IB 32 pts)
Nottingham – ABB–BBB (Neuro Pharmacol) (IB 32 pts)
Queen's Belfast – ABB/BBBb (Biomed Sci)
Reading – 320 pts (Biomed Sci) (IB 30–32 pts)
Southampton – ABB–BBB (Biomed Sci) (IB 32 pts)
Stirling – ABB 2nd yr entry (Ecol; Aquacult)
Surrey – check with University 320–340 pts (Vet Biosci) (IB 34–32 pts)
Sussex – AAB–ABB (Biomed Sci) (IB 32–36 pts)
Swansea – ABB (Biol Sci Joint Hons) (IB 32–34 pts)
Warwick – ABB (Biol Sci) (IB 34 pts)
York – ABB (Ecol Cons Env) (IB 32 pts)

300 pts **Aberdeen** – BBB 1st yr entry (Biol)
Abertay Dundee – BBB 2nd yr entry (Foren Sci)
Aston – BBC–BBB (Infec Immun) (IB 30 pts)
Birmingham – BBB (Biomed Mat Sci) (IB 30 pts)
Bradford – optional transfer for some to Medicine at Leeds 300 pts (Clin Sci)
Dundee – BCC 1st yr entry (Biol Chem Drug Dscvry) (IB 30 pts)
Essex – 300–260 pts inc BB–CC with Biol (Biol Sci 3yr) (IB 32–28 pts)
Heriot-Watt – BBB (Biol Sci (Fd Sci))
Keele – inc BC (Biomed Sci; Neuro)
Kent – 300 pts (Biol Anth) (IB 31 pts)
Lancaster – ABB–BBB (Biomed Sci) (IB 30 pts)
Liverpool – BBB (inc biol+sci) (Biovet Sci) (IB 32 pts)
London (QM) – 300–320 pts (Biomed Sci) (IB 28–32 pts)
London (RVC) – BBB (Biovet Sci)
London (St George's) – BBB (Biomed Sci) (IB 28 pts)
London Met – 300 pts (Biomed Sci)
Northumbria – 300 pts (Foren Sci; Biomed Sci)
Queen's Belfast – BBB–BBC (Biol Sci)
Sussex – BBB–BBC (Mol Genet)

280 pts **Aberystwyth** – BBB (Biol Sci) (IB 24–26 pts)
Bangor – (Biomed Sci)
Brighton – 280 pts (Ecol Biogeog)
Bristol UWE – 280–320 pts (Biol Sci)
Brunel – BBC (Biomed Sci (Immun)) (IB 30 pts HL 5 biol)
Essex – 280 pts (Biomed Sci) (IB 28–26 pts)
Glamorgan – 280 pts (Foren Sci)
Kent – BBC–BBB (Biomed Sci) (IB 31–34 pts HL 14–15 pts)

Leeds Trinity (UC) – 280 pts (Foren Psy)
Lincoln – (inc biol) 280 pts (Biovet Sci)
Middlesex – 280 pts (Biomed Sci)
Nottingham Trent – 280 pts (Biomed Sci)
Oxford Brookes – BBC (Biol Sci) (IB 30 pts)
Plymouth – 280 pts (Biol Sci) (IB 26 pts)
Stirling – BBC 1st yr entry (Ecol; Aqua)
Strathclyde – BBC (Foren Biol) (IB 26 pts)
Swansea – 280 pts (Med Sci Hum) (IB 30 pts)
Teesside – 280 pts (Foren Biol)
Ulster – 280 pts (Biomed Sci)

260 pts Bangor – 260–320 pts (Ecol) (IB 28 pts)
Bradford – 260–280 pts (Bioarch) (IB 28 pts)
Brighton – BCC (Biol Sci) (IB 28 pts)
Bristol UWE – 260–300 pts (App Biomed Sci)
Cardiff (UWIC) – 260 pts (Biomed Sci)
Central Lancashire – (Foren Sci)
Dundee – BCC 1st year entry (Neuro) (IB 30 pts)
Hull – 260–300 pts (Biomed Sci; Foren Sci Crimin)
Keele – 260–300 pts (Foren Sci) (IB 26–28 pts)
Liverpool John Moores – 260–300 pts (Biomed Sci; Foren Sci)
Nottingham Trent – 260 pts (Foren Biol)
Portsmouth – 260 pts (Biomed Sci; App Biomed Sci)
Sheffield Hallam – 260 pts (Biomed Sci BSc)
Staffordshire – 260 pts (Foren Biol) (IB 28 pts)

245 pts Abertay Dundee – CCC 245 pts (Biomed Sci)

240 pts Aberdeen – CCC 240 pts 1st yr entry (Ecol) (IB 28 pts)
Cardiff (UWIC) – 240 pts (Spo Biomed Nutr)
Coventry – 240 pts (Biomed Sci; Biol Foren Sci)
De Montfort – 240 pts (Biomed Sci) (IB 28 pts)
Greenwich – 240–300 pts (Biomed Sci)
Hertfordshire – 240 pts (Biomed Sci)
Huddersfield – 240 pts (Foren Analyt Sci)
Lincoln – 240 pts (Foren Sci)
London Met – 240 pts (Biol Sci)
Manchester Met – 240 pts (Biomed Sci Foren Biol) (IB 27 pts)
Nescot – CCC (App Biol Sci)
Nottingham Trent – 240 pts (Biol Sci)
Portsmouth – 240–280 pts (Foren Biol)
Robert Gordon – CCC (Foren Sci)
Roehampton – 240–300 pts (Biol Sci; Biomed Sci)
Wolverhampton – 240 pts (Biomed Sci)

220 pts Abertay Dundee – CCD 1st yr entry (Foren Sci)
Edinburgh Napier – 220 pts (Biol Sci)
Hull – 220–280 pts (Ecol)
Lincoln – 220 pts (Biomed Sci)
Manchester Met – 220 pts (Foren Sci) (IB 26 pts)
Middlesex – 220–280 pts (Spo Biomed)
Sheffield Hallam – 220 pts (Foren Biosci)
Sunderland – 220 pts (Biomed Sci)
Westminster – CC minimum (Biomed Sci) (IB 26 pts)
Worcester – 220–240 pts (Ecol) (IB 26 pts)

200 pts Anglia Ruskin – (Foren Sci; App Biomed Sci; Biomed Sci; Ecol Cons)
Bedfordshire – 200 pts (Biomed Sci; Med Sci; Foren Sci)
Canterbury Christ Church – 200 pts (Biosci courses; Foren Sci)

Central Lancashire – 200–240 pts (Foren Biol)
Chester – 200 pts (Biomed Sci) (IB 30 pts)
Derby – 200 pts (Foren Sci)
East London – 200 pts (Biomed Sci; Foren Sci)
Edinburgh Napier – 200 pts (Biomed Sci)
Glyndŵr – 200 pts (Foren Sci; Foren Sci Crim Just)
Kingston – 200 pts (Biomed Sci)
London South Bank – 200 pts (App Sci)
Salford – 200 pts (Biomed Sci) (IB 24 pts)
West London – 200 pts (Foren Sci)
Wolverhampton – 200 pts (Foren Sci; Foren Mol Biol)

180 pts **De Montfort** – 180 pts (Foren Sci) (IB 24 pts)
Glasgow Caledonian – DDD (Foren Invstg; Cell Mol Biol; Biomed Sci)
Sunderland – 180 pts (Foren Pharml Sci)

160 pts **Abertay Dundee** – CC (Foren Psychobiol)
Essex – 160 pts inc DD (Biol Sci 4yr) (IB 24 pts)
Leeds Met – 160 pts (Biomed Sci courses)
London South Bank – 160 pts (Foren Sci)
Robert Gordon – CC (App Biomed Sci) (IB 24 pts)
SAC (Scottish CAg) – CC (App Biosci)

140 pts **West Scotland** – CD (Foren Sci)

80 pts **East London** – 80 pts (Extd Hlth Biosci)
Glasgow Caledonian – EE (Biol Sci)
London (Birk) – for under 21s (over 21 varies) p/t (Biol Sci Biomed)

Alternative offers
See **Chapter 7** and **Appendix 1** for grades/UCAS Tariff points information for the International Baccalaureate, Scottish Highers/Advanced Highers, the Welsh Baccalaureate, the Irish Leaving Certificate, the Cambridge Pre-U Diploma, the Advanced Diploma and the Extended Project.

EXAMPLES OF FOUNDATION DEGREES IN THE SUBJECT FIELD
Aston; Brighton; Bristol UWE; Cornwall (Coll); Glyndŵr; Hertfordshire; Hull (Coll); Kent; London (QM); Myerscough (Coll); Nescot; Nottingham Trent; Petroc; Plymouth; Plymouth City (Coll); Preston (Coll); Riverside Halton (Coll); Sheffield (Coll); Staffordshire; Truro (Coll); West London; Weymouth (Coll); Wigan and Leigh (Coll); Worcester; Writtle (Coll); York (Coll).

CHOOSING YOUR COURSE (SEE ALSO CH. 1)
Some course features
Brighton (Biol Sci) A sandwich placement in Year 3 is optional. Specialist fields include animal sciences, ecology, forestry and countryside management.
Bristol (Immun) One of eight Cellular and Molecular Medicine courses, with flexibility to transfer between programmes as students' scientific interests develop. All have option for a year in industry.
Lancaster (Biol Sci) Opportunity to mix and match subjects such as genetics, biomedicine, land environment and ecology.
Leeds (Biol Sci) Students may transfer to any other course in the Faculty in Year 2.
Leicester The Biological Sciences programme offers specialist options in biochemistry, genetics, microbiology, physiology with pharmacology or zoology. All courses have a common first year with specialist decisions made in year 2.
Liverpool (Biol Sci) A broad programme, with option in first two years to specialise by transferring to any one of a range of courses in the subject field, eg Ecology, Genetics, Molecular Biology.
Warwick (Biol Sci) Specialisations in genetics, microbiology, cell biology, virology and environmental resources.
Westminster (Biol Sci) Students plan their programme with tutors through the course, combining core subjects (eg cell science, physiology) with option modules from a wide range of bioscience modules.

Universities and colleges teaching quality See www.qaa.ac.uk; http://unistats.direct.gov.uk.

Top research universities and colleges (RAE 2008) Oxford (Biochemistry); Manchester; Sheffield; Dundee; Bristol (Biochemistry); London (RH); York; Imperial London; London (King's); Leeds; Cambridge; Edinburgh.

Examples of sandwich degree courses see also **Biology**. Brighton; Bristol UWE.

ADMISSIONS INFORMATION

Number of applicants per place (approx) Aston (Biomed Sci) 8; Bristol 8, (Neuro) 10; Cardiff 8; Durham 11; East Anglia (Biol Sci) 15; Edinburgh 8; Essex 8; Lancaster (Biol Sci) 12; Leeds (Med Sci) 25; Leicester 10; London (King's) 7; London (QM) 8; London (St George's) 15; Newcastle 14; Nottingham 11; Southampton 8; Stirling 7; York 9.

Advice to applicants and planning the UCAS personal statement Read scientific journals and try to extend your knowledge beyond the A-level syllabus. Discuss your special interests, for example, ecology, microbiology, genetics or zoology (read up thoroughly on your interests since questions could be asked at interview). Voluntary attendance on courses, work experience, voluntary work, holiday jobs. Demonstrate good oral and written communication skills and be competent at handling numerical data. Interest in the law for Forensic Science courses. See **Appendix 4**.

Misconceptions about this course **Anglia Ruskin** (Foren Sci) Students are not aware that modules in management and quality assurance are taken as part of the course. **Birmingham** We offer a range of degree labels each with different UCAS codes, for example Biol Sci Genet, Biol Sci Microbiol: all have the same first year and students can freely transfer between them. It is not necessary to apply for more than one except Biol Sci Euro. (Med Sci) Applicants often use this course as an insurance for a vocational course (usually Medicine). If they are unsuccessful for their first choice, they occasionally find it difficult to commit themselves to Medical Sciences and do not perform as well as their academic performance would predict. **Cardiff** Some students mistakenly believe that they can transfer to Medicine. **De Montfort** (Foren Sci) Students are often unaware of how much of the work is analytical biology and chemistry: they think they spend their time visiting crime scenes. **London (St George's)** It is not possible to transfer to Medicine after the first year of the Biomedical Science course. Students may be able to transfer to Year 3 of the Medical course on completion of the BSc degree. **Swansea** (Med Sci Hum) Some applicants think the course is a form of medical training – it isn't, but it is relevant to anyone planning graduate entry for courses in Medicine or paramedical careers. (Biol Sci deferred entry) Some applicants think that this is a degree in its own right. In fact, after the first year, students have to choose one of the other degrees offered by the School of Biological Sciences. This course allows students an extra year in which to consider their final specialisation.

Selection interviews **Yes** Bangor, Bristol UWE, Durham, Essex, Greenwich, Hull, London (RH), London (UCL), London South Bank, Manchester, Newcastle, Nottingham, Nottingham Trent, Oxford (Biol Sci) 38%, Oxford Brookes, Stirling, Strathclyde, Sunderland, Surrey (Biomed Sci), Sussex, Swansea (Med Sci Hum), Warwick; **Some** Anglia Ruskin, Aston, Birmingham, Bristol, Cardiff, Cardiff (UWIC), De Montfort, Derby, East Anglia, Kent, Liverpool John Moores, London (St George's), Roehampton, Salford, Sheffield, Sheffield Hallam, Staffordshire, Wolverhampton, York.

Interview advice and questions You are likely to be asked about your main interests in biology and your choice of specialisation in the field of biological sciences or, for example, about the role of the botanist, specialist microbiologist in industry, your understanding of biotechnology or genetic engineering. Questions likely to be asked on field courses attended. If you have a field course workbook, take it to interview. See also **Chapter 6**. **London (St George's)** (Biomed Sci) What career path do you envisage for yourself with this degree? **Oxford** No written or work tests. Interviews are rigorous but sympathetic; successful entrants average 38.8%. Applicants are expected to demonstrate their ability to understand whatever facts they have encountered and to discuss a particular aspect of biology in which they are interested (interviews rigorous but sympathetic). What problems does a fish face under water? Are humans still evolving?

Reasons for rejection (non-academic) **Oxford** He appeared to have so much in his head that he tended to express his ideas in too much of a rush. He needs to slow down a bit and take more time to select points that are really pertinent to the questions.

AFTER-RESULTS ADVICE

Offers to applicants repeating A-levels Higher Bristol, Bristol UWE, Glasgow Caledonian, Hull, London (St George's), Newcastle, St Andrews, Sheffield; **Possibly higher** Aston, Essex, Lancaster, Manchester Met; **Same** Abertay Dundee, Aberystwyth, Anglia Ruskin, Birmingham, Birmingham City, Bolton, Cardiff, Cardiff (UWIC), Chester, Chichester, De Montfort, Derby, Durham, East Anglia, East London, Edinburgh Napier, Exeter, Glasgow, Harper Adams (UC), Heriot-Watt, Huddersfield, Kingston, Leeds, Lincoln, Liverpool Hope, Liverpool John Moores, London (RH), Oxford Brookes, Plymouth, Portsmouth, Robert Gordon, Roehampton, Salford, Sheffield Hallam, Stirling, West London, West Scotland, Wolverhampton, Worcester, York.

GRADUATE DESTINATIONS AND EMPLOYMENT (2007/8 HESA)

See also **Biology**.

Forensic Science and Archaeology graduates surveyed 1255 **Employed** 510

Career note Degrees in biological science subjects often lead graduates into medical, pharmaceutical, veterinary, food and environmental work, research and education, in both the public and private sectors (see also **Biology**). Sandwich courses are offered at a number of institutions enabling students to gain paid experience in industry and commerce, often resulting in permanent employment on graduation. In recent years there has been a considerable increase in the number of Biomedical Science courses designed for students interested in taking a hands-on approach to studying the biology of disease. However, students should be warned that the ever-popular Forensic Science courses may not always pave the way to jobs in this highly specialised field.

OTHER DEGREE SUBJECTS FOR CONSIDERATION

Biochemistry; Biology; Biotechnology; Botany; Chemistry; Consumer Sciences; Ecology; Environmental Health; Environmental Science; Genetics; Genomics; Immunology; Microbiology; Pharmaceutical Sciences; Pharmacology; Pharmacy; Physiology; Plant Sciences; Psychology; Sport and Exercise Science; Toxicology; Virology; Zoology.

BIOLOGY

(including **Applied, Cancer, Conservation, Environmental, Forensic, Human, Marine** and **Molecular Biology**; see also **Animal Sciences, Biological Sciences, Biotechnology, Environmental Sciences/Studies, Microbiology, Plant Sciences, Zoology**)

The science of biology is a broad and rapidly developing subject that increasingly affects our lives. Biologists address the challenges faced by human populations such as disease, conservation and food production, and the continuing advances in such areas as genetics and molecular biology that have applications in medicine and agriculture.

Useful websites www.societyofbiology.org; www.scienceyear.com; www.bbsrc.ac.uk; see also **Biochemistry**.

NB The points totals shown to the left of the institutions are for ease of reference only. It must not be assumed that Tariff points are always used by institutions or that they can be substituted for an offer in grades. The level of an offer is not necessarily indicative of the quality of a course.

COURSE OFFERS INFORMATION

Subject requirements/preferences GCSE Mathematics and English stipulated in some cases. **AL** Biology and chemistry important, other science subjects may be accepted. Two and sometimes three mathematics/science subjects required including biology.

NB In 2012 universities and colleges will differ in their use of GCE AL/AS unit grade information, A* grades, the Extended Project (EPQ), the Advanced Diploma and the Cambridge Pre-U examination when considering applicants and making offers. An EPQ may be accepted in place of an AS subject. Check websites of universities and colleges for the latest offers information.

Your target offers and examples of courses provided by each institution

380 pts **Bristol** – A*AA–AAB (Biol Maths) (IB 37–35 pts)

Cambridge – A*AA college offers may vary (Nat Sci (Biol Biomed Sci)) (IB 34–38 pts)

Edinburgh – A*AA 2nd yr entry (Evol Biol) (IB 38 pts)

360 pts **Bristol** – AAA–AAB (Biol) (IB 37–35 pts)

Durham – AAA (Nat Sci (Biol))

Edinburgh – AAA–ABB 1st yr entry (Mol Biol) (IB 37–32 pts)

Sheffield – AAA (Biol Yr Abrd)

340 pts **Bath** – AAB–ABB (Mol Cell Biol) (IB 34 pts)

Bristol – AAB–BBB (Palae Evol) (IB 36 pts HL 665–666)

Cardiff – AAB–ABB 340–320 pts (Biology)

Exeter – AAB–BBB (Mol Biol) (IB 34–29 pts)

Heriot-Watt – AAB 2nd year entry (Biol Sci (Microbiol))

Imperial London – AAB (Biol Fr/Ger/Span Sci) (IB 38 pts)

Manchester – AAB–BBB (Dev Biol courses) (IB 32–35 pts)

Newcastle – AAB–BBB (App Biol) (IB 32–35 pts HL biol 6)

Reading – AAB–ABBb (Psy Biol)

St Andrews – AAB–AAA (Biol courses) (IB 35–38 pts)

Sheffield – AAB (Biol MBiolSci; Biol Cons Biodiv)

Southampton – AAA–ABB (Mar Biol) (IB 36–30 pts)

320 pts **Aberdeen** – ABB 2nd yr entry (Biol; Cons Biol)

Bath – ABB (Biol) (IB 34 pts)

Birmingham – ABB–BBB (Palaeoenv) (IB 32–34 pts)

Bristol – ABB (Cncr Biol) (IB 33 pts HL 665)

Dundee – ABB 2nd yr entry (Microbiol) (IB 34 pts)

Durham – AAB–ABB (Biol Ind) (IB 34 pts)

East Anglia – ABB (Microbiol) (IB 32 pts HL 555)

Glasgow – ABB (Mar Frshwtr Biol) (IB 32 pts)

Lancaster – BBB–ABB 320 pts (Biol courses) (IB 30 pts)

Leeds – ABB–BBB 320–300 pts (Ecol Env Biol) (IB 34–32 pts)

Liverpool – ABB–BBB (Microbiol) (IB 33–30 pts)

London (RH) – ABB (Biol Psy)

Nottingham – ABB–BBB (Biol) (IB 32–34 pts)

Queen's Belfast – ABB/BBBb (Hum Biol; Mar Biol)

Sheffield – ABB (Biol Cons Biol Modn Lang) (IB 35 pts)

Southampton – ABB (Mar Biol Ocean) (HL 18–16 pts)

Sussex – ABB (Biol) (IB 34 pts)

Swansea – ABB (Mar Biol) (IB 33 pts)

Warwick – ABB (Chem Biol) (IB 34 pts)

York – ABB (Mol Cell Biol) (IB 32 pts)

300 pts **Aberdeen** – BBB 1st yr entry (Cons Biol; Mar Biol; Biol)

Aberystwyth – (Biol) (IB 26 pts)

Aston – BBC–BBB (App Hum Biol) (IB 30 pts)

Bristol UWE – 300 pts (Cons Biol)

Dundee – BBB (Mathem Biol) (IB 32 pts)

Essex – 300 pts (Mol Cell Biol) (IB 32–28 pts)

Heriot-Watt – BBB 1st yr entry (Biol Sci (Microbiol))

Keele – inc BC (Biol courses) (IB 26–28 pts)

Kent – BBB (Biol courses) (IB 28–30 pts HL 13–14 pts)

London (QM) – 300 pts (Biol Psy) (IB 28–32 pts)

Loughborough – 300 pts (Hum Biol) (IB 32–34 pts)

Newcastle – BBB (Mar Biol Ocean) (IB 32 pts HL biol 5)

Nottingham – BBB–BCC (Env Biol) (IB 24–30 pts)

For a quick reference offers calculator, fold out the inside back cover.

Plymouth – 300–360 pts (Mar Biol courses) (IB 28 pts)
Queen's Belfast – BBB (Mol Biol)
Sheffield – BBB (Biol Arch)
280 pts **Aberystwyth** – (Hum Biol Spo Sci) (IB 26 pts)
Bangor – (Biol MBiol)
Bristol UWE – 280–320 pts (Foren Biol; Hum Biol; Spo Biol (IB 26–28 pts))
Gloucestershire – 280 pts (Biol)
Northumbria – 280 pts (Biol Foren Biol)
Oxford Brookes – BBC (Cell Mol Biol) (IB 30 pts)
Plymouth – 280 pts (Env Biol) (IB 26 pts)
Staffordshire – 280 pts (Bioinformatics)
Stirling – BBC 1st year entry (Biol courses) (IB 26 pts)
Strathclyde – BBC (Foren Biol) (IB 26 pts)
Teesside – 280 pts (Foren Biol)
260 pts **Aberystwyth** – 260–300 pts (Plnt Biol) (IB 26 pts)
Bangor – 260–320 pts (Mar Biol Zool) (IB 28 pts)
Bournemouth – 260 pts (App Biol Hlth; App Biol)
Cardiff (UWIC) – 260 pts (Biomed Sci (Mol Biol))
Dundee – BCC 1st yr entry (Microbiol) (IB 30 pts)
Glasgow Caledonian – BCC (Hum Biol Sociol Psy) (IB 24 pts)
Hull – 260–300 pts (Biol; Hum Biol)
Liverpool Hope – 260–300 pts (Biol)
Liverpool John Moores – 260–300 pts (Biol) (IB 24 pts)
Nottingham Trent – 260 pts (Foren Biol)
Portsmouth – 260–300 pts (Mar Biol)
Sheffield Hallam – 260 pts (Hum Biol; Biol)
Ulster – 260 pts (Biology) (IB 28 pts)
Wolverhampton – 260–320 pts (Hum Biol)
240 pts **Bangor** – 240 pts (Mar Biol Ocean) (IB 28 pts)
Bolton – 240 pts (Biol courses)
Brighton – CCC/BCD (Env Biol Educ) (IB 28 pts)
Canterbury Christ Church – 240 pts (Env Biol courses) (IB 24 pts)
Cumbria – 240 pts (Cons Biol)
Glamorgan – 240–280 pts (Int Wldlf Biol)
Hertfordshire – 240 pts (Mol Biol Genet)
Huddersfield – 240 pts (Med Biol; Biol (Mol Cell))
Hull – 240–280 pts (Mar Frshwtr Biol)
Lincoln – 240 pts (Cons Biol)
Portsmouth – 240–280 pts (Foren Biol)
Roehampton – 240–300 pts (Biol Sci)
Worcester – 240–280 pts (Anim Biol)
230 pts **Edinburgh Napier** – 230 pts (Mar Frshwtr Biol; Foren Biol)
220 pts **Bath Spa** – 220–260 pts (Biol courses)
Chester – 220–240 pts (Biol) (IB 24 pts)
Edge Hill – 220–260 pts (Biology)
Glamorgan – 220–260 pts (Biol; Hum Biol; Foren Biol)
Greenwich – 220 pts (Hum Biosci) (IB 24 pts)
Hull – 220–280 pts (Cstl Mar Biol)
Liverpool John Moores – 220–280 pts (Psy Biol) (IB 24 pts)
Manchester Met – 220–260 pts (Cons Biol) (IB 28 pts)
Northampton – 220–260 pts (Biol; App Cons Biol)
Nottingham Trent – 220 pts (Zoo Biol) (IB 26 pts)
Westminster – CCD (Mol Biol Genet) (IB 28 pts)
Worcester – 220–240 pts (Hum Biol) (IB 25 pts)

200 pts **Anglia Ruskin** – (Biol courses)
Central Lancashire – 200–240 pts (Foren Biol)
Chester – 200–240 pts (Foren Biol) (IB 30 pts)
Derby – 200–240 pts (Cons Biol) (IB 28 pts)
East London – 200 pts (App Biol; Hum Biol courses)
Kingston – 200–280 pts (Biol; Hum Biol courses; Cell Mol Biol)
Salford – 200 pts (Biol courses)
Staffordshire – 200–260 pts (Hum Biol) (IB 28 pts)
Wolverhampton – 200 pts (Genet Mol Biol; Microbiol)
180 pts **Kingston** – 180–280 pts (Foren Biol)
160 pts **Essex** – 160 pts inc DD (Mar Biol) (IB 24 pts)
Leeds Met – 160 pts (Biomed Sci (Hum Biol)) (IB 24 pts)
Queen Margaret – 160 pts (Hum Biol) (IB 26 pts)
140 pts **West Scotland** – CD (Biol courses)
120 pts **London South Bank** – 120 pts (Biosci (Hum Biol) (Microbiol)) (IB 24 pts)
West Scotland – CD (Env Biol)
80 pts **London (Birk)** – for under 21s (over 21s varies) p/t (Mol Biol)

Alternative offers
See **Chapter 7** and **Appendix 1** for grades/UCAS Tariff points information for the International Baccalaureate, Scottish Highers/Advanced Highers, the Welsh Baccalaureate, the Irish Leaving Certificate, the Cambridge Pre-U Diploma, the Advanced Diploma and the Extended Project.

EXAMPLES OF FOUNDATION DEGREES IN THE SUBJECT FIELD
Anglia Ruskin; Bedfordshire; Blackpool and Fylde (Coll); Bournemouth; Cornwall (Coll); Harlow (Coll); Nottingham Trent; Truro (Coll). Other courses offered See also **Biological Sciences**.

CHOOSING YOUR COURSE (SEE ALSO CH. 1)
Some course features
Bangor (Biol) Some students take a 3–6-month exchange programme in Europe or the USA.
Cardiff Biochemistry, Biological Sciences and Biology courses have a common first year with the option to change at the end of Year 1.
Gloucestershire A hands-on Biology course with an emphasis on laboratory projects and field work. A short placement is included.
Leeds (Biol) An optional year in industry is offered.
London (UCL) The degrees in Biology, Environmental Biology, Human Genetics and Zoology have a common first year with the opportunity to change degrees within the department.
Nottingham (Biol) A comprehensive modern treatment of microbial, plant, animal and human biology.
Swansea (Biol) A deferred choice course enables students to choose their final degree subjects in Year 2.

Universities and colleges teaching quality See www.qaa.ac.uk; http://unistats.direct.gov.uk.

Top research universities and colleges (RAE 2008) See **Biological Sciences**.

Examples of sandwich degree courses Aston; Bath; Bradford; Bristol; Bristol UWE; Cardiff; Coventry; De Montfort; East London; Edinburgh Napier; Glamorgan; Harper Adams (UC); Hertfordshire; Huddersfield; Kent; Kingston; Leeds; Liverpool John Moores; London South Bank; Loughborough; Manchester; Manchester Met; Middlesex; Northumbria; Nottingham Trent; Plymouth; Reading; Sheffield Hallam; Surrey; Teesside; Ulster; West Scotland; York.

ADMISSIONS INFORMATION
Number of applicants per place (approx) Aberdeen 8; Aberystwyth 5; Aston 6; Bath 7; Birmingham 3; Bradford 7; Bristol 9; Cardiff 8; Dundee 6; Durham 11; Exeter 6; Hull 4; Imperial London 4; Kent 10; Leeds 6; Leicester 15; London (RH) 5; Newcastle (Mar Biol) 15; Nottingham 9; Oxford Brookes 13;

Salford 3; Southampton (Mar Biol Ocean) 6, (Biol) 7; Stirling 15; Sussex 4; Swansea (Mar Biol) 8, (Biol) 4; York 5.

Advice to applicants and planning the UCAS personal statement See **Biochemistry**, **Biological Sciences** and **Appendix 4**. **York** Advanced Diploma not generally accepted.

Misconceptions about this course **Sussex** Many students think that a Biology degree limits you to being a professional scientist which is not the case. **York** Some fail to realise that chemistry beyond GCSE is essential. Mature students often lack the confidence to consider the course.

Selection interviews **Yes** Bangor, Bath, Birmingham, Bradford (informal, after offer), Cambridge, Durham, East Anglia, Essex, Hertfordshire, Imperial London, Kent, Kingston, London (RH), London (UCL), London South Bank, Nottingham (depends on application), SAC (Scottish CAg), Sheffield Hallam, Southampton, Staffordshire, Surrey, Swansea, Writtle (Coll); **Some** Anglia Ruskin, Aston, Bath Spa, Derby, Dundee, Liverpool John Moores, Roehampton, Salford, Sheffield, Stirling, Wolverhampton, York.

Interview advice and questions Questions are likely to focus on your studies in biology, on any work experience or any special interests you may have in biology outside school. In the past, questions have included: Is the computer like a brain and, if so, could it ever be taught to think? What do you think the role of the environmental biologist will be in the next 40–50 years? Have you any strong views on vivisection? You have a micro-organism in the blood: you want to make a culture. What conditions should be borne in mind? What is a pacemaker? What problems will a giraffe experience? How does water enter a flowering plant? Compare an egg and a potato. Discuss a family tree of human genotypes. Discuss fish farming in Britain today. See also **Chapter 6**. **Liverpool John Moores** Informal interview. It is useful to bring samples of coursework to the interview. **York** Why Biology? How do you see your future?

Reasons for rejection (non-academic) **Bath Spa** Poor mathematical and scientific knowledge.

AFTER-RESULTS ADVICE
Offers to applicants repeating A-levels **Higher** Cardiff, East London, St Andrews, Strathclyde; **Possibly higher** Aston, Bath, Bradford, Durham, Leeds, London (RH), Nottingham, Portsmouth; **Same** Aberystwyth, Anglia Ruskin, Bangor, Bedfordshire, Brunel, Chester, Derby, Dundee, Edinburgh Napier, Heriot-Watt, Hull, Liverpool John Moores, London (UCL), London South Bank, Loughborough, Manchester Met, Newcastle, Oxford Brookes, Plymouth, Roehampton, Salford, Sheffield, Southampton, Staffordshire, Stirling, Teesside, Ulster, Wolverhampton, York.

GRADUATE DESTINATIONS AND EMPLOYMENT (2007/8 HESA)
Graduates surveyed 3125 **Employed** 1010 **In further study** 945 **Assumed unemployed** 325

Career note Some graduates go into research, but many will go into laboratory work in hospitals, food laboratories, agriculture, the environment and pharmaceuticals. Others go into teaching, management and other professional and technical areas.

OTHER DEGREE SUBJECTS FOR CONSIDERATION
Anatomy; Biochemistry; Biological Sciences; Biotechnology; Chemistry; Dentistry; Ecology; Environmental Health; Environmental Science/Studies; Food Science; Genomics; Health Studies; Medicine; Midwifery; Nursing; Nutrition; Optometry; Orthoptics; Pharmaceutical Sciences; Pharmacology; Pharmacy; Physiology; Physiotherapy; Plant Sciences; Radiography; Speech and Language Therapy; Zoology.

BIOTECHNOLOGY

(including **Medical Engineering**; see also **Biological Sciences, Biology, Engineering (Medical), Microbiology, Technologies**)

Biotechnology is a multidisciplinary subject which can include chemistry, biological sciences, microbiology, genetics and chemical engineering. Medical engineering involves the design, installation, maintenance and provision of technical support for diagnostic, therapeutic and other clinical equipment used by doctors, nurses and other clinical healthcare workers.

Biomedical engineering applies the principles of engineering, medicine and science to medical technologies used in the diagnosis, prognosis, monitoring and treatment of ill and injured people.

Useful websites www.bbsrc.ac.uk; www.scienceyear.com; www.abcinformation.org.

NB The points totals shown to the left of the institutions are for ease of reference only. It must not be assumed that Tariff points are always used by institutions or that they can be substituted for an offer in grades. The level of an offer is not necessarily indicative of the quality of a course.

COURSE OFFERS INFORMATION

Subject requirements/preferences GCSE Mathematics and science subjects required. **AL** Courses vary but one, two or three subjects from chemistry, biology, physics and mathematics may be required.

NB In 2012 universities and colleges will differ in their use of GCE AL/AS unit grade information, A* grades, the Extended Project (EPQ), the Advanced Diploma and the Cambridge Pre-U examination when considering applicants and making offers. An EPQ may be accepted in place of an AS subject. Check websites of universities and colleges for the latest offers information.

Your target offers and examples of courses provided by each institution

360 pts **Bristol** – AAA–ABB (Bioch Mol Biol Biotech) (IB 35 pts)
Edinburgh – AAA 2nd yr entry (Biotech) (IB 36 pts)
Imperial London – AAA (Biomat Tiss Eng) (IB 38–42 pts)
London (UCL) – AAA+AS–AAB+AS (Biotech) (IB 36–38 pts)
Manchester – AAA–AAB (Biotech (Ent) (Ent Ind)) (IB 35 pts)

340 pts **Cardiff** – AAB–ABB (Biotech)
City – AAB 340 pts (Biomed Eng BEng) (IB 30 pts)
Imperial London – AAB 340 pts (Bioeng) (IB 34 pts HL chem biol 6)
Leeds – AAB (Med Eng MEng) (IB 36 pts HL 17 pts)
London (QM) – 340 pts (Med End MEng) (IB 34 pts)
Newcastle – AAB (Bioproc Eng) (IB 36 pts HL chem maths 5)
Surrey – AAB 340 pts (Med Eng MEng) (IB 34–32 pts)

320 pts **Aberdeen** – ABB 2nd yr entry (Biotech) (IB 30 pts)
Birmingham – ABB (Biotech) (IB 32–34 pts)
Edinburgh – ABB 1st yr entry (Biotech) (IB 32 pts)
Glasgow – ABB (Biomed Eng MEng) (IB 32 pts)
Liverpool – ABB–BBB (Microbl Biotech) (IB 33–30 pts)
Newcastle – ABB (Biotech Ind) (IB 30–32 pts)
Sheffield – ABB (Biomed Eng) (IB 35 pts)
Strathclyde – ABB (Pros Orthot) (IB 34 pts)

300 pts **Aberdeen** – BBB 1st yr entry (Biotech) (IB 28 pts)
Birmingham – BBB (Biomed Mat Sci) (IB 30 pts)
Bradford – 300 pts (Med Eng MEng)
Glasgow – BBB (Biomed Eng BEng)
Nottingham – BBB–BCC (Biotech) (IB 28-32 pts)
Sheffield – BBB–BBC (Biomat Sci Tiss Eng BEng)
Surrey – BBB 300 pts (Med Eng BEng) (IB 30–32 pts)

280 pts **London (QM)** – 280 pts (Med Eng BEng) (IB 28 pts)
Northumbria – 280 pts (Biotech) (IB 28 pts)
Oxford Brookes – BBC (Biotech) (IB 30 pts)
Reading – 280 pts (Biomed Eng Cyber) (HL 555)
Salford – 280 pts (Pros Orthot) (IB 24 pts)
260 pts **Bradford** – 260 pts (App Biotech)
Bristol UWE – 260–320 pts (Biotech)
Sheffield Hallam – 260 pts (Biotech)
Ulster – 260 pts (Biomed Eng)
240 pts **Bradford** – 240 pts (Med Eng BEng)
Hertfordshire – 240 pts (Biotech)
220 pts **Edinburgh Napier** – 220 pts (Microbiol Biotech)
Westminster – CCD (Biotech) (IB 26 pts)
200 pts **East London** – 200 pts (Med Biotech)
160 pts **Wolverhampton** – 160–220 pts (Biotech) (IB 24 pts)
140 pts **West Scotland** – CD 140 pts (App Biosci)

Alternative offers
See **Chapter 7** and **Appendix 1** for grades/UCAS Tariff points information for the International Baccalaureate, Scottish Highers/Advanced Highers, the Welsh Baccalaureate, the Irish Leaving Certificate, the Cambridge Pre-U Diploma, the Advanced Diploma and the Extended Project.

EXAMPLES OF FOUNDATION DEGREES IN THE SUBJECT FIELD
Edinburgh Napier.

CHOOSING YOUR COURSE (SEE ALSO CH. 1)
Some course features
Leeds (Med Eng) The course combines engineering science, biological science and medicine. It has study abroad and work placement opportunities and strong links with industry.
Manchester (Biotech) A common first year covering several life science subjects provides the opportunity to change at a later stage.
Newcastle Twelve degrees covering the biomedical and biomolecular sciences have a common first year allowing the flexibility to make a final choice at the end of Stage 1.
Northumbria (Biotech) Main focus of course is on molecular biotechnology, including molecular biology, immunology and bioinformatics.
Wolverhampton (Biotech) Specialisation in gene manipulation, plant or microbial biotechnology.

Universities and colleges teaching quality See www.qaa.ac.uk; http://unistats.direct.gov.uk.

Examples of sandwich degree courses Bradford; Bristol; Bristol UWE; Cardiff; Edinburgh Napier; Manchester; Northumbria; Reading; Sussex.

ADMISSIONS INFORMATION
Number of applicants per place (approx) Birmingham 6; Bristol 9; Cardiff 4; Imperial London 4; Leeds 7; London (UCL) 4; Strathclyde 4.

Advice to applicants and planning the UCAS personal statement See **Biological Sciences** and **Biochemistry**. See also **Appendix 4**.

Selection interviews Yes Bradford, Imperial London, Leeds, Strathclyde, Surrey; **Some** Cardiff, Wolverhampton.

Interview advice and questions See **Biology** and **Biological Sciences**. See also **Chapter 6**.

AFTER-RESULTS ADVICE
Offers to applicants repeating A-levels Possibly higher Nottingham; **Same** Cardiff, Leeds, Liverpool John Moores, Wolverhampton.

GRADUATE DESTINATIONS AND EMPLOYMENT (2007/8 HESA)

Graduates surveyed 45 **Employed** 25 **In further study** 15 **Assumed unemployed** 5

Medical Technology graduates surveyed 1010 **Employed** 875 **In further study** 20 **Assumed unemployed** 25

Career note Biotechnology, biomedical and biochemical engineering opportunities exist in medical, agricultural, food science and pharmaceutical laboratories. Some Bioengineering graduates apply for graduate medical courses and obtain both engineering and medical qualifications.

OTHER DEGREE SUBJECTS FOR CONSIDERATION

Agriculture; Biochemistry; Biological Sciences; Biomedicine; Chemistry; Food Technology; Genetics; Materials Science and Technology; Microbiology; Molecular Biology; Pharmacology.

BUILDING and CONSTRUCTION

(including **Building Design, Building Services Engineering, Building Surveying, Construction, Fire Risk Engineering, Fire Safety Management;** for **Architectural Technology** see **Architecture;** see also **Architecture, Engineering (Civil), Housing, Surveying**)

The building and construction industry covers a wide range of activities and is closely allied to civil, municipal and structural engineering and quantity surveying. One branch of the industry covers building services engineering, a career which involves specialised areas such as heating, acoustics, lighting, refrigeration and air conditioning. Many Building, Construction, Building Surveying and Building Services Engineering courses include industrial placements and are accredited by professional bodies such as the Chartered Institute of Building, the Royal Institution of Chartered Surveyors and the Engineering Council.

Useful websites www.ciob.org.uk; www.cibse.org; www.cskills.org.

NB The points totals shown to the left of the institutions are for ease of reference only. It must not be assumed that Tariff points are always used by institutions or that they can be substituted for an offer in grades. The level of an offer is not necessarily indicative of the quality of a course.

COURSE OFFERS INFORMATION

Subject requirements/preferences **GCSE** English, mathematics and science usually required. **AL** Physics, mathematics or a technical subject may be required for some courses.

NB In 2012 universities and colleges will differ in their use of GCE AL/AS unit grade information, A* grades, the Extended Project (EPQ), the Advanced Diploma and the Cambridge Pre-U examination when considering applicants and making offers. An EPQ may be accepted in place of an AS subject. Check websites of universities and colleges for the latest offers information.

Your target offers and examples of courses provided by each institution

340 pts **Heriot-Watt** – AAB 2nd yr entry (Bld Surv) (IB 35 pts)
 Leeds – AAB (Civ Eng Constr Mgt courses) (IB 36 pts HL 17 pts)
 Manchester – AAB–BBB (Blt Nat Env Comb St) (IB 35–32 pts)
320 pts **Brunel** – BBC (Mech Eng Bld Serv MEng/BEng) (IB 32 pts)
 London (UCL) – BBB+AS (Proj Mgt Constr) (IB 32 pts)
 Newcastle – ABB/BBB (Surv Map Sci) (IB 32 pts)
300 pts **Bristol UWE** – 300–340 pts (Bld Surv) (IB 24–28 pts)
 Kingston – 300 pts (Bld Surv) (IB 32 pts)
 Loughborough – 300 pts (Commer Mgt Quant Surv) (IB 32 pts)
 Reading – 300–320 pts (Constr Mgt Surv)
 Ulster – 300 pts (Constr Eng Mgt) (IB 25–32 pts)
280 pts **Aston** – 260–300 pts (Constr Proj Mgt) (IB 29 pts)
 Brighton – BBC (Constr Mgt) (IB 28 pts)

Heriot-Watt – BBC 1st yr entry (Bld Surv) (IB 31 pts)
Loughborough – 280 pts (Constr Eng Mgt) (IB 30 pts)
Northumbria – 280 pts (Bld Surv) (IB 25 pts)
Nottingham – BBC (Sust Blt Env) (IB 30 pts)
Nottingham Trent – 280 pts (Bld Surv) (IB 25–30 pts)
Salford – 280 pts (Constr Mgt; Constr Proj Mgt; Bld Surv)
Westminster – BBC (Constr Mgt) (IB 26 pts)

270 pts **Anglia Ruskin** – 270 pts (Bld Surv)
Glasgow Caledonian – 270 pts (Bld Surv; Bld Serv Eng; Constr Mgt; Fire Rsk Eng)
Liverpool John Moores – 270 pts (Bld Serv Eng)
Sheffield Hallam – 270 pts (Bld Surv)

260 pts **Birmingham City** – 260 pts (Bld Surv) (IB 30 pts)
Central Lancashire – 260 pts (Fire Eng) (IB 28 pts)
Oxford Brookes – BCC (Constr Mgt) (IB 31 pts)
Plymouth – 260 pts (Bld Surv Env) (IB 27 pts)
Ulster – 260 pts (Bld Eng Mats) (IB 32 pts)

245 pts **Edinburgh Napier** – 245 pts (Bld Surv; Constr Proj Mgt)

240 pts **Bolton** – 240 pts (Constr)
Central Lancashire – 240–260 pts (Bld Serv Sust Eng) (IB 24 pts)
Coventry – 240 pts (Bld Serv Eng BEng) (IB 27 pts)
Glamorgan – 240–280 pts (Bld Serv Eng)
Greenwich – 240 pts (Constr Bus Mgt) (IB 24 pts)
Leeds Met – 240 pts (Bld Surv) (IB 28 pts)
Liverpool John Moores – 240 pts (Bld Serv Eng Proj Mgt; Constr Mgt)
Newport – 240 pts (Bld St)
Northumbria – 240–280 pts (Bld Proj Mgt) (IB 25 pts)
Nottingham Trent – 240 pts (Prop Mgt Constr) (IB 24 pts)
Plymouth – 240 pts (Constr Mgt Env) (IB 26 pts)
Wolverhampton – 240 pts (Bld Surv) (IB 26 pts)

230 pts **Central Lancashire** – 230 pts (Bld Surv)
Coventry – 230 pts (Bld Surv; Quant Surv Commer Mgt; Constr Mgt)
Sheffield Hallam – 230 pts (Constr Mgt)

220 pts **Bristol UWE** – 220–280 pts (Constr Mgt)
Glamorgan – 220–260 pts (Proj Mgt (Constr))
London South Bank – 220 pts (Prop Mgt (Bld Surv)) (IB 24 pts)

200 pts **Glyndŵr** – 200 pts (Bld St (Constr) (Mntnce Mgt))
Huddersfield – 200 pts (Constr Proj Mgt)
Portsmouth – 200–260 pts (Constr Eng Mgt) (IB 24 pts)

180 pts **Derby** – 180–240 pts (Constr Mgt) (IB 26 pts)
Greenwich – 180 pts (Bld Surv) (IB 24 pts)
Plymouth – 180 pts (Env Constr Surv) (IB 24 pts)

160 pts **Central Lancashire** – 160 pts (Fire Sfty Risk Mgt)
Glasgow Caledonian – CC (Bld Surv Eng)
Kingston – 160 pts (Constr Mgt) (IB 32 pts)
Robert Gordon – CC (Constr Des Mgt) (IB 24 pts)
Swansea Met – 160–360 pts (Constr Mgt; Proj Constr Mgt; Bld Cons Mgt)
Wolverhampton – 160–220 pts (Constr Mgt) (IB 24 pts)

150 pts **West London** – 150 pts (Blt Env courses) (IB 24 pts)

120 pts **Colchester (Inst)** – 120 pts (Constr Mgt)
Southampton Solent – 120 pts (Constr Mgt)

Alternative offers

See **Chapter 7** and **Appendix 1** for grades/UCAS Tariff points information for the International Baccalaureate, Scottish Highers/Advanced Highers, the Welsh Baccalaureate, the Irish Leaving Certificate, the Cambridge Pre-U Diploma, the Advanced Diploma and the Extended Project.

EXAMPLES OF FOUNDATION DEGREES IN THE SUBJECT FIELD

Bedfordshire; Blackburn (Coll Univ Centre); Bolton; Bournemouth; Bradford; Brighton; Central Lancashire; Colchester (Inst); Cornwall (Coll); Cumbria; Derby; Ealing, Hammersmith and West London (Coll); East London; Glamorgan; Glyndŵr; Greenwich; Huddersfield; Kent; Kingston; Northampton; Northumbria; Suffolk (Univ Campus); Swansea Met; West London; West Nottinghamshire (Coll); Westminster City (Coll); Weymouth (Coll); Wolverhampton.

CHOOSING YOUR COURSE (SEE ALSO CH. 1)

Some course features

Aston Construction and Construction Project Management courses have a common first year; sandwich course has good industrial contacts.

Heriot-Watt (Constr Proj Mgt) Three options are offered in Project Management, Surveying or Building Services.

Loughborough (Constr Eng Mgt) Course sponsored by industry. Two six-month placements of industrial training.

Northumbria The Foundation degree route enables entry to Architectural Technology, Building Services Engineering or Surveying, Construction Management, Estate Management or Quantity Surveying.

Plymouth The course is accredited by the Chartered Institute of Building and focuses on the environmental and sustainability performance of buildings.

Reading Students taking Construction Management, Quantity Surveying and Building Surveying follow the same course for two years, choosing the specialism in Year 3.

Universities and colleges teaching quality See www.qaa.ac.uk; http://unistats.direct.gov.uk.

Top research universities and colleges (RAE 2008) See **Architecture**.

Examples of sandwich degree courses Aston; Bristol UWE; Brunel; Cardiff; Edinburgh Napier; Glasgow Caledonian; Kingston; Leeds Met; London South Bank; Loughborough; Northumbria; Nottingham Trent; Oxford Brookes; Plymouth; Sheffield Hallam; Ulster; Wolverhampton.

ADMISSIONS INFORMATION

Number of applicants per place (approx) Bristol UWE (Constr Mgt) 5; Edinburgh Napier 8; Glamorgan 3; Glasgow Caledonian 6; Heriot-Watt 6; Kingston 4; London (UCL) 4; Loughborough 4; Northumbria 6; Salford (Bld Surv) 6; Strathclyde 5.

Advice to applicants and planning the UCAS personal statement Details of work experience with any levels of responsibility should be included. Make contact with any building organisation to arrange a meeting with staff to discuss careers in building. Give evidence of your ability to work in a team and give details of any personal achievements in technological areas and work experience. Building also covers civil engineering, surveying, quantity surveying etc and these areas should also be explored. See also **Appendix 2**.

Misconceptions about this course Loughborough Some students fail to realise that the degree includes law, finance, economics and management plus constructional technology.

Selection interviews Yes Brunel, Derby, Glamorgan, Glasgow Caledonian, Greenwich, Kingston, Liverpool John Moores, London South Bank, Loughborough, Plymouth, Robert Gordon, Sheffield Hallam, Staffordshire, Westminster; **Some** Anglia Ruskin, Birmingham City, Brighton, Salford.

Interview advice and questions Work experience in the building and civil engineering industries is important and you could be expected to describe any building project you have visited and any problems experienced in its construction. A knowledge of the range of activities to be found on a building site will be expected, for example the work of quantity and land surveyors and of the various building trades. See also **Chapter 6. Loughborough** The applicant should show an understanding of the role of the quantity surveyor.

Reasons for rejection (non-academic) Inability to communicate. Lack of motivation. Indecisiveness about reasons for choosing the course. **Loughborough** Applicant more suited to hands-on rather than an academic course.

AFTER-RESULTS ADVICE

Offers to applicants repeating A-levels Higher Liverpool John Moores, Strathclyde; **Possibly higher** Bristol UWE; **Same** Birmingham City, Bolton, Brighton, Coventry, Heriot-Watt, Huddersfield, Kingston, London (UCL), Loughborough, Northumbria, Robert Gordon, Swansea Met.

GRADUATE DESTINATIONS AND EMPLOYMENT (2007/8 HESA)

Graduates surveyed 1560 **Employed** 885 **In further study** 110 **Assumed unemployed** 215

Career note There is a wide range of opportunities within the building and construction industry for building technologists and managers, particularly stemming from the construction projects for the 2012 Olympic Games in London. This subject area also overlaps into surveying, quantity surveying, civil engineering, architecture and planning and graduates from all these subjects commonly work together as members of construction teams.

OTHER DEGREE SUBJECTS FOR CONSIDERATION

Architectural Technology; Architecture; Civil Engineering; Property Planning and Development; Quantity Surveying; Surveying.

BUSINESS AND MANAGEMENT COURSES

(see also **Business and Management Courses (International and European), Business and Management Courses (Specialised), Hospitality and Hotel Management, Human Resource Management, Leisure and Recreation Management/Studies, Marketing, Retail Management, Tourism and Travel**)

Business degrees attract more applicants than any other degree subject, with a further rise in the past year for places on a wide range of programmes. Financial studies form part of most courses, in addition to sales, marketing, human resources management and general management. Since this is a vocational subject, some work experience in the field is generally required prior to application. Many courses offer industrial placements, in some cases in the USA, Australia and New Zealand and, for those students with an A-level in a language (and in some cases a good GCSE), placements abroad are possible.

Useful websites www.civilservice.gov.uk/jobs/faststream; www.bized.co.uk; www.icsa.org.uk; www.oft.gov.uk; www.adassoc.org.uk; www.cipr.co.uk; www.ismm.co.uk; www.export.org.uk; www.ipsos-mori.com; www.capitaresourcing.co.uk; www.tax.org.uk; www.hmrc.gov.uk; www.camfoundation.com; www.shell-livewire.org; www.ibconsulting.org.uk; www.managers.org.uk; www.cipd.co.uk; www.inprad.org; www.managementhelp.com.

NB The points totals shown to the left of the institutions are for ease of reference only. It must not be assumed that Tariff points are always used by institutions or that they can be substituted for an offer in grades. The level of an offer is not necessarily indicative of the quality of a course.

COURSE OFFERS INFORMATION

Subject requirements/preferences GCSE Mathematics and English often at grade A or B required. **AL** Mathematics required for some courses. In some cases grades A, B or C may be required.

NB In 2012 universities and colleges will differ in their use of GCE AL/AS unit grade information, A* grades, the Extended Project (EPQ), the Advanced Diploma and the Cambridge Pre-U examination when considering applicants and making offers. An EPQ may be accepted in place of an AS subject. Check websites of universities and colleges for the latest offers information.

Your target offers and examples of courses provided by each institution
410 pts London (King's) – AAAb **or** AAaab (Bus Mgt) (IB 36 pts HL 665)
390 pts Warwick – AABb (Mgt) (IB 38 pts)

380 pts **Bristol** – A*AA–ABB (Mgt Acc/Econ/Fin/Law) (IB 38–34 pts)

360 pts **Bath** – AAA (Bus Admin) (IB 38 pts)

Cambridge – competitive entry after 2 **or** 3 yrs of another Cambridge course (Mgt St) (IB 38–42 pts)

Durham – AAA–ABB (Bus) (IB 34 pts)

Exeter – AAA–AAB (Mgt courses) (IB 36–34 pts)

Imperial London – contact the department A*AA (Mgt Bioch/Biol/Biotech/Chem/Elec Eng)

Lancaster – AAA–AAB (Mgt courses) (IB 34–36 pts)

Leeds – AAA–AAB (Mgt) (IB 35 pts HL 17 pts)

St Andrews – AAA (Mgt Sci) (IB 38 pts)

340 pts **Aston** – 340–320 pts (Mgt Strat) (IB 34 pts)

Birmingham – AAB–ABB (Bus Mgt courses) (IB 36 pts)

Bournemouth – 340 pts (Bus St)

Cardiff – AAB (Bus Mgt) (IB 35 pts)

City – AAA (Mgt) (IB 35 pts)

Glasgow – AAB–ABB (Bus Mgt courses) (IB 32-34 pts)

Lancaster – 340 pts (Org Mgt; Proj Mgt)

Leeds – AAB (Mgt Trans St) (IB 35 pts HL 17 pts)

London (RH) – AAB (Mgt) (IB 35 pts)

London LSE – AAB (Mgt Sci) (IB 37 pts HL 766)

Loughborough – AAB (Maths Mgt) (IB 36 pts)

Manchester – AAB–ABB (Mgt courses) (IB 33–35 pts)

Newcastle – AAB (Bus Mgt) (IB 34 pts)

Nottingham – AAB (Mgt St) (IB 32 pts)

Southampton – AAB (Mgt Sci courses) (IB 34 pts HL 17 pts)

320 pts **Durham** – ABB (Bus Fin) (IB 34 pts)

Essex – 320 pts (Bus Mgt) (IB 32 pts)

Leicester – ABB (Mgt St Pol) (IB 30 pts)

Liverpool – ABB (Law Bus) (IB 32 pts)

London (QM) – ABB 320–360 pts (Bus Mgt) (IB 32 pts)

Loughborough – ABB–AAC (Geog Mgt)

Northumbria – ABB 320 pts (Bus St; Bus Mgt)

Queen's Belfast – ABB–BBBb (Bus Mgt)

Reading – ABB (Bus Mgt) (IB 33 pts)

Sheffield – ABB (Bus Mgt Inf Mgt) (IB 33 pts)

Staffordshire – 320 pts (Bus Law) (IB 26 pts)

Strathclyde – ABB (Mgt) (IB 32 pts)

Surrey – 320–300 pts (Bus Mgt) (IB 34–32 pts)

Sussex – ABB (Bus (Fin) (Mark)) (IB 34 pts)

York – ABB (Acc Bus Fin Mgt) (IB 34 pts)

300 pts **Aberdeen** – BBB (Mgt St courses) (IB 30 pts)

Aberystwyth – 300 pts (Bus Mgt (Law)) (IB 32 pts)

Bournemouth – 300 pts (Des Bus Mgt)

Brunel – 300–350 pts (Bus Mgt (Acc/Mark))

Coventry – 300 pts (Law Bus)

East Anglia – BBB–BBC (Bus Mgt) (IB 30–32 pts)

Edinburgh – Check with Ad Tutor BBB (Bus St courses)

Heriot-Watt – BBB 2nd yr entry (Bus Mgt Ind)

Huddersfield – 300–280 pts (Entre Bus) (IB 26 pts)

Kent – 300 pts (Mgt Sci) (IB 33 pts HL 15 pts)

Oxford Brookes – BBB (Bus Comb Hons) (IB 31 pts)

Plymouth – 300–360 pts (Law Bus)

Stirling – BBB 2nd yr entry (Bus St; Mgt; Mgt Sci)

Westminster – BBB 300 pts (Bus St courses) (IB 28 pts)

280 pts **Aberystwyth** – 280 pts (Bus Mgt) (IB 27 pts)
Birmingham City – 280 pts (Bus courses) (IB 32 pts)
Brighton – BBC 280 pts (Bus Mgt courses) (IB 30 pts)
Bristol UWE – 280–340 pts (Mgt) (IB 26–32 pts)
Edge Hill – 280 pts (Bus Mgt St; Bus Mgt (Acc) (HR Mgt) (Int Bus) (Mark))
Gloucestershire – 280–300 pts (Bus Mgt)
Hull – 280 pts (Mgt) (IB 28 pts)
Keele – Flexible offers 280–320 pts inc BB/AB (Bus Mgt) (IB 28–32 pts)
Kent – 280 pts (Bus St)
Kingston – 280–320 pts (Bus Sys Mgt; Bus Mgt; Bus St; Bus Ops Mgt)
Leeds Trinity (UC) – (Bus Mgt; Bus)
Liverpool John Moores – 280 pts (Bus St)
Loughborough – 280 pts (Trans Bus Mgt) (IB 30 pts)
Northumbria – 280 pts (Bus joint courses)
Portsmouth – 280–300 pts (Bus Admin; Bus St)
Swansea – 280 pts (Bus Mgt courses)
Worcester – 280 pts (Bus courses) (IB 25 pts)

260 pts **Bangor** – 260–280 pts (Bus Soc Admin) (IB 28 pts)
Bolton – 260 pts (Bus Mgt)
BPP (UC) – 260 pts (Bus St; Bus St Fin)
Cardiff (UWIC) – 260 pts (Bus Mgt St courses) (IB 24 pts)
Coventry – 260–280 pts (Bus Mgt) (IB 24 pts)
Dundee – BCC (Bus Mgt) (IB 30 pts)
Glamorgan – 260 pts (Bus Mgt; Bus Ent)
Heriot-Watt – BCC 1st yr entry (Bus Mgt Ind; Bus Admin)
Hertfordshire – 260–300 pts (Bus St; Mgt)
Lincoln – 260 pts (Bus Mgt; Bus St; Mgt)
Liverpool Hope – 260 pts (Bus Mgt)
Liverpool John Moores – 260 pts (Marit Bus Mgt)
Nottingham Trent – 260 pts (Bus; Bus Mgt Acc Fin)
Plymouth – 260 pts (Marit Bus courses) (IB 26 pts)
Portsmouth – 260–280 pts (Bus Ent Dev)
Salford – BCC 260 pts (Bus Mgt St) (IB 28–32 pts)
Staffordshire – 260 pts (Bus St courses) (IB 26 pts)
Stirling – BCC 1st yr entry (Mgt Sci) (IB 28–30 pts)
Ulster – 260 pts (Bus joint courses; Bus St courses)
Westminster – BCC (Bus) (IB 28 pts)

240 pts **Abertay Dundee** – CCC 240 pts 2nd yr entry (Bus St)
Buckingham – 240 pts (Bus Mgt courses; Bus Ent)
Canterbury Christ Church – 240 pts (Bus St; Bus Mgt)
Central Lancashire – 240–280 pts (Bus St courses (38)) (IB 24 pts)
Chester – 240–260 pts (Mgt courses) (IB 30 pts)
Chichester – CCC (Bus St) (IB 26 pts)
City – 240 pts (Air Trans Mgt) (IB 31 pts)
De Montfort – 240–280 pts (Bus courses (13)) (IB 24–28 pts)
Derby – 240 pts (Bus St) (IB 26 pts)
Edinburgh Napier – 240 pts (Bus courses)
Glasgow Caledonian – CCC (Bus St) (IB 24 pts)
Leeds Met – 240 pts (Bus Mgt) (IB 28 pts)
London Met – 240–300 pts (Bus courses; Mgt)
Manchester Met – 240 pts (Bus courses) (IB 24–28 pts)
Middlesex – 240–280 pts (Bus Mark)
Newport – 240 pts (Bus Ldrshp Bus Ent Dev; Bus Law; Bus St)
Robert Gordon – CCC (Mgt courses) (IB 26 pts)
Roehampton – 240–280 pts (Bus Mgt courses)

Higher Education

Aspire • Achieve • Succeed

For more information about
Foundation Degrees at The College call

01202 205180

email: heunit@thecollege.ac.uk
www.thecollege.co.uk/highereducation

Business and Information Technology

Chris was a mature student and had been working for several years before deciding to gain higher level qualifications. Chris gained a first in the Foundation Degree and then progressed to Bournemouth University on the BSc Hons (Top-up) before progressing to the Masters at BU.

Chris commented

" *I decided on the Foundation Degree as I had been out of education for several years. I found the pace manageable with the workload increasing as our confidence grew.*

The facilities are excellent and the tutors brilliant, they are always accessible and there to support you. I also found that the content of the course was relevant, up-to-date and varied, teaching you a wide range of skills which have proved invaluable. The courses prepare you for a wide variety of career options, including Computer Programming, Database Administration or Project Management. Foundation Degrees are the ideal vehicle for progression to further study or employment and the skills I learnt have proved invaluable. **"**

	Sheffield Hallam – 240 pts (Bus courses)
	Winchester – 240–280 pts (Bus Mgt courses) (IB 24 pts)
230 pts	**Edinburgh Napier** – 230 pts (Bus St courses)
220 pts	**Bath Spa** – 220–260 pts (Bus Mgt courses)
	Chester – 220–260 pts (Mgt) (IB 24 pts)
	Northampton – 220–260 pts (Bus Entre) (IB 24 pts)
	Oldham (Coll Univ Centre) – 220–300 pts (Bus Mgt)
	Southampton Solent – 220 pts (Bus courses (20))
	Sunderland – 220–360 pts (Bus St; Bus HR Mgt; App Mgt)
	Teesside – 220 pts (Bus Mgt; Bus St)
	Wolverhampton – 220 pts (Bus Mgt)
	York St John – 220–260 pts (Bus Mgt courses) (IB 24 pts)
200 pts	**Anglia Ruskin** – 200 pts (Bus Mgt)
	Bedfordshire – 200 pts (Bus St) (IB 24 pts)
	Bradford – 200 pts (Bus Mgt St)
	Bucks New – 200–240 pts (Bus courses; Int Ftbl Bus Mgt)
	Coventry – 200 pts (Bus Inf Tech) (IB 24 pts)
	Doncaster (Coll Univ Centre) – 200 pts (Bus Mgt)
	East London – 200 pts (Bus Mgt) (IB 24 pts)
	Glyndŵr – 200 pts (Bus Mgt)
	Middlesex – 200–300 pts (Bus Mgt)
	Queen Margaret – BB/CCD (Bus Mgt) (IB 26 pts)
	Royal (CAg) – 200–240 pts (Bus Mgt)
	Suffolk (Univ Campus) – 200 pts (Bus Mgt FdA) (IB 24 pts)
	West London – 200 pts (Bus St)
	Writtle (Coll) – 200–360 pts (Bus Mgt) (IB 28 pts)

180 pts **Abertay Dundee** – DDD (Mgt) (IB 24 pts)
Greenwich – 180–160 pts (Bus St) (IB 24 pts)
Harper Adams (UC) – 180–220 pts (Bus Mgt Mark)
Newman (UC) – 180–260 pts (Mgt St courses)
160 pts **Anglia Ruskin** – 160 pts (Bus Econ)
Bradford (Coll Univ Centre) – 2 A2 GCEs (not General Studies) 160 pts
(Bus Admin)
London South Bank – 160 pts (Mgt Comb courses) (IB 24 pts)
SAC (Scottish CAg) – CC (Rur Bus Mgt)
St Mary's Twickenham (UC) – 160–200 pts (Mgt St)
South Essex (Coll) – 160 pts (Bus St)
Swansea Met – DD 160–360 pts (Bus St Fin/Psy)
West Scotland – CC (Bus; Mgt)
140 pts **Trinity Saint David** – 140–360 pts (Bus Mgt courses)
120 pts **Blackburn (Coll Univ Centre)** – 120 pts (Bus St)
Grimsby (IFHE) – 120–240 pts (Bus courses)
Llandrillo Cymru (Coll) – 120 pts (Mgt Bus) (IB 24 pts)
Northbrook (Coll) – 120 pts (Bus Admin)
Norwich City (Coll) – 120–240 pts (Bus Mgt)
80 pts **Croydon (Coll)** – 80–100 pts (Bus courses)
Greenwich (Sch Mgt) – 80–120 pts (Bus Mgt IT)
Holborn (Coll) – 80 pts (Bus Admin)
Kensington Bus (Coll) – 80 pts (Bus St)
London (Birk) – for under 21s (over 21s varies) p/t (Mgt)
UHI Millennium Inst – CC (Bus Mgt)

Open University – contact +44 (0)845 300 6090 **or** www.openuniversity.co.uk/you
(Bus St)
Regents Bus Sch London – check with School (Bus courses)

Alternative offers
See **Chapter 7** and **Appendix 1** for grades/UCAS Tariff points information for the International
Baccalaureate, Scottish Highers/Advanced Highers, the Welsh Baccalaureate, the Irish Leaving
Certificate, the Cambridge Pre-U Diploma, the Advanced Diploma and the Extended Project.

EXAMPLES OF FOUNDATION DEGREES IN THE SUBJECT FIELD
Askham Bryan (Coll); Bedfordshire; Bexley (Coll); Birmingham (UC); Blackburn (Coll Univ Centre);
Blackpool and Fylde (Coll); Bolton; Bournemouth; Bournemouth and Poole (Coll); Bradford; Brighton;
Bristol City (Coll); Bristol UWE; Central Lancashire; Colchester (Inst); Cornwall (Coll); Croydon (Coll); De
Montfort; Doncaster (Coll Univ Centre); Duchy (Coll); Durham New (Coll); Ealing, Hammersmith and
West London (Coll); East London; Edge Hill; Farnborough (CT); Glamorgan; Gloucestershire; Glyndŵr;
Greenwich; Grimsby (IFHE); Harper Adams (UC); Hertfordshire; K (Coll); Kirklees (Coll); Knowsley
(CmC); Lakes (Coll); Leeds Met; Liverpool John Moores; London South Bank; Manchester (Coll); Mid-
Cheshire (Coll); Middlesex; NEW (Coll); Newcastle (Coll); North Lindsey (Coll); Northampton;
Northbrook (Coll); Nottingham New (Coll); Plymouth; Riverside Halton (Coll); Royal (CAg); St Helens
(Coll); Sheffield (Coll); Sheffield Hallam; Somerset (CAT); South Devon (Coll); South Essex (Coll); South
Kent (Coll); Southampton Solent; Suffolk (Univ Campus); Wakefield (Coll); Warwickshire (Coll);
Westminster Kingsway (Coll); Writtle (Coll); York (Coll).

CHOOSING YOUR COURSE (SEE ALSO CH. 1)
Some course features
Bath (Bus Admin) A popular and highly respected sandwich course with placements in the UK and
abroad.
Brunel (Bus Mgt) Three-year or four-year sandwich courses allowing for specialisation in
management, accounting, business systems or marketing.

Business
at Hull and Harrogate College

Higher Education

Our Business, Computing and Professional Development faculty offers everything from Business Information Technology and Network Management courses to Professional Graduate Certificates in Education and Business Management options.

Students can choose to study at our campus in Hull or at the renowned Harrogate International Business School.

Hull Campus:
01482 598744
Or visit: **www.hull-college.ac.uk/HE**

Harrogate Campus:
01423 878211
Or visit: **www.harrogate.ac.uk/HE**

De Montfort (Bus Mgt Ent) Course focuses on entrepreneurship and business practice, researching and developing new business opportunities and ideas, with an optional paid placement year.

London LSE (Mgt) Course has compulsory modules in economics, psychology, accounting and finance and marketing. (Mgt Sci) Course focuses on quantitative analysis, decision-making and economic and social issues. Operational research and statistics are taken in Years 2 and 3.

Nottingham (Mgt St) Core modules include organisation studies, entrepreneurship, accounting, business computing, business, business ethics, human resource management and economics. French, German, Spanish or Chinese Studies can be selected as major/minor combinations.

Oxford Brookes (Bus Mgt) Course aimed at students not wanting to specialise in any particular area of business or are undecided. At the end of the first year, students can opt for one of the named Business degrees.

Southampton (Mgt Sci) Courses allow for specialisation in mathematical or non-mathematical aspects of management including accounting and finance, languages, entrepreneurship and music.

Winchester (Bus Mgt) Optional pathway to BA in Business Management with Public Service Management. Modules include quality management and customer care, local government, public administration and European culture and institutions.

Universities and colleges teaching quality See www.qaa.ac.uk; http://unistats.direct.gov.uk.

Top research universities and colleges (RAE 2008) (Business and Management Studies) Imperial London; Cambridge; Cardiff; Bath; London (King's); London LSE; Oxford; Lancaster; Warwick; Manchester; Strathclyde; Leeds; Nottingham; Aston; Loughborough; Sheffield.

Examples of sandwich degree courses Abertay Dundee; Aberystwyth; Aston; Bath; Birmingham (UC); Birmingham City; Bournemouth; Bradford; Brighton; Bristol UWE; Brunel; Central Lancashire; City; Coventry; De Montfort; Edinburgh Napier; Glamorgan; Glasgow Caledonian; Gloucestershire; Greenwich; Harper Adams (UC); Hertfordshire; Huddersfield; Hull; K (Coll); Kingston; Lancaster; Leeds

Met; Lincoln; Liverpool John Moores; London (QM); Loughborough; Manchester; Manchester Met; Middlesex; Newcastle; Northumbria; Nottingham Trent; Oxford Brookes; Plymouth; Portsmouth; Reading; Royal (CAg); Sheffield Hallam; Southampton Solent; Staffordshire; Surrey; Swansea Met; Teesside; Ulster; Warwickshire (Coll); West Scotland; Westminster; Wolverhampton.

ADMISSIONS INFORMATION

Number of applicants per place (approx) Abertay Dundee (Bus St) 4; Aberystwyth 3; Anglia Ruskin 5; Aston (Bus Mgt) 12, (Mgt) 5; Bangor 4; Bath (Bus Admin) 7; Birmingham 28; Birmingham (UC) 5; Blackpool and Fylde (Coll) 2; Bolton 3; Bournemouth 30; Bradford 12; Bristol 28; Brunel 12; Canterbury Christ Church 20; Cardiff 8; Central Lancashire 15; City (Bus St) 17, (Mgt Sys) 6; Colchester (Inst) 2; De Montfort (Bus Mgt) 5; Edge Hill 4; Glasgow Caledonian 18; Heriot-Watt 5; Hertfordshire 10; Huddersfield 5; Hull (Bus St) 19, (Mgt) 10; Hull (Coll) 3; Kent 30; Kingston 50; Leeds 27, (Mgt St) 16; Leeds Trinity (UC) 3; Llandrillo Cymru (Coll) 2; London (King's) 25, (Mgt Sci) 12; London (RH) 9; London LSE (Mgt) 23; London Met 10; London South Bank 4; Loughborough 5; Manchester Met (Bus St) 26; Middlesex 12; Newcastle 27, (Bus Mgt) 40; Northumbria 10; Oxford Brookes 40; Plymouth 4; Portsmouth 10, (Bus Admin) 7, (Bus St) 6; Regents Bus Sch London 25; Robert Gordon 5; Salford (Bus St) 9, (Mgt Sci) 2; Southampton Solent 13; Strathclyde 12; Sunderland 20; Surrey (Bus Mgt) 6; Swansea Met 7; Teesside (Bus St) 4; Warwick 22; West London 4; West Scotland 5; Westminster 12; Winchester 4; Wolverhampton 7; York 6; York St John 3.

Advice to applicants and planning the UCAS personal statement There are many different kinds of businesses and any work experience is almost essential for these courses. This should be described in detail: for example, size of firm, turnover, managerial problems, sales and marketing aspects, customers' attitudes. Any special interests in business management should also be included, for example, personnel work, purchasing, marketing. Give details of travel or work experience abroad and, for international courses, language expertise and examples of leadership and organising skills. Reference can be made to any particular business topics you have studied in the *Financial Times*, *The Economist* and the business sections in the weekend press. Applicants need to be sociable, ambitious, team players. Say why you are interested in the course, identify your academic strengths, your personal strengths and interests. Check information on the websites of the Chartered Institute of Public Relations, the Chartered Institute of Marketing and the Chartered Institute of Personnel and Development. See **Appendix 4**; see also **Accountancy/Accounting**.

Misconceptions about this course Aberystwyth Students are unaware that the course addresses practical aspects of business. **Salford** (Mgt Sci) Students should appreciate that the courses are fairly mathematical. **York** A previous study of management, IT or languages at A-level is necessary.

Selection interviews Yes Birmingham City, Bradford, Coventry, Doncaster (Coll Univ Centre), Durham, Edge Hill, Euro Bus Sch London, Glamorgan, Glasgow Caledonian, Hull, Kent (mature and Access students), London Met, Middlesex, Northumbria, Nottingham Trent, Plymouth, Robert Gordon, Roehampton, Sheffield Hallam, Sir Gâr (Coll), Strathclyde, Swansea, Teesside, Trinity Saint David, West London, West Thames (Coll), York; **Some** Abertay Dundee, Aberystwyth, Anglia Ruskin, Bath, Bath Spa, Blackpool and Fylde (Coll), Brighton, Buckingham, Cardiff (UWIC), Chichester, City, De Montfort, Derby (Int Bus), East Anglia, Greenwich, Kent, Leeds, Lincoln, Liverpool John Moores, Manchester Met, Salford, South Kent (Coll), Southampton, Staffordshire, Stirling, Sunderland, Warwick, Winchester, Wolverhampton.

Interview advice and questions Any work experience you describe on the UCAS application probably will be the focus of questions which could include topics covering marketing, selling, store organisation and management and customer problems. Personal qualities are naturally important in a career in business, so be ready for such questions as: What qualities do you have which are suitable and important for this course? Describe your strengths and weaknesses. Why should we give you a place on this course? Is advertising fair? What qualities does a person in business require to be successful? What makes a good manager? What is a cash-flow system? What problems can it cause? How could supermarkets improve customer relations? See also **Chapter 6**. **Buckingham** Why Business? How do you see yourself in five years' time? Have you had any work experience? If so,

BSc (Hons) Business Studies
BSc (Hons) Business Studies with Finance

Your first step to a successful business career

A business degree with BPP develops your business operation skills and knowledge, preparing you for a successful future as a leader of commerce.

BPP tutors bring their professional experience into the classroom, immersing you in the latest business developments, and our elective focused course structure and professional skills courses allow you to specialise your learning – meaning when you graduate from BPP, you can hit the ground running within your chosen field.

Course details

Length of programme: 2-7 years

Start dates: January & September

Study Centres: London (City), Manchester*, Birmingham*, Swindon** and online

Admission requirements: 260 UCAS points plus a minimum grade C in GCSE Maths and English

* Subject to validation ** BSc Business Studies only

Top businesses trust BPP – we are the exclusive study provider to many of the FTSE 100 companies

For more information on starting your business career with a BPP degree, visit: **www.bpp.com/ug** tel: **0845 077 5036**

---

discuss. **Wolverhampton** Mature students with no qualifications will be asked about their work experience.

Reasons for rejection (non-academic) Hadn't read the prospectus. Lack of communication skills. Limited commercial interest. Weak on numeracy and problem-solving. Lack of interview preparation (no questions). Lack of outside interests. Inability to cope with a year abroad. The candidate brought his parent who answered all the questions. See also **Marketing**. **Aberystwyth** Would have trouble fitting into the unique environment of Aberystwyth. Casual approach to learning. **Bournemouth** The Business Studies course is very popular. **Surrey** Hesitation about the period abroad.

AFTER-RESULTS ADVICE

Offers to applicants repeating A-levels Higher Bradford, Bristol UWE, Brunel, Greenwich, Hertfordshire, Kingston, Lancaster, Liverpool, Manchester Met, St Andrews, Sheffield, Strathclyde, Teesside; **Same** Abertay Dundee, Aberystwyth, Anglia Ruskin, Aston, Bath, Bath Spa, Birmingham City, Bolton, Bournemouth, Brighton, Brunel, Buckingham, Cardiff, Cardiff (UWIC), Chester, Chichester, De Montfort, Derby, Durham, East Anglia, East London, Glasgow, Gloucestershire, Harper Adams (UC), Huddersfield, Hull, Kent, Leeds, Lincoln, Liverpool Hope, Liverpool John Moores, Loughborough, Newman (UC), Northumbria, Oxford Brookes, Portsmouth, Robert Gordon, Roehampton, Royal (CAg), Salford, Sheffield Hallam, Staffordshire, Stirling, Suffolk (Univ Campus), Sunderland, Surrey, Trinity Saint David, Ulster, West London, West Scotland, Winchester, Wolverhampton, Worcester, York, York St John.

GRADUATE DESTINATIONS AND EMPLOYMENT (2007/8 HESA)

Business Studies graduates surveyed 8130 **Employed** 4730 **In further study** 650 **Assumed unemployed** 775

Management Sciences graduates surveyed 3380 **Employed** 1935 **In further study** 310 **Assumed unemployed** 325

Career note The majority of graduates enter trainee management roles in business-related and administrative careers, many specialising in some of the areas listed below. In 2005/6 the main graduate destinations were in finance, property development, wholesale, retail and manufacturing.

OTHER DEGREE SUBJECTS FOR CONSIDERATION

Accountancy; Banking; Business Information Technology; E-Business; Economics; Estate Management; Finance; Hospitality Management; Housing Management; Human Resource Management; Insurance; Leisure Management; Logistics; Marketing; Public Administration; Retail Management; Sports Management; Surveying.

BUSINESS AND MANAGEMENT COURSES (INTERNATIONAL AND EUROPEAN)

(including **Business** and **Management Courses with Languages**; see also **Business and Management Courses, Business and Management Courses (Specialised), Hospitality and Hotel Management, Human Resource Management, Leisure and Recreation Management/Studies, Marketing, Retail Management, Tourism and Travel**)

Similar to Business and Management Courses, this subject area focuses on business but with more of an international theme. Studying or taking part in an industrial placement abroad is another highlight of this subject area.

Useful websites See **Business and Management Courses**.

NB The points totals shown to the left of the institutions are for ease of reference only. It must not be assumed that Tariff points are always used by institutions or that they can be substituted for an offer in grades. The level of an offer is not necessarily indicative of the quality of a course.

COURSE OFFERS INFORMATION

Subject requirements/preferences GCSE Mathematics and English often at grade A or B required. **AL** A language will be stipulated for most courses in this subject area. In some cases grades A, B or C may be required.

NB In 2012 universities and colleges will differ in their use of GCE AL/AS unit grade information, A* grades, the Extended Project (EPQ), the Advanced Diploma and the Cambridge Pre-U examination when considering applicants and making offers. An EPQ may be accepted in place of an AS subject. Check websites of universities and colleges for the latest offers information.

Your target offers and examples of courses provided by each institution
390 pts Warwick – A*AA–AAAb (Int Mgt) (IB 38 pts)
360 pts Exeter – AAA–AAB (Bus St Euro) (IB 36–33 pts)
Lancaster – AAA (Bus St (St Abrd); Mgt Org (St Abrd))
Leeds – AAA (Int Bus)
Manchester – AAA–ABB (Int Mgt Am Bus St) (IB 35–34 pts)
340 pts Bath – AAB (Int Bus Span) (IB 34–36 pts)
Birmingham – AAB–ABB (Euro Bus Mgt) (IB 34-36 pts)
Cardiff – AAB (Bus Mgt Euro Lang/Jap) (Ib 35 pts)
Lancaster – 340 pts (Int Bus) (IB 34 pts)
Liverpool – AAB (Int Bus) (IB 32 pts)
London (RH) – AAB (Mgt Int Bus) (IB 35 pts)
Loughborough – AAB 340 pts (Int Bus) (IB 36 pts)
Newcastle – AAB (Int Bus Mgt) (IB 34 pts)
Nottingham – AAB (Mgt St Chin St/Fr/Ger/Span; Mgt As St; Int Bus – China campus)
Reading – AAB (Int Mgt Bus Admin Fr/Ger/Ital) (HL 666)
Southampton – AAB–ABB (Mgt Sci Fr/Ger/Span)
Surrey – ABB 340 pts (Bus Mgt Fr/Ger/Span) (IB 34 pts)

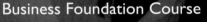

320 pts **Aston** – 320–340 pts (Int Bus Fr/Ger/Span) (IB 34 pts)
Bournemouth – 320 pts (Int Bus)
Essex – 320 pts (Bus Mgt Mdn Lang) (IB 28–29 pts)
London (QM) – 320 pts (Bus Mgt Fr/Ger/Hisp St/Russ)
Queen's Belfast – ABB–BBBb (Int Bus Fr/Ger) (IB 32 pts)
Sheffield – ABB–BBC (Fr/Ger/Russ Bus Mgt) (IB 33–30 pts)
Sussex – ABB (Bus (Int Bus))
Swansea – ABB–BBB (Int Bus; Int Mgt Sci N Am/Euro; Int Mgt Sci Lang; Int Bus Mgt (Austr) (Euro) (Lang) (N Am))
300 pts **Brunel** – 300–360 pts (Int Bus) (IB 32 pts)
Dundee – 300 pts 2nd yr entry (Int Bus Lang) (IB 34 pts)
Edinburgh – Check with Ad. tutor BBB (Int Bus Lang)
Keele – 300–360 pts (Int Bus)
Kent – 300 pts (Hisp St Bus Admin) (IB 33 pts)
Oxford Brookes – BBB (Int Bus courses)
Sheffield – BBB–BBC (Bus Mgt Kor St/Chin/Jap/Fr/Ger/Hisp St) (IB 33–30 pts)
Strathclyde – BBB–BBC (Int Bus Modn Lang)
Westminster – BBB 300 pts (Int Bus) (IB 28 pts)
280 pts **Aberystwyth** – 280 pts (Bus Mgt Lang) (IB 27 pts)
Brighton – BBC 280 pts (Int Bus)
Bristol UWE – 280–340 pts (Int Bus St Span; Int Bus St)
Edge Hill – 280 pts (Chin St Bus) (IB 24 pts)
Gloucestershire – 280–300 pts (Int Bus St)
Heriot-Watt – BBC (Int Bus Mgt Fr/Ger/Span)
Kingston – 280–320 pts (Int Bus Law) (IB 25 pts)
Northumbria – 280 pts (Int Bus Mgt) (IB 25 pts)
Portsmouth – 280–300 pts (Int Bus St; Euro Bus courses)
Stirling – BBC (Int Mgt Intcult St)
Suffolk (Univ Campus) – 280 pts (Bus Mgt BA)
Swansea – 280–300 pts (Int Bus Mgt)
260 pts **Aberdeen** – BCC (Euro Mgt St)
Bangor – 260–300 pts (Bus St Fr/Ger)
Coventry – 260–280 pts (Int Bus Mgt) (IB 28 pts)
Hertfordshire – 260–300 pts (Int Mgt)
Lincoln – 260 pts (Euro Bus; Int Bus)
Staffordshire – 260 pts (Int Bus Mgt) (IB 24 pts)
240 pts **Bradford** – 240 pts (Int Bus Mgt)
Cardiff (UWIC) – 240 pts (Int Bus Mgt) (IB 24 pts)
Central Lancashire – 240–280 pts (Int Bus) (IB 28 pts)
Chester – 240–280 pts (Int Bus) (IB 24 pts)
Glasgow Caledonian – CCC (Int Bus) (IB 24 pts)
Liverpool – 240–260 pts (Bus St Hisp St) (IB 30 pts HL lang 6)
Liverpool John Moores – 240 pts (Int Bus St Chin/Fr/Jap/Span) (IB 24 pts)
London Met – 240 pts (Int Bus Mgt) (IB 28 pts)
Manchester Met – 240 pts (Int Bus) (IB 27 pts)
Nottingham Trent – CCC 240 pts (Int Bus Fr) (IB 24 pts)
Robert Gordon – CCC (Int Bus Mgt)
Roehampton – 240–280 pts (Int Bus) (IB 26 pts)
Salford – 240–260 pts (Bus Mgt (Int)) (IB 28 pts)
Sheffield Hallam – 240 pts (Int Bus St; Int Bus St Lang; Int Bus St Tour)
Ulster – 240 pts (Euro St Bus) (IB 24 pts)
230 pts **Edinburgh Napier** – 230 pts (Bus St Lang; Int Bus)
220 pts **Hull** – 220 pts (Int Bus)
Leeds Met – 220 pts (Langs Int Bus) (IB 26 pts)
Northampton – 220–260 pts (Bus Fr/Ger)

For a quick reference offers calculator, fold out the inside back cover.

Teesside – 220 pts (Int Bus Mgt)
Wolverhampton – 220–240 pts (Int Bus Mgt; Bus Fr)
200 pts **Anglia Ruskin** – 200 pts (Int Bus)
Bedfordshire – 200 pts (Int Bus St)
De Montfort – 200–240 pts (Int Bus Glob) (IB 24 pts)
East London – 200 pts (Int Bus courses) (IB 24 pts)
Hull (Coll) – 200 pts (Int Bus)
Middlesex – 200–300 pts (Bus St Fr/Ger/Ital/Span; Int Bus; Int Bus (Arbc) (Mand) (Russ) (Span))
Plymouth – 200–240 pts (Int Bus Econ) (IB 24 pts)
York St John – 200–240 pts (Int Bus)
180 pts **Abertay Dundee** – DDD (Int Mgt) (IB 24 pts)
Anglia Ruskin – 180–200 pts (Int Mgt) (IB 24 pts)
120 pts **Southampton Solent** – 120–220 pts (Int Bus Mgt)

Euro Bus Sch London – contact School (Int Bus courses)
Open University – contact +44 (0)845 300 6090 or www.openuniversity.co.uk/you (Bus St Fr/Span)
Regents Bus Sch London – check with School (Glob Bus Mgt; Glob Bus Des Mgt)

Alternative offers
See **Chapter 7** and **Appendix 1** for grades/UCAS Tariff points information for the International Baccalaureate, Scottish Highers/Advanced Highers, the Welsh Baccalaureate, the Irish Leaving Certificate, the Cambridge Pre-U Diploma, the Advanced Diploma and the Extended Project.

EXAMPLES OF FOUNDATION DEGREES IN THE SUBJECT FIELD
Askham Bryan (Coll); Bedfordshire; Bexley (Coll); Birmingham (UC); Blackburn (Coll Univ Centre); Blackpool and Fylde (Coll); Bolton; Bournemouth; Bradford; Brighton; Bristol City (Coll); Bristol UWE; Central Lancashire; Colchester (Inst); Cornwall (Coll); Croydon (Coll); De Montfort; Doncaster (Coll Univ Centre); Duchy (Coll); Durham New (Coll); Ealing, Hammersmith and West London (Coll); East London; Edge Hill; Farnborough (CT); Glamorgan; Gloucestershire; Glyndŵr; Greenwich; Grimsby (IFHE); Harper Adams (UC); Hertfordshire; K (Coll); Kirklees (Coll); Knowsley (CmC); Lakes (Coll); Leeds Met; Liverpool John Moores; London South Bank; Manchester (Coll); Mid-Cheshire (Coll); Middlesex; NEW (Coll); Newcastle (Coll); North Lindsey (Coll); Northampton; Northbrook (Coll); Nottingham New (Coll); Plymouth; Riverside Halton (Coll); Royal (CAg); St Helens (Coll); Sheffield (Coll); Sheffield Hallam; Somerset (CAT); South Devon (Coll); South Essex (Coll); South Kent (Coll); Southampton Solent; Suffolk (Univ Campus); Wakefield (Coll); Warwickshire (Coll); Westminster Kingsway (Coll); Writtle (Coll); York (Coll).

CHOOSING YOUR COURSE (SEE ALSO CH. 1)
Some course features
De Montfort (Bus Mgt Ent) Course focuses on entrepreneurship and business practice, researching and developing new business opportunities and ideas, with an optional paid placement year.
Oxford Brookes (Bus Mgt) Course aimed at students not wanting to specialise in any particular area of business or are undecided. At the end of the first year, students can opt for one of the named Business degrees.

Universities and colleges teaching quality See www.qaa.ac.uk; http://unistats.direct.gov.uk.

Top research universities and colleges (RAE 2008) (Business and Management Studies) Imperial London; Cambridge; Cardiff; Bath; London (King's); London LSE; Oxford; Lancaster; Warwick; Manchester; Strathclyde; Leeds; Nottingham; Aston; Loughborough; Sheffield.

Examples of sandwich degree courses Abertay Dundee; Aberystwyth; Aston; Bath; Birmingham (UC); Birmingham City; Bournemouth; Bradford; Brighton; Bristol UWE; Brunel; Central Lancashire; City; Coventry; De Montfort; Edinburgh Napier; Glamorgan; Glasgow Caledonian; Gloucestershire; Greenwich; Harper Adams (UC); Hertfordshire; Huddersfield; Hull; K (Coll); Kingston; Lancaster; Leeds Met; Lincoln; Liverpool John Moores; London (QM); Loughborough; Manchester; Manchester Met; Middlesex; Newcastle; Northumbria; Nottingham Trent; Oxford Brookes; Plymouth; Portsmouth;

Reading; Royal (CAg); Sheffield Hallam; Southampton Solent; Staffordshire; Surrey; Swansea Met; Teesside; Ulster; Warwickshire (Coll); West Scotland; Westminster; Wolverhampton.

ADMISSIONS INFORMATION

Number of applicants per place (approx) Abertay Dundee (Bus St) 4; Aberystwyth 3; Anglia Ruskin 5; Aston (Int Bus) 6, (Int Bus Econ) 8; Bangor 4; Bath (Int Mgt Lang) 14; Birmingham 28; Birmingham (UC) 5; Blackpool and Fylde (Coll) 2; Bolton 3; Bradford 12; Bristol 28; Brunel 12; Canterbury Christ Church 20; Cardiff 8; Central Lancashire 15; Colchester (Inst) 2; Derby (Int Bus) 4; Edge Hill 4; Glasgow Caledonian 18; Heriot-Watt 5; Hertfordshire 10; Huddersfield 5; Hull (Coll) 3; Hull (Scarborough) 3; Kent 30; Kingston 50; Leeds 27; Leeds Trinity (UC) 3; Liverpool John Moores (Int Bus) 16; Llandrillo Cymru (Coll) 2; London (King's) 25; London (RH) 9; London Met 10; London South Bank 4; Loughborough 5; Manchester Met (Int Bus) 8; Middlesex 12; Newcastle 27, (Int Bus Mgt) 25; Northumbria 10; Oxford Brookes 40; Plymouth 4; Portsmouth 10, (Int Bus) 5; Regents Bus Sch London 25; Robert Gordon 5; Sheffield Hallam (Int Bus) 6; Southampton Solent 13; Strathclyde 12, (Int Bus Modn Lang) 6; Sunderland 20; Swansea Met 7; Warwick 22; West London 4; West Scotland 5; Westminster 12; Winchester 4; Wolverhampton 7; York 6; York St John 3.

Advice to applicants and planning the UCAS personal statement See **Business and Management Courses**.

Misconceptions about this course Aston (Int Bus Fr) Not two separate disciplines – the two subjects are integrated involving the study of language in a business and management context.

Selection interviews Yes Birmingham City, Bradford, Coventry, Doncaster (Coll Univ Centre), Durham, Edge Hill, Euro Bus Sch London, Glamorgan, Glasgow Caledonian, Hull, Kent (mature and Access students), London Met, Middlesex, Northumbria, Nottingham Trent, Plymouth, Robert Gordon, Roehampton, Sheffield Hallam, Sir Gâr (Coll), Strathclyde, Swansea, Teesside, Trinity Saint David, West London, West Thames (Coll), York; **Some** Abertay Dundee, Aberystwyth, Anglia Ruskin, Bath, Bath Spa, Blackpool and Fylde (Coll), Brighton, Buckingham, Cardiff (UWIC), Chichester, City, De Montfort, Derby (Int Bus), East Anglia, Greenwich, Kent, Leeds, Lincoln, Liverpool John Moores, Manchester Met, Salford, South Kent (Coll), Staffordshire, Stirling, Sunderland, Warwick, Winchester, Wolverhampton.

Interview advice and questions See **Business and Management Courses. Wolverhampton** Mature students with no qualifications will be asked about their work experience.

Reasons for rejection (non-academic) See **Business and Management Courses. Bournemouth** The Business Studies course is very popular. **Surrey** Hesitation about the period abroad.

AFTER-RESULTS ADVICE

Offers to applicants repeating A-levels Higher Bradford, Bristol UWE, Brunel, Greenwich, Hertfordshire, Kingston, Lancaster, Liverpool, Manchester Met, St Andrews, Sheffield, Strathclyde, Teesside; **Same** Aberystwyth, Anglia Ruskin, Aston, Bath, Birmingham City, Bournemouth, Brighton, Buckingham, Cardiff, Cardiff (UWIC), Chester, Chichester, De Montfort, Derby, Durham, East Anglia, Gloucestershire, Huddersfield, Hull, Kent, Leeds, Lincoln, Liverpool Hope, Liverpool John Moores, Loughborough, Northumbria, Oxford Brookes, Robert Gordon, Roehampton, Royal (CAg), Salford, Sheffield Hallam, Staffordshire, Stirling, Suffolk (Univ Campus), Sunderland, Surrey, Ulster, West London, Winchester, Wolverhampton, Worcester, York, York St John.

GRADUATE DESTINATIONS AND EMPLOYMENT (2007/8 HESA)

Business Studies graduates surveyed 8405 **Employed** 4330 **In further study** 810 **Assumed unemployed** 925

Management Sciences graduates surveyed 3655 **Employed** 1945 **In further study** 380 **Assumed unemployed** 370

Career note See **Business and Management Courses**.

OTHER DEGREE SUBJECTS FOR CONSIDERATION

Accountancy; Banking; Business Information Technology; E-Business; Economics; Estate Management; Finance; Hospitality Management; Housing Management; Human Resource Management; Insurance;

Leisure Management; Logistics; Marketing; Public Administration; Retail Management; Sports Management; Surveying.

BUSINESS AND MANAGEMENT COURSES (SPECIALISED)

(including **Advertising, E-Commerce, Entrepreneurship, Operations Management, Public Relations** and **Publishing**; see also **Business and Management Courses, Business and Management Courses (International and European), Hospitality and Hotel Management, Human Resource Management, Leisure and Recreation Management/Studies, Marketing, Retail Management, Tourism and Travel**)

This subject contains courses that are business and management related but which allow students to focus on business within a particular area such as agriculture, media, extreme sports or creative events to give a few examples.

Useful websites See **Business and Management Courses**.

NB The points totals shown to the left of the institutions are for ease of reference only. It must not be assumed that Tariff points are always used by institutions or that they can be substituted for an offer in grades. The level of an offer is not necessarily indicative of the quality of a course.

COURSE OFFERS INFORMATION

Subject requirements/preferences GCSE Mathematics and English often at grade A or B required. **AL** Mathematics required for some courses. In some cases grades A, B or C may be required. (**Publishing**) English required for some courses.

NB In 2012 universities and colleges will differ in their use of GCE AL/AS unit grade information, A* grades, the Extended Project (EPQ), the Advanced Diploma and the Cambridge Pre-U examination when considering applicants and making offers. An EPQ may be accepted in place of an AS subject. Check websites of universities and colleges for the latest offers information.

Your target offers and examples of courses provided by each institution
360 pts **Ulster** – AAA (Comm Adv Mark)
340 pts **Lancaster** – AAB–ABB (Org St Psy) (IB 32 pts)
Southampton – AAB (Mgt Entre) (IB 34 pts HL 17)
320 pts **Loughborough** – 320 pts (Inf Mgt Bus St) (IB 32 pts)
Newcastle – ABB (Agri-Bus Mgt) (IB 34 pts)
Northumbria – 320 pts (Adv Mgt)
300 pts **Aston** – BBB 300 pts (Tech Ent Mgt) (IB 32 pts)
Bournemouth – 300 pts (PR; Des Bus Mgt)
Huddersfield – 300 pts (PR)
Manchester – ABC (Tex Tech (Bus Mgt)) (IB 32 pts)
Oxford Brookes – BBB (Pub Media) (IB 29 pts)
280 pts **Coventry** – 280–300 pts (Disas Mgt Emer Plan)
De Montfort – 280 pts (Adv)
Harper Adams (UC) – 280 pts (Agric Frm Bus Mgt)
Huddersfield – 280 pts (Adv Mark Comm; Adv Media)
Loughborough – 280–300 pts (Air Trans Mgt) (IB 30 pts)
Worcester – 280 pts (Mark Adv PR)
260 pts **Aberdeen** – BCC–CCC (Entre)
Birmingham City – 260–280 pts (Bus Adv) (IB 30–32 pts)
Central Lancashire – 260–300 pts (PR)
Coventry – 260–280 pts (Disas Mgt; Disas Reconstr Dev; Adv Bus; Adv Media)
De Montfort – 260 pts (Mark Mgt)

Huddersfield – 260 pts (Air Trans Log Mgt; Trans Mgt)
Leeds Met – 260 pts (PR courses)
Lincoln – 260 pts (Adv courses)
Liverpool John Moores – 260 pts (PR Fr/Chin/Jap/Span; Mgt Trans Log)
Portsmouth – 260–300 pts (Bus Ent Sys)
Queen Margaret – 260 pts (PR Media)
Stirling – BCC (Pblc Mgt Admin)
240 pts **Central Lancashire** – 240–280 pts (Adv Mark Comm) (IB 28 pts)
Chester – 240 pts (PR) (IB 24 pts)
City – CCC 240 pts (Air Trans Op) (IB 26 pts)
Edinburgh Napier – 240 pts (Comm Adv PR)
Kingston – 240–280 pts (Env Haz Disas Mgt)
London Met – 240 pts (Avn Mgt; Arts Mgt)
London South Bank – 240 pts (Arts Mgt)
Manchester Met – 240 pts (Bus Ent PR) (IB 27 pts)
Robert Gordon – CCC (Comm PR) (IB 26 pts)
Sheffield Hallam – 240–260 pts (PR courses)
Southampton Solent – 240 pts (Adv)
Sunderland – 240 pts (PR)
Ulster – 240 pts (Adv courses)
Winchester – 240–280 pts (Arts Mgt) (IB 24 pts)
220 pts **Birmingham (UC)** – 220 pts (Evnt Mgt)
Edge Hill – 220–260 pts (PR)
Falmouth (UC) – 220 pts (Crea Evnts Mgt)
London Met – 220 pts (Adv Mark Comm)
Northampton – 220–260 pts (Adv courses; Bus Entre)
Plymouth – 220–240 pts (Cru Mgt)
Queen Margaret – 220 pts (PR Mark)
Southampton Solent – 220–240 pts (Evnts Mgt courses; Cru Ind Mgt)
Staffordshire – 220 pts (Adv Brnd Mgt)
200 pts **Birmingham (UC)** – 200 pts (Fd Media Comm Mgt)
Bucks New – 200–240 pts (Bus Adv Mgt; PR Mark Comm; Airln Mgt; Airpt Mgt)
East London – 200 pts (Adv)
Middlesex – 200–280 pts (Adv PR Media)
Salford – 200 pts inc Art C (Adv Des)
Teesside – 200–260 pts (PR) (IB 24-28 pts)
West London – 200 pts (Airln Airpt Mgt; Adv; PR)
180 pts **Liverpool (LIPA)** – BC 180 pts (Mus Thea Enter Mgt)
160 pts **Bedfordshire** – 160–240 pts (PR; Adv Mark Comm)
Central Lancashire – 160 pts (Fire Sfty Risk Mgt)
Southampton Solent – 160 pts (Fash Mgt Mark)
Wolverhampton – 160–220 pts (PR courses)
80 pts **Arts London** – 80 pts (PR)

Open University – contact +44 (0)845 300 6090 **or** www.openuniversity.co.uk/you (Bus Law)

Alternative offers
See **Chapter 7** and **Appendix 1** for grades/UCAS Tariff points information for the International Baccalaureate, Scottish Highers/Advanced Highers, the Welsh Baccalaureate, the Irish Leaving Certificate, the Cambridge Pre-U Diploma, the Advanced Diploma and the Extended Project.

EXAMPLES OF FOUNDATION DEGREES IN THE SUBJECT FIELD
Askham Bryan (Coll); Bedfordshire; Bexley (Coll); Birmingham (UC); Blackburn (Coll Univ Centre); Blackpool and Fylde (Coll); Bolton; Bournemouth; Bradford; Brighton; Bristol City (Coll); Bristol UWE; Central Lancashire; Colchester (Inst); Cornwall (Coll); Croydon (Coll); De Montfort; Doncaster (Coll Univ

Centre); Duchy (Coll); Durham New (Coll); Ealing, Hammersmith and West London (Coll); East London; Edge Hill; Farnborough (CT); Glamorgan; Gloucestershire; Glyndŵr; Greenwich; Grimsby (IFHE); Harper Adams (UC); Hertfordshire; K (Coll); Kirklees (Coll); Knowsley (CmC); Lakes (Coll); Leeds Met; Liverpool John Moores; London South Bank; Manchester (Coll); Mid-Cheshire (Coll); Middlesex; NEW (Coll); Newcastle (Coll); North Lindsey (Coll); Northampton; Northbrook (Coll); Nottingham New (Coll); Plymouth; Riverside Halton (Coll); Royal (CAg); St Helens (Coll); Sheffield (Coll); Sheffield Hallam; Somerset (CAT); South Devon (Coll); South Essex (Coll); South Kent (Coll); Southampton Solent; Suffolk (Univ Campus); Wakefield (Coll); Warwickshire (Coll); Westminster Kingsway (Coll); Writtle (Coll); York (Coll).

CHOOSING YOUR COURSE (SEE ALSO CH. 1)

Some course features
De Montfort (Bus Mgt Ent) Course focuses on entrepreneurship and business practice, researching and developing new business opportunities and ideas, with an optional paid placement year.
Oxford Brookes (Bus Mgt) Course aimed at students not wanting to specialise in any particular area of business or are undecided. At the end of the first year, students can opt for one of the named Business degrees.
Southampton (Mgt Sci) Courses allow for specialisation in mathematical or non-mathematical aspects of management including accounting and finance, languages, entrepreneurship and music.
Winchester (Bus Mgt) Optional pathway to BA in Business Management with Public Service Management. Modules include quality management and customer care, local government, public administration and European culture and institutions.

Universities and colleges teaching quality See www.qaa.ac.uk; http://unistats.direct.gov.uk.

Top research universities and colleges (RAE 2008) (Business and Management Studies) Imperial London; Cambridge; Cardiff; Bath; London (King's); London LSE; Oxford; Lancaster; Warwick; Manchester; Strathclyde; Leeds; Nottingham; Aston; Loughborough; Sheffield.

Examples of sandwich degree courses Abertay Dundee; Aberystwyth; Aston; Bath; Birmingham (UC); Birmingham City; Bournemouth; Bradford; Brighton; Bristol UWE; Brunel; Central Lancashire; City; Coventry; De Montfort; Edinburgh Napier; Glamorgan; Glasgow Caledonian; Gloucestershire; Greenwich; Harper Adams (UC); Hertfordshire; Huddersfield; Hull; K (Coll); Kingston; Lancaster; Leeds Met; Lincoln; Liverpool John Moores; London (QM); Loughborough; Manchester; Manchester Met; Middlesex; Newcastle; Northumbria; Nottingham Trent; Oxford Brookes; Plymouth; Portsmouth; Reading; Royal (CAg); Sheffield Hallam; Southampton Solent; Staffordshire; Surrey; Swansea Met; Teesside; Ulster; Warwickshire (Coll); West Scotland; Westminster; Wolverhampton.

ADMISSIONS INFORMATION

Number of applicants per place (approx) Abertay Dundee (Bus St) 4; Aberystwyth 3; Anglia Ruskin 5; Aston (Bus Mgt) 12, (Int Bus) 6, (Mgt) 5, (Int Bus Econ) 8; Bangor 4; Bath (Bus Admin) 7, (Int Mgt Lang) 14; Birmingham 28; Birmingham (UC) 5; Blackpool and Fylde (Coll) 2; Bolton 3; Bournemouth (PR) 10; Bradford 12; Bristol 28; Brunel 12; Canterbury Christ Church 20; Cardiff 8; Central Lancashire 15; Colchester (Inst) 2; Edge Hill 4; Edinburgh Napier (Pub) 7; Glasgow Caledonian 18; Heriot-Watt 5; Hertfordshire 10; Huddersfield 5; Hull (Coll) 3; Kent 30; Kingston 50; Leeds 27; Leeds Trinity (UC) 3; Llandrillo Cymru (Coll) 2; London (King's) 25; London (RH) 9; London Met 10; London South Bank 4; Loughborough 5; Middlesex 12; Newcastle 27; Northumbria 10; Oxford Brookes 40; Plymouth 4; Portsmouth 10; Regents Bus Sch London 25; Robert Gordon 5; Southampton Solent 13; Strathclyde 12; Sunderland 20; Swansea Met 7; Warwick 22; West London 4; West Scotland 5; Westminster 12; Winchester 4; Wolverhampton 7; York 6; York St John 3.

Advice to applicants and planning the UCAS personal statement There are many different kinds of businesses and any work experience is almost essential for these courses. This should be described in detail: for example, size of firm, turnover, managerial problems, sales and marketing aspects, customers' attitudes. Any special interests in business management should also be included, for example, personnel work, purchasing, marketing. Give details of travel or work experience abroad and, for international courses, language expertise and examples of leadership and organising skills.

Reference can be made to any particular business topics you have studied in the *Financial Times, The Economist* and the business sections in the weekend press. Applicants need to be sociable, ambitious, team players. Say why you are interested in the course, identify your academic strengths, your personal strengths and interests. Check information on the websites of the Chartered Institute of Public Relations, the Chartered Institute of Marketing and the Chartered Institute of Personnel and Development. See **Appendix 4**; see also **Accountancy/Accounting**.

Misconceptions about this course Loughborough (Pub Engl) That this is a course in Journalism: it is not!

Selection interviews Yes Birmingham City, Bradford, Coventry, Doncaster (Coll Univ Centre), Durham, Edge Hill, Euro Bus Sch London, Glamorgan, Glasgow Caledonian, Hull, Kent (mature and Access students), London Met, Middlesex, Northumbria, Nottingham Trent, Plymouth, Robert Gordon, Roehampton, Sheffield Hallam, Sir Gâr (Coll), Strathclyde, Swansea, Teesside, Trinity Saint David, West London, West Thames (Coll), York; **Some** Abertay Dundee, Aberystwyth, Anglia Ruskin, Bath, Bath Spa, Blackpool and Fylde (Coll), Brighton, Buckingham, Cardiff (UWIC), Chichester, City, De Montfort, Derby (Int Bus), East Anglia, Greenwich, Kent, Leeds, Lincoln, Liverpool John Moores, Manchester Met, Salford, Staffordshire, Stirling, Sunderland, Warwick, Winchester, Wolverhampton.

Interview advice and questions See **Business and Management Courses. Loughborough** (Pub Engl) No tests at interview. We seek students with an interest in information issues within society.

Reasons for rejection (non-academic) See **Business and Management Courses. Bournemouth** The Business Studies course is very popular.

AFTER-RESULTS ADVICE
Offers to applicants repeating A-levels Higher Bradford, Bristol UWE, Brunel, Greenwich, Hertfordshire, Kingston, Lancaster, Liverpool, Manchester Met, Sheffield, Strathclyde, Teesside; **Same** Aberystwyth, Anglia Ruskin, Aston, Bath, Birmingham City, Bournemouth, Brighton, Buckingham, Cardiff, Cardiff (UWIC), Chester, Chichester, De Montfort, Derby, Durham, East Anglia, Gloucestershire, Huddersfield, Hull, Kent, Leeds, Lincoln, Liverpool Hope, Liverpool John Moores, Loughborough, Northumbria, Oxford Brookes, Robert Gordon, Roehampton, Royal (CAg), Salford, Sheffield Hallam, Staffordshire, Stirling, Suffolk (Univ Campus), Sunderland, Surrey, Ulster, West London, Winchester, Wolverhampton, Worcester, York, York St John.

GRADUATE DESTINATIONS AND EMPLOYMENT (2007/8 HESA)
Publicity graduates surveyed 445 **Employed** 280 **In further study** 20 **Assumed unemployed** 30

Publishing graduates surveyed 80 **Employed** 40 **In further study** 10 **Assumed unemployed** 10

Career note The majority of graduates enter trainee management roles in business-related and administrative careers, many specialising in some of the areas listed below. In 2005/6 the main graduate destinations were in finance, property development, wholesale, retail and manufacturing.

OTHER DEGREE SUBJECTS FOR CONSIDERATION
Accountancy; Banking; Business Information Technology; E-Business; Economics; Estate Management; Finance; Hospitality Management; Housing Management; Human Resource Management; Insurance; Leisure Management; Logistics; Marketing; Public Administration; Retail Management; Sports Management; Surveying.

CELTIC, IRISH, SCOTTISH AND WELSH STUDIES
(including **Cornish Studies** and **Gaelic Studies**)

Irish, Scottish, Gaelic, Welsh, Breton, Manx, Cornish, Gaulish and Celtiberian languages are all included in this subject area. Courses may also include the history and civilisation of the Celtic peoples.

Useful websites www.byig-wlb.org.uk; http://new.wales.gov.uk; www.bbc.co.uk/wales; www.daltai.com; www.eisteddfod.org.uk; www.digitalmedievalist.com; www.gaelic-scotland.co.uk.

NB The points totals shown to the left of the institutions are for ease of reference only. It must not be assumed that Tariff points are always used by institutions or that they can be substituted for an offer in grades. The level of an offer is not necessarily indicative of the quality of a course.

COURSE OFFERS INFORMATION

Subject requirements/preferences GCSE A foreign language or Welsh may be required. **AL** Welsh may be required for some courses.

NB In 2012 universities and colleges will differ in their use of GCE AL/AS unit grade information, A* grades, the Extended Project (EPQ), the Advanced Diploma and the Cambridge Pre-U examination when considering applicants and making offers. An EPQ may be accepted in place of an AS subject. Check websites of universities and colleges for the latest offers information.

Your target offers and examples of courses provided by each institution
380 pts **Cambridge** – A*AA college offers may vary (A-Sxn Nrs Celt) (IB 40–42 pts)
360 pts **Oxford** – AAA (Celt courses)
340 pts **Glasgow** – AAB (Gael courses) (IB 34 pts)
300 pts **Cardiff** – 300 pts (Welsh)
         Edinburgh – BBB (Scot Ethnol) (IB 34 pts HL 555)
         Queen's Belfast – BBB–BBCb (Irish Celt St courses)
         Swansea – BBB (Welsh courses)
280 pts **Cardiff** – BBC (Welsh Ital/Span; Welsh Relig St)
260 pts **Aberystwyth** – 260 pts (Celt St) (IB 28 pts)
         Liverpool – BCC (Ir St Pol) (IB 27 pts)
240 pts **Aberdeen** – CCC (Celt Civ courses; Celt St courses; Gael St courses)
         Aberystwyth – 240 pts (Welsh Celt Langs) (IB 28 pts)
         Bangor – 240–260 pts (Welsh Hist – also available in Welsh)
         St Mary's Twickenham (UC) – 240 pts (Ir St courses)
         Ulster – 240 pts (Ir courses)
220 pts **Cardiff (UWIC)** – 220 pts (Educ St Welsh)
200 pts **Glamorgan** – 200–240 pts (Prof Welsh courses)
180 pts **UHI Millennium Inst** – DDD 180 pts (Gael; Gael Lang Cult; Gael Trad Mus; Gael Media St)

Alternative offers
See **Chapter 7** and **Appendix 1** for grades/UCAS Tariff points information for the International Baccalaureate, Scottish Highers/Advanced Highers, the Welsh Baccalaureate, the Irish Leaving Certificate, the Cambridge Pre-U Diploma, the Advanced Diploma and the Extended Project.

CHOOSING YOUR COURSE (SEE ALSO CH. 1)

Some course features
Aberystwyth There are beginners' courses for those with no previous knowledge of Welsh or Celtic languages. (Welsh Celt Langs) One or more Celtic languages, together with Welsh, are studied, with a semester spent in Brittany or Ireland.
Bangor (Welsh Hist Arch) The course focuses on the development of Wales over the centuries, the changing nature of society and settlements, and the historical context of contemporary Wales.
Edinburgh In addition to studying the cultures of Ireland and Wales, Scottish Gaelic is offered on the course in Celtic Studies.
Queen's Belfast (Ir Celt) The course focuses on modern Irish language and literature and contemporary Irish culture and society, but also provides a study of Old and Middle Irish, Scottish Gaelic, Welsh and Cornish. Students spend at least six weeks in the Gaeltacht.
UHI Millennium Inst The only degree in Scotland delivered entirely through Gaelic.

Universities and colleges teaching quality See www.qaa.ac.uk; http://unistats.direct.gov.uk.

Top research universities and colleges (RAE 2008) (Celtic studies) Cambridge; Ulster; Aberystwyth; Swansea; Cardiff; Glasgow; Bangor; Edinburgh.

ADMISSIONS INFORMATION

Number of applicants per place (approx) Aberystwyth 6; Bangor 8; Cambridge 2; Cardiff 2; Exeter 5; St Mary's Twickenham (UC) 3; Swansea 7.

Advice to applicants and planning the UCAS personal statement Interests in this field largely develop through literature, museum visits or archaeology which should be fully described in the UCAS application.

Selection interviews Yes Aberystwyth; **No** St Mary's Twickenham (UC).

Interview advice and questions Past questions have included: Why do you want to study this subject? What specific areas of Celtic culture interest you? What do you expect to gain by studying unusual subjects? See **Chapter 6**.

AFTER-RESULTS ADVICE

Offers to applicants repeating A-levels Higher Glasgow (AAA); **Same** Aberystwyth, Bangor, Cardiff, Swansea.

GRADUATE DESTINATIONS AND EMPLOYMENT (2007/8 HESA)

Graduates surveyed 150 **Employed** 45 **In further study** 60 **Assumed unemployed** 10

Career note See **Combined Courses** and **Languages**.

OTHER DEGREE SUBJECTS FOR CONSIDERATION

Anthropology; Archaeology; History.

CHEMISTRY

(see also **Biochemistry, Engineering (Chemical), Pharmacy and Pharmaceutical Sciences**)

There is a shortage of applicants for this subject despite the fact that it is the basis of a wide range of careers in the manufacturing industries. These focus on such areas as pharmaceuticals, medicine, veterinary science and health, agriculture, petroleum, cosmetics, plastics, the food industry, colour chemistry and aspects of the environment such as pollution and recycling.

Useful websites www.rsc.org; www.chem.ox.ac.uk/vrchemistry.

NB The points totals shown to the left of the institutions are for ease of reference only. It must not be assumed that Tariff points are always used by institutions or that they can be substituted for an offer in grades. The level of an offer is not necessarily indicative of the quality of a course.

COURSE OFFERS INFORMATION

Subject requirements/preferences GCSE English, mathematics/science subjects usually required. A/B grades often stipulated by popular universities. **AL** Two science subjects including chemistry required.

NB In 2012 universities and colleges will differ in their use of GCE AL/AS unit grade information, A* grades, the Extended Project (EPQ), the Advanced Diploma and the Cambridge Pre-U examination when considering applicants and making offers. An EPQ may be accepted in place of an AS subject. Check websites of universities and colleges for the latest offers information.

Your target offers and examples of courses provided by each institution

380 pts **Cambridge** – A*AA college offers may vary (Nat Sci (Chem)) (IB 38–42 pts HL 766–777)

Oxford – A*AA (Chem) (IB 38–40 pts)

360 pts **Bristol** – AAA–ABB (Chem courses) (IB 35–33 pts HL 665)

Durham – AAA (Nat Sci (Chem))

Edinburgh – AAA–ABB (Chem courses) (IB 37–32 pts)

Imperial London – AAA (Chem Fr Sci)
London (UCL) – AAA–AAB (Medcnl Chem) (IB 32–36 pts)
St Andrews – AAA inc chem (Chem Geol) (IB 36 pts)
York – AAA–ABB (Chem Res Env) (IB 32 pts)
340 pts **Aston** – AAB (MChem Chem)
Cardiff – AAB–ABB 340–320 pts (Chem courses MChem)
Durham – AAA–AAB (Chem Courses) (36 pts)
Exeter – AAB–BBB (Biol Medicin Chem) (IB 34–30 pts)
Nottingham – AAB–BBB (Medcnl Biol Chem) (IB 34–32 pts)
St Andrews – AAB (Chem Maths) (IB 36 pts)
Sheffield – AAB (Chem Am) (IB 33 pts)
Southampton – AAB–ABB (Chem Maths) (IB 34–32 pts)
Sussex – AAB–ABB (Chem MChem BSc) (IB 34–36 pts)
Warwick – AAB (Chem MChem)
320 pts **Aberdeen** – ABB–BBB (Chem; Biomed Mat Chem; Chem Off Ind; Env Chem)
Bath – ABB (Chem Drug Dscvry) (IB 34 pts HL chem 6)
Birmingham – ABB–BBC (Chem MSci; Chem Analyt Chem)
Cardiff – ABB–BBB 320–300 pts (Chem BSc)
East Anglia – ABB–BBB (Cheml Phys) (IB 31 pts)
Glasgow – ABB (Chem Medcnl Chem) (IB 32 pts)
Lancaster – 320-340 pts (Env Chem courses MChem) (IB 32–34 pts)
Leeds – ABB–BBB (Nanotech) (IB 32 pts)
Leicester – ABB–BBC (Chem MChem) (IB 30–32 pts)
Liverpool – ABB–BBB (Chem MChem) (IB 33–28 pts)
Manchester – ABB (Chem Pat Law)
Newcastle – ABB–BBB (Chem N Am/Euro) (IB 32 pts HL chem 6)
Queen's Belfast – ABB (Chem MSci)
Reading – ABB–BBB (Chem courses MChem)
St Andrews – ABB (Cheml Sci) (IB 31–34 pts)
Sheffield – ABB (Chem Euro) (IB 32–35 pts)
Sussex – ABB–BBB (Chem BSc) (IB 32–34 pts)
Warwick – ABB (Chem BSc)
300 pts **Aberdeen** – ABB–BBB (Medcnl Chem)
Aston – BBB (Chem BSc)
Birmingham – BBB (Chem Pharmacol) (IB 31 pts HL chem 5 HL chem 5)
Bristol UWE – 300 pts (Foren Chem) (IB 27 pts)
Dundee – BCC 1st yr entry (Biol Chem Drug Dscvry) (IB 30 pts)
East Anglia – BBB (Env Chem) (IB 31 pts)
Heriot-Watt – BBB 1st yr entry (Chem Nanotech) (IB 28 pts)
Keele – 300 pts (Chem courses) (IB 26–28 pts)
Kent – BBB–BBC (Foren Chem) (IB 33–31 pts)
Liverpool – BBB (Chem Ocean) (IB 31 pts)
London (QM) – 300 pts (Chem courses) (IB 26–28 pts)
Loughborough – 300–320 pts (Chem BSc) (IB 32 pts)
Northumbria – 300 pts (Chem MChem) (IB 26 pts)
Plymouth – 300–280 pts (Analyt Chem) (IB 28 pts)
Surrey – 300–320 pts (Medcnl Chem) (IB 30 pts)
280 pts **Brighton** – BBC 280 pts (Pharml Chem Sci) (IB 30 pts)
Central Lancashire – (Foren Chem)
Huddersfield – 280 pts (Chem Bioch)
Leicester – BBC (Chem BSc) (IB 30–28 pts)
Liverpool – BBC (Chem Foren Analys) (IB 28 pts HL chem 5)
Loughborough – 280–300 pts (Chem Foren Analys) (IB 32 pts)
Northumbria – 280 pts (Pharml Chem) (IB 25 pts)
Nottingham Trent – 280–260 pts (Chem MChem/BSc)

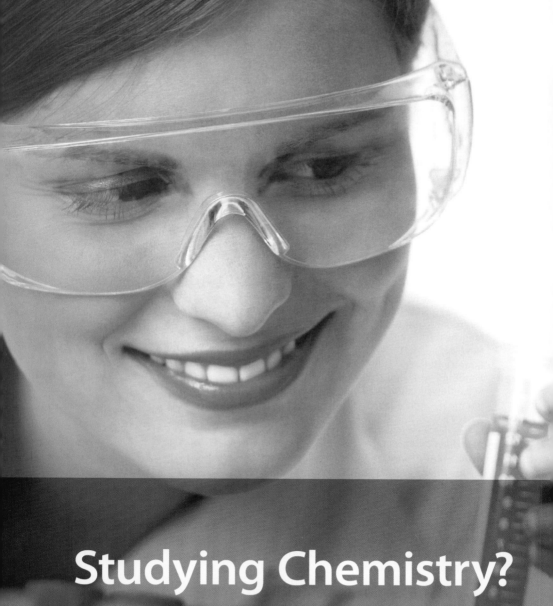

Studying Chemistry?
Join RSC ChemNet today

Latest chemistry news, information and support

RSC ChemNet membership offers a wide range of services and support for chemistry students

Join RSC ChemNet, the Royal Society of Chemistry network for 16-18 year olds studying chemistry. Receive regular mailings updating you on the latest advances in chemistry and the support of the RSC chemistry community. Members also have the opportunity to explore chemistry in the real world by attending local and national RSC ChemNet events.

- **Chemistry World and ChemNet News**
  Read about cutting-edge research, news analysis, features, careers information and events

- **Specialist information**
  Receive advice on scientific careers and assistance with the UCAS application process

- **MyRSC: Online Chemistry Network**
  Join groups, explore blogs and connect with other RSC ChemNet members

- **Visits to universities and industry**
  Experience what life is like as a student and see what careers are available to chemistry graduates

- **National events**
  Attend 'Meet the Universities' to help make university choices and the RSC's online careers fair, ChemCareers

- **Support and advice**
  Talk to university ChemSocs and RSC Local Sections about their own personal experiences in chemistry

www.rsc.org/chemnet
Registered Charity Number 207890

Queen's Belfast – BBC (Medcnl Chem; Chem Foren Analys; Chem BSc)
Strathclyde – BBC 2nd yr entry (Chem Drug Dscvry) (IB 28 pts)
260 pts **Bradford** – BCC (Chem Pharml Foren Sci) (IB 28 pts)
Brighton – BCC (Analyt Chem Bus) (IB 30 pts)
Central Lancashire – 260 pts (Chem)
Heriot-Watt – BBC (Chem Mats) (IB 28 pts)
Liverpool John Moores – 260 pts (App Chem Pharml Sci) (IB 24 pts)
Nottingham Trent – 260 pts (Pharml Medicin Chem)
Plymouth – 260 pts (Chem)
Queen's Belfast – BCC (Chem Euro)
Reading – 260–300 pts (Chem BSc; Chem Arch; Chem Educ)
240 pts **Bangor** – 240–260 pts (Mar Chem) (IB 28 pts)
Greenwich – 240 pts (Chem)
Huddersfield – 240 pts (Chem)
Hull – 240 pts (Chem Mol Med; Chem Nano)
London Met – 240 pts (Chem)
Manchester Met – 240–280 pts (Pharml Chem)
Teesside – 240–280 pts (Chem)
220 pts **Glamorgan** – 220–260 pts (Foren Chem)
200 pts **Kingston** – 200–280 pts (Chem MChem; Chem BSc; App Chem)
160 pts **Manchester Met** – 160–240 pts (Foren Chem) (IB 24 pts)
140 pts **West Scotland** – CD (Chem; Medcnl Chem)
120 pts **Arts London** – 120 pts (Cos Sci)
80 pts **London (Birk)** – for under 21s (over 21s varies) p/t (Chem)

Open University – contact +44 (0)845 300 6090 **or** www.openuniversity.co.uk/you (Nat Sci)

Alternative offers
See **Chapter 7** and **Appendix 1** for grades/UCAS Tariff points information for the International Baccalaureate, Scottish Highers/Advanced Highers, the Welsh Baccalaureate, the Irish Leaving Certificate, the Cambridge Pre-U Diploma, the Advanced Diploma and the Extended Project.

EXAMPLES OF FOUNDATION DEGREES IN THE SUBJECT FIELD
London Met.

CHOOSING YOUR COURSE (SEE ALSO CH. 1)
Some course features
Birmingham Single Honours or major/minor courses which link chemistry with business, environmental science, pharmacology or psychology.
Durham Chemistry is offered as a Single or Joint Honours course or as part of the Natural Sciences programme.
Leeds Industrial bursary scheme for students.
London (UCL) MSc and BSc courses are common in the first two years after which a choice can be made. MSc courses provide greater depth and are aimed at those wishing to follow a scientific career.
Loughborough Strong links with industry for sandwich courses.
Manchester A range of course options including placements in industry, Europe and North America.
Warwick MSc and BSc courses are common in the first two years after which a choice can be made. MSc courses provide greater depth and are aimed at those wishing to follow a scientific career.
York Sponsorships and sandwich courses available.

Universities and colleges teaching quality See www.qaa.ac.uk; http://unistats.direct.gov.uk.

Top research universities and colleges (RAE 2008) Cambridge; Nottingham; Oxford; Edinburgh; St Andrews; Bristol; Imperial London; Leeds; Warwick; York; Liverpool; Manchester; Sheffield.

Examples of sandwich degree courses Aston; Bangor; Bath; Bradford; Cardiff; Dundee; Glamorgan; Kingston; Liverpool John Moores; Loughborough; Manchester; Manchester Met; Northumbria; Nottingham Trent; Queen's Belfast; St Andrews; Surrey; Sussex; Teesside; West Scotland; York.

ADMISSIONS INFORMATION

Number of applicants per place (approx) Bangor (Mar Chem) 3, (Chem) 6; Bath 7; Bradford (Chem Pharml Foren Sci) 10; Bristol 5; Durham 6; Edinburgh 5; Heriot-Watt 6; Hull 7; Imperial London 3; Kingston 4; Leeds 3; Leicester 9; London (QM) 3; London (UCL) 5; Newcastle 5; Nottingham (Chem Mol Phys) 4, (Chem) 8; Oxford (success rate 63%); Southampton 7; Surrey 3; York 5.

Advice to applicants and planning the UCAS personal statement Extend your knowledge beyond your exam studies by reading scientific journals and keeping abreast of scientific developments in the news. Discuss any visits to chemical firms and laboratories, for example, pharmaceutical, food science, rubber and plastic, paper, photographic, environmental health. See also **Appendix 4**.

Misconceptions about this course Many students do not fully appreciate the strengths of a Chemistry degree for any career despite the fact that graduates regularly go into a diverse range of careers. **Durham** Students fail to realise that they require mathematics and that physics is useful.

Selection interviews Yes Bangor, Bath, Bristol, Cambridge, Coventry, Durham, Greenwich, Huddersfield, Hull, Keele (mature students only), Kingston, London (UCL), London Met, Loughborough, Newcastle, Northumbria, Nottingham, Nottingham Trent, Oxford (success rate 39%), Sheffield, Surrey, Warwick, York; **Some** Aston, Cardiff, Dundee, East Anglia, Liverpool John Moores, Plymouth; **No** Bristol UWE, Southampton.

Interview advice and questions Be prepared for questions on your chemistry syllabus and aspects that you enjoy the most. In the past a variety of questions have been asked, for example: Why is carbon a special element? Discuss the nature of forces between atoms with varying intermolecular distances. Describe recent practicals. What is acid rain? What other types of pollution are caused by the human race? What is an enzyme? What are the general properties of benzene? Why might sciences be less popular among girls at school? What can a mass spectrometer be used for? What would you do if a river turned bright blue and you were asked how to test a sample? What would be the difference between metal and non-metal pollution? See also **Chapter 6**. **Bath** Why Chemistry? Discuss the practical work you are doing. **Oxford** No written or work tests. Evidence required of motivation and further potential and a capacity to analyse and use information to form opinions and a willingness to discuss them. **York** Discuss your favourite areas of chemistry, some of your extra-curricular activities, your preferred learning styles – for example, small tutorials of four or fewer, lectures.

Reasons for rejection (non-academic) Didn't attend interview. Rude and unco-operative. Arrived under influence of drink. Poor attitude and poor commitment to chemistry. Incomplete, inappropriate, illegible, illiterate personal statements. **Southampton** Applicants called for interview are not normally rejected.

AFTER-RESULTS ADVICE

Offers to applicants repeating A-levels Higher Bangor, Dundee, Hull, Leeds, Northumbria, Nottingham, St Andrews, Warwick; **Possibly higher** Coventry, Edinburgh, Newcastle; **Same** Aston, Bath, Bristol (no offer if first-time grades are low), Cardiff, Durham, East Anglia, Greenwich, Heriot-Watt, Huddersfield, Keele, Kingston, Liverpool John Moores, London (UCL), London Met, Loughborough, Plymouth, Sheffield, Surrey.

GRADUATE DESTINATIONS AND EMPLOYMENT (2007/8 HESA)

Graduates surveyed 2125 **Employed** 685 **In further study** 865 **Assumed unemployed** 195

Career note A large number of chemistry graduates choose to go on to further study as well as into scientific careers in research, analysis or development. Significant numbers also follow careers in a wide range of areas in management, teaching and retail work.

OTHER DEGREE SUBJECTS FOR CONSIDERATION

Agriculture; Biochemistry; Biological Sciences; Biomedical Science; Chemical Engineering; Environmental Science; Forensic Science; Genetics; Materials Science; Medicine; Microbiology; Oceanography; Pharmacology; Pharmacy.

CHINESE

(including **Korean**; see also **Asia-Pacific Studies, Languages**)

Oriental languages are not necessarily difficult languages but they differ considerably in their writing systems which present their own problems for the new student. Even so, Chinese is not a language to be chosen for its novelty and students should have a strong interest in China and its people. It is a country with a high economic growth rate and there are good opportunities for graduates, an increasing number being recruited by firms based in East Asia. Other opportunities exist in diplomacy, aid work and tourism throughout China, Taiwan and Mongolia as well as most non-scientific career areas in the UK.

Useful websites www.cilt.org.uk; www.iol.org.uk; www.bbc.co.uk/languages; www.china.org.cn/english; www.languageadvantage.com; www.languagematters.co.uk; www.reed.co.uk/multilingual; www.chineseculture.about.com.

NB The points totals shown to the left of the institutions are for ease of reference only. It must not be assumed that Tariff points are always used by institutions or that they can be substituted for an offer in grades. The level of an offer is not necessarily indicative of the quality of a course.

COURSE OFFERS INFORMATION

Subject requirements/preferences GCSE A language is required. **AL** A modern language is usually required.

NB In 2012 universities and colleges will differ in their use of GCE AL/AS unit grade information, A* grades, the Extended Project (EPQ), the Advanced Diploma and the Cambridge Pre-U examination when considering applicants and making offers. An EPQ may be accepted in place of an AS subject. Check websites of universities and colleges for the latest offers information.

Your target offers and examples of courses provided by each institution

380 pts Cambridge – A*AA college offers may vary (As Mid E St (Chin St)) (IB 39–42 pts)

360 pts Manchester – AAA–AAB (Chin Jap MML)
         Oxford – AAA (Chin) (IB 38–42 pts)

340 pts Birmingham – AAA–AAB (Int Bus Mand Chin) (IB 36-38 pts)
         London (SOAS) – AAB (Chin (Modn Class)) (IB 36 pts HL 666)
         Manchester – AAB–BBB (Chin Ling) (IB 35–30 pts)
         Nottingham – AAB–BBB (Contemp Chin St) (IB 32 pts)

320 pts Leeds – ABB (21 joint Hons Chin courses) (IB 34 pts)
         London (SOAS) – ABB (Kor) (IB 34 pts)
         Manchester – ABB–BBC (Chin Jap BA)
         Newcastle – ABB (Chin/Jap Cult St) (IB 32 pts)
         Sheffield – ABB (Chin St Hist)

300 pts Edinburgh – BBB (Int Bus Chin) (IB 34 pts HL 555)
         Manchester – BBB–BBC (Chin Scrn St) (IB 30 pts)
         Newcastle – ABC/BBB (Ling Chin/Jap) (IB 32 pts HL engl 5)
         Sheffield – BBB–BBC (Chin St Fr/Ger/Jap/Russ/Span)
         Westminster – BBB (Jrnl Contemp Chin St) (IB 32 pts)

280 pts Edge Hill – 280 pts (Engl Chin St) (IB 24 pts)
         Sheffield – BBC (Mus Chin St)
         Westminster – BBC (Int Rel Chin)

260 pts Central Lancashire – 260–300 pts (Bus Mgt Chin) (IB 28 pts)
         Liverpool John Moores – 260 pts (PR Chin)
         Nottingham Trent – 260 pts (Chin Glob St) (IB 24 pts)

240 pts Liverpool John Moores – 240 pts (Int Bus St Chin)

180 pts Trinity Saint David – 180–240 pts (Chin St Anth; Chin St Phil; Chin St Relig St)

Alternative offers

See **Chapter 7** and **Appendix 1** for grades/UCAS Tariff points information for the International Baccalaureate, Scottish Highers/Advanced Highers, the Welsh Baccalaureate, the Irish Leaving Certificate, the Cambridge Pre-U Diploma, the Advanced Diploma and the Extended Project.

CHOOSING YOUR COURSE (SEE ALSO CH. 1)

Some course features

Edinburgh (Chin) This is an intensive language course in Mandarin Chinese and Modern Standard (colloquial) Chinese. Year 3 is spent in China.

Leeds (Chin Int Rel) Year 2 spent in China taking language courses at a university in Beijing, Tianjin or Taipei. Students expected to reach a high standard of language ability.

London (SOAS) (Chin (Modn Class)) Course designed to give broad understanding of Chinese culture, past and present, through its language, history and literature. In Years 3 and 4 students can choose to specialise in either modern or classical China.

Manchester (Chin St) Course covers both language (Mandarin) and culture, society, economics, politics and international relations.

Newcastle (Chin/Jap Cult St) Course provides language tuition in either language.

Sheffield (Mus Chin St) Dual Honours course allows students to design their own Music programme, specialising in composition, dissertation or performance. Chinese Studies involves intensive language learning (from scratch or with some prior knowledge). Year 2 at Nanjing University, and modules in Chinese business, literature, history and the environment.

Trinity Saint David (Chin St) A broad course covering the language, culture, politics, economics, philosophy and religions of China. There is a four-month placement at a Chinese university.

Universities and colleges teaching quality See www.qaa.ac.uk; http://unistats.direct.gov.uk.

Top research universities and colleges (RAE 2008) (Asian Studies) London (SOAS); Oxford; Cambridge; Leeds; Manchester; Nottingham; Westminster.

Examples of sandwich degree courses Westminster.

ADMISSIONS INFORMATION

Number of applicants per place (approx) Leeds 5; London (SOAS) 8; Westminster 18.

Advice to applicants and planning the UCAS personal statement It will be necessary to demonstrate a knowledge of China, its culture, political and economic background. Visits to the Far East should be mentioned, with reference to any features which have influenced your choice of degree course. See also **Appendix 4** under **Languages**.

Selection interviews Yes Cambridge, Leeds, London (SOAS), Oxford.

Interview advice and questions You will be expected to convince the admissions tutor why you want to study the language. Your knowledge of Chinese culture, politics and society in general, and of Far Eastern problems, could also be tested. See also **Chapter 6**.

Reasons for rejection (non-academic) Oxford His language background seemed a little weak and his written work not as strong as that of other applicants. At interview he showed himself to be a dedicated hard-working young man but lacking in the imagination, flexibility and the intellectual liveliness needed to succeed on the course.

AFTER-RESULTS ADVICE

Offers to applicants repeating A-levels Higher Leeds.

GRADUATE DESTINATIONS AND EMPLOYMENT (2007/8 HESA)

Graduates surveyed 80 **Employed** 30 **In further study** 20 **Assumed unemployed** 5

Career note See **Languages**.

OTHER DEGREE SUBJECTS FOR CONSIDERATION

Traditional Chinese Medicine; other Oriental languages.

CLASSICAL STUDIES/CLASSICAL CIVILISATION

(see also **Archaeology, Classics, Greek, History (Ancient), Latin**)

Classical Studies and Classical Civilisation courses cover the literature, history, philosophy and archaeology of Ancient Greece and Rome. A knowledge of Latin or Greek is not necessary for many courses, but check subject requirements carefully.

Useful websites www.britishmuseum.org; see also **History** and **History (Ancient)**.

NB The points totals shown to the left of the institutions are for ease of reference only. It must not be assumed that Tariff points are always used by institutions or that they can be substituted for an offer in grades. The level of an offer is not necessarily indicative of the quality of a course.

COURSE OFFERS INFORMATION

Subject requirements/preferences GCSE English and a foreign language often required. **AL** A modern language is required for joint language courses. Relevant subjects include classical civilisation, English literature, archaeology, Latin, Greek.

NB In 2012 universities and colleges will differ in their use of GCE AL/AS unit grade information, A* grades, the Extended Project (EPQ), the Advanced Diploma and the Cambridge Pre-U examination when considering applicants and making offers. An EPQ may be accepted in place of an AS subject. Check websites of universities and colleges for the latest offers information.

Your target offers and examples of courses provided by each institution

360 pts Exeter – AAA–AAB (Class St courses) (IB 36 pts)
       London (King's) – AAB+AS (Class St Byz Modn Gk St) (IB 36 pts HL 665)
       Warwick – AAbc (Class Civ) (IB 36 pts)

340 pts Bristol – AAB–ABB (Class St Phil) (IB 35–33 pts)
       Glasgow – AAB (Class (Class Civ)) (IB 30 pts)
       London (King's) – AAB+AS (Class St Film St) (IB 36 pts HL 665)
       London (UCL) – ABB+AS (Anc Wrld St Class) (IB 34-36 pts)
       Manchester – AAB–BBB (Comb St courses) (IB 35–32 pts)
       Newcastle – AAB (Class St Engl) (IB 35 pts HL Engl 6)
       St Andrews – AAB (Class St courses) (IB 36 pts)

320 pts Birmingham – ABB–BBB (Class Lit Civ joint courses) (IB 32 pts)
       Leeds – ABB–BBB (Class Civ; Class Lit Russ Civ; Rom Civ Russ Civ; Gk Civ courses)
       London (RH) – ABB (Class St Dr) (IB 34 pts)
       Manchester – ABB–BBB (Class St) (IB 33–32 pts)
       Newcastle – ABB (Class St) (IB 32 pts)
       Nottingham – ABB (Class Civ Phil) (IB 34 pts)
       Swansea – ABB (Class Civ joint courses)

300 pts Edinburgh – BBB–AAA (Class St; Class Arch Gk)
       Kent – 300–340 pts (Class Arch St courses) (IB 33 pts)
       Leeds – ABB–BBB (Rom Civ Courses) (IB 32–33 pts)
       Liverpool – ABB–BBB (Class St Modn Lang) (IB 30 pts)
       Nottingham – ABC/BBB (Class Civ Art Hist) (IB 32 pts)
       Reading – 300–340 pts (Class St Engl Lit) (IB 30 pts)

240 pts Roehampton – 240–320 pts (Class Civ courses)

180 pts Trinity Saint David – 180–240 pts (Class St courses)

 80 pts London (Birk) – for under 21s (over 21s varies) p/t (Class St)

Alternative offers

See **Chapter 7** and **Appendix 1** for grades/UCAS Tariff points information for the International Baccalaureate, Scottish Highers/Advanced Highers, the Welsh Baccalaureate, the Irish Leaving Certificate, the Cambridge Pre-U Diploma, the Advanced Diploma and the Extended Project.

CHOOSING YOUR COURSE (SEE ALSO CH. 1)

Some course features
Birmingham (Class Lit Civ) Broad course covering literature, history, drama, politics, philosophy, art, religion and science.
Durham Three courses (Classical Past, Ancient History and Classics) have a common first year.
London (King's) (Class St) One language option module (Greek or Latin) to be taken in Year 1.
London (RH) (Class St) Option courses in Year 1 include Greek law, Roman Egypt, the built environment and women in classical antiquity.
Manchester (Class St) Greek or Latin options available including beginners' courses.

Universities and colleges teaching quality See www.qaa.ac.uk; http://unistats.direct.gov.uk.

Top research universities and colleges (RAE 2008) See **Classics**.

ADMISSIONS INFORMATION

Number of applicants per place (approx) Birmingham 3; Bristol 9; Durham (Class Past) 10; Exeter 3; Leeds 7; London (RH) 4; Manchester (Class St) 4; Newcastle 8; Nottingham 6; Reading 10; Swansea 5; Trinity Saint David 2; Warwick 23.

Advice to applicants and planning the UCAS personal statement Discuss any A-level work and what has attracted you to this subject. Describe visits to classical sites or museums and what impressed you.

Misconceptions about this course Birmingham (Class Lit Civ) A study of classics at school is not necessary although while many people catch the classics bug by doing classical civilisation at A-level, others come to classics through reading the myths or seeing the plays and being fascinated by them. For others the inter-disciplinary nature of the subject attracts them – literature, drama, history, politics and philosophy. **Exeter** (Class St) This is not a language degree. There is no requirement for either A-level Latin or Greek.

Selection interviews Yes Birmingham, Durham, Kent, London (RH), Newcastle, Nottingham, Trinity Saint David; **Some** Bristol, Warwick.

Interview advice and questions In the past questions have included: What special interests do you have in Classical Studies/Classics? Have you visited Greece, Rome or any other classical sites or museums and what were your impressions? These are the types of questions to expect, along with those to explore your knowledge of the culture, theatre and architecture of the period. See also **Chapter 6**. **Birmingham** (Class Lit Civ) The programme includes some language study and, if applicants do not have a GCSE in a foreign language, we ask them to do a short language aptitude test. Interview questions are likely to focus on your reading interests (not necessarily classical texts!) and your own reflections on them. We are interested in your ability to think for yourself and we want to be sure that you are someone who will enjoy three years of reading and talking about books. **Swansea** Reasons for choosing the subject and how the student hopes to benefit from the course.

Reasons for rejection (non-academic) Birmingham Lukewarm interest in the subject. Lack of clear idea why they wanted to do this degree.

AFTER-RESULTS ADVICE

Offers to applicants repeating A-levels Higher Glasgow (AAA), Nottingham, St Andrews, Warwick; **Same** Birmingham, Bristol, Durham, Exeter, Leeds, London (RH), Newcastle.

GRADUATE DESTINATIONS AND EMPLOYMENT (2007/8 HESA)

Graduates surveyed 660 **Employed** 225 **In further study** 210 **Assumed unemployed** 65

Career note As with other non-vocational subjects, graduates enter a wide range of careers. In a small number of cases this may be subject-related with work in museums and art galleries. However, much will depend on how the student's interests develop during the undergraduate years and career planning should start early.

How to read the Subject Tables: **Chapter 7**

OTHER DEGREE SUBJECTS FOR CONSIDERATION
Archaeology; Ancient History; Classics; Greek; History; History of Art; Latin; Philosophy.

CLASSICS
(see also Classical Studies/Classical Civilisation, Greek, Latin)

Classics courses focus on a study of Greek and Latin but may also include topics related to ancient history, art and architecture, drama and philosophy. These subjects are also frequently offered in joint courses.

Useful websites www.classicspage.com; www.classics.ac.uk; www.cambridgescp.com; www.bbc.co.uk/history/ancient/greeks; www.bbc.co.uk/history/ancient/romans.

NB The points totals shown to the left of the institutions are for ease of reference only. It must not be assumed that Tariff points are always used by institutions or that they can be substituted for an offer in grades. The level of an offer is not necessarily indicative of the quality of a course.

COURSE OFFERS INFORMATION
Subject requirements/preferences GCSE English and a foreign language usually required. Grades A*/A/B may be stipulated. **AL** Check courses for Latin/Greek requirements.

NB In 2012 universities and colleges will differ in their use of GCE AL/AS unit grade information, A* grades, the Extended Project (EPQ), the Advanced Diploma and the Cambridge Pre-U examination when considering applicants and making offers. An EPQ may be accepted in place of an AS subject. Check websites of universities and colleges for the latest offers information.

Your target offers and examples of courses provided by each institution
380 pts **Cambridge** – A*AA college offers may vary (Modn Mediev Langs (Class Lat) (Class Gk)) (IB 38–42 pts))
360 pts **Bristol** – AAA–AAB (Class) (IB 37–35 pts)
     Exeter – AAA–AAB (Classics) (IB 36–31 pts HL Lat/Gk 6)
     London (King's) – AAB+AS (Classics) (IB 36 pts HL 665)
     Oxford – AAA (Class Orntl St) (IB 38–40 pts)
     Warwick – AABc (Classics) (IB 36–32 pts)
340 pts **Durham** – AAB (Class; Class Past)
     London (UCL) – ABBe (Class Abrd) (IB 34 pts)
     Nottingham – AAB (Class) (IB 34 pts)
     St Andrews – AAB (Class courses) (IB 36 pts)
320 pts **Leeds** – ABB (Classics A/B)
     Liverpool – ABB (Classics) (IB 30 pts)
     London (RH) – ABB (Classics) (IB 34 pts)
     Manchester – ABB–BBB (Class Anc Hist) (IB 33–32 pts)
     Newcastle – AAB–ABB (Classics) (IB 32-36 pts)
     Reading – 320–340 pts (Classics) (IB 32–34 pts)
     Swansea – ABB (Classics)
300 pts **Edinburgh** – BBB (Hist Class)
200 pts **Trinity Saint David** – 200 pts (Classics)
  80 pts **London (Birk)** – for under 21s (over 21s varies) p/t (Classics)

Alternative offers
See **Chapter 7** and **Appendix 1** for grades/UCAS Tariff points information for the International Baccalaureate, Scottish Highers/Advanced Highers, the Welsh Baccalaureate, the Irish Leaving Certificate, the Cambridge Pre-U Diploma, the Advanced Diploma and the Extended Project.

CHOOSING YOUR COURSE (SEE ALSO CH. 1)
Some course features
Bristol (Class) Greek and Latin languages are studied for the first two years plus option topics from literature, art, philosophy, political, social and cultural history.
Cambridge (Class Gk Lat) Latin or Greek A-levels not required for the four-year course.
Liverpool (Class) 50% of the course consists of language study (Greek or Latin) including beginners' level. The remainder is a study of literature, art, history and archaeology.
Newcastle (Class) A concentration on the study of Greek and Latin languages and literature.
Oxford Course II (Latin or Greek) requires no formal qualifications.
St Andrews (Class) A wide range of related subjects is offered as part of the Single Honours course and a wide choice of complementary courses from other departments.

Universities and colleges teaching quality See www.qaa.ac.uk; http://unistats.direct.gov.uk.

Top research universities and colleges (RAE 2008) (including Classics, Ancient History, Byzantine and Modern Greek Studies) Cambridge; Oxford; London (UCL); London (King's); Durham; Warwick; Exeter; Manchester; Bristol; St Andrews.

ADMISSIONS INFORMATION
Number of applicants per place (approx) Bristol 14; Cambridge 2; Durham (Class) 8, (Class Past) 10; Leeds 4; London (King's) 6; London (RH) 6; Manchester (Class) 10, (Class Anc Hist) 8; Newcastle 14; Nottingham 6; Oxford 2; Swansea 6; Trinity Saint David 5.

Advice to applicants and planning the UCAS personal statement Describe any visits made to classical sites or museums, or literature which you have read and enjoyed. Discuss any significant aspects which impressed you. Classics is an interdisciplinary subject and universities are looking for people who are versatile, imaginative and independently minded, so all types of extra-curricular activities (drama, music, philosophy, creative arts, politics, other languages and cultures) will be relevant. See also **Classical Studies/Classical Civilisation**.

Misconceptions about this course While Classics can appear irrelevant and élitist, universities aim to assist students to leave with a range of transferable skills that are of importance to employers.

Selection interviews **Yes** Cambridge, London (RH), London (UCL), Newcastle, Oxford (Class) 45%, (Class Eng) 20%, (Class Mod Lang) 33%, Swansea; **Some** Bristol, Warwick; **No** Durham, Leeds, St Andrews.

Interview advice and questions What do you think it means to study Classics? Do you think Classics is still a vital and central cultural discipline? What made you apply to study Classics at this university? There are often detailed questions on the texts which the students have read, to find out how reflective they are in their reading. See also **Classical Studies/Classical Civilisation** and **Chapter 6**.
Cambridge What would happen if the Classics department burned down? Do you think feminism is dead? Emma has become a different person since she took up yoga. Therefore she is not responsible for anything she did before she took up yoga. Discuss. **Oxford** Written tests to demonstrate ability in linguistics, competence in translation. Use of dictionaries not permitted. Classics and English applicants take the English Admissions Test.

Reasons for rejection (non-academic) Did not demonstrate a clear sense of why they wanted to study Classics rather than anything else.

AFTER-RESULTS ADVICE
Offers to applicants repeating A-levels **Higher** Leeds, Nottingham, St Andrews; **Same** Cambridge, Durham, Newcastle, Swansea.

GRADUATE DESTINATIONS AND EMPLOYMENT (2007/8 HESA)
See **Classical Studies/Classical Civilisation**.

Career note See **Classical Studies/Classical Civilisation**.

OTHER DEGREE SUBJECTS FOR CONSIDERATION

See **Classical Studies/Classical Civilisation**.

COMBINED COURSES

(including **Arts Management** and **Cultural Studies**; see also **Art and Design (General)**)

Many different subjects are offered in combined or modular arrangements. These courses are particularly useful for those applicants who have difficulty in deciding on one specialist subject to follow, allowing students to mix and match according to their interests and often enabling them to embark on new subjects.

Useful websites www.artscouncil.org.uk; www.scottisharts.org.uk; www.arts.org.uk; www.arts professional.co.uk; www.culturalstudies.net.

NB The points totals shown to the left of the institutions are for ease of reference only. It must not be assumed that Tariff points are always used by institutions or that they can be substituted for an offer in grades. The level of an offer is not necessarily indicative of the quality of a course.

COURSE OFFERS INFORMATION

Subject requirements/preferences GCSE English, mathematics or science and foreign language may be required by some universities. **AL** Some joint courses may require a specified subject.

NB In 2012 universities and colleges will differ in their use of GCE AL/AS unit grade information, A* grades, the Extended Project (EPQ), the Advanced Diploma and the Cambridge Pre-U examination when considering applicants and making offers. An EPQ may be accepted in place of an AS subject. Check websites of universities and colleges for the latest offers information.

Your target offers and examples of courses provided by each institution
The offers listed below are average offers. Specific offers will vary depending on the relative popularity of each subject. Check with the admissions tutor of your selected institution.

430 pts **London (King's)** – A*AAb/A*Aaab (Librl Arts) (IB 38 HL 666)
360 pts **Durham** – The offers listed are average offers. Specific offers will vary depending on the popularity of the subjects in combination. AAA (Comb Arts/Soc Sci BA) (IB 38 pts)
    Exeter – AAA–ABB (Flex Comb Hons)
    London (UCL) – AAA (Arts Sci)
    Newcastle – AAA (Comb Hons BA) (IB 34 pts HL 555+)
340 pts **Glasgow** – AAB (Hum) (IB 32 pts)
    Imperial London – NB: Hum subjs and lang courses can be taken alongside main subjs AAB (Comb Chem/Biol Fr/Ger/Span)
    Liverpool – AAB–BBB (Comb Hons) (IB 30–35 pts)
320 pts **Cardiff** – ABB 320 pts (Cult Crit joint Hons)
    East Anglia – ABB–BBB (Cult Lit Pol) (IB 35 pts)
    Newcastle – ABB (Chin Cult St) (IB 32 pts)
    Nottingham – ABB (Cult Sociol) (IB 34 pts)
    Strathclyde – ABB–ABC (Arts Soc Sci)
    Surrey – ABB–BBB (Sociol Cult Media) (IB 32 pts)
300 pts **Aston** – 300–320 pts (Comb Hons)
    Edinburgh – BBB (Hum Soc Sci) (IB 34 pts)
    Kent – 300 pts (Cult St) (IB 33 pts HL 15 pts)
    Leeds – BBB (Cult St Fr/Ger/Ital/Jap/Port/Russ) (IB 32 pts)
    Oxford Brookes – BBB (Dr Comb Hons) (IB 33 pts)
    St Andrews – BBB (General Arts/Sci MA/BSc) (IB 32 pts)
280 pts **Birmingham City** – 280 pts (Comb St)
    Brighton – BBC (Glob Hist Pol Cult) (IB 30 pts)
    Bristol UWE – 280–340 pts (Media Cult St)

Essex – 280 pts (Humanities)
Lancaster – 280 pts (Comb Tech)
London (Gold) – BBC (Soc Cult St)
260 pts **Cardiff (UWIC)** – 260 pts (Engl Contemp Media)
Central Lancashire – 260–300 pts (Comb Hons) (IB 28 pts)
Coventry – 260–280 pts (Comb St)
Hertfordshire – 260 pts (Hum) (IB 24–26 pts)
Hull – 260 pts (Media Cult Soty) (IB 28 pts)
Nottingham – BCC 260 pts (Humanities)
Westminster – BCC (Comb Soc Sci (Cult St)) (IB 28 pts)
Winchester – 260–300 pts (Arts Mgt Dr; Arts Mgt Choreo Dance)
240 pts **Aberdeen** – CCC (Arts Soc Sci) (IB 28 pts)
Bath Spa – 240–300 pts (Crea Arts courses)
Canterbury Christ Church – CCC 240 pts (Media Cult St Comb Hons) (IB 24 pts)
Chester – 240 pts (Comb Hons)
Cumbria – 240 pts (Contemp App Arts)
Dundee – CCC 240 pts (Arts Soc Sci) (IB 29 pts)
Edinburgh Napier – 240 pts (Cstmd Prog Cult St)
Heriot-Watt – CCC/BCE (Comb St BSc)
Leeds Trinity (UC) – 240 pts (Hum)
London Met – 240 pts (Arts Mgt joint courses; Arts Mgt Evnts Mgt; Arts Mgt Thea St; Arts Mgt)
London South Bank – 240 pts (Arts Mgt)
Surrey – 240 pts (Hum) (IB 26 pts)
Worcester – 240 pts (Media Cult St Sociol) (IB 26 pts)
220 pts **Bath Spa** – 220–260 pts (Cult St Hist)
Bradford – 220 pts (Comb St BSc)
De Montfort – 220–240 pts (Arts Fstvl Mgt Dance; Arts Fstvl Mgt Dr St)
Kingston – 220 pts (Vis Mat Cult)
Northampton – 220 pts (Joint Hons)
200 pts **East London** – 200 pts (Cult St courses) (IB 27 pts)
Hertfordshire – 200–240 pts (Joint Hons Prog)
Middlesex – 200–300 pts (Mus Arts Mgt)
Roehampton – 200–280 pts (Hum; Comb Hons)
180 pts **Derby** – 180–240 pts (Joint Hons courses)
Liverpool (LIPA) – BC 180 pts (Mus Thea Enter Mgt)
160 pts **Bournemouth Arts (UC)** – 160 pts (Arts Evnt Mgt)
Glamorgan – 160–260 pts (Comb St)
Greenwich – 160 pts (Comb Hons)
Keele – 160 pts (Comb courses Fdn Yr)
120 pts **Wirral Met (Coll)** – DD 120 pts (Cult St (Comb St))
80 pts **London (Birk)** – for under 21s (over 21s varies) p/t (Hum Engl/Fr/Ger; Hum Hisp St; Hum Hist Art; Hum Hist; Hum Media St; Hum Phil)

Open University – contact +44 (0)845 300 6090 **or** www.openuniversity.co.uk/you (Hum Engl/Fr/Ger/Span)
Wigan and Leigh (Coll) – Contact college (Comb Hons)

Alternative offers
See **Chapter 7** and **Appendix 1** for grades/UCAS Tariff points information for the International Baccalaureate, Scottish Highers/Advanced Highers, the Welsh Baccalaureate, the Irish Leaving Certificate, the Cambridge Pre-U Diploma, the Advanced Diploma and the Extended Project.

EXAMPLES OF FOUNDATION DEGREES IN THE SUBJECT FIELD
Bedfordshire; Canterbury Christ Church; Colchester (Inst); Norwich (UCA); Suffolk (Univ Campus); Truro (Coll).

CHOOSING YOUR COURSE (SEE ALSO CH. 1)

Some course features

Birmingham (Media Cult Soty) A study of media and cultural analysis covering national and transnational interests in Europe today.

Cardiff (Cult Crit) Course covers all aspects of society's practices, for example literature, entertainment, buildings, artefacts.

East London (Cult St) Exploration of social and political issues and the media.

Kent (Cult St) A study of popular culture, the arts and everyday life in the context of the social sciences and humanities.

Leeds (Cult St) Course focuses on languages of texts, images, bodies, technologies, spaces and power, the possibilities for radical changes and the constraints and failures of modernity.

Manchester Met (Cult St Comb Hons) Opportunity for exchange study visit to USA in second year.

Nottingham (Cult Sociol) Course based on aspects of philosophy, sociology, history, linguistics and politics.

Universities and colleges teaching quality See www.qaa.ac.uk; http://unistats.direct.gov.uk.

Top research universities and colleges (RAE 2008) (Cultural Studies) See **Communication Studies/ Communication**.

ADMISSIONS INFORMATION

Number of applicants per place (approx) Birmingham 9; Dundee (average) 13; Durham (Comb Arts) 7; Heriot-Watt 3; Leeds 15; Liverpool 6; Newcastle 7; Strathclyde 9.

Advice to applicants and planning the UCAS personal statement Refer to chosen subject tables.
Bath Spa (Crea Arts) Looks for personal statements which clarify relevant work done outside the school syllabus (eg creative writing). **De Montfort** Give information about practical experience and a personal interest in one or more areas of the arts. Show a mature attitude on arts/culture and be an original thinker. **Liverpool** (Comb Hons) We look for evidence of a broad interest across a range of subjects.

Misconceptions about this course Bath Spa (Crea Arts) Some applicants wish to specialise in one subject not realising it is a Joint Honours course. **Liverpool** (Comb Hons) Some students deterred because they believe that the course is too general. This is not so. The degree certificate shows the names of the two subjects taken to Honours degree level.

Selection interviews Yes Aberdeen, Bath Spa, Bristol UWE, De Montfort, Dundee, Durham, London Met, Manchester Met, Roehampton, St Mary's Twickenham (UC), Worcester; **Some** Bath Spa (Comb courses inc Drama), Bournemouth Arts (UC), Liverpool.

Interview advice and questions Questions will focus on your chosen subjects. See under separate subject tables. See also **Chapter 6**. **De Montfort** What do you understand to be the role of the Arts Council of England? What recent arts events have you seen/enjoyed?

Reasons for rejection (non-academic) Lack of clarity of personal goals.

AFTER-RESULTS ADVICE

Offers to applicants repeating A-levels Higher Glamorgan, St Andrews; **Possibly higher** Bristol UWE, Leeds, Newcastle, Roehampton, St Mary's Twickenham (UC); **Same** Bath Spa, Birmingham, De Montfort, Derby, Durham, Greenwich, Leicester, Liverpool, London Met, Manchester Met, Worcester.

GRADUATE DESTINATIONS AND EMPLOYMENT (2007/8 HESA)

Career note Graduates enter a wide range of careers covering business and administration, retail work, education, transport, finance, community and social services. Work experience during undergraduate years will help students to focus their interests.

OTHER DEGREE SUBJECTS FOR CONSIDERATION

See **Social Sciences/Studies**.

COMMUNICATION STUDIES/COMMUNICATION

(see also **Art and Design (General), Computer Courses, Engineering (Communications), Film, Radio, Video and TV Studies, Media Studies, Speech Pathology/Sciences/Therapy**)

Some courses combine academic and vocational studies, whilst others may be wholly academic or strictly vocational. The subject thus covers a very wide range of approaches concerning communication which should be carefully researched before applying.

Useful websites www.camfoundation.com; www.coi.gov.uk; www.aejmc.org.

NB The points totals shown to the left of the institutions are for ease of reference only. It must not be assumed that Tariff points are always used by institutions or that they can be substituted for an offer in grades. The level of an offer is not necessarily indicative of the quality of a course.

COURSE OFFERS INFORMATION

Subject requirements/preferences GCSE English and mathematics grade A–C may be required. **AL** No specific subjects required.

NB In 2012 universities and colleges will differ in their use of GCE AL/AS unit grade information, A* grades, the Extended Project (EPQ), the Advanced Diploma and the Cambridge Pre-U examination when considering applicants and making offers. An EPQ may be accepted in place of an AS subject. Check websites of universities and colleges for the latest offers information.

Your target offers and examples of courses provided by each institution
360 pts **Ulster** – AAA (Comm Adv Mark)
340 pts **Liverpool** – AAB (Engl Comm St) (IB 36 pts HL Engl 7)
  London (Gold) – AAB–ABB (Media Comm) (IB 34 pts)
  Newcastle – AAB (Media Comm Cult St) (IB 32 pts)
320 pts **Bournemouth** – 320 pts (Comm Media) (IB 32 pts)
  Cardiff – ABB (Engl Lang Comm) (IB 32 pts)
  City – ABB 320 pts (Hum Comm) (IB 32 pts)
  Leeds – ABB (Comm) (IB 33 pts)
  Leicester – ABB 320 pts (Comm Media Soty) (IB 30 pts)
  Liverpool – ABB (Comm Bus St) (IB 33 pts)
  Loughborough – ABB (Comm Media St) (IB 34 pts)
300 pts **Kingston** – BBB (Engl Lang Comm Jrnl)
  Northumbria – 300 pts (Fash Comm) (IB 25 pts)
280 pts **Birmingham City** – 280 pts (Media Comm courses)
  Bristol UWE – 280–340 pts (Mark Comm)
  Glamorgan – 280–320 pts (Media Comm courses)
  Gloucestershire – 280–300 pts (Media Comm Cult courses)
  Hertfordshire – 280–260 pts (Comm courses)
  London Met – 280 pts (Comms courses) (IB 28 pts)
  Oxford Brookes – BBC–ABB (Comm courses) (IB 30 pts)
260 pts **Brunel** – BCC 260 pts (Comm Media St) (IB 29 pts)
  Central Lancashire – 260–300 pts (Comm St Pop Cult Comb courses) (IB 28 pts)
  Glasgow Caledonian – BCC (Media Comm) (IB 24 pts)
  Keele – 260–320 pts (Media Comm Cult courses)
  Lincoln – 260 pts (Comms)
  Newman (UC) – 260 pts (Media Comm courses)
  Nottingham Trent – 260 pts (Comm Soty)
  Ulster – BCC 260 pts (Comm courses) (IB 24 pts)
240 pts **Coventry** – 240–280 pts (Comm Cult Media) (IB 27 pts)
  Edinburgh Napier – 240 pts (Comm Adv PR)
  Manchester Met – 240-280 pts (Cult Inf Comms)

Robert Gordon – CCC (Comm PR) (IB 26 pts)
Sheffield Hallam – 240 pts (PR Comm)
Southampton Solent – 240 pts (Media Comms)
220 pts **Bath Spa** – 220–280 pts (Media Comms) (IB 24 pts)
Chester – 220–260 pts (Comm St) (IB 24 pts)
200 pts **Anglia Ruskin** – 200 pts (Comm St courses) (IB 24 pts)
Bedfordshire – 200 pts (Media Prac (Mass Comm))
East London – 200 pts (Comm St) (IB 24 pts)
Glyndŵr – 200 pts (Media Comms courses)
Middlesex – 200–300 pts (Jrnl Comms)
190 pts **Buckingham** – 190–240 pts (Comm Media Jrnl courses) (IB 24 pts)
180 pts **Greenwich** – 180 pts (Media Comm) (IB 24 pts)

Alternative offers
See **Chapter 7** and **Appendix 1** for grades/UCAS Tariff points information for the International Baccalaureate, Scottish Highers/Advanced Highers, the Welsh Baccalaureate, the Irish Leaving Certificate, the Cambridge Pre-U Diploma, the Advanced Diploma and the Extended Project.

EXAMPLES OF FOUNDATION DEGREES IN THE SUBJECT FIELD
Blackpool and Fylde (Coll); Oxford Brookes; Ravensbourne; Truro (Coll); see also **Film, Radio, Video and TV Studies** and **Media Studies**.

CHOOSING YOUR COURSE (SEE ALSO CH. 1)
Some course features
Anglia Ruskin Pathways in Communications Studies and Media Studies.
Chester A theoretical and partly practical course with a six-week placement in Year 2.
Middlesex A communications course with a strong media focus.
Sheffield Hallam Focus on concepts and theories in cultural studies, linguistics, psychology and sociology. Professional expertise is possible by choosing modules in film, media and fine art.
Ulster Course includes one-to-one communication, language and communication, communication within and between social groups, mass communication and communication research. Course emphasis on students' own communication skills and inter-personal effectiveness.

Universities and colleges teaching quality See www.qaa.ac.uk; http://unistats.direct.gov.uk.

Top research universities and colleges (RAE 2008) (Communication, Cultural and Media Studies) Westminster; East Anglia; London (Gold); Cardiff; East London; London (RH); Sussex; Nottingham Trent; Ulster; Lincoln; Sunderland; Stirling.

Examples of sandwich degree courses Birmingham City; Bournemouth; Bristol UWE; Brunel; Central Lancashire; Edinburgh Napier; Gloucestershire; Greenwich; Hertfordshire; Huddersfield; Leeds Met; Nottingham Trent; Ulster.

ADMISSIONS INFORMATION
Number of applicants per place (approx) Brunel 9; Cardiff 6; Leicester 9; Manchester 5.

Advice to applicants and planning the UCAS personal statement Applicants should be able to give details of any work experience/work shadowing/discussions they have had in the media including, for example, in newspaper offices, advertising agencies, local radio stations or film companies (see also **Media Studies**). **Huddersfield** Critical awareness. Willingness to develop a range of communication skills including new technologies. **London (Gold)** Interest in a study in depth of media theory plus some experience in media practice. **Manchester Met** Motivation more important than grades.

Selection interviews **Yes** Brunel, Buckingham, Coventry, Glamorgan, Glasgow Caledonian, Leicester, Middlesex, Southampton Solent, Ulster; **Some** Anglia Ruskin, Cardiff, Chester, Huddersfield (rarely), London (Gold) (mature students), Sheffield Hallam (mature students).

Interview advice and questions Courses differ in this subject and, depending on your choice, the questions will focus on the type of course, either biased towards the media, or towards human communication by way of language, psychology, sociology or linguistics. See also separate subject tables and **Chapter 6**.

Reasons for rejection (non-academic) Unlikely to work well in groups. Poor writing. Misguided application, for example more practical work wanted. Poor motivation. Inability to give reasons for choosing the course. More practice needed in academic writing skills. Wrong course choice, wanted more practical work.

AFTER-RESULTS ADVICE
Offers to applicants repeating A-levels **Possibly higher** Coventry; **Same** Brunel, Cardiff, Chester, Huddersfield, Loughborough, Nottingham Trent, Robert Gordon, Sheffield Hallam.

GRADUATE DESTINATIONS AND EMPLOYMENT (2007/8 HESA)
See **Business and Management Courses (Specialised)**, **Marketing** and **Media Studies**.

Career note Graduates have developed a range of transferable skills in their courses which open up opportunities in several areas. There are obvious links with openings in the media, public relations and advertising.

OTHER DEGREE SUBJECTS FOR CONSIDERATION
Advertising; Art and Design; Cultural Studies; Digital Communications; English; Film, Radio, Video and TV Studies; Information Studies; Journalism; Languages; Linguistics; Marketing; Media Studies; Psychology; Public Relations; Speech Sciences.

COMMUNITY STUDIES/DEVELOPMENT
(see also **Health Sciences/Studies, Nursing and Midwifery, Social and Public Policy and Administration, Social Work**)

These courses cover aspects of community social issues, for example housing, food, health, the elderly, welfare rights and counselling and features of community development such as education, arts, sport and leisure. Work experience is very important. Most courses will lead to professional qualifications.

Useful websites www.csv.org.uk; www.infed.org/community.

NB The points totals shown to the left of the institutions are for ease of reference only. It must not be assumed that Tariff points are always used by institutions or that they can be substituted for an offer in grades. The level of an offer is not necessarily indicative of the quality of a course.

COURSE OFFERS INFORMATION
Subject requirements/preferences **GCSE** English and mathematics grade A–C may be required at some institutions. **AL** No specific subjects required. **Other** Minimum age 19 plus youth work experience for some courses. Health and CRB checks required for some courses.

NB In 2012 universities and colleges will differ in their use of GCE AL/AS unit grade information, A* grades, the Extended Project (EPQ), the Advanced Diploma and the Cambridge Pre-U examination when considering applicants and making offers. An EPQ may be accepted in place of an AS subject. Check websites of universities and colleges for the latest offers information.

Your target offers and examples of courses provided by each institution
320 pts **Manchester** – ABB–BCC (App Commun Yth Wk St)
300 pts **Edinburgh** – BBB (Commun Educ)
       Glasgow – BBB (Commun Dev)

280 pts **London Met** – 280 pts (Commun Sctr Mgt)
260 pts **Manchester Met** – 260 pts (Commun Arts courses) (IB 26 pts)
 Strathclyde – 260–240 pts (Commun Arts)
240 pts **Birmingham City** – 240 pts (Commun App Dance Thea)
 Bournemouth – 240 pts (Commun Dev)
 Newport – 240 pts (Yth Commun Wk)
 Sheffield Hallam – 240 pts (Spo Commun Dev)
 Winchester – 240–280 pts (Chld Yth Commun St courses) (IB 24 pts)
220 pts **Bishop Grosseteste (UC)** – 220 pts (Dr Commun)
 Coventry – 220 pts (App Commun Soc St)
 Dundee – AB/CCC (Commun Lrng Dev) (IB 29 pts)
 Sunderland – 220 pts (Commun Yth St)
200 pts **Bolton** – 200 pts (Commun Hlth Wlbng; Commun St)
 Cardiff (UWIC) – 200 pts (Yth Commun Educ)
 Central Lancashire – 200 pts (Commun Ldrshp)
 East London – 200 pts (Educ Commun Dev; Commun Serv Ent; Yth Commun Wk)
 Gloucestershire – 200 pts (Hlth Commun Soc Cr courses)
 Huddersfield – 200 pts (Hlth Commun St)
 Ulster – 200 pts (Commun Yth Wk)
180 pts **Bolton** – 180 pts (App Commun St)
 UCP Marjon – 180 pts (Commun Prac courses; Commun Wk; Yth Commun Wk)
160 pts **De Montfort** – 160 pts (Yth Commun Dev)
140 pts **Leeds Met** – 140 pts (Yth Wk Commun Dev)
100 pts **Newport** – 100–120 pts (Commun Hlth Wlbng)
 80 pts **Cumbria** – 80 pts (Yth Commun Wk)
 Derby – 80–120 pts (App Commun Yth St)
 London (Birk) – for under 21s (over 21s varies) p/t (Commun St)

Alternative offers
See **Chapter 7** and **Appendix 1** for grades/UCAS Tariff points information for the International Baccalaureate, Scottish Highers/Advanced Highers, the Welsh Baccalaureate, the Irish Leaving Certificate, the Cambridge Pre-U Diploma, the Advanced Diploma and the Extended Project.

EXAMPLES OF FOUNDATION DEGREES IN THE SUBJECT FIELD
Bradford; Cornwall (Coll); De Montfort; Derby; Durham New (Coll); Glyndŵr; Grimsby (IFHE); Kent; Leeds Met; Lincoln; Llandrillo Cymru (Coll); Newcastle (Coll); Newport; Northampton; Northumberland (Coll); Norwich (UCA); Sheffield Hallam; Somerset (CAT); South Devon (Coll); Staffordshire Reg Fed (SURF); Truro (Coll); Walsall (Coll); Warwickshire (Coll); Wirral Met (Coll); Wolverhampton; Worcester; York (Coll).

CHOOSING YOUR COURSE (SEE ALSO CH. 1)
Some course features
Bolton A wide range of specialist modules and work experience in Years 2 and 3.
Derby A vocational course leading to careers in community and youth work.
Edinburgh Course focuses on adult education, community work, community arts and youth work and people's participation in all aspects of community life. Practice placement blocks in Years 2 and 3, and concurrent practice placements in Year 4.
Newport An initial qualifying course leading to a recognised youth work programme.

Universities and colleges teaching quality See www.qaa.ac.uk; http://unistats.direct.gov.uk.

ADMISSIONS INFORMATION
Number of applicants per place (approx) Liverpool John Moores 2; Manchester Met 8; UCP Marjon 7.

Advice to applicants and planning the UCAS personal statement You should describe work you have done with people (elderly or young), particularly in a caring capacity, such as social work, or with the elderly or young children in schools, nursing, hospital work, youth work, community or charity work. You should also describe any problems arising and how staff dealt with them. See **Appendix 4**. **UCP Marjon** Strong multi-cultural policy. English as a Foreign Language teaching offered.

Selection interviews Yes Bradford, Derby, Huddersfield (in groups), Manchester Met, Strathclyde; **Some** Liverpool John Moores.

Interview advice and questions This subject has a vocational emphasis and work experience, or even full-time work in the field, will be expected. Community work varies considerably so, depending on your experiences, you could be asked about the extent of your work and how you would solve the problems which occur. See also **Chapter 6**. **Derby** Take us through your experience of youth and community work. What are the problems facing young people today?

Reasons for rejection (non-academic) Insufficient experience. Lack of understanding of community and youth work. Uncertain career aspirations. Incompatibility with values, methods and aims of the course. No work experience.

AFTER-RESULTS ADVICE
Offers to applicants repeating A-levels Same Liverpool John Moores, UCP Marjon.

GRADUATE DESTINATIONS AND EMPLOYMENT (2007/8 HESA)
See **Social Work**.

Career note Social and welfare areas of employment provide openings for those wanting to specialise in their chosen field of social work. Other opportunities will also exist in educational administration, leisure and outdoor activities.

OTHER DEGREE SUBJECTS FOR CONSIDERATION
Communication Studies; Education; Health and Social Care; Nursing; Politics; Psychology; Social Policy and Administration; Social Work; Sociology; Youth Studies.

COMPUTER COURSES

(including **Artificial Intelligence, Business Information Systems, Computer Networks, Computer Science, Digital Computing, E-Commerce, Information Technology** and **Web Management**; see also **Communication Studies/Communication, Information Management and Librarianship, Media Studies, Technologies**)

Computer courses are popular and provide graduates with good career prospects. Courses vary in content and in the specialisations offered which may include software engineering, programming languages, artificial intelligence, data processing and graphics. Many universities offer sandwich placements in industry and commerce.

Useful websites www.bcs.org; www.intellectuk.org; www.e-skills.com; www.iap.org.uk.

NB The points totals shown to the left of the institutions are for ease of reference only. It must not be assumed that Tariff points are always used by institutions or that they can be substituted for an offer in grades. The level of an offer is not necessarily indicative of the quality of a course.

COURSE OFFERS INFORMATION
Subject requirements/preferences GCSE Mathematics usually required. A*/A/B grades may be stipulated for some subjects. **AL** Mathematics, a science subject or computer science required for some courses. **Cambridge** (Churchill, Magdalene) Uses STEP as part of offers; (Gonville and Caius) AEA mathematics required (see **Chapter 6**).

NB In 2012 universities and colleges will differ in their use of GCE AL/AS unit grade information, A* grades, the Extended Project (EPQ), the Advanced Diploma and the Cambridge Pre-U

examination when considering applicants and making offers. An EPQ may be accepted in place of an AS subject. Check websites of universities and colleges for the latest offers information.

Your target offers and examples of courses provided by each institution

380 pts Cambridge – A*AA college offers may vary (Comp Sci) (IB 38–42 pts HL 766–777)
Imperial London – A*mathsAA (Comp (Artif Intel) (Biol Med) (Gms Vis Interact)) (IB 39 pts)
London (UCL) – AAA+AS–AAB+AS (Comp Sci Int) (IB 36–38 pts)
Oxford – A*AA (Comp Sci) (IB 38–42 pts)

360 pts Bath – AAA (Comp Sci) (IB 36 pts HL maths 6)
Bristol – AAA–AAB (Comp Sci Electron Abrd) (IB 35 pts HL 665)
Durham – AAA (Nat Sci (Comp Sci))
Edinburgh – AAA 2nd yr entry (Comp Sci courses) (IB 36 pts)
Manchester – AAA–AAB (Soft Eng) (IB 37–35 pts)
St Andrews – AAA–AAB 360 pts (Intnet Comp Sci courses) (IB 36–40 pts)
Southampton – AAA–AAB (Comp Sci Imag Multim Sys) (IB 33 pts)
Warwick – AAA–AAAb (Phil Comp Sci) (IB 38 pts)

340 pts Aston – 300–340 pts (Bus Comp IT) (IB 34 pts)
Bath – AAB 340 pts (Comp Sci Jap/Bus/Maths/Fr/Ger/Mand Chin/Span) (IB 36 pts HL maths 6)
Birmingham – AAB (Comp Sci)
Brighton – AAB (Comp Sci 4 yr; Bus Comp Sys 4 yr)
Bristol – AAB (Comp Sci Electron MEng) (IB 35 pts)
Durham – AAB (Comp Sci) (IB 36 pts)
Exeter – AAA–AAB (Comp Sci Artif Intel) (IB 34–29 pts HL Maths 6)
Lancaster – AAB–BBB (Comp Sci courses) (IB 31 pts)
Leeds – AAB (Comp courses) (IB 36 pts HL 17 pts)
London (King's) – AAB+AS **or** AA/BB+AS (Comp Sci) (IB 34 pts)
London (RH) – 300–340 pts (Comp Sci courses) (IB 30 pts)
Loughborough – AAB–AAA (Comp Sci MSci) (IB 34 pts HL 5 maths)
Queen's Belfast – AAB–BBB (Comp Sci courses)
Reading – 340–300 pts (Comp Sci courses)
Surrey – 340 pts (Comp Sci Eng) (IB 34 pts)
Warwick – AAB **or** Aabb (Comp Bus St) (IB 36 pts)
York – AAB–ABB (Comp Sys Soft Eng)

320 pts Aston – 320–280 pts (Comp Sci courses) (IB 29–33 pts)
Cardiff – ABB (Comp Maths) (IB 32 pts)
City – 320–280 pts (Bus Comp Sys) (IB 28 pts)
Durham – ABB (Comp)
East Anglia – ABB 320 pts (Comp Graph) (IB 30–32 pts)
Edinburgh – ABB 1st yr entry (Artif Intel courses) (IB 34 pts)
Glasgow – ABB (Comp Sci courses) (IB 32 pts)
Kent – 320 pts (Web Comp) (IB 32 pts)
Leicester – ABB–BBB (Comp Sci courses)
Liverpool – ABB (Intnet Comp) (IB 33 pts)
London (QM) – 320–280 pts (Comp Sci courses MSc)
Loughborough – ABB–AAB (Comp Sci BSc) (IB 30 pts HL 5 maths)
Newcastle – ABB/ACC (Comp Sci (Gms Vrtl Envs) (Net Sys Intnet Tech)) (IB 30 pts HL maths 6)
Reading – 320 pts (Cyber) (IB 33 pts)
Sheffield – ABB–BBB (Comp courses) (IB 33 pts)
Strathclyde – ABB 2nd yr entry (Bus Inf Sys) (IB 28 pts)
Sussex – ABB–BBB (inc gr 7) (Mus Inform) (IB 32–34 pts)
Swansea – ABB 320-280 pts (Comp Sci courses)

300 pts Aberdeen – BBB (Inf Sys Mgt)
Aberystwyth – 300 pts (Comp Sci) (IB 26–28 pts)

TAKE CONTROL OF YOUR FUTURE

Computing at Brunel

Information is the key to success
Discover how to manage it: technically, professionally, and profitably.
We offer the following BSc (Hons) degrees as three-year standard courses
or four-year sandwich courses with a year in industry:

- Computer Science
- Computer Science
  (Artificial Intelligence)
- Computer Science
  (Digital Media and Games)
- Computer Science
  (Network Computing)
- Computer Science
  (Software Engineering)

- Information Systems
- Information Systems
  (Business)
- Information Systems
  (e-Commerce)
- Information Systems
  (Human Computer Interaction)
- Information Systems
  (Social Web)

Brunel
UNIVERSITY
L O N D O N

Make your choice count

www **www.brunel.ac.uk/discug**
✉ **comp.ug.admissions@brunel.ac.uk**
☎ **01895 267808**

Bournemouth – 300 pts (Foren Comp)
Brunel – Contact admissions office (Gms Des courses)
East Anglia – BBB 300 pts (Comp Sci courses BSc)
Essex – 300 pts (Comp Maths) (IB 29 pts)
Heriot-Watt – BBB 1st yr entry (Comp Sci courses)
Keele – 300 pts inc BC (Comp Sci courses) (IB 26–28 pts)
London (Gold) – BBB (Crea Comp; Comp Sci; Interact Des)
Loughborough – BBB–ABB 300–340 pts (Artif Intel) (IB 34 pts)
Nottingham – BBB (Soft Sys) (IB 32 pts)
Queen's Belfast – BBB (Comp Sci BEng)

280 pts **Abertay Dundee** – BBC (Comp Arts; Comp Gms Tech)
Aberystwyth – 280 pts (Mbl Wrbl Comp) (IB 26–28 pts)
Aston – 280–320 pts (Multim Comp) (IB 29 pts)
Birmingham City – 280 pts (Comp Net Scrty; Comp Sci; Foren Comp)
Brighton – BBC 280 pts (Soft Eng) (IB 28 pts)
Bristol UWE – 280–320 pts (Web Des)
Brunel – BBC (Comp Sci Soft Eng; Inf Sys; Inf Sys Bus; Inf Sys e-Commer; Inf Sys (Hum Comp
    Interact); Inf Sys Soc Web)
Glamorgan – 280–320 pts (Comp Gms Dev)
Heriot-Watt – BBC 2nd yr entry (IT)
Lincoln – 280 pts (Comp Sci)
Loughborough – BBC–ABB 280–320 pts (Comp Mgt) (IB 30 pts)
Newcastle – BBC (Inf Sys Mgt) (IB 28 pts)
Northumbria – 280 pts (Comp Sci; Comp Gms Des Prod; Comp Foren; Ethl Hack Comp Scrty)
Oxford Brookes – BBC (Comp Sci courses) (IB 29 pts)
Salford – 280 pts (Comp; Intnet Comp)
Westminster – BBC (Comp Sci) (IB 28 pts)

260 pts   **Bolton** – 240–260 pts (Gms Des; Intnet Comm Net)
           Bristol UWE – 260 pts (Foren Comp)
           Brunel – BCC (inc C at AS maths) (Fin Comp) (IB 29 pts)
           Dundee – BCC 1st yr entry (Comp Cog Sci) (IB 30 pts)
           Glamorgan – 260–300 pts (Comp Foren; Comp Sci)
           Kingston – 260–280 pts (Comp Sci courses)
           Liverpool Hope – 260 pts (Comp courses)
           Liverpool John Moores – 260 pts (Comp Gms Tech)
           London (QM) – 260 pts (Comp Sci courses BSc) (IB 32 pts)
           Portsmouth – 260 pts (Comp Sci; Comp; Web Tech)
           Teesside – 260–320 pts (Comp Gms Prog; Comp Gms Des; Comp Gms Art)
           Ulster – 260 pts (Comp Sci; Comp Sci (Embd Comp) (Intel Sys) (Mbl Comp) (Robot))
245 pts   **Edinburgh Napier** – 245 pts (Comp courses)
240 pts   **Aberdeen** – CCC 1st yr entry (Artif Intel)
           Abertay Dundee – CCC (Ethl Hack Cntrms)
           Bangor – 240–280 pts (Comp Sci; Comp Sci Bus)
           Bradford – 240–260 pts (Comp courses)
           Bristol UWE – 240–200 pts (Comp App Maths) (IB 28–30 pts)
           Buckingham – CCC 240 pts (Comp courses)
           Canterbury Christ Church – 240 pts (Comp courses)
           Central Lancashire – 240 pts (Comp courses)
           Cumbria – 240 pts (App Comp)
           De Montfort – 240 pts (Comp courses)
           Derby – 180–240 pts (Comp/IT courses)
           Edge Hill – 240 pts (Comp courses)
           Glamorgan – 240–280 pts (Comp Sys Scrty; Comp Net)
           Glasgow Caledonian – CCC (Net Sys Sprt)
           Huddersfield – 240–260 pts (Comp Sci; Comp)
           Liverpool John Moores – 240 pts (Comp Foren) (IB 24 pts)
           London Met – 240–280 pts (Comp courses)
           Manchester Met – 240–280 pts (Mbl Comp; Comp Sci; Artif Intel)
           Newport – 240–260 pts (Comp courses; Comp Gms Des)
           Nottingham Trent – 240–280 pts (Comp Sci courses; Comp Sys (Foren Scrty); Comp St)
           Plymouth – 240–280 pts (Comp courses)
           Roehampton – 240–320 pts (Comp courses)
           Salford – 240–260 pts (Comp Sci) (IB 25–30 pts)
           Sheffield Hallam – 220–240 pts (Comp)
           Staffordshire – 240 pts (Foren Comp)
           Sunderland – 240–360 pts (Comp Foren; Comp Sci; Ethl Hack Scrty Sys Des; Net Comp; Bus Comp)
           Westminster – 240 pts (Mbl Web Comp) (IB 28 pts)
           Worcester – 240–260 pts (Comp courses)
220 pts   **Bristol UWE** – 220–240 pts (Comp Scrty)
           Coventry – 220 pts (Comp Net Comm Tech)
           Dundee – CCD 2nd yr entry (Comp Sci)
           Gloucestershire – 220 pts (Comp)
           Manchester Met – 220 pts (Comp Mus Tech courses) (IB 26 pts)
           Northampton – 220–260 pts (Comp courses)
           Stirling – CCD (Comp Sci courses) (IB 26–30 pts)
           Teesside – 220–280 pts (Comp Sci)
           West Scotland – CCD (Comp Gms Tech)
200 pts   **Bedfordshire** – 200 pts (Comp Sci; Comp Net; Mbl Comp)
           Bristol UWE – 200–240 pts (Computing)
           Bucks New – 200–240 pts (Gms Dev; Comp courses)
           Chester – 200–240 pts (Comp) (IB 24 pts)

Coventry – 200–240 pts (Comp Sci; Crea Comp)
East London – 200 pts (Bus Inf Sys)
Glyndŵr – 200 pts (Comp Net Mgt Scrty; Comp; Comp Gms Dev)
Hertfordshire – 200–300 pts (Comp Sci courses)
Hull – 200–280 pts (Comp Sci; Comp Bus Inform; Web Des Dev)
Kingston – 200–280 pts (Comp Graph Tech)
Middlesex – 200–280 pts (Foren Comp; Comp Sci; Comp Net)
Portsmouth – 200–280 pts (Comp courses)
Suffolk (Univ Campus) – 200 pts (App Comp)
West Anglia (Coll) – 200 pts (Comp Sc)
York St John – 200–240 pts (IT courses)

180 pts **Bangor** – 180–200 pts (Bus ICT)
Newman (UC) – 180–240 pts (IT courses)

160 pts **Bradford (Coll Univ Centre)** – CC (inc English and maths) 160 pts (Bus Comp Sol)
Greenwich – 160–180 pts (Comp courses)
Leeds Met – 160–200 pts (Gms Des) (IB 24–26 pts)
London South Bank – 160 pts (Comp courses)
Robert Gordon – CC 160–180 pts (Inf Sys Tech) (IB 24 pts)
Southampton Solent – 160 pts (Bus IT; Comp)
West Scotland – CC–CD (Comp Net; Comp; Multim Tech)
Wolverhampton – 160–220 pts (Comp Sci courses; Comp courses; IT Scrty)

150 pts **Anglia Ruskin** – 150 pts (Comp Sci)

140 pts **Blackpool and Fylde (Coll)** – 140–360 pts (Comp Sci)

120 pts **Colchester (Inst)** – 120 pts (Comp Sol (Net/Intnet))
Swansea Met – 120–360 pts (Comp Net)

80 pts **Farnborough (CT)** – 80–200 pts (Computing)
Havering (Coll) – 80–120 pts (Comp Sys)
London (Birk) – for under 21s (over 21s varies) p/t (Inf Sys Mgt)

Open University – contact +44 (0)845 300 6090 **or** www.openuniversity.co.uk/you (Comp IT; Comp Bus/Des/Maths/Psy/Stats; ICT)

Alternative offers
See **Chapter 7** and **Appendix 1** for grades/UCAS Tariff points information for the International Baccalaureate, Scottish Highers/Advanced Highers, the Welsh Baccalaureate, the Irish Leaving Certificate, the Cambridge Pre-U Diploma, the Advanced Diploma and the Extended Project.

EXAMPLES OF FOUNDATION DEGREES IN THE SUBJECT FIELD

Bath City (Coll); Bath Spa; Bedfordshire; Blackpool and Fylde (Coll); Bournemouth; Bradford; Brighton; Bristol City (Coll); Bucks New; Central Lancashire; Chesterfield (Coll); Colchester (Inst); Cornwall (Coll); Croydon (Coll); Cumbria; De Montfort; Doncaster (Coll Univ Centre); Durham New (Coll); Ealing, Hammersmith and West London (Coll); East Anglia; East Berkshire (Coll); East London; Edge Hill; Farnborough (CT); Glamorgan; Glyndŵr; Greenwich; Grimsby (IFHE); Highbury Portsmouth (Coll); Huddersfield; Kent; Kingston; Kirklees (Coll); Lakes (Coll); Leeds (CAD); Leeds Met; Llandrillo Cymru (Coll); London Met; London South Bank; Manchester (Coll); Merton (Coll); Mid-Cheshire (Coll); NEW (Coll); Newcastle (Coll); Newport; Northbrook (Coll); Northumbria; Nottingham New (Coll); Oxford Brookes; Plymouth; Queen's Belfast; Ravensbourne; Riverside Halton (Coll); St Helens (Coll); Salford; Sheffield (Coll); Sheffield Hallam; Shrewsbury (CAT); Somerset (CAT); South Devon (Coll); South Essex (Coll); Southampton Solent; Staffordshire Reg Fed (SURF); Stockport (Coll); Stockton Riverside (Coll); Stoke on Trent (Coll); Suffolk (Univ Campus); Sunderland; Teesside; Truro (Coll); Tyne Met (Coll); Warrington (Coll); West Cheshire (Coll); Westminster Kingsway (Coll); Wigan and Leigh (Coll); Wiltshire (Coll); Wolverhampton; York (Coll).

CHOOSING YOUR COURSE (SEE ALSO CH. 1)

Some course features
Abertay Dundee (Ethl Hack Cntrms) An unusual course, designed in collaboration with computer security companies and is expected to be accredited by the British Computer Society.

Brighton The Computing programme offers a wide range of different degrees with the final choice being made at the end of the first semester.

Reading A course is offered in Computer Science and Cybernetics involving applications with human activities and systems.

Salford The degree courses in Computer Science, Computing, Information and Intelligent Systems and Software Engineering share a common first year with final decisions on specialisation taking place in Year 2.

Southampton Transfer between Computing courses is possible up to the end of Year 2.

Warwick Students can apply for a place in the Erasmus programme or similar programme for study in an overseas university or salaried employment in industry.

Universities and colleges teaching quality See www.qaa.ac.uk; http://unistats.direct.gov.uk.

Top research universities and colleges (RAE 2008) (Computer Science and Informatics) Cambridge; Imperial London; Southampton; Edinburgh; Oxford; London (UCL); Manchester; Nottingham; Glasgow; Liverpool; Lancaster; Leeds.

Examples of sandwich degree courses Aberystwyth; Aston; Bath; Birmingham City; Bournemouth; Bradford; Brighton; Bristol UWE; Brunel; Cardiff; City; Coventry; De Montfort; Derby; East London; Edinburgh Napier; Glamorgan; Glasgow Caledonian; Gloucestershire; Greenwich; Hertfordshire; Huddersfield; Kent; Kingston; Leeds Met; Lincoln; Liverpool John Moores; London South Bank; Loughborough; Manchester; Manchester Met; Northumbria; Nottingham Trent; Oxford Brookes; Plymouth; Portsmouth; Queen's Belfast; Reading; Salford; Sheffield Hallam; Southampton Solent; Staffordshire; Surrey; Teesside; Ulster; West Scotland; Westminster; Wolverhampton; Worcester; York.

ADMISSIONS INFORMATION

Number of applicants per place (approx) Abertay Dundee 2; Aberystwyth 8; Aston (Bus Comp IT) 12; Bath 5; Birmingham 7; Bournemouth 8; Bradford 13; Bristol 8; Bristol UWE 4; Brunel 10; Buckingham 6; Cambridge 3; Cardiff 5; City 10; Coventry 10; Derby 3; Dundee 6; Durham 10; East Anglia (Maths Comp) 7; Edinburgh 4; Essex 2; Exeter 10; Glasgow Caledonian 8; Glyndŵr 3; Heriot-Watt 6; Hull (Comp Sci) 6; Imperial London 6; Kent 8; Kingston 10; Lancaster 5; Leeds 10; Leicester 13; Lincoln 5; Liverpool John Moores 3; London (King's) 20; London (QM) 6; London (RH) 5; Loughborough (CT) 2; Manchester Met 10, (Bus IT) 8; Newcastle 7; Northumbria 4; Nottingham 8; Nottingham Trent 4; Oxford Brookes 18; Plymouth 12; Portsmouth 6; Robert Gordon 3; Roehampton 3; Sheffield Hallam 5; Southampton 10; Staffordshire 4; Stirling 6; Strathclyde 16; Surrey 9; Swansea 5; Teesside 4; Warwick 11; York 9.

Advice to applicants and planning the UCAS personal statement Your computer and programming interests in and outside school or college should be described. It is also useful to give details of any visits, work experience and work shadowing relating to industrial or commercial organisations and their computer systems. (See **Appendix 4**.) Give details of your interests in, and knowledge of computer hardware, software and multimedia packages. Contact the Chartered Institute for IT for information.

Misconceptions about this course That anyone who plays computer games or uses a word processor can do a degree in Computer Studies. Some think Computing degrees are just about programming; in reality, programming is only one, albeit essential, part of computing. **Aston** (Bus Comp IT) 60% business, 40% computing and IT; compulsory placement year in industry. **City** (Bus Comp Sys) Some applicants think that it is a Business degree: it is a Computing degree focused on computing in business. **London (QM)** There are many misconceptions – among students, teachers and careers advisers – about what computer science entails. The main one is to confuse it with what schools call information and communication technology which is about the use of computer applications. Computer science is all about software – ie programming – and will generally only cover a limited study of hardware.

Selection interviews Yes Bath, Blackburn (Coll Univ Centre), Bradford, Bristol UWE, Brunel, Buckingham, Cambridge, Cardiff, City, Coventry, Cumbria, Durham, Edinburgh, Edinburgh Napier,

Glamorgan, Hertfordshire, Hull, Imperial London, Kingston, Liverpool Hope, London (Gold), London (QM), London (UCL), London South Bank, Loughborough, Newcastle, Newport, Northampton, Northbrook (Coll), Nottingham, Nottingham Trent, Oxford (Comp Sci) 19%, Plymouth, Portsmouth, Sheffield Hallam, Southampton, Surrey, West London, Wigan and Leigh (Coll), York; **Some** Abertay Dundee, Aberystwyth, Anglia Ruskin, Birmingham City, Blackpool and Fylde (Coll), Brighton, Chichester, Dundee, East Anglia, Exeter, Liverpool John Moores, London Met, Manchester Met, Salford, Staffordshire, Sunderland, Warwick (5–10%).

Interview advice and questions While A-level computer studies is not usually required, you will be questioned on your use of computers and aspects of the subject which interest you. How do you organise your homework/social life? What are your strengths and weaknesses? Do you have any idea of the type of career you would like? See also **Chapter 6**. **Cambridge** Why is the pole-vaulting world record about 6.5m and why can't it be broken? **City** The aim of the interview is to obtain a full picture of the applicant's background, life experiences etc, before making an offer. **York** No tests. Questions for discussion at the whiteboard are usually mathematical or are about fundamental computer science such as sorting.

Reasons for rejection (non-academic) Little practical interest in computers/electronics. Inability to work as part of a small team. Mismatch between referee's description and performance at interview. Unsatisfactory English. Can't communicate. Inability to convince interviewer of the candidate's worth. Incoherent, unmotivated, arrogant and without any evidence of good reason. **London (QM)** Misunderstanding of what computer science involves as an academic subject – especially in personal statements where some suggest that they are interested in a course with business and administrative skills. Lack of sufficient mathematics. Computer science is a mathematical subject and we cannot accept applicants who are unable to demonstrate good mathematical skills. **Southampton** Lack of motivation; incoherence; carelessness.

AFTER-RESULTS ADVICE
Offers to applicants repeating A-levels **Higher** Brighton, De Montfort, Greenwich, Kingston, St Andrews, Surrey, Sussex, Warwick; **Possibly higher** Bath, Bristol UWE, Edinburgh, Lancaster, Leeds, Newcastle, Oxford Brookes, Portsmouth, Sheffield, Teesside; **Same** Abertay Dundee, Aberystwyth, Anglia Ruskin, Aston, Blackpool and Fylde (Coll), Brunel, Buckingham, Cambridge, Cardiff, Cardiff (UWIC), Chichester, City, Derby, Dundee, Durham, East Anglia, East London, Exeter, Farnborough (CT), Huddersfield, Hull, Kent, Lincoln, Liverpool, Liverpool Hope, Liverpool John Moores, London (RH), London (UCL), London South Bank, Loughborough, Manchester Met, Newman (UC), Northumbria, Nottingham Trent, Robert Gordon, Salford, Sheffield Hallam, Staffordshire, Suffolk (Univ Campus), Sunderland, Ulster, West London, Wolverhampton, Worcester, York.

GRADUATE DESTINATIONS AND EMPLOYMENT (2007/8 HESA)
Computer Science graduates surveyed 5440 **Employed** 2680 **In further study** 700 **Assumed unemployed** 920

Information Systems graduates surveyed 1580 **Employed** 735 **In further study** 175 **Assumed unemployed** 285

Artificial Intelligence graduates surveyed 40 **Employed** 20 **In further study** 5 **Assumed unemployed** 5

Career note A high proportion of graduates go to work in the IT sector with some degrees leading towards particular fields (usually indicated by the course title). Significant areas include software design and engineering, web and internet-based fields, programming, systems analysis and administration.

OTHER DEGREE SUBJECTS FOR CONSIDERATION
Business Studies; Communications Engineering; Computer Engineering; Electrical and Electronic Engineering; Geographical Information Systems; Information Studies; Mathematics; Physics; Software Engineering.

CONSUMER STUDIES/SCIENCES

(including **Consumer Product Design** and **Trading Standards**; see also **Food Science/Studies and Technology, Hospitality and Hotel Management**)

Consumer Studies courses involve topics such as food and nutrition, shelter, clothing, community studies and consumer behaviour and marketing. Trading Standards courses focus on consumer law, contract law, food law, weights and measures, criminal investigation, fraud, counterfeit, and fair trading. Accredited by the Trading Standards Institute, they can lead to careers as trading standards officers.

Useful websites www.which.co.uk; www.tradingstandards.gov.uk.

NB The points totals shown to the left of the institutions are for ease of reference only. It must not be assumed that Tariff points are always used by institutions or that they can be substituted for an offer in grades. The level of an offer is not necessarily indicative of the quality of a course.

COURSE OFFERS INFORMATION

Subject requirements/preferences **GCSE** Mathematics and English usually required. **AL** No specific subjects required.

NB In 2012 universities and colleges will differ in their use of GCE AL/AS unit grade information, A* grades, the Extended Project (EPQ), the Advanced Diploma and the Cambridge Pre-U examination when considering applicants and making offers. An EPQ may be accepted in place of an AS subject. Check websites of universities and colleges for the latest offers information.

Your target offers and examples of courses provided by each institution
300 pts **Reading** – 300 pts (Consum Bhv Mark) (HL 655)
260 pts **Reading** – 260 pts (Consum Electron) (HL 555)
240 pts **Edinburgh Napier** – CCC 240–230 pts (Mark Mng Consum St)
  London Met – 240 pts (Fd Consum St courses)
  Manchester Met – 240 pts (Tr Stnds) (IB 27 pts)
  Teesside – 240 pts (Tr Stnds Consum Prot)
  Ulster – CCC 240 pts (Consum St)
220 pts **Harper Adams (UC)** – 220 pts (Fd Consum St; Consum St)
200 pts **Abertay Dundee** – CDD (Fd Consum Sci)
  Birmingham (UC) – 200 pts (Fd Consum Mgt) (IB 24 pts)
  Manchester Met – 200 pts (Consum Mark) (IB 29 pts)
180 pts **Cardiff (UWIC)** – 180 pts (Consum Tr Stnds) (IB 28 pts)

Alternative offers
See **Chapter 7** and **Appendix 1** for grades/UCAS Tariff points information for the International Baccalaureate, Scottish Highers/Advanced Highers, the Welsh Baccalaureate, the Irish Leaving Certificate, the Cambridge Pre-U Diploma, the Advanced Diploma and the Extended Project.

CHOOSING YOUR COURSE (SEE ALSO CH. 1)
Some course features
Cardiff (UWIC) The theme of the course (accredited by Trading Standards Institute) is of consumer protection, quality, law and trading standards. Graduates with a 2:2 degree are eligible for training as trading standards officers via the Diploma in Consumer Affairs and Trading Standards.
Coventry (Consum Prod Des) The four-year course covers the field of industrial design related to household products with an emphasis on styling and ergonomics. Towards the end of Year 3 students may apply for an industrial placement.
Manchester Met (Consum Mark) Course covers communications, brand design, consumer behaviour, retailing and buying. The course is validated by the Chartered Institute of Marketing.
Reading (Consum Bhv Mark) Course focuses on marketing, psychology, economics and research methods, with a wide range of optional modules from across the University including management, languages, politics and sociology.

Universities and colleges teaching quality See www.qaa.ac.uk; http://unistats.direct.gov.uk.

Examples of sandwich degree courses Birmingham (UC); Cardiff (UWIC); Harper Adams (UC); Manchester Met.

ADMISSIONS INFORMATION
Number of applicants per place (approx) Birmingham (UC) 2; Cardiff (UWIC) 5; London Met 5; Manchester Met 4; Queen Margaret 3.

Advice to applicants and planning the UCAS personal statement Relevant work experience or work shadowing in, for example, business organisations, restaurants, cafes, or the school meals service, would be appropriate. (See also **Hospitality and Hotel Management** and **Dietetics**.) Details may be obtained from the Institute of Consumer Sciences – see **Appendix 4**.

Selection interviews **Yes** Teesside; **Some** Manchester Met.

Interview advice and questions Questions will stem from your special interests in this subject and in the past have included: What interests you in consumer behaviour? What are the advantages and disadvantages? What is ergonomics? What do you understand by the term sustainable consumption? What world or national news has annoyed, pleased or upset you? What relevance do textiles and dress have to home economics? How would you react in a room full of fools? See also **Chapter 6**. **Queen Margaret** Very informal interviews covering work experience and career aspirations.

AFTER-RESULTS ADVICE
Offers to applicants repeating A-levels **Same** Manchester Met, Queen Margaret, Ulster.

GRADUATE DESTINATIONS AND EMPLOYMENT (2007/8 HESA)
Career note The various specialisms involved in these courses allow graduates to look for openings in several career areas, for example, food quality assurance, trading standards, consumer education and advice. Many graduates enter business administration and careers in particularly retailing, evaluating new products and liaising with the public.

OTHER DEGREE SUBJECTS FOR CONSIDERATION
Biological Sciences; Business Studies; Dietetics; Environmental Health; Food Science; Health Studies; Hospitality Management; Marketing; Nutrition; Psychology; Retail Management.

DANCE/DANCE STUDIES
(see also **Drama**)

Every aspect of dance can be studied in the various courses on offer as well as the theoretical, educational, historical and social aspects of the subject.

Useful websites www.arts.org.uk; www.cdet.org.uk; www.ballet.co.uk; www.ndta.org.uk.

NB The points totals shown to the left of the institutions are for ease of reference only. It must not be assumed that Tariff points are always used by institutions or that they can be substituted for an offer in grades. The level of an offer is not necessarily indicative of the quality of a course.

COURSE OFFERS INFORMATION
Subject requirements/preferences **GCSE** English usually required. Practical dance experience essential. **AL** No specific subjects required. **Other** CRB checks required for some courses: check websites.

NB In 2012 universities and colleges will differ in their use of GCE AL/AS unit grade information, A* grades, the Extended Project (EPQ), the Advanced Diploma and the Cambridge Pre-U examination when considering applicants and making offers. An EPQ may be accepted in place of an AS subject. Check websites of universities and colleges for the latest offers information.

Your target offers and examples of courses provided by each institution

340 pts Leeds – ABB–AAB (Thea Perf) (IB 36 pts)

320 pts Kingston – 320–360 pts (Dance courses)

300 pts Leeds – BBB (Perf Des) (IB 32 pts)

Salford – 300 pts (Perf Arts) (IB 31 pts)

280 pts Brighton – Fdn Dip required+interview+portfolio BBC (Perf Vis Arts (Thea) (Dance))

Chichester – BBC 280–300 pts (Dance Dr) (IB 28 pts)

Cumbria – BBC 280 pts (Dance Perf Musl Thea Perf) (IB 30 pts)

Edge Hill – offer may be altered based on audition 280 pts (Dance Dr courses) (IB 24 pts)

Middlesex – 280 pts (Dance Perf) (IB 24 pts)

Northumbria – 280 pts (Dance Choreo) (IB 25 pts)

Roehampton – 280–340 pts (Dance St) (IB 25 pts)

Surrey – 280–300 pts (Dance Cult Prof Trg) (IB 30–28 pts)

260 pts Bath Spa – 260–300 pts (Crea Writ Dance) (IB 24 pts)

De Montfort – 260 pts (Dance) (IB 24 pts)

Lincoln – 260 pts (Dance; Dance Dr)

Liverpool Hope – 260–280 pts (Dance courses) (IB 25 pts)

London Met – 260 pts (Perf Arts)

Strathclyde – 260–240 pts (Commun Arts)

Winchester – 260–300 pts (Choreo Dance) (IB 25 pts)

240 pts Bath Spa – 240–280 pts (Dance Comb Hons) (IB 24 pts)

Canterbury Christ Church – 240 pts (Dance Educ) (IB 24 pts)

Cardiff (UWIC) – 240 pts (Dance) (IB 24 pts)

Chester – 240–280 pts (Dance) (IB 24 pts)

Coventry – 240 pts (Dance Thea Prof Prac) (IB 27 pts)

De Montfort – 260–240 pts (Perf Arts) (IB 24 pts)

Falmouth (UC) – 240 pts (Dance) (IB 24 pts)

Liverpool John Moores – 240–280 pts (Dance) (IB 24 pts)

Teesside – 240–280 pts (Dance) (IB 24 pts)

220 pts Central Lancashire – 220–260 pts (Dance Perf Teach)

Northampton – 220–260 pts (Dance Joint Hons) (IB 24 pts)

Plymouth – 220 pts (Dance Thea) (IB 24 pts)

Sunderland – 220–360 pts (Dance)

Ulster – 220 pts (Dance Mus) (IB 24 pts)

York St John – 220–260 pts (Dance) (IB 24 pts)

200 pts Bucks New – 200–240 pts (Dance Perf) (IB 24 pts)

Doncaster (Coll Univ Centre) – (Dance Prac)

East London – 200 pts (Prof Dance Musl Thea) (IB 24 pts)

Manchester Met – 200–260 pts (Dance Comb Hons) (IB 28 pts)

West London – 200 pts (Dance)

Wolverhampton – 200 pts (Dance)

180 pts Derby – 180–240 pts (Dance Mov St courses) (IB 26 pts)

Greenwich – 180 pts (Dance Thea Perf) (IB 24 pts)

Liverpool (LIPA) – BC 180 pts (Commun Dance)

160 pts Brighton – CC 160 pts (Contemp Dance)

80 pts Grimsby (IFHE) – 80 pts (Perf Dance)

London (RAc Dance) – 80 pts (Ballet Educ)

Royal Scottish (RSAMD) – 80 pts min (Modn Ballet)

Colchester (Inst) – (Dance Perf) Contact Institute

Northern (Sch Contemp Dance) – Check with School (Dance)

Alternative offers

See **Chapter 7** and **Appendix 1** for grades/UCAS Tariff points information for the International Baccalaureate, Scottish Highers/Advanced Highers, the Welsh Baccalaureate, the Irish Leaving Certificate, the Cambridge Pre-U Diploma, the Advanced Diploma and the Extended Project.

EXAMPLES OF FOUNDATION DEGREES IN THE SUBJECT FIELD

Bath Spa; Bedfordshire; Blackpool and Fylde (Coll); Bournemouth; Bournemouth Arts (UC); Bradford; Brighton; Bristol City (Coll); Bucks New; Colchester (Inst); Cornwall (Coll); Craven (Coll); Cumbria; Exeter (Coll); Farnborough (CT); Hereford (CA); Hertfordshire; Huddersfield; Hull (Coll); Kirklees (Coll); Leeds City (Coll); Leeds Met; Manchester (Coll); Middlesex; NEW (Coll); Newcastle (Coll); Northbrook (Coll); Norwich City (Coll); Nottingham New (Coll); Plymouth; Rotherham (CAT); Sheffield (Coll); South Devon (Coll); St Helens (Coll); Staffordshire Reg Fed (SURF); Suffolk (Univ Campus); Teesside; Truro (Coll); West London; Wigan and Leigh (Coll).

CHOOSING YOUR COURSE (SEE ALSO CH. 1)

Some course features

Edge Hill (Dance) Topics covered include dance analysis, applied dance, dance production and dance techniques.

Kingston (Dance) Two themes – movement improvisation and key dance skills and a study of British dance in modern muticultural Britain.

Leeds (Dance) Contemporary choreography is a key area of the course to provide a focus on making and performing dance.

Surrey (Dance Cult) Focus on dance of the 20th and 21st centuries, on dance techniques (including ballet, kathak, contemporary, and African people's dance), together with choreography and dance policy and practice.

Universities and colleges teaching quality See www.qaa.ac.uk; http://unistats.direct.gov.uk.

Top research universities and colleges (RAE 2008) See **Drama**.

ADMISSIONS INFORMATION

Number of applicants per place (approx) Chichester 6; De Montfort (Dance) 13, (Perf Arts) 9; Derby 12; Liverpool (LIPA) 24; Liverpool John Moores 3; Middlesex 12; Northern (Sch Contemp Dance) 6; Roehampton 17; Surrey 5; Trinity Laban Consv 5; York St John 3.

Advice to applicants and planning the UCAS personal statement Full details should be given of examinations taken and practical experience in contemporary dance or ballet. Refer to your visits to the theatre and your impressions. You should list the dance projects in which you have worked, productions in which you have performed and the roles. State any formal dance training you have had and the grades achieved. Applicants need to have dedication, versatility, inventiveness and individuality, practical experience of dance, theoretical ability and language competency. **Bath Spa** Dance experience outside education should be mentioned.

Misconceptions about this course That Performing Arts is only an acting course: it also includes music.

Interview advice and questions Nearly all institutions will require auditions or interviews or attendance at a workshop. The following scheme required by **Liverpool (LIPA)** may act as a guide:

1 Write a short essay (500 words) on your own views and experience of dance.
   (i)   You should take into account the following.
   (ii)   Your history and how you have developed physically and intellectually in your run-up to applying to LIPA.
   (iii) Your main influences and what inspires you.
   (iv)   What you want to gain from training as a dancer.
   (v)   Your ideas on health and nutrition as a dancer, taking into account gender and physicality.
2 All candidates must prepare **two** practical audition pieces.
   (i)   Whatever you like, in whatever style you wish, as long as the piece does not exceed two minutes (please note: panel will stop anyone exceeding this time-limit). There will be no pianist at this part of the session, so if you're using music please bring it with you on a cassette tape. This devised piece should be created through you and this means that you should feel comfortable with it and that it expresses something personal about you. You should wear your regular practice clothes for your presentation.
   (ii)   You must prepare a song of your own choice. An accompanist is provided, but you must provide the sheet music for your song, fully written out for piano accompaniment and in the key you wish to sing (the accompanist will **not** transpose at sight). **Important** Do NOT choreograph your song. You should expect to sit on a high stool or stand when singing for the audition.
3 Additionally, all candidates will participate in a class given on the day of audition.
   (i)   Please ensure that you are dressed appropriately for class with clothing you are comfortable in but allows your movement to be seen. In preparing the practical elements of the audition, please remember that audition panels are not looking for a polished performance. The panel will be looking for candidates' ability to make a genuine emotional and physical connection with the material that they are presenting which shows clear intent and focus.

Remember that it is in your best interest to prepare thoroughly. Nerves inevitably play a part in any audition and can undermine even the best-prepared candidate. Your best defence is to feel confident in your preparation. See also **Chapter 6**. **Chichester** Applicants will be asked to prepare a set-piece in advance and to perform the piece in front of a group. **De Montfort** (Perf Arts) Practical workshops in dance and theatre plus a written paper. **Salford** (Perf Arts) Audition and interview. **Surrey** Applicants invited to spend a day at the university for interview and a practical class to assess dance skills. An audition fee may be charged. **Wolverhampton** Audition in the form of a dance class

Reasons for rejection (non-academic) Applicants more suitable for an acting or dance school course than a degree course. No experience of dance on the UCAS application. Limited dance skills. **Surrey** Inadequate dance background. Had not seen/read about/done any dance.

AFTER-RESULTS ADVICE
Offers to applicants repeating A-levels Same Chester, Chichester, De Montfort (Perf Arts), Liverpool John Moores, Salford, Surrey, Trinity Laban Consv, Winchester, Wolverhampton, York St John.

GRADUATE DESTINATIONS AND EMPLOYMENT (2007/8 HESA)
Graduates surveyed 595 **Employed** 250 **In further study** 95 **Assumed unemployed** 40

Career note Teaching is the most popular career destination for the majority of graduates. Other opportunities exist as dance animators working in education or in the community to encourage activity and participation in dance. There is a limited number of openings for dance or movement therapists who work with the emotionally disturbed, the elderly or physically disadvantaged.

OTHER DEGREE SUBJECTS FOR CONSIDERATION
Arts Management; Drama; Education (Primary); Music; Performance Studies; Physical Education; Sport and Exercise Science.

DENTISTRY

(including **Dental Technology, Dental Hygiene, Equine Dental Science** and **Oral Health Science**)

Dentistry involves the treatment and prevention of a wide range of mouth diseases from tooth decay and gum disease to mouth cancer. Courses in Dentistry/Dental Surgery cover the basic medical sciences, human disease, clinical studies and clinical dentistry. The amount of patient contact will vary between institutions but will be considerable in all Dental Schools. Intercalated courses in other science subjects are offered on most courses.

Useful websites www.bda.org; www.bdha.org.uk; www.dla.org.uk.

NB The points totals shown to the left of the institutions are for ease of reference only. It must not be assumed that Tariff points are always used by institutions or that they can be substituted for an offer in grades. The level of an offer is not necessarily indicative of the quality of a course.

COURSE OFFERS INFORMATION
Subject requirements/preferences **GCSE** English, mathematics and science subjects required in most cases for Dentistry courses. A*/A/B grades stipulated in certain subjects by many dental schools. **AL** Chemistry plus biology or a science subject usually required for Dentistry: see offers lines below. (Dntl Tech, Oral Hlth Sci) Science subject required or preferred. **Other** Many dental schools use admissions tests (eg UKCAT: see **Chapter 6**). Evidence of non-infectivity or hepatitis-B immunisation required and all new dental students screened for hepatitis-C. CRB check at enhanced level is also required.

NB In 2012 universities and colleges will differ in their use of GCE AL/AS unit grade information, A* grades, the Extended Project (EPQ), the Advanced Diploma and the Cambridge Pre-U examination when considering applicants and making offers. An EPQ may be accepted in place of an AS subject. Check websites of universities and colleges for the latest offers information.

Your target offers and examples of courses provided by each institution
420 pts **Queen's Belfast** – AAAa (inc AL/AS chem A+1 subj from biol, maths, phys) (Dnstry) (IB 37 pts HL 666)
400 pts **Birmingham** – AAA–AABab (Dnstry) (IB 36 pts)
390 pts **London (King's)** – AAAa–BBBc **or** AAaaa–BBbbb +UKCAT (inc AL chem/biol) (Dnstry) (IB 36 pts HL 665)
London (QM) – AABb +UKCAT (inc 2ALs chem/biol/sci subj **or** chem/biol bb) (Dnstry) (IB 36 pts HL 665)
Manchester – AAA +UKCAT (Dnstry) (IB 34 pts)
360 pts **Bristol** – AAA (inc chem+ other lab-based sci) (Dnstry) (IB 39 pts HL 666)
Dundee – AAA +UKCAT (inc biol+2 subj from chem/phys/maths) (Dnstry courses) (IB 37 pts)
Leeds – AAA (inc AL chem, biol) (Dntl Srgy) (IB 35 pts HL chem biol 6)
Liverpool – AAA (inc chem/biol+1 subj not gen st **or** crit thinking)) (Dntl Srgy) (IB 36 pts (inc chem/biol 6) HL chem biol 6)

Newcastle – AAA (inc chem and biol) (Dnstry) (IB 35 pts HL chem biol 6)

Sheffield – AAA (Dntl Srgy) (IB 35 pts)

340 pts **Cardiff** – AAB +UKCAT (inc chem/biol+2 sci subj (5yr course); (Fdn Dnstry) (IB 34 pts HL chem 5)

Glasgow – AAB (AS bbb min) +UKCAT (inc chem+phys/maths/biol) (Dnstry) (IB 34 pts)

320 pts **Manchester** – ABB +UKCAT (2 arts+sci subj) (Dnstry pre-dental entry) (IB 33 pts)

300 pts **Birmingham** – BBB (Dntl Hyg Thera) (IB 30 pts)

Edinburgh – Check with Ad tutor BBB (Oral Hlth Sci) (IB 32 pts)

Manchester – BBB–BCC (Oral Hlth Sci)

280 pts **Bristol UWE** – 280 pts (Eqn Dntl Sci)

London (QM) – 280 pts (Dntl Mat BEng) (IB 26–28 pts)

260 pts **Dundee** – BCC (Oral Hlth Sci)

Liverpool – BCC inc sci subj (Dntl Hyg Dntl Thera) (IB 27 pts)

240 pts **Manchester Met** – 240 pts inc 2AL inc sci/tech (Dntl Tech)

Portsmouth – 240 pts (Dntl Hyg Dntl Thera)

180 pts **Cardiff (UWIC)** – 180 pts inc CD one in sci subj (Dntl Tech)

160 pts **Cardiff** – CC (Dip Dntl Hyg; Dip Dntl Thera)

Sheffield – CC (Dntl Hyg Dntl Thera Dip)

80 pts **Portsmouth** – 80 pts (Dntl Nurs)

NB The following universities/dental schools offer shortened (usually four years) courses in Dentistry/Dental Surgery for graduates with at least 2.1 degrees in specified subjects. GCE A-level subjects and grades are also specified. Check with universities: **Aberdeen, Central Lancashire, Liverpool, London (King's), (QM), Peninsula (MS).**

Alternative offers

See **Chapter 7** and **Appendix 1** for grades/UCAS Tariff points information for the International Baccalaureate, Scottish Highers/Advanced Highers, the Welsh Baccalaureate, the Irish Leaving Certificate, the Cambridge Pre-U Diploma, the Advanced Diploma and the Extended Project.

EXAMPLES OF FOUNDATION DEGREES IN THE SUBJECT FIELD

Bedfordshire (Dntl Nurs; Dntl Prac Mgt); Bristol UWE (Eqn Dntl St); De Montfort (Dntl Tech); Essex (Oral Hlth Sci); Northampton (Dntl Nurs).

CHOOSING YOUR COURSE (SEE ALSO CH. 1)

Some course features

Birmingham Basic sciences are covered in Years 1 and 2, and clinical studies in Years 3, 4 and 5.

Bristol Basic sciences are covered in Years 1 and 2, and clinical studies in Years 3, 4 and 5.

Cardiff Clinical teaching starts at an early stage.

Leeds Focus on clinical dentistry from the outset.

Liverpool Clinical skills introduced from Year 2.

London (King's) Main components cover the basic sciences, diagnosis and treatment of oral and dental conditions and clinical dentistry. These are vertically integrated with a larger component of basic sciences at the beginning and a larger clinical component at the end.

London (QM) Clinical skills introduced from Year 2.

Manchester Clinical skills introduced from Year 2.

Newcastle Basic sciences are covered in Years 1 and 2, and clinical studies in Years 3, 4 and 5.

Queen's Belfast Basic sciences are covered in Years 1 and 2, and clinical studies in Years 3, 4 and 5.

Sheffield Main components cover the basic sciences, diagnosis and treatment of oral and dental conditions and clinical dentistry. These are vertically integrated with a larger component of basic sciences at the beginning and a larger clinical component at the end.

Universities and colleges teaching quality See www.qaa.ac.uk; http://unistats.direct.gov.uk.

Top research universities and colleges (RAE 2008) Manchester; London (QM); London (King's); Sheffield; Bristol; Cardiff; Leeds; Newcastle; London (UCL).

For a quick reference offers calculator, fold out the inside back cover.

ADMISSIONS INFORMATION

Number of applicants per place (approx) Birmingham 10, (Dntl Hyg Thera) 17, International applicants 129 (no quota); Bristol 9 (Pre dental 22; Dentistry); Cardiff 14; Cardiff (UWIC) (Dntl Tech) 1; Dundee 8, (Pre-Dental) 5; Edinburgh (Oral Hlth Sci) 10 places every 2nd yr; Glasgow 7; Leeds 11. 5; Liverpool 15; London (King's) 128 places (offers to 1 in 5 applicants); London (QM) 18, (300 interviewed and 200 offers made); Manchester 11, (Pre-Dental) 21, (Oral Hlth Sci) 18, (Dentistry) 10; Manchester Met 16; Newcastle 12; Portsmouth 2; Queen's Belfast 5; Sheffield 16 (interviews not held for non-EU students: 3 accepted each year).

Numbers of applicants (**a** UK **b** EU (non-UK) **c** non-EU **d** mature) Bristol **a**633 **b**633 **c**83 **d**148; Glasgow **a**437 **b**45 **c**70 **d**79; Leeds **a**877 **b**42 **c**97 **d**158; Liverpool **a**704 **b**46 **c**73 **d**143; London (King's) **a**137 **b**137 **c**25; Manchester **a**1290 **b**81 **c**152 **d**331.

Advice to applicants and planning the UCAS personal statement UCAS applications listing four choices only should be submitted by 15 October. Applicants may add up to two alternative (non-Dentistry) courses. However, if they receive offers for these courses and are rejected for Dentistry, they will not be considered for Dentistry courses in Clearing if they perform better than expected in the examinations.

On your UCAS application show evidence of your manual dexterity, work experience and awareness of problems experienced by dentists. Details should be provided of discussions with dentists and work shadowing in dental surgeries. Employment (paid or voluntary) in any field, preferably dealing with people in an environment widely removed from your home or school, could be described. Discuss any specialised fields of dentistry in which you might be interested. See also **Appendix 4**. **Bristol** Applications are not segregated by type of educational institution. Candidates are assessed on general presentation. At least 20 days of work experience is expected, if possible in different fields of dentistry. Re-sit candidates only considered if they failed to get the grades by a small margin and they had originally placed Bristol as their first firm choice. **Cardiff** Applicants must be able to demonstrate (a) evidence of, and potential for, high academic achievement, (b) an understanding of the demands of dental training and practice, (c) a caring and committed attitude towards people, (d) a willingness to accept resonsibility, (e) an ability to communicate effectively, (f) evidence of broad social, cultural or sporting interests. **Glasgow** Applicants invited to submit portfolio as evidence of their suitability. This will be assessed against the BDS Person Specification available from the Dental School. Candidates who do not submit a portfolio are not invited to selection interview. **London (King's)** School activities desirable, for example, general reading, debating, theological interests. Community activities very desirable. General activities desirable, for example, sport, first-aid, handiwork (which can be shown at interview to demonstrate manual dexterity). Work shadowing and paid or voluntary work very desirable (check website). **Manchester** Resit offers normally only made to students who firmly accepted an offer the previous year. Resit offers AAA. Applicants are required to have observed a general dental practitioner at work before applying; a minimum of two weeks is expected. **Newcastle** Applications from students with disabilities welcomed.

Misconceptions about this course Cardiff (UWIC) (Dntl Tech) Some think that the course allows them to practise as a dentist. Some think the degree is entirely practical.

Selection interviews (Dentistry) Most dental schools will interview candidates. **Yes** Birmingham (400–450 applicants and only 50% of applicants get through the initial sort), Bristol, Cardiff, Dundee, Glasgow, Leeds, London (King's), London (QM), Newcastle, Sheffield; **Some** Cardiff (UWIC), Dundee (Other Dental courses), Portsmouth (Other Dental courses).

Interview advice and questions Dental work experience or work shadowing is essential (check with university websites) and, as a result, questions will be asked on your reactions to the work and your understanding of the different types of treatment that a dentist can offer. In the past questions at interview have included: What is conservative dentistry? What does integrity mean? Do you think the first-year syllabus is a good one? What qualities are required by a dentist? What are prosthetics, periodontics, orthodontics? What causes tooth decay? Questions asked on the disadvantages of being a dentist, the future of dentistry and how you could show that you are manually dexterous. Other questions on personal attributes and spare time activities. What are the careers within the profession open to dentists? Questions on the future of dentistry (preventative and cosmetic dentistry), the problems facing dentists, the skills needed and the advantages and disadvantages of fluoride in water. How do you relax? How do you cope with stress? See also **Chapter 5**. **Bristol** All candidates called for interview must attend in order to be considered for a place; 200 are selected for interview for the five-year course and 15 for the six-year course. Offers are made to 180 and six respectively. An essay is set on a dental subject and will be assessed for spontaneity, written content and clear thought processes. Candidates at interview are assessed on general presentation, response to questions, knowledge of dentistry, evidence of teamwork, leadership, general interests, manual dexterity and good eyesight (a practical test is taken). Examples of practical work, for example, art work, needlework etc may be taken to interview as evidence of manual dexterity. **Leeds** The interview assesses personality, verbal and communication skills and knowledge of dentistry. **London (King's)** 220 applicants are interviewed of whom 180 will receive offers. All applicants receiving offers will have been interviewed. Applicants complete a questionnaire prior to interview and the interviews last about 20 minutes. Applicants may take to interview any examples of practical work, for example, art, woodwork, needlework etc as evidence of manual dexterity.

Reasons for rejection (non-academic) Lack of evidence of a firm commitment to dentistry. Lack of breadth of interests. Lack of motivation for a health care profession. Unprofessional attitude. Poor manual dexterity. Poor communication skills. Poor English. Lack of evidence of ability to work in groups. Not for the faint-hearted! More interested in running a business and making money than in caring for people. **Cardiff (UWIC)** (Dntl Tech) Target numbers need to be precise so the course fills at a late stage.

Mature students The following universities/dental schools offer shortened (usually four years) courses in Dentistry/Dental Surgery for graduates with at least 2.1 degrees in specified subjects. GCE A-level subjects and grades are also specified. Check with universities: Aberdeen, Central Lancashire, Liverpool, London (King's), (QM), Peninsula (MS).

AFTER-RESULTS ADVICE
Offers to applicants repeating A-levels **Higher** Bristol (AAA), Cardiff (preference given to students who previously applied), Dundee, Leeds (very few), Manchester (AAA – only to previous applicants who firmly accepted offer of a place); **Same** Cardiff (UWIC) (Dntl Tech), Queen's Belfast.

GRADUATE DESTINATIONS AND EMPLOYMENT (2007/8 HESA)
Graduates surveyed (Clinical) 720 **Employed** 645 **In further study** 5 **Assumed unemployed** 5

Career note The great majority of Dental Technology graduates gain employment in this career with job opportunities excellent in both the UK and Europe. There are openings in the NHS, commercial dental laboratories and the armed services.

OTHER DEGREE SUBJECTS FOR CONSIDERATION
Anatomy; Biochemistry; Biological Sciences; Biomedical Materials Science; Chemistry; Medical Sciences; Medicine; Nursing; Optometry; Pharmacy; Physiology; Physiotherapy; Radiography; Speech Therapy/Sciences; Veterinary Medicine/Science.

DEVELOPMENT STUDIES
(see also **International Relations, Politics, Town and Country Planning**)

Development Studies courses are multi-disciplinary and cover a range of subjects including economics, geography, sociology, social anthropology, politics, natural resources, with special reference to countries overseas.

Useful websites www.devstud.org.uk; www.dfid.gov.uk; www.ids.ac.uk; see also **Politics**.

NB The points totals shown to the left of the institutions are for ease of reference only. It must not be assumed that Tariff points are always used by institutions or that they can be substituted for an offer in grades. The level of an offer is not necessarily indicative of the quality of a course.

COURSE OFFERS INFORMATION

Subject requirements/preferences GCSE Mathematics, English and a foreign language may be required. **AL** Science or social science subjects may be required or preferred for some courses.

NB In 2012 universities and colleges will differ in their use of GCE AL/AS unit grade information, A* grades, the Extended Project (EPQ), the Advanced Diploma and the Cambridge Pre-U examination when considering applicants and making offers. An EPQ may be accepted in place of an AS subject. Check websites of universities and colleges for the latest offers information.

Your target offers and examples of courses provided by each institution

380 pts **Bath** – A*AA (Econ Int Dev) (IB 38 pts HL 766)
360 pts **London (SOAS)** – AAA (Dev Econ) (IB 38 pts HL 766)
320 pts **Leeds** – ABB 320 pts (Int Dev courses) (IB 34 pts HL 16 pts)
        Manchester – ABB (Dev St Sociol) (IB 31 pts)
        Sussex – ABB–BBB (Dev St courses) (IB 32–34 pts)
300 pts **Birmingham** – BBB–BCC (Af St Dev) (IB 30-32 pts)
        East Anglia – BBB 300 pts (Int Dev Env Soty) (IB 31 pts)
280 pts **Bradford** – 280 pts (Dev Pce St) (IB 30 pts)
240 pts **Chester** – 240 pts (Int Dev St courses (Comb))
        London Met – 240 pts (Int Dev; Int Dev Int Rel)
220 pts **Leeds Met** – 220 pts (Glob Dev Pce St; Glob Dev Int Rel)
        Northampton – 220–260 pts (Third Wrld Dev courses)
200 pts **East London** – 200 pts (Int Dev Third Wrld NGO Mgt)
180 pts **Derby** – 180–240 pts (Int Rel Glob Devl; Third Wrld Dev courses)
  80 pts **London (Birk)** – for under 21s (over 21s varies) p/t (Dev St)

Alternative offers
See **Chapter 7** and **Appendix 1** for grades/UCAS Tariff points information for the International Baccalaureate, Scottish Highers/Advanced Highers, the Welsh Baccalaureate, the Irish Leaving Certificate, the Cambridge Pre-U Diploma, the Advanced Diploma and the Extended Project.

CHOOSING YOUR COURSE (SEE ALSO CH. 1)

Some course features
Bradford Development Studies is offered with Economics or Peace Studies.
Derby (Int Rel Glob Dev) Course explores environmental, geographical, political, social, cultural and economic aspects of international relations and global development. Visits to key development organisations.
Leeds This is an interdisciplinary degree course with opportunity to study a second subject alongside (such as Geography or Politics). Depending on first year grade average (2.1) and on second subject, there are opportunities to study abroad in, for example, Ghana or Turkey in Year 2.
Manchester (Dev St) Students start to specialise in Year 2, choosing options from 10 study areas; in Year 3 they take a single or a joint specialisation with another area of study, for example, politics, economics.
Sussex Development Studies is also offered with French or Spanish, Geography, Economics, International Relations and Sociology.

Universities and colleges teaching quality See www.qaa.ac.uk; http://unistats.direct.gov.uk.

Top research universities and colleges (RAE 2008) Oxford; Manchester; East Anglia; Bath; London (SOAS); Birmingham.

ADMISSIONS INFORMATION

Number of applicants per place (approx) Bradford 6; East Anglia 8; Leeds 8.

Admissions tutors' advice Discuss aspects of development studies which interest you, for example in relation to geography, economics, politics. Interests in Third World countries should be mentioned. Knowledge of current events.

Advice to applicants and planning the UCAS personal statement Some students think that Development Studies has something to do with property, with plants or with childhood. It is none of these and is about international processes of change, development, progress and crisis.

Interview advice and questions Since this is a multi-disciplinary subject, questions will vary considerably. Initially they will stem from your interests and the information given on your UCAS application and your reasons for choosing the course. In the past, questions at interview have included: Define a Third World country. What help does the United Nations provide in the Third World? Could it do too much? What problems does the United Nations face in its work throughout the world? Why Development Studies? What will you do in your Gap Year, and what do you want to achieve? See also **Chapter 5**.

AFTER-RESULTS ADVICE
Offers to applicants repeating A-levels Same East Anglia.

GRADUATE DESTINATIONS AND EMPLOYMENT (2007/8 HESA)
Career note The range of specialisms offered on these courses will encourage graduates to make contact with and seek opportunities in a wide range of organisations, not necessarily limited to the Third World and government agencies.

OTHER DEGREE SUBJECTS FOR CONSIDERATION
Economics; Environmental Science/Studies; Geography; Government; International Relations; Politics; Sociology; Sustainable Development.

DIETETICS
(see also **Food Science/Studies and Technology, Nutrition**)

In addition to the scientific aspects of dietetics covering biochemistry, human physiology, food and clinical medicine, students are also introduced to health promotion, psychology, counselling and management skills. Accredited Dietetics courses qualify graduates for registration with the Health Professions Council and to practise as a dietitian in the National Health Service. (See **Appendix 4**.)

Useful websites www.nutrition.org; www.bda.uk.com; www.dietetics.co.uk.

NB The points totals shown to the left of the institutions are for ease of reference only. It must not be assumed that Tariff points are always used by institutions or that they can be substituted for an offer in grades. The level of an offer is not necessarily indicative of the quality of a course.

COURSE OFFERS INFORMATION
Subject requirements/preferences GCSE English, mathematics and science usually required. **AL** Biology and/or chemistry may be required. **Other** Health and CRB checks required and possible immunisation against hepatitis-B for practice placements.

NB In 2012 universities and colleges will differ in their use of GCE AL/AS unit grade information, A* grades, the Extended Project (EPQ), the Advanced Diploma and the Cambridge Pre-U examination when considering applicants and making offers. An EPQ may be accepted in place of an AS subject. Check websites of universities and colleges for the latest offers information.

Your target offers and examples of courses provided by each institution
340 pts London (King's) – ABB+AS (Nutr Diet) (IB 34 pts)
320 pts Nottingham – ABB–BBB (Nutr (Diet) MNutr) (IB 32–34 pts)
        Surrey – ABB–BBB 320–300 pts (Nutr Diet) (IB 34–32 pts)
300 pts London Met – 300 pts (Hum Nutr Diet) (IB 28 pts)
        Ulster – see Ch 5 +HPAT 300 pts (Diet)
280 pts Chester – 280 pts (Nutr Diet) (IB 30 pts)

Hertfordshire – 280 pts inc chem B biol C (Diet)
Plymouth – 280 pts (Diet) (IB 31 pts)
260 pts **Cardiff (UWIC)** – 260 pts (Hum Nutr Diet)
Coventry – 260 pts (Diet)
Glasgow Caledonian – BCC (Human Nutri Diet)
Leeds Met – BCC (Diet) (IB 24 pts HL 5 chem)
240 pts **Bath Spa** – 240–280 pts (Diet Hlth)
Robert Gordon – CCC 240 pts (Nutr Diet) (IB 28 pts)
200 pts **Queen Margaret** – 200 pts (Diet)

Alternative offers
See **Chapter 7** and **Appendix 1** for grades/UCAS Tariff points information for the International Baccalaureate, Scottish Highers/Advanced Highers, the Welsh Baccalaureate, the Irish Leaving Certificate, the Cambridge Pre-U Diploma, the Advanced Diploma and the Extended Project.

CHOOSING YOUR COURSE (SEE ALSO CH. 1)
Some course features
Bath Spa (Diet Hlth) Course focuses on the impact of diet, nutrition and lifestyle on health. It is not a Dietetics course and is aimed at students without a science background.
Hertfordshire Three-year course leading to registration with the Health Professions Council to practise as a dietitian.
London (King's) Clinical placements in Years 2, 3 and 4.
Nottingham This is a four-year Master of Nutrition course. Graduates with a 2.1 degree in relevant subjects such as Biochemistry accepted into Year 3 to train as dietitians.
Plymouth Supervised clinical practice in Year 2.
Surrey A professional training year is included.

Universities and colleges teaching quality See www.qaa.ac.uk; http://unistats.direct.gov.uk.

Examples of sandwich degree courses Cardiff (UWIC); Glasgow Caledonian; Leeds Met; Surrey; Ulster.

ADMISSIONS INFORMATION
Number of applicants per place (approx) Glasgow Caledonian 11; Nottingham 7; Queen Margaret 5; Surrey 1.

Advice to applicants and planning the UCAS personal statement Discuss the work with a hospital dietitian and describe fully work experience gained in hospital dietetics departments or with the schools meals services, and the problems of working in these fields. Admissions tutors expect applicants to have at least visited a dietetics department, and to be outgoing with good oral and written communication skills. Contact the British Dietetic Association (see **Appendix 4**). **Bath Spa** £1000 scholarships available.

Interview advice and questions Your knowledge of a career in dietetics will be fully explored and questions will be asked on your work experience and how you reacted to it. See also **Chapter 6**.

AFTER-RESULTS ADVICE
Offers to applicants repeating A-levels **Possibly higher** Glasgow Caledonian.

GRADUATE DESTINATIONS AND EMPLOYMENT (2007/8 HESA)
Career note Dietitians are professionally trained to advise on diets and aspects of nutrition and many degree courses combine both subjects. They may work in the NHS as hospital dietitians collaborating with medical staff on the balance of foods for patients, or in local health authorities working with GPs, or in health centres or clinics dealing with infant welfare and ante-natal problems. In addition, dietitians advise consumer groups in the food industry and government and may be involved in research. Courses can lead to professional registration: check with admissions tutors.

OTHER DEGREE SUBJECTS FOR CONSIDERATION

Biological Sciences; Biochemistry; Biology; Consumer Studies; Food Science; Health Studies; Hospitality Management; Human Nutrition; Nursing; Nutrition.

DRAMA

(including **Performing Arts/Studies, Theatre Arts, Theatre Studies** and **Theatre Design**; see also Art and Design (General), Dance/Dance Studies)

Drama courses are popular, with twice as many women as men applying each year. Lack of confidence in securing appropriate work at the end of the course, however, tends to encourage many applicants to bid for joint courses although these are usually far more competitive since there are fewer places available. Most schools of acting and drama provide a strong vocational bias whilst university drama departments offer a broader field of studies combining theory and practice. The choice of course will depend on personal preferences, either practical or theoretical, or a combination of both.

Useful websites www.equity.org.uk; www.abtt.org.uk; www.thestage.co.uk; www.uktw.co.uk; www. ukperformingarts.co.uk; www.arts.org.uk; www.stagecoach.co.uk.

NB The points totals shown to the left of the institutions are for ease of reference only. It must not be assumed that Tariff points are always used by institutions or that they can be substituted for an offer in grades. The level of an offer is not necessarily indicative of the quality of a course.

COURSE OFFERS INFORMATION

Subject requirements/preferences GCSE English usually required. **AL** English, drama, theatre studies may be required or preferred. (Theatre Arts) English, theatre studies or drama may be required for some courses. **Other** CRB clearance required for some courses: check websites.

NB In 2012 universities and colleges will differ in their use of GCE AL/AS unit grade information, A* grades, the Extended Project (EPQ), the Advanced Diploma and the Cambridge Pre-U examination when considering applicants and making offers. An EPQ may be accepted in place of an AS subject. Check websites of universities and colleges for the latest offers information.

Your target offers and examples of courses provided by each institution
390 pts **Warwick** – AABb–ABBb (Engl Thea St) (IB 36 pts)
380 pts **Cambridge** – A*AA college offers may vary (Educ Engl Dr)
360 pts **Bristol** – AAA–AAB (Dr Fr/Ger/Ital St (4 yr)) (IB 37–35 pts)
　　　　　Exeter – AAA–ABB (Dr) (IB 36–31 pts)
340 pts **Birmingham** – AAB–ABB (Dr courses) (IB 34 pts)
　　　　　East Anglia – AAB–BBB (Script Perf) (IB 33–31 pts)
　　　　　Glasgow – AAB (Thea St courses) (IB 34 pts)
　　　　　Lancaster – ABB (Thea St courses) (IB 31 pts)
　　　　　Leeds – ABB–AAB (Thea Perf) (IB 36 pts)
　　　　　London (QM) – 340 pts (Dr) (IB 32 pts)
　　　　　London (RH) – AAB–ABB (Dr Phil/Phil) (IB 35 pts)
　　　　　Loughborough – 340 pts (Dr Engl/Engl) (IB 34 pts HL Engl, Thea St)
　　　　　Manchester – See *Advice to applicants and planning the UCAS personal statement*
　　　　　　　AAB–BBB (Dr courses) (IB 35–32 pts)
　　　　　Sussex – AAB–ABB (Dr courses) (IB 34–36 pts)
320 pts **London (QM)** – 320 pts (Film St Dr) (IB 32 pts)
　　　　　Surrey – ABB–BBB (Thea St) (IB 32 pts)
　　　　　York – ABB (Writ Dir Perf) (IB 31 pts)
300 pts **Bristol UWE** – 300–340 pts (Dr courses)
　　　　　Brunel – Contact admissions office (Thea Crea Writ; Thea Engl; Thea Film TV St; Thea Gms Des; Thea Mus; Thea Snc Arts)

ABOUT THE NCDT

The National Council for Drama Training is a partnership of employers in the theatre, broadcast and media industry, employee representatives and training providers.

It exists to act as a champion for the industry by working to optimise support for professional drama training and education, embracing change and development. It works to safeguard the highest standards and provides a credible process of quality assurance through accreditation for vocation drama courses in further and higher education in the UK.

Accreditation aims to give students confidence that the courses they choose are recognised by the drama profession as being relevant to the purposes of their employment; and that the profession has confidence that the people they employ who have completed these courses have the skills and attributes required for the continuing health of the industry.

HISTORY

The National Council for Drama Training (NCDT) was established in 1976 following the publication of the Gulbenkian Foundation report Going on the Stage into professional training for drama. NCDT has been supported by the performing arts industry and charged with maintaining standards at the nation's top drama schools. Over nearly thirty years, NCDT has been providing assurance for students, their parents and funders that courses approved by NCDT are preparing students for careers in the drama profession.

COUNCIL

Council takes on a strong strategic role within the industry in order to optimise support for the professional drama training and education.

RESEARCH AND DEVELOPMENT

Between only 2% and 10% of all the students who apply for a place at drama school actually succeed in getting onto accredited courses. NCDT is looking to identify the factors that contribute to students success at audition and to use the data that we collect to gain a better understanding of the routes into accredited training and performing experiences and other important social and geographical data ever collected in the sector. it is expected to provide evidence to support advocacy arguments for increased funding, particularly for outreach and pre-audition development projects.

NCDT gathers robust graduate destinations data. The purpose of this is of tracking graduates is to show that accredited training has a much higher incidence of quality graduate destinations than non-accredited courses, where on average only one in ten enters the profession (THES, 16 April 2004). Value to providers in developing self-assessment and informing curriculum and allows NCDT to determine benchmark standards in order to assist in the decision whether to accredit new courses. It provided the first detailed map of how new performers engage with the labour market in the performing arts and demonstrates the link between quality training and employment patterns. The championing of quality graduate destinations increases the awareness and attractiveness of accredited courses in the recruitment of new students, including profiling role models to potential students from ethnic minorities or with disabilities.

Except for those at the top of the profession, performers earn comparatively low salaries. Most have to undertake alternative employment between engagements.

Despite the gloomy statistics, the personal rewards involved in a career in drama can be immense. How many people can claim they're making a living doing something they really want to do?

TRAINING

The Acting profession is increasingly competitive and work even for those who are trained is sporadic. Self belief, perseverance and confidence are vital but you do need to be realistic. For example, actors work professionally an average of 11.3 weeks of the year. Except for those at the top of the profession performers earn comparatively low salaries and most have to undertake temporary periods of alternative employment between engagements.

If you are at school and are desperate to act or want to get into Stage Management/Technical Theatre you should be aware that the advice of the industry is to stay within mainstream education before applying to drama school. Drama Schools only take students from the age of 18 and often have academic entry requirements and because of the precarious nature of a career in drama, students are advised to take full advantage of their general education and obtain as high a standard of academic qualifications as possible. Maturity is also essential and it is not unusual for schools to suggest younger applicants re-audition after a Gap Year.

For those who do aspire to an acting career it is not all bad news. Despite the gloomy statistics the personal rewards involved can be immense – how many people can claim they are making a living doing something they really want to do?

If you are determined to succeed it makes sense to have as many advantages as possible and Vocational training on a course accredited by NCDT is one of the greatest advantages of all. Over 1,500 students enter training on NCDT accredited courses each year. If you are thinking seriously about a career in performance, you should consider attending professional training at a drama school.

Training will give you the opportunity to showcase to the right people (agents, casting directors, theatre and television companies), so vital to securing that all-important first job. It is also important to realise that actors, stage managers and theatre technicians need professional skills and most will have up to three years of professional vocational training to acquire the skills needed to do their jobs and maintain a life-long career. A report carried out by the Institute of Manpower Studies on behalf of the Arts Council of England found that 86% of actors working in the profession had received formal professional training.

If you are thinking of training in Stage Management a recent study showed an almost 100% employment rate for graduates from NCDT Stage Management and Technical Theatre accredited courses.

Graduates of accredited courses, who are legally entitled to work in the UK, also qualify for full Equity membership on completion of their course.

It is important to make a distinction between vocational training courses and the vast number of performing arts courses on offer at UK universities. The Higher Education Funding Council for England funds over 2,100 degree courses with Drama or Theatre in the title. These courses may appear to have a connection with the industry, but most do not. University courses are generally more academic and do not aim to train people as actors. For more information on University drama courses contact the Standing Conference of University Drama Departments http://art.ntu.ac.uk/scudd.

A one-year course accredited by NCDT may be a suitable choice for those who have already completed a drama or theatre studies degree.

http://www.ncdt.co.uk/

West Side Story
Photo Mark Dean

GUILDFORD SCHOOL OF ACTING

GSA has built an international reputation for excellence in training for actors and technicians in all areas of theatre and the recorded media.

Situated in brand new building at the University of Surrey, GSA offers the very best vocational training in Acting, Musical Theatre and Professional Production Skills with courses ranging from National Diplomas and Foundation Degrees through to Post Graduate qualifications in Acting, Musical Theatre and Practice of Voice and Singing. We currently offer both funded places as well as private ones.

New state of the art facilities for Production, film making, a number of theatres and a very special creative community make GSA a top choice amongst candidates wishing to train for the performing arts industry.

From September 2011 GSA will be offering the only full-time Foundation Course in Musical Theatre at an accredited drama school. In addition GSA offers a Part-time evening course for students who intend to complete their A Levels prior to applying for full-time training.

These new courses complement GSA's existing Saturday School and well subscribed Summer Schools.

GSA also offers a full syllabus for Musical Theatre Singing Examinations ranging from Grades 1 – 8 through to Diploma, Licentiate and Fellowship level.

Current high profile graduates include Tom Chambers, Brenda Blethyn OBE, Celia Imrie, Michael Ball, Bill Nighy, Chloe Hart, Chris Geere, Ellie Paskell, Claire Cooper, Rob Kazinsky, Ian Kelsey and Justin Fletcher MBE

Virtually every West End show features performers who trained at GSA. Current students have performed at the Olivier Awards ceremony, the opening of G-Live, Guildford, The Festival of Remembrance at The Royal Albert Hall and numerous other prestigious events.

www.gsauk.org

Rose Bruford (Coll) – 240–280 pts (Am Thea Arts; Euro Thea Arts; Actg)

Salford – 240 pts (Engl Dr Perf St)

Worcester – 240–300 pts (Dr; Dr Perf)

220 pts Bath Spa – 220–300 pts (Dr St Educ) (IB 24 pts)

Bishop Grosseteste (UC) – 220 pts (Dr Commun)

Falmouth (UC) – 220 pts (Thea)

Northampton – 220–260 pts (Dr courses; Actg)

Queen Margaret – 220 pts (Cstm Des Constr) (IB 28 pts)

Sunderland – 220–360 pts (Dr courses) (IB 31 pts)

UCP Marjon – 220 pts (Dr Crea Writ)

York St John – 220–260 pts (Thea)

200 pts Bucks New – 200–240 pts (Perf Arts)

Central Lancashire – 200–260 pts (Contemp Thea Perf; Actg)

Cumbria – 200-280 pts (Dr Perf Tech Thea)

Doncaster (Coll Univ Centre) – (Contemp Perf Prac)

East London – 200 pts (Thea St)

Glyndŵr – 200 pts (Thea TV Perf)

St Mary's Twickenham (UC) – 160–200 pts (Dr Physl Thea) (IB 28 pts)

Southampton Solent – 200 pts (Cmdy Writ Perf; Perf)

West London – 200 pts (Actg)

Wolverhampton – Check with Ad Tutor 200 pts (Dr Film St)

180 pts Bedfordshire – 180 pts (Perf Arts; Thea Prof Prac)

Derby – 180–240 pts (Thea Arts courses) (IB 26 pts)

Greenwich – 180 pts (Dr courses)

Liverpool (LIPA) – 180 pts (Commun Dr)

Staffordshire – 180–220 pts (Dr Perf Thea Arts; Thea St Tech Stg Prod)

Swansea Met – 180–360 pts (Perf Arts)

UCP Marjon – 180 pts (Dr Educ St)

160 pts Bishop Grosseteste (UC) – 160 pts (Educ St Dr)

Central Lancashire – 160–260 pts (Mus Thea)

Grimsby (IFHE) – interview+audition 160 pts (Perf (Dr))

London (Central Sch SpDr) – CC (Actg courses)

London South Bank – CC 160 pts (Dr Perf St; Thea Prac Crea Prodg)

Reading – 160 pts (Thea Arts Educ Df St) (IB 24 pts)

Rose Bruford (Coll) – 160 pts (Actr Mushp)

St Mary's Twickenham (UC) – 160–200 pts (Dr App Thea) (IB 28 pts)

140 pts Birmingham City – 140 pts (Actg; Actg (Musl Thea))

120 pts Blackpool and Fylde (Coll) – 120–300 pts (Musl Thea)

Royal Welsh (CMusDr) – 120–200 pts (Actg; Stg Mgt; Thea Des)

100 pts Guildhall (Sch Mus Dr) – 100 pts (Act; Stg Mgt Tech Thea)

80 pts and below (Some Theatre Schools and Drama departments do not select on the basis of academic qualifications)

ALRA – 80 pts and below (Actg)

Arts Educ Sch – entry by audition; contact Admissions Tutor (Musl Thea)

Arts London – interviewÐ+portfolio+audition (Actg; Dir; Perf Des Prac)

Arts London (CFash) – (Cstm Tech Effct Mkup)

Bournemouth Arts (UC) – 80 pts (Actg)

Bristol Old Vic (Thea Sch) – interview (Prof Stg Mgt)

Croydon (Coll) – 80–100 pts (Des Crft Stg Scrn)

Essex – EE+audition 80 pts (Actg; Actg Contemp Thea)

GSA Conservatoire – audition (Actg; Musl Thea)

LAMDA – interview + audition (Prof Actg; Stg Mgt Tech Thea)

London (Birk) – (Thea Dr St)

London (RADA) – interview (Tech Thea Stg Mng)

London (RADA) – audition (Actg)

Actors, directors, stage managers & technicians
from all over the world choose to train at LAMDA.

Discover why...

THE LONDON
ACADEMY OF
MUSIC AND
DRAMATIC ART

150
ANNIVERSARY

THREE YEAR ACTING COURSE
BA (Hons) in Professional Acting

TWO YEAR ACTING COURSE
Foundation Degree in Professional Acting*

TWO YEAR STAGE MANAGEMENT & TECHNICAL THEATRE COURSE
Foundation Degree in Stage Management & Technical Theatre*

ONE YEAR CLASSICAL ACTING COURSE
Postgraduate Diploma in Classical Acting

All of LAMDA's higher education courses are validated by the University of Kent. The Academy's two and three-year courses are accredited by the National Council for Drama Training.

*Students who successfully complete the Foundation Degree in Professional Acting or Stage Management & Technical Theatre at the required level, and who choose to do so, may apply to progress to a one-year top-up BA (Hons) Theatre Arts or BA (Hons) Theatre Production degree course respectively.

With an exciting range of non-higher education options also available, including a One Year Foundation Course for students considering a career in the performing arts, there's something to inspire and challenge you at LAMDA.

For further information, please contact LAMDA at admissions@lamda.org.uk, visit www.lamda.org.uk or call 020 8834 0506.

Conservatoire for Dance and Drama

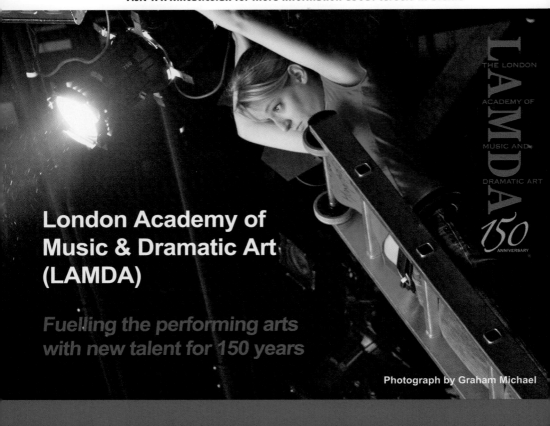

London Academy of Music & Dramatic Art (LAMDA)

Fuelling the performing arts with new talent for 150 years

THE LONDON ACADEMY OF MUSIC AND DRAMATIC ART

150 ANNIVERSARY

Photograph by Graham Michael

LAMDA is one of the world's leading drama schools. We offer exceptional vocational training to students of promise in the performing arts. Our acting course graduates can be found in the West End, Broadway, Hollywood and the UK's flagship theatre companies, as well as on television and radio. Our stage management and technical graduates also thrive across the global entertainment industry and in an extraordinary range of other managerial positions.

As an affiliate of the Conservatoire for Dance & Drama, LAMDA receives funding from the Higher Education Funding Council for England (HEFCE). This means that eligible UK/EU students are able to access loans to assist with their tuition fees and maintenance costs. In addition, LAMDA and the Conservatoire have a range of scholarships and bursaries available to ensure that the most talented students can access the Academy's training, regardless of their financial circumstances. Further details are available online at **www.lamda.org.uk**

LAMDA offers four full-time higher education accredited courses in acting and stage management & technical theatre – all of which are validated by the University of Kent. Believing the arts should be accessible to everyone, we also offer a rich mix of other programmes to ensure that whatever your ability or experience, there is a course at the Academy to suit you.

Our training is based on 150 years of experience in the business. We help aspiring actors, directors, designers, stage managers and technicians to acquire the technique and creativity necessary to succeed in these highly competitive professions. We achieve this through a first-class teaching faculty, including both experienced tutors and visiting specialists.

By inviting current professionals to work with our students, we ensure that whatever they are striving for – be it a career in theatre, on screen or behind the scenes – we have the industry connections to help them take those important first steps. Students on our full-time acting courses receive regular talks from leading agents and casting directors to prepare them for entry into the profession. Our stage management and technical theatre course students undertake enviable industry placements – enabling them to learn on the job and impress future employers. This is just one of the reasons why all of our stage management and technical students who

actively seek employment find relevant work within a few weeks of graduation.

Whichever course you choose at LAMDA, classes are conducted in small groups and progress is encouraged through conversation, practice and example. With a minimum of 35 contact hours a week, the training is as tough as the industry in which you hope to work. It is delivered, however, in a warm and supportive environment, where individual talent is nurtured and teamwork is key.

We audition and/or interview everyone who submits their application (directly to LAMDA, not via UCAS) by the advertised deadline, providing they meet the age requirements for the training. As all of our courses are vocational, we do not ask prospective students for specific academic qualifications or grades. We just ask for talent, passion and a commitment to learn.

The dramatic arts are a combination of craft, talent and inspiration. For 150 years, LAMDA has offered training that teaches the craft, nurtures the talent and frees the imagination. For further information, please contact admissions@lamda.org.uk, visit www.lamda.org.uk or call 020 8834 0506.

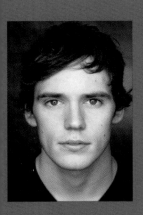

" After studying performing arts at college, I knew I needed to go to drama school to further my training. When I did the rounds of auditions, LAMDA stood out immediately. It was a well-respected school, but also very down-to-earth. People say, "You don't pick your school, your school picks you." I feel very lucky that the Academy chose me. "

2009 LAMDA graduate, Sam Claflin.
Credits include: *Any Human Heart* (Channel 4),
Pirates of the Caribbean: On Stranger Tides & United (BBC).

London Mountview (Ac Thea Arts) – audition (Perf Musl Thea; Actg; Tech Thea)
Royal Scottish (RSAMD) – 80 pts min b (Contemp Perf Prac; Actg; Tech Prod Arts)
Trinity Laban Consv – (Dance Thea)

Alternative offers
See **Chapter 7** and **Appendix 1** for grades/UCAS Tariff points information for the International Baccalaureate, Scottish Highers/Advanced Highers, the Welsh Baccalaureate, the Irish Leaving Certificate, the Cambridge Pre-U Diploma, the Advanced Diploma and the Extended Project.

EXAMPLES OF FOUNDATION DEGREES IN THE SUBJECT FIELD
Arts London (Wimb CA); Bath Spa; Bedfordshire; Blackpool and Fylde (Coll); Bournemouth; Bournemouth and Poole (Coll); Bournemouth Arts (UC); Bradford; Bristol City (Coll); Bucks New; Chichester; Colchester (Inst); Cornwall (Coll); Craven (Coll); Cumbria; Exeter (Coll); Farnborough (CT); Greenwich; Hereford (CA); Hertfordshire; Huddersfield; Hull (Coll); Kirklees (Coll); Leeds City (Coll); Leeds Met; Manchester (Coll); NEW (Coll); Newcastle (Coll); Northbrook (Coll); Norwich City (Coll); Nottingham New (Coll); Rose Bruford (Coll); Rotherham (CAT); St Helens (Coll); Sheffield (Coll); South Devon (Coll); South Essex (Coll); Staffordshire Reg Fed (SURF); Suffolk (Univ Campus); Sunderland; Teesside; Truro (Coll); Wigan and Leigh (Coll).

CHOOSING YOUR COURSE (SEE ALSO CH. 1)
Some course features
Anglia Ruskin (Drama) The course content depends on the options chosen, for example dramatic performance, technical theatre, drama in theory and practice, directing and TV drama.
Bedfordshire (Perf Arts) Focus on dance and theatre.
Brunel (Drama) A strong practical emphasis.
De Montfort (Perf Arts) A highly practical programme covering acting, directing, dance, film, arts management and community education.
Edge Hill (Drama) Options in directing, design, writing, educational or community drama.

For a quick reference offers calculator, fold out the inside back cover.

Bristol Old Vic Theatre School

An Affiliate of the Conservatoire for Dance & Drama

The Bristol Old Vic Theatre School provides the premier, conservatoire level drama training in the South West of England. For over sixty years the School has enjoyed a national and international reputation for excellence. Students are selected solely on the basis of talent.

All training courses are designed to provide students with the necessary skills and experience to sustain professional careers in their chosen area of work. Students are taught in a 'producing-house' environment, working to industry standards. All staff have considerable professional backgrounds in their area of specialism. There is an outstanding employment record from all courses, with many past students becoming movers and shakers in their field.

The Courses

3 year Professional Acting BA (Hons)

Broad and comprehensive training and preparation for professional performance in theatre, radio, television and film.

2 year Professional Acting (FdA)

Specially modified to provide as much as is possible in a reduced time. Less opportunity for "performance-under-tuition" and less time to experiment.

1 Year Professional Acting

Offers an opportunity for mature, professionally experienced students.

1 year Professional Acting for overseas students (Cert HE)

An intensive three-term (33 weeks) training in the core-skills, techniques and approaches to acting on stage.

3 year Professional Stage Management BA

Provides a broad-based training, combining theatre production skills with television and radio drama experience.

2 Year Professional Stage Management (FdA)

Long established training in theatre production skills offers a fast track course for more mature students.

1 year Theatre Production Management (PG Dip)

A one year course for only two students who will have previous training in a practical theatre discipline and/or have worked professionally in a stage management or technical theatre department.

1 year Theatre Arts Management (PG Dip)

A one year course for two students who will normally have previous training in a practical theatre discipline and/or professional experience in a theatre environment.

2 year Costume (FdA & BA Hons top up)

An intensive vocational and highly practical course for four students per year covering all aspects of costume work.

1 year Scenic Art (PG Dip)

Entirely practical, intensive, three-term course. Students will have a high level of painting and drawing skills.

4 term Theatre Design (MA)

The only course of its kind in the U.K. which is set in a Theatre School and integrated with a producing company, training designers in a realistic environment, working closely with directors, actors and technicians.

4 term Drama Directing (MA)

A four term course for up to four students with the career aim of directing drama. Students come from a very wide range of backgrounds but must have previous directing experience.

Higher Education

Aspire • Achieve • Succeed

For more information about
Foundation Degrees at The College call

01202 205180

email: heunit@thecollege.ac.uk
www.thecollege.co.uk/highereducation

Performing Arts - Contemporary Theatre

Leeanne first joined The Bournemouth and Poole College on leaving school and has now progressed onto the Foundation Degree.

Leeanne commented

" After watching my sister in a performance whilst she was studying at The Bournemouth and Poole College, I decided to follow in her footsteps and came to college to study Performing Arts. Having left school with very few qualifications it's been a wonderful experience to carry on my studies up to university level, especially as I am the first person in my family who has gone into higher education. I love the people here and being on stage is great fun. We get to perform a lot of shows each year. The tutors are absolutely amazing and although the theory work is often hard they are always around to support you and I'm learning something new every day. When I finish my studies I would like to become a teacher, as well as auditioning for stage parts and I'd really like to travel. "

Lincoln (Drama) A balanced course covering acting, directing, history and technical aspects.
Liverpool Hope (Crea Perf Arts) There are two main strands – artistic and vocational. The course covers drama, music, dance, visual art, writing and work-related skills.
London (RH) (Int Thea) Practical and theoretical studies, with study in Australia. Year's study abroad also possible in other programmes.
Loughborough (Drama) Six optional modules in Years 2 and 3.
Newport (Perf Arts) Performance for film, radio, TV, theatre and drama.

Universities and colleges teaching quality See www.qaa.ac.uk; http://unistats.direct.gov.uk.

Top research universities and colleges (RAE 2008) (Drama, Dance and Performing Arts) Warwick (Film and TV Studies); Roehampton (Dance); London (QM); St Andrews; Manchester; Bristol; Glasgow; Exeter; London (RH).

ADMISSIONS INFORMATION

Number of applicants per place (approx) Aberystwyth 10; Arts London (Actg) 32, (Dir) 10; Birmingham 15; Bishop Grosseteste (UC) 4; Bristol 19; Brunel 9; Chester 14; Cumbria 4; De Montfort (Perf Arts) 5; East Anglia 13; Edge Hill 8; Essex 15; Exeter 20; Glamorgan 6; Huddersfield 5; Hull 16, (Scarborough) 2; Hull (Coll) 2; Kent 24; Lancaster 18; Leeds 10; Liverpool (LIPA) (Perf Arts (Actg)) 48; Liverpool John Moores 10; London (Central Sch SpDr) (Thea Prac) 5; London (Gold) 28; London (RH) 10; London Met 20; London Mountview (Ac Thea Arts) (Ac Thea Arts) (Musl Thea) 8; Loughborough 6; Manchester (Dr) 6, (Dr Engl Lit) 8; Manchester (Coll) 10; Manchester Met 48; Middlesex 26; Northampton 3; Northumbria 25; Nottingham Trent 4; Queen Margaret 4; Reading 17; Roehampton 6; Royal Welsh (CMusDr) (Actg) 50, (Stg Mgt) 10; Warwick 18; Winchester (Dr) 6; Worcester 4; York 4; York St John 9.

How to read the Subject Tables: **Chapter 7**

COURSE OFFERS INFORMATION

Subject requirements/preferences AL Mathematics and chemistry required. See also **Engineering/ Engineering Sciences**.

NB In 2012 universities and colleges will differ in their use of GCE AL/AS unit grade information, A* grades, the Extended Project (EPQ), the Advanced Diploma and the Cambridge Pre-U examination when considering applicants and making offers. An EPQ may be accepted in place of an AS subject. Check websites of universities and colleges for the latest offers information.

Your target offers and examples of courses provided by each institution

380 pts Cambridge – A*AA college offers may vary 2nd yr entry only via Eng **or** Nat Sci (Cheml Eng) (IB 38–42 pts HL 766–777)

Imperial London – A*mathsAA (Cheml Eng Yr Abrd) (IB 39 pts H maths chem phys 6 pts)

360 pts Edinburgh – Check with Ad Tutor AAA 2nd yr entry (Struct Fire Sfty Eng) (IB 36 pts)

London (UCL) – AAA-AAB (Bioch Eng MEng) (IB 36-38 pts)

Manchester – AAA–AAB (Petrol Eng) (IB 35 pts)

Oxford – AAA (Eng Sci (Cheml Eng)) (IB 38–40 pts)

340 pts Aston – AAB–AAA (Cheml Eng MEng) (IB 32 pts)

Bath – AAB (Cheml Eng MEng) (IB 36 pts HL maths chem 6)

Birmingham – AAB (Cheml Ener Eng) (IB 32–34 pts)

Leeds – AAB (Cheml Pharml Eng) (IB 36 pts HL 17 pts)

London (UCL) – AAB-ABB (Bioch Eng BEng) (IB 34-36 pts)

Loughborough – 340 pts (Cheml Eng Mgt (5 yr sandwich)) (IB 36 pts HL maths, phys chem 17 pts)

Newcastle – AAB (Biopharml Tech MEng) (IB 36 pts HL maths chem 5)

Nottingham – AAB–ABB (Cheml Eng Env Eng) (IB 32 pts)

Sheffield – AAB–ABB (Cheml Eng Modn Lang) (IB 32–33 pts)

Strathclyde – AAB (Cheml Eng MEng) (IB 34 pts)

320 pts Bath – AAB-ABB (Cheml Bioproc Eng) (IB 34 pts HL maths chem 6)

Edinburgh – Check with Ad Tutor ABB 1st yr entry (Struct Fire Sfty Eng) (IB 34 pts)

Lancaster – ABB 320 pts (Nucl Eng) (IB 30 pts)

Loughborough – 320 pts (Cheml Eng Env Prot) (IB 34 pts)

Newcastle – ABB (Biopharml Tech BEng) (IB 34 pts HL chem maths 5)

Nottingham – ABB (Cheml Eng MEng/BEng) (IB 32 pts)

Queen's Belfast – ABB (Cheml Eng MEng)

Strathclyde – ABB-AAC (App Chem Cheml Eng MSci) (IB 34 pts)

Surrey – ABB–BBB (Cheml Eng inc Fdn Yr) (IB 30 pts)

300 pts Aberdeen – BBB 300 pts (Cheml Eng MEng)

Aston – BBB–ABB (Cheml Eng BEng)

Heriot-Watt – BBB (Brew Distil)

Strathclyde – BBB (Cheml Eng BEng) (IB 31 pts)

Swansea – BBB (Cheml Bioproc Eng BEng)

280 pts Queen's Belfast – BBC (Cheml Eng BEng)

Teesside – 280 pts (Cheml Eng) (IB 30 pts)

270 pts Glasgow Caledonian – 270 pts (Fire Rsk Eng)

260 pts Central Lancashire – 260 pts (Fire Eng) (IB 28 pts)

240 pts Huddersfield – 240–280 pts (Chem Cheml Eng)

Newport – 240 pts (Fire Sfty Eng)

Portsmouth – 240 pts (Petrol Eng)

230 pts London South Bank – 230 pts (Petrol Eng) (IB 24 pts)

160 pts Central Lancashire – 160 pts (Fire Sfty Risk Mgt)

140 pts West Scotland – CD (Cheml Eng BSc)

Alternative offers See **Chapter 7** and **Appendix 1** for grades/UCAS Tariff points information for the International Baccalaureate, Scottish Highers/Advanced Highers, the Welsh Baccalaureate, the Irish Leaving Certificate, the Cambridge Pre-U Diploma, the Advanced Diploma and the Extended Project.

Engineering your future – Why chemical is the way to go...
By Matt Stalker

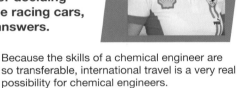

Chemical engineers are considered to be the problem-solvers of the science and engineering community. Whether it's working out how to make industrial processes more environmentally friendly or deciding which fuels are best suited to Formula One racing cars, chemical engineers have usually got the answers.

If you're reading this, you're probably already thinking about studying chemical engineering at university.

It's a career path that offers variety, travel and outstanding earning potential – 2010 chemical engineering graduates got an average starting salary of £28,000/y, the third highest in the UK. Chemical Engineering is all about changing raw materials into useful, everyday products in a safe and cost effective way. For example, did you know that petrol, plastics and synthetic fibres such as polyester and nylon, all come from oil?

Chemical Engineers understand how to alter the chemical, biochemical or physical state of a substance, to create everything from face creams to fuels.

Whynotchemeng.com is a website that's full of information about chemical engineering. Whether you're trying to better understand what chemical engineers do on a day-to-day basis, which companies employ chemical engineers or you need to find out which universities offer chemical engineering degree courses, whynotchemeng can help.

Since the campaign's launch, volunteers have visited hundreds of schools and colleges throughout the UK and played a key role in the staggering rise in number of students choosing to study chemical engineering at UK universities. Last year, a record intake of over 1800 students chose to start studying the subject at university.

Companies such as BP, Shell, Sellafield, Tate and Lyle, Foster Wheeler, MW Kellogg and Davy Process all employ chemical engineering graduates in a wide range of roles.

Because the skills of a chemical engineer are so transferable, international travel is a very real possibility for chemical engineers.

Lisa Lilley studied chemical engineering at university and later gained a PhD in combustion chemistry. She's now Shell's Formula One Project Manager and is responsible for the day-to-day management of the Ferrari Formula One project: "Chemical engineers need to keep their eyes open and be ready to adopt and exploit across different disciplines. Formula One plays an important role in the rapid development and testing of some of the new biofuel technologies," she explained.

Al Sacco is another chemical engineer and he's got further than most...much further. Al spent time working for NASA and has been into space, spending three weeks doing research into Earth's orbit!

"When people ask how far chemical engineering has taken me, I can tell them that it's taken me into space – it doesn't get much further than that!" said Al.

Whilst a chemical engineering degree isn't certain to take you as far as Al, it's a door-opening degree that equips graduates with an outstanding grasp of project management, design and how industrial processes operate. So maybe it's time to think...whynotchemeng?

Links
www.whynotchemeng.com
www.icheme.org

0039_11

CHOOSING YOUR COURSE (SEE ALSO CH. 1)
Some course features
Aberdeen Close contacts with the oil and gas industries.
Birmingham One third of the course with Business Management is devoted to management subjects.
Heriot-Watt Direct entry to Year 2 depending on A-level results. Courses have a common structure up to Year 3 allowing for a change in specialisation.
London (UCL) The MEng course leads directly to Chartered Engineer status. Students taking the BEng course will need to complete a period of further training to achieve this.
Newcastle Stages 1 and 2 are common for all nine courses in the department.
Nottingham Mining can be combined with Chemical Engineering.

Universities and colleges teaching quality See www.qaa.ac.uk; http://unistats.direct.gov.uk.

Top research universities and colleges (RAE 2008) Cambridge; Imperial London; Manchester; London (UCL); Birmingham; Sheffield; Newcastle; Bath.

Examples of sandwich degree courses Aston; Bath; London South Bank; Loughborough; Manchester; Queen's Belfast; Surrey; Teesside.

ADMISSIONS INFORMATION
Number of applicants per place (approx) Aston 4; Bath 8; Birmingham 8; Heriot-Watt 8; Huddersfield 7; Imperial London 4, (MEng) 4; Leeds 9; London (UCL) 8; Loughborough 7; Newcastle (MEng/BEng) 6; Nottingham 6; Sheffield 14; Strathclyde 6; Surrey 5; Swansea 3.

Misconceptions about this course Surrey That chemical engineering is chemistry on a large scale: physics is as applicable as chemistry.

Selection interviews Yes Bath, Cambridge, Imperial London, Leeds, London (UCL), London South Bank, Newcastle, Nottingham, Oxford, Surrey, Sussex, Teesside; **Some** Loughborough.

Interview advice and questions Past questions have included the following: How would you justify the processing of radioactive waste to people living in the neighbourhood? What is public health engineering? What is biochemical engineering? What could be the sources of fuel and energy in the year 2020? Discuss some industrial applications of chemistry. Regular incidents occur in which chemical spillage and other problems affect the environment. Be prepared to discuss these social issues. See also **Chapter 6**. **Imperial London** Interviews can be conducted in South East Asia if necessary.

Reasons for rejection (non-academic) See **Engineering/Engineering Sciences**.

AFTER-RESULTS ADVICE
Offers to applicants repeating A-levels Higher Swansea; **Possibly higher** Bath, Leeds, London South Bank, Queen's Belfast; **Same** Aston, Birmingham, Cambridge, Loughborough, Newcastle, Nottingham, Sheffield, Surrey, Teesside.

GRADUATE DESTINATIONS AND EMPLOYMENT (2007/8 HESA)
Graduates surveyed 450 **Employed** 215 **In further study** 110 **Assumed unemployed** 55

Career note Chemical engineering is involved in many aspects of industry and scientific development. In addition to the oil and chemical-based industries, graduates enter a wide range of careers including the design and construction of chemical process plants, food production, pollution control, environmental protection, energy conservation, waste recovery and recycling, medical science, health and safety, and alternative energy sources.

OTHER DEGREE SUBJECTS FOR CONSIDERATION
Biochemistry; Biotechnology; Chemistry; Colour Chemistry; Cosmetic Science; Environmental Science; Food Science and Technology; Materials Science; Mathematics; Nuclear Engineering; Physics.

ENGINEERING (CIVIL)

(including **Architectural, Coastal, Disaster Management, Environmental, Offshore, Structural** and **Transportation Engineering**; see also **Building and Construction, Environmental Sciences/Studies**)

Civil engineering is concerned with the science and art of large-scale projects. This involves the planning, design, construction, maintenance and environmental assessment of roads, railways, bridges, airports, tunnels, docks, offshore structures, dams, high rise buildings and other major works. Specialist courses may also involve water, drainage, irrigation schemes and waste engineering, traffic and coastal engineering.

Useful websites www.ice.org.uk; www.engc.org.uk; www.enginuity.org.uk.

Engineering Council statement *See* **Engineering/Engineering Sciences**.

NB The points totals shown to the left of the institutions are for ease of reference only. It must not be assumed that Tariff points are always used by institutions or that they can be substituted for an offer in grades. The level of an offer is not necessarily indicative of the quality of a course.

COURSE OFFERS INFORMATION

Subject requirements/preferences See **Engineering/Engineering Sciences**.

NB In 2012 universities and colleges will differ in their use of GCE AL/AS unit grade information, A* grades, the Extended Project (EPQ), the Advanced Diploma and the Cambridge Pre-U examination when considering applicants and making offers. An EPQ may be accepted in place of an AS subject. Check websites of universities and colleges for the latest offers information.

Your target offers and examples of courses provided by each institution

380 pts **Cambridge** – A*AA college offers may vary (Eng (Part II specialism Civ Eng)) (IB 38–42 pts)
Imperial London – A*mathsAA (Civ Eng Yr Abrd) (IB 38 pts)
London (UCL) – A*AA+AS–AAA+AS (Civ Eng) (IB 38–39 pts)

360 pts **Bath** – AAA (Civ Eng) (IB 36 pts HL maths 6)
Birmingham – AAA–AAB (Civ Eng Bus Mgt) (IB 30–34 pts)
Bristol – AAA (Civ Eng Euro) (IB 37 pts HL 666)
Edinburgh – Check with Ad Tutor AAA 2nd yr entry (Civ Eng MEng/BEng) (IB 36 pts)
Newcastle – AAA–BBB (Civ Struct Eng) (IB 36 pts HL maths 5)
Nottingham – AAA–BBB (Civ Env Eng MEng/BEng) (IB 36 pts)
Oxford – AAA (Civ Eng) (IB 38–40 pts)
Southampton – AAA (Civ Eng Archit) (IB 36 pts)
Swansea – AAA–BBB (Civ Eng MEng/BEng)

340 pts **Bristol UWE** – 340 pts (Archit Env Eng)
Cardiff – AAB–BBB 340 pts (Electron Comm Eng) (IB 30–32 pts)
City – AAB 340 pts (Civ Eng) (IB 30 pts)
Durham – AAB (Civ Eng) (IB 36 pts)
Glasgow – AAB–BBB (Civ Eng MEng/BEng; Civ Eng Archit MEng/BEng)
Leeds – AAB (Archit Eng) (IB 36 pts HL 17 pts)
Loughborough – AAB–ABB (Civ Eng MEng/BEng) (IB 34 pts)
Manchester – AAB–ABB (Civ Eng N Am) (IB 35–33 pts)
Newcastle – AAB (Off Eng MEng) (IB 37 pts HL maths phys 5)
Sheffield – AAB-BBB (Struct Eng Archit) (IB 32–33 pts)
Warwick – ABB (Civ Eng (Sust)) (IB 34–36 pts)

320 pts **Brighton** – ABB (Civ Eng MEng) (IB 28 pts)
Brunel – ABB +AS/EPQ b 320–370 pts (Mech Eng Bld Serv MEng; Civ Eng Sust) (IB 34 pts)
Edinburgh – Check with Ad Tutor ABB 1st yr entry (Civ Eng BEng)
Exeter – AAB–BBB (Civ Env Eng) (IB 29–30 pts)
Liverpool – ABB–BCC (Civ Struct Eng) (IB 35 pts)
Newcastle – ABB/BBB (Off Eng BEng) (IB 32–34 pts HL maths phys 5)
Queen's Belfast – ABB (Struct Eng Archit MEng)

Strathclyde – ABB–BBB (Civ Eng MEng/BEng; Archit Eng MEng/BEng)
Surrey – ABB–BBB (Civ Eng MEng/BEng)
300 pts **Aberdeen** – BBB (Civ Env Eng) (IB 24 pts)
Anglia Ruskin – 300 pts (Civ Eng)
Birmingham – BBB (Civ Eng Fdn Yr) (IB 28 pts)
Bradford – 300 pts (Civ Struct Eng MEng) (IB 28–32 pts)
Brighton – BBB (Civ Env Eng BEng) (IB 32 pts)
Dundee – BBB–CCC (Civ Eng Mgt MEng/BEng)
Edinburgh Napier – BBB 300 pts (Civ Trans Eng MEng; Civ Eng)
Glasgow – BBB (Civ Eng BEng) (IB 28 pts)
Liverpool – BBB–ABB (Civ Eng MEng/BEng) (IB 35 pts)
280 pts **City** – 280–320 pts (Civ Eng Surv BEng/MEng) (IB 30–32 pts)
London (QM) – 280-340 pts (Sust Ener Eng)
Loughborough – 280 pts (Archit Eng Des Mgt) (IB 30 pts)
Teesside – 280 pts (Civ Eng Disas Mgt) (IB 30 pts)
270 pts **Glasgow Caledonian** – 270 pts (Fire Rsk Eng)
Liverpool John Moores – 270 pts (Civ Eng)
Ulster – 270–320 pts (Civ Eng (Tech Ops) BSc)
260 pts **Coventry** – 260–320 pts (Civ Struct Eng BEng/MEng; Civ Eng Mgt)
Glasgow Caledonian – BCC (Env Civ Eng)
Heriot-Watt – BCC–ABC (Civ Eng Struct Eng BEng) (IB 35 pts)
Salford – 260–300 pts (Civ Archit Eng) (IB 35 pts)
240 pts **Bolton** – 240 pts (Civ Eng)
Bradford – 240 pts (Civ Struct Eng BEng) (IB 26 pts)
Dundee – CCC 1st yr entry (Civ Eng; Civ Eng Mgt)
Edinburgh Napier – 240 pts (Civ Trans Eng; Civ Eng)
Glamorgan – 240–300 pts (Civ Eng BSc/BEng)
Greenwich – 240 pts (Civ Eng; Civ Eng Proj Mgt; Civ Eng Wtr Env Mgt)
Huddersfield – 240-300 pts (Civ Eng)
Newport – 240 pts (Civ Constr Eng)
Portsmouth – 240–300 pts (Civ Eng BEng/MEng)
225 pts **East London** – 225 pts (Civ Eng BEng) (IB 26 pts)
220 pts **Bristol UWE** – 220–260 pts (Civ Eng BSc) (IB 24–28 pts)
Edinburgh Napier – 220 pts (Civ Eng BSc; Civ Tmbr Eng)
Nottingham Trent – 220–260 pts (Civ Eng St BSc) (IB 24 pts)
Sunderland – 220 pts (Ener Eng)
200 pts **Abertay Dundee** – CDD 200 pts (Civ Eng) (IB 26 pts)
Anglia Ruskin – 200 pts (Civ Eng BSc) (IB 26 pts)
East London – 200 pts (Civ Eng Surv)
Glamorgan – 200–300 pts (Civ Eng Int St)
Staffordshire – 200–240 pts (Env Eng)
Suffolk (Univ Campus) – 200 pts (Civ Eng)
180 pts **Liverpool John Moores** – 180 pts (Civ Eng St)
Plymouth – 180–260 pts (Civ Eng BEng/BSc; Civ Cstl Eng BEng/BSc)
160 pts **Kingston** – 160–280 pts (Civ Eng)
Sheffield Hallam – 160 pts (Ener Eng)
Swansea Met – 160–360 pts (Civ Eng Env Mgt; Constr Mgt)
West Scotland – CC–CD (Civ Eng)
Wolverhampton – 160–220 pts (Civ Eng)
140 pts **London South Bank** – 140–240 pts (Civ Eng) (IB 24 pts)
Robert Gordon – CD (Constr Des Mgt (Civ Eng)) (IB 24 pts)
100 pts **Derby** – 100–200 pts (Blt Env)
Leeds Met – 100–200 pts (Civ Eng St; Civ Eng)
80 pts **Bolton** – 80 pts (Civ Eng inc Fdn Yr)
Salford – 80 pts (Civ Eng inc Fnd Yr)

Alternative offers See **Chapter 7** and **Appendix 1** for grades/UCAS Tariff points information for the International Baccalaureate, Scottish Highers/Advanced Highers, the Welsh Baccalaureate, the Irish Leaving Certificate, the Cambridge Pre-U Diploma, the Advanced Diploma and the Extended Project.

EXAMPLES OF FOUNDATION DEGREES IN THE SUBJECT FIELD
Bedfordshire; Blackburn (Coll Univ Centre); Bolton; Bristol UWE; Derby; Glamorgan; Kent; Kingston; Northampton; Nottingham Trent; Somerset (CAT); Suffolk (Univ Campus); Swansea Met.

CHOOSING YOUR COURSE (SEE ALSO CH. 1)
Some course features
Cardiff The first year is common to all nine Engineering programmes.
Durham A common course for Years 1 and 2 and then two years specialising in the chosen discipline.
Exeter A multidisciplinary first year before specialising in Year 2.
Liverpool John Moores Projects include highways, railways, airports, flood control and sports stadia.
Portsmouth Opportunities for language study and vacation training in France, Germany and Spain.
Southampton Options to take a year in industry or Europe.

Universities and colleges teaching quality See www.qaa.ac.uk; http://unistats.direct.gov.uk.

Top research universities and colleges (RAE 2008) Imperial London; Swansea; Cardiff; Nottingham; Newcastle; Southampton; Sheffield; Bristol; Dundee.

Examples of sandwich degree courses Bath; Bradford; Brighton; Cardiff; City; Coventry; East London; Glamorgan; Kingston; London South Bank; Loughborough; Nottingham Trent; Portsmouth; Queen's Belfast; Salford; Southampton; Surrey; Teesside; Ulster; West Scotland.

ADMISSIONS INFORMATION
Number of applicants per place (approx) Abertay Dundee 8; Bath 13; Birmingham 6; Bradford (BEng) 5; Bristol 10; Brunel 4; Cardiff 5; City 11; Coventry 10, (Civ Eng) 11; Dundee 5; Durham 8; Edinburgh Napier 4; Glamorgan 6; Glasgow Caledonian 4; Greenwich 11; Heriot-Watt 7; Imperial London 4; Kingston 8; Leeds 10; Liverpool John Moores 16; London (UCL) 5; London South Bank 5; Loughborough 6; Newcastle 11, (Off Eng) 9; Nottingham 6; Nottingham Trent 11; Plymouth 3; Portsmouth 3; Queen's Belfast 6; Salford 5; Sheffield 7; Southampton 8; Strathclyde 4; Surrey 5; Swansea 3; Teesside 6; West Scotland 4; Wolverhampton 3.

Advice to applicants and planning the UCAS personal statement See **Engineering/Engineering Sciences**. Also read the magazine *The New Civil Engineer* and discuss articles which interest you on your application. See also **Appendix 4**.

Selection interviews Yes Bath, Brighton, Bristol, Brunel, Cambridge, Coventry, Durham, Edinburgh Napier, Glamorgan, Greenwich, Heriot-Watt, Imperial London, Kingston, Leeds, London (UCL), London South Bank, Loughborough, Newcastle, Nottingham, Oxford, Queen's Belfast, Southampton, Surrey, Sussex, Warwick; **Some** Abertay Dundee, Anglia Ruskin, Cardiff, Dundee, Nottingham Trent, Salford.

Interview advice and questions Past questions have included: Why have you chosen Civil Engineering? Have you contacted the Institution of Civil Engineers/Institution of Structural Engineers? How would you define the difference between the work of a civil engineer and the work of an architect? What would happen to a concrete beam if a load were applied? Where would it break and how could it be strengthened? The favourite question: Why do you want to be a civil engineer? What would you do if you were asked to build a concrete boat? Do you know any civil engineers? What problems were faced in building the Channel Tunnel? See also **Chapter 6**. **Cambridge** Why did they make mill chimneys so tall?

Reasons for rejection (non-academic) Lack of vitality. Lack of interest in buildings, the built environment or in civil engineering. Poor communication skills. See also **Engineering/Engineering Sciences**.

AFTER-RESULTS ADVICE

Offers to applicants repeating A-levels Higher East London, Kingston, Liverpool John Moores, Nottingham, Queen's Belfast, Teesside, Warwick; **Possibly higher** Portsmouth, Southampton; **Same** Abertay Dundee, Bath, Birmingham, Bradford, Brighton, Bristol, Cardiff, City, Coventry, Dundee, Durham, Greenwich, Heriot-Watt, Leeds, London (UCL), London South Bank, Loughborough, Newcastle, Nottingham Trent, Salford, Sheffield, Wolverhampton.

GRADUATE DESTINATIONS AND EMPLOYMENT (2007/8 HESA)

Graduates surveyed 1715 **Employed** 875 **In further study** 240 **Assumed unemployed** 230

Career note The many aspects of this subject will provide career directions for graduates with many openings with local authorities and commercial organisations.

OTHER DEGREE SUBJECTS FOR CONSIDERATION

Architecture; Building; Surveying; Town and Country Planning.

ENGINEERING (COMMUNICATIONS)

(including **Mobile Communications**; see also **Communication Studies/Communication, Engineering (Electrical and Electronic)**)

Communications Engineering impacts on many aspects of the engineering and business world. Courses overlap considerably with Electronic, Computer, Digital, Media and Internet Engineering and provide graduates with expertise in such fields as telecommunications, mobile communications and microwave engineering, optoelectronics, radio engineering and internet technology. Sandwich courses and sponsorships are offered by several universities.

Useful websites See **Computer Courses** and **Engineering (Electrical and Electronic)**.

Engineering Council Statement: See **Engineering/Engineering Sciences**.

NB The points totals shown to the left of the institutions are for ease of reference only. It must not be assumed that Tariff points are always used by institutions or that they can be substituted for an offer in grades. The level of an offer is not necessarily indicative of the quality of a course.

COURSE OFFERS INFORMATION

Subject requirements/preferences See **Engineering/Engineering Sciences**.

NB In 2012 universities and colleges will differ in their use of GCE AL/AS unit grade information, A* grades, the Extended Project (EPQ), the Advanced Diploma and the Cambridge Pre-U examination when considering applicants and making offers. An EPQ may be accepted in place of an AS subject. Check websites of universities and colleges for the latest offers information.

Your target offers and examples of courses provided by each institution

380 pts **London (UCL)** – AAA+AS–ABB+AS (Electron Eng Comm Eng) (IB 34–38 pts)

360 pts **Edinburgh** – Check with Ad Tutor AAA–AAB (Electron Elec Eng (Comms))
Southampton – AAA (Electron Eng Wrlss Comms) (IB 36 pts)
Surrey – AAA (Electron Sat Eng MEng) (IB 34–32 pts)
Swansea – AAA–AAB (Telecomm Eng MEng)

340 pts **Bath** – AAB (Electron Comm Eng MEng) (IB 36 pts HL maths phys 6)
Birmingham – AAB–ABB (Electron Comm Eng) (IB 32–36 pts)
Bristol – AAB (Electron Comm Eng courses) (IB 35 pts)
City – AAB 340 pts (Telecomm) (IB 30 pts)
Durham – AAB (Comm Eng MEng) (IB 36 pts)
Leeds – AAB (Electron Comm Eng) (IB 36pts HL 17 pts)
London (QM) – 340 pts (Comm Eng MEng) (IB 34 pts)
Newcastle – AAB (Electron Comm MEng) (IB 36 pts HL maths phys 5)

Nottingham – AAB–BBB (Electron Comm Eng) (IB 30 pts)
Sheffield – AAB–ABB (Electron Comms Eng) (IB 33–35 pts)
Surrey – AAB (Electron Sat Eng)
Warwick – AAB–ABB (Electron Eng (Comm) MEng) (IB 36 pts)
York – AAB–ABB (Electron Comm Eng MEng)

320 pts **Brunel** – ABB 320 pts (Comm Net Eng MEng) (IB 33 pts HL maths 6)
Kent – 320 pts (Electron Comm Eng MEng)
Lancaster – ABB–BBB (Elec Comm Sys MEng/BEng) (IB 30 pts)
Liverpool – ABB–BBB (Electron Comm Eng MEng/BEng) (IB 34 pts)
London (QM) – 320–360 pts (Telecomm Eng) (IB 34 pts)
Newcastle – ABB (Electron Comm BEng) (IB 32 pts HL maths phys 5)
Swansea – ABB–BBB 320 pts (Telecomm Eng BEng)

300 pts **Aberdeen** – BBB (Electon Eng Comm)
Bath – BBB (Electron Comm BEng) (IB 34 pts)
Bradford – BBB 300 pts (Electron Telecomm Intnet Eng MEng) (IB 28–32 pts)
Brighton – BBB/ABC (Dig Electron Comp Comm MEng)
Essex – 300 pts (Telecomm Eng) (IB 29 pts)
Lancaster – BBB 300 pts (Comm Sys Elec) (IB 30 pts)
Leicester – AAB–ABB/BBB–BBC 340–300 pts (Comm Electron Eng MEng/BEng)
(IB 32 pts)
Portsmouth – 300–360 pts (Comm Sys MEng)
Warwick – BBB (Electron Eng (Comm) BEng) (IB 34 pts)
York – BBB–BBC (Electron Comm BEng) (IB 32 pts)

280 pts **Aston** – BBB 280–320 pts (Comm Eng) (IB 29 pts)
Birmingham City – 280 pts (Telecomm Net)
Brighton – BBC (Dig Electron Comp Comm BEng)
Brunel – BBC 280–320 pts (Comm Net Eng BEng) (IB 30 pts)
City – 280 pts (Multim) (IB 28 pts)
Glamorgan – 280–320 pts (Electron Comm Eng; Mbl Telecomm)
London (QM) – 280 pts (Comm Eng BEng) (IB 28 pts)

260 pts **Hertfordshire** – 260-320 pts (Dig Comm Electron BEng)
London (QM) – 260–300 pts (Telecomm Eng BEng)

245 pts **Edinburgh Napier** – 245 pts (Electron Comm Eng)

240 pts **Bradford** – 240 pts (Electron Telecomm Intnet Eng BEng) (IB 26 pts)
Central Lancashire – 240 pts (Dig Sgnl Imag Proc) (IB 26 pts)
De Montfort – 240 pts (Electron Eng Comm)
Greenwich – 240 pts (Comm Sys)
Huddersfield – 240 pts (Electron Comm Eng)
London Met – 240 pts (Electron Comm Eng)
Newport – 240 pts (Electron Comm Eng)
Nottingham Trent – 240 pts (ICT)
Plymouth – 240 pts (Electron Comm Eng)
Portsmouth – 240–300 pts (Comm Sys BEng)

220 pts **Coventry** – 220 pts (Comp Net Comm Tech; Comm Eng)
East London – 220 pts (Elec Electron Eng (Comm))
London South Bank – 220–240 pts (Telecomm Comp Net Eng)

200 pts **Glyndŵr** – 200 pts (Rad Prod Comm)
London Met – 200 pts (Comm Sys) (IB 28 pts)

160 pts **Blackburn (Coll Univ Centre)** – 160 pts (Dig Comm)
Kingston – 160–280 pts (Comm Sys)
Wolverhampton – 160–220 pts (Electron Comm Eng)

Alternative offers See **Chapter 7** and **Appendix 1** for grades/UCAS Tariff points information for the International Baccalaureate, Scottish Highers/Advanced Highers, the Welsh Baccalaureate, the Irish Leaving Certificate, the Cambridge Pre-U Diploma, the Advanced Diploma and the Extended Project.

EXAMPLES OF FOUNDATION DEGREES IN THE SUBJECT FIELD
Plymouth.

CHOOSING YOUR COURSE (SEE ALSO CH. 1)
Some course features
Durham A common course for Years 1 and 2 and then two years specialising in the chosen discipline.
Leicester Communications and Electronic Engineering combined. Options to study for a year in industry or in Europe.
London (QM) There are 16 degree programmes offered in the Department of Electronic Engineering, and there is some flexibility and overlap.
Portsmouth A Foundation Year can lead to a number of Engineering and Technological degree courses.

Universities and colleges teaching quality See www.qaa.ac.uk; http://unistats.direct.gov.uk.

Examples of sandwich degree courses Aston; Bath; Bradford; Brunel; Central Lancashire; Glamorgan; Kingston; Manchester Met; Northumbria; Plymouth; Portsmouth; Surrey; Westminster; York.

ADMISSIONS INFORMATION
Number of applicants per place (approx) Birmingham 10; Bradford 9; Bristol 2; Coventry 7; Hull 8; London Met 5; London South Bank 3; Northumbria 7; Plymouth 4; York (average) 8.

Advice to applicants and planning the UCAS personal statement See **Engineering (Electrical and Electronic)**. See also **Appendix 4**.

Selection interviews Yes Bradford, Bristol, Hertfordshire, Kent, London Met, London South Bank, Sunderland.

Interview advice and questions See **Engineering (Electrical and Electronic)**.

Reasons for rejection (non-academic) See **Engineering (Electrical and Electronic)**.

AFTER-RESULTS ADVICE
Offers to applicants repeating A-levels Same Loughborough.

GRADUATE DESTINATIONS AND EMPLOYMENT (2007/8 HESA)
See **Engineering (Electrical and Electronic)** and **Engineering/Engineering Sciences**.

Career note Many commercial organisations offer opportunities in the specialist areas described at the top of this table. Work placements and sandwich courses have, in the past, resulted in over 60% of graduates gaining employment with their firms.

OTHER DEGREE SUBJECTS FOR CONSIDERATION
Computer Science; Engineering (Computer, Control, Electrical, Electronic, Systems); Physics.

ENGINEERING (COMPUTER, CONTROL, SOFTWARE and SYSTEMS)

The design and application of modern computer systems is fundamental to a wide range of disciplines which also include electronic, software and computer-aided engineering. Most courses give priority to reinforcing the essential transferable skills' consisting of management techniques, leadership skills, literacy, presentation skills, business skills and time management. At many universities Computer Engineering is offered as part of a range of Electronics degree programmes when the first and even the second year courses are common to all students, who choose to specialise later. A year in industry is a common feature of many of these courses.

Useful websites See **Computer Courses and Engineering/Engineering Sciences**.

Engineering Council statement See **Engineering/Engineering Sciences**.

NB The points totals shown to the left of the institutions are for ease of reference only. It must not be assumed that Tariff points are always used by institutions or that they can be substituted for an offer in grades. The level of an offer is not necessarily indicative of the quality of a course.

COURSE OFFERS INFORMATION

Subject requirements/preferences See **Engineering/Engineering Sciences**.

NB In 2012 universities and colleges will differ in their use of GCE AL/AS unit grade information, A* grades, the Extended Project (EPQ), the Advanced Diploma and the Cambridge Pre-U examination when considering applicants and making offers. An EPQ may be accepted in place of an AS subject. Check websites of universities and colleges for the latest offers information.

Your target offers and examples of courses provided by each institution

380 pts   Cambridge – Yrs 3 and 4 specialisation via Engineering Tripos A*AA college offers may vary (Eng (Inf Comp Eng)) (IB 38–42 pts)
Edinburgh – Check with Ad Tutor A*AA 2nd yr entry (Electron Comp Sci) (IB 38 pts)
Imperial London – A*mathsAA (Inf Sys Eng Yr Abrd) (IB 38 pts)
Manchester – A*AA (Comp Sys Eng courses) (IB 35–33 pts)

360 pts   Edinburgh – Check with Ad Tutor AAA 2nd yr entry (Electron Soft Eng MEng) (IB 36 pts)
Oxford – AAA (Inf Eng) (IB 38–42 pts)
Southampton – AAA (Comp Sci Artif Intel) (IB 34 pts)
Warwick – AAA (Comp Sys) (IB 36 pts)

340 pts   Aberystwyth – 340 pts (Soft Eng MEng) (IB 28 pts)
Bath – AAB (Comp Sys Eng MEng) (IB 36 pts HL maths phys 6)
Birmingham – AAB–ABB (Comm Sys Eng) (IB 32–36 pts)
Bristol – AAB (Comp Sci Electron MEng) (IB 35 pts)
Glasgow – AAB (Faster Route Microcomp Sys Eng MEng)
Leeds – AAB (Electron Comm Eng) (IB 36pts HL 17 pts)
London (QM) – 340 pts (Comp Eng MEng) (IB 34 pts)
Loughborough – AAB 340 pts (Sys Eng MEng) (IB 35 pts)
Newcastle – AAB (Electron Comp Eng MEng) (IB 36 pts HL maths phys 5)
Strathclyde – AAB (Comp Electron Sys MEng)
Warwick – AAB (Comp Inf Eng MEng) (IB 35–37 pts)
York – AAB–ABB (Comp Sys Soft Eng; Comp Sci Embd Sys; Electron Comp Eng MEng)

320 pts   Brunel – ABB + AS 320-370 pts (Electron Comp Eng MEng) (IB 33 pts)
Cardiff – AAB–ABB (Comp Sys Eng MEng) (IB 30 pts)
Durham – ABB (Soft Eng Euro St)
Edinburgh – Check with Ad Tutor ABB 1st yr entry (Electron Soft Eng MEng) (IB 32 pts)
Glasgow – ABB (Microcomp Sys Eng MEng)
Lancaster – ABB 320 pts (Comp Sys Eng MEng) (IB 30 pts HL 16 pts)
Leicester – ABB (Soft Electron Eng MEng)
Liverpool – ABB (Soft Dev BSc) (IB 34 pts)
Newcastle – ABB (Electron Comp Eng BEng) (IB 32 pts HL maths phys 5)
Reading – 320 pts (Comp Sci Cyber MEng; Cyber)
Sheffield – ABB 320 pts (Soft Eng) (IB 33 pts)
Strathclyde – ABB (Soft Eng BEng) (IB 32 pts)
Surrey – 320–340 pts (Dig Media Eng MEng)

300 pts   Aberdeen – BBB (Electron Comp Eng MEng) (IB 30 pts)
Bangor – 300–320 pts (Comp Sys Eng)
Bath – BBB (Comp Sys Eng BEng) (IB 34 pts HL maths phys 6)
Bournemouth – 300 pts (Soft Eng; Soft Prod Des; Soft Eng Mgt)

Bradford – BBB 300 pts (Electron Telecomm Intnet Eng MEng) (IB 28–32 pts)
Brighton – BBB/ABC (Dig Electron Comp Comm MEng)
East Anglia – BBB 300 pts (Soft Eng) (IB 31 pts)
Essex – 300 pts (Soft Eng) (IB 32 pts)
Glamorgan – 300–320 pts (Comp Sys Eng MEng)
Glasgow – BBB (Microcomp Sys Eng BEng; Electron Soft Eng)
Heriot-Watt – ABC 2nd yr entry (Comp Electron)
Kingston – 300 pts (MComp Soft Eng)
Liverpool – BBB (Comp Sci Electron Eng BEng) (IB 32 pts)
London (QM) – 300–340 pts (Dig Aud Mus Sys Eng) (IB 34 pts)
Loughborough – BBB 300 pts (Electron Comp Sys Eng (BEng)) (IB 35 pts)
Newcastle – BBB/ABC (Comp Sci (Soft Eng) BEng) (IB 32 pts HL maths phys 5)
Portsmouth – 300–360 pts (Comp Eng MEng) (IB 30 pts)
Reading – 300–340 pts (Soft Eng) (IB 30 pts)
Strathclyde – BBB (Comp Electron Sys BEng)
Warwick – BBB (Comp Inf Eng BEng) (IB 34 pts)
Westminster – BBB (Comp Sys Eng MEng) (IB 32 pts))
York – BBB–BBC (Dig Media Sys; Electron Comp Eng BEng)
280 pts **Aberystwyth** – 280 pts (Spc Sci Robot) (IB 27 pts)
Aston – 280–320 pts (Multim Comp) (IB 29 pts)
Brighton – BBC (Dig Electron Comp Comm BEng)
Cardiff – BBC 280 pts (Comp Sys Eng BEng) (IB 30 pts)
Central Lancashire – 280 pts (Comp Aid Eng MEng)
City – BCC 280 pts (Comp Sys Eng BEng) (IB 28 pts)
Glamorgan – 280–320 pts (Comp Sys Eng BEng)
Kent – 280–300 pts (Comp Sys Eng)
Lancaster – BBC (Comp Sys Eng BEng) (IB 28 pts HL 14 pts)
Leicester – BBC (Soft Electron Eng)
Liverpool John Moores – 280–240 pts (Comp Eng)
London (QM) – 280 pts (Comp Eng BEng) (IB 28 pts)
Loughborough – BBC 280–300 pts (Comp Sys Eng) (IB 32 pts)
Northumbria – 280 pts (Comp Net Tech)
Oxford Brookes – BBC (Soft Eng) (IB 29 pts)
Plymouth – 280 pts (Comp Sys Net)
Westminster – BBC (Comp Sys Eng BEng) (IB 30 pts)
260 pts **Brunel** – BCC (Comp Sys Eng BEng) (IB 29 pts)
Heriot-Watt – BCC 1st yr entry (Comp Electron)
Liverpool John Moores – 260 pts (Soft Eng)
London (QM) – 260–280 pts (Intnet Eng) (IB 30 pts)
Oxford Brookes – BBC (Comp Aid Mech Eng) (IB 30 pts)
Portsmouth – 260 pts (Comp Eng BSc)
Reading – 260 pts (Sys Eng) (IB 30 pts)
240 pts **Bangor** – 240–260 pts (Comp Sys Eng BEng)
Bolton – 240 pts (Electron Comp Eng; Comp Aid Eng)
Bradford – 240 pts (Electron Telecomm Intnet Eng BEng) (IB 26 pts)
Bristol UWE – CCC (Soft Eng) (IB 24–28 pts)
Central Lancashire – 240 pts (Comp Aid Eng BEng)
Coventry – 240 pts (Soft Eng)
Edinburgh Napier – 240 pts (Electron Comp Eng)
Greenwich – 240 pts (Comp Sys Soft Eng; Soft Eng MEng)
Huddersfield – 240 pts (Comp Sys Eng) (IB 26 pts)
Newport – 240 pts (Robot Intel Sys Eng)
Nottingham Trent – 240 pts (Comp Sys Eng)
Plymouth – 240 pts (Comp Sys Eng)

Portsmouth – 240–280 pts (Comp Eng BEng) (IB 28 pts)
Sheffield Hallam – 240 pts (Soft Eng)
230 pts **Edinburgh Napier** – 230 pts (Embd Comp Sys)
220 pts **Hull** – 220–260 pts (Comp Sys Eng)
Robert Gordon – 220–240 pts (Comp Net Mgt Des)
Teesside – 220–280 pts (Soft Dev)
200 pts **Aberystwyth** – 200 pts (Intnet Comp)
Bradford – 200–240 pts (Soft Eng BEng)
Coventry – 200 pts (Comp Hard Soft Eng; Sys Eng; Vrtl Eng)
East London – 200 pts (Soft Eng)
Heriot-Watt – CDD 1st yr entry (Comp Electron BEng)
Hertfordshire – 200 pts (Comp Sci (Soft Eng) BSc)
Northampton – 200–240 pts (Comp (Comp Sys Eng))
Sheffield Hallam – 200 pts (Comp Net Eng)
180 pts **Greenwich** – 180 pts (Comp Sys Soft Eng BSc)
170 pts **Glasgow Caledonian** – CD/DDE 170 pts (Comp Eng; Comp Aid Mech Eng)
London South Bank – 170 pts (Comp Sys Net)
160 pts **Bedfordshire** – 160 pts (Comp Sci Soft Eng)
Greenwich – 160 pts (Embd Comp Sys)
Kent – 160 pts (Comp Sys Eng inc Fdn Yr)
Sheffield Hallam – 160 pts (Comp Aid Eng Des)
South Essex (Coll) – 160 pts (Net Tech)
Southampton Solent – 160 pts (Comp Sys Net)
West Scotland – CC–CD (Comp Net)
Wolverhampton – 160–220 pts (Comp Sci (Soft Eng))
120 pts **London South Bank** – 120 pts (Comp Aid Eng)
Swansea Met – 120–340 pts (Comp Sys Electron)

Alternative offers See **Chapter 7** and **Appendix 1** for grades/UCAS Tariff points information for the International Baccalaureate, Scottish Highers/Advanced Highers, the Welsh Baccalaureate, the Irish Leaving Certificate, the Cambridge Pre-U Diploma, the Advanced Diploma and the Extended Project.

EXAMPLES OF FOUNDATION DEGREES IN THE SUBJECT FIELD
Bedfordshire; Bournemouth; Manchester (Coll); Swansea Met.

CHOOSING YOUR COURSE (SEE ALSO CH. 1)
Some course features
Bristol UWE (Comp Sys Integ) A practical course covering all aspects of computer systems, but also focuses on networks, CPU architecture and embedded systems development.
Cardiff The first year is common to all nine Engineering programmes.
Durham (MEng courses) A common course for Years 1 and 2 and then two years specialising in one of four streams, with a major design project (from design to manufacture) in Year 3.
Heriot-Watt The Software Engineering course involves a study of computer science in the first three years followed in Year 4 and 5 by specialist studies in software technology.
London (QM) The MEng programme covers all the material of the BEng programme with more time spent on professional development and advanced studies.
Plymouth Four final year pathways from which to choose your specialisation.

Universities and colleges teaching quality See www.qaa.ac.uk; http://unistats.direct.gov.uk.

Top research universities and colleges (RAE 2008) See **Computer Courses**.

Examples of sandwich degree courses Bath; Brighton; Bristol UWE; Brunel; Cardiff; City; Coventry; Greenwich; Hertfordshire; Kingston; Liverpool John Moores; London South Bank; Loughborough; Manchester; Manchester Met; Portsmouth; Queen's Belfast; Sheffield Hallam; Staffordshire; Surrey; Teesside; York.

ADMISSIONS INFORMATION

Number of applicants per place (approx) Birmingham 10; Birmingham City 6; Bournemouth 3; Bradford 6; Bristol 4; Bristol UWE 12; Cardiff 6; Central Lancashire 12; Coventry 2; Durham 6; East Anglia 4; Edinburgh 3; Huddersfield 2; Imperial London 5; Kent 5; Lancaster 12; Liverpool John Moores 2; London South Bank 3; Loughborough 17; Sheffield 10; Sheffield Hallam 8; Southampton 4; Staffordshire 5; Stirling 7; Strathclyde 7; Surrey (MEng, BEng) 3; Swansea Met 4; Teesside 3; Westminster 5; York 3 ave.

Advice to applicants and planning the UCAS personal statement See **Computer Courses** and **Engineering (Electrical and Electronic)**. See also **Appendix 4**.

Selection interviews Yes Bath, Bradford, Cardiff, Durham, East Anglia, Glamorgan, Hertfordshire, Huddersfield, Kent, Liverpool John Moores, London South Bank, Nottingham Trent, Sheffield Hallam, Swansea Met, Westminster, York; **Some** Exeter, Loughborough, Manchester;

Interview advice and questions See **Computer Courses** and **Engineering (Electrical and Electronic)** and **Chapter 6**.

Reasons for rejection (non-academic) Lack of understanding that the course involves engineering. See also **Computer Courses** and **Engineering (Electrical and Electronic)**.

AFTER-RESULTS ADVICE

Offers to applicants repeating A-levels Higher Bristol, Strathclyde, Warwick, York; **Possibly higher** City, Huddersfield, Sheffield; **Same** Bath, Birmingham, Coventry, East Anglia, Exeter, Lancaster, Liverpool John Moores, London South Bank, Loughborough, Salford, Teesside, Ulster.

GRADUATE DESTINATIONS AND EMPLOYMENT (2007/8 HESA)

Software Engineering graduates surveyed 590 **Employed** 280 **In further study** 70 **Assumed unemployed** 125

Career note Career opportunities extend right across the whole field of electronics, telecommunications, control and systems engineering.

OTHER DEGREE SUBJECTS FOR CONSIDERATION

Computer Science; Computing; Engineering (Aeronautical, Aerospace, Communications, Electrical and Electronic); Mathematics; Media (Systems/Engineering/Technology); Physics.

ENGINEERING (ELECTRICAL and ELECTRONIC)

(see also **Engineering (Acoustics and Sound)**, **Engineering (Aeronautical and Aerospace)**, **Engineering (Communications)**, **Technologies**)

Electrical and Electronic Engineering courses provide a sound foundation for those looking for a career in electricity generation and transmission, communications or control systems, including robotics. All courses cater for students wanting a general or specialist Engineering education and options should be considered when choosing degree courses. These could include optoelectronics and optical communication systems, microwave systems, radio frequency engineering and circuit technology. Many courses have common first years, allowing transfer in Year 2. Most universities and colleges have good industrial contacts and can arrange industrial placements, in some cases abroad.

Useful websites www.theiet.org; www.engc.org.uk; www.enginuity.org.uk.

Engineering Council statement See **Engineering/Engineering Sciences**.

NB The points totals shown to the left of the institutions are for ease of reference only. It must not be assumed that Tariff points are always used by institutions or that they can be substituted for an offer in grades. The level of an offer is not necessarily indicative of the quality of a course.

COURSE OFFERS INFORMATION

Subject requirements/preferences See **Engineering/Engineering Sciences**.

NB In 2012 universities and colleges will differ in their use of GCE AL/AS unit grade information, A* grades, the Extended Project (EPQ), the Advanced Diploma and the Cambridge Pre-U examination when considering applicants and making offers. An EPQ may be accepted in place of an AS subject. Check websites of universities and colleges for the latest offers information.

Your target offers and examples of courses provided by each institution

380 pts **Cambridge** – A*AA college offers may vary (Eng (Elec Inf Sci) (Elec Electron Eng)) (IB 38–42 pts)

Imperial London – A*mathsAA (Elec Electron Eng Yr Abrd) (IB 38 pts)

London (UCL) – AAA+AS–ABB+AS (Electron Eng Comm Eng) (IB 34–38 pts)

370 pts **Brunel** – ABB +AS 370 pts (Electron Elec Eng) (IB 33 pts)

360 pts **City** – AAA 360 pts (Ener Eng) (IB 32 pts HL maths 6)

Durham – AAA (Electron Eng MEng) (IB 38 pts)

Edinburgh – Check with Ad Tutor AAA 2nd yr entry (Elec Eng Renew Ener) (IB 36 pts)

Leeds – AAA (Electron Nano MEng/BEng)

Oxford – AAA (Elec Eng) (IB 38–42 pts)

Southampton – AAA (Electron Eng Mbl Scr Sys) (IB 36 pts HL 18 pts)

Strathclyde – AAA (Elec Ener Sys MEng) (IB 36 pts)

Surrey – AAA (Electron Comp Eng MEng; Electron Sat Eng MEng)

340 pts **Bath** – AAB (Elec Pwr Eng MEng) (IB 36 pts HL maths phys 6)

Birmingham – AAB–ABB (Electron Comm Eng) (IB 32–36 pts)

Bristol – AAB (Comp Sci Electron) (IB 35 pts)

Cardiff – AAB–BBB 340 pts (Electron Comm Eng) (IB 30–32 pts)

City – AAB 340 pts (Elec Electron Eng BEng) (IB 30 pts)

Durham – AAB (Electron Eng BEng)

Edinburgh – Check with Ad Tutor AAB–ABB 1st yr entry (Elec Eng Renew Ener) (IB 32 pts)

Exeter – AAB–ABB (Electron Eng Comp Sci) (IB 30–29 pts)

Glasgow – AAB (Faster Route Electron Elec Eng MEng)

Leeds – AAB (Electron Comm Eng) (IB 36pts HL 17 pts)

London (QM) – 340 pts (Electron Eng courses MEng) (IB 34 pts)

Loughborough – AAB (Electron Elec Eng MEng) (IB 35 pts)

Manchester – AAB (Mecha Eng) (IB 35–33 pts)

Newcastle – AAB (Electron Comm MEng) (IB 36 pts HL maths phys 5)

Nottingham – AAB–BBB (Electron Eng courses) (IB 30–32 pts)

Sheffield – AAB–ABB (Electron Eng courses) (IB 32–35 pts)

Strathclyde – AAB (Electron Elec Eng Bus St MEng) (IB 36 pts)

Surrey – AAB (Electron Sat Eng)

Swansea – AAB–ABB (Nanoelectron MEng)

Warwick – AAB–ABB (Electron Eng MEng) (IB 35–37 pts)

York – AAB–ABB (Electron Eng MEng; Electron Eng Nano MEng; Electron Comm Eng MEng; Electron Comp Eng MEng)

320 pts **Bristol UWE** – 320 pts (Elec Electron Eng MEng) (IB 28–30 pts)

Brunel – ABB + AS 320–370 pts (Electron Comp Eng MEng) (IB 33 pts)

Cardiff – ABB 320 pts (Elec Electron Eng MEng) (IB 30 pts)

Dundee – ABB 2nd yr entry (Electron Eng Mgt MEng; Electron Elec Eng MEng)

Exeter – ABB–BBB (Elec Electron Eng BEng) (IB 26–30 pts)

Glasgow – ABB (Electron Elec Eng MEng)

Hertfordshire – 320 pts (Dig Comms Electron MEng)

Lancaster – ABB (Mecha Eng MEng) (IB 30 pts)

Leicester – ABB (Elec Electron Eng courses MEng) (IB 32 pts)

Liverpool – ABB (Med Electron Instr MEng) (IB 34 pts)

Newcastle – ABB–BBB (Electron Eng) (IB 34 pts HL maths phys 5)

Queen's Belfast – ABB (Elec Electron Eng MEng) (IB 31–32 pts)
Strathclyde – ABB (Elec Ener Sys BEng) (IB 32 pts)
Surrey – ABB 320 pts (Electron Eng BEng)
Sussex – ABB–BBC (Elec Electron Eng MEng; Electron Eng)

300 pts **Aberdeen** – BBB 300 pts (Electron Photon) (IB 30 pts)
Aston – BBB (Electron Eng Comp Sci; Elec Electron Eng; Electromech Eng)
Bath – BBB (Electron Comm Eng BEng) (IB 34 pts)
Brighton – BBB/ABC (Dig Electron Comp Comm MEng)
Brunel – BCC +AS/EPQ c 300 pts (Electron Microelec Eng) (IB 28 pts)
Dundee – BBB 1st yr entry (Phys Microelectron) (IB 32 pts)
Essex – 300 pts (Electron Eng) (IB 29 pts)
Glasgow – BBB (Elec Electron Eng BEng)
Heriot-Watt – ABC 2nd yr entry (Elec Electron Eng MEng) (IB 28 pts)
Kent – 300 pts (Electron Comm Eng BEng) (IB 33 pts)
Lancaster – BBB (Mecha Eng BEng) (IB 29 pts)
Liverpool – BBB (Elec Eng Electron courses) (IB 28 pts)
Loughborough – BBB–AAB (Electron courses) (IB 35 pts)
Newcastle – BBB (Elec Electron Eng BEng) (IB 32 pts HL maths phys 5)
Plymouth – 300 pts (Elec Electron Eng MEng) (IB 26 pts)
Portsmouth – 300 pts (Electron Elec Eng MEng)
Reading – 300 pts (Electron Eng Cyber) (IB 29–32 pts)
Sheffield – BBB–BCC (Elec Eng) (IB 32 pts)
Sheffield Hallam – 300 pts (Elec Electron Eng MEng)
Southampton – BBB (Eng Fdn Yr (Elec/Electron/Electromech)) (IB 30 pts HL 16 pts)
Swansea – 300 pts (Electron Elec Eng MEng)
Warwick – BBB (Electron Eng BEng) (IB 34 pts)
Westminster – BBB (Electron Eng MEng) (IB 32 pts)
York – BBB–BBC (Electron Eng Nano BEng) (IB 32 pts)

280 pts **Brighton** – BBC (Dig Electron Comp Comm BEng)
Bristol UWE – 280–300pts (MEng Electron Eng) (IB 28–30 pts)
Cardiff – BBC 280 pts (Elec Electron Eng) (IB 28 pts)
Dundee – BBB 2nd yr entry (Electron Eng Mgt BEng)
Glamorgan – 280–320 pts (Elec Electron Eng; Electron Eng; Ltg Des Tech)
Hull – 280–320 pts (Electron Eng MEng)
Leicester – BBC (Elec Electron Eng courses BEng) (IB 30 pts)
Liverpool John Moores – 280 pts (Elec Electron Eng MEng)
London (QM) – 280 pts (Elec Electron Eng courses BSc)
Queen's Belfast – BBC–BCC (Elec Electron Eng BEng) (IB 29–30 pts)
Teesside – 280 pts (Elec Electron Eng) (IB 30 pts)
Westminster – BBC (BEng Electron Eng)

260 pts **Heriot-Watt** – BCC 260 pts 1st yr entry (Elec Electron Eng courses)
Hertfordshire – 260 pts (Elec Electron Eng BEng)
Manchester Met – 260 pts (Electron Sys Des) (IB 24 pts)
Northumbria – 260–280 pts (Elec Electron Eng)
Plymouth – 260–300 pts (Elec Electron Eng BEng)
Reading – 260 pts (Electron Eng Cyber BEng; Electron Eng)
Robert Gordon – BCC (Electron Elec Eng MEng)
Strathclyde – BCC 1st yr entry (Electron Elec Eng courses) (IB 30 pts)
Swansea – BCC 260 pts (Electron Elec Eng BEng; Med Eng; Elec Eng)
Ulster – 260 pts (Electron Comp Sys; Electron Eng BEng)

245 pts **Edinburgh Napier** – 245 pts (Elec Eng; Electron Elec Eng; Electron Comm Eng)
240 pts **Bangor** – 240–260 pts (Electron Eng MEng/BEng)
Bolton – 240 pts (Electron Comp Eng)
Bradford – 240 pts (Elec Electron Eng; Med Eng)
Brighton – CCC/BCD (Elec Electron Eng) (IB 28 pts)

Central Lancashire – 240 pts (Electron Eng)
De Montfort – 240 pts (Electron Eng; Electron Eng (Telecomm) (Broad Sys))
Dundee – 240 pts (Electron Eng Phys BEng) (IB 28 pts)
Greenwich – 240 pts (Electron Eng BEng; Elec Eng)
Huddersfield – 240–280 pts (Electron Eng MEng)
Liverpool John Moores – 240 pts (Elec Electron Eng BEng)
London Met – 240 pts (Electron Comm Eng)
Newport – 240 pts (Elec Eng; Electron Comm Eng)
Plymouth – 240 pts (Electron Comm Eng; Elec Electron Eng BSc)
Sheffield Hallam – 240 pts (Elec Electron Eng BEng)
Staffordshire – 240 pts (Elec Eng BEng; Electron Eng)
Sunderland – 240 pts (Electron Elec Eng)

230 pts **Glasgow Caledonian** – BC 230 pts (Elec Pwr Eng; Electron Eng)
220 pts **East London** – 220 pts (Elec Electron Eng BEng; Elec Electron Eng (Contr) (Pwr) (Comms))
Hull – 220–260 pts (Electron Eng BEng)
Robert Gordon – CCD (Electron Elec Eng BEng) (IB 26 pts)
200 pts **Bangor** – 200 pts (Electron (Hard Sys) BSc)
Coventry – 200 pts (Electron Eng; Elec Sys Eng)
Derby – 200–240 pts (Elec Electron Eng)
Glyndŵr – 200 pts (Elec Electron Eng; Aero Electron Eng; Perf Car Electron Tech)
Heriot-Watt – CDD 1st yr entry (Elec Electron Eng courses BEng)
London Met – 200 pts (Electron)
170 pts **London South Bank** – 170 pts (Elec Electron Eng)
160 pts **Sussex** – CC (Elec Electron Eng + Fdn Yr)
140 pts **Glasgow Caledonian** – CD (Electron Eng BSc)
Robert Gordon – CD (Elec Electron Eng BSc)
120 pts **Glamorgan** – 120–160 pts (Elec Electron Eng BSc)
Sheffield Hallam – 120 pts (Electron Elec Eng BSc)
Southampton Solent – 120 pts (Electron Eng BSc)
Swansea Met – 120–340 pts (Comp Sys Electron)

Alternative offers See **Chapter 7** and **Appendix 1** for grades/UCAS Tariff points information for the International Baccalaureate, Scottish Highers/Advanced Highers, the Welsh Baccalaureate, the Irish Leaving Certificate, the Cambridge Pre-U Diploma, the Advanced Diploma and the Extended Project.

EXAMPLES OF FOUNDATION DEGREES IN THE SUBJECT FIELD

Arts London; Bedfordshire; Bolton; Bournemouth; Bournemouth and Poole (Coll); Brighton; De Montfort; Exeter (Coll); Farnborough (CT); Glamorgan; Greenwich; Havering (Coll); Hertfordshire; Leeds Met; London South Bank; Manchester (Coll); Newcastle (Coll); Northbrook (Coll); Plymouth; Ravensbourne; St Helens (Coll); South Cheshire (Coll); Southampton Solent; Swansea Met; Walsall (Coll); West London; York (Coll).

CHOOSING YOUR COURSE (SEE ALSO CH. 1)

Some course features
Bath After a common two-year introduction covering electronics, communications, electrical engineering, mathematics and design, students specialise in Years 3 and 4, choosing from a range of optional and core modules. Individual and group project and design work and placement opportunities are key features of these modular courses.
Exeter A multidisciplinary first year before specialising in Year 2.
Leicester Options to study for a year in industry, in Europe or the USA.
London (QM) The MEng and BEng courses include modules on telecoms, programming, digital systems, multimedia systems, wireless networks and video and image processing.
London (UCL) (Electron Eng Nanotech) Course has solid foundation of traditional electronics and specialisation in Years 3 and 4 in fast-developing field of nanotechnology (a research specialisation at UCL).

Loughborough There is a common first year for all students in the Department, followed by a choice of five degrees.

Manchester (Electron Sys Eng) Course focuses on embedded computer systems, for example in engine management systems, MP3 players and mobile phones, with emphasis on system design.

Universities and colleges teaching quality See www.qaa.ac.uk; http://unistats.direct.gov.uk.

Top research universities and colleges (RAE 2008) (Electrical and Electronic Engineering) Leeds; Surrey; Bangor; Manchester; Imperial London; Sheffield (Automatic Control and Systems Engineering); Southampton; London (UCL); Glasgow; Bath.

Examples of sandwich degree courses Aston; Bath; Birmingham City; Bournemouth; Bradford; Brighton; Bristol UWE; Brunel; Cardiff; Central Lancashire; City; Coventry; De Montfort; East London; Glamorgan; Glasgow Caledonian; Hertfordshire; Huddersfield; Leicester; Liverpool John Moores; London Met; London South Bank; Loughborough; Manchester Met; Northumbria; Plymouth; Portsmouth; Queen's Belfast; Reading; Sheffield Hallam; Staffordshire; Sunderland; Surrey; Teesside; Ulster; Westminster; York.

ADMISSIONS INFORMATION

Number of applicants per place (approx) Aston 6; Bath 8; Birmingham 18; Birmingham City 11; Bolton 3; Bournemouth 3; Bradford (Elec Electron Eng) 8; Bristol 5; Bristol UWE 8; Cardiff 7; Central Lancashire 4; City 10; Coventry 8; De Montfort 1; Derby 8; Dundee 5; Edinburgh Napier 8; Glamorgan 2; Glasgow Caledonian 5; Greenwich 10; Heriot-Watt 6; Hertfordshire 7; Huddersfield 5; Hull 8; Kent 5; Kingston 8; Lancaster 7; Leeds 15; Leicester 15; Lincoln 8; Liverpool John Moores 2; London (UCL) 9; London South Bank 5; Manchester Met 5; Newcastle 9; Northumbria 7; Nottingham 8; Plymouth 22; Portsmouth 4; Robert Gordon 3; Salford 5; Sheffield 15; Sheffield Hallam 2; Southampton 8; Staffordshire 7; Strathclyde 7; Sunderland 6; Surrey (BEng) 6, (MEng) 3; Swansea 3; Teesside 4; Warwick 8; Westminster 5; York 5.

Advice to applicants and planning the UCAS personal statement Enthusiasm for the subject, for example career ambitions, hobbies, work experience, attendance at appropriate events, competitions etc. Evidence of good ability in mathematics and also a scientific mind. Applicants should show that they can think creatively and have the motivation to succeed on a demanding course. See also **Engineering/Engineering Sciences** and **Appendix 4**.

Selection interviews Yes Aston, Bangor (Electron Eng only), Bath, Bournemouth, Bradford, Bristol, Bristol UWE, Brunel, Cambridge, Central Lancashire, De Montfort, Derby, Durham, Essex, Heriot-Watt, Hertfordshire, Huddersfield, Hull, Imperial London, Kingston, Lancaster, Liverpool, London (UCL), London South Bank, Newcastle, Nottingham, Oxford, Plymouth, Portsmouth, Queen's Belfast, Southampton, Strathclyde, Sunderland, Surrey, West London, Westminster, York; **Some** Anglia Ruskin, Brighton, Cardiff, Dundee, Kent, Leicester, Liverpool John Moores, Loughborough, Salford, Staffordshire.

Interview advice and questions Past questions have included: How does a combustion engine work? How does a trumpet work? What type of position do you hope to reach in five to ten years' time? Could you sack an employee? What was your last physics practical? What did you learn from it? What are the methods of transmitting information from a moving object to a stationary observer? Wire bending exercise – you are provided with an accurate diagram of a shape that could be produced by bending a length of wire in a particular way. You are supplied with a pair of pliers and the exact length of wire required and you are given 10 minutes to reproduce as accurately as possible the shape drawn. A three-minute talk had to be given on one of six subjects (topics given several weeks before the interview); for example, The best is the enemy of the good'. Is there a lesson here for British industry? I was asked to take my physics file and discuss some of my conclusions in certain experiments.' Explain power transmission through the National Grid. How would you explain power transmission to a friend who hasn't done physics? See also **Chapter 6**. **York** Questions based on a mathematical problem.

Reasons for rejection (non-academic) Poor English. Inability to communicate. Frightened of technology or mathematics. Poor motivation and work ethic. Better suited to a less specialised engineering/science course. Some foreign applicants do not have adequate English. See also **Engineering/Engineering Sciences**. **Surrey** Can't speak English (it has happened!).

AFTER-RESULTS ADVICE

Offers to applicants repeating A-levels Higher Brighton, Central Lancashire, Greenwich, Huddersfield, Kingston, Newcastle, Queen's Belfast, Strathclyde, Warwick; **Possibly higher** Aston, City, De Montfort, Derby, Glasgow, Hertfordshire, London Met, Portsmouth, Sheffield; **Same** Anglia Ruskin, Bangor, Bath, Birmingham, Bolton, Bradford, Cardiff, Coventry, Dundee, Durham, Hull, Kent, Leeds, Liverpool, Liverpool John Moores, London South Bank, Loughborough, Northumbria, Nottingham (usually), Nottingham Trent, Robert Gordon, Salford, Southampton, Staffordshire, Surrey, West London, Wolverhampton, York.

GRADUATE DESTINATIONS AND EMPLOYMENT (2007/8 HESA)

Graduates surveyed 1920 **Employed** 885 **In further study** 335 **Assumed unemployed** 275

Career note Electrical and Electronic Engineering is divided into two main fields – heavy current (electrical machinery, distribution systems, generating stations) and light current (computers, control engineering, telecommunications). Opportunities exist with many commercial organisations.

OTHER DEGREE SUBJECTS FOR CONSIDERATION

Computer Science; Engineering (Aeronautical, Communications, Computer, Control); Mathematics; Physics.

ENGINEERING (MANUFACTURING)

(see also Engineering/Engineering Sciences)

Manufacturing engineering is sometimes referred to as production engineering. It is a branch of the subject concerned with management aspects of engineering such as industrial organisation, purchasing, and the planning and control of operations. Manufacturing Engineering courses are therefore geared to providing the student with a broad-based portfolio of knowledge in both the technical and business areas.

Useful websites www.engc.org.uk; www.imeche.org; www.enginuity.org.uk.

Engineering Council statement *See* **Engineering/Engineering Sciences**.

NB The points totals shown to the left of the institutions are for ease of reference only. It must not be assumed that Tariff points are always used by institutions or that they can be substituted for an offer in grades. The level of an offer is not necessarily indicative of the quality of a course.

COURSE OFFERS INFORMATION

Subject requirements/preferences See **Engineering/Engineering Sciences**.

NB In 2012 universities and colleges will differ in their use of GCE AL/AS unit grade information, A* grades, the Extended Project (EPQ), the Advanced Diploma and the Cambridge Pre-U examination when considering applicants and making offers. An EPQ may be accepted in place of an AS subject. Check websites of universities and colleges for the latest offers information.

Your target offers and examples of courses provided by each institution
380 pts Cambridge – A*AA college offers may vary (Eng (Manuf Eng)) (IB 38–42 pts)
360 pts Bath – AAA (Spo Eng) (IB 36 pts HL maths phys 6)
　　　　　Loughborough – AAA (Innov Manuf Eng) (IB 33 pts)
340 pts Durham – AAB (Des Manuf Mgt) (IB 36 pts)
　　　　　Glasgow – AAB (Prod Des Eng) (IB 32 pts)
　　　　　Liverpool – AAB (Mech Eng Bus MEng) (IB 35 pts HL maths phys Engl 5)
　　　　　Newcastle – AAB (Mech Manuf Eng) (IB 34 pts)

Nottingham – AAB (Manuf Eng Mgt MEng) (IB 30 pts)
Strathclyde – AAB (Prod Des Eng MEng) (IB 36 pts)
Warwick – AAB–ABB (Manuf Mech Eng MEng) (IB 35–37 pts)
320 pts **Leeds** – ABB (Prod Des) (IB 34 pts HL 16 pts)
Nottingham – ABB (Prod Des Manuf MEng; Manuf Eng Mgt BEng)
Strathclyde – ABB (Prod Des Eng BEng) (IB 32 pts)
300 pts **Aston** – BBB 280–320 pts (Sust Prod Des) (IB 29 pts)
Loughborough – BBB (Manuf Eng)
280 pts **Birmingham City** – 280 pts (Mgt Manuf Sys) (IB 28 pts)
Bristol UWE – 280–320 pts (Aerosp Manuf Eng)
Brunel – BBC +AS/EPQ c 280–320 pts (Ind Des Tech) (IB 32 pts)
Liverpool John Moores – 280 pts (Auto Prod Dev)
Nottingham – BBC (Prod Des Manuf BEng) (IB 30–32 pts)
Queen's Belfast – BBC–BCC (Manuf Eng BEng) (IB 29–30 pts)
245 pts **Edinburgh Napier** – CCC 245 pts (Prod Des Eng)
240 pts **Bradford** – 240 pts (Ind Eng) (IB 26 pts)
Greenwich – 240 pts (Manuf Sys Eng BEng)
Huddersfield – 240 pts (Prod Des Dev)
Newport – 240 pts (Mech Manuf Eng)
230 pts **Glasgow Caledonian** – 230 pts (Manuf Sys Eng)
200 pts **Glamorgan** – 200–240 pts (Mech Manuf Eng BSc)
Portsmouth – 200 pts (Prod Des Innov)
Southampton Solent – 200 pts (Mech Des)
180 pts **Plymouth** – 180 pts (Mech Des Manuf BSc) (IB 24 pts)
Southampton Solent – 180 pts (Manuf Mech Eng)
160 pts **Loughborough** – 160–200 pts (Manuf Eng Mgt inc Fdn Yr) (IB 25 pts)
Swansea Met – 160–360 pts (Manuf Sys Eng)
80 pts **Greenwich** – 80 pts (Manuf Sys Eng inc Fdn Yr)
Portsmouth – 80 pts (Eng Tech inc Fdn Yr (Mech Manuf Eng))
Southampton Solent – 80 pts (Mech Des inc Fdn Yr)

Alternative offers See **Chapter 7** and **Appendix 1** for grades/UCAS Tariff points information for the International Baccalaureate, Scottish Highers/Advanced Highers, the Welsh Baccalaureate, the Irish Leaving Certificate, the Cambridge Pre-U Diploma, the Advanced Diploma and the Extended Project.

EXAMPLES OF FOUNDATION DEGREES IN THE SUBJECT FIELD
Blackpool and Fylde (Coll); Brighton; Bristol City (Coll); Exeter (Coll); Havering (Coll); Myerscough (Coll); Somerset (CAT); Sunderland; Swansea Met; York (Coll).

CHOOSING YOUR COURSE (SEE ALSO CH. 1)
Some course features
Greenwich The degree programme in Manufacturing Systems Engineering shares the first two years with Mechanical Engineering, opening doors to a wide range of engineering technologies, eg aeronautical, automotive and process engineering.
Loughborough Courses include an industrial placement year leading to both a degree and a Diploma in Industrial Studies.
Newcastle Mechanical or Manufacturing Engineering is an option which is chosen after the first two years.
Nottingham (Manuf Eng Mgt) Management and business modules support studies in engineering science and design.

Universities and colleges teaching quality See www.qaa.ac.uk; http://unistats.direct.gov.uk.

Top research universities and colleges (RAE 2008) See **Engineering (Mechanical)**.

Examples of sandwich degree courses Aston; Bath; Birmingham City; Bradford; Brunel; Glamorgan; Glasgow Caledonian; London South Bank; Loughborough; Queen's Belfast; Staffordshire; Ulster.

ADMISSIONS INFORMATION

Number of applicants per place (approx) Aston 6; Bath 18; Huddersfield 1; Loughborough 6; Nottingham 5; Strathclyde 8; Warwick 8.

Advice to applicants and planning the UCAS personal statement Work experience or work shadowing in industry should be mentioned. See **Engineering/Engineering Sciences**. See also **Appendix 4**.

Selection interviews Yes Cambridge, Nottingham, Strathclyde; **Some** Loughborough.

Interview advice and questions Past questions include: What is the function of an engineer? Describe something interesting you have recently done in your A-levels. What do you know about careers in manufacturing engineering? Discuss the role of women engineers in industry. Why is a disc brake better than a drum brake? Would you be prepared to make people redundant to improve the efficiency of a production line? See also **Chapter 6**.

Reasons for rejection (non-academic) Mature students failing to attend interview are rejected. One applicant produced a forged reference and was immediately rejected. See also **Engineering/ Engineering Sciences**.

AFTER-RESULTS ADVICE

Offers to applicants repeating A-levels Higher Strathclyde; **Same** Cambridge, Huddersfield, Loughborough, Nottingham.

GRADUATE DESTINATIONS AND EMPLOYMENT (2007/8 HESA)

Graduates surveyed 500 **Employed** 235 **In further study** 75 **Assumed unemployed** 75

Career note Graduates with experience in both technical and business skills have the flexibility to enter careers in technology or business management.

OTHER DEGREE SUBJECTS FOR CONSIDERATION

Business Studies; Computer Science; Engineering (Electrical, Mechanical); Physics; Technology.

ENGINEERING (MECHANICAL)

(including **Agricultural Engineering**, **Automotive Engineering** and **Motorsport Engineering**)

Mechanical Engineering is one of the most wide-ranging engineering disciplines. All courses involve the design, installation and maintenance of equipment used in industry. Several universities include a range of Engineering courses with a common first year allowing students to specialise from Year 2. Agricultural Engineering involves all aspects of off-road vehicle design and maintenance of other machinery used in agriculture.

Useful websites www.imeche.org; www.engc.org.uk; www.iagre.org.

Engineering Council statement *See* **Engineering/Engineering Sciences**.

NB The points totals shown to the left of the institutions are for ease of reference only. It must not be assumed that Tariff points are always used by institutions or that they can be substituted for an offer in grades. The level of an offer is not necessarily indicative of the quality of a course.

COURSE OFFERS INFORMATION

Subject requirements/preferences (Product Design courses) Design technology or art may be required or preferred. See also **Engineering/Engineering Sciences**.

NB In 2012 universities and colleges will differ in their use of GCE AL/AS unit grade information, A* grades, the Extended Project (EPQ), the Advanced Diploma and the Cambridge Pre-U examination when considering applicants and making offers. An EPQ may be accepted in place of an AS subject. Check websites of universities and colleges for the latest offers information.

Your target offers and examples of courses provided by each institution

400 pts **Imperial London** – A*mathsAA (Mech Nucl Eng courses) (IB 38 pts)

380 pts **Bath** – A*AA (Manuf Eng) (IB 35–37 pts HL maths phys 6)
Cambridge – A*AA college offers may vary (Eng (Mech Eng)) (IB 38–42 pts)
London (UCL) – A*AA+AS–ABB+AS (Mech Eng MEng) (IB 36–38 pts)
Oxford – A*AA (Mech Eng) (IB 38–42 pts)

370 pts **Brunel** – 370 pts (Mech Eng Aero) (IB 34 pts)

360 pts **Bath** – AAA (Auto Eng) (IB 35–37 pts HL maths phys 6)
Birmingham – AAA (Mech Mat Eng MEng) (IB 34–36 pts)
Bristol – AAA–AAB (Mech Eng) (IB 35 pts)
City – AAA 360 pts (Mech Eng) (IB 32 pts)
Edinburgh – Check with Ad Tutor AAA 2nd yr entry (Elec Mech Eng) (IB 36 pts)
London (UCL) – AAA+AS–AAB+AS (Mech Eng BEng) (IB 34–38 pts)
Loughborough – AAA (Mech Eng courses MEng) (IB 34 pts)
Southampton – AAA (Mech Eng Sust Ener Sys) (IB 36 pts)
Strathclyde – AAA (Mech Eng Mat Eng MEng) (IB 36 pts)

340 pts **Aston** – AAB 340 pts (Mech Eng MEng) (IB 32 pts)
Bath – AAB (Integ Mech Elec Eng) (IB 35–37 pts HL maths phys 6)
Birmingham – AAB (Mech Mat Eng BEng) (IB 34 pts)
Cardiff – ABB 340 pts (Mech Eng MEng) (IB 34 pts HL 5)
Durham – AAB (Mech Eng BEng; Mech Eng MEng)
Edinburgh – Check with Ad Tutor AAB–ABB 1st yr entry (Elec Eng Renew Ener) (IB 32 pts)
Exeter – AAB–BBB (Min Eng) (IB 30–34 pts)
Glasgow – AAB (Mech Des Eng MEng) (IB 32 pts)
Leeds – AAB (Mecha Robot) (IB 36 pts HL 17 pts)
Liverpool – AAB (Mecha Robot Sys MEng) (IB 35 pts HL maths phys Engl 5)
London (QM) – 340 pts (Des Inn MEng) (IB34 pts)
Loughborough – AAB (Auto Eng MEng) (IB 36 pts)
Manchester – AAB (Mech Eng Mgt) (IB 35–33 pts)
Newcastle – AAB (Mech Eng Mathem Mdl) (IB 36 pts HL maths phys 5)
Nottingham – AAB (Mech Eng MEng) (IB 30–34 pts)
Sheffield – AAB (Mech Eng Lang) (IB 32 pts HL maths 6)
Strathclyde – AAB (Mech Eng Fin Mgt BEng) (IB 32 pts)
Surrey – AAB 340 pts (Med Eng MEng) (IB 34–32 pts)
Warwick – AAB–ABB (Manuf Mech Eng MEng) (IB 35–37 pts)

320 pts **Brunel** – ABB +AS/EPQ b 320–370 pts (Mech Eng Bld Serv MEng) (IB 30 pts)
City – 320 pts (Auto Mtrspo Eng MEng) (IB 30 pts)
Edinburgh – Check with Ad. Tutor ABB 1st yr entry (Elec Mech Eng) (IB 32 pts)
Exeter – ABB–BBB (Mech Eng BEng) (IB 32–29 pts)
Glasgow – ABB (Mech Eng Aero BEng) (IB 30 pts)
Glasgow (SA) – Check with Ad Tutor ABB (Prod Des Eng MEng)
Hertfordshire – 320 pts (Auto Eng Mtrspo MEng) (IB 30 pts)
Lancaster – ABB (Mecha MEng) (IB 30 pts)
Leicester – ABB (Mech Eng courses MEng) (IB 32 pts)
Manchester – ABB (Mech Eng) (IB 33 pts)
Nottingham – ABB–BBB (Mech Eng BEng)
Oxford Brookes – ABB (Mech Eng MEng; Mtrspo Eng MEng)
Queen's Belfast – ABB (Mech Manuf Eng MEng) (IB 31–32 pts)
Sheffield – ABB (Mech Sys Eng MEng) (IB 32 pts HL maths 6)
Strathclyde – ABB (Spo Eng) (IB 34 pts)
Sussex – ABB–BBC (Mech Eng) (IB 30–34 pts)
Swansea – 320–380 pts (Mech Eng MEng; Med Eng)

300 pts **Aberdeen** – BBB (Mech Eng Euro St BEng/MEng) (IB 30–28 pts)
Aston – BBB 300 pts (Mech Eng BEng) (IB 29 pts)
Bradford – 300 pts (Mech Auto Eng MEng) (IB 28–32 pts)

Coventry – 300 pts (Auto Eng MEng)
Dundee – BBB 300 pts 2nd yr entry (Mech Eng)
Glasgow – BBB (Mech Eng Euro) (IB 30 pts)
Glasgow (SA) – Check with Ad Tutor BBB (Prod Des Eng BEng)
Greenwich – 300 pts (Mech Eng MEng/BEng)
Harper Adams (UC) – 300 pts (Agric Eng) (IB 30 pts)
Heriot-Watt – BBB (Mech Ener Eng MEng; Mech Eng courses)
Huddersfield – 300 pts (Auto Eng MEng; Mech Eng MEng)
Lancaster – BBB (Mecha BEng) (IB 28 pts)
Liverpool – BBB (Mech Eng BEng; Mech Mat Eng; Mech Eng Bus BEng; Mecha Robot Sys BEng)
Loughborough – BBB–ABC (Mech Eng courses BEng; Mech Eng inc Fdn; Auto Eng)
Newcastle – BBB (Mech Eng inc Fdn Yr BEng) (IB 30 pts HL maths phys 5)
Oxford Brookes – BBC (Mech Eng BEng)
Plymouth – 300 pts (Mech Eng MEng) (IB 30 pts)
Portsmouth – 300 pts (Mech Eng MEng) (IB 30 pts)
Queen's Belfast – BBB (Agric Tech)
Salford – 300 pts (Mech Eng MEng) (IB 32 pts)
Sheffield – BBB 300 pts (Fdn Mech Eng)
Sheffield Hallam – 300 pts (Mech Eng MEng)
Surrey – BBB 300 pts (Mech Eng BEng) (IB 27 pts)
Ulster – 300 pts (Mech Eng)

280 pts **Aberdeen** – BBC 280 pts 2nd yr entry (Petrol Eng) (IB 26 pts)
Bristol UWE – 280–300 pts (Mtrspo Eng) (IB 28–30 pts)
Brunel – BBC (Mech Eng BEng) (IB 30 pts)
Cardiff – BBC (Mech Eng BEng) (IB 28 pts)
Central Lancashire – 280 pts (Mtrspo Eng MEng)
City – BBC 280 pts (Auto Mtrspo Eng BEng) (IB 28 pts)
Hull – 280–320 pts (Mech Eng MEng; Mech Med Eng MEng)
Leicester – BBC (Mech Eng BEng) (IB 30 pts)
Liverpool John Moores – 280 pts (Mech Eng MEng; Mech Mar Eng MEng)
London (QM) – 280 pts (Mech Eng BEng) (IB 28 pts)
Oxford Brookes – BBC (Mtrspo Eng BEng)
Strathclyde – BBC (Elec Mech Eng BEng) (IB 30 pts)
Teesside – 280 pts (Mech Eng)

260 pts **Birmingham City** – 260–280 pts (Auto Eng) (IB 28 pts)
Brighton – BCC–BBD (Auto Eng) (IB 30 pts)
Coventry – 260 pts (Mech Eng; Auto Eng)
Edinburgh Napier – 260 pts (Mech Eng MEng)
Hertfordshire – 260 pts (Auto Eng BEng; Mech Eng; Auto Eng Mtrspo BEng)
Liverpool John Moores – 260 pts (Mech Mar Eng BEng; Auto Eng)
Manchester Met – 260 pts (Mech Eng (Auto Contr) (Auto Eng)) (IB 26 pts)
Northumbria – 260–280 pts (Mech Eng)
Plymouth – BCC 260 pts (Mar Tech BEng) (IB 27 pts)
Robert Gordon – BCC-CCC (Mech Off Eng)
Salford – 260 pts (Mech Eng BEng) (IB 30 pts)
Swansea – BCC 260 pts (Med Eng)
Ulster – 260 pts (Mech Eng)

240 pts **Bolton** – 240 pts (Autombl Eng; Mech Eng)
Bradford – 240 pts (Mech Veh Tech) (IB 26 pts)
Central Lancashire – 240 pts (Mtrspo Eng BEng) (IB 24 pts)
Coventry – 240 pts (Mtrspo courses)
De Montfort – 240 pts (Mech Eng; Mecha)
Dundee – CCC (Mech Eng BEng (4 yr Hons))
Harper Adams (UC) – 240 pts (Off Rd Veh Des)

Huddersfield – 240 pts (Auto Tech) (IB 26 pts)
Kingston – 240 pts (Mech Eng BEng)
Liverpool John Moores – 240 pts (Mech Eng)
Newport – 240 pts (Mech Manuf Eng)
Oxford Brookes – BCC–CCD (Auto Eng)
Portsmouth – 240 pts (Mech Eng BEng) (IB 28 pts)
Robert Gordon – CCC (Mech Eng BEng) (IB 26 pts)
Staffordshire – 240 pts (Mecha; Mech Eng)
230 pts **Glasgow Caledonian** – BC 230 pts (Mech Electron Sys Eng)
220 pts **Aberdeen** – CCD 220 pts 1st yr entry (Petrol Eng) (IB 22 pts)
Heriot-Watt – CCD (Mech Eng BEng; Auto Eng; Mech Ener Eng)
Hull – 220–260 pts (Mech Eng BEng; Mech Med Eng BEng)
London South Bank – 220 pts (Mech Eng BEng; Mecha)
Sheffield Hallam – 220–280 pts (Mech Comp Aid Eng)
Sunderland – 220 pts (Mech Eng) (IB 32 pts)
200 pts **Coventry** – 200 pts (Mech Eng BSc; Mtrspo Eng BEng)
Dundee – CDD (Mech Eng BEng (3 yr non-Hons)) (IB 28 pts)
Glamorgan – 200–240 pts (Mech Manuf Eng BSc)
Glyndŵr – 200 pts (Perf Car Electron Tech; Aero Mech Eng; Mtrspo Des Mgt)
Hertfordshire – 200 pts (Auto Tech Mgt BSc) (IB 24–26 pts)
Portsmouth – 200–240 pts (Mech Manuf Eng) (IB 24 pts)
Southampton Solent – 200 pts (Mech Des)
Wolverhampton – 200 pts (Mech Eng)
180 pts **Greenwich** – 180 pts (Mech Eng Tech)
Plymouth – 180 pts (Mech Eng Comp Aid Des) (IB 24 pts)
170 pts **Glasgow Caledonian** – DDE 170 pts (Mecha)
160 pts **Blackburn (Coll Univ Centre)** – 160 pts (Mech Eng; Mecha)
Harper Adams (UC) – 160–180 pts (Agric Eng Mark Mgt BSc) (IB 24 pts)
Kingston – 160 pts (Mtrcycl Eng; Mech Eng; Auto Eng; Mtrspo Eng)
Sheffield Hallam – 160 pts (Mech Eng; Mech Des Eng; Auto Des Tech; Mech Auto Eng)
Sussex – CC (Eng inc Fdn Yr) (IB 28 pts)
West Scotland – CC (Mtrspo Des Eng)
140 pts **Robert Gordon** – CD (Mech Eng BSc)
120 pts **Glamorgan** – 120–160 pts (Mecha Eng BSc)
Northumbria – 120 pts (Mech Eng inc Fdn Yr)
Sheffield Hallam – 120 pts (Mech Des Eng BSc)
Swansea Met – 120–360 pts (Auto Eng; Mtrspo Eng Des; Mtrcycl Eng)
80 pts **Swansea Met** – 80–340 pts (Mech Manuf Eng 4 yrs)

Alternative offers See **Chapter 7** and **Appendix 1** for grades/UCAS Tariff points information for the International Baccalaureate, Scottish Highers/Advanced Highers, the Welsh Baccalaureate, the Irish Leaving Certificate, the Cambridge Pre-U Diploma, the Advanced Diploma and the Extended Project.

EXAMPLES OF FOUNDATION DEGREES IN THE SUBJECT FIELD
Bath; Blackburn (Coll Univ Centre); Blackpool and Fylde (Coll); Brighton; Bristol City (Coll); Bristol UWE; Derby; Exeter (Coll); Glyndŵr; Greenwich; Havering (Coll); Kingston; Loughborough (Coll); Myerscough (Coll); Oxford Brookes; Plymouth; Queen's Belfast; Sheffield Hallam; Somerset (CAT); South Cheshire (Coll); Staffordshire; Sunderland; Swansea Met; Warwickshire (Coll). (Agricultural Engineering) Bicton (Coll); Harper Adams (UC).

CHOOSING YOUR COURSE (SEE ALSO CH. 1)
Some course features
Brunel (Mech Eng) Course combines fundamental elements of mechanical engineering and design with study in associated disciplines including computing, electronics, environment and energy systems. All courses emphasise importance of industrial and commercial insight and awareness.

Cardiff The first year is common to all Engineering programmes. Core subjects include mathematics, dynamics, properties of materials, electrical engineering, electronics and business management. Option to study French or German or Spanish.

Durham A common course for Years 1 and 2 and then two years specialising in the chosen discipline.

Exeter A multidisciplinary first year before specialising in Year 2. Emphasis on design skills practice and development.

Leicester Options to study for a year in industry, in Europe or the USA.

Newcastle Eleven mechanical engineering options with common first and second years for all students.

Salford (MEng Mech Eng) Programme has broad engineering themes built around study of transport, energy, structures and communication

Strathclyde (MEng Mech Eng) Opportunity for year abroad in either Year 3 or 5.

Surrey Mechanical, medical and aerospace programmes have a common first year allowing for a final choice of degree in Year 2.

Universities and colleges teaching quality See www.qaa.ac.uk; http://unistats.direct.gov.uk.

Top research universities and colleges (RAE 2008) (Mechanical, Aeronautical and Manufacturing Engineering) Imperial London; Sheffield; Bristol (Aerospace Engineering); Greenwich; Nottingham; Leeds; Loughborough; Birmingham; Cardiff.

Examples of sandwich degree courses Aston; Bath; Birmingham City; Bradford; Brighton; Bristol UWE; Brunel; Cardiff; Central Lancashire; City; Coventry; De Montfort; East London; Glamorgan; Glasgow Caledonian; Harper Adams (UC); Hertfordshire; Huddersfield; Kingston; Leicester; Liverpool John Moores; London (QM); London South Bank; Loughborough; Manchester Met; Northumbria; Oxford Brookes; Plymouth; Portsmouth; Queen's Belfast; Salford; Sheffield Hallam; Staffordshire; Sunderland; Surrey; Teesside; Ulster; West Scotland.

ADMISSIONS INFORMATION

Number of applicants per place (approx) Abertay Dundee 4; Aston 8; Bath (MEng) 13; Birmingham 6; Bradford 4; Brighton 10; Bristol 8; Bristol UWE 17; Brunel 12; Cardiff 8; City 13; Coventry 8; Dundee 5; Durham 8; Glamorgan 6; Glyndŵr 4; Heriot-Watt 9; Hertfordshire 10; Huddersfield 1; Hull 11; Kingston 8; Lancaster 8; Leeds 15; Leicester 11; Liverpool 6; Liverpool John Moores (Mech Eng) 2; London (QM) 6; London South Bank 4; Loughborough 8, (Mech Eng) 12, (Auto Eng) 7; Manchester Met 6, (Mech Eng) 6; Newcastle 10; Northumbria 4; Nottingham 8; Plymouth 6; Portsmouth 6; Sheffield 10; Southampton 8; Staffordshire 6; Strathclyde 6; Surrey 9; Teesside 7; Warwick 8; Westminster 11.

Advice to applicants and planning the UCAS personal statement Work experience; hands-on skills. An interest in solving mathematical problems related to physical concepts. Enjoyment in designing mechanical devices or components. Interest in engines, structures, dynamics or fluid flow and efficient use of materials or energy. Apply to the Year in Industry Scheme (www.yini.org.uk) for placement. Scholarships are available to supplement the scheme. See **Engineering/Engineering Sciences**. See also **Appendix 4**.

Misconceptions about this course Loughborough Although organised by the Wolfson School of Manufacturing and Mechanical Engineering, the degree does not include manufacturing.

Selection interviews Yes Aston, Birmingham, Bolton, Bradford, Brighton, Bristol, Brunel, Cambridge, Cardiff, Durham, Harper Adams (UC), Hertfordshire, Huddersfield, Imperial London, Kingston, Lancaster, Leeds, Leicester, Liverpool John Moores, London (QM), London South Bank, Loughborough (Auto Eng), Manchester Met, Newcastle, Nottingham, Oxford, Queen's Belfast, Sheffield, Sheffield Hallam, Strathclyde, Sunderland, Surrey, Sussex; **Some** Blackpool and Fylde (Coll), Dundee, Liverpool, Staffordshire.

Interview advice and questions Past questions include: What mechanical objects have you examined and/or tried to repair? How do you see yourself in five years' time? What do you imagine you would be doing (production, management or design engineering)? What engineering interests do you have? What qualities are required to become a successful mechanical engineer? Do you like sixth

form work? Describe the working of parts on an engineering drawing. How does a fridge work? What is design in the context of mechanical engineering? What has been your greatest achievement to date? What are your career plans? See also **Engineering/Engineering Sciences** and **Chapter 6**.
Hertfordshire All interviewees receive a conditional offer. Provide an example of working as part of a team, meeting a deadline, working on your own.

Reasons for rejection (non-academic) See **Engineering/Engineering Sciences**.

AFTER-RESULTS ADVICE
Offers to applicants repeating A-levels **Higher** Brighton, Dundee, Kingston, Newcastle, Queen's Belfast, Swansea, Warwick; **Possibly higher** City, Huddersfield; **Same** Aston, Bath, Bradford, Bristol, Brunel, Coventry, Derby, Durham, East London, Edinburgh Napier, Harper Adams (UC), Heriot-Watt, Leeds (usually), Lincoln, Liverpool, Liverpool John Moores, London South Bank, Loughborough, Manchester Met, Northumbria, Nottingham, Nottingham Trent, Oxford Brookes, Sheffield, Sheffield Hallam, Southampton, Staffordshire, Sunderland, Surrey, Teesside, Wolverhampton.

GRADUATE DESTINATIONS AND EMPLOYMENT (2007/8 HESA)
Graduates surveyed 2180 **Employed** 1140 **In further study** 330 **Assumed unemployed** 285

Career note Mechanical Engineering graduates have a wide choice of career options. Apart from design and development of plant and machinery, they are also likely to be involved in production processes and working at various levels of management. Mechanical engineers share interests such as structures and stress analysis with civil and aeronautical engineers, and electronics and computing with electrical and software engineers.

OTHER DEGREE SUBJECTS FOR CONSIDERATION
Engineering (Aeronautical/Aerospace, Building, Computer (Control, Software and Systems), Electrical/ Electronic, Manufacturing, Marine); Materials Science; Mathematics; Physics; Product Design; Technologies.

ENGINEERING (MEDICAL)

(including **Clinical Engineering, Medical Electronics** and **Instrumentation, Mechanical** and **Medical Engineering, Medical Physics, Medical Product Design, Product Design for Medical Devices** and **Rehabilitation Engineering;** see also **Biotechnology**)

Biomedical Engineering lies at the interface between engineering, mathematics, physics, chemistry, biology and clinical practice. This makes it a branch of engineering that has the most direct effect on human health. It is a rapidly expanding inter-disciplinary field that applies engineering principles and technology to medical and biological problems. Biomedical engineers work in fields as diverse as neuro-technology, fluid mechanics of the blood and respiratory systems, bone and joint biomechanics, biosensors, medical imaging, synthetic biology and biomaterials. These can lead to novel devices such as joint replacements and heart valves, new surgical instruments, rehabilitation protocols and even prosthetic limbs.

NB The points totals shown to the left of the institutions are for ease of reference only. It must not be assumed that Tariff points are always used by institutions or that they can be substituted for an offer in grades. The level of an offer is not necessarily indicative of the quality of a course.

COURSE OFFERS INFORMATION
Subject requirements/preferences **GCSE** Mathematics and science subjects, chemistry and/or biology an advantage but not essential. Design and technology for Product Design courses.

NB In 2012 universities and colleges will differ in their use of GCE AL/AS unit grade information, A* grades, the Extended Project (EPQ), the Advanced Diploma and the Cambridge Pre-U

examination when considering applicants and making offers. An EPQ may be accepted in place of an AS subject. Check websites of universities and colleges for the latest offers information.

Your target offers and examples of courses provided by each institution

360 pts **Imperial London** – AAA (Biomat Tiss Eng) (IB 38–42 pts)
Liverpool – AAA (Med Eng) (IB 30 pts)
London (UCL) – AAA–ABB (Med Phys) (IB 34–36 pts)

340 pts **Birmingham** – AAB (Mech Eng (Biomed)) (IB 32–34 pts)
Cardiff – AAB (Mech Eng Med Eng MEng) (IB 34 pts inc maths HL5)
City – AAB 340 pts (Biomed Eng BEng) (IB 30 pts)
Exeter – AAB–ABB (Phys Med Apps) (IB 34–31 pts)
Leeds – AAB (Med Eng MEng) (IB 36 pts HL 17 pts)
London (King's) – AAB+AS (Phys Med Apps) (IB 36 pts)
London (QM) – 340 pts (Med End MEng) (IB 34 pts)
Manchester – AAB (Biomed Sci) (IB 35–32 pts)
Queen's Belfast – AAB (Phys Med Apps MSci)
Surrey – AAB 340 pts (Med Eng MEng) (IB 34–32 pts)

320 pts **Cardiff** – ABB (Mech Eng Med Eng BEng) (IB 32 pts inc maths HL5)
London (UCL) – Contact admissions office (Sci Eng New Med)
Reading – 320 pts (Biomed Eng)
Sheffield – ABB (Biomed Eng) (IB 35 pts)

300 pts **Bradford** – 300 pts (Med Eng MEng)
Glasgow – BBB (Med Eng BEng)
Queen's Belfast – BBB (Phys Med Apps BSc)
Sheffield – BBB–BBC (Biomat Sci Tiss Eng BEng)

280 pts **London (QM)** – 280–260 pts (Biomat Sci Eng BEng) (IB 28 pts)
Reading – 280 pts (Biomed Eng Cyber) (HL 555)

260 pts **Ulster** – 260 pts (Biomed Eng)

240 pts **Bradford** – 240 pts (Med Eng BEng)

Alternative offers

See **Chapter 7** and **Appendix 1** for Grades/UCAS Tariff points information for the International Baccalaureate, Scottish Highers/Advanced Highers, the Welsh Baccalaureate, the Irish Leaving Certificate, the Cambridge Pre-U Diploma, the Advanced Diploma and the Extended Project.

CHOOSING YOUR COURSE (SEE ALSO CH. 1)

Some course features

Cardiff A long-standing Medical Engineering course blending engineering knowledge with biomechanical applications. Lectures delivered by research-active biomechanists, clinicians and industrialists.

London (UCL) (Medical Physics) Graduates have an Institute of Physics accredited degree with a range of careers open to students not committed to a career in medical physics. Those taking this subject usually train to be an NHS medical physicist, seek a position in industry or take a higher degree.

Swansea BEng and MEng courses are offered with a year in industry. The courses are taught in an integrated College of Engineering with parts of the course taught in the Medical School.

Universities and colleges teaching quality See www.qaa.ac.uk; http://unistats.direct.gov.uk.

Examples of sandwich degree courses Cardiff; Swansea (One year paid employment. MEng students have the opportunity to spend a year in a European University).

ADMISSIONS INFORMATION

Number of applicants per place (approx) Cardiff 4; London (UCL) 6; Swansea 5.

Advice to applicants and planning the UCAS personal statement **Cardiff** An appreciation of the typical careers available within medical engineering and an interest in engineering and anatomy would be preferable. **London (UCL)** Evidence of interest in medical physics/physics eg visits to hospitals or internships.

Selection interviews Yes Cardiff (all applicants), London (UCL); **Some** Swansea (Not usually except for applicants not fitting their usual academic profile).

Interview advice and questions London (UCL) Searching questions at interview. Test may be included.

AFTER-RESULTS ADVICE
Offers to applicants repeating A-levels Same Cardiff, Liverpool, London (UCL), Swansea.

GRADUATE DESTINATIONS AND EMPLOYMENT (2007/8 HESA)
Career note High rate of graduate employment. Money Magazine ranks Biomedical Engineering No. 1 for job growth prospects for the next ten years.

ENGLISH
(including **Creative Writing**; see also **Languages, Linguistics, Literature**)

English courses continue to be extremely popular and competitive. They are an extension of school studies in literature and language and may cover topics ranging from Anglo-Saxon literature to writing in the present day. Most courses, however, will focus on certain areas such as the Medieval or Renaissance periods of literature or on English language studies. Admissions tutors will expect students to have read widely outside their A-level syllabus.

Useful websites www.bl.uk; www.lrb.co.uk; www.literature.org; www.bibliomania.com; www.online-literature.com.

NB The points totals shown to the left of the institutions are for ease of reference only. It must not be assumed that Tariff points are always used by institutions or that they can be substituted for an offer in grades. The level of an offer is not necessarily indicative of the quality of a course.

COURSE OFFERS INFORMATION
Subject requirements/preferences GCSE English Language, and English Literature required and a foreign language may be preferred. Grades may be stipulated. **AL** English with specific grades usually stipulated. Modern languages required for joint courses with languages.

NB In 2012 universities and colleges will differ in their use of GCE AL/AS unit grade information, A* grades, the Extended Project (EPQ), the Advanced Diploma and the Cambridge Pre-U examination when considering applicants and making offers. An EPQ may be accepted in place of an AS subject. Check websites of universities and colleges for the latest offers information.

Your target offers and examples of courses provided by each institution
390 pts   **London (King's)** – ABB+AS **or** AB/BB+3AS (Hisp St Engl) (IB 32 pts)
380 pts   **Cambridge** – A*AA college offers may vary (Educ Engl) (IB 38–42 pts)
          London (UCL) – AAA+AS (Engl) (IB 38 pts)
360 pts   **Birmingham** – AAA (Engl Crea Writ) (IB 36 pts)
          Bristol – AAA–ABB no pts offer (Engl Class St) (IB 38–37 pts)
          Cardiff – AAA (Engl Lit courses; Cult Crit Engl Lang)
          Durham – AAA (Engl Lit Phil) (IB 37 pts)
          East Anglia – AAB–BBB (Engl Lit)
          Exeter – AAA–AAB (Engl Fr) (IB 36–33 pts)
          London (King's) – AAAb–AAaab (Class St Engl)
          Manchester – AAA–ABB (Engl Lit courses) (IB 37–35 pts)
          Newcastle – AAA (Engl Lit) (IB 35 pts)
          Oxford – AAA (Hist Engl) (IB 38–42 pts)
          St Andrews – AAA (Engl courses) (IB 38 pts)

Sheffield – AAA (Engl Lit) (IB 35–32 pts)
Southampton – AAA (Engl Phil) (IB 34 pts HL 18)
Sussex – AAA–AAB (Engl courses)
Warwick – AAA–AAB (Engl courses)
York – AAA–AAB (Engl Lang Ling) (IB 36 pts)

340 pts **Durham** – AAB (Educ St Engl Lit; Comb Hons Arts (Engl))
East Anglia – AAB–BBB (Engl Lit Dr)
Exeter – AAB–ABB (Engl Fr/Ger/Ital/Russ/Span) (IB 34–36 pts)
Glasgow – AAB (Scot Lit) (IB 34 pts)
Lancaster – AAB–ABB 340–320 pts (Engl Lang Crea Writ) (IB 32–34 pts)
Leeds – ABB–AAB (Engl Lit Thea St) (IB 36 pts HL Engl 6)
Leicester – AAB–ABB (Engl courses)
Liverpool – AAB (Engl Comm St) (IB 36 pts HL Engl 7)
London (RH) – AAB–ABB (Engl Fr/Ger/Ital) (IB 33 pts)
Loughborough – AAB–ABB 340 pts (Engl; Engl Spo Sci; Hist Engl)
Manchester – AAB–BBC (Engl Lang Chin; Engl Lang Scrn St; Engl Lang Russ; Lang Lit Comm)
Newcastle – AAB (Engl Lang Lit) (IB 35 pts HL Engl 6)
Nottingham – AAB–ABB (Engl Crea Writ) (IB 34–36 pts)
Sheffield – AAB (Engl Lang Ling)

320 pts **Birmingham** – ABB (Engl Lang courses; Modn Langs Engl Lang)
Bournemouth – 320 pts (Engl)
Cardiff – ABB (Engl Lang Fr/Ger)
Kent – 320–340 pts (Engl Am Lit joint courses)
Leeds – ABB (Class Lit Engl) (IB 33 pts)
Liverpool – ABB (Engl Hisp St) (IB 30 pts)
London (Gold) – ABB (Engl Compar Lit)
London (King's) – BBB+AS **or** BB+3AS (Port Braz St Engl) (IB 32 pts)
London (QM) – 320–340 pts (Engl Film St) (IB 32 pts)
Newcastle – ABB (Engl Lang) (IB 34 pts HL Engl 6)
Nottingham – ABB (Engl Russ E Euro Civ)
Oxford Brookes – ABB–BBB (Engl courses) (IB 34 pts)
Queen's Belfast – ABB–BBBb (Engl courses)
Sheffield – ABB (Engl Lang Sociol)
Southampton – ABB (Engl Mus) (IB 32 pts)
Strathclyde – ABB (Engl courses) (IB 34 pts)
Surrey – ABB 320 pts (Engl Lit; Engl Lit Crea Writ)
Swansea – ABB–BBB (Engl Lit Lang St)

300 pts **Aberdeen** – BBB (Celt Civ Engl) (IB 30 pts)
Aberystwyth – 300 pts (Engl Lit Crea Writ) (IB 30 pts)
Aston – 300–340 pts (Engl Lang Fr/Ger) (IB 32–33 pts)
Brighton – 300 pts (Engl Lit) (IB 28–30 pts)
Brunel – Contact admissions office (Thea Crea Writ; Thea Engl; Gms Des Crea Writ)
Buckingham – BBB 300 pts (Engl Lit courses) (IB 27 pts)
Cardiff – BBB (Engl Lang Ital/Welsh)
Edinburgh – Check with Ad Tutor BBB (Engl Lang)
Essex – 300 pts (Engl Lang Lit) (IB 29 pts)
Gloucestershire – 280–300 pts (Engl Lit; Engl Lang)
Hertfordshire – 300 pts (Engl Lit courses)
Keele – 300–320 pts (Engl Am Lit) (IB 30–32 pts)
Kent – 300–320 pts (Engl Lit) (IB 33–35 pts)
Kingston – BBB (Engl Lang Comm Jrnl)
London (Gold) – BBB (Engl Dr)
Northumbria – 300 pts (Engl Lit; Engl Lang Lit; Engl Lit Crea Writ)
Oxford Brookes – BBB (Engl Comb Hons) (IB 33 pts)
Reading – 300–360 pts (Engl Lit courses) (IB 31–32 pts)

BA English

Joint honours also available with
Theatre
Music
Creative Writing
Film and Television Studies
Games Design

BA Creative Writing

Joint honours also available with
Theatre
English
Games Design

Find out more about the School of Arts at www.brunel.ac.uk

Brunel
UNIVERSITY
LONDON

Roehampton – 300–340 pts (Engl Lit; Crea Writ courses)
Stirling – BBB 2nd yr entry (Engl St)

280 pts Birmingham City – 280 pts (Engl Dr; Engl Lit; Engl Crea Writ; Engl Lang St)
Brunel – BBC (Crea Writ) (IB 30 pts)
Edge Hill – 280 pts (Engl; Crea Writ courses; Engl Lang courses; Engl Lit courses)
Huddersfield – 280–320 pts (Engl St; Engl Lang; Engl Lit courses; Engl Lit Crea Writ)
Hull – 280–320 pts (Engl; Engl Am Lit Cult)
Loughborough – 280–300 pts (Pub Engl) (IB 32–35 pts)
Manchester Met – 280 pts (Engl Am Lit)
Oxford Brookes – BBC/BBcc/BCbb (Engl Lang Comm) (IB 30 pts)
Salford – 280 pts (Engl Lit Jrnl; Engl Film St)

260 pts Bath Spa – 260-300 pts (Crea Writ courses)
Bristol UWE – 260–320 pts (Engl courses)
Cardiff (UWIC) – 260 pts (Engl Crea Writ; Engl Dr)
Coventry – 260–280 pts (Engl; Engl Jrnl St)
De Montfort – 260 pts (Engl; Engl Lang courses; Crea Writ joint Hons)
Dundee – BCC 1st yr entry (Engl courses)
Hertfordshire – 260–280 pts (Engl Lang Comm courses)
Lincoln – 260 pts (Engl; Engl Pol)
Liverpool – BCC (Ir St Engl)
Liverpool Hope – 260 pts (Engl Lang courses; Engl Lit courses)
Liverpool John Moores – 260 pts (Crea Writ courses; Engl courses)
London Met – 260 pts (Crea Writ Engl Lit; Crea Writ; Engl Lit)
Newport – 260 pts (Engl courses)
Nottingham Trent – 260–280 pts (Engl; Engl Comm Soty; Engl Crea Writ)
Plymouth – 260 pts (Engl courses)
Salford – 260–240 pts (Engl Lit Engl Lang) (IB 31 pts)

Stirling – BCC 1st year entry (Engl St)
Westminster – CCC–BCC (Engl Lang) (IB 30 pts)
Winchester – 260–300 pts (Crea Writ courses) (IB 24–26 pts)

240 pts **Anglia Ruskin** – 240 pts (Engl courses; Engl Lang courses; Writ courses)
Bangor – 240–300 pts (Engl courses; Engl Lang courses)
Bolton – 240 pts (Media Writ Prod) (IB 24 pts)
Bradford – 240 pts (Engl)
Buckingham – CCC 240 pts (Engl St courses)
Canterbury Christ Church – 240 pts (Engl courses; Engl Lang Comm courses)
Central Lancashire – 240–260 pts (Engl Lang St; Jrnl Engl Lit)
Chester – 240–280 pts (Crea Writ courses) (IB 30 pts)
Chichester – CCC–BCC (Engl Crea Writ) (IB 28–30 pts)
Leeds Trinity (UC) – (Engl; Engl Hist; Engl Media; Engl Writ)
London South Bank – 240 pts (Engl Dr Perf; Engl Crea Writ)
Manchester Met – 240–280 pts (Engl; Engl Crea Writ courses)
Portsmouth – 240–300 pts (Engl Lang courses; Engl Lit courses; Crea Media Writ)
Sheffield Hallam – 240–280 pts (Engl; Engl Educ St; Crea Writ)
Southampton Solent – 240 pts (Engl Adv; Engl PR)
Suffolk (Univ Campus) – 240 pts (Engl)
Teesside – 240–280 pts (Engl St; Engl St Crea Writ)
UCP Marjon – 240–260 pts (Engl Lit courses; Crea Writ courses; Engl Lang Ling)
Ulster – 240–260 pts (Engl Int Dev; Engl courses)
Worcester – 240–260 pts (Engl Lang courses; Engl Lit St courses)
York St John – 240–220 pts (Engl courses: Crea Writ)

220 pts **Bishop Grosseteste (UC)** – 220 pts (Engl Lit; Educ St Engl)
Edinburgh Napier – 220 pts (Engl; Engl Film)
Falmouth (UC) – 220 pts (Engl Media St; Engl Crea Writ)
Glamorgan – 220–280 pts (Engl Lit; Crea Prof Writ; Engl Lang)
Kingston – 220–360 pts (Engl Lang Comm courses; Engl Lit; Crea Writ courses)
Leeds Met – 220–180 pts (Engl Lit; Engl Hist)
Northampton – 220–260 pts (Engl courses; Crea Writ courses)
Suffolk (Univ Campus) – 220 pts (Engl Hist)
Sunderland – 220–300 pts (Engl; Engl Crea Writ; Engl Dr; Engl Lang Lit; Engl St courses)

200 pts **Blackburn (Coll Univ Centre)** – 200–240 pts (Engl courses; Engl (Lang Lit St))
Blackpool and Fylde (Coll) – 200 pts (Engl Lang Lit Writ)
Bolton – 200 pts (Engl)
Bucks New – 200–240 pts (Crea Writ; Script)
Central Lancashire – 200–240 pts (Engl Lang Ling)
Cumbria – 200–240 pts (Engl courses; Crea Writ Jrnl)
Doncaster (Coll Univ Centre) – 200 pts (Engl courses)
East London – 200 pts (Engl Lang courses; Engl Lit courses; Crea Prof Writ courses)
Glyndŵr – 200 pts (Engl; Engl Crea Writ; Engl Media Comms)
Middlesex – 200–300 pts (Engl Lit courses; Engl Lang Lit)
Newman (UC) – 200–240 pts (Engl courses)
Peterborough (Reg Coll) – 200 pts (Hist Engl; Engl Sociol)
Southampton – 200 pts (Cmdy Writ Perf)
Southampton Solent – 200 pts (Cmdy Writ Perf)
York St John – 200–280 pts (Engl courses)

180 pts **Aberystwyth** – 180 pts (Inf Lib St Engl Lit)
Bedfordshire – 180–220 pts (Engl courses; Crea Writ)
Derby – 180–240 pts (Engl courses; Crea Writ courses; Media Writ courses)
Greenwich – 180 pts (Engl courses; Crea Writ courses)
St Mary's Twickenham (UC) – 180–200 pts (Engl courses; Crea Writ)
Staffordshire – 180–220 pts (Script) (IB 28 pts)
Trinity Saint David – 180–240 pts (Engl Lit courses; Engl Modn Lit courses)

For a quick reference offers calculator, fold out the inside back cover.

160 pts **Norwich City (Coll)** – 160 pts (Engl)
UHI Millennium Inst – CC (Lit)
Wolverhampton – 160–220 pts (Engl courses; Crea Prof Writ courses)
120 pts **Arts London** – 120 pts (Mag Pub)
Grimsby (IFHE) – 120–240 pts (Engl St)
Trinity Saint David – 120–360 pts (Engl courses; Crea Writ courses)
80 pts **London (Birk)** – for under 21s (over 21s varies) p/t (Engl)

Alternative offers
See **Chapter 7** and **Appendix 1** for grades/UCAS Tariff points information for the International Baccalaureate, Scottish Highers/Advanced Highers, the Welsh Baccalaureate, the Irish Leaving Certificate, the Cambridge Pre-U Diploma, the Advanced Diploma and the Extended Project.

EXAMPLES OF FOUNDATION DEGREES IN THE SUBJECT FIELD
Greenwich; Plymouth.

CHOOSING YOUR COURSE (SEE ALSO CH. 1)
Some course features
Cardiff (UWIC) English can be taken with Creative Writing, Drama or Popular Culture.
Durham English Literature is a wide-ranging course focusing on poetry, drama and the novel in Year 1 with modules on selected themes. Years 2 and 3 enable students to follow their special interest. Joint courses are offered with History and Philosophy and the subject can be studied in combined honours in Arts.
East Anglia The School of English Literature and Creative Writing offers a wide range of courses including American and EMglish Literature, English Literature and Drama. There are also courses in English Literature with Creative Writing, English and Comparative Literature, and Literature and joint courses with History, Drama, American Literature. Politics, Film, Philsophy and Art History. Degree courses in Linguistics are also offered.
Liverpool English Language and Literature can be studied from its origins in the Anglo-Saxon period to the modern period, covering all the major literary and linguistic developments. Optional courses are available in the second and third years. There are also seven joint courses with English including Communication Studies, languages, History and Philosophy.
Manchester Nineteen courses are offered involving English Language and Literature. The courses focus on language and the entire range of English literature. A large number of joint courses are offered with Drama, Languages, Philosophy and Linguistics. There is also a course in Language, Literacy and Communication. (High research rating).
Middlesex Thirteen English courses are offered covering English language, English Literature and Creative Writing.
Nottingham The English Studies course covers the entire range of English literature from its beginnings to the 20th century and also medieval and modern English language. English Studies can also be taken with, for example, Latin, Philosophy, Theology and Hispanic Studies. There is also a unique course in Viking Studies covering language, literature, history and archaeology.

Universities and colleges teaching quality See www.qaa.ac.uk; http://unistats.direct.gov.uk.

Top research universities and colleges (RAE 2008) (English Language and Literature) York; London (QM); Edinburgh; Manchester; Exeter; Oxford; Nottingham; Cambridge; De Montfort; Leeds; Warwick; Glasgow; St Andrews; Queen's Belfast; Liverpool; Newcastle.

Examples of sandwich degree courses Brighton; East London; Glamorgan; Huddersfield; Lancaster; Loughborough; Nottingham Trent; Oxford Brookes; Westminster.

ADMISSIONS INFORMATION
Number of applicants per place (approx) Bangor 5; Bath Spa 8; Birmingham 7, (Engl Educ) 4; Birmingham City 9; Blackpool and Fylde (Coll) 2; Bristol 22, (Engl Dr) 45; Bristol UWE 4; Brunel 10; Buckingham 2; Cambridge (A-Sxn Nrs Celt) 2, (Engl) 4. 9; Cardiff (Engl Lit) 6; Central Lancashire 10;

Chester 20; Chichester 4; Cumbria 24; De Montfort 7; Derby 6; Dundee 6; Durham 20; East Anglia (Engl Lit Dr) 22, (Engl Lit Crea Writ) 17, (Engl St) 12; Edge Hill 4; Exeter 13; Glamorgan 8; Gloucestershire 35; Glyndŵr 2; Hertfordshire 6; Huddersfield 5; Hull 14; Hull (Coll) 1; Kingston 6; Lancaster 12; Leeds 10; Leeds Trinity (UC) 7; Leicester 6; Liverpool (Engl Comm St) 7; London (Gold) 9; London (King's) (Engl Film) 15; London (QM) 9; London (RH) 9; London (UCL) 13; London South Bank 5; Loughborough 40; Manchester (Engl Lit) 11, (Engl Lang) 7; Manchester Met 7; Middlesex 8; Newman (UC) 3; Northampton 3; Nottingham 22; Nottingham Trent 21; Oxford (success rate 25%), (Magdalen) 15; Oxford Brookes 15; Portsmouth 8; Reading 11; Roehampton 5; Salford 12; Sheffield 12; Sheffield Hallam 4; Southampton 4; Stirling 9; Sunderland 10; Swansea Met 4; Teesside 5; Trinity Saint David 4; Warwick 15, (Engl Thea) 26; Winchester 3; York 8; York St John 3.

Advice to applicants and planning the UCAS personal statement Applicants should read outside their subject. Details of any writing you have done (for example poetry, short stories) should be provided. Theatre visits and play readings are also important. Keep up to date by reading literary and theatre reviews in the national newspapers (keep a scrapbook of reviews for reference). Evidence is needed of a good writing style. Favourite authors, spare-time reading. Ability to write lucidly, accurately and succinctly. Evidence of literary enthusiasm. General interest in communications – verbal, visual, media. **Manchester** Due to the detailed nature of entry requirements for English Literature and American Studies courses, we are unable to include full details in the prospectus. For complete and up-to-date information on our entry requirements for these courses, please visit our website at www.manchester.ac.uk/ugcourses.

Misconceptions about this course Birmingham City The study of English language means descriptive linguistics – the course won't necessarily enable students to speak or write better English. **Buckingham** Native speakers of English often do not realise that the EFL degree courses are restricted to non-native speakers of English. **East Anglia** (Engl Lit Crea Writ) This is not simply a creative writing course: English literature is the predominant element. **Liverpool** (Engl Comm St) The course is not a training in journalism, although some students go on to work in the press, radio or TV.

Selection interviews Yes Bangor (mature students), Brunel, Cambridge, Canterbury Christ Church, Exeter, Gloucestershire, Huddersfield, Hull, Hull (Coll), Kingston, Lancaster, Leeds Trinity (UC), London (Gold), London (RH), London South Bank, Middlesex, Newcastle, Newport, Oxford (Engl) 27%, (Engl Econ Mgt) 11%, (Engl Lang Lit) 21%, (Engl Mod Lang) 16%, Portsmouth, Reading, Roehampton, Trinity Saint David, Warwick; **Some** Bangor, Bath Spa, Birmingham City, Blackburn (Coll Univ Centre), Blackpool and Fylde (Coll), Bristol, Cardiff (UWIC), Chester, De Montfort, Derby, Dundee, East Anglia, Leeds, Liverpool (Engl Comm St), London (King's), London Met, Loughborough, Salford, Southampton, Swansea Met, Truro (Coll), Wolverhampton.

Interview advice and questions Questions will almost certainly be asked on set A-level texts and any essays which have been submitted prior to the interview. You will also be expected to have read outside your A-level subjects and to answer questions about your favourite authors, poets, dramatists etc. Questions in the past have included: Do you think that class discussion plays an important part in your English course? What is the value of studying a text in depth rather than just reading it for pleasure? What is the difference between satire and comedy? Are books written by women different from those written by men? Why would you go to see a production of *Hamlet*? What are your views on the choice of novels for this year's Booker Prize? Short verbal tests and a précis may be set. See also **Chapter 6. Buckingham** It is useful to know if there is any particular reason why students want a particular programme; for example, for the TEFL degree is a member of the family a teacher? **Cambridge** We look for interviewees who respond positively to ideas, can think on their feet, engage intelligently with critical issues and sustain an argument. If they don't evince any of these we reject them. What books are bad for you? **East Anglia** (Engl Lit Dr) How do you reconcile yourself to an academic interest in literature on the one hand and the belief in practical performance on the other? Interviews are accompanied by auditions. **Leeds** Interview questions based on information supplied in the personal ststement. One third of the applicants are interviewed. Academic ability; current reading interests. **Liverpool** (Engl Comm St) General questions only. Reading interests, general interests, career ambitions. **London (King's)** Interview questions are based on the information in the personal statement. Applicants are asked to prepare a short literary text which will be discussed at interview. **London (UCL)** The interview will focus on an ability to discuss literature in terms of language, plot, characters and genre. Following the interview applicants will be asked to write a critical commentary on an example of unseen prose or verse. **Oxford** Is there a difference between innocence and naivety? If you could make up a word, what would it be? Why? Do you think Hamlet is a bit long? No? Well I do. Is the Bible a fictional work? Was Shakespeare a rebel? **Roehampton** Samples of work taken to interview and discussed. **Warwick** We may ask students to sight-read or to analyse a text. **York** Written essays are required to be submitted at interview.

Reasons for rejection (non-academic) Some are well-informed about English literature – others are not. Inability to respond to questions about their current studies. Lack of enthusiasm for the challenge of studying familiar subjects from a different perspective. Must be able to benefit from the course. Little interest in how people communicate with each other. They don't know a single thing about our course. **Bangor** We reject those who decline interviews. **Bristol** Not enough places to make offers to all those whose qualifications deserve one. **Cambridge** See **Interview advice and questions**. **East Anglia** (Engl Am Lit) Personal statement unconvincing in its commitment to American literature. (Other courses) Poor examples of work submitted. **Leeds** Unsuitable predictions. **Liverpool** (Engl Comm St) Student more suited to a practical course. Ungrammatical Personal Statement. **Oxford** (1) The essay she submitted was poorly written, careless and reductive and, in general, lacking in attention to the subject. She should be encouraged to write less and think more about what she is saying. She seems to put down the first thing that comes into her head. (2) We had the feeling that he rather tended to dismiss texts which did not satisfy the requirements of his personal canon and that he therefore might not be happy pursuing a course requiring the study of texts from all periods. (3) In her essay on Bronte she took a phrase from Arnold which was metaphorical (to do with hunger) and applied it literally, writing at length about the diet of the characters. **Reading** None. If they have reached the interview we have already eliminated all other factors. **Sheffield Hallam** Apparent lack of eagerness to tackle all three strands of the course (literature, language and creative writing). **Southampton** Insufficient or patchy academic achievement. Applicants coming from non-standard academic backgrounds are assessed in terms of their individual situations.

AFTER-RESULTS ADVICE
Offers to applicants repeating A-levels Higher Sheffield Hallam, Southampton (varies), Warwick; **Possibly higher** Lancaster, Newcastle, Oxford Brookes; **Same** Bangor, Birmingham City, Blackpool and Fylde (Coll), Bristol, Cambridge, Cardiff, Cardiff (UWIC), Chester, Chichester, Cumbria, De Montfort, Derby, Dundee, Durham, East Anglia, Edge Hill, Hull, Leeds, Leeds Trinity (UC), Liverpool, Liverpool Hope, London (Gold), London (RH), Loughborough, Manchester Met, Newman (UC), Newport, Nottingham, Nottingham Trent, Portsmouth, Reading, Roehampton, St Mary's Twickenham (UC), Salford, Sheffield, Staffordshire, Stirling, Suffolk (Univ Campus), Trinity Saint David, Ulster, Winchester, Wolverhampton, York, York St John.

GRADUATE DESTINATIONS AND EMPLOYMENT (2007/8 HESA)
English graduates surveyed 7675 **Employed** 2880 **In further study** 1795 **Assumed unemployed** 725

Creative Writing graduates surveyed 620 **Employed** 210 **In further study** 80 **Assumed unemployed** 105

Career note English graduates work in the media, management, public and social services, business, administration and IT, sales retail, the cultural industries and the teaching profession. Those who have undertaken courses in creative writing could aim for careers in advertising, public relations, journalism or publishing.

OTHER DEGREE SUBJECTS FOR CONSIDERATION
Communication Studies; Drama; Language courses; Linguistics; Literature; Media Studies.

ENVIRONMENTAL SCIENCES/STUDIES

(including **Conservation, Ecology, Environmental Health** and **Environmental Management**; see also **Biological Sciences, Biology, Engineering (Civil), Geography, Geology/Geological Sciences, Marine/Maritime Studies, Town and Country Planning**)

Environmental Science/Studies courses need to be considered with care as, depending on their content and specialisms, they lead to very different careers. Environmental Health courses usually focus on the training of environmental health officers whilst Environmental Studies or Science degrees cover a range of subjects with options which may include biology, geography, geology, oceanography, chemistry, legal, social and political issues.

Useful websites www.cieh.org; www.ends.co.uk; www.enn.com; www.iagre.org.uk; www.defra.gov.uk; www.socenv.org.uk; www.ies-uk.org.uk; www.noc.soton.ac.uk.

NB The points totals shown to the left of the institutions are for ease of reference only. It must not be assumed that Tariff points are always used by institutions or that they can be substituted for an offer in grades. The level of an offer is not necessarily indicative of the quality of a course.

COURSE OFFERS INFORMATION

Subject requirements/preferences GCSE English, mathematics and a science (often chemistry or biology) usually required. **AL** One or two science subjects are usually stipulated; mathematics may be required. Meteorology Mathematics, physics and another science may be required sometimes with specified grades, eg **Reading** mathematics and physics grade B.

NB In 2012 universities and colleges will differ in their use of GCE AL/AS unit grade information, A* grades, the Extended Project (EPQ), the Advanced Diploma and the Cambridge Pre-U examination when considering applicants and making offers. An EPQ may be accepted in place of an AS subject. Check websites of universities and colleges for the latest offers information.

Your target offers and examples of courses provided by each institution

380 pts **Edinburgh** – Check with Ad Tutor A*AA 2nd yr entry (Ecol Sci) (IB 36 pts)
London (UCL) – AAA+AS–ABB+AS (Env Geog) (IB 34–38 pts)

360 pts **Birmingham** – AAA (Env Geosci Int Yr) (IB 34–38 pts)
East Anglia – AAA–AAB (Meteor Ocean courses MSci) (IB 34–33 pts HL 666 inc maths)
Imperial London – AAA 360 pts (Env Geosci)
Leeds – AAA (Env Mgt (Int)) (IB 38 pts)
St Andrews – AAA (Env Biol Goog)

340 pts **Bristol** – AAB–ABB (Env Geosci) (IB 35 pts)
Cardiff – AAB–ABB (Ecol) (IB 34 pts)
East Anglia – AAB (Clim Sci BSc N Am) (IB 33 pts HL 555)
Exeter – AAB–BBB (Renew Ener) (IB 34–29 pts)
Imperial London – AAB (Ecol Env Biol) (IB 38 pts)
Lancaster – AAB 340 pts (Ecol Abrd)
London (QM) – 340 pts (Env Geog) (IB 32 pts)
London LSE – AAB (Env Plcy Econ) (IB 37 pts HL 666)
Manchester – AAB–BBB (Blt Nat Env courses) (IB 32–35 pts)
St Andrews – AAB (Sust Dev MA) (IB 36 pts)
Sheffield – AAB (Ecol BSc) (IB 33 pts)
Southampton – AAB (Env Sci MEnvSci) (IB 34 pts)

320 pts **Birmingham** – ABB–BBC (Env Geosci) (IB 28–34 pts)
Durham – ABB (Env Geosci) (IB 34 pts)
East Anglia – ABB–BBB (Meteor Ocean BSc) (IB 32–31 pts)
Edinburgh – Check with Ad Tutor ABB–AAA 1st yr entry (Ecol Sci) (IB 32-37 pts)
Glasgow – ABB (Env Chem Geog) (IB 32 pts)
Lancaster – ABB 320 pts (Env Biol Abrd)
Leeds – ABB–BBB 320–300 pts (Ecol Env Biol) (IB 34–32 pts)
Liverpool – ABB–BBB (Ecol Env) (IB 33–30 pts HL biol 6)

London LSE – ABB (Env Plcy Econ) (IB 37 pts HL 666)
Loughborough – 320 pts (Cheml Eng Env Prot) (IB 34 pts)
Newcastle – ABB–BBB (Env Sci) (IB 32 pts)
Nottingham – ABB–BBB (Env Sci Cert Euro St) (IB 34–32 pts)
Reading – 320 pts (Env Sci MEnv) (IB 31 pts)
St Andrews – ABB (Env Geosci courses) (IB 30–32 pts)
Southampton – AAB–ABB (Env Sci BSc) (IB 34–32 pts)
Stirling – ABB 2nd yr entry (Ecol)
Sussex – ABB–BBC (Ecol Cons) (IB 32–34 pts)
Warwick – ABB (Env Biol) (IB 34 pts)
York – ABB-BBB (Env Geog)

300 pts **Aberdeen** – BBB 300 pts 2nd yr entry (Env Sci; Anim Ecol; Ecol; Wldlf Mgt)
Aberystwyth – 300 pts (Env Sci) (IB 28 pts)
Birmingham – BBB (Env Sci) (IB 30–32 pts)
Bristol UWE – 300 pts (Cons Biol)
Cardiff – BBB 300 pts (Ecol) (IB 32 pts)
Edinburgh – Check with Ad Tutor BBB 1st yr entry (Env Arch) (IB 32 pts)
Essex – 300–260 pts (Ecol) (IB 26–28 pts)
Lancaster – BBB 300 pts (Sust Eng BEng)
Leeds – BBB (Env Mgt BA) (IB 32 pts)
Liverpool – BBB 300pts (Env Mgt)
London (QM) – 300–340 pts (Glob Chng Env Econ Dev) (IB 32 pts)
London (RH) – BBB (Env Geol BSc) (IB 32 pts HL 6)
Manchester – BBB (Env St) (IB 32 pts)
Nottingham – BBB–BCC (Env Biol) (IB 24–30 pts)
Plymouth – BBB 300–360 pts (Mar Biol Cstl Ecol) (IB 24 pts)
Queen's Belfast – BBB (Env Biol) (IB 30 pts)
Reading – 300 pts (Meteor Clim)
Warwick – BBB (Biol Sci (Env Res)) (IB 32 pts)

280 pts **Bangor** – 280–320 pts (Env Sci MEnvSci) (IB 28 pts)
Brighton – BBC (Env Sci) (IB 28 pts)
Bristol UWE – 280 pts (Geog Env Mgt) (IB 28 pts)
Coventry – 280–300 pts (Clim Chng Sust; Geog Nat Haz)
Huddersfield – 280 pts (Bus St Env Mgt)
Keele – 280–300 pts (Env Sust; App Env Sci)
Manchester – BBC (Env Mgt)
Northumbria – 280 pts (Env Mgt; Env Hlth)
Oxford Brookes – BBC (Env Sci courses) (IB 30 pts)
Staffordshire – 280 pts (Env Cons) (IB 24 pts)
Stirling – BBC 1st yr entry (Env Sci; Cons Sci; Ecol)
Ulster – 280 pts (Env Hlth) (IB 32 pts)

260 pts **Bangor** – 260–320 pts (Ecol) (IB 28 pts)
Bournemouth – 260 pts (Env Foren) (IB 28 pts)
Bristol UWE – 260–300 pts (Env Sci) (IB 24–28 pts)
Liverpool Hope – 260 pts (Env Biol Comb; Env Mgt Comb)
Strathclyde – BCC 1st yr entry (Env Hlth)

240 pts **Aberdeen** – CCC 240 pts 1st yr entry (Ecol) (IB 28 pts)
Bangor – 240–260 pts (Env Chem) (IB 28 pts)
Bolton – 240 pts (Env St courses)
Bournemouth – 240 pts (Ecol Wldlf Cons)
Brighton – CCC/BCD 240–280 pts (Env Biol Educ)
Canterbury Christ Church – 240 pts (Env Sci courses)
Chester – 240 pts (Nat Haz Mgt)
De Montfort – 240 pts (Grn Ener Tech)
Dundee – CCC (Env Sci; Env Sci Geog; Int Bus Env Sust; Renew Ener)

Glasgow Caledonian – CCC (Env Mgt Plan)
Greenwich – 240 pts (Env Sci) (IB 24 pts)
Hertfordshire – 240 pts (Env Mgt courses) (IB 24–26 pts)
Hull – 240–300 pts (Env Mgt)
Kingston – 240–280 pts (Env Mgt; Env Sci; Env Haz Disas Mgt; Sust Dev; App Env Geol)
Liverpool John Moores – 240 pts (Pblc Hlth (Env))
Plymouth – 240–280 pts (Env Sci) (IB 28 pts)
Portsmouth – 240–300 pts (Mar Env Sci; Env Sci)
Roehampton – 240–300 pts (Biol Sci)
Teesside – 240–280 pts (Env Sci)
Worcester – 240–280 pts (Env Sci)

230 pts **Sheffield Hallam** – 230 pts (Env Mgt; Env Cons)
220 pts **Bangor** – 220–260 pts (Mar Env St) (IB 28 pts)
Bath Spa – 220–260 pts (Env Sci)
Bradford – 220–240 pts (Geog Env Mgt)
Cardiff (UWIC) – 220 pts (Env Hlth)
Central Lancashire – 220–240 pts (Env Mgt)
Coventry – 220–240 pts (Env Hlth) (IB 27 pts)
Edge Hill – 220 pts (Env Sci)
Edinburgh Napier – 220 pts (Ecotour; Env Biol)
Harper Adams (UC) – 220–240 pts (Cntry Env Mgt)
Hull – 220–280 pts (Ecol; Env Sci)
Liverpool John Moores – 220–260 pts (Out Educ)
Manchester Met – 220–240 pts (Ecol Cons) (IB 27 pts)
Northampton – 220–260 pts (Env Sci (Clim Chng) (Lnd Ecol) (Wst Mgt)) (IB 24 pts)
Nottingham Trent – 220 pts (Wldlf Cons)
Ulster – 220 pts (Env Sci courses) (IB 24 pts)
Worcester – 220–240 pts (Cons Ecol; Ecol)

200 pts **Glyndŵr** – 200 pts (Renew Ener Sust Tech)
Kingston – 200–280 pts (Env St courses)
Leeds Met – 200 pts (Pblc Hlth Env Hlth) (IB 26 pts)
Middlesex – 200–280 pts (Env Pblc Hlth)
Nottingham Trent – 200 pts (Env Sci)
Salford – 200 pts (Wldlf Prac Cons; Env Mgt; Env Hlth)

180 pts **Derby** – 180–240 pts (Env Haz)
Salford – 180 pts (Env Geog) (IB 24 pts)
Southampton Solent – 180 pts (Geog Env St)
Trinity Saint David – 180–240 pts (Arch (Env)) (IB 26 pts)
Writtle (Coll) – 180 pts (Cons Env (Biol Surv))

160 pts **London South Bank** – 160 pts (Urb Env Plan)
SAC (Scottish CAg) – CC (Sust Env Mgt)
Swansea Met – 160–340 pts (Env Cons)
UHI Millennium Inst – CC (Sust Rural Dev)
Wolverhampton – 160 pts (Env Hlth)

Open University – contact +44 (0)845 300 6090 **or** www.openuniversity.co.uk/you (Env St)

Alternative offers

See **Chapter 7** and **Appendix 1** for grades/UCAS Tariff points information for the International Baccalaureate, Scottish Highers/Advanced Highers, the Welsh Baccalaureate, the Irish Leaving Certificate, the Cambridge Pre-U Diploma, the Advanced Diploma and the Extended Project.

EXAMPLES OF FOUNDATION DEGREES IN THE SUBJECT FIELD

Askham Bryan (Coll); Bournemouth; Cumbria; Glyndŵr; Leeds City (Coll); Manchester (Coll); Nottingham Trent; Suffolk (Univ Campus); Writtle (Coll).

CHOOSING YOUR COURSE (SEE ALSO CH. 1)

Some course features

Birmingham Specialisation in four pathways (applied ecology, water in the environment, atmospheric processes and earth surface processes) follows a broad first year Environmental Science course. There are also courses in Environmental Management and Environmental Geoscience.

Brighton The Environmental Sciences course involves a study of the human and physical environment, ecology, energy and pollution. There are also degrees in Environmental Hazards, covering geography, health, pollution and human hazards, and Earth and Ocean Science, Environmental Biology and Ecology and Biogeography.

Coventry The Environmental Health course covers food, health and safety and leads to professional status as an Environmental Health Officer.

Kingston Pathways in Environmental Science include ecology, conservation and resource management. Options include languages, business and human geography. Enviromental Studies is offered with a range of subjects including Business Management. There are also degree courses in Natural History, Environmental Hazards and Disaster Management.

Liverpool Hope Environmental Management is offered as part of a combined honours (BA/BSc) programme. Popular combinations incude Geography, Sport Studies and Sport Development.

London (UCL) European Social and Political Studies is a four-year degree that combines the study of one or two European languages (from Dutch, French, German, Italian, Russian, Scandinavian languages and Spanish) with a chosen humanities or social science specialisation including Anthropology, Economics, Geography, History, Law, Philosophy or Politics. The third year is spent abroad. Degree courses are also offered in East European Studies with Bulgarian, Czech, Slovak, Finnish, Hungarian, Polish, Romanian, Serbian, and Ukrainian.

Manchester The Environmental Science degree programme enables students to specialise in their particular fields of interest within biology, earth sciences, chemistry or biology. The course in Environmental Studies offers similar topics but deals more with the relationship between humans and their environment. Entrance scholarships available.

Newcastle The Environmental Science course covers management, ecology, tropical environments and biological conservation. Courses are also offered in Countryside Management and Rural Studies.

Universities and colleges teaching quality See www.qaa.ac.uk; http://unistats.direct.gov.uk.

Top research universities and colleges (RAE 2008) (Geography and Environmental Studies) Bristol; Cambridge; Durham; Oxford; London (QM); Leeds; London (King's); London (UCL); London LSE; Sheffield; London (RH); Aberystwyth; London (Birk); Reading; East Anglia; Manchester; Southampton.

(Earth Systems and Environmental Sciences) Cambridge; Oxford; London (UCL); Bristol; London (RH).

Examples of sandwich degree courses Bangor; Birmingham; Bradford; Brighton; Bristol UWE; Cardiff; Cardiff (UWIC); Coventry; Edinburgh Napier; Glasgow Caledonian; Harper Adams (UC); Hertfordshire; Kingston; Liverpool John Moores; Loughborough; Manchester Met; Nottingham Trent; Reading; Salford; Southampton Solent; Teesside; Ulster; West Scotland; Wolverhampton.

ADMISSIONS INFORMATION

Number of applicants per place (approx) Abertay Dundee 5; Aberystwyth 3; Bangor 3; Bath Spa 2; Birmingham 5; Bournemouth 4; Bradford 3; Bristol 7; Bristol UWE 1; Cardiff (UWIC) 4; Coventry 9; De Montfort 9; Dundee 6; Durham 5; East Anglia 7; Edinburgh 1; Essex 3; Glamorgan 1; Glasgow Caledonian 1; Gloucestershire 11; Glyndŵr 3; Greenwich 2; Harper Adams (UC) 5; Hertfordshire 5; Hull 8; Kingston 3; Lancaster 11; Leeds (Env Sci Ener) 2; Liverpool John Moores 5; London (King's) 5; London (RH) 8; London LSE 8; Manchester Met (Env Sci) 5; Northampton 4; Northumbria 8; Nottingham 6; Nottingham Trent 3; Oxford Brookes 13; Plymouth 8; Portsmouth 5; Roehampton 3; Salford 8; Sheffield Hallam 8; Southampton 5; Stirling 10; Strathclyde 1; Trinity Saint David 3; Ulster 16; Wolverhampton 2; Worcester 7; York 4.

Advice to applicants and planning the UCAS personal statement 'We want doers, not just thinkers' is one comment from an admissions tutor. Describe any field courses which you have attended; make an effort to visit one of the National Parks. Discuss these visits and identify any particular aspects which impressed you. Outline travel interests. Give details of work as a conservation volunteer and other outside-school activities. Strong communication skills, people-oriented work experience. Watch your spelling and grammar! What sparked your interest in Environmental Science? Discuss your field trips. (Env Hlth courses) A basic knowledge of environmental health as opposed to environmental sciences. Work experience in an environmental health department is looked upon very favourably. See also **Appendix 4**. **Lancaster** Two A level subjects required from biology, chemistry, computing, environmental science, geography or geology.

Misconceptions about this course **Bangor** Students should note that only simple mathematical skills are required for this course. **Leeds** (Ener Env Sci) Note that the course is closer to environmental technology than to environmental science. **Southampton** This is not just a course for environmentalists, for example links with BP, IBM etc. **Wolverhampton** This is a course in Environmental Science, not Environmental Studies: there is a difference. **York** (Env Econ Env Mgt) Some students worry that the economics part of the course will be too difficult, which is not the case.

Selection interviews Yes Bradford, Bristol UWE, Cambridge, Coventry, Durham, Glamorgan, Gloucestershire, Greenwich, Harper Adams (UC) (advisory), Hertfordshire, Kingston, Manchester Met, Newcastle, Newport, Nottingham, Nottingham Trent, Oxford Brookes, Sheffield Hallam, Strathclyde, Sussex, Trinity Saint David; **Some** Anglia Ruskin, Bangor, Bath Spa, Birmingham, Cardiff (UWIC), Derby, Dundee, East Anglia, London (King's), Plymouth, Salford, Southampton, Staffordshire, York.

Interview advice and questions Environmental issues are constantly in the news, so keep abreast of developments. You could be asked to discuss any particular environmental problems in the area in which you live and to justify your stance on any environmental issues on which you have strong opinions. See also **Chapter 6**. **Bath Spa** Questions on school work, current affairs and field courses. **East Anglia** Can you display an informed interest in any aspect of environmental science?

Reasons for rejection (non-academic) Inability to be aware of the needs of others.

AFTER-RESULTS ADVICE

Offers to applicants repeating A-levels Higher Greenwich, Lancaster, London (King's), Nottingham, Nottingham Trent, Strathclyde; **Possibly higher** Aberystwyth, Bradford, Northumbria; **Same** Bangor, Birmingham, Brighton, Cardiff (UWIC), Derby, Dundee, East Anglia, Leeds, Liverpool John Moores, Manchester Met, Plymouth, SAC (Scottish CAg), Salford, Southampton, Ulster, Wolverhampton.

GRADUATE DESTINATIONS AND EMPLOYMENT (2007/8 HESA)

Graduates surveyed 810 **Employed** 290 **In further study** 185 **Assumed unemployed** 100

Career note Some graduates find work with government departments, local authorities, statutory and voluntary bodies in areas like land management and pollution control. Others go into a range of non-scientific careers.

OTHER DEGREE SUBJECTS FOR CONSIDERATION

Biological Sciences; Biology; Chemistry; Earth Sciences; Environmental Engineering; Geography; Geology; Meteorology; Ocean Sciences/Oceanography; Town and Country Planning.

EUROPEAN STUDIES

(see also **French, German, International Relations, Languages, Russian and East European Studies**)

European Studies is an increasingly popular subject and in many cases offers the language student an opportunity to study modern languages within the context of a European country (for example, economics, politics, legal, social and cultural aspects). In these courses there is usually a strong emphasis on the written and spoken word. It is important to note, also, that many courses in other subjects offer the opportunity to study in Europe.

Useful websites www.europa.eu; www.eaces.net; www.britishcouncil.org/erasmus; see also **Languages**.

NB The points totals shown to the left of the institutions are for ease of reference only. It must not be assumed that Tariff points are always used by institutions or that they can be substituted for an offer in grades. The level of an offer is not necessarily indicative of the quality of a course.

COURSE OFFERS INFORMATION

Subject requirements/preferences GCSE English and a foreign language for all courses and possibly mathematics. Grades may be stipulated. **AL** A modern language usually required.

NB In 2012 universities and colleges will differ in their use of GCE AL/AS unit grade information, A* grades, the Extended Project (EPQ), the Advanced Diploma and the Cambridge Pre-U examination when considering applicants and making offers. An EPQ may be accepted in place of an AS subject. Check websites of universities and colleges for the latest offers information.

Your target offers and examples of courses provided by each institution

400 pts   **London (UCL)** – A*AA+AS (Euro Soc Pol St) (IB 39 pts)
360 pts   **Bath** – AAA–ABB (Modn Langs Euro St) (IB 34 pts HL lang 6)
　　　　　　Exeter – AAA–AAB (Bus Econ Euro St) (IB 30–32 pts)
　　　　　　Lancaster – AAA 360 pts (Euro Leg St) (IB 32 pts HL 17–18 pts)
　　　　　　London (King's) – AAB+AS–AAA+AS(Fr) (Euro St (Fr/Ger/Span)) (IB 34 pts)
　　　　　　Newcastle – AAA–ABB (Gov EU St) (IB 32–36 pts)
340 pts   **Birmingham** – AAB–ABB (Euro Pol Soty Econ) (IB 33–36 pts)
　　　　　　Glasgow – AAB (Cnt E Euro St) (IB 34 pts)
　　　　　　Lancaster – AAB (Euro Mgt Fr/Ger/Ital/Span)
　　　　　　Manchester – AAB–BBC (Euro St Modn Lang (Fr/Ger/Ital/Port/Russ/Span)) (IB 33–30 pts)
　　　　　　Sussex – AAB–ABB (Pol Contemp Euro St) (IB 34–36 pts)
320 pts   **Cardiff** – ABB–BBB (EU St) (IB 33 pts)
　　　　　　East Anglia – ABB–BBB (Int Rel Euro Pol) (IB 35 pts)
　　　　　　Kent – 320 pts (Euro Econ; Euro Cult)
　　　　　　Leeds – ABB (Euro Pol) (IB 34 pts)
　　　　　　Leicester – ABB (Euro St) (IB 28–30 pts)
　　　　　　London (RH) – ABB–BBB (Euro St Fr/Ger/Ital/Span)
　　　　　　Nottingham – ABB (Modn Euro St) (IB 32 pts)
　　　　　　Southampton – ABB 320 pts (Langs Contemp Euro St) (IB 32 pts)
　　　　　　Sussex – ABB–BBB (Euro St courses)
　　　　　　Swansea – ABB (Geog Euro St)
300 pts   **Aberdeen** – BBB (Euro St) (IB 28 pts)
　　　　　　Aston – 300–320 pts (Euro St Fr/Ger/Span) (IB 31–33 pts)
　　　　　　Birmingham – BBB 300 pts (Modn Langs Euro St (Soty Cult Hist) (Pol)) (IB 32 pts)
　　　　　　Bristol UWE – 300–340 pts (Euro Int Law) (IB 26–32 pts)
　　　　　　Dundee – BBB–CCC 300–240 pts (Euro St courses) (IB 29 pts)
　　　　　　Edinburgh – BBB–AAA (Modn Euro Lang EU St)
　　　　　　Essex – 300 pts (Euro St Pol) (IB 27 pts)
　　　　　　Loughborough – 300–320 pts (Euro St) (IB 32 pts)
　　　　　　Nottingham – BBB–BBC (Euro St courses) (IB 32 pts)
　　　　　　Reading – 300–320 pts (Euro St; Euro Cult Hist)
　　　　　　Strathclyde – BBB–BCC (Civ Eng Euro St) (IB 30–34 pts)
280 pts   **Kent** – 280 pts (Euro St (Soc Sci) courses) (IB 28–32 pts)
　　　　　　London (QM) – 280 pts (Euro St courses) (IB 32 pts)
　　　　　　Portsmouth – 280–300 pts (Euro Bus (Fr/Ger/Span); Euro St)
　　　　　　Stirling – BBC (Euro Film Media) (IB 32 pts)
260 pts   **Dundee** – BCC 260 pts 1st yr entry (Euro Pol) (IB 30 pts)
　　　　　　Nottingham Trent – 260 pts (Euro St courses) (IB 24 pts)

240 pts **Manchester Met** – 240 pts (Int Bus (Euro Mgt)) (IB 27 pts)
        Ulster – 240 pts (Euro St courses) (IB 24 pts)
220 pts **Manchester Met** – 220 pts (Euro St Comb Hons)
200 pts **Portsmouth** – 200–280 pts (Euro St Int Rel)

        Open University – contact +44 (0)845 300 6090 **or** www.openuniversity.co.uk/you (Euro St)

Alternative offers
See **Chapter 7** and **Appendix 1** for grades/UCAS Tariff points information for the International Baccalaureate, Scottish Highers/Advanced Highers, the Welsh Baccalaureate, the Irish Leaving Certificate, the Cambridge Pre-U Diploma, the Advanced Diploma and the Extended Project.

CHOOSING YOUR COURSE (SEE ALSO CH. 1)
Some course features
Aberystwyth The four-year BA course in European Studies combines a European language (French, German or Spanish) with a study of European economic, political and legal institutions. There are also separate degree courses in European Languages, European History and European Politics.
Aston The European Studies programme is a joint or combined honours course offering a choice between French or German and topics covering the history and development of the European Union, European law, current affairs and international relations. European Studies is also offered with Business Administration, Public Policy and Management, and Sociology. There is a one year placement year following Year 2.
East Anglia In the School of International and European Studies a foundation (first) year leads to a wide range of options.
Essex European Studies is offered with a range of subjects including French, German, Italian, Spanish, and Politics and Economics. Beginners courses are possible and it is possible to transfer between courses.
Hertfordshire The European Studies programme offers courses with 12 other subjects such as Business, Health Studies, Biology, Geography, Law, Sports Studies and Tourism.
Portsmouth European Studies is a three-year course covering European history, culture and a specialist knowledge of EU policy of a particular European country. Language study is optional. European Studies can be taken with International Relations, Law or languages.
Southampton The Contemporary Europe degree comprises a study of the history and politics of Europe and European Union institutions, with options in economics, history, law or politics. Two European languages are studied from French, German or Spanish. Portuguese is offered as a minor language. Scholarships available.
Sussex There is a degree in International Relations and Contemporary European Studies. The latter can be taken as part of a joint degree or as a minor subject.

Universities and colleges teaching quality See www.qaa.ac.uk; http://unistats.direct.gov.uk.

Top research universities and colleges (RAE 2008) Southampton; Sussex; Birmingham; Portsmouth; Cardiff; Bath; Liverpool; Aberystwyth.

ADMISSIONS INFORMATION
Number of applicants per place (approx) Aberystwyth 10; Aston 5; Cardiff 5; Dundee 6; Durham 2; East Anglia 11; Hull 6; Kent 11; Lancaster 9; Leicester 15; London (King's) 7; London (UCL) 2; London South Bank 6; Loughborough 4; Northumbria 7; Nottingham 6; Nottingham Trent 12; Portsmouth 5.

Advice to applicants and planning the UCAS personal statement Try to identify an interest you have in the country relevant to your studies. Visits to that country should be described. Read the national newspapers and magazines and keep up to date with political and economic developments. Show your interest in the culture and civilisation of Europe as a whole, through, for example, European travel. Show your motivation for choosing the course and give details of your personal achievements and any future career plans, showing your international awareness and perspective.

Selection interviews **Yes** Durham, East Anglia, Hull, London (Gold), London Met, London South Bank, Stirling, Sussex; **Some** Cardiff, Dundee, Kent (not usually), Liverpool John Moores, Loughborough, Portsmouth.

Interview advice and questions Whilst your interest in studying a language may be the main reason for applying for this subject, the politics, economics and culture of European countries are constantly in the news. You should keep up-to-date with any such topics concerning your chosen country and be prepared for questions. A language test may occupy part of the interview. See also **Chapter 6**. **Loughborough** No tests. Interview designed to inform students about the course.

Reasons for rejection (non-academic) Poor powers of expression. Lack of ideas on any issues. Lack of enthusiasm.

AFTER-RESULTS ADVICE
Offers to applicants repeating A-levels **Higher** Aberystwyth, East Anglia; **Same** Aston, Cardiff, Dundee, Liverpool John Moores, London South Bank, Loughborough.

GRADUATE DESTINATIONS AND EMPLOYMENT (2007/8 HESA)
See also **Languages** and separate language tables.

Graduates surveyed 185 **Employed** 85 **In further study** 45 **Assumed unemployed** 10

Career note See **Languages**.

OTHER DEGREE SUBJECTS FOR CONSIDERATION
Business and Management; History; International Relations; Politics; Language courses.

FILM, RADIO, VIDEO and TV STUDIES

(see also **Art and Design (Graphic Design), Communication Studies/Communication, Engineering (Acoustics and Sound), Media Studies, Photography**)

A wide range of courses in this field are on offer although applicants should be aware that many courses cover theoretical or historical aspects of the subject. Students wishing to follow courses with practical applications must check with the institution beforehand to determine how much time in the course is spent on actual film-making or video production.

Useful websites www.bfi.org.uk; www.film.com; www.allmovie.com; www.bksts.com; www.imdb.com; www.fwfr.com; www.bafta.org; www.movingimage.us; www.britfilms.com; www.filmsite.org; www.festival-cannes.com/en; www.bbc.co.uk/jobs; http://rogerebert.suntimes.com; www.radiostudiesnetwork.org.uk.

NB The points totals shown to the left of the institutions are for ease of reference only. It must not be assumed that Tariff points are always used by institutions or that they can be substituted for an offer in grades. The level of an offer is not necessarily indicative of the quality of a course.

COURSE OFFERS INFORMATION
Subject requirements/preferences **GCSE** English usually required. Courses vary, check prospectuses. **AL** English may be stipulated for some courses.

NB In 2012 universities and colleges will differ in their use of GCE AL/AS unit grade information, A* grades, the Extended Project (EPQ), the Advanced Diploma and the Cambridge Pre-U examination when considering applicants and making offers. An EPQ may be accepted in place of an AS subject. Check websites of universities and colleges for the latest offers information.

Your target offers and examples of courses provided by each institution
390 pts Warwick – AABb (Film Lit)
360 pts London (King's) – AAB+AS (Film St) (IB 34 pts)

340 pts **East Anglia** – AAB–BBB (Span Film TV) (IB 31–33 pts)
Exeter – AAB–ABB (Film St Fr/Ger/Ital/Russ/Span) (IB 34–32 pts)
Glasgow – AAB (Film TV St courses) (IB 34 pts)
Kent – 340 pts (Film St) (IB 35–33 pts)
Leicester – AAB (Modn Langs Film St) (IB 30–32 pts)
St Andrews – AAB (Film St Scot Hist) (IB 32 pts)
Southampton – AAB–ABB (Film Span) (IB 34 pts HL 17 pts)
Sussex – AAB–BBB (Film St) (IB 32–36 pts)

320 pts **Aberystwyth** – 260–320 pts (Film TV St courses) (IB 24–26 pts)
Birmingham – ABB (Modn Lang Film St)
Bournemouth – 320 pts (Script Film TV)
Bristol UWE – 320–340 pts (Film St Dr/Engl/Media)
Kent – 320 pts (Film St Hist Phil Art; Film St Comp; Film St Engl Am Postcol Lit)
Lancaster – ABB–BBB (Film St Engl Lit) (IB 29–30 pts)
London (QM) – 320 pts (Compar Lit Film St) (IB 32 pts)
London (RH) – ABB–ABbb (Film TV St)
Nottingham – ABB (Film TV St Russ) (IB 32 pts)
St Andrews – ABB (Psy Film St) (IB 32 pts)
Westminster – ABB (Film TV Prod) (IB 30 pts)
York – ABB (Writ Dir Perf) (IB 31 pts)

300 pts **Aberdeen** – BBB (Film Vis Cult) (IB 28 pts)
Aberystwyth – 260–300 pts (Scngrph St courses) (IB 24–26 pts)
Birmingham City – 260–300 pts (Film Prod Tech)
Brunel – Contact admissions office (Thea Film TV St; Thea Gms Des)
Essex – BBB 320–300 pts (Hist Film St) (IB 34–32 pts)
Hertfordshire – 280–300 pts (Film TV (Fctn) (Doc) (Enter); Engl Lang Comm Film)
Leeds – BBB (Cnma Photo) (IB 32 pts)
Leicester – BBB (Film St Engl) (IB 30–32 pts)
Liverpool – BBB (inc B/C lang) (Film St (Euro) Lang) (IB 30 pts)
Queen Margaret – 300 pts (Stg Scrn)
Queen's Belfast – BBB–BBCb (Film St courses)
Reading – 300–340 pts (Engl Lit Film Thea; Film Thea)
Surrey – BBB 300 pts (Film St; Film St Crea Writ)
Swansea – BBB 300 pts (Scrn St joint courses)

280 pts **Birmingham City** – 260–280 pts (TV Tech Prod)
Brunel – Contact admissions office (Engl Film TV St; Gms Des Engl)
Edge Hill – 280 pts (Film St)
Glamorgan – 280–320 pts (Film Vid; Film St)
Gloucestershire – 280–300 pts (Film St; Dig Film Prod; Film St Crea Writ)
Leeds Trinity (UC) – (Film St; Film TV St)
Lincoln – 280 pts (Film TV; Film TV Jrnl joint courses)
Liverpool John Moores – 280–320 pts (Film St Crea Writ)
London Met – 240–280 pts (Film Broad Prod)
Manchester Met – 280 pts (Engl Film)
Northumbria – 280 pts (Film TV St)
Oxford Brookes – BBC (Film St Jap St) (IB 30 pts)
Reading – 280–300 pts (Film Thea (Ger)) (IB 32 pts)
Sheffield Hallam – 280 pts (Film Media Prod)
Staffordshire – 280 pts (Film Prod Tech Mgt; Film Prod Mus Tech)
Stirling – BBC (Glob Cnma Cult) (IB 32 pts)

260 pts **Bangor** – 260–300 pts (Film St courses)
Birmingham City – 260–280 pts (Media Comm (Rad Prod) (TV Vid))
Bradford – 260 pts (TV Prod)
Brunel – Contact admissions office (Gms Des Snc Arts)
Central Lancashire – 260–300 pts (Film TV Scrnwrit; Film Prod)

For a quick reference offers calculator, fold out the inside back cover.

BA Film and Television Studies

Joint honours also available with
Theatre
Music
English
Games Design

BA Joint Honours Games Design

with
Film and Television Studies
Music
Sonic Arts
Creative Writing
English
Theatre

Find out more about the School of Arts at
www.brunel.ac.uk

Brunel
UNIVERSITY
L O N D O N

Dundee – BCC (Engl Film St)
Hull – 260–300 pts (Film St courses)
London Met – 260 pts (Film St)
Middlesex – see Admissions Tutor 260 pts (TV Prod)
Newport – 260 pts (Doc Film TV)
Queen Margaret – 260 pts (Film Media)
Stirling – BCC (Film Media courses)

240 pts **Brighton** – CCC (Mov Imag) (IB 28 pts)
Canterbury Christ Church – CCC–BCC (Film Rad TV St (Film/Rad/TV/Broad/Animat))
Chester – 240–280 pts (TV Prod courses) (IB 24 pts)
Cumbria – 240 pts (Film TV Prod; Film St Joint Hons)
De Montfort – 240 pts (Photo Vid)
Edinburgh (CA) – 240 pts (Film TV)
Edinburgh Napier – 240 pts (Photo Film)
Lincoln – 240 pts (Doc Prod)
Manchester Met – 240–280 pts (Contemp Film Vid; Film TV St; Film TV Cult St)
Nottingham Trent – 240 pts (Des Film TV; Film TV Joint Hons)
Portsmouth – 240–300 pts (Film St courses)
Roehampton – 240–320 pts (Film)
Sheffield Hallam – 240 pts (Film St)
Southampton Solent – 240 pts (Film TV St; Film; Engl Film; Scrnwrit; TV Vid Prod; TV Std Prod)
Sunderland – 240 pts (Film Media (TV Rad); Dig Film Prod; Media Prod (TV Rad))
Ulster – 240 pts (Film St courses)
Winchester – 240–280 pts (Film Cnma Tech; Film St)
Worcester – 240–300 pts (Film St)

220 pts **Bath Spa** – 220–280 pts (Film Scrn St courses)
Bournemouth – 220 pts (Film Prod Cnma)
Falmouth (UC) – 220 pts (Film)
Huddersfield – 220 pts (Dig Film Vis Efcts Prod; Film Animat Mus Ent)
Kingston – 220–360 pts (Film St courses)
Northampton – 220–260 pts (Film TV St courses)
Sunderland – 220–280 pts (Engl Film; Film Media; TV St)
Teesside – 220–260 pts (Film TV Prod; Broad Media Prod)
Worcester – 220–300 pts (Scrnwrit)
York St John – 220–260 pts (Film TV Prod)

200 pts **Bucks New** – 200–240 pts (Film TV Prod)
Creative Arts – 200 pts (Dig Film Scrn Arts) (IB 30 pts)
East London – 200 pts (Film St; Film Vid (Theor Prac))
Glyndŵr – 200 pts (Des (Crea Lens Media); Rad Prod Comm; TV)
Leeds Met – 200 pts (Film Mov Imag Prod)
Middlesex – 200–300 pts (Film St; Film Media Cult St)
Portsmouth – 200–280 pts (TV Film Prod; TV Broad)
Staffordshire – 200 pts (Adv Commer Film Prod)
Swansea Met – 200 pts (Doc Vid; Vid Arts)
West London – 200 pts (Film Vid Prod Film St)
Wolverhampton – 200 pts (Film St courses)

180 pts **Anglia Ruskin** – 180–220 pts (Film St; Film TV Prod)
Derby – 180–240 pts (Film TV St)
St Mary's Twickenham (UC) – 180–200 pts (Film Pop Cult)
Trinity Saint David – 180–300 pts (Film St Welsh; Film St Theol)
West Scotland – BC–CC (Film Scrnwrit; Broad Prod)

160 pts **Bedfordshire** – 160 pts (TV Prod)
Bolton – 160 pts (Film Prod Adv Mus Ind)
Bournemouth Arts (UC) – 160 pts (Film Prod; Animat Prod)
London South Bank – 160 pts (Film St; Dig Film Vid)
South Essex (Coll) – 160 pts (TV Prod Scrn Media)
Southampton Solent – 160 pts (Outsd Broad (Prod Ops))
Suffolk (Univ Campus) – 160 pts (Film Media St)

120 pts **Arts London** – 120 pts (Film TV)
Southampton Solent – 120–160 pts (Snd Film TV Gms)

80 pts **Royal Scottish (RSAMD)** – 80 pts min (Dig Film TV)

Keele – new course – contact University (Film St)

Alternative offers
See **Chapter 7** and **Appendix 1** for grades/UCAS Tariff points information for the International Baccalaureate, Scottish Highers/Advanced Highers, the Welsh Baccalaureate, the Irish Leaving Certificate, the Cambridge Pre-U Diploma, the Advanced Diploma and the Extended Project.

EXAMPLES OF FOUNDATION DEGREES IN THE SUBJECT FIELD
Bournemouth; Bournemouth and Poole (Coll); Bucks New; Cleveland (CAD); Colchester (Inst); Croydon (Coll); Cumbria; Derby; Falmouth (UC); Farnborough (CT); Glamorgan; Grimsby (IFHE); Hull (Coll); Leeds Met; Leicester (Coll); Manchester (Coll); Newcastle (Coll); Norwich (UCA); Norwich City (Coll); Nottingham New (Coll); St Helens (Coll); South Cheshire (Coll); South Essex (Coll); Stockport (Coll).

CHOOSING YOUR COURSE (SEE ALSO CH. 1)
Some course features
Bradford Film Studies is a largely theoretical course. 20% of the time is spent on practical work.
Bucks New The Film and TV Production course covers camera work, lighting, sound and editing. A creative production-based course is also offered in Digital Film Art. There is also a scriptwriting course.

East Anglia Emphasis on the history and theory of film with practical units offered in Years 2 and 3. Study abroad available in Europe, USA and Australia.

Essex Film Studies is a broad course focusing on the social and historical aspects of the media. It is offered as a joint programme with History of Art, Literature or History and American Studies.

Hertfordshire These degrees are offered in Film and Television specialising in Fiction Documentary or Entertainment. There are also degrees in Screen Cultures with Media. There is also a course in Special Effects.

Manchester Courses are offered in Film Studies which can be combined with Media and Cultural Studies, Creative Writing or Video. There are also courses in TV Journalism and Production.

Manchester Met Practical work is the main focus of the Contemporary Film and Video programme whilst the other degree courses on offer here are predominantly critical and textual academic studies.

Oxford Brookes Studies can be taken as a Single Honours course or combined with one of nine other subjects including Japanese language, Marketing or Music.

Portsmouth (Film St) The course allows students to combine their interests in reading, writing and the use of language.

Reading The Film, Theatre and Television course integrates practical work, a critical study of film and theatre and the historical and social significance of television.

Southampton Solent (Film Vid Tech) Practical production units in film and digital video-making alongside academic study.

York (Film TV Prod) This new BSc course combines practical production work with theoretical and historical understanding, involving students in a wide range of technical roles.

Universities and colleges teaching quality See www.qaa.ac.uk; http://unistats.direct.gov.uk.

Top research universities and colleges (RAE 2008) See **Drama**.

Examples of sandwich degree courses See **Media Studies**.

ADMISSIONS INFORMATION

Number of applicants per place (approx) Bournemouth 30; Bournemouth Arts (UC) 9; Brunel 10; Canterbury Christ Church 50; Cardiff 11; Central Lancashire 5; East Anglia (Film Engl St) 7, (Film Am St) 5; Kent 30; Leicester 9; Leicester (Coll) 5; Liverpool John Moores 17; London Met 7; Portsmouth 20; Sheffield Hallam 60; Southampton 5; Southampton Solent 7; Staffordshire 31; Stirling 12; Warwick 18; Westminster 41; York 4; York St John 6.

Advice to applicants and planning the UCAS personal statement **Bournemouth Arts (UC)** Any experience in film-making (beyond home videos) should be described in detail. Knowledge and preferences of types of films and the work of some producers should be included on the UCAS application. Read film magazines and other appropriate literature to keep informed of developments. Show genuine interest in a range of film genres and be knowledgeable about favourite films, directors and give details of work experience or film projects undertaken. You should also be able to discuss the ways in which films relate to broader cultural phenomena, social, literary, historical. See also **Appendix 4**.

Misconceptions about this course That an A-level film or media studies is required; it is not. That it's Film so it's easy! That the course is all practical work. Some applicants believe that these are Media courses. Some applicants believe that Film and TV Studies is a training for production work. **Bournemouth Arts (UC)** (Animat Prod) This is not a Film Studies course but a course based on traditional animation with supported computer image processing. **De Montfort** Some believe that this is a course in practical film-making: it is not, it is for analysts and historians. **Winchester** That graduation automatically leads to a job in broadcasting!

Selection interviews Most institutions will interview some applicants in this subject. **Yes** Bournemouth, Bournemouth Arts (UC), Brunel, Canterbury Christ Church, Chichester, Liverpool John Moores, Newport, York, York St John; **Some** East Anglia, Southampton, Staffordshire, Wolverhampton.

Interview advice and questions Questions will focus on your chosen field. In the case of films be prepared to answer questions not only on your favourite films but on the work of one or two directors you admire and early Hollywood examples. See also **Chapter 6**. **Bournemouth** (TV Script Film) Successful applicants will be required to submit a 20-page screenplay. A good applicant will have the ability to discuss media issues in depth, to have total commitment to TV and video production and will have attempted to make programmes. **Bournemouth Arts (UC)** Written piece prior to interview. Questions at interview relevant to the portfolio/reel. **Staffordshire** We assess essay-writing skills.

Reasons for rejection (non-academic) Not enough drive or ambition. No creative or original ideas. Preference for production work rather than practical work. Inability to articulate the thought process behind the work in the applicant's portfolio. Insufficient knowledge of media affairs. Lack of knowledge of film history. Wrong course choice, wanted more practical work.

AFTER-RESULTS ADVICE
Offers to applicants repeating A-levels Higher Bournemouth Arts (UC), Glasgow, Manchester Met; **Same** De Montfort, East Anglia, Liverpool Hope, St Mary's Twickenham (UC), Staffordshire, Stirling, Winchester, Wolverhampton, York St John.

GRADUATE DESTINATIONS AND EMPLOYMENT (2007/8 HESA)
Cinematics and Photography graduates surveyed 2290 **Employed** 980 **In further study** 135 **Assumed unemployed** 370

Career note Although this is a popular subject field, job opportunities in film, TV and radio are limited. Successful graduates frequently have gained work experience with companies during their undergraduate years. The transferable skills (verbal communication etc) will open up other career opportunities.

OTHER DEGREE SUBJECTS FOR CONSIDERATION
Animation; Communication Studies; Creative Writing; Media Studies; Photography.

FINANCE

(including **Banking, Financial Services, Insurance**; see also **Accountancy/Accounting**)

Financial Services courses provide a comprehensive view of the world of finance and normally cover banking, insurance, investment, building societies, international finance, accounting and economics. Major banks offer sponsorships for some of the specialised Banking courses.

Useful websites www.cii.co.uk; www.secinst.co.uk; www.financialadvice.co.uk; www.efinancialnews.com; www.worldbank.org; www.ifslearning.ac.uk; www.ft.com.

NB The points totals shown to the left of the institutions are for ease of reference only. It must not be assumed that Tariff points are always used by institutions or that they can be substituted for an offer in grades. The level of an offer is not necessarily indicative of the quality of a course.

COURSE OFFERS INFORMATION
Subject requirements/preferences GCSE Most institutions will require English and mathematics grade C minimum. **AL** Mathematics may be required or preferred.

NB In 2012 universities and colleges will differ in their use of GCE AL/AS unit grade information, A* grades, the Extended Project (EPQ), the Advanced Diploma and the Cambridge Pre-U examination when considering applicants and making offers. An EPQ may be accepted in place of an AS subject. Check websites of universities and colleges for the latest offers information.

Your target offers and examples of courses provided by each institution
380 pts **Bristol** – A*AA–ABB (Econ Fin) (IB 33–37 pts)
           Exeter – A*AA–AAB (Econ Fin)
           London (UCL) – A*AA–AAA (Eng Bus Fin MEng) (IB 38–39 pts)
360 pts **London (RH)** – AAA–AAB (Fin Bus Econ) (IB 32 pts)

London (UCL) – AAA–AAB (Eng Bus Fin BEng) (IB 36–38 pts)
Manchester – A*AB–AAA (Maths Fin) (IB 35 pts)
Newcastle – AAA–AAB (Bus Acc Fin) (IB 34–38 pts)
Reading – 340–360 pts (Fin Invest Bank)
340 pts Aston – 320–340 pts (Fin) (IB 34 pts)
Birmingham – AAB 340 pts (Mny Bank Fin Lang) (IB 34–36 pts)
Cardiff – AAB (Bank Fin Euro Lang) (IB 35 pts)
City – AAB (Rl Est Fin Invest) (IB 35 pts)
Glasgow – AAB (Fin courses) (IB 34 pts)
Kent – AAB (Law Acc Fin) (IB 36 ps)
Lancaster – AAB 340–360 pts (Fin Mgt St) (IB 32–36 pts)
Leeds – AAB (Fin courses) (IB 35 pts HL 17 pts)
London (QM) – AAB (Econ Fin) (IB 36 pts HL maths 5)
Loughborough – AAB (Fin Maths) (IB 34 pts HL 6 maths)
Manchester – AAB (Econ Fin) (IB 35–34 pts)
Newcastle – AAB (Fin Bus Econ) (IB 34 pts)
Nottingham – AAB (Fin Acc Mgt) (IB 34 pts)
Reading – 340 pts (Invest Fin Prop)
Sheffield – AAB–ABB (Acc Fin Mgt Econ) (IB 33 pts)
Southampton – AAB–AAA (Econ Fin) (IB 34 pts)
Surrey – AAB 340 pts (Phys Fin MPhys)
320 pts Bournemouth – 320 pts (Fin Bus; Econ Fin)
Brunel – BBC +AS/EPQ c 320 pts (Econ Bus Fin) (IB 32 pts)
Durham – ABB (Bus Fin) (IB 34 pts)
East Anglia – ABB–BBB (Bus Fin Econ) (IB 32 pts)
Essex – 320 pts (Fin Maths) (IB 34 pts)
Kingston – 320 pts (Acc Fin)
Lancaster – ABB (Fin Maths) (IB 32–34 pts)
Leicester – ABB (Bank Fin) (IB 32 pts)
Liverpool – ABB (Maths Fin) (IB 33 pts)
Newcastle – ABB (Fin Maths) (IB 34-36 pts)
Queen's Belfast – ABB–BBBb (Fin) (IB 32 pts)
Salford – ABB–BBB 320–300 pts (Law Fin)
Strathclyde – ABB (Fin courses) (IB 34 pts)
Surrey – ABB (Phys Fin BSc)
Sussex – ABB–BBB (Fin Bus)
Swansea – 320 pts (Fin Econ)
300 pts Aberdeen – BBB (Fin courses) (IB 28 pts)
Aberystwyth – 280–260 pts (Bus Fin)
Heriot-Watt – ABC–BBB (Bus Fin)
Kent – 300 pts (Acc Fin courses)
Lincoln – 300 pts (Fin courses) (IB 28 pts)
Northumbria – 300 pts (Fin Invest Mgt)
Plymouth – 300 pts (Maths)
Salford – 300 pts (Law Fin) (IB 28 pts)
280 pts Brighton – BBC 280–320 pts (Bus Mgt Fin) (IB 30 pts)
Bristol UWE – 280–340 pts (Econ (Mny Bank Fin)) (IB 24–28 pts)
Brunel – BBC (Fin Acc) (IB 32–33 pts)
De Montfort – 280 pts (Fin; Fin Mgt)
Hull – 280 pts (Fin Mgt courses)
Keele – 280-340 pts inc BB/AB (Fin courses) (IB 28–30 pts)
Nottingham Trent – 280 pts (Fin Maths; Econ Fin Bank)
Oxford Brookes – BBC (Econ Fin Int Bus) (IB 29 pts)
Portsmouth – 280 pts (Fin)
Salford – 280 pts (Prop Mgt Invest)

ifs School of Finance
Incorporated by Royal Charter

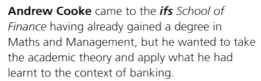

Andrew Cooke came to the **ifs** *School of Finance* having already gained a degree in Maths and Management, but he wanted to take the academic theory and apply what he had learnt to the context of banking.

'The qualification has a big focus on understanding the fundamentals of banking and areas such as core credit skills, which underpins everything a bank does. The importance of such skills has been highlighted by the credit crunch and is key to understanding liquidity issues and managing risk.'

Andrew played tribute to the standard of teaching he received at the **ifs**: 'The tutors on the course were incredibly supportive and really ensured the content was "alive" and tailored to the fast-paced environment of banking.'

Andrew is an Associate in Leveraged Finance at HSBC.

Rongrong Huo joined the **ifs** *School of Finance* to further her career and gain a specialist professional qualification in the banking industry.

'Although I'd already gained a Master's degree in Management and Finance, I found the **ifs** programme most relevant to my career as a working banking professional.

The course is ideally designed to prepare you to deal with the everyday realities of banking with applied credit analysis and risk management central features of the programme. This, together with the strategic, big picture focus of the programme gives wider career options and is, in my experience, invaluable to building a long-term career in banking.'

Rongrong is Manager in International Propositions for Corporate and Structured Banking at HSBC.

www.ifslearning.ac.uk/BSc

324 | Finance

270 pts **Glasgow Caledonian** – 270 pts (Rl Est Econ Invest)
260 pts **Bangor** – 260–300 pts (Bank Fin; Mgt Bank Fin)
Birmingham City – 260 pts (Acc Fin; Bus Fin)
Brunel – BCC (inc C at AS maths) (Fin Comp) (IB 29 pts)
Coventry – 260–320 pts (Fin Invest)
Dundee – BCC (Fin) (IB 30 pts)
Hertfordshire – 260 pts (Fin courses)
Lincoln – 260 pts (Bus Fin)
Portsmouth – 260–280 pts (Fin Bus; Int Fin Tr)
Staffordshire – 260 pts (Fin)
Stirling – 260 pts (Mny Bank Fin) (IB 30 pts)
Winchester – 260–300 pts (Bus Mgt Fin Econ)
240 pts **Aberdeen** – CCC (Fin Hisp St) (IB 30 pts)
Bradford – check with University 240 pts (Fin Plan)
Buckingham – 240–200 pts (Acc Fin Mgt)
Derby – 240 pts (Bus Fin) (IB 26 pts)
Edinburgh Napier – 240 pts (Fin Serv)
Glasgow Caledonian – CCC (Fin Invest Risk)
London Met – 240 pts (Bank; Bank Fin; Fin; Fin Servs; Fin Econ)
Manchester Met – 240–280 pts (Fin Mgt)
Plymouth – 240 pts (Int Fin; Fin Econ)
Sheffield Hallam – 240 pts (Bus Fin Mgt)
Stirling – CCC (Fin)
Suffolk (Univ Campus) – 240 pts (Bus Mgt Fin)
Teesside – 240 pts (Bus Fin)
220 pts **Hertfordshire** – 220–260 pts (Fin)
Huddersfield – 220–280 pts (Bus Fin Serv)
Leeds Met – 220 pts (Acc Fin) (IB 24 pts)
Northampton – 220–260 pts (Finance)
Southampton Solent – 220 pts (Bus Mgt Fin)
Sunderland – 220 pts (Fin Mgt courses)
200 pts **Bucks New** – 200–240 pts (Acc Fin; Bus Fin)
East London – 200 pts (Fin Mny Bank)
York St John – 200–240 pts (Bus Mgt (Fin))
180 pts **Abertay Dundee** – DDD (Fin Bus)
Greenwich – 180–220 pts (Econ Bank)
160 pts **Bradford (Coll Univ Centre)** – 160 pts (Fin Serv)

IFS – check with School (Bank Prac Mgt)

Alternative offers
See **Chapter 7** and **Appendix 1** for grades/UCAS Tariff points information for the International Baccalaureate, Scottish Highers/Advanced Highers, the Welsh Baccalaureate, the Irish Leaving Certificate, the Cambridge Pre-U Diploma, the Advanced Diploma and the Extended Project.

EXAMPLES OF FOUNDATION DEGREES IN THE SUBJECT FIELD
Blackburn (Coll Univ Centre); Blackpool and Fylde (Coll); Bournemouth; Cardiff (UWIC); Cornwall (Coll); Croydon (Coll); Cumbria; Glamorgan; Hertfordshire; Highbury Portsmouth (Coll); IFS; K (Coll); Kensington Bus (Coll); Leeds Met; Manchester (Coll); Northbrook (Coll); Salford; Sheffield (Coll); South Kent (Coll); Suffolk (Univ Campus); Truro (Coll); West Cheshire (Coll); West London; Westminster Kingsway (Coll); Weymouth (Coll); Wirral Met (Coll).

CHOOSING YOUR COURSE (SEE ALSO CH. 1)
Some course features
Brighton (Fin Invest) The course in Finance and Investment shares a common first year with the Economics and Finance degree, making transfers possible.

Durham A course in Business Finance covering economics, management, marketing and international money. It shares a first year with Accountancy and Business degrees with options to transfer at the end of the year.
Nottingham Trent An 'in company' Retail Banking degree is offered.
Reading Courses are offered in Finance and Investment Banking or Property Investment. Internships can be arranged during summer vactations.
Surrey The course in Financial Services Management is designed to match the needs of industry and can be taken to include a Professional Training year adding considerably to employment prospects.

Universities and colleges teaching quality See www.qaa.ac.uk; http://unistats.direct.gov.uk.

Top research universities and colleges (RAE 2008) See **Accountancy/Accounting**.

Examples of sandwich degree courses Abertay Dundee; Bath; Birmingham City; Bournemouth; Brighton; Bristol UWE; Brunel; City; Coventry; De Montfort; Glamorgan; Gloucestershire; Hertfordshire; Huddersfield; Kingston; Lancaster; Leeds Met; London Met; Loughborough; Manchester Met; Middlesex; Nottingham Trent; Plymouth; Portsmouth; Sheffield Hallam; Surrey; Swansea Met; Teesside; Westminster; Wolverhampton; Worcester.

ADMISSIONS INFORMATION
Number of applicants per place (approx) Aberystwyth 4; Bangor 10; Birmingham 3; Birmingham City 13; Bristol UWE 4; Buckingham 4; Cardiff 10; Central Lancashire 6; City 10; Dundee 5; Durham 4; Glamorgan 3; Loughborough 35; Manchester 22; Middlesex 3; Northampton 3; Portsmouth 4; Sheffield Hallam 4.

Advice to applicants and planning the UCAS personal statement Visits to banks or insurance companies should be described, giving details of any work experience or work shadowing done in various departments. Discuss any particular aspects of finance etc which interest you. See also **Appendix 4**.

Misconceptions about this course Many applicants believe that they can only enter careers in banking and finance when they graduate in fact, business and industry provide wide-ranging opportunities.

Selection interviews Yes Buckingham (pref), Huddersfield; **Some** Dundee, Staffordshire, Stirling; **No** City.

Interview advice and questions Banking involves both high street and merchant banks, so a knowledge of banking activities in general will be expected. In the past mergers have been discussed and also the role of the Bank of England in the economy. The work of the accountant may be discussed. See also **Chapter 6**.

Reasons for rejection (non-academic) Lack of interest. Poor English. Lacking in motivation and determination to complete the course.

AFTER-RESULTS ADVICE
Offers to applicants repeating A-levels Higher Glasgow; **Possibly higher** Bangor; **Same** Birmingham, Birmingham City, Bradford, Cardiff, City, Dundee, Edinburgh Napier, London Met, Loughborough, Northumbria, Stirling.

GRADUATE DESTINATIONS AND EMPLOYMENT (2007/8 HESA)
Graduates surveyed 1120 **Employed** 435 **In further study** 160 **Assumed unemployed** 140

Career note Most graduates enter financial careers. Further study is required to qualify as an accountant and to obtain other professional qualifications, eg Institute of Banking.

OTHER DEGREE SUBJECTS FOR CONSIDERATION
Accountancy; Actuarial Studies; Business Studies; Economics.

FOOD SCIENCE/STUDIES and TECHNOLOGY

(see also **Agricultural Sciences/Agriculture, Biochemistry, Consumer Studies/Sciences, Dietetics, Hospitality and Hotel Management, Nutrition**)

Biochemistry, microbiology, dietetics, human nutrition, food processing and technology are components of Food Science courses as well as being degree courses in their own right (and appropriate alternative courses). The study depends for its understanding on a secure foundation of several pure sciences – chemistry and two subjects from physics, mathematics, biology, botany or zoology. Only students offering subjects from these fields are likely to be considered. Food Technology covers the engineering aspects of food processing and management. A number of bursaries are offered by the food industry. Check with admissions tutors. See also **Appendix 4**.

Useful websites www.scienceyear.com; www.sofht.co.uk; www.ifst.org; www.defra.gov.uk; www.iagre.org.

NB The points totals shown to the left of the institutions are for ease of reference only. It must not be assumed that Tariff points are always used by institutions or that they can be substituted for an offer in grades. The level of an offer is not necessarily indicative of the quality of a course.

COURSE OFFERS INFORMATION

Subject requirements/preferences GCSE English, mathematics and a science. **AL** One or two mathematics/science subjects; chemistry may be required.

NB In 2012 universities and colleges will differ in their use of GCE AL/AS unit grade information, A* grades, the Extended Project (EPQ), the Advanced Diploma and the Cambridge Pre-U examination when considering applicants and making offers. An EPQ may be accepted in place of an AS subject. Check websites of universities and colleges for the latest offers information.

Your target offers and examples of courses provided by each institution

340 pts **Newcastle** – AAB–ABB (Fd Hum Nutr) (IB 32–35 pts)

320 pts **Surrey** – ABB–BBB (Fd Sci Microbiol) (IB 32–28 pts)

300 pts **Heriot-Watt** – BBB 1st yr entry (Fd Sci Tech Mgt; Biol Sci (Fd Sci))
Leeds – BBB (Fd St Nutr) (IB 32 pts HL 15 pts)
Nottingham – BBB–BCC (Fd Microbiol) (IB 24–30 pts)
Queen's Belfast – BBB (Fd Qual Sfty Nutr) (IB 32 pts)
Reading – 300 pts (Fd Sci)
Surrey – BBB–BBC (Nutr Fd Sci) (IB 32–28 pts)

280 pts **Brighton** – BBC (Vit Oeno) (IB 30 pts)
Leeds Trinity (UC) – (Nutr Fd)
Northumbria – 280 pts (Fd Sci Nutr) (IB 25 pts)
Reading – 280 pts (Fd Tech) (IB 30 pts)

260 pts **Glasgow Caledonian** – BCC (Fd Biosci)
Liverpool John Moores – 260 pts (Home Econ (Fd Des Tech))

240 pts **Cardiff (UWIC)** – 240 pts (Pblc Hlth Nutr)
London Met – 240 pts (Fd Consum St courses)
Royal (CAg) – 200-240 pts (Fd Prod Sply Mgt)
Sheffield Hallam – 240–200 pts (Fd Mark Mgt)
Teesside – 240 pts (Fd Nutr Hlth Sci)
Ulster – 240 pts (Fd Nutr)

220 pts **Bath Spa** – 220–280 pts (Fd Nutr) (IB 24 pts)
Coventry – 220–240 pts (Fd Sci Nutr)
Harper Adams (UC) – 220 pts (Consum St)
Huddersfield – 220 pts (Fd Nutr Hlth)

200 pts **Abertay Dundee** – CDD (Fd Consum Sci; Fd Nutr Hlth; Fd Prod Des)
Birmingham (UC) – 200 pts (Fd Consum Mgt) (IB 24 pts)

Glasgow – AAB (Fr courses) (IB 30 pts)
Imperial London – AAB 340 pts (Biol Fr Sci)
Lancaster – AAB (Euro Mgt (Fr)) (IB 34 pts)
Manchester – ABB–AAB (Fr courses) (IB 35–30 pts)
St Andrews – AAB–AAA (Fr courses) (IB 36 pts)
Sheffield – AAB 340 pts (Law Fr; Mech Eng Fr)
Southampton – AAB–ABB (Fr courses) (IB 32 pts)
Warwick – AAB (Fr coursse) (IB 36 pts)

320 pts **Bath** – ABB (Modn Lang Euro St (Fr and Ital/Russ/Ger)) (IB 34 pts HL Fr 6)
East Anglia – ABB–BBB (Transl Interp Dbl Hons Langs) (IB 32-31 pts)
Essex – 320 pts (Econ Fr) (IB 34 pts)
Kent – 320–300 pts (Fr (Lic de Let); Fr Single/Joint Hons)
Lancaster – ABB–BBB (Fr St courses) (IB 30 pts)
Leeds – AAB–ABC (Fr courses) (IB 34 pts HL Fr 6)
Leicester – ABB (Fr Engl; Fr Ital joint courses)
London (Inst in Paris) – ABB (Fr St)
London (QM) – 320–340 pts (Fr courses) (IB 32 pts HL Fr 6)
London (RH) – ABB–BBB (Fr courses) (IB 32 pts HL Fr 6)
Newcastle – 320 pts (Fr; Fr Bus St)
Nottingham – AAB–BBB (Fr courses)
Sheffield – ABB (Fr courses except under **340 pts**) (IB 36–32 pts)
Strathclyde – ABB (Fr courses)
Surrey – ABB–BBB (Fr courses; Lang Transl courses)
Sussex – ABB–BBB (Fr courses) (IB 32–34 pts)
Warwick – AAB–ABB (Fr St; Fr Thea St; Fr Int St)
York – ABB (Fr courses except under **360 pts**) (IB 32 pts)

300 pts **Aberdeen** – BBB (Fr courses) (IB 28 pts)
Aston – BBB–ABB 300–320 pts (Fr courses except under **340 pts**) (IB 31–33 pts)
Birmingham – BBB (Fr Maths) (IB 30–32 pts)
Cardiff – ABC (Fr Ger) (IB 30 pts)
Coventry – 300 pts (Law Fr)
East Anglia – BBB–BBC (Transl Media Fr/Span 3 yrs) (IB 31–30 pts)
Edinburgh – BBB (Fr courses)
Essex – 300 pts (Euro St Fr) (IB 30 pts)
Heriot-Watt – BBB (App Langs Transl (Fr/Ger); Langs (Interp Transl) (Fr/Ger) (Ger/Span))
Liverpool – ABB–BBB (Fr courses) (IB 30 pts HL Fr 6)
Newcastle – ABC/BBB (Ling Fr) (IB 32 pts)
Northumbria – 300–280 pts (Fr Bus; Int Bus Mgt Fr)
Queen's Belfast – BBB–BBCb (Fr courses)
Reading – 300–320 pts (Fr courses) (IB 28 pts)
Salford – 300 pts (Modn Lang Transl Interp St (Fr) (Ger) (Ital) (Port)
Sheffield Hallam – 300 pts (Int Bus St Fr)
Swansea – ABB–BBB 300 pts (Fr courses)
Westminster – BBB–CCC (Fr courses) (IB 28 pts)

280 pts **Aberystwyth** – 240–280 pts (Fr courses) (IB 29 pts)
Manchester Met – 280 pts (Fr + 2nd Lang) (IB 29 pts)

260 pts **Central Lancashire** – 260-300 pts (Fr Comb Hons)
Hull – 260–300 pts (Fr Joint courses; Fr courses)
Nottingham Trent – 260–280 pts (Fr Euro St; Fr Comm Soty; Fr Media)
Oxford Brookes – BBC–BCC (Fr Comb Hons courses) (IB 30 pts)

240 pts **Bangor** – 240–260 pts (Fr courses)
Canterbury Christ Church – 240 pts (Fr courses) (IB 24 pts)
Chester – 240 pts (Fr courses) (IB 24 pts)
Coventry – 240–260 pts (Fr courses except under **300 pts**)
Liverpool John Moores – 240 pts (P Educ Fr; Fr PR; Int Bus St Fr)

Manchester Met – 240–280 pts (Fr St) (IB 28 pts)
Sheffield Hallam – 240 pts (Mark Fr; Tour Fr)
Stirling – CCC (Fr Comp Sci) (IB 28 pts)
Ulster – 240 pts (Fr courses)
Winchester – 240–280 pts (Fr P Teach)
220 pts Kingston – 220–360 pts (Fr courses)
Leeds Met – 220 pts (Fr Int Rel; Fr Glob Dev; Fr PR; Fr Mark; Fr Tour Mgt)
Northampton – 220–260 pts (Fr courses)
200 pts Portsmouth – 200–280 pts (Fr St)
190 pts Buckingham – 190–300 pts (Fr courses 2yr)
 80 pts London (Birk) – for under 21s (over 21s varies) p/t (Fr Ger; Fr Span; Fr Mgt; Fr St)
London LSE – optional course offered by the language centre check with admissions tutor
((Fr/Ger/Span/Russ))

Alternative offers
See **Chapter 7** and **Appendix 1** for grades/UCAS Tariff points information for the International Baccalaureate, Scottish Highers/Advanced Highers, the Welsh Baccalaureate, the Irish Leaving Certificate, the Cambridge Pre-U Diploma, the Advanced Diploma and the Extended Project.

CHOOSING YOUR COURSE (SEE ALSO CH. 1)
Some course features
Bangor A three-language Honours course is offered with languages chosen from French, German, Italian or Spanish. This is an exclusively practical language course, two semesters being spent at universities appropriate to the languages chosen.
Bath (Euro St Modn Langs) French is studied with a second, equally weighted, language. The course has a contemporary focus and a wide range of options.
Cardiff (Fr) The course has a vocational emphasis, and the opportunity to sit the Paris Chamber of Commerce examination and to gain a French language qualification recognised in France.
Chester French can be studied as a Single Honours degree or as part of a Combined Honours programme.
Heriot-Watt (Langs (Interp Transl) (App Langs Transl)) Both degrees enable two main foreign languages to be studied to the same level throughout the course: the second language can be studied either from beginners' or post-beginners' level.
Leeds A large department offering a range of single, combined and major/minor courses.
Salford (Modn Langs Transl Interp St) Three languages are chosen from French, German, Italian, Portuguese, Spanish, and English as a Foreign Language.

Universities and colleges teaching quality See www.qaa.ac.uk; http://unistats.direct.gov.uk.

Top research universities and colleges (RAE 2008) Oxford; London (King's); Warwick; Cambridge; Aberdeen; St Andrews; Sheffield; Nottingham; Kent; Leeds; Exeter; London (UCL).

ADMISSIONS INFORMATION
Number of applicants per place (approx) Aston 6; Bangor 4; Bath (Euro St Modn Langs) 6; Birmingham 5; Bradford 3; Bristol 7; Cardiff 6; Central Lancashire 5; Durham 8; Exeter 8; Huddersfield 3; Hull 12; Kent 10; Kingston 4; Lancaster 7; Leeds (Joint Hons) 8; Leicester (Fr Ital) 5; Liverpool 5; Liverpool John Moores 8; London (Inst in Paris) 9; London (King's) 9; London (RH) 5; London (UCL) 8; Manchester Met 13; Middlesex 6; Newcastle 17; Northampton 3; Nottingham 16; Oxford Brookes 8; Portsmouth 20; Roehampton 5; Warwick 7; York 8.

Advice to applicants and planning the UCAS personal statement Visits to France (including exchange visits) should be described, with reference to any particular cultural or geographical features of the region visited. Providing information about your contacts with French friends and experience in speaking the language are also important. Express your willingness to work/live/travel abroad and show your interests in French life and culture. Read French newspapers and magazines and keep up-to-date with news stories etc. See also **Appendix 4**.

Misconceptions about this course Leeds See **Languages**. **Swansea** Some applicants are not aware of the range of subjects which can be combined with French in our flexible modular system. They sometimes do not know that linguistics and area studies options are also available as well as literature options in French.

Selection interviews Yes Bangor, Birmingham, Cambridge, Canterbury Christ Church, Durham, East Anglia (after offer), Essex, Exeter, Heriot-Watt, Huddersfield, Hull, Kingston, Lancaster, Liverpool, Liverpool John Moores, London (RH), London (UCL), Oxford, Portsmouth, Reading, Surrey, Sussex, Warwick; **Some** Brighton, Leeds.

Interview advice and questions Questions will almost certainly be asked on your A-level texts, in addition to your reading outside the syllabus – books, magazines, newspapers etc. Part of the interview may be conducted in French and written tests may be involved (see **Chapter 6**). **Leeds** See **Languages**.

Reasons for rejection (non-academic) Unstable personality. Known alcoholism. Poor motivation. Candidate unenthusiastic, unmotivated, ill-informed about the nature of the course (had not read the prospectus). Not keen to spend a year abroad.

AFTER-RESULTS ADVICE
Offers to applicants repeating A-levels Higher Aberystwyth, Bristol (Fr), Glasgow, Leeds, Oxford Brookes, Warwick; **Possibly higher** Aston (Fr; Fr Ger); **Same** Aston, Bradford, Brighton, Bristol (Phil Fr; Fr Lat), Chester, Durham, East Anglia, Lancaster, Liverpool, London (RH), Newcastle, Nottingham (Fr Ger; Fr Lat), Sheffield, Surrey, Sussex, Ulster.

GRADUATE DESTINATIONS AND EMPLOYMENT (2007/8 HESA)
Graduates surveyed 1360 **Employed** 570 **In further study** 335 **Assumed unemployed** 100

Career note See **Languages**.

OTHER DEGREE SUBJECTS FOR CONSIDERATION
European Studies; International Business Studies; Literature; other language tables.

GENETICS
(see also Biological Sciences, Microbiology)

Over the years genetics, the science of heredity, has developed into a detailed and wide-ranging science. It involves, on the one hand, population genetics, and on the other, molecular interactions. Studies may therefore cover microbial, plant, animal and human genetics.

Useful websites www.genetics.org; www.nature.com/genetics; www.genetics.org.uk; see also **Biological Sciences**.

NB The points totals shown to the left of the institutions are for ease of reference only. It must not be assumed that Tariff points are always used by institutions or that they can be substituted for an offer in grades. The level of an offer is not necessarily indicative of the quality of a course.

COURSE OFFERS INFORMATION
Subject requirements/preferences GCSE English, mathematics and science subjects. **AL** Chemistry and/or biology are usually required or preferred.

NB In 2012 universities and colleges will differ in their use of GCE AL/AS unit grade information, A* grades, the Extended Project (EPQ), the Advanced Diploma and the Cambridge Pre-U examination when considering applicants and making offers. An EPQ may be accepted in place of an AS subject. Check websites of universities and colleges for the latest offers information.

Your target offers and examples of courses provided by each institution

380 pts **Cambridge** – A*AA college offers may vary (Nat Sci (Genet)) (IB 38–42 pts)
360 pts **Edinburgh** – AAA 2nd yr entry (Genet)
Glasgow – AAA (Genet fast route) (IB 38 pts HL 665)
London (UCL) – AAAe–AABe (Biol Sci (Genet) (Hum Genet)) (IB 34–36 pts)
Manchester – AAA–ABB (Genet Modn Lang) (IB 35–32 pts)
340 pts **Cardiff** – AAB–ABB (Genetics) (IB 34 pts)
London (King's) – AAB+AS (Pharmacol Mol Genet) (IB 34 pts HL 5 chem biol)
Nottingham – AAB–BBB (Bioch Genet)
Sheffield – AAB–ABB (Bioch Genet) (IB 33 pts)
320 pts **Birmingham** – ABB (Bioch (Genet)) (IB 32–34 pts)
East Anglia – ABB–BBB (Mol Biol Genet) (IB 32–31 pts)
Glasgow – ABB (Genet) (IB 32 pts)
Leicester – ABB (Biol Sci (Genet)) (IB 32 pts)
Liverpool – ABB–BBB (Genet Comb Hons) (IB 33–30 pts HL biol 6)
Newcastle – ABB (Genet) (IB 32 pts)
Nottingham – ABB–BBB (Hum Genet) (IB 32 pts)
Warwick – ABB (Biol Sci (Mol Genet)) (IB 34 pts)
York – ABB (Genet Ind) (IB 32 pts)
300 pts **Aberdeen** – BBB (Genet; Genet (Immun); Genet Psy)
Birmingham – BBB (Biol Sci (Genet))
Edinburgh – BBB 1st yr entry (Genet) (IB 30 pts)
Essex – 260–300 pts inc BB–BC (Genet 3 yrs) (IB 30 pts)
Lancaster – BBB (Bioch Genet) (IB 29 pts)
Leeds – AAB–BBB (Genet) (IB 34–32 pts HL 15–16 pts)
London (QM) – 300–320 pts (Med Genet) (IB 28 pts)
Queen's Belfast – BBB–BBC (Genet) (IB 28 pts)
Sussex – BBB–BBC (Mol Genet)
Swansea – 300–320 pts (Genet; Med Genet; Genet Bioch)
280 pts **Aberystwyth** – 280–300 pts (Genet Bioch) (IB 26 pts)
Brunel – BBC (Biomed Sci (Genet)) (IB 30 pts HL 5 biol)
260 pts **Dundee** – BCC 1st year entry (Mol Genet) (IB 30 pts)
220 pts **Westminster** – CCD (Mol Biol Genet) (IB 28 pts)
200 pts **Anglia Ruskin** – 200 pts (Genet Microbiol)
London Met – 200-240 pts (Genet) (IB 28 pts)
Wolverhampton – 200 pts (Genet Mol Biol)
160 pts **Essex** – inc DD 160 pts (Genet 4 yrs) (IB 24 pts)
Westminster – CC (Mol Biol Genet 4 yrs inc Fdn) (IB 26 pts)

Alternative offers
See **Chapter 7** and **Appendix 1** for grades/UCAS Tariff points information for the International Baccalaureate, Scottish Highers/Advanced Highers, the Welsh Baccalaureate, the Irish Leaving Certificate, the Cambridge Pre-U Diploma, the Advanced Diploma and the Extended Project.

CHOOSING YOUR COURSE (SEE ALSO CH. 1)
Some course features
Brunel Genetics is offered as part of the Biomedical Sciences programme.
Liverpool Modules are offered in genetic engineering, human and medical genetics. The year in industry/research enables students to work in the UK, Europe or the USA.
London (UCL) After a common first year for all Biological Sciences students, Genetics and Human Genetics are two of the degree specialisms offered for the following years of the BSc and MSci courses. The Genetics programme focuses on genomic, evolutionary and population genetics, while cytology, pre-natal diagnosis and genetic counselling are options in the Human Genetics programme.
Manchester Transfer possible between most life sciences degree programmes at the end of the first year; students can also opt on, or off, sandwich placement year, and a foundation year is also available.

Nottingham Human Genetics is offered as a three- or four-year programme.
York Genetics is available as a specialist degree programme in the Biology degree programme, with an opportunity to spend a year abroad or in industry.

Universities and colleges teaching quality See www.qaa.ac.uk; http://unistats.direct.gov.uk.

Top research universities and colleges (RAE 2008) See **Biological Sciences**.

Examples of sandwich degree courses Bristol UWE; Brunel; Cardiff; Huddersfield; Sussex; York; see also **Biological Sciences**.

ADMISSIONS INFORMATION
Number of applicants per place (approx) Cardiff 8; Dundee 5; Leeds 7; Leicester (all Biol Sci courses) 10; Newcastle 8; Nottingham 6; Swansea 7; Wolverhampton 4; York 9.

Advice to applicants and planning the UCAS personal statement See **Biological Sciences**.

Misconceptions about this course **York** Some fail to realise that chemistry (beyond GCSE) is essential to an understanding of genetics.

Selection interviews **Yes** Cambridge, Liverpool, Swansea; **Some** Anglia Ruskin, Cardiff, Dundee, Wolverhampton, York.

Interview advice and questions Likely questions will focus on your A-level science subjects, particularly biology, why you wish to study genetics, and on careers in genetics. See also **Chapter 6**.

AFTER-RESULTS ADVICE
Offers to applicants repeating A-levels **Higher** Aberystwyth, Leeds, Newcastle, Nottingham, Swansea; **Same** Anglia Ruskin, Cardiff, Dundee, London (UCL), Wolverhampton, York.

GRADUATE DESTINATIONS AND EMPLOYMENT (2007/8 HESA)
Graduates surveyed 295 **Employed** 85 **In further study** 125 **Assumed unemployed** 30

Career note See **Biological Sciences**.

OTHER DEGREE SUBJECTS FOR CONSIDERATION
Biochemistry; Biological Sciences; Biology; Biotechnology; Human Sciences; Immunology; Life Sciences; Medical Biochemistry; Medical Biology; Medicine; Microbiology; Molecular Biology; Natural Sciences; Physiology; Plant Sciences.

GEOGRAPHY
(including **Meteorology**; see also **Environmental Sciences/Studies**)

Students following BA and BSc Geography courses often choose options from the same range of modules, but the choice of degree will depend on the arts or science subjects taken at A-level (or equivalent). The content and focus of courses will vary between universities and could emphasise the human, physical, economic or social aspects of the subject.

Useful websites www.metoffice.gov.uk; www.ccw.gov.uk; www.rgs.org; www.ordnancesurvey.co.uk; www.geographical.co.uk; www.nationalgeographic.com; www.cartography.org.uk; www.naturalengland.org.uk; www.geography.org.uk; www.thepowerofgeography.co.uk; www.spatial-literacy.org; www.gis.com.

NB The points totals shown to the left of the institutions are for ease of reference only. It must not be assumed that Tariff points are always used by institutions or that they can be substituted for an offer in grades. The level of an offer is not necessarily indicative of the quality of a course.

COURSE OFFERS INFORMATION

Subject requirements/preferences GCSE Geography usually required. Mathematics/sciences often required for BSc courses. **AL** Geography is usually required for most courses. Mathematics/science subjects required for BSc courses. (Meteorology) Mathematics, physics and another science may be required sometimes with specified grades, eg **Reading** mathematics and physics grade B.

NB In 2012 universities and colleges will differ in their use of GCE AL/AS unit grade information, A* grades, the Extended Project (EPQ), the Advanced Diploma and the Cambridge Pre-U examination when considering applicants and making offers. An EPQ may be accepted in place of an AS subject. Check websites of universities and colleges for the latest offers information.

Your target offers and examples of courses provided by each institution

380 pts **Cambridge** – college offers may vary A*AA (Geog) (IB 38–42 pts)
London (UCL) – AAA+AS–ABB+AS (Econ Geog) (IB 34–38 pts)

360 pts **Bristol** – AAA–ABB (Geog Euro) (IB 37–36 pts)
Durham – AAA (Nat Sci Geog; Geog BA/BSc; Geog Comb Hons)
East Anglia – AAA–AAB (Meteor Ocean Abrd) (IB 34–33 pts)
Exeter – AAA–AAB (Geog Euro St) (IB 34–31 pts)
Glasgow – AAA faster route (Geog courses) (IB 38 pts)
Leeds – AAA (Meteor; Meteor Clim Sci Int)
Manchester – AAA–AAB (Geog Int St) (IB 36 pts)
Nottingham – AAA–ABB (Geog Chin St) (IB 32–36 pts)
Oxford – AAA (Geog) (IB 38–40 pts)
St Andrews – AAA (Geog Mgt) (IB 36 pts)

340 pts **Birmingham** – AAB–ABB (Geog BA/BSc) (IB 32–34 pts)
Durham – AAB (Educ St (Geog))
Hull – 320–340 pts (Geog MPhys)
Lancaster – AAB 340 pts (Physl Geog Abrd)
Leeds – AAB (Geog BA)
London (King's) – ABB+AS (Geography) (IB 32 pts)
London (QM) – 340 pts (Physl Geog) (IB 32 pts)
London LSE – AAB (Geog Econ) (IB 37 pts)
Loughborough – AAB–ABB (Geog Spo Mgt) (IB 34 pts)
Manchester – AAB–ABB (Geog)
Newcastle – AAB (Geog BA/BSc) (IB 32 pts HL geog 6)
Nottingham – AAA–ABB (Geog BA/BSc) (IB 32–36 pts)
St Andrews – AAB (Geog Mid E St) (IB 32–36 pts)
Sheffield – AAB (Geog Plan) (IB 33 pts)
Southampton – AAB–ABB (Geog Ocean) (IB 36–30 pts)
Strathclyde – AAB 2nd yr entry (Geog) (IB 34 pts)
Sussex – AAB–ABB (Geog Ecol) (IB 32–34 pts)

320 pts **Aberystwyth** – 320 pts (Geog) (IB 30 pts)
Birmingham (UC) – ABB (Geog) (IB 32–34 pts)
Cardiff – ABB (Mar Geog) (IB 32 pts)
East Anglia – ABB–BBB (Meteor Ocean courses except under **360 pts**)
Exeter – ABB–BBB (Cons Biol Geog; Geog Engl; Geog Euro Mgt)
Glasgow – ABB (Geog courses BA) (IB 32 pts)
Lancaster – ABB (Geog; Physl Geog; Hum Geog; Geog (Env Chng))
Leeds – ABB (Geog Mgt) (IB 34 pts HL 16 pts)
Leicester – ABB (Geog Geol)
Liverpool – ABB (Geol Physl Geog) (IB 32 pts)
London (RH) – 320 pts (Physl Geog Geol) (IB 37 pts HL 666)
London (SOAS) – ABB (Geog Joint Hons BA/BSc) (IB 34 pts)
Loughborough – ABB–AAC (Geog Mgt)
Newcastle – 320 pts (Rur St) (IB 28–30 pts)

Reading – 320 pts (Meteor) (IB 34–31 pts)
Strathclyde – ABB 1st yr entry (Geog)
Swansea – ABB (Geog; Geog Econ; Geog Geoinf; Geog Euro St)
York – ABB-BBB (Env Geog)

300 pts **Aberdeen** – BBB (Geog (Arts) (Sci); Geog Inf Sys)
Brighton – BBB (Geog Geol) (IB 30 pts)
Edinburgh – BBB–AAA (Geog Soc Anth) (IB 32 pts)
Keele – 300 pts (Geosci) (IB 26–30 pts)
Leeds – BBB (Geog Trans Plan BSc; Meteor Atmos Sci; Geog Geol)
Liverpool – BBB (Geog Arch) (IB 30 pts)
Manchester – BBB (Geog Geol)
Newcastle – BBB–BBC (Geog Inf Sci) (IB 30–32 pts)
Reading – 300 pts (Meteor Clim)
Southampton – ABB–BBB (Arch Geog) (IB 32–30 pts)
Stirling – BBB 2nd yr entry (Geog)

280 pts **Brighton** – BBC (Env Haz) (IB 28 pts)
Bristol UWE – 280–300 pts (Geog Plan) (IB 26–32 pts)
Coventry – 280–300 pts (Disas Mgt Emer Plan; Geog BA/BSc; Glob Sust; Clim Chng; Geog; Geog Nat Haz)
Gloucestershire – 280–300 pts (Geog courses)
Northumbria – 280 pts (Geog Env Mgt) (IB 28 pts)
Oxford Brookes – BBC (Geog Comb Hons) (IB 29 pts)
Portsmouth – 280 pts (Geog BA/BSc; Hum Geog; Physl Geog; Env Geog)
Queen's Belfast – BBC–BCCb (Arch Palae Geog; Geog Euro; Geog)
Sheffield Hallam – 280 pts (Geog Plan; Geog)
Staffordshire – 200–280 pts (Geog joint courses) (IB 28 pts)
Worcester – 280–300 pts (Physl Geog courses) (IB 25 pts)

260 pts **Bournemouth** – 260 pts (App Geog) (IB 28 pts)
Coventry – 260–280 pts (Disas Mgt; Disas Reconstr Mgt)
Dundee – BCC (Geog Plan) (IB 29 pts)
Hull – 260–320 pts (Geog Spo Sci; Physl Geog BSc; Hum Geog)
Liverpool Hope – 260 pts (Geog courses)
Liverpool John Moores – 260-300 pts (Geog)
Manchester Met – 260 pts (Physl Geog) (IB 24 pts)
Plymouth – 260–280 pts (Geog BA/BSc; Geog Media Arts; Geog Lang; Geog Tour Mgt)

240 pts **Aberdeen** – CCC (Geog Hisp St) (IB 30 pts)
Bangor – 240–320 pts (Geog) (IB 28 pts)
Bath Spa – 240–280 pts (Geog)
Canterbury Christ Church – 240 pts (Geog courses)
Chester – 240 pts (Geog courses) (IB 24 pts)
Edge Hill – 240 pts (Biogeog; Geotour)
Leeds Met – 240 pts (Hum Geog; Hum Geog Plan)
Northampton – 240–280 pts (Physl Geog; Geog)
Nottingham Trent – 240 pts (Geog) (IB 24 pts)
Ulster – 240–260 pts (Geog; Geog Educ; Ir Geog; Geog Langs)
Worcester – 240–300 pts (Geog)

220 pts **Bangor** – 220–260 pts (Cstl Geog) (IB 28 pts)
Bath Spa – 220–300 pts (Geog Inf Sys)
Bradford – 220–240 pts (Geog; Geog Env Mgt; Physl Env Geog; Geog Arch)
Edge Hill – 220–280 pts (Geog)
Glamorgan – 220–280 pts (Geog; Hum Geog; Physl Geog)
Greenwich – 220 pts (Geog BA/BSc)
Hertfordshire – 220 pts (Geog courses)
Liverpool John Moores – 220–260 pts (Geog BSc/BA; Physl Geog)
Northampton – 220–260 pts (Hum Geog)

Sunderland – 220 pts (Geog Educ)
Ulster – 220–240 pts (Geog Int Dev)
200 pts **Central Lancashire** – 200–240 pts (Geog BA/BSc; Env Haz Sci Plcy Mgt)
East London – 200 pts (Geog Inf Sys)
Kingston – 200–280 pts (Geog Joint Hons; Hum Geog Joint Hons; Geog Inf Sys Joint Hons)
Nottingham Trent – 200–220 pts (Physl Geog)
180 pts **Derby** – 180–240 pts (Geog courses)
St Mary's Twickenham (UC) – 180 pts (Geog courses)
Salford – 180 pts (Geog BA/BSc) (IB 24 pts)
Southampton Solent – 180 pts (Geog Env St; Geog Mar St)
160 pts **Bishop Grosseteste (UC)** – 160 pts (Educ St Geog)
Wolverhampton – 160–220 pts (Geog courses)
80 pts **London (Birk)** – for under 21s (over 21s varies) p/t (Geog Env)

Alternative offers
See **Chapter 7** and **Appendix 1** for grades/UCAS Tariff points information for the International Baccalaureate, Scottish Highers/Advanced Highers, the Welsh Baccalaureate, the Irish Leaving Certificate, the Cambridge Pre-U Diploma, the Advanced Diploma and the Extended Project.

EXAMPLES OF FOUNDATION DEGREES IN THE SUBJECT FIELD
Bournemouth.

CHOOSING YOUR COURSE (SEE ALSO CH. 1)
Some course features
East Anglia (MSci Meteor Ocean) A new (2010) four-year course integrates a study of the Earth's oceans and atmosphere, their interactions and external influences on them and is run jointly by the Schools of Environmental Sciences and Mathematics, together with the School of Computing.
Lancaster The Geography degree schemes are flexible so students can specialise in human geography, physical geography, or geography, or study an outside related subject, in the second and third years. There are study abroad opportunities and an option to teach geography in a local school.
Newcastle Geography can be taken in the Combined Studies degree with three other subjects in Stage 1 and two in Stage 2.
Reading A leading university for the study of meteorology with opportunities for placement at the University of Oklahoma, equally renowned for this subject.

Universities and colleges teaching quality See www.qaa.ac.uk; http://unistats.direct.gov.uk.

Top research universities and colleges (RAE 2008) See **Environmental Science/Studies**.

Examples of sandwich degree courses Aberystwyth; Bradford; Cardiff; Coventry; Glamorgan; Hertfordshire; Kingston; Loughborough; Manchester Met; Nottingham Trent; Oxford Brookes; Plymouth; Queen's Belfast; Salford; Ulster; Wolverhampton.

ADMISSIONS INFORMATION
Number of applicants per place (approx) Aberystwyth 3; Birmingham 6; Bristol 15; Bristol UWE 10; Cambridge 3; Cardiff 5; Central Lancashire 3; Chester 10; Coventry 12; Derby 4; Dundee 5; Durham 8; East Anglia (Meteor Ocean) 7; Edge Hill 8; Edinburgh 8; Exeter 10; Glamorgan 5; Gloucestershire 40; Greenwich 2; Hull 10; Kent 15; Kingston 7; Lancaster 13; Leeds 12; Leicester 5; Liverpool 3; Liverpool John Moores 6; London (King's) 5; London (QM) 5; London (RH) 7; London (SOAS) 5; London LSE 8; Loughborough 6, (Geog Spo Sci) 20; Newcastle 14; Newman (UC) 2; Northampton 4; Northumbria 16; Nottingham 7; Portsmouth (Geog) 5; St Mary's Twickenham (UC) 4; Salford 3; Sheffield (BA) 13, (BSc) 10; Southampton (Geog) 7; Staffordshire 10; Strathclyde 8; Swansea 5; Wolverhampton 2; Worcester 5.

Advice to applicants and planning the UCAS personal statement Visits to, and field courses in, any specific geographical region should be fully described. Study your own locality in detail and get in touch with the area Planning Office to learn about any future developments. Read geographical magazines and describe any special interests you have – and why. Awareness of world issues and travel experience.

Misconceptions about this course Birmingham Some students think that the BA and BSc Geography courses are very different: in fact they do not differ from one another. All course options are available for both degrees. **East Anglia** (Meteor Ocean) Some applicants don't realise that the course is a very mathematical and physics-based subject. **Liverpool** Some applicants assume that a BSc course restricts them to physical geography modules. This is not so since human geography modules can be taken. Some students later specialise in human geography.

Selection interviews Yes Bristol UWE, Cambridge, Canterbury Christ Church, Central Lancashire, Coventry, Durham (essential for overseas applicants), East Anglia, Edge Hill, Greenwich, Kingston, London (King's), London (QM), London (RH), London (SOAS), London (UCL), Manchester Met, Northumbria, Oxford (Geog) 27%; **Some** Bath Spa, Bristol, Cardiff, Dundee, Liverpool, Loughborough, Newcastle, Nottingham, Salford, Southampton, Staffordshire.

Interview advice and questions Geography is a very broad subject and applicants can expect to be questioned on their syllabus and those aspects which they find of special interest. Some questions in the past have included: What fieldwork have you done? What are your views on ecology? What changes in the landscape have you noticed on the way to the interview? Explain in simple meteorological terms today's weather. Why are earthquakes almost unknown in Britain? What is the value of practical work in geography to primary school children? (BEd course) What do you enjoy about geography and why? Are there any articles of geographical importance in the news at present? Discuss the current economic situation in Britain and give your views. Questions on the Third World, on world ocean currents and drainage and economic factors world-wide. Expect to comment on local geography and on geographical photographs and diagrams. See **Chapter 6**. **Cambridge** What do you think about those who regard global warming as nonsense? Are Fair-Trade bananas really fair? Imagine you are hosting the BBC radio show on New Year's day, what message would you send to listeners? **Liverpool** Looks for why students have chosen Geography and the aspects of the subject they enjoy. **Oxford** Is nature natural? **Southampton** Applicants selected on academic ability only.

Reasons for rejection (non-academic) Lack of awareness of the content of the course. Failure to attend interview. Poor general knowledge. Lack of geographical awareness. **Hull** (BSc) Usually insufficient science background. **Liverpool** Personal statement gave no reason for choosing Geography.

AFTER-RESULTS ADVICE

Offers to applicants repeating A-levels Higher Bournemouth, Glasgow, Hull, Kingston, Nottingham, St Andrews, Sussex (Geog Lang); **Possibly higher** Edinburgh; **Same** Aberystwyth, Birmingham, Bradford, Brighton, Bristol, Cardiff, Chester, Coventry, Derby, Dundee, Durham, East Anglia, Edge Hill, Lancaster, Leeds (applicants consider which A-levels to resit for the BSc course), Liverpool, Liverpool Hope, Liverpool John Moores, London (RH), London (SOAS), Loughborough, Manchester Met, Newcastle, Newman (UC), Newport, Northumbria, Oxford Brookes, St Mary's Twickenham (UC), Salford, Southampton, Staffordshire, Ulster, Wolverhampton.

GRADUATE DESTINATIONS AND EMPLOYMENT (2007/8 HESA)

Human and Social Geography graduates surveyed 1970 **Employed** 785 **In further study** 515 **Assumed unemployed** 150

Physical Geography graduates surveyed 2460 **Employed** 950 **In further study** 640 **Assumed unemployed** 210

Career note Geography graduates enter a wide range of occupations, many in business and administrative careers. Depending on specialisations, areas could include agriculture, forestry, hydrology, transport, market research and retail. Teaching is also a popular option.

OTHER DEGREE SUBJECTS FOR CONSIDERATION

Agriculture; Anthropology; Civil Engineering; Countryside Management; Development Studies; Environmental Engineering/Science/Studies; Forestry; Geology; Geomatic Engineering; Surveying; Town Planning; Urban Land Economics; Urban Studies.

GEOLOGY/GEOLOGICAL SCIENCES

(including **Earth Sciences, Geophysics** and **Geoscience**; see also **Astronomy and Astrophysics, Environmental Sciences/Studies**)

Topics in Geology courses include the physical and chemical constitution of the earth, exploration geophysics, oil and marine geology (oceanography) and seismic interpretation. Earth Sciences cover geology, environmental science, physical geography and can also include business studies and language modules. No previous knowledge of geology is required for most courses.

Useful websites www.geolsoc.org.uk; www.bgs.ac.uk; www.noc.soton.ac.uk; www.scicentral.com; www.cardiff.ac.ukearth/degreeprogrammes/index/html.

NB The points totals shown to the left of the institutions are for ease of reference only. It must not be assumed that Tariff points are always used by institutions or that they can be substituted for an offer in grades. The level of an offer is not necessarily indicative of the quality of a course.

COURSE OFFERS INFORMATION

Subject requirements/preferences GCSE English, mathematics and a science required. **AL** One or two mathematics/science subjects usually required. Geography may be accepted as a science subject.

NB In 2012 universities and colleges will differ in their use of GCE AL/AS unit grade information, A* grades, the Extended Project (EPQ), the Advanced Diploma and the Cambridge Pre-U examination when considering applicants and making offers. An EPQ may be accepted in place of an AS subject. Check websites of universities and colleges for the latest offers information.

Your target offers and examples of courses provided by each institution

380 pts Cambridge – A*AA college offers may vary (Nat Sci (Geol)) (IB 38–42 pts)
London (UCL) – AAAe–AABe (Earth Sci Pal) (IB 34–38 pts)
Oxford – A*AA (Earth Sci (Geol)) (IB 38–42 pts))

360 pts Birmingham – AAA (Res App Geol Int Yr) (IB 34–38 pts)
Cardiff – AAA (Geol (Int) MESci) (IB 35 pts)
East Anglia – AAA–AAB (Meteor Ocean courses MSci) (IB 34–33 pts HL 666 inc maths)
Edinburgh – AAA–ABB (Geophys Meteor) (IB 37–32 pts)
Glasgow – AAA (Faster route) (Earth Sci) (IB 38 pts HL 665)
Imperial London – AAA 360 pts (Geol; Geol Geophys; Petrol Geosci; Env Geosci)
Leeds – AAA (Geol Sci (Int)) (IB 36 pts HL 18 pts)
Southampton – AAA–ABB (Geophys) (IB 32–36 pts)

340 pts Bristol – AAB–BBB (Palae Evol) (IB 36 pts HL 665–666)
Cardiff – AAB (Explor Res Geol MESci) (IB 34 pts)
East Anglia – AAB (Clim Sci BSc N Am) (IB 33 pts HL 555)
Glasgow – ABB (Arch Earth Sci) (IB 32 pts)
Lancaster – AAB–ABB 340–320 pts (Earth Env Sci Abrd) (IB 32–34 pts)
Leicester – AAB (App Env Geol MGeol; Geol Geophys MGeol; Geol Pal; Geol MGeol)
Liverpool – AAB (Geol Geophys) (IB 35 pts)
Manchester – AAB–ABB (Geochem) (IB 32 pts)

320 pts Birmingham – ABB–BBC (Env Geosci) (IB 28–34 pts)
Cardiff – ABB (Earth Sci) (IB 30–32 pts)
Durham – ABB (Env Geosci) (IB 34 pts)
East Anglia – ABB–BBB (Meteor Ocean BSc) (IB 32–31 pts)
Exeter – ABB–BBB (Eng Geol Geotech) (IB 30–28 pts)
Glasgow – ABB (Env Biogeochem) (IB 32 pts)
Lancaster – ABB (Earth Sci Geog) (IB 29 pts)
Leicester – ABB (Geol BSc)
Liverpool – ABB (Geophys (Geol)) (IB 30 pts)
London (RH) – ABB (Geoscience)
St Andrews – ABB (Env Geosci courses) (IB 30–32 pts)

Southampton – ABB (Geol BSc) (IB 30 pts HL 16 pts)

Swansea – ABB (Phys Earth Sci)

300 pts **Aberdeen** – BBB 2nd yr entry (Arch Geosci) (IB 32 pts)

Aberystwyth – 300 pts (Env Earth Sci) (IB 28 pts)

Brighton – BBB (Geog Geol) (IB 30 pts)

Cardiff – BBB (Explor Res Geol BSc)

Edinburgh – Check with admissions tutor BBB 1st yr entry (Geol MESci) (IB 34 pts)

Keele – 300 pts (Geosci) (IB 26–30 pts)

Leeds – BBB (Geophys Sci) (IB 32 pts HL 16 pts)

Leicester – BBB (Geol Phys) (IB 28–30 pts)

London (RH) – BBB (Geol) (IB 38 pts HL 66)

Plymouth – 300 pts (Geol MGeol)

Southampton – BBB (Geophysl Sci) (IB 30 pts HL 16 pts)

280 pts **Brighton** – BBC 280 pts (Geol) (IB 28 pts)

Plymouth – 280 pts (Mar Geosci)

260 pts **Brighton** – BBC (Earth Ocn Sci) (IB 28 pts)

Plymouth – 260pts (Physl Geog Geol BSc)

240 pts **Glamorgan** – 240 pts (Geol courses)

Kingston – 240–280 pts (Env Haz Disas Mgt; Earth Sys Sci; App Geol courses; Geol; App Env Geol)

Portsmouth – 240–300 pts (Geol Haz; Pal Evol)

220 pts **Bangor** – 220–260 pts (Geol Ocean) (IB 28 pts)

200 pts **Derby** – 200–240 pts (Geol)

140 pts **West Scotland** – CD (App Biosci Earth Sci)

80 pts **London (Birk)** – for under 21s (over 21s varies) p/t (Geol; Env Geol; Earth Sci)

Open University – contact +44 (0)845 300 6090 **or** www.openuniversity.co.uk/you (Geol St)

Alternative offers

See **Chapter 7** and **Appendix 1** for grades/UCAS Tariff points information for the International Baccalaureate, Scottish Highers/Advanced Highers, the Welsh Baccalaureate, the Irish Leaving Certificate, the Cambridge Pre-U Diploma, the Advanced Diploma and the Extended Project.

CHOOSING YOUR COURSE (SEE ALSO CH. 1)

Some course features

Cardiff (Explor Res Geol) Course provides a grounding in applied geology and the evaluation and exploration of the Earth's natural resources. During the second summer, an industrial placement is offered with an exploration company in the UK or overseas. Option to spend Year 3 in the USA or Australia on the MESci courses.

East Anglia A strong department of Environmental Sciences incorporating courses in Geophysical Sciences with opportunities to study abroad and in industry. A new range of integrated masters' degrees is introduced in 2010 and includes a new MSci in Climate Science.

Exeter Camborne School of Mines is a leader in the field of Engineering Geology and Geotechnics and Mining Engineering. £2000 scholarships are offered on the basis of academic excellence, together with some sponsorships.

Leeds Geological and Geophysical Sciences can be studied with placements in Europe or worldwide or with industrial placement.

Universities and colleges teaching quality See www.qaa.ac.uk; http://unistats.direct.gov.uk.

Top research universities and colleges (RAE 2008) See **Environmental Science/Studies**.

Examples of sandwich degree courses Cardiff; Glamorgan; Greenwich; Kingston; West Scotland.

ADMISSIONS INFORMATION

Number of applicants per place (approx) Aberystwyth 5; Bangor 4; Birmingham 4; Bristol 7; Cardiff 6; Derby 4; Durham 4; East Anglia 7; Edinburgh 5; Exeter 5; Imperial London 5; Kingston 19, (Earth

Sys Sci) 3; Leeds 8; Leicester 5; Liverpool 5; London (RH) 5; London (UCL) 3; Oxford 1. 2; Plymouth 7; Portsmouth (Eng Geol Geotech) 2, (Goel) 2; Southampton 5.

Advice to applicants and planning the UCAS personal statement Visits to any outstanding geological sites and field courses you have attended should be described in detail. Apart from geological formations, you should also be aware of how geology has affected humankind in specific areas in the architecture of the region and artefacts used. Evidence of social skills could be given. See also **Appendix 4**.

Misconceptions about this course East Anglia Many applicants fail to realise that environmental earth science extends beyond geology to the links between the solid earth and its behaviour and society in general. **London (UCL)** Environmental geoscience is sometimes mistaken for environmental science; they are two different subjects.

Selection interviews Yes Birmingham, Cambridge, Durham, Edinburgh, Kingston, Liverpool, London (RH), Oxford (Geol) 46%, Southampton, Sunderland; **Some** Aberystwyth (mature students only), Derby, East Anglia.

Interview advice and questions Some knowledge of the subject will be expected and applicants could be questioned on specimens of rocks and their origins. Past interviews have included questions on the field courses attended, and the geophysical methods of exploration in the detection of metals. How would you determine the age of this rock (sample shown)? Can you integrate a decay curve function and would it help you to determine the age of rocks? How many planes of crystallisation could this rock have? What causes a volcano? What is your local geology? See **Chapter 6**. **Oxford** (Earth Sci) Candidates may be asked to comment on specimens of a geological nature, based on previous knowledge of the subject.

Reasons for rejection (non-academic) Misconceptions about the course. **Exeter** Outright rejection uncommon but some applicants advised to apply for other programmes.

AFTER-RESULTS ADVICE
Offers to applicants repeating A-levels Higher Bristol, St Andrews; **Possibly higher** Cardiff, Portsmouth; **Same** Aberystwyth, Derby, Durham, East Anglia, Leeds, London (RH), Plymouth, Southampton.

GRADUATE DESTINATIONS AND EMPLOYMENT (2007/8 HESA)
Graduates surveyed 890 **Employed** 295 **In further study** 275 **Assumed unemployed** 110

Career note Areas of employment include mining and quarrying, the oil and gas industry, prospecting and processing.

OTHER DEGREE SUBJECTS FOR CONSIDERATION
Archaeology; Civil and Mining Engineering; Environmental Science; Geography; Meteorology; Oceanography; Physics.

GERMAN
(see also **European Studies, Languages**)

Language, literature, practical language skills or a broader study of Germany and its culture (European Studies) are alternative study approaches. See also **Appendix 4** under Languages.

Useful websites www.cilt.org.uk; www.goethe.de; www.bbc.co.uk/languages; www.iol.org.uk; http://languageadvantage.com; www.languagematters.co.uk; www.reed.co.uk/multilingual; www.deutsch-online.com; www.faz.net; www.sueddeutsche.de; http://europa.eu; www.gslg.org.uk; www.amgs.org.uk; www.wigs.ac.uk.

NB The points totals shown to the left of the institutions are for ease of reference only. It must not be assumed that Tariff points are always used by institutions or that they can be substituted for an offer in grades. The level of an offer is not necessarily indicative of the quality of a course.

COURSE OFFERS INFORMATION

Subject requirements/preferences GCSE English and German are required. **AL** German required usually at a specified grade.

NB In 2012 universities and colleges will differ in their use of GCE AL/AS unit grade information, A* grades, the Extended Project (EPQ), the Advanced Diploma and the Cambridge Pre-U examination when considering applicants and making offers. An EPQ may be accepted in place of an AS subject. Check websites of universities and colleges for the latest offers information.

Your target offers and examples of courses provided by each institution

420 pts **London (King's)** – A*AA+AS (Ger Hist) (IB 39 pts HL 6 ger hist)

380 pts **Cambridge** – A*AA college offers may vary (Modn Mediev Lang (Ger))

360 pts **Bath** – AAA–ABB (Int Mgt Ger) (IB 36 pts)
Birmingham – AAA +LNAT (Law Ger)
Bristol – AAA–ABB (Pol Ger) (IB 37–33 pts)
Glasgow – AAA (Ger courses) (IB 36 pts)
Imperial London – AAA (Chem Ger Sci)
London (King's) – AAB+AS (Ger Hist/Phil/Mus) (IB 32 pts)
London (UCL) – AAB+AS–BBB+AS (Ger courses) (IB 32–36 pts)
Manchester – AAA–AAB (Ger Chin MML) (IB 35–37 pts)
Nottingham – AAA +LNAT (Law Ger)
Oxford – AAA (Ger courses)
St Andrews – AAA–AAB (Ger courses)

350 pts **Warwick** – 350 pts (Fr Ger St)

340 pts **Bath** – AAB (Comp Sci Ger) (IB 34–36 pts)
Bristol – AAB-BBC (Ger courses except under **360 pts**)
Cardiff – AAB (Cult Crit Ger) (IB 30 pts)
Durham – AAB (Comb Hons (Ger); Modn Langs (Ger))
East Anglia – AAB (Law Euro Leg Sys) (IB 33 pts)
Exeter – AAB–ABB (Int Rel Ger) (IB 29 pts)
Imperial London – AAB (Biol Ger Sci)
Lancaster – AAB 340 pts (Euro Mgt (Ger)) (IB 34 pts)
Manchester – AAB–BBC (Ger St) (IB 30–35 pts)
Reading – AAB (Int Mgt Bus Admin Ger)
Sheffield – AAB (Mech Eng Ger) (IB 35 pts)
Southampton – AAB (Ger courses) (IB 34–32 pts)
Warwick – AAB–BBB (Ger St courses) (IB 32–34 pts)

320 pts **Bath** – ABB (Modn Langs Euro St (Ger and Fr/Ital/Russ/Span); Ger Fr/Ital/Span)
Kent – 320 pts (Ger Joint Hons courses) (IB 31–35 pts)
Leeds – ABB–BBB (Ger courses)
London (King's) – BBB+AS–BCC+AS (Ger courses) (IB 32 pts)
London (RH) – ABB **or** BBB (inc ger) (Ger courses) (IB 32 pts HL lang 6)
Newcastle – ABB (Ling Ger) (IB 32 pts HL Ger 6)
Sheffield – ABB–BBB (Ger courses) (IB 32–33 pts)
Surrey – ABB–BBB (Ger courses) (IB 32 pts)
Sussex – ABB–BBB (Ger courses)
York – ABB (Ger courses) (IB 32 pts)

300 pts **Aberdeen** – BBB (Ger courses) (IB 28 pts)
Aston – 300–320 pts (Ger courses except under **320 pts**)
Birmingham – BBB (Ger St courses) (IB 32–34 pts)
Cardiff – except under 340 pts ABB–BBB (Ger courses)
Dundee – BBB (Psy Ger; Scot Hist Ger)
Edinburgh – BBB (Ger courses)
Essex – 300–320 pts (Ger St Modn Lang) (IB 30 pts)
Heriot-Watt – BBB (Langs (Interp Transl) (Fr/Ger) (Ger/Span)) (IB 28 pts)
Liverpool – BBB (Ger courses) (IB 30 pts)

London (QM) – 300–340 pts (Ger courses) (IB 32–36 pts)
Nottingham – ABC–BBB (Ger Mus) (IB 32 pts)
Reading – 300–320 pts (Ger courses except under 320 pts) (IB 28 pts)
Salford – 300 pts (Ger courses; Ger with 2nd Lang; Modn Lang Transl Interp St (Fr) (Ger) (Ital) (Port)
Swansea – BBB (Ger courses)
Westminster – BBB 300 pts (Int Bus Ger) (IB 28 pts)

280 pts **Aberystwyth** – 280–300 pts (Ger courses) (IB 27 pts)
Hull – 280–300 pts (Dr Ger; Phil Ger)
Northumbria – 280–300 pts (Ger Bus) (IB 26 pts)
Portsmouth – 280 pts (Euro Bus (UK Ger))
Westminster – BBC (Int Rel Ger)

260 pts **Central Lancashire** – 260 – 300 pts (Ger Comb Hons)
Dundee – BCC (Ger courses except under **300 pts**)
Hull – 260–300 pts (Ger St; Ger Mark; Ger Mgt)
Nottingham Trent – 260 pts (Ger Euro St; Ger Glob St; Ger Media)
Westminster – BCC (Ger courses)

240 pts **Bangor** – 240–260 pts (Ger courses)
Chester – 240 pts (Ger courses) (IB 30 pts)
Manchester Met – 240 pts (Ger Fr/Ital/Span) (IB 28 pts)
Ulster – 240 pts (Ger courses)

220 pts **Leeds Met** – 220 pts (Ger Glob Dev; Ger Int Rel; Ger Mark; Ger Tour Mgt)
Sunderland – 220–360 pts (Ger Comb courses)

200 pts **Anglia Ruskin** – 200 pts (Int Bus (Berlin))
Portsmouth – 200–280 pts (German Studies)

80 pts **London (Birk)** – for under 21s (over 21s varies) p/t (Ger Mgt; Modn Ger St)
London LSE – optional course offered by the language centre check with admissions tutor (Fr/Ger/Span/Russ)

Alternative offers
See **Chapter 7** and **Appendix 1** for grades/UCAS Tariff points information for the International Baccalaureate, Scottish Highers/Advanced Highers, the Welsh Baccalaureate, the Irish Leaving Certificate, the Cambridge Pre-U Diploma, the Advanced Diploma and the Extended Project.

CHOOSING YOUR COURSE (SEE ALSO CH. 1)
Some course features
Bangor German is offered with two other languages from French, Italian and Spanish.
Durham (Modn Lang) Students take core language module each year and options from a range of modules, including film, history, literature, translation, interpreting and cultural studies.
East Anglia German can be taken as part of the Law course with European Legal Systems.
Heriot-Watt The course focuses on practical language skills, linguistics and translation studies, communication studies and European studies.
Salford The only university to offer a course combining media, a language and business studies.

Universities and colleges teaching quality See www.qaa.ac.uk; http://unistats.direct.gov.uk.

Top research universities and colleges (RAE 2008) (German, Dutch and Scandinavian languages) Oxford; Cambridge; London (King's); Leeds; London (UCL); Durham; London (RH); St Andrews; Manchester; Birmingham.

ADMISSIONS INFORMATION
Number of applicants per place (approx) Aston 4; Bangor 6; Birmingham 6; Bradford 6; Bristol 7; Cardiff 6; Central Lancashire 2; Durham 4; East Anglia 4; Exeter 4; Heriot-Watt 10; Hull 12; Kent 10; Lancaster 7; Leeds (Joint Hons) 8; Leicester 4; London (King's) 5; London (QM) 6; London (RH) 5; London (UCL) 4; Newcastle 6; Nottingham 5; Portsmouth 5; Salford 5; Staffordshire 5; Stirling 6; Surrey 2; Swansea 4; Warwick (Ger Bus St) 16, (Ger) 8; York 6.

Advice to applicants and planning the UCAS personal statement Describe visits to Germany or a German-speaking country and the particular cultural and geographical features of the region. Contacts with friends in Germany and language experience should also be mentioned, and if you are bilingual, say so. Read German newspapers and magazines and keep up-to-date with national news.

Misconceptions about this course Leeds See **Languages**. **Swansea** Some students are afraid of the year abroad, which is actually one of the most enjoyable parts of the course.

Selection interviews Yes Bangor, Birmingham (short conversation in German), Bradford, Cambridge, Durham, East Anglia, Exeter, Heriot-Watt, Hull, Liverpool, London (RH), London (UCL), Newcastle, Oxford, Sheffield, Southampton, Surrey (always); **Some** Cardiff, Leeds, Portsmouth, Swansea.

Interview advice and questions Questions asked on A-level syllabus. Part of the interview may be in German. What foreign newspapers and/or magazines do you read? Questions on German current affairs, particularly politics and reunification problems, books read outside the course, etc. See **Chapter 6. Leeds** See **Languages**.

Reasons for rejection (non-academic) Unstable personality. Poor motivation. Insufficient commitment. Unrealistic expectations. Not interested in spending a year abroad.

AFTER-RESULTS ADVICE
Offers to applicants repeating A-levels Higher Birmingham, Glasgow, Leeds, Warwick; **Same** Aston, Cardiff, Chester, Durham, East Anglia, London (RH), Newcastle (not always), Nottingham, Salford, Surrey, Swansea, Ulster, York.

GRADUATE DESTINATIONS AND EMPLOYMENT (2007/8 HESA)
Graduates surveyed 490 **Employed** 200 **In further study** 115 **Assumed unemployed** 45

Career note See **Languages**.

OTHER DEGREE SUBJECTS FOR CONSIDERATION
East European Studies; European Studies; International Business Studies.

GREEK
(see also **Classical Studies/Classical Civilisation, Classics, Languages, Latin**)

Courses are offered in Ancient and Modern Greek, covering the language and literature from ancient times to the present day. Classics and Classical Studies courses (see separate tables) also focus on Greek language and literature, and many provide the opportunity to learn Greek (and/or Latin) from scratch.

Useful websites www.greek-language.com; www.arwhead.com/Greeks; www.greekmyth.org; www.fhw.gr; www.culture.gr; www.greeklanguage.gr.

NB The points totals shown to the left of the institutions are for ease of reference only. It must not be assumed that Tariff points are always used by institutions or that they can be substituted for an offer in grades. The level of an offer is not necessarily indicative of the quality of a course.

COURSE OFFERS INFORMATION
Subject requirements/preferences GCSE English and a foreign language required. Greek required by some universities. **AL** Latin, Greek or a foreign language may be specified by some universities.

NB In 2012 universities and colleges will differ in their use of GCE AL/AS unit grade information, A* grades, the Extended Project (EPQ), the Advanced Diploma and the Cambridge Pre-U examination when considering applicants and making offers. An EPQ may be accepted in place of an AS subject. Check websites of universities and colleges for the latest offers information.

Your target offers and examples of courses provided by each institution
380 pts Cambridge – A*AA college offers may vary (Modn Mediev Lang (Class Gk)) (IB 38–42 pts)
360 pts London (King's) – AABe (Gk Engl) (IB 36 pts)
          Oxford – AAA (Modn Gk courses)

340 pts **Durham** – AAB (Class (Gk/Lat Lang option); Comb Hons Arts (Gk))
Exeter – AAB–ABB (Gk Arbc St) (IB 34–31 pts)
Glasgow – AAB (Gk courses)
London (King's) – ABB+AS (Modn Gk Port Braz St) (IB 36 pts)
London (UCL) – ABB+AS (Gk Lat) (IB 31 pts)
Newcastle – AAB (Comb St (Gk)) (IB 34 pts)
St Andrews – AAB (Gk courses) (IB 36 pts)
320 pts **Leeds** – ABB (Arbc Gk Civ) (IB 33 pts)
London (RH) – ABB 320 pts (Gk; Gk Ital; Fr/Ger Gk)
Manchester – ABB–BBB (Gk Engl Lit) (IB 33–32 pts)
Nottingham – ABB (Gk (Anc))
Swansea – ABB–BBB 320–300 pts (Gk)
300 pts **Edinburgh** – BBB–AAA (Phil Gk) (IB 34 pts HL 555)
Leeds – BBB (Gk Civ Theol Relig St) (IB 32 pts)
200 pts **Trinity Saint David** – 200–300 pts (Gk courses)

Alternative offers
See **Chapter 7** and **Appendix 1** for grades/UCAS Tariff points information for the International Baccalaureate, Scottish Highers/Advanced Highers, the Welsh Baccalaureate, the Irish Leaving Certificate, the Cambridge Pre-U Diploma, the Advanced Diploma and the Extended Project.

CHOOSING YOUR COURSE (SEE ALSO CH. 1)
Some course features
Durham Classics courses have a common first year which allows the student to begin or continue a study of Greek.
Edinburgh (Gk St) The course covers archaeology, art, literature of Greek civilisation, with an intensive Greek course in the first term for beginners.
London (King's) The Modern Greek with English course focuses on studying the classical world through reading ancient texts in the original Greek. A-level Greek is required for entry.
Nottingham (Gk (Anc)) The course combines Greek language learning throughout (no prior knowledge required) with a study of Greek literature, history, society and culture. Intensive language study is provided so at each level of the course students can read texts in the original Greek.

Universities and colleges teaching quality See www.qaa.ac.uk; http://unistats.direct.gov.uk.

Top research universities and colleges (RAE 2008) See **Classics**.

ADMISSIONS INFORMATION
Number of applicants per place (approx) Leeds 2; London (King's) 3.

Advice to applicants and planning the UCAS personal statement See **Classical Studies/Classical Civilisation**.

Selection interviews Yes Cambridge, London (RH).

Interview advice and questions Questions asked on A-level syllabus. Why do you want to study Greek? What aspects of this course interest you? (Questions will develop from answers.) See also **Chapter 6**.

Reasons for rejection (non-academic) Poor language ability.

AFTER-RESULTS ADVICE
Offers to applicants repeating A-levels Higher St Andrews; **Same** Leeds.

GRADUATE DESTINATIONS AND EMPLOYMENT (2007/8 HESA)
Classical Greek graduates surveyed 5 **Employed** 5 **In further study** 0 **Assumed unemployed** 0

Career note See **Languages**.

OTHER DEGREE SUBJECTS FOR CONSIDERATION
Ancient History; Classical Studies; Classics; European Studies; Philosophy.

HEALTH SCIENCES/STUDIES

(including **Audiology, Chiropractic, Orthoptics, Osteopathy, Paramedic Science**; see also **Community Studies/Development, Nursing and Midwifery, Pharmacology, Pharmacy and Pharmaceutical Sciences, Physiotherapy, Radiography, Social Sciences/Studies, Speech Pathology/Sciences/Therapy**)

Health Sciences/Studies is a broad subject-field which offers courses covering both practical applications concerning health and well-being (some of which border on nursing) and also the administrative activities involved in the promotion of health in the community. Also included are some specialised careers which include Chiropractic, involving the healing process by way of manipulation, mainly in the spinal region, and Osteopathy in which joints and tissues are manipulated to correct abnormalities. Audiology is concerned with the treatment and diagnosis of hearing and balance disorders while Prosthetics involves the provision and fitting of artificial limbs and Orthotics is concerned with making and fitting braces, splints and special footwear to ease pain and to assist movement.

Useful websites www.rsph.org.uk; www.bmj.com; www.reflexology.org; www.baap.org.uk; www.chiropractic-uk.co.uk; www.osteopathy.org.uk; www.who.int; www.csp.org.uk; www.scienceyear.com; www.intute.ac.uk.

NB The points totals shown to the left of the institutions are for ease of reference only. It must not be assumed that Tariff points are always used by institutions or that they can be substituted for an offer in grades. The level of an offer is not necessarily indicative of the quality of a course.

COURSE OFFERS INFORMATION

Subject requirements/preferences GCSE English, mathematics and a science important or essential for some courses. **AL** Mathematics, chemistry or biology may be required for some courses. **Other** Health checks and CRB clearance required for many courses.

NB In 2012 universities and colleges will differ in their use of GCE AL/AS unit grade information, A* grades, the Extended Project (EPQ), the Advanced Diploma and the Cambridge Pre-U examination when considering applicants and making offers. An EPQ may be accepted in place of an AS subject. Check websites of universities and colleges for the latest offers information.

Your target offers and examples of courses provided by each institution
340 pts **Exeter** – AAB–ABB (Clin Sci)
          London (UCL) – ABB+AS–BBB+AS (Audiol) (IB 32–34 pts)
320 pts **Aston** – ABB (Audiol)
          Glamorgan – 320 pts (MChiro Chiropractic)
          Glasgow – ABB (Spo Med) (IB 32 pts)
          Leeds – ABB (Audiol)
          Manchester – ABB–BBB (Audiol) (IB 33–30 pts)
          Southampton – ABB (Audiol) (IB 32 pts)
          Strathclyde – ABB (Pros Orthot) (IB 34 pts)
          Surrey – ABB (inc AL Sci) (Paramed St)
300 pts **Bradford** – optional transfer for some to Medicine at Leeds 300 pts (Clin Sci)
          Bristol – BBB (Audiol) (IB 32 pts)
          Essex – 300–280 pts (Hlth St Sociol) (IB 32–30 pts)
          Glamorgan – 300 pts (Chiropractic)
          Glasgow – BBB (Hlth Soc St)
          Manchester – BBB–BCC (Oral Hlth Sci)
          Sheffield – BBB (Orthoptics) (IB 32 pts)
          Surrey – BBB (Op Dept Pr)

Health & Science
at Hull and Harrogate College

HC UK Hull College Group

Higher Education

Hull College Group offers students the opportunity to study towards several Foundation Degrees in Health and Science within our excellent suite of laboratory facilities.

The main areas of study are in Biomedicine, Counselling, Criminology and Working with Young People, Children's Care, Learning and Development and Playwork.

Hull Campus:
01482 **598744**
Or visit: www.hull-college.ac.uk/HE

Harrogate Campus:
01423 **878211**
Or visit: www.harrogate.ac.uk/HE

280 pts **Anglo-Euro (Coll Chiro)** – (Hum Sci (Chiropractic))
Bangor – 280–230 pts (Med Sci)
Brit Coll Ost Med – BBC (inc Biol, Chem) 280 pts (M. Ost)
British Sch Ost – BBC (inc Biol and 1 other science) 280 pts (Osteopathy)
Brunel – BBC (Biomed Sci (Immun)) (IB 30 pts HL 5 biol)
De Montfort – 280 pts (Audiol)
Durham – check with Admissions Tutor BBC (Hlth Hum Sci) (IB 30 pts)
Essex – 280–300 pts (Hlth St) (IB 32–30 pts)
Hertfordshire – 280 pts (Paramed Sci)
Nescot – 280 pts (Ost Med)
Northumbria – 280 pts (Env Hlth)
Plymouth – 280–320 pts (Tox Hlth) (IB 26 pts)
Salford – 280 pts (Pros Orthot) (IB 24 pts)
Swansea – BBC 280 pts (Audiol)
Worcester – 280 pts (Hlth Psy)

260 pts **Brunel** – BCC (Occ Thera) (IB 29 pts)
Central Lancashire – 260–300 pts (Df St courses) (IB 28 pts)
Dundee – BCC (Oral Hlth Sci)
Edge Hill – 260 pts (Hlth Soc Wlbng)
Hull – BCC (Glob Hlth Hum Rlf)
Kent – 260 pts (Hlth Soc Cr) (IB 33 pts)
Leeds Trinity (UC) – 260 pts (Hlth Prom Dev)
Lincoln – 260 pts (Hlth Soc Cr)
Liverpool – BCC 260 pts (Orthoptics) (IB 28 pts)
Liverpool Hope – 260 pts (Hlth Nutr Fit)
Liverpool John Moores – 260 pts (Env Hlth)
Manchester Met – 260–240 pts (Env Hlth)

For a quick reference offers calculator, fold out the inside back cover.

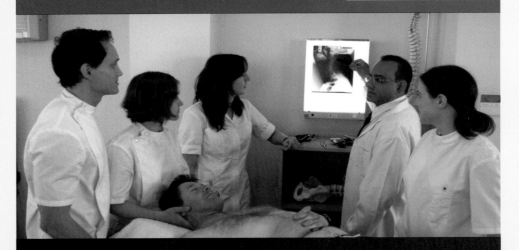

BCOM: internationally regarded as a world leader in osteopathy

The British College of Osteopathic Medicine (BCOM), based in London, is internationally regarded as one of the world's best specialist osteopathic education institutions. Founded in 1936 by the famous naturopathic osteopath, Stanley Lief, BCOM has become a world leader in osteopathic education and research with the most full-time academic staff in any UK osteopathic college. It was also the first institution in the UK to offer an osteopathic honours degree and to achieve a landmark "approval without conditions" recognition from the General Osteopathic Council (GOsC). In 2008, BCOM launched its much-praised four year **undergraduate Masters in Osteopathy**.

0207 435 6464
bcom.ac.uk

BCOM offers the most advanced research facilities in Europe; the only specialist college to provide cutting-edge on-site human-performance and hydrotherapy laboratories. Founder of the International Conference on Advances in Osteopathic Research, BCOM fosters a strong research environment and works to instil a research ethos into BCOM graduates.

BRITISH COLLEGE OF
BCOM
OSTEOPATHIC MEDICINE

The British College of Osteopathic Medicine
Accredited by the General Osteopathic Council
Registered Charity No 312907

Nottingham Trent – 260 pts (Exer Nutr Hlth)
Queen Margaret – 260–280 pts (Hlth Psy)
Sheffield – BCC (Hlth Hum Sci) (IB 29 pts)
Ulster – 260 pts (Hlth Soc Cr Plcy)

240 pts **Arts London (CFash)** – 240 pts (Cos Sci)
Bath Spa – 240–280 pts (Diet Hlth)
Bristol – CCC (Df St) (IB 28 pts)
Central Lancashire – 240 pts (Hlth St courses)
Chester – 240 pts (Hlth Soc Cr)
Coventry – 240 pts (Hum Biosci)
Edge Hill – 240 pts (Wmns Hlth)
European Sch Ost – 240 pts (Osteopathy)
Glamorgan – 240–280 pts (Hlth Soc Cr)
Leeds Met – 240 pts (Ost)
London Met – 240 pts (Herb Medcnl Sci)
Middlesex – contact University 2–3 AL 240–280 pts (Trad Chin Med)
Teesside – 240 pts (Fd Nutr Hlth Sci)

220 pts **Bangor** – 220–260 pts (Hlth Soc Cr)
Bath Spa – 220–280 pts (Hlth St courses)
Central Lancashire – 220 pts (Sex Hlth St)
Coventry – 220–240 pts (Env Hlth) (IB 27 pts)
Hertfordshire – 220–260 pts (Hlth St joint courses)
Kingston – 220–280 pts (Exer Nutr Hlth)
Northampton – 220–260 pts (Hlth St courses; Hum Biosci)
St Mary's Twickenham (UC) – 220 pts (Hlth Exer Physl Actvts)
Southampton Solent – 220 pts (Hlth Exer Physl Actvt; Hlth Prom Fit)
Sunderland – 220 pts (Commun Hlth; Hlth Soc Cr)
UCP Marjon – 220 pts (Hlth Exer Physl Actvt)
Westminster – CCD (Hlth Sci (Nutr Thera)) (IB 26 pts)
York St John – 220–240 pts (Hlth Prac)

200 pts **Birmingham City** – 200 pts (Hlth Wlbng)
Bolton – 200 pts (Commun Hlth Wlbng)
Bradford – 200 pts (Clin Sci Fdn)
Canterbury Christ Church – 200 pts (Hlth St courses)
Cardiff (UWIC) – 200 pts (Complem Thera)
De Montfort – 200 pts (Pharml Cos Sci)
East London – 200 pts (Fit Hlth; Hlth Prom; Hlth St)
Gloucestershire – 200 pts (Hlth Commun Soc Cr courses)
Glyndŵr – 200 pts (Complem Med Prac; Chin Med)
Greenwich – 200 pts (Complem Thera)
Huddersfield – 200 pts (Hlth Commun St)
Hull – 200 pts (Educ St Hlth St)
Middlesex – contact University 200–300 pts (Herb Med)
Nottingham Trent – 200 pts (Hlth Soc Cr courses)
Oldham (Coll Univ Centre) – 200–220 pts (Hlth Commun St)
Oxford Brookes – BBB (Ost)
Plymouth – 200 pts (Hlth Soc Cr St)
Roehampton – 200–260 pts (Hlth Hum Sci)
Salford – 200 pts (Env Hlth) (IB 24 pts)
Sheffield Hallam – 200 pts (Pblc Hlth Nutr)
Suffolk (Univ Campus) – 200 pts (Hlth Wlbng)
West London – 200 pts (Hlth St)

180 pts **Derby** – 180–200 pts (Hlth Soc Cr)
Greenwich – 180 pts (Pblc Hlth)
Manchester Met – 180 pts (Soc Chng (Hlth Soc Cr))

160 pts **Abertay Dundee** – CC 168 pts (Mntl Hlth Cnslg)
Anglia Ruskin – 160 pts (Pblc Hlth)
Colchester (Inst) – 160 pts (Hlth Soc Cr)
Cumbria – 160 pts (Complem Thera)
De Montfort – 160 pts (Hlth St)
Leeds Met – 160 pts (Pblc Hlth; Hlth Cr Sci; Acpntr)
London Met – 160 pts (Hlth Prom)
UHI Millennium Inst – CC (Hlth St)
Westminster – CCD (Hlth Sci (Herb Med)) (IB 26 pts)
Wolverhampton – 160–220 pts (Hlth St Soc Cr; Hlth St; Df St)

100 pts **Newport** – 100–120 pts (Commun Hlth)

Brighton – indiv offers may vary Check with University (Acpntr St; Ost)
Brit Coll Ost Med – contact Admissions Tutor (Dip Ost; Dip Naturopathy)
Open University – contact +44 (0)845 300 6090 **or** www.openuniversity.co.uk/you (Hlth Soc Cr)

Alternative offers

See **Chapter 7** and **Appendix 1** for grades/UCAS Tariff points information for the International Baccalaureate, Scottish Highers/Advanced Highers, the Welsh Baccalaureate, the Irish Leaving Certificate, the Cambridge Pre-U Diploma, the Advanced Diploma and the Extended Project.

EXAMPLES OF FOUNDATION DEGREES IN THE SUBJECT FIELD

(See also **Social and Public Policy and Administration**) Bedfordshire; Blackburn (Coll Univ Centre); Bradford; Brighton; Bristol City (Coll); Bristol UWE; Bucks New; Cardiff (UWIC); Central Lancashire; Chichester; Cornwall (Coll); Coventry; Cumbria; Durham New (Coll); East London; Edge Hill; Farnborough (CT); Greenwich; Grimsby (IFHE); Harper Adams (UC); Hereford (CA); Hopwood Hall (Coll); Huddersfield; Hugh Baird (Coll); Hull (Coll); Kendal (Coll); Kingston; Kirklees (Coll); Leeds Trinity (UC); Lincoln; Loughborough (Coll); Manchester (Coll); Newport; Norwich City (Coll); Plymouth; Portsmouth; Riverside Halton (Coll); St Helens (Coll); Stockton Riverside (Coll); Stratford upon Avon (Coll); Suffolk (Univ Campus); Swansea (Coll); Truro (Coll); Wakefield (Coll); West London; Wigan and Leigh (Coll); York St John.

CHOOSING YOUR COURSE (SEE ALSO CH. 1)

Some course features

Aberdeen The Health Sciences programme is based in the Medical School and combines courses on social, life and medical sciences. In the third year students are attached to a health or social care agency in the community.

Bath Spa Health Studies is a part of the Combined Honours programme. In addition to health subjects the course covers education, public health, child, disability and mental health.

Brunel Human Health is one of five options chosen at the end of Year 1 as part of the Biomedical Sciences programme.

Essex (Hlth Hum Sci) A multi-disciplinary course involving a study of psychology, sociology and biology relevant to health and communication skills.

Universities and colleges teaching quality See www.qaa.ac.uk; http://unistats.direct.gov.uk.

Top research universities and colleges (RAE 2008) (Allied Health Professions and Studies) London (UCL); Lancaster; Surrey; Bristol UWE; Hull; Cardiff; Swansea; Glasgow; Strathclyde; Queen's Belfast.

ADMISSIONS INFORMATION

Number of applicants per place (approx) Anglo-Euro (Coll Chiro) 1; Bangor 2; Bath Spa 1; Bournemouth 4; Bristol (Audiol) 5, (Df St) 2; Brit Coll Ost Med 5; Brunel 2; Central Lancashire 6; Chester 6; Chichester 5; Cumbria 4; European Sch Ost 3; Liverpool John Moores 10; London Met 7; Manchester 18; Manchester Met 10; Middlesex 4; Northampton 3; Portsmouth 12; Roehampton 10; Salford 8; Southampton 4; Swansea 1; Worcester 3.

UNIVERSITY OF
Southampton

Leading healthcare. Learn with the best

The University of Southampton, Faculty of Health Sciences is one of the leading schools for nursing and midwifery, offering:

- Cutting edge, research led teaching
- Excellent connections with the NHS
- Varied and interesting practice experiences
- Supportive and friendly environment

For more information visit
www.facebook.com/SouthamptonUni.
HealthSciences
Tel: +44 (0)23 8059 5500
www.southampton.ac.uk/healthsciences

Admissions tutors' advice You should describe any work with people you have done, particularly in a caring capacity, for example, working with the elderly, nursing, hospital work. Show why you wish to study this subject. You should give evidence of your ability to communicate and to work in a group. Evidence needed of applicants' understanding of the NHS and health care systems. Osteopathy applicants should provide clear evidence of why they want to work as an osteopath: work shadowing in an osteopath's practice is important and should be described. Give details of any work using your hands.

Advice to applicants and planning the UCAS personal statement There is a mistaken belief that Health Science courses include nursing.

Misconceptions about this course Bangor (Hlth Soc Cr) This is an administration course, not a nursing course. **Brit Coll Ost Med** Some students think that we offer an orthodox course in medicine. **European Sch Ost** Some applicants think we teach in French: we do not although we do have a franchise with a French school based in St Etienne and a high percentage of international students. All lectures are in English. Applicants should note that cranial osteopathy – one of our specialisms – is only one aspect of the programme.

Selection interviews Yes Birmingham, Bristol, Central Lancashire, Chichester, Coventry, European Sch Ost, Glamorgan, Middlesex, Nottingham Trent, Southampton, Worcester; **Some** Abertay Dundee, Bath Spa, Canterbury Christ Church, Cardiff (UWIC) (Complem Thera), Derby, Huddersfield (mature students), Liverpool John Moores, Salford, Swansea.

Interview advice and questions Courses vary considerably and you are likely to be questioned on your reasons for choosing the course at that university or college. If you have studied biology then questions are possible on the A-level syllabus and you could also be asked to discuss any work experience you have had. (Osteopathy) What personal qualities would you need to be a good osteopath? What have you done that you would feel demonstrates a sense of responsibility? What would you do if you were not able to secure a place on an Osteopathy course this year? See **Chapter 6**. **Liverpool John Moores** Interviews are informal. It would be useful for you to bring samples of coursework to the interview.

Reasons for rejection (non-academic) Some students are mistakenly looking for a professional qualification in, for example, occupational therapy, nursing. **Coventry** Inadequate mathematics.

AFTER-RESULTS ADVICE
Offers to applicants repeating A-levels Same Abertay Dundee, Aston, Bangor, Brighton, Chester, Derby, European Sch Ost, Huddersfield, Lincoln, Liverpool John Moores, Nottingham Trent (Hlth Env), Roehampton, Salford, Surrey, Swansea.

For a quick reference offers calculator, fold out the inside back cover.

GRADUATE DESTINATIONS AND EMPLOYMENT (2007/8 HESA)

See also under **Biotechnology**, **Dentistry**, **Medicine**, **Nursing and Midwifery**, **Nutrition** and **Optometry**.

Complementary Medicine graduates surveyed 590 **Employed** 340 **In further study** 20 **Assumed unemployed** 40

Aural and Oral Sciences graduates surveyed 580 **Employed** 425 **In further study** 15 **Assumed unemployed** 40

Career note Graduates enter a very broad variety of careers depending on their specialism. Opportunities exist in the public sector, for example, management and administrative positions with health and local authorities and in health promotion.

OTHER DEGREE SUBJECTS FOR CONSIDERATION

Audiology; Biological Sciences; Biology; Community Studies; Consumer Studies; Dentistry; Dietetics; Medicine; Nursing; Nutrition; Occupational Therapy; Optometry; Physiotherapy; Psychology; Podiatry; Radiography; Speech Therapy; Sport Science.

HISTORY

(including **Heritage Management** and Medieval Studies; see also **History (Ancient)**, **History (Economic and Social)**, **History of Art**)

Degrees in History cover a very broad field with many courses focusing on British and European history. However, specialised History degrees are available which cover other regions of the world and, in addition, all courses will offer a wide range of modules.

Useful websites www.english-heritage.org.uk; www.historytoday.com; www.genealogyarchives.com; www.historynet.com; www.archives.org.uk; www.royalhistoricalsociety.org; www.nationalarchives.gov. uk; www.historesearch.com.

NB The points totals shown to the left of the institutions are for ease of reference only. It must not be assumed that Tariff points are always used by institutions or that they can be substituted for an offer in grades. The level of an offer is not necessarily indicative of the quality of a course.

COURSE OFFERS INFORMATION

Subject requirements/preferences **GCSE** English and a foreign language may be required or preferred. **AL** History usually required at a specified grade. (Medieval Studies) History or English literature required for some courses. (Viking Studies) English or history.

NB In 2012 universities and colleges will differ in their use of GCE AL/AS unit grade information, A* grades, the Extended Project (EPQ), the Advanced Diploma and the Cambridge Pre-U examination when considering applicants and making offers. An EPQ may be accepted in place of an AS subject. Check websites of universities and colleges for the latest offers information.

Your target offers and examples of courses provided by each institution

410 pts **London (King's)** – AAAb (Hist courses) (IB 36–37 pts)
400 pts **London (UCL)** – A*AA+AS–AAA+AS (Hist Yr Abrd) (IB 38–39 pts)
        Warwick – AAAc (Hist courses) (IB 37–38 pts)
380 pts **Cambridge** – college offers may vary A*AA (Educ Hist) (IB 38–42 pts)
360 pts **Bristol** – AAA–AAB (Hist) (IB 34–35 pts)
        Durham – AAA (Engl Lit Hist) (IB 37 pts)
        Exeter – AAA–ABB 360–340 pts (Hist Arbc St) (IB 36–31 pts)
        Leeds – AAA–AAB (History) (IB 37 HL 18 pts hist 7)
        London LSE – AAA (Int Rel Hist) (IB 38 pts HL 766)
        Manchester – AAA–AAB (Hist Am St) (IB 32–37 pts)
        Newcastle – AAA–AAB (Hist Arch) (IB 37 pts)
        Nottingham – AAA (Hist Pol) (IB 38 pts)

Oxford – AAA (Anc Modn Hist) (IB 38–42 pts)
St Andrews – AAA (History) (IB 37 pts)
Sheffield – AAA (Int Hist Pol; History)
Sussex – AAA–AAB (Engl Hist) (IB 36–34 pts)
York – AAA (Hist Engl) (IB 36 pts)

340 pts **Birmingham** – AAB–ABB (War St)
Cardiff – AAB (Modn Hist Pol; Hist)
Durham – AAB (Educ St (Hist))
East Anglia – AAB–ABB (Hist Land Arch) (IB 32–34 pts)
Glasgow – AAB (Hist) (IB 34 pts)
Kent – 340 pts (Hist Phil) (IB 33 pts)
Lancaster – AAB 340 pts (History)
Leicester – AAB (Hist) (IB 34 pts)
Liverpool – AAB (Hist) (IB 33 pts HL hist 6)
London (QM) – AAB 340 pts (Modn Contemp Hist) (IB 32 pts)
London (RH) – AAB (Hist courses) (IB 36 pts)
Manchester – AAB–BBB (Mediev St; Hist St courses; Modn Hist Econ)
Newcastle – AAB (History) (IB 35 pts HL hist 6 pts)
Reading – 340–360 pts (Hist Int Rel) (IB 32 pts HL 666)
St Andrews – AAB (Scot Hist courses) (IB 36–38 pts)
Sheffield – AAB (Int Hist Int Pol) (IB 35–32 pts)
Southampton – AAB (Modn Hist Pol) (IB 34 pts)
Sussex – AAB–BBB (Hist; Hist Anth; Hist Film St; Hist Lang)

320 pts **Cardiff** – ABB (Hist Welsh Hist) (IB 28–30 pts)
Kent – 320 pts (War St) (IB 33 pts)
Lancaster – ABB 320 pts (Hist Mus) (IB 30 pts)
Leeds – ABB (Hist joint courses) (IB 35–37 pts)
Leicester – AAB 320 pts (Engl Hist) (IB 34 pts)
Liverpool – ABB (Modn Hist Pol) (IB 33 pts)
London (Gold) – ABB (Hist Anth) (IB 32 pts HL 766)
London (SOAS) – ABB (Hist courses) (IB 30–32 pts)
London (UCL) – ABB (Jew Hist) (IB 34 pts)
Loughborough – 320 pts (Hist)
Northumbria – 320 pts (Hist) (IB 26 pts)
Nottingham – ABB (Hist Contemp Chin St)
Queen's Belfast – ABB–BBBb (Hist)
Strathclyde – ABB (History) (IB 34 pts)
Swansea – ABB (Hist)

300 pts **Aberystwyth** – 320–300 pts (Modn Contemp Hist) (IB 30 pts)
Brunel – 260–300 pts (History) (IB 31 pts)
East Anglia – BBB (Am Engl Hist) (IB 31 pts HL hist 5)
Edinburgh – BBB (Soc Hist) (IB 34 pts)
Essex – 300–320 pts (Soc Cult Hist) (IB 32 pts)
Gloucestershire – 280–300 pts (Hist)
Hull – 300–260 pts (Hist; Hist Marit Hist; Hist Soc Hist)
Keele – 300–320 pts (Am St Hist) (IB 28–30 pts)
Leicester – BBB (Hist Arch) (IB 34 pts)
Liverpool – BBB (Hist Fr/Ger/Hisp St/Ital/Irish St)
Northumbria – 300 pts (Engl Lit Hist) (IB 26 pts)
Nottingham – ABC (Hist Russ)
Oxford Brookes – BBB/BBbb/Abb (Hist courses) (IB 32 pts)
Sheffield – BBB (Hist joint courses) (IB 32 pts)

280 pts **Brighton** – BBC (Hist Des Cult Soty) (IB 30 pts)
Bristol UWE – 280–320 pts (Int Hist Int Pol) (IB 28–30 pts)
Edge Hill – 280 pts (Hist courses) (IB 24 pts)

Hertfordshire – 280 pts (Hist courses)
Huddersfield – 280–320 pts (Hist)
Nottingham Trent – 280 pts (History)
Roehampton – 280–320 pts (Hist courses) (IB 26 pts)
Suffolk (Univ Campus) – 280 pts (Hist)
Teesside – 280 pts (Hist courses) (IB 24 pts)

260 pts **Brighton** – BCC (Engl Lit Commun Hist) (IB 30 pts)
Buckingham – 260 pts (Engl Lit Hist) (IB 27 pts)
Central Lancashire – 260–300 pts (Hist)
Chichester – BCC (Hist courses) (IB 28 pts)
Coventry – 260–280 pts (Hist courses)
Dundee – BCC (Bus Econ Mark Hist) (IB 29 pts HL 15 pts)
Glamorgan – 260–300 pts (Hist courses)
Hull – 300 pts (Am St Hist)
Keele – 260–320 pts (Hist courses) (IB 28–30 pts)
Lincoln – 240 pts (Engl Hist)
Liverpool – BCC (Ir St Hist) (IB 27 pts)
Liverpool Hope – 260 pts (Hist courses)
Liverpool John Moores – 260 pts (Hist)
London Met – 260 pts (Hist courses)
Manchester Met – 240 pts from full ALs (Modn Hist) (IB 26 pts)
Newman (UC) – 260 pts (Hist courses) (IB 24 pts)
Newport – 260 pts (Hist; Engl Hist)
Nottingham Trent – 260 pts (Hist joint courses)
Stirling – BCC 1st yr entry (Hist Jrnl St) (IB 28 pts)
Westminster – BCC/BB (Engl Lit Hist) (IB 28 pts)
Winchester – 260–300 pts (Hist Mediev Wrld) (IB 24 pts)

240 pts **Aberdeen** – BBB (Scot St)
Bangor – 240–280 pts (Welsh Hist Arch) (IB 28 pts)
Bolton – 240 pts (History)
Bournemouth – 240 pts (Arch Prehist; Herit Cons)
Bradford – 240 pts (Hist Pol; Modn Euro Hist)
Canterbury Christ Church – 240 pts (Hist courses)
Central Lancashire – 240 pts (Modn Wrld Hist)
Chester – 240–280 pts (History)
De Montfort – 240 pts (Hist Joint Hons) (IB 24 pts)
Greenwich – 240 pts (Hist)
Leeds Trinity (UC) – 240 pts (History)
Lincoln – 240 pts (Cons Restor; Hist; Hist Pol)
Plymouth – 240 pts (Hist courses) (IB 27 pts)
Portsmouth – 240–300 pts (Engl Hist) (IB 25 pts)
Salford – 240 pts (Contemp Mltry Int Hist) (IB 27 pts)
Sheffield Hallam – 240 pts (Hist)
Ulster – CCC 240 pts (Irish Hist courses; Hist courses)
Worcester – 240–300 pts (Hist courses) (IB 24 pts)

220 pts **Bath Spa** – 220–280 pts (Hist) (IB 24 pts)
Kingston – 220–320 pts (Hist Joint Hons) (IB 30 pts)
Sunderland – 220–360 pts (Hist; Hist Pol; Hist Media St courses)
York St John – 220–260 pts (Hist courses) (IB 24 pts)

200 pts **Anglia Ruskin** – 200 pts (Hist; Hist Engl)
Cumbria – 200 pts (History)
East London – 200 pts (Hist courses)
Glyndŵr – 200 pts (Hist; Hist Engl)
Northampton – 220–260 pts (Hist courses) (IB 24 pts)
Trinity Saint David – 200–300 pts (Church Hist; Hist courses; Mediev St)

180 pts **Derby** – 180–240 pts (Hist courses)
Leeds Met – 180 pts (Hist)
Salford – 180–200 pts (Contemp Hist Pol) (IB 27 pts)
Staffordshire – 180–220 pts (Modn Hist courses)

160 pts **Bishop Grosseteste (UC)** – 160 pts (Educ St Hist)
St Mary's Twickenham (UC) – 160–200 pts inc BC (Hist courses)
UHI Millennium Inst – CC (Hist Pol)
Wolverhampton – 160–220 pts (Hist; War St)

140 pts **Bishop Grosseteste (UC)** – 140 pts (Herit St)

 80 pts **London (Birk)** – for under 21s (over 21s varies) p/t (Hist; Hist Arch)
Staffordshire – 80–220 pts (Int Hist courses)
West Anglia (Coll) – 80–160 pts (Engl Hist; Sociol Hist)

Alternative offers

See **Chapter 7** and **Appendix 1** for grades/UCAS Tariff points information for the International Baccalaureate, Scottish Highers/Advanced Highers, the Welsh Baccalaureate, the Irish Leaving Certificate, the Cambridge Pre-U Diploma, the Advanced Diploma and the Extended Project.

EXAMPLES OF FOUNDATION DEGREES IN THE SUBJECT FIELD
Bath Spa; Blackpool and Fylde (Coll); Cumbria; Truro (Coll); Winchester.

CHOOSING YOUR COURSE (SEE ALSO CH. 1)
Some course features

Kent History can be taken with an optional deferred subject. The Single Honours programme provides the opportunity of a work placement in a museum, a cathedral workshop or a year abroad in Europe.
Leicester A very large department offering specialisms in a wide range of subjects. The subject is also part of the Combined Studies programme in which, from a choice of 17 subjects, two subjects are studied for three years and one subject for two years.
Manchester The History programme enables students to study course units across the whole range of history topics including the history of science. There are opportunities to spend part of the course studying abroad.
Ulster In addition to the Single Honours course, History is offered as a joint course (two subjects) or under the Combined Arts programme when students choose three subjects in Year 1 continuing with a study of two subjects or one major and one minor subject.

Universities and colleges teaching quality See www.qaa.ac.uk; http://unistats.direct.gov.uk.

Top research universities and colleges (RAE 2008) Imperial London; Essex; Kent; Liverpool; Oxford; Warwick; Cambridge; London (UCL); London (Birk); Southampton; Hertfordshire; London LSE; Sheffield.

ADMISSIONS INFORMATION
Number of applicants per place (approx) Aberystwyth 6; Anglia Ruskin 4; Bangor 6; Bath Spa 6; Birmingham 8, (E Medit Hist) 3, (War St) 4; Bournemouth (Herit Cons) 3; Bristol 13; Bristol UWE 6; Brunel 6; Buckingham 10; Cambridge 3; Cardiff 7; Central Lancashire 5; Chichester 4; Cumbria 5; De Montfort 10; Dundee 6; Durham 15; East Anglia 8; Edge Hill 8; Exeter 9; Gloucestershire 26; Glyndŵr 2; Huddersfield 4; Hull 5; Kent 12; Kingston 6; Lancaster 11; Leeds 12; Leeds Trinity (UC) 14; Leicester 7; Liverpool 6; London (Gold) 6; London (King's) 10; London (QM) 5; London (RH) 9; London (UCL) 13; London LSE 19; London Met 2; Manchester 5; Manchester Met 8; Middlesex 10; Newcastle 13; Newman (UC) 2; Northampton 4; Nottingham 20; Oxford Brookes 25; Portsmouth 5; Roehampton 3; St Mary's Twickenham (UC) 5; Sheffield Hallam 21; Southampton 5; Staffordshire 8; Stirling 2; Teesside 4; Trinity Saint David 6; Warwick 17; York 7; York St John 3.

Advice to applicants and planning the UCAS personal statement Show your passion for the past! Visits to places of interest should be mentioned, together with any particular features which impressed you. Read historical books and magazines outside your A-level syllabus. Mention these and describe any special areas of study which interest you. (Check that these areas are covered in the courses for which you are applying!) **Manchester** Due to the detailed nature of entry requirements for History courses, we are unable to include full details in the prospectus. For complete and up-to-date information on our entry requirements for these courses, please visit our website at www.manchester.ac.uk/ugcourses.

Misconceptions about this course Students sometimes under-estimate the amount of reading required. **Lincoln** Some students expect the subject to be assessed only by exams and essays. It is not – we use a wide range of assessment methods. **Liverpool John Moores** Some applicants think that they have to study ancient and medieval history as well as modern; we actually only cover post-1750 history. **Stirling** Some applicants think that we only teach British history. We also cover European, American, African and Environmental History.

Selection interviews Yes Bangor, Birmingham (E Medit Hist), Bishop Grosseteste (UC), Brighton, Bristol, Brunel, Cambridge, Canterbury Christ Church, Edge Hill, Essex, Hertfordshire, Hull, Lancaster, Leeds Trinity (UC), Lincoln (Cons Restor), London (King's), London (QM), London (RH), London (UCL), London Met, London South Bank, Middlesex, Oxford (Hist) 29% (Hist Mod Lang) 18%, Oxford Brookes, Portsmouth, Roehampton, Sussex, Warwick; **Some** Anglia Ruskin, Bath Spa, Buckingham, Cardiff, Chichester, De Montfort, Dundee, Exeter, Huddersfield, Kent, Lincoln, Liverpool, London LSE (rarely), Salford, Sheffield Hallam, Southampton, Staffordshire, Trinity Saint David, Winchester, Wolverhampton, York.

Interview advice and questions Questions are almost certain to be asked on those aspects of the history A-level syllabus which interest you. Examples of questions in previous years have included: Why did imperialism happen? If a Martian arrived on Earth what aspect of life would you show him/her to sum up today's society? Has the role of class been exaggerated by Marxist historians? What is the difference between power and authority and between patriotism and nationalism? Did Elizabeth I have a foreign policy? What is the relevance of history in modern society? Who are your favourite monarchs? How could you justify your study of history to the taxpayer? See **Chapter 6**. **Cambridge** How would you compare Henry VIII to Stalin? In the 1920s did the invention of the Henry Ford car lead to a national sub-culture or was it just an aspect of one? Is there such a thing as 'race'? Should historians be allowed to read sci-fi novels? **Cumbria** Questions about interest in research, analysis, argument, information gathering, future plans after study, motivation. **De Montfort** Why History? Why is history important? **Oxford** Questions on submitted work and the capacity to think independently. What are the origins of your name? Why are you sitting in this chair? **Sheffield** Written work may be required. **Swansea** We ask applicants to explain something – a hobby, an historical problem or a novel. The subject is less important than a coherent and enthusiastic explanation.

Reasons for rejection (non-academic) Personal statements which read like job applications, focusing extensively on personal skills and saying nothing about the applicant's passion for history. Poor use of personal statement combined with predicted grades. Little commitment and enthusiasm. No clear reason for choice of course. Little understanding of history. Absence or narrowness of intellectual pursuits. Deception or concealment on the UCAS application. Knowledge of 19th century history (chosen subject) did not have any depth. Unwillingness to learn. Narrow approach to subject. Failure to submit requested information. **Birmingham** Commitment insufficient to sustain interest over three years. **London (King's)** Inability to think analytically and comparatively. **London (UCL)** The vast majority of applications are of a very high standard, many applicants being predicted AAA grades. We view each application as a complete picture, taking into account personal statement, reference and performance at any interview as well as actual and predicted academic performance. There is no single rule by which applicants are selected and therefore no single reason why they are rejected. **Nottingham** No discrimination against Oxbridge applicants.

AFTER-RESULTS ADVICE

Offers to applicants repeating A-levels Higher Exeter, Glasgow, Huddersfield, Leeds, Liverpool, St Andrews, Trinity Saint David, Warwick; **Possibly higher** Aberystwyth, Birmingham, Cambridge, Portsmouth; **Same** Anglia Ruskin, Bangor, Bristol, Buckingham, Cardiff, Chester, Chichester, De Montfort, Dundee, Durham, East Anglia, Edge Hill, Hull, Kent, Lancaster, Lincoln, Liverpool Hope, Liverpool John Moores, London (QM), London (RH), London (SOAS), Newcastle, Newman (UC), Newport, Nottingham Trent, Oxford Brookes, Roehampton, St Mary's Twickenham (UC), Staffordshire, Stirling, Suffolk (Univ Campus), Winchester, Wolverhampton, York, York St John.

GRADUATE DESTINATIONS AND EMPLOYMENT (2007/8 HESA)

Graduates surveyed 6295 **Employed** 2215 **In further study** 1715 **Assumed unemployed** 600

Career note Graduates enter a broad spectrum of careers. Whilst a small number seek positions with museums and galleries, most will enter careers in management, public and social services and retail as well as the teaching profession.

OTHER DEGREE SUBJECTS FOR CONSIDERATION

Ancient History; Anthropology; Archaeology; Economic and Social History; Government; History of Art; International Relations; Medieval History; Politics.

HISTORY (ANCIENT)

(see also **Archaeology, Classical Studies/Classical Civilisation, History**)

Ancient History covers the Greek and Roman world, the social, religious, political and economic changes taking place in the Byzantine period and the medieval era which followed.

Useful websites www.royalhistoricalsociety.org; www.guardians.net; www.arwhead.com/Greeks; www.ancientworlds.net; www.bbc.co.uk/history/ancient; www.historesearch.com/ancient.html.

NB The points totals shown to the left of the institutions are for ease of reference only. It must not be assumed that Tariff points are always used by institutions or that they can be substituted for an offer in grades. The level of an offer is not necessarily indicative of the quality of a course.

COURSE OFFERS INFORMATION

Subject requirements/preferences GCSE A foreign language or classical language may be required. **AL** History or classical civilisation may be preferred subjects.

NB In 2012 universities and colleges will differ in their use of GCE AL/AS unit grade information, A* grades, the Extended Project (EPQ), the Advanced Diploma and the Cambridge Pre-U examination when considering applicants and making offers. An EPQ may be accepted in place of an AS subject. Check websites of universities and colleges for the latest offers information.

Your target offers and examples of courses provided by each institution

400 pts **London (UCL)** – A*AAe–AAAe (Anc Hist) (IB 36 pts)

360 pts **Durham** – AAA–AAB (Anc Mediev Modn Hist; Anc Hist Comb Hons)
Exeter – AAA–ABB (Anc Hist Arch) (IB 34–29 pts)
London (King's) – AAB+AS (Anc Hist) (IB 32 pts)
London (UCL) – A*AAe–AAAe (Anc Hist Egypt) (IB 36 pts)
Oxford – AAA (Anc Hist Class Arch)
St Andrews – AAA–AAB (Anc Hist) (IB 35 pts)
Warwick – ABBc–BBBc (Anc Hist Class Arch) (IB 32–36 pts)

340 pts **Bristol** – AAB (Anc Hist) (IB 35 pts)
Durham – AAB–ABB (Anc Hist Arch) (IB 32 pts)
London (UCL) – ABB+AS (Anc Wrld St) (IB 34 pts)
Newcastle – AAB–BBC (Anc Hist Arch) (IB 30–35 pts)
St Andrews – AAB (Anc Hist Arch) (IB 36 pts)

320 pts **Birmingham** – ABB (Anc Hist) (IB 34 pts)
Cardiff – ABB (Anc Hist; Anc Mediev Hist; Anc Hist Cult Crit)
Liverpool – ABB (Egyptology) (IB 34 pts)
Manchester – ABB–BBB (Anc Hist Arch) (IB 33–32 pts)
Newcastle – ABB (Anc Hist) (IB 32 pts)
Nottingham – ABB (Vkg St) (IB 32 pts)
Swansea – AAB–BBB (Egypt Class Civ)

300 pts **Cardiff** – BBB (Anc Hist Welsh)
Edinburgh – check with Admissions Tutor BBB (Anc Hist; Anc Hist Class Arch; Anc Hist Gk/Lat; Anc Mediev Hist)

Leicester – ABB–BBB (Anc Hist Hist)
Queen's Belfast – BBB–BBCb (Anc Hist courses)
Reading – 300–320 pts (Anc Hist; Anc Hist Hist)
280 pts **Reading** – 280–360 pts (Anc Hist Arch)
180 pts **Trinity Saint David** – 180–200 pts (Anc Mediev Hist; Anc Hist)

Alternative offers
See **Chapter 7** and **Appendix 1** for grades/UCAS Tariff points information for the International Baccalaureate, Scottish Highers/Advanced Highers, the Welsh Baccalaureate, the Irish Leaving Certificate, the Cambridge Pre-U Diploma, the Advanced Diploma and the Extended Project.

CHOOSING YOUR COURSE (SEE ALSO CH. 1)
Some course features
Birmingham (Anc Hist) Course focuses on social history and the lives, work, trade and leisure of everyday people from around 1000 BC to AD 1500.
Cardiff (Anc Hist) Archaeological modules can be studied as well as language modules in Greek or Latin at beginners and advanced levels.
Leicester (Anc Hist Arch) The course centres on Ancient Greece and Rome, with particular reference to the interpretation of classical texts and material remains. There is an optional module in classical and post-classical Latin.
Swansea Egyptian language study is essential for Egyptology students but optional for the Ancient History and Egyptology course. Students use the resources of the Egypt Centre, with over 3000 Egyptian antiquities.

Universities and colleges teaching quality See www.qaa.ac.uk; http://unistats.direct.gov.uk.

Top research universities and colleges (RAE 2008) See **Classics**.

ADMISSIONS INFORMATION
Number of applicants per place (approx) Birmingham 7; Bristol 12; Cardiff 4; Durham 12; Leicester 32; London (RH) 3; Manchester 6; Newcastle 10; Nottingham 10; Oxford 2.

Advice to applicants and planning the UCAS personal statement Any information about experience of excavation or museum work should be given. Visits to Greece and Italy to study archaeological sites should be described. Show your interest in, for example, Ancient Egypt developed through, for example reading, television and the Internet. Be aware of the work of the career archaeologist, for example, sites and measurement officers, field officers and field researchers (often specialists in pottery, glass, metalwork). See also **History**.

Misconceptions about this course **Liverpool** (Egypt) Some students would have been better advised looking at V400 Archaeology or VV16 Ancient History and Archaeology, both of which offer major pathways in the study of Ancient Egypt.

Selection interviews **Yes** Birmingham, Durham, Leeds, London (RH), Oxford (Anc Hist) 21%; **Some** Cardiff, Newcastle.

Interview advice and questions See **History**.

Reasons for rejection (non-academic) **Liverpool** (Egypt) Egyptology used to fill a gap on the UCAS application. Applicant misguided in choice of subject.

AFTER-RESULTS ADVICE
Offers to applicants repeating A-levels **Same** Birmingham, Cardiff, Durham, Newcastle.

GRADUATE DESTINATIONS AND EMPLOYMENT (2007/8 HESA)
See **History**.

Career note See **History**.

OTHER DEGREE SUBJECTS FOR CONSIDERATION
Anthropology; Archaeology; Classical Studies; Classics; Greek; History of Art; Latin.

HISTORY (ECONOMIC and SOCIAL)

(see also **History**)

Economic and Social History is a study of societies and economies and explores the changes that have taken place in the past and the causes and consequences of those changes. The study can cover Britain, Europe and other major powers.

Useful websites www.royalhistoricalsociety.org; www.ehs.org.uk; see also **Economics** and **History**.

NB The points totals shown to the left of the institutions are for ease of reference only. It must not be assumed that Tariff points are always used by institutions or that they can be substituted for an offer in grades. The level of an offer is not necessarily indicative of the quality of a course.

COURSE OFFERS INFORMATION

Subject requirements/preferences GCSE Mathematics usually required and a language may be preferred. **AL** History preferred.

NB In 2012 universities and colleges will differ in their use of GCE AL/AS unit grade information, A* grades, the Extended Project (EPQ), the Advanced Diploma and the Cambridge Pre-U examination when considering applicants and making offers. An EPQ may be accepted in place of an AS subject. Check websites of universities and colleges for the latest offers information.

Your target offers and examples of courses provided by each institution
430 pts **Warwick** – A*AA–AAAb (Econ Econ Hist) (IB 38 pts)
360 pts **York** – AAA (Hist Econ) (IB 36 pts)
340 pts **Glasgow** – AAB (Econ Soc Hist) (IB 34 pts)
        London LSE – AAB (Econ Hist Econ) (IB 37 pts HL 666)
        York – AAB (Econ Econ Hist) (IB 36 pts H666)
320 pts **Birmingham** – ABB (Econ Soc Hist) (IB 32 pts)
        Lancaster – ABB (Soc Hist)
        Swansea – ABB–BBB 320–300 pts (Econ Soc Hist; Econ Hist Econ)
300 pts **Edinburgh** – check with Admissions Tutor BBB (Econ Hist; Econ Soc Hist; Econ Soc Hist Env St)
        Essex – 300–320 pts (Soc Cult Hist) (IB 32 pts)
        Liverpool – BBB (Hist (Soc Econ)) (IB 30 pts)
280 pts **Aberystwyth** – 300 pts (Hist Soc Econ Hist) (IB 30 pts)
220 pts **Manchester Met** – 220 pts (Econ Soc Hist)

Alternative offers
See **Chapter 7** and **Appendix 1** for grades/UCAS Tariff points information for the International Baccalaureate, Scottish Highers/Advanced Highers, the Welsh Baccalaureate, the Irish Leaving Certificate, the Cambridge Pre-U Diploma, the Advanced Diploma and the Extended Project.

CHOOSING YOUR COURSE (SEE ALSO CH. 1)

Some course features
Birmingham The course in History and Social Science offers a study of two social sciences from economics, sociology, politics and psychology.
Manchester The subject features in three degree courses within the overall Economic and Social Studies programme of 28 degree courses. All students follow a general and broad course in Year 1 specialising in their chosen field in Years 2 and 3.
Warwick (Econ Econ Hist) The course combines economic analysis with an historical understanding of economic development and policies, the causes of economic flutuations and unemployment, the conditions for exchange rate flexibility and European integration.

Universities and colleges teaching quality See www.qaa.ac.uk; http://unistats.direct.gov.uk.

ADMISSIONS INFORMATION

Number of applicants per place (approx) Birmingham 3; Liverpool 3; London LSE (Econ Hist) 3, (Econ Hist Econ) 5; York 8.

For a quick reference offers calculator, fold out the inside back cover.

Advice to applicants and planning the UCAS personal statement See **History**.

Selection interviews **Yes** Aberystwyth, Birmingham, Liverpool, Warwick (rarely).

Interview advice and questions See **History**.

AFTER-RESULTS ADVICE
Offers to applicants repeating A-levels **Higher** Warwick, York; **Possibly higher** Liverpool.

GRADUATE DESTINATIONS AND EMPLOYMENT (2007/8 HESA)
See **History**.

Career note See **History**.

OTHER DEGREE SUBJECTS FOR CONSIDERATION
Economics; Government; History; Politics; Social Policy and Administration; Sociology.

HISTORY OF ART
(see also **History**)

History of Art (and Design) courses differ slightly between universities although most will focus on the history and appreciation of European art and architecture from the 14th to 20th centuries. Some courses also cover the Egyptian, Greek and Roman periods and at **London (SOAS)**, Asian, African and European Art. The history of all aspects of design and film can also be studied in some courses. There has been an increase in the popularity of these courses in recent years.

Useful websites www.artchive.com; www.artcyclopedia.com; www.artguide.org; www.artefact.co.uk; www.fine-art.com; www.nationalgallery.org.uk; www.britisharts.co.uk; www.tate.org.uk.

NB The points totals shown to the left of the institutions are for ease of reference only. It must not be assumed that Tariff points are always used by institutions or that they can be substituted for an offer in grades. The level of an offer is not necessarily indicative of the quality of a course.

COURSE OFFERS INFORMATION
Subject requirements/preferences **GCSE** English required and a foreign language usually preferred. **AL** History is preferred for some courses.

NB In 2012 universities and colleges will differ in their use of GCE AL/AS unit grade information, A* grades, the Extended Project (EPQ), the Advanced Diploma and the Cambridge Pre-U examination when considering applicants and making offers. An EPQ may be accepted in place of an AS subject. Check websites of universities and colleges for the latest offers information.

Your target offers and examples of courses provided by each institution
380 pts Cambridge – A*AA college offers may vary (Hist Art) (IB 40–42 pts)
360 pts Bristol – AAA–ABB (Hist Art Fr/Ger/Ital/Port/Russ/Span) (IB 37–33 pts)
　　　London (Court) – AAA (Hist Art) (IB 30 pts)
　　　London (UCL) – AABe (Hist Art Mat St) (IB 34 pts)
　　　Oxford – AAA (Hist Art) (IB 38–40 pts)
　　　Warwick – AABc–ABBc (Hist Art Fr St) (IB 32–34 pts)
340 pts East Anglia – AAB–BBB (Hist Hist Art; Hist Art Gllry Musm St)
　　　St Andrews – AAB (Art Hist Mgt) (IB 34–40 pts)
　　　York – AAB (Hist Art) (IB 32–34 pts)
320 pts Birmingham – ABB (Modn Langs Hist Art) (IB 34 pts)
　　　Essex – 320–300 pts (Film St Hist Art) (IB 34–32 pts)
　　　Glasgow – AAB (Hist Art courses) (IB 30 pts)
　　　London (Gold) – ABB (Hist Art)
　　　Manchester – ABB–BBB (Hist Art Modn Lang) (IB 33–32 pts)
　　　Nottingham – ABB–BBB (Art Hist Engl St) (IB 34 pts)
　　　Sussex – ABB–BBB (Art Hist Cult St) (IB 32–34 pts)

300 pts **Aberdeen** – BBB (Hist Art courses)
    Edinburgh – BBB–AAA (Hist Art Hist Mus) (IB 34 pts HL 555)
    Kent – check with Admissions Tutor 280–300 pts (Hist Phil Art; Hist Phil Art Cult St; Hist Phil
       Art Class Arch St)
    Leeds – ABB–BBB (Hist Art Theol Relig St) (IB 32 pts)
    Leicester – BBB–ABB (Hist Art; Hist Art (EU); Hist Art Engl)
    Nottingham – BBB–ABC (Art Hist) (IB 32 pts)
280 pts **Brighton** – BBC (Hist Des Cult Soty) (IB 30 pts)
    Essex – 300 pts (Hist Art Modn Langs) (IB 30 pts))
    Hull – 280–300 pts (Hist Hist Art; Engl Hist Art; Hist Art Dr)
    London (SOAS) – ABB–BBB (Hist Art courses) (IB 30 pts)
    Nottingham – BBC (Arch Art Hist) (IB 30 pts)
    Oxford Brookes – BBB–BBC (Hist Art Anth; Hist Art Pub Media; Hist Hist Art)
    Reading – 280–300 pts (Art Hist Art Archit)
260 pts **Aberystwyth** – 260 pts (Art Hist Fine Art; Art Hist; Musm Gllry St)
240 pts **Lincoln** – 240 pts (Cons Restor)
    Liverpool John Moores – 240 pts (Hist Art Musm St)
    Manchester Met – 240 pts (Hist Art Des)
    Plymouth – 240 pts (Art Hist)
    Roehampton – 240–320 pts (Photo Art Hist)
220 pts **Kingston** – 220 pts (Hist Art Des Film) (IB 30 pts)
200 pts **Central Lancashire** – interview 200–250 pts (Contemp Vis Arts (Hist Theor))
    Swansea Met – 200–220 pts (Art Hist)
  80 pts **London (Birk)** – for under 21s (over 21s varies) p/t (Hist Art)

Alternative offers
See **Chapter 7** and **Appendix 1** for grades/UCAS Tariff points information for the International
Baccalaureate, Scottish Highers/Advanced Highers, the Welsh Baccalaureate, the Irish Leaving
Certificate, the Cambridge Pre-U Diploma, the Advanced Diploma and the Extended Project.

CHOOSING YOUR COURSE (SEE ALSO CH. 1)
Some course features
Aberystwyth (Art Hist) The course combines the study of art history and visual culture. In the second
and third years students choose from a wide range of core and optional modules, including history of
graphic art, history of photography, contemporary art and Renaissance art.
Kent (Hist Phil Art) The course has streams in art history, contemporary arts, philosophy of art or
photographic studies.
Leeds (Hist Art Musm St) An unusual course focusing on art history, fine art and museum and gallery
collections and country houses, with opportunities for related work experience.
Leicester (Hist Art) A wide range of supplementary subjects (including languages) can be studied
including practical art which explores artistic techniques and problems.
Manchester (Hist Art) A study of art history, visual culture, architecture and theory from antiquity to
the present day. The course focuses mainly on European art but there are opportunities to study non-
Western cultures.
Manchester Met (Hist Art Des) Course has a studio practice unit.

Universities and colleges teaching quality See www.qaa.ac.uk; http://unistats.direct.gov.uk.

Top research universities and colleges (RAE 2008) (History of Art, Architecture and Design)
Glasgow; London (Court); East Anglia; Sussex; Manchester; York; Birmingham; London (UCL); Essex;
Nottingham; London (Birk); Warwick.

ADMISSIONS INFORMATION
Number of applicants per place (approx) Aberystwyth 9; Birmingham 14; Brighton 8; Cambridge 4;
East Anglia 7; Essex 5; Kent 3; Kingston 4; Leeds 29; Leicester 6; London (Gold) 10; London (SOAS) 4;
Manchester 3; Manchester Met 10; Nottingham 10; York 4.

For a quick reference offers calculator, fold out the inside back cover.

Advice to applicants and planning the UCAS personal statement Applicants for History of Art courses should have made extensive visits to art galleries, particularly in London, and should be familiar with the main European schools of painting. Evidence of lively interest required. Discuss your preferences and say why you prefer certain types of work or particular artists. You should also describe any visits to museums and any special interests in furniture, pottery or other artefacts. (See also **Appendix 4**) **London (Court)** A-levels in history, history of art, English, and modern European languages are the most relevant, however other subjects are considered. Art offered as an A-level should include a history of art paper.

Misconceptions about this course Kent The History of Art is not a practical course in fine arts. **York** Students do not need a background in art or art history. It is not a course with a studio element in it.

Selection interviews Yes Brighton, Cambridge, East Anglia (majority), London (UCL), Manchester Met, Oxford (Hist Art) 16%, Warwick; **Some** Bristol, Buckingham, Kent.

Interview advice and questions Some universities set slide tests on painting and sculpture. Those applicants who have not taken history of art at A-level will be questioned on their reasons for choosing the subject, their visits to art galleries and museums and their reactions to the art work which has impressed them. See **Chapter 6. Kent** Do they visit art galleries? Have they studied art history previously? What do they expect to get out of the degree? Sometimes they are given images to compare and discuss.

Reasons for rejection (non-academic) Poorly presented practical work. Students who do not express any interest or enthusiasm in contemporary visual arts are rejected.

AFTER-RESULTS ADVICE
Offers to applicants repeating A-levels Possibly higher St Andrews; **Same** Aberystwyth, East Anglia, Kent, Leeds, Warwick, York.

GRADUATE DESTINATIONS AND EMPLOYMENT (2007/8 HESA)
Career note Work in galleries, museums and collections will be the objective of many graduates, who should try to establish contacts by way of work placements and experience during their undergraduate years. The personal skills acquired during their studies, however, open up many opportunities in other careers.

OTHER DEGREE SUBJECTS FOR CONSIDERATION
Art; Archaeology; Architecture; Classical Studies; Photography.

HORTICULTURE

(including **Garden Design**; see also **Agricultural Sciences/Agriculture, Landscape Architecture, Plant Sciences**)

Horticulture is a broad subject area covering amenity or landscape horticulture, production horticulture and retail horticulture.

Useful websites www.iagre.org; www.rhs.org.uk; www.horticulture.org.uk.

NB The points totals shown to the left of the institutions are for ease of reference only. It must not be assumed that Tariff points are always used by institutions or that they can be substituted for an offer in grades. The level of an offer is not necessarily indicative of the quality of a course.

COURSE OFFERS INFORMATION
Subject requirements/preferences GCSE Mathematics sometimes required. **AL** A science subject may be required or preferred for some courses.

NB In 2012 universities and colleges will differ in their use of GCE AL/AS unit grade information, A* grades, the Extended Project (EPQ), the Advanced Diploma and the Cambridge Pre-U examination when considering applicants and making offers. An EPQ may be accepted in place of an AS subject. Check websites of universities and colleges for the latest offers information.

Your target offers and examples of courses provided by each institution
300 pts **Aberdeen** – BBB 1st yr entry (Plnt Soil Sci) (IB 28 pts)
200 pts **Bristol UWE** – 200–240 pts (Amen Hort Mgt) (IB 28 pts)
180 pts **Greenwich** – 180 pts (Commer Hort; Medcnl Hort)
160 pts **Hadlow (Coll)** – CC 160 pts (Gdn Des; Commer Hort; Medcnl Hort)
           SAC (Scottish CAg) – CC (Hort Plntsmn; Hort)
           Worcester – 160 pts (Hort)
140 pts **Writtle (Coll)** – 140 pts (Grn Spc Mgt)
100 pts **Writtle (Coll)** – 100–200 pts (Hort; Hort (Plntsmn) (Tree Mgt) (Glob Crop Prot); Hort Bus Mgt)

           Myerscough (Coll) – (Hort (Top-up); Commer Flor Des (Top-up)) Check with College
           Warwickshire (Coll) – [contact college] (Hort)

Alternative offers
See **Chapter 7** and **Appendix 1** for grades/UCAS Tariff points information for the International Baccalaureate, Scottish Highers/Advanced Highers, the Welsh Baccalaureate, the Irish Leaving Certificate, the Cambridge Pre-U Diploma, the Advanced Diploma and the Extended Project.

EXAMPLES OF FOUNDATION DEGREES IN THE SUBJECT FIELD
Askham Bryan (Coll); Bicton (Coll); Bolton; Bournemouth; Brighton; Bristol UWE; Glyndŵr; Greenwich; Harper Adams (UC); Myerscough (Coll); Northop (Coll); Nottingham Trent; Plymouth; South Devon (Coll); Sparsholt (Coll); Warwickshire (Coll); Wolverhampton; Worcester; Writtle (Coll).

CHOOSING YOUR COURSE (SEE ALSO CH. 1)
Some course features
Bristol UWE (Amen Hort Mgt) Course lasts four years including a one-year work placement. Alternatively, two years on a Foundation degree can be followed by one year to the BA degree.
SAC (Scottish CAg) (Hort Plntsmn) The course combines a study of the diversity of plants and their cultivation, with practical horticultural skills, and is delivered in partnership with the Royal Botanic Garden, Edinburgh.
Worcester (Hort) Course based at Pershore College and enables students to gain practical experience in the horticultural industry in the UK or overseas at the end of the first and second years.
Writtle (Coll) The College, the largest provider of horticultural education in the country, encourages students to take a sandwich placement during their course, in the UK or overseas. Twelve-month practical training placements are available with the Royal Horticultural Society.

Examples of sandwich degree courses Greenwich; Writtle (Coll).

ADMISSIONS INFORMATION
Number of applicants per place (approx) Greenwich 4; SAC (Scottish CAg) 1; Writtle (Coll) 3.

Advice to applicants and planning the UCAS personal statement Practical experience is important and visits to botanical gardens (the Royal Botanic Gardens, Kew or Edinburgh and the Royal Horticultural Society gardens at Wisley) could be described. Contact your local authority offices for details of work in parks and gardens departments. See also **Appendix 4**.

Misconceptions about this course Greenwich (Commer Hort) Students are unaware of the scope of this degree. The course covers commercial horticulture – plants, plant products, ornamentals, bedding plants, hardy trees and shrubs, salads, vegetables, fruit and organic crops from production to marketing.

Selection interviews Yes Greenwich, SAC (Scottish CAg), Worcester.

Interview advice and questions Past questions have included: How did you become interested in horticulture? How do you think this course will benefit you? Could you work in all weathers? What career are you aiming for? Are you interested in gardening? Describe your garden. What plants do you grow? How do you prune rose trees and fruit trees? Are there any EU policies at present affecting the horticulture industry? Topics relating to the importance of science and horticulture. See **Chapter 6**.

AFTER-RESULTS ADVICE
Offers to applicants repeating A-levels **Same** Greenwich, SAC (Scottish CAg).

GRADUATE DESTINATIONS AND EMPLOYMENT (2007/8 HESA)
See **Agricultural Sciences/Agriculture**.

Career note Graduates seeking employment in horticulture will look towards commercial organisations for the majority of openings. These will include positions as growers and managers with fewer vacancies for scientists involved in research and development and advisory services.

OTHER DEGREE SUBJECTS FOR CONSIDERATION
Agriculture; Biology; Crop Science; Ecology; Forestry; Landscape Architecture; Plant Sciences.

HOSPITALITY and HOTEL MANAGEMENT

(including **Events Management**; see also **Business and Management Courses, Business and Management Courses (International and European), Business and Management Courses (Specialised), Consumer Studies/Sciences, Food Science/Studies and Technology, Leisure and Recreation Management/Studies, Tourism and Travel**)

Courses cover the full range of skills required for those working in the industry. Specific studies include management, food and beverage supplies, equipment design, public relations and marketing. Depending on the course, other topics may include events management, tourism and the international trade.

Useful websites www.baha.org.uk; www.cordonbleu.net; www.instituteofhospitality.org; www.people1st.co.uk.

NB The points totals shown to the left of the institutions are for ease of reference only. It must not be assumed that Tariff points are always used by institutions or that they can be substituted for an offer in grades. The level of an offer is not necessarily indicative of the quality of a course.

COURSE OFFERS INFORMATION
Subject requirements/preferences **GCSE** English and mathematics usually required together with a foreign language for International Management courses. **AL** No specified subjects.

NB In 2012 universities and colleges will differ in their use of GCE AL/AS unit grade information, A* grades, the Extended Project (EPQ), the Advanced Diploma and the Cambridge Pre-U examination when considering applicants and making offers. An EPQ may be accepted in place of an AS subject. Check websites of universities and colleges for the latest offers information.

Your target offers and examples of courses provided by each institution
320 pts **Strathclyde** – ABB (Hspty Tour Mgt)
300 pts **Bournemouth** – 300 pts (Evnt Mgt)
         Surrey – 300 pts (Int Hspty Tour Mgt) (IB 30–32 pts)
280 pts **Bournemouth** – 280 pts (Hspty Mgt)
         Hertfordshire – 280–300 pts (Evnt Mgt)
         Plymouth – 280 pts (Evnt Mgt)
260 pts **Brighton** – BCC (Int Hspty Mgt) (IB 28 pts)
         Gloucestershire – 260 pts (Evnt Mgt) (IB 26–30 pts)
         Oxford Brookes – BCC (Int Hspty Mgt) (IB 29 pts)

Salford – BCC 260 pts (Hspty Mgt) (IB 26 pts)
Staffordshire – 260 pts (Evnt Mgt)
240 pts **Canterbury Christ Church** – 240 pts (Evnt Mgt)
Cardiff (UWIC) – 240 pts (Hspty Mgt courses; Evnts Mgt; Int Tour Hspty Mgt)
Central Lancashire – 240–280 pts (Evnt Mgt)
Chichester – CCC (Evnt Mgt courses)
Coventry – 240–260 pts (Evnt Mgt)
De Montfort – 240 pts (Arts Fstvl Mgt)
Edinburgh Napier – 240–230 pts (Fstvl Evnts Mgt courses)
Glamorgan – 240–280 pts (Evnt Mgt)
Gloucestershire – 240–260 pts (Hspty Mgt)
Huddersfield – 240–260 pts (Evnt Mgt)
Leeds Met – 240 pts (Hspty Ldrshp Mgt)
Liverpool John Moores – 240–280 pts (Evnt Mgt)
London Met – 240 pts (Evnts Mgt Mus Media Mgt)
Manchester Met – 240–260 pts (Int Hspty Mgt) (IB 28 pts)
Robert Gordon – CCC (Evnt Mgt)
Sheffield Hallam – 240–260 pts (Evnt Mngt)
Ulster – 240 pts (Leis Evnts Mgt)
Winchester – 240–280 pts (Evnt Mgt)
230 pts **Edinburgh Napier** – 230–240 pts (Hspty Tour Mgt; Hspty Mgt Entre)
220 pts **Birmingham (UC)** – 220 pts (Evnt Mgt)
Central Lancashire – 220 pts (Hspty Mgt)
De Montfort – 220–240 pts (Arts Fstvl Mgt Dr St)
Derby – 180–240 pts (Hspty Mgt)
London Met – 220–240 pts (Mus Media Mgt; Evnt Spo Mgt)
Northampton – 220–260 pts (Enter Mark)
Plymouth – 220–240 pts (Cru Mgt)
Portsmouth – 220 pts (Hspty Mgt; Hspty Mgt Tour)
Southampton Solent – 220 pts (Evnt Mgt; Evnt Mgt (Spo) (Tour))
Sunderland – 220 pts (Evnt Mgt; Int Tour Hspty Mgt)
200 pts **Birmingham (UC)** – 200–220 pts (Hspty Bus Mgt; Hspty Fd Mgt; Hspty Tour Bus Admin)
Bucks New – 200–240 pts (Evnt Fstvl Mgt; Corp Evnts Conf Mgt)
Chester – 200-240 pts (Evnts Mgt)
East London – 200 pts (Evnt Mgt courses)
Huddersfield – 200 pts (Hspty Mgt Modn Lang)
Manchester Met – 240–260 pts (Hspty Evnts Mgt) (IB 28 pts)
Queen Margaret – 200 pts (Hspty Tour Mgt; Int Hspty Mgt; Evnts Mgt)
Suffolk (Univ Campus) – 200 pts (Evnt Mgt)
West London – 200 pts (Hosp Mgt Fd St; Hspty Mgt; Evnts Mgt Hspty; Culn Arts Mgt; Evnts Mgt Tour)
Wolverhampton – 200 pts (Evnts Mgt; Int Hspty Mgt)
180 pts **Greenwich** – 180 pts (Evnt Mgt)
Huddersfield – 180 pts (Hspty Mgt Tour Leis)
Leeds Met – 180–200 pts (Enter Mgt)
160 pts **Bedfordshire** – 160 pts min (Evnt Mgt)
Bournemouth Arts (UC) – 160 pts (Arts Evnt Mgt)
De Montfort – 160–240 pts (Evnts Mgt; Prof Culn Arts)
Derby – 160–240 pts (Evnt Mgt; Prof Culn Arts)
Glasgow Caledonian – CC (Enter Evnt Mgt)
Robert Gordon – CC 160 pts (Int Hspty Mgt) (IB 24 pts)
West Scotland – CC (Evnt Mgt)
140 pts **Blackpool and Fylde (Coll)** – 140 pts (Hspty Mgt)
120 pts **Colchester (Inst)** – DD 120 pts (Mgt Hspty)
Llandrillo Cymru (Coll) – 120 pts (Htl Hspty Mgt)

Alternative offers
See **Chapter 7** and **Appendix 1** for grades/UCAS Tariff points information for the International Baccalaureate, Scottish Highers/Advanced Highers, the Welsh Baccalaureate, the Irish Leaving Certificate, the Cambridge Pre-U Diploma, the Advanced Diploma and the Extended Project.

EXAMPLES OF FOUNDATION DEGREES IN THE SUBJECT FIELD
Birmingham (UC); Bishop Grosseteste (UC); Blackburn (Coll Univ Centre); Blackpool and Fylde (Coll); Bournemouth; Bradford; Brighton; Bristol City (Coll); Bromley (CFHE); Bucks New; Cardiff (UWIC); Central Lancashire; Cornwall (Coll); Greenwich; Guildford (Coll); Highbury Portsmouth (Coll); Loughborough (Coll); Manchester (Coll); Newcastle (Coll); Norwich City (Coll); Nottingham New (Coll); Plymouth; Salford; South Devon (Coll); Stratford upon Avon (Coll); Suffolk (Univ Campus); Ulster; Warrington (Coll); Warwickshire (Coll); Westminster Kingsway (Coll).

CHOOSING YOUR COURSE (SEE ALSO CH. 1)
Some course features
Edinburgh Napier (Fstvl Evnts Mgt courses) Students learn how to plan, design, market, operate and develop events and how they can be used to help local economies. There are opportunities to study a European language and to study abroad.
Manchester Met The wide range of courses includes options in culinary arts and licensed retail management.
Oxford Brookes (Int Hspty Mgt) A Single Honours course with a paid placement year and opportunities to study abroad. In addition, Hospitality Management can be studied as part of the Combined Honours programme.
Surrey Opportunities for professional training places with leading UK and overseas companies.

Examples of sandwich degree courses Birmingham (UC); Bournemouth; Brighton; Cardiff (UWIC); Central Lancashire; Derby; Edinburgh Napier; Gloucestershire; Huddersfield; Leeds Met; Manchester Met; Oxford Brookes; Portsmouth; Sheffield Hallam; Sunderland; Surrey; Ulster; Wolverhampton.

ADMISSIONS INFORMATION
Number of applicants per place (approx) Bournemouth 9; Cardiff (UWIC) 12; Central Lancashire 8; Edinburgh Napier 17; London Met 10; Manchester Met (Hspty Mgt) 12, (Hspty Mgt Tour) 20; Middlesex 4; Oxford Brookes 9; Portsmouth 10; Robert Gordon 3; Strathclyde 8; Surrey 12.

Advice to applicants and planning the UCAS personal statement Experience in dealing with members of the public is an important element in this work which, coupled with work experience in cafés, restaurants or hotels, should be described fully. All applicants are strongly recommended to obtain practical experience in catering or hotel work. Admissions tutors are likely to look for experience in industry and for people who are ambitious, sociable and team players. See also **Appendix 4**.

Misconceptions about this course Cardiff (UWIC) (Hspty Mgt) The course is not about cooking! We are looking to create managers, not chefs.

Selection interviews Yes Cardiff (UWIC); **Some** Manchester Met, Portsmouth, Robert Gordon, Surrey; **No** Bucks New, Salford.

Interview advice and questions Past questions have included: What books do you read? What do you know about hotel work and management? What work experience have you had? What kind of job do you have in mind when you have qualified? How did you become interested in this course? Do you eat in restaurants? What types of restaurants? Discuss examples of good and bad restaurant organisation. What qualities do you have which make you suitable for management? See **Chapter 6**.

Reasons for rejection (non-academic) Lack of suitable work experience or practical training. Inability to communicate. Lack of awareness of workload, for example shift working, weekend work. **Cardiff (UWIC)** Students looking specifically for licensed trade courses or a cookery course. **Oxford Brookes** Lack of commitment to the hotel and restaurant industry.

AFTER-RESULTS ADVICE

Offers to applicants repeating A-levels Higher Bournemouth, Huddersfield, Oxford Brookes, Surrey; **Same** Brighton, Cardiff (UWIC), Manchester Met, Salford, Strathclyde, Suffolk (Univ Campus), Ulster, West London, Wolverhampton.

GRADUATE DESTINATIONS AND EMPLOYMENT (2007/8 HESA)
Including **Leisure** and **Tourism**

Graduates surveyed 2500 **Employed** 1470 **In further study** 180 **Assumed unemployed** 240

Career note These business-focused hospitality programmes open up a wide range of employment and career opportunities in both hospitality and other business sectors. The demand for employees has been high in recent years. Events Management is currently a growth area with graduates working in sports and the arts, tourist attractions, hospitality, business and industry.

OTHER DEGREE SUBJECTS FOR CONSIDERATION
Business; Consumer Studies; Dietetics; Food Science; Health Studies; Leisure and Recreation Management; Management; Tourism and Travel.

HOUSING

(see also **Building and Construction, Surveying, Town and Country Planning**)

These courses prepare students for careers in housing management although topics covered will also be relevant to other careers in business and administration. Modules will be taken in housing, law, finance, planning policy, public administration and construction.

Useful websites www.housingcorp.gov.uk; www.communities.gov.uk/housing; www.rtpi.org.uk; www.freeindex.co.uk/categories/property/construction/Property_Development.

NB The points totals shown to the left of the institutions are for ease of reference only. It must not be assumed that Tariff points are always used by institutions or that they can be substituted for an offer in grades. The level of an offer is not necessarily indicative of the quality of a course.

COURSE OFFERS INFORMATION
Subject requirements/preferences GCSE English and mathematics required. **AL** No specified subjects.

NB In 2012 universities and colleges will differ in their use of GCE AL/AS unit grade information, A* grades, the Extended Project (EPQ), the Advanced Diploma and the Cambridge Pre-U examination when considering applicants and making offers. An EPQ may be accepted in place of an AS subject. Check websites of universities and colleges for the latest offers information.

Your target offers and examples of courses provided by each institution
280 pts **Staffordshire** – 280 pts (Sust Commun)
240 pts **London South Bank** – 240 pts (Hous St; Sust Commun)
           Ulster – 240 pts (Hous Mgt)
230 pts **Sheffield Hallam** – 230 pts (Hous Prof St)
200 pts **Birmingham City** – 200 pts (Prof Hous St)
           Middlesex – 200–300 pts (Hous St)
140 pts **Cardiff (UWIC)** – 140 pts (Hous (Supptd Hous/Hous Plcy Prac))

Alternative offers
See **Chapter 7** and **Appendix 1** for grades/UCAS Tariff points information for the International Baccalaureate, Scottish Highers/Advanced Highers, the Welsh Baccalaureate, the Irish Leaving Certificate, the Cambridge Pre-U Diploma, the Advanced Diploma and the Extended Project.

EXAMPLES OF FOUNDATION DEGREES IN THE SUBJECT FIELD

Anglia Ruskin; Birmingham City; Blackburn (Coll Univ Centre); Bradford; Bristol UWE; Glyndŵr; Grimsby (IFHE); Middlesex; St Helens (Coll).

CHOOSING YOUR COURSE (SEE ALSO CH. 1)

Some course features
Cardiff (UWIC) (Hous (Supptd Hous)) The course involves social, emotional and/or lifestyle support for a variety of client needs, for example, learning disabilities, mental health, vulnerable people.
London South Bank (Hous St) The course focuses on the policy, management and economic aspects of housing, and on housing in the European context.
Sheffield Hallam A long-established course with work placement in Year 3 and the option to study a European language.
Ulster (Hous Mgt) The course, involving research, practical placements and links with practitioners, focuses on how housing management affects individuals in society, on the built environment, housing needs and the development and implementation of housing policy. The course links to others in the built environment, including Environmental Health, Construction Engineering and Management.

ADMISSIONS INFORMATION

Number of applicants per place (approx) Cardiff (UWIC) 1; Sheffield Hallam 2.

Advice to applicants and planning the UCAS personal statement An interest in people, housing problems, social affairs and the built environment is important for this course. Contacts with local housing managers (through local authority offices or housing associations) are important. Describe any such contacts and your knowledge of the housing types and needs in your area. The planning department in your local council office will be able to provide information on the various types of developments taking place in your locality and how housing needs have changed during the past 50 years. See also **Appendix 4**.

Misconceptions about this course Applicants do not appreciate that the course is very close to social work/community work and is most suitable for those wishing to work with people.

Selection interviews Some Birmingham City, Cardiff (UWIC).

Interview advice and questions Since the subject is not studied at school, questions are likely to be asked on reasons for choosing this degree. Other past questions include: What is a housing association? Why were housing associations formed? In which parts of the country would you expect private housing to be expensive and, by comparison, cheap? What is the cause of this? Have estates of multi-storey flats fulfilled their original purpose? If not, why not? What causes a slum? What is an almshouse? See **Chapter 6**. **Sheffield Hallam** An informal discussion of the course focusing on the student's interest in housing and any experience of working with the public.

Reasons for rejection (non-academic) Lack of awareness of current social policy issues.

AFTER-RESULTS ADVICE

Offers to applicants repeating A-levels Same Birmingham City, Cardiff (UWIC), London South Bank, Sheffield Hallam.

GRADUATE DESTINATIONS AND EMPLOYMENT (2007/8 HESA)

Career note Graduates aiming for openings in housing will be employed mainly as managers with local authorities; others will be employed by non-profit-making housing associations and trusts and also by property companies owning blocks of flats.

OTHER DEGREE SUBJECTS FOR CONSIDERATION

Architecture; Building; Business Studies; Community Studies; Environmental Planning; Estate Management; Property Development; Social Policy and Administration; Social Studies; Surveying; Town Planning; Urban Regeneration.

HUMAN RESOURCE MANAGEMENT

(see also **Business and Management Courses, Business and Management Courses (International and European), Business and Management Courses (Specialised)**

This is one of the many branches of the world of business and has developed from the role of the personnel manager. HR managers may be involved with the induction and training of staff, disciplinary and grievance procedures, redundancies and equal opportunities issues. In large organisations some HR staff may specialise in one or more of these areas. Work experience dealing with the public should be stressed in the UCAS personal statement.

Useful websites www.hrmguide.co.uk; www.humanresourcemanagement.co.uk.

NB The points totals shown to the left of the institutions are for ease of reference only. It must not be assumed that Tariff points are always used by institutions or that they can be substituted for an offer in grades. The level of an offer is not necessarily indicative of the quality of a course.

COURSE OFFERS INFORMATION

Subject requirements/preferences GCSE English and mathematics at C or above. **AL** No subjects specified.

NB In 2012 universities and colleges will differ in their use of GCE AL/AS unit grade information, A* grades, the Extended Project (EPQ), the Advanced Diploma and the Cambridge Pre-U examination when considering applicants and making offers. An EPQ may be accepted in place of an AS subject. Check websites of universities and colleges for the latest offers information.

Your target offers and examples of courses provided by each institution

360 pts Leeds – AAA (HR Mgt) (IB 33 pts HL 16 pts)
340 pts Aston – 320–340 pts (HR Mgt) (IB 34 pts)
        Cardiff – AAB (Bus Mgt (HR))
        London (RH) – AAB (Mgt HR) (IB 35 pts)
        Manchester – AAB (Mgt (HR)) (IB 35–34 pts)
320 pts Bath – ABB–BBC (Sociol HR Mgt) (IB 32 pts)
        Bournemouth – 320 pts (Bus St (HR Mgt))
        Lancaster – ABB (Mgt Org (HR Mgt)) (IB 30 pts)
        London LSE – ABB (HR Mgt Emp Rel) (IB 37 pts HL 666)
        Staffordshire – 320 pts (Law (HR Mgt))
        Sussex – ABB (Bus Hum Res Mgt)
        Ulster – ABB (Law HR Mgt) (IB 26 pts)
300 pts Essex – 300 pts (Mark HR Mgt)
        Heriot-Watt – BBB 2nd yr entry (Mgt HR Mgt)
        Hertfordshire – 300 pts (Bus HR; HR Mand)
        Stirling – BBB 2nd yr entry (HR Mgt)
        Strathclyde – BBB (HR Mgt) (IB 32 pts)
280 pts Gloucestershire – 280 pts (Bus Mgt (HR Mgt))
        Keele – 280–340 pts (HR Mgt courses) (IB 28–30 pts)
        Kingston – 280–320 pts (HR Mgt) (IB 31 pts)
        Northumbria – BBC 280 pts (HR Mgt) (IB 28 pts)
260 pts Birmingham City – 260–280 pts (PR HR Mgt) (IB 28 pts)
        Coventry – 260–280 pts (HR Mgt)
        Edge Hill – 260 pts (Bus Mgt HR Mgt)
        Heriot-Watt – BCC 1st yr entry (Mgt HR Mgt) (IB 28–30 pts)
        Hertfordshire – 260 pts (HR Mgt)
        Lincoln – 260 pts (HR Mgt Mark; HR Mgt PR)
        Staffordshire – 260 pts (HR Mgt)
        Stirling – BCC 1st yr entry (HR Mgt) (IB 30 pts)

Winchester – 260–300 pts (Bus Mgt HR Mgt)
Worcester – 260 pts (HR Mgt courses)
240 pts **Bradford** – 240 pts (Bus Mgt (HR Mgt))
Bristol UWE – 240–300 pts (Bus St HR Mgt)
Cardiff (UWIC) – 240 pts (Bus Mgt St HR Mgt)
Chichester – CCC (HR Mgt)
Cumbria – 240 pts (Bus HR Mgt)
De Montfort – 240 pts (HR Mgt courses)
Derby – 240 pts (HR Mgt)
Glamorgan – 240–280 pts (HR Mgt)
Liverpool John Moores – 240 pts (HR Mgt)
Manchester Met – 240 pts (HR Mgt; HR Mgt Comb Hons)
Newport – 240 pts (Bus (HR Mgt))
Nottingham Trent – 240 pts (Bus Mgt HR)
Portsmouth – 240 pts (HR Mgt; HR Mgt Psy)
Robert Gordon – CCC (Mgt HR Mgt)
Roehampton – 240–280 pts (Bus Mgt (HR Mgt))
Sheffield Hallam – 240 pts (Bus HR Mgt)
Ulster – 240 pts (Adv HR Mgt; HR Mgt Mark)
Westminster – CCC (Bus HR Mgt) (IB 28 pts)
Wolverhampton – 240 pts (Mark HR Mgt)
230 pts **Edinburgh Napier** – 230 pts (Acc HR)
220 pts **Central Lancashire** – 220 pts (HR Mgt Comb Hons) (IB 28 pts)
Leeds Met – 220 pts (Bus HR Mgt)
London Met – 220 pts (HR Mgt courses)
Northampton – 220–260 pts (HR Mgt courses)
Southampton Solent – 220 pts (Bus Mgt (HR Mgt))
Sunderland – 220–360 pts (Bus HR Mgt)
Wolverhampton – 220–240 pts (HR Mgt Law)
200 pts **Anglia Ruskin** – 200 pts (HR Mgt) (IB 24 pts)
Bedfordshire – 200 pts (Int HR Mgt)
Bucks New – 200–240 pts (HR Mgt; Bus HR Mgt)
Canterbury Christ Church – 200 pts (HR Mgt Bus; HR Mgt Mark)
East London – 200 pts (HR Mgt)
Middlesex – 200–240 pts (Bus HR Mgt; HR Mgt; HR Mgt Mark)
Suffolk (Univ Campus) – 200 pts (Bus HR Mgt)
Wolverhampton – 200–240 pts (HR Mgt)
180 pts **Abertay Dundee** – DDD (HR Mgt)
Greenwich – 180 pts (HR Mgt courses)
160 pts **Bradford (Coll Univ Centre)** – 160 pts (HR Mgt)
London South Bank – 160 pts (HR Mgt Mark)
West Scotland – CC (HR Mgt)
120 pts **Blackburn (Coll Univ Centre)** – 120 pts (HR Mgt)
Norwich City (Coll) – 120 pts (Bus Mgt (HR Mgt))
Swansea Met – DD (HR Mgt)
 80 pts **Euro Bus Sch London** – 80 pts (Int Bus HR Mgt 2 Langs)

Alternative offers
See **Chapter 7** and **Appendix 1** for grades/UCAS Tariff points information for the International Baccalaureate, Scottish Highers/Advanced Highers, the Welsh Baccalaureate, the Irish Leaving Certificate, the Cambridge Pre-U Diploma, the Advanced Diploma and the Extended Project.

EXAMPLES OF FOUNDATION DEGREES IN THE SUBJECT FIELD
Croydon (Coll); Glamorgan; Glyndŵr; Hertfordshire; Leeds Met; Middlesex; Plymouth.

CHOOSING YOUR COURSE (SEE ALSO CH. 1)

Some course features

Bath The course with Sociology has a compulsory placement year.

Cardiff Human Resources is an option within the Business programme which offers several specialist routes. The course provides the flexibility for students to transfer between degree programmes in the first year.

Lancaster (Mgt Org (HR Mgt)) The course focuses on social scientific concepts and an analysis of HR techniques, including recruitment, motivation, development and strategic planning. Students can opt to spend third year in industry.

London LSE (HR Mgt Emp Rel) This is a three-year full-time course with options from the first year which include economics, statistics, sociology, psychology, government, anthropology, information technology and language.

Portsmouth Optional industrial placement in Year 3.

Universities and colleges teaching quality See www.qaa.ac.uk; http://unistats.direct.gov.uk.

Examples of sandwich degree courses Aston; Bath; Birmingham City; Bournemouth; Bradford; Bristol UWE; Coventry; De Montfort; East London; Edinburgh Napier; Glamorgan; Gloucestershire; Hertfordshire; Lancaster; Leeds Met; Lincoln; Liverpool John Moores; London Met; Northumbria; Plymouth; Portsmouth; Sheffield Hallam; Staffordshire; Sunderland; Swansea Met; Ulster; West Scotland; Westminster; Wolverhampton; Worcester.

ADMISSIONS INFORMATION

Number of applicants per place (approx) Anglia Ruskin 10; Aston 10; London LSE 16 (see also **Business and Management Courses**).

Advice to applicants and planning the UCAS personal statement See under **Business and Management Courses**.

Selection interviews Yes De Montfort; **Some** Anglia Ruskin. See also **Business and Management Courses**.)

Interview advice and questions See under **Business and Management Courses**.

Reasons for rejection (non-academic) See under **Business and Management Courses**.

AFTER-RESULTS ADVICE

Offers to applicants repeating A-levels Higher Anglia Ruskin.

GRADUATE DESTINATIONS AND EMPLOYMENT (2007/8 HESA)

Graduates surveyed 485 **Employed** 235 **In further study** 55 **Assumed unemployed** 55

Career note See under **Business and Management Courses**.

OTHER DEGREE SUBJECTS FOR CONSIDERATION

Business Studies; Information Systems; Management Studies/Sciences; Marketing; Psychology; Retail Management; Sociology; Sports Management.

HUMAN SCIENCES/HUMAN BIOSCIENCES

Human Sciences is a multi-disciplinary study relating to biological and social sciences and focuses on social and cultural behaviour. Topics range from genetics and evolution to health, disease, social behaviour and industrial societies.

Useful websites www.scienceyear.com; www.becominghuman.org; see also **Biology** and **Geography**.

NB The points totals shown to the left of the institutions are for ease of reference only. It must not be assumed that Tariff points are always used by institutions or that they can be substituted for an offer in grades. The level of an offer is not necessarily indicative of the quality of a course.

COURSE OFFERS INFORMATION

Subject requirements/preferences **GCSE** Science essential and mathematics usually required. **AL** Chemistry/biology usually required or preferred for some courses.

NB In 2012 universities and colleges will differ in their use of GCE AL/AS unit grade information, A* grades, the Extended Project (EPQ), the Advanced Diploma and the Cambridge Pre-U examination when considering applicants and making offers. An EPQ may be accepted in place of an AS subject. Check websites of universities and colleges for the latest offers information.

Your target offers and examples of courses provided by each institution

360 pts **London (UCL)** – AAA–AAB (Hum Sci) (IB 36 pts)
        Oxford – AAA (Hum Sci) (IB 38–40 pts)
340 pts **Exeter** – AAB–BBB (Hum Biosci) (IB 34 pts)
        London (King's) – ABB+AS (Hum Sci) (IB 34 pts)
        Sussex – AAB–ABB (Hum Sci) (IB 34–36 pts)
300 pts **Sheffield** – BBB (Hum Comm Sci) (IB 32 pts)
280 pts **Durham** – check with Admissions Tutor BBC (Hlth Hum Sci) (IB 30 pts)
        Loughborough – 280–300 pts (Ergonomics) (IB 30–32 pts)
        Plymouth – 280–320 pts (Hum Biosci) (IB 26 pts)
260 pts **Northumbria** – 260 pts (Hum Biosci) (IB 24 pts)
        Sheffield – BCC (Hlth Hum Sci) (IB 29 pts)
240 pts **Bolton** – 240 pts (Hum Sci courses)
        Coventry – 240 pts (Hum Biosci)
        Roehampton – 240–300 pts (Biol Sci)
220 pts **Northampton** – 220–260 pts (Hum Biosci courses)
200 pts **Roehampton** – 200–260 pts (Hlth Hum Sci)
        West London – 200 pts (Hum Sci pre-Med Yr 1: optional transfer to Med at London (UCL)) (IB 30 pts)
180 pts **Bradford** – 180–220 pts (Interd Hum St)
        Glasgow Caledonian – BCC (Hum Biosci)

Alternative offers
See **Chapter 7** and **Appendix 1** for grades/UCAS Tariff points information for the International Baccalaureate, Scottish Highers/Advanced Highers, the Welsh Baccalaureate, the Irish Leaving Certificate, the Cambridge Pre-U Diploma, the Advanced Diploma and the Extended Project.

CHOOSING YOUR COURSE (SEE ALSO CH. 1)

Some course features
Bradford (Interd Hum St) The course covers philosophy, psychology and sociology.
Exeter The subject is taught equally between the Schools of Biosciences and Sport and Health Sciences and has a strong scientific element.
London (UCL) (Hum Sci) The course combines biological and social studies and covers such topics as anatomy, physiology, genetics, anthropology, geography and psychology.
Loughborough (Ergon) The course deals with human reactions to technical and social environments, and includes anatomy, physiology, bio-mechanics, human psychology, the principles of design and organisational behaviour.
Oxford (Hum Sci) The degree focuses on the biological, social and cultural aspects of human life. A-level or AS-level biology or mathematics may be helpful but are not a requirement.
Sussex (Hum Sci) The core of the degree is made up of anthropology, biology, psychology, linguistics and philosophy.

ADMISSIONS INFORMATION

Number of applicants per place (approx) Bradford 7; Oxford 4–5.

Advice to applicants and planning the UCAS personal statement See **Biology** and **Anthropology**. See also **Appendix 2**.

Selection interviews Yes London (UCL), Oxford (Hum Sci) 31%.

Interview advice and questions Past questions have included: What do you expect to get out of a degree in Human Sciences? Why are you interested in this subject? What problems do you think you will be able to tackle after completing the course? Why did you drop PE as an A-level given that it's relevant to Human Sciences? How do you explain altruism, given that we are surely programmed by our genes to be selfish? How far is human behaviour determined by genes? What do you think are the key differences between animals and human beings? See **Chapter 6**. **Oxford** Are there too many people in the world?

AFTER-RESULTS ADVICE
Offers to applicants repeating A-levels Information not available from institutions.

GRADUATE DESTINATIONS AND EMPLOYMENT (2007/8 HESA)
Career note As a result of the multi-disciplinary nature of these courses, graduates could focus on openings linked to their special interests or look in general at the scientific and health sectors. Health administration and social services work and laboratory-based careers are some of the more common career destinations of graduates.

OTHER DEGREE SUBJECTS FOR CONSIDERATION
Anthropology; Biology; Community Studies; Environmental Sciences; Life Sciences; Psychology; Sociology.

INFORMATION MANAGEMENT and LIBRARIANSHIP

(including **Information Systems/Technology**; see also **Computer Courses, Media Studies**)

Information Management and Library Studies covers the very wide field of information. Its organisation, retrieval, indexing, computer and media technology, classification and cataloguing are all included in these courses.

Useful websites www.aslib.co.uk; www.ukoln.ac.uk; www.cilip.org.uk; www.bl.uk.

NB The points totals shown to the left of the institutions are for ease of reference only. It must not be assumed that Tariff points are always used by institutions or that they can be substituted for an offer in grades. The level of an offer is not necessarily indicative of the quality of a course.

COURSE OFFERS INFORMATION
Subject requirements/preferences GCSE English, mathematics and occasionally a foreign language. **AL** No specified subjects.

NB In 2012 universities and colleges will differ in their use of GCE AL/AS unit grade information, A* grades, the Extended Project (EPQ), the Advanced Diploma and the Cambridge Pre-U examination when considering applicants and making offers. An EPQ may be accepted in place of an AS subject. Check websites of universities and colleges for the latest offers information.

Your target offers and examples of courses provided by each institution
340 pts **East Anglia** – AAB–BBB (Hist Art Gllry Musm St)
Exeter – AAB–BBB (IT Mgt Bus) (IB 34–29 pts HL Maths 6)
Leeds – AAB 340 pts (IT)
London (UCL) – ABB+AS (Inf Mgt Bus) (IB 34 pts)
Manchester – AAB (IT Bus)

320 pts Lancaster – ABB 320 pts (Inf Comm Sys MSci) (IB 30 pts)
Loughborough – 320 pts (Inf Mgt Bus St) (IB 32 pts)
Reading – 320–300 pts (IT; App IT; Bus IT)
Southampton – ABB (Inf Tech Org)
300 pts Aberdeen – BBB (Inf Sys Mgt; Ind Plmt)
Keele – 300 pts (IT Mgt Bus)
Lancaster – BBB 300 pts (Inf Comm Sys BSc) (IB 29 pts)
Loughborough – BBB–AAB (IT Mgt Bus) (IB 32 pts)
Sheffield – BBB (Inf Mgt) (IB 32 pts)
280 pts Brighton – BBC (Musm Herit St) (IB 28 pts)
Bristol UWE – 280–300 pts (IT Mgt Bus)
Greenwich – 280 pts (ICT Bus)
Heriot-Watt – BBC 2nd yr entry (Inf Sys courses)
London (QM) – 280 pts (ICTs; ICTs Bus Env)
Loughborough – 280 pts (Inf Mgt Comp) (IB 30 pts)
260 pts Aberystwyth – 260 pts (Musm Gllry St)
Birmingham City – 260 pts (ICT)
Glamorgan – 260–300 pts (IT)
Kent – 260 pts (IT courses; Bus IT courses)
Liverpool Hope – 260 pts (IT)
Newport – 260 pts (Inf Scrty)
Oxford Brookes – BCC (IT Mgt Bus)
Plymouth – 260 pts (IT Mgt)
240 pts Bradford – 200–240 pts (ICT courses)
Cardiff (UWIC) – 240 pts (Int Inf Sys Mgt)
Chichester – CCC (IT courses)
De Montfort – 240 pts (ICT)
Essex – CCC 240 pts (Musm Pr)
Heriot-Watt – CCC 1st yr entry (Inf Sys courses)
Huddersfield – 240 pts (ICT)
Lincoln – 240 pts (Des Exhib Mus)
Liverpool John Moores – 240 pts (Bus Mgt Inf)
Northumbria – 240 pts (Electron Pub Inf Mgt) (IB 24 pts)
Nottingham Trent – 240 pts (Bus Inf Mgt)
Plymouth – 240 pts (Bus Econ Inf Mgt)
Worcester – 240 pts (IT Educ)
220 pts Bristol UWE – 220–260 pts (Bus Inf Sys)
Gloucestershire – 220 pts (IT)
Kingston – 220 pts (Musm Gllry St)
Manchester Met – 220 pts (Libshp; Inf Mgt)
Stirling – CCD 1st yr entry (Inf Sys) (IB 26 pts)
200 pts Aberystwyth – 200 pts (Inf Lib St) (IB 26 pts)
Chester – 200–240 pts (Inf Sys Mgt) (IB 24 pts)
Chichester – CDD (IT Mgt Bus)
East London – 200 pts (Inf Scrty Sys; ICT Int Dev)
195 pts Glasgow Caledonian – 195 pts inc CC (IT Mgt Bus)
180 pts Greenwich – 180 pts (ICT)
Wolverhampton – 180 pts (Trvl Bus Inf Mgt)
160 pts Bedfordshire – 160 pts (Inf Sys)
Greenwich – 160 pts (Bus Inf Sys; Bus IT; IT Scrty)
Southampton Solent – 160 pts (Bus Inf Sys; ICT; Knwl Mgt)
West Scotland – CC (Inf Mgt)
Wolverhampton – 160 pts (IT Mgt)

Aberystwyth – Contact University (Hist Arcvl St)

Alternative offers

See **Chapter 7** and **Appendix 1** for grades/UCAS Tariff points information for the International Baccalaureate, Scottish Highers/Advanced Highers, the Welsh Baccalaureate, the Irish Leaving Certificate, the Cambridge Pre-U Diploma, the Advanced Diploma and the Extended Project.

EXAMPLES OF FOUNDATION DEGREES IN THE SUBJECT FIELD

Edge Hill; Peterborough (Reg Coll); Truro (Coll).

CHOOSING YOUR COURSE (SEE ALSO CH. 1)

Some course features

Aberystwyth This leading department offers courses in Information and Library Studies by way of 15 specialist joint subjects. There is also a unique course in Historical and Archival Studies in addition to courses in Museum and Gallery Studies.

Bradford Information and Communication Technology can be taken with a range of subjects including business, marketing, media and law.

Brighton Core subjects in the Library Studies and Information course focus on the library and community, knowledge and records, and library management; heavy use is made of computing and media technologies. There is also a choice of specialist studies from media resources, bibliographical studies and computer studies, electronic publishing, newspaper publishing, school libraries and picture archives. Short practical placements in this three-year course take place each year. An Information Management course is offered. It gives a business context for the organisation, retrieval and management of information.

Manchester Met Information and Communications is a modular course, and offers the basic core subjects covering management, information systems, retrieval and information technology. Special studies in Year 3 provide flexibility to cover areas of special interest to students. These include working in academic, business and commercial communities. Students are required to undertake two periods of placement, each of five weeks' duration. Courses in Information and Communications, and Information Management are also offered.

Universities and colleges teaching quality See www.qaa.ac.uk; http://unistats.direct.gov.uk.

Top research universities and colleges (RAE 2008) Sheffield; London (King's); London (UCL); Wolverhampton; City; Robert Gordon; Glasgow; Brunel; Loughborough; Edinburgh Napier.

Examples of sandwich degree courses Bristol UWE; Loughborough; Northumbria; Nottingham Trent; Plymouth; Staffordshire; West Scotland.

ADMISSIONS INFORMATION

Number of applicants per place (approx) Aberystwyth 4; London (UCL) 7; Loughborough 5; Manchester Met 4; Sheffield 30; Southampton 5.

Advice to applicants and planning the UCAS personal statement Work experience or work shadowing in local libraries is important but remember that reference libraries provide a different field of work. Visit university libraries and major reference libraries and discuss the work with librarians. Describe your experiences in the personal statement. See also **Appendix 4**.

Misconceptions about this course Read the prospectus carefully. The course details can be confusing. Some courses have a bias towards the organisation and retrieval of information, others towards information systems technology.

Selection interviews **Yes** London (UCL), Loughborough, Southampton.

Interview advice and questions Past questions include: What is it about librarianship that interests you? Why do you think you are suited to be a librarian? What does the job entail? What is the role of the library in school? What is the role of the public library? What new developments are taking place in libraries? Which books do you read? How often do you use a library? What is the Dewey number for the history section in the library? (Applicant studying A-level History.) See **Chapter 6**.

AFTER-RESULTS ADVICE
Offers to applicants repeating A-levels **Higher** Loughborough; **Same** Sheffield.

GRADUATE DESTINATIONS AND EMPLOYMENT (2007/8 HESA)
Graduates surveyed 205 **Employed** 105 **In further study** 25 **Assumed unemployed** 25

Career note Graduates in this subject area and in communications enter a wide range of public and private sector jobs where the need to process information as well as to make it easily accessible and user-friendly, is very high. Areas of work could include web content, design and internet management and library management.

OTHER DEGREE SUBJECTS FOR CONSIDERATION
Business Information Systems; Communication Studies; Computer Science; Geographic Information Systems; Media Studies.

INTERNATIONAL RELATIONS

(including **International Development**, **Peace Studies** and **War Studies**; see also **Development Studies, European Studies, Politics**)

A strong interest in international affairs is a prerequisite for these courses which often allow students to focus on a specific area such as African, Asian, West European politics.

Useful websites www.sipri.org; www.un.org; www.un.int; www.irc-online.org; see also **Politics**.

NB The points totals shown to the left of the institutions are for ease of reference only. It must not be assumed that Tariff points are always used by institutions or that they can be substituted for an offer in grades. The level of an offer is not necessarily indicative of the quality of a course.

COURSE OFFERS INFORMATION
Subject requirements/preferences **GCSE** English; a foreign language usually required. **AL** No specified subjects. (War Studies) History may be required.

NB In 2012 universities and colleges will differ in their use of GCE AL/AS unit grade information, A* grades, the Extended Project (EPQ), the Advanced Diploma and the Cambridge Pre-U examination when considering applicants and making offers. An EPQ may be accepted in place of an AS subject. Check websites of universities and colleges for the latest offers information.

Your target offers and examples of courses provided by each institution
430 pts **Warwick** – A*AA–AAAb (Econ Pol Int St) (IB 38 pts)
400 pts **London (King's)** – A*AA+AS–A*Aaa+AS (War St courses) (IB 39 pts)
380 pts **Bath** – A*AA (Econ Int Dev) (IB 38 pts HL 766)
         London (UCL) – A*AA+AS (Int Rel)
360 pts **Bath** – AAA (Pol Int Rel) (IB 38 pts)
         Durham – AAA (Int Rel) (37 pts)
         Exeter – AAA–ABB (Int Rel) (IB 36–33 pts)
         London (RH) – AAA–ABB 360–320 pts (Hist Int Rel) (IB 32–35 pts)
         Nottingham – AAA (Int Rel Glob Is) (IB 38 pts)
         St Andrews – AAA (Int Rel courses) (IB 38 pts)
340 pts **Birmingham** – AAB–ABB (War St)
         Exeter – AAB–ABB (Int Rel Fr/Ger/Ital/Russ/Span) (IB 31–34 pts)
         London (QM) – AAB 340 pts (Int Rel) (IB 32 pts)
         London LSE – AAB (Int Rel) (IB 37 pts HL 666)
         Loughborough – ABB–AAB (Hist Int Rel) (IB 32–34 pts)
         Manchester – AAB–ABB (Pol Int Rel) (IB 35–34 pts)

Sheffield – AAB (Int Rel Pol)
Southampton – AAB–ABBb 340 pts (Pol Int Rel) (IB 34 pts)
Sussex – AAB–ABB (Int Rel Contemp Euro St) (IB 34–36 pts)
York – AAB (Pol Int Rel) (IB 36 pts)

320 pts **Birmingham** – ABB (Int St Lang) (IB 32 pts)
East Anglia – ABB–BBB (Int Rel Int Dev courses) (IB 31–32 pts)
Essex – 320 pts (Int Rel) (IB 34 pts)
Hull – 320 pts (Pol Int Rel) (IB 34–36 pts)
Kent – 320 pts (War St) (IB 33 pts)
Lancaster – ABB (Int Rel courses) (IB 30 pts)
Leeds – ABB (Int Rel Chin/Ital/Jap/Port/Russ/Span) (IB 34 pts HL 16 pts)
Leicester – ABB (Int Rel Hist; Int Rel)
Liverpool – ABB 320 pts (Int Rel)
London (Gold) – ABB (Int St) (IB 28 pts)
Surrey – ABB (Law Int St) (IB 32 pts)
Ulster – ABB (Law Int Pol) (IB 26 pts)

300 pts **Aberdeen** – BBB (Pol Int Rel)
Aston – 300–320 pts (Int Rel Pol) (IB 31–33 pts)
City – BBB 300 pts (Int Pol Sociol)
Edinburgh – BBB–AAA (Int Rel) (IB 34 pts)
Keele – 300–320 pts (Int Rel) (IB 28–30 pts)
Loughborough – 300–320 pts (Int Rel)
Queen's Belfast – BBB–BBCb (Int Pol Cnflct St)
Reading – 300–320 pts (Int Rel courses)
Swansea – BBB 300 pts (Int Rel; Int Rel Welsh; Int Rel Am St; War Soty)

280 pts **Aberdeen** – BBB (Pol Int Rel) (IB 28 pts)
Aberystwyth – 280–300 pts (Int Rel) (IB 28 pts)
Bradford – 280 pts (Int Rel Scrty St) (IB 30 pts)
Brighton – BBC (Hum: War Cnflct Modnty) (IB 28 pts)
Nottingham Trent – 280 pts (Int Rel)
Oxford Brookes – BBC–BCC/BBcc (Int Rel courses) (IB 31 pts)
Stirling – BBC (Pol (Int Pol))
Westminster – BBC (Int Rel Chin)

260 pts **Bristol UWE** – 260–300 pts (Int Rel courses) (IB 26–32 pts)
Brunel – BCC (Int Pol) (IB 29 pts)
Coventry – 260–280 pts (Int Rel; Int Rel Pol)
De Montfort – 260 pts (Int Rel; Int Rel Pol)
Keele – 260–320 pts (Int Rel Joint Hons)
Lincoln – 260 pts (Crimin Int Rel)
Nottingham Trent – 260 pts (Glob St Joint Hons; Int Rel Joint Hons)
Westminster – BCC (Int Rel Arbc) (IB 28 pts)

240 pts **Buckingham** – 240 pts (Int St)
Canterbury Christ Church – 240 pts (Pol Int Rel; Int Rel Joint/Comb Hons)
Chester – 240 pts (Int Dev St) (IB 24 pts)
Kingston – 240–360 pts (Int Rel courses)
Lincoln – 240 pts (Int Rel courses)
London Met – 240 pts (Int Rel Pce Cnflct St; Int Rel Law)
London South Bank – 240 pts (Int Pol)
Plymouth – 240–300 pts (Int Rel courses) (IB 26 pts)
Portsmouth – 240–300 pts (Int Rel) (IB 24–25 pts)
Salford – 240 pts (Jrnl War St) (IB 31 pts)
Sheffield Hallam – 240 pts (Int Rel)
Ulster – 240 pts (Int Pol)
Winchester – 240–280 pts (Pol Glob St)

220 pts **Leeds Met** – 220 pts (Glob Dev Int Rel; Pce St Int Rel)
200 pts **East London** – 200 pts (Int Pol)
        Portsmouth – 200–280 pts (Int Dev St)
180 pts **Derby** – 180–240 pts (Int Rel Glob Devl; Thrd Wrld Dev)
        Greenwich – 180 pts (Int St)
        Staffordshire – 180 pts (Int Rel courses)
160 pts **Wolverhampton** – 160–220 pts (War St courses)
        Open University – contact +44 (0)845 300 6090 **or** www.openuniversity.co.uk/you (Int St)

Alternative offers
See **Chapter 7** and **Appendix 1** for grades/UCAS Tariff points information for the International Baccalaureate, Scottish Highers/Advanced Highers, the Welsh Baccalaureate, the Irish Leaving Certificate, the Cambridge Pre-U Diploma, the Advanced Diploma and the Extended Project.

CHOOSING YOUR COURSE (SEE ALSO CH. 1)
Some course features
Cardiff There is also a Joint degree in Politics and International Relations with Turin University.
East London (Int Dev: Thrd Wrld NGO Mgt) An interdisciplinary course, this draws on economics, politics, sociology, history and cultural studies to focus on the role of NGOs, their functions and relationships. Students are encouraged to travel to Africa, Asia, Central and Latin America; there is also a final-year work placement scheme.
London (King's) A unique range of courses in War Studies includes topics in strategy, security and intelligence.
London LSE The subject can be taken as a Single Honours degree or jointly with History. High percentage of international students.

Top research universities and colleges (RAE 2008) See **Politics**.

Examples of sandwich degree courses Aston; Loughborough; Nottingham Trent; Oxford Brookes; Plymouth; Portsmouth; Surrey.

ADMISSIONS INFORMATION
Number of applicants per place (approx) Aberystwyth 6; Birmingham 10; De Montfort 6; Derby 3; Exeter 8; Leeds 13; London (King's) 6; London LSE (Int Rel) 21; Nottingham 5; Portsmouth 2; Reading 5; Southampton (Int Rel) 6.

Advice to applicants and planning the UCAS personal statement Describe any special interests you have in the affairs of any particular country. Contact embassies for information on cultural, economic and political developments. Follow international events through newspapers and magazines. Give details of any voluntary work you have done. **London (King's)** Substantial experience required in some area of direct relevance to War Studies. **St Andrews** Give reasons for choice of course and evidence of your interest.

Misconceptions about this course Some students think that this degree will give direct entry into the Diplomatic Service.

Selection interviews Yes Birmingham, London (King's), London Met, Nottingham Trent; **Some** De Montfort, Kent, Wolverhampton.

Interview advice and questions Applicants are likely to be questioned on current international events and crises between countries. See **Chapter 6**. **Nottingham Trent** Be prepared to be challenged on your existing views!

AFTER-RESULTS ADVICE
Offers to applicants repeating A-levels Same Chester, De Montfort, Exeter, Lincoln, Wolverhampton.

GRADUATE DESTINATIONS AND EMPLOYMENT (2007/8 HESA)
See **Politics**.

Career note See **Politics**.

OTHER DEGREE SUBJECTS FOR CONSIDERATION

Development Studies; Economics; European Studies; Government; Politics.

ITALIAN

(see also Languages)

The language and literature of Italy will feature strongly on most Italian courses. The majority of applicants have no knowledge of Italian. They will need to give convincing reasons for their interest and to show that they have the ability to assimilate language quickly. See also **Appendix 4** under Languages.

Useful websites http://europa.eu; www.italia.gov.it; www.bbc.co.uk/languages; http://language advantage.com; www.sis.ac.uk; www.italianstudies.org; www.languagematters.co.uk; www.reed.co. uk/multilingual; see also **Languages**.

NB The points totals shown to the left of the institutions are for ease of reference only. It must not be assumed that Tariff points are always used by institutions or that they can be substituted for an offer in grades. The level of an offer is not necessarily indicative of the quality of a course.

COURSE OFFERS INFORMATION

Subject requirements/preferences GCSE English and a foreign language required. **AL** Italian may be required for some courses.

NB In 2012 universities and colleges will differ in their use of GCE AL/AS unit grade information, A* grades, the Extended Project (EPQ), the Advanced Diploma and the Cambridge Pre-U examination when considering applicants and making offers. An EPQ may be accepted in place of an AS subject. Check websites of universities and colleges for the latest offers information.

Your target offers and examples of courses provided by each institution

380 pts **Cambridge** – A*AA college offers may vary (Modn Mediev Lang (Ital)) (IB 38–42 pts)
360 pts **Bath** – AAA–ABB (Modn Langs Euro St) (IB 34 pts HL lang 6)
        Durham – AAA–AAB (Modn Langs (Ital)) (IB 33–34 pts)
        London (UCL) – AAB+AS–ABB+AS (Ital Des) (IB 34–36 pts)
        Manchester – AAA–AAB (Ital Russ MML) (IB 35–37 pts)
340 pts **Bath** – AAB–ABB (Ital courses) (IB 34–36 pts)
        Bristol – AAB–BBC (Ital Russ) (IB 35 pts)
        Exeter – AAB–ABB (Modn Euro Langs) (IB 29 pts)
        Glasgow – AAB (Ital courses) (IB 34 pts)
        Liverpool – AAB–BBB (Ital Comb Hons) (IB 36–30 pts)
        London (UCL) – AAB (Ital) (36 pts)
        Reading – 340–360 pts (Hist Ital)
        St Andrews – AAB (Ital courses) (IB 36 pts)
        Sheffield – AAB (Mech Eng Ital)
320 pts **Birmingham** – ABB–BBC (Ital Joint Hons) (IB 34 pts)
        Bristol – ABB-BBC (Ital courses) (35 pts)
        Cardiff – ABB–BBB (Ital courses)
        Lancaster – ABB–BBB (Ital courses) (IB 29–30 pts)
        Leicester – ABB (Ital joint courses) (IB 30 pts)
        London (RH) – ABB–BBB (Ital courses) (IB 32 pts HL lang 6)
        Manchester – ABB–BBC (Ital Chin BA; Ital Russ BA; Ital Ling)
        Strathclyde – ABB (Ital courses)
        Sussex – ABB–BBB (Ital courses)
        Warwick – ABB (Ital Euro Lit) (IB 32–34 pts)
300 pts **Edinburgh** – check with Ad tutor BBB (Ital Class) (IB 34 pts)
        Essex – 300–320 pts (Ital courses) (IB 30 pts)

Kent – 300–320 pts (Ital Joint Hons) (IB 33–35 pts)
Leeds – ABC–BBB (Ital joint courses) (IB 34 pts HL 16 pts)
Liverpool – BBB (Comm St Ital) (IB 30 pts)
Manchester – BBB–BCC (Ital St) (IB 32–28 pts)
Reading – 300–320 pts (Ital Class St; Ital Hist Art)
Salford – 300 pts (Euro Langs (Ital+2 Langs); Modn Lang St (Ital))
280 pts **Bangor** – 280 pts (Law Ital) (IB 28 pts)
Birmingham – BBC (Ital St) (IB 30–32 pts)
Essex – 280 pts (Ital St Modn Langs) (IB 28 pts)
Manchester – BBC (Ital Jap BA)
Reading – 280–360 pts (Arch Ital)
260 pts **Hertfordshire** – 260 pts (Ital courses)
Hull – 260–300 pts (Ital St; Ital Mgt; Ital Transl St; Ital Mark)
Nottingham Trent – 260 pts (Ital Joint Hons)
240 pts **Bangor** – 240–280 pts (Ital Joint Hons) (IB 26–28 pts)
Edinburgh Napier – 240 pts (Langs Intercult Comm)
Manchester Met – 240 pts (Ital Comb Hons) (IB 26 pts)
Portsmouth – 240–300 pts (App Langs)
180 pts **Greenwich** – 180 pts (Ital Comb courses) (IB 24 pts)
160 pts **Euro Bus Sch London** – CC Check with school (Int Bus Ital)

Alternative offers
See **Chapter 7** and **Appendix 1** for grades/UCAS Tariff points information for the International Baccalaureate, Scottish Highers/Advanced Highers, the Welsh Baccalaureate, the Irish Leaving Certificate, the Cambridge Pre-U Diploma, the Advanced Diploma and the Extended Project.

CHOOSING YOUR COURSE (SEE ALSO CH. 1)
Some course features
Bangor Italian can be studied with two other languages or with Law, Journalism or Media Studies.
Bath Italian is taken with a second European language as part of the European Studies course.
Hull In addition to modern language combinations, Italian can be studied with a choice from 17 other subjects.
Reading The History with Italian degree does not involve a year abroad.

Universities and colleges teaching quality See www.qaa.ac.uk; http://unistats.direct.gov.uk.

Top research universities and colleges (RAE 2008) Cambridge; Leeds; Warwick; Reading; Oxford; Bristol; Manchester; Birmingham; London (UCL); Exeter.

ADMISSIONS INFORMATION
Number of applicants per place (approx) Birmingham 5; Bristol 3; Cardiff 3; Hull 8; Lancaster 8; Leeds 3; London (RH) 4.

Advice to applicants and planning the UCAS personal statement Describe any visits to Italy and experience of speaking the language. Interests in Italian art, literature, culture, society and architecture could also be mentioned. Read Italian newspapers and magazines and give details if you have a bilingual background. Give evidence of your interest and your reasons for choosing the course. See also **Appendix 4** under Languages.

Misconceptions about this course Leeds See **Languages**.

Selection interviews Yes Birmingham (majority receive offers), London (RH), Oxford; **Some** Cambridge.

Interview advice and questions Past questions include: Why do you want to learn Italian? What foreign newspapers or magazines do you read (particularly if the applicant has taken A-level Italian)? Have you visited Italy? What do you know of the Italian people, culture, art? See **Chapter 6**. **Leeds** See **Languages**.

AFTER-RESULTS ADVICE
Offers to applicants repeating A-levels Higher Birmingham, Glasgow, Warwick; **Same** Cardiff, Hull, Leeds.

GRADUATE DESTINATIONS AND EMPLOYMENT (2007/8 HESA)
Graduates surveyed 220 **Employed** 95 **In further study** 50 **Assumed unemployed** 25

Career note See **Languages**.

OTHER DEGREE SUBJECTS FOR CONSIDERATION
European Studies; International Business Studies; other languages.

JAPANESE
(see also Asia-Pacific Studies, Languages)

A strong interest in Japan and its culture is expected of applicants. A number of four-year joint courses are now offered, all of which include a period of study in Japan. Potential employers are showing an interest in Japanese. Students report that 'it is not a soft option'. They are expected to be firmly committed to a Japanese degree (for example, by listing only Japanese on the UCAS application), to have an interest in using their degree in employment and to be prepared for a lot of hard work. See **Appendix 2** under Languages.

Useful websites www.cilt.org.uk; www.iol.org.uk; www.bbc.co.uk/languages; http://language advantage.com; www.languagematters.co.uk; www.reed.co.uk/multilingual; www.japanese-online. com; www.japaneselifestyle.com.au; www.thejapanesepage.com; www.japanesestudies.org.uk.

NB The points totals shown to the left of the institutions are for ease of reference only. It must not be assumed that Tariff points are always used by institutions or that they can be substituted for an offer in grades. The level of an offer is not necessarily indicative of the quality of a course.

COURSE OFFERS INFORMATION
Subject requirements/preferences GCSE Edinburgh: English and a foreign language usually required. **AL** Modern language required for some courses.

NB In 2012 universities and colleges will differ in their use of GCE AL/AS unit grade information, A* grades, the Extended Project (EPQ), the Advanced Diploma and the Cambridge Pre-U examination when considering applicants and making offers. An EPQ may be accepted in place of an AS subject. Check websites of universities and colleges for the latest offers information.

Your target offers and examples of courses provided by each institution
380 pts **Cambridge** – A*AA college offers may vary (As Mid E St (Jap)) (IB 38–42 pts)
360 pts **Exeter** – AAA-AAB (Flex Comb Hons Minor (jap beginners))
  Oxford – AAA (Japanese) (IB 38–40 pts)
340 pts **Bath** – AAB 340 pts (Comp Sci Jap/Bus/Maths/Fr/Ger/Mand Chin/Span) (IB 36 pts HL maths 6)
  Birmingham – AAB-ABB (Econ Jap) (IB 32–34 pts)
  London (SOAS) – AAA-AAB (Jap St) (IB 36 pts)
  Manchester – AAB-BBB (Jap St) (IB 35–30 pts)
  Southampton – AAB (Modn Langs) (IB 34 pts HL 17 pts)
320 pts **Cardiff** – ABB (Fr/Ger/Ital Jap) (IB 32 pts)
  Leeds – ABB (Jap courses) (IB 34 pts HL 16 pts)
  London (SOAS) – ABB (Jap) (IB 30 pts)
  Manchester – ABB-BBC (Ling Jap) (IB 35–30 pts)
  Newcastle – ABB-ABC (Ling Jap) (IB 32 pts)
  Sheffield – ABB (Jap St courses) (IB 32 pts)

300 pts **East Anglia** – BBB–BBC (Jap)
　　　　　Edinburgh – check with Admissions Tutor BBB (Jap Ling) (IB 34 pts)
　　　　　Oxford Brookes – BBB–BBbb (Jap St; Jap St Comb Hons)
280 pts **Leeds** – BBC (Chin St Jap)
260 pts **Central Lancashire** – 260–300 pts (Jap Comb Hons courses) (IB 26 pts)
240 pts **Liverpool John Moores** – 240 pts (Int Bus St Jap) (IB 26 pts)

Alternative offers
See **Chapter 7** and **Appendix 1** for grades/UCAS Tariff points information for the International Baccalaureate, Scottish Highers/Advanced Highers, the Welsh Baccalaureate, the Irish Leaving Certificate, the Cambridge Pre-U Diploma, the Advanced Diploma and the Extended Project.

CHOOSING YOUR COURSE (SEE ALSO CH. 1)
Some course features
Cardiff Courses are offered with Business or a choice of four European languages.
Manchester (Jap Scrn St) The course combines Japanese language and culture with core course units in understanding film, its history and pre-history, and its development across other media including television, DVD and the internet. The third year is spent abroad.
Newcastle (Jap Cult St) Course covers language, sociology, anthropology and Modern East and South East Asian History.
Sheffield Japanese can be studied in combination with 13 other subjects including Chinese, Korean and Business Management.

Universities and colleges teaching quality See www.qaa.ac.uk; http://unistats.direct.gov.uk.

Examples of sandwich degree courses Oxford Brookes.

ADMISSIONS INFORMATION
Number of applicants per place (approx) Cardiff 8; London (SOAS) 9; Sheffield 10.

Advice to applicants and planning the UCAS personal statement Discuss your interest in Japan and your reasons for wishing to study the language. Know Japan, its culture and background history. Discuss any visits you have made or contacts with Japanese nationals. See also **Appendix 4** under Languages. **Leeds** See **Languages**.

Selection interviews **Yes** Cambridge, Oxford, Southampton; **Some** Leeds.

Interview advice and questions Japanese is an extremely demanding subject and applicants are most likely to be questioned on their reasons for choosing this degree. They will be expected also to have some knowledge of Japanese culture, history and current affairs. See **Chapter 6**.

Reasons for rejection (non-academic) Insufficient evidence of genuine motivation.

GRADUATE DESTINATIONS AND EMPLOYMENT (2007/8 HESA)
Graduates surveyed 90 **Employed** 35 **In further study** 10 **Assumed unemployed** 15

Career note See **Languages**.

OTHER DEGREE SUBJECTS FOR CONSIDERATION
Asia-Pacific Studies; International Business Studies; Oriental Languages; South East Asia Studies.

LANDSCAPE ARCHITECTURE
(including **Garden Design** and **Landscape Design** and **Management**; see also **Agricultural Sciences/Agriculture, Horticulture**)

Landscape architecture is a specialised branch of architecture for which an ability in art and design is sought and for some of these courses a portfolio of art work may be required. Courses focus on the design of the environment and surrounding buildings. Landscape architecture should not be confused with the work of a garden centre.

Useful websites www.landscape.co.uk; www.laprofession.org.

NB The points totals shown to the left of the institutions are for ease of reference only. It must not be assumed that Tariff points are always used by institutions or that they can be substituted for an offer in grades. The level of an offer is not necessarily indicative of the quality of a course.

COURSE OFFERS INFORMATION
Subject requirements/preferences GCSE English, geography, art and design, mathematics and at least one science usually required. **AL** Preferred subjects for some courses include biology, geography, environmental science. A portfolio may also be required.

NB In 2012 universities and colleges will differ in their use of GCE AL/AS unit grade information, A* grades, the Extended Project (EPQ), the Advanced Diploma and the Cambridge Pre-U examination when considering applicants and making offers. An EPQ may be accepted in place of an AS subject. Check websites of universities and colleges for the latest offers information.

Your target offers and examples of courses provided by each institution
360 pts   **Sheffield** – AAA + portfolio (Archit Land) (IB 37 pts)
340 pts   **Leicester** – AAB (Modn Langs Film St) (IB 30–32 pts)
280 pts   **Birmingham City** – 280 pts (Land Archit) (IB 26 pts)
          Edinburgh (CA) – BBC (Land Archit) (IB 30 pts)
          Gloucestershire – 280–300 pts (Land Archit)
          Kingston – 280 pts (Land Plan) (IB 28 pts)
          Leeds Met – 280–320 pts (Land Archit)
          Manchester Met – 280–300 pts (Land Archit) (IB 28 pts)
          Sheffield – BBC (Land Archit Ecol) (IB 30 pts)
240 pts   **Greenwich** – 240–230 pts (Land Archit)
          Leeds Met – 240–280 pts (Gdn Art Des)
200 pts   **Writtle (Coll)** – 200–360 pts (Land Gdn Des; Gdn Des Restor Mgt)
180 pts   **Writtle (Coll)** – 180 pts (Grn Spc Mgt Hort (Tree Mgt))
160 pts   **Hadlow (Coll)** – CC 160 pts (Land Mgt; Gdn Des; Sust Land Mgt)
          Writtle (Coll) – 160 pts (Land Archit)
120 pts   **Southampton Solent** – 120 pts (Gdn Des)

Alternative offers
See **Chapter 7** and **Appendix 1** for grades/UCAS Tariff points information for the International Baccalaureate, Scottish Highers/Advanced Highers, the Welsh Baccalaureate, the Irish Leaving Certificate, the Cambridge Pre-U Diploma, the Advanced Diploma and the Extended Project.

EXAMPLES OF FOUNDATION DEGREES IN THE SUBJECT FIELD
Askham Bryan (Coll); Bishop Burton (Coll); Bournemouth; Brighton; CAFRE; Capel Manor (Coll); Cumbria; East Anglia; Falmouth (UC); Glyndŵr; Greenwich; Guildford (Coll); Harper Adams (UC); Hereford (CA); Moulton (Coll); Myerscough (Coll); Northampton; Northop (Coll); Sparsholt (Coll); Warwickshire (Coll); Writtle (Coll).

CHOOSING YOUR COURSE (SEE ALSO CH. 1)
Some course features
Birmingham City (Land Archit) The course is accredited by the Landscape Institute and combines a strong study of design with a focus on environmental and cultural issues and technical skills.
Gloucestershire Joint Honours courses are offered with relevant subjects such as geography, garden design, landscape management and heritage management.
Manchester Met The three-year BA course can be followed by a one-year Bachelor of Landscape Architecture for those wanting to enter the profession of landscape architecture. The course focuses

on the design of outdoor space and includes a European study tour and offers study opportunities in American and European universities.

Sheffield A multi-disciplinary course providing a comprehensive training in landscape architecture with a specialism in either planning or ecology. The Ecology pathway focuses on habitat restoration, urban regeneration and green technologies, while the Planning pathway centres on the political, social and economic facors of urban and rural environments.

Universities and colleges teaching quality See www.qaa.ac.uk; http://unistats.direct.gov.uk.

Examples of sandwich degree courses Edinburgh (CA); Writtle (Coll).

ADMISSIONS INFORMATION
Number of applicants per place (approx) Edinburgh (CA) 7; Gloucestershire 9; Greenwich 3; Kingston 4; Manchester Met 9; Writtle (Coll) 5.

Advice to applicants and planning the UCAS personal statement Knowledge of the work of landscape architects is important. Arrange a visit to a landscape architect's office and try to organise some work experience. Read up on historical landscape design and visit country house estates with examples of outstanding designs. Describe these visits in detail and your preferences. Membership of the National Trust could be useful. See also **Appendix 4**.

Selection interviews Yes Gloucestershire, Greenwich, Manchester Met, Sheffield, Writtle (Coll); **Some** Birmingham City.

Interview advice and questions Applicants will be expected to have had some work experience and are likely to be questioned on their knowledge of landscape architectural work and the subject. Historical examples of good landscaping could also be asked for. See **Chapter 6**.

Reasons for rejection (non-academic) Lack of historical knowledge and awareness of current developments. Poor portfolio.

AFTER-RESULTS ADVICE
Offers to applicants repeating A-levels Same Birmingham City, Edinburgh (CA), Greenwich, Manchester Met.

GRADUATE DESTINATIONS AND EMPLOYMENT (2007/8 HESA)
Graduates surveyed 170 **Employed** 70 **In further study** 40 **Assumed unemployed** 25

Career note Opportunities at present in landscape architecture are good. Openings exist in local government or private practice and may cover planning, housing, and conservation.

OTHER DEGREE SUBJECTS FOR CONSIDERATION
Architecture; Art and Design; Environmental Planning; Forestry; Horticulture.

LANGUAGES

(including **Hebrew** and **Modern Languages**; see also **African and Caribbean Studies, Asia-Pacific Studies, Chinese, English, European Studies, French, German, Greek, Italian, Japanese, Latin, Linguistics, Russian and East European Studies, Scandinavian Studies, Spanish**)

Modern Language courses usually offer three main options: a single subject degree commonly based on literature and language, a European Studies course, or two-language subjects which can often include languages different from those available at school (such as Scandinavian Studies, Russian and the languages of Eastern Europe, the Middle and Far East).

Useful websites www.iol.org.uk; www.iti.org.uk; http://europa.eu; www.cilt.org.uk; www.bbc.co.uk/languages; http://languageadvantage.com; www.omniglot.com; www.languagematters.co.uk; www.reed.co.uk/multilingual.

NB The points totals shown to the left of the institutions are for ease of reference only. It must not be assumed that Tariff points are always used by institutions or that they can be substituted for an offer in grades. The level of an offer is not necessarily indicative of the quality of a course.

COURSE OFFERS INFORMATION

Subject requirements/preferences GCSE English and a modern language required. In some cases grades A and/or B may be stipulated. **AL** A modern foreign language required usually with a specified grade.

NB In 2012 universities and colleges will differ in their use of GCE AL/AS unit grade information, A* grades, the Extended Project (EPQ), the Advanced Diploma and the Cambridge Pre-U examination when considering applicants and making offers. An EPQ may be accepted in place of an AS subject. Check websites of universities and colleges for the latest offers information.

Your target offers and examples of courses provided by each institution

410 pts **London (King's)** – AAAb/AAab+AS (Hist Port Braz St) (IB 38 pts HL 6 hist)

380 pts **Cambridge** – A*AA college offers may vary (Modn Mediev Lang) (IB 38–42 pts)
London (UCL) – AAA+AS–BBB+AS (Modn Lang) (IB 32–38 pts)

360 pts **Bath** – AAA (Euro St Modn Langs Fr/Span) (IB 36 pts)
Bristol – see separate language tables AAA–ABB (Fr) (IB 32–30 pts)
Durham – AAA–AAB (Modn Langs)
London (UCL) – AAA–ABB (Lang Cult) (IB 34–38 pts)
Oxford – AAA (Modn Lang Ling) (IB 38–40 pts)
St Andrews – AAA–AAB (Modn Lang courses) (IB 38–40 pts)

340 pts **Bristol** – AAB–BBC 340 pts (Russ) (IB 35–30 pts HL 655)
Cardiff – AAB–ABB (Euro Langs)
Exeter – see separate language tables AAB–ABB (Comb Lang courses)
Leicester – AAB (Modn Langs Film St) (IB 30–32 pts)
London (SOAS) – AAB (Chin) (IB 30 pts)
Manchester – AAB–BBC (Lang Lit Comm)
Manchester – AAB–BBB (Comb St courses) (IB 35–32 pts)
Southampton – AAB (Modn Langs) (IB 34 pts HL 17 pts)
York – AAB–ABB (Ling courses) (IB 34 pts)

320 pts **Bath** – ABB–BBB (Modn Langs Euro St courses except under 360 pts) (IB 34–32 pts)
Birmingham – ABB 320 pts (Modn Langs joint courses) (IB 32–34 pts)
Bristol – see separate language tables ABB–BCC (Ger) (IB 29–35 pts)
Hull – ABB 320 pts (Law Fr/Ger Law Lang)
Lancaster – ABB 320 pts (Euro Langs Mgt St)
Leeds – see separate language tables ABB–BBB (Modn Langs Joint Hons)
Leicester – ABB (Modn Lang St) (IB 28–30 pts)
Liverpool – ABB (Modn Euro Langs) (IB 30 pts)
London (RH) – ABB–BBB (Multiling St) (IB 32 pts)
London (SOAS) – ABB (Viet) (IB 30 pts)
Newcastle – ABB (Modn Langs Mgt St) (IB 32 pts HL Fr/Ger/Span 6)
Nottingham – ABB–ABC/BBB (Fr Russ) (IB 32 pts)
Sheffield – ABB (Modn Langs) (IB 32 pts HL lang 6)
Southampton – ABB (Lang Soty) (IB 32 pts)
Surrey – ABB–BBB 320–300 pts (Langs St) (IB 34-32 pts)
Swansea – ABB–BBB (Transl; Lang courses; Lang Comm)

300 pts **Aberdeen** – BBB (Langs Lit Scot) (IB 30 pts)
Aston – 300–320 pts (Modn Langs courses) (IB 31–33 pts)
Birmingham – BBB 300 pts (Modn Langs Euro St (Soty Cult Hist) (Pol)) (IB 32 pts)
East Anglia – BBB (Langs Mgt St)
Edinburgh – check with Admissions Tutor BBB–AAA (Modn Euro Langs EU St (2 langs from Fr/Ger/Ital/Rus/Scan St/Span)) (IB 34 pts)

Lancaster – BBB (Euro Langs Film St) (IB 29 pts)
Leeds – ABC/BBB (Thai SE As St) (IB 32 pts)
London (QM) – 300 pts (Fr/Ger/Russ Euro St; Modn Langs)
London (UCL) – BBB+AS (Dutch courses) (IB 32 pts)
Salford – 300–280 pts (Modn Lang Ling; Modn Lang Ling; Euro Langs; Modn Langs)
Strathclyde – BBB–BBC (Int Bus Modn Lang)
280 pts **East Anglia** – BBC (Transl Media Fr/Span 4 yrs; Modn Langs 4 yrs)
Essex – 280 pts (Lang St) (IB 30 pts)
Heriot-Watt – BBC (App Langs Transl; Langs (Interp Transl); Int Mgt Langs)
Roehampton – 280–340 pts (Modn Langs Transl Interp)
260 pts **Aberystwyth** – 260 pts (Rmnc Langs) (IB 29 pts)
Bristol UWE – 260–300 pts (Int Bus Lang)
Hull – 260–280 pts (Modn Lang St; Modn Langs)
Nottingham Trent – 260 pts (Modn Langs courses; Chin/Fr/Ger/Ital/Span courses)
Ulster – 260 pts inc BC (Lang Ling Comm; Lang Ling PR)
Westminster – BCC (Transl St) (IB 28 pts)
240 pts **Aberdeen** – CCC 1st yr entry (Euro Langs 20th Cent Cult)
Bangor – 240 pts (Fr/Ger/Ital/Span Joint Hons)
Coventry – 240–260 pts (Span)
Glamorgan – 240–280 pts (App Lang St)
London Met – 240 pts (App Transl)
Manchester Met – 240 pts (Joint Hons Langs)
Plymouth – 240 pts (Int Bus Modn Langs) (IB 24 pts)
Portsmouth – 240–300 pts (App Langs; Comb Modn Langs)
Sheffield Hallam – 240 pts (Bus St Langs Fr/Ger/Span; Langs Tour)
Stirling – CCC (Euro Langs Psy) (IB 28 pts)
230 pts **Edinburgh Napier** – 230 pts (Lang Joint courses)
220 pts **Leeds Met** – 220 pts (Lang St)
200 pts **Middlesex** – 200–240 pts (Transl; Int Bus Langs)
180 pts **Central Lancashire** – 180–200 pts (Modn Langs courses)
160 pts **Greenwich** – 160 pts (Int St Lang Cult)
West Scotland – CC (Langs Fr/Span)
Wolverhampton – 160–220 pts (Interp (Brit Sign Lang Engl))

Open University – contact +44 (0)845 300 6090 **or** www.openuniversity.co.uk/you (Modn Lang St)

Alternative offers
See **Chapter 7** and **Appendix 1** for grades/UCAS Tariff points information for the International Baccalaureate, Scottish Highers/Advanced Highers, the Welsh Baccalaureate, the Irish Leaving Certificate, the Cambridge Pre-U Diploma, the Advanced Diploma and the Extended Project.

CHOOSING YOUR COURSE (SEE ALSO CH. 1)
Some course features
See separate language tables.
Coventry Modern Language programmes offer French and Spanish (not ab initio). There are optional placements of one year.
Durham The modern languages offered are French, German, Russian and Spanish (all post A-level), with beginners courses in Arabic, Italian, Russian and Spanish, and options in Croatian and Serbian for Russian students. Catalan and Persian are also available. (High research rating – Fr)
Edinburgh Language courses are offered in Arabic, Celtic, Chinese, French, German, Greek, Italian, Japanese, Latin, Persian, Portuguese, Russian, Sanskrit, Scandinavian Studies (Danish, Swedish, Norwegian) and Spanish. (High research rating – Fr/Ger) There is also a Modern Language degree (two subjects).

Glasgow Czech, French, German, Greek, Italian, Latin, Polish, Portuguese, Russian, Hispanic Studies, Spanish, and Slavonic and Eastern European Studies are offered. There are also courses in Gaelic and Celtic. (High research rating – Fr)

Surrey Language courses focus on contemporary language in business, culture and society and cover French, German, Russian and Spanish.

Universities and colleges teaching quality See www.qaa.ac.uk; http://unistats.direct.gov.uk.

Top research universities and colleges (RAE 2008) See separate language tables.

ADMISSIONS INFORMATION

Number of applicants per place (approx) Aston 4; Bangor 5; Birmingham 5; Brighton 4; Bristol 15; Bristol UWE 4; Cambridge 3; Cardiff 6; Durham 6; East Anglia 15; Heriot-Watt 5; Huddersfield 12; Lancaster 10; Leeds (Joint Hons) 8; Leicester 6; Liverpool 5; Newcastle 22; Northumbria 4; Roehampton 3; Salford 6; Swansea 4; Wolverhampton 10; York 4.

Advice to applicants and planning the UCAS personal statement Discuss any literature studied outside your course work. Students applying for courses in which they have no previous knowledge (for example, Italian, Portuguese, Modern Greek, Czech, Russian) would be expected to have done a considerable amount of language work on their own in their chosen language before starting the course. See also **Appendix 4**.

Misconceptions about this course Leeds (Joint Hons) Some applicants think that studying languages means studying masses of literature – wrong. At Leeds, generally speaking, it's up to you; you study as much or as little literature as you choose. Residence abroad does not inevitably mean a university course (except where you are taking a language from scratch). Paid employment is usually another option.

Selection interviews Yes Aston, Cambridge, Coventry, Durham, East Anglia, Heriot-Watt, Hertfordshire, Huddersfield, Liverpool (Open Day invitation), London (RH), Oxford (Mod Lang) 32% (Mod Lang Ling) 27%, Roehampton; **Some** Brighton, Bristol UWE, Leeds, Salford, Swansea.

Interview advice and questions See **Chapter 6**. **Bangor** All applicants invited for interview after offer when a lower offer may be made. **Cambridge** Think of a painting of a tree. Is the tree real? **Leeds** (Joint Hons) Give an example of something outside your studies that you have achieved over the past year. **London (RH)** Conversation in the appropriate language.

Reasons for rejection (non-academic) Lack of commitment to spend a year abroad. Poor references. Poor standard of English. No reasons for why the course has been selected. Poor communication skills. Incomplete applications, for example missing qualifications and reference.

AFTER-RESULTS ADVICE

Offers to applicants repeating A-levels Higher Bristol UWE; **Possibly higher** Aston; **Same** Bangor (usually), Birmingham, Bristol, Durham, East Anglia, Leeds, Liverpool, Newcastle, Nottingham Trent, Salford, Stirling, Wolverhampton, York.

GRADUATE DESTINATIONS AND EMPLOYMENT (2007/8 HESA)

See separate language tables.

Career note The only career-related fields for language students are teaching, which attracts some graduates, and the demanding work of interpreting and translating, to which only a small number aspire. The majority will be attracted to work in management and administration, financial services and a host of other occupations which may include the social services, law and property development.

OTHER DEGREE SUBJECTS FOR CONSIDERATION

Communication Studies; Linguistics; Modern Languages Education/Teaching.

LATIN

(see also **Classical Studies/Classical Civilisation, Classics, Greek, Languages**)

Latin courses provide a study of the language, art, religion and history of the Roman world. This table should be read in conjunction with the **Classical Studies/Classical Civilisation** and **Classics** tables.

Useful websites www.thelatinlibrary.com; www.la.wikipedia.org; www.arlt.co.uk.

NB The points totals shown to the left of the institutions are for ease of reference only. It must not be assumed that Tariff points are always used by institutions or that they can be substituted for an offer in grades. The level of an offer is not necessarily indicative of the quality of a course.

COURSE OFFERS INFORMATION

Subject requirements/preferences GCSE English, a foreign language and Latin may be stipulated. **AL** Check courses for Latin requirement.

NB In 2012 universities and colleges will differ in their use of GCE AL/AS unit grade information, A* grades, the Extended Project (EPQ), the Advanced Diploma and the Cambridge Pre-U examination when considering applicants and making offers. An EPQ may be accepted in place of an AS subject. Check websites of universities and colleges for the latest offers information.

Your target offers and examples of courses provided by each institution
380 pts **Cambridge** – A*AA college offers may vary (Modn Mediev Lang (Class Lat)) (IB 38–42 pts)
360 pts **Exeter** – AAA–ABB (Lat Arbc St) (IB 36–31 pts)
          London (King's) – AABe-BBB (Lat Engl)
          Oxford – AAA (Classics) (IB 38–42 pts)
          Warwick – ABBc (Engl Lat Lit)
340 pts **Exeter** – AAB–ABB (Fr Lat) (IB 34–31 pts)
          Glasgow – AAB (Latin) (IB 34 pts)
          London (UCL) – AAB (Lat Gk) (IB 36 pts)
          St Andrews – AAB (Lat Maths) (IB 36 pts)
320 pts **Leeds** – ABB (Lat Phil; Lat Theol Relig St; Lat Russ)
          London (RH) – ABB (Engl Lat) (IB 34 pts)
          Manchester – ABB–BBB (Lat; Lat Fr/Ital/Span; Lat Engl Lit; Lat Ling)
          Nottingham – ABB (Engl St Lat) (IB 32 pts)
          Swansea – ABB (Class Civ Lat)
300 pts **Edinburgh** – check with Admissions Tutor BBB (Anc Hist Lat) (IB 34 pts)
200 pts **Trinity Saint David** – 200–300 pts (Lat Arch) (IB 24 pts)

Alternative offers
See **Chapter 7** and **Appendix 1** for grades/UCAS Tariff points information for the International Baccalaureate, Scottish Highers/Advanced Highers, the Welsh Baccalaureate, the Irish Leaving Certificate, the Cambridge Pre-U Diploma, the Advanced Diploma and the Extended Project.

CHOOSING YOUR COURSE (SEE ALSO CH. 1)

Some course features
Edinburgh An intensive Latin course is offered to beginners.
Exeter (Lat) The course focuses on the language and society of Rome, with modules in literature, history and culture, and translation from set books from and into Latin.
Leeds Joint Honours Latin students focus on Latin language and literature, and do intensive beginners' Latin course. There may be opportunities for study abroad.
St Andrews Latin is available as a Single Honours degree or in a wide range of Joint Honours courses. The Single Honours course combines Latin language study (beginners' and post A-level/ Highers) with an in-depth reading and understanding of Latin classics and other texts.
Swansea Latin is offered as a Joint Honours course with Ancient History, Classical Civilisation or Modern Languages.
Trinity Saint David Latin is offered at beginners', intermediate and advanced levels.

Universities and colleges teaching quality See www.qaa.ac.uk; http://unistats.direct.gov.uk.

Top research universities and colleges (RAE 2008) See **Classics**.

ADMISSIONS INFORMATION
Number of applicants per place (approx) Leeds 2; Manchester 5; Nottingham 6; Trinity Saint David 6.

Advice to applicants and planning the UCAS personal statement See **Classical Studies/Classical Civilisation** and **Classics**.

Selection interviews Yes Cambridge, Exeter, London (RH), London (UCL), Nottingham, Oxford, Trinity Saint David.

Interview advice and questions See **Classical Studies/Classical Civilisation** and **Classics**.

AFTER-RESULTS ADVICE
Offers to applicants repeating A-levels Higher Leeds, St Andrews, Warwick.

GRADUATE DESTINATIONS AND EMPLOYMENT (2007/8 HESA)
Graduates surveyed 10 **Employed** 0 **In further study** 5 **Assumed unemployed** 0

Career note Graduates enter a broad range of careers within management, the media, commerce and tourism as well as social and public services. Some graduates choose to work abroad and teaching is a popular option.

OTHER DEGREE SUBJECTS FOR CONSIDERATION
Ancient History; Archaeology; Classical Studies; Classics.

LATIN AMERICAN STUDIES
(including **Hispanic Studies**; see also **American Studies, Spanish**)

Latin American courses provide a study of Spanish and of Latin American republics, covering both historical and present-day conditions and problems. Normally a year is spent in Latin America.

Useful websites www.iol.org.uk; www.bbc.co.uk/languages; http://languageadvantage.com; www.languagematters.co.uk; www.reed.co.uk/multilingual; www.cilt.org.uk; www.latinworld.com; www.wola.org; www.latinamericalinks.com; www.latinamericanassoc.org; see also **Languages** and **Spanish**.

NB The points totals shown to the left of the institutions are for ease of reference only. It must not be assumed that Tariff points are always used by institutions or that they can be substituted for an offer in grades. The level of an offer is not necessarily indicative of the quality of a course.

COURSE OFFERS INFORMATION
Subject requirements/preferences GCSE Aberdeen: English, mathematics or science and a foreign language. English and a foreign language required by most universities. **AL** Spanish may be required for some courses.

NB In 2012 universities and colleges will differ in their use of GCE AL/AS unit grade information, A* grades, the Extended Project (EPQ), the Advanced Diploma and the Cambridge Pre-U examination when considering applicants and making offers. An EPQ may be accepted in place of an AS subject. Check websites of universities and colleges for the latest offers information.

Your target offers and examples of courses provided by each institution
410 pts London (King's) – AAAb/AAab+AS (Hist Port Braz St) (IB 38 pts HL 6 hist)
390 pts London (King's) – ABB+AS **or** AB/BB+3AS (Hisp St Engl) (IB 32 pts)
360 pts London (King's) – ABB+AS/AAbb+AS (Hisp St) (IB 34 pts HL 6 span)
       London (UCL) – AAB+AS–ABB+AS (Hisp St) (IB34–36 pts)

340 pts **Glasgow** – AAB (Hisp St) (IB 34 pts)
   London (King's) – ABB+AS **or** ABbb+AS (Hisp St Port Braz St) (IB 34 pts HL 6 span)
   Manchester – AAB–ABC (Span Port Lat Am St)
   Southampton – AAB (Span Lat Am St) (IB32 pts)
320 pts **Birmingham** – ABB–BBB (Hisp St Joint Hons)
   Bristol – ABB–BBC (Hisp St) (IB 30–33 pts)
   Kent – 320 pts (Hisp St Film St) (IB 35 pts)
   Leeds – ABB–AAB (Hisp Lat Am St) (IB 34 pts HL 16 pts)
   London (QM) – 320–340 pts (Hisp St courses) (IB 32 pts)
   Newcastle – ABB (Span Port Lat Am St) (IB 32 pts HL Span 6)
   Nottingham – ABB–ABC (Hisp St) (IB 34 pts)
   Sheffield – ABB (Hisp St Pol)
300 pts **Aberdeen** – BBB (Hisp St (Lat Am) (Spn)) (IB 30 pts)
   Birmingham – BBB (Hisp St) (IB 32 pts)
   Essex – 300 pts (Lat Am St Bus Mgt; Lat Am St)
   Liverpool – BBB–ABB (Lat Am Hisp St) (IB 32 pts)
   Manchester – BBB–BBC (Lat Am St Scrn St)
   Nottingham – ABC/BBB (Hisp St Hist) (IB 32 pts)
   Sheffield – ABB–BBB (Hisp St Jap) (IB 32 pts)
260 pts **Hull** – 260–300 pts (Hisp St Relig)
   London Met – 260 pts (Span Lat Am St; Lat Am St joint courses)
240 pts **Aberdeen** – CCC (Fin Hisp St) (IB 30 pts)
200 pts **Portsmouth** – 200–280 pts (Span Lat Am St)

Alternative offers
See **Chapter 7** and **Appendix 1** for grades/UCAS Tariff points information for the International Baccalaureate, Scottish Highers/Advanced Highers, the Welsh Baccalaureate, the Irish Leaving Certificate, the Cambridge Pre-U Diploma, the Advanced Diploma and the Extended Project.

CHOOSING YOUR COURSE (SEE ALSO CH. 1)
Some course features
Birmingham (Hisp St) The first two years of the course focus on Spanish language skills and Hispanic literature and culture. The third year is spent in Spain or Latin America while the fourth year centres on students' individual programme interests, for example advanced translation skills or cultural studies.
Liverpool (Hisp St) Three Iberian Romance languages (Catalan, Portuguese or Galician) are studied in addition to the main degree of Spanish. The degree programme also focuses on Spanish, Portuguese, Galician and Latin American culture.
London (UCL) (Hisp St) Course combines a study of Spanish language with courses in film history and literature. (Lat Am St) The course focuses on a study of Spanish and Portuguese and the literature and history of Spain, Portugal and Latin America.
Portsmouth (Span Lat Am Dev St) Students study the language and culture of contemporary Latin American societies, taking Spanish throughout the course. Half the placement year is in Spain and the other half at a partner institution in Latin America.

Top research universities and colleges (RAE 2008) See **Spanish**.

ADMISSIONS INFORMATION
Number of applicants per place (approx) Essex 3; Liverpool 3; Newcastle 25; Nottingham 7; Portsmouth 5.

Advice to applicants and planning the UCAS personal statement Visits and contacts with Spain and Latin American countries should be described. An awareness of the economic, historical and political scene of these countries is also important. Information may be obtained from respective embassies.

Selection interviews **Yes** Newcastle; **Some** Portsmouth.

Interview advice and questions Past questions include: Why are you interested in studying Latin American Studies? What countries related to the degree course have you visited? What career are you planning when you finish your degree? Applicants taking Spanish are likely to be asked questions on their syllabus and should also be familiar with some Spanish newspapers and magazines. See **Chapter 6**.

AFTER-RESULTS ADVICE

Offers to applicants repeating A-levels **Higher** Essex; **Same** Newcastle, Portsmouth.

GRADUATE DESTINATIONS AND EMPLOYMENT (2007/8 HESA)

Career note See **Languages**.

OTHER DEGREE SUBJECTS FOR CONSIDERATION

American Studies; Brazilian; Portuguese; Spanish.

LAW

(including **Criminology** and **Criminal Justice**; see also **Social Sciences/Studies**)

Law courses are usually divided into two parts. Part I occupies the first year and introduces the student to criminal and constitutional law and the legal process. Thereafter many different specialised topics can be studied in the second and third years. The course content is very similar for most courses. Applicants are advised to check with universities for their current policies concerning their use of the National Admissions Test for Law (LNAT). See Subject requirements/preferences below and also **Chapter 5**.

Useful websites www.barcouncil.org.uk; www.ilex.org.uk; www.lawcareers.net; www.lawsociety.org. uk; www.cps.gov.uk; www.hmcourts-service.gov.uk; www.lawscot.org.uk; www.lawsoc-ni.org; www. rollonfriday.com; www.lnat.ac.uk.

NB The points totals shown to the left of the institutions are for ease of reference only. It must not be assumed that Tariff points are always used by institutions or that they can be substituted for an offer in grades. The level of an offer is not necessarily indicative of the quality of a course.

COURSE OFFERS INFORMATION

Subject requirements/preferences GCSE Many universities will expect high grades. Manchester Requirements are often higher than normal – minimum of five A-grades. **AL** Arts, humanities, social sciences and sciences plus languages for courses combined with a foreign language. **All universities** Applicants offering art and music A-levels should check whether these subjects are acceptable.

NB In 2012 universities and colleges will differ in their use of GCE AL/AS unit grade information, A* grades, the Extended Project (EPQ), the Advanced Diploma and the Cambridge Pre-U examination when considering applicants and making offers. An EPQ may be accepted in place of an AS subject. Check websites of universities and colleges for the latest offers information.

The National Admissions Test for Law (LNAT) may be required by universities other than those indicated in the table below – check university websites and prospectuses and see also **Chapter 5**.

Your target offers and examples of courses provided by each institution

410 pts London (King's) – The National Admissions Test for Law (LNAT) may be required by universities other than those indicated in the table list – check university websites a AAAb-AABb (3 ALs) AA–AB (2ALs) + LNAT (Law) (Law) (IB 38 pts HL 555–554)

400 pts Warwick – AAAc +LNAT (Law 3yr/4yr) (IB 36–38 pts)

390 pts Warwick – AAB–AAAb/c (Euro Law)

380 pts Cambridge – college offers may vary (see **Ch. 5**) A*AA (Law) (IB 38–42 pts)

London (UCL) – AAA+AS +LNAT (Law Fr/Ger/Hisp/Ital) (IB 38 pts)

The College of Law

'I'm looking for a really thorough grounding in law that will also actually prepare me for my professional career. I want the best of both worlds to make sure I'm ready to be a lawyer.'

**A focused law degree
for focused individuals**

**Book your law degree
open day now**
college-of-law.co.uk/degree
0800 289 997

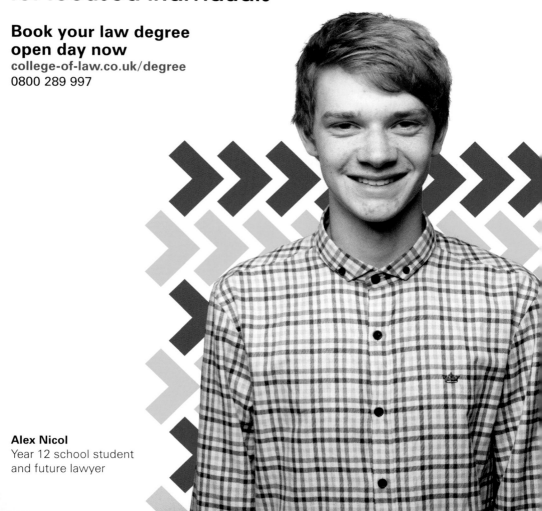

Alex Nicol
Year 12 school student
and future lawyer

The College of Law
a focused law degree for focused individuals

A new undergraduate law degree

From September 2012 The College of Law is offering students a new professional law degree for undergraduates. The LL.B has the sole aim that students learn the law in a professional and realistic context: how the law affects clients, and how lawyers think about and use the law to represent their clients' interests. It's more than "learning the law", it's learning **how** to **be** a lawyer, and enjoying the most relevant and rounded education to prepare for a professional career in law.

The College's law degree will be academically challenging, and set in a real-world context from the start, so students can best understand how the law applies to individuals and businesses.

About The College of Law

The College of Law is acknowledged as the UK's leading professional law school. With many years of experience and unrivalled contacts within the legal profession, no other law school can match The College of Law for its reputation and commitment to preparing future lawyers for the fast-moving world of modern law.

More than 7,500 students take the postgraduate courses each year – the Graduate Diploma in Law for non-law graduates, the Legal Practice Course for aspiring solicitors and the Bar Professional Training Course for prospective barristers. This is because The College's unique mix of face-to-face teaching in small group workshops which reflect working in legal practice, along with market leading online learning, deliver better results. All of The College's tutors are qualified lawyers who can pass on their experience of working in practice. This unique combination ensures that their students get the best possible preparation for a career in law.

The College of Law develops self-reliant, confident future lawyers for the modern world of law. The new Bachelor of Laws (LL.B) degree is their first step.

The College's specialist law careers service

Employability is at the heart of everything The College of Law does. The College understands that in the new era of higher university tuition fees, students will want to be assured that they have the best possible chance of securing a job in their chosen profession. The College has the best team of specialist legal careers advisors in the business, offering personalised, face-to-face guidance on the recruitment process and how to succeed. It's no surprise that 88%* of students who pass the Legal Practice Course have training contracts or other legal work within the first few months of graduation.

based on known records of students successfully completing their studies in 2009.

Seriously well connected

The legal services sector is one of the fastest growing and most dynamic parts of the economy, offering a wide range of careers whether as solicitors or barristers, in-house legal advisors, business managers or legal service entrepreneurs.

The College of Law has exclusive training arrangements with 30 major law firms, including three of the world's largest, work with 94 of the top 100 UK law firms and have thriving relationships with hundreds of regional firms. Internationally The College of Law has connections with a growing list of world class organisations including the International Bar Association, the British Council, Northwestern University School of Law in Chicago, Renmin University of China Law School and IE Law School in Spain.

"This is extremely positive news which I am sure will deliver a high quality and particularly focused offering which will be attractive to many students wishing to prepare for a career in the legal profession. This is highly innovative and is bound to cause many traditional providers to take a fresh look at how tertiary education in areas such as law is provided in the future".

Michael Shaw,
Managing Partner, Cobbetts LLP

A choice of locations

The College of Law has centres across the country (London, Bristol, Guildford, Birmingham, Chester, Manchester and York) offering the widest choice of location of any law school. Initially students will be able to study their law degree in London, Birmingham or Chester, but whichever centre they choose they can be sure of the same high standards of tuition, support and facilities. Find out about each of the centres, and watch a short video, on their website: **college-of-law.co.uk/centres**

Accommodation

The College of Law aims to offer all first-year students accommodation close to the centre at which they are studying. Check the website for more details.

Each centre has an accommodation database and student services department to assist students in finding accommodation for their second year.

The Future Lawyers Association

The College's Future Lawyers Association is a unique free-to-join resource for aspiring modern lawyers, and students can join from age 14. They will get access to useful information on a career in law and what they need to do to succeed.
college-of-law.co.uk/futurelawyers

The City Law School
CITY UNIVERSITY LONDON

World-class legal educatic
in the heart of Londe

Your route to Professional Legal Practice

The City Law School, part of **City University London**, is one of London's major law schools. With three levels of study: undergraduate, postgraduate and professional, we offer courses suitable for every step of your legal career.

Our high quality courses are delivered by leading academics and practitioners from around the world and each course is fully accredited by the relevant professional body.

Our 'real-world' experience and student focussed approach will ensure that you develop the legal knowledge and skills you'll need to excel in practice.

Undergraduate:
> LLB Law

Postgraduate:
> Graduate Entry LLB
> Graduate Diploma in Law
> LLM in EU Commercial Law
> LLM in International Banking and Finance
> LLM / M.Jur in International Commercial Law
> LLM in International Competition Law

> LLM in International Energy Litigation
> LLM in Maritime Law (UK)
> LLM in Maritime Law (Greece)
> LLM in Criminal Litigation
> LLM in Civil Litigation and Dispute Resolution
> PhD, MPhil or LLM by Research

Professional:
> Legal Practice Course
> Bar Professional Training Course
> LLM in Professional Legal Practice
> LLM in Professional Legal Skills
> CPD courses

FOR MORE INFORMATION AND TO APPLY CONTACT US:
☎ +44 (0)20 7040 3309
law@city.ac.uk
www.city.ac.uk/law

Please quote the following reference when contacting us: DCO311

www.city.ac.uk/law

The City Law School
CITY UNIVERSITY LONDON

World-class legal education
in the heart of London

The best bar none...

"I've secured a pupillage at Ten Old Square and, following studying at City, I am confident that I will be able to hit the ground running."

Leon Pickering
Graduate Diploma in Law 2008/9 / Bar Vocational Course 2009/10

"I went to Oxford University, initially intending to be an academic... however friends of mine looked like they were having so much fun at the Bar that I jumped ship.

I found City's location to be absolutely unparalleled – it's inside one of the Inns of Court at Gray's Inn. Living in London also makes it so easy to go on mini-pupillages and vacation schemes – nowhere else can match this.

The teaching at the School is excellent. Everyone was very interested in who I was and what I wanted to do: it didn't feel like a sausage factory.

Thanks to some great support and advice I've been able to secure a pupillage at Ten Old Square. Following studying at City, I am confident that I will be able to hit the ground running."

The City Law School is one of London's major law schools and offers an impressive range of fully accredited legal courses. Our BPTC delivers outstanding training for future barristers and equips you with key legal skills and networking opportunities to pursue a successful career at the Bar.

FOR MORE INFORMATION AND TO APPLY CONTACT US:

☎ +44 (0)20 7040 3309

✉ law@city.ac.uk

🖱 www.city.ac.uk/law

Please quote the following reference when contacting us: DCO311

400 | Law

London LSE – A*AA (Law) (IB 38 pts HL 766/666)
Warwick – AABc (Law Bus St)
360 pts **Birmingham** – AAA + good LNAT (Law Fr/Ger) (IB 36 pts)
Bristol – AAA +LNAT (Law Fr/Ger Law) (IB 37 pts HL 666)
Cardiff – AAA (Law; Crimin Law)
City – AAA (Law) (IB 35 pts)
Durham – AAA +LNAT (Law) (IB 37 pts)
East Anglia – AAA (Law Am Law) (IB 35 pts)
Exeter – AAA–AAB (Law (Euro)) (IB 36–34 pts)
Lancaster – AAA 360 pts (Euro Leg St) (IB 32 pts HL 17–18 pts)
Leeds – AAA +LNAT (Law Fr) (IB 38 pts HL 18 pts)
Leicester – AAA (Law; Law Fr Law Lang; Maîtrise Engl Fr Law)
Liverpool – AAA (Law) (IB 35 pts)
London (QM) – AAA (Engl Euro Law) (IB 36 pts HL 666)
London (SOAS) – AAA (Law) (IB 38 pts HL 766)
Manchester – AAA (Law Crimin) (IB 37–35 pts)
Newcastle – AAA (Law) (IB 38 pts HL 666)
Nottingham – AAA +LNAT (Law Fr/Ger/Span Law) (IB 40 pts HL 7 in subj)
Oxford – AAA +LNAT (Law Euro Law) (IB 39 pts)
Queen's Belfast – AAA–AABa (Cmn Civ Law Fr/Span) (IB 34 pts HL 666)
Sheffield – AAA (Law (Euro Int)) (IB 37 pts HL 666)
Southampton – AAA–AAB (Law (Marit Law)) (IB 36 pts HL 18 pts)
Sussex – AAA–ABB (Law Contemp Euro St) (IB 36 pts)
York – AAA (Law) (IB 36 pts)
350 pts **Warwick** – BBBb (Law Sociol)
340 pts **Aberystwyth** – 340 pts (Law) (IB 32 pts)
Aston – AAB 320–340 pts (Law Mgt) (IB 34 pts)
Brunel – AAB (Law) (IB 35 pts)
Cardiff – AAB (Law Pol/Soc) (IB 34 pts)
East Anglia – AAB (Law) (IB 33 pts)
Essex – AAB (Law Hum Rts) (IB 36 pts)
Glasgow – AAB +LNAT (Law courses)
Keele – 340–360 pts (Law (Single Hons))
Kent – AAB (Euro Leg St) (IB 33 pts)
Lancaster – AAB 340 pts (Law Crimin)
Leeds – AAB (Law Acc) (IB 38 pts)
London (Birk) – interview + reasoning test (p/t Accelerated Law) AAB (Law)
London (QM) – 340 pts (Law Pol) (IB 32 pts)
Manchester – AAB (Law Pol)
Reading – AAB (Law; Law Leg St Euro)
Sheffield – AAB (Law Crimin; Law Fr/Ger/Span)
Strathclyde – AAB (LLB (Scots) Law; Law Modn Lang)
Sussex – AAB–ABB (Law Int Rel) (IB 34–36 pts)
320 pts **Bournemouth** – 320 pts (Law; Law Tax; Bus Law; Enter Law)
Cardiff – ABB (Law Fr/Ger)
Dundee – ABB (Law Fr/Ger/Span)
Durham – ABB (Sociol Law)
East Anglia – ABB (Law Fr Law Lang) (IB 32 pts)
Huddersfield – 320–300 pts (Bus Law; Law)
Hull – ABB 320 pts (Law; Law Fr/Ger Law Lang; Law Pol; Law Lit)
Keele – 320 pts (Dual Hons Law)
Kingston – 320 pts (Law; Law Crimin)
Liverpool – ABB (Law Bus) (IB 32 pts)
London Met – 320–280 pts (LLB Law Int Dev; Law Int Rel)
Manchester – ABB (Chem Pat Law)

For a quick reference offers calculator, fold out the inside back cover.

Manchester Met – ABB 320 pts (Law)
Northumbria – ABB 320 pts (Law (Exempting)) (IB 32 pts)
Portsmouth – 320 pts (Law; Law Crimin)
Salford – check with Admissions Tutor 320 pts (Law) (IB 31 pts)
Staffordshire – 320 pts (Law LLB; Spo Law; Bus Law)
Strathclyde – ABB (Acc Bus Law)
Surrey – ABB 320 pts (Law Fr/Ger/Span Law) (IB 34 pts)
Swansea – Contact univ for joint courses AAB 320 pts (Law Bus) (IB 34 pts)
Ulster – ABB (Law Acc; Law Int Pol; Law HR Mgt; Law Ir; Law Mark)
Westminster – ABB–ABC (Law) (IB 32 pts)

300 pts **Aberdeen** – BBB (Law) (IB 34 pts)
Aberystwyth – 300 pts (Bus Mgt (Law)) (IB 32 pts)
BPP (UC) – 300 pts (LLB Bus Law (Hons); LLB Law (Hons))
Bradford – 300 pts (Law; Bus St Law)
Bristol UWE – 300–340 pts (Law; Law (Euro Int))
Buckingham – 300 pts (Law Pol)
Cardiff – BBB (Law Welsh; Law Arbc/Chin/Jap)
Central Lancashire – BBB (Law Arbc; Law LLB)
Coventry – 300 pts (Law; Law Bus; Law Fr/Span)
De Montfort – 300 pts (Law)
Derby – 300 pts (Law; Law Crimin; Law (Bus/Int/Soc Pblc))
Edinburgh – BBB–AAA (Law courses)
Glamorgan – 300–340 pts (Law; Crim Law; Commer Law)
Glasgow Caledonian – BBB (Law)
Heriot-Watt – ABC–BBB 300 pts (Bus Law courses) (IB 29 pts)
Huddersfield – 300 pts (Law Acc)
Nottingham Trent – 300–280 pts (Law Bus) (IB 24 pts)
Oxford Brookes – BBB (Law courses) (IB 32 pts)
Plymouth – 300–360 pts (Law; Law Bus; Int Rel Law)
Salford – 300 pts (Law Crim) (IB 29 pts)
Stirling – BBB (Law LLB)
Westminster – ABC (Law Fr) (IB 30 pts)

280 pts **Aberystwyth** – 280 pts (Euro Leg St) (IB 32 pts)
Bangor – 280 pts (Law courses) (IB 28 pts)
Birmingham City – 280 pts (Law Bus Law) (IB 26 pts)
Brighton – BBC 280 pts (Law Bus) (IB 30 pts)
Gloucestershire – 280–300 pts (Law)
Kingston – 280–320 pts (Int Bus Law) (IB 25 pts)
Lincoln – 280 pts (Law; Law Fin; Law Bus)
Liverpool John Moores – 280 pts (Law) (IB 30 pts)
Nottingham Trent – 280 pts (Law Crimin)
Robert Gordon – BBC (Law) (IB 28 pts HL engl 5)
Teesside – 280 pts (Law; Law Pol)

260 pts **Abertay Dundee** – BCC (Law LLB)
Bolton – 260 pts (Law; Law Comb Hons)
Canterbury Christ Church – 260–200 pts (Law) (IB 24 pts)
Coventry – 260–280 pts (Law Int St)
Cumbria – 260 pts (Law)
Edge Hill – 260 pts (Law; Law Crim; Law Mgt)
Edinburgh Napier – 260 pts (LLB Law)
Hertfordshire – 260–300 pts (Law)
Leeds Met – 260 pts (Law; Law Crim)
Liverpool Hope – 260 pts (Comb Hons Law)
Manchester Met – 260 pts (Leg St Comb Hons)
Portsmouth – 260–300 pts (Law Euro St; Law Int Rel; Law Bus)

Robert Gordon – BCC (Law Mgt) (IB 27 pts HL Engl 5)
Sheffield Hallam – 260 pts (Law; Law Crimin; Law Maîtrise Fr; Bus Law)
Stirling – BCC (Law) (IB 30 pts)
Sunderland – 260–360 pts (Law (Qualifying))
Winchester – 260–300 pts (Law Comb Hons; Law)

240 pts **Anglia Ruskin** – 240 pts (LLB Law)
Bradford (Coll Univ Centre) – 240 pts (Law Soc Welf; Mark Law)
Bucks New – 240–280 pts (Law; Bus Law)
Canterbury Christ Church – 240 pts (Leg St courses)
Cardiff (UWIC) – 240 pts (Bus Mgt St Law)
Central Lancashire – 240 pts (Law Crimin)
Chester – 240–300 pts (Law Crimin) (IB 24 pts)
East London – 240 pts (Law)
London Met – 240 pts (Law BA)
London South Bank – 240 pts (Law LLB)
Newport – 240 pts (Bus Law courses; Acc Law)
Northampton – 240–260 pts (Law courses) (IB 24 pts)
Plymouth – 240–280 pts (Marit Bus Marit Law)
Stirling – CCC (Bus Law) (IB 30 pts)

230 pts **Edinburgh Napier** – 230 pts (Acc Law)

228 pts **Glasgow Caledonian** – Check with university 228 pts inc BC (Bus Law)

220 pts **Anglia Ruskin** – 220 pts (Psy Law; Bus Law)
Blackburn (Coll Univ Centre) – 220 pts (Commer Law; Crim Law)
Northampton – 220–260 pts (Law Joint Hons)
Southampton Solent – 220–200 pts (Law Bus Mgt)
Sunderland – 220–360 pts (Law joint courses)

200 pts **Bedfordshire** – 200 pts (Acc Law) (IB 24 pts)
Doncaster (Coll Univ Centre) – 200 pts (Crim Just)
London Met – 200–280 pts (Bus Law courses)
Middlesex – 200–300 pts (Law)
Wolverhampton – 200 pts (Law; Law Phil)

180 pts **Cumbria** – 180–200 pts (Crim Law)
Derby – 180–200 pts (Law joint courses)
Greenwich – 180 pts (Law LLB) (IB 24 pts)

160 pts **Bedfordshire** – 160 pts (Law) (IB 24 pts)
St Mary's Twickenham (UC) – 160–200 pts (Bus Law)
West Scotland – CC (Law)
Wolverhampton – 160–220 pts (Bus Law)

120 pts **Grimsby (IFHE)** – 120–240 pts (Law)

80 pts **Croydon (Coll)** – 80–100 pts (Law)
Holborn (Coll) – 80 pts (Law)

London (Birk) – degree reqd (not Law) interview+reasoning test for under 21s (over 21s varies) p/t (Accelerated Law)
Open University – contact +44 (0)845 300 6090 **or** www.openuniversity.co.uk/you (Law)

Alternative offers See **Chapter 7** and **Appendix 1** for grades/UCAS Tariff points information for the International Baccalaureate, Scottish Highers/Advanced Highers, the Welsh Baccalaureate, the Irish Leaving Certificate, the Cambridge Pre-U Diploma, the Advanced Diploma and the Extended Project.

EXAMPLES OF FOUNDATION DEGREES IN THE SUBJECT FIELD

Blackpool and Fylde (Coll); Bournemouth; Bournemouth and Poole (Coll); Bristol City (Coll); Croydon (Coll); Exeter (Coll); Glyndŵr; Kingston; Nottingham New (Coll); Peterborough (Reg Coll); Portsmouth; Shrewsbury (CAT); Southampton Solent; Truro (Coll); Walsall (Coll); Weston (Coll).

CHOOSING YOUR COURSE (SEE ALSO CH. 1)

Some course features

Anglia Ruskin The Law degree is under revision. An integrated LLB/LPC degree is also planned for students seeking to qualify as a solicitor.

Aston The Law with Management programme is a qualifying Law degree focusing on business skills.

Bournemouth All Law degrees have a common first year, with specialisation options made at the end. A minimum of 40 weeks is spent in industry.

Chester Core subjects are offered to fulfil the requirements for a Qualifying Law Degree, covering contract, land, European Community, constitutional and administrative law, crime and tort. Students acheiving a 2:2 are guaranteed a place on the Legal Practice Course.

Dundee English Law and Scots Law are both offered.

Edinburgh Twelve joint courses with Law are offered including accountancy, business studies and languages.

Exeter (Law (Euro)) The fourth year is spent either at Rennes following a French Maîtrise en Droit programme or at Saabrucken following the German Magister programme. Graduates obtain a dual qualification, are exempt from the academic stages of UK professional training and are ready for the aptitude test to practise as a lawyer in France or Germany.

Huddersfield There is a Law (Exempting) course enabling students to qualify as a solicitor by incorporating the legal practice course in Years 3 and 4 (subject to an appropriate training contract). Degree courses are also offered in Law and Accountancy and Business Law.

Kent The Law course is designed to enable students to gain the necessary exemptions from the Law Society examinations. Other Law courses include English and French/German/Spanish/Italian Law. There is a law clinic enabling students to practise law under the supervision of solicitors. (High research rating)

London (King's) English Law can be studied with American, French, German or Australian Law. Transfers to these programmes take place only after completion of the first year.

London (UCL) Law can be studied with another legal system with a year spent at a host university in Australia, Singapore, Hong Kong, or, for the European degree, in France, Germany, Italy or Spain.

Universities and colleges teaching quality See www.qaa.ac.uk; http://unistats.direct.gov.uk.

Top research universities and colleges (RAE 2008) London LSE; London (UCL); Oxford; Durham; Nottingham; Kent; Cambridge; Cardiff; Queen's Belfast; Edinburgh; London (QM); Reading; Strathclyde; Ulster; Birmingham.

Examples of sandwich degree courses Abertay Dundee; Aston; (compulsory) Birmingham City; Bournemouth; Bradford; Brighton; Brunel; City; De Montfort; Edinburgh Napier; Hertfordshire; Huddersfield; Lancaster; Nottingham Trent; Plymouth; Surrey; Teesside; Westminster.

ADMISSIONS INFORMATION

Number of applicants per place (approx) Abertay Dundee 3; Aberystwyth 8; Anglia Ruskin 10; Aston 10; Bangor 3; Birmingham 4; Birmingham City 20; Bournemouth 9; Bradford 2; Bristol 9; Bristol UWE 27; Brunel 2; Buckingham 3; Cambridge 7; Cardiff 12; Central Lancashire 36; City 23; Coventry 15; De Montfort 6; Derby 7; Dundee 6; Durham 14; East Anglia 14; East London 13; Edinburgh 5; Edinburgh Napier 7; Essex 26; Exeter 15; Glamorgan 3; Glasgow 8; Glasgow Caledonian 10; Huddersfield 10; Hull 15; Kent 11; Kingston 25; Lancaster 8; Leeds 15; Leicester 9; Liverpool 10; Liverpool John Moores 10; London (King's) 14; London (QM) 17; London (SOAS) 8; London (UCL) 21; London LSE 14; London Met 13; London South Bank 4; Manchester 8; Manchester Met 21; Middlesex 25; Newcastle 13; Northampton 4; Northumbria 12; Nottingham 9; Nottingham Trent 15; Oxford Brookes 18; Plymouth 14; Robert Gordon 4; Sheffield 16; Sheffield Hallam 6; Southampton 7; Southampton Solent 5; Staffordshire 16; Strathclyde (Law) 10; Sussex 10; Teesside 3; Warwick 20; West London 18; Westminster 29; Wolverhampton 12; York 8.

Advice to applicants and planning the UCAS personal statement Visit the law courts and take notes on cases heard. Follow leading legal arguments in the press. Read the law sections in the Independent, Times and the Guardian. Discuss the career with lawyers and, if possible, obtain work shadowing in lawyers' offices. Describe these visits and experiences and indicate any special areas of law which interest you. (Read *Learning the Law* by Glanville Williams.) Commitment is essential to the study of law as an academic discipline, not necessarily with a view to taking it up as a career.

When writing to admissions tutors, especially by email, take care to present yourself well: text language is not acceptable. You should use communication as an opportunity to demonstrate your skill in the use of English. Spelling mistakes, punctuation errors and bad grammar suggest that you will struggle to develop the expected writing ability (see **Misconceptions about this course**) and may lead to your application being rejected. When writing to an admissions tutor do not demand an answer immediately or by return or urgently. If your query is reasonable the tutor will respond without such urging. Adding these demands is bad manners and suggests that you are doing everything at the last minute and increases your chances of a rejection.

The criteria for admission are: motivation and capacity for sustained and intense work; the ability to analyse and solve problems using logical and critical approaches; the ability to draw fine distinctions, to separate the relevant from the irrelevant; the capacity for accurate and critical observation, for sustained and cogent argument; creativity and flexibility of thought and lateral thinking; competence in English; the ability to express ideas clearly and effectively, a willingness to listen and to be able to give considered responses. See also **Appendix 4**.

Misconceptions about this course **Aberystwyth** Some applicants believe that all Law graduates enter the legal profession – this is incorrect. **Birmingham** Students tend to believe that success in the law centres on the ability to learn information. Whilst some information does necessarily have to be learnt, the most important skills involve (a) developing an ability to select the most relevant pieces of information and (b) developing the ability to write tightly argued, persuasively reasoned essays on the basis of such information. **Bristol** Many applicants think that most of our applicants have been privately educated: the reverse is true. **Derby** Many applicants do not realise the amount of work involved to get a good degree classification.

Selection interviews Approximately four well-qualified candidates apply for every place on undergraduate Law courses in the UK and the National Admissions Test for Law (LNAT) is used by a number of universities (see **Your target offers and examples of courses provided by each institution** and **Chapter 5**). **Yes** Aberystwyth, Anglia Ruskin, Birmingham, Bristol, Bristol UWE, Buckingham, Cambridge, Canterbury Christ Church, Central Lancashire, Coventry, Durham, East London, Edinburgh Napier, Essex, Exeter, Glasgow, Lancaster, Liverpool, Liverpool John Moores, London (King's), London (UCL), London South Bank, Northumbria, Nottingham, Oxford (Course 1) 18% (Course 2) 10%, Queen's Belfast, Southampton Solent, Surrey, Teesside, Warwick, York; **Some** Bangor, Cardiff (Law Lang), Derby, Dundee, East Anglia, Huddersfield, Kent (mature/Access students), Nottingham Trent (mature students), Oxford Brookes (mature students), Sheffield Hallam, Southampton (mature students), Staffordshire, Sunderland; **No** Sussex.

Interview advice and questions Law is a highly competitive subject and applicants will be expected to have a basic awareness of aspects of law and to have gained some work experience, on which they are likely to be questioned. It is almost certain that a legal question will be asked at interview and applicants will be tested on their responses. Questions in the past have included: What interests you in the study of law? What would you do to overcome the problem of prison overcrowding if you were (a) a judge (b) a prosecutor (c) the Prime Minister? What legal cases have you read about recently? What is jurisprudence? What are the causes of violence in society? A friend bought a bun which, unknown to him, contained a stone. He gave it to you to eat and you broke a tooth. Could you sue anyone? Have you visited any law courts? What cases did you see? A person arrives in England unable to speak the language. He lights a cigarette in a restaurant where smoking is not allowed. Can he be charged and convicted? What should be done in the case of an elderly person who steals a bar of soap? What, in your opinion, would be the two basic laws in Utopia? Describe, without using your hands, how you would do the butterfly stroke. What would happen if there were no law? Should we legalise euthanasia? If you could change any law, what would it be? How would you implement the changes? If a person tries to kill someone using black magic, are they guilty of attempted murder? If a jury uses a ouija board to reach a decision, is it wrong? If so, why? Jane attends a university interview. As she enters the building she sees a diamond brooch on the floor.

She hands it to the interviewer who hands it to the police. The brooch is never claimed. Who is entitled to it? Jane? The interviewer? The police? The University authorities? The Crown? Mr Grabbit who owns the building?

For joint courses: what academic skills are needed to succeed? Why have you applied for a joint degree? Where does honesty fit into law? See also **Chapter 5**. **Cambridge** Logic questions. If I returned to the waiting room and my jacket had been taken and I then took another one, got home and actually discovered it was mine, had I committed a crime? If the interviewer pulled out a gun and aimed it at me, but missed as he had a bad arm, had he committed a crime? If the interviewer pulled out a gun and aimed it at me, thinking it was loaded but, in fact, it was full of blanks and fired it at me with the intention to kill, had he committed a crime? Which of the three preceding situations are similar and which is the odd one out? If a law is immoral, is it still a law and must people abide by it? For example, when Hitler legalised the systematic killing of Jews, was it still law? **Oxford** Should the use of mobile phones be banned on public transport? Is wearing school uniform a breach of human rights? If you could go back in time to any period of time, when would it be and why? Would you trade your scarf for my bike, even if you have no idea what state it's in or if I even have one? Is someone guilty of an offence if they did not set out to commit a crime but ended up doing so? Does a girl-scout have a political agenda?

Reasons for rejection (non-academic) 'Dreams' about being a lawyer! Poorly informed about the subject. Badly drafted application. Under-estimate of work load. Poor communication skills. **Manchester Met** Some were rejected because they were obviously more suited to Psychology.

AFTER-RESULTS ADVICE
Offers to applicants repeating A-levels **Higher** Aberystwyth, Bristol UWE, Coventry, Dundee, Essex, Glamorgan, Glasgow, Hull, Leeds, London Met, Manchester Met, Newcastle, Nottingham, Oxford Brookes, Queen's Belfast, Sheffield, Sheffield Hallam, Strathclyde, Warwick; **Possibly higher** Liverpool; **Same** Anglia Ruskin, Bangor, Birmingham, Bradford, Brighton, Bristol, Brunel, Cardiff, De Montfort, Derby, Durham, East Anglia, Huddersfield, Kingston, Lincoln, Liverpool Hope, Liverpool John Moores, Northumbria, Nottingham Trent, Staffordshire, Stirling, Sunderland, Surrey, Wolverhampton.

GRADUATE DESTINATIONS AND EMPLOYMENT (2007/8 HESA)
Graduates surveyed 8265 **Employed** 2105 **In further study** 3515 **Assumed unemployed** 525

Career note Many graduates seek to practise in the legal profession after further training. However, a Law degree provides a good starting point for many other careers in industry, commerce and the public services. The study of consumer protection can lead to specialisation and qualification as a trading standards officer.

OTHER DEGREE SUBJECTS FOR CONSIDERATION
Criminology; Economics; Government; History; International Relations; Politics; Social Policy and Administration; Sociology.

LEISURE and RECREATION MANAGEMENT/STUDIES
(see also **Business and Management Courses, Business and Management Courses, (International and European), Business and Management Courses (Specialised), Hospitality and Hotel Management, Sports Sciences/Studies, Tourism and Travel**)

The courses cover various aspects of leisure and recreation. Specialist options include recreation management, tourism and countryside management, all of which are offered as individual degree courses in their own right. There is also an obvious link with Sports Studies, Physical Education and Tourism and Travel courses. See also **Appendix 4**.

Useful websites www.ispal.org.uk; www.bized.co.uk; www.leisuremanagement.co.uk; www.baha.org.uk; www.leisureopportunities.co.uk; www.recmanagement.com; www.isrm.co.uk; www.uksport.gov.uk; www.london2012.com.

NB The points totals shown to the left of the institutions are for ease of reference only. It must not be assumed that Tariff points are always used by institutions or that they can be substituted for an offer in grades. The level of an offer is not necessarily indicative of the quality of a course.

COURSE OFFERS INFORMATION

Subject requirements/preferences GCSE Normally English and mathematics grades A–C. **AL** No specified subjects. **Other** CRB clearance and health checks required for some courses.

NB In 2012 universities and colleges will differ in their use of GCE AL/AS unit grade information, A* grades, the Extended Project (EPQ), the Advanced Diploma and the Cambridge Pre-U examination when considering applicants and making offers. An EPQ may be accepted in place of an AS subject. Check websites of universities and colleges for the latest offers information.

Your target offers and examples of courses provided by each institution

300 pts **Manchester** – BBB–BBC (Mgt Leis) (IB 30–28 pts)
280 pts **Bournemouth** – 280 pts (Leis Mark) (IB 30 pts)
         Brighton – BBC (Spo Leis Mgt) (IB 30 pts)
         Bristol UWE – 280–300 pts (Spo Exer Mgt)
         Cardiff (UWIC) – 280 pts (Spo Mgt)
         Gloucestershire – 280 pts (Leis Spo Mgt)
         Salford – 280–300 pts (Spo Leis Mgt) (IB 26 pts)
260 pts **Liverpool Hope** – 260 pts (Dance and Tour; Media Comm Tour; Mus Tour)
240 pts **Aberystwyth** – 240 pts (Cntry Recr Tour) (IB 28 pts)
         Central Lancashire – 240–280 pts (Spo Mgt)
         Creative Arts – 240 pts (Leis Jrnl) (IB 30 pts)
         Edinburgh Napier – 240–230 pts (Fstvl Evnts Mgt courses)
         Glamorgan – 240–280 pts (Spo Mgt)
         Manchester Met – 240 pts (Leis Mgt (Spo Dev) (Out Actvts)) (IB 28 pts)
         Sheffield Hallam – 240 pts (Evnts Leis Mgt)
         Stranmillis (UC) – CCC 240 pts (Hlth Leis St)
         Suffolk (Univ Campus) – 240 pts (Leis Mgt)
         Ulster – 240 pts (Leis Evnts Mgt)
         Worcester – 240 pts (Out Advntr Ldrshp Mgt)
220 pts **Cumbria** – 220 pts (Out St; Out Ldrshp)
         Harper Adams (UC) – 220–240 pts (Advntr Recr Mgt; Leis Tour Mgt)
         Southampton Solent – 220–240 pts (Extrm Spo Mgt)
200 pts **Bolton** – 200 pts (Spo Leis Mgt) (IB 20 pts)
         Bucks New – 200–240 pts (Golf St)
180 pts **Hull** – 180 pts (Spo Leis Mgt courses)
160 pts **Derby** – 160–240 pts (Spo Psy Out Recr)
         SAC (Scottish CAg) – CC 160 pts (Out Prsts Mgt)
         Swansea Met – 160–360 pts (Leis Mgt)

Alternative offers
See **Chapter 7** and **Appendix 1** for grades/UCAS Tariff points information for the International Baccalaureate, Scottish Highers/Advanced Highers, the Welsh Baccalaureate, the Irish Leaving Certificate, the Cambridge Pre-U Diploma, the Advanced Diploma and the Extended Project.

EXAMPLES OF FOUNDATION DEGREES IN THE SUBJECT FIELD

(see also **Tourism and Travel**) Aberystwyth; Blackpool and Fylde (Coll); Bournemouth; Bucks New; Chichester; Colchester (Inst); Cornwall (Coll); Cumbria; Derby; Duchy (Coll); Edge Hill; Glamorgan; Guildford (Coll); Harper Adams (UC); Leeds City (Coll); Liverpool (CmC); Loughborough (Coll); Manchester (Coll); Myerscough (Coll); Newcastle (Coll); Norwich City (Coll); Salford; Sheffield (Coll); Wirral Met (Coll); Writtle (Coll); Yorkshire Coast (CFHE).

CHOOSING YOUR COURSE (SEE ALSO CH. 1)

Some course features

Birmingham (UC) The Adventure Tourism Management course involves studies in commercial and risk management, options include modern languages, sports international and nature tourism.

Brighton (Spo Leis Mgt) The course has options in sport psychology, performance and marketing.

Creative Arts (Leis Jrnl) This unique course is taught alongside the Sports Journalism and the Motoring Journalism courses. A multimedia degree, it targets the leisure magazine sector and specialist sports and leisure websites and has particular strengths in practical production training.

Cumbria (Out St; Out Ldrshp) The courses involve climbing, canoeing, sailing and mountaineering and are based in the centre of the Lake District.

Harper Adams (UC) The courses include Adventure Recreation Management, Tourism and Leisure Managment.

Southampton Solent Courses focus on principles of coaching, event and activity safety and operations, customer service management, leisure marketing and business management.

Trinity Saint David A broad course in Outdoor Education is available which includes work placement. Cultural Tourism is available with 16 other subjects.

UCP Marjon Single and combined courses can be taken with Outdoor Adventure.

Universities and colleges teaching quality See www.qaa.ac.uk; http://unistats.direct.gov.uk.

Top research universities and colleges (RAE 2008) See **Sports Sciences/Studies**.

Examples of sandwich degree courses Aberystwyth; Bournemouth; Brighton; Gloucestershire; Harper Adams (UC); Ulster.

ADMISSIONS INFORMATION

Number of applicants per place (approx) Brighton 10; Cardiff (UWIC) 3; Gloucestershire 7; Hull 3; Liverpool John Moores 3; SAC (Scottish CAg) 4.

Advice to applicants and planning the UCAS personal statement Work experience, visits to leisure centres and national parks and any interests you have in particular aspects of leisure should be described, for example, art galleries, museums, countryside management, sport. An involvement in sports and leisure as a participant or employee is an advantage. See also **Appendix 4**.

Misconceptions about this course The level of business studies in leisure management courses is higher than many students expect.

Selection interviews Some Creative Arts, Liverpool John Moores, Salford.

Interview advice and questions In addition to sporting or other related interests, applicants will be expected to have had some work experience and can expect to be asked to discuss their interests. What do you hope to gain by going to university? See **Chapter 6**.

Reasons for rejection (non-academic) Poor communication or presentation skills. Relatively poor sporting background or knowledge.

AFTER-RESULTS ADVICE

Offers to applicants repeating A-levels Same Cardiff (UWIC), Liverpool John Moores, Salford.

GRADUATE DESTINATIONS AND EMPLOYMENT (2007/8 HESA)

See **Hospitality and Event Management**.

Career note Career opportunities exist in public and private sectors within leisure facilities, health clubs, the arts, leisure promotion, marketing and events management. Some graduates work in sports development and outdoor activities.

OTHER DEGREE SUBJECTS FOR CONSIDERATION

Business Studies; Events Management; Hospitality Management; Sports Studies; Tourism.

LINGUISTICS

(see also **English, Languages**)

Linguistics covers the study of language structure and function, and also includes areas such as children's language, slang, language handicap, advertising language, language styles and the learning of foreign languages.

Useful websites www.iol.org.uk; www.cal.org; http://web.mit.edu/linguistics; www.applij. oxfordjournals.org; www.lsadc.org; www.sil.org; www.baal.org.uk.

NB The points totals shown to the left of the institutions are for ease of reference only. It must not be assumed that Tariff points are always used by institutions or that they can be substituted for an offer in grades. The level of an offer is not necessarily indicative of the quality of a course.

COURSE OFFERS INFORMATION

Subject requirements/preferences GCSE English required and a foreign language preferred. **AL** English may be required or preferred for some courses.

NB In 2012 universities and colleges will differ in their use of GCE AL/AS unit grade information, A* grades, the Extended Project (EPQ), the Advanced Diploma and the Cambridge Pre-U examination when considering applicants and making offers. An EPQ may be accepted in place of an AS subject. Check websites of universities and colleges for the latest offers information.

Your target offers and examples of courses provided by each institution

380 pts Cambridge – (Part II subject, taken after Part I in another, usually language–related, subject). College offers may vary A*AA (Modn Mediev Lang (Ling)) (IB 38–42 pts)
London (UCL) – AAA–ABB (Ling) (IB 34–38 pts)

360 pts Oxford – AAA (Modn Lang Ling) (IB 38–40 pts)
York – AAA–AAB (Engl Lang Ling) (IB 36 pts)

340 pts Lancaster – AAB 340 pts (Ling Psy) (IB 31 pts)
Manchester – AAB–BBB (Ling courses) (IB 35–30 pts)
Southampton – AAB (Fr/Ger/Span Ling St) (IB 32 pts)
St Andrews – AAB–ABB (Engl Ling)
York – AAB–ABB (Ling courses) (IB 34 pts)

320 pts Kent – 320–340 pts (Engl Lang Ling)
Lancaster – ABB 320 pts (Socioling) (IB 30 pts)
Leeds – ABB (Ling joint courses) (IB 34 pts HL 16 pts)
London (SOAS) – ABB (Ling courses) (IB 36 pts)
Newcastle – ABB (Ling Fr/Ger/Span) (IB 32 pts HL Engl 5)
Queen's Belfast – ABB–BBCb (Ling Joint Hons)

300 pts Aberdeen – BBB (Lang Ling courses) (IB 30 pts)
Edinburgh – BBB–AAA (Ling Soc Anth) (IB 34 pts H555)
Essex – 300 pts (Engl Lang Ling) (IB 32 pts)
London (QM) – BBB 300 pts (Fr Ling) (IB 32 pts)
Newcastle – ABC/BBB (Ling Chin/Jap) (IB 32 pts HL engl 5)
Roehampton – 300–340 pts (Engl Lang Ling)
Sheffield – ABB–BBB (Ling courses) (IB 32–35 pts)

280 pts Brighton – BBC (Engl Lang Ling) (IB 28 pts)
Westminster – CCC (Russ Ling)

260 pts Bangor – 260–320 pts (Ling Engl Lang; Ling Engl Lit)
Bristol UWE – 260–300 pts (Engl Lang Ling) (IB 26–32 pts)
Central Lancashire – 260–300 pts (Engl Lang Ling Comb Hons)
Nottingham Trent – 260 pts (Ling Joint Hons)
Ulster – 260 pts (Ling PR) (IB 24 pts)
Westminster – BCC/BB (Ling Crea Writ) (IB 30 pts)

240 pts **Bangor** – 240–280 pts (Ling)
Manchester Met – 240 pts (Fr/Ger/Ital/Span Ling; Comb Hons Ling)
220 pts **Salford** – 220–300 pts (Ling courses)
Sunderland – 220 pts (Ling courses)
UCP Marjon – 220 pts (Engl Lang Ling Educ St)
160 pts **Wolverhampton** – 160–220 pts (Ling courses)
 80 pts **London (Birk)** – no A-level reqs for under 21s (over 21s varies) p/t (Ling Lang)

Alternative offers
See **Chapter 7** and **Appendix 1** for grades/UCAS Tariff points information for the International Baccalaureate, Scottish Highers/Advanced Highers, the Welsh Baccalaureate, the Irish Leaving Certificate, the Cambridge Pre-U Diploma, the Advanced Diploma and the Extended Project.

CHOOSING YOUR COURSE (SEE ALSO CH. 1)
Some course features
Edinburgh The University is regarded as a world leader in the study of linguistics. Opportunity to take an MA in Linguistics or as the lead subject combined with a second subject.
Lancaster (Ling N Am) The course focuses on the sound, grammar and meaning systems of different languages, and has a wide range of options. Study in a North American institution may be possible.
Leeds Linguistics and Phonetics can be taken as a single subject, a major subject or as part of a Joint Honours programme.
London (QM) (Compar Lit Ling) Students divide their time between the two subjects, the former making connections with literature and film, music, the visual arts and popular culture.

Universities and colleges teaching quality See www.qaa.ac.uk; http://unistats.direct.gov.uk.

Top research universities and colleges (RAE 2008) London (QM); Edinburgh; York; Essex; Sheffield; Wolverhampton; London (UCL); Manchester; Lancaster; Central Lancashire; Cambridge; Bristol UWE.

ADMISSIONS INFORMATION
Number of applicants per place (approx) Bangor 3; East London 3; Essex 1; Lancaster 12; Leeds 12; York 11.

Advice to applicants and planning the UCAS personal statement Give details of your interests in language and how it works, and about your knowledge of languages and their similarities and differences.

Selection interviews Yes Brighton, Cambridge, East London, Essex, Lancaster, Newcastle, Reading; **Some** Salford, Sheffield.

Interview advice and questions Past questions include: Why do you want to study Linguistics? What does the subject involve? What do you intend to do at the end of your degree course? What answer do you give to your parents or friends when they ask why you want to study the subject? How and why does language vary according to sex, age, social background and regional origins? See also **Chapter 6**.

Reasons for rejection (non-academic) Lack of knowledge of linguistics. Hesitation about the period to be spent abroad.

AFTER-RESULTS ADVICE
Offers to applicants repeating A-levels Higher Essex; **Same** Brighton, Leeds, Newcastle, Salford, York.

GRADUATE DESTINATIONS AND EMPLOYMENT (2007/8 HESA)
Graduates surveyed 505 **Employed** 205 **In further study** 100 **Assumed unemployed** 55

Career note Students enter a wide range of careers, with information management and editorial work in publishing offering some interesting and useful outlets.

OTHER DEGREE SUBJECTS FOR CONSIDERATION

Cognitive Science; Communication Studies; Education Studies; English; Psychology; Speech Sciences.

LITERATURE

(see also **English**)

This is a very broad subject introducing many aspects of the study of literature and aesthetics. Courses will vary in content. Degree courses in English and foreign languages will also include a study of literature.

Useful websites www.lrb.co.uk; www.literature.org; www.bibliomania.com; www.bl.uk; www.acla.org; http://icla.byu.edu.

NB The points totals shown to the left of the institutions are for ease of reference only. It must not be assumed that Tariff points are always used by institutions or that they can be substituted for an offer in grades. The level of an offer is not necessarily indicative of the quality of a course.

COURSE OFFERS INFORMATION

Subject requirements/preferences **GCSE** English and a foreign language usually required. **AL** English may be required or preferred for some courses.

NB In 2012 universities and colleges will differ in their use of GCE AL/AS unit grade information, A* grades, the Extended Project (EPQ), the Advanced Diploma and the Cambridge Pre-U examination when considering applicants and making offers. An EPQ may be accepted in place of an AS subject. Check websites of universities and colleges for the latest offers information.

Your target offers and examples of courses provided by each institution
390 pts **Warwick** – AABb (Film Lit; Engl Lit)
360 pts **Durham** – AAA (Engl Lit) (IB 37 pts)
East Anglia – AAB–BBB (Engl Lit)
London (King's) – AAB+AS (Compar Lit Film St) (IB 35 pts)
Warwick – AAA–AAAb (Phil Lit) (IB 36–38 pts)
340 pts **Cardiff** – AAB (Cult Lit courses) (IB 33–34 pts)
East Anglia – AAB–BBB (Art Hist Lit) (IB 31–33 pts)
Glasgow – AAB (Scot Lit) (IB 34 pts)
Manchester – AAB–ABB (Lit St Dr App Engl St) (IB 35–32 pts)
St Andrews – AAB (Compar Lit)
320 pts **Essex** – 320–300 pts (Lit Sociol) (IB 29 pts)
London (Gold) – ABB (Engl Compar Lit)
London (QM) – 320 pts (Russ Compar Lit) (IB 32 pts)
London (RH) – ABB–BBB (Compar Lit Cult courses) (IB 32 pts)
Warwick – ABB (Ital Euro Lit) (IB 32–34 pts)
300 pts **Aberdeen** – BBB (Lit Wrld Cntxt)
Buckingham – BBB 300 pts (Engl Lit courses) (IB 27 pts)
Edinburgh – check with Admissions Tutor BBB (Scot Lit Scot Hist)
Essex – 300 pts (Lit Myth) (IB 29 pts)
Hertfordshire – 300 pts (Engl Lit courses)
Kent – 300–320 pts (Compar Lit St courses) (IB 28 pts)
London (Gold) – BBB (Media Modn Lit; Engl Am Lit)
Reading – 300–320 pts (Engl Lit Euro Lit Cult)
280 pts **Aberystwyth** – 280 pts (Engl Lit) (IB 30 pts)
Birmingham City – 280 pts (Engl Lit courses)
Edge Hill – 280 pts (Engl Lit courses)
260 pts **Stirling** – BCC 260 pts (Engl St Scot Lit)
240 pts **Aberystwyth** – 240 pts (Ir Lang Lit)
Ulster – 240 pts (Ir Lang Lit)

Worcester – 240–260 pts (Engl Lit St courses)
200 pts **Blackpool and Fylde (Coll)** – 200 pts (Engl Lang Lit Writ)
Trinity Saint David – 200 pts (Welsh Engl Lit)

Staffordshire – contact University (Lit Contemp Cult)

Alternative offers
See **Chapter 7** and **Appendix 1** for grades/UCAS Tariff points information for the International Baccalaureate, Scottish Highers/Advanced Highers, the Welsh Baccalaureate, the Irish Leaving Certificate, the Cambridge Pre-U Diploma, the Advanced Diploma and the Extended Project.

EXAMPLES OF FOUNDATION DEGREES IN THE SUBJECT FIELD
Bath Spa; Truro (Coll); Winchester.

CHOOSING YOUR COURSE (SEE ALSO CH. 1)
Some course features
Glasgow (Scot Lit) Course covers poetry, drama, fiction and prose of Scotland in English and Scots from the 14th century to the present day.
London (Gold) (Engl Compar Lit) There is an option to specialise in the literature of other countries, for example America, Europe, the Caribbean.
Reading (Engl Lit Euro Lit Cult) The course explores the inter-relationship between the literatures and cultures of different European countries to gain a comparative perspective on English literature, culture and history. All works are in translation for those without foreign language skills.
Ulster (Ir Lang Lit) Course focuses on an in-depth study of the literary and historical traditions of Gaelic Ireland from the Bardic period to the present day and gaining a high level of competence in written and spoken Irish. Applicants need at least grade C (or equivalent) in A-level Irish.

Top research universities and colleges (RAE 2008) See **English**.

ADMISSIONS INFORMATION
Number of applicants per place (approx) East Anglia 12; Essex 4.

Advice to applicants and planning the UCAS personal statement See **English**. **Kent** Interest in literatures other than English.

Misconceptions about this course Kent Some students think that a foreign language is required – it is not.

Selection interviews Yes Trinity Saint David.

Interview advice and questions See **English**. See also **Chapter 6**. **Kent** Which book would you take on a desert island, and why? What is the point of doing a Literature degree in the 21st century?

Reasons for rejection (non-academic) Kent Perceived inability to think on their feet.

GRADUATE DESTINATIONS AND EMPLOYMENT (2007/8 HESA)
Graduates surveyed 115 **Employed** 40 **In further study** 30 **Assumed unemployed** 15

Career note Students enter a wide range of careers, with information management and editorial work in publishing offering some interesting and useful outlets. See Arts; English; Linguistics; Welsh and Celtic Studies.

MARINE/MARITIME STUDIES

(including **Oceanography**; see also **Environmental Sciences/Studies, Naval Architecture**)

Marine and Maritime Studies can involve a range of subjects such as marine business, technology, navigation, nautical studies, underwater rescue and transport.

Useful websites www.bized.co.uk; www.british-shipping.org; www.uk-sail.org.uk; www.rya.org.uk; www.royalnavy.mod.uk; www.sstg.org; www.noc.soton.ac.uk; www.nautinst.org; www.mcsuk.org; www.nmm.ac.uk; www.imo.org; www.mcga.gov.uk.

NB The points totals shown to the left of the institutions are for ease of reference only. It must not be assumed that Tariff points are always used by institutions or that they can be substituted for an offer in grades. The level of an offer is not necessarily indicative of the quality of a course.

COURSE OFFERS INFORMATION
Subject requirements/preferences GCSE Mathematics and science are required for several courses. **AL** Science or mathematics will be required or preferred for some courses.

NB In 2012 universities and colleges will differ in their use of GCE AL/AS unit grade information, A* grades, the Extended Project (EPQ), the Advanced Diploma and the Cambridge Pre-U examination when considering applicants and making offers. An EPQ may be accepted in place of an AS subject. Check websites of universities and colleges for the latest offers information.

Your target offers and examples of courses provided by each institution

360 pts **East Anglia** – AAA–AAB (Meteor Ocean courses MSci) (IB 34–33 pts HL 666 inc maths)
Southampton – AAA–ABB (Ocean courses MOcean) (IB 36–33 pts)

340 pts **Cardiff** – AAB–ABB (Mar Geosci courses)
Heriot-Watt – AAB 2nd yr entry (App Mar Biol)
Newcastle – AAB (Sml Crft Tech MEng) (IB 37 pts HL maths phys 5)
Southampton – AAB (Ship Sci) (IB 36 pts HL 18)

320 pts **Cardiff** – ABB (Mar Geog) (IB 32 pts)
East Anglia – ABB–BBB (Meteor Ocean BSc) (IB 32–31 pts)
Liverpool – ABB 320 pts (Ocn Clim) (IB 30 pts)
Newcastle – ABB/BBB (Off Eng BEng) (IB 32–34 pts HL maths phys 5)
Swansea – ABB (Mar Biol) (IB 33 pts)

300 pts **Aberdeen** – BBB 300 pts (Electron Ocnc Instr) (IB 30 pts)
Essex – 300–260 pts inc BB–CC (Mar Biol) (IB 32–28 pts)
Heriot-Watt – BBB 1st yr entry (App Mar Biol)
Liverpool – BBB 300 pts (Ocn Sci) (IB 30 pts)
Newcastle – BBB (Mar Zool) (IB 32 pts HL biol 6)
Plymouth – BBB 300–360 pts (Mar Biol Ocean) (IB 24 pts)
Southampton – BBB (Ocn Chem) (IB 32 pts HL 15 pts)

280 pts **Plymouth** – 280 pts (Mar Geosci)

260 pts **Bangor** – 260–320 pts (Mar Biol Zool) (IB 28 pts)
Bournemouth – 260 pts (Mar Arch; Mar Cstl Mgt)
Brighton – BBC (Earth Ocn Sci) (IB 28 pts)
Hull – 260–300 pts (Aqua Zool)
Liverpool John Moores – 260 pts (Marit Bus Mgt)
Plymouth – BCC 260 pts (Mar Tech BEng) (IB 27 pts)
Portsmouth – 260–300 pts (Mar Biol)

240 pts **Bangor** – 240–260 pts (Mar Chem) (IB 28 pts)
Coventry – 240 pts (Auto Trans Des (Boat))
Hull – 240–280 pts (Mar Frshwtr Biol)
Liverpool John Moores – 240 pts (Marit St; Naut Sci)
Plymouth – 240–280 pts (Env Sci (Marit Cons); Marit Bus Marit Law; Ocn Explor; Ocn Sci)
Portsmouth – 240–300 pts (Mar Env Sci)
UHI Millennium Inst – AA–DD (Mar Sci)

220 pts **Bangor** – 220–260 pts (Cstl Geog) (IB 28 pts)
Hull – 220–280 pts (Cstl Mar Biol)
Plymouth – 220–240 pts (Cru Mgt)
Southampton Solent – 220 pts (Wtrspo St Mgt)
Ulster – 220 pts (Mar Sci) (IB 24 pts)

200 pts **Plymouth** – 200 pts (Surf Sci Tech; App Mar Spo Sci; Mar St (Navig) (Ocn Ycht) (Merch Shp))
180 pts **Plymouth** – 180 pts (Mar Cmpstes Tech)
South Tyneside (Coll) – 180 pts (Mar Ops)
Southampton Solent – 180 pts (Ycht Prod Surv; Ycht Pwrcrft Des)
160 pts **Essex** – 160 pts inc DD (Mar Biol) (IB 24 pts)
120 pts **Southampton Solent** – 120 pts (Marit Bus; Ship Port Mgt)

Alternative offers
See **Chapter 7** and **Appendix 1** for grades/UCAS Tariff points information for the International Baccalaureate, Scottish Highers/Advanced Highers, the Welsh Baccalaureate, the Irish Leaving Certificate, the Cambridge Pre-U Diploma, the Advanced Diploma and the Extended Project.

EXAMPLES OF FOUNDATION DEGREES IN THE SUBJECT FIELD
Blackpool and Fylde (Coll); Bournemouth; Cornwall (Coll); Liverpool John Moores; Plymouth; South Tyneside (Coll); Southampton Solent; Suffolk (Univ Campus).

CHOOSING YOUR COURSE (SEE ALSO CH. 1)
Some course features
Bangor A large department covering marine sciences, coastal geography and ocean sciences.
Liverpool John Moores (Marit St) A broad-based programme for students with a general interest in ships and sea, with a wide range of optional maritime subjects (for example, freight operations, navigation, marine engineering, meteorology, international trade and finance). Students can build their own degree course as their interests develop, based on core modules such as port and cargo operations, management of people and goods, management science and law. Part of the final year can be spent in Norway and all Maritime courses have an optional placement year.
Plymouth (App Mar Spo Sci) A unique course involving the study of human performance, equipment use and design, the nature of the marine environment and practical work. An optional professional diving module is available in the second year.
Southampton Solent Unique courses in Yacht and Powercraft Design and Yacht Production and Surveying.

Universities and colleges teaching quality See www.qaa.ac.uk; http://unistats.direct.gov.uk.

Examples of sandwich degree courses Blackpool and Fylde (Coll); Bournemouth; Cornwall (Coll); Liverpool John Moores; Plymouth; South Tyneside (Coll); Southampton Solent; Suffolk (Univ Campus).

ADMISSIONS INFORMATION
Number of applicants per place (approx) Glasgow 2; Liverpool John Moores (Marit St) 3; Southampton 6; Southampton Solent (Ocean) 6, (Ocn Chem) 6.

Advice to applicants and planning the UCAS personal statement This is a specialised field and, in many cases, applicants will have experience of marine activities. Describe these experiences, for example, sailing, snorkelling, fishing. See also **Appendix 4**.

Selection interviews Yes Southampton, UHI Millennium Inst.

Interview advice and questions Most applicants will have been stimulated by their studies in science or will have strong interests or connections with marine activities. They are likely to be questioned on their reasons for choosing the course. See **Chapter 6**.

AFTER-RESULTS ADVICE
Offers to applicants repeating A-levels Same Bangor, Liverpool John Moores, Plymouth, UHI Millennium Inst.

GRADUATE DESTINATIONS AND EMPLOYMENT (2007/8 HESA)
Maritime Technology graduates surveyed 75 **Employed** 45 **In further study** 10 **Assumed unemployed** 10

Ocean Sciences graduates surveyed 815 **Employed** 405 **In further study** 165 **Assumed unemployed** 180

Career note This subject area covers a wide range of vocational courses, each offering graduates an equally wide choice of career openings in either purely scientific or very practical areas.

OTHER DEGREE SUBJECTS FOR CONSIDERATION

Biology; Civil Engineering; Environmental Studies/Sciences; Geography; Marine Engineering; Marine Transport; Naval Architecture; Oceanography.

MARKETING

(including **Public Relations**; see also **Business and Management Courses, Business and Management Courses (International and European), Business and Management Courses (Specialised), Retail Management**)

Marketing courses are very popular and applications should include evidence of work experience or work shadowing. Marketing is a subject also covered in most Business Studies courses and in specialist (and equally relevant) courses such as Leisure Marketing and Food Marketing, for which lower offers are often made. Most courses offer the same subject content.

Useful websites www.adassoc.org.uk; www.cim.co.uk; www.camfoundation.com; www.ipa.co.uk; www.ipsos-mori.com; www.marketingstudies.net; www.marketingtoday.com.

NB The points totals shown to the left of the institutions are for ease of reference only. It must not be assumed that Tariff points are always used by institutions or that they can be substituted for an offer in grades. The level of an offer is not necessarily indicative of the quality of a course.

COURSE OFFERS INFORMATION

Subject requirements/preferences **GCSE** English and mathematics. **AL** No specified subjects required.

NB In 2012 universities and colleges will differ in their use of GCE AL/AS unit grade information, A* grades, the Extended Project (EPQ), the Advanced Diploma and the Cambridge Pre-U examination when considering applicants and making offers. An EPQ may be accepted in place of an AS subject. Check websites of universities and colleges for the latest offers information.

Your target offers and examples of courses provided by each institution

360 pts **Exeter** – AAA–AAB (Mgt Mark) (IB 36–33 pts)
Lancaster – AAA 360 pts (Mark Mgt Abrd) (IB 32 pts)
Leeds – AAA–AAB (Mgt Mark) (IB 35 pts HL 17 pts)
Ulster – AAA (Comm Adv Mark)

340 pts **Cardiff** – AAB (Bus Mgt (Mark))
Lancaster – AAB 340 pts (Adv Mark) (IB 34 pts)
London (RH) – AAB (Mgt Mark) (IB 35 pts)
Loughborough – AAB (Rtl Mark Mgt) (36 pts)
Manchester – AAB (Mgt (Mark))
Southampton – AAB (Int Mark) (IB 34 pts HL 17)

320 pts **Aston** – AAB–AAA 320–340 pts (Mark) (IB 34 pts HL 665)
Bournemouth – 320 pts (Bus St Mark)
Dundee – ABB 2nd yr entry (Bus Econ Mark MA/BSc)
Essex – 320 pts (Mgt Mark) (IB 34 pts)
Lancaster – ABB 320 pts (Mark Psy) (IB 30 pts)
Liverpool – ABB (Mark) (IB 32 pts)
Newcastle – ABB (Mark Mgt) (IB 34 pts)
Northumbria – ABB 320 pts (Mark Mgt)
Strathclyde – ABB (Mark courses)

Sussex – ABB (Mark Mgt)

Swansea – ABB–BBB (Bus Mgt (Mark))

300 pts **Bournemouth** – 300 pts (Adv Mark Comm; Mark; PR)

Brunel – 300–350 pts (Bus Mgt (Mark)) (IB 32 pts)

Heriot-Watt – ABC (Bus Mgt Mark)

Hertfordshire – 300 pts (Mark Comb courses)

Huddersfield – 300 pts (Mark Brnd Mgt; Mark; Mark PR)

Kent – 300 pts (Bus Admin (Mark)) (IB 33 pts)

Northumbria – 300 pts (Fash Mark)

Nottingham Trent – 300 pts (Fash Mark Brnd; Fash Comm Prom)

Oxford Brookes – BBB (Bus Mark Mgt)

Reading – 300 pts (Bus Stats Mark) (IB 36 pts)

280 pts **Bournemouth** – 280 pts (Leis Mark) (IB 30 pts)

Brighton – BBC (Bus Mgt Mark)

Bristol UWE – 280–340 pts (Mark Comm)

De Montfort – 280 pts (Adv)

Edge Hill – 280 pts (Mark)

Gloucestershire – 280–300 pts (Mark Mgt Brnd; Mark Adv Comms; PR)

Harper Adams (UC) – 280 pts (Agric Mark)

Hertfordshire – 280 pts (Mark)

Hull – 280 pts (Mgt Mark; Mark courses)

Keele – 280–340 pts (Mark courses)

Kingston – 280 pts (Mark Mgt) (IB 31 pts)

Leeds Trinity (UC) – (Media Mark; Bus Mark)

Manchester Met – 280 pts (Int Fash Mark) (IB 30 pts)

Northumbria – 280 pts (Bus Mark) (IB 25 pts)

Portsmouth – 280–300 pts (Mark; Mark Psy)

Royal (CAg) – 280–300 pts (Prop Agncy Mark)

Stirling – BBC (Rtl Mark)

Worcester – 280 pts (Adv; Bus Mark; Mark Adv PR; Bus Mgt Mark; Mark)

260 pts **Aberystwyth** – 260 pts (Mark courses) (IB 27 pts)

Bangor – 260–300 pts (Mark Fr/Ger/Ital/Span)

Birmingham City – 260–280 pts (Mark Adv PR) (IB 24 pts)

Bolton – 260 pts (Bus Mgt (Mark)) (IB 24 pts)

Brighton – BCC (Trav Tour Mark) (IB 28 pts)

Coventry – 260–280 pts (Mark; Adv Mark)

Lincoln – 260–280 pts (Mark; Mark PR)

Liverpool Hope – 260 pts (Mark courses) (IB 25 pts)

Liverpool John Moores – 260 pts (Mark)

Plymouth – 260 pts (Mark) (IB 26 pts)

Staffordshire – BCC (Mark Mgt)

Stirling – BCC (Mark)

Ulster – 260 pts (Mark)

Westminster – BCC (Mark Comms) (IB 28 pts)

240 pts **Bradford** – 240 pts (Mark) (IB 24 pts)

Buckingham – 240 pts (Mark Psy) (IB 26 pts)

Canterbury Christ Church – CCC (Mark Acc)

Cardiff (UWIC) – 240 pts (Mark Mgt)

Central Lancashire – 240–280 pts (Adv Mark Comm) (IB 28 pts)

Chester – 240 pts (Mark; PR; Adv)

Chichester – CCC (Mark) (IB 26 pts)

Coventry – 240–260 pts (Spo Mark)

De Montfort – 240 pts (Mark; Int Mark Bus; Mark Mgt)

Derby – 240 pts (Int Mark Mgt) (IB 26 pts)

Edinburgh Napier – 240–230 pts (Mark Mgt; Mark Dig Media)

For a quick reference offers calculator, fold out the inside back cover.

Glamorgan – 240–280 pts (Mark) (IB 24 pts)
Glasgow Caledonian – CCC (Fash Mark)
Leeds (CAD) – 240 pts (Crea Adv)
Liverpool John Moores – 240 pts (Bus PR)
London Met – 240 pts (PR)
Manchester Met – 240 pts (Spo Mark Mgt) (IB 26–28 pts)
Newport – 240 pts (Mark) (IB 24 pts)
Nottingham Trent – 240 pts (Mark Des Comm; Bus Mgt Mark)
Plymouth – 240 pts (Bus Econ Mark) (IB 24 pts)
Robert Gordon – CCC 240 pts (Mgt Mark)
Roehampton – 240–280 pts (Mark; Mark Multim)
Salford – 240 pts (Bus St Mark Mgt)
Sheffield Hallam – 240–200 pts (Bus Mark; Fd Mark Mgt; Mark Rtl)
Southampton Solent – 240 pts (PR Comm)
Suffolk (Univ Campus) – 240 pts (Bus Mgt Mark)
Wolverhampton – 240 pts (Mark HR Mgt)
230 pts **Greenwich** – 230–240 pts (PR)
220 pts **Creative Arts** – 220–260 pts (Fash Mgt Mark) (IB 24 pts)
Falmouth (UC) – 220 pts (Adv; PR)
Leeds Met – 220 pts (Mark; Mark Adv Mgt; Spo Mark PR; PR Mark)
Northampton – 220–260 pts (Enter Mark; Mark; Mark Psy; Mark Joint Hons; Adv)
Southampton Solent – 220–240 pts (Mark Adv Mgt; Mark Evnt Mgt)
Sunderland – 220–360 pts (Bus Mark Mgt)
York St John – 220–260 pts (Mark Mgt)
200 pts **Anglia Ruskin** – 200 pts (Mark)
Bedfordshire – 200 pts (Mark; Mark Media Prac)

Birmingham (UC) – 200 pts (Mark Mgt; Mark Evnts Mgt)
Bucks New – 200–240 pts (PR Mark Comm; Mark; Bus Mark Mgt)
East London – 200 pts (Mark; Adv)
Glyndŵr – 200 pts (Bus Mark)
Middlesex – 200–280 pts (Mark; Adv PR Media)
Queen Margaret – BB/CCD (Mark Mgt)
Teesside – 200–260 pts (PR) (IB 24-28 pts)
West London – 200 pts (Mark Bus)
180 pts **Abertay Dundee** – DDD (Mark Bus)
Greenwich – 180 pts (Adv Mark Comm; Mark)
Harper Adams (UC) – 180–240 pts (Agri-Fd Mark Bus St; Bus Mgt Mark)
160 pts **Bedfordshire** – 160–240 pts (PR; Adv Mark Comm)
Euro Bus Sch London – CC Contact school (Int Bus Mark Lang)
London South Bank – 160–240 pts (Mark Comb courses)
Swansea Met – 160 pts (Mark Mgt)
West Scotland – CC (Int Mark)
Wolverhampton – 160–220 pts (Mark Mgt; PR)
100 pts **Holborn (Coll)** – Check with Ad Tutor (Bus Mark)

Regents Bus Sch London – check with School (Glob Mark Mgt)

Alternative offers
See **Chapter 7** and **Appendix 1** for grades/UCAS Tariff points information for the International Baccalaureate, Scottish Highers/Advanced Highers, the Welsh Baccalaureate, the Irish Leaving Certificate, the Cambridge Pre-U Diploma, the Advanced Diploma and the Extended Project.

EXAMPLES OF FOUNDATION DEGREES IN THE SUBJECT FIELD

Arts London; Bath Spa; Bedfordshire; Birmingham (UC); Bournemouth; Bournemouth and Poole (Coll); Central Lancashire; Cornwall (Coll); Croydon (Coll); Glamorgan; Glyndŵr; Grimsby (IFHE); Guildford (Coll); Harper Adams (UC); Kirklees (Coll); Leeds (CAD); Manchester (Coll); Nottingham New (Coll); Plymouth; Salford; Sheffield (Coll); Somerset (CAT); Southampton Solent; Truro (Coll); Writtle (Coll).

CHOOSING YOUR COURSE (SEE ALSO CH. 1)

Some course features
Bournemouth The course covers advertising communications, media and marketing methods with a six week placement with an advertising agency.
Brunel Marketing is offered as a pathway in the Business and Management programme and can be taken as a three-year full-time or four-year sandwich course.
Lancaster (Mark Mgt) There is a one-year work placement between the second and third years.
Loughborough (Rtl Mark Mgt) The third year is spent on a salaried business placement as a trainee manager in a UK retail or marketing organisation.
Manchester Met A full-time or sandwich course, the latter with placments in the UK and abroad. Special features include a study of the fashion business, fashion products and the world-wide fashion industry.
Northumbria The course integrates fashion design with the fashion business and marketing.
Oxford Brookes (Mark Mgt) The course can be taken as a Single Honours degree or combined with one of 18 other subjects.
Portsmouth (Mark) The course is recognised by the Chartered Institute of Marketing. The four-year sandwich course involves a paid marketing placement.
Westminster Students are expected to find employment for a period during the course, ideally abroad. Work placement officers have contacts with institutions overseas.

Universities and colleges teaching quality See www.qaa.ac.uk; http://unistats.direct.gov.uk.

For a quick reference offers calculator, fold out the inside back cover.

Examples of sandwich degree courses Abertay Dundee; Aston; Birmingham City; Bournemouth; Bradford; Brighton; Bristol UWE; Brunel; Central Lancashire; De Montfort; Glamorgan; Gloucestershire; Greenwich; Harper Adams (UC); Hertfordshire; Huddersfield; Lancaster; Leeds Met; Liverpool John Moores; Manchester Met; Newcastle; Northumbria; Nottingham Trent; Plymouth; Portsmouth; Sheffield Hallam; Staffordshire; Swansea Met; Ulster; Westminster; Wolverhampton; Worcester.

ADMISSIONS INFORMATION

Number of applicants per place (approx) Abertay Dundee 6; Aberystwyth 3; Anglia Ruskin 5; Aston 9; Birmingham City 4; Bournemouth 10; Brunel 10; Central Lancashire 13; De Montfort 3; Derby 5; Glasgow Caledonian 15; Harper Adams (UC) 3; Huddersfield 7; Lancaster 28; Lincoln 3; London Met 10; Northampton 4; Northumbria 8; Nottingham Trent 2; Plymouth 12; Portsmouth 4; Staffordshire 6; Stirling 10; Teesside 3.

Advice to applicants and planning the UCAS personal statement See **Business and Management Courses**. See also **Appendix 4**.

Selection interviews **Yes** Harper Adams (UC) (advisory), Manchester Met, Middlesex, Northbrook (Coll), Writtle (Coll); **Some** Abertay Dundee, Aberystwyth, Anglia Ruskin, Aston, Buckingham, De Montfort, Queen Margaret, Staffordshire.

Interview advice and questions Past questions include: What is marketing? Why do you want to take a Marketing degree? Is sales pressure justified? How would you feel if you had to market a product which you considered to be inferior? See **Chapter 6**. **Buckingham** What job do you see yourself doing in five years' time?

Reasons for rejection (non-academic) Little thought of reasons for deciding on a Marketing degree. Weak on numeracy and problem-solving. Limited commercial awareness. Poor inter-personal skills. Lack of leadership potential. No interest in widening their horizons, either geographically or intellectually. 'We look at appearance, motivation and the applicant's ability to ask questions.' Not hungry enough. Limited understanding of the career. No clear reasons for wishing to do the course.

AFTER-RESULTS ADVICE

Offers to applicants repeating A-levels **Same** Abertay Dundee, Aberystwyth, Anglia Ruskin, Aston, Buckingham, De Montfort, Lincoln, Manchester Met, Queen Margaret, Staffordshire.

GRADUATE DESTINATIONS AND EMPLOYMENT (2007/8 HESA)

Graduates surveyed 2220 **Employed** 1285 **In further study** 175 **Assumed unemployed** 235

Career note See **Business and Management Courses**.

OTHER DEGREE SUBJECTS FOR CONSIDERATION

Advertising; Art and Design; Business courses; Communications; Graphic Design; Psychology; Public Relations.

MATERIALS SCIENCE/METALLURGY

Materials Science is a broad subject which mainly covers physics, chemistry and engineering at one and the same time! From its origins in metallurgy, materials science has now moved into the processing, structure and properties of materials – ceramics, polymers, composites and electrical materials. Materials science and metallurgy are perhaps the most misunderstood of all careers and applications for degree courses are low with very reasonable offers. Valuable bursaries and scholarships are offered by the Institute of Materials, Minerals and Mining (check with Institute – see **Appendix 4**). Polymer Science is a branch of materials science and is often studied in conjunction with Chemistry and covers such topics as polymer properties and processing relating to industrial applications with, for example, plastics, paints, adhesives. Other courses under this heading include Fashion and Leather Technology. See also **Appendix 4**.

Useful websites www.scienceyear.com; www.eef.org.uk/uksteel; www.iom3.org; www.noisemakers. org.uk; www.imm.org.

NB The points totals shown to the left of the institutions are for ease of reference only. It must not be assumed that Tariff points are always used by institutions or that they can be substituted for an offer in grades. The level of an offer is not necessarily indicative of the quality of a course.

COURSE OFFERS INFORMATION

Subject requirements/preferences GCSE (for Engineering/Science courses) Science/mathematics subjects. **AL** Mathematics, physics and/or chemistry required for most courses. (Polymer Science) Mathematics and/or physics usually required; design technology encouraged.

NB In 2012 universities and colleges will differ in their use of GCE AL/AS unit grade information, A* grades, the Extended Project (EPQ), the Advanced Diploma and the Cambridge Pre-U examination when considering applicants and making offers. An EPQ may be accepted in place of an AS subject. Check websites of universities and colleges for the latest offers information.

Your target offers and examples of courses provided by each institution

380 pts **Cambridge** – A*AA college offers may vary (Nat Sci (Mat Sci)) (IB 38–42 pts)
Oxford – A*AA (Mat Sci)

360 pts **Imperial London** – AAA (Mat Sci Eng MEng; Biomat Tiss Eng; Mat Nucl Eng)
London (UCL) – AABe (Hist Art Mat St) (IB 34 pts)
Oxford – AAA (Mat Econ Mgt) (IB 38–40 pts)
Southampton – AAA (Mech Eng Advnc Mat MEng) (IB 36 pts)

340 pts **Exeter** – AAB–ABB (Mat Eng MEng) (IB 34–31 pts)
Imperial London – AAB (Mat Mgt BEng; Mats; Mat Sci Eng)
Leeds – AAB (Cheml Mat Eng) (IB 36 pts HL 17 pts)
London (QM) – 340 pts (Mat Sci Eng MEng) (IB 34 pts)
Loughborough – 340 pts (Auto Mat MEng) (IB 32 pts)
Manchester – AAB–ABC (Biomed Mat Sci) (IB 35–32 pts)
Newcastle – AAB (Mech Mat Eng MEng) (IB 36 pts)
St Andrews – AAB 2nd yr entry (Chem Mat Chem) (IB 34 pts)
Sheffield – AAB (Mat Sci Eng Yr in Jap) (IB 33–30 pts)
Strathclyde – AAB (Mech Eng Mat Eng MEng) (IB 36 pts)

320 pts **Birmingham** – ABB (Spo Mat Sci) (IB 32 pts)
Exeter – ABB–BBB (Mat Eng BEng) (IB 32–29 pts)
Liverpool – ABB (Mech Mat Eng BEng) (IB 30 pts)
Manchester – ABB–ABC (Tex Sci Tech) (IB 34–33 pts)
Sheffield – ABB (Metal) (IB 30–33 pts)
Swansea – ABB–BBB (Mat Sci Eng MEng)

300 pts **Aberdeen** – BBB (Mech Eng Mat BEng/MEng) (IB 30–28 pts)
Birmingham – BBB (Biomed Mat Sci) (IB 30 pts)
Bradford – 300 pts (Med Eng MEng)
Edinburgh – Check with Ad Tutor BBB (Chem Mat Chem) (IB 32 pts)
Liverpool – BBB (Mat Eng BEng; Mat Des Manuf)
Loughborough – 300 pts (Des Eng Mat) (IB 28–30 pts)
Nottingham – BBB–BCC (Biomed Mat Sci) (IB 28–32 pts)
Sheffield – ABC/BBB (Aerosp Mat BEng) (IB 30–33 pts)

280 pts **Birmingham City** – 280–260 pts (Fash Des Gmnt Tech)
London (QM) – 280 pts (Mat Sci Eng BEng) (IB 28 pts)

260 pts **Central Lancashire** – 260 pts (Fire Eng) (IB 28 pts)
Heriot-Watt – BBC (Fash Tech)
London (QM) – 260 pts (Mat Sci Eng BSc) (IB 26 pts)
Northampton – 260 pts (Mat Tech (Lea))
Swansea – 260 pts (Mat Sci Eng BEng)

240 pts **Bradford** – 240 pts (Med Eng BEng)
De Montfort – 240 pts (Fash Tech)
Edinburgh Napier – 240 pts (Poly Eng)
Manchester Met – 240 pts (Fash Des Tech)
200 pts **London Met** – 200 pts (Poly Eng)
Manchester Met – 200 pts (Tex)
180 pts **Plymouth** – 180 pts (Mar Cmpstes Tech)

Alternative offers
See **Chapter 7** and **Appendix 1** for grades/UCAS Tariff points information for the International Baccalaureate, Scottish Highers/Advanced Highers, the Welsh Baccalaureate, the Irish Leaving Certificate, the Cambridge Pre-U Diploma, the Advanced Diploma and the Extended Project.

EXAMPLES OF FOUNDATION DEGREES IN THE SUBJECT FIELD
Bradford; Bucks New; De Montfort; Kirklees (Coll); Leeds (CAD); Leeds Met; Leicester (Coll); Liverpool (CmC); London Met; London UCK (Coll); West Anglia (Coll).

CHOOSING YOUR COURSE (SEE ALSO CH. 1)
Some course features
Birmingham Courses are offered in Mechanical and Materials Science, Metallurgy/Materials Engineering, Materials Science and Technology and Biomedical Science (artificial hip joints, heart valves, contact lenses etc). There is also a course in Sports Science and Materials Technology.
Imperial London All Materials courses are the same for all students in the first two years, with specialisation in t in the final year, with additional options including management, finacne and languages. One-year relevant placements for MEng students.
London (QM) (Dntl Mat) MEng and BEng programmes focus on maxillofacial anatomy, biomaterials, dental materials and materials properties and structures. The MEng fourth year has advanced topics in ceramics and biomaterials with an optional one-year industrial placement after the third year.
London Met Three-year degree courses are offered in Polymer Engineering and in Polymer Science.
Loughborough The Materials Engineering programme allows students to develop either Materials Engineering or Business Management options in the final year. There is an optional third year in Europe or in industry. There are also courses in Automotive Materials. Scholarships available.
Manchester The Materials Science programme focuses on engineering aspects whilst the Biomedical Materials Science programme can be taken with or without industrial experience. The Biomedical Materials Science course covers cell structure, anatomy, tissue interaction and drug release systems. There are also courses in Textile Sciences and Technology. Entrance scholarships.
Northampton (Mat Tech (Lea)) This course is unique. The University is the UK's leading provider of leather technology courses, and is the only one to have a tannery.
Sheffield In this Materials Science and Engineering course options exist in ceramic science, polymer science, glass and metal science: these subjects are also offered as specialist degrees. Admission can also be by way of Physical Sciences since final degree course decisions between Materials Science or Physics or Chemistry can be delayed. Courses in Metal Science, Ceramic Science, Glass Science, and also Polymer Science and Engineering are also offered.

Universities and colleges teaching quality See www.qaa.ac.uk; http://unistats.direct.gov.uk.

Top research universities and colleges (RAE 2008) (Metallurgy and Materials) Cambridge; Liverpool; Kent; Oxford; Manchester; Birmingham; Sheffield; Imperial London; Swansea; London (QM).

Examples of sandwich degree courses Loughborough; Manchester; Plymouth; Portsmouth.

ADMISSIONS INFORMATION
Number of applicants per place (approx) Birmingham 8; Imperial London 3; Liverpool 3; Manchester Met 7; Nottingham 7; Southampton 8; Swansea 4.

Advice to applicants and planning the UCAS personal statement Read scientific and engineering journals and describe any special interests you have. Try to visit chemical or technological installations (rubber, plastics, glass etc) and describe your visits. See also **Appendix 4**.

Misconceptions about this course Students are generally unaware of what this subject involves or the opportunities within the industry.

Selection interviews Yes Birmingham, Imperial London, Oxford (Mat Sci) 44%, (Mat Sci Econ Mgt) 44%; **Some** Leeds.

Interview advice and questions Questions are likely to be based on A/AS-level science subjects. Recent examples include: Why did you choose Materials Science? How would you make each part of this table lamp (on the interviewer's desk)? Identify this piece of material. How was it manufactured? How has it been treated? (Questions related to metal and polymer samples.) What would you consider the major growth area in materials science? See **Chapter 6**. **Birmingham** We try to gauge understanding; for example, an applicant would be unlikely to be questioned on specific facts, but might be asked what they have understood from a piece of coursework at school. **Oxford** Tutors look for an ability to apply logical reasoning to problems in physical science and an enthusiasm for thinking about new concepts in science and engineering.

AFTER-RESULTS ADVICE
Offers to applicants repeating A-levels Higher Swansea; **Same** Birmingham, Leeds (CAD), Liverpool, Manchester Met.

GRADUATE DESTINATIONS AND EMPLOYMENT (2007/8 HESA)
Metallurgy graduates surveyed 25 **Employed** 5 **In further study** 10 **Assumed unemployed** 0

Polymer graduates surveyed 420 **Employed** 265 **In further study** 20 **Assumed unemployed** 45

Materials Science and Technology graduates surveyed 245 **Employed** 100 **In further study** 75 **Assumed unemployed** 25

Career note Materials scientists are involved in a wide range of specialisms in which openings are likely in a range of industries. These include manufacturing processes in which the work is closely linked with that of mechanical, chemical, production and design engineers.

OTHER DEGREE SUBJECTS FOR CONSIDERATION
Aerospace Engineering; Biotechnology; Chemistry; Dentistry; Engineering Sciences; Mathematics; Mechanical Engineering; Medical Engineering; Plastics Technology; Physics; Product Design and Materials; Prosthetics and Orthotics; Sports Technology.

MATHEMATICS
(including **Mathematical Sciences/Studies**; see also **Statistics**)

Mathematics at degree level is an extension of A-level mathematics, covering pure and applied mathematics, statistics, computing, mathematical analysis and mathematical applications. Mathematics is of increasing importance and is used in the simplest of design procedures and not only in applications in the physical sciences and engineering. It also plays a key role in management, economics, medicine and the social and behavioural sciences.

Useful websites www.ima.org.uk; www.gchq.gov.uk/codebreaking; www.orsoc.org.uk; www. scienceyear.com; www.m-a.org.uk; www.mathscareers.org.uk; www.imo.math.ca; www.bmoc.maths. org; www.maths.org; www.ukmt.org.uk.

NB The points totals shown to the left of the institutions are for ease of reference only. It must not be assumed that Tariff points are always used by institutions or that they can be substituted for an offer in grades. The level of an offer is not necessarily indicative of the quality of a course.

12; Leeds (Maths) 5, (Maths Fin) 4; Leicester 14; Liverpool 5; London (Gold) 5; London (King's) 8; London (QM) 5; London (RH) 8; London (UCL) 8; London LSE (Maths Econ) 11, (Bus Maths Stats) 10; London Met 3; Manchester Met 3; Middlesex 5; Newcastle 7; Northumbria 7; Nottingham Trent 7; Oxford Brookes 21; Plymouth 8; Portsmouth 7; Sheffield 5; Sheffield Hallam 3; Southampton 9–10; Strathclyde 6; Surrey 7; Warwick 6; York 6.

Advice to applicants and planning the UCAS personal statement Any interests you have in careers requiring mathematical ability could be mentioned – for example, engineering, computers (hardware and software) and business applications. Show determination, love of mathematics and an appreciation of the rigour of the course. Give details of your skills, work experience, positions of responsibility. A variety of non-academic interests to complement the applicant's academic abilities preferred. For non-UK students fluency in oral and written English required. **Manchester** Unit grades may form part of an offer. **Warwick** Offers for courses in Statistics (MORSE, Mathematics and Statistics) may include achievement requirements in selected unit grades. Check University website for latest information. See also **Appendix 4**.

Misconceptions about this course London (QM) Some believe that a study of mechanics is compulsory – it is not. **Surrey** Maths is not just about calculations: it focuses on reasoning, logic and applications. **York** Further maths is not required.

Selection interviews Yes Aberystwyth, Bath, Birmingham, Bishop Grosseteste (UC), Bristol UWE, Brunel, Cambridge, Cardiff, Central Lancashire, City, Coventry, Durham, East London, Essex, Exeter, Glamorgan, Heriot-Watt, Imperial London, Kent, Kingston, Lancaster, Leeds, Liverpool, Liverpool John Moores, London (Gold), London (King's), London (RH), London (UCL), London Met, Manchester Met, Newcastle, Northampton, Northumbria, Nottingham, Oxford (Maths) 20% (Maths Comp Sci) 31% (Maths Phil) 25% (Maths Stats) 17%, Reading, Salford, Sheffield, Southampton, Sussex, Warwick, York; **Some** Brighton, Bristol, East Anglia, Greenwich, London LSE (rarely), Loughborough.

Interview advice and questions Questions are likely to be asked arising from the information you have given in your UCAS application and about your interests in the subject. Questions in recent years have included: How many ways are there of incorrectly setting up the back row of a chess board? A ladder on a rough floor leans against a smooth wall. Describe the forces acting on the ladder and give the maximum possible angle of inclination possible. There are three particles connected by a string; the middle one is made to move – describe the subsequent motion of the particles. What mathematics books have you read outside your syllabus? Why does a ball bounce? Discuss the work of any renowned mathematician. Balance a pencil on your index fingers and then try to move both towards the centre of the pencil. Explain what is happening in terms of forces and friction. See **Chapter 6**. **Cambridge** If you could spend half an hour with any mathematician past or present, who would it be? **Oxford** (Maths Phil) What makes you think I'm having thoughts? What was the most beautiful proof in A-level mathematics? I am an oil baron in the desert and I need to deliver oil to four different towns which happen to lie in a straight line. In order to deliver the correct amount to each town I must visit each town in turn, returning to my warehouse in between each visit. Where would I position my warehouse in order to drive the shortest possible distance? Roads are no problem since I have a friend who will build me as many roads as I like for free. **Southampton** Personal statements generate discussion points. Our interviews are informal chats and so technical probing is kept low key.

Reasons for rejection (non-academic) Usually academic reasons only. Lack of motivation. We were somewhat uneasy about how much mathematics he will remember after a Gap Year running a theatre in South Africa. **Birmingham** A poorly-written and poorly-organised personal statement.

AFTER-RESULTS ADVICE
Offers to applicants repeating A-levels Higher Brighton, Coventry, Essex, Glasgow, London Met, Salford, Strathclyde, Surrey, Swansea, Warwick; **Possibly higher** Cambridge (Hom), Durham, Lancaster, Leeds, Newcastle, Sheffield; **Same** Aberystwyth, Aston, Bath, Birmingham, Bristol, Brunel, Chester, East Anglia, Liverpool, Liverpool Hope, London (RH), Loughborough (usually), Manchester Met, Nottingham, Nottingham Trent, Oxford Brookes, Sheffield Hallam, Southampton, Stirling, Ulster, Wolverhampton, York.

GRADUATE DESTINATIONS AND EMPLOYMENT (2007/8 HESA)
See also **Statistics**.

Mathematics graduates surveyed 3630 **Employed** 1225 **In further study** 1035 **Assumed unemployed** 390

Operational Research graduates surveyed 40 **Employed** 20 **In further study** 5 **Assumed unemployed** 0

Career note Graduates enter a range of careers. Whilst business, finance and retail areas are popular options, mathematicians also have important roles in the manufacturing industries. Mathematics offers the pleasure of problem-solving, the satisfaction of a rigorous argument and the most widely employable non-vocational degree subject. A student's view: 'Maths trains you to work in the abstract, to think creatively and to come up with concrete conclusions.' These transferable skills are much sought-after by employers. Employment prospects are excellent, with high salaries.

OTHER DEGREE SUBJECTS FOR CONSIDERATION
Accountancy; Actuarial Studies; Astronomy; Astrophysics; Computer Science; Economics; Engineering Sciences; Operational Research; Physics; Statistics.

MEDIA STUDIES

(including **Broadcasting** and **Journalism**; see also **Art and Design (General)**, **Communication Studies/Communication**, **Computer Courses**, **Engineering (Acoustics and Sound)**, **Film**, **Radio**, **Video and TV Studies**, **Information Management and Librarianship**, **Photography**)

Intending Media applicants need to check course details carefully since this subject area can involve graphic design, illustration and other art courses as well as the media in the fields of TV, radio and journalism. Courses in Journalism include block and day release, evening/weekend magazine journalism, and photo-journalism. Full details can be obtained by referring to www.nctj.com/courses.

Useful websites www.bbc.co.uk/jobs; www.newspapersoc.org.uk; www.ppa.co.uk; http://careers. thomsonreuters.com; www.arts.org.uk; www.nctj.com; www.ipa.co.uk; www.camfoundation.com; www.mediastudies.com.

NB The points totals shown to the left of the institutions are for ease of reference only. It must not be assumed that Tariff points are always used by institutions or that they can be substituted for an offer in grades. The level of an offer is not necessarily indicative of the quality of a course.

COURSE OFFERS INFORMATION
Subject requirements/preferences **GCSE** English and mathematics often required. **AL** No specified subjects required.

NB In 2012 universities and colleges will differ in their use of GCE AL/AS unit grade information, A* grades, the Extended Project (EPQ), the Advanced Diploma and the Cambridge Pre-U examination when considering applicants and making offers. An EPQ may be accepted in place of an AS subject. Check websites of universities and colleges for the latest offers information.

Your target offers and examples of courses provided by each institution

340 pts **Cardiff** – AAB-ABB (Jrnl Media Cult St) (IB 36 pts)
City – 340 pts (Jrnl; Jrnl Soc Sci)
East Anglia – AAB–BBB (Media St)
Glasgow – AAB (Arts Media Inform) (IB 34 pts)
London (Gold) – AAB-ABB (Media Comm) (IB 34 pts)
Newcastle – AAB (Media Comm Cult St) (IB 32 pts)
Strathclyde – AAB (Jrnl Crea Writ courses)
320 pts **Birmingham** – ABB–BBB (Media Cult Soty courses) (IB 32–34 pts)
Bournemouth – 320 pts (Multim Jrnl; Multim Bus Entre; Comm Media)

Keele Chemistry, physics, biology (dual science award acceptable, grades BB minimum), English language and mathematics at grade B minimum. A broad spread of subjects is expected with a minimum of four at grade A.

Lancaster See **Liverpool**

Leeds Six subjects at grade B minimum including English, mathematics, chemistry and biology or dual science award.

Leicester English language and sciences (including chemistry) or dual science award.

Liverpool Nine subjects grades A–C, including dual science (or biology, chemistry and physics), English language and mathematics at grade B minimum.

London (King's) Grade B (minimum) in chemistry, biology and physics (or dual science award), English and mathematics.

London (QM) Six subjects at AB minimum grades including English, mathematics and science subjects.

London (St George's) Six subjects at AB minimum grades including English, mathematics and science subjects.

London (UCL) English and mathematics at grade B minimum.

Manchester Seven subjects with five at grades A/A*. Chemistry, biology and physics required at either AS or **GCSE** grade C minimum, with English and mathematics at grade B minimum.

Newcastle At least five subjects with grades AAAAB to include English, mathematics and either biology, chemistry, physics or dual science award.

Nottingham Six subjects at geade A/A* to include biology, chemistry and physcis or dual science award. (Grade A AS physics can compensate for a B at **GCSE**.)

Oxford Chemistry, mathematics, biology and physics or dual science award acceptable.

Peninsula (MS) Seven subjects at grades A/B including biology, chemistry or physics or dual science award, English and mathematics or dual science award.

Queen's Belfast Chemistry, biology, mathematics and either physics or dual science award.

St Andrews Chemistry, biology, mathematics and physics. If mathematics and biology are not offered at A2 then each must have been passed at grade B or higher. English is required at grade B or higher.

Sheffield At least six subjects at grade A. English, mathematics, chemistry and a science required.

Southampton Seven subjects at grade B or above including English, mathematics and dual science award or equivalent. (Widening Access course BM6) Five **GCSE**s at grade C including English, mathematics and dual science award or equivalent. (Students join the five-year programme on completion of Year Zero.)

AL See **Your target offers and examples of courses provided by each institution** below. Candidates applying for A104 courses at **Bristol, Cardiff, Dundee, East Anglia, Edinburgh, London (King's), Manchester, Sheffield** and **Southampton** are not accepted if they are offering more than one laboratory-based subject (check with University). **Cambridge (Emmanuel)** AEA in one science subject when only two are taken may be required. **London (UCL)** Mathematics and further mathematics will not both be counted towards three AL subjects. **Other requirements** See **Health Requirements** below; CRB clearance is also required.

NB Home and EU-funded students applying for entry to Medicine are required by many universities to sit either the UKCAT or BMAT tests before applying. See Your target offers and examples of courses provided by each institution below, Chapter 6 and Chapter 5 for further information.

NB In 2012 universities and colleges will differ in their use of GCE AL/AS unit grade information, A* grades, the Extended Project (EPQ), the Advanced Diploma and the Cambridge Pre-U examination when considering applicants and making offers. An EPQ may be accepted in place of an AS subject. Check websites of universities and colleges for the latest offers information.

Your target offers and examples of courses provided by each institution

420 pts **Queen's Belfast** – AAAa +UKCAT (inc AL chem+sci/maths subj; AS biol b min) (Med 5 yrs) (IB 37 pts HL 666)

410 pts **East Anglia** – AAAb–AABb +UKCAT (inc AL A biol) (Med 5 yrs) (IB 33–34 pts HL 666)

Edinburgh – AAAb +UKCAT (inc AL chem+1 from maths/phys/biol; AS biol min) (Med 5/6 yrs) (IB 37 pts HL 766)

Hull York (MS) – AAAb +UKCAT (inc chem, biol) (Medicine) (IB 36 pts HL 665)

Imperial London – AAAb +BMAT (inc AL biol/chem+sci/maths) (Medicine) (HL 655)

Liverpool – AAAb (inc chem+biol at AL/AS) 410 pts (Med 6 yrs) (IB 38 pts HL 676)

London (King's) – AAAb **or** AAaab +UKCAT (inc AL chem/biol **or** AS b chem/biol) (Medicine 5 yrs) (IB 38 pts HL 655)

London (QM) – AAAb +UKCAT (inc chem and/or biol to at least AS b with 1 of these (or both) to A2 +1 other sci) (Med 5 yrs) (IB 36 pts HL 665)

London (St George's) – AAAb +UKCAT (inc chem+biol) (Medicine 5 yrs) (HL 665)

390 pts **Lancaster** – (application through Liverpool University. See Admissions Information below) AABB (inc chem+biol at AL/AS) 390 pts (Medicine)

London (UCL) – AAA+AS (inc AL chem+biol) (Med 6 yrs) (IB 38 pts HL 6 biol 6 chem 6)

380 pts **Cambridge** – A*AA +BMAT college offers may vary (inc AL biol/chem/maths/phys; chem reqd at least at AS; some colleges may require 3 sci ALs) (Med 6 yrs) (IB 38–42 pts)

360 pts **Birmingham** – AAA (inc AL chem+1 from biol/maths/phys; AS biol grade b if not offered at AL: hum biol acceptable) 360 pts (Med 5 yrs)

Brighton and Sussex (MS) – A*AB–AAA (inc AS biol/chem) +AL 360 pts (Medicine 5 yrs) (IB 37 pts HL 17 pts)

Cardiff – AAB +UKCAT (inc 2 subjs from chem, biol, phys, stats inc chem/biol at AS if not at AL) (Med 6 yrs) (IB 36 pts HL 18 pts)

Dundee – AAA (Med 6 yrs Pre-Med Year) (IB 34 pts HL 766)

Durham – Offered through a partnership between Newcastle and Durham Universities. (Only Phase I of II available at Durham) AAA +UKCAT (inc AL chem/biol pref 1 non-sci at AL/AS) (Medicine 2 yr) (IB 38 pts HL chem 6)

Keele – 360 pts (inc AL chem biol + 1 from maths/phys + 1 from a rigorous academic subj if only 2 sci subjs are offered) (Medicine) (IB 34 pts)

Leeds – AAA +UKCAT (inc chem + biol) (Med 5 yrs) (IB 36 pts HL chem 6)

Leicester – AAA +UKCAT 3AL **or** 340–400 pts +UKCAT (inc 4AS in yr 12 inc A chem, biol at AL/AS) (Med 5 yrs) (IB 36 pts HL chem biol 6)

London (King's) – AAA–BCC + UKCAT (Ext Med degree prog 6 yrs)

Manchester – AAA +UKCAT (inc AL chem+1 from biol/hum biol/phys/maths +1 other subj) (Med 5 yrs)

Newcastle – Offered through a partnership between Newcastle and Durham Universities AAA +UKCAT (inc AL chem/biol pref 1 non-sci at AL/AS) (Medicine 5 yrs) (IB 38 pts HL chem 6)

Nottingham – AAA + UKCAT (inc AL chem+biol) (Med 5 yrs) (IB 36 pts)

Oxford – AAA +BMAT (inc AL chem+1 from biol/phys/maths) (Med 6 yrs) (IB 38–40 pts)

Peninsula (MS) – AAA (Med 5 yrs) (IB 36 pts)

Sheffield – AAA (inc AB chem+sci subjs) (Med) (IB 34 pts HL 666)

Southampton – AAA (Wide access BCC) + UKCAT (inc AS chem+biol **or** AL chem) (Med 5 yrs) (IB 36 pts HL 18)

340 pts **Aberdeen** – AAB +UKCAT (chem required+1 from biol/maths/phys +1 other) (Med 5 yrs) (IB 36 pts HL 666)

Bristol – AAB (Med 6 yrs Pre-Med Yr)

Glasgow – AAB +UKCAT (inc AL chem+1 subj from maths/phys/bio pref; 4AS in yr 12; pts not accepted) (Med 5 yrs) (IB 36 pts)

St Andrews – AAB–AAA (inc AL chem+biol/maths/phys) (Med 5 yrs Fdn Yr 6 yrs) (IB 37 pts HL 766)

320 pts **London (UCL)** – Contact admissions office (Sci Eng New Med; Sci Mgt New Med)

Manchester – ABB (Med Fdn Yr 6 yrs)

260 pts Southampton – BCC (Med (Widening Access))
220 pts London (St George's) – Check with Ad Tutor 220 pts (Fdn Med)
West London – CCD (inc C min chem) (Hum Sci (Pre-Med option))

Medicine Foundation courses These are designed for students who have demonstrated high academic potential but who have taken non-science subjects or a combination including no more than one of biology, chemistry and physics.

Alternative offers See **Chapter 7** and **Appendix 1** for grades/UCAS Tariff points information for the International Baccalaureate, Scottish Highers/Advanced Highers, the Welsh Baccalaureate, the Irish Leaving Certificate, the Cambridge Pre-U Diploma, the Advanced Diploma and the Extended Project.

OTHER HIGHER EDUCATION COURSES IN THE SUBJECT FIELD
Foundation and other courses (contact the institutions for details) Brighton and Sussex (MS) (260 pts), Cardiff (370 pts), Coventry, Hertfordshire (Paramed Sci), London (King's), London (St George's) (Nat Sci ABBc), Portsmouth.

CHOOSING YOUR COURSE (SEE ALSO CH. 1)
Some course features
NB See **Chapter 6** for details of admissions tests to be taken **before** application.

Aberdeen Phase 1 covers the fundamentals of medical sciences followed in Phase 2 by the principles of clinical medicine. Clinical Teaching and Patient contact from Year 1. An intercalated BSc Medical Sciences degree is offered with placements across the Highlands and Islands.

Brighton Brighton and Sussex Medical School students are members of both universities. The course offers an integrated programme of academic and clinical experience with students working with patients from the first term. From Year 3, students are based at the Royal Sussex County Hospital in Brighton. Experience of Medical Practice in different medical settings in the UK or abroad takes place in Year 4.

Keele The five year course has five themes, which run through the course: (a) scientific basis of medicine (b) clinical communication (c) individual communication and population health (d) quality and efficiency in healthcare and (e) ethics, personal and professional development. There is also a Health Foundation year.

London (St George's) The MBBS has been designed to enhance the integration between scientific and clinical disciplines and to develop self-directed learning skills.

Newcastle Phase 1 (two years) of the medical course is taken either at Newcastle or Stockton. Students come into contact with patients at the start of their course, being attached to a family doctor and accompanying them on some of their rounds. Clinical applications are emphasised throughout the course alongside basic sciences. Students not taking science subjects may apply for the pre-medical course. See also **Durham**.

Oxford The course in Medicine lasts six years. The pre-clinical course lasts three years. This is followed by the clinical course, which is based in the John Radcliffe Hospital. A significant part of this course is examined by continuous assessment.

St Andrews Medical Sciences is a three-year degree course and leads to the ordinary degree of BSc in three years or to an honours degree in four years. Studies cover molecular biochemistry, human anatomy and human physiology. Half of graduates progress to a clinical place at Manchester University Medical School to follow the three-year clinical course, the remainder have a place at one of the four medical schools in Scotland, almost a third at Edinburgh.

Universities and colleges teaching quality See www.qaa.ac.uk; http://unistats.direct.gov.uk.

Top research universities and colleges (RAE 2008) (Pre-clinical and Human Biological Sciences) Oxford; London (UCL); Manchester; London (QM); London (King's); Bristol; Liverpool; Sussex. Hospital-based Clinical subjects Edinburgh; Cambridge; London (UCL); Oxford; Imperial London; London (King's); Birmingham; London (QM); Aberdeen; Manchester; Newcastle; Southampton; Bristol.

ADMISSIONS INFORMATION
Number of applicants per place (approx) Bristol 14; Peninsula (MS) 11.

Numbers of applicants (**a** UK **b** EU (non-UK) **c** non-EU **d** mature) Aberdeen **a**1513 for 162 places **b**1513 for 162 places **c**270 for 13 places (preference given to applicants from countries unable to provide a medical training); Birmingham **a**5 **b**25 Grad entry 12; Brighton and Sussex (MS) **a**10 **c**10; Cambridge **a**5; Cardiff **a**20 (6-year course) **c**22 (preference given to applicants from countries not providing a medical training); Dundee **a**7 (Pre-Med yr 11); East Anglia **a**7; Edinburgh **a**11 (international applicants not normally called for interview); Glasgow **a**6 **c**20; Hull York (MS) **a**130 **b**130 **c**10; Imperial London **a**7 **c**25; Leeds **a**2156 **b**97 **c**352 **d**488; Leicester **a**10; Liverpool **a**8; London (King's) **a**311 **b**311 places **c**25 places; London (QM) **a**8 **c**20; London (St George's) **a**3200 **b**250 **c**260 **d**1950; Manchester **a**7 **c**10; Newcastle **a**10 (Pre-Med yr 27) **c**14; Nottingham **a**9 **c**15; Oxford **a**26% success rate **c**10; Queen's Belfast **a**4 **c** (a small number of places are allocated); Sheffield **a**17 (For six-year courses the number of applicants per place averages 30); St Andrews **a**8; London (UCL) **c**24.

Admissions tutors' advice Policies adopted by all medical schools are very similar. However, a brief outline of the information provided by admissions tutors is given below. Further information should be obtained direct from institutions. Applicants wishing to contact medical schools should do so either by letter or by telephone and not by e-mail.

Aberdeen Applicants must take the UKCAT in the year of application. This also applies to those students seeking deferred entry and those who are reapplying. In the past, students with scores between 513 and 776 have been called for interview. Interviews for some applicants. Applicants to show a knowledge of the core qualities required by doctors and evidence of teamwork and non-academic pursuits. Overseas applicants may be interviewed abroad. Interviews last about 15 minutes. Most offers made in March. Points equivalent results not accepted. Re-sits not normally accepted. International students English language entry requirement (or equivalent): IELTS 7.0. Minimum age on entry 17 years 5 months. Clinical teaching and patient contact in Year 2.

Birmingham Non-academic interests and extra-curricular activities noted in addition to academic factors. General studies not accepted, but points equivalent results may be accepted. Interviews last about 15 minutes with three interviewers – a GP, a surgeon and a student. Approximately 1000 called for interview; 10% take a year off which does not jeopardise the chances of an offer but candidates must be available for interview. Re-sit candidates who failed by a small margin are only considered in exceptional circumstances. Transfers of undergraduates from other medical schools not considered. International applicants must show a good standard of written and spoken English.

Brighton and Sussex (MS) An average UKCAT score is considered an advantage, a lower score is not regarded as a disadvantage. General studies not accepted. No offers made without an interview. Interviews last about 15 minutes with three selectors. Students are members of both universities. Years 3–5 take place in the Medical Education Centre at the Royal Sussex Hospital in Brighton. Clinical experience from Year 1.

Bristol No places offered without an interview. Top 10% of applicants called for interview lasting 15 minutes, remainder grouped into three categories: 'high reserve', 'hold' and 'unsuccessful' – some from the first two categories will be interviewed. Full details of the interview process are offered on the Bristol website. Widening participation panel considers appropriate candidates, 50 of whom will be interviewed. Criteria for selection: realistic and academic interest in medicine, commitment to helping others, wide range of interests, contribution to school/college activities, personal achievements. Interview criteria: reasons for wanting to study Medicine, awareness of current developments, communication skills, self-confidence, enthusiasm and determination to study, ability to cope with stress, awareness of the content of the course and career. General studies not acceptable. Deferred entry welcomed but applicants must be available for interview. Points equivalent results not accepted. International students English language requirement (or equivalent): IELTS 7.0.

Cambridge Some colleges insist on three science/maths subjects (Christs, Downing, Jesus, Magdalene, Newnham, Peterhouse, St John's, Trinity). Normally two interviews, each of 20 minutes each. Films of interviews on www.cam.ac.uk/admissions/undergraduate/interviews. Gap Year acceptable but for positive reasons. Clinical studies from Year 4; 50% of students continue at the Cambridge Clinical School (Addenbrooke's Hospital).

Cardiff Great emphasis placed on evidence of a caring nature and exposure to hospital/health environments. Applicant's comment: 'Two interviewers and a 15-minute interview. Mainly questions on "Why Medicine?" Very helpful students'. Points-equivalent results not accepted. Clinical studies from Year 1.

Dundee Preference given to candidates who achieve the right grades at the first sitting. A system of mini interviews has been introduced which enable students separate opportunities to sell themselves. Deferred entry acceptable. Clinical attachments in Year 4.

Durham (see also **Newcastle**) The medical course is offered in partnership with Newcastle University. Study is at Queen's Campus, Stockton. Preference given to applicants with relevant work experience in caring environment, hospital, voluntary capacity or through previous employment. Particular interest in recruiting local students, either school leavers or mature students. Interviews at Stockton with two selectors; may include a written personal qualities assessment test (PQA). Graduate applicants with a 2(ii) degree are not accepted even if they possess a Masters degree or a PhD. Applicants from non-EU countries must apply to Newcastle where there is a quota of places for overseas students. Clinical contact begins in Year 1.

East Anglia Criteria include academic requirements, capacity to cope with self-directed learning, team work, responsibility, motivation. Interview regarded as the acid test; seven stations are used for the interviews, candidates visit each station for one question with six minutes at each station. Two scenario questions, see www.med.uea.ac.uk/mbbs/mbbs application). English entry requirements IELTS 7.5. Clinical experience from Year 1.

Edinburgh All examination grades must be achieved at the first sitting; only in extenuating circumstances will re-sits be considered. Equal weighting given to academic and non-academic criteria. Non-academic criteria score based on personal qualities and skills, evidence of career exploration prior to application, breadth and level of non-academic achievements and interests. Work experience and work shadowing viewed positively but the admissions panel recognise that not all applicants have equal opportunities to gain such experience. Most school-leaving applicants are not interviewed. Graduate and mature applicants may be interviewed; 202 places available, one in seven receive an offer. International applicants not normally called for interview. Clinical experience from Year 1.

Glasgow General studies not accepted. Formal work experience expected. (Work experience scheme operated by staff at Monklands Hospital, Lanarkshire.) All interviews held in Glasgow including those for overseas students. Interviewers assess candidates' performance on five points (i) knowledge of the medical course and experience of self-directed learning, (ii) experience of teamwork, (iii) communication skills, (iv) understanding of a medical career, (v) enthusiasm and commitment to medicine. Only in extenuating circumstances (family illness etc) will second-time applications be considered. Points-equivalent results not accepted. Feedback available to all candidates who fail to achieve admission. Transfers from other medical schools not accepted. Clinical experience from Year 1.

Hull York (MS) Students apply to HYMS not to Hull or York universities. Students allocated places at Hull or York by ballot in Years 1 and 2. Non-EU applicants English language (or equivalent requirement) IELTS 7.0. Transfers from other medical schools not accepted. Disabilities listed on UCAS application do not affect the assessment of the application; 600 called for interview, 340 offered places. Interviews of 20 minutes with two people. Article to be read beforehand, with a question to follow. Formally structured interviews exploring academic ability, motivation, understanding of healthcare issues, communication skills, conscientiousness, empathy, tolerance and maturity. Questions are drawn from a bank of possible topics (available online prior to interview). Re-sits acceptable but with higher grades. Feedback to unsuccessful candidates after February. Clinical placements from Year 1.

Imperial London Fifteen-minute interviews with panel of four or five selectors. Not aimed at being an intimidating experience – an evaluation of motivation, capacity to deal with stress, evidence of working as a leader and team member, ability to multitask, likely contribution to university life, communication skills and maturity. Admissions tutor's comment: 'We look for resourceful men and women with wide interests and accomplishments, a practical concern for others and for those who will make a contribution to the life of the school and hospital. 'Results within two weeks. Re-sit candidates must have applied to Imperial School of Medicine previously, have achieved at least CCC and have predictions of AAA in the winter re-sit examinations and have extenuating circumstances to explain previous failure in the referee's statement. Candidates may also write directly to the School. Clinical contact in Year 1.

Keele Keele is no longer in partnership with the Manchester Medical School. All applications are now submitted to Keele. There are 130 places available, 10 for international students. There are three entry routes for Medicine: there is a Health Foundation Year (A104) for home and international applicants without the science A-levels required for the five-year course (chemistry or biology and one subject from chemistry, biology, mathematics or physics) and with grades of AAB not including chemistry beyond GCSE) although A-level biology is acceptable with non-science A-levels. Four GCSEs are also required at grades A/A* including English and mathematics at grade C or above. Successful completion of this course gives automatic entry to Year 1 of the five-year Medicine degree; 10 places are available on the graduate entry course for home/EU applicants who enter directly into Module 2 of the five-year course. Graduates must offer a 2i honours degree or better in a biomedically-related science for entry to this course although applicants with other backgrounds can be successful with appropriate prior study and preparation for GAMSAT. Resit candidates must achieve AAA. English requirement for international applicants is IELTS 7.0.

Lancaster The University delivers the curriculum of the Medical School of Liverpool University, with the academic base at Lancaster University and clinical placements in Lancashire and Cumbria. To apply, use Liverpool University's UCAS code and see www.liv.ac.uk/sme for course and application information.

Leeds Admissions tutors' comment: 'Consider your motivation carefully – we do!' Good verbal, non-verbal and presentational skills required. Candidates should: (i) be able to report on some direct experience of what a career in medicine is about; (ii) show evidence of social activities on a regular basis (eg, part-time employment, organised community experiences); (iii) show evidence of positions of responsibility and interests outside medical and school activities. Gap Years encouraged but candidates must be available for interview, 20% of all applicants interviewed. Points equivalent results not accepted. International students English language requirement (or equivalent): IELTS 7.5. Re-applications accepted from students who have achieved the right grades. Re-sits only considered in exceptional circumstances and with good supporting evidence; offer AAA. Transfers from other medical schools not encouraged. Clinical practice begins in Year 4.

Leicester Final award is a combined degree from both universities. Interview lasts 20 minutes with two selectors (one doctor and one final-year medical student; both have had interview training). Interview not an academic test. Selectors each score independently on motivation, communication skills and suitability for a career in medicine. Gap Years acceptable. Re-sits considered only in exceptional circumstances; offer AAA. Transfers from other medical schools not accepted. Clinical work commences in Year 1.

Liverpool Fifty medical places for the five-year medical course are offered at Lancaster University. Students follow the Liverpool curriculum and graduate with a Liverpool degree. Applications are made to Liverpool University (Code L41, course code 105). Evidence required of healthcare experience. Gap Year acceptable for positive reasons but applicants must be available for interview. Gap Year not possible for overseas students. First year Foundation programme offered for under-qualified international students. English language requirement (or equivalent): IELTS 7.5. Clinical contact from Year 1.

London (King's) Personal statement a significant factor in selection. Emphasis placed on appreciation of academic, physical and emotional demands of the course, commitment, evidence of working in a caring environment, communication skills and interaction with the general public. Approximately 1200 applicants (35%) called for interview. Clinical contact in Year 1.

London (QM) Personal statement a significant factor in selection. 'You are expected to write your own, with an honest reflection of your strengths and interests and you will be closely questioned on this statement at interview. We don't want people who are simply good at science. High grades are no guarantee of a place. For interview applicants are ranked by their UKCAT score – no predetermined scores. Interview of 15–20 minutes. Re-sits only considered in exceptional cases; offer AAAb. Clinical experience from Year 1.

London (St George's) Applicants must be taking A-level chemistry and biology (or one to A-level and the other to AS-level). You will be required to complete your A-levels within two years of study and be predicted between BBC and AAA and have taken a fourth distinct AS-level in which you have achieved (or are predicted) a B. If not, your application will be unsuccessful. However, if you are predicted AABb and have at least 416 pts from 8 subjects at GCSE including mathematics, English and dual award science (ie average of grade A) then you will be called for interview. All applicants expected to have work experience in a medical environment. No offers without an interview – predicted grades important in selecting candidates for interview. Four selectors and an interview of 15–20 minutes. Some students who are not predicted to get the grades of the offer are also interviewed and considered for a place. Transfers from other medical schools rare. International students English language requirement (or equivalent): IELTS 7.0. Deferred entry welcomed. Clinical experience commences in Year 3. (Fdn Med) This course is for mature non-graduate students only.

London (UCL) Three selectors interview applicants, each interview lasting 15–20 minutes; 30% of applicants interviewed. Qualities sought include motivation, awareness of scientific and medical issues, ability to express and defend opinions, maturity and individual strengths. Deferred entry for good reason is acceptable. Repeat applications only considered if candidate has previously received and held a firm offer from Royal Free or University College Medical School. Minimum age of entry 18 years. Transfers from other medical schools not accepted. International students may take the University Preparation Certificate for Science and Engineering (UPCSE) which is the minimum entry requirement for entry to Medicine. Clinical attachments start in Year 3.

Manchester Minimum age of entry 17 years; 341 places. Interviews with three selectors last about 15 minutes. Mitigating circumstances regarding the health or disposition of the candidate should appear on the referee's report. If you feel unwell before the interview inform the admissions tutor and the interview will be re-scheduled; pleas of infirmity cannot be accepted after the interview! Candidates should be aware of the advantages and disadvantages of problem-based learning and opinions may be asked. Ethical questions may be raised. Decisions will be made by the end of March. Re-sit offers only made to applicants who received an offer after interview the previous year and who marginally failed to achieve the required grades; increasingly such offers are only made in the light of extenuating circumstances. Second-time applicants should include their previous UCAS number on their statement. Clinical attachments from Year 3.

Newcastle (see also **Durham**) 225 places at Newcastle; 102 places at Durham. Applicants' comments (Durham): 'Two interviewers and a 25 minute interview. Very relaxed interview. Stockton campus small. Good community spirit but some way from Durham'; (Newcastle): 'I had an interview with two selectors who had a gentle, helpful manner. I didn't feel under pressure but felt stretched'. Retakes not considered except in special circumstances. Deferred entry accepted. Consideration given to candidates who have overcome significant disadvantages (eg caring for parents with ill health). Clinical experience from Year 3.

Nottingham Critical thinking and general studies not acceptable. Candidates requesting deferred entry are expected to undertake a constructive year. No offers are made without an interview. Candidates receive preliminary online questionnaire to be completed. Interviews 15 minutes with two selectors. Re-sit applicants who have previously applied will be reconsidered but only in extenuating circumstances. Deferred entry acceptable. International students English language requirement (or equivalent): IELTS 7.0. No transfers accepted from other medical schools. Clinical experience from Year 1. Applicant's comments: 'I had one interview. There were two interviewers: the first asked me questions based on my personal statement, the second asked no scientific questions, focusing on the problems of the NHS and asking how I would deal with certain problems. He finally asked me to convince him why he should offer me a place.'

Oxford Critical thinking and general studies are not acceptable. Biology is recommended at AS-level. 425 applicants called for interview on the basis of academic performance, test score and information on the application form. Ratio of interviewees to places approximately 2.5 to 1. No student admitted without an interview. All colleges use a common set of selection criteria. Candidate's comment (Lincoln College): 'Two interviewers and two interviews. Questions covered my hobbies and social life, and scientific topics to test my logical train of thought. A great university, but it's not the be-all and end-all if you don't get in'. Clinical experience commences in Year 4.

Peninsula (MS) In the first two years students will be based at either the Exeter or Plymouth universities, allocation taking place on a random basis. Qualities sought on the application and at interview: (i) integrity and honesty; (ii) motivation and commitment; (iii) empathy and non-judgemental attitudes; (iv) communication and listening skills; (v) teamwork; (vi) ability to cope with stress; (vii) problem-solving skills; (viii) awareness of one's strengths and weaknesses; (ix) reflectiveness; (x) suitable approach to life and people. Applicant's comment: 'I was asked to stand in the middle of the room and to demonstrate my commitment to Medicine in one minute! They then asked me to write my responses to a series of questions.' Clinical skills training commences in the first year.

Queen's Belfast Majority of applicants are school-leavers; 95% from Northern Ireland. When considering applicants' GCSE performance, the best nine subjects will be scored on the basis of 4 points for an A* and 3 points for an A. Points will also be given or deducted on each UKCAT paper. Offers for resitting applicants will be restricted. These applicants will have been expected to have missed their offer by one grade. A proportion of candidates will be called for interview. Interviews last about 15 minutes. A small number of places are allocated to non-EU applicants. Number of places restricted for re-sit applicants who have narrowly missed an offer at Queen's. Clinical experience from Year 1.

Sheffield Applications processed between October and end of March. Candidates may send additional information concerning extenuating circumstances or health problems. Interviews last 20 minutes with up to three selectors. Candidates re-sitting for the first time may be considered: offer AAA. Gap Year acceptable; medicine-related work very helpful. Clinical experience from Year 1.

Southampton Only mature, non-graduate applicants are selected for interview. All applicants should show in their UCAS personal statement and reference that they are (i) self-motivated and have initiative, (ii) literate and articulate, (iii) able to interact successfully with others, (iv) that they have learnt from their experiences with people in health and social care settings. Deferred entry accepted. Candidates who wish to change their year of entry should submit requests before mid-March. Patient contact from Year 1.

St Andrews Medical Science students take full three-year programme leading to BSc (Hons), followed by clinical studies at Manchester University. Interviews last about 20 minutes with two or three selectors. Special attention given to international students and those who achieve qualifications at more than one sitting. As far as possible the interview panel will reflect the gender and ethnic distribution of candidates for interview.

Warwick Graduate entry only to Medicine.

Advice to applicants and planning the UCAS personal statement (See also **Admissions tutors' advice**)
Nearly all universities now require either the UKCAT or BMAT entry tests to be taken before applying for Medicine. Check websites (www.ukcat.ac.uk; www.bmat.org.uk) for details of test dates and test centres and with universities for their requirements. It is essential that you check for the latest information before applying and that you give yourself plenty of time to make arrangements for sitting these tests (see also **Chapter 6**).

Admissions tutors look for certain personal qualities (see **Admissions information** above) and these will emerge in your personal statement, at the interview and on your school or college reference. There should be evidence of scientific interest, commitment, enthusiasm, determination, stability, self-motivation, ability to organise your own work, interest in the welfare of others, communication skills, modesty (arrogance and over-confidence could lead to rejection!), breadth of interest, leadership skills, stamina, good physical and mental health.

Some kind of first–hand experience in a medical setting is almost obligatory for those applying for Medicine (see also under **Admissions tutors' advice**). Depending on your personal contacts in the medical profession, this could include observing operations (for example, orthopaedic surgery), working in hospitals and discussing the career with your GP. Remember that your friends and relatives may have medical conditions that they would be willing to discuss with you – and all this will contribute to your knowledge and show that you are informed and interested. Read medical and scientific magazines and keep up–to–date with important current issues – AIDS, swine 'flu, assisted dying, abortion. Community work, clubs, societies, school and social activities should be mentioned. Show that you have an understanding of the role of health professionals in society and the social factors that influence health and disease. And finally, a comment from one admissions tutor 'Don't rush around doing things just for your CV. If you are a boring student, be an incredibly well–read boring student! You can play netball, rugby, hockey, make beautiful music and paint with your feet, but if you fail to get the grades you'll be rejected. '

Misconceptions about this course **Liverpool** Some applicants think that three science subjects at A-level are required to study Medicine – wrong! **London (St George's)** That you should be white, middle class and male: 60% of medical students are now female and 53% of our students are not white.

Selection interviews All medical schools interview candidates. See **Admissions tutors' advice** and also **Chapter 6**. **Yes** Oxford (13%).

Interview advice and questions Questions will vary between applicants, depending on their UCAS statements and their A/AS-level subjects. Questions are likely to relate to A-level specific subjects, general medicine topics and unconnected topics (see also **Admissions tutors' advice**). The following questions will provide a guide to the range of topics covered in past interviews. Outline the structure of DNA. What is meant by homeostasis? Is a virus a living organism? What has been the most important advance in biology in the last 50 years? What interests you about (i) science, (ii) biology, (iii) chemistry? Why did you choose the particular AS/A-level subjects you are doing? Why do you want to study Medicine/become a doctor? Do you expect people to be grateful? Why do you want to study here? Why should we take you? What do you do to relax? What do you do when you have three or four things to do, and they are all equally urgent? How do you balance work and all the outside activities you do? Do you agree with the concept of Foundation hospitals? What do you think about polyclinics? Do you think NHS doctors and staff should be able to take private patients? If you were in charge of finances for a large health authority, what would be your priorities for funding? If you had to decide between saving the life of a young child and that of an old person, what would you do? Would you treat lung cancer patients who refuse to give up smoking? What do you understand by 'gene therapy'? Can you give any examples? In your opinion what is the most serious cause for concern for the health of the UK? What do you want to do with your medical degree? What do you think the human genome project can offer medicine? Should we pay for donor organs? Where do you see yourself in 15 years' time? What was the last non-technical book you read? What is your favourite piece of classical music? List your top five novels. What is your favourite play? What politician do you admire the most? Who made the most valuable contribution to the 20th century? Why do you think research is important? Why is teamwork important? What do you think about the NHS's problems?? Do you think that sport is important? What did you gain from doing work experience in a nursing home? What were the standards like? How does the medical profession deal with social issues? What societies will you join at university? How could you compare your hobby of rowing with medicine? Do you agree that it is difficult to balance the demands of being a doctor with those of starting a family? In doing a medical course, what would you find the most emotionally challenging aspect? How would you cope with emotional strain? What do you think about going to war with Iraq? Who should have priority for receiving drugs in a 'flu epidemic/ pandemic? How would you deal with the death of a patient? What are stem cells? Why are they controversial? How is cloning done? What constitutes a human being? Describe an egg. How can you measure intelligence? How do we combat genetic diseases? How are genes actually implanted? What do you want to talk about? If you were a cardiothoracic surgeon, would you perform a heart by-pass operation on a smoker? What are the negative aspects of becoming a doctor? At some interviews essays may be set, eg (i) 'A scientific education is a good basis for a medical degree: discuss'; (ii) 'Only drugs that are safe and effective should be prescribed to patients: discuss'. Occasionally applicants at interview may be given scenarios to discuss (see **East Anglia** under **Admissions tutors' advice**). See **Chapter 6**. **Oxford** Tell me about drowning. What do you think of assisted suicide? Would you give a 60-year-old woman IVF treatment? When are people dead?

Reasons for rejection (non-academic) Insufficient vocation demonstrated. No steps taken to gain practical experience relevant to medicine. Doubts as to the ability to cope with the stress of a medical career. Not enough awareness about the career. Lack of knowledge about the course. Applicant appears dull and lacking in enthusiasm and motivation. Lacking a caring, committed attitude towards people. No evidence of broad social, cultural or sporting interests or of teamwork. Poor or lack of communication skills. Arrogance. Over-confident at interview. Unrealistic expectations about being a doctor.

Age at entry Applicants must be 17 years old on 30 September of the year of entry. However, some medical schools stipulate 17 years 6 months, and a small number stipulate 18 years. Those considering entry at 17 would probably be advised to take a Gap Year.

Health requirements Medical schools require all students to have their immunity status for hepatitis B, tuberculosis and rubella checked on entry. Offers are usually made subject to satisfactory health screening for hepatitis B. In line with advice from the General Medical Council, students will not be admitted to courses who are found to be e-antigen positive when screened within the first week of the course. Candidates accepting offers should assure themselves of their immunity status.

Mature students Medical schools usually accept a small number of mature students each year. However, several, if not the majority, reject applicants over 30 years of age. Some medical schools accept non-graduates although A-level passes at high grades are usually stipulated. The majority of applicants accepted are likely to be graduates with a first or upper second honours degree. **Birmingham** Maximum age at entry is 30 years. **Bristol** Maximum age at entry is 30 years. **Leeds** Maximum age at entry is 30 years. Applicants should hold the required A-level grades or a high class science degree; 15–20 places. **Southampton** 36 places available, maximum age 40; GCSE mathematics, physics, biology or double science required. Applicants with nursing qualifications should hold two grade B A-levels including chemistry. Mature students taking Access courses must achieve 70% in A2 chemistry.

Advice to graduate applicants Graduate applicants are considered by all medical schools. At some medical schools the Graduate Australian Medical Schools Admission Test (GAMSAT) and the Medical Schools Admissions Test (MSAT) are now being used to assess the aptitude of prospective applicants. Applicants, for example, at Peninsula (MS) are selected on the basis of three criteria: (i) an Honours degree at 2.2 or above; (ii) the GAMSAT score; (iii) performance at interview. All applicants must be EU students. **London (St George's)** Some students think that science graduates are the only ones to do well in GAMSAT: 40% of those on the course do not have a science degree or A-levels; however, work experience is essential.

GRADUATE DESTINATIONS AND EMPLOYMENT (2007/8 HESA)
Graduates surveyed 5020 **Employed** 4810 **In further study** 20 **Assumed unemployed** 5

Career note Applicants should also bear in mind that while most doctors do work in the NHS, either in hospital services or in general practice, not a few graduates choose to work in other fields such as public health, pharmacology, the environment, occupational medicine with industrial organisations, the armed services and opportunities abroad.

OTHER DEGREE SUBJECTS FOR CONSIDERATION
Biomedical/Medical Materials Science; Biology; Biotechnology; Clinical Sciences; Dentistry; Dietetics; Genetics; Health Sciences; Immunology; Medical Biochemistry; Medical Engineering; Medical Microbiology; Medical Physics; Medical Product Design; Medical Sciences; Medicinal Chemistry; Midwifery; Nursing; Nutrition; Occupational Therapy; Optometry; Osteopathy; Pharmacology; Pharmacy; Physiology; Physiotherapy; Psychology; Radiography; Speech Sciences; Sports Medicine; Veterinary Medicine; Virology – and Law! (The work of doctors and lawyers is similar: both are required to identify the relevant information – clinical symptoms or legal issues!)

MICROBIOLOGY

(see also Biological Sciences, Biology, Biotechnology, Genetics)

Microbiology is a branch of biological science specialising in the study of micro-organisms: bacteria, viruses and fungi. The subject covers the relationship between these organisms and disease and industrial applications such as food and drug production, waste-water treatment and future biochemical uses.

Useful websites www.scienceyear.com; www.sgm.ac.uk; www.nature.com/micro; www.microbes. info; www.asm.org; www.microbiol.org; see also Biochemistry, Biological Sciences and Biology.

NB The points totals shown to the left of the institutions are for ease of reference only. It must not be assumed that Tariff points are always used by institutions or that they can be substituted for an offer in grades. The level of an offer is not necessarily indicative of the quality of a course.

COURSE OFFERS INFORMATION

Subject requirements/preferences GCSE English and mathematics and science subjects. **AL** One or two mathematics/science subjects including chemistry and/or biology, required or preferred; grades sometimes specified.

NB In 2012 universities and colleges will differ in their use of GCE AL/AS unit grade information, A* grades, the Extended Project (EPQ), the Advanced Diploma and the Cambridge Pre-U examination when considering applicants and making offers. An EPQ may be accepted in place of an AS subject. Check websites of universities and colleges for the latest offers information.

Your target offers and examples of courses provided by each institution

380 pts **Cambridge** – A*AA (Biomed Eng option yrs 3–4)

360 pts **Glasgow** – AAA Faster route (Microbiol) (IB 38 pts HL 665)

340 pts **Birmingham** – AAB–BBB (Biol Sci (Microbiol)) (IB 32–34 pts)
Cardiff – AAB–ABB (Microbiology) (IB 32 pts HL 55 biol chem)
Heriot-Watt – AAB 2nd year entry (Biol Sci (Microbiol))
Imperial London – AAB 340 pts (Microbiology) (IB 36 pts HL 66)
Manchester – AAB–BBB (Microbiol Modn Lang) (IB 33–35 pts)
Sheffield – AAB–ABB (Genet Microbiol) (IB 35–33 pts)
Strathclyde – AAB 2nd yr entry (Immun Microbiol)

320 pts **Bristol** – ABB (Microbiol) (IB 32 pts HL 655)
Dundee – ABB 2nd yr entry (Microbiol) (IB 34 pts)
East Anglia – ABB (Microbiol) (IB 32 pts HL 555)
Glasgow – ABB–BBC (Microbiol) (IB 32 pts)
Leeds – ABB–BBB 320–300 pts (Microbiol Virol) (IB 34–32 pts HL 16–15 pts)
Leicester – ABB (Biol Sci (Microbiol)) (IB 32 pts HL 66)
Liverpool – ABB–BBB (Microbl Biotech) (IB 33–30 pts)
Newcastle – ABB (Biomed Sci + Med Microbiol) (IB 32 pts)
Surrey – ABB–BBB (Bioch (Tox)) (IB 32–28 pts)

300 pts **Aston** – BBC–BBB (Infec Immun) (IB 30 pts)
Heriot-Watt – BBB 1st yr entry (Biol Sci (Microbiol))
Nottingham – BBB (Microbiol Cert Euro St) (IB 28 pts)
Queen's Belfast – BBB (Microbiol) (IB 28 pts HL 555)
Reading – 300 pts (Microbiology)
Strathclyde – BBB 1st yr entry (Immun Microbiol)
Warwick – BBB (Med Microbiol Virol) (IB 32 pts)

280 pts **Aberystwyth** – 280–320 pts (Zool Microbiol)
Strathclyde – BBC 2nd yr entry (Bioch Microbiol)

260 pts **Bradford** – 260 pts (Biomed Sci (Med Microbiol))
Dundee – BCC 1st yr entry (Microbiol) (IB 30 pts)

Staffordshire – 260 pts (Bioch Microbiol) (IB 28 pts)
Strathclyde – BCC 1st year entry (Bioch Microbiol)
240 pts **Bristol UWE** – 240–300 pts (Microbiol)
Huddersfield – 240 pts (Microbl Sci)
London Met – 240 pts (Microbiol)
Manchester Met – 240 pts (Microbiol)
220 pts **Edinburgh Napier** – 220 pts (Microbiol Biotech)
Nottingham Trent – 220 pts (Biol Sci (Microbiol))
Westminster – CCD (Microbiology)
200 pts **Anglia Ruskin** – 200 pts (Genet Microbiol)
East London – 200 pts (Med Microbiol)
Wolverhampton – 200 pts (Microbiol)
180 pts **Glasgow Caledonian** – DDD (Microbiol)
140 pts **West Scotland** – CD (App Biosci Microbiol)
120 pts **London South Bank** – 120 pts (Biosci (Microbiol))

Alternative offers
See **Chapter 7** and **Appendix 1** for grades/UCAS Tariff points information for the International Baccalaureate, Scottish Highers/Advanced Highers, the Welsh Baccalaureate, the Irish Leaving Certificate, the Cambridge Pre-U Diploma, the Advanced Diploma and the Extended Project.

EXAMPLES OF FOUNDATION DEGREES IN THE SUBJECT FIELD
St Helens (Coll).

CHOOSING YOUR COURSE (SEE ALSO CH. 1)
Some course features
Aston (Infec Immun) Course is included in the Biology programmes and offers a placement year in industry.
Cardiff Modules offered in medical microbiology, genetic manipulation, ecology and microbial physiology and biochemistry.
Manchester Met Units cover medical microbiology, food and health, genetics and biological risk management. A 12 month placement is offered in Year 3.
Nottingham Special topics in virology, molecular biology, and food and environmental microbiology. Northern Food scholarships offered.

Universities and colleges teaching quality See www.qaa.ac.uk; http://unistats.direct.gov.uk.

Top research universities and colleges (RAE 2008) See **Biological Sciences**.

Examples of sandwich degree courses Aston; Bristol; Bristol UWE; Cardiff; De Montfort; Glamorgan; Leeds; London South Bank; Manchester; Nottingham Trent; West Scotland. See also **Biochemistry and Biological Sciences**.

ADMISSIONS INFORMATION
Number of applicants per place (approx) Aberystwyth 5; Bradford 6; Bristol 5; Cardiff 4; Dundee 5; Leeds 7; Liverpool 3; Nottingham 7; Strathclyde 10; Surrey 4; Swansea 5; Wolverhampton 4.

Advice to applicants and planning the UCAS personal statement Relevant experience, particularly for mature students. See **Biological Sciences** and also **Appendix 4**.

Selection interviews **Yes** Bristol, London South Bank, Nottingham (depends on application), Surrey, Swansea; **Some** Aberystwyth (mature applicants only), Cardiff, Leeds, Wolverhampton.

Interview advice and questions Examples of past questions include: Is money spent on the arts a waste? How much does the country spend on research and on the armed forces? Discuss reproduction in bacteria. What do you particularly like about your study of biology? What would you like to do after your degree? Do you have any strong views on vivisection? Discuss the differences between the courses you have applied for. What important advances have been made in the biological field recently? How would you describe microbiology? Do you know anything about the diseases caused by micro-organisms? What symptoms would be caused by which particular organisms? See **Chapter 6**.

AFTER-RESULTS ADVICE

Offers to applicants repeating A-levels Higher Bristol, Strathclyde, Swansea, Warwick; **Possibly higher** East Anglia, Nottingham; **Same** Aberystwyth, Anglia Ruskin, Bradford, Cardiff, Leeds, Liverpool, Wolverhampton.

GRADUATE DESTINATIONS AND EMPLOYMENT (2007/8 HESA)

Graduates surveyed 430 **Employed** 140 **In further study** 160 **Assumed unemployed** 40

Career note See **Biology**.

OTHER DEGREE SUBJECTS FOR CONSIDERATION

Animal Sciences; Biochemistry; Biological Sciences; Biology; Biotechnology; Genetics; Medical Sciences; Medicine; Molecular Biology; Pharmacology; Physiology.

MUSIC

(including **Music Technology**; see also **Technologies**)

Theory and practice are combined to a greater or lesser extent in most university Music courses and from which about 50% or more of graduates will go on to non-music careers. However, courses are also offered by Conservatoires and Schools of Music where the majority of applicants are aiming to become professional musicians. For these courses the ability to perform on an instrument is more important than academic ability and offers are therefore likely to be lower. See also **Appendix 2**. Some applications are made through the Conservatoires Admissions Service (CUKAS): see **Chapter 6** for details.

Useful websites www.arts.org.uk; www.communitymusic.org; www.ism.org; www.bpi-med.co.uk; www.roh.org.uk; www.nyo.org.uk; www.bbc.co.uk/youngmusican; www.cukas.ac.uk.

NB The points totals shown to the left of the institutions are for ease of reference only. It must not be assumed that Tariff points are always used by institutions or that they can be substituted for an offer in grades. The level of an offer is not necessarily indicative of the quality of a course.

COURSE OFFERS INFORMATION

Subject requirements/preferences GCSE A foreign language and mathematics may be required. A good range of As and Bs for popular universities. **AL** Music plus an instrumental grade usually required.

NB In 2012 universities and colleges will differ in their use of GCE AL/AS unit grade information, A* grades, the Extended Project (EPQ), the Advanced Diploma and the Cambridge Pre-U examination when considering applicants and making offers. An EPQ may be accepted in place of an AS subject. Check websites of universities and colleges for the latest offers information.

Your target offers and examples of courses provided by each institution

380 pts **Cambridge** – A*AA college offers may vary (Mus) (IB 38–42 pts HL 766–777)
        Imperial London – A*mathsAA (Phys St Musl Perf) (IB 38 pts. HL 666)
        London (King's) – AAA+AS **or** AAaab (Mus) (IB 38 pts HL mus 7)
360 pts **Durham** – AAA (Comb Arts Mus) (IB 37 pts)
        Manchester – AAA–AAB inc gr 8D inst/voice, gr 6 piano (Mus Dr) (IB 35 pts)
        Oxford – AAA (Music) (IB 38–42 pts)
        Southampton – AAA (Maths Mus) (IB 36 pts HL 18 pts)
        Warwick – AAA (Mus)

BA Music
Joint honours also available with
Theatre
English
Games Design
Film and Television Studies

BA Sonic Arts
Joint honours also available with
Games Design
Theatre

BMus Musical Performance

BMus Musical Composition

Find out more about the School of Arts at www.brunel.ac.uk

Brunel
UNIVERSITY
L O N D O N

340 pts **Birmingham** – AAB (Mus courses) (IB 36 pts)
Bristol – AAB–BBB (inc ABRSM gr 5 piano) (Mus Fr/Ger/Ital) (IB 35–30 pts)
Cardiff – AAB–BBB (inc gr 8 theor+gr 8 prac) (Mus Welsh) (IB 33 pts)
Durham – AAB (Mus; Educ St Mus)
Glasgow – AAB–ABB (+ gr 8 ABRSM) (Mus courses MA) (IB 32–34 pts)
Leeds – AAB + gr. 5 ABRSM (Mus Multim Electron) (IB 36 pts HL 17 pts)
Newcastle – AAB–ABB (Mus courses) (IB 35 pts HL mus 5)
Surrey – AAB 340 pts (Mus Snd Rec (Tonmeister))

320 pts **City** – ABB–BBC (Mus)
Leeds – ABB (Pop Wrld Mus) (IB 33 pts)
Liverpool – ABB 320 pts (Mus Pop Mus) (IB 33 pts)
London (Gold) – ABB (Mus Comp) (IB 32 pts)
London (RH) – ABB (inc gr 7 instr) 320 pts (Mus Pol St) (IB 35 pts HL mus 6)
Nottingham – ABB (Music BA) (IB 34 pts)
Oxford Brookes – ABB (Mus Psy)
Sheffield – ABB (Mus) (IB 35–30 pts)
Southampton – ABB (Accoust Mus) (IB 32 pts HL 16 pts)
Surrey – (inc gr 7) 320 pts (Mus) (IB 32 pts)
Sussex – ABB–BBB (inc gr 7) (Mus Inform) (IB 32–34 pts)
York – ABB (Mus) (IB 34 pts HL mus 6)

300 pts **Aberdeen** – BBB (Mus BMus; Mus St courses)
Bournemouth – 300 pts (Mus Aud Tech)
Brunel – Contact admissions office (Thea Mus; Thea Snc Arts)
East Anglia – BBB–BBC ABRSM Gr 8 (Mus Tech) (IB 30 pts)
Edinburgh – BBB–AAA (Hist Art Hist Mus) (IB 34 pts HL 555)
Kent – 300 pts (Mus Tech)

Lancaster – BBB–BBC 300–280 pts (Mus Tech) (IB 28–29 pts)
London (SOAS) – BBB (Mus St; Mus Arbc; Mus Dev St; Mus Jap)
Newcastle – BBB (Folk Trad Mus BMus) (IB 32 pts)
Queen's Belfast – BBB–BBCb (Mus Tech) (IB 29 pts HL 655)
Roehampton – 300–360 pts (P Educ Mus)
Sheffield – BBB–BBC (Mus Hisp St; Mus E As St)
Surrey – BBB (inc gr 5 theory) (Crea Mus Tech) (IB 32 pts)
York – BBB (Mus Tech Sys BEng)

280 pts **Birmingham City** – 280 pts (Mus Tech) (IB 30 pts)
Brighton – BBC (Dig Mus Snd Arts)
Bristol UWE – 280 pts (Aud Mus Tech; Crea Mus Tech; Mus Sys Eng)
Brunel – BBC (inc AL mus) (Mus) (IB 30 pts)
Glamorgan – 280–320 pts (Pop Mus; Pop Mus Tech)
Gloucestershire – 280 pts (Pop Mus; Mus Media Mgt)
Huddersfield – 280–300 pts (Mus Dr; Mus Tech; Mus; Mus Jrnl)
Leeds (CMus) – BBC 280 pts (Mus Prod)
Oxford Brookes – BBC (Snd Tech Dig Mus)
Salford – 280 pts (Mus) (IB 30 pts)
Stranmillis (UC) – BBC (Mus Educ)
Teesside – 280 pts (Mus Tech)

260 pts **Bangor** – 260–300 pts (Mus) (IB 28 pts)
Bolton – 260 pts (Mus Cr Ind Bus)
Brunel – Contact admissions office (Gms Des Snc Arts)
Cumbria – 260–280 pts (Musl Thea Perf courses)
Edge Hill – 260–280 pts (Mus Snd Dr; Media Mus Snd)
Hull – (inc gr 7 **or** above on 1st study instr/voice) 260–300 pts (Mus Fr/Ger/Ital/Span) (IB 28 pts)
Keele – 260–320 pts (Mus courses; Mus Tech)
Lincoln – 260 pts (Aud Prod)
Liverpool (LIPA) – 260 pts (Mus; Mus (Perf Arts); Snd Tech)
Liverpool Hope – 260–320 pts (Mus courses)
Liverpool John Moores – 260 pts (Pop Mus St)
Manchester Met – 260 pts (Crea Mus Prod; Mus Comb Hons; Pop Mus courses)
Strathclyde – BCC (App Mus)

240 pts **Anglia Ruskin** – 240 pts (Mus; Mus Dr; Aud Tech Crea Mus Tech)
Bath Spa – (+ gr 8) 240–300 pts (Crea Mus Tech)
Bradford – 240 pts (Media St Mus Tech)
Canterbury Christ Church – 240 pts (Mus courses)
Chester – 240–280 pts (Pop Mus courses)
Coventry – 240 pts (Mus Perf Prof Prac; Mus Cmpsn Prof Prac; Mus Tech)
De Montfort – 240 pts (Mus Tech Innov; Mus Tech; Mus Tech Perf)
Edinburgh Napier – 240 pts (Pop Mus)
Hull – 240 pts (Crea Mus Tech courses)
Hull (Coll) – BCC–CCC 240 pts (Crea Mus Tech courses)
Kingston – 240–360 pts (Mus; Mus Tech)
Leeds (CMus) – 240 pts (Mus; Mus Jazz; Pop Mus St)
Leeds Met – 240 pts (Music Perf/Prod)
Northampton – 240–280 pts (Pop Mus courses)
Plymouth – 240 pts (P Mus BEd)
Royal Scottish (RSAMD) – Offered jointly with University of Glasgow check with College (Mus BEd)
Southampton Solent – 240 pts (Mus Prom; Pop Mus Jrnl)
Staffordshire – 240–280 pts (Crea Mus Tech; Mus Tech; e-Mus)
Swansea Met – 240 pts (Mus Tech)
Ulster – 240–280 pts (Mus; Mus Dance; Mus Ir; Mus Psy)

220 pts **Creative Arts** – 220 pts (Mus Jrnl)
Falmouth (UC) – 220 pts (Crea Mus Tech)
Hertfordshire – 220–260 pts (Mus Cmpsn Tech; Mus Tech)
London Met – 220–240 pts (Mus Media Mgt)
Oxford Brookes – CCD (Mus; Mus Comb Hons)
Plymouth – 200 pts (Music)
Sunderland – 220–360 pts (Mus courses)
Teesside – 220–280 pts (Contemp Mus Crea)
York St John – 220–260 pts (Mus courses)

200 pts **Bedfordshire** – 200 pts (Mus Tech) (IB 24 pts)
Bucks New – 200–240 pts (Aud Mus Prod; Mus Arts Mgt; Mus Mgt Arst Dev)
Doncaster (Coll Univ Centre) – 200 pts (Crea Mus Tech)
East London – 200 pts (Mus Cult (Theor Prod))
London Met – 200–240 pts (Musl Instr courses)
Middlesex – 200–300 pts (Mus Arts Mgt; Jazz; Mus Perf; Mus Comp)
Portsmouth – 200–280 pts (Mus Snd Tech)
UCP Marjon – 200 pts (Live Mus)
West London – 200 pts (Mus Tech courses)
Wolverhampton – 200 pts (Mus; Mus Pop Mus; Mus Tech)

180 pts **Derby** – 180–240 pts (Pop Mus Prod joint courses)
Liverpool (LIPA) – BC 180 pts (Mus Thea Enter Mgt)
Reading – 180 pts (Ed St P Mus)
UHI Millennium Inst – DDD 180 pts (Gael Trad Mus)

160 pts **Bishop Grosseteste (UC)** – DDE 160 pts (Educ St Mus)
Central Lancashire – 160–260 pts (Mus Thea; Mus Prac; Mus Prod; Mus Prod Arts)
Chichester – DDD 160-200 pts (Mus joint courses)
Colchester (Inst) – BD 160 pts (Mus; Musl Thea)
Grimsby (IFHE) – 160 pts (Crea Mus)
Rose Bruford (Coll) – 160 pts (Mus Tech)
Southampton Solent – 160 pts (Audio Tech)
Truro (Coll) – 160 pts (Contemp Wrld Jazz)
West Scotland – CC (Mus Tech; Commer Mus)
Westminster – CC (Commer Mus) (IB 24 pts)

150 pts **West London** – 150 pts (Pop Mus Perf)

120 pts **Blackpool and Fylde (Coll)** – 120–300 pts (Musl Thea)
RCMus – Check with Ad. Tutor 120 pts (Mus)

100 pts and below **Birmingham City** – 80 pts (Jazz; Mus)
Guildhall (Sch Mus Dr) – 100 pts (Thea; Mus)
Havering (Coll) – contact the College (Mus Prac Tech)
London (RAcMus) – Contact the Academy EE (Mus BMusD)
Manchester (RNCM) – Check with College 80 pts (Mus Bmus; Mus)
Royal Scottish (RSAMD) – check with College (Mus; Scot Mus BA; Mus Thea)
Royal Welsh (CMusDr) – contact College and apply direct (Pop Mus; Perf Prod)
Trinity Laban Consv – Check with Ad. Tutor (inc gr 8) (Perf BMus; Perf St MMus)
UHI Millennium Inst – Contact admissions (Pop Mus Perf)

Alternative offers

See **Chapter 7** and **Appendix 1** for grades/UCAS Tariff points information for the International Baccalaureate, Scottish Highers/Advanced Highers, the Welsh Baccalaureate, the Irish Leaving Certificate, the Cambridge Pre-U Diploma, the Advanced Diploma and the Extended Project.

EXAMPLES OF FOUNDATION DEGREES IN THE SUBJECT FIELD

Bath Spa; Bournemouth; Brighton; Bucks New; Canterbury Christ Church; Central Lancashire; Colchester (Inst); Creative Arts; Exeter (Coll); Farnborough (CT); Hereford (CA); Hull (Coll); Kent; Leeds City (Coll); Manchester (Coll); Newcastle (Coll); North Lindsey (Coll); Northbrook (Coll); Norwich City (Coll);

Nottingham New (Coll); Plymouth; Rotherham (CAT); St Helens (Coll); South Essex (Coll); South Tyneside (Coll); Suffolk (Univ Campus); Sunderland; Truro (Coll); West Anglia (Coll); West London; Westminster City (Coll).

CHOOSING YOUR COURSE (SEE ALSO CH. 1)

Some course features

Bournemouth The Music and Audio Technology course focuses on the application of hardware and software technologies to create music. There is a 40 week placement in Year 3.

Brighton The course in Music Performance and Visual Art utilises the visual art/music interface with close links between dance, theatre and music. There is also a Digital Music degree in which music is studied relating to computers and electronic instruments, and a course in Music Production.

Chichester The Music degree has four strands – Performance and Direction, Composing, Arranging and Improvising, Style and Genre, History and Culture. There are also courses in Musical Theatre, Performing Arts, Commercial Music.

Edinburgh Music is a three-year or four-year honours course. In each year the curriculum is broadly divided between composition, history and practical studies. Options are introduced in the third year and include electronic music but also cover music technology and acoustics. There is also a BMus course in Music Technology.

Greenwich A degree in Entertainment Technologies and Music Production is offered to school leavers. There is a Creative Production and Technology course for students who have completed a HND in Music and who intend to pursue careers in the music industry.

Hertfordshire Courses are offered in Composition and Technology, Sound Design Technology and Entertainment Industry Management, which has three pathways in studio production, entertainment industry and the classical music industry. There are also over 15 joint courses with Electronic Music.

Liverpool Hope A large number of combined courses with music are offered in which students can specialise in popular or classical music. BA (QTS) students specialise in the latter.

Liverpool John Moores A very broad course in Popular Music Studies includes some work experience. There is also a course in Audio and Music Production.

Teesside Three-year full-time or four-year sandwich courses are offered in Digital Music and Music Software Development.

UCP Marjon The course in Live Music provides a programme of study focusing on performance technology and media work.

Universities and colleges teaching quality See www.qaa.ac.uk; http://unistats.direct.gov.uk.

Top research universities and colleges (RAE 2008) London (RH); Birmingham; Manchester; Southampton; Cambridge; London (King's); Sheffield; Oxford; York; Newcastle; Nottingham.

Examples of sandwich degree courses Birmingham City; Bournemouth; Bristol UWE; Brunel; City; Glamorgan; Gloucestershire; Hertfordshire; Huddersfield; London Met; Portsmouth; Staffordshire; Surrey; Teesside.

ADMISSIONS INFORMATION

Number of applicants per place (approx) Aberystwyth 5; Anglia Ruskin 5; Bangor 4; Bath Spa 8; Birmingham 8; Bristol 12; Brunel 7; Cambridge 3, (Hom) 4; Cardiff 6; Chichester 4; City 7; Colchester (Inst) 4; Cumbria 7; Durham 5; East Anglia 12; Edinburgh 11; Edinburgh Napier 3; Glasgow 4; Huddersfield 2; Hull 21; Kingston 18; Lancaster 8; Leeds 18; Liverpool 9; Liverpool (LIPA) 12; London (Gold) 7; London (King's) 10; London (RAcMus) 7; London (RH) 7; London (SOAS) 4; London Met 10; Manchester (RNCM) 8; Middlesex 23; Newcastle 24; Northampton 3; Northumbria 12; Nottingham 7; Oxford Brookes 12; Queen's Belfast 6; RCMus 10; Roehampton 4; Rose Bruford (Coll) 15; Royal Scottish (RSAMD) 6; Salford 5; Southampton 5; Strathclyde 15; Surrey 6, (Tonmeister) 12; Trinity Laban Consv 4; Ulster 8; Worcester 8; York 8; York St John 2.

Advice to applicants and planning the UCAS personal statement In addition to your ability and expertise with your chosen musical instrument(s), it is also important to know your composers and to take a critical interest in various kinds of music. Reference should be made to these, visits to concerts listed and any special interests indicated in types of musical activity, for example, opera, ballet. Work with orchestras, choirs and other musical groups should also be included and full details given of any competitions entered and awards obtained. See **Chapter 5** for details of applications for Music courses at Conservatoires. **Guildhall (Sch Mus Dr)** International applicants sending extra documentation from overseas must make sure that for Customs purposes they indicate that they will pay any import tax charged. **London (Gold)** We encourage students to bring examples of their written and creative work. **Royal Welsh (CMusDr)** Evidence of performance-related experience, eg youth orchestras, solo work, prizes, scholarships etc. Our course is a conservatoire course as opposed to a more academic university course. We offer a very high standard of performance tuition balanced with academic theory modules. **Surrey** (Snd Rec (Tonmeister)) Demonstration of motivation towards professional sound recording.

Misconceptions about this course Cardiff Some mistakenly think that the BMus scheme is either performance-based or something inferior to the principal music-based degree. **Salford** (Pop Mus Rec) This is not a specialised music technology degree: it is a music degree with specialisation in music technology and production. Specialisation can be significant in Year 3. BTEC Popular Music students must be prepared for the rigours of an academic degree. Some students expect the course to make them famous! **Surrey** Some believe that the Music course is exclusively performance-based (the course includes substantial academic and compositional elements).

Selection interviews Most institutions, plus audition to include a performance of a prepared piece (or pieces) on main instrument. **Yes** Doncaster (Coll Univ Centre), Guildhall (Sch Mus Dr) (Interviews mostly held at the School but also at Newcastle and in the USA.), Oxford (Music) 38%; **Some** Anglia Ruskin, Bath Spa, Bucks New, Cardiff, Coventry (Proforma used prior to interview – some students rejected at this stage), Liverpool (LIPA), Staffordshire (Mus Tech), Surrey.

Interview advice and questions
NB See also **Chapter 5** under Music.

Anglia Ruskin In addition to A-levels, we also require Grade 7 (good pass, first study) plus Grade 5 minimum keyboard standard.

Bangor Offer depends on proven ability in historical or compositional fields plus acceptable performance standard. Options include music therapy, recording techniques, jazz.

Bath Spa Some candidates interviewed. Required to perform and sight-read on main instrument, and given aural and critical listening tests. Discussion of previous performing, composing and academic experience. (Fdn Commer Mus) All applicants must submit a self-composed audio prior to interview. (Mus Tech) Applicants will be required to submit an audio portfolio demonstrating technical and creative skills.

Bristol (Mus Fr/Ger/Ital) No in-depth interviews; candidates invited to Open Days.

Cambridge (St Catharine's) At interview candidates may have to undergo some simple keyboard or aural tests (such as harmonisation of an unseen melody or memorisation of a rhythm). More importantly, they will have to comment on some unseen musical extracts from a stylistic and analytical point of view. Candidates are asked to submit some examples of work before the interview, from the fields of harmony and counterpoint, history, and analysis; they are also encouraged to send any other material such as compositions, programme notes or an independent essay on a subject of interest to the candidate. (Taking the STEP examination is not a requirement for admission.) Above all this, though, the main prerequisite for reading Music at St Catharine's is an academic interest in the subject itself.

Canterbury Christ Church Associated Board examinations in two instruments (or one instrument and voice); keyboard competence essential, particularly for the BEd course.

Colchester (Inst) Great stress laid on candidate's ability to communicate love of the subject.

Cumbria Admission by live performance or on tape. QTS applicants interviewed for teaching suitability. See **Chapter 6**.

Durham Grade 6 piano (Associated Board), a foreign language (GCSE grade A–C), A-level music grade B required.

East Anglia Only unusual and mature candidates are interviewed. Applicants are expected to perform music with insight and show genuine intellectual curiosity about music and its cultural background. At interview candidates will be asked to perform on their principal instrument. Those who play orchestral instruments or sing will also be expected to play simple music on the piano. At interview we look for applicants with proficiency in instrumental or vocal performance (preferably at Grade 8 standard or above), range of experience of music of many types and an intelligent attitude towards discussion.

Edinburgh Napier Most candidates are called for interview, although very well qualified candidates may be offered a place without interview. All are asked to submit samples of their work. Associated Board Grade 7 on piano is usually expected.

Huddersfield Have an open and inquisitive outlook with regard to all aspects of music from performing to composing, musicology to listening. Candidates auditioned on their principal instrument or voice. They will be asked about playing technique, interpretation and interests.

Hull (Coll) Good instrumental grades can improve chances of an offer and of confirmation in August. Students are not normally required to attend an audition/interview. Decisions will be made according to the information supplied on the UCAS application. Successful applicants will be invited to attend a departmental Open Day. We welcome applications from mature students and those with unconventional qualifications: in such cases an interview may be required.

Kingston Associated Board Grade 8 on main instrument is required, with at least Grade 4 on a keyboard instrument (where this is not the main instrument). Audition and interview may be required. Candidates with non-standard qualifications are interviewed and asked to bring samples of written work.

Lancaster Grade 8 Associated Board required on an instrument or voice and some keyboard proficiency (Grade 6) usually expected. We do not accept candidates without interview. For the Music degree, instrumental or vocal skills equivalent to Grade 8 required. For Music Technology, applicants should hold music theory Grade 5 or be able to demonstrate the ability to read a score. Applicants wishing to take practical studies will need instrumental or vocal skills equivalent to Grade 8.

Leeds Intending students should follow an academic rather than practical-oriented A-level course. The University is experimenting with abandoning the formal interview in favour of small group Open Days for those holding offers made on the UCAS information, to focus on a practical exchange of information relevant to the applicant's decision to accept or reject the offer. Grade 8 Associated Board on an instrument is a normal expectation.

Leeds (CMus) There will be an audition and an essay on music theory.

Liverpool (LIPA) In addition to performing in orchestras etc, give details of any compositions you have completed (the number and styles). Instrumentalists (including vocalists) should describe any performance/gig experience together with any musical instrument grades achieved. (Mus) Candidates should prepare two pieces of contrasting music to play on their chosen instrument. Candidates who have put song-writing/composition as either first or second choice should have a cassette, CD or minidisc of their work to play to the panel. (Snd Tech) Applicants must prepare a critical review of a sound recording of their choice which highlights the technical and production values that they think are the most important. Examples of recorded work they have undertaken should also be available at interview eg on CD, cassette or DAT. (Mus Perf Arts) Applicants should have A levels (or equivalent) and have completed Grade 5 Music Theory before the course commences.

London (Gold) The interview will include an aural discussion of music and the personal interests of the applicant.

London (RAcMus) All candidates are called for audition, and those who are successful are called for a further interview; places are offered later, subject to the minimum GCSE requirements being achieved. (BMus) Applicants sit a 50-minute written paper, and may also be tested on keyboard and aural performance.

For a quick reference offers calculator, fold out the inside back cover.

320 pts **Newcastle** – ABB/BBB (Sml Crft Tech BEng) (IB 32–34 pts HL maths phys 5)
　　　　 Strathclyde – ABB (Nvl Archit Sml Crft Eng) (IB 32 pts)
300 pts **Newcastle** – BBB (Mar Tech BEng) (IB 32 pts HL maths phys 5)
280 pts **Liverpool John Moores** – 280 pts (Mech Mar Eng MEng)
260 pts **Liverpool John Moores** – 260 pts (Mech Mar Eng BEng)
　　　　 Plymouth – BCC 260 pts (Mar Tech BEng) (IB 27 pts)
240 pts **Coventry** – 240 pts (Auto Trans Des (Boat))
　　　　 Liverpool John Moores – 240 pts (Naut Sci BSc)
200 pts **Plymouth** – 200 pts (Mar St (Ocn Ycht))
180 pts **South Tyneside (Coll)** – 180 pts (Mar Eng)
　　　　 Southampton Solent – 180 pts (Ycht Prod Surv; Ycht Pwrcrft Des)

Alternative offers
See **Chapter 7** and **Appendix 1** for grades/UCAS Tariff points information for the International Baccalaureate, Scottish Highers/Advanced Highers, the Welsh Baccalaureate, the Irish Leaving Certificate, the Cambridge Pre-U Diploma, the Advanced Diploma and the Extended Project.

EXAMPLES OF FOUNDATION DEGREES IN THE SUBJECT FIELD
Blackpool and Fylde (Coll); Cornwall (Coll); Liverpool John Moores; Plymouth City (Coll); South Devon (Coll); Southampton Solent.

CHOOSING YOUR COURSE (SEE ALSO CH. 1)
Some course features
Newcastle (Mar Tech; Off Eng; Sml Crft Tech; Nvl Archit) All MEng and BEng courses take a common Stage 1 first year and then follow their specialised degree programmes. Transfer is possible between MEng courses and to the Marine Technology BEng degree.
Southampton Solent (Ycht Pwrcrft Des) The course is fully accredited by the Royal Institution of Naval Architects. A foundation year is available.
Strathclyde (Nvl Archit) A broad-based engineering course covering engineering science, flotation and stability, ship and offshore structures design. Topics also include resistance and propulsion, ship structural analysis, marine engineering systems, business and management. Some opportunities for sponsorship and work experience.

Top research universities and colleges (RAE 2008) (Naval Architecture and Marine Engineering) Glasgow; Strathclyde.

ADMISSIONS INFORMATION
Number of applicants per place (approx) Newcastle 9; Southampton 4.

Advice to applicants and planning the UCAS personal statement Special interests in this subject area should be described fully. Visits to shipyards and awareness of ship design from the Mary Rose in Portsmouth to modern speedboats should be fully explained and the problems noted. See also **Engineering/Engineering Sciences** and **Marine/Maritime Studies**. See also **Appendix 4**.

Selection interviews Yes Newcastle, Southampton.

Interview advice and questions Because of the highly vocational nature of this subject, applicants will naturally be expected to discuss any work experience and to justify their reasons for choosing the course. See **Chapter 6**.

AFTER-RESULTS ADVICE
Offers to applicants repeating A-levels Higher Newcastle.

GRADUATE DESTINATIONS AND EMPLOYMENT (2007/8 HESA)
Graduates surveyed 30 **Employed** 20 **In further study** 5 **Assumed unemployed** 5

Career note A small proportion of naval architects work in the shipbuilding and repair industry, others are involved in the construction of oil rigs or may work for ship-owning companies. There are also a number of firms of marine consultants employing naval architects as managers or consultants.

OTHER DEGREE SUBJECTS FOR CONSIDERATION

Aeronautical Engineering; Civil Engineering; Electrical/Electronic Engineering; Geography; Marine Biology; Marine Engineering; Marine/Maritime Studies; Marine Technology; Mechanical Engineering; Oceanography; Physics; Shipping Operations; Transport Management.

NURSING and MIDWIFERY

(including **Paramedic Science**; see also **Biological Sciences, Community Studies/Development, Health Sciences/Studies**)

Nursing and Midwifery courses are designed to equip students with the scientific and caring skills demanded by medical science in the 21st century. Courses follow a similar pattern with an introductory programme of study covering clinical skills, nursing practice and the behavioural and social sciences. Thereafter, specialisation starts in adult, child or mental health nursing, or with patients with learning disabilities. Throughout the three-year course students gain extensive clinical experience in hospital wards, clinics, accident and emergency and high-dependency settings. UCAS handles applications for Nursing degree and diploma courses.

Useful websites www.scicentral.com; www.nhscareers.nhs.uk; www.nursingtimes.net; see also **Health Sciences/Studies** and **Medicine**.

NB The points totals shown to the left of the institutions are for ease of reference only. It must not be assumed that Tariff points are always used by institutions or that they can be substituted for an offer in grades. The level of an offer is not necessarily indicative of the quality of a course.

COURSE OFFERS INFORMATION

Subject requirements/preferences GCSE English and a science subject. Mathematics required at several universities. **AL** Science subjects required for some courses. **Other** requirements All applicants holding firm offers will require an occupational health check and Criminal Records Bureau (CRB) clearance and are required to provide documentary evidence that they have not been infected with hepatitis-B. (Paramed Sci) Full clean manual UK driving licence with at least a provisional C1 category.

NB In 2012 universities and colleges will differ in their use of GCE AL/AS unit grade information, A* grades, the Extended Project (EPQ), the Advanced Diploma and the Cambridge Pre-U examination when considering applicants and making offers. An EPQ may be accepted in place of an AS subject. Check websites of universities and colleges for the latest offers information.

Your target offers and examples of courses provided by each institution

Abbreviations used in this table A – Adult; C – Child; LD – Learning Disability; MH – Mental Health

340 pts **Southampton** – AAB (Midwif)
320 pts **Nottingham** – ABB (Nurs Sci MNursSci) (IB 27 pts)
Surrey – ABB (inc AL Sci) (Paramed St)
Surrey – ABB (Midwif)
300 pts **Birmingham** – BBB (Nurs A/MH) (IB 30–34 pts)
Bournemouth – 300 pts (Midwifery)
Bristol UWE – 300 pts (Midwif)
Cumbria – 300 pts (Midwif)
Edinburgh – BBB–AAA (Nurs St) (IB 34–35 pts HL 555)
Glasgow – BBB (Nurs A/C/LD/MH)
Leeds – BBB (Midwif; Nurs A/C/LD/MH)
London (King's) – BBCe (Nurs A/C/MH)
Manchester – BBB 300 pts (Midwif)
Southampton – BBC 300–280 pts (Nurs A/C/LD/MH)
Swansea – BBB 300 pts (Midwif)
280 pts **Bradford** – 280 pts (Midwif St)
East Anglia – 280 pyd (Midwif)

Hertfordshire – 280 pts (Paramed Sci)
Liverpool – BBC (Nursing) (IB 28 pts)
Northumbria – 280 pts (Midwif St)
Oxford Brookes – BBC–CCC (Nurs A)
Sheffield Hallam – 280 pts (Midwif)
Stirling – BBC (Midwif)
Suffolk (Univ Campus) – 280 pts (Midwif; Nurs A/C/MH)
Swansea – BBC–BBB 290 pts (Nurs A/C/MH)
Ulster – 280 pts (Nurs A/MH)
York – BBC (Nurs Prac A/C/LD/MH) (IB 28 pts)
260 pts **Bournemouth** – 260 pts (Nurs A/C/LD/MH)
Brighton – BBC (Nurs A/C/MH)
Coventry – 260 pts (Midwif)
East Anglia – BCC (Nurs A/C/LD/MH)
Edge Hill – BCC 260 pts (Nurs A/C/MH/LD; Midwif)
Huddersfield – BCC 260 pts (Midwif St)
Kingston – BCC (Midwif)
Manchester – BCC (Nurs A/C/MH) (IB 28 pts)
Northumbria – 260 pts (Nurs A/C/LD/MH) (IB 24 pts)
Nottingham – BCC (Nurs A/C/MH) (IB 28 pts)
Queen's Belfast – BC/CCD (with relevant subj) **or** BB/CCC (without relevabt subj) (Nurs A/C/LD/MH)
Salford – 260–280 pts (Midwif)
Teesside – BCC 260–360 pts (Midwif)
240 pts **Bangor** – CCC 240 pts (Midwif)
Birmingham City – CCC 240 pts (Nurs A/C/LD/MH; Midwif)
Brighton – CCC (Midwif) (IB 28 pts)
Canterbury Christ Church – CCC (Midwifery)
Cardiff – CCC 240 pts (Midwif) (IB 26 pts)
Central Lancashire – 240 pts (Midwif)
Coventry – CCC 240 pts (Nurs A/C/LD/MH) (IB 27–28 pts)
Cumbria – CCC 240 pts (Nurs A/MH)
De Montfort – CCC 240 pts (Nurs A/C; Midwif)
Glamorgan – 240–280 pts (Midwif)
Hertfordshire – 240 pts (Nurs)
Kingston – 240 pts (Nurs/ Registered Nurs)
Lincoln – CCC 240 pts (Nurs A)
Liverpool John Moores – 240–260 pts (Nurs A/MH; Midwif)
Oxford Brookes – CCC (Nurs)
Plymouth – CCC 240 pts (Paramed Practnr)
Queen's Belfast – BCC/CCD (with relevant subj)/BB/CCC (without relevant subj) (Midwif)
Robert Gordon – CCC–BC (Nurs A/C/MH)
Staffordshire – CCC 240 pts (Nurs Prac A/C/MH; Midwif Prac)
Teesside – CCC 240 pts (Nurs St A/C/MH)
Worcester – 240 pts (Midwif)
220 pts **Bedfordshire** – 220 pts (Midwif)
Central Lancashire – 220 pts (Nurs Pre Reg)
Leeds Met – 220 pts (Nurs A/MH)
Northampton – 220–260 pts (Midwif)
Queen Margaret – 220 pts (Nurs)
Salford – 220 pts (Prof St Nurs Soc Wk) (IB 26 pts)
200 pts **Anglia Ruskin** – 200 pts (Midwifery)
Bangor – 2AL 200 pts (Nurs A/C/MH/LD)
Bedfordshire – 200 pts (Nurs A/C/LD/MH)
Bristol UWE – 200–240 pts (Nurs A/C/MH/LD) (IB 24 pts)

Central Lancashire – 200 pts (Nurs A/C/MH)
Chester – 200–240 pts (Nurs A/C/LD/MH; Midwif)
Coventry – 200 pts (Paramed Sci)
Glyndŵr – 200 pts (Nurs)
Hull – 200 pts (Nurs A/C/MH/LD)
Manchester Met – 200 pts (Nurs A/MH)
Northampton – 200–220 pts (Nurs A/C/MH/LD)
Plymouth – 200–240 pts (Midwif; Nurs A/C/MH)
West London – 200 pts (Midwif)
Wolverhampton – 200 pts (Nurs A/C/MH)

180 pts **Edinburgh Napier** – 180 pts (Nurs A/C/MH/LD; Midwif)
Greenwich – 180-200 pts (Nurs A/C/LD/MH; Midwif)
Sheffield Hallam – 180–200 pts (Nurs St A/C/MH)

160 pts **Abertay Dundee** – Check with ad tutor CC (Nurs MH)
Anglia Ruskin – 160 pts (Nurs A/C/LD/MH)
Bristol UWE – Check with ad tutor 160 pts (Paramed Pr)
Dundee – check with Ad Tutor CC–DD (Midwif)
Glasgow Caledonian – check with admissions tutor CC 160 pts (Midwif)
Keele – 160–200 pts (Nurs A/C/MH/LD)
London South Bank – CC (MH Nurs Soc Wk)
Oxford Brookes – CCC (Nurs MH)
Robert Gordon – check with Admissions Tutor CC (Midwif)
West London – 160–200 pts (Nurs A/C/MH/LD)
Worcester – CC (Nurs A/C/MH)

120 pts **Bucks New** – 120 pts (Nurs A/C/MH)
West Scotland – CD 120 pts (Nurs A/C/MH; Midwif)

Open University – contact +44 (0)845 300 6090 **or** www.openuniversity.co.uk/you (Nurs Prac)

Alternative offers
See **Chapter 7** and **Appendix 1** for grades/UCAS Tariff points information for the International Baccalaureate, Scottish Highers/Advanced Highers, the Welsh Baccalaureate, the Irish Leaving Certificate, the Cambridge Pre-U Diploma, the Advanced Diploma and the Extended Project.

EXAMPLES OF FOUNDATION DEGREES IN THE SUBJECT FIELD
Bournemouth; Bristol UWE; Cornwall (Coll); Coventry; Cumbria; East London; Essex; Greenwich; Grimsby (IFHE); Liverpool John Moores; London (St George's); South Devon (Coll); Wigan and Leigh (Coll); Worcester.

CHOOSING YOUR COURSE (SEE ALSO CH. 1)
Some course features
Anglia Ruskin There is a common element of Nursing for all specialised areas that cover nursing fields in Child, Adult, Mental Health and Learning Disabilities. There is also a BSc Midwifery degree course.
Bedfordshire Obstetrics, midwifery, the midwife practitioner, women's health, ethics and law are all covered in the Nursing degree. Specialisation is offered in Adult, Children's and Mental Health Nursing. A Midwifery course is also provided.
Hertfordshire (Paramed Sci) The course runs over four extended academic years and leads to qualifying and registering as a professional paramedic. Theoretical studies are interspersed with clinical practice placements. The third year is a sandwich/practice year when students are paid employees of the London Ambulance Service NHS Trust.
Liverpool The nursing degree is a three-year course leading to the degree (BNurs), with opportunities to specialise in district nursing, health visiting, clinical nursing, research or cancer nursing.

UNIVERSITY OF
Southampton

The University of Southampton is training the next generation of professionals in nursing, midwifery and other health sciences.

The Times newspaper ranked us number one in England in its influential survey of university departments; our impressive research portfolio in nursing and midwifery won us second place in the UK's latest independent assessment of research quality (RAE 2008).

Our vision is to create a world-class environment of learning and discovery. Improving health outcomes and transforming health care drives our ambitions locally, nationally and globally. Practitioners who train at Southampton are well-placed to become expert clinicians and leaders across health and social care.

Our academic staff work together in multidisciplinary research groups tackling challenging issues such as cancer, palliative and end of life care, rehabilitation and the organisation of care.

www.southampton.ac.uk/healthsciences

Swansea Nursing students in Wales are paid by a bursary from the NHS Wales Bursary Scheme. It is not means tested. The courses covers Adult, Child and Mental Health Nursing, prior to which a common foundation course is offered. There is also a Midwifery degree.

Universities and colleges teaching quality See www.qaa.ac.uk; http://unistats.direct.gov.uk.

Top research universities and colleges (RAE 2008) Manchester; Southampton; Ulster; York; City; Hertfordshire; Leeds; Nottingham; Stirling.

ADMISSIONS INFORMATION

Number of applicants per place (approx) Abertay Dundee 10; Anglia Ruskin 10; Bangor 10; Birmingham 8; Birmingham City 15; Bournemouth 9; Brighton 3; Bristol UWE 27; Cardiff 12, (non-EU) 6; Central Lancashire (Midwif) 14; City (Nurs MH) 4, (Nurs C) 8, (Midwif) 5; Cumbria 8; De Montfort 10; Glasgow Caledonian 12; Glyndŵr 4; Huddersfield (Midwif St) 10; Hull 10; Leeds (Midwif) 12; Liverpool John Moores (Nurs) 5; London (King's) 4; London South Bank 16; Middlesex 10; Northampton 17; Northumbria 16; Nottingham 3; Queen Margaret 3; Salford 10, (Midwif) 11; Sheffield Hallam 8; Southampton (Nurs) 15, (Midwif) 25; Staffordshire (Midwif Prac) 10; Surrey 10; Swansea 10; York (Nurs) 8, (Midwif Prac) 2.

Advice to applicants and planning the UCAS personal statement Experience of care work – for example in hospitals, old people's homes, children's homes – is important. Describe what you have done and what you have learned. Read nursing journals in order to be aware of new developments in the treatment of illnesses. Note, in particular, the various needs of patients and the problems they experience. Try to compare different nursing approaches with, for example, children, people with learning disabilities, old people and terminally ill people. If you under-performed at GCSE, give reasons. If you have had work experience or a part-time job, describe how your skills have developed, for example responsibility, communication, team-building, organisational skills. How do you spend your spare time? Explain how your interests help with stress and pressure. See also **Appendix 4**. Admission is subject to eligibility for an NHS bursary. Contact NHS Student Grants Unit, tel 01253 655655.

Misconceptions about this course That Nursing programmes are not demanding. Midwives and nurses don't do shift work and are not involved in travelling! **City** Midwives are only involved at the birth stage and not at the ante-natal and post-natal stages, or in education and support.

Selection interviews Most institutions **Yes** Anglia Ruskin, Birmingham, Bournemouth (Midwif), Brighton, Cardiff, City, East Anglia, Hertfordshire, Sheffield Hallam, Surrey, Swansea, Wolverhampton, York; **Some** Abertay Dundee, Bucks New, Salford.

Interview advice and questions Past questions have included: Why do you want to be a nurse? What experience have you had in nursing? What do you think of the nurses' pay situation? Should nurses go on strike? What are your views on abortion? What branch of nursing most interests you? How would you communicate with someone who can't speak English? What is the nurse's role in the community? How should a nurse react in an emergency? How would you cope with telling a patient's relative that the patient was dying? Admissions tutors look for communication skills, team interaction and the applicant's understanding of health/society-related subjects. Some applicants have difficulty with maths – multiplication and division – used in calculating dosage for medicines. See **Chapter 6**. **London South Bank** What do you understand by equal opportunities? **Swansea** What is your perception of the role of the nurse? What qualities do you have that would be good for nursing?

Reasons for rejection (non-academic) Insufficient awareness of the roles and responsibilities of a midwife or nurse. Lack of motivation. Poor communication skills. Lack of awareness of nursing developments through the media. (Detailed knowledge of the NHS or nursing practice not usually required.) Failed medical. Unsatisfactory health record. Not fulfilling the hepatitis B requirements or police check requirements. Poor preparation for the interview. Too shy. Only wants nursing as a means to something else, for example commission in the armed forces. Too many choices on the UCAS application, for example Midwifery, Physiotherapy, Occupational Therapy. No care experience. **Birmingham** No work experience. **De Montfort** No insight as to nursing as a career or the various branches of nursing. **Swansea** Poor communication skills.

AFTER-RESULTS ADVICE

Offers to applicants repeating A-levels Higher Bristol UWE, Cardiff, Hull, Liverpool John Moores (Midwif); **Same** De Montfort, Huddersfield, Liverpool John Moores, London South Bank, Queen Margaret, Salford, Staffordshire, Stirling, Suffolk (Univ Campus), Surrey, Swansea, Wolverhampton.

GRADUATE DESTINATIONS AND EMPLOYMENT (2007/8 HESA)

Graduates surveyed 5350 **Employed** 4225 **In further study** 55 **Assumed unemployed** 125

Career note The majority of graduates aim to enter the nursing profession.

OTHER DEGREE SUBJECTS FOR CONSIDERATION

Audiology; Biological Sciences; Biology; Community Studies; Dietetics; Education; Health Studies; Medicine; Nutrition; Occupational Therapy; Optometry; Pharmacology; Pharmacy; Physiotherapy; Podiatry; Psychology; Radiography; Social Policy and Administration; Social Work; Sociology; Speech Therapy; Veterinary Nursing.

NUTRITION

(see also **Dietetics, Food Science/Studies and Technology**)

Nutrition attracts a great deal of attention in society and whilst controversy, claim and counter-claim seem to focus daily on the merits and otherwise of food, it is, nevertheless, a scientific study in itself. Courses involve topics relating to diet, health, nutrition and food policy and are designed to prepare students to enter careers as specialists in nutrition and dietetics.

Useful websites www.nutrition.org.uk; www.nutritionsociety.org; see also under **Dietetics**.

NB The points totals shown to the left of the institutions are for ease of reference only. It must not be assumed that Tariff points are always used by institutions or that they can be substituted for an offer in grades. The level of an offer is not necessarily indicative of the quality of a course.

COURSE OFFERS INFORMATION

Subject requirements/preferences GCSE Mathematics and science usually required. **AL** Science subjects required for most courses, biology and/or chemistry preferred.

NB In 2012 universities and colleges will differ in their use of GCE AL/AS unit grade information, A* grades, the Extended Project (EPQ), the Advanced Diploma and the Cambridge Pre-U examination when considering applicants and making offers. An EPQ may be accepted in place of an AS subject. Check websites of universities and colleges for the latest offers information.

Your target offers and examples of courses provided by each institution

340 pts **London (King's)** – ABB+AS (Nutr Diet) (IB 34 pts)
Newcastle – AAB–ABB (Fd Hum Nutr) (IB 32–35 pts)
320 pts **Glasgow** – ABB (Physiol Spo Sci Nutr) (IB 32 pts)
Leeds – ABB 320 pts (Nutrition)
London (King's) – BBB+AS (Nutrition) (IB 32 pts)
Nottingham – ABB–BBB (Nutr (Diet) MNutr) (IB 32–34 pts)
Surrey – ABB–BBB 320–300 pts (Nutr Diet) (IB 34–32 pts)
300 pts **Aberdeen** – BBB 300 pts (Edu P Hlth Nutr)
Leeds – BBB (Fd St Nutr) (IB 32 pts HL 15 pts)
London Met – 300 pts (Hum Nutr Diet) (IB 28 pts)
Nottingham – BBB–BBC (Nutr Fd Sci (Euro St)) (IB 28–32 pts)
Queen's Belfast – BBB (Fd Qual Sfty Nutr) (IB 32 pts)
Reading – BBB 300 pts (Nutri Fd Sci)
Surrey – BBB–BBC 300–280 pts (Nutrition)

280 pts **Leeds Trinity (UC)** – (Nutr Fd; Spo Hlth Exer Nutr)

Northumbria – 280–300 pts (Fd Sci Nutr; Spo Exer Nutr) (IB 25 pts)

Oxford Brookes – BBC (Nutr) (IB 30 pts)

Plymouth – 280–300 pts (Exer Nutr Hlth; Pblc Hlth Nutr)

Worcester – 280 pts (Hum Nutr)

260 pts **Bournemouth** – BCC 260 pts (Nutri) (28 pts)

Cardiff (UWIC) – 260 pts (Hum Nutr Diet)

Edge Hill – BCC 260 pts (Nutri Hlth)

Glasgow Caledonian – BCC (Human Nutri Diet)

Leeds Met – BCC (Diet) (IB 24 pts HL 5 chem)

Liverpool Hope – 260 pts (Hlth Nutr Comb Hons) (IB 25 pts)

Liverpool John Moores – 260 pts (Fd Nutr)

Nottingham Trent – 260 pts (Exer Nutr Hlth)

240 pts **Aberdeen** – CCC (Hlth Sci (Hlth Nutr))

Bath Spa – 240–280 pts (Hum Nutr)

Cardiff (UWIC) – 240 pts (Pblc Hlth Nutr; Spo Biomed Nutr)

Central Lancashire – 240–280 pts (Hum Nutri)

Chester – BCC 240 pts (Hum Nutr)

London Met – CCC 240 pts (Pblc Hlth Nutr)

Newport – 240 pts (Hlth Exerc Nutr)

Robert Gordon – CCC 240 pts (Nutr Diet) (IB 28 pts)

Staffordshire – 240 pts (Spo Exer Nutr)

Suffolk (Univ Campus) – 240 pts (Nutr Hum Hlth)

Teesside – 240 pts (Fd Nutr Hlth Sci)

Ulster – CCC 240 pts (Hum Nutr)

220 pts **Bath Spa** – 220–280 pts (Fd Nutr) (IB 24 pts)

Coventry – 220–240 pts (Fd Sci Nutr; Exer Nutr Hlth)

Glamorgan – 220–260 pts (Actvty Commun Hlth) (IB 28 pts)

Greenwich – 220–240 pts (Hum Nutr)

Huddersfield – 220 pts (Fd Nutr Hlth; Nutr Pblc Hlth)

Lincoln – 220 pts (Hum Nutr)

Middlesex – 220 pts (Spo Exer Sci (Spo Nutr))

Westminster – CCD (Nutr Exer Sci) (IB 26 pts)

200 pts **Abertay Dundee** – CDD (Fd Nutr Hlth)

Birmingham City – 200 pts (Nutri Sci)

Kingston – 200–280 pts (Nutr Spo Sci; Nutr; Hum Biol Nutr; Bioch Nutr)

Leeds Met – 200 pts (Nutr Pblc Hlth)

London Met – 200-240 pts (Hum Nutr) (IB 28 pts)

London South Bank – CDD 200 pts (Fd Nutr)

Manchester Met – 200–240 pts (Hum Nutr) (IB 27 pts)

Roehampton – 200–240 pts (Nutr Hlth)

Sheffield Hallam – 200 pts (Pblc Hlth Nutr; Nutr Hlth Lfstl)

180 pts **Abertay Dundee** – 180 pts (Spo Exer Nutr) (IB 26 pts)

Harper Adams (UC) – 180–220 pts (Fd Nutr Wlbng)

160 pts **Queen Margaret** – 160 pts (Nutr)

Robert Gordon – CC (Nutr)

St Mary's Twickenham (UC) – 160–200 pts (Nutr courses)

100 pts **Bradford (Coll Univ Centre)** – 100-140 pts (Diet Nutr Hlth)

Alternative offers

See **Chapter 7** and **Appendix 1** for grades/UCAS Tariff points information for the International Baccalaureate, Scottish Highers/Advanced Highers, the Welsh Baccalaureate, the Irish Leaving Certificate, the Cambridge Pre-U Diploma, the Advanced Diploma and the Extended Project.

EXAMPLES OF FOUNDATION DEGREES IN THE SUBJECT FIELD
CAFRE; Duchy (Coll); Glamorgan.

CHOOSING YOUR COURSE (SEE ALSO CH. 1)
Some course features
London (King's) The BSc course is a modular programme with specialised options including diet, disease, obesity, antioxidants and cancer. There is a four year Nutrition and Dietetics course with clinical placements in Year 2, 3 and 4, leading to qualification as a dietician.
Newcastle (Fd Hum Nutr) Stages 1 and 2 focus on biology and biological chemistry, with an emphasis on nutrition and food science. After a work placement, Stage 3 covers nutrition, health and disease, biotechnology in the food industry, plants as food, and sport and exercise nutrition.
Reading (Nutr Fd Sci) Course is normally four years with a placement year in Year 3.
Sheffield Hallam (Pblc Hlth Nutr) Course includes business elements covering human resources and project management.

Top research universities and colleges (RAE 2008) (**Nutritional Sciences**; see also **Agricultural Sciences/Agriculture**.) London (King's).

Examples of sandwich degree courses Cardiff (UWIC); Coventry; Glamorgan; Glasgow Caledonian; Harper Adams (UC); Huddersfield; Kingston; Leeds Met; London South Bank; Manchester Met; Newcastle; Northumbria; Queen's Belfast; Reading; Sheffield Hallam; Surrey; Teesside; Ulster.

ADMISSIONS INFORMATION
Number of applicants per place (approx) Cardiff (UWIC) 5; Glasgow Caledonian 8; Liverpool John Moores 10; London (King's) 6; London Met 9; London South Bank 5; Newcastle 5; Nottingham 7; Robert Gordon 4; Surrey 5.

Advice to applicants and planning the UCAS personal statement Information on relevant experience, reasons for wanting to do the degree and careers sought would be useful. See also **Dietetics** and **Appendix 4**. **Surrey** Overseas students not eligible for Nutrition and Dietetics course.

Misconceptions about this course Some applicants do not realise that this is a science course.

Selection interviews **Yes** London Met, London South Bank, Nottingham (depends on application), Robert Gordon, Surrey; **Some** Liverpool John Moores, Roehampton.

Interview advice and questions Past questions have focused on scientific A-level subjects studied and aspects of subjects enjoyed by the applicants. Questions then arise from answers. Extensive knowledge expected of nutrition as a career and candidates should have talked to people involved in this type of work, for example dietitians. They will also be expected to discuss wider problems such as food supplies in developing countries and nutritional problems resulting from famine. See **Chapter 6**. **Liverpool John Moores** Interviews are informal. It would be useful for you to bring samples of coursework to the interview.

AFTER-RESULTS ADVICE
Offers to applicants repeating A-levels **Possibly higher** Nottingham; **Same** Liverpool John Moores, Manchester Met, Roehampton, St Mary's Twickenham (UC), Surrey.

GRADUATE DESTINATIONS AND EMPLOYMENT (2007/8 HESA)
Graduates surveyed 750 **Employed** 405 **In further study** 90 **Assumed unemployed** 60

Career note Nutritionists work in retail, health promotion and sport whilst others specialise in dietetics.

OTHER DEGREE SUBJECTS FOR CONSIDERATION
Biological Sciences; Biology; Consumer Studies; Dietetics; Food Sciences; Health Studies/Sciences.

OCCUPATIONAL THERAPY

Contrary to common belief, occupational therapy is not an art career although art and craftwork may be involved as a therapeutic exercise. Occupational therapists assess the physical, mental and social needs of ill or disabled people and help them regain lost skills and manage their lives to the best of their circumstances. Most courses include anatomy, physiology, physical rehabilitation, psychology, sociology, mental health and ethics. Selectors look for maturity, initiative, enterprise, tact, sound judgement and organising ability.

Useful websites www.cot.co.uk; www.otdirect.co.uk.

NB The points totals shown to the left of the institutions are for ease of reference only. It must not be assumed that Tariff points are always used by institutions or that they can be substituted for an offer in grades. The level of an offer is not necessarily indicative of the quality of a course.

COURSE OFFERS INFORMATION

Subject requirements/preferences GCSE English, mathematics and science grade A–C. **AL** A social science or science subjects required or preferred for most courses. **Other** All applicants need to pass an occupational health check and obtain Criminal Records Bureau (CRB) clearance.

NB In 2012 universities and colleges will differ in their use of GCE AL/AS unit grade information, A* grades, the Extended Project (EPQ), the Advanced Diploma and the Cambridge Pre-U examination when considering applicants and making offers. An EPQ may be accepted in place of an AS subject. Check websites of universities and colleges for the latest offers information.

Your target offers and examples of courses provided by each institution
340 pts **Bristol UWE** – 340 pts (Occ Thera)
320 pts **Cardiff** – ABB (Occ Thera)
            Southampton – ABB (Occ Thera) (IB 32 pts HL 16)
300 pts **Bournemouth** – 300 pts (Occ Thera) (IB 28 pts)
            Ulster – (See Ch. 5) BBB +HPAT (Occ Thera) (IB 25 pts)
280 pts **Northumbria** – 280 pts (Occ Thera)
            Oxford Brookes – BBC 280 pts (Occ Thera)
270 pts **Glyndŵr** – 270 pts (Occ Thera)
260 pts **Brunel** – BCC (Occ Thera) (IB 29 pts)
            Coventry – 260 pts (Occ Thera)
            East Anglia – BBC (Occ Thera)
            York St John – 260 pts (Occ Thera) (IB 24 pts)
240 pts **Bradford** – CCC (Occ Thera) (IB 24 pts)
            Canterbury Christ Church – 240 pts (Occ Thera)
            Cumbria – 240 pts (Occ Thera)
            Derby – 240 pts (Occ Thera) (IB 26 pts)
            Huddersfield – CCC 240 pts (Occ Thera)
            Liverpool – CCC 240 pts (Occ Thera) (IB 26 pts)
            Northampton – 240–280 pts (Occ Thera) (IB 24 pts)
            Plymouth – 240 pts (Occ Thera) (IB 27 pts)
            Robert Gordon – CCC 240 pts (Occ Thera) (IB 26 pts)
            Salford – 240 pts (Occ Thera)
            Sheffield Hallam – 240 pts (Occ Thera)
            Teesside – 240–280 pts (Occ Thera)
230 pts **Queen Margaret** – 230 pts (Occ Thera)
160 pts **Glasgow Caledonian** – CC (Occ Thera)
            London South Bank – 160 pts (Occ Thera) (IB 24 pts)

            Brighton – p/t, indiv offers may vary, NHS bursaries are available for all courses. Check
                with University (Occ Thera)

UNIVERSITY OF
Southampton

"I came to Southampton because it is one of the most respected Universities for health sciences. With my degree, I hope to work with injured soldiers in developing world countries. The University offers so many extra-curricular opportunities, there is simply not enough hours in the day. I love the fitness classes at the Jubilee Sports Centre and have kept my first aid certificate up-to-date with the Royal Yachting Association (RYA). I am also on the committee for the University Symphonic Wind Orchestra and play the flute. The library is one of the main attractions of this uni – it is huge. I often go there to work on essays with my friends because there are no distractions and you have all the books you could need."

Lydia Pavia | Occupational Therapy

www.southampton.ac.uk/healthsciences

Alternative offers
See **Chapter 7** and **Appendix 1** for grades/UCAS Tariff points information for the International Baccalaureate, Scottish Highers/Advanced Highers, the Welsh Baccalaureate, the Irish Leaving Certificate, the Cambridge Pre-U Diploma, the Advanced Diploma and the Extended Project.

CHOOSING YOUR COURSE (SEE ALSO CH. 1)
Some course features
See also **Health Sciences/Studies**.

Brunel (Occ Thera) Course can also be taken as a four- to six-year part-time course.
East Anglia (Occ Thera) Practice placements in hospitals and the community. Advanced units in Year 3 include paediatrics and orthotics.
Liverpool (Occ Thera) Six placements take place throughout the course. 1000 hours required in practice settings for professional registration.

Universities and colleges teaching quality See www.qaa.ac.uk; http://unistats.direct.gov.uk.

ADMISSIONS INFORMATION
Number of applicants per place (approx) Canterbury Christ Church 5; Cardiff 10; Coventry 15; Cumbria 20; Derby 5; East Anglia 5; Northampton 4; Northumbria 4; Oxford Brookes 12; Queen Margaret 7; Robert Gordon 6; Salford 5; Sheffield Hallam 7; Southampton 7; Ulster 13; York St John 5.

Advice to applicants and planning the UCAS personal statement Contact your local hospital and discuss this career with the occupational therapists. Try to obtain work shadowing experience and make notes of your observations. Describe any such visits in full (see **Reasons for rejection (non-academic)**). Applicants are expected to have visited two occupational therapy departments, one in a physical or social services setting, one in the mental health field. Good interpersonal skills. Breadth and nature of health-related work experience is important. Also skills, interests (for example, sports, design). Applicants should have a high standard of communication skills and experience of working with people with disabilities. See also **Appendix 4**. **York St John** Contact with the profession essential; very competitive course.

Selection interviews Most institutions. **Yes** East Anglia.

Interview advice and questions Since this a vocational course, work experience is nearly always essential and applicants are likely to be questioned on the types of work involved and the career. Some universities may use admissions tests: check websites and see **Chapter 6**.

Reasons for rejection (non-academic) Poor communication skills. Lack of knowledge of occupational therapy. Little evidence of working with people. Uncertain about their future career. Lack of maturity. Indecision regarding the profession. **Salford** Failure to function well in groups and inability to perform practical tasks.

AFTER-RESULTS ADVICE
Offers to applicants repeating A-levels Same Derby, Salford, York St John.

GRADUATE DESTINATIONS AND EMPLOYMENT (2007/8 HESA)
Career note Occupational therapists (who work mostly in hospital departments) are involved in the rehabilitation of those who have required medical treatment and involve the young, aged and, for example, people with learning difficulties.

OTHER DEGREE SUBJECTS FOR CONSIDERATION
Audiology; Community Studies; Dietetics; Education; Health Studies/Sciences; Nursing; Nutrition; Physiotherapy; Podiatry; Psychology; Radiography; Social Policy and Administration; Social Work; Sociology; Speech Sciences.

OPTOMETRY (OPHTHALMIC OPTICS)
(including **Ophthalmic Dispensing** and **Orthoptics**)

Optometry courses (which are increasingly popular) lead to qualification as an optometrist (previously known as an ophthalmic optician). They provide training in detecting defects and diseases in the eye and in prescribing treatment with, for example, spectacles, contact lenses and other appliances to correct or improve vision. Orthoptics includes the study of general anatomy, physiology and normal child development and leads to a career as an orthoptist. This involves the investigation, diagnosis and treatment of binocular vision and other eye conditions. The main components of degree courses include the study of the eye, the use of diagnostic and measuring equipment and treatment of eye abnormalities. See also **Appendix 4**.

Useful websites www.optical.org; www.orthoptics.org.uk.

NB The points totals shown to the left of the institutions are for ease of reference only. It must not be assumed that Tariff points are always used by institutions or that they can be substituted for an offer in grades. The level of an offer is not necessarily indicative of the quality of a course.

COURSE OFFERS INFORMATION
Subject requirements/preferences GCSE Good grades in English and science subjects usually required. **AL** Science subjects required for all Optometry courses. Mathematics usually acceptable.

NB In 2012 universities and colleges will differ in their use of GCE AL/AS unit grade information, A* grades, the Extended Project (EPQ), the Advanced Diploma and the Cambridge Pre-U examination when considering applicants and making offers. An EPQ may be accepted in place of an AS subject. Check websites of universities and colleges for the latest offers information.

Your target offers and examples of courses provided by each institution

360 pts **Aston** – AAA (Optom) (IB 34–35 pts)
Cardiff – AAA (Optometry) (IB 34 pts)

340 pts **Bradford** – AAB 340 pts (Optometry) (IB 33 pts)
City – AAB (Optometry) (IB 35 pts)
Glasgow Caledonian – AAB (Optom)
Manchester – AAB (Optometry) (IB 35 pts)
Ulster – AAB 340 pts (Optometry) (IB 37 pts)

320 pts **Anglia Ruskin** – ABB (Optom) (IB 33 pts HL chem biol maths 6)

300 pts **Sheffield** – BBB (Orthoptics) (IB 32 pts)

260 pts **Liverpool** – BCC 260 pts (Orthoptics) (IB 28 pts)

200 pts **Anglia Ruskin** – 200 pts (Oph Disp)

160 pts **Glasgow Caledonian** – CC (Oph Disp)

120 pts **Bradford (Coll Univ Centre)** – 1 A level in Biol, Phys, Chem **or** Maths 120–160 pts (Oph Disp Mgt)

Alternative offers
See **Chapter 7** and **Appendix 1** for grades/UCAS Tariff points information for the International Baccalaureate, Scottish Highers/Advanced Highers, the Welsh Baccalaureate, the Irish Leaving Certificate, the Cambridge Pre-U Diploma, the Advanced Diploma and the Extended Project.

EXAMPLES OF FOUNDATION DEGREES IN THE SUBJECT FIELD
City; Nottingham Castle (Coll).

CHOOSING YOUR COURSE (SEE ALSO CH. 1)
Some course features
Aston The course offers an integration of teaching and professional practice and a hospital placement scheme.
Bradford Placements take place after graduation during the Pre-registration Year.
Cardiff This is a three-year course after which graduates undertake a one-year pre-registration course.
City Extensive patient contact takes place in Year 3.

Universities and colleges teaching quality See www.qaa.ac.uk; http://unistats.direct.gov.uk.

Top research universities and colleges (RAE 2008) Aston (Optometry); City (Biomedical and Vision Sciences); Cardiff (Optometry and Vision Science).

ADMISSIONS INFORMATION
Number of applicants per place (approx) Anglia Ruskin 12; Aston 7; Bradford 6; Cardiff 13; City 11; Glasgow Caledonian 9.

Numbers of applicants (a UK **b** EU (non-UK) **c** non-EU **d** mature) Anglia Ruskin **a**431 **b**431; Aston **a**700 **b**50 **c**70 **d**10; Bradford **a**600 **b**600 **c**90; Glasgow Caledonian **a**548 **c**23.

Advice to applicants and planning the UCAS personal statement For Optometry courses contact with optometrists is essential, either work shadowing or gaining some work experience. Make notes of your experiences and the work done and report fully on the UCAS application on why the career interests you. See also **Appendix 4**.

Selection interviews **Yes** Bradford, City, Glasgow Caledonian; **Some** Anglia Ruskin, Aston, Cardiff.

Interview advice and questions Optometry is a competitive subject requiring applicants to have had some work experience on which they will be questioned. See **Chapter 6**. **Anglia Ruskin** Why will you make a good optometrist? Describe the job.

AFTER-RESULTS ADVICE
Offers to applicants repeating A-levels **Higher** City; **Possibly higher** Aston; **Same** Anglia Ruskin, Cardiff.

GRADUATE DESTINATIONS AND EMPLOYMENT (2007/8 HESA)
Graduates surveyed 480 **Employed** 350 **In further study** 15 **Assumed unemployed** 10

Career note The great majority of graduates enter private practice either in small businesses or in larger organisations (which have been on the increase in recent years). A small number work in eye hospitals. Orthoptists tend to work in public health and education dealing with children and the elderly.

OTHER DEGREE SUBJECTS FOR CONSIDERATION
Health Studies; Nursing; Occupational Therapy; Physics; Physiotherapy; Radiography; Speech Studies.

PHARMACOLOGY
(including **Toxicology**; see also **Biological Sciences, Health Sciences/Studies**)

Pharmacology is the study of drugs and medicines and courses focus on physiology, biochemistry, toxicology, immunology, microbiology and chemotherapy. Pharmacologists are not qualified to work as pharmacists. Toxicology involves the study of the adverse effects of chemicals on living systems. See also **Appendix 4** under **Pharmacology**.

Useful websites www.thebts.org; www.scienceyear.com; www.pharmacology.com.

NB The points totals shown to the left of the institutions are for ease of reference only. It must not be assumed that Tariff points are always used by institutions or that they can be substituted for an offer in grades. The level of an offer is not necessarily indicative of the quality of a course.

COURSE OFFERS INFORMATION
Subject requirements/preferences GCSE English, science and mathematics. **AL** Chemistry and/or biology required for most courses.

NB In 2012 universities and colleges will differ in their use of GCE AL/AS unit grade information, A* grades, the Extended Project (EPQ), the Advanced Diploma and the Cambridge Pre-U examination when considering applicants and making offers. An EPQ may be accepted in place of an AS subject. Check websites of universities and colleges for the latest offers information.

Your target offers and examples of courses provided by each institution

380 pts	**Cambridge** – A*AA college offers may vary (Nat Sci (Pharmacol)) (IB 38–42 pts HL 766–777)
360 pts	**London (UCL)** – AAA–AAB (Pharmacol) (IB 36–38 pts)
	Manchester – AAA–AAB (Pharmacol Modn Lang) (IB 35–32 pts)
340 pts	**Leeds** – AAB–BBB (Pharmacol) (IB 36–32 pts HL 17–15 pts)
	London (King's) – AAB+AS (Physiol Pharmacol) (IB 34 pts HL 5 chem biol)
	Newcastle – AAB/BBB (Pharmacol) (IB 32 pts HL chem biol 5)
320 pts	**Bath** – ABB (Pharmacol) (IB 34 pts HL 666)
	Bristol – ABB (Pharmacol Ind) (IB 33 pts HL 665 inc 2 sci)
	Glasgow – ABB (Pharmacol) (IB 32 pts)
	Leicester – ABB (Biol Sci (Physiol Pharmacol)) (IB 32–34 pts)
	Nottingham – ABB–BBB (Neuro Pharmacol) (IB 32 pts)
	Surrey – ABB–BBB (Bioch (Pharmacol))
300 pts	**Birmingham** – BBB (Chem Pharmacol) (IB 31 pts HL chem 5 HL chem 5)
	Cardiff – BBB 300 pts (Med Pharmacol) (IB 32 pts)
	Edinburgh – check with Admissions Tutor BBB 1st yr entry (Pharmacology) (IB 30 pts)
	Liverpool – BBB–ABB (Medcnl Chem Pharmacol) (IB 32 pts)
	Newcastle – BBB (Drug Dev BEng) (IB 36 pts)
	Southampton – BBB (Pharmacol)
280 pts	**Nottingham Trent** – 280 pts (Pharmacol)
	Plymouth – 280–320 pts (Tox Hlth) (IB 26 pts)
	Strathclyde – BBC (Bioch Pharmacol)

260 pts **Bradford** – 260 pts (Biomed Sci (Pharmacol)) (IB 28 pts)
Dundee – BCC 1st year entry (Bioch Pharmacol) (IB 30 pts)
Glasgow Caledonian – BCC (Pharmacol)
Nottingham Trent – 260 pts (Biol Sci (Pharmacol))
Sheffield Hallam – 260 pts (Pharml Sci)
240 pts **Aberdeen** – CCC (Immun Pharmacol) (IB 28 pts)
Central Lancashire – 240–260 pts (Physiol Pharmacol)
Coventry – 240 pts (Med Pharmacol Sci)
Hertfordshire – 240 pts (Pharmacol; Pharmacol Euro/N Am)
London Met – 240 pts (Pharmacol)
Middlesex – contact University 2–3 AL 240–280 pts (Trad Chin Med)
Portsmouth – 240 pts (Pharmacol)
220 pts **Huddersfield** – 220 pts (Pharml Sci)
Westminster – CCD/CC (Physiol Pharmacol) (IB 26 pts)
200 pts **De Montfort** – 200 pts (Pharml Cos Sci)
East London – 200 pts (Tox courses) (IB 24 pts)
Kingston – 200–280 pts (Pharmacol; Pharmacol Bus)
Wolverhampton – 200 pts (Pharmacol)
165 pts **Queen Margaret** – 165 pts (App Pharmacol)
160 pts **Leeds Met** – 160 pts (Biomed Sci (Physiol Pharmacol))

Alternative offers

See **Chapter 7** and **Appendix 1** for grades/UCAS Tariff points information for the International Baccalaureate, the Scottish Highers/Advanced Highers, the Welsh Baccalaureate, the Irish Leaving Certificate, the Cambridge Pre-U Diploma, the Advanced Diploma and the Extended Project.

CHOOSING YOUR COURSE (SEE ALSO CH. 1)

Some course features

Coventry The course in Medical and Pharmacological Sciences focuses on a study of pharmacology and physiology and applications in medicine. It can be taken with a year in professional placement.
Kingston There is an optional sandwich year in full-time employment.
London (King's) A single honours degree is offered in Pharmacology. In the first two years the focus is on physiology, biochemistry and pharmacology. In the third year, specialist topics include toxicology, immunology and environmental pharmacology. See also **Biological Sciences**.
Newcastle (Drug Dev) This new course focuses on science and engineering, covering chemistry, genetics, biology and pharmacology as well as bioprocessing for the large-scale manufacture of biopharmaceuticals.
Portsmouth The Pharmacology course has a common first year with Biomedical Science. This is a three year full-time or four-year sandwich course and includes a study of physiology, biochemistry and chemistry to support studies in pharmacology. Overall the course has a biochemical focus towards modern pharmacology with an emphasis on pharmacology in all three years.
Southampton The Pharmacology degree is based on both physiology and biochemistry and looks at the design of drugs and their biological effects. A one year placement is possible.

Universities and colleges teaching quality See www.qaa.ac.uk; http://unistats.direct.gov.uk.

Examples of sandwich degree courses (including Pharmaceutical Sciences, Pharmacology and Pharmacy) Bath (Pharmacol); Bradford (Pharm); Bristol (Pharmacol); Cardiff (Pharmacol); Coventry (Pharm Sci); De Montfort (Pharml Cos Sci); East London (Pharmacol); Hertfordshire (Pharml Sci); Huddersfield (Pharml Sci); Kingston (Pharml Sci; Pharmacol); London Met (Pharmacol); Manchester (Pharmacol); Manchester Met (Physiol Pharmacol St); Nottingham Trent (Pharmacol); Sheffield Hallam (Pharml Sci); Southampton (Pharmacol).

ADMISSIONS INFORMATION

Number of applicants per place (approx) Bath 6; Birmingham 6; Bradford 20; Bristol 8; Cardiff 8; Dundee 5; East London 4; Hertfordshire 10; Leeds 7; Liverpool 5; London (King's) 6; Portsmouth 4; Southampton 8; Strathclyde 10; Wolverhampton 4.

Advice to applicants and planning the UCAS personal statement Contact with the pharmaceutical industry is important in order to be aware of the range of work undertaken. Read pharmaceutical journals (although note that Pharmacology and Pharmacy courses lead to different careers). See also **Pharmacy**. **Bath** Interests outside A-level studies. Important to produce evidence that there is more to the student than A-level ability. **Bristol** Be aware that a Pharmacology degree is mainly biological rather than chemical although both subjects are important.

Misconceptions about this course Mistaken belief that Pharmacology and Pharmaceutical Sciences is the same as Pharmacy and that a Pharmacology degree will lead to work as a pharmacist.

Selection interviews Yes Bath, Birmingham (don't be anxious – this is an opportunity for you to see us!), Cambridge, Newcastle; **Some** Cardiff, Dundee, Portsmouth.

Interview advice and questions Past questions include: Why do you want to do Pharmacology? Why not Pharmacy? Why not Chemistry? How are pharmacologists employed in industry? What are the issues raised by anti-vivisectionists on animal experimentation? Questions relating to the A-level syllabus in chemistry and biology. See **Chapter 6**.

Reasons for rejection (non-academic) Confusion between Pharmacology, Pharmacy and Pharmaceutical Sciences. One university rejected two applicants because they had no motivation or understanding of the course (one had A-levels at AAB!). Insurance against rejection for Medicine. Lack of knowledge about pharmacology as a subject.

AFTER-RESULTS ADVICE
Offers to applicants repeating A-levels Higher Bristol, Glasgow, Leeds; **Same** Bath, Bradford, Cardiff, Dundee, Portsmouth.

GRADUATE DESTINATIONS AND EMPLOYMENT (2007/8 HESA)
Pharmacology, Toxicology and Pharmacy graduates surveyed 2200 **Employed** 1365 **In further study** 270 **Assumed unemployed** 85

Career note The majority of pharmacologists work with the large pharmaceutical companies involved in research and development. A small number are employed by the NHS in medical research and clinical trials. Some will eventually diversify and become involved in marketing, sales and advertising.

OTHER DEGREE SUBJECTS FOR CONSIDERATION
Biochemistry; Biological Sciences; Biology; Biotechnology; Chemistry; Life Sciences; Medical Biochemistry; Medicinal Chemistry; Microbiology; Natural Sciences; Pharmaceutical Sciences; Pharmacy; Physiology; Toxicology.

PHARMACY and PHARMACEUTICAL SCIENCES
(including Herbal Medicine; see also Biochemistry, Chemistry, Health Sciences/Studies)

Pharmacy is the science of medicines, involving research into chemical structures and natural products of possible medicinal value, the development of dosage and the safety testing of products. This table also includes information on courses in Pharmaceutical Science (which should not be confused with Pharmacy) which is a multi-disciplinary subject covering chemistry, biochemistry, pharmacology and medical issues. Pharmaceutical scientists apply their knowledge of science and the biology of disease to the design and delivery of therapeutic agents. Note: All Pharmacy courses leading to MPharm are four years. Only Pharmacy degree courses accredited by the Royal Phamaceutical Society of Great Britain lead to a qualification as a pharmacist. Check prospectuses and websites.

Useful websites www.pharmweb.net; www.scienceyear.com; www.pharmacycareers.org; www.chemistanddruggist.co.uk.

NB The points totals shown to the left of the institutions are for ease of reference only. It must not be assumed that Tariff points are always used by institutions or that they can be substituted for an offer in grades. The level of an offer is not necessarily indicative of the quality of a course.

COURSE OFFERS INFORMATION

Subject requirements/preferences GCSE English, mathematics and science subjects. **AL** Chemistry and one or two other sciences required for most courses.

NB In 2012 universities and colleges will differ in their use of GCE AL/AS unit grade information, A* grades, the Extended Project (EPQ), the Advanced Diploma and the Cambridge Pre-U examination when considering applicants and making offers. An EPQ may be accepted in place of an AS subject. Check websites of universities and colleges for the latest offers information.

Your target offers and examples of courses provided by each institution

340 pts **Aston** – AAB–ABB (Pharm MPharm) (IB 34 pts)
Bath – AAB (Pharm MPharm) (IB 36 pts HL 666)
Cardiff – AAB–ABB (Pharm MPharm) (IB 34 pts HL chem 6 +1 sci)
London (King's) – AAB+AS–Aabbe (Pharm MPharm) (IB 34 pts HL 655)
Manchester – AAB–ABB (Pharm MPharm) (IB 35 pts HL 766)
Nottingham – ABB–AAB (Pharm MPharm) (IB 36 pts)
Queen's Belfast – AAB–ABBa (Pharm MPharm) (IB 34 pts HL 666)
Ulster – 340 pts (Pharm)

320 pts **Brighton** – ABB (Pharm MPharm) (IB 34 pts HL 5 chem)
East Anglia – AAB–ABB (Pharm MPharm) (IB 31–32 pts)
Hertfordshire – 320 pts (Pharm MPharm)
Leicester – ABB (Pharml Chem Ind)
London (Sch Pharm) – AAB–ABB (Pharm MPharm) (IB 32 pts HL 655)
Strathclyde – ABB–BBB (Pharm MPharm)

300 pts **Bradford** – 300 pts (Pharm MPharm) (IB 30 pts)
Central Lancashire – 300 pts (Pharm) (IB 32 pts)
De Montfort – 300 pts (Pharm MPharm)
East Anglia – BBB (Pharml Chem)
Huddersfield – 300–340 pts (Pharm MPharm)
Keele – BBB (Pharm MPharm) (IB 32 pts)
Kent – BBB 300 pts (Pharm MPharm) (IB 32 pts)
Kingston – 300 pts (Pharm MPharm)
Liverpool John Moores – 300 pts (Pharm MPharm)
Loughborough – 300 pts (Medcnl Pharml Chem BSc) (IB 34 pts)
Portsmouth – BBB (Pharm MPharm) (IB 30 pts)
Reading – BBB (Pharm MPharm)
Robert Gordon – BBB (Pharm MPharm)
Sunderland – 300–360 pts (Pharm MPharm)
Wolverhampton – 300–360 pts (Pharm MPharm)

280 pts **Brighton** – BBC 280 pts (Pharml Chem Sci) (IB 30 pts)
London (QM) – 280 pts (Pharml Chem) (IB 28 pts)
Northumbria – 280 pts (Pharml Chem) (IB 25 pts)

260 pts **Bradford** – BCC (Chem Pharml Foren Sci) (IB 28 pts)
Leicester – BCC (Pharml Chem) (IB 30 pts)
Nottingham Trent – 260 pts (Pharml Medicin Chem)
Sheffield Hallam – 260 pts (Pharml Sci)

240 pts **Bradford** – 240 pts (Pharml Mgt)
Greenwich – 240–220 pts (Pharml Sci)
Hertfordshire – 240 pts (Pharml Sci)
Hull – 240–300 pts (Pharml Sci)
London Met – 240 pts (Pharml Sci)
Manchester Met – 240–280 pts (Pharml Chem)

220 pts **Huddersfield** – 220 pts (Pharml Sci)

200 pts **De Montfort** – 200 pts (Pharml Cos Sci)
East London – 200 pts (Herb Med)
Kingston – 200–280 pts (Pharml Sci)

Middlesex – contact University 200–300 pts (Herb Med)
Wolverhampton – 200–260 pts (Pharml Sci)
160 pts Westminster – CCD (Hlth Sci (Herb Med)) (IB 26 pts)
140 pts West Scotland – CD (Pharml Sci)

Alternative offers
See **Chapter 7** and **Appendix 1** for grades/UCAS Tariff points information for the International Baccalaureate, Scottish Highers/Advanced Highers, the Welsh Baccalaureate, the Irish Leaving Certificate, the Cambridge Pre-U Diploma, the Advanced Diploma and the Extended Project.

EXAMPLES OF FOUNDATION DEGREES IN THE SUBJECT FIELD
Aston; Birmingham Met (Coll); Kent; (Medway Sch Pharm) Kingston; Merton (Coll); Preston (Coll); Sunderland City (Coll).

CHOOSING YOUR COURSE (SEE ALSO CH. 1)
Some course features
Aston One of the largest pharmacy schools which includes hospital-based clinical teaching.
Brighton (Pharm) Studies include behavioural sciences, social pharmacy, health promotion and business studies reflecting the changing role of the pharmacist.
East Anglia (Pharm) Professional placements begin in Year 1.
Hertfordshire (Pharml Sci) Students not meeting the normal entry requirements can apply for an Extended degree which leads to Year 1 entry.
Keele Hospital, industrial and community placements take place throughout the course.

Universities and colleges teaching quality See www.qaa.ac.uk; http://unistats.direct.gov.uk.

Top research universities and colleges (RAE 2008) Nottingham; Manchester; London UCK (Coll) (Sch Pharm); Bath; Queen's Belfast; East Anglia; London (King's); Strathclyde; Bradford; Cardiff.

Examples of sandwich degree courses See **Pharmacology**.

ADMISSIONS INFORMATION
Number of applicants per place (approx) Aston 10; Bath 6; Bradford 10; Brighton 24 (apply early); Cardiff 5; De Montfort 14; Liverpool John Moores (Pharm) 7; London (King's) 15, (Sch Pharm) 6; Nottingham 8; Portsmouth 20; Robert Gordon 11; Strathclyde 10; Sunderland 20.

Numbers of applicants (a UK **b** EU (non-UK) **c** non-EU **d** mature) Aston **a**1400 **b**100 **c**300 **d**180; Bradford **a**1200 **b**1200 **c**200.

Advice to applicants and planning the UCAS personal statement Work experience and work shadowing with a retail and/or hospital pharmacist is important, and essential for Pharmacy applicants. Read pharmaceutical journals, extend your knowledge of well known drugs and antibiotics. Read up on the history of drugs. Attendance at open days or careers conference. See also **Appendix 4**. **Manchester** Students giving preference for Pharmacy are likely to be more successful than those who choose Pharmacy as an alternative to Medicine or Dentistry.

Misconceptions about this course That a degree in Pharmaceutical Science is a qualification leading to a career as a pharmacist. It is not: it is a course which concerns the application of chemical and biomedical science to the design, synthesis and analysis of pharmaceuticals for medicinal purposes. See also **Pharmacology**.

Selection interviews Yes Bath, Bradford, Brighton, Bristol, De Montfort, East Anglia, Liverpool John Moores, London UCK (Coll) (Sch Pharm), Manchester (most), Nottingham, Robert Gordon, Strathclyde, Wolverhampton; **Some** Aston, Cardiff, Portsmouth.

Interview advice and questions As work experience is essential for Pharmacy applicants, questions are likely to focus on this and what they have discovered. Other relevant questions could include: Why do you want to study Pharmacy? What types of work do pharmacists do? What interests you about the Pharmacy course? What branch of pharmacy do you want to enter? Name a drug – what do you know about it (formula, use etc)? Name a drug from a natural source and its use. Can you think of another way of extracting a drug? Why do fungi destroy bacteria? What is an antibiotic? Can you name one and say how it was discovered? What is insulin? What is its source and function? What is diabetes? What type of insulin is used in its treatment? What is a hormone? What drugs are available over the counter without prescription? What is the formula of aspirin? What is genetic engineering? See also **Chapter 6**. **Bath** Informal and relaxed; 400 approx selected for interview – very few rejected at this stage. **Cardiff** Interviews cover both academic and vocational aspects; candidates must reach a satisfactory level in both areas. **Liverpool John Moores** What are the products of a reaction between an alcohol and a carboxylic acid? **Manchester** Candidates failing to attend interviews will have their applications withdrawn. The majority of applicants are called for interview.

Reasons for rejection (non-academic) Poor communication skills. Poor knowledge of pharmacy and the work of a pharmacist.

AFTER-RESULTS ADVICE

Offers to applicants repeating A-levels Higher Bradford, Cardiff, De Montfort, Liverpool John Moores, London UCK (Coll) (Sch Pharm) AAB, Nottingham (offers rarely made), Portsmouth, Queen's Belfast, Strathclyde; **Possibly higher** Aston, Robert Gordon; **Same** Bath, Brighton, East Anglia, Sunderland, Wolverhampton.

GRADUATE DESTINATIONS AND EMPLOYMENT (2007/8 HESA)

See **Pharmacology**.

Career note The majority of Pharmacy graduates proceed to work in the commercial and retail fields, although opportunities also exist with pharmaceutical companies and in hospital pharmacies. There are also opportunities in agricultural and veterinary pharmacy.

OTHER DEGREE SUBJECTS FOR CONSIDERATION

Biochemistry; Biological Sciences; Biology; Biotechnology; Chemistry; Drug Development; Life Sciences; Medicinal Chemistry; Microbiology; Natural Sciences; Pharmacology; Physiology.

PHILOSOPHY

(see also **Psychology**)

Philosophy is one of the oldest and most fundamental disciplines, which examines the nature of the universe and humanity's place in it. Philosophy seeks to discover the essence of the mind, language and physical reality and discusses the methods used to investigate these topics.

Useful websites www.iep.utm.edu; www.philosophypages.com; www.philosophy.eserver.org; see also **Religious Studies**.

NB The points totals shown to the left of the institutions are for ease of reference only. It must not be assumed that Tariff points are always used by institutions or that they can be substituted for an offer in grades. The level of an offer is not necessarily indicative of the quality of a course.

COURSE OFFERS INFORMATION

Subject requirements/preferences GCSE English and mathematics. A foreign language may be required. **AL** No specific subjects except for joint courses.

NB In 2012 universities and colleges will differ in their use of GCE AL/AS unit grade information, A* grades, the Extended Project (EPQ), the Advanced Diploma and the Cambridge Pre-U examination when considering applicants and making offers. An EPQ may be accepted in place of an AS subject. Check websites of universities and colleges for the latest offers information.

Your target offers and examples of courses provided by each institution
440 pts Warwick – See Advice to applicants and planning the UCAS personal statement below
and **Chapter 5**. A*AAa–AABa (Maths Phil) (IB 39 pts HL maths 6)
400 pts Oxford – A*A*A (Maths Phil) (IB 38–42 pts)

390 pts **Warwick** – A*AAb-AAAb (PPE) (IB 38–40 pts)
380 pts **Bristol** – A*AA–AAB (Maths Phil) (IB 36 pts HL 666)
　　　　　Cambridge – A*AA college offers may vary (Phil) (IB 40–42 pts)
　　　　　London (King's) – AAA+AS **or** AAaa+AS (War St Phil) (IB 38 pts)
　　　　　London (UCL) – AAA+AS–AAB+AS (Phil Hist Art) (IB 36–38 pts)
　　　　　Oxford – A*AA (Phys Phil) (IB 38–42 pts)
360 pts **Birmingham** – AAA–AAB (Maths Phil) (IB 34–38 pts)
　　　　　Bristol – AAA–ABB (Phil Theol) (IB 37–33 pts HL 665)
　　　　　Durham – AAA (Phil Psy) (IB 38–40 pts)
　　　　　London (King's) – AAB+AS (Phys Phil) (IB 36 pts HL maths phys 5)
　　　　　London LSE – AAA (Phil Lgc Sci Meth) (IB 38 pts HL 766)
　　　　　Nottingham – AAA–AAB (Maths Phil) (IB 38 pts)
　　　　　Oxford – AAA (PPE) (IB 38–40 pts)
　　　　　St Andrews – AAA–AAB (Phil courses) (IB 36-40 pts)
　　　　　Warwick – AAA–AAAb (Phil Comp Sci) (IB 38 pts)
　　　　　York – AAA (Phil Pol Econ)
340 pts **Bristol** – AAB–ABB (Class St Phil) (IB 35–33 pts)
　　　　　East Anglia – AAB–BBB (PPE) (IB 32–31 pts)
　　　　　Exeter – AAA–AAB (Phil Pol Econ; Phil Langs)
　　　　　Glasgow – AAB (Phil BSc courses) (IB 34–32 pts)
　　　　　Leeds – AAB (Mnd Knwl) (IB 35 pts)
　　　　　Liverpool – AAB–ABB (Maths Phil) (IB 35 pts HL 555)
　　　　　London (Birk) – AAB (Phil)
　　　　　London (King's) – AAB+AS-Abbbe (Rel Phil Eth)
　　　　　London (RH) – AAB–ABB (Mus Phil; Phil; Anc Hist Phil; Dr Phil; Langs Phil)
　　　　　Manchester – AAB–BBB (Phil Comb St courses) (IB 35–32 pts)
　　　　　Queen's Belfast – AAB–ABBa (PPE)
　　　　　St Andrews – AAB (Phil Theol St) (IB 36 pts)
　　　　　Sheffield – AAB–ABB (Ling Phil courses) (IB 32–35 pts)
　　　　　Southampton – AAB–ABB (Phil Pol) (IB 34 pts HL 16 pts)
　　　　　Sussex – AAB–ABB (Hist Phil) (IB 34–36 pts)
　　　　　Swansea – AAB (PPE)
320 pts **Birmingham** – ABB (Phil Joint Hons) (IB 32–34 pts)
　　　　　Cardiff – ABB (Phil Sociol) (IB 32 pts)
　　　　　Dundee – ABB 320 pts 2nd yr entry (Art Phil Contemp Prac) (IB 34 pts)
　　　　　Essex – 300–320 pts (Phil Law) (IB 29 pts)
　　　　　Hull – 320 pts (Phil BA)
　　　　　Kent – 320 pts (Phil Pol) (IB 31–35 pts)
　　　　　Lancaster – ABB 320 pts (Hist Phil) (IB 32 pts)
　　　　　Leeds – ABB–BBC (Phil joint courses) (IB 32 pts)
　　　　　Newcastle – ABB (Phil St) (IB 32 pts HL 555)
　　　　　Nottingham – ABB (Fr/Ger Phil) (IB 32 pts)
　　　　　Reading – 320–340 pts (Phil courses)
　　　　　Sheffield – ABB–BBB (Bib St Phil) (IB 35–32 pts)
300 pts **Aberdeen** – BBB (Nat Phil (Phys)) (IB 30 pts HL 15 pts)
　　　　　East Anglia – BBB (Phil Film St) (IB 31 pts)
　　　　　Edinburgh – BBB–AAA (Phil Gk) (IB 34 pts HL 555)
　　　　　Essex – 300–320 pts (PPE) (IB 29 pts)
　　　　　Keele – 300–320 pts (Phil joint courses) (IB 25 pts)
　　　　　Lancaster – BBB–BBC 300–280 pts (Eth Phil Relig) (IB 29 pts)
　　　　　Liverpool – BBB (Phil Fr/Ger/Hisp St/Ital) (IB 30 pts)
　　　　　Queen's Belfast – BBB–BBCb (Phil courses) (IB 29 pts HL 655)
280 pts **Bristol UWE** – 280–300 pts (Engl Phil)
　　　　　Gloucestershire – 280–300 pts (Relig Phil Eth)
　　　　　Hertfordshire – 280 pts (Phil Crea Writ; Phil Media Cult; Phil)

For a quick reference offers calculator, fold out the inside back cover.

Hull – 280–300 pts (Phil Langs) (IB 30 pts)
London (Hey) – 280 pts (Psy Phil)
Oxford Brookes – BBC–ABB (Phil Comb Hons courses)
Roehampton – 280–340 pts (Phil courses)
260 pts Bristol UWE – 260–300 pts (Phil; Phil Media Cult St; Phil Jrnl)
Dundee – BCC (Am St Phil) (IB 29 pts)
Liverpool Hope – 260–320 pts (Phil Eth courses) (IB 25 pts)
London Met – 260 pts (Phil Bus Econ; Phil Hist)
Manchester Met – 220–260 pts (Phil joint courses)
Newman (UC) – 260 pts (Phil Relig Eth courses; Phil Theol courses)
Nottingham Trent – 260 pts (Phil Media; Phil Langs; Phil Euro St)
240 pts Bradford – 240 pts (Phil)
Dundee – CCC 240 pts 1st yr entry (Art Phil Contemp Prac)
Stirling – CCC (Comp Sci Phil)
220 pts Bath Spa – 220–280 pts (Phil Eth)
Northampton – 220–260 pts (Phil; Phil Joint Hons)
200 pts Anglia Ruskin – 200 pts (Phil; Phil Dr; Phil Engl)
Central Lancashire – 200–240 pts (Phil Comb Hons; Phil)
180 pts Bradford – 180–220 pts (Interd Hum St (Phil Engl Psy Sociol))
Greenwich – 180 pts (Phil Langs)
Staffordshire – 180–220 pts (Phil courses)
Trinity Saint David – 180–240 pts (Phil Joint Hons)
160 pts St Mary's Twickenham (UC) – 160–200 pts (Phil Joint Hons)
Wolverhampton – 160–220 pts (Phil Sociol; Relig St Phil; War St Phil)

Open University – contact +44 (0)845 300 6090 **or** www.openuniversity.co.uk/you
(Pol Phil Econ)

Alternative offers
See **Chapter 7** and **Appendix 1** for grades/UCAS Tariff points information for the International Baccalaureate, Scottish Highers/Advanced Highers, the Welsh Baccalaureate, the Irish Leaving Certificate, the Cambridge Pre-U Diploma, the Advanced Diploma and the Extended Project.

CHOOSING YOUR COURSE (SEE ALSO CH. 1)
Some course features
Exeter A large number of combined honours courses are offered in Philosophy including options with modern languages in which a year is spent abroad. Other programmes also allow for a year of study in Europe, North America and Australia.
London (Hey) One of the largest faculties. Philosophy can also be studied with Theology, Psychology or Religion and Ethics.
Manchester Philosophy is a broad course covering the main subject topics such as the philosophy of modern religion, modern political thought, psychology, law and a language. Philosophy is also offered with Politics.
Oxford Brookes Philosophy can be studied as a single subject or with a range of joint subjects including Anthropology, Molecular Biology, European Culture and Society, Fine Art, Mathematics, Psychology, Sociology and Theology.
York A single honours and a range of integrated courses can be studied on an 'Equal' basis in which Philosophy is taken with English, French, German, History, Linguistics, Sociology, Mathematics and Physics. A Politics, Philosophy and Economics course is also offered. See also **Combined courses**.

Universities and colleges teaching quality See www.qaa.ac.uk; http://unistats.direct.gov.uk.

Top research universities and colleges (RAE 2008) London (UCL); St Andrews; London (King's); Sheffield; Reading; Cambridge (Hist Phil Sci); London LSE; Oxford; Stirling; Bristol; Essex; London (Birk); Nottingham; Leeds; Middlesex; Edinburgh.

ADMISSIONS INFORMATION

Number of applicants per place (approx) Birmingham 6; Bradford 7; Bristol 19; Cambridge 6; Cardiff 8; Dundee 6; Durham (all courses) 14; East Anglia 6; Hull 19; Kent 9; Lancaster 6; Leeds 10; Liverpool 5; London (Hey) 4; London (King's) 6; London LSE 11; London Met 3; Manchester 10; Middlesex 8; Northampton 3; Nottingham 7; Oxford (success rate 44%, (PPE) 29%); Sheffield 6; Southampton 7; Staffordshire 8; Trinity Saint David 4; Warwick 9; York 6.

Advice to applicants and planning the UCAS personal statement Read Bertrand Russell's *Problems of Philosophy*. Refer to any particular aspects of philosophy which interest you (check that these are offered on the courses for which you are applying). Since Philosophy is not a school subject, selectors will expect applicants to have read around the subject. Explain what you know about the nature of studying philosophy. Say what you have read in philosophy and give an example of a philosophical issue that interests you. Universities do not expect applicants to have a wide knowledge of the subject, but evidence that you know what the subject is about is important.

Misconceptions about this course Applicants are sometimes surprised to find what wide-ranging Philosophy courses are offered.

Selection interviews Yes Birmingham, Bristol (mature students), Cambridge, Durham, Kingston, Lancaster, Leeds, Liverpool, London (Hey), London (UCL), Newcastle, Oxford (Phil Mod Lang) 24% (PPE) 18% (Phil Theol) 6%, Southampton, Staffordshire, Trinity Saint David, Warwick; **Some** Cardiff, Dundee, Hull, London LSE (rare), York.

Interview advice and questions Philosophy is a very wide subject and initially applicants will be asked for their reasons for their choice and their special interests in the subject. Questions in recent years have included: Is there a difference between being tactless and being insensitive? Can you be tactless and thin-skinned? Define the difference between knowledge and belief. Was the vertical distortion of El Greco's paintings a product of a vision defect? What is the point of studying philosophy? What books on philosophy have you read? Discuss the work of a renowned philosopher. What is a philosophical novel? Who has the right to decide your future – yourself or another? What do you want to do with your life? What is a philosophical question? John is your husband, and if John is your husband then necessarily you must be his wife; if you are necessarily his wife then it is not possible that you could not be his wife; so it was impossible for you not to have married him – you were destined for each other. Discuss. What is the difference between a man's entitlements, his deserts and his attributes? What are morals? A good understanding of philosophy is needed for entry to degree courses, and applicants are expected to demonstrate this if they are called to interview. As one admissions tutor stated, 'If you find Bertrand Russell's *Problems of Philosophy* unreadable – don't apply!' See also **Chapter 6**. **Cambridge** If you were to form a government of philosophers what selection process would you use? Is it moral to hook up a psychopath (whose only pleasure is killing) to a really stimulating machine so that he can believe he is in the real world and kill as much as he likes? **Oxford** If you entered a teletransporter and your body was destroyed and instantly recreated on Mars in exactly the same way with all your memories intact etc, would you be the same person? Tutors are not so much concerned with what you know as how you think about it. Evidence required concerning social and political topics and the ability to discuss them critically. (PPE) Is being hungry the same thing as wanting to eat? Why is there not a global government? What do you think of teleport machines? Should there be an intelligence test to decide who should vote? **York** Do human beings have free will? Do we perceive the world as it really is?

Reasons for rejection (non-academic) Evidence of severe psychological disturbance, criminal activity, drug problems (evidence from referees' reports). Lack of knowledge of philosophy. **Oxford** He was not able to explore his thoughts deeply enough or with sufficient centrality. **York** No evidence of having read any philosophical literature.

AFTER-RESULTS ADVICE

Offers to applicants repeating A-levels Higher Bristol (Phil Econ), Essex, Glasgow, Leeds, Nottingham (in some cases), Warwick; **Same** Birmingham, Bristol, Cardiff, Dundee, Durham, East

Anglia, Hull, Liverpool Hope, Newcastle, Newport, Nottingham (in some cases), Nottingham Trent, St Mary's Twickenham (UC), Southampton, Staffordshire, Stirling, Wolverhampton, York.

GRADUATE DESTINATIONS AND EMPLOYMENT (2007/8 HESA)
Graduates surveyed 1590 **Employed** 580 **In further study** 415 **Assumed unemployed** 195

Career note Graduates have a wide range of transferable skills that can lead to employment in many areas, eg management, public administration, publishing, banking and social services.

OTHER DEGREE SUBJECTS FOR CONSIDERATION
Divinity; History and Philosophy of Science; History of Art; Human Sciences; Psychology; Religious Studies; Science; Theology.

PHOTOGRAPHY
(see also Art and Design (General), Art and Design (Fine Art), Film, Radio, Video and TV Studies, Media Studies)

Photography courses offer a range of specialised studies involving commercial, industrial and still photography, portraiture and film, digital and video work. Increasingly this subject is featuring in Media courses. See also **Appendix 4**.

Useful websites http://hub. the-aop.org; www.rps.org; www.bjp-online.com.

NB The points totals shown to the left of the institutions are for ease of reference only. It must not be assumed that Tariff points are always used by institutions or that they can be substituted for an offer in grades. The level of an offer is not necessarily indicative of the quality of a course.

COURSE OFFERS INFORMATION
Subject requirements/preferences GCSE Art and/or a portfolio usually required. **AL** One or two subjects may be required, including an art/design or creative subject. Most institutions will make offers on the basis of a portfolio of work.

NB In 2012 universities and colleges will differ in their use of GCE AL/AS unit grade information, A* grades, the Extended Project (EPQ), the Advanced Diploma and the Cambridge Pre-U examination when considering applicants and making offers. An EPQ may be accepted in place of an AS subject. Check websites of universities and colleges for the latest offers information.

Your target offers and examples of courses provided by each institution
320 pts **Glasgow (SA)** – ABB (Fine Art (Photo))
300 pts **Huddersfield** – 300 pts (Photo)
        Leeds – BBB (Cnma Photo) (IB 32 pts)
280 pts **Birmingham City** – 280 pts (Media Comm (Media Photo))
        Brighton – BBC (Photo)
        Glamorgan – 280–320 pts (Photo)
        Gloucestershire – 280–300 pts (Photojrnl Doc Photo)
        London Met – 280 pts (Fine Art (Photo))
        Northumbria – 280 pts (Contemp Photo Prac)
        Nottingham Trent – 280 pts (Photo Photo Euro)
        Roehampton – 280–340 pts (Photo joint courses) (IB 25 pts)
        Sheffield Hallam – 280 pts (Photo)
260 pts **Coventry** – 260 pts (Photo) (IB 26 pts)
240 pts **Bolton** – 240 pts (Photo; Photo Comb Hons)
        Bournemouth – 240 pts (Photography)
        Bradford – 240 pts (Photo Dig Media)
        Canterbury Christ Church – 240 pts (Photo Joint Hons) (IB 24 pts)
        Central Lancashire – 240–260 pts (Photo; Photo Jrnl; Photo Fash Brnd Prom)
        Chester – 240 pts (Photo Comb courses)

Cumbria – 240 pts (Photo) (IB 30 pts)
De Montfort – 240 pts (Photo Vid)
Edinburgh (CA) – 240 pts (Photography)
Edinburgh Napier – 240 pts (Photo Film)
Kent – contact admissions 240 pts (Photo BA (top-up))
Lincoln – 240 pts (Contemp Lns Media courses)
Newport – 240–260 pts (Doc Photo; Photo Fash Adv; Photo Art)
Plymouth – 240 pts (Photog) (IB 24 pts)
Suffolk (Univ Campus) – 240 pts (Photo Dig Media; Photo)
Ulster – 240 pts (Photo)

220 pts **Anglia Ruskin** – 220 pts (Photo)
Middlesex – 220 pts (Photo)
Northampton – 220–260 pts (Photo Prac)
Staffordshire – 220 pts (Photo; Photo Phil; Fine Art (Photo))
Sunderland – 220–360 pts (Photo)

200 pts **Bristol UWE** – 200 pts (Photo)
Creative Arts – 200 pts (Photo) (IB 30 pts)
East London – 200 pts (Photo courses)
Hereford (CA) – 200 pts (Photo)
Nescot – 200 pts (Photo Imag)
Portsmouth – 200–280 pts (Fdn Art (Photo)) (IB 25 pts)
Swansea Met – 200–360 pts (Photo Arts)
West London – 200 pts (Photo Dig Imag)
Westminster – BB (Photo Arts)
Wolverhampton – 200 pts (Photo)

180 pts **Derby** – 180–240 pts (Commer Photo) (IB 20 pts)
Hertfordshire – 180 pts (Photo Media)
Staffordshire – 180–220 pts (Photojrnl)

160 pts **Blackpool and Fylde (Coll)** – 160 pts (Wldlf Photo)
Colchester (Inst) – 160 pts (Photo)
Robert Gordon – 160 pts (Photo Electron Media) (IB 24 pts)
Sir Gâr (Coll) – 160 pts (Photo PR)
Southampton Solent – 160–200 pts (Fash Photo; Photo)
Westminster – CC (Photo Dig Imag) (IB 26 pts)

160pts **Bedfordshire** – 160 pts (Photo Vid Art)

120 pts **Blackburn (Coll Univ Centre)** – 120 pts (Photo Media)
Bournemouth Arts (UC) – 120 pts (Photo)
Cleveland (CAD) – 120 pts (Photo)
Grimsby (IFHE) – 120–240 pts (Commer Photography)
Northbrook (Coll) – 120 pts (Contemp Photo Arts (Prac))
South Essex (Coll) – 120–160 pts (Photo)
South Nottingham (Coll) – 120–200 pts (Photo Dig Imag)
Stockport (Coll) – 120 pts (Photo)

100 pts **London South Bank** – 100 pts (Dig Photo)

Arts London – contact admissions (Photo)
Falmouth (UC) – contact admissions (Press Edit Photo; Mar Nat Hist Photo))
Kingston – contact admissions office (Photo)
Manchester Met – (Photo) contact admissions
Norwich (UCA) – CCc (Photo)
Ravensbourne – contact admissions (Dig Photo)

Alternative offers
See **Chapter 7** and **Appendix 1** for grades/UCAS Tariff points information for the International Baccalaureate, Scottish Highers/Advanced Highers, the Welsh Baccalaureate, the Irish Leaving Certificate, the Cambridge Pre-U Diploma, the Advanced Diploma and the Extended Project.

For a quick reference offers calculator, fold out the inside back cover.

EXAMPLES OF FOUNDATION DEGREES IN THE SUBJECT FIELD

Anglia Ruskin; Arts London; Bath Spa; Bedfordshire; Blackburn (Coll Univ Centre); Blackpool and Fylde (Coll); Bournemouth Arts (UC); Brighton; Bristol City (Coll); Bucks New; Cleveland (CAD); Cornwall (Coll); Exeter (Coll); Farnborough (CT); Gloucestershire; Greenwich; Grimsby (IFHE); Guildford (Coll); Hereford (CA); Hertfordshire; Hull (Coll); Kirklees (Coll); Leeds (CAD); Manchester (Coll); Mid-Cheshire (Coll); Nescot; Nottingham New (Coll); Plymouth (CA); Sheffield (Coll); St Helens (Coll); Staffordshire Reg Fed (SURF); Truro (Coll).

CHOOSING YOUR COURSE (SEE ALSO CH. 1)

Some course features
Falmouth (UC) Specialist courses in Press, Marine and Natural History Photography are also offered.
Nottingham Trent Courses in Photography are offered focusing on social documentary, art practice, fashion work or with a year in Europe.
Westminster (Clin Photo) The only full-time degree in clinical photography in the UK, it combines a study of photography and digital imaging with science, anatomy, physiology, biology and clinical practice. Work-based learning in a clinical setting forms a large part of the course.

Universities and colleges teaching quality See www.qaa.ac.uk; http://unistats.direct.gov.uk.

Examples of sandwich degree courses Birmingham City; Portsmouth; Staffordshire.

ADMISSIONS INFORMATION

Number of applicants per place (approx) Arts London 10; Birmingham City 6; Blackpool and Fylde (Coll) 3; Bournemouth Arts (UC) 7; Cleveland (CAD) 2; Derby 20; Edinburgh Napier 33; Falmouth (UC) 3; Newport 2; Nottingham Trent 4; Plymouth 2; Plymouth (CA) 7; Portsmouth 4; Staffordshire 3; Stockport (Coll) 6; Swansea Met 12.

Advice to applicants and planning the UCAS personal statement Discuss your interest in photography and your knowledge of various aspects of the subject, for example, digital, video, landscape, medical, wildlife and portrait photography. Read photographic journals to keep up-to-date on developments, particularly in photographic technology. You will also need first-hand experience of photography and to be competent in basic skills. See also **Appendix 4**. **Derby** (Non-UK students) Fluency in written and spoken English important. Portfolio of work essential.

Misconceptions about this course Some believe that courses are all practical work with no theory. **Cumbria** They didn't realise the facilities were so good! **Kirklees (Coll)** Some applicants think that it's a traditional photography course. It's as digital as the individual wants it to be.

Selection interviews Most institutions will interview applicants and expect to see a portfolio of work.

Interview advice and questions Questions relate to the applicant's portfolio of work which, for these courses, is of prime importance. Who are your favourite photographers? What is the most recent exhibition you have attended? Have any leading photographers influenced your work? Questions regarding contemporary photography. Written work sometimes required. See **Chapter 6**.

Reasons for rejection (non-academic) Lack of passion for the subject. Lack of exploration and creativity in practical work. Poorly presented portfolio.

AFTER-RESULTS ADVICE

Offers to applicants repeating A-levels Same Birmingham City, Blackpool and Fylde (Coll), Chester, Cumbria, Manchester Met, Nottingham Trent, Staffordshire.

GRADUATE DESTINATIONS AND EMPLOYMENT (2007/8 HESA)

See **Film, Radio, Video and TV Studies**.

Career note Opportunities for photographers exist in a range of specialisms including advertising and editorial work, fashion, medical, industrial, scientific and technical photography. Some graduates also go into photojournalism and other aspects of the media.

OTHER DEGREE SUBJECTS FOR CONSIDERATION
Art and Design; Digital Animation; Film, Radio, Video and TV Studies; Media Studies; Moving Image; Radiography.

PHYSICAL EDUCATION

(including **Including Coaching**; see also **Sports Sciences/Studies**)

Physical Education courses are very popular and unfortunately restricted in number. Ability in gymnastics and involvement in sport are obviously important factors. See also **Appendix 2**.

Useful websites www.afpe.org.uk; www.uksport.gov.uk; see also **Education Studies** and **Teacher Training**.

NB The points totals shown to the left of the institutions are for ease of reference only. It must not be assumed that Tariff points are always used by institutions or that they can be substituted for an offer in grades. The level of an offer is not necessarily indicative of the quality of a course.

COURSE OFFERS INFORMATION
Subject requirements/preferences GCSE English, mathematics and a science. **AL** PE, sports studies and science are preferred subjects and for some courses one of these may be required. **Other** Enhanced Disclosure (criminal record check) before starting the course. Declaration of Health usually required.

NB In 2012 universities and colleges will differ in their use of GCE AL/AS unit grade information, A* grades, the Extended Project (EPQ), the Advanced Diploma and the Cambridge Pre-U examination when considering applicants and making offers. An EPQ may be accepted in place of an AS subject. Check websites of universities and colleges for the latest offers information.

Your target offers and examples of courses provided by each institution
340 pts **Brighton** – AAB 340–380 pts (PE QTS) (IB 36 pts)
320 pts **Birmingham** – ABB–BBB (Spo PE Coach Sci)
  Brighton – ABB (Spo Coach) (IB 32 pts)
300 pts **Bangor** – 300-260 pts (Spo Sci (PE))
  Cardiff (UWIC) – 300 pts (Spo PE)
  East Anglia – BBB (PE Spo)
  Edge Hill – 300 pts (PE Sch Spo)
  Edinburgh – BBB (PE) (IB 34 pts HL 555)
  Roehampton – 300–360 pts (P Educ (PE) QTS)
  Stranmillis (UC) – BBB (PE Educ)
280 pts **Brunel** – 280 pts (Spo Coach)
  Gloucestershire – 280–300 pts (Spo Coach Spo Sci)
  Leeds Met – 280–260 pts (PE; Spo Coach)
  Newman (UC) – 280–320 pts (Ely Yrs P Educ PE; Ely Chld P Educ PE)
  Northumbria – 280 pts (Spo Coach) (IB 25 pts)
  Oxford Brookes – BBC (PE)
  Sheffield Hallam – 280 pts (PE Yth Spo)
  Wolverhampton – 280 pts (PE QTS P)
  Worcester – 280 pts (PE Comb Hons)
260 pts **Bangor** – 260-280 pts (Spo Hlth PE)
  Bristol UWE – 260–300 pts (Spo Coach) (IB 26–28 pts)
  Brunel – 260–300 pts (BSc S PE)
  Canterbury Christ Church – 260 pts (PE Spo Exer Sci)
  Cardiff (UWIC) – 260 pts (Educ St Spo Physl Actvt) (IB 28 pts)
  Chichester – CCC–BCC (Spo Coach)
  Manchester Met – 260 pts (Exer PE Comb Hons; Coach St Comb Hons)

Sheffield Hallam – 260 pts (Spo Dev Coach)
Southampton Solent – 260 pts (Spo Coach)
Stirling – BCC (Spo St PE Educ) (IB 30 pts)
240 pts **Bedfordshire** – 240–320 pts (PE QTS S)
Central Lancashire – 240-280 pts (Spo Coach)
Cumbria – 240 pts (PE QTS P/S)
Glyndŵr – 240 pts (Spo Coach)
Greenwich – 240 pts (Spo Sci Coach)
Hull – 240 pts (Spo Coach Perf)
Leeds Trinity (UC) – 240 pts (PE P Spo Dev)
Lincoln – 240 pts (Spo Dev Coach)
Liverpool John Moores – 240–280 pts (Spo Dev PE; PE QTS P/S; Educ St PE)
London Met – 240 pts (Spo Sci Coach)
Newport – 240 pts (Spo Coach)
Plymouth – 240 pts (P PE)
UCP Marjon – 240 pts (Coach PE; PE S Educ)
220 pts **East London** – 220 pts (Spo Coach)
Kingston – 220 pts (Spo Coach)
Liverpool John Moores – 220–260 pts (Out Educ PE)
UCP Marjon – 220 pts (Chld PE)
York St John – 220–260 pts (Phys Ed Spo Coach)
200 pts **Bedfordshire** – 200 pts (Spo Sci Coach)
Bolton – 200 pts (Spo Sci Coach)
180 pts **Abertay Dundee** – 180 pts (Spo Coach)
Anglia Ruskin – 180 pts (Spo Coach PE)
St Mary's Twickenham (UC) – 180–200 pts (PE QTS S)
Staffordshire – 180–240 pts (PE Yth Spo Coach)
160 pts **Bishop Grosseteste (UC)** – 160 pts (Educ St Spo)
Derby – 160–240 pts (Spo Coach/Dev/Psy)
SAC (Scottish CAg) – CC (Spo Dev Coach)
St Mary's Twickenham (UC) – 160 pts (Coach Sci)
140 pts **Bishop Burton (Coll)** – 140 pts (Eqn Spo Coach)
100 pts **Bucks New** – 100–200 pts (Spo Coach)

Alternative offers
See **Chapter 7** and **Appendix 1** for grades/UCAS Tariff points information for the International Baccalaureate, Scottish Highers/Advanced Highers, the Welsh Baccalaureate, the Irish Leaving Certificate, the Cambridge Pre-U Diploma, the Advanced Diploma and the Extended Project.

CHOOSING YOUR COURSE (SEE ALSO CH. 1)
Some course features
Birmingham (Spo PE Coach Sci) A practical and theoretical programme in sport, physical education and leisure with a placement module in education or the leisure industry.
Chichester (PE QTS S) Course covers games, gymnastics, dance, aquatic, athletic fitness and health and outdoor adventure activities. Placements take place in Years 2 and 3 and the final year.
Liverpool John Moores Courses are offered for those wanting to train as PE teachers or with specialist studies in sport development and management.
UCP Marjon (Coach PE) Course covers coach and sport education and also leads to a PGCE in PE teaching.

Top research universities and colleges (RAE 2008) See **Sports Sciences/Studies**.

ADMISSIONS INFORMATION
Number of applicants per place (approx) Bangor 19; Birmingham 5; Brunel 10; Chichester 5; Edge Hill 40; Leeds Trinity (UC) 33; Liverpool John Moores 4; Newman (UC) 5; Sheffield Hallam 60; St Mary's Twickenham (UC) 9; UCP Marjon 18; Worcester 31.

Advice to applicants and planning the UCAS personal statement Ability in gymnastics, athletics and all sports and games is important. Full details of these activities should be given on the UCAS application – for example, teams, dates and awards achieved, assisting in extra-curricular activities. Involvement with local sports clubs, health clubs, summer camps, Gap Year. Relevant experience in coaching, teaching, community and youth work. **Liverpool John Moores** Commitment to working with children and a good sports background.

Selection interviews Most institutions. In most cases, applicants will take part in physical education practical tests and games/gymnastics, depending on the course. The results of these tests could affect the level of offers. See **Chapter 6**.

Interview advice and questions The applicant's interests in physical education will be discussed, with specific questions on, for example, sportsmanship, refereeing, umpiring and coaching. Questions in the past have also included: What qualities should a good netball goal defence possess? How could you encourage a group of children into believing that sport is fun? Do you think that physical education should be compulsory in schools? Why do you think you would make a good teacher? What is the name of the education minister? **Liverpool John Moores** Questions on what the applicant has gained or learned through experiences with children.

Reasons for rejection (non-academic) Poor communication and presentational skills. Relatively poor sporting background or knowledge. Lack of knowledge about the teaching of physical education and the commitment required. Lack of ability in practicalities, for example, gymnastics, dance when relevant. Poor self-presentation. Poor writing skills.

AFTER-RESULTS ADVICE
Offers to applicants repeating A-levels Same Liverpool John Moores, Newman (UC), St Mary's Twickenham (UC).

GRADUATE DESTINATIONS AND EMPLOYMENT (2007/8 HESA)
Career note The majority of graduates go into education although, depending on any special interests, they may also go on into the sport and leisure industry.

OTHER DEGREE SUBJECTS FOR CONSIDERATION
Coach Education; Exercise and Fitness; Exercise Physiology; Human Biology; Leisure and Recreation; Physiotherapy; Sport and Exercise Science; Sport Health and Exercise; Sport Studies/Sciences; Sports Coaching; Sports Development; Sports Engineering; Sports Psychology; Sports Therapy.

PHYSICS
(see also Astronomy and Astrophysics)

There is a considerable shortage of applicants for Physics courses. Many courses have flexible arrangements to enable students to follow their own interests and specialisations, for example circuit design, microwave devices, cosmology, medical physics, solid state electronics.

Useful websites www.scienceyear.com; www.scicentral.com; www.ipem.org.uk; www.iop.org; www.noisemakers.org.uk; www.NewScientistJobs.com; www.physics.org; www.nature.com/physics.

NB The points totals shown to the left of the institutions are for ease of reference only. It must not be assumed that Tariff points are always used by institutions or that they can be substituted for an offer in grades. The level of an offer is not necessarily indicative of the quality of a course.

COURSE OFFERS INFORMATION
Subject requirements/preferences GCSE English, mathematics and science. **AL** Physics and mathematics are required for most courses.

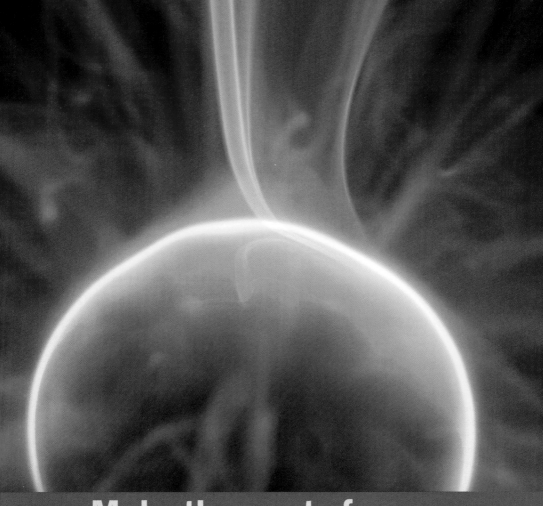

Make the most of your potential as a physicist

Whether you're at school, college, university or have already embarked on your career, find out how the Institute of Physics can help you.

www.iop.org/careers

Thinking about physics?

If you are considering studying physics at university, then why not find out more about what is available from the Institute of Physics.

Physics on Course

Physics on Course is your indispensible guide to physics courses in higher education. Updated annually, *Physics on Course* lists all accredited undergraduate physics degree courses in the UK and Ireland, including the grades that you need to get onto the course. E-mail **education@iop.org** to order your free print copy.

MyPhysicsCourse

New for 2011 is MyPhysicsCourse, the online version of *Physics on Course*. MyPhysicsCourse is a comprehensive, searchable online database of accredited physics degree courses. So whether you want to search by location, or browse astrophysics degrees visit **www.myphysicscourse.org**.

Free membership for 16–19 students

Aged 16–19 and studying physics? Join the Institute of Physics for free and receive:

- Regular updates on what's new in physics
- Exam and university guidance
- Information about careers in physics
- The chance to interact with other young physicists

By joining IOP you will become part of the UK's largest physics community and you will also get full access to the members' magazine *Physics World* online and *physicsworld.com* as well as lots of other exclusive 16–19 member offers.
Find out more and join at **www.iop.org/16-19**.

The Institute of Physics is a scientific charity devoted to increasing the practice, understanding and application of physics. It has a worldwide membership of around 40 000 and is a leading communicator of physics-related science to all audiences, from specialists through to government and the general public.

IOP Institute of Physics

University of Salford
A Greater Manchester University

PHYSICSALFORD
What will you achieve?

AT SALFORD WE'RE TAKING A DIFFERENT APPROACH TO PHYSICS, HELPING YOU ACHIEVE, INVENT AND DISCOVER MORE IN LIFE.

BY CAPITALISING ON THE STRENGTHS WITHIN THE UNIVERSITY WE ARE ABLE TO OFFER A RANGE OF SPECIALISED PHYSICS DEGREES:

- BSc (Hons)/MPhys (Hons) Physics
- BSc (Hons)/MPhys (Hons) Physics with Acoustics
- MPhys (Hons) Physics with Studies in North America
- BSc (Hons) Physics with Pilot Studies
- BSc (Hons)/MPhys (Hons) Physics with a Foundation Year
- BSc (Hons)/MPhys (Hons) Pure and Applied Physics

The University of Salford campus is just a mile and a half from Manchester city centre, giving you the best of both worlds - a friendly, safe environment but just minutes away from all the fun and opportunities of a big city.

For a prospectus contact us:
T: 0161 295 4545
www.cse.salford.ac.uk/physics

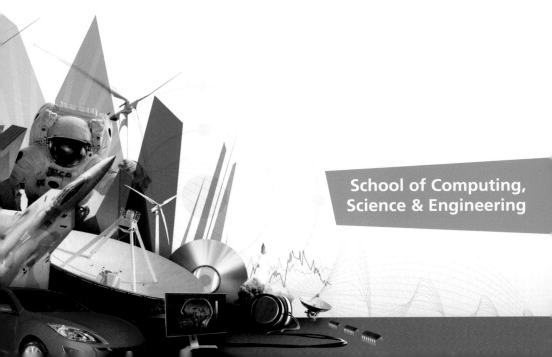

School of Computing, Science & Engineering

University of Salford
A Greater Manchester University

Physics has changed at Salford
- come and find out how

As a Salford physics graduate you will have no shortage of skills. As well as being highly numerate, analytical and logical, the chances are that you'll also be a creative thinker, meticulous, excellent at problem solving and project management - skills that are relevant in any work environment.

A unique part of the Salford physics degree, recently re-designed in partnership with the Institute of Physics, is our emphasis on employer engagement.

An important part of your degree will feature guest lectures from professional physicists from organisations such as; BDP Acoustics, Pilkington, the Royal Navy, Salford Royal Hospital, Nuvia and OpTIC Technium. You will hear about real-life situations and stories of individuals working in industries where physics graduates are sought after and also participate in problem solving activities related to their industry.

We also recognise that physics is a practical as well as a theoretical subject and understand the importance of relating theory taught in lectures to the practicals in the labs. Our curriculum is designed so that relevant practical laboratory classes are taught alongside the core lectures. Not only will this help you understand the concepts more easily, but it makes your learning more interesting too!

As well as teaching you on a day to day basis, your physics lecturers at Salford will be active researchers engaged in a diverse range of projects, meaning your lessons will be up-to-date and relevant to current issues in modern society.

Examples of our current research areas include:

- Improving the performance of solar energy conversion
- The development of new hydrogen storage materials for use in cars
- Understanding radiation damage in materials for fusion reactors
- Complexity theory and applications e.g. used in forecasting climate change and the stock market
- The development of biomaterials for medical applications.

We hold a number of physics open days, which includes a campus tour, throughout the year. Visit our website to find out more.

www.cse.salford.ac.uk/physics

School of Computing
Science & Engineering

NB In 2012 universities and colleges will differ in their use of GCE AL/AS unit grade information, A* grades, the Extended Project (EPQ), the Advanced Diploma and the Cambridge Pre-U examination when considering applicants and making offers. An EPQ may be accepted in place of an AS subject. Check websites of universities and colleges for the latest offers information.

Your target offers and examples of courses provided by each institution

440 pts **Warwick** – See Advice to applicants and planning the UCAS personal statement below and **Chapter 5**. A*AAa (Maths Phys) (IB 39 pts HL maths 6)

420 pts **Imperial London** – A*A*A* (Maths App Maths Phys)

380 pts **Bath** – A*AA–AAA (Nat Sci) (IB 34–38 pts)
Bristol – A*AA–AAB (Maths Phys) (IB 36 pts HL 666)
Cambridge – A*AA college offers may vary (Nat Sci (Phys) (Physl Sci) (Astro)) (IB 38–42 pts HL 766–777)
Edinburgh – A*AA 2nd yr entry (Phys) (IB 38 pts)
Imperial London – A*mathsAA (Phys Theor Phys) (IB 38 pts HL 666)
London (King's) – AAA+AS (Maths Phys) (IB 38 pts H maths 6)
Manchester – A*AA–AAA (Phys Astro) (IB 37–33 pts)
Oxford – A*AA (Phys Phil) (IB 38–42 pts)

360 pts **Birmingham** – AAA–AAB (Phys courses) (IB 32–34 pts)
Bristol – AAA–AAB (Phys Astro) (IB 37–35 pts HL maths phys 6)
Durham – AAA (Maths Phys Joint Hons BSc/MSci) (IB 37 pts HL 6 maths phys)
East Anglia – AAA (Nat Sci BSc) (34 pts)
Edinburgh – AAA–ABB (Geophys) (IB 37–32 pts)
Exeter – AAA–AAB (Phys courses)
Glasgow – AAA (Phys Astro Faster Route)
Leeds – AAA–AAB (Phys Astro) (IB 36–34 pts HL maths phys 6)
Leicester – AAA–AAB (Phys Nano Tech BSc/MPhys) (IB 34 pts)
Liverpool – AAA–ABB (Astro MPhys) (IB 27 pts HL maths phys 6)
London (King's) – AAB+AS (Phys Phil) (IB 36 pts HL maths phys 5)
London (RH) – AAA–ABB (Phys Prtcl Phys) (IB 36 pts)
London (UCL) – AAB+AS–ABB+AS (Theor Phys) (IB 34–36 pts HL 6 maths phys)
Manchester – A*AA–AAA (Phys Phil) (IB 37–33 pts)
Nottingham – AAA–AAB (Phys courses) (IB 34–36 pts)
St Andrews – AAA (Lgc Phil Sci Phys) (IB 38 pts)
Warwick – AAA–AAB (Phys Bus St) (IB 36 pts)

340 pts **Bath** – AAB–ABB (Phys courses) (IB 34–36 pts HL maths phys 5–6)
Bristol – AAB–ABB (Cheml Phys) (IB 34 pts HL 665 maths phys chem)
Cardiff – AAB–ABB (Phys Maths) (IB 32 pts HL 6 maths phys)
Edinburgh – AAB–ABB (Mathem Phys) (IB 34 pts)
Exeter – AAB–ABB (Phys Aus/N Am/NZ) (IB 34–31 pts)
Lancaster – AAB–AAA 340-360 pts (Phys Prtcl Phys Cosmo BSc) (IB 34-36 pts)
Liverpool – AAB–BBB (Phys Nucl Sci) (IB 26 pts)
London (King's) – AAB+AS (Phys Med Apps) (IB 36 pts)
Newcastle – AAB (Nat Sci) (IB 34 pts)
Queen's Belfast – AAB (Phys MSci; Phys Med Apps MSci; Theor Phys)
Sheffield – AAB–ABB (Phys Med Phys) (IB 33 pts)
Southampton – AAB (Phys Spc Sci) (IB 36–34 pts)
Surrey – AAB 340 pts (Phys MPhys; Phys Nucl Astro MPhys; Phys Sat Tech MPhys; Phys Fin MPhys)
Sussex – AAB–ABB (Phys Astro) (IB 32–36 pts)
Swansea – 340 pts (Phys MPhys; Theor Phys)
York – AAB–ABB (Maths Phys) (IB 34–32 pts)

320 pts **Aberdeen** – ABB (Phys Comp Sys Mdl)
Central Lancashire – ABB (Comp Phys; Maths Phys)
Glasgow – ABB (Phys Theor Phys) (B 32 pts)

Leeds – ABB (Hist Phil Sci (Phys); Chem Phys)
Liverpool – ABB (Mathem Phys MMath) (IB 32 pts)
London (QM) – 320 pts (Phys Prtcl Phys MSci) (HL maths phys 6)
Loughborough – ABB–AAB (Spo Sci Phys) (IB 30 pts)
Strathclyde – ABB–BBB (Phys QTS) (IB 30–32 pts)
Surrey – ABB (Phys Fin BSc)
Sussex – AAB–BBB (Phys) (IB 34 pts)
York – ABB (Phys Astro BSc)

300 pts **Aberdeen** – BBB (Nat Phil (Phys)) (IB 30 pts HL 15 pts)
Cardiff – BBB (Astro; Theor Comput Phys)
Dundee – BBB (Electron Eng Phys MEng) (IB 28–32 pts)
Heriot-Watt – BBB (Phys courses)
Keele – 300–320 pts (Phys courses)
Liverpool John Moores – BBB (Phys Astron) (IB 24–28 pts)
London (QM) – 300 pts (Phys Prtcl Phys BSc) (IB 30pts HL maths phys 6)
Nottingham Trent – 260–300 pts (Phys; Phys Astro; Phys Nucl Tech)
Queen's Belfast – BBB (Phys BSc; Phys Med Apps BSc)
Salford – 300 pts (Phys Acoust MPhys)
Swansea – 300 pts (Phys BSc; Phys Nano; Phys Spo Sci)

280 pts **Central Lancashire** – 280–320 pts (Astro)
Hertfordshire – 280 pts (Phys courses)
Kent – BBC (Phys Astro) (IB 30 pts)
Queen's Belfast – BBB (Phys Comp Sci)
West Scotland – BBC (Phys Nucl Tech)

260 pts **Hull** – 260–320 pts (App Phys BSc; Phys; Phys Nano)

240 pts **Aberdeen** – CCC 240 pts (Phys Langs; Phys Geol)

Aberystwyth – 240 pts (Spc Sci Robot) (IB 27 pts HL phys comp-sci maths 5)
Coventry – 240 pts (Ind Phys)
220 pts **Nottingham Trent** – 220 pts (Phys Foren Apps)
Portsmouth – 220 pts (App Phys)
200 pts **Glamorgan** – 200 pts (Astron)
160 pts **Canterbury Christ Church** – 160 pts (Integ Sci)
Salford – 160 pts (Phys Fdn Yr)
140 pts **West Scotland** – CD–DD **or** bbc (Phys)

Liverpool John Moores – Check with university (Astro MPhys)
Open University – contact +44 (0)845 300 6090 **or** www.openuniversity.co.uk/you
(Phys Sci)

Alternative offers
See **Chapter 7** and **Appendix 1** for grades/UCAS Tariff points information for the International Baccalaureate, Scottish Highers/Advanced Highers, the Welsh Baccalaureate, the Irish Leaving Certificate, the Cambridge Pre-U Diploma, the Advanced Diploma and the Extended Project.

EXAMPLES OF FOUNDATION DEGREES IN THE SUBJECT FIELD
Cumbria; Hull (Coll); Nottingham Trent.

CHOOSING YOUR COURSE (SEE ALSO CH. 1)
Some course features
Bath After a first year on the Natural Sciences programme or the Mathematics and Physics course it is possible to transfer to Single Honours Physics in Year 2.
Durham Several courses are offered which include Theoretical Physics and Astronomy. Physics can also be taken jointly with seven other subjects and is also offered as part of the Natural Sciences programme.

THE UNIVERSITY *of York*

Study Physics at THE University of the Year

The University of York is regularly in the Top10 of national league tables, and is the Times Higher Education 'University of the Year 2010'.

2010
THE AWARDS
UNIVERSITY OF THE YEAR

Why is it the right place for you to study physics?

We pride ourselves on the quality of the undergraduate experience we offer – as seen in our many satisfied graduates. York has an enviable reputation for having high standards and yet being friendly and welcoming for students from all backgrounds, so anyone has the opportunity to excel.

What can you study?

We have a flexible modular system, offering degrees in Physics, Physics with Astrophysics, Theoretical Physics, Maths and Physics, Physics with Philosophy and Physics with Business Management. All are available as either 3-year BSc and 4-year MPhys, and with an option for a 'year in Europe'. Transfers between degrees are allowed in the 1st year.

How do you study?

We teach via a mix of traditional lectures, small group tutorials, laboratories, workshops and projects. All our students carry out an in-depth research project in their final year – often thought to be the best part of the degree!

How can you find out more?

Why not come along to one of our Open Days, read our undergraduate booklet or visit the website http://www.york.ac.uk/physics ? You can also email any questions to physics-undergraduate-admissions@york.ac.uk .

Kent The Physics course allows considerable flexibility and enables students to defer their choice between Physics and other degree programmes in the Faculty until the end of the first year. Physics can also be studied with Astrophysics, Forensic Science, Astronomy and Space Science.
Loughborough An optional year in paid employement is offered either in the UK or abroad.
Warwick A central core of physics and mathematics is taken by all Physics students, ensuring flexibility and freedom of choice in the courses that follow in the second and third years. Mathematics and Physics, and Physics and Business Studies courses are also available.

Universities and colleges teaching quality See www.qaa.ac.uk; http://unistats.direct.gov.uk.

Top research universities and colleges (RAE 2008) Lancaster; Cambridge; Nottingham; St Andrews; Bath; Edinburgh; Durham; Imperial London; Sheffield; London (UCL); Glasgow; Birmingham; Exeter; Sussex.

Examples of sandwich degree courses Bath; Bristol; Hertfordshire; Loughborough; Nottingham Trent; Surrey; West Scotland.

ADMISSIONS INFORMATION
Number of applicants per place (approx) Bath 6; Birmingham 6; Bristol 9; Cardiff 4, (Phys Astron) 6; Dundee 5; Durham 6; Edinburgh 9; Exeter 5; Heriot-Watt 5; Hull 7; Imperial London 3; Kent 8; Lancaster 8; Leeds 7; Leicester 7; Liverpool 4; London (King's) 7; London (QM) 6; London (RH) 9; London (UCL) 6; Loughborough 6; Nottingham 10; Salford 5; Southampton 6; Strathclyde 5; Surrey 5; Swansea 3; Warwick 8; York 5.

Advice to applicants and planning the UCAS personal statement Work experience should be mentioned, together with interests in maths and physics. Admissions tutors look for potential, enthusiasm and interest in the subject. The Institute of Physics can provide information on the work of the physicist. An awareness of the range of careers in which physics is involved should also be

mentioned on the UCAS application, together with an explanation of any particular interests and details of books read on physics or mathematics (not science fiction!), and attendance at courses, for example, summer schools or day conferences for physics or engineering. See **Appendix 4**.

Selection interviews **Yes** Bath, Birmingham, Cambridge, Durham, Exeter, Heriot-Watt, Hull, Imperial London, Lancaster, Liverpool, London (QM), London (RH), Loughborough, Nottingham, Oxford (Phys) 24% (Phys Phil) 20%, Sheffield, Strathclyde, Surrey, Swansea, Warwick, York; **Some** Cardiff, Dundee, East Anglia, Salford.

Interview advice and questions Questions will almost certainly focus on those aspects of the physics A/AS-level course which the student enjoys. See **Chapter 6**. **Bristol** Why Physics? Questions on mechanics, physics and pure maths. Given paper and calculator and questions asked orally; best to take your own calculator. Tutors seek enthusiastic and highly motivated students and the physicist's ability to apply basic principles to unfamiliar situations.

AFTER-RESULTS ADVICE
Offers to applicants repeating A-levels **Higher** Bristol, Glasgow, St Andrews, Warwick; **Possibly higher** Aberystwyth, Hull, Leeds, Loughborough, York; **Same** Birmingham, Cardiff, Dundee, Durham, East Anglia, Exeter, Lancaster, Leicester, Liverpool, Salford, Swansea.

GRADUATE DESTINATIONS AND EMPLOYMENT (2007/8 HESA)
Graduates surveyed 1825 **Employed** 470 **In further study** 760 **Assumed unemployed** 220

Career note Many graduates go into scientific and technical work in the manufacturing industries. However, in recent years, financial work, management and marketing have also attracted many seeking alternative careers.

OTHER DEGREE SUBJECTS FOR CONSIDERATION
Astronomy; Astrophysics; Computer Science; Earth Sciences; Engineering subjects; Geophysics; Materials Science and Metallurgy; Mathematics; Meteorology; Natural Sciences; Oceanography; Optometry; Radiography.

PHYSIOLOGY
(see also **Anatomical Science/Anatomy, Animal Sciences, Psychology**)

Physiology is a study of body function. Courses in this wide-ranging subject will cover the central nervous system, special senses and neuro-muscular mechanisms, and body-regulating systems such as exercise, stress and temperature regulation.

Useful websites www.scienceyear.com; www.physoc.org; www.physiology.org; see also **Biological Sciences**.

NB The points totals shown to the left of the institutions are for ease of reference only. It must not be assumed that Tariff points are always used by institutions or that they can be substituted for an offer in grades. The level of an offer is not necessarily indicative of the quality of a course.

COURSE OFFERS INFORMATION
Subject requirements/preferences GCSE Science and mathematics at grade A. **AL** Two science subjects are usually required; chemistry and biology are the preferred subjects. **Other** requirements **Oxford** (Biomed Sci) Applicants take the BioMedical Admissions Test (BMAT) (see **Chapter 6**).

NB In 2012 universities and colleges will differ in their use of GCE AL/AS unit grade information, A* grades, the Extended Project (EPQ), the Advanced Diploma and the Cambridge Pre-U examination when considering applicants and making offers. An EPQ may be accepted in place of an AS subject. Check websites of universities and colleges for the latest offers information.

Your target offers and examples of courses provided by each institution

380 pts **Cambridge** – college offers may vary A*AA (Nat Sci (Physiol Dev Neuro)) (IB 38–42 pts)
360 pts **Edinburgh** – A*AA 2nd yr entry (Physiol) (IB 38 pts)
Leeds – AAA–BBB (Hum Physiol) (IB 32 pts)
Manchester – AAA–AAB (Physiol Modn Lang) (IB 35–32 pts)
Oxford – AAA +BMAT (Biomed Sci) (IB 38–42 pts)
340 pts **Cardiff** – AAB–ABB 340–320 pts (Biomed Sci (Physiol)) (IB 34 pts)
London (King's) – AAB+AS (Physiol Pharmacol) (IB 34 pts HL 5 chem biol)
320 pts **Aberdeen** – ABB–BCC (Physiol Ind)
Bristol – ABB (Physiol Sci) (IB 33 pts HL 6–5 inc sci)
Glasgow – ABB (Physiol Psy) (IB 32 pts)
Leeds – ABB–BBB (Spo Sci Physiol) (IB 32–34 HL 16–15 pts)
Leicester – ABB (Biol Sci (Physiol Pharmacol)) (IB 32–34 pts)
Liverpool – ABB–BBB (Physiol) (IB 31 pts)
Newcastle – ABB (Physiol Sci) (IB 32 pts)
280 pts **Ulster** – 280 pts (Clin Physiol courses)
260 pts **Dundee** – BCC 1st year entry (Bioch Physiol Sci) (IB 30 pts)
Edinburgh Napier – BCC 260 pts (Spo Exer Sci (Exer Physiol))
Wolverhampton – 260–320 pts (Hum Physiol)
240 pts **Aberdeen** – 240 pts (Physiol)
Central Lancashire – 240–260 pts (Physiol Pharmacol)
Hertfordshire – 240 pts (Physiol)
Leeds – CCC (Clin Physiol (Cardio))
Manchester Met – 240–280 pts (Physiol (Phys Actvt Hlth)) (IB 32 pts)
220 pts **Wolverhampton** – 220–240 pts (Clin Physiol)
200 pts **Manchester Met** – 200–280 pts (Clin Physiol; App Biomed Sci (Clin))
160 pts **Leeds Met** – 160 pts (Physiol Pharm)

Alternative offers
See **Chapter 7** and **Appendix 1** for grades/UCAS Tariff points information for the International Baccalaureate, Scottish Highers/Advanced Highers, the Welsh Baccalaureate, the Irish Leaving Certificate, the Cambridge Pre-U Diploma, the Advanced Diploma and the Extended Project.

EXAMPLES OF FOUNDATION DEGREES IN THE SUBJECT FIELD
Middlesex; Nescot.

CHOOSING YOUR COURSE (SEE ALSO CH. 1)
Some course features
See also **Biological Sciences**.

Bristol In the first two years Physiology is studied with two other subjects, for example anatomy, pharmacology, psychology, philosophy or a language.
Leeds (Hum Physiol) Course has an optional year in industry or abroad.
Leicester (Med Physiol) Students with first class performance in the first year can apply to transfer to Medicine. Study abroad through the Erasmus scheme is also possible, and a four-year sandwich course is also available.
Newcastle The Biomedical Sciences programme offers seven science subjects, all of which have a common first year. The decision to take Physiology, or any other subject, takes place in Year 2.

Universities and colleges teaching quality See www.qaa.ac.uk; http://unistats.direct.gov.uk.

Top research universities and colleges (RAE 2008) See **Biological Sciences**.

Examples of sandwich degree courses Bristol UWE; Cardiff; Manchester Met; Wolverhampton.

ADMISSIONS INFORMATION
Number of applicants per place (approx) Bristol 6; Cardiff 8; Dundee 5; Leeds 4; Leicester 5; Liverpool 10; London (King's) 5; Newcastle 6.

Advice to applicants and planning the UCAS personal statement See **Anatomical Science/ Anatomy** and **Biological Sciences**.

Selection interviews **Yes** Cambridge, Leeds, Newcastle, Oxford; **Some** Bristol, Cardiff, Dundee.

Interview advice and questions Past questions include: What made you decide to do a Physiology degree? What experimental work have you done connected with physiology? What future career do you have in mind? What is physiology? Why not choose Medicine instead? What practicals do you do at school? See **Chapter 6**. **Cardiff** Interviewer expects to see outside interests and ability to mix with people as well as an interest in biological sciences. **Oxford** Over 85% of applicants interviewed. What food (out of choice) was the best to eat before an interview?

AFTER-RESULTS ADVICE
Offers to applicants repeating A-levels **Higher** Bristol, Glasgow, Leeds, Leicester, Newcastle, St Andrews; **Same** Cardiff, Dundee.

GRADUATE DESTINATIONS AND EMPLOYMENT (2007/8 HESA)
See **Anatomical Science/ Anatomy**.

Career note See **Biology**.

OTHER DEGREE SUBJECTS FOR CONSIDERATION
Anatomy; Biochemistry; Biological Sciences; Biotechnology; Dentistry; Genetics; Health Studies; Medicine; Microbiology; Nursing; Optometry; Pharmacology; Radiography; Sports Science.

PHYSIOTHERAPY
(see also **Health Sciences/Studies**)

Physiotherapists work as part of a multi-disciplinary team with other health professionals and are involved in the treatment and rehabilitation of patients of all ages and with a wide variety of medical problems. On successful completion of the three-year course, graduates are eligible for State Registration and Membership of the Chartered Society of Physiotherapy. (See **Appendix 2**)

Useful websites www.csp.org.uk; www.thephysiotherapysite.co.uk; www.nhscareers.nhs.uk; www.physiotherapy.co.uk.

NB The points totals shown to the left of the institutions are for ease of reference only. It must not be assumed that Tariff points are always used by institutions or that they can be substituted for an offer in grades. The level of an offer is not necessarily indicative of the quality of a course.

COURSE OFFERS INFORMATION
Subject requirements/preferences **GCSE** English, mathematics and science subjects. Many universities stipulate A/B grades in specific subjects. **AL** One or two science subjects are required. **Other** requirements Occupational health check and Criminal Records Bureau (CRB) clearance.

NB In 2012 universities and colleges will differ in their use of GCE AL/AS unit grade information, A* grades, the Extended Project (EPQ), the Advanced Diploma and the Cambridge Pre-U examination when considering applicants and making offers. An EPQ may be accepted in place of an AS subject. Check websites of universities and colleges for the latest offers information.

Your target offers and examples of courses provided by each institution
370 pts **Southampton** – ABBb 370 pts (Physio) (IB 33 pts)
340 pts **Bournemouth** – 340 pts (Physiotherapy)
Cardiff – AAB (Physiotherapy) (IB 27 pts)
Queen Margaret – AAB 340 pts (Physiotherapy)
330 pts **Coventry** – see Advice to applicants and planning the UCAS personal statement 330 pts
(inc A2 Biol C **or** above) (Physio)

320 pts   **Birmingham** – ABB 320 pts (Physio) (IB 34 pts)
　　　　Bristol UWE – 320–360 pts (Physio)
　　　　Brunel – ABB (Physiotherapy) (IB 33 pts)
　　　　Central Lancashire – ABB (Physio) (IB 30 pts)
　　　　East Anglia – ABB (Physio) (IB 31 pts)
　　　　Huddersfield – ABB (Physio)
　　　　Keele – ABB (Physiotherapy) (IB 27 pts)
　　　　London (King's) – ABB+AS **or** AB/BB+3AS (Physio) (IB 32 pts HL 5 in 2 sci)
　　　　London (St George's) – ABB 320 pts (Physio)
　　　　Northumbria – 320 pts (inc B in Health Sci subj) (Physio) (IB 32 pts)
　　　　Nottingham – ABB (Physio) (IB 34 pts HL biol 6)
　　　　Oxford Brookes – ABB/ABbb (Physio)
300 pts   **Brighton** – BBB (Physio) (IB 34 pts)
　　　　Cumbria – 300 pts (Physio)
　　　　East London – 300 pts (Physio) (IB 26 pts)
　　　　Glasgow Caledonian – BBB (Physio)
　　　　Hertfordshire – 300 pts (Physio)
　　　　Kingston – 300 pts (Physio)
　　　　Liverpool – 300 pts (Physio) (IB 30 pts)
　　　　Manchester Met – 300 pts (Physio)
　　　　Plymouth – 300 pts (Physio)
　　　　Robert Gordon – BBB (Physio) (IB 32 pts)
　　　　Salford – BBB 300 pts (Physio) (IB 32 pts)
　　　　Sheffield Hallam – 300 pts (Physio)
　　　　Teesside – 300 pts (Physio)
　　　　Ulster – see Ch 5 BBB+HPAT (Physio)
　　　　York St John – 300 pts (Physiotherapy)
280 pts   **Bradford** – BBC 280 pts (Physio) (IB 32 pts)
　　　　Leeds Met – 280 pts (Physio)
180 pts   **London South Bank** – 180 pts (Physio)

Alternative offers
See **Chapter 7** and **Appendix 1** for grades/UCAS Tariff points information for the International Baccalaureate, Scottish Highers/Advanced Highers, the Welsh Baccalaureate, the Irish Leaving Certificate, the Cambridge Pre-U Diploma, the Advanced Diploma and the Extended Project.

EXAMPLES OF FOUNDATION DEGREES IN THE SUBJECT FIELD
Salford.

CHOOSING YOUR COURSE (SEE ALSO CH. 1)
Some course features
NHS bursaries are available for all Physiotherapy courses.

East London Physiotherapy is available as full-time, or part-time university-based courses, or as full-time situated learning where one third of the course is practice-based and two-thirds is university-based.
Hertfordshire (Physiotherapy) One third of the course is spent on practice placements in hospitals and health care units.
Nottingham (Physiotherapy) 32 weeks of supervised clinical practice split into eight four-week blocks take place in Years 2 and 3.
Southampton A four-year part-time course is offered to school leavers.

Universities and colleges teaching quality See www.qaa.ac.uk; http://unistats.direct.gov.uk.

ADMISSIONS INFORMATION
Number of applicants per place (approx) Birmingham 9; Bradford 22; Brighton 30, (places for overseas candidates) 6; Bristol UWE 12; Brunel 11; Cardiff 17; Coventry 15; East Anglia 14; East

London 10; Glasgow Caledonian 12; Hertfordshire 13; Huddersfield 18; Kingston 9; Liverpool 20; London (King's) 16; Manchester 18; Northumbria 37; Queen Margaret 11; Robert Gordon 13; Salford 28; Sheffield Hallam 12; Southampton 15; Teesside 33; Ulster 12.

Advice to applicants and planning the UCAS personal statement Visits to, and work experience in, hospital physiotherapy departments are important although many universities publicly state that this is not necessary. However, with the level of competition for this subject I would regard this as doubtful (see **Reasons for rejection**). Applicants must demonstrate a clear understanding of the nature of the profession. Give details of voluntary work activities. Take notes of the work done and the different aspects of physiotherapy. Explain your experience fully on the UCAS application. Outside interests and teamwork are considered important. Good communication skills. Observation placement within a physiotherapy department. See also **Appendix 4**. **Coventry** The University of Leicester part-delivers a BSc Physiotherapy degree. This course is a Coventry University degree that has 30 places based at the Leicester campus. Teaching takes place at Leicester and Coventry. Students are admitted by Coventry but live and mostly study at Leicester. **Manchester Met** We need to know why you want to be a physiotherapist. We also look for work shadowing a physiotherapist or work experience in another caring role. Evidence is also required of good communication skills, ability to care for people and of teamwork and leadership. **Salford** Essential for applicants to seek experience in as wide a range of settings as possible.

Misconceptions about this course Some applicants think that physiotherapy has a sports bias.

Selection interviews Yes Most institutions including Birmingham, Bradford, Brighton, Coventry, East Anglia, East London, Huddersfield, Nottingham, Robert Gordon, Salford, Sheffield Hallam; **Some** Brunel (mature students), Cardiff (mature students), Kingston, Queen Margaret, Southampton (mature students; who are asked to write about their life experience).

Interview advice and questions Physiotherapy is one of the most popular courses at present and work experience is very important, if not essential. A sound knowledge of the career, types of treatment used in physiotherapy and some understanding of the possible problems experienced by patients will be expected. Past interview questions include: How does physiotherapy fit into the overall health care system? If one patient was a heavy smoker and the other not, would you treat them the same? What was the most emotionally challenging thing you have ever done? Give an example of teamwork in which you have been involved. Why should we make you an offer? What is chiropractic? What is osteopathy? See **Chapter 6**.

Reasons for rejection (non-academic) Lack of knowledge of the profession. Failure to convince the interviewers of a reasoned basis for following the profession. Failure to have visited a hospital physiotherapy unit. Lack of awareness of the demands of the course. Other subjects listed on the UCAS application. **Birmingham** Poor communication skills. Lack of career insight. **Bristol UWE** Applicants re-sitting A-levels are not normally considered. **Cardiff** Lack of knowledge of physiotherapy; experience of sports injuries only.

AFTER-RESULTS ADVICE
Offers to applicants repeating A-levels Higher Bristol UWE (candidates who fail at interview will not normally be reconsidered), East Anglia, East London, Glasgow Caledonian, Kingston, Teesside; **Same** Coventry, Queen Margaret, Salford, Southampton.

GRADUATE DESTINATIONS AND EMPLOYMENT (2007/8 HESA)
Career note The professional qualifications gained on graduation enable physiotherapists to seek posts in the Health Service where the majority are employed. A small number work in the community health service, particularly in rural areas, whilst others work in residential homes. In addition to private practice, there are also some opportunities in professional sports clubs.

OTHER DEGREE SUBJECTS FOR CONSIDERATION
Anatomy; Audiology; Biological Sciences; Health Studies; Leisure and Recreation; Nursing; Occupational Therapy; Osteopathy; Physical Education; Psychology; Sport Science/Studies.

PLANT SCIENCES

(including **Botany**; see also **Biological Sciences, Biology, Horticulture**)

Plant Sciences cover such areas as plant biochemistry, plant genetics, plant conservation and plant geography. Botany encompasses all aspects of plant science and also other subject areas including agriculture, forestry and horticulture. Botany is basic to these subjects and others including pharmacology and water management. As with other biological sciences, some universities introduce Plant Sciences by way of a common first year with other subjects.

Useful websites www.kew.org; www.anbg.gov.au; www.scienceyear.com; www.botany.net; www. botany.org.

NB The points totals shown to the left of the institutions are for ease of reference only. It must not be assumed that Tariff points are always used by institutions or that they can be substituted for an offer in grades. The level of an offer is not necessarily indicative of the quality of a course.

COURSE OFFERS INFORMATION

Subject requirements/preferences GCSE Mathematics if not offered at A-level. **AL** One or two science subjects are usually required.

NB In 2012 universities and colleges will differ in their use of GCE AL/AS unit grade information, A* grades, the Extended Project (EPQ), the Advanced Diploma and the Cambridge Pre-U examination when considering applicants and making offers. An EPQ may be accepted in place of an AS subject. Check websites of universities and colleges for the latest offers information.

Your target offers and examples of courses provided by each institution
380 pts Cambridge – A*AA college offers may vary (Nat Sci (Plnt Sci)) (IB 38–42 pts)
360 pts Manchester – AAA–ABB (Plnt Sci Ind) (IB 35–32 pts)
340 pts Birmingham – AAB–BBB (Biol Sci (Plnt Biol)) (IB 32 pts)
  Imperial London – AAB 340 pts (Plant Biol) (IB 38 pts HL 665)
  Sheffield – ABB–AAB (Plnt Sci courses) (IB 35–33 pts)
320 pts East Anglia – ABB (Plnt Sci MSci) (IB 32 pts)
  Glasgow – ABB (Plnt Sci) (IB 32 pts)
300 pts Aberdeen – BBB 1st yr entry (Plnt Soil Sci) (IB 28 pts)
  Edinburgh – BBB (Plnt Sci) (IB 30 pts)
  Nottingham – BBB–BBC (Plnt Sci (Euro St)) (IB 28–32 pts)
260 pts Aberystwyth – 260–300 pts (Plnt Biol) (IB 26 pts)
240 pts Aberdeen – CCC 1st yr entry (Plnt Biol) (IB 28 pts)
  Worcester – 240–280 pts (Biol (Plnt Sci))
220 pts Myerscough (Coll) – 220 pts (Arbor)

Alternative offers
See **Chapter 7** and **Appendix 1** for grades/UCAS Tariff points information for the International Baccalaureate, Scottish Highers/Advanced Highers, the Welsh Baccalaureate, the Irish Leaving Certificate, the Cambridge Pre-U Diploma, the Advanced Diploma and the Extended Project.

CHOOSING YOUR COURSE (SEE ALSO CH. 1)
Some course features
See also **Biology** and **Horticulture**.

Aberystwyth After a common first year focusing on plant structure, function, physiology and classification, students can tailor their degree scheme through their choice of module options. Field studies in northern Spain and western Ireland are available.
Birmingham Plant Biology is an option in the Biological Sciences programme. Specialisation can take place at the beginning of the course or in Year 2.
East Anglia It is possible to start on the flexible Biological Sciences programme in which modules are chosen depending on the student's preference.

Top research universities and colleges (RAE 2008) See **Biological Sciences**.

Examples of sandwich degree courses Manchester.

ADMISSIONS INFORMATION

Number of applicants per place (approx) Edinburgh 6; Glasgow 4; Nottingham 7; Sheffield 5.

Advice to applicants and planning the UCAS personal statement Visit botanical gardens. See **Biological Sciences**. See also **Appendix 2**.

Selection interviews **Yes** Cambridge, Nottingham (depends on application).

Interview advice and questions You are likely to be questioned on your biology studies, your reasons for wishing to study Plant Sciences and your ideas about a possible future career. In the past questions have been asked about Darwin's theory of evolution, photosynthesis and DNA and the value of gardening programmes on TV! See **Chapter 6**.

AFTER-RESULTS ADVICE

Offers to applicants repeating A-levels **Possibly higher** Nottingham; **Same** Birmingham, Sheffield.

GRADUATE DESTINATIONS AND EMPLOYMENT (2007/8 HESA)

Graduates surveyed 20 **Employed** 10 **In further study** 5 **Assumed unemployed** 5

Career note See **Biology** and **Horticulture**.

OTHER DEGREE SUBJECTS FOR CONSIDERATION

Agriculture; Biochemistry; Biological Sciences; Biology; Crop Science (Agronomy); Ecology; Food Science; Forestry; Herbal Medicine; Horticulture; Landscape Architecture; Traditional Chinese Medicine.

PODIATRY (CHIROPODY)

Podiatry is a relatively new term for chiropody and deals with the management of disease and disorders of the ankle and foot. Podiatrists diagnose nail, skin and movement problems, devise treatment plans and carry out treatment for all age groups. Courses lead to state registration and some work shadowing prior to application is preferred by admissions tutors.

Useful websites www.feetforlife.org; www.nhscareers.nhs.uk; www.podiatrynetwork.com; www.podiatrytoday.com; www.podiatrychannel.com.

NB The points totals shown to the left of the institutions are for ease of reference only. It must not be assumed that Tariff points are always used by institutions or that they can be substituted for an offer in grades. The level of an offer is not necessarily indicative of the quality of a course.

COURSE OFFERS INFORMATION

Subject requirements/preferences **GCSE** Mathematics and science subjects. **AL** Biology usually required or preferred. **Other** requirements Hepatitis B, tuberculosis and tetanus immunisation; Criminal Records Bureau (CRB) clearance (a pre-existing record could prevent a student from participating in the placement component of the course and prevent the student from gaining state registration).

NB In 2012 universities and colleges will differ in their use of GCE AL/AS unit grade information, A* grades, the Extended Project (EPQ), the Advanced Diploma and the Cambridge Pre-U examination when considering applicants and making offers. An EPQ may be accepted in place of an AS subject. Check websites of universities and colleges for the latest offers information.

Your target offers and examples of courses provided by each institution
300 pts Huddersfield – 300 pts (Pod)
Southampton – BBB (Pod) (IB 28 pts)
Ulster – (See Ch. 5) BBB +HPAT (Pod) (IB 25 pts)

260 pts   **Brighton** – BCC 260 pts (Pod) (IB 28 pts)
240 pts   **East London** – 240 pts (Pod Med) (IB 26 pts)
          Queen Margaret – 240 pts (Pod) (IB 26 pts)
          Salford – 240 pts (Pod) (IB 24 pts)
220 pts   **Birmingham Met (Coll)** – 220 pts (Podiatry)
          Cardiff (UWIC) – CCD 220 pts (Podiatry)
          Northampton – 220–260 pts (Pod) (IB 24 pts)
200 pts   **Plymouth** – 200 pts (Pod) (IB 27 pts)
160 pts   **Durham New (Coll)** – 160 pts (Pod)
          Glasgow Caledonian – CC (Pod)

Alternative offers
See **Chapter 7** and **Appendix 1** for grades/UCAS Tariff points information for the International Baccalaureate, Scottish Highers/Advanced Highers, the Welsh Baccalaureate, the Irish Leaving Certificate, the Cambridge Pre-U Diploma, the Advanced Diploma and the Extended Project.

EXAMPLES OF FOUNDATION DEGREES IN THE SUBJECT FIELD
Salford.

CHOOSING YOUR COURSE (SEE ALSO CH. 1)
Some course features
NHS bursaries are available for all Podiatry courses. See also **Health Sciences/Studies**.

Northampton Students manage their own patient cases during the course.
Plymouth Supervised placements in NHS Trusts from Year 1.
Southampton A modular programme with six units studied in each semester, these include local anaesthesia and prescription-only medicines.

Universities and colleges teaching quality See www.qaa.ac.uk; http://unistats.direct.gov.uk.

ADMISSIONS INFORMATION
Number of applicants per place (approx) Birmingham Met (Coll) 4; Cardiff (UWIC) 8; Huddersfield 2–3; Northampton 2; Salford 3; Southampton 4.

Advice to applicants and planning the UCAS personal statement Visit a podiatrist's clinic to gain work experience/work shadowing experience. Applicants need the ability to communicate with all age ranges, to work independently, to be resourceful and to possess a focussed approach to academic work. Admissions tutors look for evidence of an understanding of podiatry, some work experience, good people skills, and effective communication. Mature applicants must include an academic reference (not an employer reference). See also **Appendix 4**.

Misconceptions about this course Cardiff (UWIC) Prospective students are often not aware of the demanding requirements of the course: 1000 practical clinical hours augmented by a rigorous academic programme. Applicants are often unaware that whilst the elderly are a significant sub-population of patients with a variety of foot problems, increasingly the role of the podiatrist is the diagnosis and management of biomechanical/developmental disorders as well as the management of the diabetic or rheumatoid patient and those who require surgical intervention for nail problems. **Huddersfield** Many people think that podiatry is limited in its scope of practice to treating toe nails, corns and calluses: FALSE. As professionals, we do treat such pathologies but the scope of practice is much wider. It now includes surgery, biomechanics, sports injuries, treating children and high risk patients. Because offers are low it is considered an easier course than, for example, Physiotherapy: FALSE. The course is academically demanding in addition to the compulsory clinical requirement.

Selection interviews Most institutions **Yes** Huddersfield, Southampton; **Some** Cardiff (UWIC).

Interview advice and questions Past questions include: Have you visited a podiatrist's surgery? What do your friends think about your choice of career? Do you think that being a podiatrist could cause you any physical problems? With which groups of people do podiatrists come into contact? What are your perceptions of the scope of practice of podiatry? What transferable skills do you think you will need? See **Chapter 6**. **Cardiff (UWIC)** What made you consider podiatry as a career? Have you researched your career choice and where did you find the information? What have you discovered and has this altered your original perception of podiatry? What personal characteristics do you think you possess which might be useful for this work?

Reasons for rejection (non-academic) Unconvincing attitude; poor communication and inter-personal skills; lack of motivation; medical condition or physical disabilities which are incompatible with professional practice; no knowledge of chosen profession; lack of work experience.

AFTER-RESULTS ADVICE
Offers to applicants repeating A-levels Same Cardiff (UWIC), Huddersfield, Salford.

GRADUATE DESTINATIONS AND EMPLOYMENT (2007/8 HESA)
Career note Many state-registered podiatrists are employed by the NHS whilst others work in private practice or commercially run clinics.

OTHER DEGREE SUBJECTS FOR CONSIDERATION
Audiology; Biological Sciences; Health Studies; Nursing; Occupational Therapy; Osteopathy; Physiotherapy.

POLITICS

(including **Government**; see also **Development Studies, International Relations, Social Sciences/ Studies**)

Politics is often described as the study of 'who gets what, where, when and how'. Courses have become increasingly popular in recent years and usually cover the politics and government of the major powers. Because of the variety of degree courses on offer, it is possible to study the politics of almost any country in the world.

Useful websites http://europa.eu; www.fco.gov.uk; www.psa.ac.uk; www.parliament.uk; www.whitehouse.gov; www.amnesty.org; www.direct.gov.uk; www.un.org; www.un.int.

NB The points totals shown to the left of the institutions are for ease of reference only. It must not be assumed that Tariff points are always used by institutions or that they can be substituted for an offer in grades. The level of an offer is not necessarily indicative of the quality of a course.

COURSE OFFERS INFORMATION
Subject requirements/preferences GCSE English, mathematics and a foreign language may be required. **AL** No subjects specified; history useful but an arts or social science subject an advantage.

NB In 2012 universities and colleges will differ in their use of GCE AL/AS unit grade information, A* grades, the Extended Project (EPQ), the Advanced Diploma and the Cambridge Pre-U examination when considering applicants and making offers. An EPQ may be accepted in place of an AS subject. Check websites of universities and colleges for the latest offers information.

Your target offers and examples of courses provided by each institution
400 pts **London (King's)** – A*AA+AS–A*Aaa+AS (War St courses) (IB 39 pts)
London (UCL) – A*AA+AS (Euro Soc Pol St) (IB 39 pts)
390 pts **Warwick** – AABb (Pol courses)
380 pts **Bristol** – A*AA–ABB (Pol Econ)
Cambridge – A*AA college offers may vary (Pol Psy Sociol (PPS)) (IB 38–42 pts HL 766–777)
360 pts **Bath** – AAA (Euro Lang Pol) (IB 34–36 pts)
Bristol – AAA–AAB (Pol Fr/Ger/Ital/Port/Russ/Span) (IB 37–34 pts HL 666)
Durham – AAA (PPE) (IB 38 pts)

Exeter – AAA–ABB (Int Rel) (IB 36–33 pts)
London (SOAS) – AAA (Pol Dev St) (IB 34 pts)
London LSE – AAA (Gov Hist) (IB 38 pts HL 766)
Newcastle – AAA–BBB (Pol Econ) (IB 35 pts)
Nottingham – AAA (Int Rel Glob Is) (IB 38 pts)
Oxford – AAA (Hist Pol) (IB 38–42 pts)
St Andrews – AAA (Pol courses) (IB 38 pts)
York – AAA (Hist Pol) (IB 36 pts)

340 pts **Birmingham** – AAB–ABB (War St)
East Anglia – AAB–BBB (PPE) (IB 32–31 pts)
Essex – AAB 340–300 pts (Law Pol) (IB 36 pts)
Exeter – AAB–ABB (Pol Law) (IB 34–29 pts)
Glasgow – AAB (Pol; Pol Langs; Pol Psy; Pol Bus Mgt)
Leeds – AAB (Pol) (IB 36 pts HL 17 pts)
London (QM) – 340 pts (Pol Bus Mgt) (IB 32 pts)
London (UCL) – AAB–ABB (Pol)
London LSE – AAB (Pol Phil) (IB 37 pts)
Loughborough – AAB (Econ Pol) (IB 32 pts)
Manchester – AAB–ABB (Pol Int Rel) (IB 35–34 pts)
Newcastle – AAB–BBB (Gov EU St) (IB 32–36 pts)
Nottingham – AAB (Pol) (IB 36 pts)
Queen's Belfast – AAB–ABBa (PPE)
Sheffield – AAB (Int Pol E As St) (IB 35 pts)
Southampton – ABB–AAB (Pol courses) (IB 34 pts)
Sussex – AAB–ABB (Pol courses) (IB 34–36 pts)
Swansea – AAB (PPE)
York – AAB–ABB (Soc Pol Sci) (IB 34–32 pts)

320 pts **Cardiff** – ABB–AAB 320 pts (Pol courses) (IB 35 pts)
Durham – ABB (Pol Sociol)
East Anglia – ABB–BBB (Cult Lit Pol) (IB 35 pts)
Hull – 320–340 pts (Glob Gov) (IB 34 pts)
Kent – 320 pts (Pol Int Rel courses) (IB 32 pts)
Lancaster – ABB 320 pts (Pol Int Rel) (IB 30 pts)
Leeds – ABB 320 pts (Int Dev courses) (IB 34 pts HL 16 pts)
Leicester – ABB (Pol Econ)
Liverpool – ABB (Pol Int Bus) (IB 33 pts)
London (Gold) – ABB (Econ Pol Pblc Pol) (IB 28 pts)
London (RH) – AAB 320 pts (Pol Int Rel) (IB 34–32 pts)
Nottingham – ABB (Pol Am St; Euro Pol)
Strathclyde – ABB (Pol courses) (IB 34 pts)
Swansea – ABB–BBB (Pol; Pol Soc Hist; Pol Langs; Pol Comms)
Ulster – ABB (Law Int Pol) (IB 26 pts)

300 pts **Aberdeen** – BBB (Pol Int Rel)
Aston – BBB–ABB 300–320 pts (Pol Int Rel) (IB 32–33 pts)
Buckingham – 300 pts (Law Pol)
City – BBB 300 pts (Int Pol) (IB 32 pts)
Edinburgh – BBB–AAA (Pol) (IB 34 pts HL 555)
Essex – 300–320 pts (Pol Sociol) (IB 32–36 pts)
Leicester – BBB (Hist Pol)
Loughborough – 300–340 pts (Pol Int Rel) (IB 32 pts)
Northumbria – 300 pts (Pol) (IB 26 pts)
Queen's Belfast – BBB–BBCb (Pol joint courses) (IB 29 pts HL 655)
Reading – 300–320 pts (Pol)
Surrey – BBB 300 pts (Pol Plcy St) (IB 32 pts)
Swansea – BBB 300 pts (War Soty)

280 pts **Aberystwyth** – 280 pts (Pce Cnflct Scrty) (IB 27–28 pts)
Bradford – BBC 280 pts (Pol; Pol Pce St; Pol Law)
Brighton – BBC (Pol Crimin)
Oxford Brookes – BBC–BCC/BBcc (Pol courses) (IB 31 pts)
Salford – 280 pts (Pol Arbc)
Stirling – BBC (Pol; Pol (Int Pol); PPE)

260 pts **Bristol UWE** – 260–300 pts (Pol; Engl Pol)
Brunel – 260–300 pts (Pol Hist) (IB 31 pts)
Central Lancashire – 260–300 pts (Pol; Pol Int Rel)
Coventry – 260–280 pts (Int Rel Pol; Int Rel)
Dundee – BCC (Pol courses) (HL 555)
Huddersfield – 260–280 pts (Pol; Pol Contemp Hist; Pol Media)
Keele – 260–320 pts (Am St Pol; Pol; Mus Pol)
Liverpool Hope – 260 pts (Pol; Pol Tour; Pol Geog)
Nottingham Trent – 260 pts (Pol Hist; Pol Int Rel)

240 pts **Bangor** – 240–260 pts (Pol Soc Sci)
Buckingham – 240 pts (Pol Econ Law)
Canterbury Christ Church – 240 pts (Pol Gov; Pol Glob Gov courses; Pol courses)
Chester – 240 pts (Pol courses)
London Met – 240 pts (Pol; Pol Bank; Pol Pce Cnflct St)
London South Bank – 240 pts (Int Pol courses)
Plymouth – 240 pts (Pol)
Ulster – CCC 240 pts (Pol Soc Plcy) (IB 24 pts)
Westminster – CCC–BBC (Pol) (IB 28 pts)
Worcester – 240-280 pts (Pol Ppl Pwr)

220 pts **Kingston** – 220–360 pts (Pol Jrnl; Int Rel; Pol App Econ)
Manchester Met – 220–240 pts (Pol courses; Int Pol courses)
Northampton – 220–260 pts (Pol; Pol Joint Hons)
Sunderland – 220–300 pts (Contemp Hist Pol; Pol courses)
Winchester – 260–300 pts (Pol Glob St courses) (IB 24 pts)

200 pts **De Montfort** – 200–260 pts (Pol; Pol Hist; Pol Jrnl; Pol Int Rel)
East London – 200 pts (Int Pol courses)
Leeds Met – 200–220 pts (Pol; Pol Int Rel; Glob Dev Pol; Pce St Pol)
Lincoln – 200–260 pts (Pol; Crimin Pol; Int Rel Pol)
Middlesex – 200–300 pts (Int Pol St courses)
Portsmouth – 200–300 pts (Pol; Pol Sociol)
Sheffield Hallam – 200 pts (Pol Sociol)
Wolverhampton – 200 pts (Pol Phil)

180 pts **Derby** – 180–240 pts (Int Rel courses)
Salford – 180–280 pts (Pol) (IB 29 pts)
Staffordshire – 180 pts (Int Rel courses)

160 pts **Greenwich** – 160–180 pts (Pol) (IB 24 pts)
Wolverhampton – 160–220 pts (Pol Hist)

140 pts **West Scotland** – CD (Soc Sci (Pol))

Open University – +44(0)8453006090 **or** www.openuniversity.co.uk/you

Alternative offers

See **Chapter 7** and **Appendix 1** for grades/UCAS Tariff points information for the International Baccalaureate, Scottish Highers/Advanced Highers, the Welsh Baccalaureate, the Irish Leaving Certificate, the Cambridge Pre-U Diploma, the Advanced Diploma and the Extended Project.

CHOOSING YOUR COURSE (SEE ALSO CH. 1)

Some course features

Bangor Political and Social Sciences is offered as a three-year course, which includes modules in psychology, economic and social issues, European and American topics.

Chester The International Development Studies course focuses on socio-economic, political, cultural and environmental aspects, exploring the Third World and comparisons between rich and poor, urban and rural and contemporary and historical. A Politics course in being validated.

Essex The Department of Government offers a wide range of courses in two main degrees, Politics and International Relations and Politics. Over 30 specialist options are available covering world politics, democracy and human rights. Twelve other joint courses are also available.

Kent The Department offers two main programmes – Politics, Politics and International Relations, also with French, German and Italian and an optional year in Finland, Japan or the Czech Republic. Other courses include British and American Policy Studies, European Politics, Industrial Relations, Human Resource Management and War Studies.

Universities and colleges teaching quality See www.qaa.ac.uk; http://unistats.direct.gov.uk.

Top research universities and colleges (RAE 2008) (Politics and International Studies) Essex; Sheffield; Aberystwyth; Oxford; London LSE; London (UCL); London (SOAS); Sussex (Int Rel); Warwick; Exeter; Nottingham; Manchester; Cambridge.

Examples of sandwich degree courses Aston; Bath; Brunel; Coventry; De Montfort; Huddersfield; Lancaster; Leeds Met; Loughborough; Nottingham Trent; Oxford Brookes; Plymouth; Portsmouth; Surrey; Westminster.

ADMISSIONS INFORMATION

Number of applicants per place (approx) Aberystwyth 4; Aston 4; Bath 2; Birmingham 6; Bradford 10; Bristol 14; Brunel 5; Buckingham 2; Cardiff 14; Cardiff (UWIC) 3; De Montfort 6; Dundee 6; Durham (all courses) 11; East Anglia 15; Exeter 8; Hull 11, (PPE) 20; Kent 14; Lancaster 14; Leeds 18; Leicester 11; Liverpool 9; Liverpool John Moores 6; London (QM) 10; London (SOAS) 5; London LSE (Gov) 17, (Gov Econ) 10, (Gov Hist) 17; London Met 5; Loughborough 4; Newcastle 9; Northampton 4; Nottingham 5; Nottingham Trent 3; Oxford (PPE) 7; Oxford Brookes 12; Portsmouth 6; Salford 7; Southampton 6; Staffordshire 10; Stirling 9; Swansea 3; Warwick 10; York 8.

Advice to applicants and planning the UCAS personal statement Study the workings of government in the UK, Europe and other areas of the world, such as the Middle East, the Far East, America and Russia. Describe visits to the Houses of Commons and Lords and the debates taking place. Attend council meetings – county, town, district, village halls. Describe these visits and agendas. Read current affairs avidly. Be aware of political developments in the major countries and regions of the world including the Middle East, South America, the UK, Europe, USA, China, Korea and Russia. Keep abreast of developments in theatres of war, for example, Afghanistan. Explain your interests in detail. **Aberystwyth** We look for degree candidates with a strong interest in political and social issues and who want to inquire into the way in which the world is organised politically, socially and economically. **De Montfort** Demonstration of active interest in current affairs and some understanding of how politics affects our daily lives.

Misconceptions about this course Aberystwyth Many students believe that they need to study politics at A-level for Politics courses – this is not the case. **Cardiff (UWIC)** Some consider that Politics is a narrow subject, only relevant to those who want a political career. **De Montfort** Some applicants believe that a Politics course only covers the mechanics of government and parliament.

Selection interviews Yes Bath (mature students), Birmingham, Cambridge, Durham, Exeter, Huddersfield, Hull, Leeds (Pol Parl St), Leicester, Liverpool, London (Gold), London (SOAS), London Met, London South Bank, Nottingham, Oxford, Portsmouth, Sheffield, Sussex, Swansea, Ulster, Warwick; **Some** Aberystwyth, Bristol, Cardiff (UWIC), De Montfort, Dundee, Liverpool John Moores, London LSE, Loughborough, Salford, Staffordshire, York.

Interview advice and questions Questions may stem from A/AS-level studies but applicants will also be expected to be up-to-date in their knowledge and opinions of current events. Questions in recent years have included: What constitutes a 'great power'? What is happening at present in the Labour Party? Define capitalism. What is a political decision? How do opinion polls detract from democracy? Is the European Union a good idea? Why? What are the views of the present government on the European Union? What is a 'spin doctor'? Are politicians hypocrites? See also **Chapter 6**. **De Montfort** Why Politics? What political issues motivate your interests, for example environmentalism, human rights?

AFTER-RESULTS ADVICE
Offers to applicants repeating A-levels Higher Essex, Glasgow, Leeds, Newcastle, Nottingham, Warwick, York; **Possibly higher** Hull, Lancaster, Oxford Brookes, Swansea; **Same** Aberystwyth, Birmingham, Bristol, Buckingham, Cardiff (UWIC), De Montfort, Dundee, Durham, East Anglia, Lincoln, Liverpool Hope, Liverpool John Moores, London (SOAS), London Met, London South Bank, Loughborough, Nottingham Trent, Portsmouth, Salford, Staffordshire, Stirling, Sussex, Wolverhampton.

GRADUATE DESTINATIONS AND EMPLOYMENT (2007/8 HESA)
Graduates surveyed 3620 **Employed** 1355 **In further study** 870 **Assumed unemployed** 390

Career note The transferable skills gained in this degree open up a wide range of career opportunities. Graduates seek positions in management, public services and administration and in some cases in political activities.

OTHER DEGREE SUBJECTS FOR CONSIDERATION
Development Studies; Economics; Government; History; International Relations; Public Policy and Administration; Social Policy and Administration; Sociology.

PSYCHOLOGY

(including Behavioural Science, Cognitive Sciences, Counselling and Neuroscience; see also Animal Sciences, Biological Sciences, Philosophy, Physiology, Social Sciences/Studies)

Psychology is a very popular subject, with the number of applications rising by 40,000 in the last ten years. The study attracts three times more women than men. It covers studies in development, behaviour, perception, memory, language, learning, personality as well as social relationships and abnormal psychology. Psychology is a science and you will be involved in experimentation and statistical analysis. The degree is usually offered as a BSc or a BA course and there are many similarities between them. The differences are in the elective subjects which can be taken in the second and third years. It is not a training to enable you to psycho-analyse your friends – psychology is not the same as psychiatry!

To qualify as a chartered psychologist (for which a postgraduate qualification is required) it is necessary to obtain a first degree (or equivalent) qualification which gives eligibility for both Graduate Membership (GM) and the Graduate Basis for Registration (GBR) of the British Psychological Society (BPS). A full list of courses accredited by the British Psychological Society is available on the Society's website www.bps.org.uk. The website also provides careers information and information about all the qualifications needed for careers in the wide-ranging field of psychology. (See **Appendix 4**.)

Behavioural Science covers the study of animal and human behaviour and offers an overlap between Zoology, Sociology, Psychology and Biological Sciences. Psychology, however, also crosses over into Education, Management Sciences, Human Resource Management, Counselling, Public Relations, Advertising, Artificial Intelligence, Marketing, Retail and Social Studies.

Useful websites www.psychology.org; www.bps.org.uk; www.socialpsychology.org; www.psychcentral.com.

NB The points totals shown to the left of the institutions are for ease of reference only. It must not be assumed that Tariff points are always used by institutions or that they can be substituted for an offer in grades. The level of an offer is not necessarily indicative of the quality of a course.

RADIOGRAPHY

(including **Medical Imaging** and **Radiotherapy**; see also **Health Sciences/Studies**)

Many institutions offer both Diagnostic and Therapeutic Radiography but applicants should check this, and course entry requirements, before applying. Information on courses is also available from the Society of Radiographers (see **Appendix 4**). **Diagnostic Radiography** The demonstration on film (or other imaging materials) of the position and structure of the body's organs using radiation or other imaging media. **Therapeutic Radiography** The planning and administration of treatment for patients suffering from malignant and non-malignant disease using different forms of radiation. Courses lead to state registration.

Useful websites www.sor.org; www.radiographycareers.co.uk; www.nhscareers.nhs.uk.

NB The points totals shown to the left of the institutions are for ease of reference only. It must not be assumed that Tariff points are always used by institutions or that they can be substituted for an offer in grades. The level of an offer is not necessarily indicative of the quality of a course.

COURSE OFFERS INFORMATION

Subject requirements/preferences **GCSE** Five subjects including English, mathematics and a science subject (usually at one sitting). **AL** One or two sciences required; mathematics may be acceptable. (Radiotherapy) One science subject required for some courses. Psychology may not be considered a science subject at some institutions. **Other** requirements Applicants required to have an occupational health check and a Criminal Records Bureau (CRB) clearance. Visit to, or work experience in, a hospital imaging department often required/expected.

NB In 2012 universities and colleges will differ in their use of GCE AL/AS unit grade information, A* grades, the Extended Project (EPQ), the Advanced Diploma and the Cambridge Pre-U examination when considering applicants and making offers. An EPQ may be accepted in place of an AS subject. Check websites of universities and colleges for the latest offers information.

Your target offers and examples of courses provided by each institution

320 pts **Exeter** – ABB–BBC (Med Imag (Diag Radiog)) (IB 32–28 pts)

300 pts **London (St George's)** – BBB (Diag Radiog)
Ulster – (See **Ch. 5**) BBB +HPAT (Radiog (Diag) (Ther)) (IB 25 pts)

280 pts **Bradford** – 280 pts (Diag Radiog)
Cardiff – 280 pts (Radiog (Diag Radiog Imag)) (IB 24 pts)
City – BBC 280 pts (Radiog (Diag Imag); Radiog (Radioth Oncol))
Salford – 280 pts (Diag Radiog) (IB 30 pts)
Suffolk (Univ Campus) – 280 pts (Diag Radiog; Radiog (Diag))

260 pts **Cardiff** – 260 pts (Radiothera Onc) (IB 24 pts)
Glasgow Caledonian – BCC (Rdtn Onc Sci; Diag Imag Sci)
Hertfordshire – 260 pts (Radiothera Onc)
Leeds – BBC (Radiog (Diag))
Liverpool – BCC (Radiothera) (IB 28 pts)
London (St George's) – BCC (Ther Radiog)
Sheffield Hallam – BCC 260 pts (Diag Radiog)

240 pts **Birmingham City** – CCC 240 pts (Diag Radiog)
Bristol UWE – 240–280 pts (Diag Imag; Radiothera) (IB 26 pts)
Cumbria – 240 pts (Diag Radiog)
Robert Gordon – CCC 240 pts (Diag Radiog) (IB 26 pts)
Teesside – 240–300 pts (Diag Radiog)

220 pts **Portsmouth** – 220–300 pts (Diag Radiog; Ther Radiog)
Sheffield Hallam – 220 pts (Radiothera Onc)

200 pts **Canterbury Christ Church** – Check with Ad. Tutor 200 pts (Diag Radiog)

Derby – 200–240 pts (Diag Radiog)
Queen Margaret – 200 pts (Diag Radiog; Ther Radiog)
160 pts **Hertfordshire** – 160–240 pts (Diag Radiog Imag)
London South Bank – 160–180 pts (Diag Radiog; Thera Radiog)

Alternative offers
See **Chapter 7** and **Appendix 1** for grades/UCAS Tariff points information for the International Baccalaureate, Scottish Highers/Advanced Highers, the Welsh Baccalaureate, the Irish Leaving Certificate, the Cambridge Pre-U Diploma, the Advanced Diploma and the Extended Project.

EXAMPLES OF FOUNDATION DEGREES IN THE SUBJECT FIELD
Anglia Ruskin; City; Portsmouth; Salford.

CHOOSING YOUR COURSE (SEE ALSO CH. 1)
Some course features
Cardiff The year is divided into seven academic and seven clinical blocks. Placements are in radiography departments throughout South Wales.
City A Foundation degree in Radiotherapy Practice is offered.
Cumbria Fifty-four weeks of clinical placements in the three-year course are spent in hospitals in northern England. Students' preferences are taken into account.
Exeter (Med Imag (Diag Radiog)) This is a specialist course leading to a career as a diagnostic radiographer.
Portsmouth There is a seven-week exchange programme working in hospitals in Hong Kong.

Universities and colleges teaching quality See www.qaa.ac.uk; http://unistats.direct.gov.uk.

ADMISSIONS INFORMATION
Number of applicants per place (approx) Birmingham City (Radiothera) 8; Bradford 8; Cardiff 3; Derby 6; Glasgow Caledonian 7; Hertfordshire (Diag Radiog Imag) 8; Leeds 10; Liverpool 13; London (St George's) 7; London South Bank 9; Portsmouth 10; Robert Gordon 5; Salford 10; Sheffield Hallam 8, (Radiothera Onc) 3; Southampton 5; Suffolk (Univ Campus) 3; Teesside 10.

Advice to applicants and planning the UCAS personal statement Contacts with radiographers and visits to the radiography departments of hospitals should be discussed in full on the UCAS application. See also **Appendix 4**. **Birmingham City** Evidence needed of a visit to at least one imaging department or oncology (radiotherapy) department before completing the UCAS application. Evidence of good research into the career. **Liverpool** Choice between therapeutic and diagnostic pathways should be made before applying. **Salford** Selectors look for evidence of communication skills, teamwork, work experience in public areas.

Misconceptions about this course There is often confusion between radiotherapy and diagnostic imaging and between diagnostic and therapeutic radiography.

Selection interviews **Yes** Birmingham City, Cardiff, City, Derby, Hertfordshire, London South Bank, Portsmouth, Queen Margaret, Salford, Sheffield Hallam; **Some** London (St George's).

Interview advice and questions All applicants should have discussed this career with a radiographer and visited a hospital radiography department. Questions follow from these contacts. Where does radiography fit into the overall health care system? See **Chapter 6**.

Reasons for rejection (non-academic) Lack of interest in people. Poor communication skills. Occasionally students may be unsuitable for the clinical environment, for example, they express a fear of blood and needles; poor grasp of radiography as a career. Unable to meet criteria for employment in the Health Service, for example, health factors, criminal convictions, severe disabilities.

AFTER-RESULTS ADVICE
Offers to applicants repeating A-levels **Higher** London (St George's); **Same** Derby, Salford.

GRADUATE DESTINATIONS AND EMPLOYMENT (2007/8 HESA)

Career note Most radiographers work in the NHS in hospital radiography departments undertaking diagnostic or therapeutic treatment. Others work in private healthcare.

OTHER DEGREE SUBJECTS FOR CONSIDERATION

Audiology; Forensic Engineering; Health Studies; Medical Physics; Nursing; Occupational Therapy; Physics; Podiatry; Speech Sciences.

RELIGIOUS STUDIES

(including Biblical Studies, Divinity, Jewish Studies and Theology)

Religious Studies courses cover four degree course subjects: Religious Studies, Divinity, Theology and Biblical Studies. The subject content of these courses varies and students should check prospectuses carefully. They are not intended as training courses for church ministry; an adherence to a particular religious denomination is not a necessary qualification for entry. (NB Religious studies is an acceptable second or third A-level for any non-scientific degree course.)

Useful websites www.guardian.co.uk/religion; www.cwmission.org; www.miraclestudies.net; www.academicinfo.net/religindex.html; www.theologywebsite.com; www.jewishstudies.org; www.jewishstudies.virtualave.net; www.jewfaq.org; www.virtualreligion.net; www.jis.oxford journals.org.

NB The points totals shown to the left of the institutions are for ease of reference only. It must not be assumed that Tariff points are always used by institutions or that they can be substituted for an offer in grades. The level of an offer is not necessarily indicative of the quality of a course.

COURSE OFFERS INFORMATION

Subject requirements/preferences GCSE English and mathematics. For teacher training, English and mathematics and science. AL Religious studies or theology may be required or preferred for some courses.

NB In 2012 universities and colleges will differ in their use of GCE AL/AS unit grade information, A* grades, the Extended Project (EPQ), the Advanced Diploma and the Cambridge Pre-U examination when considering applicants and making offers. An EPQ may be accepted in place of an AS subject. Check websites of universities and colleges for the latest offers information.

Your target offers and examples of courses provided by each institution
380 pts **Cambridge** – A*AA college offers may vary (Educ Relig St BA) (IB 38–42 pts)
360 pts **Bristol** – AAA–AAB (Phil Theol) (IB 37–33 pts)
　　　　 Durham – AAA (Theol Phil)
　　　　 Oxford – AAA (Theol Orntl St) (IB 38–40 pts)
　　　　 St Andrews – AAA–AAB (Heb) (IB 30 pts)
340 pts **Birmingham** – AAB–BBB (Hist Art Theol)
　　　　 Bristol – AAB–BBB (Theol Relig St) (IB 35–32 pts)
　　　　 Durham – AAB (Theol; Theol (Euro St))
　　　　 Glasgow – AAB (Theol Relig St) (IB 34 pts)
　　　　 London (King's) – ABB+AS–BBB+AS (Theol)
　　　　 St Andrews – AAB (Bib St) (IB 32 pts)
320 pts **Exeter** – ABB–BBB (Theol courses) (IB 34–29 pts)
　　　　 Kent – 320–280 pts (Relig St Hist; Relig St Phil)
　　　　 Leeds – ABB–BBB (Theol Relig St)
　　　　 London (UCL) – ABB (Jew Hist) (IB 34 pts)
　　　　 Manchester – AAB–ABB (St Relig Theol) (IB 33–32 pts)
　　　　 Nottingham – ABB–BBB (Theol courses) (IB 34 pts)
　　　　 Sheffield – ABB–BBB (Bib St Phil) (IB 35–32 pts)

300 pts **Aberdeen** – BBB (Theol, Div, Relig St) (IB 30 pts)
Birmingham – BBB (Theol)
Cardiff – BBB 300 pts (Relig Theol St)
Edinburgh – BBB-AAA (Div) (IB 26–28 pts)
Essex – 300–320 pts (Phil Rel Eth)
Lancaster – BBB (Relig St Sociol) (IB 28–29 pts)
Nottingham – ABC (Theol) (IB 32 pts)
Queen's Belfast – BBB–BBCb (Div) (IB 29 pts)

280 pts **Birmingham** – BBC (Islam St) (IB 30 pts)
Cardiff – BBC 280 pts (Relig St Ital/Span)
Gloucestershire – 280–300 pts (Relig Phil Eth)
London (Hey) – 280 pts (Phil Relig Eth) (IB 28–32 pts)
London (SOAS) – BBC (St Relig)
Oxford Brookes – BBC/BBcc/BCbc (Relig Theol)
Roehampton – 280–360 pts (Theol Rel St) (25 pts)
Stirling – BBC–CCC (Relig St Comb Hons)
Stranmillis (UC) – BBC (Relig St Educ)
Winchester – 280–320 pts (Theol Relig St; Relig St Arch; Relig St Bus Mgt)

260 pts **Chester** – 260 pts (Theol Relig St) (IB 24 pts)
Chichester – BCC 260 pts (Theol Rel)
Huddersfield – 260 pts (Relig Educ)
Liverpool Hope – 260 pts (Theol Relig St)
Newman (UC) – 260 pts (Theol courses)

240 pts **Bangor** – 240–300 pts (Relig St; Theol courses BA/BD)
Canterbury Christ Church – 240 pts (Theol courses; Relig St courses)
Chester – 240–260 pts (Relig St) (IB 24 pts)
Edge Hill – 240 pts (Rel Educ QTS)
Hull – 240–280 pts (Relig courses)
Leeds Trinity (UC) – (Relig St)

220 pts **Bath Spa** – 220–280 pts (St Relig)
Newport – 220–260 pts (Relig St; Relig St Joint Hons)
York St John – 220–260 pts (Theol Relig St)

200 pts **Central Lancashire** – 200–300 pts (Islam St Comb Hons; Relig Cult Soty Comb Hons)
Cumbria – 200 pts (Relig St)
Leeds Trinity (UC) – 200 pts (Theol)
Middlesex – 200–300 pts (Educ Rel St)
Wolverhampton – 160–200 pts (Relig St courses)

180 pts **Trinity Saint David** – 180–240 pts (Theol courses; Relig St courses; Islam St; Div)

160 pts **Bishop Grosseteste (UC)** – 160 pts (Educ St Theol)
St Mary's Twickenham (UC) – 160–200 pts (Theol Relig St)
UHI Millennium Inst – AA–DD (Theol St)

140 pts **Islamic Advanced St (Coll)** – 140–220 pts (Islam St)

Alternative offers
See **Chapter 7** and **Appendix 1** for grades/UCAS Tariff points information for the International Baccalaureate, Scottish Highers/Advanced Highers, the Welsh Baccalaureate, the Irish Leaving Certificate, the Cambridge Pre-U Diploma, the Advanced Diploma and the Extended Project.

EXAMPLES OF FOUNDATION DEGREES IN THE SUBJECT FIELD
Newman (UC); York St John.

CHOOSING YOUR COURSE (SEE ALSO CH. 1)
Some course features
Birmingham (Islam St) The course provides a critical investigation of Islamic history with options in Arabic, Islamic law and introductions to Christianity and Judaism.

Durham (Theol) The course combines aspects of philosophy, history and social sciences and includes a detailed study of the Old and New Testaments.

Edinburgh MA and Honours and BA General degrees are offered in Religious Studies and Divinity. There is also a Bachelor of Divinity course equipping students for the ordained ministry.

Lancaster (Relig St) A distinguished course offering core and over 40 optional modules in such diverse areas as Islam, Sanskrit, pilgrimage, practical anthropology, myth and mysticism. There is a second year placement programme in the USA and an optional four-week summer course in India.

Sheffield (Bib St) The only course in England looking at the development of the Bible and its place in contemporary society, politics, art, film, literature and music.

Universities and colleges teaching quality See www.qaa.ac.uk; http://unistats.direct.gov.uk.

Top research universities and colleges (RAE 2008) (Theology, Divinity and Religious Studies) Durham; Aberdeen; Cambridge; Oxford; London (UCL); Manchester; Sheffield; Edinburgh; Nottingham.

ADMISSIONS INFORMATION

Number of applicants per place (approx) Bangor 5; Birmingham 4; Bristol 9; Cambridge 2; Chichester 6; Cumbria 12; Durham 6; Edinburgh 3; Exeter 7; Glasgow 4; Hull 10; Kent 13; Lancaster 6; Leeds 4; Leeds Trinity (UC) 4; Liverpool Hope 6; London (Hey) 4; London (King's) 6; Middlesex 4; Newman (UC) 2; Nottingham 10; Sheffield 7; Trinity Saint David 7; Winchester 6; York St John 2.

Advice to applicants and planning the UCAS personal statement An awareness of the differences between the main religions is important as is any special research you have done to help you decide on your preferred courses. Interests in the religious art and architecture of various periods and styles should be noted. Applicants should have an open-minded approach to studying a diverse range of religious traditions.

Misconceptions about this course Some students think that you must be religious to study Theology – in fact, people of all faiths and none study the subject. A study of religions is not Christian theology. **Leeds** Some applicants are not aware of the breadth of the subject. We offer modules covering New Testament, Christian theology, Islamic studies, Hinduism, Buddhism, Sikhism, Christian ethics, sociology of religion.

Selection interviews Yes Cambridge, Chester, Durham, Edinburgh, Glasgow, Hull, Lancaster, Leeds, Leeds Trinity (UC), London (Hey), London (SOAS), Nottingham, Oxford (Theol) 38%, Oxford Brookes, Sheffield, Trinity Saint David, Winchester; **Some** Bristol, Cardiff, Southampton.

Interview advice and questions Past questions have included: Why do you want to study Theology/ Biblical Studies/Religious Studies? What do you hope to do after obtaining your degree? Questions relating to the A-level syllabus. Questions on current theological topics. Do you have any strong religious convictions? Do you think that your religious beliefs will be changed at the end of the course? Why did you choose Religious Studies rather than Biblical Studies? How would you explain the miracles to a 10-year-old? (BEd course). Do you agree with the National Lottery? How do you think you can apply theology to your career? See **Chapter 6**. **Cambridge** There is a Christian priest who regularly visits India and converted to a Hindu priest. When he is in England he still practises as a Christian priest. What problems might this pose? Do you believe we should eradicate Christmas on the basis that it offends other religious groups? **Oxford** The ability to defend one's opinions and willingness to engage in a lively dialogue are both important.

Reasons for rejection (non-academic) Students not attending Open Days may be rejected. Too religiously conservative. Failure to interact. Lack of motivation to study a subject which goes beyond A-level. **Cardiff** Insufficiently open to an academic study of religion.

AFTER-RESULTS ADVICE

Offers to applicants repeating A-levels Higher Hull, Manchester, St Andrews; **Possibly higher** Cambridge (Hom); **Same** Bangor, Birmingham, Cardiff, Chester, Durham, Glasgow, Greenwich,

Lancaster, Leeds, Liverpool Hope, London (SOAS), Nottingham, St Mary's Twickenham (UC), Sheffield, Stirling, Trinity Saint David, Winchester, Wolverhampton, York St John.

GRADUATE DESTINATIONS AND EMPLOYMENT (2007/8 HESA)
Graduates surveyed 1140 **Employed** 360 **In further study** 385 **Assumed unemployed** 80

Career note Although a small number of graduates may regard these courses as a preparation for entry to religious orders, the great majority enter other careers, with teaching particularly popular.

OTHER DEGREE SUBJECTS FOR CONSIDERATION
Community Studies; Education; History; Philosophy; Psychology; Social Policy and Administration; Social Work.

RETAIL MANAGEMENT

(see also **Business and Management Courses, Business and Management Courses (International and European), Business and Management Courses (Specialised), Marketing**)

This subject attracts a large number of applicants each year and it is necessary to have work experience before applying. The work itself varies depending on the type of retail outlet. After completing their courses graduates in a large department store will be involved in different aspects of the business, for example supervising shop assistants, warehouse and packing staff. They could also receive special training in the sales of particular goods, for example food and drink, clothing, furniture. Subsequently there may be opportunities to become buyers. In more specialised shops, for example shoes, fashion and food, graduates are likely to work only with these products, with opportunities to reach senior management.

Useful websites www.brc.org.uk; www.retailweek.com; www.theretailbulletin.com; www.retailcareers.co.uk; www.retailchoice.com; www.nrf.com.

NB The points totals shown to the left of the institutions are for ease of reference only. It must not be assumed that Tariff points are always used by institutions or that they can be substituted for an offer in grades. The level of an offer is not necessarily indicative of the quality of a course.

COURSE OFFERS INFORMATION
Subject requirements/preferences GCSE English and mathematics at grade C or above. **AL** No subjects specified.

NB In 2012 universities and colleges will differ in their use of GCE AL/AS unit grade information, A* grades, the Extended Project (EPQ), the Advanced Diploma and the Cambridge Pre-U examination when considering applicants and making offers. An EPQ may be accepted in place of an AS subject. Check websites of universities and colleges for the latest offers information.

Your target offers and examples of courses provided by each institution
340 pts Loughborough – AAB (Rtl Mark Mgt) (36 pts)
320 pts Manchester – apply early ABB–ABC (Fash Tex Rtl) (IB 34–33 pts)
300 pts Surrey – BBB 300 pts (Bus Rtl Mgt) (IB 30 pts)
Westminster – BBB 300 pts (Bus St Rtl) (IB 28 pts)
280 pts Birmingham City – 280 pts (Fash Rtl Mgt) (IB 28 pts)
Bournemouth – 280 pts (Rtl Mgt)
Brighton – BBC (Rtl Mark) (IB 28 pts)
Heriot-Watt – BBC (Fash, Mark Rtl)
Huddersfield – 280 pts (Rtl Mark Mgt)
Stirling – BBC (Rtl Mark)
240 pts Canterbury Christ Church – 240 pts (Bus Mgt (Rtl))
Cardiff (UWIC) – 240 pts (Mark Mgt)

Central Lancashire – 240–280 pts (Rtl Mgt Comb Hons) (IB 28 pts)
De Montfort – 240 pts (Rtl Buy (Fash) (Tex); Rtl Mgt)
Leeds Met – 240 pts (Rtl Mark Mgt)
Manchester Met – 240–260 pts (Hspty Lic Rtl Mgt)
Robert Gordon – CCC (Rtl Mgt) (IB 24 pts)
Roehampton – 240–280 pts (Bus Mgt (Rtl Mgt Mark))
Ulster – 240 pts (Bus Rtl St; Comp Rtl St)
220 pts **London Met** – 220 pts (Rtl Mgt courses)
Northampton – 220–260 pts (Rtl Joint Hons)
200 pts **Bucks New** – 200–240 pts (Bus Rtl Mgt)

Alternative offers
See **Chapter 7** and **Appendix 1** for grades/UCAS Tariff points information for the International Baccalaureate, Scottish Highers/Advanced Highers, the Welsh Baccalaureate, the Irish Leaving Certificate, the Cambridge Pre-U Diploma, the Advanced Diploma and the Extended Project.

EXAMPLES OF FOUNDATION DEGREES IN THE SUBJECT FIELD
Arts London; Bedfordshire; Birmingham (UC); Blackburn (Coll Univ Centre); Bournemouth; Brighton; Cornwall (Coll); Exeter (Coll); Grimsby (IFHE); Kent; Middlesex; Norwich City (Coll); Plymouth; Suffolk (Univ Campus); Wolverhampton.

CHOOSING YOUR COURSE (SEE ALSO CH. 1)
Some course features
Birmingham City (Fash Rtl Mgt) The course focuses on the global fashion industry and design management. It includes fabric sourcing, pattern cutting and manufacturing, and fashion forecasting.
Bournemouth (Rtl Mgt) The course has paid industrial placements and overseas opportunities.
Loughborough (Rtl Mark Mgt) This four-year sandwich course includes a placement year leading to a Diploma in Professional Studies. Retailers are closely involved throughout and provide lectures, case studies, skills workshops and company visits.
Queen Margaret (Rtl Mgt) Course options in the third year include e-marketing, advertising and marketing communications, fashion marketing and market planning.
Surrey (Rtl Mgt) A long-established course with industrial work placements and high graduate employment.

Universities and colleges teaching quality See www.qaa.ac.uk; http://unistats.direct.gov.uk.

Examples of sandwich degree courses Bournemouth; Bradford; Brighton; Central Lancashire; De Montfort; Huddersfield; Manchester Met.

ADMISSIONS INFORMATION
Number of applicants per place (approx) See also **Business and Management Courses**. Bournemouth 8; Manchester Met 10.

Advice to applicants and planning the UCAS personal statement See also **Business and Management Courses**. **Manchester Met** (Rtl Mark Mgt) Evidence of working with people or voluntary work experience (department unable to assist with sponsorships).

Misconceptions about this course See **Business and Management Courses**.

Selection interviews See **Business and Management Courses**.

Interview advice and questions See **Business and Management Courses**.

Reasons for rejection (non-academic) See **Business and Management Courses**.

GRADUATE DESTINATIONS AND EMPLOYMENT (2007/8 HESA)
Career note Majority of graduates work in business involved in marketing and retail work. Employment options include brand design, product management, advertising, PR, sales and account management.

OTHER DEGREE SUBJECTS FOR CONSIDERATION

Business Studies; Consumer Sciences/Studies; E-Commerce; Human Resource Management; Psychology; Supply Chain Management.

RUSSIAN and EAST EUROPEAN STUDIES

(including **Bulgarian, Croatian, Czech, Finnish, Georgian, Hungarian, Polish, Romanian, Russian** and **Serbian**; see also **European Studies, Languages**)

East European Studies cover a wide range of the less popular language courses and should be considered by anyone with a love of and gift for languages. Many natural linguists often devote themselves to one of the popular European languages studied up to A-level, when their language skills could be extended to the more unusual languages, thereby increasing their future career opportunities.

Useful websites www.basees.org.uk; www.iol.org.uk; www.bbc.co.uk/languages; http://languageadvantage.com; www.languagematters.co.uk; www.reed.co.uk/multilingual; www.cilt.org.uk.

NB The points totals shown to the left of the institutions are for ease of reference only. It must not be assumed that Tariff points are always used by institutions or that they can be substituted for an offer in grades. The level of an offer is not necessarily indicative of the quality of a course.

COURSE OFFERS INFORMATION

Subject requirements/preferences GCSE A foreign language. **AL** One or two modern languages may be stipulated.

NB In 2012 universities and colleges will differ in their use of GCE AL/AS unit grade information, A* grades, the Extended Project (EPQ), the Advanced Diploma and the Cambridge Pre-U examination when considering applicants and making offers. An EPQ may be accepted in place of an AS subject. Check websites of universities and colleges for the latest offers information.

Your target offers and examples of courses provided by each institution

380 pts **Cambridge** – college offers may vary A*AA (Modn Mediev Lang (Russ)) (IB 38–42 pts HL 776–777)

360 pts **London (UCL)** – AAA–ABB (Russ St) (IB 32 pts)
Manchester – AAA–AAB (Russ Span) (IB 35–37 pts)
Oxford – AAA (Engl Russ) (IB 38–42 pts)
St Andrews – AAA–AAB (Econ Russ) (IB 32 pts)

340 pts **Bristol** – AAB–BBC 340 pts (Russ) (IB 35–30 pts HL 655)
Durham – AAB 340 pts (Modn Langs (Russ +1–2 Langs)) (IB 34 pts)
Exeter – AAB–ABB (Int Rel Russ) (IB 29 pts)
Glasgow – AAB (Cnt E Euro St) (IB 34 pts)

320 pts **Bath** – ABB–BBB (Euro St Modn Lang (Russ Fr/Ger/Span)) (IB 34 pts HL lang 6)
Birmingham – ABB–BBB 320 pts (Russ St Joint Hons)
London (SOAS) – ABB (Georg)
London (UCL) – ABB (Russ Hist) (IB 32 pts)
Manchester – ABB–BBC (Russ Port) (IB 30–33 pts)

300 pts **Edinburgh** – check with ad tutor BBB (Russ St Hist Art) (IB 34 pts)
London (QM) – 300–340 pts (Russ Pol) (IB 32 pts)
Manchester – BBB–BCC (Russ Scrn St) (IB 32–28 pts)
Nottingham – ABC–BBB (Serb Cro St) (IB 28–30 pts)
Sheffield – BBB–BBC (Russ Bus Mgt) (IB 30–33 pts)
Westminster – CCC–BBB (Russ courses)

280 pts **Leeds** – BBC (Russ A/B courses) (IB 32 pts)

200 pts **Middlesex** – 200–300 pts (Int Bus Russ)

160 pts **Euro Bus Sch London** – CC check with Bus Sch (Int Bus (Russ))
 80 pts **London LSE** – optional course offered by the language centre check with admissions tutor
((Fr/Ger/Span/Russ))

Alternative offers
See **Chapter 7** and **Appendix 1** for grades/UCAS Tariff points information for the International Baccalaureate, Scottish Highers/Advanced Highers, the Welsh Baccalaureate, the Irish Leaving Certificate, the Cambridge Pre-U Diploma, the Advanced Diploma and the Extended Project.

CHOOSING YOUR COURSE (SEE ALSO CH. 1)
Some course features
See also **Languages**.

Durham Russian is only offered as one of two or three other subjects in the Combined Honours course.
Glasgow At all levels language tuition is given by Russian native language speakers.
London LSE Full degrees in languages are not offered by LSE, but Russian Language and Society can be taken as a degree option on most undergraduate courses.
Nottingham Beginners' courses are offered in Russian which can also be combined with another subject taken from the very wide range available, from Serbo-Croat to Contemporary Chinese Studies.

Universities and colleges teaching quality See www.qaa.ac.uk; http://unistats.direct.gov.uk.

Top research universities and colleges (RAE 2008) (Russian, Slavonic and East European languages) Manchester; Oxford; Sheffield; Cambridge; Bristol; Nottingham; Exeter.

ADMISSIONS INFORMATION
Number of applicants per place (approx) Birmingham 3; Bristol 7; Durham 7; Leeds 3; London (UCL) (E Euro St Bulg) 1; Nottingham 5.

Advice to applicants and planning the UCAS personal statement Visits to Eastern Europe should be mentioned, supported by your special reasons for wishing to study the language. A knowledge of the cultural, economic and political scene could be important. Fluent English important for non-UK students. Evidence of wide reading, travel and residence abroad. See also **Appendix 4** under Languages.

Selection interviews Yes Cambridge, Durham, Exeter, London (UCL), Oxford; **Some** Nottingham.

Interview advice and questions Since many applicants will not have taken Russian at A-level, questions often focus on their reasons for choosing a Russian degree, and their knowledge of, and interest in, Russia. Those taking A-level Russian are likely to be questioned on the course and on any reading done outside A-level work. East European Studies applicants will need to show some knowledge of their chosen country/countries and any specific reasons why they wish to follow the course. See also **Chapter 6**. **Leeds** See **Languages**.

Reasons for rejection (non-academic) Lack of perceived commitment for a demanding ab initio subject.

AFTER-RESULTS ADVICE
Offers to applicants repeating A-levels Higher Bristol, Glasgow, Leeds, St Andrews; **Same** Durham.

GRADUATE DESTINATIONS AND EMPLOYMENT (2007/8 HESA)
Graduates surveyed 125 **Employed** 55 **In further study** 30 **Assumed unemployed** 15

Career note See **Languages**.

OTHER DEGREE SUBJECTS FOR CONSIDERATION
Economics; European Studies; International Relations; Linguistics; Politics; other languages.

SCANDINAVIAN STUDIES

(see also **Languages**)

Scandinavian Studies provides students who enjoy languages with the opportunity to extend their language expertise to learn a modern Scandinavian language – Danish, Norwegian or Swedish – from beginner's level to Honours level in four years, including a year in Scandinavia. The three languages are very similar to each other and a knowledge of one makes it possible to access easily the literature and cultures of the other two. Viking Studies includes Old Norse, runology and archaeology.

Useful websites www.cilt.org.uk; www.iol.org.uk; www.bbc.co.uk/languages; http://language advantage.com; www.languagematters.co.uk; www.reed.co.uk/multilingual; www.scandinaviahouse. org; www.scandinavianstudy.org; www.nordicstudies.com.

NB The points totals shown to the left of the institutions are for ease of reference only. It must not be assumed that Tariff points are always used by institutions or that they can be substituted for an offer in grades. The level of an offer is not necessarily indicative of the quality of a course.

COURSE OFFERS INFORMATION

Subject requirements/preferences GCSE Foreign language preferred for all courses. **AL** A modern language may be required.

NB In 2012 universities and colleges will differ in their use of GCE AL/AS unit grade information, A* grades, the Extended Project (EPQ), the Advanced Diploma and the Cambridge Pre-U examination when considering applicants and making offers. An EPQ may be accepted in place of an AS subject. Check websites of universities and colleges for the latest offers information.

Your target offers and examples of courses provided by each institution
380 pts **Cambridge** – A*AA college offers may vary (A-Sxn Nrs Celt) (IB 40–42 pts)
360 pts **London (UCL)** – AAB+AS–BBB+AS (Scand St Hist) (IB 32–36 pts)
320 pts **London (UCL)** – ABB–BBB (Vkg St) (IB 32–36 pts)
         Nottingham – ABB (Vkg St) (IB 32 pts)
300 pts **Edinburgh** – Check with Ad. Tutor BBB–AAA (Celt Scand St) (IB 34 pts HL 555)

Alternative offers
See **Chapter 7** and **Appendix 1** for grades/UCAS Tariff points information for the International Baccalaureate, Scottish Highers/Advanced Highers, the Welsh Baccalaureate, the Irish Leaving Certificate, the Cambridge Pre-U Diploma, the Advanced Diploma and the Extended Project.

CHOOSING YOUR COURSE (SEE ALSO CH. 1)

Some course features
See also **Languages**.

Cambridge (A-Sxn Nrs Celt) Old Norse is offered as part of this degree.
Edinburgh Beginners are provided with a concentrated course in the spoken and written language of their choice from Danish, Norwegian or Swedish. Year 3 is spent in a university in one of the Scandinavian countries.
London (UCL) Danish, Icelandic, Norwegian and Swedish are taught from scratch on the Scandinavian Studies courses. Icelandic and one other Scandinavian language are taught on the Icelandic course. No prior knowledge of the languages is required.
Nottingham (Vkg St) Course covers languages, literature, history and archaeology.

Universities and colleges teaching quality See www.qaa.ac.uk; http://unistats.direct.gov.uk.

Top research universities and colleges (RAE 2008) See **German**.

ADMISSIONS INFORMATION

Number of applicants per place (approx) London (UCL) 3.

Advice to applicants and planning the UCAS personal statement Visits to Scandinavian countries could be the source of an interest in studying these languages. You should also be aware of cultural, political, geographical and economic aspects of Scandinavian countries. Knowledge of these should be shown in your statement.

Selection interviews Yes Cambridge.

Interview advice and questions Applicants in the past have been questioned on why they have chosen this subject area, on their visits to Scandinavia and on their knowledge of the country/ countries and their people. Future career plans are likely to be discussed. See **Chapter 6**.

Reasons for rejection (non-academic) One applicant didn't know the difference between a noun and a verb.

GRADUATE DESTINATIONS AND EMPLOYMENT (2007/8 HESA)
Graduates surveyed 10 **Employed** 5 **In further study** 0 **Assumed unemployed** 0

Career note See **Languages**.

OTHER DEGREE SUBJECTS FOR CONSIDERATION
Archaeology; European History/Studies; History; other modern languages, including, for example, Russian and East European languages.

SOCIAL and PUBLIC POLICY and ADMINISTRATION

(see also Community Studies/Development, Sociology, Social Work)

Social Policy is a multi-disciplinary degree that combines elements from sociology, political science, social and economic history, economics, cultural studies and philosophy. It is a study of the needs of society and how best to provide such services as education, housing, health and welfare services.

Useful websites www.lga.gov.uk; www.ippr.org.uk; www.swap.ac.uk.

NB The points totals shown to the left of the institutions are for ease of reference only. It must not be assumed that Tariff points are always used by institutions or that they can be substituted for an offer in grades. The level of an offer is not necessarily indicative of the quality of a course.

COURSE OFFERS INFORMATION
Subject requirements/preferences GCSE English and mathematics normally required. **AL** No subjects specified.

NB In 2012 universities and colleges will differ in their use of GCE AL/AS unit grade information, A* grades, the Extended Project (EPQ), the Advanced Diploma and the Cambridge Pre-U examination when considering applicants and making offers. An EPQ may be accepted in place of an AS subject. Check websites of universities and colleges for the latest offers information.

Your target offers and examples of courses provided by each institution
350 pts Queen's Belfast – BBBb/BBCb (Soc Plcy courses)
340 pts Birmingham – AAB–ABB (Soc Plcy Pol)
　　　　 Bristol – AAB–ABB (Soc Plcy Pol)
　　　　 Glasgow – AAB (Pblc Plcy courses)
　　　　 Loughborough – AAB (Econ Soc Pol) (IB 34 pts)
　　　　 Warwick – BBBc–BBCc (Sociol (Soc Plcy))
320 pts Bath – ABB–BBC (Soc Plcy) (IB 34 pts)
　　　　 Birmingham – ABB–BBB (Plan Soc Plcy Joint Hons)
　　　　 Leeds – ABB–BBB (Soc Plcy courses) (IB 32 pts HL 15 pts)
　　　　 London LSE – ABB (Soc Plcy Gov) (IB 36–37 pts)
　　　　 Loughborough – 320 pts (Crimin Soc Plcy) (IB 32 pts)
　　　　 Nottingham – ABB (Sociol Soc Plcy) (IB 34 pts)

Sheffield – ABB–BBC (Soc Plcy Sociol) (IB 32 pts)
Southampton – ABB (Sociol Soc Plcy) (IB 33 pts)
300 pts **Aston** – BBB. 300–320 pts (Pblc Plcy Mgt courses) (IB 31–33 pts)
Bristol – ABC–BBB (Soc Plcy Sociol) (IB 32 pts)
Cardiff – BBB (Soc Plcy)
Edinburgh – BBB–AAA (Soc Plcy Law)
Leeds – ABC (Soc Plcy) (IB 30 pts HL 14 pts)
Liverpool – BBB (Sociol Soc Plcy) (IB 30 pts)
Loughborough – 300 pts (Soc Pol Crim)
Nottingham – BBB (Soc Wk Soc Plcy) (IB 32 pts)
Swansea – BBB (Soc Hist Soc Plcy) (IB 30 pts)
York – BBB (Soc Plcy) (IB 30 pts)
280 pts **Bangor** – 280 pts (Law Soc Plcy)
Birmingham – BBC (Soc Plcy Joint Hons) (IB 30–32 pts)
Brighton – BBC (Crimin Soc Plcy) (IB 30 pts)
Kent – 280–320 pts (Soc Plcy Law Welf) (IB 31–33 pts)
Leeds – BBC (Soc Pol Sociol) (IB 30 pts HL 14 pts)
Lincoln – 280–260 pts (Psy Soc Plcy; Crimin Soc Plcy)
London Met – 280 pts (Soc Plcy Joint Hons)
260 pts **Liverpool Hope** – 260 pts (Soc Plcy courses)
240 pts **Central Lancashire** – 240 pts (Soc Plcy Comb Hons)
Lincoln – 240 pts (Soc Plcy)
Stirling – CCC–BBB (Soc Plcy) (IB 28 pts)
Ulster – 240 pts (Soc Plcy; Soc Plcy Pol; Soc Plcy Econ)
220 pts **Anglia Ruskin** – 220–260 pts (Crimin Soc; Soc Plcy Law)
Bangor – 220–260 pts (Soc Plcy Joint Hons courses except under **280 pts**)
Bradford – 220 pts (Soc Plcy Sociol) (IB 24 pts)
Worcester – 220–260 pts (Soc Welf)
200 pts **De Montfort** – 200 pts (Pblc Plcy Joint Hons)
Glyndŵr – 200 pts (Pblc Soc Plcy)
Manchester Met – 200 pts (Pblc Serv; Pblc Mgt St)
180 pts **Salford** – 180–240 pts (Cnslg St Soc Plcy) (IB 24 pts)
160 pts **London South Bank** – 160 pts (Soc Plcy; Euro Plcy St courses; Int Soc Plcy)
Swansea Met – 160 pts (Pblc Serv)
Wolverhampton – 160–220 pts (Soc Cr Soc Plcy; Soc Plcy Df St; Soc Plcy Pol; Sociol Soc Plcy)
140 pts **Anglia Ruskin** – 140 pts (Soc Plcy)
West Scotland – CD (Soc Plcy)

Open University – contact +44(0)845 300 6090 **or** www.openuniversity.co.uk/you (Soc Plcy Sociol)

Alternative offers
See **Chapter 7** and **Appendix 1** for grades/UCAS Tariff points information for the International Baccalaureate, Scottish Highers/Advanced Highers, the Welsh Baccalaureate, the Irish Leaving Certificate, the Cambridge Pre-U Diploma, the Advanced Diploma and the Extended Project.

EXAMPLES OF FOUNDATION DEGREES IN THE SUBJECT FIELD
Anglia Ruskin; Bath; Bedfordshire; Bishop Burton (Coll); Bishop Grosseteste (UC); Blackburn (Coll Univ Centre); Blackpool and Fylde (Coll); Bournemouth; Bournemouth and Poole (Coll); Bradford; Brighton; Bristol City (Coll); Bristol UWE; City; Colchester (Inst); Cornwall (Coll); Coventry; Craven (Coll); Cumbria; De Montfort; Derby; Duchy (Coll); Durham New (Coll); East London; Edge Hill; Essex; Exeter (Coll); Farnborough (CT); Glamorgan; Gloucestershire; Glyndŵr; Greenwich; Grimsby (IFHE); Havering (Coll); Hertfordshire; Hopwood Hall (Coll); Huddersfield; Kent; Kirklees (Coll); Lakes (Coll); Lancaster; Leeds City (Coll); Leeds Met; Leeds Trinity (UC); Lincoln; Llandrillo Cymru (Coll); Manchester (Coll); Newman (UC); Newport; Northumberland (Coll); Norwich City (Coll); Nottingham Trent; Peterborough (Reg Coll);

Plymouth; Riverside Halton (Coll); Ruskin Oxford (Coll); St Helens (Coll); Sheffield (Coll); Sir Gâr (Coll); Somerset (CAT); Staffordshire; Stockport (Coll); Stranmillis (UC); Sunderland; Sunderland City (Coll); Truro (Coll); Tyne Met (Coll); Uxbridge (Coll); Walsall (Coll); Warwickshire (Coll); West Anglia (Coll); Westminster Kingsway (Coll); Weymouth (Coll); Wigan and Leigh (Coll); Wirral Met (Coll); Wolverhampton; Worcester; Worcester (CT); York (Coll); York St John.

CHOOSING YOUR COURSE (SEE ALSO CH. 1)
Some course features
Anglia Ruskin (Soc Plcy courses) In addition to an optional semester abroad in Year 2 there is also an internship module in which students can gain vocational experience with an organisation.
Kent (Soc Plcy Pblc Sctr Mgt) Course has an option to study a language and many other subjects in Year 1.
London LSE (Soc Plcy) An outside option of special interest to the student is taken in each year of the course. A module in Social Psychology is offered for students taking courses in Social Policy and Criminology.
Sheffield (Soc Plcy Crimin) There is a Year Abroad scheme in the USA and Australia.

Universities and colleges teaching quality See www.qaa.ac.uk; http://unistats.direct.gov.uk.

Top research universities and colleges (RAE 2008) See **Social Work**.

Examples of sandwich degree courses Aston; Bath; Central Lancashire; De Montfort; Loughborough; Middlesex.

ADMISSIONS INFORMATION
Number of applicants per place (approx) Aston 8; Bangor 6; Bath 6; Birmingham 5; Bristol 3; Cardiff 4; Central Lancashire 6; De Montfort 5; Kent 5; Leeds 10; London LSE (Soc Plcy) 4, (Soc Plcy Sociol) 8, (Soc Plcy Econ) 7, (Soc Plcy Gov) 14; Loughborough 5; Manchester Met 4; Middlesex 12; Nottingham 3; Southampton 6; Stirling 11; Swansea 6; York 3.

Advice to applicants and planning the UCAS personal statement Careers in public and social administration are covered by this subject; consequently a good knowledge of these occupations and contacts with the social services should be discussed fully on your UCAS application. Gain work experience if possible. (See **Appendix 4** for contact details of some relevant organisations.) **Aston** The course is specially tailored for students aiming for careers in NHS management, the civil service and local government. **Bangor** Ability to communicate and work in a group. **York** Work experience, including voluntary work relevant to social policy.

Misconceptions about this course York Some applicants imagine that the course is vocational and leads directly to social work – it does not. Graduates in this field are well placed for a wide range of careers.

Selection interviews Yes Birmingham, London LSE, Swansea; **Some** Anglia Ruskin, Bangor, Bath (mature applicants), Cardiff, Kent, Leeds (mature students), Loughborough, Salford, Southampton, York.

Interview advice and questions Past questions have included: What relevance has history to social administration? What do you understand by 'public policy'? What advantage do you think studying social science gives when working in policy fields? How could the image of public management of services be improved? Applicants should be fully aware of the content and the differences between all the courses on offer, why they want to study Social Policy and their career objectives. See **Chapter 6**.

Reasons for rejection (non-academic) Some universities require attendance when they invite applicants to Open Days (check). Lack of awareness of current social issues. See also **Social Work**. **Bath** Applicant really wanted Business Studies: evidence that teacher, careers adviser or parents are pushing the applicant into the subject or higher education.

AFTER-RESULTS ADVICE
Offers to applicants repeating A-levels Higher Glasgow, Leeds; **Same** Anglia Ruskin, Bangor, Bath, Birmingham, Brighton, Cardiff, Loughborough, Salford, Southampton, York.

GRADUATE DESTINATIONS AND EMPLOYMENT (2007/8 HESA)
Graduates surveyed 965 **Employed** 425 **In further study** 130 **Assumed unemployed** 100

Career note See **Social Sciences/Studies**.

OTHER DEGREE SUBJECTS FOR CONSIDERATION
Behavioural Science; Community Studies; Criminology; Economic and Social History; Economics; Education; Government; Health Studies; Human Resource Management; Law; Politics; Psychology; Social Work; Sociology; Women's Studies.

SOCIAL SCIENCES/STUDIES

(including **Combined Social Sciences, Criminology, Criminal Justice** and **Human Rights**; see also **Education Studies, Health Sciences/Studies, Law, Politics, Psychology, Teacher Training**)

Most Social Sciences/Studies courses take a broad view of aspects of society, for example, economics, politics, history, social psychology and urban studies. Applied Social Studies usually focuses on practical and theoretical preparation for a career in social work. These courses are particularly popular with mature students and some universities and colleges offer shortened degree courses for those with relevant work experience.

Useful websites www.csv.org.uk; www.intute.ac.uk.

NB The points totals shown to the left of the institutions are for ease of reference only. It must not be assumed that Tariff points are always used by institutions or that they can be substituted for an offer in grades. The level of an offer is not necessarily indicative of the quality of a course.

COURSE OFFERS INFORMATION
Subject requirements/preferences GCSE Usually English and mathematics; a science may be required. **AL** No subjects specified. **Other** requirements A Criminal Records Bureau (CRB) check and relevant work experience required for some courses.

NB In 2012 universities and colleges will differ in their use of GCE AL/AS unit grade information, A* grades, the Extended Project (EPQ), the Advanced Diploma and the Cambridge Pre-U examination when considering applicants and making offers. An EPQ may be accepted in place of an AS subject. Check websites of universities and colleges for the latest offers information.

Your target offers and examples of courses provided by each institution
360 pts **Durham** – AAA (Comb Hons Soc Sci) (IB 37 pts)
          Exeter – AAA (Flex Comb Hons Sociol)
340 pts **Essex** – 340–300 pts (Crimin) (IB 34–32 pts)
          Glasgow – AAB (App Soc Sci)
          Lancaster – AAB 340 pts (Law Crimin)
          London (UCL) – AAB–ABB (Soc Sci)
          Manchester – AAB (Criminology) (IB 33 pts)
320 pts **Bath** – ABB–BBC (Soc Sci) (IB 32–34 pts)
          Birmingham – ABB (Hist Soc Sci) (IB 33 pts)
          Cardiff – ABB–BBB (Crimin; Crimin Sociol; Crimin Educ)
          Durham – ABB (Crimin) (IB 34 pts)
          Kent – 320–280 pts (Crimin Joint Hons) (IB 33–31 pts)
          Leeds – ABB (Crim Just Crimin) (IB 34 pts)
          London LSE – ABB (Soc Plcy Crimin) (IB 36–37 pts)
          Loughborough – 320 pts (Crimin Soc Plcy) (IB 32 pts)
          Manchester – ABB–BCC (App Commun Yth Wk St)
          Queen's Belfast – ABB–BBBb (Criminology)
          Sheffield – ABB (Soc Plcy Crimin) (IB 33 pts)
          Southampton – ABB–BBBb (Crim Anth)

Staffordshire – 320 pts (Crimin)
Strathclyde – ABB–ABC (Arts Soc Sci)
Surrey – ABB (Crimin Sociol)
300 pts Cardiff – BBB (Soc Sci)
De Montfort – 300 pts (Law Hum Rts Soc Just)
Edinburgh – BBB (Hum Soc Sci) (IB 34 pts)
Gloucestershire – 300 pts (Crimin)
Lancaster – BBB (Crimin Sociol) (IB 29 pts)
Leicester – BBB (Crimin)
London (RH) – BBB (Crimin Sociol)
Stirling – BBB 2nd yr entry (Crimin)
Ulster – 300 pts (Crimin Crim Just)
280 pts Aberystwyth – 280 pts (Hum Rts) (32 pts)
Brighton – BBC (Crimin Soc Plcy) (IB 30 pts)
Bristol UWE – 280–320 pts (Crimin; Crimin Jrnl)
City – BBC 280 pts (Crimin Sociol) (IB 30 pts)
Liverpool John Moores – 280 pts (Crim Just)
Northumbria – 280 pts (Crimin Foren Sci) (IB 25 pts)
Nottingham Trent – 280 pts (Law Crimin)
Salford – 280–240 pts (Crimin; Crimin Cult St)
York – BBC (App Soc Sci) (IB 30 pts)
260 pts Bolton – 260 pts (Crimin Foren Psy)
Central Lancashire – 260–300 pts (Comb Soc Sci)
Coventry – 260 pts (Crimin; Crimin Psy; Crimin Law)
Derby – 260 pts (Crim Just)
Hull – 260–300 pts (Crimin courses)
Keele – 260–320 pts (Crimin courses) (IB 32 pts)
Lincoln – 260 pts (Crimin Int Rel; Crimin; Crimin Hist)
Liverpool Hope – 260 pts (Crimin)
Liverpool John Moores – 260 pts (Crimin)
Manchester Met – 260 pts (Crimin; Justice courses)
Middlesex – 260 pts (Plcg)
Plymouth – 260–300 pts (Crimin Crim Just St courses)
Swansea – 260–320 pts (Crimin Soc Plcy; Crim Psy; Crimin Crim Just)
Westminster – BCC/BB (Soc Sci) (IB 28 pts)
245 pts Glasgow Caledonian – CCC 245 pts (Soc Sci (Crimin); Soc Sci)
240 pts Bangor – 240–260 pts (Crimin Crim Just) (IB 28 pts)
Birmingham City – 240 pts (Crimin Sociol; Crim Invstg; Crimin Scrty St; Crimin Plc)
Brighton – CCC (App Soc Sci) (IB 28 pts)
Bristol UWE – 240–320 pts (Crimin Joint Hons)
Central Lancashire – 240–260 pts (Crimin Joint Hons; Law Crimin; Eth Hum Rts)
East London – 240 pts (Crimin Crim Just)
Hastings (Univ Centre) – CCC/BCD 240–280 pts (App Soc Sci) (IB 28 pts)
London Met – 240 pts (Crimin Media St)
Newport – 240 pts (Soc Welf; Crimin Crim Just; Soc St Cnslg St)
Portsmouth – 240–300 pts (Crimin Psy; Crimin Foren St)
Roehampton – 240–280 pts (Crimin)
Sheffield Hallam – 240 pts (Crimin; Crimin Sociol)
Southampton Solent – 240 pts (Crimin; Crim Invstg Psy)
Stirling – CCC 1st yr entry (Crimin) (IB 28 pts)
Suffolk (Univ Campus) – 240 pts (Crimin; Crimin Yth St)
Teesside – 240–220 pts (Crimin courses; Yth St)
Wolverhampton – 240 pts (Crim Just Crimin)
220 pts Anglia Ruskin – 220–280 pts (Crimin courses) (IB 30 pts)
Chester – 220–260 pts (Crimin Comb courses) (IB 30 pts)

Edge Hill – 220–260 pts (Crimin Crim Just courses)
Kingston – 220–320 pts (Crimin Joint Hons; Hum Rts Joint Hons)
Northampton – 220–260 pts (Crimin)
Sunderland – 220 pts (Crimin)
Worcester – 220–260 pts (Soc Welf)

200 pts **Canterbury Christ Church** – 200 pts (App Crimin courses) (IB 24 pts)
Central Lancashire – 200 pts (Crimin Crim Just; Hum Rts)
Coventry – 200 pts (Yth Wk)
Cumbria – 200–240 pts (Soc Sci Crimin)
De Montfort – 200 pts (App Crimin; App Crimin Foren Sci)
Doncaster (Coll Univ Centre) – 200 pts (Crim Just; App Soc Sci)
Glyndŵr – 200 pts (Crim Just)
Huddersfield – 200 pts (Soc Sci)
Kent – 200 pts (Crim Just St) (IB 27 pts)
Lincoln – 200 pts (Soc Sci)
London Met – 200 pts (Crimin Yth St)
Middlesex – 200–280 pts (Glob Soc Sci; Crim Just Crimin; Crimin Psy; Yth Just)
Nottingham Trent – 200 pts (Yth St)
Oldham (Coll Univ Centre) – 200 pts (Soc Sci)
Sheffield Hallam – 200 pts (Pol Crimin; App Soc Sci)
Staffordshire – 200 pts (Crim Dvnc Soty)
West London – 200 pts (Crimin Sociol)
Wolverhampton – 200 pts (Crim)

180 pts **Blackburn (Coll Univ Centre)** – 180–200 pts (Soc Sci)
Derby – 180–240 pts (Crimin Joint Hons)
Havering (Coll) – 180 pts (Soc Sci Hum)
Leeds Met – 180 pts (Soc Sci) (IB 24 pts)

160 pts **Abertay Dundee** – CC 168 pts (Soc Sci)
Bedfordshire – 160 pts (Crimin; App Soc St)
Bucks New – 160–200 pts (Plc St; Crimin)
Glamorgan – 160–200 pts (Crimin Crim Just; Crimin Foren Sci; Crimin Comb Hons)
Greenwich – 160 pts (Yth Commun St; Crimin)
London (Gold) – CC (App Soc Sci Commun Dev Yth Wk)
London South Bank – CC 160 pts (Crimin Soc Plcy; Citzn St courses)
Robert Gordon – CC (App Soc Sci)
South Essex (Coll) – 160 pts (Soc St)
UHI Millennium Inst – CC (Soc Sci)
Wolverhampton – 160–220 pts (Policing)
Worcester – 160 pts (Yth Commun Serv)

150 pts **Swansea Met** – 150 pts (Pblc Admin)
140 pts **West Scotland** – CD (Soc Sci)
120 pts **Cornwall (Coll)** – 120 pts (Comb Soc Sci)
Grimsby (IFHE) – 120 pts (Crimin St)

Liverpool Hope – contact University (App Soc Sci)
Open University – contact +44(0)845 300 6090 **or** www.openuniversity.co.uk/you (Crimin
Psy St; Soc Sci Econ; Soc Sci Geog; Soc Sci Media St; Soc Sci Pol; Soc Sci Psy St)

Alternative offers

See **Chapter 7** and **Appendix 1** for grades/UCAS Tariff points information for the International
Baccalaureate, Scottish Highers/Advanced Highers, the Welsh Baccalaureate, the Irish Leaving
Certificate, the Cambridge Pre-U Diploma, the Advanced Diploma and the Extended Project.

EXAMPLES OF FOUNDATION DEGREES IN THE SUBJECT FIELD

(See also **Social and Public Policy and Administration**) Barnfield (Coll); Bath; Bedford (Coll);
Bedfordshire; Blackburn (Coll Univ Centre); Blackpool and Fylde (Coll); Boston (Coll); Bournemouth;

Bradford; Brighton; Bristol City (Coll); Canterbury Christ Church; Central Lancashire; Croydon (Coll); Cumbria; De Montfort; Derby; Duchy (Coll); Exeter (Coll); Grantham (Coll); Grimsby (IFHE); Hartlepool (CFE); Huddersfield; Hull (Coll); Leeds City (Coll); Leicester; Leicester (Coll); Liverpool Hope; London Met; Newcastle (Coll); Newman (UC); Newport; Northampton; Northbrook (Coll); Nottingham Castle (Coll); Nottingham Trent; Oaklands (Coll); Open University; Oxford and Cherwell Valley (Coll); Oxford Brookes; Peterborough (Reg Coll); Plymouth; Plymouth City (Coll); Portsmouth; Runshaw (Coll); Ruskin Oxford (Coll); St Helens (Coll); Sir Gâr (Coll); South Tyneside (Coll);Staffordshire Reg Fed (SURF); Stratford upon Avon (Coll); Sunderland City (Coll); Sussex Downs (Coll); Teesside; Truro (Coll); Warrington (Coll); West Anglia (Coll); Winchester; Worcester; York St John; Yorkshire Coast (CFHE).

CHOOSING YOUR COURSE (SEE ALSO CH. 1)

Some course features

Canterbury Christ Church Courses are offered in Social Work and Police Studies, the latter offered in conjunction with the Kent Police. There are also courses in Child and Youth Studies and in Applied Criminology.

Central Lancashire Degree courses in Criminology, Deaf Studies and joint British Sign Language, Human Rights, Race and Ethnic Studies and Social Policy are offered on the combined honours and joint programmes. The University offers a unit degree scheme that includes courses from economics, psychology and sociology.

Huddersfield There are courses in Criminology, Health and Community Studies and Police Studies and Youth Work. A three-year course is also offered leading to a degree and a Diploma in Social Work. The degree in Social Sciences covers Sociology, Politics, Psychology and Criminology.

Newcastle Social Studies provides a degree in Social Policy and Social Anthropology and covers most fields of importance in contemporary sociology. A degree is also offered in Social Work.

Universities and colleges teaching quality See www.qaa.ac.uk; http://unistats.direct.gov.uk.

Top research universities and colleges (RAE 2008) See **Social Work**.

Examples of sandwich degree courses Bath; Gloucestershire.

ADMISSIONS INFORMATION

Number of applicants per place (approx) Abertay Dundee 1; Bangor 2; Bath 6; Bradford 15; Cornwall (Coll) 2; Coventry 7; Cumbria 4; De Montfort 1; Durham 3; East London 10; Edge Hill 5; Edinburgh 12; Glasgow Caledonian 9; Hull 5; Kingston 5; Leicester (Crimin) 9; Liverpool 13; London (King's) 5; London LSE (all progs) 14; London South Bank 3; Manchester Met 10; Middlesex 26; Northampton 5; Nottingham Trent 2; Portsmouth 3; Roehampton 6; Salford 12; Sheffield Hallam 7; Southampton 6; Staffordshire 2; Sunderland 11; Swansea 8; West Scotland 5; Westminster 14; Winchester 3; York 5.

Advice to applicants and planning the UCAS personal statement The Social Sciences/Studies subject area covers several topics. Focus on these (or some of these) and state your main areas of interest, outlining your work experience, personal goals and motivation to follow the course. Show your interest in current affairs and especially in social issues and government policies.

Misconceptions about this course Cornwall (Coll) That students transfer to Plymouth at the end of Year 1: this is a three-year course in Cornwall.

Selection interviews Yes Anglia Ruskin, Bangor, Birmingham, Brunel, Coventry, Cumbria, Doncaster (Coll Univ Centre), Durham, East London, Edge Hill, Essex, Glasgow Caledonian, Hull, Kingston, London South Bank, Newcastle, Newport, Nottingham Trent, Oxford, Roehampton, Salford, Sunderland, West London, Westminster; **Some** Abertay Dundee, Bath (mature students), Bristol, Cornwall (Coll), East Anglia, Robert Gordon, Staffordshire, Winchester, York.

Interview advice and questions Past questions have included: Define democracy. What is the role of the Church in nationalistic aspirations? Does today's government listen to its people? Questions on current affairs. How would you change the running of your school? What are the faults of the Labour Party/Conservative Party? Do you agree with the National Lottery? Is money from the National Lottery well spent? Give examples of how the social services have failed. What is your understanding of the social origins of problems? See also **Chapter 6**.

Reasons for rejection (non-academic) Stated preference for other institutions. Incompetence in answering questions.

AFTER-RESULTS ADVICE

Offers to applicants repeating A-levels Higher Essex, Glasgow, Salford (possibly), Swansea; **Same** Abertay Dundee, Anglia Ruskin, Bangor, Bradford, Chester, Cornwall (Coll), Coventry, Cumbria, Durham, East Anglia, Gloucestershire, Leeds, Liverpool, London Met, London South Bank, Manchester Met, Newport, Nottingham Trent, Roehampton, Sheffield Hallam, Staffordshire, Stirling, Winchester, Wolverhampton.

GRADUATE DESTINATIONS AND EMPLOYMENT (2007/8 HESA)

Graduates surveyed 745 **Employed** 360 **In further study** 115 **Assumed unemployed** 85

Career note Graduates find careers in all aspects of social provision, for example health services, welfare agencies such as housing departments, the probation service, police forces, the prison service, personnel work and residential care and other careers not necessarily linked with their degree subjects.

OTHER DEGREE SUBJECTS FOR CONSIDERATION

Business Studies; Community Studies; Economics; Education; Geography; Government; Health Studies; Law; Politics; Psychology; Public Administration; Social Policy; Social Work; Sociology; Urban Studies.

SOCIAL WORK

(see also Community Studies/Development, Social and Public Policy and Administration)

Social Work courses (which lead to careers in social work) have similarities to those in Applied Social Studies, Social Policy and Administration, Community Studies and Health Studies. If you are offered a place on a Social Work course which leads to registration as a social worker, you must undergo the Criminal Records Bureau (CRB) disclosure check. You will also have to provide health information and certification. Check for full details of training and careers in social work with the General Social Care Council (see **Appendix 4**). Students from England receive full payment of fees and student bursaries from the General Social Care Council.

Useful websites www.gscc.org.uk; www.swap.ac.uk; www.ageconcern.org.uk; www.samaritans.org; www.ccwales.org.uk; www.sssc.uk.com; www.niscc.info; www.socialworkandcare.co.uk.

NB The points totals shown to the left of the institutions are for ease of reference only. It must not be assumed that Tariff points are always used by institutions or that they can be substituted for an offer in grades. The level of an offer is not necessarily indicative of the quality of a course.

COURSE OFFERS INFORMATION

Subject requirements/preferences GCSE English and mathematics usually required. **AL** No subjects specified. **Other** An Enhanced Criminal Records Bureau check and an occupational health check required. Check also minimum age requirements.

NB In 2012 universities and colleges will differ in their use of GCE AL/AS unit grade information, A* grades, the Extended Project (EPQ), the Advanced Diploma and the Cambridge Pre-U examination when considering applicants and making offers. An EPQ may be accepted in place of an AS subject. Check websites of universities and colleges for the latest offers information.

Your target offers and examples of courses provided by each institution
320 pts Brunel – 320 pts (Soc Wk) (IB 32 pts)
        Queen's Belfast – ABB (Soc Wk)
        Sussex – ABB–BBB (Soc Wk) (IB 34 pts)
300 pts Bath – BBB (Soc Wk App Soc St) (IB 32 pts)
        Birmingham – BBB (Soc Wk)

East Anglia – BBB–ABB (Soc Wk) (IB 30 pts)
Edinburgh – BBB–AAA (Soc Wk) (IB 34 pts)
Lancaster – BBB 300 pts (Soc Wk) (IB 28 pts)
Leeds – BBB (Soc Wk)
Nottingham – BBB (Soc Wk Soc Plcy) (IB 32 pts)
Strathclyde – BBB (Soc Wk) (IB 28 pts)
Ulster – BBB 300 pts (Soc Wk)
280 pts **Bournemouth** – 280 pts (Soc Wk) (IB 30 pts)
Bucks New – 280 pts (Soc Wk)
Coventry – 280 pts (Soc Wk)
Gloucestershire – 280–300 pts (Soc Wk)
Kent – 280 pts (Soc Wk) (IB 31 pts)
London (Gold) – BBC (Soc Wk) (IB 30 pts)
London Met – 280 pts (Soc Wk)
Oxford Brookes – BBC (Soc Wk)
Salford – 280 pts (Soc Wk St)
Sheffield – BBC (Soc Wk) (IB 30 pts)
York – BBC (Soc Wk) (IB 30 pts)
260 pts **Bradford** – 260 pts (Soc Wk)
Edge Hill – 260–280 pts (Soc Wk)
Keele – 260–280 pts (Soc Wk) (IB 26–28 pts)
Liverpool Hope – 260 pts (Soc Work)
Liverpool John Moores – 260 pts (Soc Wk)
London (RH) – 260 pts (Soc Wk)
Northumbria – 260 pts (Soc Wk)
Swansea – BCC (Soc Wk)
Wiltshire (Coll) – 260 pts (Soc Wk)
Winchester – 260–300 pts (Soc Cr St courses)
240 pts **Anglia Ruskin** – 240 pts (Soc Wk)
Chester – 240 pts (Soc Wk) (IB 24 pts)
Chichester – CCC (Soc Wk) (IB 28 pts)
De Montfort – 240 pts (Soc Wk)
Dundee – CCC (Soc Wk)
Glamorgan – 240–280 pts (Soc Wk)
Hertfordshire – 240 pts (Soc Wk)
Huddersfield – 240 pts (Soc Wk)
Hull – 240–260 pts (Soc Wk)
Kingston – 240 pts (Soc Wk)
Lincoln – 240 pts (Soc Wk)
Middlesex – 240–280 pts (Soc Wk)
NEW (Coll) – 240 pts (Soc Wk)
Newport – 240 pts (Soc Wk)
Nottingham Trent – CCC 240 pts (Soc Wk)
Robert Gordon – CCC 240 pts (Soc Wk)
Stirling – CCC (Soc Wk)
Suffolk (Univ Campus) – 240 pts (Soc Wk)
Sunderland – 240 pts (Soc Wk)
Teesside – 240 pts (Soc Wk)
220 pts **Bangor** – 220–260 pts (Soc Wk) (IB 28 pts)
Glyndŵr – 220–260 pts (Soc Wk)
Northampton – 220–260 pts (Soc Cr courses; Soc Wk)
Worcester – 220–260 pts (Soc Welf courses)
200 pts **Birmingham City** – 200–240 pts (Soc Wk)
Bristol UWE – 200–240 pts (Soc Wk)
Canterbury Christ Church – 200–240 pts (Soc Wk) (IB 24 pts)

Cumbria – 200 pts (Soc Wk)
East London – 200 pts (Soc Wk)
Leeds Met – 200 pts (Soc Wk)
Manchester Met – 200 pts (Soc Wk) (IB 24 pts)
Plymouth – 200 pts (Soc Wk)
Portsmouth – 200–260 pts (Soc Wk)
Sheffield Hallam – 200 pts (Soc Wk)
Southampton Solent – 200 pts (Soc Wk)
West London – 200 pts (Soc Wk)

180 pts **Durham New (Coll)** – 180 pts (Soc Wk)
Greenwich – 180 pts (Soc Wk)
Liverpool (CmC) – 180 pts (Soc Wk)
Staffordshire – 180–240 pts (Soc Wk)
UCP Marjon – 180 pts (Chld Welf Soty; Wk Chld Yng Ppl; Commun Wk; Yth Commun Wk)

160 pts **Bedfordshire** – 160 pts (Soc Wk; Hlth Soc Cr)
Bradford (Coll Univ Centre) – CC (Soc Wk)
Cardiff (UWIC) – 160 pts (Soc Wk; Hlth Soc Cr)
Central Lancashire – CC (Soc Wk)
Chester – 160–200 pts (Chr Yth Wk; Mslm Yth Wk)
Colchester (Inst) – 160 pts (Hlth Soc Cr)
Cornwall (Coll) – 160 pts (Soc Wk)
Glasgow Caledonian – CC (Soc Wk)
London (Gold) – CC (App Soc Sci Commun Dev Yth Wk)
London South Bank – 160 pts (Soc Wk)
Roehampton – 160–200 pts (Hlth Soc Cr)
South Essex (Coll) – 160 pts (Soc Wk)
Wolverhampton – 160–220 pts (Soc Wk)

140 pts **West Scotland** – CD (Soc Wk)
80 pts **Derby** – 80–120 pts (App Soc Wk)
Havering (Coll) – check with admissions tutor 80 pts (Soc Wk)
Stockport (Coll) – check with admissions tutor 80 pts (Soc Wk)

Open University – www.openuniversity.co.uk/you (Soc Wk)
Trinity Saint David – contact admissions (Yth Commun Wk)

Alternative offers See **Chapter 7** and **Appendix 1** for grades/UCAS Tariff points information for the International Baccalaureate, Scottish Highers/Advanced Highers, the Welsh Baccalaureate, the Irish Leaving Certificate, the Cambridge Pre-U Diploma, the Advanced Diploma and the Extended Project.

EXAMPLES OF FOUNDATION DEGREES IN THE SUBJECT FIELD
See **Social and Public Policy and Administration**.

CHOOSING YOUR COURSE (SEE ALSO CH. 1)
Some course features
Brunel Students are required to attend university and placements each day between 9am and 5pm. Placements are in Years 2 and 3, occupying 2½ to 3 days each week, with the remaining time at university.
Coventry The course covers law, human growth and development, communication skills and partnership working.
East Anglia (Soc Wk) 200 days spent on placements with social work agencies.

Universities and colleges teaching quality See www.qaa.ac.uk; http://unistats.direct.gov.uk.

Top research universities and colleges (RAE 2008) (**Social Work** and **Social Policy and Administration**) London LSE; Bath; Leeds; Kent; Edinburgh; York; City; Oxford; Sheffield; Lancaster; Keele; Birmingham; London South Bank; Nottingham Trent; Sussex.

Examples of sandwich degree courses Bath.

ADMISSIONS INFORMATION

Number of applicants per place (approx) Bangor 8; Bath 8; Birmingham 13; Bradford 10; Coventry 22; Dundee 6; London Met 27; Northampton 7; Nottingham Trent 6; Sheffield Hallam 4; Southampton 10; Staffordshire 3.

Advice to applicants and planning the UCAS personal statement The statement should show motivation for social work, relevant work experience, awareness of the demands of social work and give relevant personal information, for example disabilities. Awareness of the origins of personal and family difficulties, commitment to anti-discriminatory practice. Most applicants for these courses will have significant experience of a statutory care agency or voluntary/private organisation providing a social work or social care service. See also **Social and Public Policy and Administration** and **Appendix 2**.

Selection interviews Yes Anglia Ruskin, Bangor, Birmingham, Bradford, Brunel, Chichester, Coventry, Liverpool Hope, Nottingham, Nottingham Trent, Portsmouth, Robert Gordon, Salford, Sheffield Hallam, Staffordshire, West London, Wolverhampton, York; **Some** Cardiff (UWIC), Dundee.

Interview advice and questions What qualities are needed to be a social worker? What use to you think you will be to a society as a social worker? Why should money be spent on prison offenders? Your younger brother is playing truant and mixing with bad company. Your parents don't know. Would you do? See also **Social and Public Policy and Administration** and **Chapter 6**.

Reasons for rejection (non-academic) Criminal convictions.

AFTER-RESULTS ADVICE

Offers to applicants repeating A-levels Same Bangor, Lincoln, Liverpool Hope, Salford (Coll), Staffordshire, Suffolk (Univ Campus), Wolverhampton.

GRADUATE DESTINATIONS AND EMPLOYMENT (2007/8 HESA)

Graduates surveyed 3690 **Employed** 2505 **In further study** 190 **Assumed unemployed** 215

Career note See **Social Sciences/Studies**.

OTHER DEGREE SUBJECTS FOR CONSIDERATION

Community Studies; Conductive Education; Criminology; Economics; Education; Health Studies; Law; Psychology; Public Sector Management and Administration; Social Policy; Sociology; Youth Studies.

SOCIOLOGY

(see also Anthropology, Social and Public Policy and Administration)

Sociology is the study of social organisation, social structures, systems, institutions and practices. Courses are likely to include the meaning and structure of, for example, race, ethnicity and gender, industrial behaviour, crime and deviance, health and illness. **NB** Sociology is not a training course for social workers, although some graduates take additional qualifications to qualify in social work.

Useful websites www.britsoc.co.uk; www.asanet.org; www.sociology.org.uk; www.sociology.org.

NB The points totals shown to the left of the institutions are for ease of reference only. It must not be assumed that Tariff points are always used by institutions or that they can be substituted for an offer in grades. The level of an offer is not necessarily indicative of the quality of a course.

COURSE OFFERS INFORMATION

Subject requirements/preferences GCSE English and mathematics usually required. **AL** No subjects specified.

NB In 2012 universities and colleges will differ in their use of GCE AL/AS unit grade information, A* grades, the Extended Project (EPQ), the Advanced Diploma and the Cambridge Pre-U

examination when considering applicants and making offers. An EPQ may be accepted in place of an AS subject. Check websites of universities and colleges for the latest offers information.

Your target offers and examples of courses provided by each institution

380 pts **Cambridge** – A*AA college offers may vary (Pol Psy Sociol (PPS)) (IB 38–42 pts HL 766–777)

360 pts **Durham** – AAA (Comb Hons Soc Sci) (IB 37 pts)

350 pts **Warwick** – BBBb (Hist Sociol; Fr Sociol; Law Sociol)

340 pts **Glasgow** – AAB (Sociol courses) (IB 34 pts)
Southampton – AAB (Phil Sociol) (IB 34 pts HL 17 pts)

320 pts **Bath** – ABB–BBC (Sociol HR Mgt) (IB 32 pts)
Birmingham – BBB–ABB (Sociol Phil) (IB 32 pts)
Bristol – ABB (Theol Sociol) (IB 33 pts)
Cardiff – ABB (Sociol Jrnl; Soc Phil App Eth)
Durham – ABB (Anth and Sociol) (IB 34 pts HL 17–19 pts)
East Anglia – ABB–BBB (Soty Cult Media) (IB 31–32 pts)
Essex – 320–300 pts (Sociol Law) (IB 30–32 pts)
Lancaster – ABB 320 pts (Socioling) (IB 30 pts)
London (Gold) – ABB (Hist Sociol)
London LSE – ABB (Sociol) (IB 36 pts)
Loughborough – 320–330 pts (Econ Sociol)
Manchester – ABB–BBB (Sociol courses) (IB 34–33 pts)
Nottingham – ABB (Sociol) (IB 34 pts)
Southampton – ABB–BBBb 320–350 pts (Sociol) (IB 32 pts HL 16 pts)
Strathclyde – ABB–ABC (Sociol)
Surrey – ABB–BBB (Sociol Cult Media) (IB 32 pts)
Sussex – ABB–BBB (Sociol Int Dev) (IB 32 pts)

300 pts **Aberdeen** – BBB (Sociol courses)
Aston – BBB–ABB 300 pts (Sociol courses) (IB 32–33 pts)
Birmingham – BBB–AAB (Sociol Soc Plcy) (IB 32 pts)
Brunel – 300–350 pts (Psy Sociol) (IB 33 pts)
Cardiff – BBB (Sociol; Soc Plcy Sociol; Sociol Welsh)
City – BBB 300 pts (Sociol Psy) (IB 32 pts)
Edinburgh – BBB–AAA (Sociol Soc Econ Hist; Sociol Soc Anth)
Exeter – BBB–AAB (Sociol Fr/Ger/Ital/Russ/Span) (IB 29–28 pts)
Lancaster – BBB 300 pts (Sociol) (IB 29 pts)
Leeds – BBB (Sociol Theol Relig St) (IB 32 pts HL 15 pts)
Leicester – BBB (Media Sociol) (IB 28–30 pts)
Liverpool – BBB–BBC (Crimin Sociol) (IB 30 pts)
London (Gold) – BBB (Media Sociol) (IB 28 pts)
Loughborough – 300 pts (Sociol) (IB 32 pts)
Newcastle – BBB (Pol Sociol) (IB 32 pts)
Northumbria – 300 pts (Sociol courses)
Queen's Belfast – BBB–BBCb (Sociol courses)
Sheffield – BBB (Sociol courses) (IB 30–33 pts)
Stirling – BBB 2nd yr entry (Sociol Soc Plcy)
York – BBB (Sociol; Sociol Soc Psy; Sociol Educ)

280 pts **City** – BBC 280 pts (Sociol) (IB 30 pts)
Gloucestershire – 280 pts (Sociol; Engl Lit Sociol)
Kent – 280–300 pts (Sociol Econ) (IB 31–33 pts)
Oxford Brookes – BBC (Sociol courses) (IB 31 pts)
Salford – 280–240 pts (Sociol Cult St) (IB 29 pts)

260 pts **Brighton** – BCC (Sociol Engl Lit) (IB 28 pts)
Brunel – 260–300 pts (Anth Sociol; Sociol Media St) (IB 31–32 pts)

For a quick reference offers calculator, fold out the inside back cover.

Coventry – 260–280 pts (Sociol; Sociol Psy; Sociol Crimin)
Huddersfield – 260 pts (Sociol; Sociol Educ)
Hull – 260–300 pts (Sociol Anth courses)
Keele – 260–320 pts (Sociol courses) (IB 30 pts)
Liverpool John Moores – 260 pts (Sociol)
Manchester Met – 260–240 pts (Sociol Comb Hons) (IB 24 pts)
Plymouth – 260–300 pts (Sociol)
Westminster – BCC/BB (Sociol) (IB 28 pts)

240 pts **Bath Spa** – 240–280 pts (Sociol)
Birmingham City – 240 pts (Sociol; Sociol Crimin; Sociol Psy)
Bradford – 240 pts (Sociol)
Bristol UWE – 240–300 pts (Hist Sociol) (IB 28 pts)
Bucks New – 240–280 pts (Psy Sociol)
Canterbury Christ Church – 240 pts (Sociol courses)
Central Lancashire – 240 pts (Sociol courses)
Hastings (Univ Centre) – CCC/BCD 240–280 pts (Sociol Commun Hist) (IB 28 pts)
Kingston – 240 pts (Sociol)
Leeds Met – 240 pts (Psy Socty)
London South Bank – 240 pts (Int Pol Sociol)
Newport – 240 pts (Sociol; Sociol Yth Just; Sociol Soc Welf; Sociol Crim)
Northampton – 240–280 pts (Sociol)
Nottingham Trent – 240 pts (Sociol)
Portsmouth – 240–300 pts (Sociol; Sociol Media St; Sociol Psy)
St Mary's Twickenham (UC) – 240 pts (Sociol)
Stirling – CCC 1st yr entry (Sociol Soc Plcy) (IB 28 pts)
Suffolk (Univ Campus) – 240 pts (Sociol Yth St; Sociol Crimin)
Ulster – 240 pts (Sociol; Sociol Ir Hist; Sociol Commun Dev)

220 pts **Bangor** – 220–260 pts (Sociol Crimin Joint Hons) (IB 24 pts)
Bath Spa – 220–260 pts (Sociol Comb courses)
Chester – 220–260 pts (Sociol)
Edge Hill – 220–260 pts (Sociol; Sociol Chld Yth St; Engl Sociol; Hist Sociol)
Glamorgan – 220–260 pts (Sociol Educ; Sociol Hist)
Liverpool John Moores – 220 pts (Sociol Crimin)
Queen Margaret – 220 pts (Psy Sociol)
Sheffield Hallam – 220 pts (Sociol; App Soc Sci (Psy Sociol))
Sunderland – 220 pts (Sociol courses)
Teesside – 220 pts (Sociol; Sociol Yth St; Sociol Pol)
Worcester – 220–260 pts (Sociol)

200 pts **Anglia Ruskin** – 200 pts (Sociol; Sociol Engl; Sociol Media St)
Bucks New – 200–240 pts (Psysoc St)
Canterbury Christ Church – 200 pts (Sociol Soc Sci courses)
Derby – 200–220 pts (Sociol Joint Hons; Sociol)
Leeds Met – 200–180 pts (Crimin Sociol; Pol Sociol)
London Met – 200 pts (Sociol)
Middlesex – 200–280 pts (Sociol)
Roehampton – 200–240 pts (Sociol courses)
Staffordshire – 200 pts (Sociol courses)
West London – 200 pts (Crimin Sociol)

180 pts **Bedfordshire** – 180–220 pts (Crimin Sociol)

160 pts **Abertay Dundee** – CC 168 pts (Sociol)
East London – 160–200 pts (Sociol courses)
Greenwich – 160 pts (Sociol courses)
London South Bank – CC (Sociol)
Wolverhampton – 160–220 pts (Sociol Pol; Relig St Sociol; Sociol)

140 pts **West Scotland** – CD (Sociol)

Alternative offers
See **Chapter 7** and **Appendix 1** for grades/UCAS Tariff points information for the International Baccalaureate, Scottish Highers/Advanced Highers, the Welsh Baccalaureate, the Irish Leaving Certificate, the Cambridge Pre-U Diploma, the Advanced Diploma and the Extended Project.

EXAMPLES OF FOUNDATION DEGREES IN THE SUBJECT FIELD
Blackburn (Coll Univ Centre); Bradford; De Montfort; London Met; Plymouth; Truro (Coll); Winchester.

CHOOSING YOUR COURSE (SEE ALSO CH. 1)
Some course features
Bristol In the first year of the Sociology course students choose two additional subjects from the Faculties of Social Sciences and the Arts. There are joint programmes combining with Philosophy, Social Policy and Theology. Sociology can also be taken with study abroad.
Edinburgh Sociology, the discipline which examines the relationship between individuals and society, is offered as a single honours course or with Social Anthropology, Politics, South Asian Studies or Economic History.
Kent A single honours course is offered. In Part II, core courses are taken, including social analysis of industrial societies and research practices in sociology, as well as optional third-year courses such as the sociology of politics, education, knowledge, sex, gender and the family.
Leeds In the first year of the Sociology degree social, intellectual and cultural trends in the 19th and 20th centuries are studied together with computing skills. Social processes and institutions form the core subjects in Year 2, and in Year 3 options are taken from a wide range of topics from which students are asked to choose two for further research.
London LSE A module in Social Psychology is offered for students taking courses in Sociology.

Universities and colleges teaching quality See www.qaa.ac.uk; http://unistats.direct.gov.uk.

Top research universities and colleges (RAE 2008) Manchester; Essex; London (Gold); York; Lancaster; Surrey; Edinburgh; Warwick; Cardiff; Exeter; Oxford; Cambridge.

Examples of sandwich degree courses Aston; Bath; Brunel; Middlesex; Northumbria; Nottingham Trent; Surrey.

ADMISSIONS INFORMATION
Number of applicants per place (approx) Aston 8; Bangor 1; Bath 7; Birmingham 8; Birmingham City 12; Bristol 8; Brunel 24; Cardiff 5; Cardiff (UWIC) 4; City 11; Durham 13; East Anglia 15; East London 8; Exeter 5; Gloucestershire 8; Greenwich 5; Hull 11; Kent 10; Kingston 9; Lancaster 12; Leeds 14; Leicester 4; Liverpool 9; Liverpool John Moores 10; London (Gold) 5; London LSE 10; London Met 3; Loughborough 10; Northampton 3; Northumbria 18; Nottingham 7; Plymouth 9; Portsmouth 12; Roehampton 4; Sheffield Hallam 7; Southampton 4; Staffordshire 10; Sunderland 5; Surrey 6; Warwick 20; Worcester 5; York 5.

Advice to applicants and planning the UCAS personal statement Show your ability to communicate and work as part of a group and your curiosity about issues such as social conflict and social change between social groups. Discuss your interests in sociology on the personal statement. Demonstrate an intellectual curiosity about sociology and social problems. (International students) Good command of written and spoken English required. See **Social Sciences/Studies**.

Misconceptions about this course Some applicants believe that all sociologists want to become social workers. **Birmingham** Students with an interest in crime and deviance may be disappointed that we do not offer modules in this area. **London Met** That it is the stamping ground of student activists and has no relevance to the real world.

Selection interviews **Yes** Aston, Birmingham City, Brunel, Cambridge, City, Derby, Durham, East London, Exeter, Hull, Lancaster, Leeds, Leicester, Liverpool, London (Gold), Loughborough, Newcastle, Nottingham, Portsmouth, St Mary's Twickenham (UC), Surrey, Warwick; **Some** Anglia Ruskin, Bath (mature applicants), Bath Spa, Birmingham (mature applicants), Bristol, Cardiff, Kent, Liverpool John Moores, London Met, Nottingham Trent, Salford, Sheffield Hallam, Southampton, Staffordshire.

Interview advice and questions Past questions have included: Why do you want to study Sociology? What books have you read on the subject? How do you see the role of women changing in the next 20 years? See also **Chapter 6**. **London Met** Questions will focus on existing level of interest in the subject and the applicant's expectations about studying.

Reasons for rejection (non-academic) Evidence of difficulty with written work. Non-attendance at open days (find out from your universities if your attendance will affect their offers). 'In the middle of an interview for Sociology a student asked us if we could interview him for Sports Studies instead!' See also **Social and Public Policy and Administration**. **Durham** No evidence of awareness of what the course involves. **London Met** References which indicated that the individual would not be able to work effectively within a diverse student group; concern that the applicant had not put any serious thought into the choice of subject for study.

AFTER-RESULTS ADVICE
Offers to applicants repeating A-levels **Higher** Brunel, East London, Essex, Glasgow, Hull, Newcastle, Nottingham Trent, Warwick, York; **Possibly higher** Leeds, Liverpool, Portsmouth; **Same** Aston, Bangor, Bath, Birmingham, Birmingham City, Bristol, Cardiff, Coventry, Derby, Durham, Gloucestershire, Kingston, Lancaster, Liverpool John Moores, London Met, Loughborough, Northumbria, Roehampton, St Mary's Twickenham (UC), Salford, Sheffield Hallam, Southampton, Staffordshire.

GRADUATE DESTINATIONS AND EMPLOYMENT (2007/8 HESA)
Graduates surveyed 4095 **Employed** 1740 **In further study** 615 **Assumed unemployed** 410

Career note See **Social Sciences/Studies**.

OTHER DEGREE SUBJECTS FOR CONSIDERATION
Anthropology; Economic and Social History; Economics; Education; Geography; Government; Health Studies; History; Law; Politics; Psychology; Social Policy; Social Work.

SPANISH

(including **Hispanic Studies** and **Portuguese**; see also **Languages, Latin American Studies**)

Spanish can be studied by focusing on the language and literature of Spain. Broader courses in Hispanic Studies (see also **Latin American Studies**) are available which also include Portuguese and Latin American studies. See also **Appendix 4** under Languages.

Useful websites www.donquijote.co.uk; http://europa.eu; www.cilt.org.uk; www.iol.org.uk; www. bbc.co.uk/languages; http://languageadvantage.com; www.languagematters.co.uk; www.reed.co.uk/multilingual; www.studyspanish.com; www.spanishlanguageguide.com; see also **Latin American Studies**.

NB The points totals shown to the left of the institutions are for ease of reference only. It must not be assumed that Tariff points are always used by institutions or that they can be substituted for an offer in grades. The level of an offer is not necessarily indicative of the quality of a course.

COURSE OFFERS INFORMATION
Subject requirements/preferences **GCSE** English, mathematics or science and a foreign language. **AL** Spanish required for most courses.

NB In 2012 universities and colleges will differ in their use of GCE AL/AS unit grade information, A* grades, the Extended Project (EPQ), the Advanced Diploma and the Cambridge Pre-U examination when considering applicants and making offers. An EPQ may be accepted in place of an AS subject. Check websites of universities and colleges for the latest offers information.

Your target offers and examples of courses provided by each institution
380 pts Cambridge – A*AA college offers may vary (Modn Mediev Langs (Span) (Port)) (IB 38–42 pts HL 766–777)

London (UCL) – AAA+AS–BBB+AS (Modn Langs (Span)) (IB 32–38 pts)
Warwick – AABc (Hist Lit Cult Am) (IB 36 pts)

360 pts **Bath** – AAA–ABB (Modn Langs Euro St) (IB 34 pts HL lang 6)
Bristol – AAA–ABB (Hist Art Span/Port) (IB 37–34 pts)
Imperial London – AAA (Chem Span Sci) (IB 38 pts)
London (King's) – ABB+AS/AAbb+AS (Hisp St) (IB 34 pts HL 6 span)
London (RH) – AAA (Econ Span)
Manchester – AAA–AAB (Span Chin/Jap MML) (IB 35–37 pts)
Nottingham – AAA–AAB (Econ Hisp St) (IB 38 pts)
Oxford – AAA (Span courses) (IB 38–42 pts)
Queen's Belfast – AAA–AABa (Cmn Civ Law Fr/Span) (IB 34 pts HL 666)
St Andrews – AAA (Span) (IB 38 pts)

340 pts **Birmingham** – AAB (Port Mny Bank Fin) (IB 34–36 pts)
Bristol – AAB–BBC (Span courses except under **360 pts**) (IB 30–33 pts)
East Anglia – AAB–BBB (Span Film TV) (IB 31–33 pts)
Exeter – AAB–ABB (Film St Fr/Ger/Ital/Russ/Span) (IB 34–32 pts)
Glasgow – AAB (Hisp St) (IB 34 pts)
Imperial London – AAB (Biol Span Sci) (IB 38 pts)
London (King's) – ABB+AS **or** ABbb+AS (Hisp St Port Braz St) (IB 34 pts HL 6 span)
London (UCL) – ABB+AS (Hisp St Modn Gk St) (IB 34 pts)
St Andrews – AAB–AAA (Int Rel Span) (IB 38 pts)
Southampton – AAB (Span Port Lat Am St) (IB 34 pts)
Surrey – AAB (Bus Mgt Span)
Sussex – AAB–ABB (Dev St Span) (IB 34–36 pts)

320 pts **Bath** – ABB–BBB (Span Fr/Ger/Ital/Russ) (IB 34 pts HL lang 6)
Birmingham – ABB (Port Joint Hons)
Bristol – ABB–BBC (Hisp St) (IB 30–33 pts)
Cardiff – ABB (Span) (IB 30 pts)
Exeter – ABB–BBB (Sociol Span) (IB 32–29 pts)
Kent – 320 pts (Hisp St) (IB 35 pts)
Leeds – ABB–AAB (Hisp Lat Am St) (IB 34 pts HL 16 pts)
Leicester – ABB (Span Engl) (IB 28–30 pts)
London (QM) – 320–340 pts (Hisp St; Hisp St Geog; Hisp St Pol; Hisp St Ctln Lang)
London (RH) – ABB–BBB (Span Int Rel) (IB 32 pts)
Newcastle – ABB (Span Port Lat Am St) (IB 32 pts HL Span 6)
Nottingham – ABB–ABC (Span Contemp Chin St) (IB 34 pts)
Strathclyde – ABB (Span courses)
Surrey – ABB (Span)
York – ABB (Span) (IB 32 pts)

300 pts **Aberdeen** – BBB (Span courses)
Aston – 300–320 pts (Span Comb Hons) (IB 31–33 pts)
Birmingham – BBB (Hisp St) (IB 32 pts)
Cardiff – BBB–ABB (Span courses) (IB 30 pts)
Coventry – 300 pts (Law Span)
East Anglia – BBB–BBC (Transl Media Fr/Span 3 yrs) (IB 31–30 pts)
Edinburgh – Check with Ad. Tutor BBB (Span Port EU St; Span Engl Lit; Span Class; Hisp St Hist)
Essex – 300 pts (Port St Modn Langs) (IB 30 pts)
Heriot-Watt – BBB (Langs (Interp Transl) (Fr/Ger) (Ger/Span)) (IB 28 pts)
Hertfordshire – 300 pts (Mark Span; Tour Span)
Lancaster – BBB–ABB 300–320 pts (Span St Mus) (IB 30 pts)
Liverpool – BBB 300 pts (Hisp St courses) (IB 30 pts)
Manchester – BBB–AAA (Span courses except under 360 pts) (IB 30–33 pts)
Northumbria – 300 pts (Span Bus) (IB 26 pts)

Queen's Belfast – BBB–BBCb (Span St; Span Port St)
Salford – 300 pts (Law Span) (IB 30 pts)
Sheffield – BBB (Hisp St courses) (IB 35–32 pts)
Swansea – BBB 300 pts (Span Pol; Span Comp Sci)
280 pts **Aberystwyth** – 280 pts (Span courses) (IB 29 pts)
Hull – 280–300 pts (Span courses)
Portsmouth – 280 pts (Euro Bus (Span))
Roehampton – 280–320 pts (Span Media Cult)
260 pts **Central Lancashire** – 260-300 pts (Span Comb courses)
Dundee – BCC (Span courses)
London Met – 260 pts (Span)
Nottingham Trent – 260 pts (Media Span; Span Ital)
Oxford Brookes – BCC (Span minor field) (IB 30 pts)
Westminster – BCC–BBB (Span courses) (IB 28 pts)
240 pts **Bangor** – 240–280 pts (Span courses)
Buckingham – 240–300 pts (Psy Span; Span Mark)
Coventry – 240–260 pts (Span; Span Bus; Span Int Rel)
Edinburgh Napier – 240 pts (Span courses)
Kingston – 240–320 pts (Span courses) (IB 25–27 pts)
Liverpool John Moores – 240 pts (Int Bus St Span)
Manchester Met – 240 pts (Span St; Span Comb Hons)
Plymouth – 240–260 pts (Span courses)
Sheffield Hallam – 240 pts (Int Bus Span; Span Mark; Span Tour)
Stirling – CCC (Span Psy) (IB 28 pts)
220 pts **Chester** – 220–260 pts (Span courses)
Hertfordshire – 220–260 pts (Hist Span)
Leeds Met – 220 pts (Span PR; Span Glob Dev)
Sunderland – 220 pts (Span Comb Hons)
Ulster – 220–240 pts (Euro St Span; Span Comp; Span Acc; Span Rtl St)
200 pts **Glamorgan** – 200–260 pts (Bus Span; Engl Span; Law Span)
Middlesex – 200–280 pts (Span Int Bus)
Portsmouth – 200–280 pts (Span St)
180 pts **Abertay Dundee** – 180 pts (Bus Span)
Greenwich – 180–160 pts (Span courses)
160 pts **Euro Bus Sch London** – CC Check with Bus Sch (Int Bus Span)
80 pts **London (Birk)** – for under 21s (over 21s varies) p/t (Span Lat Am St; Span Port)
London LSE – optional course offered by the language centre check with admissions tutor (Fr/Ger/Span/Russ)

Alternative offers
See **Chapter 7** and **Appendix 1** for grades/UCAS Tariff points information for the International Baccalaureate, Scottish Highers/Advanced Highers, the Welsh Baccalaureate, the Irish Leaving Certificate, the Cambridge Pre-U Diploma, the Advanced Diploma and the Extended Project.

CHOOSING YOUR COURSE (SEE ALSO CH. 1)
Some course features
East Anglia For particularly able students, Spanish courses are offered over three years, not the usual four-year course.
Heriot-Watt Spanish can be taken with Interpreting and Translating, International Management and Teaching English to Speakers of Other Languages.
London (King's) The University offers a very wide range of courses covering Hispanic, Portuguese and Brazilian Studies.
London Met There is an Open Language programme offered to students to continue a study of a preferred language irrespective of their chosen degree course (see also **Languages**).

Warwick (Hist Lit Cult Ams) A four-year interdisciplinary course, with the third year spent at a university in the Americas. Spanish language is taught throughout, with beginners following an introductory course in Year 1, and students with A-level Spanish taking one more advanced course. There are opportunities to study Spanish American literature as poetry.

Universities and colleges teaching quality See www.qaa.ac.uk; http://unistats.direct.gov.uk.

Top research universities and colleges (RAE 2008) (Iberian and Latin American languages) Nottingham; Cambridge; London (King's) (Port); London (Birk); Durham; London (QM); Leeds; St Andrews; Newcastle; Queen's Belfast.

ADMISSIONS INFORMATION
Number of applicants per place (approx) Birmingham 9; Bristol 7; Cardiff 3; Exeter 5; Hull 14; Leeds 10; Liverpool 3; London (King's) 6; London (QM) 5; London (UCL) 6; Middlesex 2; Newcastle 12; Nottingham 7; Portsmouth 4; Salford 5.

Advice to applicants and planning the UCAS personal statement Visits to Spanish-speaking countries should be discussed. Study the geography, culture, literature and politics of Spain (or Portugal) and discuss your interests in full. Further information could be obtained from embassies in London. See also **Appendix 4** under **Languages**.

Selection interviews Yes Cambridge, Hull, London (RH), London (UCL), Nottingham, Oxford; **Some** Cardiff, Leeds, Roehampton, Swansea.

Interview advice and questions Candidates offering A-level Spanish are likely to be questioned on their A-level work, their reasons for wanting to take the subject and on their knowledge of Spain and its people. Interest in Spain important for all applicants. Student Comment: Mostly questions about the literature I had read and I was given a poem and asked questions on it.' Questions were asked in the target language. There were two interviewers for the Spanish interview; they did their best to trip me up and to make me think under pressure by asking aggressive questions. See **Chapter 6**.

AFTER-RESULTS ADVICE
Offers to applicants repeating A-levels Higher Glasgow, Leeds; **Same** Cardiff, Chester, Hull, Liverpool, London (RH), Newcastle, Nottingham, Roehampton, Swansea.

GRADUATE DESTINATIONS AND EMPLOYMENT (2007/8 HESA)
Spanish graduates surveyed 840 **Employed** 355 **In further study** 185 **Assumed unemployed** 55

Portuguese graduates surveyed 40 **Employed** 15 **In further study** 5 **Assumed unemployed** 5

Career note See **Languages**.

OTHER DEGREE SUBJECTS FOR CONSIDERATION
International Business Studies; Latin American Studies; Linguistics; see other Language tables.

Speech Pathology/Sciences/Therapy

(including **Deaf Studies**; see also **Communication Studies/Communication, Health Sciences/ Studies**)

Speech Pathology/Sciences/Therapy is the study of speech defects caused by accident, disease or psychological trauma. These can include failure to develop communication at the usual age, voice disorders, physical and learning disabilities and stammering. Courses lead to qualification as a speech therapist. This is one of many medical courses. See also **Medicine** and **Appendix 4**.

Useful websites www.rcslt.org; www.speechteach.co.uk; www.asha.org.

NB The points totals shown to the left of the institutions are for ease of reference only. It must not be assumed that Tariff points are always used by institutions or that they can be substituted for an offer in grades. The level of an offer is not necessarily indicative of the quality of a course.

COURSE OFFERS INFORMATION

Subject requirements/preferences **GCSE** English language, modern foreign language and biology/ dual award science at grade B or above. **AL** At least one science subject; biology may be stipulated, psychology and English language may be preferred. **Other** requirements Criminal Records Bureau (CRB) and occupational health checks essential for speech sciences/speech therapy applicants.

NB In 2012 universities and colleges will differ in their use of GCE AL/AS unit grade information, A* grades, the Extended Project (EPQ), the Advanced Diploma and the Cambridge Pre-U examination when considering applicants and making offers. An EPQ may be accepted in place of an AS subject. Check websites of universities and colleges for the latest offers information.

Your target offers and examples of courses provided by each institution
380 pts **London (UCL)** – AAA+AS–ABB+AS (Sp Sci) (IB 36–37 pts)
340 pts **Manchester** – AAB (Sp Lang Thera) (IB 33 pts)
Queen Margaret – 340 pts (Sp Lang Thera) (IB 32 pts)
320 pts **East Anglia** – ABB–BBB (Sp Lang Thera) (IB 31 pts HL 666)
Newcastle – ABB (Sp Lang Sci) (IB 35 pts HL 555 biol 6)
Reading – 320 pts (Sp Lang Thera)
Sheffield – ABB **or** ABab (Sp Sci) (IB 33 pts)
Strathclyde – ABB (Sp Lang Path) (IB 32 pts)
300 pts **Cardiff (UWIC)** – BBB 300–320 pts (Sp Lang Thera) (IB 25 pts)
City – BBB (Sp Lang Thera) (IB 32 pts HL 555)
Essex – 300 pts (Engl Lang Lang Acq Diso) (IB 29 pts)
Leeds Met – BBB (Clin Lang Sci (Sp Lang Thera)) (IB 32 pts)
Manchester Met – BBB (Sp Path Thera; Psy Sp Path)
Sheffield – BBB (Hum Comm Sci) (IB 32 pts)
UCP Marjon – 300 pts (Sp Lang Thera)
Ulster – BBB +HPAT (Sp Lang Thera)
280 pts **Birmingham City** – 280 pts (Sp Lang Thera) (IB 36 pts)
De Montfort – BBC 280 pts (Hum Comm (Sp Lang Thera)) (IB 28 pts)
260 pts **Central Lancashire** – 260–300 pts (Df St courses) (IB 28 pts)
240 pts **Bristol** – CCC (Df St) (IB 28 pts)
160 pts **Reading** – 160 pts (Thea Arts Educ Df St) (IB 24 pts)
Wolverhampton – 160–220 pts (Ling Df St courses)

Alternative offers
See **Chapter 7** and **Appendix 1** for grades/UCAS Tariff points information for the International Baccalaureate, Scottish Highers/Advanced Highers, the Welsh Baccalaureate, the Irish Leaving Certificate, the Cambridge Pre-U Diploma, the Advanced Diploma and the Extended Project.

EXAMPLES OF FOUNDATION DEGREES IN THE SUBJECT FIELD
Portsmouth.

CHOOSING YOUR COURSE (SEE ALSO CH. 1)
Some course features
Cardiff (UWIC) Course includes a module in bi-lingual studies which focuses on the needs of multi-cultural and multi-lingual groups.
London (UCL) Clinical work begins in the first year. Organised clinical placements take place throughout the course, mostly in London and south-east England.
Manchester Met Placements are four and eight weeks and may be anywhere in the Manchester region, so temporary accommodation may be needed.

Reading (Sp Lang Thera) Clinics are run on campus in collaboration with the local authority. The course involves the use of computer-assisted analyses of language.

Sheffield (Sp Sci) Course leads to qualification as a speech therapist. (Hum Comm Sci) Focuses on the use of speech and language and how the process fails, for example in autism and dyslexia, but is not a professional qualification in speech therapy.

Universities and colleges teaching quality See www.qaa.ac.uk; http://unistats.direct.gov.uk.

Top research universities and colleges (RAE 2008) (Language and Communication Science) City.

ADMISSIONS INFORMATION

Number of applicants per place (approx) Birmingham City 28; Cardiff (UWIC) 10; City 16; De Montfort 5; London (UCL) 9; Manchester 13; Manchester Met 21; Newcastle 23; Queen Margaret 12.

Advice to applicants and planning the UCAS personal statement Contact with speech therapists and visits to their clinics are an essential part of the preparation for this career. Discuss your contacts in full, giving details of any work experience or work shadowing you have done and your interest in helping people to communicate, showing evidence of good 'people skills'. See also **Appendix 4** and **Chapter 6. Manchester** Selectors look for some practical experience with individuals who have communication or swallowing difficulties. (International students) Good English required because of placement periods.

Misconceptions about this course Some students fail to differentiate between speech therapy, occupational therapy and physiotherapy. They do not realise that to study speech and language therapy there are academic demands, including the study of linguistics, psychology, medical sciences and clinical dynamics, so the course is intensive. **Cardiff (UWIC)** Some are under the impression that good grades are not necessary, that it is an easy option and one has to speak with a standard pronunciation.

Selection interviews Yes De Montfort, London (UCL), Manchester Met, Queen Margaret, Sheffield, UCP Marjon.

Interview advice and questions Have you visited a speech therapy clinic? What made you want to become a speech therapist? What type of speech problems are there? What type of person would make a good speech therapist? Interviews often include an ear test (test of listening ability). What did you see when you visited a speech and language therapy clinic? See also **Chapter 6. Cardiff (UWIC)** Interviewees must demonstrate an insight into communication problems and explain how one speech sound is produced.

Reasons for rejection (non-academic) Insufficient knowledge of speech and language therapy. Lack of maturity. Poor communication skills. Written language problems.

AFTER-RESULTS ADVICE

Offers to applicants repeating A-levels Higher Birmingham City, Cardiff (UWIC); **Possibly higher** Manchester Met; **Same** City, De Montfort, Newcastle.

GRADUATE DESTINATIONS AND EMPLOYMENT (2007/8 HESA)

Career note Speech therapists work mainly in NHS clinics, some work in hospitals and others in special schools or units for the mentally or physically handicapped. The demand for speech therapists is high.

OTHER DEGREE SUBJECTS FOR CONSIDERATION

Audiology; Communication Studies; Deaf Studies; Education; Health Studies; Linguistics; Psychology.

SPORTS SCIENCES/STUDIES

(see also **Leisure and Recreation Management/Studies, Physical Education**)

In addition to the theory and practice of many different sporting activities, Sports Sciences/Studies courses also cover the psychological aspects of sports and of sports business administration. The geography, economics and sociology of recreation may also be included. The England and Wales Cricket Board has introduced the Universities Centres of Cricketing Excellence scheme (UCCE). Details can be obtained from the following centres of excellence: Cambridge Centre www.mccuniversities. org/cambridge; Cardiff/Glamorgan Centre www.mccuniversities.org/cardiff-glamorgan; Durham Centre www.mccuniversities.org/durham; Leeds/Bradford Centre www.mccuniversities.org/leeds-bradford; Loughborough Centre www.mccuniversities.org/loughborough; Oxford Centre www.mccuniversities. org/oxford. See also **Appendix 4**.

Useful websites www.isrm.co.uk; www.uksport.gov.uk; www.laureus.com; www.wsf.org.uk; www.sta. co.uk; www.olympic.org; www.sportscotland.org.uk; www.baha.org.uk; www.planet-science.com; www.london2012.com.

NB The points totals shown to the left of the institutions are for ease of reference only. It must not be assumed that Tariff points are always used by institutions or that they can be substituted for an offer in grades. The level of an offer is not necessarily indicative of the quality of a course.

COURSE OFFERS INFORMATION

Subject requirements/preferences GCSE English, mathematics and, often, a science subject; check prospectuses. **AL** Science required for Sport Science courses. PE required for some Sport Studies courses. **Other** requirements Enhanced Criminal Records Bureau (CRB) disclosure required for many courses. Evidence of commitment to sport.

NB In 2012 universities and colleges will differ in their use of GCE AL/AS unit grade information, A* grades, the Extended Project (EPQ), the Advanced Diploma and the Cambridge Pre-U examination when considering applicants and making offers. An EPQ may be accepted in place of an AS subject. Check websites of universities and colleges for the latest offers information.

Your target offers and examples of courses provided by each institution

360 pts **Bath** – AAA (Spo Eng) (IB 36 pts HL maths phys 6)
Birmingham – AAA–AAB 360–340 pts (Spo Exer Sci) (IB 36 pts)
Birmingham – AAA–AAB (Maths Spo Sci) (IB 34–38 pts HL maths 6)
Exeter – AAA–AAB (Psy Spo Exer Sci) (IB 36–33 pts)
Loughborough – AAA–AAB (Spo Tech) (IB 36 pts)

340 pts **Bath** – AAB (Coach Educ Spo Dev) (IB 35 pts)
Birmingham – AAB (App Glf Mgt St) (IB 34–36 pts)
Exeter – AAB–BBB (Hum Biosci) (IB 34 pts)
Loughborough – AAB–ABB 340 pts (Engl Spo Sci)
Loughborough – 340–320 pts (Spo Mgt) (IB 34–32 pts)
Sheffield – AAB (Spo Eng; Mtr Spo Eng Mgt)

320 pts **Bournemouth** – 320 pts (Spo Mgt; Spo Dev Coach Sci)
Brighton – ABB (Spo Exer Sci) (IB 32 pts)
Cardiff (UWIC) – 320 pts (Spo Exer Sci) (IB 25 pts)
Central Lancashire – ABB–BBB (Spo Jrnl) (IB 32 pts)
Durham – ABB (Sport) (IB 32–30 pts)
Glasgow – ABB (Spo Med) (IB 32 pts)
Leeds – ABB–BBB (Spo Exer Sci) (IB 32–34 HL 16–15 pts)
Strathclyde – ABB (Spo Eng) (IB 34 pts)
Ulster – ABB (Spo Exer Sci)

320 pts **Birmingham** – ABB (Spo Mat Sci) (IB 32-34 pts)
Brighton – ABB (Spo Coach) (IB 32 pts)
Loughborough – ABB–AAB (Spo Sci Phys) (IB 30 pts)
Ulster – ABB (Spo Sci)

300 pts   **Bangor** – 300–260 pts (Spo Hlth Exer Sci; Spo Sci Psy)

Cardiff (UWIC) – 300 pts (Spo PE; Spo Condit Rehab Msg)

Edinburgh – BBB–AAA (Spo Recr Mgt) (IB 32 pts)

Essex – 300–340 pts (Spo Sci Biol) (IB 30–28 pts)

Glamorgan – 300 pts (Spo Psy)

Gloucestershire – 300 pts (Spo Dev)

Hertfordshire – 300 pts (Spo Thera; Spo Exer Sci; Spo St)

Kent – 300 pts (Spo Thera Hlth Fit) (IB 33 pts)

Leeds Met – 300–260 pts (Spo Exer Sci) (IB 25 pts)

Loughborough – 300 pts (Chem Spo Sci BSc) (IB 34 pts)

Salford – 300 pts (Spo Rehab) (IB 29 pts)

Sheffield Hallam – 300–280 pts (Spo Exer Sci; Spo Sci Perf Coach)

Southampton – BBB (Spo St) (IB 30 pts)

Swansea – BBB 300 pts (Spo Sci)

280 pts   **Bristol UWE** – 280–320 pts (Spo Biol) (IB 26–28 pts)

Bristol UWE – 280 pts (Eqn Spo Sci) (IB 24 pts)

Brunel – 280–300 pts (Mgt Spo Dev) (IB 32 pts)

Cardiff (UWIC) – 280 pts (Spo Dev; Spo Mgt)

Central Lancashire – 280–300 pts (Spo Sci)

Edge Hill – 280 pts (Spo Exer Psy)

Edinburgh – Check with Ad. Tutor BBC (App Spo Sci) (IB 32 pts)

Glamorgan – BBC (Spo Sci Rgby; Spo Exer Sci; Spo St)

Gloucestershire – 280–300 pts (Spo Thera; Spo Sci, Spo Educ)

Huddersfield – 280 pts (Spo Mark PR; Spo Jrnl; Spo Prom Mark)

Leeds Trinity (UC) – 280 pts (Spo Jrnl)

Northumbria – 280–300 pts (Spo Exer Nutr) (IB 25 pts)

Oxford Brookes – BBC–BBB (Spo Exer Sci) (IB 30 pts)

Portsmouth – 280 pts (Spo Dev; Spo Exer Sci)

Salford – 280–300 pts (Spo Leis Mgt) (IB 26 pts)

Strathclyde – BBC (Spo Physl Actvt)

Teesside – 280–300 pts (Spo Thera)

Worcester – 280 pts (Spo Thera; Spo St; Spo Bus Mgt)

260 pts   **Aberystwyth** – 260 pts (Spo Exer Sci) (IB 28 pts)

Bangor – 260-280 pts (Spo Hlth PE)

Bournemouth – 260 pts (Exer Sci)

Brighton – BCC (Spo St)

Bristol UWE – 260–300 pts (Spo Coach) (IB 26–28 pts)

Central Lancashire – 260–300 pts (Spo Psy; Spo Tech)

Coventry – 260–280 pts (Spo Tour)

Dundee – BCC (Spo Biomed)

Edge Hill – 260–280 pts (Spo Thera; Spo Dev; Spo Exer Sci)

Kent – 260 pts (Spo Exer Mgt) (IB 29 pts)

Liverpool Hope – 260 pts (Spo Psy; Spo St)

Manchester Met – 260–280 pts (Coach St) (IB 28 pts)

Newman (UC) – 260–280 pts (Spo St courses)

Sheffield Hallam – 260 pts (Spo Dev Coach; Spo Coach)

Stirling – BCC (Spo Exer Sci) (IB 30 pts)

Swansea – 260 pts (Spo Mats)

Teesside – 260 pts (Spo Exer Psy; Spo Exer; Spo Exer (Coach Sci) (App Exer Sci))

Ulster – 260 pts (Spo Tech) (IB 24 pts)

240 pts   **Aberdeen** – CCC (Spo Exer Sci BSc; Spo St (Exer Hlth); App Spo Sci Educ)

Aberystwyth – 240 pts (Eqn Hum Spo Sci) (IB 28 pts)

Bedfordshire – 240 pts (Spo Exer Sci)

Canterbury Christ Church – 240 pts (Spo courses)

Cardiff (UWIC) – 240 pts (Spo Biomed Nutr)
Central Lancashire – 240–280 pts (Spo Coach)
Chester – 240–280 pts (Spo Exer Sci courses) (IB 24 pts)
Chichester – CCC 240–300 pts (Spo Coach Sci; Spo Exer Psy)
Coventry – 240–260 pts (Spo Mark; Spo Mgt; Spo Thera)
Cumbria – 240 pts (Spo St; Spo Mgt; Spo Exer Sci; Coach Spo Dev)
Edinburgh Napier – 240–260 pts (Spo Tech)
Glamorgan – 240–280 pts (Spo Mgt; Spo Dev)
Glyndŵr – 240 pts (Spo Coach; Spo Exer Sci)
Greenwich – 240 pts (Spo Sci; Spo Sci Coach)
Hull – 240–280 pts (Spo Exer Sci; Spo Rehab)
Leeds Met – 240–200 pts (Spo Bus Mgt; Spo Leis Cult) (IB 24–28 pts)
Lincoln – 240 pts (Eq Spo Sci)
Liverpool John Moores – 240–280 pts (Spo courses)
Manchester Met – 180 pts from full ALs (Psy Spo Exer)
Robert Gordon – 240 pts (Spo Exer Sci)
Roehampton – 240–280 pts (Spo Sci Comb Hons; Spo Exer Sci)
St Mary's Twickenham (UC) – 240 pts (Spo Coach Sci; Spo Rehab; Spo Sci)
Salford – 240–260 pts (App Spo Sci courses)
UCP Marjon – 240 pts (App Spo Sci Coach courses)
Winchester – 240–280 pts (Spo Coach Dev; Spo Mgt)
220 pts **Birmingham (UC)** – 220 pts (Spo Thera)
Central Lancashire – 220–260 pts (Spo St; Spo PR)
East London – 220 pts (Spo Coach)
Kingston – 220–280 pts (Spo Sci; Spo Analys Coach)

Lincoln – 220–280 pts (Spo Mark)
Middlesex – 220 pts (Spo Exer Sci)
Myerscough (Coll) – 220 pts (Sportsturf Sci Mgt)
Northampton – 220–260 pts (Spo Exer Sci; Spo Dev; Spo Mark)
Nottingham Trent – 220–280 pts (Coach Spo Sci) (IB 28 pts)
Nottingham Trent – 220 pts (Eqn Spo Sci)
St Mary's Twickenham (UC) – 220 pts (Clin Exer Sci)
Southampton Solent – 220 pts (Wtrspo St Mgt)
Sunderland – 220–300 pts (Spo Exer Dev; Spo Exer Sci; Spo St)
Teesside – 220 pts (Spo Mgt)
UCP Marjon – 220 pts (Spo Dev; Out Advntr Educ St)
York St John – 220–260 pts (Spo Soty Dev; Spo Sci Perf Condit; Spo Sci Injry Mgt)

200 pts **Bedfordshire** – 200 pts (Spo Sci Coach)
Bolton – 200–240 pts (Spo Rehab; Spo Dev; Spo Sci Coach)
Bristol UWE – 200–240 pts (Spo Bus Mgt) (IB 24 pts)
Bucks New – 200–240 pts (Spo Mgt Coach St; Spo Mgt Ftbl St)
Central Lancashire – 200–220 pts (Mtr Spo)
East London – 200 pts (Spo Dev)
London Met – 200–240 pts (Spo Sci; Spo Dance Thera)
Middlesex – 200–220 pts (Spo Rehab)
Plymouth – 200 pts (Surf Sci Tech; App Mar Spo Sci)
Sheffield Hallam – 200 pts (Spo Bus Mgt; Spo Tech)
Suffolk (Univ Campus) – 200–240 pts (Spo Exer Sci)

180 pts **Abertay Dundee** – DDD (Spo Exer courses)
Anglia Ruskin – 180 pts (Spo Sci) (IB 24 pts)
Derby – 180–240 pts (Spo Exer St)
Staffordshire – 180–240 pts (Spo St; Spo Exer Sci)
Warwickshire (Coll) – 180 pts (Spo Sci)
Wolverhampton – 180–200 pts (Spo Mgt)

160 pts **Bedfordshire** – 160–240 pts (App Spo St)
Bishop Grosseteste (UC) – 160 pts (Educ St Spo)
London South Bank – CC 160 pts (Spo Exer Sci)
South Essex (Coll) – 160 pts (Spo St)
Swansea Met – 160 pts (Pblc Serv)

140 pts **Writtle (Coll)** – 140–240 pts (Spo Exer Perf courses)

120 pts **Colchester (Inst)** – 120 pts (Mgt Spo)
Swansea Met – 120 pts (Spo Mgt; Spo Exer Sci)

80 pts **Farnborough (CT)** – 80 pts (Spo Sci (Exer Hlth Mgt))

Myerscough (Coll) – (Mtrspo Mgt Log (Top-up)) Check with College

Alternative offers
See **Chapter 7** and **Appendix 1** for grades/UCAS Tariff points information for the International Baccalaureate, Scottish Highers/Advanced Highers, the Welsh Baccalaureate, the Irish Leaving Certificate, the Cambridge Pre-U Diploma, the Advanced Diploma and the Extended Project.

EXAMPLES OF FOUNDATION DEGREES IN THE SUBJECT FIELD

Arts London (CComm); Askham Bryan (Coll); Bath; Bath City (Coll); Bedfordshire; Birmingham (UC); Bishop Burton (Coll); Blackpool and Fylde (Coll); Bournemouth; Bradford; Brighton; Bristol UWE; Bucks New; Cardiff (UWIC); Central Lancashire; Chester; Chesterfield (Coll); Chichester; Colchester (Inst); Cornwall (Coll); Coventry; Cumbria; Doncaster (Coll Univ Centre); Duchy (Coll); Durham New (Coll); East Anglia; Edge Hill; Exeter (Coll); Farnborough (CT); Glamorgan; Grimsby (IFHE); Hertfordshire; Hopwood Hall (Coll); Huddersfield; Hull (Coll); Kirklees (Coll); Leeds City (Coll); Leeds Trinity (UC); Lincoln; Llandrillo Cymru (Coll); London Met; London South Bank; Loughborough (Coll); Manchester (Coll); Mid-Cheshire (Coll); Middlesex; Milton Keynes (Univ Centre); Myerscough (Coll); Neath Port

Talbot (Coll); Nescot; Newcastle (Coll); Newport; North Lindsey (Coll); Petroc; Plymouth; Reaseheath (Coll); Riverside Halton (Coll); St Helens (Coll); Sheffield (Coll); Somerset (CAT); South Devon (Coll); South Nottingham (Coll); Southgate (Coll); Sunderland; Sunderland City (Coll); Teesside; Truro (Coll); Tyne Met (Coll); Ulster; Wakefield (Coll); Warwickshire (Coll); West London; Wigan and Leigh (Coll); Wolverhampton; Worcester (CT); Writtle (Coll); York (Coll).

CHOOSING YOUR COURSE (SEE ALSO CH. 1)

Some course features

Birmingham (Spo Mat Sci) This course focuses on the design and materials used in the manufacture of sports equipment. Research placements are offered during summer vacations.

Brighton (Spo Jrnl) A placement project takes place in the final year. The course is accredited by the National Council for the Training of Journalists with graduates receiving the Certificate in Newspaper Journalism.

Brunel After a common first year students select their preferred specialisation in administration, coaching, exercise and fitness, physical education or a multi-disciplinary route.

Central Lancashire A wide range of sport and related courses are provided, some specialising in Adventure Sports and Motor Sport.

Exeter (Hum Biosci) The course combines molecular biology and biochemistry with exercise and sports science, including biomechanics and human exercise physiology.

Loughborough The University has a national and international reputation in sport, leisure management and physical education.

Top research universities and colleges (RAE 2008) (Sports-related studies) Birmingham; Loughborough; Bristol; Liverpool John Moores; Stirling; Bath; Leeds Met; Brunel; Bangor; Exeter; Leeds.

Examples of sandwich degree courses Bath; Bournemouth; Brighton; Bristol UWE; Brunel; Coventry; Glamorgan; Gloucestershire; Hertfordshire; Huddersfield; Kingston; London Met; London South Bank; Loughborough; Nottingham Trent; Sheffield Hallam; Swansea Met; Ulster; Warwickshire (Coll); Wolverhampton; Writtle (Coll).

ADMISSIONS INFORMATION

Number of applicants per place (approx) Aberystwyth 5; Bangor 15; Bath (Coach Educ Spo Dev) 8; Birmingham 7; Brunel 6; Canterbury Christ Church 30; Cardiff (UWIC) 10; Chichester 4; Cumbria 14, (Spo St) 6; Durham 6; Edinburgh 11; Exeter 23; Gloucestershire 8; Kingston 13; Leeds 25; Leeds Trinity (UC) 35; Liverpool John Moores 4; Loughborough 20; Manchester Met 16; Northampton 4; Northumbria 30; Nottingham Trent 8; Portsmouth 12; Roehampton 8; St Mary's Twickenham (UC) 4; Salford 30; Sheffield Hallam 7; South Essex (Coll) 1; Southampton 8; Staffordshire 12; Stirling 10; Strathclyde 28; Sunderland 2; Swansea 6; Teesside 15; Winchester 5; Wolverhampton 4; Worcester 10; York St John 4.

Advice to applicants and planning the UCAS personal statement See also **Physical Education**. See also **Appendix 4**. **Cardiff (UWIC)** A strong personal statement required which clearly identifies current performance profile and indicates a balanced lifestyle. **Salford** Previous experience in a sporting environment will be noted. Previous study is preferred in biology/human biology, physics, chemistry, physical education/sports studies. Psychology is preferred. Other comments (Coach Sci) For these courses applicants must have proven coaching skills to gain a place. (Spo Sci) These are lab-based courses examining the physical stress of sport on the human body. A sound scientific aptitude is required. Although professional sporting qualifications and high level practical experience cannot take the place of scientific entry qualifications, they will be considered in any borderline applicants holding a conditional offer. Comment on any coaching or competitive experience.

Misconceptions about this course Bath (Spo Exer Sci) This is not a sports course with a high component of practical sport: it is a science programme with minimal practical sport. (Coach Educ Spo Dev) This is not necessarily a course for elite athletes. **Birmingham** (App Glf Mgt St) Applicants do not appreciate the academic depth required across key areas (it is, in a sense, a multiple Honours course – business management, sports science, coaching theory, materials science). **Sheffield Hallam** (Spo Tech) Some applicants expect an engineering course! **Swansea** (Spo Sci) Applicants underestimate the quantity of maths on the course. Many applicants are uncertain about the differences between Sports Studies and Sports Science.

Selection interviews Yes Bath, Birmingham, Cumbria, Durham, Edinburgh, Leeds, Leeds Trinity (UC), Nottingham Trent, Sheffield Hallam; **Some** Anglia Ruskin, Cardiff (UWIC), Chichester, Derby, Liverpool John Moores, Roehampton, St Mary's Twickenham (UC), Salford, Sheffield Hallam, Staffordshire, Wolverhampton.

Interview advice and questions Applicants' interests in sport and their sporting activities are likely to be discussed at length. Past questions include: How do you strike a balance between sport and academic work? How many, and which, sports do you coach? For how long? Have you devised your own coaching programme? What age-range do you coach? Do you coach unsupervised? See **Chapter 6. Loughborough** A high level of sporting achievement is expected

Reasons for rejection (non-academic) Not genuinely interested in outdoor activities. Poor sporting background or knowledge. Personal appearance. Inability to apply their science to their specialist sport. Illiteracy. Using the course as a second option to physiotherapy. Arrogance. Expectation that they will be playing sport all day. When the course is explained to them some applicants realise that a more arts-based course would be more appropriate.

AFTER-RESULTS ADVICE
Offers to applicants repeating A-levels Higher Swansea; **Same** Cardiff (UWIC), Chichester, Derby, Dundee, Lincoln, Liverpool John Moores, Loughborough, Plymouth, Roehampton, St Mary's Twickenham (UC), Salford, Sheffield Hallam, Staffordshire, Stirling, Sunderland, Winchester, Wolverhampton, York St John.

GRADUATE DESTINATIONS AND EMPLOYMENT (2007/8 HESA)
Graduates surveyed 5735 **Employed** 2495 **In further study** 947 **Assumed unemployed** 405

Career note Career options include sport development, coaching, teaching, outdoor centres, sports equipment development, sales, recreation management and professional sport.

OTHER DEGREE SUBJECTS FOR CONSIDERATION
Anatomy; Biology; Human Movement Studies; Leisure and Recreation Management; Nutrition; Physical Education; Physiology; Physiotherapy; Sports Equipment Product Design.

STATISTICS
(see also **Mathematics**)

Statistics has mathematical underpinnings but is primarily concerned with the collection, interpretation and analysis of data. Statistics are used to analyse and solve problems in a wide range of areas, particularly in the scientific, business, government and public services.

Useful websites www.rss.org.uk; www.statistics.gov.uk.

NB The points totals shown to the left of the institutions are for ease of reference only. It must not be assumed that Tariff points are always used by institutions or that they can be substituted for an offer in grades. The level of an offer is not necessarily indicative of the quality of a course.

COURSE OFFERS INFORMATION
Subject requirements/preferences GCSE English and mathematics. **AL** Mathematics required for all courses.

NB In 2012 universities and colleges will differ in their use of GCE AL/AS unit grade information, A* grades, the Extended Project (EPQ), the Advanced Diploma and the Cambridge Pre-U examination when considering applicants and making offers. An EPQ may be accepted in place of an AS subject. Check websites of universities and colleges for the latest offers information.

Your target offers and examples of courses provided by each institution

440 pts **Warwick** – See *Advice to applicants and planning the UCAS personal statement* below and **Chapter 5**. A*AAa–AABa (Maths OR Stats Econ (MORSE)) (IB 39 pts HL maths 6)

420 pts **Imperial London** – A*A*A* (Maths Stats Fin) (IB 38 pts HL maths phys 6)

400 pts **London (UCL)** – A*AA+AS–AAA+AS (Stats Econ Lang) (IB 39–36 pts)

Oxford – A*A*A (Maths Stats) (IB 38–40 pts)

380 pts **Bristol** – A*AA–AAA (Maths Stats) (IB 36 pts HL 666)

Manchester – A*AA–AAA (Maths Stats) (IB 36 pts)

360 pts **Bath** – AAA–AAB (Maths Stats) (IB 36 pts HL maths 6)

City – AAA 360 pts (Mathem Sci Stats) (IB 32 pts)

Durham – AAA (Nat Sci (Stats)) (IB 38–42 pts HL maths 6/7)

Glasgow – AAA Faster route (Stats courses)

London LSE – AAA (Bus Maths Stats) (IB 38 pts HL 766)

St Andrews – AAA (Lgc Phil Sci Stats) (IB 36 pts)

Southampton – AAA (Maths Stats) (IB 36 pts HL 18 pts)

340 pts **Birmingham** – AAB (Mathem Econ Stats) (IB 34 pts)

Edinburgh – AAB–ABB (Maths Stats) (IB 32 pts)

Lancaster – AAB (Maths Stats) (IB 30 pts HL maths 6)

London (QM) – 340 pts (Maths Stats MSci) (IB 34 pts)

Newcastle – AAB (Stats Mgt) (IB 34–32 pts HL maths 6)

Queen's Belfast – AAB/ABBa (Maths Stats OR)

Surrey – AAB–ABB 340–320 pts (Maths Stats) (IB 30–32 pts)

320 pts **East Anglia** – ABB–ABC (Bus Stats) (IB 32 pts HL maths 6)

Edinburgh – Check with Ad Tutor ABB–ABC (Econ Stats) (IB 32 pts)

Glasgow – ABB (Stats courses) (IB 32 pts)

Heriot-Watt – ABB (Stats Mdl)

Lancaster – ABB 320 pts (Stats BSc) (IB 30 pts HL maths 6)

Leeds – ABB–AAB (Stats; Maths Stats)

Liverpool – ABB (Maths Stats) (IB 33 pts HL maths 6)

London (QM) – 320 pts (Maths Stats) (IB 34 pts HL maths 6)

London (RH) – ABB (Maths Stats) (IB 33 pts HL maths 6)

Newcastle – ABB–AAB (Acc Stats) (IB 32–34 pts)

York – ABB–AAB (Maths Stats)

300 pts **Aberystwyth** – 300 pts (Geog Stats) (IB 29 pts)

Brunel – Contact admissions office (Maths Stats Mgt)

Heriot-Watt – BBB–ABB (Maths Stats)

Kent – 300 pts (Maths Stats) (IB 33 pts)

Queen's Belfast – ABC/ACCb (Maths Stats OR BSc)

Reading – 300 pts (Stats) (IB 36 pts)

Strathclyde – ABC–ABB (Maths Stats Fin) (IB 32 pts)

280 pts **Bristol UWE** – 280–300 pts (Statistics) (IB 26–28 pts)

Oxford Brookes – BBC (Bus Mgt Stats)

Plymouth – 280 pts (App Stats) (IB 29 pts)

260 pts **Kingston** – 260–280 pts (Act Maths Stats) (IB 26–28 pts)

Portsmouth – 260–300 pts (Maths Stats)

240 pts **Coventry** – 240 pts (Maths Stats)

Oxford Brookes – CCC (Stats) (IB 29 pts)

230 pts **Edinburgh Napier** – 230 pts (Mgt/App Stats)

220 pts **Staffordshire** – 220–280 pts (Maths App Stats) (IB 26 pts)

200 pts **Kingston** – 200–260 pts (Med Stats) (IB 26–28 pts)

London Met – 200 pts (Stats joint courses)

Middlesex – 200–280 pts (Bus Stats)

160 pts **Greenwich** – 160 pts (Stats; Maths Stats Comp; Stats Comp)

80 pts **London (Birk)** – for under 21s (over 21s varies) p/t (Stats Econ; Stats Mgt)

Alternative offers
See **Chapter 7** and **Appendix 1** for grades/UCAS Tariff points information for the International Baccalaureate, Scottish Highers/Advanced Highers, the Welsh Baccalaureate, the Irish Leaving Certificate, the Cambridge Pre-U Diploma, the Advanced Diploma and the Extended Project.

EXAMPLES OF FOUNDATION DEGREES IN THE SUBJECT FIELD
Blackpool and Fylde (Coll).

CHOOSING YOUR COURSE (SEE ALSO CH. 1)
Some course features
Kingston (Med Stats courses) An optional professional placement year is offered to students.
Warwick (MORSE) Course has a statistics specialisation in Years 3 and 4 of the BSc and MMORSE courses.

Universities and colleges teaching quality See www.qaa.ac.uk; http://unistats.direct.gov.uk.

Top research universities and colleges (RAE 2008) (Statistics and Operational Research) Oxford; Imperial London; Bristol; Warwick; Nottingham; Leeds; Kent; Southampton; Lancaster.

Examples of sandwich degree courses Bath; Coventry; Kingston; Portsmouth; Reading; Staffordshire; Surrey; Ulster; Wolverhampton.

ADMISSIONS INFORMATION
Number of applicants per place (approx) Bath 10; Coventry 3; East London 3; Heriot-Watt 6; Lancaster 11; Liverpool John Moores 6; London (UCL) 9; Newcastle 5; Southampton 10; York 5.

Advice to applicants and planning the UCAS personal statement Love mathematics, don't expect an easy life. See **Mathematics**. See also **Appendix 4**.

Selection interviews Yes Bath, Birmingham, Liverpool, Liverpool John Moores, London (UCL), Newcastle, Sheffield; **Some** Greenwich.

Interview advice and questions Questions could be asked on your A-level syllabus (particularly in mathematics). Applicants' knowledge of statistics and their interest in the subject are likely to be tested, together with their awareness of the application of statistics in commerce and industry. See **Chapter 5**.

AFTER-RESULTS ADVICE
Offers to applicants repeating A-levels Higher Kent, Leeds, Liverpool, Liverpool John Moores, Newcastle, Swansea; **Same** Birmingham.

GRADUATE DESTINATIONS AND EMPLOYMENT (2007/8 HESA)
Graduates surveyed 200 **Employed** 75 **In further study** 55 **Assumed unemployed** 15

Career note See **Mathematics**.

OTHER DEGREE SUBJECTS FOR CONSIDERATION
Accountancy; Actuarial Sciences; Business Information Technology; Business Studies; Computer Science; Economics; Financial Services; Mathematical Studies; Mathematics.

SURVEYING

(including Building and Quantity Surveying and Property Management/Development.
For Finiancial Investment in Property see under **Finance.)**

Surveying covers a very diverse range of careers and courses and following a Royal Institution of Chartered Surveyors (RICS) accredited course is the accepted way to become a Chartered Surveyor. There are three main specialisms which involve the Built Environment (Building Surveying, Project

Management and Quantity Surveying); Land Surveying (Rural, Planning, Environmental, Minerals and Waste Management); Property Surveying (Commercial and Residential Property and Valuation, Facilities Management, Arts and Antiques). Student membership of the RICS is possible. Not all the courses listed below receive RICS accreditation; check with the university or college prior to applying.

Useful websites www.rics.org/careers; www.brookes.ac.uk/schools/be/about/estates/index.

NB The points totals shown to the left of the institutions are for ease of reference only. It must not be assumed that Tariff points are always used by institutions or that they can be substituted for an offer in grades. The level of an offer is not necessarily indicative of the quality of a course.

COURSE OFFERS INFORMATION

Subject requirements/preferences GCSE English and mathematics grade A–C. **AL** No subjects specified; mathematics useful.

NB In 2012 universities and colleges will differ in their use of GCE AL/AS unit grade information, A* grades, the Extended Project (EPQ), the Advanced Diploma and the Cambridge Pre-U examination when considering applicants and making offers. An EPQ may be accepted in place of an AS subject. Check websites of universities and colleges for the latest offers information.

Your target offers and examples of courses provided by each institution
380 pts **Cambridge** – A*AA (Surv) (IB 38–42)
340 pts **Heriot-Watt** – AAB 2nd yr entry (Bld Surv) (IB 35 pts)
         Reading – 340 pts (Rur Prop Mgt)
320 pts **Ulster** – 320 pts (Quant Surv)
300 pts **Aberdeen** – BBB (Prop Spat Plan)
         Bristol UWE – 300–340 pts (Bld Surv) (IB 24-28 pts)
         Kingston – 300 pts (Prop Plan Dev) (IB 32 pts)
         Loughborough – 300 pts (Commer Mgt Quant Surv) (IB 32 pts)
         Northumbria – 300 pts (Plan Dev Surv) (IB 30 pts)
         Oxford Brookes – BBB–ABB (Rl Est Mgt) (IB 33 pts)
         Reading – 300–320 pts (Quant Surv)
         Ulster – 300 pts (Plan Prop Dev)
280 pts **Birmingham City** – 280 pts (Rl Est Mgt) (IB 27 pts)
         Brighton – BBC 280 pts (Bld Surv) (IB 28 pts)
         Heriot-Watt – BBC (Quant Surv) (IB 29-31 pts)
         Northumbria – 280 pts (Bld Surv) (IB 25 pts)
         Nottingham Trent – 280 pts (Quant Surv Constr Commer Mgt) (IB 28 pts)
         Oxford Brookes – BBC–BCC (Plan Prop Dev) (IB 30–31 pts)
         Royal (CAg) – 280–300 pts (Prop Agncy Mark)
         Salford – 280 pts (Quant Surv; Bld Surv)
         Westminster – BBC (Quant Surv) (IB 26 pts)
270 pts **Anglia Ruskin** – 270 pts (Bld Surv; Quant Surv)
         Glasgow Caledonian – 270 pts (Int Rl Est; Rl Est Bus Mgt)
         Liverpool John Moores – 270 pts (Quant Surv; Bld Surv)
         Portsmouth – 270 pts (Prop Dev Quant Surv) (IB 28 pts)
         Sheffield Hallam – 270 pts (Bld Surv; Quant Surv)
260 pts **Birmingham City** – 260 pts (Bld Surv) (IB 30 pts)
         Glamorgan – 260 pts (Rl Est Apprsl Mgt)
245 pts **Edinburgh Napier** – 245 pts (Prop Dev Val)
240 pts **Bolton** – 240 pts (Bld Surv Prop Mgt)
         Edinburgh Napier – 240–245 pts (Quant Surv)
         Greenwich – 240 pts (Constr Surv Mgt) (IB 24 pts)
         Huddersfield – 240 pts (Prop Dev)
         Leeds Met – 240 pts (Quant Surv) (IB 28 pts)
         Wolverhampton – 240 pts (Bld Surv) (IB 26 pts)

230 pts **Central Lancashire** – 230 pts (Commer Mgt Quant Surv; Bld Surv)
Coventry – 230 pts (Bld Surv; Commer Mgt; Quant Surv Commer Mgt)
Robert Gordon – 230 pts (Surv (Quant Surv))
Wolverhampton – 230 pts (Commer Mgt Quant Surv; Rl Est)
220 pts **Bristol UWE** – 220–260 pts (Rl Est (Val Mgt))
Glamorgan – 220–260 pts (Quant Surv)
Harper Adams (UC) – 220 pts (Rur Prop Mgt)
London South Bank – 220 pts (Commer Mgt (Quant Surv); Bld Surv)
200 pts **Glyndŵr** – 200 pts (Est Agncy; Est Mgt)
Wolverhampton – 200 pts (Quant Surv)
180 pts **Anglia Ruskin** – 180 pts (Prop Surv)
Derby – 180–240 pts (Prop Dev)
Greenwich – 180 pts (Bld Surv) (IB 24 pts)
150 pts **West London** – 150 pts (Blt Env (Quant Surv))

CEM – Distance Learning Course, see www.cem.ac.uk (Bld Surv; Quant Surv; Est Mgt)
Oxford Brookes – Contact the admissions office (Surv courses)

Alternative offers
See **Chapter 7** and **Appendix 1** for grades/UCAS Tariff points information for the International Baccalaureate, Scottish Highers/Advanced Highers, the Welsh Baccalaureate, the Irish Leaving Certificate, the Cambridge Pre-U Diploma, the Advanced Diploma and the Extended Project.

EXAMPLES OF FOUNDATION DEGREES IN THE SUBJECT FIELD
Anglia Ruskin (Bld Surv); Birmingham City (Coll) (Property); Bolton (Quant Surv), (Bld Surv), (Property); Bradford (Property); Brighton (Bld Surv); Glamorgan (Quant Surv), (Property); Glyndŵr (Property); Middlesex (Property); Northampton (Property); Northumbria (Quant Surv), (Bld Surv), (Property); Royal (CAg) (Property); Swansea Met (Quant Surv); West London; Wigan and Leigh (Coll) (Bld Surv).

CHOOSING YOUR COURSE (SEE ALSO CH. 1)
Some course features
Anglia Ruskin (Quant Surv) The course shares many common themes with the Building Surveying course but also focuses on management practice, project management and procurement.
Kingston (Prop Plan Dev) The course involves the study of economics, law and business.
Loughborough (Commer Mgt Quant Surv) Accredited by the RICS. Sponsorship is a condition of entry to the course. All suitable applicants are interviewed by the sponsors.
Northumbria (Bld Surv) The Foundation course enables entry to Architectural Technology, Building Services Engineering or Surveying, Construction Management, Estate Management or Quantity Surveying.
Robert Gordon Common first years for Building and Quantity Surveying students who make a final choice of subject at the beginning of Year 2. This is a feature of other universities eg Edinburgh Napier.

Universities and colleges teaching quality See www.qaa.ac.uk; http://unistats.direct.gov.uk. Check on RICS accreditation.

Examples of sandwich degree courses Bradford (Property); Coventry (Quant Surv); Kingston (Quant Surv); London South Bank (Quant Surv); Loughborough (Quant Surv); Northampton (Quant Surv); Northumbria; Nottingham Trent (Quant Surv); Oxford Brookes (Quant Surv); Robert Gordon (industrial placements may be possible); Sheffield Hallam (Quant Surv); Ulster (Quant Surv) (Property).

ADMISSIONS INFORMATION
Number of applicants per place (approx) Anglia Ruskin 2; Birmingham City (Quant Surv) 4; Cambridge 3; Edinburgh Napier (Quant Surv, all three courses) 12; Glamorgan (Quant Surv) 4, (Property) 6; Glasgow Caledonian (Quant Surv) 3; Glyndŵr (Property) 3; Greenwich (Quant Surv) 8;

Harper Adams (UC) (Property) 4; Kingston (Quant Surv) 1, (Property) 22; Liverpool John Moores (Quant Surv) 10, (Property) 15; London South Bank 2; Loughborough (Quant Surv) 9; Northumbria (Quant Surv) 17, (Property) 17; Nottingham Trent (Quant Surv) 10, (Property) 3; Oxford Brookes (Quant Surv) 4, (Property) 5; Portsmouth (Property) 5; Robert Gordon (Quant Surv) 5; Royal (CAg) (Property) 3; Salford (Quant Surv) 6, (Property) 3; Sheffield Hallam (Quant Surv) 7, (Property) 5; Westminster (Property) 10; Wolverhampton (Quant Surv) 6.

Admissions tutors' advice Nottingham Trent Candidates should demonstrate that they have researched the employment opportunities in the property and construction sectors.

Advice to applicants and planning the UCAS personal statement Surveyors work with architects and builders as well as in their own consultancies dealing with commercial and residential property. Work experience with various firms is strongly recommended depending on the type of surveying speciality preferred. Read surveying magazines. **Cambridge** Statements should be customized to the overall interests of students, not to the Land Economy Tripos specifically. **Oxford Brookes** (Non-UK students) Written and spoken English must be good. Applicants should be reflective. I am looking for at least 50–60% of the personal statement to cover issues surrounding why they want to do the course, what motivates them about the subject, how they have developed their interest, how their A levels have helped them and what they have gained from any work experience. Extra-curricular activities are useful but should not dominate the statement.

Misconceptions about this course Students underestimate the need for numerical competence.

Selection interviews Yes Birmingham City (Quant Surv), Cambridge (Property), Glamorgan (Quant Surv), (Property), Glasgow Caledonian (Quant Surv), Harper Adams (UC) (Property), Heriot-Watt (Quant Surv), (Property), Kingston (Quantity Surveying), Liverpool John Moores (Quant Surv), Loughborough (Quant Surv), Nottingham Trent (Quant Surv), Royal (CAg) (Property), Ulster (Quant Surv); **Some** Abertay Dundee, Anglia Ruskin (Quant Surv), (Property), East London (Property), Nottingham Trent (Property), Robert Gordon (Quant Surv), Salford; **No** Edinburgh Napier.

Interview advice and questions What types of work are underaken by surveyors? How do you qualify? What did you learn on your work experience? **Cambridge** (Land Econ) Questions on subsidies and the euro and economics. Who owns London? How important is the modern day church in town planning. How important are natural resources to a country? Is it more important to focus on poverty at home or abroad? Is the environment a bigger crisis than poverty? Do you think that getting involved with poverty abroad is interfering with others 'freedoms'? (The questions were based on information given in the personal statement.) See **Chapter 6**. Students sit a thinking test and a written exam. **Oxford Brookes** Interviews for applicants who are likely to be offered a place. Telephone interviews for those who cannot attend. Group exercise at interview. No offers without an interview.

Reasons for rejection (non-academic) Inability to communicate. Lack of motivation. Indecisiveness about reasons for choosing the course. **Loughborough** Applicants more suited to a practical type of course rather than an academic one. **Nottingham Trent** Incoherent and badly written application forms.

AFTER-RESULTS ADVICE

Offers to applicants repeating A-levels Higher Bolton, Nottingham Trent; **Possibly higher** Glamorgan, Liverpool John Moores; **Same** Abertay Dundee, Coventry, Edinburgh Napier, Oxford Brookes, Portsmouth, Robert Gordon, Salford.

GRADUATE DESTINATIONS AND EMPLOYMENT (2007/8 HESA)

Career note See **Building and Construction**.

OTHER DEGREE SUBJECTS FOR CONSIDERATION

Architecture; Building and Construction; Civil Engineering; Estate Management; Town Planning; Urban Studies.

TEACHER TRAINING

(see also **Education Studies, Social Sciences/Studies**)

Teacher training courses are offered in the following subject areas: Art and Design (P); Biology (P S); Business Studies (S); Chemistry (P S); Childhood (P); Computer Education (P); Creative and Performing Arts (P); Dance (P S); Design and Technology (P S); Drama (P S); English (P S); Environmental Science (P S); Environmental Studies (P); French (P S); General Primary; Geography (P S); History (P S); Maths (P S); Music (P S); Physical Education/Movement Studies (P S); Religious Studies (P); Science (P S); Sociology (P); Textile Design (P); Welsh (P).

For further information on teaching as a career see websites below and **Appendix 4** for contact details. Over 50 taster courses are offered each year to those considering teaching as a career. Early Childhood Studies has been introduced in recent years by a number of universities. The courses focus on child development, from birth to eight years of age, and the provision of education for children and their families. It is a multi-disciplinary subject and can cover social problems and legal and psychological issues. Note that many institutions listed below also offer one-year Postgraduate Certificate in Education (PGCE) courses which qualify graduates to teach other subjects.

Useful websites www.tda.gov.uk; www.gtcs.org.uk; www.gttr.ac.uk; http://educationcymru.org; www.education.gov.uk.

NB The points totals shown to the left of the institutions are for ease of reference only. It must not be assumed that Tariff points are always used by institutions or that they can be substituted for an offer in grades. The level of an offer is not necessarily indicative of the quality of a course.

COURSE OFFERS INFORMATION

Subject requirements/preferences See **Education Studies**.

NB In 2012 universities and colleges will differ in their use of GCE AL/AS unit grade information, A* grades, the Extended Project (EPQ), the Advanced Diploma and the Cambridge Pre-U examination when considering applicants and making offers. An EPQ may be accepted in place of an AS subject. Check websites of universities and colleges for the latest offers information.

Your target offers and examples of courses provided by each institution
Abbreviations used in this table: ITE – Initial Teacher Education; ITT – Initial Teacher Training; P – Primary Teaching; QTS – Qualified Teacher Status; S – Secondary Teaching; STQ – Scottish Teaching Qualification.

380 pts Cambridge – A*AA college offers may vary (Educ (Biol Sci) (Class) (Engl) (Engl Dr) (Geog) (Hist) (Maths) (Mdn Langs) (Mus) (Physl Sci) BA)

340 pts Loughborough – AAB (Maths Maths Educ)

320 pts Sussex – ABB–BBB (Engl Lang Teach) (IB 32–34 pts)

300 pts Aberdeen – BBB (Educ P; Educ S)
Brighton – BBB (P Educ BA)
Durham – BBB (P Teach Gen BA/BSc)
Edinburgh – BBB (P BEd; P PE BEd)
Glasgow – BBB (P STQ MA)
Liverpool Hope – 300 pts (P QTS Educ BA)
Roehampton – 300–360 pts (P Educ (QTS) BA/BSc)
Stranmillis (UC) – BBB (P BEd)
Strathclyde – BBB–BBC (P Ed BEd)

280 pts Brighton – BBC (S Educ courses)
Gloucestershire – 280 pts (P QTS BEd)
Leeds Trinity (UC) – BBC (P Educ (7–11) BA)
Manchester Met – 280 pts (P BA)
Northampton – 280 pts (P QTS Educ BA)

Oxford Brookes – BBC (P Educ BA)
Sunderland – 280–360 pts (P BA)
260 pts **Bristol UWE** – 260–360 pts (BA P ITE/Ely Yrs)
Brunel – 260–300 pts (BSc S PE)
Central Lancashire – 260–300 pts (Df St courses) (IB 28 pts)
Chichester – BCC (P QTS BA)
Hertfordshire – 260 pts (P BEd)
Leeds Met – 260 pts (P BA; Ely Yrs Educ QTS)
Newman (UC) – 260–320 pts (P QTS S BA)
Northumbria – 260 pts (P BA)
Nottingham Trent – BCC 260 pts (P BA)
240 pts **Anglia Ruskin** – 240 pts (P Educ BA; P Educ ITT BA)
Bangor – 240 pts (P Educ QTS BA)
Canterbury Christ Church – 240–260 pts (QTS P Educ BA; Maths S Educ QTS BSc)
Chester – 240 pts (Ely Yrs BEd; Gen P)
Cumbria – 240 pts (Ely Yrs Educ QTS; P Educ QTS BA)
Derby – 240–280 pts (BEd courses)
Edge Hill – 240–280 pts (P Educ/S Educ courses)
Hull – 240–260 pts (P QTS BA)
Liverpool John Moores – 240–280 pts (P BA/S Educ courses)
Manchester Met – 240 pts (Maths S Educ QTS BA)
Plymouth – 240 pts (P courses BEd)
Royal Scottish (RSAMD) – Offered jointly with University of Glasgow check with College (Mus BEd)
Sheffield Hallam – 240 pts (P BA)
Stirling – CCD–BCC (Primary and Seconday Teaching BA/BSc; Educ P; Educ S)
220 pts **Bedfordshire** – 220–320 pts (P Educ QTS BEd)
Chichester – CCD (Maths Teach KS 2+3) (IB 26 pts)
Dundee – AB-CCC (P Educ BEd)
Newport – 220 pts (BA P St QTS; S Des Tech)
Northampton – 220–260 pts (Ely Yrs Educ QTS)
Sunderland – 220–360 pts (S BA)
West Scotland – CCD/DDDD (P BEd)
200 pts **Central Lancashire** – + CACDP level 2 200 pts (Brit Sign Lang)
Edinburgh – BB (Des Tech BEd)
Kingston – 200 pts (P QTS BA)
Middlesex – 200-300 pts (P Educ BA)
Nottingham Trent – 200 pts (S Des Tech Educ QTS BA)
UCP Marjon – 200–240 pts (P QTS BEd)
Wolverhampton – 200–260 pts (P BEd)
180 pts **Greenwich** – 180 pts (Des Tech QTS)
Reading – 180 pts (P BA)
St Mary's Twickenham (UC) – 180–200 pts (P Educ (QTS) BA)
160 pts **Bishop Grosseteste (UC)** – CC 160 pts (P QTS BA)
London (Gold) – CC (Des Tech Educ QTS)
Sheffield Hallam – 160 pts (QTS S (Des Tech) (Sci) (Maths) BSc)
140 pts **Queen's Belfast** – Concurrent option available at St. Mary's **or** Stranmillis. Check with Ad. Tutor (Ed BEd (St Mary's (UC) or Stranmillis (UC)))

Bournemouth and Poole (Coll) – two year course for teachers and trainers without a BA (Hons) check with School (PCE BA (Hons))

Alternative offers See **Chapter 7** and **Appendix 1** for grades/UCAS Tariff points information for the International Baccalaureate, Scottish Highers/Advanced Highers, the Welsh Baccalaureate, the Irish Leaving Certificate, the Cambridge Pre-U Diploma, the Advanced Diploma and the Extended Project.

EXAMPLES OF FOUNDATION DEGREES IN THE SUBJECT FIELD

Bangor; Bath City (Coll); Bath Spa; Bedfordshire; Bishop Grosseteste (UC); Blackburn (Coll Univ Centre); Blackpool and Fylde (Coll); Bournemouth; Bradford; Brighton; Bristol City (Coll); Bristol UWE; Bucks New; Central Lancashire; Chichester; Cornwall (Coll); Cumbria; Derby; Duchy (Coll); East London; Edge Hill; Exeter (Coll); Farnborough (CT); Glamorgan; Gloucestershire; Glyndŵr; Greenwich; Grimsby (IFHE); Guildford (Coll); Havering (Coll); Hopwood Hall (Coll); Huddersfield; Kingston; Kirklees (Coll); Lakes (Coll); Leeds City (Coll); Leeds Met; Leeds Trinity (UC); London Met; Loughborough (Coll); Manchester (Coll); Mid-Cheshire (Coll); Myerscough (Coll); NEW (Coll); Newman (UC); Northbrook (Coll); Oxford Brookes; Peterborough (Reg Coll); Petroc; Plymouth; Plymouth City (Coll); Reading; Riverside Halton (Coll); Roehampton; St Mary's Twickenham (UC); Sheffield (Coll); South Cheshire (Coll); South Devon (Coll); South Essex (Coll); Southgate (Coll); Stockport (Coll); Stranmillis (UC); Stratford upon Avon (Coll); Suffolk (Univ Campus); Sunderland; Teesside; Truro (Coll); Wakefield (Coll); Warrington (Coll); West Anglia (Coll); Wigan and Leigh (Coll); Wirral Met (Coll); Worcester.

CHOOSING YOUR COURSE (SEE ALSO CH. 1)

Some course features

Chester Early years and primary teaching degrees.

Chichester Primary teacher training, and postgraduate courses in Primary and Secondary Education.

Cumbria In addition to Primary and Secondary Education courses with specialist options ICT, English, Maths and RE, there are also several options covering outdoor education and leadership.

Durham A three-year teaching course is offered at Queen's campus.

Edge Hill Primary and secondary teaching courses.

Hull BA Primary courses are offered in Biology, English, Information and Communications Technology and Mathematics; there are also courses in Education with Early Childhood Studies, Social Inclusion and Specian Needs, or Media, Culture and Societ.

Liverpool Hope Education Studies plus the option to take primary teaching courses in mathematics or modern languages.

Liverpool John Moores Early Years, Primary and Secondary Education courses are offered and also Outdoor Education and Environmental Education and Sport Development and Physical Education.

Middlesex Education Studies can be taken with a National Curriculum subject as a route to a PGCE in Primary or Secondary Education.

Top research universities and colleges (RAE 2008) See www.tda.gov.uk (England); www.shefc.ac.uk (Scotland); www.elwa.org.uk (Wales); http://unistats.direct.gov.uk. London (Inst Ed); Oxford; Cambridge; London (King's); Bristol; Leeds; Exeter; Manchester Met; Warwick; York; Durham; Sussex; Stirling.

ADMISSIONS INFORMATION

Number of applicants per place (approx) Aberystwyth 6; Anglia Ruskin 1; Bangor 5; Bath 17; Bath Spa 5; Birmingham 8; Bishop Grosseteste (UC) 12; Bristol UWE 20; Brunel (PE) 5; Cambridge 2. 5; Canterbury Christ Church 15; Cardiff (Educ) 8; Cardiff (UWIC) 3; Central Lancashire 5; Chester 25; Cumbria 5; Derby 13; Dundee 5; Durham 8; Edge Hill 17; Edinburgh (P) 3; Gloucestershire 20; Glyndŵr 15; Greenwich 3; Hull 7; Hull (Coll) 4; Kingston 9; Leeds 4; Liverpool Hope 5; Liverpool John Moores 3; London (Gold) 5, (Des Tech) 4; Manchester Met 23, (Maths) 4; Middlesex 7; Newman (UC) (S Engl) 3, (Theol) 3, (Ely Yrs) 5, (Biol) 7, (Geog) 3, (PE) 6, (Sci) 1; Northampton 7; Northumbria 8; Nottingham Trent 11; Oxford Brookes 6; Plymouth 14; Roehampton 6; St Mary's Twickenham (UC) 19; Sheffield Hallam 7, (PE) 60; Strathclyde 7; Swansea Met 10; Trinity Saint David 10; UCP Marjon 5; West Scotland 7; Winchester 4; Wolverhampton 4; Worcester 21, (Engl) 51; York 3.

Advice to applicants and planning the UCAS personal statement Any application for teacher training courses requires candidates to have experience of observation in schools and with children relevant to the choice of age range. Describe what you have learned from this. Any work with young people should be described in detail, indicating any problems which you may have seen which children create for the teacher. Applicants are strongly advised to have had some teaching practice prior to interview and should give evidence of time spent in primary or secondary school and give an analysis of activity undertaken with children. Give details of music qualifications, if any. Admissions tutors look for precise, succinct, well-reasoned, well-written statements (no mistakes!). All applicants for Initial Teacher Training (ITT) courses in England leading to Qualified Teacher Status must register provisionally with the General Teaching Council for England. Check with www.gtce.org.uk for full details. See **Chapter 6**.

Misconceptions about this course Newman (UC) That the Theology course only concentrates on the Christian/Catholic religions – all major religions are covered.

Selection interviews Check all institutions. It is a requirement that all candidates for teacher education are interviewed. **Yes** Bishop Grosseteste (UC), Bristol UWE, Brunel, Cambridge, Cardiff (UWIC), Derby, Durham, Kingston, London (Gold), Manchester Met (group interviews), Newman (UC), Nottingham Trent, Oxford Brookes, Plymouth, Stockport (Coll), Worcester, York St John; **Some** Anglia Ruskin, Bangor, Cardiff, Dundee, Lincoln, Liverpool John Moores, Roehampton, UCP Marjon, West Scotland, Winchester, York.

Interview advice and questions Questions invariably focus on why you want to teach and your experiences in the classroom. In some cases you may be asked to write an essay on these topics. Questions in the past have included: What do you think are important issues in education at present? Discussion of course work will take place for Art applicants. **Cambridge** The stage is a platform for opinions or just entertainment? **Derby** Applicants are asked about an aspect of education. **Liverpool John Moores** Discussion regarding any experience the applicant has had with children.

Reasons for rejection (non-academic) Unable to meet the requirements of written standard English. Ungrammatical personal statements. Lack of research about teaching at primary or secondary levels. Lack of experience in schools. Insufficient experience of working with people; tendency to be racist.

AFTER-RESULTS ADVICE
Offers to applicants repeating A-levels Higher Oxford Brookes, Warwick; **Possibly higher** Cumbria; **Same** Anglia Ruskin, Bangor, Bishop Grosseteste (UC), Brighton, Brunel, Cambridge, Canterbury Christ Church, Cardiff, Chester, De Montfort, Derby, Dundee, Durham, East Anglia, Lincoln, Liverpool Hope, Liverpool John Moores, London (Gold), Manchester Met, Newman (UC), Northumbria, Nottingham Trent, Roehampton, St Mary's Twickenham (UC), Stirling, Sunderland, UCP Marjon, UHI Millennium Inst, Winchester, Wolverhampton, Worcester, York, York St John.

GRADUATE DESTINATIONS AND EMPLOYMENT (2007/8 HESA)
Graduates surveyed 5935 **Employed** 4345 **In further study** 210 **Assumed unemployed** 115

OTHER DEGREE SUBJECTS FOR CONSIDERATION
Education Studies; Psychology; Social Policy; Social Sciences; Social Work.

TECHNOLOGIES

(see also **Biotechnology, Computer Courses, Engineering/Engineering Sciences, Engineering (Electrical and Electronic), Music**)

Technology covers a wide range of activities and is commonly associated with the engineering industries although there are also scientific and artistic applications. The courses listed below give an insight into the range of technology courses available and see also individual subject tables.

Useful websites www.techreview.com; www.intute.ac.uk.

NB The points totals shown to the left of the institutions are for ease of reference only. It must not be assumed that Tariff points are always used by institutions or that they can be substituted for an offer in grades. The level of an offer is not necessarily indicative of the quality of a course.

COURSE OFFERS INFORMATION
Subject requirements/preferences GCSE English and mathematics required. **AL** Mathematics and/or a science may be required.

NB In 2012 universities and colleges will differ in their use of GCE AL/AS unit grade information, A* grades, the Extended Project (EPQ), the Advanced Diploma and the Cambridge Pre-U examination when considering applicants and making offers. An EPQ may be accepted in place of an AS subject. Check websites of universities and colleges for the latest offers information.

Your target offers and examples of courses provided by each institution

360 pts **Surrey** – AAA–AAB (Spc Tech Planet Explor MEng)

340 pts **Leeds** – AAB (Avn Tech Plt St) (MEng IB 36 pts HL 17 pts)
Newcastle – AAB (Biopharml Tech MEng) (IB 36 pts HL maths chem 5)
York – AAB–ABB (Mus Tech Sys MEng)

320 pts **Birmingham** – ABB (Spo Sci Mat Tech)
Bournemouth – 320 pts (Crea Tech; Gms Tech)
Brunel – BBC +AS/EPQ c 320 pts (Multim Tech Des) (IB 31 pts)
Newcastle – ABB (Biopharml Tech BEng) (IB 34 pts HL chem maths 5)
Surrey – ABB (Spc Tech Planet Explor BEng) (IB 28 pts)

300 pts **Aston** – BBB 300 pts (Tech Ent Mgt) (IB 32 pts)
Glasgow – BBB (Technol Educ)
Manchester – ABC (Tex Tech (Bus Mgt)) (IB 32 pts)
Queen's Belfast – BBB (Agric Tech)
York – BBB (Mus Tech Sys BEng)

280 pts **Birmingham City** – 280–260 pts (Fash Des Gmnt Tech)
Bournemouth – 280 pts (Advnc Tech Bus Innov)
Bristol UWE – 280–320 pts (Tour Env Mgt) (IB 24–28 pts)
Glamorgan – 280–320 pts (Crea Tech)
Lancaster – 280 pts (Comb Tech)
Leeds – BBC (TECH Des Colour)
Suffolk (Univ Campus) – 280 pts (Radiother Onc)
Teesside – 280 pts (Sust Des Tech)

260 pts **Lincoln** – BCC 260 pts (Web Tech)
Northampton – 260 pts (Mat Tech (Lea))
Ulster – 260 pts (Tech Des)

240 pts **Bangor** – 240–280 pts (Crea Tech; Des Tech S Educ)
Bolton – 240 pts (Comp Tech)
Bristol UWE – 240–300 pts (Prod Des Tech)
De Montfort – 240 pts (Fash Tech)
Hertfordshire – 240 pts (Aerosp Tech Plt St)
Huddersfield – 240 pts (Eng Tech Mgt)
Hull – 240 pts (Crea Mus Tech)
Manchester Met – 240 pts (Fash Des Tech)
Staffordshire – 240 pts (Aero Tech; Auto Tech; Robot Tech)
Stranmillis (UC) – CCC (Tech Des Educ)
Ulster – 240–220 pts (Cln Tech)

220 pts **Liverpool John Moores** – 220–260 pts (Des Tech P S Educ)
Sunderland – 220 pts (Des Tech Educ)

200 pts **Bradford** – 200 pts (Tech Mgt; Tech Mgt BSc)
Chester – 200–240 pts (Multim Tech courses) (IB 24 pts)
Glasgow – BB (Tech Mgt)
Hertfordshire – 200 pts (Intnet Tech e-Commer; Dig Rts Tech)

180 pts **Cardiff (UWIC)** – 180 pts inc CD one in sci subj (Dntl Tech)
Derby – 180–240 pts (Snd Lt Lv Evnt Tech)
Plymouth – 180 pts (Mar Cmpstes Tech; Mar Spo Tech BSc)

160 pts **SAC (Scottish CAg)** – CC (Grn Tech)
Sheffield Hallam – 160 pts (Des Tech S Educ; Rlwy Tech)
West Scotland – CC–CD (Multim Tech)
Open University – (Tech) (contact +44(0)845 300 6090 or www.openuniversity. c)

Alternative offers
See **Chapter 7** and **Appendix 1** for grades/UCAS Tariff points information for the International Baccalaureate, Scottish Highers/Advanced Highers, the Welsh Baccalaureate, the Irish Leaving Certificate, the Cambridge Pre-U Diploma, the Advanced Diploma and the Extended Project.

EXAMPLES OF FOUNDATION DEGREES IN THE SUBJECT FIELD
Askham Bryan (Coll); Bournemouth and Poole (Coll); Central Lancashire; Milton Keynes (Univ Centre); Petroc.

CHOOSING YOUR COURSE (SEE ALSO CH. 1)
Some course features
Aston (Tech Ent Mgt) The course covers product design, computing and engineering management.
Bangor (Crea Tech) The course is made up of two-thirds core computer science modules and one-third creative industries modules; scholarship and sponsorship opportunities are avaialble on a competitive basis.
Birmingham (Spo Sci Mat Tech) The course focuses on the design and materials of sports equipment for athletes, essential to peak performance.
Newcastle (Biopharml Tech) A new course focusing on the science and processes of developing and large-scale manufacturing of biopharmaceuticals, with opportunities for an industrial placement.

Top research universities and colleges (RAE 2008) See **Engineering/Engineering Sciences** and **Materials Science/Metallurgy**.

Examples of sandwich degree courses Aston; Bradford; De Montfort; Glamorgan; Huddersfield; Sheffield Hallam; Teesside; Ulster.

ADMISSIONS INFORMATION
Number of applicants per place (approx) Aston 6.

Advice to applicants and planning the UCAS personal statement See **Engineering** courses and **Physics**.

Selection interviews **Yes** Aston, Glasgow, Staffordshire.

Interview advice and questions See **Engineering/Engineering Sciences** and **Chapter 6**.

AFTER-RESULTS ADVICE
Offers to applicants repeating A-levels **Same** Aston, Staffordshire.

GRADUATE DESTINATIONS AND EMPLOYMENT (2007/8 HESA)
See **Engineering/Engineering Sciences**.

Career note See **Engineering/Engineering Sciences**.

OTHER DEGREE SUBJECTS FOR CONSIDERATION
Architectural Technology; Biotechnology; Design Technology; Digital Technology; Engineering Sciences; Environmental Materials Technology; Fashion Technology; Food Technology; Information Technology; Internet Technology; Marine Technology; Mechanical Engineering; Motorsport Technology; Multimedia Technology; Music Technology; Nanotechnology; Sound Technology; Space Technology; Sports Technology; Web Technology.

TOURISM and TRAVEL

(see also **Business and Management Courses, Business and Management Courses (International and European), Business and Management Courses (Specialised), Hospitality and Hotel Management, Leisure and Recreation Management/Studies**)

Tourism and Travel courses are popular; some are combined with Hospitality Management which provides students with specialisms in two areas. Courses involve business studies and a detailed study of tourism and travel. Industrial placements are frequently involved and language options are often included. See also **Appendix 4**.

Useful websites www.wttc.org; www.abta.com; www.baha.org.uk.

NB The points totals shown to the left of the institutions are for ease of reference only. It must not be assumed that Tariff points are always used by institutions or that they can be substituted for an offer in grades. The level of an offer is not necessarily indicative of the quality of a course.

COURSE OFFERS INFORMATION

Subject requirements/preferences GCSE English and mathematics required. **AL** No subjects specified.

NB In 2012 universities and colleges will differ in their use of GCE AL/AS unit grade information, A* grades, the Extended Project (EPQ), the Advanced Diploma and the Cambridge Pre-U examination when considering applicants and making offers. An EPQ may be accepted in place of an AS subject. Check websites of universities and colleges for the latest offers information.

Your target offers and examples of courses provided by each institution

360 pts **Exeter** – AAA–AAB (Mgt Tour) (IB 36–33 pts)

320 pts **Strathclyde** – ABB (Hspty Tour Mgt)

300 pts **Hertfordshire** – 300 pts (Tour Mgt Tour Langs)
Kent – 2300 pts (Bus St Tour yr Ind) (IB 33 pts HL 14 pts)
Surrey – BBB 300 pts (Tour Mgt) (IB 30–32 pts)

280 pts **Bournemouth** – 280 pts (Tour Mgt)
Bristol UWE – 280–320 pts (Tour Env Mgt) (IB 24–28 pts)
Gloucestershire – 280–300 pts (Tour Mgt)
Northumbria – 280 pts (Trav Tour Mgt) (IB 28 pts)
Salford – 280 pts (Tour Mgt)

260 pts **Aberystwyth** – 260 pts (Tour Lang) (IB 28 pts)
Bolton – 260 pts (Bus Mgt (Tour); Int Tour Mgt)
Brighton – BCC (Int Tour Mgt) (IB 28 pts)
Coventry – 260–280 pts (Tour Fr/Span; Spo Tour)
Hertfordshire – 260 pts (Int Tour Mgt)
Liverpool Hope – 260 pts (Tourism)
Liverpool John Moores – 260 pts (Out Educ Advntr Tour)
Oxford Brookes – BCC (Int Tour Mgt) (IB 29 pts)
Staffordshire – 260 pts (Tour Mgt)
Westminster – 260–280 pts (Tour Plan) (IB 26 pts)

240 pts **Aberystwyth** – 240 pts (Cntry Recr Tour) (IB 28 pts)
Canterbury Christ Church – 240 pts (Tour Mgt) (IB 24 pts)
Cardiff (UWIC) – 240 pts (Tour Mgt courses; Int Tour Hspty Mgt)
Central Lancashire – 240–280 pts (Int Tour Mgt; Tour Mgt)
Chester – 240 pts (Tour Mgt) (IB 24–28 pts)
Chichester – CCC (Tour Mgt courses)
Edinburgh Napier – 240 pts (Tour Mgt; Tour Entre Mgt; Tour Mgt HR Mgt)
Glamorgan – 240–280 pts (Tour Mgt; Tour Mark)
Lincoln – 240 pts (Int Tour Mgt; Spo Tour Mgt; Tour Mgt; Tour Mark)

For a quick reference offers calculator, fold out the inside back cover.

	Liverpool John Moores – 240–280 pts (Tour Leis Mgt)
	Manchester Met – 240 pts (Tour Mgt; Tour Mgt Evnts; Tour Comb Hons)
	Plymouth – 240–220 pts (Int Tour Mgt)
	Robert Gordon – CCC (Int Tour Mgt) (IB 26 pts)
	Sheffield Hallam – 240 pts (Tour Hspty Bus Mgt)
	Suffolk (Univ Campus) – CCC 240 pts (Tour Mgt)
	Ulster – CCC 240 pts (Int Trav Tour Mgt; Int Trav Tour St Langs)
220 pts	**Birmingham (UC)** – 220 pts (Tour Bus Mgt; Int Tour Mgt; Advntr Tour Mgt)
	Edinburgh Napier – 220 pts (Ecotour)
	Harper Adams (UC) – 220–240 pts (Leis Tour)
	Hertfordshire – 220–280 pts (Tour Joint Hons)
	Hull – 220 pts (Tour Mgt; Int Tour Mgt)
	Leeds Met – 200–220 pts (Int Tour Mgt)
	London Met – 220 pts (Int Tour Mgt; Int Tour Mgt Trav Mgt)
	Northampton – 220–260 pts (Tour courses; Herit Mgt; Trav Tour Mgt courses)
	Plymouth – 220–240 pts (Cru Mgt; Tour Mgt; Bus Tour)
	St Mary's Twickenham (UC) – 160–220 pts (Tour; Tour Mgt)
	Southampton Solent – 220 pts (Out Advntr Mgt; Tour Mgt; Int Tour Mgt)
	Stirling – CCD (Tour Mgt)
	Sunderland – 220 pts (Tour Comb Hons; Tour Mgt)
	York St John – 220–260 pts (Tour Mgt; Int Tour Mgt; Tour Mgt Mark)
200 pts	**Anglia Ruskin** – 200 pts (Tour Mgt)
	Bath Spa – 180–200 pts (Tour Mgt)
	Bucks New – 200–240 pts (Tour courses)
	Chester – 200–240 pts (Tour) (IB 24–28 pts)
	East London – 200–220 pts (Int Tour Mgt)

Greenwich – 200 pts (Tour Mgt Comb Hons)
Middlesex – 200–300 pts (Int Tour Mgt)
Queen Margaret – 200 pts (Hspty Tour Mgt; Tour Mgt)
180 pts **Abertay Dundee** – DDD (Tour Mgt)
Derby – 180–240 pts (Trav Tour; Advntr Tour courses)
West London – 180 pts (Trav Tour Mgt)
160 pts **Bedfordshire** – 160–200 pts (Trav Tour; Int Tour Mgt)
London South Bank – CC 160 pts (Tour Hspty)
SAC (Scottish CAg) – CC 160 pts (Out Prsts Mgt; Fd Tour Mgt; Out Prsts Mgt; Eqn Tour Mgt; Nat Tour Mgt)
Swansea Met – 160–360 pts (Int Trav Tour Mgt; Tour Mgt)
West Scotland – CC (Tourism)
Wolverhampton – 160–200 pts (Tour Mgt)
140 pts **Blackpool and Fylde (Coll)** – 140 pts (Int Rsrt Tour Mgt)
Trinity Saint David – 140 pts (Tour; Tour Mgt)
120 pts **Grimsby (IFHE)** – 120–240 pts (Tour Bus Mgt)
Llandrillo Cymru (Coll) – 120 pts (Mgt Trav Tour)

EXAMPLES OF FOUNDATION DEGREES IN THE SUBJECT FIELD

Aberystwyth; Arts London (CComm); Bath Spa; Bicton (Coll); Birmingham (UC); Bishop Grosseteste (UC); Blackpool and Fylde (Coll); Bournemouth; Bournemouth and Poole (Coll); Brighton; Bristol City (Coll); Bucks New; Central Lancashire; Chesterfield (Coll); Colchester (Inst); Cornwall (Coll); Craven (Coll); Doncaster (Coll Univ Centre); Duchy (Coll); Ealing, Hammersmith and West London (Coll); Exeter (Coll); Greenwich; Grimsby (IFHE); Guildford (Coll); Harper Adams (UC); Hereford (CA); Hertfordshire; Hugh Baird (Coll); Hull (Coll); Leeds City (Coll); Liverpool (CmC); Llandrillo Cymru (Coll); London Met; Loughborough (Coll); Mid-Kent (Coll); Myerscough (Coll); Newcastle (Coll); North Hertfordshire (Coll); Northampton; Northampton (Coll); Northbrook (Coll); Oaklands (Coll); Pembrokeshire (Coll); Pershore (Coll); Plymouth; Plymouth City (Coll); Preston (Coll); Riverside Halton (Coll); Runshaw (Coll); Somerset (CAT); South Devon (Coll); Southgate (Coll); Sunderland; Tyne Met (Coll); Westminster Kingsway (Coll); Weston (Coll); Writtle (Coll).

CHOOSING YOUR COURSE (SEE ALSO CH. 1)

Some course features
Bristol UWE (Tour Env Mgt) Field courses are UK-based in the first year and overseas in the second. Students contribute to the costs of these. There are options to study a European language, and to take a year out on placement.
Plymouth (Cru Mgt) The course focuses on the study of cruise tourism and the management of cruise operations. There is an optional year on a cruise ship.
Southampton Solent Courses are offered in Outdoor Adventure and Watersports.
West London In addition to airline travel the course includes modules in retail travel, customer relations, human resources management and transport management.

Examples of sandwich degree courses Aberystwyth; Bedfordshire; Birmingham (UC); Bournemouth; Brighton; Bristol UWE; Cardiff (UWIC); Central Lancashire; Coventry; Glamorgan; Gloucestershire; Greenwich; Harper Adams (UC); Hertfordshire; Huddersfield; Leeds Met; Llandrillo Cymru (Coll); London Met; London South Bank; Manchester Met; Middlesex; Northumbria; Oxford Brookes; Plymouth; Portsmouth; Sheffield Hallam; Staffordshire; Sunderland; Surrey; Swansea Met; Ulster; Wolverhampton; Writtle (Coll).

ADMISSIONS INFORMATION

Number of applicants per place (approx) Aberystwyth 3; Bath Spa 5; Birmingham (UC) 10; Bournemouth 16; Derby 4; Glamorgan 8; Liverpool John Moores 10; Northumbria 6; Sheffield Hallam 12; Sunderland 2.

Advice to applicants and planning the UCAS personal statement Work experience in the travel and tourism industry is important – in agencies, in the airline industry or hotels. This work could be described in detail. Any experience with people in sales work, dealing with the public – their problems and complaints – should also be included. Travel should be outlined, detailing places visited. Genuine interest in travel, diverse cultures and people. Good communication skills required. See also **Appendix 4**.

Misconceptions about this course Bath Spa The course is not purely vocational and operational: it also involves management issues. **Wolverhampton** Some applicants are uncertain whether or not to take a Business Management course instead of Tourism Management. They should be aware that the latter will equip them with a tourism-specific knowledge of business.

Selection interviews Yes Brighton, Derby, Sunderland; **Some** Abertay Dundee, Anglia Ruskin, Lincoln, Liverpool John Moores, Salford.

Interview advice and questions Past questions have included: What problems have you experienced when travelling? Questions on places visited. Experiences of air, rail and sea travel. What is marketing? What special qualities do you have that will be of use in the travel industry? See **Chapter 6**.

Reasons for rejection (non-academic) Wolverhampton English language competence.

AFTER-RESULTS ADVICE
Offers to applicants repeating A-levels Same Abertay Dundee, Anglia Ruskin, Birmingham (UC), Chester, Derby, Lincoln, Liverpool John Moores, Manchester Met, Northumbria, St Mary's Twickenham (UC), Salford, Wolverhampton.

GRADUATE DESTINATIONS AND EMPLOYMENT (2007/8 HESA)
Graduates surveyed 1240 **Employed** 850 **In further study** 65 **Assumed unemployed** 25

Career note See **Business and Management Courses**.

OTHER DEGREE SUBJECTS FOR CONSIDERATION
Airline and Airport Management; Business Studies; Events Management; Heritage Management; Hospitality Management; Leisure and Recreation Management; Travel Management.

TOWN and COUNTRY PLANNING

(including **Environmental Planning** and **Urban Studies**; see also **Development Studies, Environmental Sciences/Studies, Housing, Transport Management and Planning**)

Town and Country Planning courses are very similar and some lead to qualification or part of a qualification as a member of the Royal Town Planning Institute (RTPI). Further information from the RTPI (see **Appendix 4**).

Useful websites www.rtpi.org.uk; www.townplanningreview.lupjournals.org.

NB The points totals shown to the left of the institutions are for ease of reference only. It must not be assumed that Tariff points are always used by institutions or that they can be substituted for an offer in grades. The level of an offer is not necessarily indicative of the quality of a course.

COURSE OFFERS INFORMATION
Subject requirements/preferences GCSE English and mathematics required. **AL** Geography may be specified.

NB In 2012 universities and colleges will differ in their use of GCE AL/AS unit grade information, A* grades, the Extended Project (EPQ), the Advanced Diploma and the Cambridge Pre-U examination when considering applicants and making offers. An EPQ may be accepted in place of an AS subject. Check websites of universities and colleges for the latest offers information.

Your target offers and examples of courses provided by each institution

340 pts **London LSE** – AAB (Env Dev) (IB 37 pts HL 666)
Reading – 340 pts (Rur Prop Mgt)
Sheffield – AAB (Geog Plan) (IB 33 pts)

320 pts **Birmingham** – ABB–BBB (Plan Econ) (IB 32–34 pts)
Bristol UWE – 320 pts (Twn Cntry Plan)
Cardiff – 300–320 pts (Geog (Hum) Plan) (IB 32 pts)
Liverpool – ABB (MPlan Twn Reg Plan)
London (UCL) – ABB (Urb Plan Des Mgt) (IB 32 pts)
Manchester – ABB (Twn Cntry Plan MTCP) (IB 32 pts)

300 pts **Bristol UWE** – 300–340 pts (Prop Dev Plan) (IB 24–28 pts)
Cardiff – 300–320 pts (Cty Reg Plan) (IB 32 pts)
Leeds – BBB (Geog Trans Plan BSc)
Liverpool – BBB (Env Plan; Urb Reg Plan)
Newcastle – BBB/BBC inc Geog (Geog Plan) (IB 30 pts)
Northumbria – 300 pts (Plan Dev Surv) (IB 30 pts)
Oxford Brookes – BBB (Cty Reg Plan MPlan) (IB 32 pts)
Queen's Belfast – BBB–BBCb (Env Plan)
Sheffield – BBB (Urb St Plan) (IB 32 pts)
Ulster – 300 pts (Urb Plan Prop Dev)

280 pts **Bristol UWE** – 280–300 pts (Geog Plan) (IB 26–32 pts)
Heriot-Watt – BBC (Urb Reg Plan)
Manchester – BBC (Cty Reg Dev) (IB 28 pts)
Sheffield Hallam – 280 pts (Geog Plan)

260 pts **Dundee** – BCC (Twn Reg Plan MA) (HL 555)
Oxford Brookes – BCC (Cts Env Des Dev) (IB 28 pts)

240 pts **Anglia Ruskin** – 240 pts (Env Plan)
Bangor – 240–280 pts (Env Plan Mgt)
Canterbury Christ Church – 240 pts (Urb Reg St)
Leeds Met – 240 pts (Hum Geog Plan)

230 pts **Sheffield Hallam** – 230 pts (Plan Trans)
220 pts **Birmingham City** – 220 pts (Plan Dev)
160 pts **London South Bank** – 160 pts (Urb Env Plan)

Alternative offers

See **Chapter 7** and **Appendix 1** for grades/UCAS Tariff points information for the International Baccalaureate, Scottish Highers/Advanced Highers, the Welsh Baccalaureate, the Irish Leaving Certificate, the Cambridge Pre-U Diploma, the Advanced Diploma and the Extended Project.

EXAMPLES OF FOUNDATION DEGREES IN THE SUBJECT FIELD

Anglia Ruskin; Birmingham City; Blackburn (Coll Univ Centre); Derby; Glyndŵr; Grimsby (IFHE); Middlesex; Northampton; Royal (CAg).

CHOOSING YOUR COURSE (SEE ALSO CH. 1)

Some course features

Bangor The Environmental Planning and Management course covers rural, urban and coastal environments and is offered in English and Welsh. The course includes two professional placements of one month.

Birmingham Two courses are offered in Urban and Regional Planning, one combined with Geography and the other with Public Policy, Government and Management in addition to which there is a joint course in Planning.

Kent Urban Studies (Social Policy) course reviews the problems of towns and cities and the various processes (political, economic, geographic and social) with a bias towards sociology or economics or social policy. There is also a course in Urban Regeneration.

Oxford Brookes Two degrees, Cities – Environment, Design and Development, and City and Regional Planning, are offered as single honours courses. The former is also available as a combined course.

Sheffield Hallam A Planning Studies course leading to a degree and a Diploma in Town Planning is offered. It also has a transport pathway that leads to a separate degree in Planning and Transport.

Universities and colleges teaching quality See www.qaa.ac.uk; http://unistats.direct.gov.uk.

Top research universities and colleges (RAE 2008) Sheffield; Cardiff; Newcastle; Leeds; Reading; Manchester; Glasgow; London (UCL).

Examples of sandwich degree courses Bristol UWE; Liverpool John Moores; Manchester Met; Newcastle; Ulster.

ADMISSIONS INFORMATION

Number of applicants per place (approx) Birmingham 2; Birmingham City 6; Bristol UWE 6; Cardiff 6; Dundee 5; London (UCL) 6; London South Bank 3; Newcastle 9; Oxford Brookes 3; Sheffield Hallam 6.

Advice to applicants and planning the UCAS personal statement Visit your local planning office and discuss the career with planners. Know plans and proposed developments in your area and any objections to them. Study the history of town planning worldwide and the development of new towns in the United Kingdom during the 20th century, for example Bournville, Milton Keynes, Port Sunlight, Welwyn Garden City, Cumbernauld, and the advantages and disadvantages which became apparent. See also **Appendix 4**. **Oxford Brookes** See entry under Surveying.

Selection interviews Yes Bristol UWE, London (UCL), London South Bank, Newcastle, Oxford Brookes (Interviews for promising applicants. No offers to applicants not interviewed); **Some** Abertay Dundee, Anglia Ruskin, Birmingham City, Cardiff, Dundee.

Interview advice and questions Since Town and Country Planning courses are vocational, work experience in a planning office is relevant and questions are likely to be asked on the type of work done and the problems faced by planners. Questions in recent years have included: If you were re-planning your home county for the future, what points would you consider? How are statistics used in urban planning? How do you think the problem of inner cities can be solved? Have you visited your local planning office? See **Chapter 6**.

Reasons for rejection (non-academic) Lack of commitment to study for a professional qualification in Town Planning.

AFTER-RESULTS ADVICE
Offers to applicants repeating A-levels Higher Bristol UWE, Newcastle; **Same** Abertay Dundee, Birmingham City, Cardiff, Dundee, London South Bank, Oxford Brookes.

GRADUATE DESTINATIONS AND EMPLOYMENT (2007/8 HESA)
Graduates surveyed 850 **Employed** 75 **In further study** 80 **Assumed unemployed** 90

Career note Town planning graduates have a choice of career options within local authority planning offices. In addition to working on individual projects on urban development, they will also be involved in advising, co-ordinating and adjudicating in disputes and appeals. Planners also work closely with economists, surveyors and sociologists and their skills open up a wide range of other careers.

OTHER DEGREE SUBJECTS FOR CONSIDERATION
Architecture; Countryside Management; Environmental Studies; Geography; Heritage Management; Housing; Land Economy; Property; Public Administration; Real Estate; Sociology; Surveying; Transport Management.

TRANSPORT MANAGEMENT and PLANNING
(including Logistics and Supply Chain Management; see also Engineering/Engineering Sciences, Town and Country Planning)

Transport Management and Planning is a specialised branch of business studies with many applications on land, sea and air. It is not as popular as the less specialised Business Studies courses but is just as relevant and will provide the student with an excellent introduction to management and its problems.

Useful websites www.cilt-international.com; www.transportweb.com; www.nats.co.uk; www.ciltuk. org.uk.

NB The points totals shown to the left of the institutions are for ease of reference only. It must not be assumed that Tariff points are always used by institutions or that they can be substituted for an offer in grades. The level of an offer is not necessarily indicative of the quality of a course.

COURSE OFFERS INFORMATION
Subject requirements/preferences GCSE English and mathematics required. Birmingham Mathematics grade B. **AL** No subjects specified.

NB In 2012 universities and colleges will differ in their use of GCE AL/AS unit grade information, A* grades, the Extended Project (EPQ), the Advanced Diploma and the Cambridge Pre-U examination when considering applicants and making offers. An EPQ may be accepted in place of an AS subject. Check websites of universities and colleges for the latest offers information.

Your target offers and examples of courses provided by each institution

340 pts Cardiff – AAB (Bus Mgt (Log Ops))
City – AAB 340 pts (Air Trans Ops Mgt BSc)
Leeds – AAB (Econ Trans St) (IB 35 pts)
300 pts Aston – 280–300 pts (Trans Mgt) (IB 32 pts)
Leeds – BBB (Geog Trans Plan BSc)

280 pts **Aston** – 280–300 pts (Log) (IB 32 pts)
Hull – 280 pts (Acc Log)
Loughborough – 280 pts (Trans Bus Mgt) (IB 30 pts)
Northumbria – 280 pts (Bus Log Sply Chn Mgt)
260 pts **Bolton** – 260 pts (Bus Mgt (Sply Chn Mgt))
City – See **Advice to applicants and planning the UCAS personal statement** below BCC 260–240 pts (Air Trans Ops ATPL) (IB 28 pts)
Huddersfield – 260 pts (Trans Des; Air Trans Log Mgt)
Hull – 260 pts (Log; Mark Log; Bus Log)
Liverpool John Moores – 260 pts (Mgt Trans Log)
240 pts **Bristol UWE** – 240–280 pts (Plan Trans)
Bucks New – 240–280 pts (Air Trans Plt Trg)
Coventry – 240 pts (Auto Trans Des (Bike/Boat/Veh/Trans))
Edinburgh Napier – 240 pts (Civ Trans Eng)
Manchester Met – 240 pts (Log Comb Hons)
230 pts **Sheffield Hallam** – 230 pts (Plan Trans courses)
220 pts **Plymouth** – 220–240 pts (Cru Mgt)
Southampton Solent – 220–240 pts (Cru Ind Mgt)
Ulster – 220 pts inc CC (Trans courses)
200 pts **Coventry** – 200 pts (Log Bus Mgt)
Huddersfield – 200–280 pts (Trans Log Mgt; Log Sply Chn Mgt; Euro Log Mgt)
Plymouth – 200 pts (Mar St (Navig) (Ocn Ycht) (Merch Shp))
180 pts **Greenwich** – 180–200 pts (Bus Prchsg Sply Chn Mgt)
120 pts **Swansea Met** – 120–160 pts (Trans Mgt; Log Sply Chn Mgt)

Bucks New – contact University (Airln Airpt Mgt)
Staffordshire – contact University (Trans Des)

Alternative offers
See **Chapter 7** and **Appendix 1** for grades/UCAS Tariff points information for the International Baccalaureate, Scottish Highers/Advanced Highers, the Welsh Baccalaureate, the Irish Leaving Certificate, the Cambridge Pre-U Diploma, the Advanced Diploma and the Extended Project.

EXAMPLES OF FOUNDATION DEGREES IN THE SUBJECT FIELD
Derby; Greenwich; Suffolk (Univ Campus).

CHOOSING YOUR COURSE (SEE ALSO CH. 1)
Some course features
Aston (Log Mgt) This is a business course focusing on the supply chain and distribution industry. There is a four-year course involving paid professional experience.
Bucks New (Air Trans Plt Trg) Students on this course will only be finally accepted on to the Commercial pilot training route at the end of a successful first year and with a Class 1 medical certificate. There is also an Airline and Airport Management course.
Liverpool John Moores (Mgt Trans Log) The course is accredited by the Chartered Institute of Logistics and Transport; there is an option for a placement/sandwich year in industry.
Loughborough (Trans Bus Mgt; Air Trans Mgt) Courses include a year in industry. French, German and Spanish modules can be selected.

Examples of sandwich degree courses Aston; Bristol UWE; City; Huddersfield; Liverpool John Moores; Loughborough; Plymouth; Sheffield Hallam; Staffordshire.

ADMISSIONS INFORMATION
Number of applicants per place (approx) Aston 5; Coventry 5; Huddersfield 5; Loughborough 11.

Advice to applicants and planning the UCAS personal statement Air, sea, road and rail transport are the main specialist areas. Contacts with those involved and work experience or work shadowing should be described in full. See also **Appendix 4**. **City** (Air Trans Ops ATPL) Applicants need a Class 1

Medical Certificate from the UK Civil Aviation Authority and preferably to have taken a pilot aptitude test before starting the course. Check with admissions.

Selection interviews Yes Huddersfield, Loughborough; **Some** Aston, Bucks New.

Interview advice and questions Some knowledge of the transport industry (land, sea and air) is likely to be important at interview. Reading around the subject is also important, as are any contacts with management staff in the industries. Past questions have included: What developments are taking place to reduce the number of cars on the roads? What transport problems are there in your own locality? How did you travel to your interview? What problems did you encounter? How could they have been overcome? See **Chapter 6**.

AFTER-RESULTS ADVICE
Offers to applicants repeating A-levels Same Aston.

GRADUATE DESTINATIONS AND EMPLOYMENT (2007/8 HESA)
Career note Many graduates will aim for openings linked with specialisms in their degree courses. These could cover air, rail, sea, bus or freight transport in which they will be involved in the management and control of operations as well as marketing and financial operations.

OTHER DEGREE SUBJECTS FOR CONSIDERATION
Air Transport Engineering; Civil Engineering; Environmental Studies; Logistics; Marine Transport; Town and Country Planning; Urban Studies.

VETERINARY SCIENCE/MEDICINE

(including **Bioveterinary Sciences** and **Veterinary Nursing**; see also **Animal Sciences**)

Veterinary Medicine/Science degrees enable students to acquire the professional skills and experience to qualify as veterinary surgeons. Courses follow the same pattern and combine a rigorous scientific training with practical experience. The demand for these courses is considerable (see below) and work experience is essential prior to application. Graduate entry programmes provide a route to qualifying as a vet to graduates with good degrees in specified subjects. See also **Appendix 4**. Veterinary Nursing honours degree courses combine both the academic learning and the nursing training required by the Royal College of Veterinary Surgeons, and can also include practice management. Foundation degrees in Veterinary Nursing are more widely available. Bioveterinary Sciences are usually three-year full-time BSc degree courses focusing on animal biology, management and disease but do not qualify graduates to work as vets. For places in Veterinary Science/Medicine, applicants may select only four universities. Applicants to the University of Cambridge Veterinary School and the Royal Veterinary College, University of London are required to sit the BioMedical Admissions Test (BMAT) (see **Chapter 6**).

Useful websites www.rcvs.org.uk; www.admissionstests.cambridgeassessment.org.uk; www.bvna. org.uk; www.spvs.org.uk.

NB The points totals shown to the left of the institutions are for ease of reference only. It must not be assumed that Tariff points are always used by institutions or that they can be substituted for an offer in grades. The level of an offer is not necessarily indicative of the quality of a course.

COURSE OFFERS INFORMATION
Subject requirements/preferences GCSE (Vet Sci/Med) Grade B English, mathematics, physics, dual science if not at A-level. **Bristol, Glasgow** Grade A or B in physics. **Bristol** Grade A in five or six subjects. **Liverpool** English, mathematics, physics, dual science grade B if not at A-level. (Vet Nurs) Five subjects including English and two science. **AL** (Vet Sci/Med) See offers below. (Vet Nurs) Biology and another science may be required. **Other** Work experience essential for Vet Sci/Med and Vet Nurs courses and preferred for other courses: check requirements. Health checks may be required.

NB In 2012 universities and colleges will differ in their use of GCE AL/AS unit grade information, A* grades, the Extended Project (EPQ), the Advanced Diploma and the Cambridge Pre-U examination when considering applicants and making offers. An EPQ may be accepted in place of an AS subject. Check websites of universities and colleges for the latest offers information.

Your target offers and examples of courses provided by each institution

390 pts **Liverpool** – AABb (inc biol+chem) (Vet Sci) (IB 36 pts HL 666)

380 pts **Cambridge** – A*AA +BMAT (inc AL in 3 sci subjs pref/AL in 2 sci) (Vet Med) (IB 38–42 pts)

360 pts **London (RVC)** – AAA–AAB+BMAT (inc AL chem+biol +1 other) (Vet Med)

340 pts **Bristol** – AAB (inc chem+biol) (Vet Sci+Pre-Vet Yr) (IB 35 pts HL 766)

        Edinburgh – AAB (inc chem+biol +maths/phys) (Vet Med) (IB 36 pts)

        Glasgow – AAB (inc A chem+biol+phys/maths AB/BA) (Vet Med) (IB 36 pts)

        Nottingham – AAB (inc biol/chem) (Vet Med+Prelim Yr) (IB 38 pts HL 76)

320 pts **Surrey** – check with University 320–340 pts (Vet Biosci) (IB 34–32 pts)

300 pts **Glasgow** – BBB (inc chem+biol+maths/phys) (Vet Biosci) (IB 32 pts)

        Harper Adams (UC) – BBB (Biovet Sci)

        Liverpool – BBB (inc biol+sci) (Biovet Sci) (IB 32 pts)

        London (RVC) – BBB (inc chem+maths/phys/biol +1 other) (Biovet Sci 3yrs BSc)

        Nottingham – Can lead to Vet Studies at St George's, Grenada BBB (Pre-Vet Cert course)

280 pts **Bristol** – BBC (inc BB biol+chem) (Vet Nurs Biovet Sci) (IB 30 pts)

        Lincoln – (inc biol) 280 pts (Biovet Sci)

260 pts **Harper Adams (UC)** – 260 pts (Vet Nurs Prac Mgt)

240 pts **Bristol UWE** – 240–280 pts (inc biol) (Biovet Sci) (IB 24 pts)

        Lincoln – CCC (1 Yr Cert Vet Med Sci for entry to Yr 1 Vet Med course at Nottingham University)

        London (RVC) – CCC (inc chem+biol) (Vet Gateway prog 1 yr)

        Middlesex – 240–280 pts (Vet Nurs)

200 pts **Bristol UWE** – 200–260 pts (inc biol) (Vet Nurs Sci) (IB 26 pts)

        Myerscough (Coll) – 200 pts (Vet Nurs)

160 pts **London (RVC)** – CC–AA (inc 2 sci pref biol) (Vet Nurs)

        Warwickshire (Coll) – 160 pts (Vet Nurs Bus Mgt; Anim Welf)

        Edinburgh Napier – 2AL offers vary (Vet Nurs)

Alternative offers

See **Chapter 7** and **Appendix 1** for grades/UCAS Tariff points information for the International Baccalaureate, Scottish Highers/Advanced Highers, the Welsh Baccalaureate, the Irish Leaving Certificate, the Cambridge Pre-U Diploma, the Advanced Diploma and the Extended Project.

EXAMPLES OF FOUNDATION DEGREES IN THE SUBJECT FIELD

Askham Bryan (Coll); Bicton (Coll); Bristol UWE Fdn Sci 100–140 pts; Duchy (Coll); Greenwich; Hadlow (Coll); Harper Adams (UC); London (RVC); Myerscough (Coll); Nottingham Trent; Reaseheath (Coll); Sparsholt (Coll); Warwickshire (Coll).

CHOOSING YOUR COURSE (SEE ALSO CH. 1)

Some course features

Author's note Veterinary Science/Medicine is the most intensely competitive subject and, as in the case of Medicine, one or two offers and three rejections are not uncommon. As a result, the Royal College of Veterinary Surgeons has raised a number of points which are relevant to applicants and advisers.

1 Every candidate for a Veterinary Medicine/Science degree course should be advised to spend a suitable period with a veterinarian in practice.

2 A period spent in veterinary work may reveal a hitherto unsuspected allergy or sensitivity following contact with various animals.

3 Potential applicants should be under no illusions about the difficulty of the task they have set themselves . . . at least five applicants for every available place . . . with no likelihood of places being increased at the present time.

4 There are so many candidates who can produce the necessary level of scholastic attainment that other considerations have to be taken into account in making the choice. In most cases, the number of GCSE grade As will be crucial. This is current practice. Headteachers' reports and details of applicants' interests, activities and background are very relevant and are taken fully into consideration . . . applicants are reminded to include details of periods of time spent with veterinary surgeons.

5 Any applicant who has not received an offer but who achieves the grades required for admission ought to get in touch, as soon as the results are known, with the schools and enquire about the prospects of entry at the Clearing stage. All courses cover the same subject topics.

Bristol UWE The degree in Veterinary Nursing Science includes 70 weeks of work placement and leads to the RCVS qualification. This course and that of Veterinary Practice Management take place at Hartpury College, Gloucester.

Edinburgh Veterinary Medicine programmes are also accredited by the American Veterinary Medical Association so graduates can practise as vets in North America.

London (RVC) (Vet Gateway) Course guarantees a place on the five-year Veterinary Medicine programme. Applicants require chemistry and biology and any other subject at A-level (except general studies) and there are other conditions for eligibility (see www.rvc.ac.uk). (BSc Biovet Sci 3 yr) Course does not qualify graduates to practise as veterinary surgeons. There is also a six-year Veterinary Medicine Combined course.

Nottingham The course which involves the Preliminary Year is for students without the required science qualifications but who have high academic achievement in non-science or vocational subjects. Successful completion of the course enables direct entry into Year 1 of the five-year course.

Surrey The degree in Veterinary Biosciences focuses on animal health and disease. There are opportunities for professional placements.

Universities and colleges teaching quality See www.qaa.ac.uk; http://unistats.direct.gov.uk.

Top research universities and colleges (RAE 2008) See **Agricultural Sciences/Agriculture**.

Examples of sandwich degree courses Bristol UWE (Vet Nurs); Harper Adams (UC) (Vet Nurs).

ADMISSIONS INFORMATION

Number of applicants per place (approx) Bristol (Vet Sci) 12, (Vet Nurs Biovet Sci) 4; Cambridge 5; Edinburgh 17; Glasgow 20; Liverpool 12; London (RVC) 5; Nottingham 11.

Numbers of applicants (**a** UK **b** EU (non-UK) **c** non-EU **d** mature) London (RVC) **a**759 **b**71 **c**156 **d**172.

Advice to applicants and planning the UCAS personal statement Applicants for Veterinary Science must limit their choices to four universities and submit their applications by 15 October. They may add up to two alternative courses. Work experience is almost always essential so discuss this in full, giving information about the size and type of practice and the type of work in which you were involved. See also **Appendix 4**. **Bristol** Evidence is needed of wide veterinary animal experience, together with evidence of initiative. **Edinburgh** Competition for places is intense: 72 places are available and only one in seven applicants will receive an offer. The strongest candidates are interviewed and are normally required to take with them an additional reference outlining recent work experience. **Liverpool** The selection process involves three areas: academic ability to cope with the course; knowledge of vocational aspects of veterinary science acquired through work experience in veterinary practice and working with animals; personal attributes that demonstrate responsibility and self-motivation. **London (RVC)** Six weeks' hands-on experience needed: two weeks in a veterinary practice; two weeks with large domestic animals; two weeks with other animals, for example riding school, zoo, kennels.

Misconceptions about this course Bristol UWE (Vet Nurs Sci) Students think that the degree qualifies them as veterinary nurses but in fact RCVS assessment/training is additional. **Liverpool** (Biovet Sci) Some applicants think that the course allows students to transfer to Veterinary Science: it does not.

Selection interviews Yes All institutions; (Vet Sci and Vet Nurs) **Some** Bristol; **No** London (RVC).

Interview advice and questions Past questions have included: Why do you want to be a vet? Have you visited a veterinary practice? What did you see? Do you think there should be a Vet National Health Service? What are your views on vivisection? What are your views on intensive factory farming? How can you justify thousands of pounds of taxpayers' money being spent on training you to be a vet when it could be used to train a civil engineer? When would you feel it your responsibility to tell battery hen farmers that they were being cruel to their livestock? What are your views on vegetarians? How does aspirin stop pain? Why does it only work for a certain length of time? Do you eat beef? Outline the bovine TB problem. Questions on A-level science syllabus. See **Chapter 6**. **Glasgow** Applicants complete a questionnaire prior to interview. Questions cover experience with animals, reasons for choice of career, animal welfare, teamwork, work experience, stressful situations.

Reasons for rejection (non-academic) Failure to demonstrate motivation. Lack of basic knowledge or understanding of ethical and animal issues.

AFTER-RESULTS ADVICE
Offers to applicants repeating A-levels **Higher** London (RVC); **Same** Bristol UWE (Vet Nurs Sci), Liverpool (candidates achieving the necessary grades are welcome to reapply); **No** Cambridge; Edinburgh Glasgow.

GRADUATE DESTINATIONS AND EMPLOYMENT (2007/8 HESA)
Graduates surveyed 615 **Employed** 505 **In further study** 15 **Assumed unemployed** 40

Career note Over 80% of veterinary surgeons work in private practice with the remainder involved in research in universities, government-financed research departments and in firms linked with farming, foodstuff manufacturers and pharmaceutical companies.

OTHER DEGREE SUBJECTS FOR CONSIDERATION
Agricultural Science; Agriculture; Animal Sciences; Biological Sciences; Biology; Dentistry; Equine Dental Science; Equine Management; Equine Studies; Medicine; Zoology.

ZOOLOGY

(including **Animal Biology**; see also **Agricultural Sciences/Agriculture, Animal Sciences, Biological Sciences, Biology**)

Zoology courses have a biological science foundation and could cover animal ecology, marine and fisheries biology, animal population, development and behaviour and, on some courses, wildlife management and fisheries.

Useful websites www.scienceyear.com; www.zsl.org/ioz; www.zsl.org; www.academicinfo.net/zoo. html.

NB The points totals shown to the left of the institutions are for ease of reference only. It must not be assumed that Tariff points are always used by institutions or that they can be substituted for an offer in grades. The level of an offer is not necessarily indicative of the quality of a course.

COURSE OFFERS INFORMATION
Subject requirements/preferences **GCSE** English and science/mathematics required or preferred. **AL** One or two sciences will be required.

NB In 2012 universities and colleges will differ in their use of GCE AL/AS unit grade information, A* grades, the Extended Project (EPQ), the Advanced Diploma and the Cambridge Pre-U examination when considering applicants and making offers. An EPQ may be accepted in place of an AS subject. Check websites of universities and colleges for the latest offers information.

Your target offers and examples of courses provided by each institution

380 pts **Cambridge** – A*AA college offers may vary (Nat Sci (Zool)) (IB 38–42 pts)

360 pts **Bristol** – AAA–ABB (Zool) (IB 34 pts HL 666)

London (UCL) – AABe–AAAe (Biol Sci (Zool)) (IB 34–36 pts)

Manchester – AAA–AAB (Zool Modn Lang) (IB 35–32 pts)

340 pts **Birmingham** – AAB–ABB (Biol Sci (Zool)) (IB 32–34 pts)

Cardiff – AAB–ABB 340–320 pts (Zoology) (IB 34 pts HL biol chem 5)

Imperial London – AAB 340 pts (Zoology) (IB 36 pts HL 66)

Manchester – AAA–AAB (Zool Ind) (IB 35–32 pts)

St Andrews – AAB (Zool) (IB 32 pts)

Sheffield – AAB (Zool MBiolSci) (IB 35 pts)

320 pts **Durham** – ABB (Zool Ind) (IB 34 pts HL 55)

Exeter – BBB–AAB (Zool courses) (IB 34 pts)

Glasgow – ABB (App Maths Zool) (IB 32 pts)

Leeds – BBB–ABB (Zool) (IB 34–32 pts HL 16–15 pts)

Leicester – ABB (Biol Sci (Zool)) (IB 32 pts)

Liverpool – BBB–ABB (Zool) (IB 33–30 pts)

London (RH) – 320 pts (Zool) (IB 34 pts)

Newcastle – ABB/BBB (Zoology) (IB 32 pts)

Reading – 320 pts (Zool)

Sheffield – ABB (Zool BSc) (IB 33 pts)

Swansea – ABB (Zoo) (IB 33 pts)

300 pts **Aberdeen** – BBB (Zool) (IB 28 pts)

Edinburgh – BBB (Zoology) (IB 30 pts)

London (QM) – BBB (Zool Aqua Biol) (IB 30 pts)

Newcastle – BBB (Mar Zool) (IB 32 pts HL biol 6)

Nottingham – BBB–ABB (Zoology MSci/BSc) (IB 32–34 pts)

Queen's Belfast – BBB (Zool) (IB 28 pts HL 555)

Southampton – BBB (3 sci)–AAB (2 sci) 300–340 pts (Zoology) (IB 32 pts HL 16 pts)

280 pts **Aberystwyth** – 280–320 pts (Zool; Zool Microbiol)

Bangor – 280–340 pts (Zoology MZool)

Stirling – BBC 1st year entry (Aqua)

260 pts **Dundee** – BCC (Zool) (IB 28 pts)

Hull – 260–300 pts (Aqua Zool; Zool)

Liverpool John Moores – 260-300 pts (Zoology)

Staffordshire – 260 pts (Anim Biol Cons)

240 pts **Bangor** – 240–280 pts (Zool Anim Bhv) (IB 28 pts)

Bolton – 240 pts (Biol (Anim Biol))

Glamorgan – 240–280 pts (Int Wldlf Biol)

Roehampton – 240–300 pts (Zool)

220 pts **Cumbria** – 220 pts (Wldlf Media)

Nottingham Trent – 220 pts (Zoo Biol) (IB 26 pts)

200 pts **Anglia Ruskin** – 200 pts (Mar Biol Nat Hist) (IB 24 pts)

Manchester Met – 200–280 pts (Wldlf Biol)

Nottingham Trent – 200pts (Anim Zool) (IB 24 pts)

180 pts **Derby** – 180–240 pts (Zool courses) (IB 26 pts)

Salford – 180–200 pts (Zool; Wldlf Cons Zoo Biol)

160 pts **Blackpool and Fylde (Coll)** – 160 pts (Wldlf Photo)

140 pts **West Scotland** – CD (App Biosci Zool)

Alternative offers

See **Chapter 7** and **Appendix 1** for grades/UCAS Tariff points information for the International Baccalaureate, Scottish Highers/Advanced Highers, the Welsh Baccalaureate, the Irish Leaving Certificate, the Cambridge Pre-U Diploma, the Advanced Diploma and the Extended Project.

EXAMPLES OF FOUNDATION DEGREES IN THE SUBJECT FIELD
See also Animal Sciences. Cornwall (Coll); Sparsholt (Coll).

CHOOSING YOUR COURSE (SEE ALSO CH. 1)
Some course features
See **Biological Sciences**.

Anglia Ruskin (Zool) Study in the USA is an option for one semester.
Durham All Biological Sciences degrees have a common first year, with transfers possible to other degrees or to Natural Sciences in the second year. The four-year Zoology degree includes an industrial placement.
Hull (Aqua Zool) Course focuses on the interface between land and water and expands on the animal biology aspects of marine and freshwater biology.
Stirling (Aqua) An exchange programme with universities in Sweden is part of the course.

Universities and colleges teaching quality See www.qaa.ac.uk; http://unistats.direct.gov.uk.

Examples of sandwich degree courses Cardiff; Durham; Exeter; Manchester; West Scotland.

ADMISSIONS INFORMATION
Number of applicants per place (approx) Aberystwyth 8; Bangor 3; Bristol 13; Cardiff 8; Durham 11; Leeds 7; Liverpool John Moores 6; London (RH) 6; Newcastle 15; Nottingham 6; Southampton 7; Swansea 6.

Advice to applicants and planning the UCAS personal statement Interests in animals should be described, together with any first-hand experience gained. Visits to zoos, farms, fish farms etc and field courses attended should be described, together with any special points of interest that you noted.

Selection interviews **Yes** Durham, Hull, Liverpool, London (RH), Newcastle; **Some** Cardiff, Derby, Dundee, Roehampton, Swansea.

Interview advice and questions Past questions have included: Why do you want to study Zoology? What career do you hope to follow on graduation? Specimens may be given to identify. Questions usually asked on the A-level subjects. See **Chapter 6**.

AFTER-RESULTS ADVICE
Offers to applicants repeating A-levels **Higher** Bristol, Hull, Leeds, Swansea; **Same** Aberystwyth, Bangor, Cardiff, Derby, Dundee, Durham, Liverpool, Liverpool John Moores, London (RH), Roehampton, Swansea.

GRADUATE DESTINATIONS AND EMPLOYMENT (2007/8 HESA)
Graduates surveyed 690 **Employed** 230 **In further study** 170 **Assumed unemployed** 85

Career note See **Biology**.

OTHER DEGREE SUBJECTS FOR CONSIDERATION
Animal Ecology; Animal Sciences; Aquaculture; Biological Sciences; Biology; Ecology; Fisheries Management; Marine Biology; Parasitology; Veterinary Science; Wildlife Management.

The choice of a subject to study (from over 50,000 degree courses) and of a university or college (from more than 300 institutions) is a major task for students living in the United Kingdom (UK). For overseas and European Union (EU) applicants it is even greater, and the decisions that have to be made need much careful planning, preferably beginning two years before the start of the course. **NB** Beware that there are some private institutions offering bogus degrees: check www.ucas.com for your university and college choices.

APPLICATIONS AND THE POINTS-BASED IMMIGRATION SYSTEM

In addition to submitting your application through UCAS (see **Chapter 5**) a new Points-based Immigration System is now in operation for overseas students. The main features of this system include:

- **Visa letters** Students will require a special 'visa letter' from their universities before being admitted. This will be sent to you by the university in time for you to apply for your visa.
- **Maintenance** Students will need to show that they are able to pay for the first year's tuition fees, plus £600 per month for accommodation and living expenses. Additional funds and regulations apply for those bringing dependants into the UK.
- **Proof of qualifications** Your visa letter will list all the qualifications that you submitted to obtain your university place and original proof will be required for these qualifications when submitting your visa application. These documents will be checked by the Home Office. Any fraudulent documents will result in your visa application being rejected and a possible ban from entering the UK for 10 years.
- **Attendance** Once you have started your course, your attendance will be monitored. Non-attending students will be reported to the UK Border Agency.

Full details can be obtained from www.ukcisa.org.uk/student/index.php.

SELECTION, ADMISSION AND FINANCE

The first reason for making early contact with your preferred institution is to check their requirements for your chosen subject and their selection policies for overseas applicants. For example, for all Art and some Architecture courses you will have to present a portfolio of work or slides. For Music courses your application often will have to be accompanied by a recording you have made of your playing or singing and, in many cases, a personal audition will be necessary. Attendance at an interview in this country is compulsory for some universities and for some courses. At other institutions the interview may take place either in the UK or with a university or college representative in your own country.

The ability to speak and write good English is essential and many institutions require evidence of competence, for example scores from the International English Language Testing System (IELTS) or from the Test of English as a Foreign Language (TOEFL) (see www.ielts.org and www.ets.org/toefl). For some institutions you may have to send examples of your written work. Each institution provides information about its English language entry requirements and a summary of this is given for each university listed below. International students should note that the recommended threshold for minimum English language requirements is IELTS 6.5–7.0. Recent research indicates that students with a lower score may have difficulty in dealing with their course.

At the end of this book you will find a directory of universities and colleges in the UK, together with their contact details. Most universities and colleges in the UK have an overseas student adviser who can advise you on these and other points you need to consider, such as passports, visas, entry certificates, evidence of financial support, medical certificates, medical insurance, and the numbers of overseas students in the university from your own country. All these details are very important and need to be considered at the same time as choosing your course and institution.

The subject tables in **Chapter 8** provide a comprehensive picture of courses on offer and of comparative entry levels. However, before making an application, other factors should be considered such as English language entry requirements (see above), the availability of English language teaching, living costs, tuition fees and any scholarships or other awards which might be offered. Detailed information about these can be obtained from the international offices in each university or college, from British higher education fairs throughout the world and from the British Council offices abroad and from websites: see www.britishcouncil.org; www.education.org.

Below is a brief summary of the arrangements made by each university in the UK for students aiming to take a full-time degree programme. The information is presented as follows:

- Institution.
- International student numbers.
- English language entry requirements for degree programmes shown in either IELTS or TOEFL scores. These vary between universities and courses. For the IELTS, scores can range from 5.5 to 7.5, and for the TOEFL computer-based test, scores can range from a minimum of 213; for the written TOEFL the usual minimum entry level is 5.0. For full details contact the university or college.
- Arrangements for English tuition.
- International Foundation courses.
- Annual tuition fees (approximate) for full-time undergraduate degree courses. Tuition fees also usually include fees for examinations and graduation. These figures are approximate and are subject to change each year. EU students pay 'home student' fees, except for those from the Channel Islands and the Isle of Man; students from the British Overseas Territories are now treated as home students for fee purposes at universities and other institutions of higher education.
- Annual living costs. These are also approximate and represent the costs for a single student over the year. The living costs shown cover university accommodation (usually guaranteed for the first year only), food, books, clothing and travel in the UK, but not travel to or from the UK. (Costs are likely to rise year by year in line with the rate of inflation in the UK, currently around 3% per year.) Overseas students are normally permitted to take part-time work for a period of up to 20 hours per week.
- Scholarships and awards for non-EU students (most universities offer awards for EU students).

UNIVERSITY INFORMATION AND FEES FOR INTERNATIONAL STUDENTS

Discussions are taking place at Government level on an increase in tuition fees from 2012. These could affect the fees charged for courses for non-EU/international students. Intending applicants should therefore check university websites before applying. The fees published below (unless otherwise stated) are those being charged to students in 2010/11.

Aberdeen International students 14%, 115 nationalities. IELTS 6.0; for Medicine 7.0. Four-week English course available in August before the start of the academic year. *Fees:* Arts subjects £9250, Science subjects £11,500, Medicine £22,500. Some scholarships and grants. *Living costs:* Living costs: £5000-£6000.

Abertay Dundee International students 10%. *English language entry requirement (or equivalent):* IELTS 5.5. Pre-sessional English course available, also full-time English course September to May and free English tuition throughout degree course. *Fees:* All courses £8150. *Living costs:* £5000–£6000. Several scholarships available, including special awards for students from India and from some countries in the Far East and the USA.

Aberystwyth A large number of international students. *English language entry requirement (or equivalent):* IELTS 6.5. Full-time tuition in English available. *Fees:* Arts subjects £8500, Science subjects £10,750, joint courses £9500. *Living costs:* £5000–£6000. Awards for students from the Far East.

Anglia Ruskin International students 21%. *English language entry requirement (or equivalent):* IELTS 5.5. A one-year International Foundation programme available. *Fees:* Arts subjects £9300, Science subjects £10,300. *Living costs:* £7000–£7500.

Arts London A large number of international students. *English language entry requirement (or equivalent):* IELTS 6.5. Courses in Fashion Promotion, Acting, Directing require IELTS 7.5. Language Centre courses in academic English for 12, 24, 34 or 36 weeks. *Fees:* Degree courses £11,900. *Living costs:* £9500–£10,500.

Aston Over 1000 students from over 80 countries, with 15% of the total student population from overseas. International Orientation programme at the beginning of the academic year. *English language entry requirement (or equivalent):* IELTS 6.0–6.5. International Foundation programme offered as a bridge to the degree courses. Pre-sessional English classes also available of five and 10 weeks duration. *Fees:* Non-Science programmes £11,700, Social Science and Computing courses £12,950, Engineering and Science courses £14,700. *Living costs:* £6000–£7000. Scholarships offered, including bursaries for Engineering and Science subjects.

Bangor Ten per cent of the student population is made up of international students from 70 countries. Lower cost of living than many other UK cities. *English language entry requirement (or equivalent):* IELTS 6.0. Pre-study English course starting September, January or April depending on level of English proficiency, leads to International Foundation course. One-month or two-month courses before starting degree course also offered. *Fees:* Arts, Humanities and Social Science courses £9120, Science courses £10,200. *Living costs:* £5700. Scholarships available.

Bath Over 1500 international students from around 100 countries. *English language entry requirement (or equivalent):* IELTS 6.0. Pre-degree language courses offered, ranging from one month to one year. *Fees:* Arts and Humanities subjects £11,000, Science and Engineering courses £14,000. *Living costs:* £7500–£8000. Scholarships and awards available, including residential awards for applicants from the Far East and Kenya.

Bath Spa Students from 40 countries. *English language entry requirement (or equivalent):* IELTS 5.5 for subjects supported by the Undergraduate Course for International Students (UCIS). Foundation courses available for students below this score. Subjects not supported by UCIS, entry level IELTS 6.0. *Fees:* £9000–£9600 (plus studio fees £200–£300 for Art and Design courses). *Living costs:* £7000–£8000.

Bedfordshire Over 3000 EU and international students. *English language entry requirement (or equivalent):* IELTS 6.0. General English programmes are offered, including a summer school. *Fees:* £9,300. *Living costs:* £6000–£7000.

Birmingham Over 4000 international students from 152 countries. *English language entry requirement (or equivalent):* IELTS 6.0. Courses in Law, Health Science, Medicine and Dentistry require IELTS 7.0. Six, 10 and 20-week English language programmes available, depending on language proficiency, ranging from IELTS 4.5 to 5.5. *Fees:* Non-laboratory subjects £10,800, laboratory subjects £13,950, clinical programmes £25,685. *Living costs:* £8000–£9000. International Foundation programme available. Awards are offered by some subject departments including Bioscience, Computer Science, Earth Sciences, Law, Psychology; there are also Engineering scholarships for students from Malaysia.

Birmingham City Large number of international students. *English language entry requirement (or equivalent):* IELTS 6.0. Pre-sessional language courses and in-session language support. Orientation programme for all students. *Fees:* £9000, Conservatoire/Acting courses £12,500–£13,000. *Living costs:* £6000–£7000. Music bursaries.

Bolton Over 500 students from 60 countries represented. *English language entry requirement (or equivalent):* IELTS 6.0. Courses start in September, some in January. Pre-sessional and in-session English tuition plus Access and Foundation programmes available in Business Management and Engineering. *Fees:* £8000 with up to £250 discount for prompt payment. *Living costs:* £7000.

Bournemouth A large number of international students. *English language entry requirement (or equivalent):* IELTS 6.0. Preparatory English programme offered, starting in January, April or July depending on applicant's level of English (entry IELTS 4.5/5.0/5.5). Several language schools in the town (see www.englishuk.com.uk or www.baselt.org.uk). Pre-sessional study skills programme also offered. *Fees:* £9500–£11,500. *Living costs:* £7500–£8500. Some subject awards available.

Bradford Over 100 countries represented (22%). *English language entry requirement (or equivalent):* IELTS 6.0. Some students may be admitted to Year 2, depending on qualifications. *Fees:* Science and

Engineering courses £11,400, other courses £9000 (lower fees for students taking a sandwich year). *Living costs:* £6000–£8500. Ten scholarships to cover the duration of the course.

Brighton Some 2000 international students from over 100 countries. *English language entry requirement (or equivalent):* IELTS 6.0 (or 5.5 for less linguistically demanding subjects). New four-year degree programme (UK4) includes preparatory year. *Fees:* £10,900–£11,500. Fixed fees possible. *Living costs:* £7000–£8000. Links with other nationals at Brighton. Merit scholarships for students from Norway and some countries in the Far East and Africa.

Bristol Approximately 1100 students from over 100 countries. *English language entry requirement (or equivalent):* IELTS 6.5 (possibly lower for some Science and Engineering subjects). *Fees:* Arts subjects £12,400, Science subjects £15,550, Clinical subjects £28,700. *Living costs:* £6500–£9000. Some bursaries and scholarships for one year from some subject departments including Law, Medicine, Dentistry and Veterinary Science.

Bristol UWE More than 1750 international students. *English language entry requirement (or equivalent):* IELTS 6.0. English language preparatory and pre-sessional courses offered. English modules can also be taken throughout your degree. *Fees:* Classroom-based subjects £10,000, laboratory subjects £10,500. *Living costs:* £6500–£9000. Some partial fee scholarships available in Computing, Mathematics and Engineering, and Law scholarships for students from the Far East, South Africa, the West Indies and North America.

Buckingham Eighty nationalities represented at this small university. *English language entry requirement (or equivalent):* IELTS 6.0. *Fees:* £3500 (approximately) per term – check with the university. *Living costs:* £6000–£7000. Tuition fee discount for students from the Bahamas, Bulgaria and India. Some scholarships for students from the Far East, Russia and Eastern Europe.

Bucks New Around 7.5% of student population are international students from 50 countries. *English language entry requirement (or equivalent):* IELTS 6.0. *Fees:* £8500–£9300. *Living costs:* £6000–£7000.

Brunel More than 2000 international students from over 110 countries. *English language entry requirement (or equivalent):* IELTS 6.0 for science/technology subjects, 7.0 for Law, 6.5 for other subjects. English language tuition offered during and before the course but only to improve existing skills. *Fees:* Non-laboratory subjects £9200, laboratory subjects £11,100. *Living costs:* £7000–£8000. Twenty bursaries offered.

Cambridge Over 1000 international undergraduate students. *English language entry requirement (or equivalent):* IELTS 7.0 overall, with minimum of 6.0 in each element. TOEFL (written) 600 (minimum) and at least 5.0 in TOEFL test of written English. *Fees:* Arts, Humanities, Language and Social Science courses £11,829–£15,480. Science and Engineering £18,000, clinical subjects £28,632, College fees £4000–£5000. *Living costs:* £6000–£7000. Awards available, also scholarships for students from Hong Kong.

Canterbury Christ Church *English language entry requirement (or equivalent):* IELTS 6.0. *Fees:* £7880–£8050. *Living costs:* £6000–£7000.

Cardiff Over 3500 international students from 100 countries. *English language entry requirement (or equivalent):* IELTS 6.0–7.0. Comprehensive selection of pre-sessional language courses from three weeks to nine months. Induction course for all students. International Foundation courses for Business, Law, Engineering, Computer Science and Health and Life Sciences. *Fees:* Arts courses £10,700, science courses £13,750. *Living costs:* £6000–£8000. Law scholarships offered on the basis of academic merit.

Central Lancashire Large international student population from many countries. *English language entry requirement (or equivalent):* IELTS 6.0. Competence in written and spoken English required on application. *Fees:* £9450–£10,450. *Living costs:* £6000–£7000.

Chester *English language entry requirement (or equivalent):* IELTS 6.0. International Foundation year available for Business Studies students. *Fees:* £7585–£8855. *Living costs:* £6000–£7000.

Chichester International students from several countries. *English language entry requirement (or equivalent):* IELTS 6.0. *Fees:* £8300–£9500. *Living costs:* £7000–£8000.

Sunderland A large number of international students. *English language entry requirement (or equivalent):* IELTS 5.5–6.0. English language tuition available. *Fees:* £8300. *Living costs:* £5500–£6500.

Surrey A large international community with 43% from the Far East. *English language entry requirement (or equivalent):* IELTS 6.0. English language courses and summer courses offered. *Fees:* £11,000–£13,750. *Living costs:* £7000–£8000. Scholarships and bursaries offered, including awards for students on Civil Engineering courses.

Sussex More than 2500 international students. *English language entry requirement (or equivalent):* IELTS 6.5. English language and study skills courses available. International Foundation courses offered, covering English language tuition and a choice from Humanities, Law, Media Studies, Social Sciences and Cultural Studies and Science and Technology. *Fees:* £10,900–£14,640, Medicine £23,678. *Living costs:* £8000–£8500. Forty international scholarships.

Swansea Students from over 100 countries. *English language entry requirement (or equivalent):* IELTS 6.0. Pre-sessional English language courses available and on-going support during degree courses. *Fees:* £9300–£11,900. *Living costs:* £5500–£6500. Some overseas scholarships and prizes.

Swansea Met *English language entry requirement (or equivalent):* IELTS 6.5. *Fees:* £8,000. *Living costs:* £5500–£6500.

Teesside Students from over 75 countries. *English language entry requirement (or equivalent):* IELTS 6.5 for Law, English and Humanities, 5.5 for Engineering, Science, Technology and Computing courses and 6.0 for all other courses. Free English courses available throughout the year while following degree programmes. International summer school available. *Fees:* £9,750 *Living costs:* £5500–£6500.

Trinity Saint David International students are well-represented at the university. More information can be found on the international student section of the website, www.trinitysaintdavid.ac.uk/en/international/aboutus/ or by contacting the international office: internationalcc@trinitysaintdavid.ac.uk. *English language entry requirement (or equivalent):* IELTS 6.0. International Foundation programme. Accommodation possible for each year at university. *Fees:* £9070. *Living costs:* £5500–£6500.

Ulster Students from over 40 countries. *English language entry requirement (or equivalent):* IELTS 5.5. *Fees:* £9,020. *Living costs:* £5500–£6500.

Warwick Over 3500 international students. *English language entry requirement (or equivalent):* IELTS 6.0 for Science courses, 6.5 for Arts courses, 6.5 for MORSE courses, and 7.0 for Social Studies and Business courses. English support available. *Fees:* £12,625-£16,000. *Living costs:* £6500–£7500. More than 20 awards available for overseas students.

West London A large number of international students. *English language entry requirement (or equivalent):* IELTS 5.0 for the International Foundation programme and 5.5 for undergraduate courses. English language support available and also pre-sessional courses. *Fees:* £7990–£9350 *Living costs:* £9500–£12,500.

West Scotland Over 1100 international students. *English language entry requirement (or equivalent):* IELTS 6.0. English language Foundation course available. *Fees:* Art based course £10,000, Science based course £10,500. *Living costs:* £6500–£7000. Some first-year scholarships.

Westminster Students from 148 countries (51% Asian). *English language entry requirement (or equivalent):* IELTS 6.0. International Foundation certificate courses available focusing on the Built Environment, Mathematics and Computing or Social Sciences and Literature. *Fees:* £9830. *Living costs:* £9500–£10,500.

Winchester Some 150 international students from 30 countries. *English language entry requirement (or equivalent):* IELTS 6.0. Language courses available. *Fees:* £8,370 *Living costs:* £7500–£8500.

Wolverhampton A large number (2500) of international students from over 100 countries. *English language entry requirement (or equivalent):* IELTS 6.0. English courses available over one or two months or longer. International student programme. *Fees:* £9,450. *Living costs:* £6000–£6500. Twenty Scholarships for Excellence offered.

Worcester *English language entry requirement (or equivalent):* IELTS 6.0. *Fees:* £8400. *Living costs:* £6000–£6500.

York Fifteen per cent of students from outside the UK. *English language entry requirement (or equivalent):* IELTS 6.0. Six-month and pre-sessional English language courses. Intensive vacation courses. *Fees:* £11,300–£14,850. *Living costs:* £6500–£7500. Several scholarships for overseas students.

York St John *English language entry requirement (or equivalent):* IELTS 6.0 (3 year degree course or 4 year course including Foundation year). *Fees:* £8500 except health related courses £11,600. *Living costs:* £6500–£7500.

BRITISH OVERSEAS TERRITORIES STUDENTS

Students from British Overseas Territories are now treated as home students for fee purposes at universities and other institutions of higher education in the UK. The territories to which this policy applies are:

British Overseas Territories Anguilla, Bermuda, British Antarctic Territory, British Indian Ocean Territory, British Virgin Islands, Cayman Islands, Falkland Islands, Montserrat, Pitcairn Islands, South Georgia and the South Sandwich Islands, St Helena and its Dependencies, Turks and Caicos Islands.

Overseas Territories of other EU member states Greenland, Faroe Islands (Denmark), Netherlands Antilles (Bonaire, Curacao, Saba, St Eustatius, St Marten), Aruba (Netherlands), New Caledonia, French Polynesia, Wallis and Futura, Mayotte, St Pierre et Miquelon (France).

SECTION 1: UNIVERSITIES

Listed below are universities in the United Kingdom that offer degree and diploma courses at higher education level. Applications to these institutions are submitted through UCAS except for part-time courses, private universities and colleges, and further education courses. For current information refer to the websites shown and also to www.ucas.com for a comprehensive list of degree and diploma courses (see **Appendix 5**).

Aberdeen This is a city-centre university on Scotland's east coast. (University of Aberdeen, Students Admissions and School Leavers, University Office, King's College, Aberdeen, Aberdeenshire, Scotland AB24 3FX. Tel 01224 272090; www.abdn.ac.uk)

Abertay Dundee The University has a modern city-centre campus. (University of Abertay Dundee, Student Recruitment Office, Kydd Building, Dundee, Fife, Scotland DD1 1HG. Tel 01382 308080; www.abertay.ac.uk)

Aberystwyth This is a coastal university with a striking campus. (Aberystwyth University, Student Welcome Centre, Penglais Campus, Aberystwyth, Ceredigion, Wales SY23 3FB. Tel 01970 622021; www.aber.ac.uk)

Anglia Ruskin The University has main campuses in Cambridge and Chelmsford and partner colleges throughout East Anglia. (Anglia Ruskin University, Contact Centre, Bishop Hall Lane, Chelmsford, Essex, England CM1 1SQ. Tel 0845 271 3333; www.anglia.ac.uk)

Arts London The University consists of four Colleges of Art and Design (Camberwell, Chelsea, Central Saint Martins (including Byam Shaw School of Art) and Wimbledon), the London College of Communication and the London College of Fashion. (University of the Arts London, 272 High Holborn, London, England C1V 7EY. Tel 020 7514 6000; www.arts.ac.uk)

Aston This University has a green campus in the centre of Birmingham with academic, sporting and social activities on site. (Aston University, The Registry (Admissions), Aston Triangle, Birmingham, England B4 7ET. Tel 0121 204 4444; www.aston.ac.uk)

Bangor The University has a central site in Bangor on the Menai Straits with partner institutions (including the Welsh College of Horticulture) throughout North Wales. (Bangor University, The Student Recruitment Unit, Bangor, Gwynedd, Wales LL57 2DG. Tel 01248 383944; www.bangor.ac.uk)

Bath The University is on a rural campus one mile from the centre of Bath, with partner colleges in Bath, Swindon and Wiltshire. (University of Bath, Recruitment and Admissions, Bath, Somerset, England BA2 7AY. Tel 01225 383019; www.bath.ac.uk)

Bath Spa This University was created in 2005 and is located on two campuses near Bath, with partner colleges in Wiltshire. (Bath Spa University, Admissions Office, Newton Park, Newton St Loe, Bath, Somerset, England BA2 9BN. Tel 01225 875624; www.bathspa.ac.uk)

Bedfordshire This University was formed in August 2006 from the merger of Luton University and the Bedford campus of De Montfort University. The main campus is in the centre of Luton, with two campuses in Bedford, and four partner colleges. (University of Bedfordshire, The Admissions Office, Park Square, Luton, Bedfordshire, England LU1 3JU. Tel 0844 848 2235; www.beds.ac.uk)

Birmingham This is a 'red-brick' university at Edgbaston to the south of the city, with a second campus at Selly Oak. (University of Birmingham, Edgbaston, Birmingham, West Midlands, England B15 2TT. Tel 0121 414 3344; www.bham.ac.uk)

Birmingham City Situated in Birmingham itself, the University has teaching sites located around the city, each focusing on one subject. Partner colleges in Birmingham and Warwickshire also offer courses. (Birmingham City University, Birmingham City University, City North Campus, Birmingham, West Midlands, England B42 2SU. Tel 0121 331 5595; www.bcu.ac.uk)

Bolton The University was created in 2005 and is based at Deane Campus, close to the town centre. (University of Bolton, Recruitment and Admissions, Deane Road, Bolton, Greater Manchester, England BL3 5AB. Tel 01204 900600; www.bolton.ac.uk)

Bournemouth The University site is in a large coastal resort, with partner colleges in the region also offering courses. (Bournemouth University, Fern Barrow, Talbot Campus, Poole, Dorset, England BH12 5BB. Tel 01202 961916; www.bournemouth.ac.uk)

Bradford The University's main campus is close to the city centre, with the School of Management two miles away. (University of Bradford, Course Enquiries Office, Richmond Road, Bradford, West Yorkshire, England BD7 1DP. Tel 0800 073 1255; www.brad.ac.uk)

Brighton Situated on the south coast, the University has campuses in Brighton and Eastbourne and partner colleges in Sussex. University-validated courses are offered at several partner colleges. (University of Brighton, The Registry (Admissions), Mithras House, Lewes Road, Brighton, East Sussex, England BN2 4AT. Tel 01273 600900; www.brighton.ac.uk)

Brighton and Sussex (MS) The campus is located at Falmer, just outside Brighton. (Brighton and Sussex Medical School, BSMS Admissions, Brighton and Sussex Medical School, University of Sussex, Brighton, East Sussex, England BN1 9PX. Tel 01273 643528; www.bsms.ac.uk)

Bristol This is a city university with halls of residence in Stoke Bishop and Clifton. (University of Bristol, Senate House, Tyndall Avenue, Bristol, England BS8 1TH. Tel 0117 928 9000; www.bristol.ac.uk)

Bristol UWE The University has four campuses in and around Bristol with an associate Faculty at Hartpury, and regional centres in Bath, Gloucestershire and Swindon. Links with the Bristol Old Vic Theatre School and the Royal West of England Academy. (University of the West of England, Bristol, Admissions Office, Frenchay Campus, Coldharbour Lane, Bristol, Somerset, England BS16 1QY. Tel 0117 965 6261; www.uwe.ac.uk)

Brunel The University has a compact campus to the west of London at Uxbridge. Brunel also validates courses at the London School of Theology. (Brunel University, Admissions Office, Uxbridge, Middlesex, England UB8 3PH. Tel 01895 265265; www.brunel.ac.uk)

Buckingham A small independent university, it has two sites within the town some 40 miles north of London offering two-year (eight-term) degrees. (University of Buckingham, Admissions Office, Hunter Street, Buckingham, Buckinghamshire, England MK18 1EG. Tel 01280 820313; www.buckingham.ac.uk)

Bucks New A new university (2007), it has two campuses in High Wycombe and one at Chalfont St Giles and links with partner colleges. (Buckinghamshire New University, Admissions, Queen Alexandra Road, High Wycombe, Buckinghamshire, England HP11 2JZ. Tel 0800 0565 660; www.bucks.ac.uk)

Cambridge The University has 31 colleges located throughout the city. Colleges: Lucy Cavendish, Murray Edwards (formerly New Hall) and Newnham (women only); the following admit both men and women undergraduates: Christ's, Churchill, Clare, Corpus Christi, Darwin, Downing, Emmanuel, Fitzwilliam, Girton, Gonville and Caius, Homerton, Hughes, Jesus, King's, Magdalene, Pembroke, Peterhouse, Queens', Robinson, St Catharine's, St John's, Selwyn, Sidney Sussex, Trinity, Trinity Hall, Wolfson. Clare Hall and Darwin admit only graduates. (University of Cambridge, Cambridge Admissions Office, Fitzwilliam House, 32 Trumpington Street, Cambridge, Cambridgeshire, England CB2 1QY. Tel 01223 333308; www.cam.ac.uk)

Canterbury Christ Church The University was created in 2005 with the main campus located near Canterbury city centre and campuses also at Broadstairs, Medway University Centre and Folkestone. (Canterbury Christ Church University, Admissions, North Holmes Road, Canterbury, Kent, England CT1 1QU. Tel 01227 782900; www.canterbury.ac.uk)

Cardiff The main (Cathays Park) campus of the University is located in the city centre, with the Heath Park campus a mile to the south. (Cardiff University, Admissions, MacKenzie House, 30–36 Newport Road, Cardiff, Glamorgan, Wales CF24 0DE. Tel 029 2087 9999; www.cardiff.ac.uk)

Cardiff (UWIC) (University of Wales Institute, Cardiff, Llandaff Campus, Western Avenue, Cardiff, Glamorgan, Wales CF5 2YB. Tel 029 2041 6070; www.uwic.ac.uk)

Central Lancashire The University is located on a small campus in the city centre with partner colleges throughout Lancashire. (University of Central Lancashire, Admissions Office, Preston, Lancashire, England PR1 2HE. Tel 01772 201201; www.uclan.ac.uk)

Chester This university was formed in 2005 and is located on a campus in Chester, with a second campus in Warrington and three partner colleges. (University of Chester, Undergraduate Admissions, Parkgate Road, Chester, Cheshire, England CH1 4BJ. Tel 01244 512528; www.chester.ac.uk)

Chichester This is a small university (2005) with campuses at Chichester and Bognor Regis. (University of Chichester, Admissions, Bognor Regis Campus, Upper Bognor Road, Bognor Regis, West Sussex, England PO21 1HR. Tel 01243 816002; www.chiuni.ac.uk)

City The University is situated in central London, with Nursing and Midwifery located at St Bartholomew's Hospital. (City University, Undergraduate Admissions Office, Northampton Square, London, England EC1V 0HB. Tel 020 7040 5060; www.city.ac.uk)

Coventry The University has a 33-acre campus in Coventry and a number of teaching centres throughout the city with courses offered in several partner colleges. (Coventry University, The Student Centre, 1 Gulson Road, Coventry, England CV1 2JH. Tel 024 7615 2525; www.coventry.ac.uk)

Creative Arts The University has five colleges – three in Kent (Canterbury, Maidstone and Rochester) and two in Surrey (Epsom and Farnham). (University for the Creative Arts, Enquiries Service, Falkner Road, Farnham, Surrey, England GU9 7DS. Tel 01252 892883; www.ucreative.ac.uk/enquiries)

Cumbria This new university (2007) was created by the merger of St Martin's College and Cumbria Institute of the Arts. There are campuses in Ambleside, Carlisle, Lancaster, Penrith and London. (University of Cumbria, Fusehill Street, Carlisle, Cumbria, England CA1 2HH. Tel 01228 616234; www.cumbria.ac.uk)

De Montfort The University has two sites in Leicester and nine associated colleges. (De Montfort University, Students Admissions, The Gateway, Leicester, England LE1 9BH. Tel 0116 255 1551; www.dmu.ac.uk)

Derby The University has two campuses: one close to Derby city centre and the second at Buxton. (University of Derby, Admissions, Kedleston Road, Derby, Derbyshire, England DE22 1GB. Tel 01332 591167; www.derby.ac.uk)

Dundee A city-centre campus, with the Medical School and School of Nursing located at Ninewells Hospital to the west of the city. (University of Dundee, Admissions and Student Recruitment, Nethergate, Dundee, Scotland DD1 4HN. Tel 01382 383838; www.dundee.ac.uk)

Durham The University has two sites, the main site in Durham city and the second, at Stockton, with two colleges on the Queen's Campus. (Durham University, Undergraduate Admissions Office, University Office, Old Elvet, Durham, England DH1 3HP. Tel 0191 334 6123; www.dur.ac.uk)

East Anglia The University is set in parkland close to Norwich. (University of East Anglia, Admissions Office, Norwich, Norfolk, England NR4 7TJ. Tel 01603 591515; www.uea.ac.uk)

East London The University has campuses in London at Stratford and Docklands. Courses are also offered at several colleges in Greater London. (University of East London, Docklands Campus, 4–6 University Way, London, England E16 2RB. Tel 020 8223 3333; www.uel.ac.uk)

Edge Hill This university (formed in 2005) has its campus in Ormskirk near Liverpool. (Edge Hill University, Academic Registry, Ormskirk, Lancashire, England L39 4QP. Tel 01695 650950; www.edgehill.ac.uk)

Edinburgh This university consists of the University Central Area in the city centre and the University King's Buildings on a site a mile to the south. (Edinburgh University, Student Recruitment and Admissions, 57 George Square, Edinburgh, Scotland EH8 9JU. Tel 0131 651 1905; www.ed.ac.uk)

Edinburgh Napier The University has seven campuses in the centre of Edinburgh and two to the south-west. (Edinburgh Napier University, Information Office, Craiglockart Campus, Edinburgh, Scotland EH14 1DJ. Tel 08452 606040; www.napier.ac.uk)

Essex The University has a parkland campus two miles from Colchester. The University and the South Essex College Partnership also provide degree schemes at the new Southend campus. The University validates degrees offered by Writtle College and by the East 15 Acting School. (University of Essex, Undergraduate Admissions, Wivenhoe Park, Colchester, Essex, England CO4 3SQ. Tel 01206 873778; www.essex.ac.uk)

Exeter The University has two sites in Exeter: the Streatham campus is the largest, and the St Luke's campus is a mile away. A third campus (University of Exeter in Cornwall campus) is situated at Penryn in Cornwall. (University of Exeter, Admissions Office, 8th Floor, Laver Building, North Park Road, Exeter, Devon, England EX4 4QE. Tel 01392 723044; www.exeter.ac.uk)

Glamorgan The University has four faculties on two campuses in Pontypridd and a faculty in Cardiff. The main campus is at Glamorgan and the new School of Creative and Cultural Industries is in Cardiff city centre. The University has partnerships with the Royal Welsh College of Music and Drama and several other colleges. (University of Glamorgan, Enquiries and Admissions Unit, Pontypridd, Glamorgan, Wales CF37 1DL. Tel 08456 434030; www.glam.ac.uk)

Glasgow The University has three campuses, two on the outskirts of Glasgow and one on the Crichton campus at Dumfries. Glasgow School of Art and the Scottish Agricultural College in Ayr are associated institutions. (University of Glasgow, Recruitment, Admissions and International Service, Fraser Building, 65 Hillhead Street, Glasgow, Strathclyde, Scotland G12 8QF. Tel 0141 330 3177; www.gla.ac.uk)

Glasgow Caledonian The University has a city-centre campus. (Glasgow Caledonian University, City Campus, Admissions Office, Cowcaddens Road, Glasgow, Scotland G4 0BA. Tel 0141 331 3334; www.gcal.ac.uk)

Gloucestershire Three campuses in Cheltenham and one in Gloucester form the University. It also has partner colleges in Gloucestershire, Herefordshire, Wiltshire and Worcestershire. (University of Gloucestershire, Student Recruitment Office, Hardwick Administration Centre, St Pauls Road, Cheltenham, Gloucestershire, England GL50 4BS. Tel 0844 801 0001; www.glos.ac.uk)

Glyndŵr This is a new university (2008), formerly North East Wales IHE, and is situated in Wrexham town centre. (Glyndŵr University, Plas Coch, Mold Road, Wrexham, Wales LL11 2AW. Tel 01978 290666; www.glyndwr.ac.uk)

Greenwich The main campus of the University is at Greenwich, a second is at Avery Hill in south London and a third is at Medway at Chatham Maritime. There are also partner colleges in east London and Kent. (University of Greenwich, Enquiry Unit, Greenwich Campus, Old Royal Naval College, Park Row, London, England SE10 9LS. Tel 0800 005 006; www.gre.ac.uk)

Heriot-Watt The University has a large parkland campus seven miles west of Edinburgh and a second campus in the Scottish Borders at Galashiels 35 miles to the south. (Heriot-Watt University, Admissions Unit, Edinburgh Campus, Edinburgh, Scotland EH14 4AS. Tel 0131 449 5111; www.hw.ac.uk)

Hertfordshire This university has two campuses in Hatfield. Courses are also offered through a consortium of four Hertfordshire colleges and the University has links with all Hertfordshire further education colleges. (University of Hertfordshire, University Admissions Service, College Lane, Hatfield, Hertfordshire, England AL10 9AB. Tel 01707 284800; www.herts.ac.uk)

Huddersfield This is a town-centre university with University Centres at Barnsley and Oldham and links to colleges of further education throughout the north of England. (University of Huddersfield, Admissions Office, Queensgate, Huddersfield, West Yorkshire, England HD1 3DH. Tel 01484 473969; www.hud.ac.uk)

Hull The main campus is in Hull, two miles from the city centre, with a smaller campus at Scarborough. (University of Hull, Admissions Service, Cottingham Road, Hull, Yorkshire, England HU6 7RX. Tel 01482 466100; www.hull.ac.uk)

Hull York (MS) The Medical School is a partnership between the Universities of Hull and York, with teaching facilities on the main campuses of both universities. (Hull York Medical School, Admissions Section, John Hughlings Jackson Building, Heslington, York, England YO10 5DD. Tel 01904 321 762; www.hyms.ac.uk)

Imperial London The College became an independent university, separate from the University of London, in 2007. The central site is in South Kensington. Medicine is based mainly at St Mary's Hospital, Paddington, Charing Cross Hospital and Hammersmith Hospital (Imperial College London, Registry, Level 3 Sherfield Building, South Kensington Campus, London, England SW7 2AZ. Tel 020 7589 5111; www.imperial.ac.uk)

Keele This is a small university on a green campus five miles from Stoke-on-Trent. (Keele University, Academic Registry, Keele, Staffordshire, England ST5 5BG. Tel 01782 734005; www.keele.ac.uk)

Kent The University has a spacious campus near Canterbury, and also campuses at Medway, Chatham and Wye, with two associate colleges (South Kent College, Mid Kent College) and two partner institutions (West Kent College, Canterbury College). (University of Kent, Admissions and Partnership Services, The Registry, Canterbury, Kent, England CT2 7NZ. Tel 01227 827272; www.kent.ac.uk)

Kingston With four campuses in and around the town and 10 partner colleges, the University has easy access to London. (Kingston University, River House, 53–57 High Street, Kingston upon Thames, Surrey, England KT1 1LQ. Tel 0844 855 2177; www.kingston.ac.uk)

Lancaster The University has a parkland site three miles south of Lancaster city centre. (Lancaster University, Undergraduate Admissions Office, Bailrigg, Lancaster, England LA1 4YW. Tel 01524 594910; www.lancs.ac.uk)

Leeds The University is sited on a campus in the centre of the city. (University of Leeds, Undergraduate Admissions Office, Leeds, West Yorkshire, England LS2 9JT. Tel 0113 243 1751; www.leeds.ac.uk)

Leeds Met The University has two campuses, one in the city and a second in Headingly on the outskirts of Leeds, and partner colleges throughout the region. (Leeds Metropolitan University, Course Enquiries Office, Civic Quarter, Leeds, West Yorkshire, England LS1 3HE. Tel 0113 812 3113; www.lmu.ac.uk)

Leicester The compact campus is located on the southern edge of the city. (University of Leicester, Admissions Office, University Road, Leicester, Leicestershire, England LE1 7RH. Tel 0116 252 5280; www.le.ac.uk)

Lincoln The Brayford and Cathedral campuses are in the city, with the Riseholme Park campus some five miles away. There is also a campus in Hull and associated colleges in Lincolnshire. (University of Lincoln, Academic Registry, Brayford Pool, Lincoln, Lincolnshire, England LN6 7TS. Tel 01522 886097; www.lincoln.ac.uk)

Liverpool The University has a large city-centre campus. (University of Liverpool, Student Recruitment and Admissions Office, Foundation Building, Brownlow Hill, Liverpool, Merseyside, England L69 7ZX. Tel 0151 794 5927; www.liv.ac.uk)

Liverpool Hope This university, created in 2005, is situated outside Liverpool. (Liverpool Hope University, Admissions Office, Hope Park, Liverpool, Merseyside, England L16 9JD. Tel 0151 291 3295; www.hope.ac.uk)

Liverpool John Moores The University has three campuses in and around Liverpool (Liverpool John Moores, Admissions and Information Officer, Byrom Street, Liverpool, Merseyside, England L3 3AF. Tel 0151 231 2021; www.livjm.ac.uk)

London (Birk) The College is situated in Bloomsbury in the London University precinct and provides part-time and evening higher education courses. (Birkbeck, University of London, Malet Street, London, England WC1E 7HX. Tel 020 7631 6000; www.bbk.ac.uk)

London (Gold) The college is located on a single campus in south-east London. (Goldsmiths, University of London, Admissions Office, Lewisham Way, New Cross, London, England SE14 6NW. Tel 020 7919 7766; www.gold.ac.uk)

London (Hey) The College is on a site in central London. (Heythrop College, University of London, Registry, Kensington Square, London, England W8 5HN. Tel 020 7795 6600; www.heythrop.ac.uk)

London (Inst Ed) (Institute of Education, University of London, 20 Bedford Way, London, England WC1H 0AL. Tel 020 7612 6000; www.ioe.ac.uk)

London (Inst in Paris) The Institute's Department of French Studies and Comparative Studies is located in central Paris and operates in partnership with Queen Mary and Royal Holloway, University of London. (University of London Institute in Paris, 9-11 rue de Constantine, 75340, Paris, France Cedex 07. Tel +33 (0) 1 44 11 73 83/76; www.ulip.lon.ac.uk)

London (King's) The College has campuses in central and south London (Strand, Waterloo and London Bridge) including the School of Medicine, the Dental Institute and the School of Biomedical and Health Sciences. (King's College, University of London, Enquiries, Strand, London, England WC2R 2LS. Tel 020 7836 5454; www.kcl.ac.uk)

London (QM) There is a city campus in the East End of London. (Queen Mary, University of London, Admissions Office, Mile End Road, London, England E1 4NS. Tel 020 7882 5511; www.qmul.ac.uk)

London (RH) There is a large campus with halls of residence situated at Egham, 19 miles west from central London and three miles of Windsor. (Royal Holloway, University of London, Admissions Office, Egham, Surrey, England TW20 0EX. Tel 01784 434455; www.rhul.ac.uk)

London (RVC) The College has campuses in London and Hertfordshire. (Royal Veterinary College, University of London, Royal College Street, London, England NW1 0TU. Tel 020 7468 5147; www.rvc.ac.uk)

London (St George's) Located on a compact site in south-west London, St George's is a specialist health sciences university, having extensive links with many hospitals and practices, and with Kingston University and Royal Holloway London. (St George's, University of London, Cranmer Terrace, London, England SW17 0RE. Tel 020 8725 2333; www.sgul.ac.uk)

London (Sch Pharm) The School has a central London site close to the London University precinct. (School of Pharmacy, University of London, 29–39 Brunswick Square, London, England WC1N 1AX. Tel 020 7753 5800; www.pharmacy.ac.uk)

London (SOAS) The College is located in Bloomsbury in the London University precinct. (School of Oriental and African Studies, University of London, Thornhaugh Street, Russell Square, London, England WC1H 0XG. Tel 020 7898 4034; www.soas.ac.uk)

London (UCL) The College is located in Bloomsbury in the London University precinct. (University College London, University of London, Gower Street, London, England WC1E 6BT. Tel 020 7679 3000; www.ucl.ac.uk)

London LSE LSE is a university specialising in the whole range of social science subjects (from Economics, Politics and Law to Sociology, Accounting and Finance). Located in the heart of London. LSE entrance examination may be required. (London School of Economics and Political Science, Undergraduate Admissions Office, Houghton Street, London, England WC2A 2AE. Tel 020 7955 7170; www.lse.ac.uk)

London Met The University has two campuses, one in north London (with the largest (new) science laboratory in Europe) and one in the City, and several partner colleges. (London Metropolitan University, Admissions Office, 166–220 Holloway Road, London, England N7 8DB. Tel 020 7133 4200; www.londonmet.ac.uk)

London South Bank The main campus of the University is in Southwark on the south bank of the Thames in London. Other campuses are at Whipps Cross in east London and at Havering in Essex. (London South Bank University, Admissions Office, 90 London Road, London, England SE1 6LN. Tel 020 7815 6100; www.lsbu.ac.uk)

Loughborough On a large rural single-site campus, the University is a mile from the town centre. (Loughborough University, Undergraduate Admissions Office, Loughborough, Leicestershire, England LE11 3TU. Tel 01509 263171; www.lboro.ac.uk)

Manchester The University has a large precinct one mile south of the city centre. (University of Manchester, Student Recruitment and Admissions, Rutherford Building, Oxford Road, Manchester, England M13 9PL. Tel 0161 306 1631; www.manchester.ac.uk)

Manchester Met The University has five sites in Manchester and one in Cheshire, at Alsager and Crewe. (Manchester Metropolitan University, Admissions Office, All Saints Building, All Saints, Manchester, Greater Manchester, England M15 6BH. Tel 0161 247 2000; www.mmu.ac.uk)

Middlesex This is a multi-campus university in north London with associate colleges in the region. (Middlesex University, Admissions Enquiries, The Burroughs, Hendon, London, England NW4 4BT. Tel 020 8411 5555; www.mdx.ac.uk)

Newcastle The University has a single campus in the city centre. (Newcastle University, Admissions Office, 6 Kensington Terrace, Newcastle-upon-Tyne, Tyne and Wear, England NE1 7RU. Tel 0191 208 3333; www.ncl.ac.uk)

Newport The University has two campuses, in Newport and Caerleon. (Newport, University of Wales, Admissions Office, Caerleon Campus, Lodge Road, Caerleon, Newport, South Wales NP18 3QT. Tel 01633 432030; www.newport.ac.uk)

Northampton The University (created in 2005) has two campuses close to the town centre. (University of Northampton, Admissions Office, Park Campus, Boughton Green Road, Northampton, Northamptonshire, England NN2 7AL. Tel 0800 358 2232; www.northampton.ac.uk)

Northumbria The University has two campuses in and around Newcastle. (Northumbria University, Ellison Place, Newcastle-upon-Tyne, Tyne and Wear, England NE1 8ST. Tel 0191 243 7420; www.northumbria. ac.uk)

Nottingham This is a large campus university to the west of the city with a second campus two miles from the city centre, and a third at Sutton Bonington for the new School of Veterinary Science and Medicine, 10 miles south of University Park. (University of Nottingham, Admissions Office, University Park, Nottingham, Nottinghamshire, England NG7 2RD. Tel 0115 951 5559; www.nottingham. ac.uk)

Nottingham Trent The University has three campuses: City site, in the centre of Nottingham, Clifton and Brackenhurst. The Clifton campus of the University is four miles from Nottingham city centre and caters for Education, Humanities and Science whilst Brackenhurst, near Southwell, focuses on land-based subjects. (Nottingham Trent University, Registry Admissions, Dryden Centre, Burton Street, Nottingham, Nottinghamshire, England NG1 4BU. Tel 0115 848 4200; www.ntu.ac.uk)

Open University This is the UK's largest university for part-time and distance-learning higher education, providing supported distance learning for undergraduate (and postgraduate) students who must be over 18. Application and registration is made direct to the OU, and not through UCAS (at present). (Open University, Student Registration and Enquiry Service, PO Box 197, Milton Keynes, Buckinghamshire, England MK7 6BJ. Tel 0845 300 6090; www.open.ac.uk)

Oxford The University has 30 colleges and seven private halls admitting undergraduates throughout the city. Colleges: Balliol, Brasenose, Christ Church, Corpus Christi, Exeter, Harris Manchester (mature students only), Hertford, Jesus, Keble, Lady Margaret Hall, Lincoln, Magdalen, Mansfield, Merton, New, Oriel, Pembroke, St Anne's, St Catherine's, St Edmund Hall, St Hilda's (women only, but has voted to admit men), St Hugh's, St John's, St Peter's, Somerville, Queen's, Trinity, University, Wadham, Worcester. Permanent Private Halls: Blackfriars, Campion Hall (men only), Greyfriars, Regent's Park College, St Benet's Hall, St Stephen's House, Wycliffe. (University of Oxford, Undergraduate Admissions Office, University Offices, Wellington Square, Oxford, Oxfordshire, England OX1 2JD. Tel 01865 288000; www. ox.ac.uk)

Oxford Brookes The University has three main campuses in and around Oxford. (Oxford Brookes University, Admissions Office, Headington Campus, Gipsy Lane, Oxford, Oxfordshire, England OX3 0BP. Tel 01865 483040; www.brookes.ac.uk)

Peninsula (MS) The College has campuses at Exeter and Plymouth Universities and teaching facilities in Truro. (Peninsula College of Medicine and Dentistry, The John Bull Building, Tamar Science Park, Research Way, Plymouth, Devon, England PL6 8BU. Tel 01752 437444; www.pms.ac.uk)

Plymouth The University has two main campuses, one in Plymouth and a second, the Peninsula Allied Health Centre, is four miles north of the main campus. Courses are also offered at eight partner colleges. (University of Plymouth, Central Admissions, Drake Circus, Plymouth, Devon, England PL4 8AA. Tel 01752 585 858; www.plymouth.ac.uk)

Portsmouth The main campus of the University is close to the town centre; courses are also taught at colleges in Hampshire and Surrey. (University of Portsmouth, Academic Registry, University House, Winston Churchill Avenue, Portsmouth, Hampshire, England PO1 2UP. Tel 023 9284 8484; www.port. ac.uk)

Queen Margaret This new university (2007) is located on a new campus on the Firth of Forth east of Edinburgh, with student accommodation on site. (Queen Margaret University, Edinburgh, The Admissions Office, Queen Margaret University Drive, Edinburgh, Scotland EH21 6UU. Tel 0131 474 0000; www.qmu. ac.uk)

Queen's Belfast The University has a large campus in the south of the city. (Queen's University Belfast, Admissions Service, University Road, Belfast, County Antrim, Northern Ireland BT7 1NN. Tel 028 9097 2727; www.qub.ac.uk)

Reading There are three campuses in the University, with the main (Whiteknights) on a rural campus at the edge of the city, and two others within walking distance. Foundation degrees are taught at two partner colleges. (University of Reading, Student Recruitment Office, PO Box 217, Reading, Berkshire, England RG6 6AH. Tel 0118 378 8619; www.rdg.ac.uk)

Richmond (Am Int Univ) The University runs British and American courses. American courses are accredited by the Middle States Commission on Higher Education, an agency recognised by the US Department of Education. Courses are also approved by the Open University and can lead to Open University Validated Awards. (Richmond, The American International University in London, Queen's Road, Richmond-upon-Thames, Surrey, England TW10 6JP. Tel 020 8332 8200; www.richmond.ac.uk)

Robert Gordon The University has two campuses in and near Aberdeen city centre. (Robert Gordon University, Admissions Office, Administration Building, Schoolhill, Aberdeen, Aberdeenshire, Scotland AB10 1FR. Tel 01224 262728; www.rgu.ac.uk)

Roehampton Established in 2004, the University is located in south-west London, close to Richmond Park, and has four Colleges: Digby Stuart, Froebel, Southlands and Whitelands. (Roehampton University, Enquiries Office, Erasmus House, Roehampton Lane, London, England SW15 5PU. Tel 020 8392 3232; roehampton.ac.uk)

St Andrews Founded in 1413, and the third oldest university in the English-speaking world, this is a town-centre university on the east coast of Scotland. (University of St Andrews, Admissions Application Centre, St Katherine's West, 16 The Scores, St Andrews, Fife, Scotland KY16 9AX. Tel 01334 462150; www.st-andrews.ac.uk)

Salford This is a city-centre campus university for all courses, except for Midwifery at Bury and Nursing at Eccles. (University of Salford, Admissions Officer, The Crescent, Salford, Greater Manchester, England M5 4WT. Tel 0161 295 4545; www.salford.ac.uk)

Sheffield The university campus is close to Sheffield's city centre. (University of Sheffield, Admissions Services, Student Services Department, 9 Northumberland Road, Sheffield, South Yorkshire, England S10 2TT. Tel 0114 222 8030; www.shef.ac.uk)

Sheffield Hallam The University has two campuses, one in the city centre, and the second two miles away. (Sheffield Hallam University, Admissions Office, City Campus, Howard Street, Sheffield, South Yorkshire, England S1 1WB. Tel 0114 225 5555; www.shu.ac.uk)

Southampton The University has five main campuses in Southampton and Winchester. (University of Southampton, University Road, Southampton, Hampshire, England SO17 1BJ. Tel 023 8059 5000; www.soton.ac.uk)

Southampton Solent The University (created in 2005) is close to Southampton city centre, and has two partner colleges. (Southampton Solent University, Student Recruitment, East Park Terrace, Southampton, Hampshire, England SO14 0YN. Tel 023 8031 9000; www.solent.ac.uk)

Staffordshire The University has campuses at Stafford, Stoke, Lichfield, Shrewsbury and several regional colleges. (Staffordshire University, Admissions, College Road, Stoke on Trent, Staffordshire, England ST4 2DE. Tel 01782 292753; www.staffs.ac.uk)

Stirling The University is situated on a large rural campus. (University of Stirling, UG Admissions Office, Stirling, Stirlingshire, Scotland FK9 4LA. Tel 01786 467044; www.stir.ac.uk)

Strathclyde The University's main campus is in Glasgow city centre, with the Jordanhill campus to the west of the city. (University of Strathclyde, 16 Richmond Street, Glasgow, Lanarkshire, Scotland G1 1XQ. Tel 0141 552 4400; www.strath.ac.uk)

Sunderland The main campus of the University is in Sunderland city centre, with the Sir Tom Cowie campus across the river accommodating the Business School and Informatics Centre. (University of Sunderland, Student Recruitment, Chester Road, Sunderland, Tyne and Wear, England SR1 3SD. Tel 0191 515 2000; www.sunderland.ac.uk)

Surrey The University has a modern campus a mile from Guildford city centre. Some foundation-year teaching takes place in local colleges. (University of Surrey, Undergraduate Admissions Office, Stag Hill, Guildford, Surrey, England GU2 7XH. Tel 01483 689906; www.surrey.ac.uk)

Sussex The University has a single site campus four miles from Brighton. (University of Sussex, Undergraduate Admissions, Sussex House, Falmer, Brighton, Sussex, England BN1 9RH. Tel 01273 678416; www.sussex.ac.uk)

Swansea The University is situated in a parkland campus outside Swansea. (Swansea University, Admissions, Singleton Park, Swansea, Wales SA2 8PP. Tel 01792 205678; www.swan.ac.uk)

Swansea Met This new (2008) university (formerly Swansea Institute) is situated in the centre of Swansea. (Swansea Metropolitan University, Admissions Office, Mount Pleasant Campus, Swansea, Wales SA1 6ED. Tel 01792 481000; www.smu.ac.uk)

Teesside This is a city-centre university, with its campus in Middlesbrough. It has links with colleges in the region. (Teesside University, Admissions Office, Middlesbrough, Tees Valley, England TS1 3BA. Tel 01642 384228; www.tees.ac.uk)

Trinity Saint David This is a new university (2010) created by the merger of the University of Wales, Lampeter, and Trinity University College with courses run at Carmarthen and Lampeter (formed from a merger between Trinity St David University and Trinity University college). (Trinity Saint David, University of Wales, Academic Registry, Lampeter, Ceredigion, Wales SA48 7ED. Tel Carmarthen – 01267 676767; Lampeter – 01570 422351; www.trinitysaintdavid.ac.uk)

UHI Millennium Inst The UHI is based on a partnership of colleges and research centres, each with its own distinctive character. Full-time undergraduate courses are provided by the following partner colleges (for addresses see Section 3). Institutions are shown by initials in the tables in Chapter 8: Argyll College (AC), Highland Theological College (HTC), Inverness College (IC), Lews Castle College (LCC),Moray College (MC), Ness Foundation (NF), North Atlantic Fisheries College (NAFC), North Highland College (NHC), Orkney College (OC), Perth College (PC), Sabhal Mor Ostaig (SMO), Scottish Association for Marine Science (SAMS), Shetland College (SC) and West Highland College (WHC). (University of the Highlands and Islands

Millennium Institute, Course Information Unit, Executive Office, Ness Walk, Inverness, Scotland IV3 5SQ. Tel 01463 279000; www.uhi.ac.uk)

Ulster The University has four campuses – Belfast, Coleraine, Jordanstown, and Magee in Londonderry. (University of Ulster, Belfast Campus, York Street, Belfast, Co. Antrim, Northern Ireland BT15 1ED. Tel 028 701 23456; www.ulster.ac.uk)

Warwick The University has a single-site campus situated three miles outside Coventry. (University of Warwick, Student Admissions Office, Coventry, West Midlands, England CV4 7AL. Tel 024 7652 3723; www.warwick.ac.uk)

West London (Formerly Thames Valley University) The University has campuses at Ealing, Reading, Slough and Brentford, and links with four sites in west London and associated colleges. (University of West London, Learning Advice Centre, St Mary's Road, Ealing, London, England W5 5RF. Tel 0800 036 8888; www.tvu.ac.uk)

West Scotland This new university (2007) was formed from the merger of the University of Paisley and Bell College. There are four campuses – Paisley, Ayr, Hamilton and Dumfries. (University of the West of Scotland, Admissions Office, High Street, Paisley, Renfrewshire, Scotland PA1 2BE. Tel 0141 8483727; www.uws.ac.uk)

Westminster The University has four campuses (Cavendish, Marylebone and Regent in central London and Harrow) and associated colleges including the British Academy of New Music. (University of Westminster, Central Admissions, 35 Marylebone Road, London, England NW1 5LS. Tel 020 7911 5020; www.westminster.ac.uk)

Winchester This is a new university (2005) close to the centre of the city with sites in Basingstoke and Bournemouth. (University of Winchester, Course Enquiries, West Hill, Winchester, Hampshire, England SO22 4NR. Tel 01962 827234; www.winchester.ac.uk)

Wolverhampton The University has two campuses in Wolverhampton and others in Walsall and Telford. (University of Wolverhampton, Admissions Unit, MX, City Campus North, Camp Street, Wolverhampton, West Midlands, England WV1 1AD. Tel 01902 321000; www.wlv.ac.uk)

Worcester This small new university (2005) is located on a campus a short distance from Worcester city centre. (University of Worcester, Admissions Office, Henwick Grove, Worcester, England WR2 6AJ. Tel 01905 855111; www.worcester.ac.uk)

York The University has a parkland campus on the outskirts of York and a second campus in the city centre. (University of York, Admissions and School Liaison, Heslington, York, North Yorkshire, England YO10 5DD. Tel 01904 433533; www.york.ac.uk)

York St John This university (created in 2006) is on a site facing York Minster, five minutes walk from York city centre. (York St John University, Lord Mayor's Walk, York, North Yorkshire, England YO31 7EX. Tel 01904 624624; www.yorksj.ac.uk)

SECTION 2: UNIVERSITY COLLEGES, INSTITUTES, AND SPECIALIST COLLEGES OF AGRICULTURE AND HORTICULTURE, ART, DANCE, DRAMA, MUSIC, OSTEOPATHY AND SPEECH

University Colleges and Institutes provide undergraduate and postgraduate courses in a wide range of subjects and are university-sector institutions. While many universities and university colleges offer courses in art, design, music, drama, agriculture, horticulture and courses connected to the land-based industries, the specialist colleges listed below provide courses at many levels, often part-time, in these separate fields.

It is important that you read prospectuses and check websites carefully and go to Open Days to find out as much as you can about these colleges and about their courses which interest you. Applications for full-time courses at the institutions listed below are through UCAS.

Abbreviations used below A = Art and Design; **Ag** = Agriculture, Animals and Land-related courses; **C** = Communication; **D** = Drama, Performing and Theatre Arts; **Da** = Dance; **F** = Fashion; **H** = Horticulture and Landscape-related courses; **M** = Music.

Academy of Live and Recorded Arts (ALRA) Studio 24, Royal Victoria Patriotic Building, John Archer Way, London, England SW18 3SX. Tel 020 8870 6475; www.alra.co.uk [**D**]

Anglo-European College of Chiropractic 13–15 Parkwood Road, Bournemouth, Dorset, England BH5 2DF. Tel 01202 436200; www.aecc.ac.uk

Anniesland College Hatfield Campus, 19 Hatfield Drive, Glasgow, Scotland G12 0YE. Tel 0141 357 3969; www.anniesland.ac.uk

Archit Assoc Sch London (Architectural Association School of Architecture, 36 Bedford Square, London, England WC1B 3ES. Tel 020 7887 4000; www.aaschool.ac.uk)

Arts Educational Schools London Cone Ripman House, 14 Bath Road, London, England W4 1LY. Tel 020 8987 6666; www.artsed.co.uk [**A**]

Arts University College at Bournemouth Wallisdown, Poole, Dorset, England BH12 5HH. Tel 01202 533011; www.aucb.ac.uk [**A**]

Askham Bryan College Askham Bryan, York, England YO23 3FR. Tel 01904 772277; www.askham-bryan. ac.uk [**Ag**]

Berkshire College of Agriculture Hall Place, Burchetts Green, Maidenhead, Berkshire, England SL6 6QR. Tel 01628 824444; www.bca.ac.uk [**Ag**]

Bishop Burton College Learner Services, York Road, Bishop Burton, East Riding of Yorkshire, England HU17 8QG. Tel 01964 553000; www.bishopb-college.ac.uk [**Ag**]

Bishop Grosseteste University College Academic Registry, Newport, Lincoln, Lincolnshire, England LN1 3DY. Tel 01522 583658; www.bishopg.ac.uk

Bristol Old Vic Theatre School 1–2 Downside Road, Clifton, Bristol, England BS8 2XF. Tel 0117 973 3535; www.oldvic.ac.uk [**D**]

British College of Osteopathic Medicine Lief House, 120–122 Finchley Road, London, England NW3 5HR. Tel 020 7435 6464; www.bcom.ac.uk

British School of Osteopathy 275 Borough High Street, Student Admissions; 020 7089 5316, London, England SE1 1JE. Tel 020 7407 0222; www.bso.ac.uk

Camberwell College of Art, University of the Arts London Peckham Road, London, England SE5 8UF. Tel 020 7514 6302; www.camberwell.arts.ac.uk [**A**]

Capel Manor College Administrative Office, Bullsmore Lane, Enfield, Middlesex, England EN1 4RQ. Tel 08456 122122; www.capel.ac.uk [**H**]

Cavendish College London 35–37 Alfred Place, London, England WC1E 7DP. Tel 020 7580 4074; www. cavendish.ac.uk

Central Saint Martins College of Art and Design, University of the Arts London Southampton Row, London, England WC1B 4AP. Tel 020 7514 7022; www.csm.arts.ac.uk [**A**]

Central School of Speech and Drama, University of London The School's main campus is at the Embassy Theatre, 15 minutes by Underground from Central London. Central School of Speech and Drama Academic Registry, Embassy Theatre, 64 Eton Avenue, London, England NW3 3HY. Tel 020 7722 8183; www.cssd. ac.uk [**D**]

Chelsea College of Art and Design, University of the Arts London 16 John Islip Street, London, England SW1P 4JU. Tel 020 7514 7751; www.chelsea.arts.ac.uk [**A**]

City and Guilds of London Art School 124 Kennington Park Road, London, England SE11 4DJ. Tel 020 7735 2306; www.cityandguildsartschool.ac.uk [**A**]

Cleveland College of Art and Design Green Lane, Linthorpe, Middlesbrough, England TS5 7RJ. Tel 01642 288000; www.ccad.ac.uk [**A**]

Colchester Institute Course Enquiries, Sheepen Road, Colchester, Essex, England CO3 3LL. Tel 01206 712777; www.colchester.ac.uk

College of Agriculture Food and Rural Enterprise (CAFRE) Greenmount Campus, 22 Greenmount Road, Antrim, County Antrim, Northern Ireland BT41 4PU. Tel 0800 028 4291; www.cafre.ac.uk [**Ag**]

College of Estate Management Whiteknights, Reading, Berkshire, England RG6 6AW. Tel 0800 019 9697; www.cem.ac.uk

Courtauld Institute of Art, University of London The Institute, together with its gallery, is located in Somerset House on the Strand in central London. The Courtauld Institute of Art. Somerset House, London, England WC2R 0RN. Tel 020 7872 0220; www.courtauld.ac.uk [**A**]

Drama Centre London (part of Central St Martin's, University of the Arts London) Saffron House, 10 Back Hill, London, England EC1R 5LQ. Tel 020 7514 8778; www.csm.arts.ac.uk/drama [**D**]

East 15 Actg Sch East 15 Acting School, Hatfields, Rectory Lane, Loughton, Essex, England IG10 3RY. Tel 020 8508 5983; www.east15.ac.uk [**D**]

Edinburgh College of Art Academic Registry, Lauriston Place, Edinburgh, Scotland EH3 9DF. Tel 0131 221 6027; www.eca.ac.uk [**A**]

European School of Osteopathy Boxley House, The Street, Boxley, Maidstone, Kent, England ME14 3DZ. Tel 01622 671558; www.eso.ac.uk

Falmouth University College (including Dartington College of Arts) Admissions Office, Woodlane, Falmouth, Cornwall, England TR11 4RH. Tel 01326 211077; www.falmouth.ac.uk

Glasgow School of Art 167 Renfrew Street, Glasgow, Scotland G3 6RQ. Tel 0141 353 4500; www.gsa.ac.uk [**A**]

Gray's School of Art, Robert Gordon University Garthdee Road, Aberdeen, Scotland AB10 7QD. Tel 01224 263600; www.rgu.ac.uk [**A**]

Guildford School of Acting, GSA Conservatoire Stag Hill Campus, Guildford, Surrey, England GU2 7XH. Tel 01483 560701; www.conservatoire.org [**D**]

Guildhall School of Music and Drama Silk Street, Barbican, London, England EC2Y 8DT. Tel 020 7628 2571; www.gsmd.ac.uk [**M**]

Harper Adams University College Admissions Office, Newport, Shropshire, England TF10 8NB. Tel 01952 815000; www.gsmd.ac.uk [**Ag**]

Hartpury College Hartpury House, Hartpury, Gloucester, England GL19 3BE. Tel 01452 702345; www.hartpury.ac.uk [**Ag**]

Heatherley School of Fine Art 75 Lots Road, London, England SW10 0RN. Tel 020 7351 4190; www.heatherleys.org [**A**]

Hereford College of Arts Folly Lane, Hereford, England HR1 1LT. Tel 01432 273359; www.hca.ac.uk [**A**]

Leeds College of Art and Design Blenheim Walk, Leeds, West Yorkshire, England LS2 9AQ. Tel 0113 202 8039; www.leeds-art.ac.uk [**A**]

Leeds College of Music 3 Quarry Hill, Leeds, West Yorkshire, England LS2 7PD. Tel 0113 222 3416; www.lcm.ac.uk [**M**]

Leeds Trinity University College Student Enquiries Office, Brownberrie Lane, Horsforth, Leeds, West Yorkshire, England LS18 5HD. Tel 0113 283 7100; www.leedstrinity.ac.uk

Liverpool Institute for Performing Arts Mount Street, Liverpool, Merseyside, England L1 9HF. Tel 0151 330 3009; www.lipa.ac.uk [**D**]

London Academy of Music and Dramatic Art 155 Talgarth Road, London, England W14 9DA. Tel 020 8834 0500; www.lamda.org.uk [**M**]

London College of Communication, University of the Arts London Elephant & Castle, London, England SE1 6SB. Tel 020 7514 6569; www.lcc.arts.ac.uk [**C**]

London College of Fashion, University of the Arts London 20 John Princes Street, London, England W1G 0BJ. Tel 0207 514 7400; www.fashion.arts.ac.uk [**F**]

Marjon, University College Plymouth St Mark and St John Admissions Office, Derriford Road, Plymouth, Devon, England PL6 8BH. Tel 01752 636890; www.marjon.ac.uk

Mountview Academy of Theatre Arts Clarendon Road, Wood Green, London, England N22. Tel 020 8881 2201; www.mountview.org.uk [**D**]

Myerscough College Myerscough Hall, St Michael's Road, Bilsborrow, Preston, Lancashire, England PR3 0RY. Tel 01995 642222; www.myerscough.ac.uk [**Ag**]

Newman University College Admissions Registrar, Genners Lane, Bartley Green, Birmingham, West Midlands, England B32 3NT. Tel 01214761181; www.newman.ac.uk

Northern School of Contemporary Dance 98 Chapeltown Road, Leeds, West Yorkshire, England LS7 4BH. Tel 0113 219 3000; www.nscd.ac.uk [**Da**]

Northop College (Part of Deeside College, formerly the Welsh College of Horticulture) Holywell Road, Northop, Flintshire, Wales CH7 6AA. Tel 01352 841000; www.deeside.ac.uk/northop/ [**H**]

Norwich University College of the Arts Admissions, Francis House, 3–7 Redwell Street, Norwich, Norfolk, England NR2 4SN. Tel 01603 610561; www.nuca.ac.uk [**A**]

Pershore College (Part of Warwickshire College.) Avonbank, Pershore, Worcestershire, England WR10 3JP. Tel 01386 552443; www.pershore.ac.uk [**H**]

Plymouth College of Art Tavistock Place, Plymouth, Devon, England PL4 8AT. Tel 01752 203434; www.plymouthart.ac.uk [**A**]

Ravensbourne 6 Penrose Way, London, England SE10 0EW. Tel 020 3040 3500; www.rave.ac.uk [**C**]

Reaseheath College Reaseheath, Nantwich, Cheshire, England CW5 6DF. Tel 01270 625131; 01270 613242; www.reaseheath.ac.uk [**Ag**]

Rose Bruford College Lamorbey Park Campus, Burnt Oak Lane, Sidcup, Kent, England DA15 9DF. Tel 020 8308 2600; www.bruford.ac.uk [**D**]

Royal Academy of Dance 36 Battersea Square, London, England SW11 3RA. Tel 020 7326 8000; www.rad.org.uk [**Da**]

Royal Academy of Dramatic Art (RADA) 62–64 Gower Street, London, England WC1E 6ED. Tel 020 7636 7076; www.rada.org [**D**]

Royal Academy of Music, University of London This is Britain's senior conservatoire, founded in 1822. (Royal Academy of Music). Marylebone Road, London, England NW1 5HT. Tel 020 7873 7373; www.ram.ac.uk [**M**]

Royal Agricultural College Stroud Road, Cirencester, Gloucestershire, England GL7 6JS. Tel 01285 652531; www.rac.ac.uk [**Ag**]

Royal Ballet School 46 Floral Street, Covent Garden, London, England WC2E 9DA. Tel 020 7836 8899; www.royal-ballet-school.org.uk [**Da**]

Royal College of Music Prince Consort Road, London, England SW7 2BS. Tel 020 7589 3643; www.rcm.ac.uk [**M**]

Royal Northern College of Music 124 Oxford Road, Manchester, England M13 9RD. Tel 0161 907 5200; www.rncm.ac.uk [**M**]

Royal Scottish Academy of Music and Drama 100 Renfrew Street, Glasgow, Scotland G2 3DB. Tel 0141 332 4101; www.rsamd.ac.uk [**M**]

Royal Welsh College of Music and Drama Castle Grounds, Cathays Park, Cardiff, Wales CF10 3ER. Tel 029 2039 1361; www.rwcmd.ac.uk **[M]**

Ruskin School of Drawing and Fine Art 74 High Street, Oxford, England OX1 4BG. Tel 01865 276940; www.ruskin-sch.ox.ac.uk **[A]**

St Mary's University College Twickenham Registry, Waldegrave Road, Strawberry Hill, Twickenham, Middlesex, England TW1 4SX. Tel 020 8240 4000; www.smuc.ac.uk

Scottish Agricultural College Student Recruitment and Admissions Office, SAC Ayr Campus, Auchincruive Estate, Ayr, Scotland KA6 5HW. Tel 0800 269453; www.sac.ac.uk **[Ag]**

Slade School of Fine Art, University College London Gower Street, London, England WC1E 6BT. Tel 020 7679 2313; www.ucl.ac.uk/slade **[A]**

Sparsholt College Hampshire Westley Lane, Sparsholt, Winchester, Hampshire, England SO21 2NF. Tel 01962 776441; www.sparsholt.ac.uk **[H]**

Stranmillis University College Academic Registry, Stranmillis Road, Belfast, Northern Ireland BT9 5DY. Tel 028 9038 4263; www.stran.ac.uk

Trinity Laban Conservatoire of Music and Dance Creekside, London, England SE8 3DZ. Tel 020 8691 8600; www.trinitylaban.ac.uk **[M]**

University Campus Suffolk Admissions Office, Waterfront Building, Neptune Quay, Ipswich, Suffolk, England IP4 1QJ. Tel 01473 338833; www.ucs.ac.uk

University College Birmingham Summer Row, Birmingham, West Midlands, England B15 2TT. Tel 0121 604 1000; www.ucb.ac.uk

Wimbledon College of Art, University of the Arts London Merton Hall Road, London, England SW19 3QA. Tel 020 7514 9641; www.wimbledon.arts.ac.uk **[A]**

Winchester School of Art, University of Southampton Park Avenue, Winchester, Hampshire, England SO23 8DL. Tel 023 8059 7141; www.wsa.soton.ac.uk **[A]**

Writtle College Lordship Road, Chelmsford, Essex, England CM1 3RR. Tel 01245 424200; www.writtle. ac.uk **[H]**

SECTION 3: UNIVERSITY CENTRES, FURTHER EDUCATION AND OTHER COLLEGES OFFERING HIGHER EDUCATION COURSES

Changes are taking place fast in this sector, with the merger of colleges and the introduction in 2009 of University Centres. These are linked to further education colleges and to one or more universities, and provide Foundation and Honours degree courses (often part-time) and sometimes postgraduate qualifications.

The following colleges appear under various subject headings in the tables in **Chapter 8** and are in UCAS for some of their courses. See prospectuses and websites for application details.

University Centres

Barnsley University Centre Church Street, Barnsley, South Yorkshire, England S70 2AN. Tel 01226 606262; www.barnsley.hud.ac.uk

Blackburn College University Centre Feilden Street, Blackburn, Lancashire, England BB2 1LH. Tel 01254 55144; Student Hotline 01254 292929; www.blackburn.ac.uk

Bradford College University Centre Admissions Office, Great Horton Road, Bradford, West Yorkshire, England BD7 1AY. Tel 01274 433333; www.bradfordcollege.ac.uk

Doncaster College and University Centre High Melton, Doncaster, England DN5 7SZ. Tel 01302 553 773; www.don.ac.uk

Milton Keynes University Centre 200 Silbury Boulevard, Milton Keynes, Buckinghamshire, England MK9 1LT. Tel 01908 684444; www.ucmk.ac.uk

Oldham College University Centre Cromwell Street, Oldham, Greater Manchester, England OL1 1BB. Tel 0800 085 0374; www.hud.ac.uk/oldham

University Centre Folkestone Mill Bay, Folkestone, Kent, England CT20 1JG. Tel 0800 804 8500; www.ucf.ac.uk

University Centre Hastings Havelock Road, Hastings, East Sussex, England TN34 1BE. Tel 08456 020607; www.uch.ac.uk

University Centre Yeovil 91 Preston Road, Yeovil, Somerset, England BA20 2DN. Tel 01935 845454; www.ucy.ac.uk

Other Further Education Colleges

Aberdeen College Gallowgate Centre, Gallowgate, Aberdeen, Scotland AB25 1BN. Tel 01224 612000; Information and Booking Centre 01224 612330; www.abcol.ac.uk

Abingdon and Witney College Abingdon Campus, Wootton Road, Abingdon, Oxfordshire, England OX14 1GG. Tel 01235 555585; www.abingdon-witney.ac.uk

Accrington and Rossendale College Broad Oak Road, Accrington, Lancashire, England BB5 2AW. Tel 01254 389933; Information and Care 01254 354354; www.accross.ac.uk

Adam Smith College St Brycedale Campus, St Brycedale Avenue, Kirkcaldy, Fife, Scotland KY1 1EX. Tel 01592 223400; Course Hotline 0800 413280; www.adamsmithcollege.ac.uk

Andover College Andover College, Charlton Road, Andover, Hampshire, England SP10 1EJ. Tel 01264 360000; www.andover.ac.uk

Angus College Keptie Road, Arbroath, Angus, Scotland DD11 3EA. Tel 01241 432600; www.angus.ac.uk

Argyll College (UHI partner college – see Section 2) West Bay, Dunoon, Argyll & Bute, Scotland PA23 7HP. Tel 08452 309969; www.argyllcollege.com

Aylesbury College Oxford Road, Aylesbury, Buckinghamshire, England HP21 8PD. Tel 01296 588588; www.aylesbury.ac.uk

Ayr College Dam Park, Ayr, Strathclyde, Scotland KA8 0EU. Tel 01292 265184; Admissions 0800 199798; www.ayrcoll.ac.uk

Banff and Buchan College Main Campus, Henderson Road, Fraserburgh, Aberdeenshire, Scotland AB43 9GA. Tel 01346 586100; www.banff-buchan.ac.uk

Barking and Dagenham College Dagenham Road, Romford, Essex, England RM7 0XU. Tel 020 8090 3020;

Barnet College Graseby House, Wood Street, Barnet, Hertfordshire, England EN5 5UJ. Tel 020 8200 8300; Enrolment/Course Information 020 8266 4000; www.barnet.ac.uk

Barnfield College New Bedford Road Campus, New Bedford Road, Luton, Bedfordshire, England LU2 7BF. Tel 01582 569500; www.barnfield.ac.uk

Barony College Parkgate, Dumfries, Dumfries and Galloway, Scotland DG1 3NE. Tel 01387 860251; www.barony.ac.uk

Basingstoke College of Technology Worting Road, Basingstoke, Hampshire, England RG21 8TN. Tel 01256 354141; www.bcot.ac.uk

Bedford College Cauldwell Street, Bedford, Bedfordshire, England MK42 9AH. Tel 01234 291000; www.bedford.ac.uk

Bexley College Tower Road, Belvedere, Kent, England DA17 6JA. Tel 01322 404000; www.bexley.ac.uk

Bicton College East Budleigh, Budleigh Salterton, Devon, England EX9 7BY. Tel 01395 562400; www.bicton.ac.uk

Birmingham Metropolitan College (incorporating Matthew Boulton College of Further and Higher Education and Sutton Coldfield College) Jennens Road, Birmingham, West Midlands, England B4 7PS. Tel 0845 155 0101; www.bmetc.ac.uk

Bishop Auckland College Woodhouse Lane, Bishop Auckland, County Durham, England DL14 6JZ. Tel 01388 443000; Course Enquiries 08000 926506; www.bacoll.ac.uk

Blackpool and the Fylde College Ashfield Road, Bispham, Blackpool, Lancashire, England FY2 0HB. Tel 01253 504343; www.blackpool.ac.uk

Borders College Head Office, Scottish Borders Campus, Nether Road, Galashiels, Borders, Scotland TD1 3HE. Tel 08700 505152; www.borderscollege.ac.uk

Boston College Skirbeck Road, Boston, Lincolnshire, England PE21 6JF. Tel 01205 365701; Course Information 01205 313218; www.boston.ac.uk

Bournemouth and Poole College Customer Enquiry Centre, North Road, Poole, Dorset, England BH14 0LS. Tel 01202 205205; www.thecollege.co.uk

Bournville College Bristol Road South, Northfield, Birmingham, West Midlands, England B31 2AJ. Tel 0121 483 1000; Course Enquiries 0121 483 1111; www.bournville.ac.uk

BPP University College of Professional Studies Ltd BPP House, Aldine Place, 142–144 Uxbridge Road, London, England W12 8AA. Tel 020 8740 2222; www.bpp.com

Bracknell and Wokingham College College Information Centre, Church Road, Bracknell, Berkshire, England RG12 1DJ. Tel 0845 330 3343; www.bracknell.ac.uk

Braintree College Church Lane, Braintree, Essex, England CM7 5SN. Tel 01376 321711; Course Enquiries 01376 557020; www.braintree.ac.uk

Bridgend College Cowbridge Road, Bridgend, Mid-Glamorgan, Wales CF31 3DF. Tel 01656 302 302; www.bridgend.ac.uk

Bridgwater College Bath Road, Bridgwater, Somerset, England TA6 4PZ. Tel 01278 455464; Course Enquiries 01278 441234; www.bridgwater.ac.uk

Brockenhurst College Lyndhurst Road, Brockenhurst, Hampshire, England SO42 7ZE. Tel 01590 625555; www.brock.ac.uk

Bromley College of Further and Higher Education Rookery Lane, Bromley, Kent, England BR2 8HE. Tel 020 8295 7000; Course Enquiries 020 8295 7001; www.bromley.ac.uk

Brooklands College Weybridge Campus, Heath Road, Weybridge, Surrey, England KT13 8TT. Tel 01932 797797; www.brooklands.ac.uk

Brooksby Melton College Melton Mowbray Campus, Ashfordby Road, Melton Mowbray, Leicestershire, England LE13 0HJ. Tel 01664 850850; Course Enquiries 01664 855444; www.brooksbymelton.ac.uk

Burnley College Princess Way, Burnley, Lancashire, England BB12 0AN. Tel 01282 733373; Student Services 01282 733333; www.burnley.ac.uk

Burton College Student Services, Lichfield Street, Burton on Trent, Staffordshire, England DE14 3RL. Tel 01283 494400; www.burton-college.ac.uk

Bury College Woodbury Centre, Market Street, Bury, Greater Manchester, England BL9 0BG. Tel 0161 280 8280; www.burycollege.ac.uk

Calderdale College Francis Street, Halifax, West Yorkshire, England HX1 3UZ. Tel Course Information 01422 399399; www.calderdale.ac.uk

Cambridge Regional College Kings Hedges Road, Cambridge, Cambridgeshire, England CB4 2QT. Tel 01223 418200; www.camre.ac.uk

Canterbury College New Dover Road, Canterbury, Kent, England CT1 3AJ. Tel 01227 811111; Learning Advice/Courses 01227 811188; www.cant-col.ac.uk

Cardonald College Mosspark Drive, Glasgow, Scotland G52 3AY. Tel 0141 272 3333; www.cardonald. ac.uk

Carlisle College Information Unit, Victoria Place, Carlisle, Cumbria, England CA1 1HS. Tel 01228 822703; www.carlisle.ac.uk

Carmel College Prescot Road, St Helens, Merseyside, England WA10 3AG. Tel 01744 452200; www. carmel.ac.uk

Carnegie College (formerly Lauder College) Pittsburgh Road, Halbeath, Dunfermline, Fife, Scotland KY11 8DY. Tel 0844 248 0155; www.carnegiecollege.ac.uk

Carshalton College Nightingale Road, Carshalton, Surrey, England SM5 2EJ. Tel 020 8544 4444; www. carshalton.ac.uk

Castle College Nottingham Maid Marian Way, Nottingham, Nottinghamshire, England NG1 6AB. Tel 08458 450500; www.castlecollege.ac.uk

CECOS London College 59 Crompton Road, London, England N1 2YT. Tel 020 7359 3316; www.cecos. co.uk

Central Bedfordshire College (formerly Dunstable College) Kingsway, Dunstable, Bedfordshire, England LU5 4HG. Tel 0845 355 2525; www.centralbeds.ac.uk

Central College of Commerce Cathedral Street, Glasgow, Scotland G1 2TA. Tel Information Unit 0141 552 3941; www.centralcollege.ac.uk

Chelmsford College 102 Moulsham Street, Chelmsford, Essex, England CM2 0JQ. Tel 01245 265611; www.chelmsford-college.ac.uk

Chesterfield College Infirmary Road, Chesterfield, Derbyshire, England S41 7NG. Tel 01246 500500; www.chesterfield.ac.uk

Chichester College Westgate Fields, Chichester, West Sussex, England PO19 1SB. Tel 01243 786321; www.chichester.ac.uk

City and Islington College The Marlborough Building, 383 Holloway Road, London, England N7 0RN. Tel 020 7700 9200; www.candi.ac.uk

City College Birmingham Fordrough Campus, 300 Bordesley Green, Birmingham, West Midlands, England B9 5NA. Tel 0121 204 0000; www.citycol.ac.uk

City College Brighton and Hove Pelham Street, Brighton, East Sussex, England BN1 4FA. Tel 01273 667788; Course Advisers 01273 667759; www.ccb.ac.uk

City College Coventry Swanswell Centre, 50 Swanswell Street, Coventry, England CV1 5DG. Tel 0800 616202; www.covcollege.ac.uk

City College Plymouth Formerly Plymouth College of Further Education. King's Road, Devonport, Plymouth, Devon, England PL1 5QG. Tel 01752 305300; www.cityplym.ac.uk

City of Bath College Student Advice Centre, Avon St, Bath, Somerset, England BA1 1UP. Tel 01225 312191; www.citybathcoll.ac.uk

City of Bristol College Ashley Down Road, Bristol, England BS7 9BU. Tel 0117 312 5000; www.cityofbristol. ac.uk

City of Sunderland College Bede Centre, Durham Road, Sunderland, Tyne and Wear, England SR3 4AH. Tel 0191 511 6000; HE Admissions 0191 511 6260; www.citysun.ac.uk

City of Westminster College Paddington Green Campus, Paddington Green, London, England W2 1NB. Tel 020 7723 8826; www.cwc.ac.uk

City of Wolverhampton College Paget Road Campus, Paget Road, Wolverhampton, West Midlands, England WV6 0DU. Tel 01902 836000; www.wolverhamptoncollege.ac.uk

Cliff College Calver, Hope Valley, Derbyshire, England S32 3XG. Tel 01246 584202; www.cliffcollege.ac.uk

Clydebank College College Square, Queens' Quay, Clydebank, Scotland G81 1BF. Tel 0141 951 7400; www.clydebank.ac.uk

Coatbridge College Kildonan Street, Coatbridge, Lanarkshire, Scotland ML5 3LS. Tel 01236 422316; Admissions 01236 436000; www.coatbridge.ac.uk

Coleg Llandrillo Cymru Llandudno Road, Rhos-on-Sea, Colwyn Bay, Wales LL28 4HZ. Tel 01492 546 666; www.llandrillo.ac.uk

Coleg Menai Ffriddoedd Road, Bangor, Gwynedd, Wales LL57 2TP. Tel 01248 370125; www.menai.ac.uk

Coleg Sir Gâr Graig Campus, Sandy Road, Pwll, Carmarthenshire, Wales SA15 4DN. Tel 01554 748000; www.colegsirgar.ac.uk

College of Haringey, Enfield and North East London Formed in 2009 from a merger between Enfield College and the College of North East London. Enfield Centre, Hertford Road, Enfield, Middlesex, England EN3 5HA. Tel 020 8442 3055; www.conel.ac.uk

College of North West London Willesden Centre, Dudden Hill Lane, London, England NW10 2XD. Tel 020 8208 5000; Course Information 020 8208 5050; www.cnwl.ac.uk

College of West Anglia King's Lynn Centre, Tennyson Avenue, King's Lynn, Norfolk, England PE30 2QW. Tel 01553 761144; www.col-westanglia.ac.uk

College Ystrad Mynach Twyn Road, Ystrad Mynach, Hengoed, Wales CF82 7XR. Tel 01443 816888; www.ystrad-mynach.ac.uk

Cornwall College Camborne Campus, Trevenson Road, Pool, Redruth, Cornwall, England TR15 3RD. Tel 01209 616161; www.cornwall.ac.uk

Craven College High Street, Skipton, North Yorkshire, England BD23 1JY. Tel 01756 791411; www.craven-college.ac.uk

Croydon College College Road, Croydon, England CR9 1DX. Tel Course Information 020 8760 5914; www.croydon.ac.uk

Cumbernauld College Town Centre, Cumbernauld, Glasgow, Strathclyde, Scotland G67 1HU. Tel 01236 731811; www.cumbernauld.ac.uk

Darlington College Central Park, Haughton Road, Darlington, England DL1 1DR. Tel 01325 503050; www.darlington.ac.uk

Dearne Valley College Manvers Park, Wath upon Dearne, Rotherham, South Yorkshire, England S63 7EW. Tel 01709 513333; www.dearne-coll.ac.uk

Derby College Prince Charles Avenue, Mackworth, Derby, Derbyshire, England DE22 4LR. Tel 01332 520200; Course enquiries 0800 028 0289; www.derby-college.ac.uk

Derwentside College Consett Campus, Front Street, Consett, County Durham, England DH8 5EE. Tel 01207 585900; www.derwentside.ac.uk

Duchy College Rosewarne Campus, Camborne, Cornwall, Wales TR14 0AB. Tel 01209 722100; www.cornwall.ac.uk/duchy

Dudley College The Broadway, Dudley, West Midlands, England DY1 4AS. Tel 01384 363000; Course Enquiries 01384 363363; www.dudleycol.ac.uk

Dumfries and Galloway College College Gate, Bankend Road, Dumfries, Scotland DG1 4FD. Tel 01387 7340001; www.dumgal.ac.uk

Dundee College Kingsway Campus, Old Glamis Road, Dundee, Scotland DD3 8LE. Tel 01382 834834; Student Services 01382 834844; www.dundeecollege.ac.uk

Ealing, Hammersmith and West London College Gliddon Road, Barons Court, London, England W14 9BL. Tel 020 8741 1688; www.wlc.ac.uk

East Berkshire College Langley Campus, Station Road, Langley, Berkshire, England SL3 8BY. Tel 0845 373 2500; www.eastberks.ac.uk

East Durham College Houghall Campus, Houghall, Durham, England DH1 3SG. Tel 0191 375 4700; www.eastdurham.ac.uk

East Riding College Beverley Campus, Gallows Lane, Beverley, East Riding of Yorkshire, England HU17 7DT. Tel 845 120 0037; www.eastridingcollege.ac.uk

East Surrey College Gatton Point, London Road, Redhill, Surrey, England RH1 2JT. Tel 01737 788444; www.esc.ac.uk

Eastleigh College Chestnut Avenue, Eastleigh, Hampshire, England SO50 5FS. Tel 023 8091 1299; www.eastleigh.ac.uk

Easton College Easton, Norwich, Norfolk, England NR9 5DX. Tel 01603 731200; www.easton-college.ac.uk

Edinburgh's Telford College 350 West Granton Road, Edinburgh, Scotland EH5 1QE. Tel 0131 559 4000; www.ed-coll.ac.uk

European Business School Inner Circle, Regent's Park, London, England NW1 4NS. Tel 020 7487 7505; www.ebslondon.ac.uk

Exeter College Hele Road, Exeter, Devon, England EX4 4JS. Tel 0845 111 6000; www.exe-coll.ac.uk

Fareham College Bishopsfield Road, Fareham, Hampshire, England PO14 1NH. Tel 01329 815200; www.fareham.ac.uk

Farnborough College of Technology Boundary Road, Farnborough, Hampshire, England GU14 6SB. Tel 01252 407040; www.farn-ct.ac.uk

Filton College Filton Avenue, Filton, Bristol, England BS34 7AT. Tel 0117 909 2297; www.filton.ac.uk

Forth Valley College Falkirk Campus, Grangemouth Road, Falkirk, Scotland FK2 9AD. Tel 01324 403000; www.forthvalley.ac.uk

Furness College Channelside, Barrow-in-Furness, Cumbria, England LA14 2PJ. Tel 01229 825017; www.furness.ac.uk

Gateshead College Baltic Campus, Baltic Business Quarter, Quarryfield Road, Gateshead, England NE8 3BE. Tel 0191 490 2246; www.gateshead.ac.uk

Glasgow College of Nautical Studies 21 Thistle Street, Glasgow, Scotland G5 9XB. Tel 0141 565 2500; www.glasgow-nautical.ac.uk

Glasgow Metropolitan College 60 North Hanover Street, Glasgow, Scotland G1 2BP. Tel 0141 566 6222; www.glasgowmet.ac.uk

Gloucestershire College (The Royal Forest of Dean College and Gloucester College have now merged.) Gloucester Campus, Llanthony Road, Gloucester, England GL2 5JQ. Tel 0845 155 2020; www.gloscol.ac.uk

Grantham College Stonebridge Road, Grantham, Lincolnshire, England NG31 9AP. Tel 01476 400200; Course Information 01476 400200; www.grantham.ac.uk

Great Yarmouth College Suffolk Road, Southtown, Great Yarmouth, Norfolk, England NR31 0ED. Tel 01493 655261; www.gyc.ac.uk

Greenwich School of Management Meridian House, Royal Hill, London, England SE10 8RD. Tel 020 8516 7800; www.greenwich-college.ac.uk

Grimsby Institute of Further and Higher Education Nuns Corner, Laceby Road, Grimsby, North East Lincolnshire, England DN34 5BQ. Tel 0800 315002; www.grimsby.ac.uk

Guildford College Stoke Park Campus, Stoke Road, Guildford, Surrey, England GU1 1EZ. Tel 01483 448500; www.guildford.ac.uk

Hackney Community College Shoreditch Campus, Falkirk Street, London, England N1 6HQ. Tel 020 7613 9123; www.tcch.ac.uk

Hadlow College Hadlow, Tonbridge, Kent, England TN11 0AL. Tel 0500 551 434; www.hadlow.ac.uk

Halesowen College Whittingham Road, Halesowen, West Midlands, England B63 3NA. Tel 0121 602 7777; www.halesowen.ac.uk

Harlow College Valizy Avenue, Harlow, Essex, England CM20 3LH. Tel 01279 868000; www.harlow-college.ac.uk

Harrow College Harrow on the Hill Campus, Lowlands Road, Harrow, Middlesex, England HA1 3AQ. Tel 020 8909 6000; www.harrow.ac.uk

Hartlepool College of Further Education Stockton Street, Hartlepool, England TS24 7NT. Tel 01429 295000; www.hartlepoolfe.ac.uk

Havering College Ardleigh Green Road, Hornchurch, Essex, England RM11 2LL. Tel 01708 455011; Course Information 01708 462 801; www.havering-college.ac.uk

Henley College Coventry Henley Road, Bell Green, Coventry, West Midlands, England CV2 1ED. Tel 024 7662 6300; www.henley-cov.ac.uk

Hereford College of Technology Folly Lane, Hereford, England HR1 1LS. Tel 0800 032 1986; www.hct.ac.uk

Hertford Regional College Ware Centre, Scotts Road, Ware, Hertfordshire, England SG12 9JF. Tel 01992 411 400; www.hrc.ac.uk

Highbury College Portsmouth Dovercourt Road, Cosham, Portsmouth, Hampshire, England PO6 2SA. Tel 023 9238 3131; www.highbury.ac.uk

Highland Theological College (UHI partner college – see Section 2) High Street, Dingwall, Scotland IV15 9HA. Tel 01349 780000; www.htc.uhi.ac.uk

Hillcroft College South Bank, Surbiton, Surrey, England KT6 6DF. Tel 020 8399 2688; www.hillcroft.ac.uk

Holborn College Woolwich Road, London, England SE7 8LN. Tel 020 7403 8080; www.holborncollege.ac.uk

Hopwood Hall College Rochdale Campus, St Mary's Gate, Rochdale, England OL12 6RY. Tel 01706 345346; www.hopwood.ac.uk

Hugh Baird College Balliol Road, Bootle, Merseyside, England L20 7EW. Tel 0151 353 4444; www.hughbaird.ac.uk

Hull College The Queen's Gardens Centre, Wilberforce Drive, Hull, England HU1 3DG. Tel 01482 598 744; www.hull-college.ac.uk

Huntingdonshire Regional College California Road, Huntingdon, England PE29 1BL. Tel 01480 379100; www.huntingdon.ac.uk

IFS School of Finance 8th Floor, Peninsular House, 36 Monument Street, London, England EC3R 8LJ. Tel 01227 829499; www.ifslearning.ac.uk

Islamic College for Advanced Studies 133 High Road, Willesden, London, England NW10 2SW. Tel 020 8451 9993; www.islamic-college.ac.uk

Isle of Wight College Medina Way, Newport, Isle of Wight, England PO30 5TA. Tel 01983 526631; www.iwcollege.ac.uk

James Watt College Finnart Street, Greenock, Scotland PA16 8HF. Tel 01475 724433; Student Information Centre 0800 587; www.jameswatt.ac.uk

Jewel and Esk College Edinburgh Campus, 24 Milton Road East, Edinburgh, Scotland EH15 2PP. Tel 0131 334 7000; Information Services 0131 334 7163; www.jec.ac.uk

K College Brook Street, Tonbridge, Kent, England TN9 2PW. Tel 0845 207 8220; www.kcollege.ac.uk

Kendal College The College of the South Lakes. Milnthorpe Road, Kendal, Cumbria, England LA9 5AY. Tel 01539 814700; www.kendal.ac.uk

Kensington College of Business Wesley House, 4 Wild Court, London, England WC2B 4AU. Tel 020 7404 6330; www.kensingtoncoll.ac.uk

Kidderminster College Market Street, Kidderminster, Worcestershire, England DY10 1LX. Tel 01562 820811; www.kidderminster.ac.uk

Kilmarnock College Holehouse Road, Kilmarnock, Strathclyde, Scotland KA3 7AT. Tel 01563 523501; www.kilmarnock.ac.uk

Kingston College Kingston Hall Road, Kingston upon Thames, Surrey, England KT1 2AQ. Tel 020 8546 2151; www.kingston-college.ac.uk

Kingston Maurward College Kingston Maurward, Dorchester, Dorset, England DT2 8PY. Tel 01305 215000; Course Enquiries 01305 215032/215025; www.kmc.ac.uk

Kirklees College (Formerly Dewsbury College) New North Road, Huddersfield, West Yorkshire, England HD1 5NN. Tel 01484 437000; www.kirkleescollege.ac.uk

Knowsley Community College Kirkby Campus, Cherryfield Drive, Kirkby, Merseyside, England L32 8SF. Tel 08451 551055; www.knowsleycollege.ac.uk

Lakes College, West Cumbria Hallwood Road, Lillyhall Business Park, Workington, Cumbria, England CA14 4JN. Tel 01946 839300; www.lcwc.ac.uk

Lambeth College 45 Clapham Common South Side, London, England SW4 9BL. Tel 020 7501 5010; Course Information 020 7501 5000; www.lambethcollege.ac.uk

Lancaster and Morecambe College Morecambe Road, Lancaster, England LA1 2TY. Tel 01524 66215; www.lmc.ac.uk

Langside College 50 Prospecthill Road, Glasgow, Scotland G42 9LB. Tel 0141 272 3600; www.langside.ac.uk

Lansdowne College 40–44 Bark Place, London, England W2 4AT. Tel 020 7616 4400; www.lansdownecollege.com

Leeds City College Thomas Danby Campus, Roundhay Road, Leeds, West Yorkshire, England LS7 3BG. Tel 0113 249 4912; www.leedscitycollege.ac.uk

Leeds College of Building North Street, Leeds, West Yorkshire, England LS2 7QT. Tel 0113 222 6000; Student Services 0113 222 6000; www.lcb.ac.uk

Leek College Stockwell Street, Leek, Staffordshire, England ST13 6DP. Tel 01538 398866; www.leek.ac.uk

Leicester College Freemen's Park Campus, Aylestone Road, Leicester, England LE2 7LW. Tel 0116 224 2240; www.leicestercollege.ac.uk

Leo Baeck College The Sternberg Centre, 80 East End Road, London, England N3 2SY. Tel 020 8349 5600; www.lbc.ac.uk

Lewisham College Lewisham Way, London, England SE4 1UT. Tel 020 8692 0353/0800 834545; www.lewisham.ac.uk

Lews Castle College Colaisde A' Chaisteil; (UHI partner college – see Section 2) Castle Grounds, Stornoway, Isle of Lewis, Scotland HS2 0XR. Tel 01851 770000; www.lews.uhi.ac.uk

Lincoln College Monks Road, Lincoln, Lincolnshire, England LN2 5HQ. Tel 01522 876000; www.lincolncollege.ac.uk

Liverpool Community College Bankfield Road, Liverpool, Merseyside, England L13 0BQ. Tel 0151 252 1515; www.liv-coll.ac.uk

London College of Business and Computing Millennium Place, 206 Cambridge Heath Road, London, England E2 9NQ. Tel 020 8983 4193; www.lcbc.com

London School of Commerce Chaucer House, White Hart Yard, London, England SE1 1NX. Tel 020 7357 0077; www.lsclondon.co.uk

Loughborough College Radmoor Road, Loughborough, Leicestershire, England LE11 3BT. Tel 0845 166 2950; www.loucoll.ac.uk

Macclesfield College Park Lane, Macclesfield, Cheshire, England SK11 8LF. Tel 01625 410000; Information/Enrolment 01625 410001; www.macclesfield.ac.uk

Merton College Morden Park, London Road, Morden, Surrey, England SM4 5QX. Tel 020 8408 6500; www.merton.ac.uk

Mid-Cheshire College Hartford Campus, Chester Road, Northwich, Cheshire, England CW8 1LJ. Tel 01606 74444; www.midchesh.ac.uk

Mid-Kent College Chatham Maritime Campus, Medway Building, Horsted Centre, Chatham, Kent, England ME4 4AG. Tel 01634 888800; www.midkent.ac.uk

Middlesbrough College Dock Street, Middlesbrough, North Yorkshire, England TS2 1AD. Tel 01642 333333; Course Information 01642 296600; www.mibro.ac.uk

Milton Keynes College Wroughton Campus, Chaffron Way Campus, Leadenhall, Milton Keynes, Buckinghamshire, England MK6 5LP. Tel 01908 684444; www.mkcollege.ac.uk

Moray College (UHI partner college – see Section 2) Moray Street, Elgin, County of Moray, Scotland IV30 1JJ. Tel 01343 576216; www.moray.ac.uk

Moulton College West Street, Moulton, Northampton, England NN3 7RR. Tel 01604 491131; www.moulton.ac.uk

Nazarene Theological College Dene Road, Didsbury, Manchester, Greater Manchester, England M20 2GU. Tel 0161 445 3063; www.nazarene.ac.uk

Neath Port Talbot College Dwr-y-Felin Road, Neath, Wales SA10 7RF. Tel 01639 648000; www.nptc.ac.uk

Nelson and Colne College Reedyford Site, Scotland Road, Nelson, Lancashire, England BB9 7YT. Tel 01282 440200; www.nelson.ac.uk

Nescot, North East Surrey College of Technology Reigate Road, Ewell, Epsom, Surrey, England KT17 3DS. Tel 020 8394 3038; www.nescot.ac.uk

NEW College (North East Worcestershire College) Redditch Campus, Peakman Street, Redditch, Worcestershire, England B98 8DW. Tel 01527 570020; www.ne-worcs.ac.uk

New College Durham Framwellgate Moor Campus, Durham, England DH1 5ES. Tel 0191 375 4000; www.newcollegedurham.ac.uk

New College Nottingham The Adams Building, Stoney Street, Nottingham, Nottinghamshire, England NG1 1NG. Tel 01159 100100; www.ncn.ac.uk

New College Stamford Drift Road, Stamford, Lincolnshire, England PE9 1XA. Tel 01780 484300; www.stamford.ac.uk

New College Swindon New College Drive, Swindon, Wiltshire, England SN3 1AH. Tel 01793 611 470; www.newcollege.ac.uk

New College Telford King Street, Wellington, Telford, Shropshire, England TF1 1NY. Tel 01952 641892; www.newcollegetelford.ac.uk

Newbury College Monks Lane, Newbury, Berkshire, England RG14 7TD. Tel 01635 845000; www.newbury-college.ac.uk

Newcastle College Rye Hill Campus, Scotswood Road, Newcastle-upon-Tyne, Tyne and Wear, England NE4 7SA. Tel 0191 200 4000; www.ncl-coll.ac.uk

Newcastle-under-Lyme College Knutton Lane, Newcastle-under-Lyme, Staffordshire, England ST5 2GB. Tel 01782 715 111; www.nulc.ac.uk

Newham College of Further Education East Ham Campus, High Street South, London, England E6 6ER. Tel 020 8257 4000; www.newham.ac.uk

North Atlantic Fisheries College (UHI partner college – see Section 2) NAFC Marine Centre, Port Arthur, Scalloway, Shetland, Scotland ZE1 0UN. Tel 01595 772000; www.nafc.ac.uk

North Glasgow College 123 Flemington Street, Springburn, Glasgow, Scotland G21 4TD. Tel 0141 630 5000; www.northglasgowcollege.ac.uk

North Hertfordshire College Monkswood Way, Stevenage, Hertfordshire, England SG1 1LA. Tel 01462 424242; Courses 01462 424242; www.nhc.ac.uk

North Highland College (UHI partner college – see Section 2) Ormlie Road, Thurso, Caithness, Scotland KW14 7EE. Tel 01847 889000; www.northhighland.ac.uk

North Lindsey College Kingsway, Scunthorpe, North Lincolnshire, England DN17 1AJ. Tel 01724 281111; www.northlindsey.ac.uk

North Nottinghamshire College Carlton Road, Worksop, Nottinghamshire, England S81 7HP. Tel 01909 504504; Student Services 01909 504500; www.nnotts-col.ac.uk

North Trafford College (See Trafford College below) Talbot Road, Stretford, Greater Manchester, England M32 0XH. Tel 01618 867070; www.trafford.ac.uk

North Warwickshire and Hinckley College Nuneaton Campus, Hinckley Road, Nuneaton, Warwickshire, England CV11 6BH. Tel 024 7624 3000; www.nwhc.ac.uk

North West Kent College Oakfield Lane, Dartford, Kent, England DA1 2JT. Tel 01322 629400; www.nwkcollege.ac.uk

Northampton College Booth Lane, Northampton, Northamptonshire, England NN3 3RF. Tel 01604 734567; www.northamptoncollege.ac.uk

Northbrook College, Sussex West Durrington Campus, Littlehampton Road, Worthing, West Sussex, England BN12 6NU. Tel 08451 556060; www.northbrook.ac.uk

Northern Regional College (Formerly North East Institute of Further and Higher Education) Ballymena Campus, Trostan Avenue Building, Ballymena, Co Antrim, Northern Ireland BT43 7BN. Tel 028 2563 6221; www.nrc.ac.uk

Northumberland College College Road, Ashington, Northumberland, England NE63 9RG. Tel 01670 841200; www.northumberland.ac.uk

Norton Radstock College South Hill Park, Radstock, Somerset, England BA3 3RW. Tel 01761 433161; www.nortcoll.ac.uk

Norwich City College Ipswich Road, Norwich, Norfolk, England NR2 2LJ. Tel 01603 773 311; www.ccn. ac.uk

Oaklands College, St Albans Smallford Campus, Hatfield Road, St Albans, Hertfordshire, England AL4 0JA. Tel 01727 737080; www.oaklands.ac.uk

Oatridge College Ecclesmachan, Broxburn, West Lothian, Scotland EH52 6NH. Tel 01506 864800; www. oatridge.ac.uk

Orkney College (UHI partner college – see Section 2) East Road, Kirkwall, Orkney, Scotland KW15 1LX. Tel 01856 569000; www.orkney.uhi.ac.uk

Orpington College The Walnuts, Orpington, Kent, England BR6 0TE. Tel 01689 899700; www.orpington. ac.uk

Otley College Otley, Ipswich, Suffolk, England IP6 9EY. Tel 01473 785543; www.otleycollege.ac.uk

Oxford and Cherwell Valley College Banbury Campus, Broughton Road, Banbury, Oxford, Oxfordshire, England OX16 9QA. Tel 01865 550550; www.ocvc.ac.uk

Pembrokeshire College (Coleg Sir Benfro) Merlins Bridge, Haverfordwest, Pembrokeshire, Wales SA61 1SZ. Tel 01437 753000; Freephone 0800 716236; www.pembrokeshire.ac.uk

Perth College (UHI partner college – see Section 2) Crieff Road, Perth, Perth and Kinross, Scotland PH1 2NX. Tel 08452 701177; www.perth.ac.uk

Peterborough Regional College Park Crescent, Peterborough, Cambridgeshire, England PE1 4DZ. Tel 0845 872 8722; www.peterborough.ac.uk

Petroc (Created through the merger of North Devon College and East Devon College in 2008.) Old Sticklepath Hill, Sticklepath, Barnstaple, Devon, England EX31 2BQ. Tel 01271 345 291; www.petroc. ac.uk

Plumpton College Ditchling Road, Near Lewes, East Sussex, England BN7 3AE. Tel 01273 890454; www. plumpton.ac.uk

Portsmouth College Tangier Road, Copnor, Portsmouth, Hampshire, England PO3 6PZ. Tel 023 9266 7521; www.portsmouth-college.ac.uk

Preston College Fulwood Campus, St Vincent's Road, Preston, Lancashire, England PR1 6AS. Tel 01772 225000; www.preston.ac.uk

Redbridge College Little Heath, Barley Lane, Romford, Essex, England RM6 4XT. Tel 020 8548 7400; www.redbridge-college.ac.uk

Redcar and Cleveland College Corporation Road, Redcar, Cleveland, England TS10 1EZ. Tel 01642 473132; www.cleveland.ac.uk

Regents Business School, London Inner Circle, Regent's Park, London, England NW1 4NS. Tel 020 7487 7505; www.rbslondon.ac.uk

Reid Kerr College Admission Unit, Renfrew Road, Paisley, Renfrewshire, Scotland PA3 4DR. Tel 0141 581 2222; Course Enquiries 0800 527343; www.reidkerr.net

Richmond-upon-Thames College Egerton Road, Twickenham, Surrey, England TW2 7SJ. Tel 020 8607 8000; www.richmond-utcoll.ac.uk

Riverside College Halton Kingsway Campus, Kingsway, Widnes, Cheshire, England WA8 7QQ. Tel 0151 257 2020; www.riversidecollege.ac.uk

Rotherham College of Arts and Technology Town Centre Campus, Eastwood Lane, Rotherham, South Yorkshire, England S65 1EG. Tel 08080 722777; www.rotherham.ac.uk

Royal Forest of Dean College (See also Gloucester College) Five Acres Campus, Bury Hill, Coleford, Gloucestershire, England GL16 7JT. Tel 01594 833416; www.rfdc.ac.uk

Royal National College for the Blind College Road, Hereford, England HR1 1EB. Tel 01432 265725; www.rncb.ac.uk

Runshaw College Adult College, Euxton Lane, Chorley, Lancashire, England PR7 6AD. Tel 01772 642040; www.runshaw.ac.uk

Ruskin College Oxford Student Enquiry Office, Walton Street, Oxford, England OX1 2HE. Tel 01865 554331; www.ruskin.ac.uk

Sabhal Mor Ostaig (UHI partner college – see Section 2) ACC, Sleat, Isle of Skye, Scotland IV44 8RQ. Tel 01471 888 304; www.smo.uhi.ac.uk

St Helens College Water Street, St Helens, Merseyside, England WA10 1PP. Tel 01744 733766; www.sthelens.ac.uk

Salford College Worsley Campus, Walkden Road, Worsley, England M28 7QD. Tel 0161 702 8272; Central Admissions 0161 211 5001; www.salford-col.ac.uk

Sandwell College Central Enquiries, Oldbury Campus, Pound Road, Oldbury, West Midlands, England B68 8NA. Tel 0800 622006; www.sandwell.ac.uk

School of Audio Engineering Institute SAE Institute Head Office, Littlemore Park, Armstrong Road, Oxford, England OX 4FY. Tel 01865 787 150; www.sae.edu

Scottish Association for Marine Science (UHI partner college – see Section 2) Dunstaffnage Marine Laboratory, Oban, Argyll, Scotland PA37 1QA. Tel 01631 559000; www.sams.ac.uk

Selby College Abbot's Road, Selby, North Yorkshire, England YO8 8AT. Tel 01757 211000; www.selby.ac.uk

Sheffield College PO Box 345, Sheffield, England S2 2YY. Tel 0114 260 2600; www.sheffcol.ac.uk

Shetland College (UHI partner college – see Section 2) Gremista, Lerwick, Shetland, Scotland ZE1 0PX. Tel 01595 771000; www.shetland.uhi.ac.uk

Shrewsbury College of Arts and Technology London Road, Shrewsbury, Shropshire, England SY2 6PR. Tel 01743 342342; www.shrewsbury.ac.uk

Shuttleworth College Old Warden Park, Biggleswade, Bedfordshire, England SG18 9DX. Tel 01767 626222; www.shuttleworth.ac.uk

Skelmersdale and Ormskirk Colleges Westbank Campus, Yewdale, Skelmersdale, Lancashire, England WN8 6JA. Tel 01695 52300; www.skelmersdale.ac.uk

Solihull College Blossomfield Road, Solihull, West Midlands, England B91 1SB. Tel 0121 678 7000; www.solihull.ac.uk

Somerset College of Arts and Technology Wellington Road, Taunton, Somerset, England TA1 5AX. Tel 01823 366366; www.somerset.ac.uk

South Birmingham College Digbeth Campus, High Street, Deritend, Digbeth, Birmingham, West Midlands, England B5 5SU. Tel 0121 694 5000; www.sbirmc.ac.uk

South Cheshire College Dane Bank Avenue, Crewe, Cheshire, England CW2 8AB. Tel 01270 654654; www.s-cheshire.ac.uk

South Devon College Vantage Point, Long Road, Paignton, Devon, England TQ2 7EJ. Tel 01803 540505; www.southdevon.ac.uk

South Downs College College Road, Waterlooville, Hampshire, England PO7 8AA. Tel 023 9279 7979; www.southdowns.ac.uk

South Essex College (Formerly South East Essex College; merged Jan 2010 with Thurrock and Basildon College) Luker Road, Southend-on-Sea, Essex, England SS1 1ND. Tel 01702 220400; www.southessex. ac.uk

South Kent College (Formerly South Kent College and West Kent College) Brook Street, Tonbridge, Kent, England TN9 2WP. Tel 0845 207 8220; www.kcollege.ac.uk

South Lanarkshire College College Way, East Kilbride, Scotland G75 0NE. Tel Student Admissions 01355 807780; www.south-lanarkshire-college.ac.uk

South Leicestershire College Station Road, Wigston, Leicestershire, England LE18 2DW. Tel 0116 264 3555; www.slcollege.ac.uk

South Nottingham College West Bridgford Centre, Greythorne Drive, West Bridgford, Nottingham, England NG2 7GA. Tel 0115 914 6400; www.snc.ac.uk

South Staffordshire College Cannock Campus, The Green, Cannock, Staffordshire, England WS11 1UE. Tel 0300 456 2424; www.southstaffs.ac.uk

South Thames College Wandsworth High Street, London, England SW18 2PP. Tel Course Enquiries 020 8918 7777; www.south-thames.ac.uk

South Tyneside College St George's Avenue, South Shields, Tyne and Wear, England NE34 6ET. Tel 0191 427 3500; www.stc.ac.uk

Southampton City College St Mary Street, Southampton, Hampshire, England SO14 1AR. Tel 023 8048 4848; www.southampton-city.ac.uk

Southern Regional College (Formerly Upper Bann Institute) Portadown Campus, 36 Lurgan Road, Portadown, Armagh, Northern Ireland BT63 5BL. Tel 028 3839 7777; www.src.ac.uk

Southgate College High Street, Southgate, London, England N14 6BS. Tel 020 8982 5050; www. southgate.ac.uk

Southport College Mornington Road, Southport, Merseyside, England PR9 0TT. Tel 01704 392704; www. southport.ac.uk

Southwark College Waterloo Centre, The Cut, London, England SE1 8LE. Tel 020 7815 1500; www. southwark.ac.uk

Stafford College Earl Street, Stafford, England ST16 2QR. Tel 01785 223 800; www.staffordcoll.ac.uk

Staffordshire University Regional Federation Partnerships Office, BL166, Blackheath Lane, Stafford, Staffordshire, England ST18 0AD. Tel 01782 294000; www.staffs.ac.uk

Stephenson College Thornborough Road, Coalville, Leicestershire, England LE67 3TN. Tel 01530 836136; www.stephensoncoll.ac.uk

Stevenson College Edinburgh Bankhead Avenue, Edinburgh, Lothian, Scotland EH11 4DE. Tel 0131 535 4600; Course Enquiries 0131 535 4700; www.stevenson.ac.uk

Stockport College Town Centre Campus, Wellington Road South, Stockport, Greater Manchester, England SK1 3UQ. Tel 0161 958 3100; www.stockport.ac.uk

Stockton Riverside College Harvard Avenue, Stockton-On-Tees, England TS17 6FB. Tel 01642 865 400; www.stockton.ac.uk

Stoke on Trent College Cauldon Campus, Stoke Road, Shelton, Stoke on Trent, Staffordshire, England ST4 2DG. Tel 01782 208208; www.stokecoll.ac.uk

Stourbridge College Hagley Road Centre, Hagley Road, Stourbridge, West Midlands, England DY8 1QU. Tel 01384 344344; www.stourbridge.ac.uk

Stow College 43 Shamrock Street, Glasgow, Scotland G4 9LD. Tel 0844 249 8585; www.stow.ac.uk

Stratford-upon-Avon College The Willows North, Alcester Road, Stratford-upon-Avon, Warwickshire, England CV37 9QR. Tel 01789 266245; www.stratford.ac.uk

Strode College Church Road, Street, Somerset, England BA16 0AB. Tel 01458 844400; www.strode-college.ac.uk

Strode's College High Street, Egham, Surrey, England TW20 9DR. Tel 01784 437506; www.strodes.ac.uk

Stroud College Stratford Road, Stroud, Gloucestershire, England GL5 4AH. Tel 01453 763424; www.stroud.ac.uk

Sussex Coast College Hastings (Formerly Hastings College of Art and Technology) Station Plaza Campus, Station Approach, Hastings, East Sussex, England TN34 1BA. Tel 01424 442222; www.hastings.ac.uk

Sussex Downs College Cross Levels Way, Eastbourne, East Sussex, England BN21 2UF. Tel 01323 637637; www.sussexdowns.ac.uk

Sutton Coldfield College (Now part of Birmingham Metropolitan College) Lichfield Road, Sutton Coldfield, West Midlands, England B74 2NW. Tel 0121 355 5671; www.bmetc.ac.uk

Swansea College Coleg Abertawe, Tycoch, Swansea, Wales SA2 9EB. Tel 01792 284000; www.swancoll.ac.uk

Swindon College North Star Campus, North Star Avenue, Swindon, Wiltshire, England SN2 1DY. Tel 0800 731 2250; www.swindon-college.ac.uk

Tameside College Beaufort Road, Ashton-under-Lyne, Greater Manchester, England OL6 6NX. Tel 0161 908 6789; www.tameside.ac.uk

Telford College of Arts and Technology Haybridge Road, Wellington, Telford, Shropshire, England TF1 2NP. Tel 01952 642237; Student Services 01952 642237; www.tcat.ac.uk

Thanet College Ramsgate Road, Broadstairs, Kent, England CT10 1PN. Tel 01843 605040; Admissions 01843 605049; www.thanet.ac.uk

The London College UCK Kensington Campus, Victoria Gardens, London, England W11 3PE. Tel 020 7243 4000; www.lcuck.ac.uk

The Manchester College (Formerly Manchester College of Art and Technology and City College Manchester) Whitworth Street, Manchester, England M11 2WH. Tel 0800 068 8585; www.themanchestercollege.ac.uk

The Oldham College Rochdale Road, Oldham, Greater Manchester, England OL9 6AA. Tel 0161 785 4000; www.oldham.ac.uk

Totton College Calmore Road, Totton, Hampshire, England SO40 3ZX. Tel 023 8087 4874; www.totton.ac.uk

Trafford College Talbot Road, Stretford, Manchester, England M32 0XH. Tel 0161 886 7000; www.trafford.ac.uk

Tresham College of Further and Higher Education Kettering Campus, Windmill Avenue, Kettering, Northamptonshire, England NN15 6ER. Tel 0845 658 8990; www.tresham.ac.uk

Truro College College Road, Truro, Cornwall, England TR1 3XX. Tel General Enquiries 01872 267000; www.trurocollege.ac.uk

Tyne Metropolitan College Embleton Avenue, Wallsend, Tyne and Wear, England NE28 9NJ. Tel 0191 229 5000; www.tynemet.ac.uk

Uxbridge College Park Road, Uxbridge, Middlesex, England UB8 1NQ. Tel 01895 853333; www.uxbridge.ac.uk

Wakefield College Margaret Street, Wakefield, West Yorkshire, England WF1 2DH. Tel 01924 789111; www.wakefield.ac.uk

Walford and North Shropshire College Oswestry Campus, Shrewsbury Road, Oswestry, Shropshire, England SY11 4QB. Tel 01691 688000; www.wnsc.ac.uk

Walsall College Wisemore Campus, Littleton Street West, Walsall, West Midlands, England WS2 8ES. Tel 01922 657000; www.walsallcollege.ac.uk

Waltham Forest College 707 Forest Road, London, England E17 4JB. Tel 020 8501 8501; www.waltham.ac.uk

Warrington Collegiate Winwick Road, Warrington, Cheshire, England WA2 8QA. Tel 01925 494494; www.warrington.ac.uk

Warwickshire College Leamington Centre, Warwick New Road, Leamington Spa, Warwickshire, England CV32 5JE. Tel 01926 318000; www.warkscol.ac.uk

West Cheshire College Chester Campus, Eaton Road, Handbridge, Chester, Cheshire, England CH4 7ER. Tel 0151 356 7800; www.west-cheshire.ac.uk

West Herts College Watford Campus, Hempstead Road, Watford, Hertfordshire, England WD17 3EZ. Tel 01923 812000; www.westherts.ac.uk

West Highland College (Formed from a merger between Lochaber and Skye and Wester Ross College; UHI partner college – see Section 2) An Aird, Fort William, Inverness-shire, Scotland PH33 6AN. Tel 01379 874000; www.lochaber.uhi.ac.uk

West Lothian College Almondvale Crescent, Livingston, West Lothian, Scotland EH54 7EP. Tel 01506 418181; Information 01506 427605; www.west-lothian.ac.uk

West Nottinghamshire College Derby Road, Mansfield, Nottinghamshire, England NG18 5BH. Tel 01623 627191; HE Enquiries 01623 413639/0800 100 3; www.wnc.ac.uk

West Suffolk College Out Risbygate, Bury St Edmunds, Suffolk, England IP33 3RL. Tel 01284 701301; www.westsuffolk.ac.uk

West Thames College London Road, Isleworth, Middlesex, England TW7 4HS. Tel 020 8326 2000; www.west-thames.ac.uk

Westminster Kingsway College St James's Park Centre, Castle Lane, London, England SW1E 6DR. Tel Information 08700 609800; www.westking.ac.uk

Weston College Knightstone Campus Weston College, Knightstone Road, Weston-super-Mare, Somerset, England BS23 2AL. Tel 01934 411411; www.weston.ac.uk

Weymouth College Cranford Avenue, Weymouth, Dorset, England DT4 7LQ. Tel 01305 761100; Course Applications 0870 060 9800/1; www.weymouth.ac.uk

Wigan and Leigh College Parsons Walk, Wigan, Greater Manchester, England WN1 1RU. Tel 01942 761111; www.wigan-leigh.ac.uk

Wiltshire College Chippenham Campus, Cocklebury Road, Chippenham, Wiltshire, England SN15 3QD. Tel 01249 464644; www.wiltshire.ac.uk

Wirral Metropolitan College Conway Park Campus, Europa Boulevard, Conway Park, Birkenhead, Merseyside, England CH41 4NT. Tel 0151 551 7777; www.wmc.ac.uk

Worcester College of Technology Deansway, Worcester, Wocestershire, England WR1 2JF. Tel 01905 725555; www.wortech.ac.uk

Yeovil College Mudford Road, Yeovil, Somerset, England BA21 4DR. Tel 01935 423921; www.yeovil.ac.uk

York College Sim Balk Lane, York, North Yorkshire, England YO23 2BB. Tel 01904 770400; www.yorkcollege.ac.uk

Yorkshire Coast College Lady Edith's Drive, Scarborough, North Yorkshire, England YO12 5RN. Tel 01723 372105; www.yorkshirecoastcollege.ac.uk

Universities in the UK accept a range of international qualifications and those which normally satisfy the minimum general entrance requirements are listed below. However, the specific levels of achievement or grades required for entry to degree courses with international qualifications will vary, depending on the popularity of the university or college and the chosen degree programme. The subject tables in **Chapter 8** provide a guide to the levels of entry to courses although direct comparisons between A-level grades and international qualifications are not always possible except for the three European examinations listed at the end of this Appendix. Students not holding the required qualifications should consider taking an International Foundation course.

International students whose mother tongue is not English and/or who have not studied for their secondary education in English will be required to pass an English test such as IELTS (International English Language Testing System) or TOEFL (the Test of English as a Foreign Language). Entry requirements vary between universities and courses. For the IELTS, scores can range from 5.5 to 7.5, for the TOEFL computer-based test scores can range from a minimum of 213, and for the TOEFL written test the minimum entry score is 5.0 (see www.ielts.org and www.ets.org/toefl).

Algeria Baccalaureate de l'Enseignement Secondaire
Argentina Completion of Year One of Licenciado/Professional Title
Australia Completion of Year 12 certificates
Austria Reifazeugnis/Maturazeugnis
Bahrain Two-year diploma or associate degree
Bangladesh Bachelor of Arts, Science and Commerce
Belgium Certificat d'Enseignement Secondaire Superieur
Bermuda Diploma of Arts and Science
Bosnia-Herzegovina Secondary School Leaving Diploma
Brazil Completion of Ensino Medio and a good pass in the Vestibular
Brunei Brunei GCE A-level
Bulgaria Diploma za Zavarshino Sredno Obrazovanie (Diploma of Completed Secondary Education)
Canada Completion of Grade 12 secondary/high school certificate or equivalent
Chile Completion of secondary education and a good pass in the Prueba de Seleccion Universitaria (formally Prueba de Conocimientos Especificos)
China Completion of one year of a Bachelor degree from a recognised university with good grades
Croatia Matura (Secondary school leaving diploma)
Cyprus Apolytirion/Lise Bitirme Diploma with good grades
Czech Republic Vysvedceni o Maturitni Zkousce/Maturita
Denmark Studentereksamen (HF), (HHX), (HTX)
Egypt Completion of year one of a Bachelor degree or two-year Diploma
Finland Ylioppilastutkinoto/Studentexamen (Matriculation certificate)
France French Baccalaureate
Gambia West African Senior Secondary Certificate Exam (WASSCE) Advanced Level
Georgia Successful completion of Year One of a Bachelor degree
Germany Abitur
Ghana West African Senior Secondary Certificate Exam (WASSCE)/A-levels
Greece Apolytirion of Eniaio Lykeio (previously Apolytirion of Lykeio)
Hong Kong A-levels/ HKALE
Hungary Erettsegi/Matura
Iceland Studentsprof

India High grades from Standard XII School Leaving examinations from certain examination boards
Ireland Irish Leaving Certificate Higher Level
Israel Bagrut
Italy Diploma Conseguito con l'Esame di Stato (formerly the Diploma di Matura) with good grades
Japan Upper Secondary School leaving diploma/Kotogakko Sotsugyo Shomeisho plus foundation year
Kenya Cambridge Overseas Higher School Certificate
Lebanon Lebanese Baccalaureate plus foundation year
Malaysia Sijil Tinggi Persekolahan Malaysia (STPM, Malaysia Higher School Certificate)
Mauritius Cambridge Overseas Higher School Certificate or A-levels
Mexico Bachillerato plus foundation year
Netherlands Voorbereidend Wetenschappelijk Onderwijs (VWO)
Nigeria Successful completion of year one of a Bachelor degree
Norway Diploma of a completed 3-year course of upper secondary education
Pakistan Bachelor degree
Poland Matura/Swiadectwo Dojrzalosci
Portugal Diploma de Ensino Secundario
Russian Federation Diploma of completed Specialised Secondary Education or successful completion of first year of Bakalav
Saudi Arabia Successful completion of first year of a Bachelor degree
Serbia and Montenegro Matura
Singapore Polytechnic Diploma or A-levels
South Korea Junior College Diploma
Spain Curso de Orientacion Universitaria (COU) with good grades
Sri Lanka A-levels
Sweden Fullstandigt Slutbetyg fran Gymnasieskolan
Taiwan Senior High school Diploma
Thailand Successful completion of year one of a Bachelor degree
Turkey Devlet Lise Diplomasi (State High School Diploma) with good grades
Uganda Uganda Advanced Certificate of Education (UACE) or East African Advanced Certificate of Education
Ukraine Successful completion of year one of Bakakavre
USA Good grades from the High School Graduation Diploma with SAT and/or APT

COMPARISONS BETWEEN A-LEVEL GRADES AND THE FOLLOWING EUROPEAN EXAMINATIONS

A-level grades	AAA	AAB	ABB	BBB	BBC	BCC
European Baccalaureate	85%	80%	75%	70%	65%	60%
French Baccalaureate	16 Bien	15 Bien	14 Bien	13 Assez Bien	12 Assez Bien	11 Assez Bien
German Abitur	1.0–1.2	1.3–1.4	1.5–1.8	1.9–2.1	2.2–2.4	2.5–2.7

APPENDIX 3
CAMBRIDGE PRE-U

Cambridge Pre-U is a new post-16 qualification developed by the University of Cambridge International Examinations (CIE). It aims to prepare students from across the world with the skills and knowledge required to make a success of their subsequent studies at university. Representatives from higher education have been involved in writing the syllabi and universities have shown great interest in the qualification.

Students can take individual Cambridge Pre-U subjects and build them up into a portfolio that suits their interests and ambitions. The structure of each Cambridge Pre-U syllabus is linear, and this differentiates it from AS- and A-levels. All the assessment takes place at the end of the two-year course. Students can take a Cambridge Pre-U subject at Subsidiary level (in other words after one year) although the result would not count towards the full (Principal) qualification. Twenty-four syllabi are now available: Mathematics, Further Mathematics, Economics, Chemistry, Physics, Biology, English, History, Geography, Business Studies, German, French, Spanish, Classical Heritage, Mandarin Chinese, Art History, Sport Science, Greek, Latin, Art and Design, Comparative Government and Politics, Psychology, Music, and Philosophy and Ethics.

Results for individual subjects are decided on a scale of 1 to 10, with a separate grade for the full Diploma. For the full Cambridge Pre-U Diploma students will offer at least three Principal subjects (some will want to offer more). The distinguishing feature is that students will have complete freedom of choice in their subjects, in other words they can specialise in, say, the natural sciences. To qualify for the full Diploma, students offer a programme that includes a core course in Global Perspectives – giving students the opportunity to engage with issues that will face every young person, wherever in the world they live and work.

While the highest grade, D1, has not been allocated a UCAS Tariff points value (at the time of this book going to press), the second highest grade (D2) in a Pre-U Principal subject is valued at 145 UCAS Tariff points compared to 140 points for the new A-level A* grade and 120 points for an A-level grade A. See the Cambridge Pre-U UCAS Tariff points table in **Appendix 1**.

Teaching of the Cambridge Pre-U started in September 2008. The first examinations took place in 2010. You can find out more about Cambridge Pre-U at www.cie.org.uk/qualifications/academic/uppersec/preu and if you are planning to apply for university in 2011/12, find out from prospectuses and websites their admissions information for Cambridge Pre-U applicants.

APPENDIX 4
PROFESSIONAL ASSOCIATIONS

Professional associations vary in size and function and many offer examinations to provide members with vocational qualifications. However, many of the larger bodies do not conduct examinations but accept evidence provided by the satisfactory completion of appropriate degree and diploma courses. When applying for courses in vocational subjects, therefore, it is important to check whether your chosen course is accredited by a professional association, since membership of such bodies is usually necessary for progression in your chosen career after graduation.

Information about careers, which you can use as background information for your UCAS application, can be obtained from the organisations below listed under the subject table headings used in **Chapter 8**. Full details of professional associations, their examinations and the degree courses accredited by them are published in *British Qualifications* (see **Appendix 5**).

Some additional organisations that can provide useful careers-related information are listed below under the subject table headings and other sources of relevant information are indicated in the subject tables of **Chapter 8** and in **Appendix 5**.

Accountancy/Accounting
Association of Accounting Technicians www.aat.org.uk
Association of Chartered Certified Accountants www.accaglobal.com
Association of International Accountants www.aiaworldwide.com
Chartered Institute of Management Accountants www.cimaglobal.com
Chartered Institute of Public Finance and Accountancy www.cipfa.org.uk
Chartered Institute of Taxation www.tax.org.uk
Institute of Accounting Technicians in Ireland www.accountingtechniciansireland.ie
Institute of Chartered Accountants in England and Wales www.icaew.com
Institute of Chartered Accountants in Ireland www.charteredaccountants.ie
Institute of Chartered Accountants of Scotland www.icas.org.uk
Institute of Financial Accountants www.ifa.org.uk
Institute of Internal Auditors www.iia.org.uk

Actuarial Science/Studies
Institute and Faculty of Actuaries www.actuaries.org.uk

Agricultural Sciences/Agriculture
Royal Agricultural Society of England www.rase.org.uk

Animal Sciences
British Horse Society www.bhs.org.uk
British Society of Animal Science www.bsas.org.uk

Anthropology
Association of Social Anthropologists of the UK and Commonwealth www.theasa.org
Royal Anthropological Institute www.therai.org.uk

Archaeology
Council for British Archaeology www.britarch.ac.uk
Institute of Field Archaeologists www.archaeologists.net

Architecture
Chartered Institute of Architectural Technologists www.ciat.org.uk
Royal Incorporation of Architects in Scotland www.rias.org.uk
Royal Institute of British Architects www.architecture.com

Art and Design
Arts Council England www.arts.org.uk
Association of Illustrators www.theaoi.com
Association of Photographers www.the-aop.org
British Association of Art Therapists www.baat.org
British Association of Paintings Conservator-Restorers www.bapcr.org.uk
British Institute of Professional Photography www.bipp.com
Chartered Society of Designers www.csd.org.uk
Crafts Council www.craftscouncil.org.uk
Design Council www.designcouncil.org.uk
Institute of Professional Goldsmiths www.ipgold.org.uk
National Society for Education in Art and Design www.nsead.org
Institue of Conservation www.icon.org.uk
Royal British Society of Sculptors www.rbs.org.uk
Scottish Arts Council www.creativescotland.com
Textile Institute www.texi.org

Astronomy/Astrophysics
Royal Astronomical Society www.ras.org.uk

Biochemistry (see also Chemistry)
Association of Clinical Biochemistry www.acb.org.uk
Biochemical Society www.biochemistry.org
British Society for Immunology http://bsi.immunology.org

Biological Sciences/Biology
British Society for Human Genetics www.bshg.org.uk
Genetics Society www.genetics.org.uk
Institute of Biomedical Science www.ibms.org
Society of Biology www.societyofbiology.org

Building
Chartered Institute of Building www.ciob.org.uk
Chartered Institution of Building Services Engineers www.cibse.org
Construction Industry Training Board (CITB) www.cskills.org

Business Courses
Chartered Institute of Personnel and Development www.cipd.co.uk
Chartered Institute of Public Relations www.cipr.co.uk
Chartered Management Institute www.managers.org.uk
Communication, Advertising and Marketing Education Foundation (CAM Foundation)
    www.camfoundation.com
Council for Administration www.cfa.uk.com
Department for Business, Innovation, and Skills www.bis.gov.uk
Institute of Administrative Management www.instam.org
Institute of Business Consulting www.ibconsulting.org.uk
Institute of Chartered Secretaries and Administrators www.icsa.org.uk
Institute of Export www.export.org.uk
Institute of Practitioners in Advertising www.ipa.co.uk
Institute of Sales and Marketing Management www.ismm.co.uk

Chemistry
Institute of Nanotechnology www.nano.org.uk
Royal Society of Chemistry www.rsc.org

Computer Courses
BCS The Chartered Institute for IT www.bcs.org
Institute for the Management of Information Systems www.imis.org.uk
Institute of Information Technology Training www.iitt.org.uk
Institution of Analysts and Programmers www.iap.org.uk

Consumer Studies/Sciences
Institute of Consumer Sciences (incorporating Home Economics) www.scenta.co.uk
Trading Standards Institute www.tradingstandards.gov.uk

Dance
Council for Dance Education and Training www.cdet.org.uk

Dentistry
British Association of Dental Nurses www.badn.org.uk
British Association of Dental Therapists www.badt.org.uk
British Dental Association www.bda.org
British Dental Hygienists' Association www.bdha.org.uk
Dental Laboratories Association www.dla.org.uk
Dental Technicians Association www.dta-uk.org
General Dental Council www.gdc-uk.org

Dietetics
British Dietetic Association www.bda.uk.com

Drama
Equity www.equity.org.uk
National Council for Drama Training www.ncdt.co.uk
Society of British Theatre Designers www.theatredesign.org.uk

Economics
Royal Economic Society www.res.org.uk

Education and Teacher Training
Department for Education www.education.gov.uk
General Teaching Council for England www.gtce.org.uk
General Teaching Council for Northern Ireland www.gtcni.org.uk
General Teaching Council for Scotland www.gtcs.org.uk
General Teaching Council for Wales www.gtcw.org.uk
Training and Development Agency for Schools www.tda.gov.uk

Engineering/Engineering Sciences
Energy Institute www.energyinst.org.uk
Engineering Council UK www.engc.org.uk
Institute for Manufacturing www.ifm.eng.cam.ac.uk
Institute of Acoustics www.ioa.org.uk
Institute of Marine Engineering, Science and Technology www.imarest.org
Institution of Agricultural Engineers www.iagre.org
Institution of Civil Engineers www.ice.org.uk
Institution of Engineering Designers www.ied.org.uk
Institution of Engineering and Technology www.theiet.org

Institution of Mechanical Engineers www.imeche.org
Nuclear Institute www.nuclearinst.com
Royal Aeronautical Society www.raes.org.uk

Environmental Science/Studies
Chartered Institute of Environmental Health www.cieh.org
Chartered Institution of Wastes Management www.ciwm.co.uk
Chartered Institution of Water and Environmental Management www.ciwem.org
Environment Agency www.environment-agency.gov.uk
Institute of Ecology and Environmental Management www.ieem.net
Institution of Environmental Sciences www.ies-uk.org.uk
Institution of Occupational Safety and Health www.iosh.co.uk
Royal Environmental Health Institute of Scotland www.rehis.org
Society for the Environment www.socenv.org.uk

Film, Radio, Video and TV Studies
British Film Institute www.bfi.org.uk
Skillset (National Training Organisation for broadcast, film, video and multimedia) www.skillset.org

Finance (including Banking and Insurance)
Chartered Institute of Bankers in Scotland www.charteredbanker.com
Chartered Institute of Loss Adjusters www.cila.co.uk
Chartered Insurance Institute www.cii.co.uk
Financial Services Skills Council www.fssc.org.uk
Institute of Financial Services www.ifslearning.ac.uk
Personal Finance Society www.thepfs.org
Securities and Investment Institute www.sii.co.uk

Food Science/Studies and Technology
Institute of Food Science and Technology www.ifst.org
Society of Food Hygiene and Technology www.sofht.co.uk

Forensic Science
Forensic Science Society www.forensic-science-society.org

Forestry
Institute of Chartered Foresters www.charteredforesters.org
Wood Technology Society www.iwsc.org.uk
Royal Forestry Society www.rfs.org.uk

Geography
British Cartographic Society www.cartography.org.uk
Royal Geographical Society www.rgs.org
Royal Meteorological Society www.rmets.org

Geology/Geological Sciences
Geological Society www.geolsoc.org.uk

Health Sciences/Studies
British Academy of Audiology http://theloop.netplan.co.uk
British and Irish Orthoptic Society www.orthoptics.org.uk
British Association of Prosthetists and Orthotists www.bapo.com
British Chiropractic Association www.chiropractic-uk.co.uk
British Occupational Hygiene Society www.bohs.org
British Osteopathic Association and General Osteopathic Council www.osteopathy.org.uk

Institute for Complementary and Natural Medicine www.i-c-m.org.uk
Institution of Occupational Safety and Health www.iosh.co.uk
Society of Homeopaths www.homeopathy-soh.org

History
Royal Historical Society www.rhs.ac.uk

Horticulture
Institute of Horticulture www.horticulture.org.uk

Hospitality and Hotel Management
Institute of Hospitality www.instituteofhospitality.org.
People 1st www.people1st.co.uk

Housing
Chartered Institute of Housing www.cih.org

Human Resource Management
Chartered Institute of Personnel and Development www.cipd.co.uk

Information Management
Association for Information Management www.aslib.co.uk
Chartered Institute of Library and Information Professionals www.cilip.org.uk

Landscape Architecture
Landscape Institute www.landscapeinstitute.org.uk

Languages
Chartered Institute of Linguists www.iol.org.uk
Institute of Translation and Interpreting www.iti.org.uk

Law
Bar Council www.barcouncil.org.uk
Faculty of Advocates www.advocates.org.uk
Institute of Legal Executives www.ilex.org.uk
Law Society www.lawsociety.org.uk
Law Society of Northern Ireland www.lawsoc-ni.org
Law Society of Scotland www.lawscot.org.uk

Leisure and Recreation Management/Studies
Institute for Sport, Parks and Leisure www.ispal.org.uk

Linguistics
British Association for Applied Linguistics www.baal.org.uk
Royal College of Speech and Language Therapists www.rcslt.org

Marine/Maritime Studies
Nautical Institute www.nautinst.org

Marketing
Chartered Institute of Marketing www.cim.co.uk
Institute of Sales and Marketing Management www.ismm.co.uk

Materials Science/Metallurgy
Institute of Materials, Minerals and Mining www.iom3.org

Mathematics
Council for Mathematical Sciences www.cms.ac.uk
Institute of Mathematics and its Applications www.ima.org.uk
London Mathematical Society www.lms.ac.uk
Mathematical Association www.m-a.org.uk

Media Studies
British Broadcasting Corporation www.bbc.co.uk/jobs
National Council for the Training of Journalists www.nctj.com
Skillset (National training organisation for broadcast, film, video and multimedia) www.skillset.org
Society for Editors and Proofreaders www.sfep.org.uk
Society of Authors www.societyofauthors.org

Medicine
British Medical Association www.bma.org.uk
General Medical Council www.gmc-uk.org
Institute for Complementary and Natural Medicine www.i-c-m.org.uk

Microbiology (see also Biological Sciences/Biology)
Society for General Microbiology www.sgm.ac.uk

Music
Incorporated Society of Musicians www.ism.org
Institute of Musical Instrument Technology www.imit.org.uk

Naval Architecture
Royal Institution of Naval Architects www.rina.org.uk

Nursing and Midwifery
Community Practitioners' and Health Visitors' Association www.unite-cphva.org
Health and Social Care in Northern Ireland www.n-i.nhs.uk
Nursing and Midwifery Council www.nmc-uk.org
Royal College of Midwives www.rcm.org.uk
Royal College of Nursing www.rcn.org.uk

Nutrition (see Dietetics)

Occupational Therapy
British Association/College of Occupational Therapists www.cot.co.uk

Optometry
Association of British Dispensing Opticians www.abdo.org.uk
British and Irish Orthoptic Society www.orthoptics.org.uk
College of Optometrists www.college-optometrists.org
General Optical Council www.optical.org

Pharmacology
British Toxicology Society www.thebts.org
Royal Pharmaceutical Society of Great Britain www.rpsgb.org.uk

Pharmacy
Royal Pharmaceutical Society of Great Britain www.rpsgb.org.uk

Photography
Association of Photographers http://hub.the-aop.org
British Institute of Professional Photography www.bipp.com
Royal Photographic Society www.rps.org

Physical Education (see Education and Teacher Training and Sports Sciences/Studies)

Physics
Institute of Physics www.iop.org
Institute of Physics and Engineering in Medicine www.ipem.org.uk

Physiotherapy
Association of Chartered Physiotherapists in Animal Therapy www.acpat.org
Chartered Society of Physiotherapy www.csp.org.uk

Plant Sciences (see Biological Sciences/Biology)

Podiatry
Society of Chiropodists and Podiatrists www.feetforlife.org

Property Management/Development
Chartered Institute of Building www.ciob.org.uk
Chartered Surveyors Training Trust www.cstt.org.uk
National Association of Estate Agents www.naea.co.uk
Royal Institution of Chartered Surveyors www.rics.org

Psychology
British Psychological Society www.bps.org.uk

Public Relations
Chartered Institute of Public Relations www.cipr.co.uk

Quantity Surveying
Chartered Institute of Building www.ciob.org.uk
Royal Institution of Chartered Surveyors www.rics.org

Radiography
Society and College of Radiographers www.sor.org

Social Work
Care Council for Wales www.ccwales.org.uk
General Social Care Council www.gscc.org.uk
Northern Ireland Social Care Council www.niscc.info
Scottish Social Services Council www.sssc.uk.com

Sociology
British Sociological Association www.britsoc.co.uk

Speech Pathology/Sciences/Therapy
Royal College of Speech and Language Therapists www.rcslt.org

Sports Sciences/Studies
British Association of Sport and Exercise Sciences www.bases.org.uk
English Institute of Sport www.eis2win.co.uk

Institute of Sport and Recreation Management www.isrm.co.uk
Scottish Institute of Sport www.sisport.com
Society of Sports Therapists www.society-of-sports-therapists.org
Sport England www.sportengland.org
Sport Scotland www.sportscotland.org.uk
Sport Wales www.sportwales.org.uk
Sports Institute Northern Ireland www.sini.co.uk
UK Sport www.uksport.gov.uk

Statistics
Royal Statistical Society www.rss.org.uk

Tourism and Travel
Institute for Sport, Parks and Leisure www.ispal.org.uk
Institute of Travel and Tourism www.itt.co.uk

Town and Country Planning
Royal Town Planning Institute www.rtpi.org.uk

Transport Management and Planning
Chartered Institute of Logistics and Transport www.ciltuk.org.uk

Veterinary Science/Medicine/Nursing
Association of Chartered Physiotherapists in Animal Therapy www.acpat.org
British Veterinary Nursing Association www.bvna.org.uk
Royal College of Veterinary Surgeons www.rcvs.org.uk
Royal Veterinary College www.rvc.ac.uk

Zoology
Royal Entomological Society www.royensoc.co.uk
Zoological Society of London www.zsl.org

Unless otherwise stated, the publications in this list are all available from Trotman Publishing (www.trotman.co.uk / 0870 900 2665).

STANDARD REFERENCE BOOKS

British Qualifications, 39th edition, Kogan Page Ltd
British Vocational Qualifications, 10th edition, Kogan Page Ltd

OTHER BOOKS AND RESOURCES

Choosing Your Degree Course & University, 12th edition, Brian Heap, Trotman Publishing
Critical Choices: Applying to University, Trotman Publishing
Destinations of Leavers from Higher Education 2007/8, Higher Education Statistics Agency Services (available from HESA)
Getting Into course guides: US & Canadian Universities, Art & Design Courses, Business & Economics Courses, Dental School, Engineering Courses, Law, Medical School, Oxford & Cambridge, Physiotherapy Courses, Psychology Courses, Veterinary School, Trotman Publishing
Guide to Student Money 2011, 16th edition, Gwenda Thomas, Trotman Publishing
Guide to UK Universities 2010, 30th edition, Klaus Boehm and Jenny Lees-Spalding, Trotman Publishing
How to Complete Your UCAS Application: 2012 Entry, Trotman Publishing
Insiders' Guide to Applying to University, 2nd edition, Karla Fitzhugh, Trotman Publishing
Into Higher Education 2009: The Higher Education Guide for People with Disabilities, Skill – The National Bureau for Students with Disabilities
Study in Europe – UK Socrates-Erasmus Student Guide, UK Socrates-Erasmus Council
Studying and Learning at University, Alan Pritchard, Sage Study Skills Series
Surviving Your First Year at University, Trotman Publishing
The Times Good University Guide 2012, John O'Leary, Times Books
University Scholarships, Awards and Bursaries, 8th edition, Brian Heap, Trotman Publishing
The Virgin 2012 Guide to British Universities, Piers Dudgeon, Virgin Publishing
Which Uni? Find the Best University for You, Karla Fitzhugh, Trotman Publishing
Your Gap Year, 6th edition, Susan Griffith, Crimson Publishing

USEFUL WEBSITES

Education, course and applications information
www.direct.gov.uk/en/EducationAndLearning
www.coursediscover.co.uk
www.britishcouncil.org/erasmus
www.hesa.ac.uk
www.opendays.com (information on university and college open days)
http://unistats.direct.gov.uk (official information from UK universities and colleges for comparing courses)
www.ucas.com

Careers information
www.armyjobs.mod.uk
www.careerseurope.co.uk
www.connexions-direct.com
www.tomarrowsengineers.org.uk
www.insidecareers.co.uk
www.isco.org.uk

www.milkround.com
www.nhscareers.nhs.uk
www.prospects.ac.uk
www.socialworkandcarejobs.co.uk
www.tda.gov.uk
www.trotman.co.uk
www.ucreative.ac.uk

Gap Years
www.gapyear.com
www.gap-year.com
www.yini.org.uk (Year in Industry)

Study overseas
www.acu.ac.uk
www.fulbright.co.uk
www.allaboutcollege.com

INDEX OF ADVERTISERS

COURSE INDEX